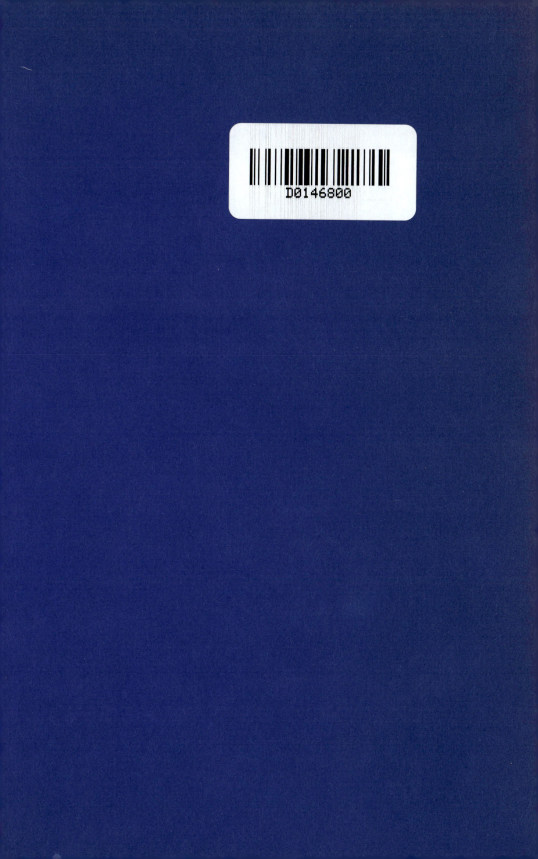

FREEDOM

A DOCUMENTARY HISTORY OF EMANCIPATION
1861–1867

SERIES II
THE BLACK MILITARY EXPERIENCE

Photographs of Private Hubbard Pryor, 44th U.S. Colored Infantry, before and after enlisting.

Source: Enclosed in Col. R. D. Mussey to Major C. W. Foster, 10 Oct. 1864, M-750 1864, Letters Received, ser. 360, Colored Troops Division, RG 94 [B-468].

FREEDOM

A DOCUMENTARY HISTORY OF
EMANCIPATION
1861–1867

SELECTED FROM THE HOLDINGS OF THE
NATIONAL ARCHIVES OF THE UNITED STATES

SERIES II
THE BLACK MILITARY EXPERIENCE

IRA BERLIN, EDITOR
JOSEPH P. REIDY, ASSOCIATE EDITOR
LESLIE S. ROWLAND, ASSOCIATE EDITOR

CAMBRIDGE UNIVERSITY PRESS

CAMBRIDGE
LONDON   NEW YORK   NEW ROCHELLE
MELBOURNE   SYDNEY

Published by the Press Syndicate of the University of Cambridge
The Pitt Building, Trumpington Street, Cambridge CB2 1RP
32 East 57th Street, New York, NY 10022, USA
296 Beaconsfield Parade, Middle Park, Melbourne 3206, Australia

© Cambridge University Press 1982

First published 1982

Printed in the United States of America

Library of Congress Cataloging in Publication Data

Main entry under title:
The Black military experience

(Freedom, a documentary history of
emancipation, 1861–1867; ser. 2)

Includes index.

1. United States – History – Civil War, 1861-
1865 – Afro-American troops – Sources.
I. Berlin, Ira, 1941-   II. Reidy,
Joseph P. (Joseph Patrick), 1948-
III. Rowland, Leslie S.   IV. Series.
E185.2.F88 vol. 2 [E492.9] 973.7'415 82-4446

ISBN 0 521 22984 7   AACR2

Contents

CONTENTS

PART 2

THE STRUCTURE OF BLACK MILITARY LIFE: LIMITS AND OPPORTUNITIES

viii

Contents

ix

Contents

Acknowledgments

AN ENTERPRISE of the scope of the Freedmen and Southern Society Project incurs numerous debts from its inception to its conclusion. With the publication of the first volume of *Freedom,* the editors would like to acknowledge the advice, support, and encouragement of numerous friends and colleagues, with the understanding that their generosity can never be fully repaid.

Our first debt is to Herbert G. Gutman. In 1975, while representing the American Historical Association on the National Historical Publications and Records Commission (NHPRC), Professor Gutman broached the idea of using the documentary format identified with the "Founding Fathers" series to write history from the perspective of the past's majority rather than its most prominent figures. The staff of the NHPRC, then under the direction of Fred Shelley, enthusiastically endorsed Gutman's proposal and the commission agreed, as a first effort, to sponsor a study of the transformation of black life during emancipation. Since then, Shelley's successor, Frank Burke, along with Roger Bruns and George Vogt, respectively director and assistant director for publications of the NHPRC, have continued to lend their support and wise counsel to the Freedmen and Southern Society Project, encouraging the editors to reshape the documentary format in ways that serve the special needs of such a novel and massive undertaking. To our sadness and regret, the NHPRC, which has stimulated some of the most important historical research during the last generation and has helped make the basic texts of the American past available to the American people, is now threatened with extinction by short-sighted budgetary considerations.

The Department of History at the University of Maryland, first under the leadership of Walter Rundell, Jr., and then Emory G. Evans, has provided a comfortable home for the project, as well as significant material support. Our colleagues at the university have been helpful and encouraging, if somewhat curious as to why some historians choose to work a double shift. We would especially like to thank Louis R. Harlan and Raymond W. Smock, editors of the Booker T. Washington Papers, who provided not only a wellspring of common-sense editorial advice, but also the reassuring example that it is possible to complete a multivolume editorial project within a single lifetime.

Between 1976 and 1979, the Freedmen and Southern Society Project made its home deep in the recesses of the National Archives building in Washington. During that time, the National Archives not only shared its already cramped quarters with the project staff, but also allowed us direct access to the stacks of the Archives. Little can be said for either the appointments of the interior of the National Archives or its climate—which has no analog anywhere in the world—but without the hospitality of the Archives and the ability to roam freely through the records, this project would not have been possible. During our residence at the Archives, the Archives-based research staff of the NHPRC and the staff of the National Archives tutored us on the organization of that great institution and the vagaries of its many record groups. Although it is impossible to thank all the men and women who answered questions, gave directions, and politely corrected ill-founded notions, we are especially grateful to Robert Clarke, Afro-American specialist; Meyer Fishbein, then director of the Military Division of the National Archives; Elaine Everly, Dale Floyd, Maida Loescher, Michael Musick, and Robert Matchett of the Navy and Old Army Branch; James Harwood, Hope Holdcamper, Michael McReynolds, and Donald Mosholder, of the Judicial and Fiscal Branch; George P. Perros of the Legislative Branch; and Mary Giunta, Anne Henry, and Diane Buncombe of the NHPRC research staff.

While working at the National Archives, two research assistants joined the editors in searching through the records and compiling the project's "primary selection." Garrine P. Laney and Gail M. Thomas, now completing doctoral work at the University of Chicago and the University of Rochester, respectively, helped expand the range of the project far beyond anything the editors could have hoped to master. Their contributions to *Freedom* are evident throughout this volume and will be evident in subsequent volumes as well.

As part of its support, the University of Maryland history department annually provided a graduate student to assist on the project, and other graduate students joined the project during summer recesses. We like to think these graduate assistants learned as much from the project as the project gained from their presence. Actually, it was a rather uneven exchange. These young scholars brought enormous energy, vitality, and a whole range of new questions to the project, which enriched it in a variety of ways. Some of the project's alumni—Cindy Aron now of the University of Virginia, Richard Richardson now of the Maryland Hall of Records, Roslyn

Acknowledgments

Wright now of the National Archives—have gone on to academic and archival careers of their own. Others—Walter Hill, Pete Hoefer, Greg LaMotta, Edna Medford, Holly Syrrakos, and Jill Zahniser—are completing graduate work at the University of Maryland and elsewhere. Still others—Carl Hinton, Earl Kelly, Lori Melucci, and Carolyn Robertson—have followed their interests in other directions. We thank them all.

In addition, over the years some twenty University of Maryland undergraduates have helped photocopy documents and maintain the project's files. We owe them a large debt of gratitude for the care and attention they gave to a job that can at best be described as tedious. We would especially like to thank Kathie Reed, who was there at the beginning and knew the rules when none existed, and Linda Sandifer, whose record for photocopying accuracy and speed stands unmatched. Susan Ezell and Lorraine Lee helped transcribe the documents, and their unfailing disposition cheered us all.

A few special thanks are due. Eric Foner, Herbert G. Gutman, James M. McPherson, Michael Musick, and Benjamin Quarles read the manuscript and made wise suggestions that saved us from numerous howlers and improved the organization and presentation. Herman Belz read Chapter 8, and Manoj K. Joshi contributed to Chapter 6. Barbara J. Fields, who joined the project as associate editor while Leslie Rowland was on leave, and Michael K. Honey, an NHPRC fellow, helped make the final editorial corrections. Being fresh when we were tired, they offered perspective on the entire enterprise and a needed fillip to push this volume into print. Michael K. Honey, Garrine P. Laney, and Joseph Mannard indexed the volume with great patience and diligence; and Walter J. Gilbert, assistant director of the University of Maryland's computer center employed the mysteries of his craft to transform crude index entries into the finished product. Edna Medford helped correct final proofs. Susan Bailey not only mastered the complexities of nineteenth-century orthography and twentieth-century word processing, but also reminded us that the social commitments reflected in these pages remain much alive today. Finally to Sara Dunlap Jackson, who appreciated the wealth of the Archives sources and who understood the need for this collection thirty years before anyone else, we owe a special debt. Not only did she lead us to material that we might otherwise never have found, but her enthusiasm, her dedication, and indeed her impatience to see this volume reach print speeded it to conclusion. We hope the dedication of this volume suggests how much she means to all of us.

I.B.

College Park   J.P.R.
October 1981   L.S.R.

Introduction

No EVENT in American history matches the drama of emancipation. More than a century later, it continues to stir the deepest emotions. And properly so. Emancipation accompanied the military defeat of the world's most powerful slaveholding class, and freed a larger number of slaves than lived in all other New World slave societies combined. Clothed in the rhetoric of biblical prophecy and national destiny and born of a bloody civil war, it accomplished a profound social revolution. That revolution destroyed forever a way of life based upon the ownership of human beings, restoring to the former slaves proprietorship of their own persons, liquidating without compensation private property valued at billions of dollars, and forcibly substituting the relations of free labor for those of slavery. In designating the former slaves as citizens, emancipation placed citizenship upon new ground, defined in the federal Constitution and thenceforth removed beyond the jurisdiction of the states. By obliterating the sovereignty of master over slave, it handed a monopoly of sovereignty to the newly consolidated nation-state. The freeing of the slaves simultaneously overturned the old regime of the South and set the entire nation upon a new course.

The death of slavery led to an intense period of social reconstruction, closely supervised by the victorious North, which lasted over a decade in many places. During this period, former slaves challenged the domination of the old masters, demanding land and the right to control their own labor. Former masters, abetted by a complaisant President, defeated the freedpeople's bid for economic independence and imposed on them new legal and extra-legal constraints. But whatever the outcome, the struggle itself confirmed the magnitude of the change. Freedpeople confronted their former masters as free laborers in a system predicated upon contractual equality between employers and employees. They gained, if only temporarily, full citizenship rights, including the right to vote and hold public office.

With emancipation in the South, the United States enacted its part in a world-wide drama. Throughout the western world and beyond, the forces unleashed by the American and French revolutions and by the industrial revolution worked to undermine political regimes based upon hereditary privilege and economic systems based upon bound labor. Slavery had already succumbed in the Northern states and in the French and British Caribbean before the American Civil War, and it would shortly do so in its remaining strongholds in Spanish and Portuguese America. Almost simultaneously with the great struggle in the United States, the vestiges of serfdom in central and eastern Europe yielded to the pressure of the age. Only small pockets in Africa and Asia remained immune, and their immunity was temporary. The fateful lightning announced by the victorious Union army was soon to strike, if it had not already struck, wherever men and women remained in bonds of personal servitude.

For all systems of bondage, emancipation represented the acid test, the moment of truth. The upheaval of conventional expectations stripped away the patina of routine, exposing the cross purposes and warring intentions that had simmered – often unnoticed – beneath the surface of the old order. In throwing off habitual restraints, freed men and women redesigned their lives in ways that spoke eloquently of their hidden life in bondage, revealing clandestine institutions, long cherished beliefs, and deeply held values. In confronting new restraints, they abandoned their usual caution in favor of direct speech and yet more direct action. Lords and serfs, masters and slaves had to survey the new social boundaries without the old etiquette of dominance and subordination as a guide. Their efforts to do so led to confrontations that could be awkward, painful, and frequently violent. The continued force of these encounters awakened men and women caught up in the drama to the realization that their actions no longer ratified old, established ways, but set radically new precedents for themselves and for future generations.

Moments of revolutionary transformation expose as at no other time the foundation upon which societies rest. While those who enjoy political power and social authority speak their minds and indulge their inclinations freely and often, their subordinates generally cannot. Only in the upheaval of accustomed routine can the lower orders give voice to the assumptions that guide their world as it is and as they wish it to be. Some of them quickly grasp the essence of the new circumstances. Under the tutelage of unprecedented events, ordinary men and women become extraordinarily perceptive and articulate, seizing the moment to challenge the assumptions of the old regime and proclaim a new social order. Even then, few take the initiative. Some – perhaps most – simply try to maintain their balance, to reconstitute a routine, to maximize gains and minimize losses as events swirl around them. But inevitably they too become swept up in the revolutionary process. Barely conscious acts and unacknowledged motives carried over from the past take on a changed significance. Attempts to stand still or turn back only hasten the process forward. At revolutionary moments all actions – those of the timid and reluctant as much as those of the bold and eager – expose to view the inner workings of society.

Because they thrust common folk into prominence, moments of revolutionary transformation have long occupied historians seeking to solve the mysteries of human society. Knowledge of the subordinate groups who have formed the majority throughout history has proved essential to an understanding of how the world works. Historians have therefore developed special methods for penetrating the often opaque histories of peasants, slaves, and wage-workers. Some have viewed them over the *longue durée,* translating glacial demographic and economic changes into an understanding of times past. Others have sought such understanding by focusing on particular events, decoding the fury of *carnaval,* the ritual of a bread riot, the terror of the "theater of death," or the tense confrontation of an industrial strike. Almost all have learned from periods of revolutionary transformation. Regardless of approach, direct testimony by the people involved has usually been a luxury. For this reason, the study of emancipation in the United States promises rich rewards not just to those specifically interested in the question but to all who seek a fuller view of the human past. Encompassing in full measure the revolutionary implications of all transitions from bondage to freedom, emancipation in the American South has left behind an unparalleled wealth of documentation permitting direct access to the thoughts and actions of the freed men and women themselves. Indeed, it provides the richest known record of any subordinate class at its moment of liberation.

THE RECORDS

As the war for Union became a war for liberty, the lives of slaves and freedpeople became increasingly intertwined with the activities of both the Union and Confederate governments. Following the war, federal agencies continued to figure prominently in the reconstruction of Southern economy and society. The records created and collected by the agencies of these governments and now housed in the National Archives of the United States provide an unrivaled manuscript source for understanding the passage of black people from slavery to freedom. Such governmental units as the Colored Troops Division of the Adjutant General's Office; the American Freedmen's

Inquiry Commission; the Union army at every level of command, from the headquarters in Washington to local army posts; army support organizations in Washington, including the Judge Advocate General's Office, the Provost Marshal General's Office, and the Quartermaster General's Office, and their subordinates in the field; the Civil War Special Agencies of the Treasury Department; individual regiments of U.S. Colored Troops; various branches of the Confederate government (whose records fell into Union hands at the conclusion of the war); the Southern Claims Commission; the Freedman's Bank; and, most important, the Bureau of Refugees, Freedmen, and Abandoned Lands all played a role in the coming of freedom. (See pp. xxxi–xxxii for a list of record groups drawn upon for the present volume.)

The missions of these agencies placed them in close contact with ordinary people of all sorts, and their bureaucratic structure provided a mechanism for the preservation of many records of people generally dismissed as historically mute. The Bureau of Refugees, Freedmen, and Abandoned Lands (Freedmen's Bureau) illustrates the point. Although the bureau often lacked resources to do more than make written note of the abuses of freedpeople brought to its attention, bureau agents scattered across the South conducted censuses, undertook investigations, recorded depositions, filed reports, and accumulated letters authored by ex-slaves and interested whites. Other agencies whose duties focused less directly upon the concerns of former slaves created thousands of similar, though more dispersed, records.

In these archival files, alongside official reports, hundreds of letters and statements by former slaves give voice to people whose aspirations, beliefs, and behavior have gone largely unrecorded. Not only did extraordinary numbers of ex-slaves, many of them newly literate, put pen to paper in the early years of freedom, but hundreds of others, entirely illiterate, gave depositions to government officials, placed their marks on resolutions passed at mass meetings, testified before courts-martial and Freedmen's Bureau courts, and dictated letters to more literate blacks and to white officials and teachers. The written record thus created constitutes an unparalleled outpouring from people caught up in the emancipation process. Predictably, many of these documents requested official action to redress wrongs committed by powerful former slaveholders who only reluctantly recognized ex-slaves as free, rarely as equal. Others, however, originated in relationships entirely outside the purview of either federal officials or white former masters and employers. They include, for example, correspondence between black soldiers and their families and between kinfolk who had been separated during slavery. That such letters fell for various reasons into the bureaucratic net of government agencies (and thus were preserved along with official records) should not obscure their deeply personal origins.

Selected out of the masses of purely administrative records, these documents convey, perhaps as no historian can, the experiences of the liberated: the quiet personal satisfaction of meeting an old master on equal terms, as well as the outrage of ejection from a segregated streetcar; the elation of a fugitive enlisting in the Union army, and the humiliation of a laborer cheated out of hard-earned wages; the joy of a family reunion after years of forced separation, and the distress of having a child involuntarily apprenticed to a former owner; the hope that freedom would bring a new world, and the fear that, in so many ways, life would be much as before. Similar records offer insight into the equally diverse reactions of planters, Union officers, and Southern yeomen—men and women who faced emancipation with different interests and expectations. Taken together, these records provide the fullest documentation of the destruction of any dependent social relationship, and the release of any people—serfs or slaves—from their dependent status and the simultaneous transformation of an entire society. As far as is known, no comparable record exists for the liberation of any group of serfs or slaves or the transformation of any people into wage workers.

However valuable, the archival records also have their problems. They are massive, repetitive, and often blandly bureaucratic. Their size alone makes research by individual scholars inevitably incomplete and often haphazard. The Freedmen's Bureau records, for example, extend to over 700 cubic feet, and they constitute a relatively small record group. The records of U.S. Army continental commands for the period spanning the Civil War era fill more than 10,000 cubic feet. In addition to their daunting volume, the bureaucratic structure of archival records creates obstacles for studies that go beyond the institutional history of particular agencies or the documentation of policy formation to examine underlying social process. Governmental practice provided the mechanism for preserving these records, but it also fragmented them in ways that can hinder historical reconstruction. Assume, for example, that a group of freedmen petition the Secretary of the Treasury complaining of a Confederate raid on a Treasury Department-supervised plantation. Their petition may be forwarded to the Secretary of War, since the army protects such plantations. He in turn passes it on to a military field commander, who sends it down the chain of command. If black soldiers provided the plantation guard, the petition may be forwarded to the adjutant general, who directed the Bureau of Colored Troops, who would then send it to a commander of a black regiment. On the other hand, if the Secretary of the Treasury wished to act himself, he could have forwarded it to a Treasury agent in the field. Augmented by additional information in the form of reports, depositions, or endorsements on the original complaint, the petition might be passed along to still other federal agencies. In the meantime, the Confederate raiders may have made a report to their commander, perhaps noting the effect of their foray on black morale. Rebel planters, anxious to regain their property, could now have their say, addressing the Confederate Secretary of War, the local commander, or the adjutant and inspector general. At any or all points, additional documents may be added and portions of the original documentation may come to rest. Only a search of the records of all these agencies can make the full story available. In part because of the scope of such an undertaking, individual scholars have been unable to avail themselves of the fullness of the Archives' resources. Research has necessarily been piecemeal and limited to one or two record groups or portions of various record groups. Only a large-scale collaborative effort could make the resources of the Archives available to the public.

THE FREEDMEN AND SOUTHERN SOCIETY PROJECT

In the fall of 1976, with a grant from the National Historical Publications and Records Commission, and under the sponsorship of the University of Maryland, the Freedmen and Southern Society Project launched a systematic search of those records at the National Archives that promised to yield material for a documentary history of emancipation. Over the course of the next three years, the editors selected more than 40,000 items, representing perhaps 2 percent of the documents they examined. Indexed and cross-referenced topically, chronologically, and geographically, this preliminary selection constituted the basis from which the documents published as *Freedom: A Documentary History of Emancipation* are selected and annotated, and from which the editors' introductory essays are written.

The editors found it imperative from the outset to be selective, centering their attention upon the wartime and postwar experiences of slaves and ex-slaves, but seeking as well to illuminate the social, economic, and political setting of the emancipation process. The formation of federal policy, for example, is not central to the project's concerns, except insofar as the preconceptions and actions of policy makers influenced the shape that freedom assumed. Therefore, the volumes published by the Freedmen and Southern Society Project will not undertake a history of the Freedmen's Bureau, the U.S. Army, the Bureau of Colored Troops, or any other governmental agency; nonetheless, documents about the operations of these agencies will be prominent when they describe activities of freedpeople and shed light upon the context in which former slaves struggled to construct their own lives. Throughout the selection process, the editors labored to reconstruct the history of the freedpeople rather than the institutions that surrounded them.

Above all, the editors have sought to delineate the central elements of the process by which men and women moved from the utter dependence slaveholders demanded but never fully received, to the independence freedpeople desired but only rarely attained. This process began with the slow breakdown of slavery on the periphery of the South and extended to the establishment of the social, economic, and political institutions that black people hoped would secure their independence. The editors have also sought to recognize the diversity of black life and the emancipation process, selecting documents that illustrate the varied experiences of former slaves in different parts of the South, who labored at diverse tasks, and who differed from one another in gender, in age, and in social or economic status. For while former slaves, like other men and women caught in the transit from slavery to freedom, wanted to enlarge their liberty and ensure their independence from their former masters, how they desired to do so and what they meant by freedom were tempered by their previous experiences as well as by the circumstances in which they were enmeshed. At the same time, the editors have been alert to the shared ideas and aspirations that American slaves carried into freedom and to those features of emancipation that were common throughout the South – and more generally still, common to all people escaping bondage. These common characteristics and the regularities of the process of emancipation connect the lives of former slaves across time and space and link them to other dependent people struggling for autonomy.

Reflecting editorial interest in a *social* history of emancipation, *Freedom* is organized thematically, following the process of emancipation. At each step the editors have selected documents that illustrate processes they believe are central to the transition from slavery to freedom. The first two series concentrate primarily upon the years of the Civil War. Series I documents the destruction of slavery, the diverse circumstances under which slaves claimed their freedom, and the wartime labor arrangements developed as slavery collapsed. Series II examines the recruitment of black men into the Union army and the experiences of black soldiers under arms. The remaining series, while drawing in part upon evidence from the war years, explore most fully the transformation of black life that followed the conclusion of armed conflict. They document the struggle for land, the evolution of new labor arrangements, relations with former masters and other whites, law and justice, violence and other extra-legal repression, geographical mobility, family relationships, education, religion, the structure and activities of the black community, and black politics in the early years of Reconstruction. The volumes are organized as follows:

Series I   Transformation: The Destruction of Slavery
Series II   The Black Military Experience
Series III Land, Capital, and Labor
Series IV   Race Relations, Violence, Law, and Justice
Series V   The Black Community: Family, Church,
            School, and Society

Topical arrangment continues within the volumes of each series as well, with each section introduced by an essay that provides background information, outlines government policy, and elaborates the larger themes. The documents are further subdivided, when relevant, to reflect distinct historical, economic, and demographic circumstances. Also reflecting the editors' predominant concern with social process, annotation—including both the notes to particular documents and the introductory essays—is designed to provide a context for the documents rather than to identify persons or places. The official character of most of the records means that vast quantities of biographical data are available for many of the army officers, Freedmen's Bureau agents, and others who cross the pages of these volumes. The editors have nonetheless decided against the time-consuming extraction of details about individuals, because to do so would divert energy from research into the larger social themes and would add little of substance to the business at hand.

In its aim, approach, and editorial universe, the Freedmen and Southern Society Project therefore differs fundamentally from most historical editing enterprises. Rather than searching out the complete manuscript record of an individual man or woman, the project examines the process of social transformation, and rather than seeking all the documentary evidence relevant to that transformation, it confines itself to the resources of the National Archives. *Freedom* endeavors to combine the strengths of the traditional interpretive monograph with the rich diversity of the documentary edition while addressing in one historical setting a central question of the human experience: how men and women strive to enlarge their freedom and secure their independence from those who would dominate their lives.

Editorial Method

THE RENDITION of nineteenth-century manuscripts into print proceeds at best along a tortuous path. Transcribing handwritten documents into a standardized, more accessible form inevitably sacrifices some of their evocative power. The scrawl penciled by a hardpressed army commander, the letters painstakingly formed by an ex-slave new to the alphabet, and the practiced script of a professional clerk all reduce to the same uncompromising print. At the same time, simply reading, much less transcribing, idiosyncratic handwriting poses enormous difficulties. The records left by barely literate writers offer special problems, although these are often no more serious than the obstacles created by better-educated but careless clerks, slovenly and hurried military officers, or even the ravages of time upon fragile paper.

The editors have approached the question of transcription with the conviction that readability need not require extensive editorial intervention and, indeed, that modernization (beyond that already imposed by conversion into type) can compromise the historical value of a document. The practical dilemmas of setting precise limits to editorial intervention, once initiated, also suggest the wisdom of restraint. In short, the editors believe that even when printing documents written by near illiterates, the desiderata of preserving immediacy and conveying the struggle of ordinary men and women to communicate intensely felt emotions outweigh any inconveniences inflicted by allowing the documents to stand as they were written. Fortunately for the modern reader, a mere passing acquaintance with the primer usually led uneducated writers to spell as they spoke, producing documents that may appear impenetrable to the eye but are perfectly understandable when read phonetically. In fact, reproduced verbatim, such documents offer intriguing evidence about the nature of the spoken language. Other writers, presumably better educated, frequently demonstrated such haphazard adherence to rules of grammar, spelling, and punctuation that their productions rival those of the semiliterate. And careless copyists or telegraph operators further garbled many documents. Both equity and convenience demand, nonetheless, that all writings by the schooled—however incoherent—be transcribed according to the same principles as those applied to the documents of the unschooled. Indeed, a verbatim rendition permits interesting observations about American literacy in the mid-nineteenth century, as well as about the talents or personalities of particular individuals.

Therefore, the textual body of each document in this volume is reproduced—to the extent permitted by modern typography—*exactly* as it appears in the original manuscript. (The few exceptions to this general principle will be noted hereafter.) The editorial *sic* is never employed: all peculiarities of syntax, spelling, capitalization, and punctuation appear in the original manuscript. The same is true of paragraph breaks, missing or incomplete words, words run together, quotation marks or parentheses that are not closed, characters raised above the line, contractions, and abbreviations. When the correct reading of a character is ambiguous (as, for example, a letter "C" written halfway between upper- and lower-case, or a nondescript blotch of punctuation that could be either a comma or a period), modern practice is followed. Illegible or obscured words that can be inferred with confidence from textual evidence are printed in ordinary roman type, enclosed in brackets. If the editors' reading is conjectural or doubtful, a question mark is added. When the editors cannot decipher a word by either inference or conjecture, it is represented by a three-dot ellipsis enclosed in brackets. An undecipherable passage of more than one word is represented in the same way, but a footnote reports the extent of the illegible material. (See p. xxx for a summary of editorial symbols.)

Handwritten letters display many characteristics that cannot be exactly reproduced on the printed page or can be printed only at considerable expense. Some adaptations are, therefore, conventional. Words underlined once in the manuscript appear in italics. Words underlined more than once are printed in small capitals. To represent printed forms with blanks filled in by hand, the words originally in print are set in small capitals and the handwritten insertions appear in lower-case, with spaces before and after to suggest the blanks in the form. Interlineations are simply incorporated into the text at the point marked by the author, with no special notation by the editors unless the interlineation represents a substantial alteration. Finally, the beginning of a new paragraph is indicated by indentation, regardless of how the author set apart paragraphs.

The editors deviate from the standard of faithful reproduction of the textual body of the document in only two significant ways. The many documents entirely bereft of punctuation require some editorial intervention for the sake of readability. However, the editors wish to avoid "silent" addition of any material, and supplying punctuation in brackets would be extremely cumbersome, if not pedantic. Therefore, the editors employ the less intrusive device of adding extra spaces at what they take to be unpunctuated sentence breaks. Although most such judgments are unambiguous, there are instances in which the placement of sentence breaks requires an interpretive decision. To prevent the ambiguity that could result if an unpunctuated or unconventionally punctuated sentence concluded at the end of a line of type, the last word of any such sentence always appears at the beginning of the next line. For technical reasons, punctuation of quotations in the endnotes and footnotes is modernized.

The second substantial deviation from verbatim reproduction of the text is the occasional publication of excerpted portions of documents. Most documents are printed in their entirety, but excerpts are taken from certain manuscripts, especially long bureaucratic reports, extensive legal proceedings, and other kinds of testimony. Editorial omission of a substantial body of material is indicated by a four-dot ellipsis centered on the page. An omission of only one or two sentences is marked by a four-dot ellipsis following the end of the preceding sentence. The endnote identifies each excerpt as such and, when significant, describes the portion of the document not printed. (See the sample document which follows this essay for a guide to the elements of a printed document, including headnote, endnote, and footnote.)

The editors intervene without notation in the text of manuscripts in two minor ways. When the author of a manuscript inadvertently repeated a word, the duplicate is omitted. Similarly, most material canceled by the author is omitted, since it usually represents false starts or ordinary slips of the pen. When, however, the editors judge that the crossed-out material reflects an important alteration of meaning, it is printed as ~~canceled type~~. Apart from these cases, no "silent" additions, corrections, or deletions are made in the textual body of documents. Instead, all editorial insertions are clearly identified by being placed in italics and in brackets. Insertions by the editors may be descriptive interpolations (such as [*In the margin*] or [*Endorsement*]); addition of words or letters omitted by the author; or correction of misspelled words and erroneous dates. Great restraint is exercised, however, in making such editorial additions: the editors intervene only when the document cannot be understood or is seriously misleading as it stands. In particular, no effort is made to correct misspelled personal and place names. When material added by the editors is conjectural, a question mark is placed within the brackets. For printed documents only (of which there are few), "silent" correction is made for jumbled letters, errant punctuation, and transpositions that appear to be typesetting errors.

While faithfully reproducing the text of documents with only minimal editorial intervention, the editors are less scrupulous with the peripheral parts of manuscripts. To print in full, exactly as in the original document, such elements as the complete return address, the full inside address, and a multiline complimentary closing would drastically reduce the number of documents that could be published. Considerations of space have, therefore, impelled the editors to adopt the following procedures. The place and date follow original spelling and punctuation, but they are placed on a single line at the beginning of the document regardless of where they appear in the manuscript. The salutation and complimentary closing, while spelled and punctuated as in the manuscript, are run into the text regardless of their positions in the original. Multiple signatures are printed only when there are twelve or fewer names. For documents with more than twelve signatures, including the many petitions bearing dozens or even hundreds of names, the editors state only the total number of signatures on the signature line, for example, [86 *signatures*], although some information about the signers is always provided in the headnote and sometimes in the endnote as well. The formal legal apparatus accompanying sworn affidavits, including the name and position of the offical who administered the oath and the names of witnesses, is omitted; the endnote, however, indicates whether an affidavit was sworn before a military officer, a Freedmen's Bureau agent, or a civil official.

The inside and return addresses create special complications. The documents in this volume come from bureaucratic, mostly military, files. Therefore both inside and return addresses often include a military rank or other title and a statement of military command and location which may run to three or more lines. Similar details usually accompany the signature as well. Considerations of space alone preclude printing such material verbatim. Furthermore, even if published in full, the addresses would not always provide for the reader enough information to identify fully the sender and recipient. Military etiquette required that a subordinate officer address his superior not directly, but through the latter's adjutant. Thus, a letter destined for a general is ordinarily addressed to a captain or lieutenant, often only by the name of that lesser officer. To bring order out of the chaos that would remain even if all addresses were printed in full, while at the same time conveying all necessary information to the reader, the editors employ a two-fold procedure. First, the headnote of each document identifies both sender and recipient – not by name, but by position, command, or other categorical label. For example, a letter from a staff assistant of the general in command of the military Department of the Gulf is labeled as originating not from "Lieutenant So-and-So" but from the "Headquarters of the Department of the Gulf." Most of the time this information is apparent in the document itself, but when necessary the editors resort to other documents, published military registers, and service records to supply the proper designations. Second, the citation of each document (in the endnote) states the military rank or other title and name of both sender and recipient exactly as given in the original document. Thus, the headnote and endnote together communicate the information from the return and inside addresses without printing those addresses in full.

Bureaucratic and especially military procedures often created document files containing letters with numerous enclosures and endorsements. While many routine endorsements served merely to transmit letters through the proper military channels, others reported the results of investigations, stated policy decisions, and issued orders. Indeed, enclosures or endorsements themselves are often valuable documents deserving publication. The editors therefore treat the material accompanying a document in one of three ways. First, some or all of such material may be printed in full along with the cover document. Second, accompanying items not published may be summarized in the endnote. Third, any accompanying material neither published nor summarized is noted in the endnote by the words "endorsements," "enclosures," "other enclosures," or "other endorsements." The editors do not, however, attempt to describe the contents or even note the existence of other documents that appear in the same file with the document being published, but were not enclosed in it or attached to it. Clerks sometimes consolidated files of related – or even unrelated – correspondence, and many such files are voluminous. The editors draw upon other documents in the same file when necessary for annotation, just as they do upon documents filed elsewhere, but the endnote is normally a guide only to the material actually enclosed in, attached to, or endorsed upon the published document.

A technical description symbol follows each document at the left, usually on the same line as the signature. The symbol describes the physical form of the manuscript, the handwriting, and the signature. (See p. xxxi for the symbols employed.)

An endnote for each document, or group of related documents, begins with a full citation which should allow the reader to locate the original among the holdings of the National Archives. The citation refers solely to the document from which the printed transcription is made; the editors have searched out neither other copies in the National Archives nor any previously published versions. Because all the documents published in *Freedom* come from the National Archives, no repository name is included in the citation statement. Record groups are cited only by their numbers. (See pp. xxxi–xxxii for a list of record group abbreviations.) For the convenience of researchers, the editors usually provide both series title and series number for each document, but readers should note that series numbers are assigned by the National Archives staff for purposes of control and retrieval, and they are subject to revision. Also for the convenience of researchers, each citation concludes with the Freedmen and Southern Society Project's own file number for that document, enclosed in brackets. In future the editors plan to microfilm all the documents accumulated during the project's search at the National Archives, along with the various geographical and topical indexes created by the staff. The project's file number for each document will thus serve as a guide both to the microfilm copy of the manuscript document and to other related documents in the project's files.

For ease of reference, the documents published in *Freedom* are numbered in sequence. Upon occasion, the editors have selected for publication several documents that taken together constitute a single episode. These documentary "clusters" are demarked at their beginning and at their conclusion by the project's logo — a broken shackle. The documents within each cluster bear alphabetical designations next to the number of the cluster.

Because *Freedom* focuses upon a subject, or a series of questions, the editors consider the function of annotation different from that required in editing the papers of an individual. While the editors seek, in the essays that introduce each section, to provide background information and interpretive context that will assist the reader in understanding the documents that follow, the documents themselves are selected and arranged to tell their own story with relatively little annotation. When the editors judge annotation to be necessary or helpful, it usually appears in the form of further information about the content of a document or about the historical events under consideration, rather than biographical identification of individuals mentioned in the document. Thus, there are few editorial notes to specific items within a document, but the endnote often describes the outcome of the case or discusses further the episode portrayed in the document. Such annotation, as well as the section essays, is based primarily upon other documents from the National Archives holdings, and those documents are cited in full, providing a further guide to related records that could not be published. Annotation is also drawn from published primary sources, and, with few exceptions, the editors rely entirely upon primary material rather than the secondary literature.

347: Discharged Maryland Black Soldier to a Freedmen's Bureau Claim Agent

Headnote*

Date and place line (reproduced as in manuscript, except printed on a single line at the top of the document regardless of location in manuscript)

Salutation (reproduced as in manuscript, except run into text regardless of location in manuscript)

Body of document (reproduced as in manuscript, except extra space added at unpunctuated sentence breaks)

Technical description of the document (see list of symbols, p. xxxi)*

Complimentary closing (reproduced as in manuscript, except run into text regardless of location in manuscript)

Signature (reproduced as in manuscript, except titles and identification omitted)

Williamsport Washington Co MD oct the 8 /66

Sir   it is With Much Pleser That I seat my self Tu Rit you a few lines Tu Now if you can Git The Bounty That is Cuming Tu us & We hear That The ar Mor for us   if The ar Pleas Tu let us Now & if you Can git it With or Discharges   if you Can I shod lik for you Tu Du so   sum of The Boys ar Giting on Esey A Bout Thear Papars & The Monney Tu   The ar so Menney After Them Tu let Them git it for Them & The Tel Them That The Can git it suner   Nomor But I still Reman you abdiant survent

Charles. P. Taylor

ALS

Charles P. Taylor to Mr. Wm. Fowler, 8 Oct. 1866, Unregistered Letters Received, ser. 1963, MD & DE Asst. Comr., RG 105[a] [A-9641].[b] Endorsement.[c]   Taylor identified himself as a former sergeant in the 4th USCI.[d]

Endnote*

a. Full citation of the document: titles and names of sender and recipient exactly as spelled in manuscript; date; and National Archives citation (see list of record group abbreviations, pp. xxxi–xxxii)

b. Freedmen and Southern Society Project file number

c. Notation of enclosures and/or endorsements that are neither published with the document nor summarized in the endnote text

d. Text of endnote

Footnotes,* if any, follow the endnote

* Elements marked with an asterisk are supplied by the editors.

Symbols and Abbreviations

[roman]   Words or letters in roman type within brackets represent editorial inference or conjecture of parts of manuscripts that are illegible, obscured, or mutilated. A question mark within the brackets indicates doubt about the conjecture.

[. . .]   A three-dot ellipsis within brackets represents illegible or obscured words that the editors cannot decipher. If there is more than one undecipherable word, a footnote reports the extent of the passage.

. . .[5]   A three-dot ellipsis and a footnote represent words or passages entirely lost because the manuscript is torn or a portion is missing. The footnote reports the approximate amount of material missing.

~~canceled~~   Canceled type represents material written and then crossed out by the author of a manuscript. This device is used only when the editors judge that the crossed-out material reflects an important alteration of meaning. Ordinarily, canceled words are omitted without notation.

[*italic*]   Words or letters in italic type within brackets represent material that is not part of the original manuscript and has been inserted by the editors. A question mark within the brackets indicates that the insertion is a conjecture.

. . . .   A four-dot ellipsis centered on the page represents editorial omission of a substantial body of material. A shorter omission, of only one or two sentences, is indicated by a four-dot ellipsis following the end of the preceding sentence.

Symbols and Abbreviations

SYMBOLS USED TO DESCRIBE MANUSCRIPTS

Symbols used to describe the handwriting, form, and signature of each document appear at the end of each document.

The first capital letter describes the handwriting of the document:
A   autograph (written in the author's hand)
H   handwritten by other than the author (for example, by a clerk)
P   printed
T   typed

The second capital letter, with lower-case modifier when appropriate, describes the form of the document:

L	letter	c	copy
D	document	p	press copy
E	endorsement	d	draft
W	wire (telegram)	f	fragment

The third capital letter describes the signature:
S   signed by the author
Sr signed with a representation in the author's name
I   initialed by the author
     no signature or representation

For example, among the more common symbols are: ALS (autograph letter, signed by author), HLS (handwritten letter, signed by author), HLSr (handwritten letter, signed with a representation), HLcSr (handwritten copy of a letter, signed with a representation), HD (handwritten document, no signature).

ABBREVIATIONS FOR RECORD GROUPS IN THE NATIONAL ARCHIVES OF THE UNITED STATES

RG 11   Record Group 11: General Records of the United States Government

RG 15   Record Group 15: Records of the Veterans Administration

RG 45   Record Group 45: Naval Records Collection of the Office of Naval Records and Library

RG 46   Record Group 46: Records of the United States Senate

RG 56   Record Group 56: General Records of the Department of the Treasury

RG 58   Record Group 58: Records of the Internal Revenue Service

RG 59   Record Group 59: General Records of the Department of State

RG 60   Record Group 60: General Records of the Department of Justice

RG 92   Record Group 92: Records of the Office of the Quartermaster General

RG 94   Record Group 94: Records of the Adjutant General's Office, 1780s–1917

RG 99   Record Group 99: Records of the Office of the Paymaster General

RG 101   Record Group 101: Records of the Office of the Comptroller of the Currency

RG 105   Record Group 105: Records of the Bureau of Refugees, Freedmen, and Abandoned Lands

RG 107   Record Group 107: Records of the Office of the Secretary of War

RG 108   Record Group 108: Records of the Headquarters of the Army

RG 109   Record Group 109: War Department Collection of Confederate Records

RG 110   Record Group 110: Records of the Provost Marshal General's Bureau (Civil War)

RG 153   Record Group 153: Records of the Office of the Judge Advocate General (Army)

RG 217   Record Group 217: Records of the United States General Accounting Office

RG 233   Record Group 233: Records of the United States House of Representatives

RG 366   Record Group 366: Records of the Civil War Special Agencies of the Treasury Department

RG 393   Record Group 393: Records of United States Army Continental Commands, 1821–1920

Symbols and Abbreviations

MILITARY AND OTHER ABBREVIATIONS THAT APPEAR FREQUENTLY IN THE DOCUMENTS

A.A.A.G.	Acting Assistant Adjutant General
A.A.G.	Assistant Adjutant General
A.C.	Army Corps
A.C.	Assistant Commissioner (Freedmen's Bureau)
Act. or Actg.	Acting
A.D.	African Descent
A.D.C.	Aide-de-Camp
Adjt.	Adjutant
Agt.	Agent
A.G.O.	Adjutant General's Office
A.Q.M.	Assistant Quartermaster
Asst.	Assistant
A.S.A.C.	Assistant Subassistant Commissioner (Freedmen's Bureau)
A.S.W.	Assistant Secretary of War
BG	Brigadier General
BGC	Brigadier General Commanding
BBG	Brevet Brigadier General
BGV	Brigadier General of Volunteers
BMG	Brevet Major General
BRFAL	Bureau of Refugees, Freedmen, and Abandoned Lands

Symbols and Abbreviations

Brig.	Brigadier
Bvt.	Brevet
Capt.	Captain
Cav.	Cavalry
C.d'A.	Corps d'Afrique
C.H.	Court House
Co.	Company
Col.	Colonel
col^d, cold., col.	colored
comdg., cmdg.	commanding
Comr.	Commissioner (Freedmen's Bureau)
C.S.	Commissary of Subsistence
C.S.	Commissioned Staff
C.S.	Confederate States
c.s.	current series
C.S.A.	Confederate States of America
Dept.	Department
Dist.	District
D.P.M.	Deputy Provost Marshal
E.M.M.	Enrolled Missouri Militia
Freedmen's Bureau	Bureau of Refugees, Freedmen, and Abandoned Lands
G.C.M.	General Court-Martial
Gen.	General
HQ, Hd. Qrs., Hdqrs.	Headquarters
Inf.	Infantry
Insp.	Inspector
inst.	*instant* (the current month of the year)
J.A.	Judge Advocate
Lt. or Lieut.	Lieutenant
Maj.	Major
MG	Major General
MGC	Major General Commanding
MGV	Major General of Volunteers
M.O.	Mustering Officer
M.S.M.	Missouri State Militia
N.C.O.	Noncommissioned Officer(s)
NCS	Noncommissioned Staff
NG	Native Guard
Obt. Servt.	Obedient Servant
P.M.	Provost Marshal
P.M.	Paymaster
P.M.G.	Provost Marshal General
Priv. or Pri.	Private

Symbols and Abbreviations

Pro. Mar. or Provo. Mar.	Provost Marshal
prox.	*proximo* (the next month of the year)
Q.M.	Quartermaster
Regt.	Regiment, regimental
RG	Record Group
R.Q.M.	Regimental Quartermaster
S.A.C.	Subassistant Commissioner (Freedmen's Bureau)
Sec. War	Secretary of War
ser.	series
Sergt. or Sgt.	Sergeant
Subasst. Comr.	Subassistant Commissioner (Freedmen's Bureau)
Supt.	Superintendent
ult.	*ultimo* (the preceding month of the year)
USCA Lt	U.S. Colored Artillery (Light)
USCA Hvy	U.S. Colored Artillery (Heavy)
USCC	U.S. Colored Cavalry
USCHA	U.S. Colored Heavy Artillery
USCI	U.S. Colored Infantry
USCLtA	U.S. Colored Light Artillery
USCT	U.S. Colored Troops
U.S.A.	U.S. Army
U.S.V.	U.S. Volunteers
V. or Vols.	Volunteers (usually preceded by a state abbreviation)
V.R.C.	Veteran Reserve Corps

The Black Military Experience, 1861–1867

FREEDOM came to most American slaves only through force of arms. The growing Northern commitment to emancipation availed nothing without victory on the battlefield. But once federal policy makers had committed the Union to abolishing slavery, the Northern armies that eroded Confederate territory simultaneously expanded the domain of freedom. The Union army perforce became an army of liberation, and as it did, both the Northern public and the freed slaves themselves demanded that the direct beneficiaries of freedom join the battle against the slaveholders' rebellion. Incorporation of black soldiers into Union ranks at once turned to Northern advantage a vast source of manpower that the Confederacy proved incapable of tapping and enhanced the antislavery character of the war. The liberating force of black enlistments weakened slavery in the loyal border states and the Union-occupied South no less than in the Confederacy, thereby extending the nation's commitment to freedom beyond the limits of the Emancipation Proclamation. Black enlistees in the border states received their freedom and, in time, guaranteed the liberty of their immediate families as well. Throughout the slave states, black enlistment and slave emancipation advanced together and, indeed, became inseparable.

Black men coveted the liberator's role, but soldiering remained a complex, ambiguous experience. If most free blacks and slaves rushed to join the Union army, others entered federal service only at the point of a bayonet. Once enlisted, ex-slaves who itched to confront their former masters on terms of equality found themselves enmeshed in another white-dominated hierarchy which, like the one they had escaped, assumed their inferiority. Organized into separate black regiments, paid at a lower rate than white soldiers, denied the opportunity to become commissioned officers, often ill-used by commanders whose mode of discipline resembled that of slavemasters, and frequently assigned to menial duties rather than battlefield roles, black soldiers learned forcefully of the continued inequities of American life. Nonetheless, the war left black soldiers with far more than their freedom. They gained new skills in regimental schools and a wider knowledge of the world in army service. Fighting and dying for the Union advanced black claims to all the rights and privileges of full citizenship. Victory over those who had previously dominated their lives bred a confidence which soldiers proudly carried into freedom and which permeated the entire black community. The successes of black soldiers in their war against discrimination within the army, however limited, politicized them and their families, preparing all blacks for the larger struggle they would face at war's end.[1]

At the beginning of the war, few Union policy makers foresaw a military role for either black freemen or bondsmen. Southern leaders and Northern abolitionists may have placed slavery at the cornerstone of the Confederacy, but Northern policy makers minimized the connection between secession and chattel bondage. In the eyes of Northern leaders and most Northern whites, the conflict would be a war for Union — not against slavery — fought by the white men of each section. Most Union army commanders followed the same line of reasoning, even after local authorities in some parts of the South

[1] This essay, like the shorter essays that introduce each section of documents, is based primarily upon the documents included in this volume and upon those in the files of the Freedmen and Southern Society Project. In organizing this volume, several other important primary and secondary sources have served as guides to the black military experience. Since they have been relied upon throughout, they are not cited at every point. Portions of the essays that lack specific footnotes should thus be understood to rest upon the documents in the remainder of the volume and upon the following sources. "The Negro in the Military Service of the United States, 1639–1886," compiled by the Adjutant General's Office between 1885 and 1888, is a valuable primary source collection. Its eight volumes are among the records of the Bureau of Colored Troops in the National Archives, and they are also available as a National Archives microfilm publication. Also useful are the annual reports of the Bureau of Colored Troops for 1863 through 1866, published in series 3 of *Official Records*: vol. 3, pp. 1111–15; vol. 4, pp. 788–90; vol. 5, pp. 137–40, 1029–31. One section of the final report of the Provost Marshal General's Bureau summarizes the laws and orders affecting the military service of black soldiers: *Official Records*, ser. 3, vol. 5, pp. 654–62. The most valuable secondary sources are Benjamin Quarles, *The Negro in the Civil War* (Boston, 1953); Dudley Taylor Cornish, *The Sable Arm: Negro Troops in the Union Army, 1861–1865* (New York, 1956); an interpretive collection of documents edited by James M. McPherson, *The Negro's Civil War: How American Negroes Felt and Acted During the War for the Union* (New York, 1965); Mary F. Berry, *Military Necessity and Civil Rights Policy: Black Citizenship and the Constitution, 1861–1868* (Port Washington, N.Y., 1977); and Leon F. Litwack, *Been in the Storm So Long: The Aftermath of Slavery* (New York, 1979), chap. 2. Three important nineteenth-century studies are those by William Wells Brown, a prominent black abolitionist, *The Negro in the American Rebellion* (Boston, 1867); and by two black Civil War veterans, George W. Williams, *A History of the Negro Troops in the War of the Rebellion, 1861–1865* (New York, 1888); and Joseph T. Wilson, *The Black Phalanx: A History of the Negro Soldiers of the United States in the Wars of 1775–1812 and 1861–65* (Hartford, 1888).

mustered a few free men of color into Native Guard units.[2] But as the Northern army confronted its enemy in the field, the indispensable role slavery played in the Confederate war effort soon became evident. Southern armies depended heavily on slave and free black labor to construct fortifications, transport materiel, tend cavalry horses, and perform camp services for both officers and enlisted men. Meanwhile, slaves on the home front raised the commercial staples necessary for foreign credit, labored in armories, shipyards, and ironworks to manufacture the weapons of war, and grew the food that fed both the army and the civilian population. Slave labor thus undergirded Confederate ability to wage war, while freeing Southern white men for battlefield service. Indeed, as Union generals probed their adversary, they found that Confederate spokesmen had made no idle boast: slavery stood at the center of Southern economy and society. The revelation gave new standing to abolitionists and their demand for emancipation. Slowly Union field commanders and then desk-bound policy makers came to see that preserving the Union required an assault upon chattel bondage.

General Benjamin F. Butler, a pugnacious politician with no previous military experience, first made the connection. Commanding the Union beachhead at Fortress Monroe in tidewater Virginia in the spring of 1861, Butler gave asylum to several runaway slaves, and, when their masters tried to reclaim the fugitive property, he sent the slaveholders packing. Initially, Butler acted out of an almost instinctive reluctance to aid the enemy. But, in a manner that came to characterize his command throughout the war, he quickly transformed his instincts into matters of high principle that flamboyantly redounded to his own and the North's benefit. Contending that slave property, like other private property, might rightfully be appropriated by the army upon grounds of military necessity, especially when such property was being employed in the enemy's cause, Butler put the fugitives to work in his quartermaster department. Shall the rebels "be allowed the use of this property against the United States," Butler asked rhetorically, "and we not be allowed its use in aid of the United States?"[3] Thus Butler established a rationale for refusing to return fugitive slaves and for turning their labor to Union advantage, while at the same time evading the question of emancipation. Without challenging their status as property, prag-

---

[2] On the Confederate free black units, see *Official Records*, ser. 1, vol. 15, pp. 556–57; *Official Records*, ser. 4, vol. 1, pp. 1087–88, and vol. 2, pp. 197, 941; Mary F. Berry, "Negro Troops in Blue and Gray: The Louisiana Native Guards, 1861–1863," *Louisiana History* 8 (Spring 1967): 165–90; and Charles H. Wesley, "Employment of Negroes as Soldiers in the Confederate Army," *Journal of Negro History* 4 (July 1919): 239–53.
[3] *Official Records*, ser. 2, vol. 1, pp. 752, 754–55.

matic federal commanders could remove escaped or captured slaves from Confederate strength and add them to the Union side. The issue was captured property used by the enemy to wage war—"contraband of war"—not freedom.

The North reveled in Butler's stroke, and the label "contrabands" adhered firmly to fugitive slaves. Other Union commanders hastened to follow Butler's lead. They increasingly perceived the value of black labor to their forces and also welcomed a solution to the problems posed by the escalating influx of fugitives into their lines. In August 1861 Congress—pressed by an upsurge in emancipationist sentiment in the North—gave legal standing to Butler's logic. The First Confiscation Act provided that a master who permitted his slave to labor in any Confederate service forfeited his claim to the slave.[4] However, as so often proved true during the war, events rapidly outran this legal position. With every advance of Union forces, slaves fled bondage and sought refuge with the Northern armies. With little regard for whether the fugitives had actually served the Confederacy, Union commanders turned the potential burden of civilian refugees into an asset by putting them to work on fortifications, on supply lines, and in personal service. Furthermore, as the war moved into its second year, support swelled for vigorous punishment of secessionists. Depriving rebels of their slaves appealed to Northerners frustrated by military stalemate and all too many defeats. Mindful of the apocalyptic vision of a vengeful God, some Northerners came to believe that their ultimate success hinged on elevating their struggle with the South to the level of high principle to demonstrate to themselves and to the world that they fought for right and justice and not for mere political or economic power. If the demands of the war sensitized Northerners to the moral necessity of freedom, the growing recognition of the evil of slavery awakened Northerners to the South's dependence on black laborers. Indeed, as the war dragged on, the rationale offered for emancipation became increasingly detached from the motives of its advocates. Abolitionists noted the military advantages of black freedom, while generals observed the immorality of slavery. Fed by a variety of sources, the argument that each captured or fugitive slave put to work within federal lines would be, in effect, a net gain of two—one gained for the Union, one lost to the Confederacy—grew in power. Increasing numbers of Northerners concluded that military as well as moral necessity demanded an end to slavery.

Emancipation inched forward during the first half of 1862. Congress legislated compensated emancipation in the District of Colum-

---

[4] U.S., *Statutes at Large, Treaties, and Proclamations*, vol. 12 (Boston, 1863), p. 319.

bia and prohibited slavery in the territories, and President Abraham Lincoln – unsuccessfully – urged the slave states still in the Union to consider gradual, compensated emancipation.[5] Then, in July 1862, the Second Confiscation Act and the Militia Act formally adopted emancipation and the employment of fugitive slave labor as weapons of war. These acts declared "forever free" all captured and fugitive slaves of rebels and authorized the mobilization of blacks in "any military or naval service for which they may be found competent."[6] If Lincoln's preliminary Emancipation Proclamation of September 1862 and the final proclamation of January 1, 1863, in effect freed no more slaves than had the Second Confiscation Act, they captured the imagination of the Northern public and elevated the Union's commitment to emancipation far beyond the level of mere expediency by adding moral weight to the Union cause. They also pledged the federal government to the full exploitation of black labor in defeating the Confederacy.[7]

Only a short step separated arguments about the value of black labor in support of the Union military to proposals that black men be used even more directly against the Confederacy. The same military and moral necessity that enlarged Northern support for emancipation pushed the question of enlisting black soldiers to the fore, and indeed, the two issues became increasingly intertwined. Once emancipation found a place on the Union escutcheon, many Northern whites demanded that the blood of blacks as well as whites be shed to purchase black freedom, some for obviously self-serving motives, others believing that black participation in the Union's victory would render the commitment to emancipation irreversible.

Still, policy makers hesitated. The prospect of arming slaves or even free blacks raised fundamental questions about the place of black people in American society, questions that went far beyond immediate demands of the war. After emancipating their slaves in the Revolutionary era, the Northern states had consigned them to the margins of society. Northern whites alternately exploited free blacks as cheap, menial laborers and urged black deportation from the United States, while consistently depriving black freepeople of the rights whites equated with freedom. Most Northern states denied blacks the right to vote or to sit on juries, and several states prohibited blacks from testifying against whites. White Americans deemed bearing arms in defense of the Republic an essential element

---

[5] *Statutes at Large*, vol. 12, pp. 376–78, 432, 538–39, 617; Abraham Lincoln, *Collected Works*, ed. Roy P. Basler (New Brunswick, N.J., 1953), vol. 5, pp. 144–46, 160–61, 317–19, 324–25, 503–4, 529–32.

[6] *Statutes at Large*, vol. 12, pp. 589–92, 597–600.

[7] *Statutes at Large*, vol. 12, pp. 1267–69; John Hope Franklin, *The Emancipation Proclamation* (Garden City, N.Y., 1963).

of citizenship, and federal legislation dating from 1792 restricted militia enrollment to white men.[8] As recently as 1859, Massachusetts Governor Nathaniel P. Banks had vetoed a law that would have incorporated black men into the state forces.[9] Blacks and their abolitionist allies challenged these proscriptions as denials of both the fundamental rights of man and the rights of citizens, and they protested racial discrimination. Thus, enlisting black men into the Union army not only would suggest a measure of equality most Northern whites refused to concede, but also would enlarge black claims to full citizenship. It challenged the racial basis of Northern society at a time when civil war threatened to redefine racial lines. For these reasons, black enlistment raised questions few Northern leaders willingly confronted. Both Congress and the Lincoln administration moved cautiously.

If Union policy makers avoided the implications of black enlistment, blacks and their allies seized them with alacrity. From the beginning of the war, Northern blacks pressed for the opportunity to serve in the army. They were joined by New England abolitionists, radical Midwestern Free Soilers, and even a few career military officers of antislavery persuasion who also saw black enlistment as a lever against slavery and racial discrimination. John A. Andrew, governor of Massachusetts, stood at the front of this group. Conscious of both the vital need for manpower and the ideological implications of arming blacks, in 1862 he began peppering the War Department with requests for permission to raise a free black regiment within his state's volunteer organization. Simultaneously, James H. Lane, veteran of the Kansas border wars and now a U.S. senator from that state, pressed for and eventually assumed similar authority. Two career army officers also lent early support to black enlistment: General John W. Phelps, a Vermont abolitionist serving in the Department of the Gulf, and General David Hunter, commander of Union operations along the coast of South Carolina, Georgia, and Florida. While the military command structure circumscribed Phelps and Hunter in ways that hardly affected Andrew or Lane, the strategic positions of the two generals and their explicit advocacy of slave – as well as free black – recruitment strengthened the bond between enlistment and emancipation.

In the summer of 1862, Phelps and Hunter, acting independently, armed fugitive slave men on their own authority and pressed for War Department recognition of their troops. Both soon ran afoul

---

[8] Leon F. Litwack, *North of Slavery: The Negro in the Free States, 1790–1860* (Chicago, 1961).

[9] Francis W. Bird, *Review of Governor Banks' Veto of the Revised Code, on Account of Its Authorizing the Enrollment of Colored Citizens in the Militia* (Boston, 1860); Adjutant General's Office, "Negro in the Military Service," pp. 946–50.

of their superiors. Phelps tangled with Butler—now in command of the Department of the Gulf—and was quickly mastered by the practiced politician. Hunter, who also barged ahead without War Department approval, disbanded his slave regiment when it failed to receive official sanction and thus could be neither uniformed nor paid. But, although Phelps and Hunter received public reprimands and reversals, events moved so quickly that their previously unacceptable policies soon won official blessing. Butler, after forcing Phelps's resignation, not only armed blacks—free blacks, rather than slaves—but also shamelessly claimed credit for initiating black enlistment. Similarly, within weeks of the dissolution of Hunter's regiment, Secretary of War Edwin M. Stanton authorized Hunter's subordinate, General Rufus Saxton, to raise several regiments among South Carolina Sea Island contrabands.

Yet the War Department's expectations in sanctioning the employment of black soldiers were different from those of Phelps or Hunter. While these radical generals had hoped to field a slave army of liberation, the department saw black enlistment as a stopgap measure to ease a temporary manpower shortage in a few critical military theaters. The War Department neither proposed large-scale black enlistment nor connected black enlistment to the emerging national emancipation policy. But, if federal policy makers were not yet fully committed to black enlistment, the organization of a few black regiments in Louisiana, South Carolina, and Kansas provided early opportunities for black men to demonstrate their eagerness to enlist and their potential as soldiers, important precedents upon which the proponents of black enlistment could draw.

Northern military setbacks in the summer and fall of 1862 reoriented Union priorities. Just as military necessity prompted Congress and President Lincoln to make emancipation the centerpiece of federal war policy, so the course of the war eroded the obstacles to universal black enlistment. Differences between the preliminary Emancipation Proclamation of September 1862 and the final proclamation of January 1863 suggest changes in Lincoln's thinking even over the brief three-month period. Whereas the former made no mention of arming emancipated slaves, the latter expressed an intention to receive slaves freed by the proclamation into military service to garrison forts and other military installations.[10] After the new year, Secretary of War Stanton

---

[10] *Statutes at Large*, vol. 12, pp. 1267–69. The final proclamation also declared that slaves emancipated by its provisions would be received into armed service on navy vessels. Congress had laid the legal foundations for black military service in the Second Confiscation Act and the Militia Act, both adopted in July 1862. The former authorized President Lincoln to employ "persons of African descent" in any way he deemed "necessary and proper for the suppression of this rebellion," organizing and deploying them as he judged best; the latter authorized

also showed greater awareness of the military advantages of arming large numbers of contrabands, as well as the need to find employment for the thousands of fugitives thronging into army camps. In March 1863, he ordered the American Freedmen's Inquiry Commission to investigate the condition of refugee slaves and report "what measures will best contribute to their protection and improvement, so that they may defend and support themselves; and also, how they can be most usefully employed in the service of the Government for the suppression of the rebellion."[11] Thus, by early 1863 the Lincoln administration had tied the question of slavery to the larger issues of the nature of the war, the impact of emancipation on American society, and the role of blacks in the war effort. These issues could not easily be separated, and the insatiable demand for soldiers forced the question of black enlistment to the fore. The previously inconceivable idea of large-scale black enlistment appeared increasingly to be common sense.

Union manpower needs gave new leverage to the proponents of black enlistment. Protracted warfare overwhelmed the War Department's initial plan to supplement the small regular army with a volunteer force. Men who had entered the army enthusiastically under Lincoln's early calls for volunteers, and who had reenlisted for additional terms of service, grew impatient with the bloody stalemate, as families suffered during their absence and the death toll mounted. The number of new volunteers plummeted, worsening the army's already serious manpower shortage. Scrambling to fill depleted Union ranks, Congress in March 1863 required systematic enrollment of all male citizens aged twenty through forty-five and provided for conscription by lottery from the enrollment lists.[12] The legislation flouted popular opposition, forced military service upon the unwilling, and fueled resistance to both the draft and the war itself. The increasing manpower demands inexorably shifted Northern perceptions of the utility of black enlistments, especially when combined with the belief that, since blacks would clearly benefit from Union victory, whites should not bear the entire burden of battle. The white potential draftee looked with increasing favor upon the idea of filling Union ranks with black men, even if he

Lincoln "to receive into the service of the United States, for the purpose of constructing intrenchments, or performing camp service, or any other labor, or any military or naval service for which they may be found competent, persons of African descent. . . ." (*Statutes at Large*, vol. 12, pp. 592, 599.)

[11] *Official Records*, ser. 3, vol. 3, p. 73.

[12] *Statutes at Large*, vol. 12, pp. 731–37. On the operation of the enrollment and conscription system and popular resistance to it, see Fred A. Shannon, *The Organization and Administration of the Union Army, 1861–1863* (Cleveland, 1928), vol. 1, pp. 295–323, and vol. 2, pp. 11–243; and Eugene C. Murdock, *Patriotism Limited, 1862–1865* (Kent, Ohio, 1967).

cared little about emancipation or disdained black people altogether. And the same manpower needs that compelled Congress to draft white men hastened a War Department commitment to enlist black men.

With Governor Andrew and others pressing the case and with black regiments already established in Louisiana, in South Carolina, and—with something less than official sanction—in Kansas, the Lincoln administration slowly, grudgingly, but irrevocably, turned to black men to redress the shortage of white soldiers. Early in 1863, Secretary of War Stanton authorized the governors of Rhode Island, Massachusetts, and Connecticut to organize black regiments. But, as if to emphasize the tentative nature of the commitment, Stanton balked when Ohio Governor David Tod asked for similar authority. Black Ohio volunteers and those of other Northern states would have to enlist in the various New England regiments.

Stanton's restriction scarcely hindered the abolitionists. Before long, Andrew and others had commissioned antislavery radical George L. Stearns to recruit black men throughout the free states. Stearns, in turn, organized citizens' committees, raised money, and hired black recruiting agents to scour the North for black enlistees. With long years of experience in the abolition movement and deep roots in Northern black communities, men like Martin R. Delany, O. S. B. Wall, John Mercer Langston, and John Jones had no trouble locating recruits and forwarding them to the regimental rendezvous in New England. Their efforts benefited from the public support of nearly all Northern black leaders, culminating in a convention of blacks from the state of New York in July 1863, which resolved that "more effective remedies ought now to be *thoroughly* tried, in the shape of warm lead and cold steel, duly administered by two hundred thousand black doctors. . . ."[13] By the summer of 1863, as the Massachusetts, Rhode Island, and Connecticut regiments filled, Stanton permitted other Northern governors to initiate black recruitment in their own states. Since black enlistees counted toward state draft quotas, most happily complied.

While authorizing free black enlistment in the North, Stanton also moved to expand recruitment of slave men in the Union-occupied South. He dispatched General Daniel Ullmann to Louisiana, assigned General Edward A. Wild to North Carolina, and sent Adjutant General Lorenzo Thomas to the upper Mississippi Valley to give slave enlistments full official sanction. Stanton charged Ullmann with raising a black brigade in the Gulf region, a task for

---

[13] *Record of Action of the Convention Held at Poughkeepsie, N.Y., July 15th and 16th, 1863, for the Purpose of Facilitating the Introduction of Colored Troops into the Service of the United States* (New York, 1863). Quotation on p. 8.

which Ullmann had been preparing in New York since the new year. Pushed by Massachusetts Governor Andrew, Stanton authorized Wild to inaugurate black recruitment in the Union's tidewater North Carolina foothold, and the Bay State general headed south to organize what became known as Wild's African Brigade. As befitted his rank, Thomas shouldered weightier responsibilities. In addition to raising black troops, Thomas would coordinate contraband policy with the Treasury Department and convince white soldiers of the virtues of black enlistment.

Thomas's appointment, embodying a shift from haphazard recruitment of blacks by interested parties and independent commanders to a systematic, centrally coordinated recruitment policy, confirmed the change in the War Department's approach. Adjutant General Thomas found skeptics aplenty within the commands of Generals Ulysses S. Grant and William T. Sherman, and Sherman, like others, would never be fully convinced. But the Union had made its commitment to arming blacks, and growing manpower demands only deepened it. In May 1863, the War Department established the Bureau of Colored Troops to regulate and supervise the enlistment of black soldiers and the selection of officers to command black regiments.[14] From the spring of 1863 to the end of the war, the federal government labored consistently to maximize the number of black soldiers.

During the summer of 1863, events on the war front and the home front enlarged the federal government's commitment to the recruitment of blacks. On the war front, Northern military victories at Gettysburg and Vicksburg arrested the Confederate offensive in the North and divided the Confederacy. The Union army's southward march – especially in the Mississippi Valley – stretched federal supply lines, brought thousands of defenseless contrabands under Union protection, and exposed large expanses of occupied territory to Confederate raiders, further multiplying the army's demand for soldiers. On the home front, these new demands sparked violent opposition to federal manpower policies. The Enrollment Act of March 1863 allowed wealthy conscripts to buy their way out of military service by either paying a $300 commutation fee or employing a substitute. Still others received hardship exemptions as specified in the act, though political influence rather than genuine need too often determined the success of many applicants. Those without money or political influence found the draft especially burdensome.[15] In July, hundreds of New Yorkers, many of them Irish immigrants, angered by the inequities of the draft, lashed out

[14] *Official Records*, ser. 3, vol. 3, pp. 215–16.
[15] See note 12.

at the most visible and vulnerable symbols of the war: their black neighbors.[16] The riot raised serious questions about the enrollment system and sent Northern politicians scurrying for an alternative to conscription. To even the most politically naive Northerners, black enlistment provided a means to defuse draft resistance at a time when the federal army's need for soldiers was increasing. At the same time, well-publicized battle achievements by black regiments at Port Hudson and Milliken's Bend, Louisiana, and at Fort Wagner, South Carolina, eased popular fears that black men could not fight, mitigated white opposition within army ranks, and stoked the enthusiasm of both recruiters and black volunteers.

However firm, official commitment to black enlistment did not of itself put black men into uniform. In the Northern free states, where recruiters had full access to the black population, the number of potential recruits was small. According to an estimate by the Superintendent of the Census, only 46,000 black men of military age resided in those states (see Table 1), so that Northern free blacks alone could not hope to meet federal manpower requirements. The largest number of black men within reach of army recruiters resided in the border slave states that had remained in the Union (Maryland, Delaware, Missouri, and Kentucky) and in those portions of the Confederate states occupied by federal forces before the end of 1862 (especially Tennessee and Louisiana). But in these areas, exempted from the Emancipation Proclamation, white unionists, many of them slaveholders, raised powerful objections to black recruitment. Fearful for their property, they alternately threatened to desert the Union and claimed unflinching devotion to the federal government in order to prevent the enlistment of slaves or even free blacks. At first federal policy makers respected such claims, especially while Confederate forces still contended for military control of these states. But, while the Lincoln administration sought to avoid alienating loyal masters, many of whom carried considerable political weight, it still desperately desired to tap these vast reserves of potential soldiers.

In each border state, and in Tennessee and Louisiana as well, the administration weighed the value of slaveholder unionism against army manpower needs. The reading of the scale varied from place to place and time to time depending on the course of the war, the nature of white unionism, and the viability of slavery. But everywhere slaves, fleeing to Union lines to offer military service in exchange for freedom, shifted the balance against their masters. Often they did so at considerable risk, for many "loyal" slaveholders would

---

[16] Adrian Cook, *The Armies of the Streets: The New York Draft Riots of 1863* (Lexington, Ky., 1974).

Table 1. Black Soldiers in the Union Army and Black Male Population of Military Age in 1860, by State

| State | Black male population, ages 18 to 45 | | | Black soldiers | |
	Free	Slave	Total	Number credited to the state	Percentage of black men ages 18 to 45
Northern free states					
Maine	272	—	272	104	
New Hampshire	103	—	103	125	
Vermont	140	—	140	120	
Massachusetts	1,973	—	1,973	3,966	
Connecticut	1,760	—	1,760	1,764	
Rhode Island	809	—	809	1,837	
New York	10,208	—	10,208	4,125	
New Jersey	4,866	—	4,866	1,185	
Pennsylvania	10,844	—	10,844	8,612	
District of Columbia[a]	1,823	—	1,823	3,269	
Ohio	7,161	—	7,161	5,092	
Indiana	2,219	—	2,219	1,537	
Illinois	1,622	—	1,622	1,811	
Michigan	1,622	—	1,622	1,387	
Wisconsin	292	—	292	165	
Minnesota	61	—	61	104	
Iowa	249	—	249	440	
Kansas	126	—	126	2,080	
Subtotal	46,150	—	46,150	37,723	
Black soldiers recruited in Confederate states but credited to Northern free states[b]				(5,052)	
Total				32,671	71
Union slave states					
Delaware	3,597	289	3,886	954	25
Maryland	15,149	16,108	31,257	8,718	28
Missouri	701	20,466	21,167	8,344	39
Kentucky	1,650	40,285	41,935	23,703	57
Total	21,097	77,148	98,245	41,719	42
Confederate slave states					
Virginia	9,309	92,119	101,428	5,919[c]	6
North Carolina	5,150	55,020	60,170	5,035	8
South Carolina	1,522	70,798	72,320	5,462	8
Florida	131	12,028	12,159	1,044	9
Georgia	583	83,819	84,402	3,486	4
Alabama	391	83,945	84,336	4,969	6
Mississippi	130	85,777	85,907	17,869	21
Louisiana	3,205	75,548	78,753	24,052	31
Texas	62	36,140	36,202	47	(less than 1)
Arkansas	22	23,088	23,110	5,526	24
Tennessee	1,162	50,047	51,209	20,133	39
Subtotal	21,667	668,329	689,996	93,542	
Black soldiers recruited in Confederate states but credited to Northern free states[b]				5,052	
Total				98,594	14
Other areas	2,041[d]	2,041	5,991[e]		
Total for all areas	90,955	745,477	836,432	178,975	21

Note: The percentage of each state's black military-age population that entered the army is merely an approximation, because fugitive slaves frequently enlisted in regiments outside their home states (the number of black soldiers credited to Kansas and the District of Columbia, for example, was notably swelled by such enlistments), and other population movements make the 1860 census figure somewhat inadequate for comparison with enlistment statistics. Because early Massachusetts, Connecticut, and Rhode Island black regiments recruited throughout the North, state-by-state computation of population percentages for the free states would be misleading; hence, only a regional percentage is given.
[a] Congress had already ended slavery in the District of Columbia at the time these population figures were compiled.
[b] Enlisted under the act of July 4, 1864, that permitted Northern state agents to recruit blacks in the Confederate states. See *Official Records*, ser. 3, vol. 5, p. 662. [c] Virginia, 5,723; West Virginia, 196.
[d] California, 1,918; Oregon, 38; Colorado, 5; Nebraska, 15; Nevada, 27; New Mexico, 16; Utah, 5; Washington, 17.
[e] Colorado Territory, 95; state or territory unknown, 5,896.
Sources: Population figures come from a report by the Superintendent of the Census, based upon the 1860 census (see pp. 87–88); the number of black soldiers credited to each state is given in the 1865 report of the Bureau of Colored Troops (*Official Records*, ser. 3, vol. 5, p. 138).

rather have seen their slaves in a shroud than in a uniform. Others tried to discourage slave flight by abusing and spitefully selling the families of black enlistees. The willingness of slaves to venture all for freedom intertwined the politics of enlistment with the politics of emancipation and, when military necessity triumphed over political expediency, enlistment effected black freedom in those areas of the South untouched by the liberating provisions of the Emancipation Proclamation.

Military need for laborers also confounded army recruitment. Army quartermasters and engineers increasingly depended on black teamsters, dockhands, and laborers to supply Union forces and construct federal fortifications.[17] The opportunity to remain near family and friends and, frequently, to earn higher and more regular pay made such employment more attractive than uniformed service to many black men. Thus, as the number of available black men shrank, the competition between quartermasters and recruiters intensified. Although the War Department resolved the problem differently at different times, this competition shaped black enlistment throughout the war.

As early as the beginning of 1864, enlistment had so undermined slavery in some places that masters who wished to retain a labor force were often compelled to acknowledge black liberty, in practice if not in principle. To prevent their slaves from running away and joining the Union army, they offered wages and other accouterments of freedom.[18] In such cases, freedom lost its power as an incentive for enlistment, and enthusiasm for military service waned. Moreover, as the war dragged on, black men, like white, learned that military service entailed considerable suffering, not only for themselves but also for their families. Many who had managed to carve out freedom and earn a living outside the army saw little reason to enlist. When the stream of black volunteers slowed, the army frequently resorted to impressment. Press gangs – sometimes composed of black soldiers – rode roughshod over potential enlistees, and conscription often became indistinguishable from kidnapping. Freedom thus brought new forms of compulsion to black life.

Blacks resisted impressment as they had resisted slavery and often forced Union commanders to modify such practices. Federal policy makers searched for more legitimate means to fill depleted army ranks. In February 1864, Congress revised the much-abused Enrollment Act, eliminating many of its inequities and also making all black men in the Union states – slaves included – subject to the for-

---

[17] For a full discussion of Union employment of black military laborers, see *Freedom: A Documentary History of Emancipation, 1861–1867*, ser. 1.

[18] For a description of the disintegration of slavery, see *Freedom: A Documentary History of Emancipation*, ser. 1.

mal procedures of enrollment and draft.[19] The revised Enrollment Act threatened Northern whites with conscription that could no longer be evaded by payment of a commutation fee, while substitutes were becoming increasingly difficult and increasingly expensive to obtain. Citizens' committees and local and state governments offered new and larger bounties to volunteers – white or black – who would fill their draft quotas. The Northern states also sought permission to recruit black men from the Confederate states, counting such recruits toward Northern state quotas and paying them sizable state bounties. Congress complied in July 1864,[20] and Northern agents spread across the Union-occupied South, impressing blacks already besieged by local army recruiters. But such activities alienated army commanders as well as blacks and obtained relatively few new recruits. In March 1865, Congress repealed the enabling legislation,[21] but the problem of impressment remained, and abusive conscription continued to the end of the war.

By the spring of 1865, black enlistment and conscription had placed 179,000 black men in the Union army, forming, together with those blacks who served in the navy, nearly 10 percent of those who served in Northern armed forces.[22] Of this number, approximately 33,000 enlisted in the Northern free states. The border slaveholding states of Delaware, Maryland, Missouri, and Kentucky offered a total of nearly 42,000, with Kentucky alone providing over half. Tennessee contributed 20,000; Louisiana, 24,000; Mississippi, nearly 18,000; and the remaining states of the Confederacy accounted for approximately 37,000 (Table 1).

The extent of black participation in the Union army varied from place to place. In some areas nearly all black men of military age served, in others hardly any. Everywhere freedom provided the most powerful stimulus to enlistment. In the border states, where slavery continued through most of the war (and, in Kentucky and Delaware, even at war's end), a large proportion of black men joined the

---

[19] U.S., *Statutes at Large, Treaties, and Proclamations*, vol. 13 (Boston, 1866), pp. 6–11.

[20] *Statutes at Large*, vol. 13, p. 379.

[21] *Statutes at Large*, vol. 13, p. 491.

[22] According to a recent study, 9,596 black men served in the Union navy during the Civil War, of whom 1,081 came from foreign countries; 3,838 from the free states (including the District of Columbia after 1862); 2,379 from the border slave states (including the District of Columbia in 1861–2); and 2,298 from the Confederate slave states. Of the border-state black sailors, roughly three-quarters were from Maryland; and of the black sailors from the Confederate states, half came from Virginia. These figures are calculated from David L. Valuska, "The Negro in the Union Navy: 1861–1865," (Ph.D. diss., Lehigh University, 1973), pp. 31, 56–57, 73–74, 83–84, 91–92, and 126. For different figures, see Herbert Aptheker, "The Negro in the Union Navy," *Journal of Negro History* 32 (Apr. 1947): 169–200.

army. Missouri's share of total black soldiers, for example, was nearly twice the state's proportion of the nation's black men, even without counting fugitive Missouri slaves who joined the army in neighboring Kansas. In Kentucky, where, beginning in early March 1865, slave volunteers could free not only themselves but also their families,[23] army service claimed nearly three-fifths of the black men of military age. Only 5 percent of the nation's black men resided in Kentucky at the start of the Civil War, and many had fled to enlist in Northern and Tennessee regiments before recruitment was finally permitted in their home state, yet the black soldiers credited to Kentucky constituted over 13 percent of the total. On the other hand, in most areas where the Union army arrived late in the war and where freedom derived from the Emancipation Proclamation, few blacks enlisted. Although Alabama and Georgia together contained 20 percent of all black men aged eighteen to forty-five, only 5 percent of all black troops enlisted within their borders. In Texas, the last Confederate state to surrender, a token forty-seven black soldiers saw Union service, from a population of over 36,000 black men of military age. This variety in the black military experience affected the struggle for freedom both during the war and in the years that followed.

Enlistment not only strengthened the bondsmen's claim to freedom; it also enhanced the freemen's claim to equality. As free blacks and their abolitionist allies had argued from the beginning of the war, Northern blacks welcomed the chance to strike at slavery as a means of acquiring all the rights of citizens. Although the figures do not allow precise calculation, in many areas of the North it appears that blacks served in higher proportion than whites. The Census Office estimated in 1863 that fewer than 10,000 black soldiers would be obtained from the free states if black men enlisted in the same proportion as white men had, yet more than three times that number served in Northern black regiments, an impressive showing even after discounting for the enlistment of some Southern fugitives and Canadian émigrés in the Northern units.[24]

---

[23] On March 3, 1865, by joint resolution, Congress provided for the freedom of the wives and children of all men serving in, or subsequently mustered into, army or navy service. (*Statutes at Large*, vol. 13, p. 571.) The Militia Act of July 1862 had earlier declared "forever free" the mothers, wives, and children of black men who had belonged to disloyal masters and then rendered service to the United States, but the freedom provision applied only if the family members were also owned by disloyal masters, effectively excluding the families of most border-state black soldiers. (*Statutes at Large*, vol. 12, p. 599.) Both Maryland and Missouri abolished slavery by state action before the March 1865 joint resolution.

[24] See *Freedom*, ser. 2: doc. 27, for the Census Office estimate. An additional 3,800 Northern blacks enlisted in the Union navy. (See note 22.)

As the North debated the issue of enlisting blacks in the Union army, a similar discussion took shape in the Southern states.[25] Measured by letters and memorials to the Confederate Secretary of War and other Southern officials, it followed the outline of the Northern debate. Like white Northerners, white Southerners – many of them slaveholders – argued that a "nigger" could stop a bullet as well as a white man; thus black enlistment would save white lives. Confident of black loyalties, some Southern whites itched to send their bondsmen against the arrogant Yankees, to authenticate the South's beneficent view of slavery. Others recoiled from the prospect of arming slaves, but their reluctance diminished once the North began recruiting black men. An enemy that stooped to such barbarism, they argued, deserved retaliation in kind. As in the North, wartime necessity added urgency to these arguments, and the call for slave enlistment grew more insistent as Confederate military fortunes deteriorated. Yet in some important respects, the Southern debate differed sharply from the Northern one. Only a handful of free people of color and no slaves pleaded for the chance to fight for Southern nationality and black bondage. Moreover, the Southern debate over arming slaves lagged well behind the Northern one. Whereas Union officials accepted some slave soldiers in 1862 and began large-scale recruitment in early 1863, Confederate authorities inaugurated slave enlistment only in the desperate spring of 1865, when the war was already lost. Northern and Southern understandings of the implications of black armed service stand most fully contrasted in the combatants' respective concerns about the difference between enlisting slaves and enlisting free blacks. While the South countenanced free black military service long before the North contemplated such a move,[26] the pressures inherent in the peculiar institution prohibited Southern consideration of arming slaves until long after the North could expediently do so and, indeed, until the whole question had become moot.

Once enlisted, black soldiers had much in common with Billy Yank or even Johnny Reb.[27] Black soldiers experienced the same desperate loneliness of men fearful for their lives and separated from family and friends. The same reveille blasted them from their bunks in the morning, and the same tattoo put them to bed at night; the same mosquitoes entered their tents in the summer, and the same wind

---

[25] See Robert F. Durden, *The Gray and the Black: The Confederate Debate on Emancipation* (Baton Rouge, La., 1972).

[26] See note 2.

[27] See Bell Irvin Wiley, *The Life of Johnny Reb: The Common Soldier of the Confederacy* (Indianapolis, 1943), and *The Life of Billy Yank: The Common Soldier of the Union* (Indianapolis, 1951).

whistled through their barracks in the winter. Like white soldiers, they enlisted expecting the glory of great battles but often found themselves wielding picks rather than swords, shovels rather than rifles. They too grumbled about long hours on the drillfield, complained about overbearing officers, and bemoaned the poor quality of army rations. And, like soldiers everywhere, they found relief in the camaraderie of the campfire.

Yet, if military life created countless similarities, the seemingly insoluble distinctions between slave and free, black and white remained as well. A white Northern private might boast of fighting for the Union and $13 a month, just as a Southern one might claim he battled for Bobby Lee and nationhood, but few black soldiers could see the war in such narrow terms.[28] Many owed their liberty to military enlistment, and most understood that the freedom of all blacks depended on Union victory. Across the field, behind the hedge, Johnny Reb might spy a money-grubbing Yankee, just as Billy Yank might see a sotted aristocrat, but black soldiers frequently confronted men who had recently sold their parents, put their sisters in the field, and scarred them with the lash, and who would gladly clap them back into bondage. Knowledge that their own freedom and that of their posterity hung in the balance made blacks Union patriots.

The timing and circumstance of black enlistment enlarged the black commitment to the Union and magnified black expectations about the rewards of military service. Entering the war at the Union's ebb, black soldiers came to believe that they had shifted the balance from the Confederate to the Union side. In return, they hoped that their participation would infuse federal emancipation policy with a commitment to racial equality. While many contemporaries – Southern as well as Northern – shared this understanding of the importance of black entry into the war, only a handful of Northern whites believed that black military service implied a commitment to equality and then, perhaps, only a commitment to equality before the law. So if blacks celebrated their acceptance into the ranks as a sign of a dramatic alteration of their place in American society, they soon learned that the changes they envisioned came slowly if at all. In fact, instead of speeding blacks down the road to racial equality, federal officials frequently formulated policies that confirmed the established pattern of invidious racial distinctions.

Union policies at all levels shaped the distinctive nature of the black military experience. Many of the policies sprang effortlessly from the historical legacy of slavery and discrimination. For ex-

---

[28] For the motivations of ordinary Union and Confederate white soldiers, see Wiley, *Billy Yank*, pp. 37–44, and *Johnny Reb*, pp. 308–15.

ample, although a few light-skinned blacks passed silently into white regiments,[29] no one ever gave serious consideration to placing white and black soldiers in the same units.[30] More commonly, Union policy respecting black soldiers evolved slowly and painfully against the backdrop of the war's changing fortunes, congressional and administrative politics, and Northern popular opinion. Whatever their origin, these policies touched all aspects of the lives of black soldiers, from their diet to their duties, from their relations with their officers to their relations with their families. But two Union policies proved particularly significant in giving form to the black military experience: excluding blacks from commissioned office and paying black soldiers less than white ones. While not necessarily more blatant in intent or effect than other discriminatory actions, these two policies fully revealed the racial inequities of federal military service. They provoked massive protests by black soldiers and their abolitionist allies and captured the attention of the general public. The questions of commissions and pay thus not only set black soldiers apart from white ones, but also encouraged black soldiers to make common cause among themselves. Although they wore the same uniform as white soldiers, observed the same articles of war, answered to the same system of military justice, and confronted the same enemy, black soldiers fought a different war. Because they struggled to end inequality as well as to save the Union, they faced enemies on two fronts, battling against the blue as well as the gray to achieve freedom and equality.

When black soldiers first entered the Union army, the breezy

[29] One Northern free black who served in a white regiment was Private Charles R. Pratt, a member of the 11th Ohio Infantry Volunteers. In August 1864, while stationed near Atlanta, Pratt applied for transfer to the black 55th Massachusetts Infantry on the following grounds: "I am a colored man, and my position as private in a white Regiment is very unpleasant. My feelings are constantly outraged by the conduct of those who have no respect for my race." A company commander in another Ohio white regiment, also stationed near Atlanta, petitioned in September 1864 for the transfer of four mulattoes ("one of them very dark") from his company to some Ohio black regiment. While assuring the Secretary of War that he favored the use of black troops, he contended that "the presence of these men cause great dissatisfaction among the white soldiers and occasion myself a great deal of trouble to keep order and quiet in the company and is I think an injustice both to myself and the men to have them where they now are." The War Department readily complied with these requests for transfer. (Priv. Charles R. Pratt to Brig. Genl. L. Thomas, 3 Aug. 1864, P-276 1864, Letters Received, ser. 360, Colored Troops Division, RG 94 [B-55]; Lieut. Henry C. Reppert to Hon. E. M. Stanton, 17 Sept. 1864, R-314 1864, Letters Received, ser. 360, Colored Troops Division, RG 94 [B-58].)

[30] In the Union navy, by contrast, black sailors served on the same ships with white sailors, probably as a result of long-standing seafaring customs. Like their counterparts in the army, however, black sailors filled the lowest ranks. See Valuska, "Negro in the Union Navy."

assurances of federal officials – from Secretary of War Stanton to local recruiters – that those who fought under the American flag would enjoy its full protection and benefits blinded all but the most prescient to the question of treatment after enlistment.[31] Thus, the first black soldiers recruited in lowcountry South Carolina and the sugar parishes of Louisiana expected to be treated like other soldiers, and at first it appeared they would be. While the appointment of black officers did not appear to be an issue in the Sea Islands, where General David Hunter organized the first slave regiment, the free colored Louisiana Native Guard units, mustered into service by General Benjamin F. Butler, served from the start under officers of their own color. These black officers, almost all free by birth, worldly, and well educated, had so impressed Butler that he readily offered them commissions in Union ranks. Recognizing the close bonds between the officers and the enlisted men, and anticipating the importance of black commissioned officers for future Union recruitment, Butler also organized a second Louisiana Native Guard regiment, with many black officers selected from men of the first regiment, and had begun recruiting a third, consisting partly of escaped slaves as well as free blacks, when his tenure as department commander ended late in 1862. As constant manpower shortages and the impressive performance of the Native Guard dispelled Butler's initial skepticism about the military aptitude of black men, his confidence in the ability of black officers to recruit and lead black troops grew.

However, Butler's successor, General Nathaniel P. Banks, considered the black officers unfit for command and determined to eliminate them from the service and replace them with whites. Banks devised a variety of stratagems, ranging from formal boards of examination to outright deception, to purge the black commissioned officers. Though a few black officers remained in the three Louisiana Native Guard regiments until mid-1864, Banks's action confirmed War Department skepticism about the advisability of commissioning black officers.

Northern blacks and antislavery proponents of black enlistment like Governor Andrew in Massachusetts and Senator Lane in Kansas also assumed that commissioned offices would follow logically upon the admission of blacks to armed service. During the summer of 1862, Lane had gone so far as to sign commissions for several black recruiters of his 1st Kansas Colored Volunteers. The War Department, however, silently refused to recognize their validity, reducing Lane's commissions to a hollow promise. Skeptical of the ability of

---

[31] For examples of early doubts of Northern blacks about equal treatment within the army, see *Christian Recorder*, 26 July 1862, 14 Feb. 1863.

black men to lead and fearful of the reaction of white soldiers to the appointment of black men to superior office, Secretary of War Stanton refused to commission black line officers throughout 1863 and 1864. During this period, blacks attained commissioned office only as chaplains and surgeons – positions with the rank of major but outside the regular chain of command. Even these appointments came grudgingly and were accompanied by a hail of abusive complaints from white officers and men.

Blacks vehemently protested the War Department's exclusionary policies. The free colored former officers of the Louisiana Native Guard spearheaded the protest, but they were soon joined by Northern free blacks and their white allies, who believed the appointment of black officers would give talented black men an opportunity to demonstrate the full capabilities of their race. Soldiers in the 54th and 55th Massachusetts infantry regiments pressed both their officers and Governor Andrew for promotion, and early in 1864 Andrew tested the War Department's determination to exclude black officers. Exercising a governor's authority over troops raised in his state, Andrew offered a lieutenancy to Sergeant Stephen A. Swails, an educated, light-skinned freeman who had compiled an exemplary military record. When the War Department blocked Andrew's action, Swails and others barraged federal authorities with demands for a favorable ruling. As the protest mounted, the battlefield valor of black soldiers, especially noncommissioned officers, steadily eroded the department's position. The combined pressure of black soldiers, Northern black abolitionists, and white proponents of black equality weakened the opposition to black officers. When a long list of prominent Republican politicans added their approval early in 1865, the War Department agreed to commission Swails. Yet, even with the end of the war in sight, the department resisted wholesale appointment of black officers and succeeded in confining their number to a mere handful and restricting their service to a few – mostly Northern – regiments. Indeed, most black officers received their commissions after the cessation of hostilities and served as officers only briefly before their regiments were mustered out.

The pay they received also distinguished black soldiers from white ones. Believing the assurances of the early army recruiters and recruitment broadsides, blacks assumed that they would receive the same remuneration as white soldiers. But the War Department ruled that the legal basis for black military service lay in the 1862 Militia Act and paid all black soldiers according to its provisions: $10 per month, minus $3 for clothing, rather than the $13 per month, plus clothing, that white privates received. Even black commissioned and noncommissioned officers received the same $7 monthly pay, so that

20

the highest-ranking black officer earned barely half the compensation of the lowest-ranking white enlisted man.[32]

Unequal pay angered black soldiers as perhaps no other Union policy did. The reduced income imposed a severe strain on families dependent upon black soldiers for their support, but the principle mattered at least as much. Blacks in the army, those recruiting soldiers, and those contemplating enlistment, as well as their abolitionist allies, viewed the discriminatory pay policy as yet another vestige of second-class citizenship and determined to eradicate it. Led by black soldiers recruited in the free states and encouraged by sympathetic white officers, several black regiments refused to accept the $7 monthly pittance, regarding it as an affront to their dignity as American soldiers. Rather than submit to inferior treatment some went over a year without pay. The 54th and 55th Massachusetts regiments even refused Governor Andrew's offer to use state funds to increase their compensation to the amount white privates received. In the meantime, they fought and died, dug fortifications and fell ill, and fumed at the progressive impoverishment of their families. By late 1863, the protest boiled over in open revolt when men in the 3rd South Carolina Volunteers under Sergeant William Walker stacked their arms and refused to perform duty until the army granted equal pay. Walker's superiors charged him with mutiny and executed him as an example to other black protesters. But Walker's death did not stem the protest. Instead, black soldiers stationed in other parts of the South began to agitate for change. Many teetered on the brink of mutiny until Congress passed an act equalizing the pay of black and white soldiers in June 1864.[33]

The War Department's inability to sustain its guarantees of equal treatment provoked no less fury than its overtly discriminatory practices. Confederate refusal to accord captured black soldiers the rights customarily due prisoners of war demanded that Union policy makers act to ensure black soldiers the most elementary protection of the flag. While numerous Union commanders from regimental officers up through President Lincoln declared their readiness to retaliate in kind if the Confederates acted on their threat to hang or enslave black prisoners, enforcing federal policy proved difficult. Even the most unambiguous evidence – such as the Confederate slaughter of black soldiers after the surrender of Fort Pillow, Tennessee – never seemed proof enough for most Union officials. The reluctance, if not refusal, of federal officers to make good their prom-

---

[32] For the pay provisions of the Militia Act, see *Statutes at Large*, vol. 12, p. 599; for the pay allotted white soldiers of various ranks, see *Revised Army Regulations*, pp. 358–63.

[33] *Statutes at Large*, vol. 13, pp. 129–30.

ise of retaliation meant that black soldiers faced dangers white ones seldom encountered. This special vulnerability of black soldiers marked another distinctive aspect of the black military experience. Knowing that death or enslavement might follow capture, they fought all the more desperately for the Union. Knowing that the federal government offered them less protection than their white counterparts, they remained alienated from the Union for which they fought and pressed for equal protection.

Other distinguishing features of black military life arose from neither explicit policy decisions nor their haphazard enforcement but from the unspoken assumptions of American race relations. Dealings between black soldiers and their officers generally followed the familiar pattern of white superiors and black subordinates and thus carried all the historic burdens of white–black relationships in the United States. But the diverse expectations both black soldiers and white officers brought to soldiering complicated the traditional pattern of American race relations still further. As committed abolitionists, some white officers volunteered to lead black troops as a means of demolishing racial stereotypes and fulfilling their own egalitarian vision. Glorying in the epithet "nigger officers," they befriended their men and promoted their cause. Other white officers accepted positions in black regiments only in quest of rapid advancement. They cared nothing for the cause of freedom or racial equality and despised their men all the more because of the stigma attached to serving with black soldiers. Few white officers of black regiments exhibited all the characteristics of either the abolitionist or the careerist; instead they combined in varying degrees attitudes derived from both seemingly contradictory positions. At each extreme, white officers exercised command in a variety of ways. Moreover, since black soldiers responded to their officers with similar diversity, the relationship between white officers and black soldiers defies easy categorization. If some black soldiers found support and comfort serving under men of antislavery conviction, others found the well-meaning paternalism of abolitionist officers more distasteful than the simple contempt of racist commanders. Black soldiers resented being treated like children no less than being treated like slaves. But whatever the specific pattern of relationships, the fact that the line of command within black regiments generally coincided with the color line added still another distinguishing element to black military life.

The complex pattern of Union policies, the often sporadic enforcement of these policies, and the unspoken assumptions that stood behind them touched all aspects of black military life. In addition to influencing relations between enlisted men and their officers, the treatment they could expect if captured, the pay they received, and their prospects for promotion from the ranks, these policies affected the nature of military justice and discipline, the care afforded sick and wounded soldiers, and the food, clothing, and equipment issued to healthy ones. Taken together, these policies sensitized black soldiers to any act that might be deemed discriminatory. In such a context, racially innocent actions inexorably acquired racial meaning. The harsh discipline white officers meted out to black subordinates in many instances may have differed little from their punishment of white inferiors. In the eyes of former slaves, however, a white man wielding a lash against a black one conveyed an unambiguous image of slavery. Just as white officers instituted policies based upon their understanding of racial differences, blacks protested against perceived abuses.

The course of the war widened the distance that Union policies had created between white and black soldiers. Because black soldiers entered the army at different times than white ones and fought in different theaters under different commanders, they came to see the war in different terms. The timing of black entry into the war suggests how these differences complemented those created by Union policies to give the black military experience its distinctive character.

By the middle of 1863, when a significant number of black troops took the field for the first time, white soldiers had been battling the rebels for over two years. Many had grown disenchanted with a war that seemed to have no end, and a considerable number evinced little sympathy for changing Union war aims – particularly emancipation. Black soldiers rarely shared this estrangement, however disillusioned they might have been by some aspects of federal policy. Having struggled for the right to bear arms in defense of their country, they were anxious to strike a blow against the slaveholding South. While many white soldiers wearied as the war dragged on, black enthusiasm grew with the Union's commitment to freedom and to the effort – however feeble and reluctant – to eliminate the most glaring racial inequities from military life.

The timing of their entry into the army affected black soldiers in other ways as well. The war made different demands on Union soldiers after 1863 than before. By the time black soldiers took the field, Confederate forces had been swept from the Mississippi Valley and parts of the Atlantic seaboard. With their removal, the Union army required large bodies of troops to secure the vast expanse of the occupied South and to protect its lengthening supply lines. No matter who composed the federal army after 1863, thousands of Union soldiers would be guarding railroad bridges and telegraph lines, manning artillery stations, constructing fortifications, and protecting contraband camps. That blacks entered the war just at the moment Union manpower needs took a new form determined much of the course of black service.

Could they fight? The question haunted the debate over black enlistment and followed black soldiers into the army. Black soldiers longed for the opportunity to test their mettle on the field of battle and thus resolve lingering doubts about their manhood and demonstrate their worthiness for full citizenship. Yet, the Union army needed large numbers of soldiers to do everything but fight. That need complemented the widespread belief that black soldiers could better handle shovels than guns and that, as the Emancipation Proclamation suggested, black soldiers should serve mainly to relieve white men for front-line duty. In many instances black soldiers found themselves serving as nothing more than uniformed laborers.

Heavy fatigue duty wore out clothing as quickly as it wore down bodies. When black soldiers exhausted their $3 monthly clothing allowance, quartermasters deducted the cost of additional clothing from their $7 monthly pay, thus salting the wound of discriminatory pay. Long days of fatigue duty strung end on end sapped the morale of black soldiers, and lack of drill compromised their military efficiency. Both they and their officers, including many antislavery champions of black enlistment, protested discriminatory labor assignments which neither military strategy nor the dignity of Union service seemed to warrant. But if they protested, they could lift but an enfeebled voice in search of public sympathy, and if black soldiers threatened mutiny, they were often too tired even to stack their arms, let alone raise them. Finally, in the face of overwhelming evidence of injustice, the most damning of which was the disproportionately high morbidity afflicting black soldiers, in June 1864 Adjutant General Thomas banned excessive fatigue duty for black troops and required that their assignments to labor details be proportionate to those of their white comrades. Many commanders ignored the order and continued to work black soldiers more like beasts of burden than like national defenders, but eventually General Thomas's command established a norm.

Just as Union policies and the course of the war distinguished the lives of black soldiers from those of white ones, so they fractured the black military experience in a variety of ways. Black soldiers brought diverse experiences and expectations to soldiering. Some had grown up in cities, attended schools taught by prominent clergymen, traveled widely, and enjoyed freedom for generations. Others had come from the tight, overwhelmingly black world of the plantation and knew little of life beyond the slave quarter. Some entered military service as young men, hardly more than children; others joined the army late in life and had children of their own. Whether black soldiers had been free men or slaves, Northerners or

Southerners, artisans or field hands; whether they had been raised among the black majority of the Carolina lowcountry or the white majority of the Northern states: all these circumstances in some measure influenced the course of black military life. Such diversity shaped the reactions of black soldiers to Union policies and affected the implementation of those policies. Free blacks, who were generally better educated and more cosmopolitan than slaves, marched into military service with hopes and aspirations different from those of slaves. While black soldiers who had just escaped bondage may well have seen military service as partial payment for their liberty — as many Union officials suggested — those who had been free before the war saw little personal gain in the reward of liberty. The inequities of black military life thus seemed particularly galling to those black soldiers who had been free. Not surprisingly, they led demands for commissioned office and monopolized those ranks after Union policy changed. Brandishing a protest tradition generations in the making and using their connections with white antislavery advocates, they initiated complaints about federal pay policies and other inequities within the army. Although soldiers who had been slaves joined these protests and initiated still others, the free black regiments generally took the lead. Regiments composed of former slaves appear to have resorted to direct action more often than did the former freemen — as Sergeant Walker's mutiny suggests — perhaps because former slaves enjoyed less complete mastery of the mechanism of formal petitioning or less confidence in its efficacy.

Differences among black soldiers extended beyond the mechanics of protest to the sources of grievance. Lack of sensitivity to distinctions among blacks frequently left white officers mystified at the variety of reactions to the same policies. When army quartermasters altered the diet of black soldiers to include more pork and corn bread, Southern-born soldiers welcomed the change, but Northern-born blacks, accustomed to beef and wheat bread, complained bitterly. In ways similar if not as dramatic, cultural differences between those who practiced skilled trades and enjoyed literacy and those who lacked skills or education affected the deployment of black soldiers and their relations with their officers and their fellow soldiers. Even within slave regiments, artisans, house servants, and other privileged bondsmen provided the bulk of the noncommissioned officers. The structure of the black community shaped the structure of black military life. Occasionally physiological differences supplemented cultural ones. Like whites, blacks raised in different disease environments had developed different immunities, so that for some black soldiers assignment to subtropical regions confirmed commonplace stereotypes about the ability of black people to survive in such areas, while it inevitably resulted in disaster for others.

Although the changing nature of the war consigned many black soldiers to labor and support duties, it sent others into fierce confrontations with the enemy. Again, the time and place of enlistment, the skills and knowledge blacks brought to soldiering, the personal temperament and political influence of particular commanders, and the Union army's need for front-line troops all helped determine who would fight and how they would fight. From the moment black soldiers entered the war, politically potent abolitionist proponents of black enlistment pressed the War Department and army field officers to send black soldiers against the enemy as a means of demonstrating that blacks could and would stand up to their former masters. At Port Hudson, Milliken's Bend, and Fort Wagner, black soldiers quickly proved that battlefield heroics knew no color line. But even after they had established their martial credentials, all black soldiers did not enjoy the same opportunity to face the enemy. Because of their earlier entry into the war and their abolitionist connections, units composed disproportionately of Louisiana and Northern freemen played a large role in the early battles, as did the first slave soldiers recruited in South Carolina and Louisiana. In the years that followed, the considerable reputations of these first regiments, as well as their strategic locations, continued to thrust them into an active combat role. For much the same reasons, other black regiments rarely engaged the enemy. In the Mississippi Valley, for example, most black soldiers saw little combat, in some measure because Union troops had already secured the region and in some measure because many of the region's commanders remained skeptical of the military abilities of blacks. Nonetheless, the changing course of the war could deprive even skeptical commanders of the luxury of excluding blacks from battle and could put black soldiers face to face with the enemy. In the final grueling operations of the eastern theater, General Ulysses S. Grant summoned every available Union soldier to assault the Confederate strongholds in Virginia. Grant's armies included the largest concentration of black soldiers engaged at any time during the war, most of them eventually organized into the Union army's only all-black army corps. In the trenches before Richmond and Petersburg, black soldiers, like white ones, dug earthworks, held the Union lines, pressed the rebel defenses, and at long last participated in the triumphant march into the capital of the vanquished Confederacy. Thus by war's end nearly all black soldiers received a taste of combat, though even then the course of the war continued to determine how they fought.

For the men who fought, the Civil War was a traumatic event that molded their lives and those of their descendants in countless ways. It elevated some to new heights of glory and power, propelling them into political and entrepreneurial careers. It shattered others. The thousands of limbless men found in all corners of America long after the shooting stopped provided grim reminders of the continuing impact of the war. For generations after the war ended, the outcome of the struggle determined the social relations, economic standing, and political allegiance of millions of Americans. That emancipation accompanied enlistment for most black soldiers heightened the impact of military service on black life. Because so many black soldiers simultaneously achieved freedom and reached maturity, the military experience took on an even larger meaning for black soldiers, their families, the black community, and, ultimately, the entire society.

Soldiering provided black men with more than legal freedom. In dramatic and undeniable ways military service countered the degradation that had undermined black self-esteem during the antebellum years. Battlefield confrontations with the slaveholding enemy exhilarated black soldiers by demonstrating in the most elemental manner the essential equality of men. But nothing more fully reveals the revolutionary impact of soldiering on black life than the transit of black men from slaves to liberators. In smashing the manacles that bound their people, black soldiers elevated themselves and transformed their own consciousness. In their own eyes, in the eyes of the black community, and, however reluctantly, in the eyes of the nation, black men gained a new standing by donning the Union blue and participating in the nation's great triumph.

A good deal of the liberating force of the black military experience derived not from great battles with the slaveholding enemy or stark confrontation with bondage but from military routine. Black soldiers savored the dignity of standing picket, with the right to challenge trespassers, no matter what their race or rank. As participants in foraging parties, they witnessed the futile anger of former masters who lost their slaves, their crops, their livestock, and even their homes to the claims of "military necessity." They gained a new sense of their own place in society while guarding captured Confederate soldiers, whose dejected demeanor and powerless situation contrasted markedly with former boasts of racial invincibility. Even the most mundane activities—the mastery of the manual of arms, the deployment of large, complicated weapons, and the execution of complex evolutions—provided new sources of pride and accomplishment.

Beyond the battlefield or even the drillfield, military service transformed the lives of black soldiers. As slaves or even freemen, blacks generally viewed the world through a narrow lens. As soldiers, they traveled broadly, met a wider variety of people, and expanded their range of experience. More important, black soldiers had occasion to see the world from positions of dominance as well as subordination. Although they continued to answer to higher authority, black soldiers frequently found themselves in circumstances where they alone commanded the field. Their new knowledge and authority burst the bonds of subservience bred by slavery and second-class citizenship. Soldiering thus granted black men far greater control over their own destiny and fostered a new self-confidence.

Skills and knowledge gained in the service enlarged this new self-confidence in numerous ways. Army schools offered black soldiers access to the printed word, an opportunity legally denied slaves and even some black freemen before the war. Black soldiers, like freedpeople generally, rushed to take advantage of book learning. Literacy not only allowed black soldiers to communicate with their families and advance into the noncommissioned ranks, but also provided the means to petition against injustice and to articulate their vision of the new world of freedom. Education in the army advanced along other lines as well. Regimental chaplains regularly tutored black soldiers in a variety of subjects, practical as well as moral. Although many chaplains filtered their message through a brand of religious paternalism that black soldiers found unpalatable, lectures on everything from standard sanitary procedures to the Constitution of the United States enlarged the world of men long kept ignorant of such subjects and encouraged them to widen their intellectual horizons. In many regiments, black soldiers joined together to build schools, to hire teachers, and to form library and debating societies.

The struggle for equality within the Union army also taught important lessons. Not only did congressional provision of equal pay and the War Department's tardy acquiescence on the question of commissioning officers stir optimism about eventual equality, but the struggle itself awakened men previously excluded from the political process to the possibilities of redressing their grievances, informed them of the means by which their goals might be achieved, and identified the federal government as a forum for obtaining justice. Northern free blacks had a long tradition of political protest, and they drew on it freely. But the tactics pioneered by Northern freemen passed quickly to slave soldiers, most of whom had no previous political experience. Before long, regiments composed of newly liberated slaves petitioned and protested with all the skill and tenacity of those whose members were freeborn, demanding that the government they fought to preserve accord them and their families the dignity and protection due to all its citizens. In so doing, former slaves learned something about the system of government under which Americans lived. They came to understand that justice depended not on the favor of a single powerful individual, but on impersonal rules and regulations which governed all citizens. For while some army officers played the petty tyrant and others willingly countenanced such autocratic behavior, behind their arbitrary actions stood a forest of regulations that ruled military life. In learning how to deal with abstract law as well as personal authority, previously enslaved black soldiers took their first steps as free men. And in the process, they not only asserted their claim to citizenship, but also broke down the barriers that distinguished freemen and bondsmen and thereby unified the black community as never before.

Military service also offered some black soldiers opportunities for advancement that far exceeded those available during the antebellum years. Although the War Department balked at commissioning black officers until late in the war, it had no objection to the appointment of blacks to the noncommissioned ranks. Indeed, the difficulties inherent in balancing the often antagonistic interests of officers and enlisted men in a highly charged racial atmosphere encouraged Union officials to turn this task over to selected black soldiers. Standing between the largely white officer corps and the black enlisted ranks, black sergeants and corporals played a role similar to that of a factory foreman or even an antebellum slave driver. While they enjoyed a considerable measure of power, their authority was never large enough to satisfy either those below or those above them in rank. Their responsibilities for assignment and discipline frequently alienated black enlisted men without gaining the approbation of white officers. But because black noncommissioned officers camped with the other enlisted men and shared their daily routine, as well as so many other common experiences, they generally gained the trust of the men they led. Black soldiers frequently took their problems to their sergeants and corporals, and these black officers assumed a leading role in presenting grievances and protests to higher authorities. Advocacy of this kind exacted a toll, as rebuffs brought reduction in rank or other punishments. But black noncommissioned officers — along with the few commissioned ones — generally gained in stature from their wartime role and transferred their positions of leadership to civilian life when the war ended.

The black military experience affected many more than those who wore the Union uniform. Soldiering altered the lives of the families of black soldiers from the moment of enlistment. In some places, enlistment ensured the safety and secured the freedom of black people. In the border states, where slavery persisted unimpeached by the Emancipation Proclamation, enlistment of husbands and fathers established the only claim to liberty for the families of black soldiers. Elsewhere, black soldiers guarded contraband camps and Union-held plantations to prevent Confederate raiders from recapturing and reenslaving loved ones. But the same act of enlistment that provided protection for some black families encouraged the abuse and confinement of others. Angry masters who vowed to take revenge upon slave women and children if black men dared to enlist had few compunctions about making good their threats.

After enlistment, the experience of black soldiers continued to shape the lives of those who remained behind. While the questions of equal pay and protection appeared in the guise of abstract justice to interested whites, these same issues touched the wives and children of black soldiers in a direct and immediate manner. After all, the treatment accorded black prisoners was a matter of life and death, and the difference between $7 and $13 a month was often the difference between subsistence and starvation for many black families. By the same token, the impoverished condition of families left at home or liable to abuse by Confederate guerrillas or former masters influenced the conduct of black soldiers. Nothing more surely moved black soldiers to protest than news of the material hardship or physical suffering of their families.

Soldiering deeply affected relations between black men and black women. Everywhere the enlistment of black soldiers designated black men as the liberators and defenders of black women and children, who, whatever their wartime service, occupied the position of defenseless dependents. Army service thus assigned an active role to black men and a passive one to black women in the process of liberation. Although black women fully participated in the destruction of slavery and the struggle for freedom, the official sanction of black men as liberators brought the sexual division between black men and women closer to the American ideal of protector and protected. The uneven impact of military life on men and women also widened the social distance between black men and black women. For if armed service – in all its various aspects – helped free black men from the world of bondage and second-class citizenship, black women enjoyed no comparable experience. Whatever changes freedom brought to the lives of black women, they rarely equaled the dramatic changes of status and experience that accompanied military duty.

The actions of black soldiers reverberated beyond the family circle. Black soldiers enthusiastically bore the news of emancipation. In carrying freedom's sword, black soldiers demonstrated that liberty was as much the product of the black man's valor as it was the white man's gift. Slaves seemed to understand this, and they welcomed black soldiers with special enthusiasm. Fugitives followed the soldiers' line of march, bondsmen and women fearful of their masters' wrath took refuge among black regiments, and everywhere crowds of blacks lined the roads to cheer. In bearing the message of liberty, black soldiers also aided the passage of black people from slavery to freedom in countless practical ways. They informed freedpeople of their newly won rights, they tutored them in the nuances of federal policy, and they elaborated on the opportunities that liberty offered. Although the message they carried – like the rumored possibility of land – often proved to be an empty promise, it encouraged freedpeople to press their former masters and, indeed, their new Yankee rulers in ways that expanded freedom.

Blacks everywhere rallied to the support of their sable arm. Associations to aid sick and wounded soldiers and to provide for the widows and orphans of the fallen sprang up throughout the North and liberated South. Formerly slave or formerly free, blacks welcomed black soldiers into their homes and onto the podium at public meetings and celebrations. They took pride in the martial accomplishments of black soldiers and shared the indignities black soldiers suffered at the hands of federal policy makers. The black and abolitionist press provided an important link between soldiers and the larger community.[34] Reports from black soldiers, mostly chaplains and noncommissioned officers, filled newspaper columns in the free states and the occupied South. They not only provided news of the whereabouts of black units for concerned families and friends, but also told tales of black soldiers in mortal combat with the slaveholding enemy, thereby allowing the larger black community to share in the destruction of slavery. The press informed blacks and antislavery whites about discriminatory Union policies, bringing the issues of unequal pay, the denial of military commissions, and the abuse of black prisoners of war to the home front. By counterpoising black battlefield heroics with the inequities of black military life, black leaders quickly put soldiering to work in the struggle for equal rights. After 1863, calls for the end of discrimination rarely failed to mention the importance of black soldiers in defending the Union. Thus for practical as well as emotional reasons, the military experience drew the black community together. Along with emancipation, victories on the issues of equal pay and black officers fueled the optimism and sharpened the political consciousness of all blacks. Although most black men would not be enfranchised until several years after the war ended, black participation in the politics of reconstruction began with enlistment in the Union army.

The black military experience imparted more than unalloyed optimism. Heroism and self-sacrifice inspired some black soldiers, but the appalling carnage, the continuing inequities of military life, and the equivocal commitment of federal officials to black advancement left others disillusioned. The experience of black soldiers warned all

[34] See, for example, the African Methodist Episcopal *Christian Recorder*, New York *Anglo-African*, *Douglass' Monthly*, New Orleans *Tribune*, Beaufort *Free South*, *National Anti-Slavery Standard*, and *Liberator*.

blacks that, at best, the Yankees were unreliable allies whose interests only occasionally coincided with those of the black community. The frequent failure of army officers to correct transparent injustices and their willingness to reject the most heart-rending protests on the cold ground of military necessity left black soldiers and civilians alike more cynical than confident about the white man's army and the white man's government. While this cynicism estranged some from the political process, it hardened others to the struggle still ahead and deepened their determination to press on. In either case, the cynicism reflected a new sophistication, an understanding that, as in slave times, black people would have to keep their own counsel, that even in the moment of triumph nothing would come easily, and that political victories often cost as much as military ones.

The influence of soldiering on black life did not end when the shooting stopped. If anything, its importance grew. Many black soldiers remained in uniform as part of the Union army of occupation, and they continued to advise freedpeople on the new demands of freedom and the workings of the world beyond the plantation. Their presence, especially when commanded by sympathetic white officers, helped to limit violence against freedpeople and to prevent newly returned Confederate veterans from running roughshod over defenseless former slaves. Military service provided a steppingstone to leadership in the black community, as it did in postwar American society generally. With wartime responsibilities behind them, black soldiers often became deeply involved in the black communities where they were stationed. Some took wives from among the local population and fully entered local community life, thereby fusing the experience of the liberator and the liberated. Drawing on their martial experience and the confidence it engendered, black soldiers framed the aspirations of many of the newly freed and also helped reconstruct the black community's institutional infrastructure to meet the demands of freedom. They frequently took the lead in organizing the black community, establishing schools, building churches, and founding fraternal societies. In the first conventions blacks held following the war, black soldiers often dominated debate. By standing armed and ready to aid black people, and by bringing knowledge and confidence to many black communities, black soldiers remained significant figures in black life after emancipation.

In much the same way that the liberating impact of the black military experience radiated out from black soldiers and their families into the larger black community, so it spread into white society as well. Abolitionist officers, many of whom had led the fight for black enlistment, provided the most important agents of the dissemination of a new racial liberality. Standing with black soldiers through the war and, to some degree, suffering from identification with black troops, their commitment to equality inside the army deepened their commitment to equality in American society generally. Many remained in the South as Freedmen's Bureau agents, Republican politicians, and schoolteachers at war's end. Others who returned to the North joined with blacks, including many who had served under their command, to form a nub of consistent support for racial equality within the Republican party. They attacked second-class citizenship within American society just as they had attacked it in the army. Pointing to the contribution of black soldiers in preserving the Union, they helped roll back the color line in the Northern states and urged a radical reconstruction of the defeated Confederacy.[35]

Indeed, even before the Radical Republicans gained control of Congress, the role of black soldiers had become an important element in arguments that black men should play an active role in governing the reconstructed slave states. In the spring of 1864, while nudging conservative Louisiana unionists into a position more consonant with changing congressional sentiment, Lincoln singled out former soldiers as one group of blacks who might be granted the suffrage.[36] In the years that followed, others – whether resisting more extensive changes in the racial status quo or urging still greater ones – drew upon black military service to make similar arguments. The black military experience thus expanded and deepened the nation's commitment to equal rights.

Perhaps no one more fully understood the role black soldiers played in inflating black aspirations and enlarging black opportunities than did members of the old master class. Even when they admitted that black soldiers acquitted themselves in an impeccable manner, former slave masters complained bitterly about the unsettling influence of black troops on the old pattern of subordination. Once freedpeople came in contact with black troops, they deferred less readily and they labored less willingly. By their presence as well as their words and actions, black soldiers convinced blacks and whites alike that the old world was gone forever.

As black soldiers and the black community gloried in the world turned upside down, former slaveholders detested the revolution and despised black soldiers as symbols of the new state of affairs. They pleaded for the removal of black soldiers from the South, complaining not only of the arrogance or misconduct of the soldiers themselves, but also of the social disruption that would certainly follow from the provo-

[35] See, for example, Norwood P. Hallowell, *The Meaning of Memorial Day* (Boston, 1896); Thomas J. Morgan, *The Negro in America and the Ideal American Republic* (Philadelphia, 1898).
[36] Lincoln, *Collected Works*, vol. 7, p. 243.

cative nature of a black military presence. Such appeals, especially when filtered through white unionists, had a powerful influence on federal officials and speeded the demobilization of many black units and the relegation of still others to distant corners of the South, far from the centers of black life. Where black soldiers remained in service, whites did not accept their presence easily, and violence between black soldiers and white civilians became commonplace.

While in the ranks of the Union army, black soldiers had protection enough. But once mustered out of service, much of that protection vanished. Black veterans became fair game for white regulators and terrorists, and, when former soldiers eluded such gangs, their families frequently became the victims of violent abuse. In some areas of the South, attacks on black soldiers and their families became full-scale pogroms.

Such assaults only confirmed the importance of the black military experience. Brutal attacks on black soldiers reemphasized the fact that at the moment of emancipation black soldiers broke the bonds of servitude and paved the way for freedom. The image of long lines of black soldiers marching through the South with slave masters fleeing at their approach spurred blacks to seek a fuller freedom and sustained them in the face of continued adversity. Throughout the postwar years, the black contribution to Union victory provided a firm basis for claims to equality, and black veterans continued to play a central role in black communities, North and South. The skills and experience black men gained during the war not only propelled many into positions of leadership and sustained the prominence of others, but also shaped the expectations and aspirations of all black people. The achievements and pride engendered by military service helped to make the new world of freedom.

PART I

Black Enlistment and the Collapse of Chattel Bondage

Early Recruitment: Lowcountry South Carolina, Georgia, and Florida; Louisiana; and Kansas

UNION occupation of Hilton Head, South Carolina, in November 1861, and New Orleans, Louisiana, in April 1862, brought the question of arming black soldiers to the fore. Abolitionist generals David Hunter in South Carolina and John W. Phelps in Louisiana envisioned a slave army of liberation assaulting the Confederacy from their respective points of command. Simultaneously, James H. Lane, the fiery senator from Kansas, pressed the War Department for permission to recruit black soldiers in his home state. Ignoring the Lincoln administration's equivocation on, if not opposition to their requests, the three men independently recruited black soldiers on their own authority. Blacks and their abolitionist allies had long pressed federal policy makers without success for black enlistment. The actions of Hunter, Phelps, and Lane made it impossible for the Lincoln administration to evade the issue any longer.[1]

LOWCOUNTRY SOUTH CAROLINA, GEORGIA, AND FLORIDA

General David Hunter itched for the opportunity to play the liberator. Appointed Commander of the Department of the South in March 1862, Hunter moved rapidly to realize his ambition.[2]

[1] Published accounts of early recruitment include: Thomas Wentworth Higginson, *Army Life in a Black Regiment* (Boston, 1869); Joseph T. Wilson, *The Black Phalanx: A History of the Negro Soldiers of the United States in the Wars of 1775–1812 and 1861–65* (Hartford, 1888), pp. 111–65; George W. Williams, *A History of the Negro Troops in the War of the Rebellion, 1861–1865* (New York, 1888), pp. 78–101; Willie Lee Rose, *Rehearsal for Reconstruction: The Port Royal Experiment* (Indianapolis, 1964), chap. 6; and Dudley Taylor Cornish, *The Sable Arm: Negro Troops in the Union Army, 1861–1865* (New York, 1956), chaps. 2, 3, & 4.
[2] Benjamin F. Thomas and Harold M. Hyman, *Stanton: The Life and Times of Lincoln's Secretary of War* (New York, 1962), pp. 234–38, esp. 236.

Whereas his predecessor, General Thomas W. Sherman, had confined blacks to the role of laborers, Hunter quickly brought black men under arms. Early in April 1862, Hunter asked the War Department for authorization to arm 50,000 blacks for service against the rebels. He requested muskets for them as well as some kind of distinctive uniform, considering red pantaloons appropriate.[3] When the department did nothing, Hunter acted on his own. In mid-April, he freed the blacks in the area around Fort Pulaski, Georgia, with the intention of putting the able-bodied to work for the quartermaster. Early the following month, Hunter proclaimed the liberation of all the slaves in South Carolina, Georgia, and Florida. President Abraham Lincoln abruptly countermanded Hunter's plan to remove the keystone of Southern society.[4] But if he could not bring the Confederate house down at once, Hunter would at least shake its foundation.

On the same day that he issued his emancipation proclamation, Hunter clarified his recruitment policy and reasserted his determination to bring former slaves into Union service. He ordered the conscription of all able-bodied black men aged eighteen to forty-five.[5] Executing the order brought the military into sharp conflict both with Treasury Department agents in charge of abandoned plantations and with former slaves, who objected to the unanticipated and unexplained impressment.

In the eyes of Treasury officials, Hunter's conscription order both obstructed their work provisioning the islands' swollen black population and jeopardized the blacks' future as freedpeople. Under Treasury Department tutelage, Sea Island blacks had grown their own food, had harvested the lucrative, long-staple cotton crops left standing in the fields by fleeing masters, and had begun to sow another year's crop of cotton and vegetables. Viewing continued production of market staples as crucial to a successful transition from slavery to freedom, the Treasury officials argued that removing the able-bodied men both threatened the islands' food supply and undermined their fledgling experiment in free labor.[6] Treasury officials also scored Hunter's policy for its debilitating effects on the morale of the newly freed slaves.

Blacks considered the prospect of impressment equally forbidding and feared it would mean permanent separation of families. Likening

---

[3] *Official Records*, ser. 1, vol. 6, pp. 263–64.

[4] *Official Records*, ser. 3, vol. 2, pp. 42–43.

[5] A.A.A.G. Ed. W. Smith to Brig. Gen. H. W. Benham, 9 May 1862, Letters Received, ser. 2255, Northern Dist. Dept. of the South, RG 393 Pt. 2 No. 130 [C-1633].

[6] The best account of conflict between military and Treasury Department authorities is Rose, *Rehearsal for Reconstruction*.

it to sale during slave times, they were naturally terrified. To some, it confirmed former masters' repeated warnings that the Yankees only intended to sell them as slaves in Cuba. Heavy-handed federal action led Sea Island blacks to wonder if they had merely exchanged their old masters for new ones.

Ignoring protesting Treasury agents and black victims alike, Hunter continued to organize his black regiment. In the summer of 1862, the House of Representatives passed a resolution requesting that Secretary of War Edwin M. Stanton furnish information about Hunter's activities. Stanton replied evasively, observing that Hunter had yet to submit a report of his operations.[7] But if Stanton evaded, Hunter relished the opportunity to pontificate. In his famous "fugitive masters" letter, he sarcastically informed Congress of precisely what he was doing and why. Yet neither his boldness nor the publicity it generated helped Hunter's immediate efforts. In August—with the War Department still unwilling to recognize and pay the regiment—he disbanded it, retaining only one company in the service.

Despite his frustration, Hunter did not abandon the plan of eventually organizing a black regiment. For the present, he relinquished control of the one remaining company to General Rufus Saxton, who had come to the islands as General Sherman's quartermaster, and whom Stanton had appointed to supervise contraband affairs in April 1862. Under Saxton, Hunter's dream of a black regiment was realized.

Hard on the heels of Hunter's disbandment of the regiment, Saxton asked Stanton for permission to recruit and arm 5,000 black quartermaster employees, whom he euphemistically termed "laborers" but whose intended use as an armed force to protect lowcountry contrabands he did not disguise.[8] Surprisingly, Stanton not only authorized the 5,000 quartermaster laborers but also an additional 5,000 black soldiers, who would "receive the same pay and rations as are allowed by law to volunteers in the service."[9] Stanton's pay guarantee removed one of the chief obstacles standing in the way of Hunter's black regiment and paved the way for the formal organization of the 1st South Carolina Volunteers in mid-October 1862. In the interim, Saxton laid plans for his regiment with both Stanton and Massachusetts Governor John A. Andrew and Andrew's abolitionist associates. Within a month of organization, Saxton named as

---

[7] *Official Records*, ser. 3, vol. 2, pp. 147–48.

[8] Mansfield French, a missionary to the freedpeople at Port Royal, detailed his own role in securing Stanton's approval of the plan to enlist black soldiers in [Mansfield French] to Brevet Major Genl. R. Saxton, 4 Sept. 1865, enclosed in M. French to Hon. E. M. Stanton, 24 Oct. 1865, W-2260 1865, Letters Received, ser. 12, RG 94 [K-570].

[9] *Official Records*, ser. 1, vol. 14, pp. 377–78.

commander of the regiment Thomas W. Higginson, radical aboli-tionist and former ally of John Brown. Despite smoldering black resentment of Hunter's earlier impressment, the regiment filled to capacity almost immediately. Higginson, like others, believed that habits of obedience developed during slavery made blacks ideal sol-diers, and he commented repeatedly that only the noblest of motives prompted his men to enlist. Early in 1863 recruitment for the 2nd South Carolina Volunteers began, followed shortly by the organiza-tion of the 3rd Volunteers.

By March 1863, voluntary enlistment in the 2nd and 3rd South Carolina Volunteers began to lag, so Hunter (who, as department commander, had superior authority to Saxton's regarding black troops) began another mandatory draft of able-bodied men and then authorized formation of the 4th South Carolina Volunteers. Hunter broadened the age distribution of eligible draftees by raising the upper limit from forty-five to fifty. More significantly, in light of opposition to his earlier draft, he tagged for conscription only un-employed contrabands.[10] However, Hunter allowed his recruiters to determine who was unemployed, and as a result they took whom-ever they pleased. Only a fine line separated conscription and kid-napping as Hunter's recruiters ransacked the islands.

In the year since the initial conscription, supervision of the leased plantations had passed out of the hands of the Treasury Department and into Saxton's care at the headquarters of contraband affairs. In the transfer, blacks employed on the plantations lost the benefit of official advocacy independent of military priorities that they had en-joyed under Treasury tutelage. Their protest was muted in the sec-ond Hunter conscription.

Black military laborers, on the other hand, did not suffer from the same lack of advocates. Their military employers objected loudly after Hunter's recruiters stripped the labor forces at several highly strategic fortifications. Stung by the protests and fearful of possible military disruption, Hunter forbade recruiters to conscript employ-ees of the engineer's department. Nonetheless, recruiters claiming ignorance of the ban continued impressing until their raid on the laborers at Fort Clinch, Florida, provoked enough furor to end the recruiters' depredations.

At the end of 1863, Hunter's successor, General Quincy A. Gill-more, began recruiting new regiments of lowcountry blacks under the auspices of the War Department's Bureau of Colored Troops, without ensuring that Saxton's regiments either reached or retained their full strength.[11] In February 1864, the South Carolina Volun-

---

[10] *Official Records*, ser. 1, vol. 14, pp. 1020–21, 429–30.
[11] *Official Records*, ser. 3, vol. 3, pp. 1183–84.

teer regiments – all still far below full strength – joined the Colored Troops organization, becoming the 33rd, 34th, and 21st U.S. Colored Infantry (the latter representing a combination of the 3rd and 4th South Carolina Volunteer regiments). With that, recruitment in the lowcountry passed entirely into the hands of recruiting officers working at large for the Bureau of Colored Troops. Despite the new organization, the concern over past abuses, and the general orders suppressing involuntary enlistments, military laborers working literally under Saxton's nose suffered summary impressment as late as May 1864.[12] Moreover, in late summer 1864, the new department commander, General John G. Foster, ordered the conscription of all "unemployed" black men of military age as well as "deserters" working on government plantations, a plan that would all but guarantee recruitment by force, as the experience of nearly two and one-half years had demonstrated.[13]

Though the South Carolina regiments enjoyed formal War Department approval, ultimately joining the Bureau of Colored Troops organization, the tentativeness of their early organization continued to plague them. As Colonel Higginson later observed, the first black man to die in the Union cause was a Sea Islander – ironically named John Brown – who fell in August 1862 fighting in conjunction with the company Hunter retained in service.[14] Yet neither Brown nor the blacks whom Hunter recruited enjoyed the distinction that their early service should have won them. The four South Carolina regiments struggled for recognition of their legitimacy until March 1865, when Congress finally conferred it.[15]

LOUISIANA

In Louisiana, initial recruitment of black soldiers followed a pattern similar to that of South Carolina. Federal forces captured New Orleans and the surrounding countryside in April 1862, long before the Lincoln administration condoned wholesale enlistment of blacks. But unlike his counterpart in South Carolina, General Benjamin F. Butler, commander of the Department of the Gulf in Louisiana, felt no

---

[12] See Lieut. T. Mahoney to Lt. Col. M. R. Morgan, 25 Apr. 1864, M-81 1864, Letters Received, ser. 4109, Dept. of the South, RG 393 Pt. 1 [C-1326]; and Lt. Timothy Mahoney to Capt. T. A. P. Champlin, 7 May 1864, M-87 1864, Letters Received, ser. 4109, Dept. of the South, RG 393 Pt. 1 [C-1326].

[13] *Official Records*, ser. 3, vol. 4, p. 621.

[14] Higginson, *Army Life*, pp. 272–77.

[15] *Official Records*, ser. 3, vol. 4, p. 1223.

need to press Washington to admit blacks to federal armed service. However, his subordinate, General John W. Phelps, recognized the strategic and political value of arming Southern slaves against their rebellious masters and urged Butler to authorize formation of such a force. Phelps pushed and Butler stalled. The confrontation between the two paralleled the struggle between Hunter and Stanton.

General Phelps, commanding U.S. forces at Camp Parapet outside of New Orleans, forced consideration of the question of enlisting black soldiers shortly after federal forces occupied southern Louisiana. A veteran army officer and antislavery advocate, Phelps boldly announced his intention to destroy slavery in a December 1861 proclamation.[16] By the following spring he openly gave refuge to runaway slaves and refused to permit their masters to reclaim them. According to planters' complaints to General Butler, Phelps permitted troops under his command to inculcate a spirit of wholesale insubordination among slaves in the area surrounding the camp. In certain cases, his soldiers reportedly meted out vengeance to planters who had mistreated their slaves. By late May 1862, such complaints prompted Butler to advise Phelps to keep his troops under better control and to harbor only those contrabands whose labor he could use.[17]

In June 1862, Phelps reiterated his opposition to slavery and recommended that the President abolish it forthwith. In the name of the suffering slaves, he urged formulation of a national policy on the future of Southern blacks.[18] Central to this policy would be emancipation and enlistment.

As Phelps argued the case for enlistment, General Butler went to equally great lengths to deny both the necessity and the wisdom of arming blacks. While not objecting to using slaves against the Confederacy, Butler contended that military conditions did not demand black troops, and, maintaining that blacks were naturally terrified of firearms, he doubted they could ever become effective soldiers. Butler expressed admiration for the mulatto officers of the former Confederate Native Guard, praising their intelligence, urbanity, and sincerity, but he nonetheless declined to accept their April 1862 offer of service in the United States Army.[19]

As the two officers tested the national political winds, neither found the currents entirely to his satisfaction. Late in July 1862, Phelps decided to force Butler's hand on the issue and proceeded to

[16] "Proclamation of Brig. Gen. Phelps to the People of the South West," 4 Dec. 1861, P-14 1861, Letters Received, ser. 1755, Dept. of the Gulf, RG 393 Pt. 1 [C-500].
[17] *Official Records*, ser. 1, vol. 15, pp. 446–47.
[18] *Official Records*, ser. 1, vol. 15, pp. 486–90.
[19] *Official Records*, ser. 1, vol. 15, pp. 441–42.

raise five companies of black troops. Butler hewed closely to the national policy against arming blacks, while at the same time pressing the War Department for additional guidance on the question. The department demurred, leaving Phelps and Butler to settle the matter themselves.

The final break came at the end of July 1862, when Phelps asked Butler for arms and equipment for the contrabands he had organized. Butler evaded the question, instead ordering Phelps to use the contrabands to cut down surrounding trees, which provided a vantage point for rebel attacks. Viewing the order as a humiliating rejection of his proposal and, even more insulting, as a suggestion that he and his officers serve as slave drivers, Phelps resigned. Butler rejected the resignation, refused to authorize Phelps's plan, and ordered him to start chopping wood. He also submitted the matter to the War Department, which took no immediate action, and Phelps's resignation stood.

From the outset, Butler and Phelps took fundamentally different positions regarding military use of blacks. Phelps envisioned arming escaped slaves in order to undermine the rebellion in the most practically and politically damaging way: by destroying the South's labor force and turning slaves against their masters. While no less committed to using every available weapon against the Confederacy, Butler preferred to use slaves as military laborers until Congress, the President, or the War Department decided to arm them. In the meantime, he found his available force of white soldiers more than adequate for the military needs of his department, and he refused to address the "vexed question" of using slaves as soldiers.

During the heat of the Phelps–Butler controversy, military manpower demands changed dramatically. Early in August 1862, a Confederate offensive forced Butler's troops to evacuate Baton Rouge and left him scrambling for more soldiers. He appealed for more men to General-in-Chief of the Army Henry W. Halleck, but to no avail. With the Native Guard's offer of service fresh in his mind, he saw a chance both to enlist at least one full regiment at a stroke and to eliminate the bitterness lingering from his confrontation with Phelps.

Butler "called on Africa," as he termed it, to relieve his shortage of men, and, as a consequence, became the first Union general successfully to organize a black regiment.[20] Butler made great capital out of that distinction and, even after leaving command of the Department of the Gulf and returning to his original command at Fortress Monroe, Virginia, he remained a prominent figure in the campaign to arm blacks. By the closing months of the war, Butler's

[20] See *Freedom*, ser. 2: doc. 127.

Army of the James, which included the only all-black army corps, contained virtually every black soldier fighting in the Virginia theater. Until he resigned his own commission in January 1865, Butler remained one of the most important military advocates of black recruitment.

Nonetheless, Butler's decision to enlist the Louisiana Native Guard did not signal his acceptance of Phelps's position. Phelps advocated arming slaves both to remove them from the side of the Confederacy and turn them against their former masters. Butler, on the other hand, mustered into service the free people of color who had earlier offered their services to the Confederacy and who, despite their changed loyalty, did not constitute the army of liberation that Phelps had envisioned. Hence the irony of the Louisiana recruitment settlement: not only did Butler claim credit for Phelps's work after he had drummed the abolitionist out of the service, but he also stripped Phelps's policy of its most radical element while placing himself in the forefront of the movement to enlist black soldiers.

KANSAS

Early recruitment in South Carolina and Louisiana proceeded under the auspices of military commanders and received formal War Department blessing by the summer of 1862. Recruitment of blacks in Kansas began without either. There, James H. Lane, grizzled veteran of the border wars and the state's newly minted United States senator, assumed that the recruiting commission issued him by the War Department in July 1862 entitled him to enlist blacks as well as whites into Union military service. And, not contenting himself with enlisting Kansas blacks, he sent agents throughout the North seeking recruits for his black regiment. Before long, complaints poured into the War Department about the detrimental effect of Lane's agents on white enlistment. Perhaps stung by such criticism, Lane attempted to affirm his right to recruit blacks. But in August and again in September, Stanton and General-in-Chief Halleck denied Lane any such authority. Nonetheless, Lane persisted and, as the governor of Kansas later observed, "The first Kansas Colored Regiment was raised in an irregular way, that is, it was done neither directly by the authorities of the State, nor by Federal Authority."[21] Indeed, Lane not only continued to muster blacks into

[21] Govr. Thos. Carney to A. Lincoln, 5 June 1863, #3175 1863, Letters Received Irregular, RG 107 [L-128].

the service under his own authority, but also appointed black recruiting agents with the promise they would serve as officers for the men they enlisted. In matters of pay and allowances, Lane vowed to treat black and white soldiers the same. Armed with such assurances, Lane's recruiters did their job well. Despite its unauthorized status, the 1st Kansas Colored Volunteers made a favorable impression when inspected in October 1862.

But Lane's singular action caused problems for his men. Receiving no pay, some simply left the regiment and were later arrested and court-martialed as deserters.[22] Others grew restless under military discipline without recognition – not to mention pay. In April 1863, Colonel James M. Williams of the 1st Kansas Colored Volunteers took the extraordinary action of relieving his men from their details on the fortifications at Camp Emancipation, Kansas, to cool their growing insubordination. Eventually the 1st Kansas Colored Volunteers received federal authorization (and, following the formation of the Bureau of Colored Troops, was renamed the 79th U.S. Colored Infantry), but the confusion of its unauthorized origins continued to plague the members of the regiment as they attempted to gain their promised commissions, equal pay and privileges, and, for many, any pay.[23] Not until January 1864 did the Bureau of Colored Troops provide pay for those who had volunteered in 1862 and then only at the lower rate black soldiers received.[24]

Because Hunter, Phelps, and Lane enlisted blacks without prior War Department approval, the earliest black regiments suffered the stain of illegitimacy throughout their existence. The men who served in these first black regiments had difficulty collecting pay, bounties, and pensions. But their pioneering role helped transform War Department policy, paving the way for the establishment of the Bureau of Colored Troops and the regular enrollment of black soldiers.

---

[22] Testimony of Sergeant Oram Miller and Corporal John McCartens, proceedings of general court-martial in the case of Private George True, 79th USCI, 2 May 1865, MM-2035, Court-Martial Case Files, ser. 15, RG 153 [H-42]. The court found True guilty of desertion and sentenced him to forfeit all pay and allowances for the period of his unauthorized absence and to return to duty.

[23] See *Freedom*, ser. 2: doc. 161, 134a–b.

[24] A.A. Genl. C. W. Foster to Col. John Williams, 16 Jan. 1864, vol. 2, pp. 113–14, Letters Sent, ser. 352, Colored Troops Division, RG 94 [B-500].

LOWCOUNTRY SOUTH CAROLINA, GEORGIA, AND FLORIDA

1: Treasury Department Special Agent to the Commander of the Department of the South

Beaufort [*S.C.*], Sunday, May 11. 1862

Sir, This evening I received from Brig. Gen. Stevens, through his adjutant, while I was at my headquarters on St. Helena Island, a circular, requesting me to aid in executing an order, issued by your command, for the collection of all negroes on the plantations, between 18 & 45, able to bear arms, – who are to be sent forthwith to Hilton Head. I issued prompt instructions to the superintendents to aid in the execution of the order, which requires the negroes to be sent to Beaufort to-morrow morning, and they are furnishing descriptive rolls of the persons required. While thus yielding ready obedience to military authority, – which must of necessity be paramount to all civil interests in your command, – I must respectfully beg leave, as the representative of another Department, to express my great regret for the order, and my reasons for such regret: –

The Treasury Department, in whose service I am, was early put in charge of the plantations. President Lincoln in an autograph note which I have with me, of date Feb. 15. 1862. desired the Secretary of the Treasury to give me such instructions in relation to the negroes here, as seemed to him judicious. Under date of Feb. 19, the Secretary gave me such instructions (a copy of which has been presented to yourself), the main purport of which is, that he desired "to prevent the deterioration of the estates, secure their best possible cultivation under the circumstances, and promote the welfare of the laborers." In this letter of instructions, he also approved a plan presented by myself for the cultivation of the plantations and the management of the negroes, in a report, a copy of which I have furnished to yourself, The War Department, under date of Feb. 18, sanctioned the enterprise, in an order to Gen. Sherman, which he made a part of General Order No. 17, dated March 8., announcing myself as General Superintendent and Director of the Negroes.

To the end aforesaid, the Treasury Department has already expended large amounts, viz, some $5000, for implements and seeds; has transported a large quantity of cotton seed from N.Y.; has purchased and sent here ninety mules and ten horses, at a cost in all of at least $15000; has forwarded me $10,000 to pay for labor, – some $3,200 of which I have expended, and shall expend some $2000 more as soon as proper pay-rolls have been made. Voluntary associations, with the sanction of the Government, have also paid salaries to the superintendents, who receive army rations; have forwarded large supplies of clothing, worth, to say the least, $10,000, if not double that amount. They have also forwarded supplies of meat for localities where we are trying to get along without rations. Schools also have been opened for the non-working population, and in the evening for those who work. With the week closing yesterday the planting of the crops has substantially closed. Some 6000 or 8000 acres, by a rough estimate, have been planted. The accurate statistics are being handed us, and I can give them in a few days. The corn, vegetables, and cotton, are up and growing. The season of cultivating has come; and without proper cultivation the crops planted will come to nothing; and the money expended by Government, as well as the labor, will be useless. All the hands, with few exceptions, now on the plantations, are useful for the cultivation of the growing crops; and only a few could be taken from them without substantial injury. Under these circumstances it is proposed to take from the plantations all able-bodied men between 18 & 45, – leaving only women and children, and old or sickly men, to cultivate the crops. There is no exception even for the ploughman or the foreman. Two thirds of the available force of the plantations, will be taken, – to say nothing of the injurious influence upon the sensitive minds and feelings of those who remain, greatly diminishing the results of their labor. Thus the public funds devoted to a work which has the sanction of the War and Treasury Departments, and the approval of the President, will have been, in a very large proportion, wasted. But the order has other than financial and industrial results. The cultivation of the plantations was a social experiment, which it was deemed important to make. It is a new and delicate one, and entitled to a fair trial. The conscription of these laborers will at once arrest it, and disorganize and defeat an enterprise now hopefully begun.

As the persons are to be taken to Hilton Head, and without their consent, I assume (though I trust under a misapprehension) that they are to be organized for military purposes without their consent. I deplore the probable effects of this on their minds. They are ignorant, suspicious, and sensitive. They have not acquired such confidence in us, – they have not so far recovered the manhood which two centuries of bondage have rooted out, – they do not, as yet, so realize that they have a country to fight for, as to make this, in my judgment, a safe way of dealing with them. I have been struck, and so have others associated with me been struck, with their indisposition to become soldiers. This indisposition will pass away; but only time and growing confidence in us will remove it.

I fear also that an enforced enlistment will give color to their masters' assurance that we were going to take them to Cuba. For these and other reasons which I have no time to give, I deplore the order which summarily calls these people to Hilton Head, there to be enrolled and enlisted. Even if they are to return, they would be excited by the trip; the families left behind would be in disorder, and all would be in suspense as to what would come next. I have grave apprehensions as to what may occur to-morrow morning, upon the execution of the order.

While thus expressing my anxious regrets, let me assure you that I have no hostility to the entirely voluntary enlistment of negroes. They should be instructed in due time and as they grow to it, in every right and duty, even that to bear arms in the common defense; and accordingly I acceded readily to the request of yours for facilities to a colored person engaged in promoting such enlistments.

I ought perhaps to add that General Saxton is hourly expected, by the McLellan, provided with new and full instructions from the War Department, to assume charge of the negroes and the plantations, and it is perhaps desirable to await these before reducing the force on the plantations, unless a controlling military exigency necessitates the reduction.

It is with pain that I see the work, with which the Treasury Department has charged me, summarily defeated, and I cannot believe it to have been the intention of the Government, having expended so much upon it, thus to leave it. On the other hand all communications received by me from Washington, affirm continued confidence in it, and the intention to promote it

While therefore yielding obedience to the order issued, I have felt compelled to state in what manner it appears to me to conflict with the policy of the Government, and the duties with which I have been charged; and in conclusion I beg leave to suggest whether it be just to deal thus with these poor people against their will. Your Obt. Svt.

HLcSr   (Signed) Edward L. Pierce

Edward L. Pierce to Maj. Gen. Hunter, 11 May 1862, enclosed in S. P. Chase to Edwin M. Stanton, 21 May 1862, Departments 454 1862, Letters Received from the President & Executive Departments, RG 107 [L-306].

2: Plantation Superintendent to a Treasury Department Special Agent

Mrs Jenkins' Plantation St Helena Island S.C. [*May 1862*]
Dr Sir   The quiet of the last sabbath evening was broken in upon,
by one, whom I shall call in this connection, an intruder Mr
Phillips — I saw that he was laboring under some excitement,
which excitement was communicated to me through the medium
of a circular from Gen Stevens, which Mr Phillips very privately
submitted for my perusal and *benefit*, with also an order from
yourself, authorizing me to act in accordance with the spirit and
letter, of the military command
    At 1/2 past 1. AM of Monday a detachment of 3 Soldiers in
command of a Corporal, were admitted to my home and quartered,
also breakfasted, in the morning. After which preparation was
made for the execution of the "order". As we left the House we
saw, where had been but a few moments before, field Hands hard
at work, nothing but Horses and Ploughs, without Drivers, and
idle Hoes. On inquiry we found that no one could tell the
whereabouts of any of the "able bodied men" — The fact was they
had "Smelt a very large Rat," and according to the expression of
an old Man on the place had found it "very necessary to go to the
woods to split Rails" — The soldiers went to the Cabins and to
the woods some 1/4 of a mile distant, and brought in all but two
of the men "capable of bearing arms." The two men had eluded
the vigilance of the Soldiers and could not be found. The people
were not told the object for which they were taken, until brought
to me. I tried to explain to them why they were to be carried
away, cheering and encouraging them by every means in my
power. All seemed disheartened and sad though none were
stubborn or used harsh words — The Soldiers used them very
kindly, and made no decided demonstration of authority. The
scene at the House was strange and affecting — Women and
children gathered around the men to say "farewell." Fathers took
the little children in their arms, while the Women gave way to
the wildest expressions of grief. When the women first came up,
several of them had axes in their hands — My foreman also carried
his ax about with him for some time, but no threat or attempt to
use them was made — (I think the axes were those which the men
had used in the woods for *Rail splitting*; but when the time came
to *march*, these were laid aside, and a moaning and weeping, such
as touches the hearts of strong men, burst forth — an evidence — and
sure witness that there is a fountain of love and humanity in the
hearts of the poor Negroes of South Carolina — that can be opened

and will overflow with the sentiments which characterise the heart of mankind, that is impressed with the image of God.

My attempts to comfort the hearts and quiet the apprehensions of the mourners were quite unsuccessful – and I left them, to join the new recruits – they "refusing to be comforted." One woman told me "she had lost all her children and friends, and now her husband was taken, and she must die uncared for." Many expressions of a like nature were made to me – while all felt and believed this to be a final seperation – My protection was claimed, but I was to "give such aid as was in my power" for the execution of the order. I reserved, by advisement of the Corporal, the foremen on all my places – At the Dr Croft Plantation but two men were taken – The others – with the foreman escaped to the Woods – having gained information in regard to the movement, from a woman who had seen the Soldiers at Mrs Jenkins place. Some of the remaining hands – protested that they would not work any longer on the Plantations – but have concluded since I have *talked* with them to go on with their labor; and a few are willing to do more than before – This "conscription" together with the manner of its execution has created a suspicion that the government have not the interest in the Negroes that it has professed, and many of them sighed, yesterday – for the "old fetters," as being better than the new liberty. My own heart well nigh failed me, and but for the desire to still sympathise with this, as they call themselves – short minded – but peculiar people – I should desire to commit my charge to some person, with a stronger mind and sterner heart than my own – It gives me pleasure to state to-day – that there is something less of the demonstration of grief than yesterday – tho their hearts are still large with thoughts of the seperation   With much respect I subscribe myself Your humble Servt

HLcSr   G. M Wells

G. M. Wells to E. L. Pierce, [May 1862], enclosed in S. P. Chase to Edwin M. Stanton, 21 May 1862, Departments 454 1862, Letters Received from the President & Executive Departments, RG 107 [L-306].

3: Commander of the Department of the South to the Secretary of War

Port Royal S° Cª June 23ʳᵈ 1862

Sir: I have the honor to acknowledge the receipt of a communication from the Adjutant General of the Army, dated

June 13th 1862, requesting me to furnish you with information
necessary to answer certain resolutions introduced in the House of
Representatives, June 9th 1862, on motion of the Hon. Mr.
Wickliffe of Kentucky, – their substance being to inquire;

1st Whether I had organized or was organizing a regiment of
"Fugitive Slaves" in this Department.

2nd Whether any authority had been given to me from the War
Department for such organization; – and

3rd Whether I had been furnished by order of the War
Department with clothing, uniforms, arms, equipments and so
forth for such a force?

Only having received the letter covering these inquiries at a late
hour on Saturday night, I urge forward my answer in time for the
Steamer sailing today (Monday), – this haste preventing me from
entering as minutely as I could wish upon many points of detail
such as the paramount importance of the subject calls for. But in
view of the near termination of the present session of Congress,
and the wide-spread interest which must have been awakened by
Mr Wickliffe's Resolutions, I prefer sending even this imperfect
answer to waiting the period necessary for the collection of fuller
and more comprehensive data.

To the First Question therefore I reply that no regiment of
"Fugitive Slaves" has been, or is being organized in this
Department. There is, however, a fine regiment of persons whose
late masters are "Fugitive Rebels," – men who everywhere fly before
the appearance of the National Flag, leaving their servants behind
them to shift as best they can for themselves. – So far, indeed,
are the loyal persons composing this regiment from seeking to
avoid the presence of their late owners, that they are now, one and
all, working with remarkable industry to place themselves in a
position to go in full and effective pursuit of their fugacious and
traitorous proprietors.

To the Second Question, I have the honor to answer that the
instructions given to Brig. Gen. T. W. Sherman by the Hon.
Simon Cameron, late Secretary of War, and turned over to me by
succession for my guidance, – do distinctly authorize me to employ
all loyal persons offering their services in defence of the Union and
for the suppression of this Rebellion in any manner I might see
fit, or that the circumstances might call for. There is no
restriction as to the character or color of the persons to be
employed, or the nature of the employment, whether civil or
military, in which their services should be used. I conclude,
therefore that I have been authorized to enlist "Fugitive Slaves" as
soldiers, could any such be found in this Department. – No such
characters, however, have yet appeared within view of our most

advanced pickets, — the loyal slaves everywhere remaining on their plantations to welcome us, aid us, and supply us with food, labor and information. — It is the masters who have in every instance been the "Fugitives", running away from loyal slaves as well as loyal soldiers, and whom we have only partially been able to see, — chiefly their heads over ramparts, or, rifle in hand, dodging behind trees, — in the extreme distance. — In the absence of any "Fugitive Master Law", the deserted Slaves would be wholly without remedy, had not the crime of Treason given them the right to pursue, capture and bring back those persons of whose protection they have been thus suddenly bereft.

To the Third Interrogatory, it is my painful duty to reply that I never have received any Specific authority for issues of clothing, uniforms, arms, equipments and so forth to the troops in question, — my general instructions from Mr Cameron to employ them in any manner I might find necessary, and the military exigencies of the Department and the country, being my only, but in my judgment, sufficient justification. Neither have I had any Specific authority for supplying these persons with shovels, spades and pick axes when employing them as laborers, nor with boats and oars when using them as lightermen, — but these are not points included in Mr. Wickliffe's Resolution. — To me it seemed that liberty to employ men in any particular capacity implied with it liberty, also, to supply them with the necessary tools; and acting upon this faith, I have clothed, equipped and armed the only loyal regiment yet raised in South Carolina.

I must say, in vindication of my own conduct, that had it not been for the many other diversified and imperative claims on my time and attention, a much more satisfactory result might have been hoped for; and that in place of only one, as at present, at least five or six well-drilled, brave and thoroughly acclimated regiments should by this time have been added to the loyal forces of the Union.

The experiment of arming the Blacks, so far as I have made it, has been a complete and even marvellous success. They are sober, docile, attentive and enthusiastic, displaying great natural capacities for acquiring the duties of the soldier. They are eager beyond all things to take the field and be led into action; and it is the unanimous opinion of the officers who have had charge of them, that in the peculiarities of this climate and Country they will prove invaluable auxiliaries, — fully equal to the similar regiments so long and successfully used by the British Authorities in the West India Islands.

In conclusion I would say it is my hope, — there appearing no possibility of other reinforcements owing to the exigencies of the

Campaign in the Peninsula, — to have organized by the end of next
Fall, and to be able to present to the Government, from forty
eight to fifty thousand of these hardy and devoted
soldiers. — Trusting that this letter may form part of your answer
to Mr Wickliffe's Resolutions, I have the honor to be, most
respectfully, Your Very Obed[r] Servt.

HLc   [*David Hunter*]

[David Hunter] to Edwin M. Stanton, 23 June 1862, vol. 10 DS, pp. 65–
69, Letters Sent, ser. 4088, Dept. of the South, RG 393 Pt. 1 {C-1481}.
On June 14, 1862, the Secretary of War had submitted to Congress an
evasive, circumlocutory reply that contrasted sharply with Hunter's forth-
right statement. He had claimed ignorance of Hunter's alleged organization
of black troops and refused to provide Congress with copies of Hunter's
orders, on the grounds that the President felt that such a step would be
"improper and incompatible with the public welfare." (*Official Records*, ser.
3, vol. 2, pp. 147–48.)

4: Superintendent of Contrabands in
the Department of the South to the Secretary of War

Beaufort South Carolina October 29th 1862.
Sir. I have the honor to report that I am organizing the 1st South
Carolina Vols. as rapidly as possible
I think you will be disappointed with regard to the number of
recruits I shall be able to obtain. I labour under many
disadvantages in this matter. In the first place, the sphere of our
operations is very limited. The Quartermaster's Department has a
large number of able-bodied men in its employ, also the Engineer
Department. All the officers servants are negroes and numbers of
others [drive] a flourishing business as fishermen, workmen on
steam-boats and for private traders   large numbers are also
employed in the Navy Department as sailors servants pilots &c.
I believe it is your intention that all these demands should be
supplied before enlisting into the U.S. Service
When the colored regiment was first organized by Genl Hunter
no provision was made for its payment and the men were
discharged after several months service receiving nothing for it   in
the mean time their families suffered   those who did not enlist in
the first regiment were receiving wages all this time. Accustomed
as these people are to having their rights disregarded this failure to
pay them for their service has weakened their confidence in our
promises for the future & makes them slow to enlist   If I could

be authorized to give them a small bounty as an evidence that they were really to be paid for their services they would all readily enlist.

Until the arrival of reinforcements shall enable Genl Mitchell to extend his lines to Charleston, I shall hardly be able to fill more than one regiment.

I find less opposition to this movement than I expected the majority in this Department are satisfied of its wisdom & propriety. I have a great many applications from all grades of officers & soldiers serving here, for positions in this regiment. I have no doubt but they will make good soldiers.

I regret to inform you that Genl Mitchell with two members of his staff are very ill with malarial fever & one member of his staff Capt Williams has already died with the same disease. I am with great respect Your obedient servant

ALS   R Saxton

Brig. Genl. R. Saxton to Hon. Edwin M. Stanton, 29 Oct. 1862, S-2104 1862, Letters Received, ser. 12, RG 94 [K-568].

5: Superintendent of Contrabands in the Department of the South to the Secretary of War

Beaufort South Carolina Jan 25th 1863

Dear Sir. I have the honor to report that the organization of the 1st Regt. of South Carolina Volunteers is now completed. The regiment is light infantry composed of ten companies of about eighty six men (each) armed with muskets, and officered by white men. In organization, drill, discipline, and morale, for the length of time it has been in service, this regiment is not surpassed by any white regiment in this Department. Should it ever be its good fortune to get into action I have no fears but it will win its own way to the confidence of those who are willing to recognize courage, and manhood, and vindicate the wise policy of the administration in putting these men into the field and giving them a chance to strike a blow for the country and their own liberty. In no regiment have I ever seen duty performed with so much cheerfulness, and alacrity, and as sentinels they are peculiarly vigilant I have never seen in any body of men such enthusiasm and deep seated devotion to their officers as exists in this. They will surely go wherever they are led. Every man is a volunteer and seems fully persuaded of the importance of his service to his

race. In the organization of this regiment I have labored under difficulties which might have discouraged one who had less faith in the wisdom of the measure, but I am glad to report that the experiment is a complete success. My belief is that when we get a footing on the main land regiments may be raised which will do more than any now in service to put an end to this rebellion   I have sent the regiment upon an expedition to the coast of Georgia the result of which I shall report for your information as soon as it returns. I have the honor also to report that I have commenced the organization of the 2nd Regt which is to be commanded by Col Montgomery   I am Sir with great respect Your Obedent Servant
ALS   R Saxton

Brig. Genl. R. Saxton to Hon. Edwin M. Stanton, 25 Jan. 1863, S-196 1863, Letters Received, RG 107 [L-161].

6A: Army Engineer to the Headquarters of the Department of the South

Fort Clinch Florida 3^{d} April 1863.
Colonel   When I was at Hilton Head, lately, you did me the honor to say that my work should be protected from the interference of men, who are enlisting and drafting soldiers for the African Regiments.

Your verbal promise was followed almost immediately by Gen. Order No. 24^{1} in wh you exempted from draft all blacks in the employ of this Dep. on permanent fortifications.

But even if you had not thus doubly secured the safety of my men, I should have been quite at ease for the present, because Col. Higginson had assured me that he would not draft any soldiers during his present expedition.

Notwithstanding this promise of the Colonel (and therefore, I believe, without his knowledge or direction) and in direct violation of Gen. Order No. 24. 19th March, from your Head Quarters – published here a week ago, the men hired by me for work on Fort Clinch have been attacked in the night by Major Strong of the 1st. So. Ca. Vol. with an armed guard and five of them have been siezed and carried away by force.

The names of these men are as follows viz: –

Jeff Houston
Peter Williams
Jake Forrester
Sam Major
John Wanton

They were siezed night before last and were forbidden permission to see me before leaving – an officer with them declaring that he "didn't care a damn for Capt. Sears; if they didn't go he would give them the bayonet." The boat left at an early hour yesterday morning, before I had ascertained anything of the matter.

My men, Colonl, *have not been drafted. They have been kidnapped in the night.* And that by men, who profess to be their peculiar friends. A panic has siezed the negroes remaining here and many of them, unless closely watched will escape to the enemy.

It is proper for me to say, that evidence exists of the complicity of the Rev. Kennedy and Mr. Helper Sup. of Contrabands, in this barbarity. If I understand the case rightly, the raid began by an attempt of Kennedy to revenge himself on Jeff Houston, a bargeman in the employ of the U.S. on Fort Clinch. Jeff is young and good looking – he is also a fascinating fiddler! Whenever, *after taps*, the Rev. Kennedy visited any of the young widowed hearts, whose lords had gone to the wars, (on missionary duty, I mean) he was sure to find Jeff consoling the best looking. Mr. Kennedy accounted this an interference with his pastoral duties. But, I am sorry to say, that Mr. Kennedy allowed himself to be led into slandering the private character of Jeff. He has more than insinuated that this exemplary young men has even penetrated the persons of several of the best looking grazing widows of colour.

I do not believe any thing of the sort. These "poor, innocent people" (I quote Mr. Heper's adjectives) would not permit anything of the kind; and besides, my man Jeff is too good to act so.

I firmly believe that his principal fault is in being better looking than Rev Kennedy and younger and more popular with the colored ladies here, than that gentleman.

If Jeff Houston is guilty of misconduct there is a proper way of punishing him; He is one of my best men – *that is why he is wanted* and a pretext may be invented for moving him away.

I do respectfully and earnestly entreat you, Colonel, to have my men returned to me.

And I do farther respectfully entreat you, with equal earnestness, to vindicate the title of a United States officer, to be considered a humane gentleman, a title so severely attacked by the barbarous conduct of Major Strong.

The accompanying paper marked A contains a statement of each individual case. I have the honor to be, Colonel, very truly & respectfully Yr Obt Sert

ALS   Alfred F. Sears

Capt. Alfred F. Sears to Lt. Col. Chas. G. Halpine, 3 Apr. 1863, enclosed in Col. Jos. R. Hawley to Lt. Col. Chas. G. Halpine, 29 Apr. 1863, H-1424 1863, Letters Received, ser. 4109, Dept. of the South, RG 393 Pt. 1 [C-1317]. Enclosure. On April 16, Colonel Thomas W. Higginson, commander of the 1st South Carolina Volunteers, wrote to the headquarters of the Department of the South on behalf of Major J. D. Strong, denying the charges of forcible impressment and expressing ignorance of the general order exempting military laborers from conscription. Higginson concluded: "It is difficult to carry out a draft without some mistakes & irregularities, and I shall be happy to aid in rectifying them, so far as possible." (Col. T. W. Higginson to Lt. Israel R. Sealy, 16 Apr. 1863, enclosed in Col. Jos. R. Hawley to Lt. Col. Chas. G. Halpine, 29 Apr. 1863, H-1424 1863, Letters Received, ser. 4109, Dept. of the South, RG 393 Pt. 1 [C-1317].)

1 Department of the South General Orders Nos. 17 and 24 figured prominently in the Fort Clinch affair. The former, issued March 6, 1863, ordered the conscription of all able-bodied black men aged eighteen to fifty. The latter, issued March 19, 1863, exempted permanent employees of the engineer's department from the provisions of General Order No. 17. (*Official Records*, ser. 1, vol. 14, pp. 1020–21, 429–30.)

6B: Affidavit of an Impressed Black Recruit

Fernandina, Fla.
twenty eighth day of April in the year Eighteen hundred Sixty-three
My name is Jacob Forrester. I live at Fernandina, Fla. I work at Fort Clinch. I am employed by Captain Sears.
About the first of the month I was at home, about eight oclock in the evening. Major Strong and Captain James, both belonging to the 1st S.C. Vols. came into the house and asked John Wanton what was his name; he told them, when the Major caught him on the shoulder and told him he wanted him to be a soldier, and I came out and he asked me what was my name. I told him; he then asked me where I was working. I told him I was working at the fort. He said it did not make any difference where I was working, he had had orders from high authorities to take us. He then took us outside the gate and had us fall in with a file of guards, fifteen or twenty men, and made us go down to the boat. After we got on the boat he asked us if we did not want to be

57

examined by the Doctor. I told him no. I did not have any need to be examined by the Doctor. I was as well as any other man, and that is all he told us until he sent us back again.

The day before I came away, Capt Rogers told us that he wanted all the recruits from Fernandina to go before the Col. I was the first one that went in; the Colonel asked me if I came of my own free will. I told him, "no Sir", I told him "I could not say I came of my own free will by the way I was taken," told him "if I wanted to be a soldier I had plenty of chances before.

He asked me "if I had my own choice what I would do; I told him I would stay home, but if I was compelled to go, I would go, for I was no better to die than any other man." These were the very words. He gave us until the next evening to study to see what was our intent.

The next evening I saw the Captain and told him it was my desire to go home and I would like to have my pass.

There is nothing else now except that he asked me if I was coming back.

his

HDSr   Jacob × Forrester

mark

Affidavit of Jacob Forrester, 28 Apr. 1863, enclosed in Col. Jos. R. Hawley to Lt. Col. Chas. G. Halpine, 29 Apr. 1863, H-1424 1863, Letters Received, ser. 4109, Dept. of the South, RG 393 Pt. 1 [C-1317]. Affidavit sworn before the Fernandina, Florida, post commander and post adjutant.

❧

7: Testimony by the Commander of a South Carolina Black Regiment before the American Freedmen's Inquiry Commission

[*Beaufort, S.C. 1863*]

. . . .

Col. McKaye. — They [*former slave soldiers*] have a habit of obedience to begin with.

Col. Higginson — I think that assists them, but it is not altogether the cause. And that brings us around to the point whether these people have any idea of justice and law. This question I asked of myself, because my fear was that they had been so accustomed to plantation discipline that they would deem all discipline to be unjust and irregular. I had read that it is impossible to get an idea of Justice into the head of a South Sea Islander, and I thought that it might be the same here, but I determined to try it with a steady hand, and try it fairly. In this respect I have been most agreably disappointed in these men, and that is a discovery that has given me more faith in their future than anything else.

Q. They have, then, a decided idea, sense and perception of law?

A. Yes, sir; I discover that they have a sense of law, and I think that the credit of it is partly due to the admirable training which military life gives of recognizing and administering law. For instance, guard duty – if it were usual to have a camp without a guard, I should institute a guard system as the best mode of educating these men. Here's an instance of their idea of law. They have been told over and over again that a guard was only to take orders from the officer of the guard or the commanding officer of the post. You cannot get a soldier in this regiment to take an order from any one else. No captain can make a soldier of his company leave his post at his order – it is as much as can be done at my order. A few days ago I tried with difficulty to make this sentinel here in front of my quarters go to camp upon an errand. I asked him to go and he refused, saying "you know, Colonel, I can't go." I told him that he certainly could; that I possessed the right to order guards off post. "Very true;" he replied, "but I can't go; if I leave this post I might as well never have been put here," and I could not make this man leave. He evidently felt a little anxious at disobeying me, but he also felt sure that he was right and would not take the risk. It was a very amusing scene to the officers, and Dr. Rogers and the major laughed heartily at the argument between me and him.

I mention this incident as a proof of their idea of law – there is no difficulty in making them understand that during the time they are on guard duty they must only obey the guard officers. Of course, at the very beginning, the first view that every recruit has is, that he must obey every officer, but it takes very little time to give them the idea clearly.

You asked in regard to the habit of obedience being favorable to military life. It is favorable and the reverse. It is unfavorable because it has not hitherto been associated in their minds with the idea of Justice – it has been a cringing obedience. Their idea of obeying their masters was not because it was wise and just, but because he was powerful and could enforce obedience. I have often had occasion to say that the best slave does not make the best soldier, but on the contrary, the habits of a soldier will never do for a slave. I have taken unwearied pains to explain to them and I think they understand that they must obey their officers simply because they are officers, and just so every officer must obey me, and I obey General Saxton and he General Hunter. They understand that thoroughly, and it therefore does not diminish their self-respect. When they first came here and had occasion to speak to me out of doors they would stand with cap in hand. I said "put on your cap and make the military salute, then assume the position of the soldier, and go on with what you have to say." I find that the men most servile in this way as a general thing make the poorest soldiers – the iron has entered them too far. When they can unlearn this servility and develope manhood they become admirable soldiers.

Q. Then as a mere preparation for the life of the citizen, the common life of the man, you think organizing them into military bodies is important?

A. I should say of unspeakable value.

Q. Have these men, as far as you have discovered, any idea, or is it easy to give them an idea, of the necessity and obligation men have to fight for their liberty?

A. I think it is very easy indeed. Some of them are indolent, are home-loving, are smart, can make more money in other ways, do not think that they should like camp life and are unwilling to volunteer. Some are selfish, and while recognizing that the thing should be done, leave somebody else to do it; but there is a general recognition that the thing has got to be done. I think the general aim and probable consequences of this war are better understood in this regiment than in any white regiment – not because the intellectual ability is equal, but because it comes home to them personally.

Q. What motive had you in the process of getting up this regiment, notwithstanding the great discouragements, for inducing these men to enlist – was it for the wages?

A. No, I do not think it was for wages; a large part of them enlisted when they felt uncertain whether they would get their pay. The men from Florida particularly, I am sure enlisted from patriotic motives, – from a love of liberty.

Q. And really it was from a desire to assist in winning their own liberty?

A. I think it was.

. . . .

HD

Excerpt from testimony of Col. Higginson, [1863], O-328 1863, Letters Received, ser. 12, RG 94 [K-81]. Topical labels in the margin are omitted.

8: Commander of the Department of the South to the Superintendent of Contrabands in the Department of the South

Hilton Head, S.C. August 29th 1864

General: I have received your letter of the 27th in relation to the enlistment of colored men for soldiers, by Col. Littlefield, which you think invades your rights as Superintendent of Contrabands.

The recent depletion of our force to send necessary reinforcements to other and more important points has rendered it necessary to collect in all the military force of the Department. Col. Littlefield is only carrying out my orders in this respect. I want to collect all the men that are capable of carrying arms to fill the ranks of the regiments that are to remain here to defend our positions. I do not see any reason why the negro women and children may not be made to cultivate the plantations now under cultivation as well as within the limits of our enemies where they are required to cultivate for their own wants, and, in addition, for their masters mistresses, and, in fact for the proportion of the rebel army fixed by tax law.

It is known that several hundred deserters are on the islands of St. Helena, Ladies Id. Paris Id. and Philips Id. These are employed on the plantations of those persons who are cultivating staples for the market. Their interests must not be suffered to interfere with the interests of the United States. There are enough exempts to attend to all the manual labor required on these private (quasi public) plantations. We must require all the able bodied men to bear arms and I trust and expect you to carry out the idea with an eye single to the interests of the U.S. and not to those of the parties who as agents of the humanitarian societies would not, when the pinch comes, give an ounce's resistance to the attacks of the enemy. Truly yours,

(Signed) J G Foster

P.S. – The new Treasury Regulations, which I have just received, seem to give the whole matter of the support of the contrabands upon the plantations into the hands of the Treasury Agents. If this be so your position as Sup't of Contrabands will be vacated, and the War Dep't should, if such be the case, withdraw its instructions to you. Yours,

HLcS

(Sg[d]) J G Foster.

M.G. Comdg. J. G. Foster to General Saxton, 29 Aug. 1864, vol. 14 DS, pp. 99–100, Letters Sent, ser. 4088, Dept. of the South, RG 393 Pt. 1 [C-1488].

LOUISIANA

9: Commander of Camp Parapet to the Headquarters of the Department of the Gulf

Camp Parapet, La. July 30th 1862.

Sir, I enclose herewith requisitions for arms, accoutrements, clothing, camp and garrison equipage etc for three regiments of Africans which I propose to raise for the defense of this point. The location is swampy and unhealthy and

The Southern loyalists are willing, as I understand, to furnish their share of the tax for the support of the war; but they should also furnish their quota of men, which they have not thus far done. An opportunity now offers of supplying the deficiency; and it is not safe to neglect opportunities in war. I think that with the proper facilities I could raise the three regiments proposed in a short time. Without holding out any inducements, or offering any reward, I have now upward of three hundred Africans organized into five companies who are all willing and ready to shew their devotion to our cause in any way that it may be put to the test. They are willing to submit to anything rather than to slavery.

Society in the South seems to be on the point of dissolution; and the best way of preventing the African from becoming instrumental in a general state of anarchy, is to enlist him in the cause of the Republic. If we reject his services, any petty military chieftain, by offering him freedom, can have them for the purpose of robbery and plunder. It is for the interests of the South as well as for the North that the African should be permitted to offer his block for the temple of Freedom. Sentiments unworthy of the MAN of the present day, worthy only of another Cain could prevent such an offer from being accepted.

I would recommend that the Cadet graduates of the present year should be sent to South Carolina and this point to organize and discipline our African levies, and that the more promising non Commissioned Officers and privates of the army be appointed as company officers to command them. Prompt and energetic efforts in this direction would probably accomplish more towards a speedy termination of the war and an early restoration of peace and amity than any other course which could be adopted   I have the honor to remain Sir, Very respectfully your obedient servant

HLS   J. W. Phelps

Brigr. Genl. J. W. Phelps to Captain R. S. Davis, 30 July 1862, #19 1862, Letters Received, ser. 1756, Dept. of the Gulf, RG 393 Pt. 1 [C-500]. Over the next three days, Phelps and General Benjamin F. Butler, Commander of the Department of the Gulf, corresponded repeatedly regarding the disposition of the contrabands whom Phelps harbored in his camp. On July 31, 1862, Butler instructed Phelps to use the contrabands to cut down the trees surrounding the camp. Phelps received Butler's letter on the same day and immediately tendered his resignation, explaining, "I am not willing to become the mere Slave-driver which you propose, having no qualifications in that way." On August 2, Butler wrote two letters in reply to Phelps's letters of July 30 and 31, refusing to accept Phelps's resignation, pointing out that the proposal to organize black troops required authorization by the President, and instructing Phelps to put the contrabands to work on the trees, as previously ordered. On August 2, Butler also submitted documents on the case to the Secretary of War. (Vol. 2 DG, pp. 234, 238–46, Letters Sent, ser. 1738, Dept. of the Gulf, RG 393 Pt. 1 [C-500].)

10: Commander of Camp Parapet to the Commander of the Department of the Gulf

Camp Parapet La: August 2nd 1862

Sir, Two communications from you of this date have this moment been received   One of them refers to the raising of volunteer or militia forces, stating that I "must desist from the formation of any negro Military Organization", and the other declaring in a spirit contrary to all usage of military service and to all the rights and liberties of a citizen of a free government, that my resignation will not be accepted by you, that a leave of absence until its acceptance by the president will not be granted me, and that I must see to it that your orders, which I could not obey without becoming a slave myself, are "faithfully and diligently executed."

It can be of but little consequence to me as to what kind of slavery I am to be subjected, whether to African slavery or to that which you thus so offensively propose for me, giving me an order wholly opposed to my convictions of right as well as of the higher scale of public necessities in the case, and insisting upon my complying with it *faithfully* and *diligently*, allowing me no room to escape with my convictions or my principles at any sacrifice that I may make. I cannot submit to either kind of slavery, and cannot therefore, for a double reason, comply with your order of the 31st of July, in complying with which I should submit to both kinds, – both to African Slavery and to that to which you resort in its defence.

63

Desirous to the last of saving the public interests involved, I appeal to your sense of justice to reconsider your decision and make the most to the cause out of the sacrifice which I offer, by granting the quiet, proper and customary action upon my resignation By refusing my request you would subject me to great inconvenience without, as far as I can see, any advantage either to yourself or to the service.

With the view of securing myself a tardy justice in the case, being remote from the capitol, where the transmission of the mails is remarkably irregular and uncertain, and in order to give you every assurance that my resignation is tendered in strict compliance with paragraph 29 of the Regulations, to be "unconditional and immediate", I herewith enclose a copy for the Adjutant General of the Army, which I desire may be forwarded to him to be laid before the President for as early action in the case as his Excellency may be pleased to accord. And as my position, sufficiently unpleasant already, promises to become much more so still by the course of action which I am sorry to find that you deem it proper to pursue, I urgently request his Excellency, by a speedy acceptance of my commission to liberate me from that sense of suffocation, from that darkling sense of bondage and enthralment which, it appears to me, like the snake around the muscles and sinews of Laocoon, is entangling and deadening the energies of the government and country, when a decisive act might cut the coils and liberate us from their baneful and fascinating influence forever.

In conclusion of this communication, and I should also hope of my services in this Department, I deem it my duty to state, lest it might not otherwise come to your notice, that several parties of the free colored men of New-Orleans have recently come to consult me on the propriety of raising one or two regiments of volunteers from their class of the population for the defence of the government and good order, and that I have recommended them to propose the measure to you, having no power to act upon it myself. I am Sir, very respectfully Your Obdt Servt

J. W. Phelps

P.S. Monday Aug 4. The Negroes increase rapidly. There are doubtless now six hundred able bodied men in camp. These, added to those who are suffering uselessly in the prisons and jails of New Orleans and vicinity, and feeding from the general stock of provisions, would make a good regiment of one thousand men who might contribute as much to the preservation of law and good order as a regiment of Caucasians, and probably much more. Now a mere burden, they might become a beneficent element of governmental power.

ALS   J. W. P

Brigr. Genl. J. W. Phelps to Major General B. F. Butler, 2 Aug. 1862, G-476 1862, Letters Received, ser. 12, RG 94 [K-27]. In the same file is Phelps's resignation letter of August 2, 1862, to the adjutant general, stating that he found it "impossible to serve in this Department without doing violence to my convictions of right and public necessity."

11: **Order by the Commander of the Department of the Gulf**

New Orleans, August 22, 1862.

GENERAL ORDERS No. 63. WHEREAS, on the 23d day of April, in the year eighteen hundred and sixty-one, at a public meeting of the free colored population of the city of New Orleans, a military organization, known as the "Native Guards" (colored), had its existence, which military organization was duly and legally enrolled as a part of the militia of the State, its officers being commissioned by THOMAS O. MOORE, GOVERNOR AND COMMANDER-IN-CHIEF of the militia of the State of Louisiana, in the form following, that is to say:

"THE STATE OF LOUISIANA. ⎫
[Seal of the State.] ⎬

"By THOMAS OVERTON MOORE, Governor of the State of Louisiana, and Commander-in-Chief of the Militia thereof.

"In the name and by the authority of the State of Louisiana:

"KNOW YE, that _____ _____, having been duly and legally elected Captain of the "Native Guards" (colored), 1st Division of the Militia of Louisiana, to serve for the term of the war,

"I do hereby appoint and commission him Captain as aforesaid, to take rank as such, from the 2d day of May, eighteen hundred and sixty-one.

"He is, therefore, carefully and diligently to discharge the duties of his office by doing and performing all manner of things thereto belonging. And I do strictly charge and require all officers, non-commissioned officers and privates under his command, to be obedient to his orders as Captain; and he is to observe and follow such orders and directions, from time to time, as he shall receive from me, or the future Governor of the State of Louisiana, or other superior officers, according to the Rules and Articles of War, and in conformity to law.

"In testimony whereof, I have caused these letters to be made patent, and the seal of the State to be hereunto annexed.

{L.S.}   'Given under my hand, at the city of Baton Rouge, on the second day of May, in the year of our Lord one thousand eight hundred and sixty-one.

[Signed] "THOS. O. MOORE.

"By the Governor:

[Signed] "P. D. HARDY, Secretary of State.
[Endorsed] "I, Maurice Grivot, Adjutant and Inspector General of
the State of Louisiana, do hereby certify that _____ _____,
named in the within commission, did, on the second day of May,
in the year 1861, deposit in my office his written acceptance of the
office to which he is commissioned, and his oath of office taken
according to law.

[Signed] "M. GRIVOT, Adjt. and Insp. Gen. La."

AND WHEREAS, such military organization elicited praise and
respect, and was complimented in General Orders for its patriotism
and loyalty, and was ordered to continue during the war, in the
words following:

"HEADQUARTERS LOUISIANA MILITIA, }
"*Adjutant General's Office, March* 24, 1862. }

"ORDER NO. 426.

"I. The Governor and Commander-in-Chief, relying implicitly
upon the loyalty of the free colored population of the City and
State, for the protection of their homes, their property, and for
Southern rights, from the pollution of a ruthless invader, and
believing that the military organization which existed prior to the
15th February, 1862, and elicited praise and respect for the
patriotic motives which prompted it, should exist for and during
the war, calls upon them to maintain their organization, and to
hold themselves prepared for such orders as may be transmitted to
them.

"II. The Colonel Commanding will report without delay to
Major General Lewis, commanding State Militia.

"By order of THOS. O. MOORE, Governor.
[Signed] "M. GRIVOT, Adjutant General."

AND WHEREAS, said military organization, by the same
order, was directed to report to Major General Lewis for service,
but did not leave the city of New Orleans when he did:

NOW, THEREFORE, the Commanding General, believing that
a large portion of this militia force of the State of Louisiana are
willing to take service in the Volunteer forces of the United States
and be enrolled and organized to "defend their homes from
ruthless invaders;" to protect their wives and children and kindred
from wrong and outrage; to shield their property from being seized
by bad men; and to defend the Flag of their native country, as
their fathers did under Jackson at Chalmette, against Packenham
and his myrmidons, carrying the black flag of "beauty and booty."

Appreciating their motives, relying upon their "well-known
loyalty and patriotism," and with "praise and respect" for these

brave men—it is ordered that all the members of the "Native Guards" aforesaid, and all other free colored citizens recognized by the first and late Governor and Authorities of the State of Louisiana as a portion of the Militia of the State, who shall enlist in the Volunteer Service of the United States, shall be duly organized by the appointment of proper officers, and accepted, paid, equipped, armed and rationed as are other Volunteer Troops of the United States, subject to the approval of the President of the United States. All such persons are required at once to report themselves at the Touro Charity Building, Front Levee Street, New-Orleans, where proper officers will muster them into the service of the United States. By command of MAJOR-GENERAL BUTLER.

PD

General Orders No. 63, Headquarters Department of the Gulf, 22 Aug. 1862, Orders & Circulars, ser. 44, RG 94 [DD-8]. All braces appear in the original.

KANSAS

12: Recruiting Officer to the Adjutant General of the Army

Harrisburg Pa Aug 4th 10.30 AM [*1862*]

Br Gen L Thomas   Persons calling themselves recruiting officers for Genl James Lanes Colored Regiments are putting out hand bills and calling meetings of colored men offering the same inducements to enlist as are granted White soldiers— This is producing the worst effect on Enlistment of Whites   cannot it be stopped at once   Will write enclosing hand bills.

HWSr   Richd J Dodge

Richd. J. Dodge to Br. Gen. L. Thomas, 4 Aug. [1862], Telegrams Collected by the Office of the Secretary of War (Bound), RG 107 [L-209].

13: Order by the Kansas Commissioner of Recruitment

Leavenworth City [*Kans.*] Aug 6 – 1862

General Orders No 2   That persons of African Descent who may desire to enter the service of the United States in this Department, shall fully understand the terms and conditions upon which they will be received into such service, Recruiting officers who are authorized under instructions from this office, to receive such persons, *Shall*, before receiving them, read to them, and in their presence, the following Sections of the "Act" Entitled an act to amend the Act calling for the Militia to execute the laws of the Union, suppress, and repel invasions" approved February twenty eight seventeen hundred and ninety five, – and the acts amendatory thereto, and, for other purposes, approved July 17 – 1862, as follows,

"SEC. 12. *And be it further enacted*, That the President be, and he is hereby, authorized to receive into the service of the United States for the purpose of constructing intrenchments or camp service, or any other labor, or any military or naval service for which they may be found competent, persons of African descent, and such persons shall be enrolled and organized under such regulations, not inconsistent with the Constitution and laws, as the President may prescribe.

SEC. 13. *And be it further enacted*, That when any man or boy of African descent, who by the laws of any State shall owe service or labor to any person who, during the present rebellion has levied war or has borne arms against the United States, or adhered to their enemies by giving them aid and comfort, shall render any such service as is provided for in this act, he, his mother, and his wife and children, shall forever thereafter be free, any law, usage or custom whatsoever to the contrary notwithstanding; *Provided*, That the mother, wife and children of such man or boy of African descent shall not be made free by the operation of this act except where such mother, wife or children owe service or labor to some person, who, during the present rebellion, has borne arms against the United States, or adhered to their enemies by giving them aid and comfort."

By order of James H. Lane Commissioner of Recruiting Dept of Kan

HD

[*Endorsement*] The law of July 17th 1862 authorises the President *only* to recieve into the military service of the U.S persons of African descent. As the President has not authorised Recruiting officers to recieve into the service of the U.S. such persons for general military purposes, the enclosed order of Genl Lane is without the authority of law. Aug 18th 1862   H. W. Halleck   Genl in Chf

General Orders No. 2, Office of Recruiting Commission, Department of Kansas, 6 Aug. 1862, enclosed in Maj. T. J. Weed to Hon. Edwin M. Stanton, 6 Aug. 1862, L-565 1862, Letters Received, RG 107 [L-21]. Another endorsement. Sections 12 and 13 of the Second Confiscation Act are in the form of a newspaper clipping attached to the handwritten order.

14: Black Recruiter to the Kansas Commissioner of Recruitment

Camp Henning near Fort Scott [*Kans.*] January 12" 1863
Dear Sir   I hope you will excuse me for putting myself before your notice at this time; But such is the case that I am Compelled to do so. According to your promise in last August you gave me permission in the presence of Co^l J M Williams   Co^l Delahay and others to raise one Company of Colored Soldiers to be officered by Colored officers. According to your permission Co^l J M. Williams did on the 18" Day of August 1862 issue to me a recruiting Commission to that effect and I now propose to send you a coppy of that Commission which I now hold and on the Streangth of which I raised my Company. (To W^{it})

Office recruiting Commissioner
Northern District Kansas
Leavenworth No 62 Delaware St August 18" 1862
W D Matthews Sir you have permission to raise one company of free Colored men for the 1st Kansas Colored Volunteers to be officered by men of Colour and all Commanders of Companies and Battalions in said Regiment will regard the same as regularly officered and will issue rations and Equipments accordingly   By order of
Genl James H. Lane
J. M. Williams
Capt 5" K V Rect^g Com

So as we three did agree to officer this Company with Colored officers So we three must agree to keep our *Sacred word*. According to the Presidents proclamation there is nothing to hinder me from being mustered in as an officer   The way in which Major Weed agrees to muster — refuseing to do it with Company [now] —   If I am mustered as a recruiting officer and fulfill the requirements of

Genl Order war department No 75^1 what is there legally to
prevent my being mustered into such Company as one of its
officers— Nothing Surely— if I Can be mustered to recruit I can
be to fight. Major Weed Says he will muster me as a recruiting
officer—but I want to be mustered as Captain of my Company as
there is no captain mustered for my Company yet and the vacancy
still exists. I wish you would let me know as soon as possible
either by letter or by Telegraph. For I am under great obligation
to these men of my Company for keeping them here as long as I
have For they think I am about to sell them out and it may Cause
some of them to be Shot which would be a great disgrace to the
Regiment. It is now with you Genl to fulfil the promise you gave
me as it was under that promise that I got the men here
Therefore I but ask for Justice regardless of my Colour—as we are
all fighting for the same great and glorious Cause of Union and
Liberty— I am that I am Yours as Companion and Royal Arch
Mason

William D. Matthews

Direct your letter or telegraph to telegraph to Leavenworth to the
Care of D W Wilder

ALS   W D M

William D. Matthews to Hon. James H. Lane, 12 Jan. 1863, filed with
K-138 1864, Letters Received, ser. 360, Colored Troops Division, RG 94
[B-91]. Another document in the file indicates that the Secretary of War
authorized Matthews's muster as an officer. (E. M. S. to U.S. Mustering
Officer, 28 Jan. 1863.) However, there is no evidence that Matthews re-
ceived a commission at this time.

1 War Department General Orders No. 75, issued July 8, 1862, authorized governors to muster recruiters as company officers at the start of a
volunteer regiment's formation. It also outlined the duties of such officers
during organization. (*Official Records*, ser. 3, vol. 2, pp. 210–11.)

15: Chief of Staff of the Department of the Missouri to the Commander of the Department of the Missouri

F^t Scott Kansas Oct 16th P.M. [1862]

General I hope that from the "mixed dish" which I send you
something of interest may be gleaned— My opportunities for
maturing & putting in shape are not the best, ergo &c—

    Yesterday afternoon in company with several officers of the Post
I rode over to "Fort Lincoln" to inspect the *negroe Regts*.

Capt. Williams – 5th Kansas Ca^{vy} – the commander & to be Co^l, provided these recruits "of African descent" are mustered as U.S. soldiers, showed me through camp and at 4 o'clk beat the assembly and had dress parade. Laying aside the question as to the policy or propriety of making soldiers of the Negroe and viewing them as machines of war, I must say that the inspection was highly satisfactory – They exhibit a proficiency in the manual and in company evolutions truly surprising and the best company is the one officered by black men. The white officers are enthusiasts and think they would rather drill & discipline black men than white. I know I have seen very many Regts longer in the service than these which would appear badly beside them. They are clothed with a lot of gray clothing which was on hand at Leavenworth where Genl Halleck confined the uniform to blue. The arms are Austrian and Prussian muskets – not good –

Genl Lane has ordered Capt Williams to consolidate the two Regts to be known as the 1st Kansas Infantry.

He has also ordered that immediately after the consolidation & muster that the Regt "move to the front" encamping at Baxter's Springs, & reporting from that point to Genl Blunt for duty – ("Baxter^s Springs" are 60 miles south of here on the road to Fort Gibson) To effect this he directs Capt Williams to make requisition for transportation, subsistence, ammunition &c.

Genl Blunt has ordered Maj Henning, Commander of the Post, at F^t Scott, to construct a telegraph line to Leavenworth and to make use of these negroes for that purpose – Lane claims that Henning cant carry out the order so far as the Negroes are concerned because he, Lane, has not yet turned them over to Gov^t & the probability is that the Regt will go to Baxter's Springs unless they become disgusted at being ordered around without any recognition from Govt and disband. This brings me to a point which Capt Williams desires laid before you. These men have been recruited with the promise that they were to fight, not work as common laborers, that they were to be treated in every way as soldiers, with like immunities &c & that they would have an opportunity to strike a blow for the freedom of their brothers. Many of them are intelligent free negroes – some having a good business at home, others leaving their families without any support; they have been kept together without pay & under but a quasi organization. They are now two months in camp and no one can tell what is to be done with them. They ask me. I am noncommittal. They ask Lane – he evades – but urges them on by adroit tactics for which he is notable. Williams says they must be mustered in some way or they will disband. They would, I think, commence the construction of this telegraph willingly if they could be *mustered*, in the hope that a time would come when they might fight. No mustering officer in this Dist will muster them without your order— You see, therefore, the question is likely to be decided by you— The scheme is one of Lane's & with him is a hobby. I think perhaps he can screw the Prest up to the point of assuming all necessary responsibility— I dont wonder that Lane is proud of his Colored Regt. No one who could see these stalwart men, with their earnest faces, in battle line but would feel similarly—

. . . .

ALS   N. P. Chipman

Excerpt from Coln. N. P. Chipman to General [Samuel R. Curtis], 16 Oct. [1862], C-46 1862, Letters Received, ser. 2593, Dept. of the MO, RG 393 Pt. 1 [C-104].

16: Commander of a Kansas Black Regiment to the Headquarters of the Department of Kansas

Camp Emancipation Near Fᵗ Scott Kansas April 21″ 1863
Sir   In view of the fact that my Command is to recieve no pay from the paymaster now paying off troops in this vicinity, and that we have for the Ten months that we have been in service, as yet not recieved one cent, and further that out of all this there seems to be a growing restlessness and insubordination, which are the natural results of these long trials and sufferings. I have taken the responsibility to order the details for the work on the fortifications in this vicinity to be discontinued from tomorrow morning in order to give my whole time to the discipline of the Regiment   I feel that this Step though irregular and unauthorised nevertheless is absolutely necessary to restrain the mutinous and insubordinate Spirit which has all along manifested itself in a Small degree in the Command (Growing out of the treatment from the Government in regard to pay) from Culminating in open anarchy and perhaps mutiny. My men feel sorely troubled and grieved about their pay and I feel that this Course taken at this Stage of the proceedings is really necessary for the interests of the General service. And I preferred to take this Course seemingly of my own accord to prevent being forced to do so. Indeed I fear trouble from desertions and other Scources But I will do all that an officer can do and hope I will by this means Secure the end I desire that is to maintain the good discipline of the Command. I

would perfer to be ordered down the Country for a Short distance
if no further to get beyond the reach of Outside influence

Hoping General that this will meet with your approbation I am
with high respects Your Obedient Servant

HLcS   J M Williams

Lt. Col. J. M. Williams to Capt. H. Q. Loring, 21 Apr. 1863, Letters
Sent, 79th USCI (new), Regimental Books & Papers USCT, RG 94 [G-
117]. In January 1864, the Bureau of Colored Troops authorized payment
of the 1st Kansas Colored Volunteers from the date of its muster. (A.A.
Genl. C. W. Foster to Col. John Williams, 16 Jan. 1864, vol. 2, pp.
113–14, Letters Sent, ser. 352, Colored Troops Division, RG 94 [B-
500].) For later pay difficulties, see *Freedom*, ser. 2: doc. 161.

Recruitment in the Free States and Free-State Recruitment in the Occupied South

FROM THE FIRST SHOTS at Sumter, a few Northerners advocated enlisting black freemen into Union ranks. These Union partisans believed that the added weight of black soldiers would crush the Confederacy and end the rebellion. But, like other prescriptions for victory, the call for black enlistment embodied deeper social and political commitments. Most of these early advocates also hoped that a black military presence would help transform the war for Union into a war for freedom and would strengthen black claims to equality. Northern blacks, many of them former slaves, shared this belief, and they pressed for an opportunity to strike out against tne South and slavery. Throughout 1861 and 1862, letters trickled into the War Department and other governmental agencies urging the organization of black regiments. But the miscellaneous nature of these memorials, the relative anonymity of their authors, and the disproportionate number of blacks among the petitioners suggest that the enlistment of blacks had yet to sink deep roots in the free states.[1]

As the war dragged on and the death toll mounted, grim necessity swelled support for the enlistment of black freemen in the North just as it encouraged slave recruitment in portions of the occupied South. Many of the new supporters of mustering black soldiers did not share the abolitionist and equalitarian commitments of the early advocates. Instead, they dwelled on the allegedly superior resistance of blacks to the rigors of soldiering in the subtropical South, and the belief that the South would use, if they were not already using, armed blacks against the North. Many frankly believed that black soldiers would make better cannon fodder than white ones. And even if Northern freemen would not or could not

[1] Published accounts of recruitment of blacks in the free states include: Luis F. Emilio, *History of the Fifty-Fourth Regiment of Massachusetts Volunteer Infantry, 1863–1865,* 2d ed. (Boston, 1894), pp. 1–34; Henry G. Pearson, *The Life of John A. Andrew, Governor of Massachusetts 1861–1865* (Boston, 1904), vol. 2, pp. 63–121; Dudley Taylor Cornish, *The Sable Arm: Negro Troops in the Union Army, 1861–1865* (New York, 1956), pp. 105–11; James M. McPherson, *The Struggle for Equality: Abolitionists and the Negro in the Civil War and Reconstruction* (Princeton, N.J., 1964), pp. 202–8.

fight, they might at least relieve white soldiers of burdensome fatigue duties. Fired by such contradictory motives, Northern opinion began to shift, and in late 1862 and early 1863 plans for black enlistment inched forward, pulled by an equalitarian alliance of white and black abolitionists and pushed by white fears of rumored conscription. Perhaps nothing more reveals the subtle shift of federal policy than the appearance of a census report estimating the number of black men of military age.

Preeminent among the advocates of enlisting Northern freemen was John A. Andrew, governor of Massachusetts and a determined foe of slavery. Upon taking office, Andrew pressed hard to muster blacks into Union ranks. Early in 1863, in the company of Wendell Phillips, Francis W. Bird, and other Massachusetts radicals, he traveled to Washington to place his case before President Abraham Lincoln and Secretary of War Edwin M. Stanton. Andrew left the capital believing that Northern blacks would soon be enlisted on the same terms as whites. Although Stanton did not share Andrew's understanding of the terms of black service, the Secretary of War soon began the process of black recruitment. In mid-January, the War Department authorized the governor of Rhode Island to muster a separate regiment of "volunteers of African descent." Soon after, Andrew received similar permission, and the 54th Massachusetts Colored Infantry began to take shape.[2]

Andrew began work at once, certain that black enlistment would aid the war against slavery in the South and caste in the North. He contacted black leaders to assure them – incorrectly it turned out – that black soldiers would receive the same protection and privileges as whites. He carefully selected white officers (one of Stanton's explicit stipulations) whose lofty social standing would counter the sure opposition that mustering black soldiers everywhere faced. In Massachusetts, blue bloods would lead black skins. And, since Massachusetts alone could not supply enough black soldiers to fill a regiment, Andrew sent abolitionist George L. Stearns outside the state to recruit black freemen and rally antislavery support. Stearns, lavishly supported by abolitionist largess, established a network of black recruiting agents throughout the North. Working on a commission basis, Martin R. Delany, John Jones, John M. Langston, and other black leaders became the primary source of enlistees for the 54th Massachusetts, the 14th Rhode Island Heavy Artillery, and the 29th Connecticut. These men, with deep roots in Northern black communities, drew on the militia companies that had been organized in Northern cities following the passage of the 1850 Fugitive Slave Act. Andrew enlisted the aid of like-minded Northern

---

[2] *Official Records*, ser. 3, vol. 3, pp. 16, 20–21, 38–39.

officials. Ohio Governor David Tod supported Andrew's efforts and urged Ohio freemen to join the Massachusetts regiment, assuring them – on Andrew's authority – that the terms of their enlistment were the same as those of white soldiers. By the end of March 1863, recruiters had filled the 54th Massachusetts, and the organization of a second black Massachusetts regiment had begun.

Andrew's success in recruiting blacks from all over the North, combined with the Union army's voracious appetite for soldiers, turned the tide of Northern opinion and placed additional pressure on policy makers to regularize black enlistment. Citizen groups composed of leading businessmen and civic leaders, often organized by the peripatetic Stearns, urged black enlistment and generously supported legislative lobbying with their time and money. Blacks continued to petition for the right to enlist, and in July black leaders from all over New York met in Poughkeepsie to press black enlistment.[3] State governors, particularly in the Midwest, evinced a growing interest in establishing separate black regiments, if only to fill their own conscription quotas. At first, Stanton urged these officials to cooperate with Andrew to ensure the success of the "experiment." But when the 54th and 55th Massachusetts reached full strength and Andrew stopped taking new recruits, Stanton's policy lost its force. Acting under the recently issued War Department General Order No. 143 and through the newly established Bureau of Colored Troops. Stanton authorized the establishment of black regiments upon request. In quick succession, the governors of Ohio, Pennsylvania, Michigan, Iowa, Wisconsin, Illinois, and Indiana asked for and received permission to muster black soldiers.[4] Only in New York, where the Democratic governor balked at the organization of a black unit, did the struggle for black enlistment continue to encounter opposition. By the end of 1863, that opposition, too, had collapsed. The question then became how soon and how many, not if, Northern freemen could be brought under arms, with Secretary of War Stanton urging on the Northern governors. Before long complaints of impressment mixed with petitions for enlistment.

By early 1864, Northern states experienced growing difficulty filling their national conscription quotas. Having long since exhausted the pool of volunteers, Congress began revising conscription laws to increase draft calls, abolish commutation, and prevent draft evasion. Northern businessmen, alarmed at the depletion of their

---

[3] *Record of Action of the Convention Held at Poughkeepsie, N.Y., July 15th and 16th, 1863, for the Purpose of Facilitating the Introduction of Colored Troops into the Service of the United States* (New York, 1863).

[4] *Negro in the Military Service*, pp. 1241–44, 1270, 1299, 1329–38, 1425–32, 1436–37, 1501, 1541, 1681, 1747, 1770, ser. 390, Colored Troops Division, RG 94.

labor force that would inevitably result from a more systematic draft, clamored for an alternative. They devised a scheme that could both fill state quotas and keep Northern laborers at their jobs by drawing on the large number of potential soldiers in the liberated South.

Under the plan, Northern states would send agents to recruit the "unemployed" men – both white and black – of the occupied South, crediting them toward Northern state draft quotas. In return, recruits would receive Northern state bounties, and agents would collect a fee for each man enlisted. In the summer of 1864, as Congress again considered the problem of raising additional troops, support for the plan grew among Northern workers who had no interest in fighting and politicians who feared repetition of the violent draft resistance that had shaken the North the previous summer. On July 4, 1864, an amendment to the 1863 enrollment act authorized just such recruitment in all the rebellious states except Arkansas, Tennessee, and Louisiana.[5]

With the passage of the act, Northern recruiters moved quickly into the Mississippi Valley, South Carolina, and northern Alabama and Georgia, the latter area but recently fallen to General William T. Sherman. Although they operated under the protective shield of the Union army, the recruiters showed little concern for the problems of field commanders and even less respect for military etiquette. Moreover, despite the color-blind provisions of the law, the recruiters aimed only to enlist blacks. In their greed to collect men and the accompanying fee, recruiters ravaged the countryside, exposing themselves and their quarry to rebel attack; demanded food, forage, and transportation from their hosts; and even went so far as to take recruits from among military laborers.

In the face of such high-handed methods, military commanders soon lost patience. Suspicions that this new policy represented a compromise with the cowardliness and lack of patriotism of Northern shirkers only fueled their anger. No officer matched Sherman in degree of contempt for Northern recruiters and the system they represented. Like many Union commanders, Sherman considered blacks more valuable to his mobile forces as laborers and teamsters than as soldiers. Despite mounting evidence to the contrary, he doubted the ability of blacks to serve effectively as soldiers. Accordingly, Sherman permitted within his lines only able-bodied men capable of fatigue work. All other blacks he turned away. His lack of confidence in black soldiers lowered his estimation of the recruiters in principle; their ransacking his labor gangs for recruits infuriated him in practice. Eventually he ordered the summary arrest of any re-

[5] *Official Records*, ser. 3, vol. 4, p. 473.

cruiter interfering with military laborers. This action and Sherman's vigorous protest to General-in-Chief Henry W. Halleck induced President Lincoln to admit his own misgivings about the recruiting system.[6]

Nonetheless, abuses continued. In the Mississippi Valley, the recruitment bounties made it attractive for blacks already enlisted under Adjutant General Lorenzo Thomas to desert their regiments and reenlist with the Northern recruiters. In South Carolina, Northern agents disrupted work details and, when blacks hesitated, kidnapped them. Yet, at times, certain military commanders themselves adopted these questionable practices and even operated in collusion with the Northern recruiters. Several officers suffered court-martial and imprisonment as a consequence.[7]

Overall, the system of allowing Northern states to fill their quotas by recruiting in the South pleased no one. It inflamed military commanders, disrupted black regiments, and further complicated black recruitment. It failed to produce recruits in numbers sufficient either to relieve Northern states of the draft or to justify its abuses. Consequently, in March 1865, Congress legislated an end to the policy.[8] The Bureau of Colored Troops later estimated that during eight months in the field, more than 1,000 Northern recruiters had brought only 5,052 black men into federal service.[9]

[6] Major Genl. W. T. Sherman to Major Genl. H. W. Halleck, 14 July 1864, M-560 1864, Letters Received, ser. 360, Colored Troops Division, RG 94 [B-51]; M.G. W. T. Sherman to Genl. Lorenzo Thomas, 21 [July] 1864, S-30 1864, Letters Received by Adjutant General L. Thomas, ser. 363, Colored Troops Division, RG 94 [V-68]; A. Lincoln to Major General Sherman, 18 July 1864, Telegrams Collected by the Office of the Secretary of War (Bound), RG 107 [L-308].

[7] Col. [Reuben D. Mussey] to Mr. McKim, 14 Aug. 1864, vol. 221 DC, pp. 31–34; Col. [Reuben D. Mussey] to Brig. Genl. W. D. Whipple, 1 Nov. 1864, vol. 221 DC, pp. 261–62; Col. [Reuben D. Mussey] to Rev. E. W. Jackson, 22 Feb. 1865, vol. 221 DC, p. 502, Letters Sent by the Commissioner, ser. 1141, Organization of U.S. Colored Troops, Dept. of the Cumberland, RG 393 Pt. 1 [C-42 & C-49].

[8] *Official Records,* ser. 3, vol. 4, p. 1226.

[9] *Official Records,* ser. 3, vol. 5, p. 662.

17: Ohio White Unionist to the Secretary of War

Cincinnati. Aug 10 1861

Dear Sir   This is to inquire of you whether the government will accept of a Regiment of infantry consisting of 1000 *colored men,* three fourths of whom are bright mulattoes, the same to be officered throughout by competent white men. I am confident from late indications that in ten days I can muster 1000 or even 1500 of those men that will do good service. they are eager and willing to fight if the opportunity is shown them. since the "Bull's Run" or Manassas affair these men are much aroused on the war subject and as they are able why not let them do the government service also? I understand that the *Rebels* had a regiment of blacks in that engagement and in the next battle we can give them black for black. I can also raise an artillery company of the same class of men and doubt not but that they will stand fire with most of our troops (not to speak disparagingly of *them*) please answer at your earliest opportunity and oblige Very Respectfully Your obt Serv't

ALS   J. L. Stevens

J. L. Stevens to Hon. Mr. Cameron, 10 Aug. 1861, S-247 1861, Letters Received Irregular, RG 107 [L-86].

18: Michigan Black Physician to the Secretary of War

Battle Creek [*Mich.*] Oct 30th 1861
Dear Sir: Having learned that in your instructions to Gen. Sherman you authorized the enrollment of colored persons I wish to solicit the privilege of raising from five to ten thousand free men to report in sixty days to take any position that may be assigned us (sharp shooters preferred). We would like white persons for superior officers. If this proposition is not accepted we will if armed & equipped by the government fight as guerillas.

Any information or instructions that may be forwarded to me immediately will be thankfully received and implicitly obeyed.

A part of us are half breed Indians and legal voters in the state of Michigan. We are all anxious to fight for the maintenance of the Union and the preservation of the principles promulgated by Pres Lincoln and we are sure of success of allowed an opportunity.

In the name of God answer immediately. Yours fraternally

ALS   G. P. Miller M.D.

G. P. Miller to Simon Cameron, 30 Oct. 1861, M-310 1861, Letters Received Irregular, RG 107 [L-88]. The War Department, although praising Miller's "patriotic spirit and intelligence," declined his offer, on the grounds that "the orders to Genl. Sherman and other officers . . . authorize the arming of colored persons only in cases of great emergency. . . ." (Thomas A. Scott to Dr. G. P. Miller, 9 Nov. 1861, vol. 47, p. 51, Letters Sent, RG 107 [L-88].)

19: Two Ohio Blacks to the Secretary of War

Cleveland O 15 Nov. 1861.

Sir: The following particulars heareafter mentioned; have been laid before the, "Hon S. P. Chase, Sec of the Tres." and his reply to us, is that "we apply to you direct.

Theirfore, we would humly and respectfuly State, that, we are Colard men, (legal voters)   all voted for the presant administration. the question now is will you allow us the poor priverlige of fighting — and (if need be dieing) to suport those in office who are our own choise. we belive that a reigement of colard men can be raised in this State, who we are sure, would make as patriotic and good Soldiers as any other.

What we ask of you is that you give us the proper athroity to rais Such a reigement, and it *can* and SHALL be done.

We could give you a Thousand names as ether signers or as refferance if required. we would however refer you to the Hon Gen Crowell, Hon R. G. Riddle, M. C. and R^{bt} Pain Esq. [. . .]¹

W. T. Boyd,
J. T. Alston

P.S. we waite your reply. Box 3501

ALS

W. T. Boyd and J. T. Alston to Hon. Simon Cameron, 15 Nov. 1861, B-288 1861, Letters Received Irregular, RG 107 [L-78].

1 Two illegible words.

20: Ohio Black to the Secretary of War

Oberlin O. Nov. 27th 1861

Sir: — Very many of the colored citizens of Ohio and other states have had a great desire to assist the government in putting down this injurious rebellion.

Since they have heard that the rebels are forming regiments of the free blacks and compelling them to fight against the Union as well as their Slaves. They have urged me to write and beg that you will receive one or more regiments (or companies) of the colored of the free States to counterbalance those employed against the Union by Rebels.

We are partly drilled and would wish to enter active service amediately.

We behold your sick list each day and Sympathize with the Soldiers and the government. We are confident of our ability to stand the hard Ships of the field and the climate So unhealthy to the Soldiers of the *North*

To prove our attachment and our will to defend the government we only ask a trial   I have the honor to remain your humble Servant

<small>ALS</small>   Wm A. Jones

Wm. A. Jones to Hon. S. Cameron, 27 Nov. 1861, J-52 1861, Letters Received Irregular, RG 107 [L-91].

21: **Two New York Abolitionists to the Secretary of War**

Lockport [*N.Y.*] Nov 30, 1861

Dear Sir: Geo W. Clark, a well known friend of Freedom and the Union, in company with myself, proposes if we shall be able to secure your approval of the measure, to raise a Regiment of Colored Men, in the North, to aid in suppressing this most wicked rebellion. A powerful auxilary can be furnished in this direction, and we are sanguine that the time has come when the inauguration of such a force would not only be approved by a vast majority of our Northern people, friendly to the Govt and the Union, but prove also an inspiration to their enthusiasm in the cause. Indeed we think no measure could prove more popular, as the South – the Rebels – have now made it their settled policy to arm not only the savages but the Free Blacks – arming these and *drilling* them to shoot down our brave Northern soldiers, while employing the bondsmen to dig trenches and build forts and furnish supplies for their murderous armies. There may be difference of opinion in regard to the propriety or policy of arming slaves and Free Blacks in the South to fight for us, but we are satisfied that there would be the most hearty approval of the policy we advocate in reference to arming the *Free Colored* men of the North. Indeed, we know, from the best of Evidence, that there is almost an impatience for the adoption of some such measure. There are thousands of stalwart, heroic, *powerful,* colored men of the Free States, and many of them Citisens, who have common rights and feel a common interest in the support of the

Union and the Govt, who would freely shed their blood in their defence, anxiously waiting to *be allowed* to share in the perils of the battle field to uphold the Flag and honor of the Nation.   Equally now as in the last War and in the War of the Revolution, we of the North are coming to think that the blood of the Colored Man in this costly sacrifice of white men's blood is an offering that the Nation should not despise.   If you shall judge it proper or expedient to authorise this proposition we will pledge ourselves to furnish a Regiment that for deeds of bravery and endurance shall not prove unworthy of the admiration of the Country and that shall do much to silence the accusations of enemies across the Ocean.   We can furnish you satisfactory references   Very Respectfully

G. W. Clark –

ALS
W. Stickney

G. W. Clark and W. Stickney to Hon. S. Cameron, 30 Nov. 1861, C-102 1861, Letters Received, ser. 496, Volunteer Service Division, RG 94 [BB-4].

22: Former Slave to the Secretary of War

London   Canada West   May 7th 1862

dear sir. please indulg me the liberty of writing you afew lines upon a subject of grave importance to your & my country   It is true I am now stoping in canada for awhile but it is not my home – & before I proceen further I must inform you of your humble correspondent.   My name is G. H. White formerly the Servant of Robert Toombs of Georgia.   M^r W^m H Seward knows something about me   I am now a minister, & am called upon By my peopel to tender to your *Hon* thir willingness to serve as soldiers in the southern parts during the summer season or longer if required.   our offer is not for speculation or self interest but for our love for the north & the government at large, & at the same time we pray god that the triumph of the north & restoration of peace if I may call it will prove an eternal overthrow of the institution of slavery which is the cause of all our trouble   if you desire to see me let me hear at an early day.   I am certain of raising a good no. in the west & in the north.   I am aquainted all thro the south for I traveled with Senator Toombs all over it nearly.   I am quite willing to spend my life in preaching against sin & fighting against the same.   Mr Seward & many other of both

white & colored know me in Washington   please let me hear from
your Hon soon   your most humble servant

Garland H. White

please excuse my bad writing as I never went to School a day in
my left. I learnd what little I know by the hardest. yet I feel
that the simplist instroment used in the right direction sometimes
accomplishs much good. I pray you in gods name to consider the
condition of your humble speaker in the distant. A man who are
free from all the calumities of your land. yet when he thinks of his
sufferring countrymen he can but feel that good might make him
instromental in your hands to the accomplishments of some
humble good. as simple as this request may seeme to you yet it
might prove one of the greatest acts of your life. an act which
might redown to your honor to the remotest generation– I want
to see my friends at port royal & other places in the South. I now
close by saying I hope to hear from you as soon as possible. I
shall not be happy till I hear from you on this very important
subject & not then if I am denied– So now my chance to do
good as I think rest altogether [*with*] you. now may the good lord
help you to make a faverorabl desition   heaven bless you & your
dear family is the prayer & your most obedient sirvant   G. H.
White   minister of the gospel   London Canada West

A Black regiment headed by the Revd Garland. H. White offers
their services in protection of the southern forts during the sickly
season

ALS

Garland H. White to E. M. Stanton, 7 May 1862, W-561 1862, Letters
Received, RG 107 [L-160].

23: Captain of a Black Militia Company to the Secretary of War

Pittsburg Penna   May 13th 1862

Dear Sir   I see that it is your intention to garrison the Southern
forts with COLORED SOLDIERS and if such be the fact I hereby
tender to you the "Fort Pitt Cadets of the City of Pittsburg for
duty   The Fort Pitt Cadets have been organized some two years
and are quite Proficient in military discipline. I can furnish you
with satisfactory reference &c. I will also pledge myself to recruit
two hundred men within thirty days after you shall have given
authority or placed an officer in this city for recruiting. The men

whom I shall recruit will be able-bodied and of unquestionable
loyalty to the United States of America. You will please be kind
enough give this your attention   I remain Your ob't serv't

                                                    Rufus Sibb Jones

P.S. Please find two extracts from city papers in regards to the
Fort Pitt cadets

ALS

Rufus Sibb Jones to Hon. Edwin M. Stanton, 13 May 1862, J-100 1862,
Letters Received, ser. 496, Volunteer Service Division, RG 94 [BB-1]. The
enclosed newspaper clippings indicate that the Fort Pitt Cadets drilled during a local celebration of West Indian Emancipation.

24: Governor of Illinois to the President

                                        Springfield Ill July 11" 62

President Lincoln — The crisis of the war and our National
existence is upon us — The time has come for the adoption of
more decisive measures   greater animus and earnestness must be
infused into our military movements — blows must be struck at
the vital part of the Rebellion — The Government should employ
every available means compatible with the rules of warfare to
subject the traitors — Summon to the standard of the Republic all
willing to fight for the Union — Let loyalty, and that alone, be
the dividing line between the nation and its foes   Generals should
not be permitted to fritter away the sinews of our brave men in
guarding the property of traitors, and in driving back into their
hands loyal blacks who offer us their labor and seek shelter with
the federal flag — Shall we sit [supinely] by and see the war sweep
[off] the youth and strength of the land and refuse aid from that
class of men who are at least worthy foes of traitors and the
murderers of our Government and of our children — Our Armies
should be directed to forward [forage] on the Enemy and to cease
paying traitors and their abettors exhorbitant exactions for food
needed by the spent and sick or hungry soldier — Mild and
conciliatory means have been tried in vain to recall the rebels to
their allegiance   The conservative policy has utterly failed to
reduce traitors to obedience, and to restore the supremacy of the
laws   They have by means of sweeping conscriptions gathered in
countless hordes and threatened to beat back and overwhelm the
Armies of the Union with blood and treason in their
hearts — They flaunt the black flag of rebellion in the face of the

Government and threaten to butcher our brave and loyal Armies
with foreign bayonets— They arm negroes and merciless savages in
their behalf— Mr Lincoln, the crisis demands greater efforts and
stearner measures Proclaim anew the good old motto of the
Republic: "Liberty and Union, now and forever, one and
inseparable" and accept the services of all loyal men, and it will be
in your power to stamp armies of the earth, irresistable armies,
that will bear banners to certain victory— In any event Ill is
already alive with beat of drum, resounding with the tread of new
recruits which will respond to your call! Adopt this policy and she
will leap like a flaming giant into the fight This policy for the
conduct of the war will render foreign intervention impossible and
the arms of the Republic invincible— It will bring the conflict to
a speedy close and secure peace on a permanent basis

HWSr   Richd Yates

Gov. Richd. Yates to President Lincoln, 11 July 1862, Telegrams Collected by the Office of the Secretary of War (Bound), RG 107 [L-205].

25: Governor of Iowa to the General-in-Chief of the Army

[*Des Moines*] Iowa August 5 1862

General   You will bear me witness I have not trouble on the
"*negro*" subject but there is as it seems to me so much good sense
in the following extract from a letter to me from one of the best
colonels this state has in the service that I have yielded to the
temptation to send it to you— It is as follows. "I hope under the
confiscation and emancipation bill just passed by Congress to
supply my regiment with a sufficient number of 'contrabands' to
do all the 'extra duty' labor of my camp. I have now *sixty men on
extra duty* as teamsters &c. whose places could just as well be filled
with *niggers*— We do not need a single negro in the army to fight
but we could use to good advantage about one hundred & fifty
with a regiment as teamsters & for making roads, chopping wood,
policing camp &c. *There are enough soldiers on extra duty in the army
to take Richmond or any other rebel city if they were in the ranks instead
of doing negro work.*"

I have but one remark to add and that in regard to the negroes
fighting— it is this—When this war is over & we have summed
up the entire loss of life it has imposed on the country I shall not
have any regrets if it is found that a part of the dead are *niggers*
and that *all* are not white men—

We will have one fine new regiment filled in this month— The order of yesterday for a draft of 300000 men for nine months is just what we want except as to length of service but that cant be helped as the law is so. Very Respectfully Your Obt Sev

ALS   Samuel J Kirkwood

Samuel J. Kirkwood to General [Henry W. Halleck], 5 Aug. 1862, K-493 1862, Letters Received, ser. 22, RG 108 [S-29].

26: Governor of Massachusetts to a Massachusetts Abolitionist

Boston, January 30th 1863.

Dear Sir: As you may have seen by the news-papers, I am about to raise a colored regiment in Massachusetts. This I cannot but regard as perhaps the most important corps to be organized during the whole war, in view of what must be the composition of our new levies; and therefore I am very anxious to organize it judiciously, in order that it may be a model for all future colored regiments. I am desirious to have for its officers—particularly its field officers—young men of military experience, of firm anti-slavery principles, ambitious, superior to a vulgar contempt for color, and having faith in the capacity of colored men for military service. Such officers must necessarily be gentlemen of the highest tone and honor; and I shall look for them in those circles of educated anti-slavery society, which next to the colored race itself have the greatest interest in the success of this experiment.

Reviewing the young men of this character I have described, now in the Massachusetts service, it occurs to me to offer the colonelcy of such a regiment to your son, Captain Shaw of the 2nd Mass. Infantry and the Lt. Colonelcy to Capt. Hallowell of Philadelphia. With my deep conviction of the importance of this undertaking in view of the fact that it will be the first colored regiment to be raised in the free States, and that its success or its failure will go far to elevate or to depress the estimation in which the character of the colored American will be held throughout this world, the command of such a regiment seems to me to be a high object of ambition for any officer.

. . . .

My mind is drawn towards Captain Shaw by many considerations. I am sure that he would attract the support, sympathy and active cooperation of many besides his immediate family and relatives. The more ardent; faithful and true

Republicans and friends of liberty would recognize in him a scion from a tree whose fruit and leaves have always contributed to the strength and healing of our generation. So also it is with Captain Hollowell. His father is a quaker gentleman of Philadelphia, two of whose sons are officers in one regiment and another is a merchant in Boston.

. . . .

HLc   [*John A. Andrew*]

[John A. Andrew] to Francis G. Shaw, 30 Jan. 1863, Negro in the Military Service, p. 1082, ser. 390, Colored Troops Division, RG 94 [B-450]. Ellipses in manuscript. War Department compilers copied this extract from a draft in Massachusetts state records.

27: Superintendent of the Census Office to the Secretary of the Interior

Washington February 11, 1863

Sir. Respecting the number of free colored persons in the United States, of the arms bearing age, I have the honor to submit tabular statements, herewith accompanying, which show the number of such persons of 18 and under 45, and, hypothetically, the proportion in the free States, which may be supposed available from this population upon the data furnished by the number of white persons who have entered the military service, from the various States and Territories. In my opinion the number of colored persons in the free States physically conditioned to bear arms, is less in a given population than the number of whites, from the fact that the Free Colored population in the North is made to hold its numbers by supply from the South, rather than by that natural increase from generation, incident to good conditions. This view is sustained by the current reports on mortality which in many instances prove the number of deaths among the free-colored to be greater than the births. The increase among this population, in Massachusetts, from 1840 to 1850 was less than 5 per cent, and from 50. to 60 less than 6. per cent. In Maine and New Hampshire, Vermont and New York, they have actually decreased, which fact taken in connection with the small aggregate increase of 12 per cent, North & South in ten years *from all causes,* proves beyond question that the race would not advance in the Northern States, but by artificial additions, and that physically it is, under its present circumstances neither equal to the slave or free population.

87

In my opinion the number of the free colored population has always been over estimated from the fact of their concentration in Cities and large Towns, and their employment in out door avocations, whereas, if employed in factories and trades and on farms they would escape observation and be almost lost sight of. I am equally convinced that while climate has much to do with their physical condition, their general mode of life incident to caste and condition has probably equal effect upon their vitality— Be the reasons what they may, the fact is evident that the Colored population in the Northern and Western States, holds an inferior place physically to the whites and could hardly be relied upon to supply proportionate numbers of able bodied men. From the tables presented, it appears that the whole number of free colored men in the United States of the arms bearing age, amounts to less than 91.000 and that they are nearly equally divided between the Free and Slave-holding States. If however we concede the probability of this class of persons enlisting for military duty in numbers proportionate to the white population they would in all the States and Territories supply eighteen regiments of 1000 men each—while the non-slave holding States and the District of Columbia would supply nearly ten regiments. The State of Maine would furnish 50 men, New Hampshire 20, Massachusetts 400, Rhode Island 160, Vermont 30, New York and and Pennsylvania could supply 4000 while in any other State but Ohio it would be impossible to raise a full regiment. I send you also, a table giving the number of Slaves in the United States, of the arm-bearing age which reaches nearly the figure of 750.000 the condition and circumstances of whom preclude all calculations as to what proportion could be made available as men at arms. I have the honor to be Very Respectfully Your ob^r Servt

HLS

Jos. C G Kennedy

Jos. C. G. Kennedy to Hon. J. P. Usher, 11 Feb. 1863, I-77 1863, Letters Received Irregular, RG 107 [L-105]. Enclosures, endorsement. The information in the tables to which Kennedy refers has been reformulated and presented in the introductory essay as Table 1.

28: Governor of Massachusetts to a Northern Black Leader

Boston, March 23. 1863.

Dear Sir: In reply to your inquiries made as to the position of colored men who may be enlisted and mustered into the volunteer service of the United States, I would say, that their position, in respect to pay, equipments, bounty, or aid and protection, when so mustered, will be precisely the same, in every particular, as that of any and all other volunteers.

I desire further to state to you, that when I was in Washington, on one occasion, in an interview with Mr Stanton, the Secretary of War, he stated in the most emphatic manner, that he would never consent that free colored men should be accepted into the service to serve as soldiers in the South until he should be assured that the Government of the United States was prepared to guarantee and defend, to the last dollar and the last man, to these men, all the rights, privileges and immunities that are given, by the laws of civilized warfare, to other soldiers. Their present acceptance and muster-in, as soldiers, pledges the honor of the Nation in the same degree and to the same rights with all other troops. They will be soldiers of the Union – nothing less and nothing different. I believe they will earn for themselves an honorable fame, vindicating their race and redeeming their future from disaspersions of the past. I am yours truly,

HLcSr   John A. Andrew.

John A. Andrew to George T. Downing, 23 Mar. 1863, Negro in the Military Service, p. 1133, ser. 390, Colored Troops Division, RG 94 [B-451]. War Department compilers copied this letter from Massachusetts state records.

29: New York Recruiting Agent to the Secretary of War

New York April 6th 1863.

Sir   Some seven weeks ago, I started on somewhat of an extensive recruiting tour and while starting recruiting offices for my cavalry regiment – I authorized the most prominent and enlightened negroes I could find to enroll their fellow bretheren and such other men as would volunteer to serve for the war as soldiers in the first Brigade of N.Y.S. Coloured Volunteers. after spending some six weeks at it I had over twenty four hundred names enrolled, and they are now anxiously awaiting some sort of recognition from the government willing and able to fight. they think that the government does not wish their services, when we are compelled to enforce the conscript law to compel men who are unwilling to fight while men that are more serviceable and can endure more hardships and fatigues than white men and they have been compelled to remain at home feeling themselves humbled and disgraced and treated with more contempt and disgrace than by the Southern Slave drivers and rebels. probably you have not thought of this matter nor seen it in the same light as it is seen and felt here by the men themselves. All I desire is from you a prompt reply as to whether you desire their services or not. if you want them send me on the requisite authority to have them mustered in   I will have them equipped clothed and drilled and after three months in camp if you see fit then to let me command them well and good   if not I will be content with knowing that I have done my country another good service. all I desire [is] the necessary authority to transport equip and subsist them for ninety days and at the end of that time I will turn over to the government as fine a body of well-drilled and disciplined troops as you or any other man ever laid eyes on. hoping my dear Sir that you will not keep me waiting for a reply I am Sir Very Respectfully Yours most truly & faithfully

Henry M Herman.

P.S. My references are the President Secy of State Hon Charles Sumner, Horace Greely, H W Beecher, and numerous others

ALS

[*Endorsement*] A.G. Office April 18th 1863   Respectfully returned to the Secretary of War

No authority has been given from this office to Major Henry M. Herman to raise colored troops

The views of the Secretary on the subject of organizing troops of this kind, have not been communicated as yet, for the guidance of the Adjutant Generals Department. Thomas M Vincent Asst. Adjt. Genl.

Major Henry M. Herman to Hon. Edwin M. Stanton, 6 Apr. 1863, H-426 1863, Letters Received, ser. 496, Volunteer Service Division, RG 94 [BB-6]. Another endorsement.

30: Northern Recruiter to the Solicitor of the War Department

Buffalo [N.Y.] April 27. 1863

My Dear friend   Your esteemed favor of the 21" inst was received in course of mail. I thank you most heartily for your kind

mention of me to Secretary Stanton and shall be careful not to
forfeit the good opinion he has of my labors.

My work still expands. A day or two since I received
permission of Gov. Gamble of Missouri, Mayor Filley of St Louis,
and Genl. Curtiss to take quietly as many men as I could get from
St. Louis, and I have already taken steps for the prosecution of my
work there. In all the large Cities of the West we are aided and
encouraged by the authorities and prominent citizens so that altho'
quiet we are enabled to act openly. Fifty four men came through
on Saturday from Cincinnati and the line of roads from that place
to Cleveland. From other points they are increasing so rapidly that
I am enabled to make my own terms with the Railroads for
transportation, one 46/100 per mile express trains. Last Evening
two prominent citizens of this place came to me with a proposition
for the use of some of these Black troops, which after a long
conference shaped itself into this proposition, that the Govt should
occupy Florida with a sufficient force of colored men to hold it,
with the promise that at the end of the war all who chose to
remain should have a grant of land, the same priviledge to be
extended to all colored persons who would emigrate. There is one
feature of the contemplated settlement of the status of this race
that always troubles me. It is the interference of the Govt with
their labor in any way. All Govt plans of working plantations is
but a modified form of slavery, under which the Black will not
improve either his mental or moral condition and will have to be
abandoned in the end; But put arms in their hands and you at
once increase their self respect and give them confidence in their
abilities to support themselves and their families. Arm One
Hundred Thousand Blacks, conscript them wherever they are to be
found, give them good white officers who will take an interest in
their welfare, colored Chaplins, and colored Surgeons as far as
competent ones can be found, tell them that as soon as they are
competent to command they shall be promoted, and you will have
an army that will put down the rebellion without further draft on
the northern Whites who will call on God to bless Abraham
Lincoln for saving them from this dreaded conscription and
effectually extirpate slavery from the land. With one hundred
thousand colored men taught the use of the musket it will not be
possible to reenslave them.

Please acertain if you can what the President and Secretary
Stanton [*think*] of the Florida plan. It would be a very popular
move among the Northern Whites who will encourage any scheme
that promises to send the black men south.

I have no doubt that I could engage most heartily all the leaders of the colored men in the north to aid it with their most energetic efforts, and it would largely increase the recruiting of these men in the free states. You know I have been cultivating these affiliations for years, and they now come in play. Truly Your friend –

HLS
George L. Stearns

George L. Stearns to William Whiting, 27 Apr. 1863, S-237 1863, Letters Received Irregular, RG 107 [L-123].

31: Governor of Ohio to a Northern Black Recruiter

Columbus, Ohio, May 16, 1863.

John M. Langston, Esq., present: Referring to our conversation of last evening, I have now to report: 1st., That the Government is desirous to obtain all the colored troops that can be raised. 2d., That the pay, bounty, clothing and term of enlistment will be the same for colored troops as for white troops. 3d., That authority has been given by the Government to Governor Andrew, of Massachusetts, to recruit colored men for the Massachusetts Brigade from all the loyal States. 4th., That as it was uncertain what number of colored men could be promptly raised in Ohio, I have advised, and still do advise, that those disposed to enter the service, promptly join the Massachusetts Regiments, Thus securing to the Government the services of Colored Men much earlier than if the attempt was made to get up regiments in each loyal State. Having requested the Governor of Massachusetts to organize the colored men from Ohio into separate companies, so far as practicable, and also to keep me fully advised of the name, age and place of residence of each, Ohio will have the full benefit of all enlistments from the State, and the recruits themselves the benefit of the State associations, to the same extent nearly as if organized into a State regiment. In addition to the benefits before recited, I believe that the State of Massachusetts pays an extra bounty of $50 to each recruit who may join the Massachusetts Brigade. No such provision was made by the laws of Ohio.

I am glad to know that you are devoting your best energies to the work of raising troops for this brigade, and trust your efforts will be highly successful.

Herewith I hand you copy of a letter to Governor Andrew; also copy of a letter recently received from General D. Hunter, from Hilton Head, highly commending the conduct of your countrymen under his command, which you are at liberty to make such use of as you may see proper.   Yours, &c.,

TLcSr   David Tod

Governor David Tod to John M. Langston, 16 May 1863, Negro in the Military Service, pp. 1242–43, ser. 390, Colored Troops Division, RG 94 [B-452]. The location of the letter from which this copy was made is not indicated. A copy of Tod's letter to Governor John A. Andrew (16 May 1863), asking that black volunteers from Ohio be organized into their own companies within the Massachusetts black regiments, appears in the same compilation, p. 1241, but the letter from General Hunter is not included.

32: Northern Black Recruiter to the Bureau of Colored Troops

Washington D.C.   Mar. 3rd 1865

Dear Sir   I desire to enter the recruiting service. I reside in Ohio. have lived in Ohio since 1846. previous to which time I lived in North Carolina. I am now 39 years old. I took charge of the Col^d recruiting service in Ohio in the spring of 1863. for the State of Massachusetts. I served in the capacity of state Ag^t to organize the colored settlements for the purpose of facilitating colored enlistments. during the time the state of Massachusetts through its agency was allowed to take recruits from the state of Ohio, or about three months. I was then appointed by Gov. Tod to superintend the (Col^d) Recruiting service in the same capacity. in which I had been serving. for the state of Massachusetts   I was employed by Gov. Tod about Four months during which time I recruited about 300. of the 5 Regiment of USC.T. in the spring of 1864 I was appointed by Gov Brough to assist in raising the 27th Reg. U.S.C.T   I was in his service three months   during a part of the time. while I was recruiting in Ohio I had the controle of the transportation & subsistance. all of which I did to the entire satisfaction of the gentlemen in authority. if not inconsistant with your orders I wish an appointment to Recruit in some part of the south with a Commission to rank as Captain   very Respectfully your obedient serv^t

ALS   O. S. B. Wall

O. S. B. Wall to Col. Foster, 3 March 1865, W-172 1865, Letters Received, ser. 360, Colored Troops Division, RG 94 [B-395]. An endorsement dated March 3, 1865, indicates that Colonel C. W. Foster of the

Bureau of Colored Troops examined Wall in person and concluded that he was well qualified to serve as a recruiting officer for black troops. In the same file are drafts of letters to the Commander of the Department of the South and to the War Department's Commissary of Musters ordering Wall's muster as a captain and his assignment to South Carolina for recruiting duty. (C. W. Foster to Brevet Major Genl. R. Saxton, 3 Mar. 1865; C. W. Foster to Capt. Henry Keteltas, 3 Mar. 1865.)

33: Chicago Newspaper Editor to the Clerk of the Senate Military Affairs Committee, Enclosing a *Chicago Tribune* Editorial

Chicago, June 15th 1863.

Friend White   Can you do anything to secure an order authorizing Gov Yates to raise a colored regiment of Illinois troops? If the authority is given the regiment will be made up. There are 300 blacks in this city alone ready to join it, but they refuse to go off to Massachusetts, and I don't blame them. Try and see Mr Stanton on this subject. Yours truly

ALS   J. Medill

[*Enclosure*]   [*Chicago*] MONDAY, JUNE 15, 1863.

AN ILLINOIS COLORED REGIMENT.

The time has come when the colored men of this State should be permitted to raise an Illinois regiment. The opposition to the employment of this species of soldiers to help put down the rebellion has in great measure ceased. It is only now and then that a Copperhead is heard to object. The army has ceased to oppose it, and the whole mass of loyal people are in favor of it.

Massachusetts broke the ice, and has shown how easily the thing can be done. The first colored regiment sailed from Boston 1,046 strong. The second regiment is nearly full, and Gov. Andrew has ordered the commencement of a third. But the blacks of other States have furnished most of the men. Two hundred and fifty have been contributed from Illinois. A squad of thirty-three, enlisted by Lewis Isbell (colored), went East on Saturday. The same recruiting agent had sent one hundred previously.

But the colored men enlist to join Massachusetts regiments very reluctantly. They are impatient to get up an *Illinois* regiment. They can see no good reason why they are refused that privilege. They want to fight for the Union, but they prefer being mustered into the service as a part of the quota of their own great State. They feel a commendable State pride. Illinois has led the van in patriotic sacrifice, and in bravery on the battle field, she yields the palm to no other State. The colored men, if given a fair chance, will prove themselves worthy of being enrolled among Illinois soldiers. They are but a handfull of population, still they can raise one thousand stalwart fighting men, who will go as far as their white officers dare lead them. Why should they not have the opportunity? A thousand blacks will save a thousand white men from being drafted. Let those who are opposed to colored men volunteering, enlist themselves; but if they decline, then let them keep their mouths shut.

The Secretary of War ought to authorize Gov. Yates to raise a regiment of black volunteers from Illinois, and we think our patriotic Governor should insist upon having that privilege. We hope he will. There are three to four hundred blacks in this city who will join such a regiment. It should be encamped here. From this point recruiting officers would visit every portion of the State where an able bodied colored man could be found, and bring him here and swear him in.

All that is needed to raise a splendid regiment is to pursue exactly the same course in respect to transportation, pay, rations, clothing and arms, as that by which sixty thousand white men were procured last summer. The process is simple and made plain by experience. If Gov. Yates obtains the permission to raise a regiment and selects a set of capable and experienced men for commissioned officers, with the right kind of man a for Colonel, and place the details in the hands of Adjutant General Fuller, we will guarantee that the colored people will produce within thirty days thereafter, as full and firm a regiment as has marched from this State — a regiment that will stand as much hardship, and fight as desperately, and kill as many rebels in battle, as any equal number of men of the purest Anglo-Saxon blood that have gone to the wars.

PD

[*Endorsement*] Referred to Captain Foster with directions to issue an order authorizing a Regiment of colored troops to be raised in Illinois —

The order to issue not to the Governor but to Major Stearns   E M Stanton

J. Medill to [Horace] White, 15 June 1863, enclosing clipping from *Chicago Tribune*, 15 June 1863, M-17 1863, Letters Received, ser. 360, Colored Troops Division, RG 94 [B-406]. On "Office of the Daily Tribune" letterhead.

34: Chairman of the Pennsylvania Supervisory Committee for Recruiting Colored Regiments to the Secretary of War

Philadelphia July 30th 1863

Sir. The Committee for supervising the recruiting Colored Troops for three years or the war, respectfully inform you that the first recruits were mustered in the 27th of June and the Regiment – 3d US Cold Troops made full 24th July: that two Companies of another regiment have also been mustered in and that efforts are being actively made to fill it with dispatch: with fine prospects of success.

The Committee beg leave to call your attention to a few facts connected with this most important subject. A Large majority of the two hundred and eighty five Gentlemen, comprising leading men of all classes who memorialize the war department to authorize these Colored Regiments to be raised in Pennsylvania, have, untill very recently, been opposed to arming men of color, and, with but few exceptions, have held opinions more favorable than adverse to the continued existance of Slavery. Their signatures are typical of the great change which the events of the past two years have wrought in the public mind.

The invitation extended to the free colored men of the nation, to enter into the service of their Country is in the opinion of the Committee the most popular war measure that the administration adopted. The Committee is lead to this conclusion: by the fact that hundreds of prominent Citizens express much regret that they had no opportunity to sign the memorial – that the Committee has been obliged to enlarge its numbers three times in order to take in those who applied to become members of it – by the voluntary and very liberal donations in money made to the Committee to enable it to defray the extraordinary expenses of recruiting not allowed by law, and by the open and hearty commendation, expressed in the City and throught the State, on the whole movement.

The Committee have held public meetings in the City and in various parts of Pennsylvania which have been large and enthusiastic, have published, addresses, circulars, posters, pamphlet and Editorials setting forth the duty of the colored race, all of which have been well received and have elicited proper responses in sympathy and aid from the white, and in recruits from the Colored race. It has daily sent single squads of Colored Troops, armed and Equipped in the U.S. uniform carrying the flag into all quarters of the city and into neighboring towns beating up recruits, and not only has the novel sight of a few colored soldiers met with no marks of disapprobation from whites, but has generally met with the strongest manifestations of approval evinced by cheers and other demonstrations. In one instance an attack was made upon the flag-bearer, who promptly felled his assailant to the earth, and then quietly resumed his march, applauded by all who witnessed the act. White soldiers have repeatedly cheered these squads of colored troops on meeting them in the streets, and whole Regiments marching to the defense of the state have cheered these Head Quarters. In every respect so far as the experience of the past few weeks enable the Committee to judge, there is not only no repugnance on the part of the white soldiers to colored Soldiers but a positive disposition to fraternize with them

There is a fact which should be prominently set forth — it is this: that the Lt Col Commanding the Camp has been able with the assistance of but three Lieutenants, to maintain perfect order among the recruits — rapidly increased from a mere squad to a full regiment, much of this is, certainly due to the character of the troops themselves, and to their previous habits of subordination. The neighbors to the Camp are unanimous in praise of the honesty and good behavior of the men when on furlough, and experienced officers of the regular army who have observed their drill and evolutions speak in favorable terms of the rapid progress they make in acquiring knowledge of their new profession.

Even the lowest classes of the Community — the class which in New York under audacious leaders, manifest diabolical hatred to the colored race, *in this city* show no positive aversion to the Enlistment of colored men as soldiers, and in some instances the classes alluded to have been known to express their satisfaction in the movement, under the impression that such enlistments would lessen their own chances of being called out. In narrating some of the recent wonderful changes in public sentiment, regarding colored troops, the Committee desires it to be distinctly understood that it does not claim to have created in the slightest degree this enlightened sentiment — the march of events has done this. The Committee, has only assisted in revealing the change boldly and plainly to the world.

The committee in connection with Major Geo L Stearns has organized an extensive agency designed to promote recruiting of

97

colored men by means of intelligent correspondents and active
recruiting agents, the fruits of which are beginning to be gathered

In Pennsylvania and in the adjacent States of New York, New
Jersey Delaware Maryland and Ohio the free colored population by
the last census was two hundred and seventy one
thousand. Doubtless it is now much larger, and if with the
aggregate, the colored population of New England and the western
states (the latter largely increased by refugees from slave states) is
computed, the total of this class cannot fall far short of four
hundred thousand, out of which, by proper efforts, at least fifty
regiments numbering forty thousand men may be recruited.

Assuming that it is the fixed purpose of the administration to
encourage the formation of as many regiments of colored troops
from the loyal states as possible, the committee would respectfully
suggest that if the concentration of efforts to procure recruits be
but for *one Camp* and for one Regiment *at a time* it will be found
most conducive to success. Philadelphia is particularly well
adapted, under the able direction and supervision of Major Stearns,
to be made the local center (outside the lines of the army) for all
operations having this object in view. It has a loyal population
largely sympathizing in the movement, and liberally subscribing to
the fund in aid of it. It is the natural center of the colored men
of the Free States — it has an organized Committee of earnest
workers, who have now perfected their machinery and know how
to proceed — and, above all, the general tone and sentiment of the
City on the subject of enlisting Colored men is far in advance of
any other metropolitan community in the Union.

. . . .

HLS   Thomas Webster

Excerpt from Thomas Webster to Hon. E. M. Stanton, 30 July 1863,
W-68 1863, Letters Received, ser. 360, Colored Troops Division, RG 94
[B-46]. A covering letter assured the Secretary of War that Webster spoke
on behalf of the entire "Supervisory Committee for Recruiting Colored
Regiments." (Thomas Webster to E. M. Stanton, 30 July 1863.) For the
remainder of the letter, see *Freedom*, ser. 2: doc. 150.

35: Commissioner for the Recruitment of Black Troops to the Secretary of War

Philadelphia Aug. 17th 1863

Sir: On the 6th of June, I offered to place, under your control, for
the service of the War Department, an Organization for Recruiting

Colored men in the Free States, which I had established at Buffalo N.Y.

This Organization consisted of Salaried Agents in most of the large cities, and Sub-agents paid a recruiting fee for the men procured by them. It was then my intention to retire from this work.

In reply you requested me to retain it for the service of the War Department and offered to make me Recruiting Commissioner for the United States with liberty to make and execute my own plans and audit the accounts of my Agents. Funds were to be placed at my disposal from the Secret Service fund of the Department. I accepted the offer and reported to you in person for duty on the 13th of June and was directed to proceed to Philadelphia and superintend the raising of Colored Troops in Pennsylvania.

This duty has been successfully performed. One Colored Regiment (3d U.S. Col Vols) of 800 men was raised in four weeks and the 6th U.S.C.V has four companies of Eighty men each. Of late the draft has interfered with recruiting, but when that is filled and colored men have no chance to be paid as substitutes I think recruiting here will be resumed here with spirit.

On the 13th of June when I applied to you for funds I was informed that you had decided to draw on the Fund for Recruiting &c of the Volunteer Army and I was directed to apply to Major Vincent for information as to the manner of accounting for such funds. From him I received information that Civilians could not be paid as Recruiting Agents of the War Department and that it would be necessary to give my agents commissions in the Volunteer regiments and afterwards detail them for Service under my orders. I also found it necessary to acquaint myself with the details of the recruiting service to enable me to decide in what manner I could connect my mode of recruiting with that Authorized by the War Department.

It soon became apparent to me that my Agents to be efficient must be as heretofore under my exclusive control, and I took measures to raise a fund by subscriptions in our large cities to defray such expenses of recruiting in the Southern States as could not legally be paid by the War Department, in which I have been very successful. Fifty Thousand dollars has been pledged for this purpose in New England and I have encouragement that all that will be wanted can be procured in other cities including New York and Philadelphia.

This fund will be sufficient for all purposes except the payment of the recruiting fee of two dollars per man authorized by law to be paid to any person who will bring an acceptable recruit to a Station.

The payment of this trifling sum to Colored men of ability will encourage them to devote themselves to the work and their advocacy of this service will create a general impression on their race favorable to the Service. Many of them will venture within the enemy's lines, prompted by hatred of slavery and the desire to earn money and we may reasonably expect soon to demoralize the Slave population everywhere within the enemy's lines. The recruiting fee will be found a powerful instrument in our hands.

On the 10th inst. having funds in my possession I notified you that I was ready for recruiting in the Southern States and the next morning proceeded to Baltimore to confer with Col. Birney. a fortnight earlier I had with his consent placed one of my Agents under his direction and advanced him funds from my private means, (his own being exhausted), to aid in the work. I was much pleased to learn from him that the aid furnished had largely increased the number of his men and he expressed the belief that with continued aid he could recruit several regiments in Maryland.

On Wednesday I called on Major Genl. Foster at Fortress Monroe who received me very Cordially and said he should be glad to have my aid in recruiting in his Department, would subsist, arm and clothe the recruits, but had no money to pay the recruiting expenses.

He referred me to Brig. Gen. Naglee at Norfolk who could give me information as to recruiting there and at Newberne.

I also called on Capt. Wilder Superintendent of Contrabands who informed me that a few weeks earlier an order was sent from Washington to Fortress Monroe, to impress all able-bodied colored men for Service in the Qr Masters Dept at Washington, and that all who could be secured had been sent forward. That many had escaped and in fright had taken to the woods where they remained preventing others from coming in. He said it would require some time to dispel their fears, that in time if the impressment was not resumed we could obtain large numbers for the Army. He also said that the number of men would be largely increased by the payment of the recruiting fee.

On Thursday I called on Brig. Gen. Naglee at Norfolk stating that I had been referred by Maj. Gen. Foster to him for information of the recruiting in Norfolk and Newberne N.C at the same time I showed him my appointment as Recruiting Commissioner. He refused to give me any information without a positive order, but volunteered advice as to other work which not being in my department I declined to receive   I was informed at Fortress Monroe that Gen. Wild had used his own funds in recruiting his Brigade.

My conclusions derived from information obtained on this trip are. That eight to ten regiments can by the use of proper means be raised in Maryland and as many more in General Fosters Department but that the officers in command of the Army are already so fully occupied with their duties that they have not sufficient time to attend to this work.

I therefore recommend that an officer of proper rank be charged with the recruiting of Colored troops in Maryland and another be sent to Gen. Fosters Department for the same duty. That they be provided in advance with the necessary funds for the payment of expenses including a fee of two dollars each for procuring recruits. That the impressment of Colored men be discontinued everywhere. The ablest of them run to the woods imparting their fears to the Slaves thus keeping them out of our lines, and we get only those who are too ignorant or indolent to take care of themselves. I feel sure we can get more men by fair enlistment, or hiring them at wages as laborers, in three months than we can by combining it with impressment.

I have been reliably informed that in General Gilmore's Department at least three hundred were frightened away by impressment, previous to his arrival are in the woods visiting the plantations by night and returning to their hiding places before daylight. They prevent the slaves from running to our lines. Col. Birney appears to be well qualified to take sole charge of recruiting in Maryland. He readily acquires the Confidence of the Negro and is a thorough organizer of a regiment.

I returned to this city on Friday last. On Saturday I received your order to report to Maj. Gen. Rosecrans. It will require a few days to arrange my affairs here and in Boston, but as soon as possible I will report myself for duty according to orders. I have the honor to be, Very Respectfully, Your Obt. Servant

HLS   George L. Stearns

Major George L. Stearns to Hon. Edwin M. Stanton, 17 Aug. 1863, filed with S-18 1863, Letters Received, ser. 360, Colored Troops Division, RG 94 [B-477].

36: Northern Black Recruiter to the Secretary of War

Chicago, Ill. Dec. 15th 1863.

Sir: The Subject and policy of Black Troops, have become of much intrest in our Country, and the effective means and method of raising them, is a matter of much importance.

In consideration of this sir, I embrace the earliest opportunity of asking the privilege of calling the attention of your Department to the fact, that as a policy in perfect harmony with the course of the President and your own enlightened views, that the Agency of intelligent competent black men adapted to the work must be the most effective means of obtaining Black Troops; because knowing and being of that people as a race, they can command such influences as is required to accomplish the object.

I have been successfully engaged as a Recruiting Agent of Black Troops, first as a Recruiting Agent for Massachusetts 54th Regt. and from the commencement as the Managing Agent in the West and South-West for Rhode Island Heavy Artillery, which is now nearly full; and now have the Contract from the State Authorities of Connecticut, for the entire West and South-West, in raising Colored Troops to fill her quota.

During these engagements, I have had associated with me, Mr. John Jones, a very respectable and responsible business colored man of this city, and we have associated ourselves permanently together, in an Agency for raising Black Troops for all parts of the Country.

We are able sir, to command all of the effective black men as Agents in the United States, and in the event of an order from your Department giving us the Authority to recruit Colored Troops in any of the Southern or sceded states, we will be ready and able to raise a Regiment, or Brigade if required, in a shorter time than can be otherwise effected.

With the belief sir, that this is one of the measures in which the claims of the Black Man may be officially recognised, without seemingly infringing upon those of other citizens, I confidently ask sir, that this humble request, may engage your early notice.

All satisfactory References will be given by both of us. I have the honor to be sir, Your most obt. Very humble servt.

M. R. Delany

HLS
M. M. Wagoner, Secry.

M. R. Delany to Hon. Secry. War, 15 Dec. 1863, D-135 1863, Letters Received, ser. 360, Colored Troops Division, RG 94 [B-393]. Delany enclosed two broadsides, portions of which are published below.

37: Recruitment Broadsides for Connecticut and Rhode Island Black Regiments

COLORED SOLDIERS!

EQUAL STATE RIGHTS!

AND MONTHLY PAY WITH WHITE MEN!!

On the 1st day of January, 1863, the President of the United States proclaimed

FREEDOM TO OVER

THREE MILLIONS OF SLAVES!

This decree is to be enforced by all the power of the Nation.   On the 21st of July last he issued the following order:—

PROTECTION OF COLORED TROOPS.

"WAR DEPARTMENT, ADJUTANT GENERAL'S OFFICE, }
WASHINGTON, July 21.   }

—" *General Order, No. 233.*

"The following order of the President is published for the information and government of all concerned:—

EXECUTIVE MANSION, WASHINGTON, July 30.

'" It is the duty of every Government to give protection to its citizens, of whatever class, color, or condition, and especially to those who are duly organized as soldiers in the public service.   The law of nations, and the usages and customs of war, as carried on by civilized powers, permit no distinction as to color in the treatment of prisoners of war as public enemies.   To sell or enslave any captured person on account of his color, is a relapse into barbarism, and a crime against the civilization of the age.

'" The Government of the United States will give the same protection to all its soldiers, and if the enemy shall sell or enslave any one because of his color, the offence shall be punished by retaliation upon the enemy's prisoners in our possession.   It is, therefore, ordered, for every soldier of the United States, killed in violation of the laws of war, a rebel soldier shall be executed; and for every one enslaved by the enemy, or sold into slavery, a rebel soldier shall be placed at hard labor on the public works, and continued at such labor until the other shall be released and receive the treatment due to prisoners of war.

'" ABRAHAM LINCOLN." '

'" By order of the Secretary of War.

'" E. D. TOWNSEND, Assistant Adjutant General." '

That the President is in earnest the rebels soon began to find out, as witness the following order from his Secretary of War:—

"WAR DEPARTMENT, WASHINGTON CITY, August 8, 1863.

" SIR :—Your letter of the 3d inst., calling the attention of this Department to the cases of Orin H. Brown, William H. Johnston, and Wm. Wilson, three colored men captured on the gunboat Isaac Smith, has received consideration.   This Department has directed that three rebel prisoners of South Carolina, if there be any such in our possession, and if not, three others, be confined in close custody and held as hostages for Brown, Johnston, and Wilson, and that the fact be communicated to the rebel authorities at Richmond.

" Very respectfully your obedient servant,

" EDWIN M. STANTON, Secretary of War.

" The Hon. GIDEON WELLES, Secretary of the Navy."

And retaliation will be our practice now—man for man—to the bitter end.

BRAVERY OF COLORED TROOPS.

Your enemies say, "oh, the negro won't fight; he's a coward naturally." A viler slander Satan never uttered through the lips of a traitor. A dozen bloody fields attest their valor. The President, in his letter to the Springfield Convention, bears witness to the fact, and says but for their bravery one of the most important victories of the war could not have been achieved.

And again: Major General Blunt, in his official report of the battle of Honey Springs, Ark., says the First Kansas colored regiment particularly distinguished themselves. They fought like veterans, and preserved their lines unbroken throughout the engagement. "Their coolness and bravery," adds General Blunt, "I have never seen surpassed. They were in the hottest of the fight, and opposed to Texas troops—twice their number—whom they completely routed. The Twentieth Texas Regiment, which fought against them, went into the fight with 300 men, and came out with only 60."

A young soldier of company K, Tenth Connecticut Volunteers, writing home to his mother an account of the late fight at James Island, says: "But for the bravery of three companies of the Massachusetts Fifty-fourth (colored), our whole regiment would have been captured. As it was, we had to double-quick in, to avoid being cut off by the rebel cavalry. *They fought like heroes.*"

But why multiply proof? None but a traitor will now deny it.

Colored Citizens:
The hour you have so long waited for has struck. Your country calls you. Instead of repelling, as hitherto, your patriotic offers, she now invites your services.

To the State of Rhode Island belongs the honor of first recognizing and rewarding your valor in the field.

The First Regiment Rhode Island Heavy Artillery, now organizing there, will consist of eighteen hundred men, all colored soldiers, commanded in part by colored officers. These forces are destined for forts and fortifications on the coast of that State, but liable to be placed by the President where most needed.

This State pays each man a cash bounty of $250
Of which you receive $75 as soon as you arrive there, and the remainder in a few days.
You will also get the United States bounty of 100

Making $350
Also $13 per month, with clothing and rations, the same as white soldiers in every respect. Besides, no man's family will be allowed to want while he is in the service. The wounded will receive pensions for life, and also the families of those who may fall. Above all, you will there be treated with respect, as soldiers and as men. *No other State gives colored men over $50 bounty.* Are you not as patriotic as others? At a numerously attended meeting in Buffalo, on the 1st, when nearly every able bodied man present volunteered, the following resolutions were unanimously passed:

Resolved, That we, the colored citizens of Buffalo, not only approve, but we regard the present as the most favorable call for colored soldiers to go as artillerymen, to defend the garrisons and harbors on the coast of the New England States from rebel pirates —those vicegerents of the devil, who, of all the foul creatures which infest and pollute the seas, they, in human shape, are the most loathsome and most to be shunned.

Resolved, That for this purpose we tender Captains Works and Engly, now present with us, our hearty approval, our co-operation, our hearty efforts, our aid and encouragement for enlisting colored soldiers.

Rally then, around the old flag. One and all lend your aid in wiping out the most wicked rebellion that ever polluted the records of heaven. The millions of your brethren still in bondage implore you to strike for their freedom. Will you heed their cry? Go, then, to the State of Rhode Island. She more than welcomes you with her bounties and her honors to enter the service of the Union in her ranks. The rebellion now totters and reels; and hereafter, when traitors will only be remembered to be cursed—with a united country and your brethren free—you will point with just pride to the part you bore, and the place you filled in the loyal Union Army. Such a record and such deeds, be assured, will be a source of proud remembrance to you and your posterity forever.

VOLUNTEERS!
COME FORWARD AND SIGN THE ROLL.

Let every Man apply in Person, if Possible.

IF NOT, WRITE TO EITHER OF THE PERSONS NAMED BELOW.

Dr. M. R. DELANY, Chicago, Ill., Head Quarters for the West, 172 Clark St.
Mr. JOHN JONES, " " Assistant.

SUB-AGENTS.
(The Illinois List is not yet complete.)

Mr. Emanuel Hersey, Quincy, Ill.   Rev. Garland H. White, Lafayette, Ind.
Mr. Joshua Highwarden, Indianapolis, Ind.   Rev. George W. Brodie, Logansport, Ind.
Mr. N. D. Thompson, 52 Pine St., Buffalo, N. Y.   Right Rev. Bishop Green.
Lewis Isbell, Traveling Agent.

☞ Either of these gentlemen, being fully authorized, will gladly give all further information, furnish you with Railroad Tickets to Rhode Island, and good board and lodging until ready to start.

PD

Recruitment broadsides [1863], enclosed in M. R. Delany to Hon. Secry. War, 15 Dec. 1863, D-135 1863, Letters Received, ser. 360, Colored Troops Division, RG 94 [B-393]. The reverse side of the first broadside (for the 29th Connecticut Volunteers) instructed volunteers to apply to "Dr. M. R. Delany, State Contractor, Head-quarters of the West and South-Western States and Territories" in Chicago or to W. F. Staines in Evansville, Indiana. The handwritten notation in the margin of the second broadside is a Bureau of Colored Troops file number.

38A: Chairman of a New York Recruitment Committee to the Secretary of War

New York Oct 12" 1863

Dear Sir: I enclose you a correspondence had between a Committee consisting of myself and others known as the Committee on "Fremont Legion" and the Governor of the State of New York relating to the organization of colored regiments. Mr Smith Requa of Albany acted as our agent in negotiating with the Governor and you will see by the enclosed letters of Mr Requa to Mr Lewis Francis of our Committee how much trouble and delay has been incurred in getting the final and definite answer of Governor Seymour which he briefly sums up in the statement that he does "not deem it advisable to give such authentications"

You will see by the enclosed letter of Senator Sumner addressed to me on the 21st June last that we have in the course pursued followed his suggestions. Should the President in view of the action of Governor Seymour see fit to grant authentications for raising colored regiments in this state I doubt not many colored men would volunteer. Several thousands have already gone from us to Rhode Island Massachusetts and Pennsylvania. There are many remaining who prefer entering the service in regiments organized at home. The rapid volunteering of the negroes south is a powerful stimulus to their friends here and if officers could be appointed who have the confidence of these men I doubt not New York would send several regiments.

We deem it proper that the whole matter be turned over to the proper authorities at Washington and we pray you to inform us whether the President is willing to grant authentications for the raising of these regiments? With great Respect Your Obt Servant

ALS   Edward Gilbert

Edward Gilbert to Hon. Edwin M. Stanton, 12 Oct. 1863, G-51 1863, Letters Received, ser. 360, Colored Troops Division, RG 94 [B-404]. Enclosed are letters from Senator Charles Sumner and Albany lobbyist Smith Requa, which indicate that the Fremont Legion Committee had turned to the federal government after New York officials rejected their petition to raise a black regiment. But President Lincoln refused to challenge state prerogatives on this matter and insisted that official authorization could come only from the governor. When the committee again petitioned Albany, Governor Horatio Seymour remained adamant in his opposition. Claiming to be "the special Friend of the Negro," he told Requa that he "opposed . . . the whole system of using Negro regiments, from principal." (Charles Sumner to [Edward Gilbert], 21 June 1863; Smith Requa to Mr. Lewis Francis, 17 Aug. 1863, 31 Aug. 1863.) The file also includes one of the petitions presented to Governor Seymour, asking the appointment of James Fairman to raise a brigade of black volunteers in New York, and a letter pointing out that if recruitment was not authorized in New York, blacks would enlist in neighboring states and not be counted toward New York's draft quota. (Edward Gilbert et al. to Horatio Seymour, 9 July 1863; Lewis Francis to Horatio Seymour, 13 Aug. 1863.)

38B: Committee Lobbyist to an Officer of a New York Recruitment Committee

Albany [N.Y.] Oct 7 1863

Dear Sir I enclose you, in addition to the Governors reply, a letter to you which I thought you might need to use in connection with Governors Letter by way of Explanation

I saw the Gov. on the day of his return 6^{oc} in afternoon, and had an interview with him, when I soon discovered that in deferrence to the change of public sentiment since my first interview, his feelings were very much modified in favour of Negro Soldiers and even went so far as to say, "that they might be used advantageously at the South," but of course, he could not, or would not recede from his former position, and he evidently thought it was a question of dobtful expediency for him to commit himself on paper, at this time, on so delicate a question. He wanted very much to leave it, with a mere verbal refusal, But of course I talked of nothing else than the document which he had promised to furnish, and made another engagement to meet him in evening at 10 O'clock— As I found him again very Busy I talked of calling again next Eve., when he concluded to write it at once.

He first wrote a simple denial of your particular application, when I reminded him he had promised to make it general so as to preclude any further applications of that nature – when, he changed a word or two, which gives it the shape I suppose you wished to have it.

It is not as definite as I was in hope he would make it, but is the best I could do with him.

He suggested that the word "Colored" as used in your petition, was not proper, or in good taste, hence he uses the word "Negro" – as expressing the Nationality, and kind of colour referred to   Of course you will appreciate, and profit by the hint from such a quarter

Hoping, with such an answer as I have been able to get for you, you will be able to accomplish your much desired object   I remain Very Respectfully Yours

ALS   Smith Requa

Smith Requa to Mr. L. Francis, 7 Oct. 1863, enclosed in Edward Gilbert to Hon. Edwin M. Stanton, 12 Oct. 1863, G-51 1863, Letters Received, ser. 360, Colored Troops Division, RG 94 [B-404]. Enclosed are Governor Seymour's rejection of a New York black regiment and Requa's description of the circumstances of his meeting with the governor. (Horatio Seymour to E. Gilbert et al., 7 Oct. 1863; Smith Requa to Mr. L. Francis, 7 Oct. 1863.)

38C: New York Union League Members to the Secretary of War, Enclosing the Governor of New York to the Union League

New York Dec^b 1st 1863

Dear Sir   On behalf of the Union League Club of this City, we respectfully ask an authorization for a regiment of colored troops to be raised in the State of New York under the auspices of that Club. We have already made an application to his Excellency Governor Seymour and have received a reply, of which we enclose a copy.

The Union League Club is composed of over five hundred of the wealthiest and most respectable citizens of New York, whose sole bond of association is an unflinching determination to support the Government.

They have subscribed a large sum to be appropriated to the raising of a colored regiment and will procure much more. They believe that by their exertions and influence they can, with the permission of the Government, put in the field a regiment worthy to stand side by side with the Fifty Fourth Massachusetts.

If we are so fortunate as to receive your authorization, we shall take immediate steps to carry out our plan, and shall endeavour to present for approval able and experienced officers whose heart is in the work   We are Sir, Very respectfully Your obedient servants

Geo. Bliss Jr
L G B Cannon

ALS

[*Enclosure*]   Albany [*N.Y.*] Nov 27th 1863

Gentlemen   I have received your communication in relation to the organization of Negro Regiments in Companies. The matter rests entirely with the War Department at Washington. I understand that permission has been given to persons in Brooklyn to raise such Regiments and I suppose therefore you can get a like authorization.

I send you a copy of a letter written by me to Mr. Rodgers of New York which covers the whole ground of your communication   Yours truly &c

Horatio Seymour

[*In another hand*] The letter referred to as enclosed is the published one stating that the State bounty will be paid to colored men.

HLcSr

Geo. Bliss Jr. and L. G. B. Cannon to Hon. E. M. Stanton, 1 Dec. 1863, enclosing Horatio Seymour to Alex. Van Rensselaer et al., 27 Nov. 63, N-41 1863, Letters Received, ser. 360, Colored Troops Division, RG 94 [B-410]. A Bureau of Colored Troops endorsement indicates that a letter was sent to George Bliss authorizing the Union League to raise a black regiment.

❧

39A: Boston Businessmen and Professionals to the Secretary of War

Boston, 10th December, 1863.

Sir   We beg leave to call your attention to the urgent necessity for some measure which will give an impulse to the recruiting of the 300,000 troops last called for.

In the free States the great numbers already drawn from the workshops and fields have seriously embarrassed many branches of the industry upon which the production of the Country depends, and it is clearly desirable to reduce the call upon such resources to the lowest point which is consistent with the vigorous prosecution of the War.

On the other hand there are large sections of the country where the rewards of industry are uncertain, where large numbers of men Black and White have been thrown out of their usual occupations, and large numbers of those *less able* are appealing to the charities of the Government and of individuals to save them from actual destruction by cold and hunger.

Sound political economy, humanity and common sense equally demand that every effort should be made to use this unemployed population as far as possible for filling our Armies instead of drawing too largely upon the well paid and productive classes of the loyal states.

The producing states can well afford to add such sums to the pay and bounties offered by Government as will relieve their citizens from at least a part of the new call and at the same time confer a positive benefit upon the loyal and persecuted people of the disaffected States from whom no Quotas have been demanded.

For these and other reasons we earnestly recommend that permission should be immediately given to the loyal states to recruit soldiers (against their Quotas) in those parts of the Rebel States within our control, both to fill up the white regiments now there and to create such Black Regiments as you may deem it expedient to authorize.

We believe that such permission will encourage recruiting in the loyal states themselves by the assurance of success which it will give, and by bringing forward the many old soldiers who are willing to enlist but who are now waiting for the most favorable moment to do so.

We believe too that much of the very embarrassing demand for charity will be provided for out of the money thus distributed.

To give full effect to the policy which we advocate it is important that stringent orders should be issued that the Black troops shall be treated *as soldiers* and only called upon for their fair share of the fatigue and police work of the whole army, and that no impressment shall be used except in those emergencies when Black and White men alike shall be forced to work or fight for their common country. We are, respectfully, Your obedient Servants

HLS   [*34 signatures*]

Amos A. Lawrence et al. to Honorable E. M. Stanton, 10 Dec. 1863, enclosed in S. Hooper to Honble E. M. Stanton, 19 Dec. [1863], H-1807 1863, Letters Received, RG 107 [L-159].

39B: Commander of the Military Division of the Mississippi to a Northern Recruiter

(Copy)   On the field Near Atlanta Ga July 30" 1864
Sir   Yours from Chattanooga July 28 is rec^d notifying me of your
appointment by your state as Lieut Col and Provost Marshal of
Georgia Alabama and Mississippi under the act of Congress
approved July 4" 1864, to recruit volunteers to be credited the
quotas of the states respectively. On applying to General Webster
at Nashville he will grant you a pass through our lines to those
states and as I have had Considerable experience in those States
would suggest recruiting Depots to be established at Macon and
Columbus Miss. Selma, Montgomery and Mobile Alabama, and
Columbus, Milledgeville, & Savannah Ga.

I do not see that the law restricts you to Black recruits, but you
are at liberty to Collect white recruits also

It is waste of time and money to open rendezvous in Northwest
Georgia for I assure you I have not seen an able bodied man black
or white there fit for a soldier who was not in this Army or the
one opposed to it.

You speak of the impression going abroad that I am opposed to
the Organization of Colored Regiments   My opinions are usually
very positive, and there is no reason why you should not know
them

Though entertaining a profound reverence for our Congress, I do
doubt their wisdom in the passage of this law.

1"   Because Civilian Agents about an Army are a nuisance!

2^d   The duty of Citizens to fight for their Country is too Sacred
an one to be peddled off by buying up the refuse of other States

3^d   It is unjust to the brave soldiers and volunteers who are
fighting as those who compose this Army do, to place them on a
par with the class of recruits you are after.

4"   The Negro is in a transition state and is not the equal of
the white man

5"   He is liberated from his bondage by act of War, and the
Armies in the field are entitled to all his assistance in labor and
fighting, *in addition* to the proper quotas of the States.

6"   This bidding and bartering for recruits, white and black has
delayed the reenforcement of our Armies, at the times when such
reenforcements would have enabled us to make our success
permanent

7"   The law is an experiment which pending War is unwise and
unsafe, and has delayed the universal draft which I firmly believe
will become necessary to overcome the wide spread resistance

offered us and I also believe the universal draft will be wise and beneficial, for under the providence of God it will seperate the Sheep from the Goats, and demonstrate what Citizens will fight for their Country and what will only talk.

No one shall infer from this that I am not a friend of the Negro as well as the white race; I contend that the treason and Rebellion of the Master, freed the Slave, and I and the armies I have commanded have conducted to safe points more negroes than those of any General Officer in the Army, but I prefer some Negroes for Pioneers, Teamsters, Cooks and Servants, others gradually to experiment in the art of the Soldier, beginning with the duties of the local Garrisons, such as we had at Memphis, Vicksburg, Natchez, Nashville, and Chattanooga; but I would not draw on the poor Race for too large a proportion of its active athletic Young men for some must remain to seek new homes and provide for the old and the young the feeble and helpless.

These are some of my peculiar notions but I assure you they are shared by a large portion of our fighting men

You may show this to the Agents of the other States, in the same business as yourself   I am &c,

HLcSr

(Signed) W. T. Sherman

Major General W. T. Sherman to John A. Spooner, 30 July 1864, enclosed in R. D. Mussey to Major [Charles W. Foster?], 2 Aug. 1864, M-583 1864, Letters Received, ser. 360, Colored Troops Division, RG 94 [B-465]. In the covering letter, Colonel Reuben D. Mussey, commissioner for the Organization of U.S. Colored Troops in middle and east Tennessee, commented on Sherman's view of Northern recruiters: "While I cannot endorse what Sherman says of the Negro – (for I think he is fully two years behind the time – and when I say two years I mean two of those century like years which we are living – I most heartily endorse and approve his detestation of that shirking from duty which resorts to 'man-peddling' and to that inevitable trouble which will rise from the various States bidding against each other."

40: Ohio Black Soldier to the President

Baltimore Maryland Guard House february 22th 1865
To His Excelency and most hily honored President   to you I look and beg of you to look at my case and take compashion on me   I have bin ronged out of my Writes   a man came to my residence

III

in mercer County ohio and told me that he had authority to get up volenteers and that he Was paying $200 dollars for one year and I thought that I would go for one year so I Went With him and then he made me drunk and sold me to another man for a substitute and did not give me any money atall and I had married a Widdow With eight children Who are depending on me for support and I am a poor colord man havent enything for them to live on except by my labor and I am in the gard house and cant do enything for them and they have had me ever since the 28 of last month and my family is suffering   in the first place they carryed me to Johnsons island then to camp Delaware and then I found out that I Was sold as a substitute and they tryed to make me be mustered in as a substitute and I Would not   then the soldiers told me that I Was right and they could not hold me and that if I Was to get out and go home that they Would not nor could not disturb me   and so the guards let me out of the camp and I Went home and stayed fore months and then a man came and taken me and put me in prison and they have had me ever since   now to your honor I beg to look on me and see in to my case   I Was born on Walnut hills near Cincinnati ohio and Was sold in tiffin ohio   I never was out of the State till I was taken a prisner   now I beg your majestys honor to take compashion on me if you please   I am glad that I have the honor of being your Excelency Servant

ALS
William Joseph Nelson

William Joseph Nelson to Mr. Abraham Lincoln, 22 Feb. 1865, N-19 1865, Letters Received, ser. 360, Colored Troops Division, RG 94 [B-176]. Endorsements indicate that Private Nelson was being held as a deserter. The disposition of the case is not indicated.

3

Recruitment in Tidewater Virginia and North Carolina; the Mississippi Valley; and Tennessee

PRESIDENT LINCOLN'S commitment, announced in the Emancipation Proclamation, to employ black soldiers in garrisoning Union fortifications intensified federal efforts to recruit black soldiers. Although still cautious, Secretary of War Edwin M. Stanton moved quickly to incorporate as many blacks as possible into Union ranks. In January 1863, Stanton ordered General Daniel Ullmann to Louisiana to build upon the earlier efforts of Generals Benjamin F. Butler and Nathaniel P. Banks and raise a brigade of black soldiers in the Department of the Gulf. In April, as Ullmann embarked for Louisiana, Stanton sent Adjutant General Lorenzo Thomas to the upper Mississippi Valley to begin recruiting blacks in the Union-occupied areas north of Vicksburg. About the same time, Stanton authorized George L. Stearns to begin black enlistment in middle and east Tennessee and – at the urging of Massachusetts Governor John A. Andrew – promoted Colonel Edward A. Wild to the rank of general with orders to recruit and command a brigade of black soldiers in tidewater North Carolina. Stanton's recruiters achieved phenomenal success, and in May 1863 the War Department created the Bureau of Colored Troops in the Adjutant General's Office to supervise recruitment and to administer the organization of newly enlisted black soldiers. The establishment of the Bureau of Colored Troops signaled the Lincoln administration's full commitment to black enlistment.[1]

TIDEWATER VIRGINIA AND NORTH CAROLINA

Massachusetts Governor John A. Andrew not only led the movement to enlist Northern free blacks in the Union army, but early on

[1] Published accounts of recruitment in the tidewater, the Mississippi Valley, and Tennessee include: Daniel Ullmann, *The Organization of Colored Troops and the Regeneration of the South* (Washington, 1868); and Dudley Taylor Cornish, *The Sable Arm: Negro Troops in the Union Army, 1861–1865* (New York, 1956), chap. 6.

he also urged the recruitment of former slaves. In October 1862, when General John A. Dix, commander of Fortress Monroe in tidewater Virginia, suggested that the contrabands who had taken refuge around the fort might be better protected if removed north, Andrew retorted that they should be armed and allowed to defend their freedom on their native ground. Nothing came of this proposal under Dix's flaccid regime, but early in 1863, when the Union army established a beachhead in the North Carolina tidewater, Andrew renewed his appeal. At first Andrew apparently desired to recruit former Virginia and North Carolina slaves in order to fill the ranks of the 54th Massachusetts. But his success in attracting Northern volunteers persuaded him to press for a separate North Carolina unit, with the example of the Massachusetts regiments serving as a stimulus to slave enlistment.

While Andrew made his case, Union officers, forced to defend their North Carolina foothold against Confederate counterattack and rebel guerrillas, armed and drilled former slaves on their own authority. Despite complaints from North Carolina unionists, including the state's newly appointed military governor, some Northern officers proposed immediate enlistment of all blacks entering Union lines.[2] And, in April 1863, in spite of the obvious lack of enthusiasm of General John G. Foster, commander of the Department of North Carolina, Secretary of War Stanton authorized a Massachusetts abolitionist, Colonel Edward A. Wild, to begin recruiting a brigade of black volunteers. Reflecting his still tentative commitment to black enlistment, Stanton carefully hedged Wild's authority. He ordered that the regiments composing the North Carolina brigade be filled sequentially and provided that if they were not filled in a "reasonable" length of time, the authorization would be revoked.[3] Like Andrew, Wild chose his officers from the Northern abolitionist vanguard, many of whom had helped to recruit the 54th Massachusetts. Within months he had enrolled the first regiment of North Carolina Colored Volunteers and by year's end Wild's "African Brigade" was in the field.

Through the summer of 1863, North Carolina remained the focus of black recruitment in the tidewater, although Andrew, through

---

[2] Mily. Gov. Edw. Stanly to Major Genl. J. G. Foster, 20 Jan. 1863, N-43 1863, Letters Received, ser. 3238, Dept. of NC & VA, RG 393 Pt. 1 [C-3083].

[3] E. M. S. to Colonel Edward A. Wild under cover to the Governor of Massachusetts, 14 Apr. 1863, W-9 1863, Letters Received, ser. 360, Colored Troops Division, RG 94 [B-418]. This letter, one of several drafts of the same order, is in a number of different hands. The last paragraph, providing a temporal limit to Wild's authority, appears to have been added by Stanton. It was sent to Wild care of Governor John Andrew of Massachusetts.

his contacts with Massachusetts officers stationed around Fortress Monroe, pressed for similar action in Virginia. So thoroughly was federal policy transformed that in July even Stanton adopted Andrew's cause. He reminded Foster, now commander of the consolidated Department of Virginia and North Carolina, that Foster's predecessor in Virginia had failed to act vigorously on the matter of black enlistment and observed firmly that he hoped Foster would "not fall into that error."[4] General Benjamin F. Butler, who replaced Foster in November 1863, needed no such prompting. Within days of his arrival at Fortress Monroe, his agents had begun enlisting former slaves into Union ranks. And within a month, he had won unprecedented War Department permission to offer black recruits a small federal bounty and had established a black cavalry unit.[5]

Butler's desire to bring former slaves under Union arms tangled with his heavy dependence on black military laborers. Two years earlier, while commander at Fortress Monroe, Butler gleefully employed as laborers the numerous fugitives coming into his lines. Now the success of his labor policy obstructed his effort to speed black enlistment. Army recruiters found that blacks who earned good wages as military laborers showed little interest in enlistment. The need for troops and the reluctance of blacks to enlist led some frustrated recruiters to force blacks into service. But, as elsewhere, impressment not only roused the ire of the black community and its Northern missionary allies; it also upset quartermasters who depended on black teamsters, mechanics, and stevedores to keep the Union army rolling. In December 1863, in an attempt to reconcile the competing claims of army recruiters and quartermasters as well as Northern missionaries and the blacks themselves, Butler issued new regulations for recruiting black soldiers, employing black laborers, and maintaining black contrabands.

Armed with Butler's pronouncement, army recruiters acted with new vigor, indeed too much vigor. The tidewater rang with howls of protest as recruiting officers dragged black men away from their jobs and families. Although Butler soon halted this heavy-handed enlistment, blacks remained wary of Yankee recruiters. At the same time, blacks in the army, like Chaplain Garland H. White, a former slave, faulted Virginia contrabands for their reluctance "to

---

[4] Edwin M. Stanton to Major General J. G. Foster, 20 July 1863, Telegrams Collected by the Office of the Secretary of War (Bound), RG 107 [L-305]. General John A. Dix commanded the Department of Virginia from June 1862 until July 15, 1863, when the Department of Virginia and North Carolina was created.

[5] Maj. Gen. B. F. Butler to Hon. Secy. of War, 29 Nov. 1863, Telegrams Collected by the Office of the Secretary of War (Bound), RG 107 [L-212].

take up arms to help to free themselves or be useful to the country." Though the attractiveness of military labor continued to outweigh considerations of armed service, particularly for men with large families, nearly 11,000 Virginia and North Carolina blacks, primarily from the tidewater, enlisted in the Union army.

THE MISSISSIPPI VALLEY

Precedent already existed for the enlistment of black soldiers in the Mississippi Valley. But the subsequent actions of General Nathaniel P. Banks, who purged black officers from Union ranks in Louisiana, and the inaction of General Ulysses S. Grant and his subordinates, who showed no interest in black enlistment in the valley above Vicksburg, obscured General Benjamin Butler's earlier enrollment of black soldiers.[6] Shortly after the new year, Stanton determined to begin anew in the Mississippi Valley. At the recommendation of President Lincoln, Stanton ordered General Daniel Ullmann, a recently released prisoner of the rebels passionately committed to the organization of black soldiers, to raise a black brigade in Louisiana. Shortly thereafter, Stanton dispatched Adjutant General Lorenzo Thomas to the upper Mississippi Valley to supervise black recruitment and to demolish lingering opposition to black service among Grant's officers and men.

During 1863, army opposition to black soldiers gradually diminished, in large measure owing to the steadfast efforts of Adjutant General Thomas, who traveled up and down the river, persuading white troops of the need to arm blacks and organizing black regiments. In the upper valley, Grant and his subordinate commanders established contraband camps at such places as Memphis, Helena, Corinth, and Holly Springs where the army provided shelter and subsistence to the growing number of fugitive slaves whose masters had abandoned their estates while seeking security within Confederate lines. When he arrived, General Thomas determined to reduce the swelling population of the camps by enlisting all the able-bodied men and settling the remaining fugitives on abandoned plantations. He envisioned a system in which black soldiers would protect their families and other fugitive slaves, who, in turn, would provide for themselves and grow market staples on the plantations. The former slaves would thus relieve the government of their support, subsidize the Union war effort, and line the Mississippi with a

[6] See *Freedom*, ser. 2: doc. 127–131.

loyal population.[7] Thomas tapped the manpower of the contraband camps with great success, organizing black regiments at Helena, Arkansas; Lake Providence, Milliken's Bend, and Goodrich's Landing, Louisiana; Grand Gulf, Mississippi; and La Grange, Tennessee, within weeks of his arrival. The fall of Vicksburg in July 1863 so increased the contraband population in the valley that he quickly raised additional regiments at Vicksburg, Natchez, and Holly Springs, Mississippi, as well as La Grange and Memphis, Tennessee. By the end of 1863, he had enlisted nearly 21,000 black soldiers, representing over thirty regiments of cavalry, heavy artillery, and infantry.[8]

In Louisiana a different pattern prevailed. There many planters claimed unionist sympathies. If they did not welcome the arrival of federal soldiers, neither did they flee. Rather, they remained on their estates and appealed to Union military authorities to protect their property and guarantee the subordination of their slaves. Both General Butler and General Banks, wishing to keep these planters loyal, agreed to ensure the subservience of the black population provided the planters paid wages to their laborers. The two generals adopted a policy of discouraging flight from the plantations by holding to a minimum the number of contraband camps and putting "vagrants" to work on public projects.[9] These policies may have secured planter loyalty and introduced the rudiments of a wage system, but they did little to meet the Union army's growing manpower needs. Unable to tap contraband camps like those lining the upper valley, army recruiters turned on the plantations. They ransacked the great estates, taking every man even remotely likely to pass the physical examination. Plantation recruitment not only threatened the planters' economic interests, but frequently left them smarting from humiliations inflicted by arrogant recruiters, who as often as not were black. The planters complained vociferously and lambasted military authorities for undermining the plantation regime. The competing manpower demands of army commanders and loyal planters framed black recruitment in the lower valley for the remainder of the war.

Even before Thomas arrived in the Mississippi Valley in April 1863, Banks had come to terms with the loyal planters. Several months earlier, responding to their pleas and those of Northern lessees, he had banned plantation recruitment throughout the Depart-

---

[7] Adjt. Genl. L. Thomas to Hon. Edwin M. Stanton, 12 Apr. 1863, enclosing Adjutant General L. Thomas, plan for the cultivation of plantations, 10 Apr. 1863, A-808 1863, Letters Received, ser. 12, RG 94 [K-62].

[8] *Official Records,* ser. 3, vol. 3, pp. 212, 214, 1189–91; *Official Army Register,* pt. 8, pp. 219–39.

[9] For a full discussion of this policy, see *Freedom,* ser. 1.

ment of the Gulf.[10] Banks, however, neither enforced the prohibition nor enunciated a general recruitment policy. In the absence of general regulations or enforcement of Banks's piecemeal policy, recruiters continued to operate virtually without restriction, persuading, cajoling, and intimidating plantation hands into the service. Moreover, Banks's feeble interdiction of plantation recruiting left enlistments in New Orleans entirely unregulated. Unlike plantation districts with their impoverished slave majorities, New Orleans boasted a prosperous class of free people of color. Many of the freemen worked as skilled artisans and shopkeepers, and some enjoyed independent wealth and the status that came with it. In addition, a large number of laborers – black and mulatto, slave and free – worked in the city's vast transportation network, including the army's quartermaster and commissary departments. Most New Orleans slaves toiled directly for their masters but others labored as hirelings, and some of the latter controlled their own time, lived out, and enjoyed a considerable measure of freedom. Recruiters ran roughshod over these distinctions, ignored passes exempting men from service, and impressed free black artisans and slave military laborers alike. When recruiters persuaded the city police to aid their overzealous attempt to round up so-called vagrants, abuses multiplied. These excesses mobilized the entire urban population against recruitment: slave owners complained about seizure of their slave property; quartermaster and commissary officers opposed disruption of their work crews; free blacks objected to being treated like slaves; and slave hirelings protested their loss of privilege. Despite such protests, the large number of draft-age men in the city proved too tempting for recruiters to resist, and periodically throughout the war collective outcries followed on the heels of recruiter depredations.

When Adjutant General Thomas arrived in the Mississippi Valley, he acknowledged the peculiarities of the Louisiana situation by leaving Banks in charge of recruitment in the lower valley but reserving the right to supersede his authority when necessary. With Thomas's blessing, during the summer of 1863 Banks created the Corps d'Afrique by consolidating the existing Louisiana Native Guard regiments with those organized since Banks assumed command.[11] But even as Banks systematized and simplified the organization of black troops in Louisiana, the War Department complicated the situation by relieving him of some of the day-to-day responsibilities of recruiting. In January 1863, the department

---

[10] *Official Records*, ser. 1, vol. 15, p. 678.
[11] *Official Records*, ser. 1, vol. 15, pp. 716–17; vol. 26, pt. 1, p. 539. Recruitment for the Corps d'Afrique remained under Banks's supervision until April 1864 when Thomas incorporated them into his larger organization of U.S. Colored Troops. (*Official Records*, ser. 3, vol. 4, pp. 214–15.)

ordered General Daniel Ullmann, a free-soil general who had impressed President Lincoln with his desire to enlist black troops, to raise a black brigade in Louisiana. After spending several months in New York City enlisting white officers, Ullmann sailed for Louisiana late in April. His arrival forced a reconsideration of Banks's recruitment policy.

War Department instructions empowered Ullmann to accept volunteers for his brigade from anywhere within the limits of the Department of the Gulf,[12] but Banks wanted Ullmann to steer clear of the planters' labor force. Ullmann bridled at such a restriction because it drastically reduced the number of potential recruits and, more important, because he considered the plantation system a travesty of free labor. While he could not challenge his superior's authority directly, Ullmann ignored the spirit of Banks's policy and looked the other way as his recruiters stripped the plantations of able-bodied men.[13] Loyal planters and Northern lessees again complained loudly. With the number of their influential friends growing – including by now Adjutant General Thomas himself – their protests took increasing effect. In May and June 1863, first Banks and then Thomas issued stern orders forbidding all further plantation recruitment. Banks informed Ullmann that the prohibition would remain in effect until President Lincoln himself ordered otherwise.[14] Lincoln, in the midst of sensitive negotiations aimed at readmitting Louisiana to the Union, had no desire to alienate the loyal planters and Northern lessees, both essential constituents in the unionist alliance. Consequently, the military's demand for recruits gave way to the politics of placating loyal planters. Nonetheless, in defiance of both Banks's instructions to Ullmann and Thomas's prohibition, recruiters continued to operate freely on the plantations.

As the summer advanced, both loyal planters and Northern lessees continued their protest. They also acquired important allies when Treasury Department officials assumed control of abandoned plantations in July.[15] Late in August 1863, under pressure from

[12] *Official Records,* ser. 3, vol. 3, pp. 14, 99–100, 102–3.

[13] Brig. General Daniel Ullmann to Brigadier General L. Thomas, 19 May 1863, Negro in the Military Service, pp. 1249–51, ser. 390, Colored Troops Division, RG 94 [B-472].

[14] M.G.C. N. P. Banks to Brig. Genl. D. Ullman, 8 May 1863, vol. 5 DG, p. 149, Letters Sent, ser. 1738, Dept. of the Gulf, RG 393 Pt. 1 [C-617]; Special Orders No. 35, 13 June 1863, L. Thomas Letters & Orders, Generals' Papers & Books, ser. 159, RG 94 [V-19].

[15] Congressional action of March 1863 put all captured and abandoned property in the insurrectionary states, except that used in waging war against the United States, under the jurisdiction of the Treasury Department. (*Official Records,* ser. 3, vol. 3, pp. 98–99.) In the Department of the Gulf, Treasury officer Benjamin F. Flanders assumed control over abandoned plantations in mid-July. (Benj. F. Flanders to Hon. S. P. Chase, 17 Sept. [1863], vol. 119, pp. 169–71, Letters Sent, 3rd Agency, RG 366 [Q-87].)

Washington, Banks finally took the decisive action regarding recruitment that he had dodged from the start. He established a commission of enrollment to supervise the recruitment, training, and education of black troops. In addition, he offered protection to the families of black soldiers and ordered that blacks found unfit for military service be conscripted as laborers.[16]

All of Banks's maneuvering still failed to ensure an adequate supply of black recruits, so, at the end of September 1863, he officially disposed of Adjutant General Thomas's and President Lincoln's injunctions and ordered the conscription of all able-bodied plantation men aged twenty to thirty.[17] Anticipating the objections of the plantation interest, he allowed substitutes for indispensable skilled laborers and promised to furnish planters with sufficient workers for the upcoming harvest. Banks's order at once regulated and legitimated plantation recruitment. Predictably enough, as the harvest season approached, planters grew increasingly anxious about labor shortages and forwarded new pleas for intercession to their well-placed friends. Now Adjutant General Thomas came to their rescue. In November he suspended Banks's order, thereby reinstating yet again the interdiction of plantation recruitment.[18]

The new year brought no upsurge in black volunteers, and the continuing need for soldiers left the army still scrounging for recruits. Complaints by New Orleans whites about large numbers of black "vagrants," both in the city and in the nearby Lake Ponchartrain area, suggested a possible solution. If the army could conscript these troublesome blacks, it might alleviate its manpower shortage, leaving the plantations untouched and simultaneously eliminating the "vagrant" problem. The ensuing campaign succeeded in scattering the "vagrants" rather than enlisting them. Moreover, it prompted angry protests in New Orleans from free black victims of the recruiters' excesses.

As the summer of 1864 waned, Banks realized that the planters' need for laborers promised to recreate the troubles of the previous harvest. As in 1863, planters pressured their advocates locally and in Washington to guarantee their labor supply. Banks again tried to balance his continued need for soldiers with the planters' seasonal labor requirements: in August 1864 he ordered the conscription of all able-bodied black men aged eighteen to forty, exempting one-fifth on each plantation to ensure planters their skilled labor force. In addition, the order provided for the recruits' temporary detachment from service, after muster, so they could work the harvest.[19]

---

[16] *Official Records*, ser. 1, vol. 26, pt. 1, p. 704.
[17] *Official Records*, ser. 1, vol. 26, pt. 1, p. 741.
[18] *Official Records*, ser. 1, vol. 26, pt. 1, p. 803.
[19] *Official Records*, ser. 1, vol. 41, pt. 2, pp. 518–19.

By early October, Banks was acting upon requests from planters for laborers, on condition that the planters, rather than the army, pay and support the furloughed recruits.[20]

Banks's new order set the stage for the most orderly conscription in the two-and-a-half-year history of Louisiana recruitment. But it came too late. In October 1864, weary of continued complaints about recruitment, General Edward R. S. Canby, commander of the Military Division of West Mississippi, which included the Department of the Gulf, prohibited all conscription in Louisiana and Arkansas.[21] But, with Canby's permission, General Stephen A. Hurlbut, Banks's successor, attempted to raise two regiments of black volunteers in New Orleans, encouraging the black officers whom Banks had purged from the Louisiana Native Guard to act as recruiters, with the promise that they could serve again as officers.[22] However, doubts about recommissioning the former Native Guard officers led Hurlbut to equivocate on his pledge. Without Hurlbut's assurance of support to the Native Guard officers, recruitment ended abruptly.

Early in 1865, with recruitment at a standstill, Hurlbut received War Department approval for a general draft to alleviate the continued shortage of soldiers.[23] Extant enrollment books suggest that many black artisans exempted under Banks's earlier conscription fell victim to this draft.[24] Like earlier conscriptions, Hurlbut's draft also spawned abuse of blacks, especially in New Orleans. As the war wound down, the need for additional recruits diminished drastically. On the first of May 1865, Adjutant General Thomas halted recruitment of black troops altogether, but not before the new draft had conscripted thousands of Louisiana blacks into the army.

In the end, the multiplicity of competing interests in Louisiana — planters, Northern lessees, contrabands, and free blacks, all claiming loyalty to the Union, as well as officials of both War and Treasury departments — foiled all efforts to formulate an orderly, consistent, and coherent recruitment policy. Nonetheless, the long Union military occupation, coupled with wholesale conscription, obtained over 24,000 black troops in Louisiana, more than from any other state.[25]

---

[20] Major Geo. B. Drake to Chaplain T. W. Conway, 3 Oct. 1864, vol. 8 DG, p. 325, Letters Sent, ser. 1738, Dept. of the Gulf, RG 393 Pt. 1 [C-726].

[21] *Official Records*, ser. 1, vol. 41, pt. 3, p. 774.

[22] *Official Records*, ser. 1, vol. 41, pt. 3, pp. 880–81.

[23] General Orders No. 2, Headquarters, Department of the Gulf, 17 Jan. 1865, and Circular No. 3, Headquarters, Department of the Gulf, 24 Jan. 1865, Orders & Circulars, ser. 44, RG 94 [DD-17].

[24] Vol. 513A/662 DG, Descriptive Roll of Troops Received at Depot General Recruiting Service, ser. 1922, General Recruiting Service, Dept. of the Gulf, RG 393 Pt. 1 [C-821].

[25] *Official Records*, ser. 3, vol. 5, p. 138.

Meanwhile, in the upper valley, Adjutant General Thomas escaped the tightrope walk that Louisiana's peculiarities forced upon Banks. In Kentucky, Tennessee, Missouri, Mississippi, Arkansas, and northern Louisiana, Thomas recruited over 69,000 black troops, primarily by tapping the steady supply of black fugitives fleeing to the Union contraband camps and freedom.[26]

TENNESSEE

Though recruitment in Tennessee, like that in the Mississippi Valley and the tidewater, began after Lincoln issued the Emancipation Proclamation, Tennessee's divided political loyalty and its strategic military position combined to produce a unique recruitment policy. Despite the state's secession, unionist forces dominated east Tennessee. Under the leadership of Senator Andrew Johnson – the only United States senator from the seceded states who did not vacate his Washington office – loyal east Tennesseans proclaimed their allegiance to the Union. Boasting a white yeoman constituency, unionists strongly opposed both secession and its underlying cause, slavery. Some slaveholders recognized the impending doom of their peculiar institution and adopted the unionist antislavery stance. Unlike anywhere else in the South, in Tennessee unionism coincided with opposition to slavery.

If the prospect of slavery's demise quickened slaveholder unionism, the course of wartime military activity hastened that demise. During 1862 and 1863, Tennessee hosted large contending armies, whose constant movements, fierce and numerous battles, and periodic redrawing of lines of occupation sundered the bonds of slavery throughout the state. Even without deliberate federal attempts to undermine slavery, the fighting perforce ensured its collapse as a functioning social system. Thousands of blacks simply fled their masters and sought safety within Union lines. A few farmed on their own, some found employment with nearby farmers or planters, but most migrated to the cities or gathered in army-organized contraband camps. Hence, Lincoln's exemption of loyal Tennessee slaveholders from the provisions of his Emancipation Proclamation could not stem the libertarian tide.

Early in 1863, determined to reduce the state's growing contraband population and counter the Confederate military threat, Senator Johnson, de facto head of Tennessee's loyal government, pro-

---

[26] *Official Records,* ser. 3, vol. 5, pp. 123–24.

posed the enlistment of blacks in the state's militia.[27] President Lincoln sympathized with Johnson's proposal and moved to expand the latter's authority with respect to employing blacks. In April 1863 Lincoln appointed Johnson military governor of Tennessee, with jurisdiction over all fugitive slaves and slaves of rebel masters.[28] Secretary of War Edwin M. Stanton encouraged Johnson to put all able-bodied blacks to work for the government. Meanwhile, in deference to Johnson's authority, the War Department's chief organizer of black troops in the Mississippi Valley, Adjutant General Lorenzo Thomas, confined his Tennessee operations to the western counties, leaving the rest of the state under Johnson's control.

Having secured such sweeping powers from the War Department, Johnson lost interest in his black militia and placed the state adjutant general in charge of the two companies organized. In consultation with General William S. Rosecrans, commander of the Nashville-based Department of the Cumberland, Johnson determined that the army needed black laborers more than black soldiers, and he proceeded to organize all available blacks into work details. Johnson had no objections to mustering such laborers formally into federal service, which he did with slaves impressed in 1862 to work on Nashville fortifications, but he delayed mustering black combatants. By the summer of 1863, Stanton had grown impatient and decided to circumvent Johnson by sending abolitionist George L. Stearns, one of the most successful Northern recruiters of black troops, to Tennessee. Early in September, armed with the rank of major and $50,000 raised by private subscription in the North, Stearns joined Rosecrans in Nashville. Modeling his operations after his successful Northern experience, Stearns hoped to spur black enlistments by employing civilian agents who would collect a fee for each recruit.[29]

Stanton's orders guided Stearns and Rosecrans. The War Secretary authorized the enlistment of slaves of loyal masters if the master consented, and made such masters eligible to collect the bounty normally paid to volunteer recruits. Stanton further approved the enlistment of slaves of loyal owners who withheld consent, provided that military necessity required such enlistments and provided that such owners received compensation. And he advised Stearns that Johnson held ultimate control over Tennessee recruitment, ordering Stearns to make his actions consistent with the governor's views. Hence, Lincoln and Stanton bolstered the loyalty of wayward slaveholding unionists by offering compensated emancipation of their draft-age men.[30]

[27] *Official Records*, ser. 3, vol. 3, p. 103.
[28] *Official Records*, ser. 3, vol. 3, pp. 122–23.
[29] *Official Records*, ser. 3, vol. 4, pp. 762–66.
[30] *Official Records*, ser. 3, vol. 3, pp. 785–87, 793, 816–17.

War Department policy carefully delimited the boundaries of Stearns's authority, but Johnson still found them too broad. He preferred that Stearns stop recruiting altogether. Johnson considered Stearns a Northern meddler, resented his intrusion, and felt that state authorities could organize recruitment with less risk of antagonizing loyal slave owners than could the Yankee abolitionist. Most of all, he objected to Stearns's determination to make former slaves into soldiers. Assuming that blacks would best serve in their familiar capacity as laborers, Johnson reasoned that he could recruit them himself without Stearns's assistance.

By late September 1863, under pressure from Lincoln, Stearns and Johnson compromised their differences. Stearns would take charge of the recruitment of black soldiers, but Johnson retained authority over their disposition. Johnson intended that such soldiers serve primarily as laborers, and Stearns had to abandon his goal of enlisting fighters, resting content in the knowledge that blacks in any military capacity dealt an irreversible blow to slavery.

While Stearns and Johnson ironed out their differences, Stearns's recruiters moved freely about, gathering recruits and sending them to Nashville for muster. In mid-September 1863, however, the battle of Chickamauga temporarily disrupted transportation facilities, and, as the number of black recruits continued to grow, Stearns decided to organize regiments at Gallatin, Shelbyville, Murfreesboro, and Clarksville as well. Slaves from Tennessee's ravaged plantation area fled to those towns, quickly filling the regiments. In addition, slaves from Kentucky's western tobacco region fled southward across the border to Clarksville both to escape bondage and to enlist.[31]

In October 1863, when the War Department placed recruitment in Tennessee, Maryland, and Missouri under the jurisdiction of the Bureau of Colored Troops, Johnson protested and Stanton quickly reaffirmed the governor's ultimate authority over Tennessee recruitment.[32] Except for three heavy artillery regiments organized in early 1864 to garrison the fortifications of Tennessee's major cities and one mobile light artillery battery, Johnson continued to adhere to his original conception of the black military role.[33] In February 1864, Reuben D. Mussey, formerly Stearns's chief assis-

---

[31] Even after black recruitment began in Kentucky in the spring of 1864, Clarksville continued to draw large numbers of Kentucky recruits. In August 1864, the head of enrollment and the draft in Kentucky estimated that some 2,000 Kentucky slaves had enlisted at Clarksville since recruitment had begun there the previous year. (Maj. W. H. Sidell to Col. R. D. Mussey, 18 Aug. 1864, vol. 3, pp. 365–66, Letters Sent & Circulars Issued, ser. 3962, KY Actg. Asst. Pro. Mar. Gen., RG 110 [R-35].)

[32] *Official Records*, ser. 3, vol. 3, pp. 860–61, 876.

[33] *Official Records*, ser. 3, vol. 4, pp. 765–66.

tant, replaced Stearns as head of black recruitment in middle and east Tennessee. Like his predecessor, Mussey opposed confining recruits to the capacity of laborers, and, before long, the course of the war forced Johnson to abandon his narrow view of the black soldier's utility. As the Union army pushed southward into Georgia during 1864, lines of supply and communication lengthened, and black troops spread out to defend them. But defending Union supply lines necessitated constant skirmishing with rebel guerrillas, and Tennessee black soldiers saw more military action than Johnson had ever envisioned. And in General George Thomas's campaign to rid the state of Confederate troops in the closing months of 1864, Tennessee black soldiers also met the enemy on the battlefield.[34]

In the process of defending supply lines and fighting rebels, black troops fanned into all corners of Tennessee, as well as northern Alabama and Georgia, and in effect served as mobile havens for fugitive slaves. With an eye to enlisting able-bodied fugitives as they entered Union lines, Mussey had potential soldiers forwarded to his central recruitment rendezvous to join other contraband recruits still moving into Union-held cities. The procedure provided for orderly enlistment of a steady supply of contraband volunteers. With rebel slavemasters having no grounds for complaint and loyal masters accepting either voluntary or compensated emancipation, Mussey's work proceeded virtually unimpeded.[35]

The combined effect of political loyalty and military emancipation distinguished Tennessee's recruitment experience from that of every other slave state. In the Mississippi Valley a strong unionist interest of loyal planters and Northern lessees insisted on federal guarantees of an adequate plantation labor force. In middle and east Tennessee, by contrast, the absence of such a functioning plantation economy enabled recruiters to enlist virtually all willing draft-age men not deployed as military laborers. In the slave states that did not secede, less extensive military operations left their slave systems comparatively untrammeled by the contending armies. Hence, no border state experienced the same rapid disintegration of slavery and consequent proliferation of contrabands prior to enlistment that Tennessee did. Moreover, even though state governments in the border states maintained nominal loyalty to the Union, Lincoln constantly had to appease elected officials and their proslavery constituents in order to strengthen their wavering loyalty to Washington. In such circumstances, the initial viability of slavery denied to recruiters the pool of contrabands available in Tennessee. Nowhere to the north or the

[34] See *Freedom*, ser. 2: doc. 221.
[35] Mussey summarized both his own and Stearns's recruitment efforts in his October 1864 report to the Bureau of Colored Troops. (*Official Records*, ser. 3, vol. 4, pp. 762–74.)

south did unionism and emancipation so successfully combine to squelch opposition to recruitment as they did in Tennessee. And except for Louisiana and Kentucky, no slave state provided more blacks to the Union army.

TIDEWATER VIRGINIA AND NORTH CAROLINA

41: Governor of Massachusetts to the Headquarters of the Department of Virginia

Copy.   Boston. October 16th 1862.

Major: I have the honor to acknowledge the receipt of your letter of Sept. 30th, accompanied by a letter from Major General Dix, together with a copy of a letter addressed to the General from the War Department at Washington. In these communications it is proposed to me to take some active measures for the reception in Massachusetts of a portion of the escaped slaves now at or about Fortress Monroe, according to a plan proposed by Major General Dix, and in which the General has obtained the acquiescence of the War Department. This plan is represented as "very desirable for reasons both military and humane." It is said that the Fortress is threatened and probably may be attacked; that, if so, these people may be "swept back into slavery," or that a hasty retreat and transportation of them will be attended inevitably with severe suffering to the helpless.

It is imperative upon me to say that, though I sympathize deeply with the humane motives upon which General Dix is seeking to act, I do not concur in any way or to any degree in the plan proposed. These same motives of humanity lead me in a different direction, and to a point where in general, as sound reasoning teaches and even in particular cases, as the case in question makes manifest, I find that the true interests of the African and Saxon are interwoven and their rights correlative as they are identical, so that the assertion and maintenance of the one become the salvation of the other. If indeed it is true that rebel hordes are coiling their traitorous length for a deadly spring upon Fortress Monroe, and that rebel Ironclads are coming down the River, and if it be true that the Union force to oppose the threatened assault is inferior to the forces that menace them, – then by listening to your proposals, I should deprive the band of heroes now under command of General Dix, and steadily awaiting the storm, of the strength of hundreds of stout arms which would be nerved with the desperation of men fighting for liberty, and I should deprive this slandered race of the praise and of the education of their manhood to be acquired in a bold struggle for their dearest rights. Here Providence has given to them a chance to complete their emancipation from Slavery by a victory over prejudice: and it is significant that if I do any thing to deny them that chance, by the same act I may visibly injure the cause of the Union Arms. I cannot bring myself to do anything to take away from the command under General Dix this great *reserved force,* as I know you would find it if you would but use it. If you are attacked, let the blacks fight to preserve their freedom! They are needed. If anything could strengthen my previous opinions on this point, it would be just such facts as you narrate in your letter. If the Negroes have wives and children to fight for in addition to their freedom, they will not show themselves insensible to their motives which have inspired all other races. It is one of their rights to strike for their dearest other rights, as all races have done. I should welcome every blow of theirs which might at once carry succor to a patriot, death to a traitor, confusion to their slanderers, renewed life to their own veins, and bring victory to our flag. —

Contemplating, however, the possibility of their removal, permit me to say that the Northern States are of all places, the worst possible to select for an asylum. These poor people, afloat upon the world, are inhabitants of a Southern climate, and have habits, and are subject to needs and to peculiarities of physical constitution accordingly. Where, then, is the prudence or the humanity of subjecting them at once to the rigors of our Northern sky, in the winter season, with the moral certainty of inflicting extreme suffering, resulting probably in disease and death? If their removal is definitely determined upon, I would take the liberty of suggesting for the asylum some Union foothold in the South, — as Hilton Head, — where they could retain their health, be trained as soldiers, and their labor be rendered economically available. For them to come here for encampment or asylum, would be to come as paupers and sufferers into a strange land and a climate trying even to its habitues, as a swarm of homeless wanderers, migrating without purpose, and not to the wilderness where the strong arm would suffice for maintenance, but to a busy community where they would be incapable of self help, — a course certain to demoralize themselves and endanger others. Such an event would be a handle to all traitors and to all persons evilly disposed. We should be told that the experiment had been tried and had failed;

that the negroes were proved worthless and incapable of taking care of themselves, when the truth would be that we had pursued the plan most eminently calculated to disable and corrupt them. I meet with pleasure the motives of humanity which have dictated your proposed plan; but from the very same feelings I must consider the plan mistaken. It is precisely because I do not wish the negroes to suffer, precisely because I would save their wives and children from perishing; precisely because I do not wish their new freedom to become liecence, corruption and infamy, that I respectfully decline to aid or countenance your plan for their transportation to the North. –

In as much as the letter of Major General Dix is accompanied by a copy of a letter from the War Department granting permission to correspond concerning the plan proposed, I deem it incumbent upon me to state that I have, since receiving your letters, conferred with that Department upon this subject, and I am sure that there is not any difference of opinion between the Department and myself thereon; nor do I find there the existence of any such apprehensions regarding the safety of General Dix's position as you seem to entertain.

I ought to add that, even were my views coincident with your own, I am, under the law absolutely powerless, in my official capacity to promote them. – I have the honor to be very Respectfully Your Ob't Servant.

HLcS

                                                  John A. Andrew

Governor John A. Andrew to Major John A. Bolles, 16 Oct. 1862, M-2035 1862, Letters Received, RG 107 [L-151]. Endorsement. In response to Andrew, General John A. Dix, commander of the Department of Virginia, defended his plan for shipping the contraband blacks north. He also asserted that blacks had no interest in fighting: "Their indisposition to take up arms is nearly universal. They say they are willing to work, but they do not wish to fight." Indeed, Dix doubted that blacks would fight for their liberty. Although the Union army had several hundred thousand men under arms in the slave states, not "the slightest disposition [has] been manifested on the part of the blacks to avail themselves of so favorable an opportunity for asserting their freedom." (Maj. Genl. John A. Dix to Governor John A. Andrew, 5 Nov. 1862, vol. 3 VaNc, pp. 405–11, Letters Sent, ser. 5046, Dept. of VA & NC, RG 393 Pt. 1 [C-3203].)

42: Deputy Provost Marshal of the 18th Army Corps to the Headquarters of the 18th Army Corps

[*New Berne, N.C.*] February 19th 1863

Colonel. I have the honor to report that Chaplain Means sent me word this morning, that the Contrabands under the charge of Palmer at the camp near Fort Totten had refused to work and were being drilled by a white soldier, I sent a guard consisting of one corporal and twelve men, and arrested about one hundred negroes, and a white man who was instructing them. I found when they were brought to the Guard House, that the Contrabands having agreed to go into a black regiment now being raised in this Department, were under the impression that they were soldiers

I immediately reported myself at Head Quarters, stated the circumstances, and awaited orders. I learned from you that no authority had been given, to any person or persons to raise a Negro regiment, but that one colored man had been told that if he procured the names of one thousand colored men, who were willing to enlist as soldiers, their services might be accepted. I also learned from you that Gen. Wessel while in command had given permission to certain negroes to drill on a certain day. You then gave me your orders which I executed as follows, viz.

I told the contrabands that no permission had yet been given for the formation of a colored regiment; that the fact that they had expressed their willingness, to fight for the United States did not release them from the performance of their duties under the direction of Chaplain Means and others in authority over them; that they must return to their labour until such time as they had permission from the proper authorities to fight for the United States.

I then released them all upon their promise to return to their work with the exception of nine whom Chaplain Means wished kept in custody until his return from Beaufort where he now is. The white soldier who was drilling them I have now in confinement in accordence with your orders. Having as I believe executed your orders to the letter, I remain Very Respectfully Your obedient Servant.

HLS   George F. Woodman

Lt. George F. Woodman to Lieut. Col. Hoffman, 19 Feb. 1863, W-31 1863, Letters Received, ser. 3238, Dept. of NC & 18th A.C., RG 393 Pt. 1 [C-3087]. Endorsement.

43: Governor of Massachusetts to the Secretary of War

Boston, April 1st 1863

Sir: I avail myself of the visit of my Secretary, Lieut. Col. Browne, to suggest the idea of the detailment of some able, brave, tried and *believing* man, as a brigadier to undertake in North Carolina the organization of the colored troops, selecting officers therefor as did Gen'l. Ullmann, for Louisiana. — I have information leading me to the belief that with the proper man to lead the movement good troops can be raised in N.C. in numbers from 2500 to 5000, now within Gen¹ Foster's lines. But it needs a *man* always for the soul of any movement — even to trundle a wheel-barrow. And the right man is the main point. My own undertaking to raise a colored regiment in Mass. was begun upon talking with you about N.C. and the difficulty of attracting negroes to join *white troops;* while it would be comparatively easy to gain large numbers to join an army in part already composed of black troops. I suggested that if you could send some colored troops down there, the result would shortly be a general attraction of the blacks to our army, unless the business of dealing with those people should be badly mismanaged. —

And if you are prepared to have it done, I believe the work is already ripe. When our regiment gets there it will be the nest egg of a brigade. The officers of the 44th. and 45th. Mass now there, will render every aid in their power. So will many others. I learn that Genl. Foster is now looking with a kind eye on black troops. — In truth, I believe within four months the idea of thus organizing colored men will be most popular throughout the North. Meanwhile I am desirous of doing what I can to bring it before the public mind by *doing* the thing which men are discussing. There is little chance for opposition after a thing is accomplished and *seems* to be *good.*

I wish to assure you — though I cant think it necessary — that I am influenced by no merely *State* policy, that is, in a *local* sense, in raising colored regiments *here.* The truth is that unless we do it, in Mass, it cannot be expected elsewhere. While, if we do it, others *will* ultimately and indeed, *soon,* follow. Thus, then, Massachusetts can help by deed and example the ripening of Northern public sentiment and at the same time can help the department to [enlist] some black troops thoroughly organized for others to rally around. If nobody else will take black men I will, with your consent. And if the U.S. Government is not prepared to organize a brigade in N.C. I would gladly take those black men who may choose to come here, receive our State bounty and be mustered in. But I prefer to see the work going on *in the South itself*, if the department will order the work to be done and direct its organization.

Brig. Genl. Frank Barlow of New York would be a very good officer to detail for such a purpose in N.C. Or if the President would permit me to name an officer, I could find a Colonel by selecting one of several whom I know, to whom a vacant brigadiership might be assigned, better fitted for such an enterprise having regard to the proper combination of intellectual and moral qualities, with military experience than any brigadier with whom I am personally familiar now in the service. I have the honor to be, Faithfully your Obt. Servt.

John A. Andrew

P.S. However, our 54th. is being raised and officered, for *active* not for *fatigue* duty, and unless active operations of a brilliant sort are contemplated in No. Carolina, in which they as a portion of the troops in that command could be allowed to engage; then I pray you to send the 54th. to So. Carolina, where, under Genl Hunter negro troops will be appreciated and allowed a place in onward and honorable movements of active war.

The officers and men are both very carefully picked. We have aimed at getting officers of high character making careful selections out of many candidates. The men are selected just as regulars would be chosen by the most careful recruiting officer. Out of 450 now in camp, there are but two in hospital. — 100 more men are awaiting inspection by Surgeon, when they also will go to camp. —

Capt. Collins (4th. U.S. Infty.) who is Chief mustering and disbursing Officer in Mass. remarked this morning that these black troops are the best lot of men whom he has seen in any regiment during his nine months experience in Massachusetts.

HLS

Gov. John A. Andrew to Hon. Edwin M. Stanton, 1 April 1863, M-138 1863, Letters Received Irregular, RG 107 [L-109].

44: Commander of the Department of North Carolina to the Secretary of War

New Berne No Ca May 5 1863

Sir   A letter from Govr Andrew of date April 1st is referred to me by the War Department under date of April 27th, I have the honor to acknowledge receipt of the same and in reply beg leave to say.

If it be the policy of the Government, and the orders of the proper authorities, I will carry out, with my best efforts, the idea of raising colored troops in this Department, but would suggest, as my opinion based on experience that, not more than one Regiment, if even that, could be raised in this Department by voluntary enlistment, and forced enlistments would of course alienate the negroes, the very object the Governor of Massachusett wishes to avoid.

I will briefly state the times and circumstances under which I have armed and used Negroes in this Department. Besides the arming of spies and scouts, which was abandoned, we armed them at "Elizabeth City" during the time that post was threatened by Guerrillas, we obtained about 80 and they did their duty well enough, but we found they could not be trusted in any outward movement or raid probably owing to their lack of discipline.

During the late attack on Washington, the Negroes applied to me for Arms, and to strengthen my lines I armed about 120 all I had arms for, they did their duty well and seemed willing to fight, the test was not applied of course, they seemed to realize that the time was one of emergency and self preservation and that they must help, but the emergency having passed they did not and do not seem willing to enlist, they wish to *work* for the Government but to live with their families. Again, here at this Post, I received a petition signed by about 120 Negroes, for arms and organization in the U.S. Service, I replied that if names or promises could be received from enough to constitute the nucleus of a Regiment, I would consider the matter and be prepared to take action on it, since then officially I have heard nothing, but unofficially hear that not more than about 300 men or names were obtained.

I wish however to state that the wishes of the Government, if ordered, will be carried out not only with obedience, (my duty as a Soldier) but with zeal and in such a way as to endeavor to make it popular, rather than antagonistic to, the feelings of the white troops.

Referring to the Postscript of Govr Andrew's letter I beg leave to say, my orders are, to act on the defensive and that therefore the 54th would not be able to participate in "active operations of a brilliant sort" and moreover that white troops can stand the climate of North Carolina very well, but that in South Carolina white troops are very liable to the malarious influences of the Climate, which of course negro troops can stand, if therefore, the

54th and other Negro Regiments could relieve white Regiments in that Department, the interests of the Service would in my opinion be doubly served   I have the honor to remain Sir Very Respectfully Your ob't Servant

HLS   J. G. Foster.

Major Genl. J. G. Foster to Hon. Edwin M. Stanton, 5 May 1863, #2371 1863, Letters Received Irregular, RG 107 [L-126]. Late in July, Secretary of War Stanton encouraged General Foster not to fall into the "error" of his predecessor, who had failed to encourage black men to come in from the plantations and enlist. (Edwin M. Stanton to Major General J. G. Foster, 20 July 1863, Telegrams Collected by the Office of the Secretary of War (Bound), RG 107 [L-305].)

45: Commander of the Army and District of North Carolina to the Adjutant General of the Army, Enclosing a Report by the District Quartermaster

Newbern, N.C., Nov 16th 1863.

Since my arrival in North Carolina, I have done all in my power to advance the recruiting of colored Soldiers, in accordance with the orders of the Dept of War.   But in spite of all exertions, this variety of recruiting is comparatively of little account, while thousands of men are thronging about our posts, with the expectation of being rationed, or rationed and paid.   Many of these render a poor equivalent to the government, who would do something as soldiers in this malarious climate.

After much observation and inquiry, I am satisfied that the government is competing with itself through the Quartermasters, Commissaries, Engineer and other Departments.   Enclosed is a list of prices paid by the Quartermaster at New Berne, which fully justifies the conclusions I have arrived at.

While such prices are paid in N.C. it will be impossible to make much headway with recruiting.[1]

These views are presented with a view to call the attention of the proper authority to the question of a judicious reduction.   Very Respectfully Your Obd[r] Serv[t]

HLS   John Peck

[Enclosure]   *[New Berne, N.C., Nov. 2, 1863]*

Report of Negroes employed by the Quartermaster's Department,
at Newberne, N.C.

In whose employ. (In charge of.)	No.	Rate of pay $ cts.	Time	How Employed.
Captain R. C. Webster, A.Q.M. (Chief Quartermaster)	167	5 00 @ 10 00 −63	month	Laborers and helpers on U.S.M.R.R.
	21	@ 2 00 8 00	day	Carpenters, Wipers, Blacksmith at Machine Shop and on R.R.
Captain Wᵐ Holden, A.Q.M. (Saw Mills & Contrabands)	668	@ 10 00 50	month	Logging, Rafting, Bridge Building, Burning Charcoal &c
	85	@ 3 00 50	day	Engineers, Fireman, Ship Carpenters &c.
	108	@ 1 50	"	Carpenters, Masons, Mechanics and Blacksmiths
Captain Geo. W. Bradley, A.Q.M. (Water Transportation)	225	15 00	month	Stevedore Gang.
Captain Jaˢ Weldon A.Q.M. (Land Transportation)	33	20 00	"	Teamsters.
	194	10 00 50	"	Laborers, Stable Men, &c
	10	@ 1 25	day.	Blacksmiths, Carpenters &c.
Captain D. Messenger A.Q.M. (Clothing Camp and G. Equipage.	8	10 00	month	Laborers in Store house
	5	1 25	day	Blacksmiths.
Total.	1524			

Remarks. The prices were originally fixed by the authority of Maj. Gen.
Burnside, upon the occupation of this place.

HDS   R. C. Webster

Maj. Genl. John Peck to Brig. Genl. L. Thomas, 16 Nov. 1863, enclosing
Captain R. C. Webster, Report of Negroes employed by the Quartermaster's Department at Newberne N.C., [2 Nov. 1863], N-84 1863, Letters Received, ser. 360, Colored Troops Division, RG 94 [B-420]. Endorsements. The "remarks" placed here at the bottom of Webster's table
appear in the manuscript table as an additional vertical column.

1 At the date of this letter, the monthly pay of black soldiers was $10,
minus $3 for clothing.

46: Order by the Commander of the Department of Virginia and North Carolina

Fort Monroe, Va., December 5th, 1863. General Orders No. 46. The recruitment of colored troops has become the settled purpose of the Government. It is therefore the duty of every officer and soldier to aid in carrying out that purpose, by every proper means, irrespective of personal predilections. To do this effectually, the former condition of the blacks, their change of relation; the new rights acquired by them; the new obligations imposed upon them; the duty of the Government to them; the great stake they have in the War; and the claims their ignorance and the helplessness of their women and children, make upon each of us, who hold a higher grade in social and political life must all be carefully considered.

It will also be taken into account that the colored soldiers have none of the machinery of "State aid" for the support of their families while fighting our battles, so liberally provided for the white soldiers, nor the generous bounties given by the State and National Governments in the loyal States—although this last is far more than compensated to the black man by the great boon awarded to him, the result of the war—Freedom for himself and his race forever!

To deal with these several aspects of this subject, so that as few of the negroes as possible shall become chargeable either upon the bounty of Government or the charities of the benevolent, and at the same time to do justice to those who shall enlist, to encourage enlistments, and to cause all capable of working to employ themselves for their support, and that of their families—either in arms or other service—and that the rights of negroes and the Government may both be protected, it is ordered:

I. In this Department, after the 1st day of December, instant, and until otherwise ordered, every able bodied colored man who shall enlist and be mustered into the service of the United States for three years or during the war, shall be paid as bounty, to supply his immediate wants, the sum of ten (10) dollars. And it shall be the duty of each mustering officer to return to these Head Quarters duplicate rolls of recruits so enlisted and mustered into the service on the 10th, 20th and last days of each month, so that the bounty may be promptly paid and accounted for.

II. To the family of each colored soldier so enlisted and mustered so long as he shall remain in the service and behave well, shall be furnished suitable subsistence, under the direction of the Superintendent of Negro Affairs, or their Assistants; and each soldier shall be furnished with a certificate of subsistence for his family, as soon as he is mustered; and any soldier deserting, or whose pay and allowances are forfeited by Court-Martial, shall be reported by his Captain to the Superintendent of the District where his family lives, and the subsistence may be stopped, – provided that such subsistence shall be continued for at least six months to the family of any colored soldier who shall die in the service by disease, wound, or battle.

III. Every enlisted colored man shall have the same uniform, clothing, arms, equipments, camp equipage, rations, medical and hospital treatment as are furnished to the United States soldiers of a like arm of the service, unless, upon request, some modification thereof shall be granted from these Head Quarters.

IV. The pay of the colored soldiers shall be ten ($10.) dollars per month, three of which may be retained for clothing. But the non-commissioned officers, whether colored or white shall have the same addition to their pay as other non-commissioned officers. It is, however, hoped and believed by the Commanding General, that Congress, as an act of justice, will increase the pay of the colored troops to a uniform rate with other troops of the United States. He can see no reason why a colored soldier should be asked to fight upon less pay than any other. The colored man fills an equal space in ranks while he lives and an equal grave when he falls.

V. It appears by returns from the several recruiting officers that enlistments are discouraged, and the Government is competing against itself, because of the payment of sums larger than the pay of colored soldiers to the colored employees in the several Staff Departments, and that, too, while the charities of the Government and individuals are supporting the families of the laborer. It is further ordered: That no officer or other person on behalf of the Government, or to be paid by the Government, on land in this Department, shall employ or hire any colored man for a greater rate of wages than ten dollars per month, or the pay of a colored soldier and rations, or fifteen dollars per month without rations, except that mechanics and skilled laborers may be employed at other rates – regard being had, however, to the pay of the soldier in fixing such rates.

VI. The best use during the war for an able-bodied colored man, as well for himself as the country, is to be a soldier; it is therefore further ordered: That no colored man, between the ages of eighteen and forty-five, who can pass the Surgeon's examination for a soldier, shall be employed on land by any person in behalf of the Government (mechanics and skilled laborers alone excepted.) And it shall be the duty of each officer or other person employing colored labor in this Department to be paid by or on behalf of the Government, to cause each laborer to be examined by the Surgeons detailed to examine colored recruits, who shall furnish the laborer with a certificate of disability or ability, as the case may be, and after the first day of January next, no employment rolls of colored laborers will be certified or passed at these Head Quarters wherein this order has not been complied with, and are not vouched for by such certificates of disability of the employees. And whenever hereafter a colored employee of the Government shall not be paid within sixty days after his wages shall become due and payable, the officer or other person having the funds to make such payment shall be dismissed the service, subject to the approval of the President.

. . . .

X. The theory upon which negroes are received into the Union lines, and employed, either as laborers or soldiers, is that every negro able to work who leaves the rebel lines, diminishes by so much the producing power of the rebellion to supply itself with food and labor necessary to be done outside of military operations to sustain its armies; and the United States thereby gains either a soldier or a producer. Women and children are received, because it would be manifestly iniquitous and unjust to take the husband and father and leave the wife and child to ill-treatment and starvation. Women and children are also received when unaccompanied by the husband and father, because the negro has the domestic affections in as strong a degree as the white man, and however far south his master may drive him, he will sooner or later return to his family.

Therefore it is ordered: That every officer and soldier of this command shall aid by every means in his power, the coming of all colored people within the Union lines; that all officers commanding Expeditions and Raids shall bring in with them all the negroes possible, affording them transportation, aid, protection and encouragement. Any officer bringing or admitting negroes within his lines shall forthwith report the same to the Superintendent of Negro Affairs within his District, so they may be cared for and protected, enlisted or set to work. Any officer, soldier or citizen who shall dissuade, hinder, prevent, or endeavor to hinder or prevent any negro from coming within the Union lines; or shall dissuade, hinder, prevent, or endeavor to prevent or hinder any negro from enlisting; or who shall insult, abuse, ridicule or interfere with, for the purpose of casting ridicule or contempt upon colored troops or individual soldiers, because they are colored, shall be deemed to be, and held liable under the several acts of Congress applicable to this subject, and be punished with military severity for obstructing recruiting. . . . .

By command of Major General Butler.
HD

General Orders No. 46, Head Quarters Dept. of Va. and North Carolina, 5 Dec. 1863, vol. 52 VaNc, General Orders Issued, ser. 5078, Dept. of VA & NC, RG 393 Pt. 1 [C-3062]. With this order Butler established the organizations (particularly the Bureau of Negro Affairs) and the procedures for recruiting black soldiers, employing black laborers, and maintaining former slaves in the tidewater region. Only the portions of the order relating to military recruitment are printed here.

47A: Virginia Freedwoman to a Northern Missionary

[*York Co., Va. December 10, 1863*]

Sir I take the liberty to pen you a few lines, stating my own case, the Soldiers have taken my Husband away, from me, on yesterday, and it was against his will, and he is not competent to bee A Soldier. he is verry delicate, and in bad health, in the Bargin, and I am not healthy myself, but if they, keep him, they leave me, and 3 children, to get along, the best we can, and one of them is now verry Sick. do try and get them to release him if you can, for they too[k] him, when he was on his way to his work. he is A shoo make by trade, his Name is James Wallis. pleas do all you can

ALS   Jane Wallis, his wife

Jane Wallis to Prof. Woodburry, [10 Dec. 1863], Letters, Orders, & Telegrams Received by Lt. Col. J. B. Kinsman, ser. 4108, Ft. Monroe VA Dept. of Negro Affairs, RG 105 [A-7838]. Endorsement.

47B: Northern Missionary to the Commander of the Department of Virginia and North Carolina

Portsmouth [*Va.*] Dec 10th 1863.

To Maj. Gen. Butler The Undersigned respectfully solicits the attention of the Commanding General to the following facts.

Soldiers, stationed at Craney Island under Col Nelson are daily making arrests of Colored Citizens, in and about Portsmouth and Norfolk, for the purpose of compelling them to volunteer in the U.S. Service.

That these men are taken from their ordinary and necessary avocations; from their houses, workshops, drays, churches, & schools and carried to Craney Island against their will, where they are urged to enlist; and if they refuse subjected to a species of torture to compel them so to do. They are forced to carry a ball, supposed to weigh forty or fifty pounds for several hours in sucession.

The undersigned would further represent; that these outrages cause much suffering among the poorer families, dependent on the daily wages of these men for support. And that it undermines and will ultimately destroy the Loyal Sentiments of the Colored people. He therefore prays the attention of the Commanding General to these abuses.

ALS   H. S. Beals

H. S. Beals to Maj. Gen. Butler, 10 Dec. 1863, Letters, Orders, & Telegrams Received by Lt. Col. J. B. Kinsman, ser. 4108, Ft. Monroe VA Dept. of Negro Affairs, RG 105 [A-7838]. General Butler ordered Lieutenant Colonel J. Burnham Kinsman, General Superintendent of Negro Affairs in the Department of Virginia and North Carolina, to investigate. Kinsman proceeded to Craney Island, where he reported that "Col Nelson has a company of Zouaves in different parts of the country; at Newport-News; Norfolk; Portsmouth and elsewheres who take men from their work or from the church or the streets; which is creating great consternation among the Negroes in Norfolk and Portsmouth; and causing them to hide for fear of impressment. . . ." (Lt. Col. J. B. Kinsman to Maj. General Butler, 12 Dec. 1863, Letters, Orders, & Telegrams Received by Lt. Col. J. B. Kinsman, ser. 4108, Ft. Monroe VA Dept. of Negro Affairs, RG 105 [A-7838].)

47C: Statement by an Impressed Virginia Black Soldier

[*Craney Island, Va.*] Jan. 2nd 1864

Statement of John Banks (Colored) in the matter of recruiting colored men, by force.

My name is John Banks, am about 24 years of age, live at the Parrish Farm, one mile this side of Newport News where I have a mother & wife.

On the 2^{d} day of Dec. 1863 I was cutting wood in the woods about a mile from my house when a number of colored soldiers, armed (probably about ten men) came upon me and asked me to enlist. I told them that I could not enlist because I was obliged to do the work for my family. They then obliged me to go to Newport News to see Capt. Montgomery, their Commanding Officer. I begged Capt. Montgomery to release me or at least to let me go home to see my family. He treated me kindly and let me go home under guard & stay about five minutes. He said he couldnt release me because he "had *orders*" to take all colored men & make them enlist, but that he would send me to Col. Nelson at Craney Island & if I didn't wish to remain the Col. would send me home the next morning. I was then sent the same day to Craney Island on a tug, surrounded by armed soldiers, just as though I was a prisoner.

Arriving at Craney Island I heard such stories of men being obliged to "tote" balls because they refused to enlist and also of their being confined in the guard house on hard bread & water, that when my enlistment papers were made out I did not dare to remonstrate but accepted the five dollars bounty and my uniform and clothing and performed the duty of a soldier. I was detailed for duty in the Quartermaster's Dept. at Norfolk five days, part of which time I was under guard, so that I could not even go to get a drink of water without an armed soldier going with me.

While at Newport News a soldier told George Marrow and me that if we didn't enlist he would put the contents of his musket into us.

At Craney Island I saw Bob Smith put into the guard house because he would not enlist.

HD

Statement of John Banks, 2 Jan. 1864, filed with N-18 1863, Letters Received, ser. 360, Colored Troops Division, RG 94 [B-20]. Sworn before an army judge advocate. According to other documents in the same file, General Benjamin F. Butler, commander of the Department of Virginia and North Carolina, who was determined to end impressment and the abuse of impressed blacks, ordered on January 9, 1864, that Colonel John A. Nelson, who directed the impressment, be dismissed from the service. That order was subject to the approval of President Lincoln, but despite Lincoln's endorsement to the contrary, the War Department apparently dismissed Nelson.

48: Black Chaplain to the Secretaries of War and State

White house Landing Va June 14th 1864

Dear sir   I take the liberty to bring before your mind some important facts imbracing the condition of the slaves now falling in our lines. I had hoped that these fugitives when leaving their Rebel masters & coming into our lines were made instrumental in the hands of your honors government to help to crush this wicked Rebellion, but to my sad supprise, I am sorry to say that while white & colored men from the north are breathing out their last breath upon the Battl field in freeing these stupit creatures, they are left Idle to rove over the country like the ox that feed the army. at the same time here are three or four colored Regts unfilled & they & their families are daily subsisted by the government — it is true they are unwilling to a great extent to take up arms to help to free themselves or be useful to the country. this you can easily account for — but when accounted for, the great question remains still the same, I.E. why should they not be made to fall in our ranks as in other states where our conquest has been made, no less than 300 are lying about this place, for you to dispose of in some way   they look as tho they would make good soldiers, please parden me for troubling you. I am your Humble servt

ALS

Garland H. White

Acting Chaplain Garland H. White to Hon. Edwin M. Stanton and Wm. H. Seward, 14 June 1864, filed with W-309 1864, Letters Received, ser. 360, Colored Troops Division, RG 94 [B-70]. White was chaplain of the 28th USCI, an Indiana black regiment.

49: Order by the Commander at Plymouth, North Carolina

To RECRUITING
Agents.

All Negroes brought inside the lines at this place, will, immediately on their arrival here, and before any papers are drawn up, enlisting them as soldiers, be reported at the Provost Office in person.

Agents are hereby notified that all "*swearing in*" of colored recruits must be done at the Provost Office at this Station, and no officer of this command will be permitted to administer that obligation to the men, except at that Office.

It must be remembered that, upon arrival within the lines of occupation of U. S. Troops, Negro Refugees become *FREE MEN*, and any misrepresentation of their situation made them with a view to their enlistment as soldiers, will be summarily punished. While it is the duty of the negro, in return for the freedom offered him, to enter the army, the practice of fraud to induce him thereto, will not be tolerated.

By command of Col. JONES FRANKLE,

WM. G. HASKELL,

Lieut. & A. A. A. Gen'l.

Dated at Head-Quarters, Station of Plymouth, }
March 9th, 1865. }

PD

Broadside, 9 Mar. 1865, vol. 176/419 VaNc, General Orders & Circulars Issued, ser. 1812, Station of Plymouth NC, RG 393 Pt. 2 No. 88 [C-3168].

Black Enlistment

THE MISSISSIPPI VALLEY

50: General-in-Chief of the Army to the Commander of the Department of the Tennessee

(Unofficial)   Washington, March 31st /63

Genl, It is the policy of the government to withdraw from the enemy as much productive labor as possible. So long as the rebels retain and employ their slaves in producing grains, &c, they can employ all the whites in the field. Every slave withdrawn from the enemy, is equivalent to a white man put *hors de combat.*

Again, it is the policy of the government to use the negroes of the South so far as practicable as a military force for the defence of forts, depts, &c. If the experience of Genl Banks near New Orleans should be satisfactory, a much larger force will be organized during the coming summer; & if they can be used to hold points on the Mississippi during the sickly season, it will afford much relief to our armies. They certainly can be used with advantage as laborers, teamsters, cooks, &c.

And it is the opinion of many who have examined the question without passion or prejudice, that they can also be used as a military force. It certainly is good policy to use them to the very best advantage we can. Like almost anything else, they may be made instruments of good or evil. In the hands of the enemy they are used with much effect against us. In our hands we must try to use them with the best possible effect against the rebels.

It has been reported to the Secretary of War that many of the officers of your command not only discourage the negroes from coming under our protection, but, by ill treatment, force them to return to their masters. This is not only bad policy in itself, but it is directly opposed to the policy adopted by the government. Whatever may be the individual opinion of an officer in regard to the wisdom of measures adopted and announced by the government, it is the duty of every one to cheerfully and honestly endeavour to carry out the measures so adopted. Their good or bad policy is a matter of opinion before they are tried; their real character can only be determined by a fair trial. When adopted by the government it is the duty of every officer to give them such a trial, and to do everything in his power to carry the orders of his government into execution.

It is expected that you will use your official and personal influence to remove prejudices on this subject, and to fully and thoroughly carry out the policy now adopted and ordered by the government. That policy is, to withdraw from the use of the enemy all the slaves you can, and to employ those so withdrawn, to the best possible advantage against the enemy.

The character of the war has very much changed within the last year. There is now no possible hope of a reconciliation with the rebels. The union party in the South is virtually destroyed. There can be no peace but that which is enforced by the sword. We must conquer the rebels, or be conquered by them. The north must either destroy the slave-oligarchy, or become slaves themselves; – the manufacturers – mere hewers of wood and drawers of water to southern aristocrats.

This is the phase which the rebellion has now assumed. We must take things as they are. The government, looking at the subject in all its aspects, has adopted a policy, and we must cheerfully and faithfully carry out that policy.

I write you this unofficial letter, simply as a personal friend, and as a matter of friendly advice. From my position here, where I can survey the entire field, perhaps I may be better able to understand the tone of public opinion, and the intentions of the Government, than you can from merely consulting the officers of your own army. Very respectfully Your obt servt

HLdS

H. W. Halleck

Genl. in Chf. H. W. Halleck to Major Genl. U. S. Grant, 31 Mar. 1863, H. W. Halleck Letters Sent, Generals' Papers & Books, ser. 159, RG 94 [V-123]. Halleck made numerous additions to the draft letter and added the entire last paragraph in his own hand.

51: Commander of a Louisiana Black Brigade to the Adjutant General of the Army

NEW ORLEANS, LOUISIANA, MAY 19th 1863.
GENERAL: I have the honor to report that, after a long voyage from New York, I arrived with my command, in this city, on the 20th–21st ult. Major General Banks being absent in the field, I immediately reported to Brigadier General Sherman, who was in command. He advised me to telegraph to General Banks and wait for his answer. I did so at once, and receiving no answer, continued to do so until the 26th, when despairing of hearing from him I sailed with the command, according to the orders of the General-in-Chief, for Baton Rouge, arriving there on the

morning of the 27th ult. After consultation with Major General
Augur, who did not think I could effect much there, I established
recruiting depots in that city, and proceeded to fit out an
expedition, comprising officers for two regiments, to establish
other depots at and in the neighborhood of Franklin, on the
Teche. On the 2d instant, the day after the above expedition had
sailed, I received a letter from Major General Banks; requesting me
to visit him as soon as possible at Opelousas. I sailed on the same
day for Algiers, and owing to the great difficulty of obtaining
transportation in this region, did not succeed in reaching
Opelousas until the night of the 4th. After full conferences with
him, he wrote me a letter, a copy of which I herewith
enclose. He also delivered to me a letter to Major General
Halleck, which I also enclose. In accordance with the suggestions
of General Banks, I have established a camp of instruction &
recruiting depots at Brashear City, ordering back to it the officers
whom I had ordered to Franklin. I have continued the depots at
Baton Rouge, and establishing my headquarters in this city, have
opened here several depots. Comparatively few of those [*recruits*]
promised me by General Banks in his letter have, as yet, arrived
at Brashear City. I presume that, in a few days, a large number
will be reported. So far, I have been obliged to depend upon
other efforts. I have now in Brashear, Baton Rouge, and this city
nineteen hundred and seventy-six men, three hundred of whom
have not been surveyed by the surgeons. I am very confident that,
in less than a fortnight, if no further obstacles are thrown in my
way, that I shall be able to report five regiments full. As I feared,
and stated to his Excellency, the President, and the Secretary of
War, before I left Washington, the contract system has been a
serious impediment. I feared at one time, that it would utterly
paralyze my efforts. Although General Banks says in his letter to
me, that "you are authorized by the Secretary of War to recruit
troops in any portion of the Department of the Gulf," yet he is
now unwilling that I should interfere with it. Of course I have
yielded to his wishes, although it completely neutralizes in this
region the moral effect of my movement. The practical operation
of the system is a virtual rendition of the negro to slavery. Proof
accumulates that in many, I should say the majority, of cases the
cruelty to his person is far greater than in his former
condition. As to his ever obtaining any wages under the system as
conducted, that is simply a farce. Had it not been for this
impediment and another, of which I proceed to speak, I could,
with ease, have raised ten thousand men in the first ten days after
my arrival. The other impediment, to which I referred, is that I
find that, excepting Major General Banks, Brigadier General

Bowen, and a few other honorable exceptions, the whole body of officials in this department, military and civil, with whom I and my officers have come into contact, seem to be opposed (some bitterly) to the policy of the government in this matter, and many have endeavored to throw every obstacle in their power in my way. I propose to make these matters, as verbally requested by the Secretary of War, the subject of a special report to him. Notwithstanding these difficulties the way is clear now to raise very large bodies of troops of this class, if the government desire it. As soon as Port Hudson shall be taken (and it looks as if it will be in a few days) a country full of negroes will be open to us, and tens of thousands can be speedily recruited. I take pleasure in saying that, whenever the negro has the opportunity, he shows the greatest willingness and alacrity to enlist. I am also exceedingly glad to have it in my power to say that he shows an aptitude and desire to learn the drill, and a cleanliness in his person and in his camp, well worthy of imitation by more pretentious soldiers. I have full confidence that he will make a soldier of which commanders may be proud. At the request of Major General Banks I intend to bring down from Brashear a force of five hundred men to cleanse and purify this city. I have the honor to remain, General, your obedient servant,

TLcSr   Daniel Ullman

Brig. General Daniel Ullman to Brigadier General L. Thomas, 19 May 1863, Negro in the Military Service, pp. 1249–51, ser. 390, Colored Troops Division, RG 94 [B-472]. Copies of the enclosures to which Ull-mann refers – letters from Banks to Ullmann acknowledging the latter's ar-rival and pledging support for his effort, and from Banks to Halleck re-porting Ullmann's arrival, both dated May 5, 1863 – appear in the same compilation, pp. 1226–28 and 1224–25.

52: Absentee Mississippi and Louisiana Planter to the Adjutant General of the Army

Staten Island [N.Y.], June 2d, 1863.
My Dear Sir: As well known and acknowledged unionists we received *strong* "protection papers" from Generals Grant and McPherson; and from Admiral Porter, but despite said "papers," our rights as loyal citizens have been rudely violated by certain parties who visited our several estates, and FORCIBLY removed nearly all the male negroes therefrom. (saving some blacks who

managed to *conceal* themselves from the "pressgang.") Now, as I am not aware that *freed* and hired negroes can be impressed for Government service (most particularly for cotton making on *hired places,*) I intend to have a very thorough investigation made of this *gross* violation of our rights, and the orders of the commanding generals, and would be much indebted if you will kindly inform me who gave authority to the *Kansas* officer who led the "impressment" expedition? for, as *you* control the "abandoned property" business, &c., I have been advised to apply to *you* for information concerning the conduct of the subordinates in your immediate Department.

Our negroes were freed and working for us on wages, and, as General Halleck issued especial orders to General Grant for our "protection," I should be glad to know by what *show* even of right or justice, our papers were thus disregarded? and, as *our* loyalty is recognized at headquarters, I intend to have this grave matter of "impressment" closely examined. In a letter from the Admiral (of very recent date) *he* is evidently in ignorance of any such scheme, as he writes, that, *our "negroes"* (who are free to choose for themselves) "will not be interfered with." I take it for granted, My Dear Sir, that *you* are in ignorance of the outrageous conduct of the officers who so exceeded the limits of their official duties, therefore, I must beg a few lines in answer, that proper steps may be taken for due inquiry into this highhanded measure. Dr. Duncan's reputation for loyalty is too well known to require any discussion of our *rights* to protection, but, if you desire any *vouchers* respecting our devoted Unionism, I must refer you to General Halleck; Mr. Seward; Mr. Thurlow Weed; General Scott; Mr. John P. Kennedy, or to a *host* of influential northerners. My husband, (Mr. Henry Duncan of Miss.) writes me of the seizure of his hired blacks, and also mentions that the "pressgang" visited his house at night; searched the quarters for their occupants; and remained on his premises until daylight. Having recently returned from a brief visit to Mississippi, I *saw for myself,* how grossly the Kansas and other troops violated the dwellings of even *Union* people, but being a Northern and loyal woman, I do not intend to be treated like a *rebel* without decided resistance. Mississippi is certainly far away, yet the mania for Cotton and money-making there is a notorious fact, and the light of justice may light up that remote district for public edification. Unless some change be made in the treatment of loyal citizens. Trusting, My Dear Sir, that you will make an examination into our claims and case, and relying on your desire to correct a grievous wrong – I remain Yours Very truly,

(signed) Mary Duncan

147

My address is "Mrs. Henry Duncan, care of Duncan, Sherman & Co. (Bankers) New York City."
P.S. – We (as a family) have *nine* estates on the river, most of them opposite Lake Providence, and they have been literally *rifled* and *stripped.*
HLcSr

Mary Duncan to General Thomas, 2 June 1863, enclosed in Adjt. Gen. L. Thomas to Brig. Gen. J. P. Hawkins, 26 June 1863, T-3 1863 supplemental, Letters Received, ser. 1756, Dept. of the Gulf, RG 393 Pt. 1 [C-548]. In the covering letter, Adjutant General Thomas instructed General Hawkins, commander of a black brigade at Millikens Bend, Louisiana: "If property has been improperly taken, it should be returned for we ought to protect our friends."

53: Company Commander to the Commander of a Louisiana Black Regiment and a Statement by an Army Recruiting Officer

Millikens Bend La July 18th /63
Sir Alow me to make a Statement in regard to the Negroes formerly owned by Henry Duncan being forced to join our Co. On the evening of April 12th Capt Bishop & I met Bill Paulds in Providence and asked him to enlist in our Co. he was trying then to get over that night to See his wife and we promised to give him a Sergeancy in the Co if he could get us 10 or 15 good men. he told us he knew of more than that number that would come if he could get over. Bishop then promised to take him over that night, as it was considered dangerous to go in day light as Gurrilles were on that side every day. At dark they Started with Ed F Brown & Lieut Voris. On the 13th I went over the *canal* with Bishop we found Bill with Several men we took their names, and on the 14th I went into camp with them 8 in all among the number was Charles Boswell, Jake Walls, Peter Home and Bob Williams. I left Bill in charge of them as he claimed to have got them all. they were all from that Side the river. On the 16th I got a skiff for Bill & Charles to cross over to take Some things to there wives they came back next morning and had got Some more men to come along. On the 18th I went up the river recruiting and was absent from camp about all the time untill 1st of May. During our Stay at Providence we gave about all the men from Duncan passes to go over and see there families, and I Saw Bishop pass Several Squads of 3 to Six out at

dark and get a Skiff for them   they would go over and be back by daylight next morning

As for forcing men to go into the Co we never even used *harsh words*. we told them as we did all others that they would be most likely kept along the river to guard the plantations where their families would be at work, as that was the understanding we had of the policy layed down by *Gen Thomas*

I deem it my duty to make the above Statement on behalf of our Deceased Captain, as the men endeavoured to make the impression on the officer examining them that Capt Bishop had forced them to come away from the plantation, which was by no means the case   I am very respectfuly Your Obedient Servant

ALS   Robt. M. Campbell

Millikins Bend La July 18ᵗʰ 1863

I Joseph L. Coppoc a Capt 8ᵗʰ Reg La Vols AD. Certify that I visited the Duncan plantations oposite Lake Providence several times about the middle of March 1863. during those visits I noticed a great dissatisfaction among the Colored people of said plantations. they complained that they were poorly cared for, over worked and had but little to eat. Their greatest desire appeared to be, to get with the Union army, and were willing and even anxious to go with it in any capacity they could be useful, and stating that their condition could not be made worse than it was at that time. One negro man in particular stated to me that he had concealed himself in a swamp for over ten days, watching for an opportunity to escape to our lines, but was detected, put in the stocks and severely whipped.

ADS   Joseph L. Coppoc

1st Lieut. Robt. M. Campbell to Col. H. Scofield, 18 July 1863, and statement by Joseph L. Coppoc, 18 July 1863, both enclosed in Lt. Geo. C. Lockwood to Lieut. Wm. E. Kuhn, 19 July 1863, L-238B 1863, Letters Received, ser. 4720, Dept. of the TN, RG 393 Pt. 1 [C-2007]. Lieutenant George C. Lockwood, an aide-de-camp at the headquarters of the Department of the Tennessee, had been ordered to investigate Mary Duncan's complaint about depredations by recruiters. In his report to department headquarters, Lockwood enclosed, in addition to the two documents above, two lists of blacks on the Duncan plantation and a report by a sergeant in Lieutenant Campbell's company, 8th Louisiana Infantry of African Descent.

54A: New Orleans Merchant to the Commander of the Department of the Gulf

New Orleans Aug [5, 1863]

General, My house servant, a negro man [aged] 40 years, while leaving my house on his way to my office, yesterday was met and seized by a squad of negro soldiers and obliged [to go] along. His hard begging for release and his protestations [that] he did not wish to go, did not avail him and his resistance [was] overcome by superior force, which compelled him to move on.

Informed today of orders having been issued for the release of all these unjust arrest and my servant having sent word to me to come out and begging me to obtain his release, I went to the place of confinement, – the Southern Press – where after seeing my servant and he expressing the wish to come with me, I requested the officer in command to allow him to go out, – when I was informed that my man had signed the enlistment roll. I enquired at once of my servant, while standing before the officer, for a confirmation of this fact, but he denied having signed any paper with his name, – but the officer refused to pass him out. Pursueing my enquiry of my servant I soon learnt, that after arrival at the press about noon yesterday, with a numerous company gathered up, he had been told "to touch the pen" but he did not know, what it had been for.

My servant feeling anxious to return to his home and not having enlisted at his own free will, I would most respectfully request for an order of release, as he has been a faithful and honest servant and is anxious to return to his home. I have the honor to be General, Your most obt serv.

ALS   C. T. Buddeck

C. T. Buddeck to Major Genl. N. P. Banks, [5] Aug. [1863], B-222 1863, Letters Received, ser. 1920, Civil Affairs, Dept. of the Gulf, RG 393 Pt. 1 [C-688]. Part of right margin is torn, accounting for the bracketed words in the first paragraph. C. P. Stone, chief of staff at Department of the Gulf headquarters, initialed the communication and noted: "I can see no reason why a colored man should be dragged into the service without his consent & without some legal formality of draft, any more than a white man – This seems to be a case of oppression."

54B: Superintendent of Negro Labor in the Department of the Gulf to the Commander of the Department of the Gulf

New Orleans. August 5th 1863.

Sir. It becomes my duty to lay before you the facts concerning an outrage committed upon a loyal citizen. Last night about 10 1/2 O'Clock a squad of Policemen (Six in number) entered the house of Mr P. Bourgeois situated near the corner of Dryades and Washington Streets and attempted to take his son Peter from the house for the purpose of making a Soldier of him.

He refused to go and was immediately set upon and cruelly beaten by the squad one of them using a knife upon him and wounding him in three different places.

They then carried him off by force despite the remonstrances of his aged Father, and put him in the Southern Cotton Press from which place he was released to-day. The family are all free mulatoes, the Father being very white with long gray hair.

The above is only one of the cases that have been brought to my notice daily for the past three weeks only that hitherto these acts were reported to me as having been committed by Negro Soldiers and last night they had the assistance of the Police. I beg you will instruct me if I can act in this matter and if so, in what manner. My office is constantly besieged by persons both white and Black (Military Officers and Civillians) Some enquiring for their servants, others for their sons and Brothers some of whom have been forcibly seized while performing important duties. The greatest consternation exists among the Colored people, and the Citizens have good reason to be indignant. Several prominent Citizens to-day informed me that their houses were forcibly entered last night and their servants taken out of bed and maltreated if they refused to accompany the Squad.

Another unpleasant feature is that the entire matter is attributed to my agency both by the white Citizens and the Negroes, and I consequently loose the confidence of the Blacks, which I have so long been striving to gain that my influence with them might be both powerfull and beneficial.

I have thus communicated the matter for your information and shall be happy to execute any instructions which I may receive. I have the honor to be Sir. Very Respectfully Your Obdt Servt.

HLS   Geo. H. Hanks

Lieut. Geo. H. Hanks to Major General N. P. Banks, 5 Aug. 1863, H-91 1863, Letters Received, ser. 1920, Civil Affairs, Dept. of the Gulf, RG 393 Pt. 1 [C-533].

54C: New Orleans Recruiter to the Commander of the Department of the Gulf

New Orleans   August 7th 1863.

Sir. It having been reported to me by several prominent suburban residents of this city, that there were many vagrant contrabands prowling about their premises, I applied to the Chief of Police for assistance in collecting them that I might be able to select such as were suitable for the military service.

Unfortunately the Police exceeded their instructions and several outrages were committed upon Citizens both white and black almost in the heart of the City a fact which could be regretted by none more than myself. I have released the Negroes whenever called upon to do so by their owners or employers and have made every apology to the parties for the inconvenience to which they had been put. Many were released by me on their own representation that they were able to support themselves. Every person that called upon Major Plumly or myself on business regarding the Negroes was courteously received by us and shown every attention in our power. They all went away pleased and satisfied with the exception perhaps of those who having found that their former slaves had voluntarily enlisted were obliged to go back without them. There are others recruiting in this city who sometimes use harsh measures to induce the negroes to enlist, and all of their outrages are ascribed to me, as situated as I am there are many who for political reasons would be only too glad to affix a stigma to my name.

Trusting that this explanation may prove satisfactory I have the honor to remain Sir. Very Respectfully Your Ob'd't Serv[t]

HLcSr   P. F. Mancosas

P. F. Mancosas to Major Genl. N. P. Banks, 7 Aug. 1863, M-372 1863, Letters Received, ser. 1756, Dept. of the Gulf, RG 393 Pt. 1 [C-533].

Black Enlistment

54D: Statements of an Anonymous New Orleans Black

[*New Orleans, La. September?* 1863]

the president Shall be Commander in Chief of the Army and navy of the united States and of the militia of the Several States when called into the actual Service of the united States

Let See if Slavery was any value   what m^r Yancy Say the number of Slaves in the Southern States estimated 3,500,000 and the were worth $1200,000 000 in gold which would be a bout $1800,000,000 in Green Backs Eighteen hundred million Dollars   the Collored population is not educated but what Great responciblity has been placeed on them   the have been Steam boat pilots ingenears and Black Smiths Coopers Carpenters Shoe makers Drivers on plantations Sugar makers porters on Steam boats and at hotels Dineing Servant Porters in Commision houses Grocery Stores Public weighers Carrige Drivers preachers of the Gospel the best Soldiers the united States Can Raise but the tel lies Sometimes and So dos all negro traders   the get Drunk and lawiers and merchants Generals and Governors and all Clases   the black men has wives and Sweet harts Jest like the white men   Some white men has Collored wives and Sweet hearts   god made all   it is not a City rule for Collored people to ride in the white peoples cars but the bed togeather   God mad all   the must all Die

it is retten that a man can not Serve two master But it Seems that the Collored population has got two a rebel master and a union master   the both want our Servises   one wants us to make Cotton and Sugar And the Sell it and keep the money   the union masters wants us to fight the battles under white officers and the injoy both money and the union   black Soldiers And white officers will not play togeathe much longer   the Constitution is if any man rebells against those united States his property Shall be confescated and Slaves declared and henceforth Set free forever   when theire is a insurection or rebllion against these united States the Constitution gives the president of the united States full power to arm as many soldiers of African decent as he deems nescesisary to Surpress the Rebellion and officers Should be black or white According to their abillitys   the Collored man Should guard Stations Garison forts and mand vessels according to his Compasitys

A well regulated militia being necessary to the cecurity of a free State the right of the people to keep and Bear arms Shall not be infringed

we are to Support the Constitution but no religious test Shall ever be required as a qualification to Any office or public trust

under the united States   the excitement of the wars is mostly keep
up from the Churches   the Say god is fighting the battle but it is
the people   But the will find that god fought our battle
once   the way to have peace is to distroy the enemy   As long as
theire is a Slave their will be rebles Against the Government of
the united States   So we must look out our white officers may be
union men but Slave holders at heart   the Are allways on hand
when theire is money but Look out for them in the battle
feild   liberty is what we want and nothing Shorter

our Southern friend tells that the are fighting for negros and
will have them   our union friends Says the are not fighting to free
the negroes   we are fighting for the union and free navigation of
the Mississippi river   very well let the white fight for what the
want and we negroes fight for what we want   there are three
things to fight for and two races of people divided into three
Classes   one wants negro Slaves   the other the union the other
Liberty   So liberty must take the day nothing Shorter   we are the
Blackest and the bravest race   the president Says there is a wide
Difference Between the black Race and the white race   But we
Say that white corn and yellow will mix by the taussels but the
black and white Race must mix by the roots as the are so well
mixed and has no tausels – freedom and liberty is the word with
the Collered people

We the people of the united States in order to form a more
perfect union Establish Justice insure domestick tranquillity
provide for the common defence promote the general wellfare and
secure the blessings of liberty to ourselves and our posterity do
ordain and establish this Constitution for the united States of
America

My Dear union masters and reble masters or friends   How are
we Slave Population to take hold of a musket under white officers
which a great part of them has been in the reble army and the
meet to hold a war Consels all to them Selves   Dear Sir I heard a
federal officer Say after the fall of Port hudson to a Collored
Soldier we will not want any more negro Soldiers   go home to
your master   i my Self went to a union lawyer on Some
Buiness   the first question are you free or Slave   Before the fall of
porthudson the white Preachers told us we were all free as any
white man and in Less time than a month after you weare taking
us up and puting in the lockups and Cotton presses giving us
nothing to eat nor nothing Sleep on And haveing negro traders for
recruting officers Drawing his Sword over us like we were
dogs   By those means you will Soon have the union north   if any
union man can deny this i will write no more   i am for the union
and liberty to all men or nothing Shorter   treason against the

united States Shall consist only in Levying ware against them or in adhering to theire enemies giving them aid and Comfort   no person Shall be convicted of treason unless on the testimoney of two witnesses to the Same overt Act or Confession in open Court   the Congress Shall Have power to declare punishment of treason but no attainder of treason Shall work Corruption of blood or forfeiture Except during the life of the person attained

Now let us see whether the Colored population will be turn back in to Slavery and the union lost or not   on the 4″ of last July it was Said to the colored population that the were all free and on the 4″ of August locked up in Cotton presses like Horses or hogs By reble watchmen and Saying to us Gen banks Says you are All free why do you not go to him and get passes   And one half of the recruiting officers is rebles taken the oath to get a living and would Sink the Government into ashes   the Scrptures says the enemy must Suffer death before we can Have peace   the fall of porthudson and vicksburg is nothing   the rebles must fall or the union must fall   Sure the Southern men Says the are not fighting for money the are fighting for negros   the northern men Say the did not com South to free the negroes but to Save the union   very well for that much   what is the colored men fighting for   if the makes us free we are happy to hear it And when we are free men and a people we will fight for our rights and liberty   we care nothing about the union   we heave been in it Slaves over two hundred And fifty years   we have made the contry and So far Saved the union and if we heave to fight for our rights let us fight under Colored officers for we are the men that will kill the Enemies of the Government   pleas let me continue

Art 173   the Slave is entirely Subject to the will of his master Who may Correct and Chastise him though not with unusal Rigor nor So as to maim or mutilate him or to expose him to the danger of loss of life or to cause his death

Art 174   the Slave is incapable of making any kind of Contract Except those which relate to own emancipation

Art 175   All that a Slave possesses belongs to his master   he Possesses nothing of his own excep his peculium that is to Say the Sum of money or movable estate which his master chooses He Should possess

Art 176   the can transmit nothing by Succession or otherwise but the Succession of free persons related to them which the would have Inherited had the been free may pass through them to such of their descendants as may have acquired their liberty before the Succession opened

A part of the Civil Code of louisiana

the united States Shall guarantee to every State in this union a

155

republican form of government and Shall protect each of them a
gainst invaison and on Aplication of the legislature. or of the
executive when the legislature. can not be convened against
Domestic violence

now is the united States government and constitution free or a
local Goverment   if it is free let us colored population muster in
to ams and garison forts guard Station and mand vessels and then
we will know wheather we are free people or not   then we will
know wheather you want to make brest works of us or not or
make us fools ornot   I heard one of most Ables and distingush
lawiers Say that the Colored population was all free and Had as
much liberty in the union as he had   in four or five days after I
went to him to get him to atend Some buiness for me he Said to
me Are you free or Slave   Sir Said i am free By your own
speeches   was you born free   no Sir Said i   we have been made
fools of from the time Butlers fleet landed hear but I have
remained At my old Stand and will untill i See what i am
dowing   I know very well that the white union men cannot put
down the rebeles for them that was not rebles Soon will be   i am
Sory that I am not able to write good   may the union forever
Stand with peace and liberty to All good people

HD   A Colored man

[*New Orleans, La. September? 1863*]

the President Shall at Stated times receive for his Services a
Compensation which Shall neither be increased or diminished
During the period for which he Shall have Been Elected and he
Shall not receive within that period Any other emolument from
the united States or any of them   Before he enters on the
execution of his office he Shall take the following oath or
Afirmation   I do Solemnly Sweare (or Affirm) that I will faithfully
execute the office of president of the united States and will to the
best of my Ability. preserve Protect and defend the Constitution of
the united States   the president Shall be commander in chief of
the Army and navy of the united States and of the miltia of the
Several States when called Into actual Service of the united States

when the president ordered three hundred thousand Colored
Soldiers to be mustered into the united States Army on the first
Day of last April if So the rebles would have fell like the
Surrender of vicksburg and porthudson

Declare freedom at onc and give us Somting to fight for   Black
Soldiers Black officers and all white rebles will Soon run them in
or out of the union

the writer was born in 18.18 feb 16"

HD   one of the union Colored friends

Statements of A Colored man and one of the union Colored friends, [Sept.?
1863], enclosed in Lt. Col. Jas. A. Hopkins to Brig. Gen. James Bowen,
2 Sept. 1863, H-99 1863, Letters Received, ser. 1920, Civil Affairs,
Dept. of the Gulf, RG 393 Pt. 1 [C-704]. Both statements are in the
same handwriting. In his covering letter, Chief of Police James A. Hopkins
reported that a policeman had found the statements "in the public Street."

55: Provost Marshal of St. Bernard Parish to the Provost Marshal General of the Department of the Gulf

St. Bernard [Parish, La.], August, 21, *1863.*
General   I have the honor to report that four negro soldiers
representing themselves as belonging to the 1st La. Native Guards
with passes signed by the A.A.G. of Brig. Gen. Ullman, came
into this parish yesterday for the alleged purpose of
recruiting. That under this guise they visited plantations of loyal
& peaceable men, putting guards over their houses, threatening to
shoot any white person attempting to leave the houses, and then
siezing horses carts & mules for the purpose of transporting men
women & children from the plantations to the city of New
Orleans. That a band of negroes thus assembled to the number of
seventy five went singing, shouting & marauding through the
Parish disturbing the peace.

The property thus siezed has mostly been returned to the proper
owners & the women & children have been advised to return [*to*]
thir several plantations.

These Recruiting negroes have promised to return in a day or
two to convey all the negroes who desire it to the City. Thus
great insubordination and confusion has been caused. Today five
more negro soldiers with passes similar to the others visited the
Plantation of Mr. E. Villerie loaded their muskets in front of his
door and demanded some colored women whom they called their
wives —

I most respectfully submit that such a method of Recruiting for
the Service of the U.S. Army is improper & await further
instructions in regard to it. Your Most Obt Servt

ALS   Geo G. Davis

Capt. Geo. G. Davis to Brig. Gen. James Bowen, 21 Aug. 1863, Letters Received, ser. 1845, Provost Marshal, Dept. of the Gulf, RG 393 Pt. 1 [C-768]. On August 23, the provost marshal general forwarded Davis's letter to departmental headquarters, remarking that parish provost marshals were "without guards to enforce order." In an endorsement on a similar letter, the commander of the Defenses of New Orleans also criticized disruptive recruitment practices: "The whole system of recruiting as practiced within the limits of these Defences by persons not connected with my command, is subversive of the first principles of good order and military discipline, and it is within my personal knowledge that these recruiting parties are not only depredating upon the community, but upon each other and the United States." He added that he held for trial the four recruiters mentioned in Davis's letter, an action General Banks, commander of the Department of the Gulf, approved. (Endorsement by B.G.C. W. H. Emory, 21 Aug. 1863, on Capt. S. W. Sawyer to Lieut. H. Kallenstroth, 21 Aug. 1863, Letters Received, ser. 1845, Provost Marshal, Dept. of the Gulf, RG 393 Pt. 1 [C-768].)

56: Supervising Special Agent of the Treasury Department to the Commander of the Department of the Gulf, Enclosing a Letter from a Plantation Manager to the Treasury Department Superintendent of Plantations

New Orleans, Septr 26th *1863.*

General. I, exceedingly, regret being compelled to lay before you an instance of flagrant violation of your order on the part of Col Kempsy, commanding 16th Reg^t Corps D'Afrique. The accompanying papers will, sufficiently, explain the offense.

I cannot refrain, General, from availing myself of the present occasion, to urge upon your consideration the vast importance of a strict enforcement of your former orders upon the subject. Both the State and the Government have a vital interest in the matter. If we lose the confidence of the negro, we shall labor in vain to secure his services in a profitable working of the plantations; the money already invested by the United States, will be irretrievably lost; the great staples of Louisiana will be ruined; the internal revenue deprived of a fruitful source of income, and society, itself, be demoralized, by rendering a large part of the population, vagabond.

If negroes are to be impressed, as described in the enclosed papers, they have lost, not gained, by the proclamation of the President. They are, nominally, free, but in reality, the most unprotected of serfs.

I invoke, General, your most effecient intervention in this
matter. I beg that the wisdom, which dictated your orders, giving
assured protection to the negro, may have the largest and fullest
operation. Touching the carts and mules, I will merely say, that
as they are my property, receipted for by me, I am confident that
you will order their immediate restoration. I have the honor to
remain, General, Very Respectfully Y^r Ob^t Servt

HLS   Benj. F. Flanders.

[*Enclosure*]
"*Copy*" Mayronne Plantation Parish St. Charles La Septr 25" 1863
Capt. Cozzens My overseer on the Payne plantation reports to me
this minute that Col Kempsey of the 16th Regiment of Colored
population last night about 11 O'Clock and took from the said
place, 2 carts and 6 Mules and 22 men and the overseer Mr.
Cozanah did show the letter of August 15" of protection but the
said Col. said his orders were of later date. now this Col. was
entreated not to take the said Hands from Government place, of
protection– His head-quarters are at Bonnett Carré point some 16
miles above this place. you will attend to this matter immediately
as the Hands taken are men we cannot do without

HLcSr   Jno. L. Murphy

Benj. F. Flanders to Maj. Genl. N. P. Banks, 26 Sept. 1863, enclosing
Jno. L. Murphy to Capt. Cozzens, 25 Sept. 1863, F-406 1863, Letters
Received, ser. 1756, Dept. of the Gulf, RG 393 Pt. 1 [C-535]. Other
enclosures.

57: Baton Rouge Free Blacks to the Provost Marshal of Baton Rouge

[*Baton Rouge, La. November 1863*]
The memorial of the undersigned free men of color, residing in
the City of Baton Rouge beg leave most respectfully to call your
attention to a hardship to which we are subjected and at the same
time to ask you to apply the remedy.
The evil we complain of is, that we are hunted up in the
streets, in the market house, and other places whilst engaged in
our daily avocations, and marched off to the Penetentiary, where
we are placed with contrabands, and forced into the service. Now
we claim to be freemen – we were born free, have lived free, and
wish to be treated as freemen.

We are aware that the Congress of the United States has passed an act requiring each state to furnish a certain proportion of troops to be regularly drafted, the ages of said troops being specified in the act— As loyal men we are ready and willing to comply with, and obey the mandate of Congress; but we respectfully submit whether we should not be placed on the same footing with others who are subject to the draft— Let our names and ages be regularly registered, and placed in the wheel, and whover of us that may be drawn will unhesitatingly shoulder arms, or furnish a substitute or pay the sum required by the act of Congress— In conclusion we beg leave to state that as a class we have always been law-abiding, and have never been backward in contributing our share towards the support of the Government under which we have lived, State, or National. We are still prepared to do so, and do assure those representing the government to whom we owe fealty that we shall always be ready to respond whenever called upon, but at the same time claim the same privileges extended to other freemen, so far as the draft is concerned— Respectfully Submitted—

HDS   [36 *signatures*]

[*Endorsement*] Provost Marshal's Office Nov 11th 1863 Respectfully forwarded for the consideration of the Genl Comdg— There are many abuses in enforcing the conscription which should be corrected—such as, arresting persons with colored soldiers—taking officers servants—employees in QM Dept—tearing up passes—arresting boys and old men—&c— Danl Pardee Lt Col & P.M.

[*Endorsement*] H^d Q^{rs} Baton Rouge Nov. 11 '63 This memorial &c is forwarded to H^d Q^r, because I have no powers in the premises,—& be cause I think it is very reasonable, & just.

Charges of even worse abuses, than mentioned by the Pro. Marshall, are constantly made against the Conscription authorities,—of corruption, receiving bribes &c Very Respectfully P. St Geo Cooke Brig. Gen. U.S.V. Cmg

[*Endorsement*] Office Com of Enrm Nov. 14 [*1863*] Respectfully referred to Lieu Col. Bangs Supt recruiting— The acts complained of are in direct violation of orders and instructions, and Gen Cooke should arrest and punish the guilty parties By order of Board John S Clark Col ADC Chairman

J. Lofficial et al. to Lieutenant Col. Pardee, [Nov. 1863], P-174 1863, Letters Received, ser. 1920, Civil Affairs, Dept. of the Gulf, RG 393 Pt. 1 [C-716]. Other endorsements.

&

58A: **Representative of Louisiana Planters to the Commander of the Division of West Mississippi**

New Orleans August 2 1864

Sir   We now enclose you a correct copy of information handed to Col Hanks[1]

Col Hanks Sir   We are informed by reliable persons that there are a great many Negroes to be found in the following places. viz.

On the Algiers side of the River beginning on the place of one Mr Rinck, about 12 miles below the City, all along the swamp to the Cut off, where one person Judge Morgan employs some one hundred prime young men. Thence always in the Swamp to Trepaniers Canal, back of Algiers, and thence in the Swamp to the back of Gretna there are some Eighteen hundred to two thousand colored men fit to bear arms.

On this side beginning back of the Barracks, and up the Gentilly Road, down to the back of the City, up to the Ponchartrain Rail Road there are some Twelve to fifteen hundred

Thence from the Ponchartrain Rail Road all along the swamp, and along the Lake shore to the back of Carrollton, and thence also along the Lake shore to the back of Kenners, and as far as the woods go beyond Kenner, thence coming back to the City all along the Jackson Rail Road, there are at least Three to five thousand.

On the ridge called La Freniere beyond Kenner along the Lake Shore and the Jackson Rail Road up to Pass Manchac, there are over One thousand, all men in the prime of life who cut wood on public and private property for a few days and then idle the balance of the time. They are those who have escaped from Plantation labor, causing their families to be supported by the Govenment, or those who work Plantations. There are also over three or four thousand Men about the City who live in idleness part of the time, and work just enough to exist. Most Respectfully Your Obt. Svt.

S. B. Bevans

New Orleans   August 2ᵈ 1864

Col Hanks in answer to the above communication stated he had at first thought he had the right of taking colored men in the City, but on further consideration he concluded he had no such right, and had therefore released some two hundred colored men who had been taken up in the City. He stated further he had no right to take any colored men either in the City of New Orleans, Baton Rouge, Thibodeaux or any other village, but that he would or could only take them on Plantations.

On my stating to him that General Canby and General Banks had both told me quite the contrary, He stated positively again that he would begin taking people from Plantations tomorrow morning, taking all between Eighteen and Forty except five per cent. He stated further that if he had the authority he could in Forty eight hours, pick up in and about the City, two thousand able bodied recruits. Under these considerations I appeal to you General for redress, feeling assured that you would not permit men shall escape who are many a burden to the Community, as the police reports daily show. Whilst industrious men are taken, who are working Crops, which pay heavy duties for the support of the Government   Most Respectfully Your Obt. Svt.

HLS

S. B. Bevans

[*Endorsement*] H^d Q^r. Mil. Div. West Miss., New Orleans, Aug. 3^d 1864. The planters who are represented by Mr Bevans, called on me on Saturday of last week, and were advised that it was the intention to interfere as little as possible with the interests of private individuals, and that, to the extent that they could indicate or secure recruits for the colored regiments from other sources, the demand upon the laborers on the plantations would be diminished. They were referred to the Commander of the Department of the Gulf, with the expression of the opinion that the proposition made by them would be as acceptable to him, as it was to me. It is now represented, that the superintendent of colored labor considers that he is constrained by the terms of the order from these Head Quarters to limit his operations to the colored laborers on the plantations. This direction was given under the impression, that the other sources of obtaining recruits had already been exhausted, and the order will be so construed as to embrace any other source, which can legitimately be made use of.

The subject is worthy of consideration, and is respectfully referred to Maj Gen. Banks, for such action as, in his judgement, may be necessary and proper. Ed. R. S. Canby Major General Com'd'g.

[*Endorsement*] Headquarters, Dept of the Gulf, N.O. Augt 3, 1864. Respectfully returned to Major General Canby, with the following statement.

Mr Bevans, Mr Davis, and other gentlemen representing the planting interest, called upon me some days since, and received the same assurances that you have given them, – that every consideration would be given to their interests consistent with the service.

Colonel Hanks has received instructions to leave upon the Plantations the Engineer, Blacksmith and Carpenter, and to take such measures as will embarass in the least possible degree the Planters. This has been received as satisfactory by those who have called upon me. We have rolls showing the exact number of men on each plantation between 18 and 40. I have directed him to leave one fifth of this number upon the plantations, consulting the employers as to the selections to be made taking care that the objects of the Government are not defeated. He has also received instructions to enlist all unemployed negroes in the City and populous neighborhoods, who are without regular employment. He will do this before the plantations are disturbed. This season being one of comparative leisure, it has been suggested to the planters that if the interests of the Government would admit it, laborers would be temporarily supplied to assist in the busy month of December. I do not think any serious embarassment will grow out of this order. N. P. Banks M.G.C.

[*Endorsement*] If the necessities do not prevent it colored laborers now taken from the plantations may be furnished during the busy period of the cotton season, upon the condition of not being paid by the Government while in the employment of the planters. Ed. R. S. Canby Maj Genl H^d Qrs. Mil. Div. West Miss., New Orleans, Aug 3^d /64.

S. B. Bevans to Maj. Genl. E. R. S. Canby, 2 Aug. 1864, B-143 1864, Letters Received, ser. 1920, Civil Affairs, Dept. of the Gulf, RG 393 Pt. 1 [C-726]. General Banks later approved the policy of furloughing enlisted recruits to work the harvest. (Major Geo. B. Drake to Chaplain T. W. Conway, 3 Oct. 1864, vol. 8 DG, p. 325, Letters Sent, ser. 1738, Dept. of the Gulf, RG 393 Pt. 1 [C-726].)

1 George H. Hanks, superintendent of Negro labor in the Department of the Gulf.

58B: Headquarters of the Department of the Gulf to the Commander of the Defenses of New Orleans and the Latter's Reply

New Orleans Aug 15th 1864

Brig Gen'l T. W. Sherman Comd'g Defences   It has been officially reported at these Headquarters, that Negroes in and about this City, Carrollton, Lakeport &c, who have respectable means of support, are being seized and enlisted in the Army

The Commanding General desires that all such be released, and only those taken who are refugees, or vagrants, or those who are without any employment. I have the honor to be Very Respectfully Your obt Sevt

HLcSr   (signed) Geo. B. Drake

New Orleans, Aug. 17 1864

Maj. Drake   Your letter of this date is rec'd and attended to.

From the enclosed papers the Major General Comdg. will perceive what steps were taken to get these 12,000 negroes into the Army. He will perceive that I districted the whole extent of Swamps described in the letter of Bevans & Co, and so arranged the matter that the whole area of swamp could be scoured in a short time. To be assured of no mistake—a copy of Bevan's & Co's letter with all the endorsements thereon was furnished each field officer entrusted with this important duty.

It is no wonder that some negroes were taken up that ought not to have been; for how is a party of soldiers to ascertain exactly whether a stray negro is employed or not, other than his own word for it; and if their words are to be taken—none or few negroes could be obtained. Very Respectfully Your Obt. Svt.

ALS   T. W. Sherman

Geo. B. Drake to Brig. Gen. T. W. Sherman, 15 Aug. 1864, enclosed in T. W. Sherman to Maj. Drake, 17 Aug. 1864, S-136 1864, Letters Received, ser. 1920, Civil Affairs, Dept. of the Gulf, RG 393 Pt. 1 [C-726]. Endorsements. The other enclosures mentioned are not in the file.

58C: New Orleans Free Blacks to the Commander of the Department of the Gulf

New Orleans August 17th 1864

The petitioners respectfully represent: That they are loyal citizens of the United States; that they are sincerely attached to the Constitution and desire sincerely the maintenance of the Unity of the National Government and its laws; that a large number of them are property-holders real and personal, and are engaged in all the pursuits of commerce, industry and trades, and thereby are taxpayers; that they are all law-abiding citizens and have always behaved themselves peacefully & decently.

The petioners represent that on the arrival of Gen. Butler they answered with the greatest dispatch to his appeal for troops in the defense of the Union flag, and two regiments sprang from among them, ready, within the space of a week, to meet the enemy of the national cause;

Your petitioners also represent that in June last 1863, in answer to the call of Georges F. Shepley then Military Governor of Louisiana the same population in the short space of *Forty-Eight hours,* raised two full regiments which were sent to the defense of this city

Now your petitioners respectfully represent that since a few days, to their great detriment and to that of their fellow citizens a large number of them are arrested in the public thoughfare, and incarcerated as criminals, while engaged in their various avocations.

Your petitioners know the feelings and hearts of their population to assure you that in case of emergency they would not be backward to offer their support and services to the National Government, as they have always done on every former occasion.

The petitioners therefore respectfully pray, that you will use of your power to cause the release of those of our population who were arrested as if they were felons or criminals.

Your petitioners further pray that you will cause the arbitrary acts to cease, and will ever pray.

HDS

Manuel Guerrier   Paul Trevigne
J. B. Roudanez   L. P. [Trévigne]
Thomas M[d] Porée F. Durousseau

Manuel Guerrier et al. to Major Gen. Nathaniel P. Banks, 17 Aug. 1864, P-109 1864, Letters Received, ser. 1920, Civil Affairs, Dept. of the Gulf, RG 393 Pt. 1 [C-738]. Written in an elaborate script on oversized paper.

59: Conscription Order for a Louisiana Plantation

Office Superintendent Negro Labor,

Department of the Gulf,

New-Orleans, August 1st, 1864.

Capt. W. E. Thrall

Provost Marshal, Parish of Lafourche

SIR—

You will require Mr. Hubert Murray to produce at your office, on or before the _____ instant, the following named men of color, and all others between the ages of 18 and 40 years, at present on Laurel Valley Plantation, to be forwarded to the general recruiting rendezvous, in accordance with General Orders No. 106

NAME.		AGE.	NAME.		AGE.
Amos Harrison	Re'd	40	Carter	gone	37
Robin	"	40	George Lee		40
Moses Wheeler	gone	38	Joseph Smith	gone	25
Wallace	Exempt	34	Billy Watson	Re'd	25
Josiah	gone x	39	Little Henry	"	22
Motley	gone	34	Fred	Exempt	28
Berry	(consumption)	38	Richard Lee	"	20
Allen	runaway gone	37	Jefferson	"	34
Albert	"	35	Harrison	"	
Guy Langmus	"	39			
William Lucas	"	40			
Isaac	Re'd	38			
Matt	gone	40			
Anderson	Re'd	38			

Very respectfully, your obdt. Servt. Geo. H. Hanks

Col. & Supt. Negro Labor.

PD

Col. Geo. H. Hanks to Capt. W. E. Thrall, 1 Aug. 1864, Records Relating to Enrollment & Draft, ser. 1876, Provost Marshal, Dept. of the Gulf, RG 393 Pt. 1 [C-812]. Printed form with handwritten insertions in two different hands.

60: Louisiana Planter to the Commander of the Division of West Mississippi

New York   August 17' 1864

General   Though not having the honor of a personal introduction to you I enclose the within letter from our mutual friend Major General Dix— General, though a citizen of the State of New York residing in this city I am the owner and Cultivator of the Woodlands plantation situated on the right bank of the Mississippi river about 40 miles below New Orleans.

This plantation is hereditary property and with all my other property was sequestrated by the Confederate Government in consequence of my firm adherence to the government of the United States. The success of our arms restored my property and since that time I have been able to live on my place which I do for six months of the year. Under the orders promulgated the last season by Major Gen Banks we have hired and punctually paid our people besides having incurred great outlay in providing all the means necessary to raise and secure our crops believing that as the Government encouraged us to sow they would allow us to reap and harvest our crop—

We now see with great alarm the recent Military order issued by command of Major Genl Banks directing the conscription of all our able bodied men between the ages of 20 & 40 years of age. This order if carried into effect at this time when the crops are just on the eve of being secured will involve the whole planting interests in ruin—

As we have acted somewhat on the implied if not absolute guarantee of our Government in the conduct of our agricultural business we humbly ask of you General that if not absolutely required by impending danger our people be allowed to remain on our places till the crop of sugar & Cotton is secured—

We have already during the last season furnished for enlistment all our able bodied hands between the ages of twenty and thirty and now to take all those between 20 and forty would leave us entirely with the weak aged and helpless—

We trust General that you will see the matter in its proper light and issue such orders as will save us, at the same time that they will best advance the interests of the General government, who in a pecuniary point of view are certainly interested to keep all the specie in the country which our production of sugar and cotton on our own soil is certain to do—

These views General are made in strict deference to your own as regards immediate danger to our country but should you be able to save the planters from ruin by allowing them to secure the crops they have raised under encouragement of Government you will confer a great favour on the agriculturalists of Louisiana— We remain, General Most Truly Yours

Bradish Johnson

P.S. I hope to be in Louisiana by the 1st of November if not earlier—

ALS

Bradish Johnson to Major General Canby, 17 Aug. 1864, J-3 1864, Letters Received, ser. 5515, Div. of West MS, RG 393 Pt. 1 [C-831]. A penciled, crossed-out endorsement in the handwriting of General Edward R. S. Canby, commander of the Division of West Mississippi, reads: "Answer—That the enrollment of laborers from the plantations has been so arranged as to produce the least possible inconvenience to the planters concerned."

61: Commander of a Black Brigade to the Headquarters of the Department of the Gulf

Morganzia, La. Oct. 24— 1864

Major: I have the honor to state that the present system of recruiting for Colored Troops has proved a failure, and does not meet the wants of the service, and I take the liberty to suggest that experience has demonstrated there is but two ways to get soldiers: First that partially adopted by the Government at the first commencement of the war in accepting by regiments and then holding the officers responsible for failure to keep full ranks.

And secondly that of the peremptory draft which when thoroughly adopted and rigidly adhered to is the best, but if we cannot have this the first will answer our purpose. The same reasons why these men should not be taken from the plantations here are equally applicable to Northern farms yet as the season is nearly over these objections loose their force.

And I request that Regimental Commanders may be authorized and directed to at once under the direction of Comdg. Genl. of Div. or Post proceed to recruit and enlist, any and all able bodied men that may offer their services and for this purpose they send officers with detachments of men and with permission to have for their own regiment all they may so acquire not to exceed the maximum allowed by law.

As strange as it may appear I have never yet been able to obtain permission to recruit for my regiment and if I had had it I long since could have acquired and maintained the maximum number but when I had a few more than the prescribed allowance they were taken away which destroyed all inducement to effort.

It has long since been demonstrated that one set of Regimental Officers will not recruit for another only in case of a General System like the present   some little may be done but nothing to be compared to what officers of regiments will do for themselves.

The disinclination of planters to have recruiting parties come upon their plantations has probably influenced the adoption of the present system more than any one thing but as I have in Ill. often gone to the houses, farms and workshops of citizens and solicited not their slaves, but thir sons to go out in defence of their country it is to be presumed we could be safely trusted with this duty here. Very respectfully

HLcSr

(Signed) H. N. Frisbie

Col. H. N. Frisbie to Major Geo. B. Drake, 24 Oct. 1864, vol. 201/412 DG, pp. 61–62, Letters Sent, ser. 1990, 1st Brigade 1st Division USCT, Dept. of the Gulf, RG 393 Pt. 2 No. 106 [C-891]. According to the chief of recruiting in the Department of the Gulf, some commanders of black regiments possessed the permission to recruit that Frisbie requested. Yet the recruiting chief opposed such departures from the norm and recommended revocation of all such authorizations given to individual commanders. (Endorsement of Capn. Sheldon Sturgeon, 5 Oct. 1864, on C. L. Dunbar to Capt. Styles, 29 Sept. 1864, Incoming Correspondence of B. F. Flanders, Group B, 3rd Agency, RG 366 [Q-65].)

62: Adjutant General of the Army to the Secretary of War

Washington, D.C. November 7, 1864

Sir: Under your special instructions, I proceeded to the Mississippi River, and organized Colored Troops. I have now the honor to report the following as the result thus far:

IOWA. (near the Missouri line)

1 Regiment of Infantry.

ARKANSAS.

6 Regiments of Infantry.

TENNESSEE.

2 Regiments of Heavy Artillery.
1 Company of Light Artillery.
2 Regiments of Infantry.

MISSISSIPPI:

1 Regiment of Cavalry.
2 Regiments of Heavy Artillery.
5 Regiments of Infantry.

LOUISIANA

1 Regiment of Cavalry.
3 Companies of Light Artillery.
6 Regiments of Infantry.

ALABAMA.

3 Regiments of Infantry.

FLORIDA.

1 Regiment of Infantry.

KENTUCKY

2 Regiments of Cavalry.
2 Regiments of Heavy Artillery.
11 Regiments of Infantry.

RECAPITULATION:

4 Regiments of Cavalry –	4,800
6 Regiments of Heavy Artillery –	10,800
4 Companies of Light Artillery –	720
40 Regiments of Infantry	40,000
Total:	56,320

All of the above Regiments were organized on the maximum standard, and when entirely complete would give the above specified number. That number was undoubtedly on the rolls, though some of the Regiments may not have been entirely full when ordered to the field, as the losses by death and other casualties were in many cases made up by recruits. At the present time the aggregate is about 50,000.

In the above enumeration I make no mention of other

Regiments organized in Tennessee, as they were raised under specific orders from the War Department, addressed to others.

No organizations were made in North Georgia, as the few negroes who came within our lines were assigned to Regiments in Tennessee.

In Louisiana only one Regiment was organized, because the Infantry Regiments raised in that state by General Banks, were limited to 500 men each, and orders were subsequently given to raise them to 1000 each. All the recruits, therefore were necessary for this purpose.

In Kentucky the number on the rolls the fifteenth of October, was about 17,000, which number would be increased to 20,000, as other organizations had been authorized and were going forward. When this number is obtained, it is recommended that no further Regiments be ordered, but that the subsequent recruits be assigned to those already in the service, to keep them up to the maximum standard.

More troops could have been put into the Army, but for the pressing demands of the several Departments on the Mississippi, and for laborers with the troops operating in the field. The number of blacks used in this way, including cooks and servants, must be very large. Most of the labor is done by this class of men, and the Forts on the Mississippi river have been mainly thrown up by them. Where white and black troops come together in the same command, the latter have to do the work. At first this was always the case, and in vain did I endeavor to correct it, contending that if they were to be made soldiers, time should be afforded for drill and discipline; and that they should have their fair share of fatigue duty. The prejudice in the Army against their employment as troops, was very great; but now, since their fighting qualities and manliness have been fully shown by the blacks, it has greatly changed.

All of these Regiments have white officers, who are selected with care, and are subject to an examination, and even a second one, if deemed necessary. Great difficulty was experienced in the early part of the work in getting medical officers, but this has been remedied by sending a Medical officer through the New England States, who induced a number of Physicians to appear for examination, and receive appointments.

The non-commissioned officers are generally appointed from White Regiments, but as intelligent blacks are found, they are made Sergeants and Corporals, and ultimately they will fill all these positions. I have the honor to be Very Respectfully Your Obedient Servant

HLc   {*Lorenzo Thomas*}

171

Adjutant General [Lorenzo Thomas] to Hon. Edwin M. Stanton, 7 Nov. 1864, L. Thomas Letters Sent, Generals' Papers & Books, ser. 159, RG 94 [V-44].

TENNESSEE

63: Military Governor of Tennessee to the Secretary of War

Nashville Sept 17 1863.

Hon. E. M. Stanton. I have made the acquaintance &c. of Maj. Stearns Asst. Adjt Genl. U.S. Vols. who is here with authority to raise negro troops in the Dept of the Cumberland. We have been taking steps in that direction & have organized the men with a double purpose first to Employ them on the Gov't works where needed & then Convert them into soldiers & have so far succeeded well. We need more laborers now than can be obtained for the prosecution of works that are indispensable to sustain the Rear of Genl Rosecrans Army. Maj Stearns proposes to organize & place them in Camp where they in fact remain idle this will to a very great extent impede the progress of the works & diminish the number of hands employed. All the Negroes will quit work when they can go into Camp & do nothing. We must Contract them for both purposes. I must be frank in stating my opinion that Maj Stearns mission with his notions will give us no aid in organization Negro Reg'ts in Tennessee. There are a number of persons running in from the other states who are anxious to raise such Reg'ts for the simple purpose of holding the offices without regard to the condition of the negro or the suppression of the rebellion. I must further state that we can organize Reg'ts in Tennessee as well as we can others & that we can find more men in Tennessee ready & willing to Command than we can raise Reg'ts to Command in Tennessee. Answer will raise negro troops & lead them to battle[1] it will have much better influence upon the public mind. We are just now beginning to organize & put the state facility in motion. It is exceedingly important for this question to be handled in such way as will do the least injury in forming a correct public Judgement at this time We hope therefore that the organization of negro Reg'ts in Tennessee will be left to the Gen'l Comd'g this Dept. & Military Governor. I would respectfully ask that the President may be furnished a copy of this telegram. An early answer is respectfully asked.

HWSr   Andrew Johnson

Andrew Johnson to Hon. E. M. Stanton, 17 Sept. 1863, Telegrams Collected by the Office of the Secretary of War (Bound), RG 107 [L-214]. In reply, Secretary of War Stanton clarified Stearns's position: "He is while in your State your subordinate bound to follow your directions and may be relieved by you whenever his action is deemed by you prejudicial. Upon your judgment in matters relating to the State of which you are Governor the Department relies in respect to whatever relates to the people whether white or black bond or free. No officer of colored troops will be appointed but in accordance with your views as the Chief State Executive. If Major Stearns can be of no aid and his presence is obnoxious he will of course be removed, whether relieved by you or not." (Edwin M. Stanton to Brigadier General Andrew Johnson, 18 Sept. 1863, Telegrams Collected by the Office of the Secretary of War (Bound), RG 107 [L-307].)

1 This sentence apparently was garbled over the wires.

64: Commissioner for the Organization of Black Troops in Tennessee to the Secretary of War

Nashville Tenn. Sept 19th 1863

Sir: I met by appointment of Gov. Johnson, M[r] East, Secy. of State. Horace Maynard M.C and D[r] Bowen, as a committee to discuss some propositions having reference to the enlistment of Colored men, and the consequent emancipation of the Slaves of this State. They agree that the slave is virtually emancipated and cannot be returned to his old position. One half or more as freed as slaves of rebels, and the rest virtually free to day.

There is a strong and defiant Anti-Slavery Sentiment here that is ripening to full expression and will soon make itself felt throughout the land. I think Tenn. will lead our northern States on this subject and pave the way for a fair settlement of this vexed question. I have a full and most cordial understanding with Gov. Johnson and expect in a week or less to commence recruiting

The Colored men are anxious to enter the Army as soon as they can be treated fairly and paid promptly, but many have been employed for months without pay, some few I am told for twelve months and they distrust the Officers who have thus neglected their duty,

The impressment is working evil in this Department. Men who

are pressed in the service are rarely enrolled and in consequence not paid. Respectfully

HLS   George L. Stearns

Major George L. Stearns to Hon. Edwin M. Stanton, 19 Sept. 1863, S-241 1863, Letters Received Irregular, RG 107 [L-118]. At this time, Governor Johnson did not share Stearns's sanguine appraisal of slavery's destruction. Rather, he proposed to President Lincoln that the Union pay a bounty of $300 per recruit to loyal masters who consented to let their slaves enlist. He viewed such a payment as "an entering wedge to emancipation," which would "paralize much opposition to recruiting slaves in Tennessee." (Mil. Gov. Andrew Johnson to A. Lincoln, 23 Sept. 1863, Telegrams Collected by the Office of the Secretary of War (Bound), RG 107 [L-211].)

65: Tennessee Slaveholders to the Secretary of War

Nashville Tenn. September 26th 1863

The undersigned, citizens of Tennessee, more or less interested in Negro Slavery, respectfully ask leave to submit the following brief Statement.

That the Negro is demoralized as a slave, we recognize as a fact. It matters not what may have been our opinions upon this subject, or whether we prefer a different state of things, the destruction of Negro Slavery in this country, is an accomplished and immutable fact, and we are willing to accept it as such. This being taken for granted then, there are two questions of vast importance presented for our decission.

First. Shall the Negro, demoralized as a slave, remain demoralized as a human being – a man – and thus become a nuisance and a trouble, or not?

Secondly. Shall he be so treated, as to become the friend, or enemy of the United States? If in our opinion, it had been the policy of our Government, to utterly demoralize him as a man, and at the same time, to make him a bitter enemy, its Military agencies could not have pursued a more effective course, so far as his treatment has come under our observation. He has been induced to leave his home, either by promises which the Government has made to him in good faith, or from the state of things, with the hope of bettering his condition, and with the desire of rendering service in return, to meet in many cases harshest treatment.

Willing to labor for the Government for low wages, he has often been pressed, and driven at the point of the bayonet, at unseasonable hours, and forced to labor without pay, or the promise of any. And in too many instances when his services have been volunteered, his treatment has been more that of a brute than of a human being. We submit that the whole policy of forcibly impressing negroes is wrong. In our opinion the true policy of the Government is to so use the Negro as to elevate him and at the same time make him its friend. That this can be done, our lifelong acquaintance with the negro enables us to speak confidently. In our opinion the sentiment of gratitude is much stronger in him, than in the white race, and he is much more susceptible to its influences. He never forgets a favor however small. His attachments are of the strongest kind, and he will endure much, and suffer much before he will desert their object.

In our opinion this trait in his character should form the basis of his treatment by the Government. In this way you make of him a fast friend, and at the same time elevate him by calling into exercise the noblest sentiment of human nature.

We are happy to believe that this is not only the true, but the adopted policy of our Government – that government towards which our allegiance has never faltered for a moment.

In view of the premises, what we have to request, is that all conscription and forcible impressment of negroes (except in cases of those guilty of crime or vagrancy) should cease by peremptory order for the present. If hereafter the exegencies of the Government should require such conscription or impressment, that it be done in a regular manner by responsible officers designated for that especial service.

Thirdly. That able bodied negro men be regularly inlisted into the service of the United States with the promise of pay and freedom, according to the laws of Congress. In this way we believe a sufficient force can be raised to supply the needs of the Government either for Military operations, or labor, and at the same time the negro will be improved and elevated.

As southern men heretofore interested either directly or indirectly in slavery, we have submitted plainly and briefly our opinions on this subject, which we deem of vital importance and ask for them a respectful consideration.

HDS   [*20 signatures*]

John W. Bowen et al. to Hon. Secretary of War, 26 Sept. 1863, B-242 1863, Letters Received, ser. 360, Colored Troops Division, RG 94 [B-26].

66: Commissioner for the Organization of Black Troops in Tennessee to the Secretary of War, Enclosing a Recruitment Notice and the Statement of an Impressed Black Recruit

Nashville Sept 25th 1863

Sir: I have at last obtained Gov. Johnson's consent to the advertisement enclosed, and have commenced recruiting with good prospects of success.

The impressment of colored men which is going on daily in an irresponsible way, will help me as soon as I establish a camp and show them they are safe inside of it. They wont be likely to desert.

The colored men here are treated like brutes, any officer who wants them I am told impresses on his own authority and it is seldom they are paid.

On sunday a large number were impressed and one was shot he died on Wednesday. I enclose the copy of a statement made to me by one of them from Zenia Ohio taken down verbatim by my clerk Gov Johnson disapproves of the impressment so he told me yet it goes on daily.

Gen. Meigs Q.M.G passed here yesterday on his way to the front. If you will order him on his return to investigate the impressment of men for various purposes, I think you will get some light on the subject. Respectfully

HLS   George L. Stearns

[*Enclosure*]   [*Nashville, Tenn. September 1863*]

HEADQUARTERS COMMISSIONER FOR THE ORGANIZATION OF U.S. COLORED TROOPS, NASHVILLE, TENN.

Colored men in the Department of the Cumberland will be enlisted into the service of the United States as soldiers, on the following terms:

1st. All freemen who will volunteer.

2d. All slaves of rebel or disloyal masters who will volunteer to enlist, will be free at the expiration of their term of service.

3d. All slaves of loyal citizens with the consent of their owners will be received into the service of the United States; such slaves will be free on the expiration of their term of service.

4th. Loyal Masters will receive a certificate of the enlistment of their slaves which will entitle them to payment of a sum not exceeding the bounty, now provided by law for the enlistment of white recruits.

5th. Colored soldiers will receive clothing, rations, and $10 per month pay. $3 per month will be deducted for clothing.

Recruiting Stations are established at Nashville, Gallatin and Murfreesboro. Other stations will be advertised when established.

PD   GEORGE L. STEARNS

[Enclosure]   *[Nashville, Tenn. September 1863]*

STATEMENT OF ARMSTEAD LEWIS OF ZENIA OHIO.

I went to the Colored Methodist Church at 11 o'Clock A.M on Sunday Sept. 20th 1863. After church while on my way home was stopped by a guard who demanded my pass   I handed it to them. They retained possession of it. They ordered me to fall in among them and I was marched around from place to place till they collected all they could get. We were then marched to a camp about 1 1/2 miles and delivered to some colored men who were placed on guard over us. They counted us and found they had 180 men. All through the afternoon and evening they kept bringing in squads   They took the passes of the men and after examining them burned them before us. At dark they put a double Guard around us and told us if we attempted to escape we would be shot down. We were left that way out in the Cold all night without tents blankets or fire and some of the men were bareheaded and some with out coats

                                                       his
HDcSr   (Signed) Armstead × Lewis
                                                      mark

Major George L. Stearns to Hon. Edwin M. Stanton, 25 Sept. 1863, enclosing recruitment notice, [Sept. 1863], and statement of Armstead Lewis, [Sept. 1863], all filed with S-18 1863, Letters Received, ser. 360, Colored Troops Division, RG 94 [B-477]. The recruitment notice appears to have been clipped from a newspaper.

67: Commissioner for the Organization of Black Troops in Tennessee to the Secretary of War, Enclosing a Letter from the Commissioner to a Boston Associate

                                        Nashville Oct. 24th 1863

Sir: I have been here five weeks since my return from the front. Immediately on my arrival I called on Gov. Johnson and in time came to a thorough understanding with him. Let me say to you I never quarrel having a much better mode of obtaining what I want. Gov. Johnson as soon as he understood me came heartily into my plans also Gen. R. S. Granger and I now have all the power and means at my command for thorough organization of these Troops.

The recruiting men and the organization of Regiments will be easily done here now that I can have Officers at the time I want them and public opinion will change slowly or rapidly as we drive on the work. I am associating mainly with slaveholders who are anxious to have the enlistment go on and they daily call at my rooms to give me information and assistance.

We have one regiment here recruited before I came   it has about 900 men but needs to be drilled. The second has a full complement of men but needs Officers. The Officers and men are good as any in the U.S.

They will become our best soldiers if you will allow me to put them in a Camp of instruction subject to *your* order

Gov. Johnson having the political control and I having the Military this Department will by next Spring give you a larger number of Colored Troops the best in the U.S. service

There are indications that we shall have men from Kentucky from slaveholders who prefer the Three Hundred Dollars in hand to a slave on the road. some have come in already and when offered their slaves or the money take the Certificate of Enlistment. Respectfully

George L. Stearns

I enclose a copy of letter to J M Forbes for your information

HLS

[*Enclosure*]   Nashville Oct. 18th 1863

Copy   For use, not for publication.

Esteemed Friend   Yours of the 11th is at hand. I don't wonder that you feel discouraged from your point of view, but let me tell you, that the President, while apparently taking one step back, really takes two forward, as you will see by the order enclosed for your private use. If you have time to read all the letters I have sent to Mr. Wellman, you will understand some of the difficulties I have had to remove. There were others which as I could not make you understand except you were here, I have not reported. All are now out of my way and the track clear. Let me sketch to you the policy of the leading slaveholding Union men of this State. They see clearly that their political and social existence *here* depends on the abolition of Slavery and the control of the

State by the Union men. Therefore they have entered most
heartily into my plans for the organization of colored regiments
and are daily in consultation with me.

Their leading propositions are,

First. That the States in rebellion, are not out of the Union,
but retain their former position subject however to the military
control, which should be extended over them as fast as the
rebellion is subdued. Any other position is fatal to the doctrine
that no State can dissolve its political relations with the other
States, and would justify secession, if the end to be attained was
justifiable.

Second. The rebels have forfeited all their rights including those
of life and property, consequently the right to participate in the
Government of the Country. The people of the rebellious States
are divided into thre classes.

1st Those who have always been loyal to the Union.

2nd Rebels who concocted and urged on the rebellion.

3^{d} The mass of voters more or less in favor of the rebellion
and followers of its leaders. Take away the power and influence of
the second class and the mass will follow the Union men who will
control this state. In time they can control all the states in
rebellion. Therefore the plan of the union men here is to enlist in
the army all the able bodied slaves in this Department and oblige
their masters to take care of the rest, for the present. To urge the
Govt to repeal all laws that create distinction between the colored
and white soldier, full pay being as necessary to enable the former
to support his family as it is to the latter. To continue the
present military Government of this State until the change of
public sentiment will enable them to control it. This control will
be necessary if the State is declared a Territory, and therefore
nothing will be gained by such action, while it will shock the
feelings of those, who having fought for the perpetuity of the
Union, would find it virtually dissolved. You need not fear that
the Govt. will falter in the policy of arming the negro. No other
course is open to it. The want of Troops and the necessity of
saving the union men will compel them to go on, although they
may halt at particular times or places. The enclosed order to Gov.
Johnson places my affairs on a firm basis and will through him,
give me the virtual control of the work. He is a very pleasant and
desirable co-worker, not caring to assume authority for its sake,
and having enough business on his hands now without interfering
in mine. As to position I care nothing   If as subordinate I can do
the work to which my soul is bound. I prefer it to power without
the means for carrying out my plans. I now expect to go home in
November and after a few days, return here with my wife,

prepared to spend the winter and aid Gov. Johnson and his friends to carry out their policy. In the meantime you had better continue to collect funds, for the fight will be long and earnest. I wrote you a few words about Brig. Gen¹ E. A. Paine. Further acquaintance with him has convinced me he has talents for the command in Missouri or all along the Mississippi, that would make his appointment very desirable to us if Secy Stanton still wants a General for that work. I wish you would enquire about him so that being satisfied you could urge his appointment to any proper place that may need a good man to carry on the work. Day by day my work advances and takes shape. We had a meeting of soldiers and citizens at the capitol on Saturday night of congratulation for the victories in Ohio, Penn. and Indiana. Gov. Johnson made a great speech in which he indicated the policy of emancipation and reconstruction in clear and unmistakable language. Freedom for all he said, must be the rule. If the rule was right, the results would be right. The rebellion had laid out all the State institutions of the South, one here another there. If in the process of reconstruction there was one that was not adapted to the new order of things, let it lie where it was. It was not now a question whether slavery should be abolished. Slavery was extinct. No man could now control his slaves against their will. The U.S. Govt. was bound by the constitution, to guarantee every state, a republican form of Government and under that power would make all necessary regulations. We want 500 000 Yankees to come to our fair State, and aid us to develope its resources. Dr. Bowen said the question had been between the man and the mule. This war had decided us in favor of the man. The rebellion had taken from him his only son. He was glad he died by the hand of God and not by the bayonet of a defender of his country. Truly Your Friend

HLcSr

(Signed) George L. Stearns.

Major George L. Stearns to Hon. Edwin M. Stanton, 24 Oct. 1863, enclosing George L. Stearns to John M. Forbes, 18 Oct. 1863, both filed with S-18 1863, Letters Received, ser. 360, Colored Troops Division, RG 94 [B-477]. The postscript on Stearns's letter to the Secretary of War is in Stearns's hand. The order that Stearns describes as enclosed in his letter to John M. Forbes is not in the file.

68: Commissioner for the Organization of Black Troops in Middle and East Tennessee to the Headquarters of U.S. Colored Troops in Tennessee

Nashville April 11th 1864.

Lieutenant   I have the honor to state that during the past week but little Recruiting has been done in that part of the State under my charge— And Col. Morgan of the 14" U.S.C.T. recruiting for the 42nd and 44th U.S.C.T. reports only 20 Recruits for the week ending Saturday last.

There several reasons for this poverty of recruiting which naturally suggest themselves— Among these are—the high price commanded by laborers as Compared with Soldiers operates disadvantageously to Recruiting— A large number of persons from the north, as well as Residents of this State, are preparing to cultivate the land this year and they are unable to get a sufficiency of able-bodied laborers for this purpose. I spoke of the higher price commanded by laborers as compared to Soldiers. The Quartermasters Schedule of prices for colored laborers in this town is $25 per month and a Ration. For doing precisely the same duty, as a soldier, and for the same Quartermaster, he will receive $10 per month. Of Course no laborer with his eyes open will join the Invalid Regiment or Regiment for "fatigue duty."

I think, too, among the intelligent Colored men of this vicinity the tardiness of the Government to accord equal pay to all its Soldiers, acts disadvantageously for Recruiting Colored Troops. The actual pay received by a Colored Soldier exclusive of rations and Clothing is $6.50 per month and that of the White Soldier who does the same duty is $13.00. In calculating this difference of pay—the actual difference is larger than the apparent—for when Colored troops are kept on fatigue duty their clothing wears out much faster than that of white troops doing ordinary field duty. It seems to me, therefore, in view of the fact that the Colored Soldier's pay is so much smaller than that of the White Soldier, peculiarly unjust to keep the men upon that sort of duty which must inevitably, as every person who has commanded a company knows reduce to a still more pitiful sum the stipend of $6.50 per month.

During the past week I received 45 applications for Commissions in Colored Troops, and referred 32 to the Examining Board

The Examining Bord at this place during the past week examined 17 applicants and passed 12   None passed higher than the grade of Captain.

The Contraband Camp at this place has about 600 men, women, & children in it.

The 16th U.S.C.T. has arrived here *en route* for Chattanooga. The 17th U.S.C.T. is here and will report for duty in the Q.M. Department.

I have found it necessary to issue the Enclosed Circular. Many applications are made to me for "Certificates of Enlistment." I am satisfied from an examination of the Enrollment Law that any owner whose Slave is enlisted is entitled to a statement of that fact and I am also satisfied that it was not the intention of General Order 329 A.G.O. 1862 [*1863*] that a compensation for his slave should be awarded to a man who has done everything – even to shooting – to prevent his slave coming to the Recruiting Office. The form of Certificate of Enlistment used by me as will be seen by the Copy enclosed – with the endorsement required by my Circular, meets the demands of the Enrollment Law and the order referred to. I have the honor Lieutenant to be Very Respy Yr obt Servt

HLcSr
                                                Signed R. D. Mussey

Capt. R. D. Mussey to Lieutenant George Mason, 11 Apr. 1864, M-25 1864, Letters Received by Adjutant General L. Thomas, ser. 363, Colored Troops Division, RG 94 [V-90]. The enclosed circular authorized enlistment of all able-bodied volunteers, including the slaves of loyal Tennessee and Kentucky slave owners; it ordered that certificates of enlistment distinguish between masters who presented their slaves for enlistment and masters who applied for certificates only after their slaves had run away to enlist; and it forbade the issue of certificates to slaveowners in Alabama, Georgia, and the Carolinas, on the ground that the Emancipation Proclamation had abolished slavery in those states. Also enclosed is a blank certificate of enlistment.

4

Recruitment in the Border States: Maryland, Missouri, and Kentucky

IN THE BORDER SLAVE STATES, fidelity to the Union united with the continued legality of slavery to make black recruitment different from that in either the North or the seceded slave states.[1] Slaveholders in Maryland, Missouri, and Kentucky won exemption from Lincoln's Emancipation Proclamation in return for their loyalty, but they recognized the precariousness of their prized institution. Understanding that slaves who served as soldiers would inevitably achieve freedom, they opposed slave recruitment as the entering wedge of emancipation. Throughout the border states, nonslaveholding whites formed a significant element in the unionist coalition. Although their importance varied from place to place – generally being least in Kentucky and greatest in Maryland – nonslaveholders everywhere cared little about recruitment as a threat to slavery. Indeed, far from sharing the slaveholders' alarm, they commonly viewed black enlistment as a means of easing the burden of federal draft quotas that fell disproportionately upon them. Thus the struggle over black recruitment not only brought border-state slaveholders into conflict with the Lincoln administration, but also stirred longstanding enmity between slaveholding and nonslaveholding whites. Eventually, the desire of blacks to serve in the Union army and the desire of both Union officials and nonslaveholding whites to have them serve triumphed over slaveholders' reservations. As slaveholders feared, the initiation of black recruitment marked the beginning of the end of slavery in each of the border states.

[1] Published accounts of recruitment in the border states include: John W. Blassingame, "The Recruitment of Negro Troops in Maryland," *Maryland Historical Magazine* 58 (Mar. 1963): 20–29, and "The Recruitment of Colored Troops in Kentucky, Maryland and Missouri, 1863–1865," *Historian* 29 (Aug. 1967): 533–45; E. Merton Coulter, *The Civil War and Readjustment in Kentucky* (Chapel Hill, N.C., 1933); William E. Parrish, *Turbulent Partnership: Missouri and the Union 1861–1865* (Columbia, Mo., 1963); and Charles Lewis Wagandt, *The Mighty Revolution: Negro Emancipation in Maryland* (Baltimore, 1964), chaps. 9 & 13.

The Black Military Experience

Beginning in June 1863, General Robert C. Schenck, commanding the Middle Department and 8th Army Corps, repeatedly urged President Lincoln to authorize enlistment of the several thousand blacks, mostly freemen, who had labored on the fortifications around Baltimore. The War Department turned to Colonel William Birney, son of antislavery politician James G. Birney, to take charge of recruitment of free blacks in Maryland. Fresh from successfully organizing two black regiments in the District of Columbia, Birney eagerly entered upon his new responsibilities, enjoying full support from General Schenck. He established recruitment headquarters in Baltimore in mid-July 1863 and in less than seven weeks filled the 4th U.S. Colored Infantry. Birney augmented his ranks by dramatically liberating from Baltimore's jails and slave pens both unruly Maryland bondsmen and slaves interned by District of Columbia owners to evade emancipation in the capital. This heady enterprise won the praise of blacks and antislavery whites alike.

Just as the slave-pen enlistments went beyond Birney's mandate to recruit free blacks, so too did the activities of the civilian agents he employed to gather potential recruits and conduct them to Baltimore for enlistment. Irate slave owners charged that Birney's agents acted indiscriminately, taking bondsmen as well as freemen, and in one county, civil authorities jailed an agent on the charge of assisting slaves to escape from their masters. As recruitment expanded to include the entire state, white opposition swelled, and rumors of armed black recruiting parties sent tremors through the slaveholding population. Maryland officials and prominent citizens hastened to protest in person and by letter to President Lincoln, the Secretary of War, and to Maryland's representatives in Washington.

Lincoln considered black recruiting parties a needless affront to loyal slaveholders, inviting violent resistance and, perhaps more important, undermining the development of emancipationist sentiment. He repeatedly denounced such methods and assured Maryland whites that no one had authority to recruit slaves. Presidential pronouncements could not stem the flow of runaway slaves anxious to secure their liberty by joining the Union army. With increasing exasperation, slave owners continued to demand an immediate halt to slave enlistments, or, failing that, the regularization of recruitment procedures and federal compensation to owners of slave enlistees.

Maryland's nonslaveholding whites took a different tack and pressed for unrestricted enlistment of slaves. Before the war, nonslaveholders had come to depend on the labor of free blacks, who constituted nearly half the state's black population in 1860. Recruitment of black freemen not only reduced the nonslaveholders' labor supply, it also artificially increased the value of slaves, whose labor they now had to hire. So long as the federal government recruited free blacks but not slaves, black enlistments benefited slaveholders at the expense of nonslaveholders. The latter attacked this inequity and insisted that even unionist slaveholders share the war's burdens. Civil authorities came to the aid of nonslaveholders, arresting free black recruits for breach of contract with their employers and threatening recruiters with arrest for enticement. When free blacks refused to be intimidated, their families were abused and their crops destroyed by opponents of enlistment.

At the end of September 1863, President Lincoln, angered by incessant reports of the violation of recruitment guidelines, ordered complete suspension of black enlistments in Maryland, pending negotiation with state officials. Secretary of War Edwin M. Stanton argued the need for additional Maryland recruits and secured Lincoln's assent to a new policy, issued as General Order No. 329 in early October. Under this order, which became the model for recruitment in the other loyal border states and in Tennessee, free blacks and slaves whose masters consented could enlist immediately, the slaves gaining freedom and their masters, if judged loyal by a special commission, receiving compensation from the government. Lincoln agreed only reluctantly to enlistment of slaves who lacked their masters' consent, a step which would effectively ensure the destruction of Maryland slavery. This expedient would not be adopted until thirty days after the opening of recruitment under Order No. 329—and then only if the number of black recruits obtained under more restrictive procedures proved inadequate.[2]

Governor Augustus W. Bradford petitioned in vain for extension of the "grace" period, as Birney launched a new recruitment drive, unprecedented in its use of armed black recruiting squads. Whites predictably resisted Birney's new thrust and even murdered one recruitment officer. Nevertheless, slaves welcomed the changed policy and fled to the recruiters to exchange bondage for military service and freedom. As long as slaves left their masters willingly and accessible recruiting parties afforded protection, the momentum could not easily be broken. Disconcerted slave owners insisted that many slaves were forced away, but Birney answered every charge of impressment with denial that he mustered in any man against his will.

By late January 1864, effective opposition to black enlistments had collapsed. While slave owners remained hostile, the majority of Maryland whites accepted the policy. Maryland emancipationists had registered impressive gains in the fall 1863 state elections, and

---

[2] *Official Records*, ser. 3, vol. 3, pp. 860–61.

large-scale slave enlistments pleased nonslaveholders (in large measure because slave recruits helped reduce the state's draft quota). But by the time whites acquiesced in slave recruitment, the number of potential black enlistees had already fallen drastically. Birney identified the remaining obstacles to further voluntary black enlistments when he argued that an equal pay policy and an extensive draft were necessary to increase the number of free black recruits, while slaves would continue to volunteer only if provision were made for the freedom and maintenance of their families. The draft aside, federal policy makers took months to see the wisdom of Birney's suggestions. Black volunteers came forward in ever smaller numbers, and charges of impressment multiplied. In a desperate effort to exempt Maryland from the draft, the state legislature in early February offered attractive bounties to free blacks and slaves, as well as whites, who enlisted before March 1.[3]

Despite the incentive of the state bounty, the prospects for further black enlistments in Maryland appeared bleak in early 1864. Birney, seeking a more active command, requested and received a transfer to the battlefront, where he led the black troops he had recruited the previous summer and fall. His position in Maryland fell to Colonel Samuel M. Bowman, who energetically set out to revive the sluggish flow of black volunteers. Bowman launched an elaborate program of mass meetings, cooperation with black ministers, and wide distribution of posters promoting enlistment. These tactics successfully procured recruits, but only by aggravating the growing labor shortage in the countryside. Bowman also secured authority to send recruiting parties to jails and slave pens to enlist all black men held under any but criminal charges.

When a state convention met in April 1864 with emancipation the chief item on its agenda, the foremost incentive to slave enlistment vanished. At the end of the month, Bowman reported unflattering prospects for further recruitment, except by outright impressment: free blacks objected to the army's unequal pay policy and slaves anticipated freedom from the state convention. Except for jail enlistments and forced recruitment, the role of military service in hastening freedom had come to an end. Promulgation of the new state constitution on November 1, 1864, formally terminated slavery in Maryland and placed black enlistments – now reduced to a mere trickle – on the same basis as in the free states.[4]

[3] Maryland, Legislature, *Laws of the State of Maryland. 1864* (Annapolis, 1864), pp. 20–23.
[4] Wagandt, *Mighty Revolution*, treats the politics of Maryland emancipation in detail.

Black Enlistment

As throughout the border South, black recruitment in Missouri was inseparable from the politics of emancipation. From the first days of the war, the emancipation issue divided Missouri unionists. The more radical contingent denounced the torpid administration of the unionist provisional governor, Hamilton R. Gamble, convinced that his policies bolstered the tottering slave regime. When General Samuel R. Curtis, commander of the Department of the Missouri during 1862 and early 1863, allied with the radicals, he earned the enmity of Governor Gamble and further divided the unionist camp. The paralyzing rift between military and civil authorities finally induced President Lincoln to try a change of military commanders. Casting about for an appropriate appointee in the spring of 1863, Lincoln at last settled upon General John M. Schofield, a St. Louis resident at the outbreak of the war and an officer who had seen action on Missouri battlefields. No sooner had Schofield assumed command in Missouri than the state convention dealt a blow to radical hopes for a speedy end to slavery, by adopting instead an ordinance of gradual emancipation. The June 1863 ordinance postponed until 1870 the beginning of the emancipation process, and its provisions guaranteed that slavery would linger at least to the end of the century. Evidently content with this limited step toward freedom, or at least convinced that it represented a significant advance, General Schofield determined not to permit army policies, especially black recruitment, to jeopardize the gradualist solution.[5]

Although Northern recruiting agents had earlier enrolled a few free blacks in St. Louis and fugitive slaves regularly left the state to enlist in Kansas, the first systematic recruitment of Missouri blacks did not begin until the summer of 1863. In July, Adjutant General Lorenzo Thomas, launching a massive recruitment drive throughout the Mississippi Valley, authorized Colonel William A. Pile, Methodist clergyman and radical commander of a St. Louis infantry unit, to enlist Missouri blacks in an Arkansas regiment. Schofield sanctioned this effort and secured Governor Gamble's consent to Pile's operations within Missouri, but only so long as Pile restricted enlistments to antebellum freemen and the slaves of disloyal masters.[6] Both Schofield and Gamble insisted that Pile neither recruit the slaves of unionists nor violate any state law. In practice, these stipulations confined Pile's recruitment activities to Missouri's tiny free

---

[5] Parrish, *Turbulent Partnership*. treats the politics of Missouri emancipation in detail.

[6] *Official Records*, ser. 3, vol. 3, pp. 328–29, 356, 525–26, 630–31.

black population and to fugitive slaves who had already collected around military camps and in the city of St. Louis.

Slaves' determination to enlist and the desire of radicals to expand recruitment and thus hasten emancipation pushed this restrictive policy to its limits. The breaking point came when Pile, under Thomas's authority, opened a recruiting rendezvous at Keokuk, Iowa, just across the Missouri line.[7] Iowa-based recruiting parties scoured northern Missouri and slaves readily enlisted. The resulting outcry from both slave owners and army officers induced General Schofield to halt all black recruitment. He exempted only General Thomas Ewing's operations in western Missouri. In August, Ewing had initiated a plan to facilitate liberation of the slaves of disloyal masters by escorting them to Kansas, where he enlisted the able-bodied men and assisted the others in obtaining employment. But Schofield cautioned Ewing to succor only those blacks whose owners were clearly subject to the confiscation acts and ordered him to return to bondage all slaves inadvertently taken from loyal masters.

Into late September 1863, Schofield continued to delay large-scale recruitment of black soldiers in Missouri. Pressed by Adjutant General Thomas to accelerate enlistments, he contended that few legally eligible recruits remained in the state and that mobile recruitment squads—which Thomas favored—inevitably spawned unauthorized enlistment of the slaves of unionists. But Schofield now acknowledged the desirability of arming black men and the inevitability of slave enlistments. He turned to Washington for advice in designing a policy that would inaugurate slave recruitment but eliminate abuses. The War Department responded with General Order No. 329, issued in early October 1863 to organize black recruitment in Maryland and Tennessee, and encouraged Schofield to propose appropriate modifications. In mid-November, he issued a general order, No. 135, authorizing immediate enlistment of slaves, regardless of owners' loyalty or consent (with promise of compensation to loyal masters). While thus broadening the scope of enlistment, the order also banned mobile recruiting squads, instead restricting recruitment to district and county provost marshals. Colonel Pile, although charged with the organization of black troops after their enlistment, lost his authority over recruitment.[8]

Missouri radicals greeted General Order No. 135 with skepticism, reflecting their suspicion of General Schofield and his cozy alliance with Governor Gamble. Certain that vigorous black recruitment would effectively destroy slavery, they doubted that the pro-

---

[7] Special Orders, No. 40, Adjutant General of the Army, 1 Aug. 1863, Negro in the Military Service, p. 1461, ser. 390, Colored Troops Division, RG 94 [B-618].

[8] *Official Records*, ser. 3, vol. 3, pp. 1009–10, 1034–36.

vost marshals would enlist slaves with zeal. Officers who had participated in the earlier recruitment, including Pile, scoffed at the idea that any system could be as effective as that of roving recruiting parties, especially parties composed of black soldiers.

These misgivings proved well founded. The inauguration of Schofield's system in late November 1863 found provost marshals already preoccupied with their duties of supervising enrollment and draft, examining substitutes, and apprehending deserters. Even the most committed marshals lacked time to devote much attention to black recruitment, and many, entirely unsympathetic to arming slaves, actively discouraged potential recruits. But even had the officers been enthusiastic, the provost marshal system entailed two serious obstacles for slaves who sought to join the army. Most important, the marshal's fixed location required that a slave flee his master and make his way to the recruitment office without protection. Slave patrols and roving guerrillas seized upon this vulnerability to recapture, abuse, and even murder would-be enlistees. Furthermore, a slave who succeeded in reaching a provost marshal's office but was rejected after physical examination had no recourse but to return to the tender mercies of the master he had just abandoned or risk apprehension as a runaway. Critics of Schofield's plan maintained that only mobile recruiters could offer slaves some measure of protection.[9]

Not content with the advantages conferred by the very structure of Schofield's recruitment system, slave owners worked to forestall slave enlistments and punish enlistees. In addition to tighter supervision and petty hindrances such as locking up clothing at night, masters wreaked a special vengeance on the families of slave recruits: they intercepted money sent by the soldiers; whipped and abused enslaved wives, children, and old folk; and burdened family members with heavy labor ordinarily performed by slave men. Despite protests by black soldiers and compassionate whites, as well as official concern that such treatment discouraged enlistments, continued legal sanction for Missouri slavery thwarted military intervention. Aware of the army's limited authority, some slave owners moved to salvage their investment by selling soldiers' families to Kentucky, where slavery yet stood undisturbed by legal action or black recruitment. Outraged at the slaveholders' audacity and moved by soldiers' pleas for redress, military commanders attempted to halt out-of-state sales. But many soldiers' families reached the slave marts of Kentucky, nonetheless.[10] Fatally

[9] Brig. Genl. Wm. A. Pile to Maj. Genl. W. S. Rosecrans, 18 Feb. 1864, Unentered Letters Received, ser. 2594, Dept. of the MO, RG 393 Pt. 1 [C-184].

[10] Schofield prohibited removal of Missouri slaves on November 10, 1863. (Extract of Special Orders No. 307, Head Quarters, Department of the Missouri, 10 Nov. 1863, filed with J-445 1864, Letters Received, RG 107 [L-46].) One

handicapped by the continued legality of slavery, sympathetic officers argued that only federal action freeing the wives and children of black soldiers would protect the families.

Amid mounting radical objections to Schofield's administration, Lincoln searched for a replacement unidentified with any one political faction. In January 1864, he settled upon General William S. Rosecrans. Sharing Schofield's opposition to free-ranging recruiting squads, Rosecrans introduced no major change in his predecessor's enlistment policy. Indeed, when Adjutant General Thomas authorized Pile to dispatch mobile recruiting officers, Rosecrans succeeded in having Thomas's order countermanded.[11] But Rosecrans did appoint provost marshals more sympathetic to black enlistments, and some of them apparently sent out recruiting squads of their own. White Missourians continued to object vehemently to such forays, especially those by black soldiers.

However cautiously Rosecrans and his predecessor regulated enlistment procedures, recruitment itself encouraged slaves to flee their masters, and they did so by the thousands. By early 1864 no effort on Rosecrans's part could disguise the fact that military recruitment had undermined Missouri slavery. In February, a large number of state legislators inadvertently acknowledged the extent to which slaves had managed to escape bondage when they requested forced enlistment of all blacks who had liberated themselves from their masters but had not entered the army. Dissolution of the master's authority, the promise of eventual compensation, and the credit of black soldiers against the state's draft quota at last persuaded many white Missourians, slaveholders included, to support black enlistment.

Ironically, the success of recruitment in undermining slavery hindered continued enlistments and created new difficulties for army recruiters. By the spring of 1864 enlistments had virtually ceased. Masters offered cash or share-crop incentives in order to retain their slaves; runaway bondsmen commanded high wages with few questions asked; and only the rare black man wished to join the army. Slave enlistments had in effect rendered the 1863 gradual emancipation ordinance irrelevant. In January 1865 Missouri whites merely ratified the collapse of slavery when a new state constitution provided for immediate emancipation.[12]

---

month later, Schofield advised the provost marshal general of the Department of the Missouri to permit removal of slaves unfit for military service, provided they consented. (Major Genl. J. M. Schofield to Lt. Col. J. O. Broadhead, 9 Dec. 1863, M-927 1864, Letters Received, ser. 2786, Provost Marshal General, Dept. of the MO, RG 393 Pt. 1 [C-198].)

[11] *Official Records*, ser. 3, vol. 4, pp. 163–66, 195–96.
[12] Parrish, *Turbulent Partnership*, chap. 9, esp. pp. 200–201.

Black Enlistment

The connection between enlistment and emancipation was nowhere more evident than in Kentucky. As the war for Union became a war for freedom and as the North turned to blacks as a source of manpower for its depleted armies, border-state slavery grew increasingly precarious. Kentucky slaveholders recognized that black recruitment would sap slavery's strength, and they resolutely demanded that federal authorities respect the legality of bondage. Because they commanded the most viable slave system in the border states and because President Lincoln feared Kentucky disunionism, they enjoyed considerable success in delaying recruitment and emancipation. But in the end, black enlistment dealt a fatal blow to slavery in Kentucky as it had in the other border states.

By the end of 1863, the federal government was fully committed to recruiting black soldiers everywhere except Kentucky. Although Kentucky boasted the largest black population among the border states, its quarter of a million slaves and ten thousand free blacks remained off limits to federal recruiters. Proslavery unionism dominated state politics and employed every channel to prevent interference with slave property. While strong unionist minorities in Maryland and Missouri had favored both emancipation and recruitment, Kentucky's unionists generally feared that any discussion of emancipation and recruitment would turn Kentucky against the Union. During 1863 the most extensive levy upon Kentucky's black manpower came in the form not of enlistment, but of impressment of slave laborers to construct federal supply lines. Although the Union army implemented impressment in only a few counties and never approached the 6,000 slaves authorized, the War Department and President Lincoln expressed satisfaction with that limited requisition and appeased Kentucky slave owners by exempting the state from their border-state recruitment program.[13]

Kentucky slaves did not share Washington's deference to the "loyal" slave interest, and they determined to seek freedom by joining the Union army. Unable to enlist at home, many seized opportunities to become soldiers in neighboring states. Throughout 1863 slave owners regularly complained that Kentucky bondsmen followed antebellum escape routes across the Ohio River to join free-state black regiments. Slave flight northward proved, moreover, to be only a harbinger of the exodus that followed the September 1863 inauguration of black recruitment in Tennessee. Over 2,000 slave men, often accompanied by their families, streamed from southern

[13] Edwin M. Stanton to Mr. President, 1 Oct. 1863, M-101 1863, Letters Received Irregular, RG 107 [L-133].

191

Kentucky's slave-dominated tobacco counties into the Clarksville, Tennessee, recruiting station. Strenuous protests by slave owners and state officials fell upon deaf ears in the War Department.[14]

With recruitment underway in every direction beyond the state's borders and Kentucky slaves determined to grasp every opportunity to escape bondage, federal authorities hinted that the time had arrived for black recruitment to begin in Kentucky as well. Federal initiatives emboldened slavery's critics within the state, especially those whites liable to the draft. They observed that local slave enlistments would secure to Kentucky the credits against its draft quota now being lost to neighboring states. However, when Adjutant General Lorenzo Thomas consulted with Governor Thomas E. Bramlette and other state leaders on the subject in late January 1864, they rebuffed his overtures, and Thomas came away persuaded that insisting upon black recruitment would endanger Kentucky's fidelity to the Union.

Congress had less patience than the adjutant general and more authority. In February 1864, amendments to the Enrollment Act provided for conscription of slaves, and the Provost Marshal General's Bureau ordered its officials to add the names of black men to the pool from which draftees would be drawn.[15] The beginning of slave enrollment in Kentucky, with the implication that a draft would soon follow, precipitated a crisis between federal and state authority. With approval of Governor Bramlette, Colonel Frank Wolford, a Kentucky military hero, publicly denounced Lincoln as a tyrant and assailed the enrollment of slaves as unconstitutional. When the War Department dismissed Wolford from the army, his popularity soared, and white Kentuckians united more than ever in opposition to federal policies. Only frenetic unionist lobbying dissuaded Governor Bramlette from ordering state officials to resist the slave enrollment. Eventually a compromise was reached. Enrollment would continue, but Kentucky blacks remained exempt from the draft so long as white volunteers filled the state's quota.[16]

Although the compromise averted a violent confrontation, the agitation it inspired had a profound effect on both slaves and their masters. Learning that recruitment was in the offing, slaves sought out provost marshals and pressed to be enlisted. The enthusiasm of bondsmen unsettled slaveholders and made the prospect of federal compensation for enlisted slaves, as promised by the Enrollment Act, more attractive. As in Maryland and Missouri, mere rumors of enlistment eroded bondage.

[14] Jos. P. Flint to Gov. Thos. E. Bramlette, 5 Sept. 1864, Letters Received, ser. 3967, KY Actg. Asst. Pro. Mar. Gen., RG 110 [R-13].
[15] *Official Records*, ser. 3, vol. 4, pp. 132, 146.
[16] *Official Records*, ser. 3, vol. 4, pp. 174–76.

Meanwhile, in Kentucky's far western counties, black enlistment had become more than rumor. Strategic considerations, especially the vital importance of securing the Mississippi River, had from the beginning of the war led the Union army to administer the area west of the Tennessee River separately from the rest of the state. The War Department, planning to garrison the river fortifications with black troops, took advantage of this segmented administration in early 1864 and opened recruitment for black artillery regiments at Columbus and Paducah. By spring, the success of that enterprise, despite protests from slave owners, increased pressure for black recruitment throughout Kentucky.[17] At the same time, laggard white enlistment undermined the state's case for exemption from slave conscription.

Recognizing the direction of developing policy, General Stephen G. Burbridge, commander of the District of Kentucky, ordered in mid-April 1864 the first enlistment of blacks throughout Kentucky. Himself a Kentuckian and a slave owner, Burbridge sought to minimize the blow to slavery and deflect white opposition. With War Department approval, his General Order No. 34 opened recruitment offices only to free blacks and to slaves at the "request" of their owners. Burbridge also restricted recruiting to provost marshals — interdicting at the outset any mobile enlistment parties organized along the lines of Colonel Birney's in Maryland and Colonel Pile's in Missouri — and required that black enlistees be immediately sent out of the state for organization and training. No armed blacks would remain at home to insult Kentucky whites or inspire insubordination among Kentucky slaves.[18]

Burbridge's effort to obtain black recruits without threatening slavery foundered, because few slaves patiently awaited their masters' approval before seeking freedom. Singly and collectively, bondsmen appeared before provost marshals, begging or even demanding to be enlisted. Sent home to seek their masters' consent or rejected because they lacked it, would-be enlistees met brutal violence at the hands of indignant whites. The extent of such attacks shocked army officials, including General Burbridge, while the slaves' readiness to enlist hinted at untapped manpower. Only a month after the opening of limited recruitment, the War Department authorized enlistment of all black volunteers, regardless of the wishes of their owners. By early June 1864, any slave who reached a recruiting office could enlist.[19]

The long pent-up tide of black volunteers almost immediately

[17] *Official Records*, ser. 3, vol. 4, pp. 60, 138, 245.
[18] *Official Records*, ser. 3, vol. 4, pp. 233–34, 248–49.
[19] *Official Records*, ser. 3, vol. 4, p. 422.

threatened to overwhelm the recruitment system. Provost marshals labored ceaselessly. The number of new black regiments outstripped the supply of white officers. At Camp Nelson, on the edge of the bluegrass region, black recruits gathered in such numbers that, even though special officers were sent to augment the regular provost marshal force, many men waited weeks before they could be enlisted.

Slaves who flocked to the recruitment centers faced numerous obstacles, and, as in Missouri, the provost marshal system itself created some of the difficulties. Unprotected until they reached the safety of a recruitment office, fugitive slave volunteers risked arrest, physical abuse, even death. Many traveled great distances by night to avoid violent encounters with outraged whites. But wherever recruitment offices were accessible, black recruits materialized in numbers that astonished even the most optimistic army officials. By late summer, over 14,000 had volunteered, and reports indicated accessions at the rate of 100 per day.[20]

The magnitude of slave enlistments persuaded Union authorities to abandon the circuitous procedures that conciliated white Kentuckians at the expense of black enlistees and the army. In the summer of 1864, Adjutant General Thomas abrogated Burbridge's policy of sending black volunteers out of the state by designating eight permanent centers within Kentucky where black volunteers would be formed into regiments. Reflecting growing commitment to black enlistments, Thomas also ordered that the soldiers at each center become, in effect, recruiting regiments, with detached squads moving through the countryside to offer protection to slave volunteers.[21] Thomas's decision to surmount the limitations of the provost marshal system by sending black recruiters directly to the farms and plantations promised to diminish white interference with slave enlistments. But the new policy announcement also preserved Thomas's ascendency in black recruitment, a role threatened by complaints from various quarters that Kentucky recruitment procedures catered too much to slaveholders. Thomas's order successfully deflected a critical report by Colonel Samuel M. Bowman, who proposed directly to the War Department that the system he had employed in Maryland would be an improvement over the Kentucky method.[22] Thomas's policy announcement notwithstanding, the new

---

[20] *Official Records*, ser. 3, vol. 4, p. 733.

[21] *Official Records*, ser. 3, vol. 4, pp. 429–30, 548.

[22] Bowman, after visiting Kentucky, reported that black recruitment "is carried on by Provost Marshals in the ordinary method of recruiting white men," that those officers — mostly Kentuckians — were "more or less influenced" by the general white opposition to black enlistments, that slave owners kept their slaves under "strict local guard," and that "none can enlist without danger of arrest or being shot." He proposed that black recruitment in Kentucky be placed under charge

system remained unrealized for many months: the demands upon black troops were so great (often regiments were hardly organized before being sent to the front or assigned to duty guarding federal installations) that few were available to man recruitment centers and roam the countryside. Nonetheless, even occasional use of mobile black recruiting parties further sped black enlistments and undermined slavery.

Ill-treatment accorded the families of black volunteers, however, threatened to temper large-scale recruitment. Masters exercised their power over slave families to forestall runaway men and to vent their wrath against those who successfully escaped. Yet the threat of abuse did not halt the flight of black men to recruiting stations. Instead, attacks on black women and children encouraged many men to take their families with them, adding black dependents to the deluge of army volunteers.

The black soldiers' families posed difficult problems for army officials. Lacking clear policy directives, recruiters initially and somewhat inadvertently created camps and "villages" of black dependents along with regiments of black soldiers. Slave owners protested, and the army itself found the hordes of women and children increasingly inconvenient. Adjutant General Thomas, torn between dedication to raising black troops and respect for the continued legality of slavery in Kentucky, formulated an approach that would recruit soldiers while leaving families in the hands of masters – thereby relieving the army of a burden and guaranteeing a slave labor force to planters and farmers. In July 1864, Thomas prohibited the entry of additional black dependents into army camps and ordered that families squatting around posts and regiments be turned out and their masters informed of the date for expulsion.[23] Ejection of black families constituted in effect their return to slavery, and black soldiers exploded with anger. Some sympathetic officers submitted to arrest rather than thus betray the confidence of their men. When irate

of "a competent officer of sufficient rank having no other command" who would send recruiting parties into every county; he predicted that "the negroes would flock to them and be protected by them." Modestly confessing that his success in Maryland could not guarantee similar accomplishments in Kentucky, where the political situation was different, Bowman indicated, however, that if the Secretary of War should choose to assign him to supervise Kentucky black recruitment, he would "go most cheerfully." (Col. S. M. Bowman to Hon. C. A. Dana, 29 July 1864, B-822 1864, Letters Received, ser. 360, Colored Troops Division, RG 94 [B-86].) Bowman made similar proposals directly to Adjutant General Thomas. In reply, Thomas outlined his own plan for mobile recruiting squads, asserted that it differed "in no important respect" from the procedures outlined by Bowman, and concluded that he had no need of Bowman's services in Kentucky. (Adjutant General L. Thomas to Colonel S. M. Bowman, 27 July 1864, A-785 1864, Letters Received, ser. 12, RG 94 [K-545].)

[23] *Official Records*, ser. 3, vol. 4, p. 474.

reports reached Washington, the War Department forced Thomas to rescind his directive and instructed him neither to encourage acceptance of black dependents into army camps nor to turn them out. Such ambiguous guidelines meant that individual commanders exercised considerable discretion in their treatment of soldiers' families. Most sought to minimize their responsibilities by discouraging or even prohibiting dependents from entering their lines. Some resorted repeatedly to forcible expulsion when families nevertheless congregated near their soldier husbands and fathers. For the most part, army treatment of black dependents steadily deteriorated during the second half of 1864, culminating in the brutal eviction of hundreds of women and children from Camp Nelson in November. Shocked by the resultant suffering, Northern missionaries and sympathetic officers publicized the army's shabby policies toward black soldiers' families, and at length the Camp Nelson refuge reopened. Through at least the end of the year, however, army ill-treatment of dependents worked to decrease black enlistments.

By late 1864, sluggish black volunteering, attributed by most observers to depletion of the black male population in areas near recruitment centers, placed new pressure upon recruiters. They increased the activities of mobile recruiting squads and frequently resorted to outright impressment.[24] Adjutant General Thomas himself had authorized forcible enlistment of black men who had escaped their masters without joining the army. Claims upon black manpower also intensified with the enforcement of repeated drafts, for black substitutes came to be highly valued both in Kentucky and in states to the north. In the clamor for substitutes, organized systems of virtual kidnapping beset Kentucky's black population. Such practices did little to attract recruits. At the same time, increasing numbers of slave owners responded to large-scale slave flight by offering wages or crop shares to bondsmen who would continue to labor in the houses, fields, and workshops. With black men apprehensive about heavy-handed impressment and many masters offering them inducements to remain at home, the prospects for further volunteering appeared dim.

Gloomy forecasts proved to be mistaken, because changes in federal policy created new incentives for black Kentuckians to take up a soldier's arms. At the beginning of March 1865, Congress passed a joint resolution that offered freedom to the wives and children of

---

[24] *Official Records,* ser. 3, vol. 4, p. 995; affidavit of Capt. Geo. H. Partridge, 16 Feb. 1865, and affidavit of Dallas Sneed, 21 Feb. 1865, both enclosed in E. H. Green to Hon. Geo. H. Yeaman, 24 Feb. 1865, filed as A-47 1866, Letters Received, ser. 360, Colored Troops Division, RG 94 [B-421].

black soldiers and of future black volunteers.[25] General John M. Palmer, new commander of the Department of Kentucky, actively enforced the law. He circulated printed orders and addressed enthusiastic meetings in black churches, inviting black men to "coin freedom" for their families. Although only a few weeks remained before the end of the war and the end of recruitment, a renewed swell of enlistments put thousands of additional Kentucky slaves into uniform. In all, nearly 24,000 Kentucky blacks – considerably more than half the state's black men of military age – joined the Union army during the thirteen months between April 1864 and May 1865.

With the war concluded, Kentucky masters still fought to keep slavery intact. Angry slaveholders used the state courts to challenge the freedom of black soldiers' families and sued for damages any person who dared to employ them. State judges obligingly pronounced the federal law unconstitutional, and the stage was set for months of conflict between military authorities and the state government regarding the status of black women and children, and indeed the status of slavery itself. Unresolved until December 1865, when the Thirteenth Amendment became part of the United States Constitution, the turmoil nonetheless revealed that black enlistments had destroyed the viability of slavery in Kentucky.

[25] *Official Records,* ser. 3, vol. 4, pp. 1219, 1228.

MARYLAND

69: Commander of the Middle Department and 8th Army Corps to the President

Baltimore July 4 1863

His Excellency Abraham Lincoln President of the United States   I have again and again in vain endeavored to get the attention of the authorities at Washington to the fact that at least one negro regiment might be raised here.   I telegraphed you some days ago on the subject and venture once more respectfully to suggest that somebody be sent here or authorized to accept the services of & organize these blacks who are now willing to be enrolled.   I have had some thousands of them at work on fortifications but will

discharge the most of them in a day or two. I had also upwards
of two hundred (200) offering today from Cambridge on the
Eastern Shore but if not accepted and organized while this spirit
prevails among them it will be difficult to get them hereafter
HWSr   Robt. C. Schenck

Maj. Genl. Robt. C. Schenck to Abraham Lincoln, 4 July 1863, Telegrams Collected by the Office of the Secretary of War (Bound), RG 107
[L-213]. Two days later, the Secretary of War informed General Schenck
that the Bureau of Colored Troops would order the organization of a black
regiment in Maryland and that Colonel William Birney had been directed
to report to Schenck for recruiting duty. (Edwin M. Stanton to Major
General Schenck, 6 July 1863, Telegrams Collected by the Office of the
Secretary of War (Bound), RG 107 [L-213].)

70: Superintendent of Maryland Black Recruitment to the Headquarters of the Middle Department and 8th Army Corps

Baltimore, July 27, 1863.
Sir, I have the honor to report that immediately on the receipt of
Special Order No. 202, of this date,[1] I proceeded to Camlin's
Slave Pen in Pratt Street, accompanied by Lieut. Sykes and
Sergeant Southworth. I considered any guard unnecessary.
   The part of the prison in which slaves are confined is a
brick-paved yard about twenty five feet in width by forty in
length, closed in on all sides. The front wall is a high brick one;
the other sides are occupied by the cells or prisons two or three
stories in height. The yard is not covered in. It is paved with
brick. A few benches, a hydrant, numerous wash tubs and clothes
lines covered with drying clothes were the only objects in it. In
this place, I found 26 men 1 boy 29 women and 3
infants. Sixteen of the men were shackled together, by couples, at
the ancles with heavy irons and one had his legs chained together
by ingeniously contrived locks connected by chains suspended to
his waist. I sent for a blacksmith and had the shackles and chains
removed.
   The following statement exhibits the names of the prisoners,
names & residence of their owners and the periods for which they
have been held in confinement:

Names.	Belongs to	Residence	Period of imprison.	Loyalty.
1. Charles Dorsey,	Thos. Worthington,	Baltimore Co.,	10 d.	Dis.
2. William Sims,	Nancy Counter,	Prince George Co.	17 months.	Disl.

3.	Samuel Davis,	W^m. H. Cleggett,	" "	4 mo.	Disl.
		Mr. Cleggett is said to have two sons in rebel army.			
4.	John Francis Toodles	Jas. Mulligan,	Prince Geo. Co.	16 mo.	Dis.
		This man has been confined in all about three years.			
5.	Henry Toodles,	Emanuel Wade,	Baltimore,	14 mos.	Dis.
6.	Henry Wilson,	Geo. Ranniker,	Balt. Co.	1 mo.	Dis.
7.	James Dent,	Alfred Osborne	Prince Geo. Co.,	22 mos.	Dis.
8.	Geo. Hammond,	Reese Hammond,	Ann Ar. Co.	24 mo.	Dis.
9.	Charles Foote,	Thos. Ristar,	Lime Kiln Bot. Balt. Co.	15 m.	Dis.
10.	Michael Fletcher	Chas. Hill,	Prince Geo. Co.	14 m.	Dis.

. . . .

These all expressed their desire to enlist in the service of the United States and were conducted to the Recruiting Office on Camden Street to be examined by the Surgeon.

In regard to the slaves of General Stewart, of the rebel army, I could not execute the order, they being confined in the Baltimore City Jail, and not in Camlin's Slave Pen.

The women are in number:

1.	Betsey Ward,	Dr. Snyder,	Georgetown,	23 m.	?
2.	Virginia West,	Mr. Cleggett,	Prince Geo. Co.	7 m.	D
3.	Ellen J. Roberson,	Eriah Hassett,	Washington,	15 mo.	?
4.	Lena Harrod,	Dr. Lewis Makel,	Georgetown,	15 m.	?
5.	Rachel Harrod (,6 yr. old)	" "	"	15 m.	?
6.	Sophia Simmons,	Wm B. Hill,	Malbern,	12 m.	?
7.	Martha Wells,	"	"	12 m.	?
8.	Susan Collins,	Hammond Dorsey,	Ellicott's Mills,	24 m.	Dis.
9.	Willie (child of Susan, & 4 mos. old)	"	born in prison.		
10.	Martha Clark,	Thos. E. Berry,	Prince Geo. Co.	12 mos.	Dis.

. . . .

These unfortunates were all liberated in accordance with your order. It appears from their statements that this slave pen has been used chiefly for the purpose of holding persons in evasion of the laws of Congress, entitled to their freedom in the District of Columbia and persons claimed as slaves by rebels or rebel sympathizers. Respectfully Submitted,

ALS

William Birney

Colonel William Birney to Lt. Col. Wm. H. Chesebrough, 27 July 1863, B-383 1863, Letters Received, ser. 2343, Middle Dept. & 8th Army Corps, RG 393 Pt. 1 [C-4127]. Omitted portions are the remainder of lists which totaled twenty-seven men and thirty-two women and children. Forty of the slaves had been confined longer than a year; three had been in jail for over two years. Two children had been born in prison, and one two-year-old child was listed as having been jailed, with his mother, for twenty-three months.

1 Paragraph 10 of Special Order 202 issued by General Robert C. Schenck, commander of the Middle Department and 8th Army Corps, on July 27,

1863 ordered: "Colonel Berney is authorized to proceed to Camlin's Slave pen in Pratt Street and enlist the slaves of Gen'l Stuart and other Rebels and Rebel sympathizers there incarcerated, in the service of the United States—and liberate all those confined there." (Vol. 54/65 8AC, p. 412, Special Orders, ser. 2354, Middle Dept. & 8th A.C., RG 393 Pt. 1 [C-4127].)

71: Baltimore Judge to the Secretary of War

Baltimore, August 15th., 1863.

Dear Sir: In obedience to your request I desire to submit in writing to you for the consideration of the War Department the following views respecting the use of the power given to the President by the act of Congress approved July 17th., 1862. There are by the Census of 1860, in Maryland, Eighty thousand free negroes and Eighty seven thousand slaves; which latter are owned or held to service by about sixteen thousand persons. The population of the State is about seven hundred and fifty thousand. The Government, as I am informed, has directed an officer of the Army, Col. Birney, (than whom in my judgement no better selection could have been made) to enlist the free blacks of the State in the service of the United States, which enlistments are proceeding with great rapidity. The objection which I have to this proceeding, in common with other non slaveholders, is one which will strike your mind with great force. To take away from the State the hearty, strong & able free blacks who now do the manual labor on the farms of the seven comparitively free counties of the State, and in the City of Baltimore, will leave those sections of the State without labor, or else compel them, the most loyal sections of the State, to hire Slave labor. This at once gives a new value to the institution which no loyal man desires should be permanent, and which it has been both hoped and conceded the war would destroy, and which, likewise, the Administration has taught us to believe it was its policy to rid us of for ever. I do not mean to assert that all slaveholders in this State are disloyal, but by far the greater portion of them are, and such as are hostile to the Government are by far the most bitter and active enemies in our midst. The course now pursued by Colonel Birney, under instructions as I understand it, viz: that of enlisting none but free persons, will double the value of slave property, as it is called, and actually indirectly put money in the hands of those hostile to the Government which is taken from the purses of the loyal non-holding people of the State. I suppose that the Government has no wish that such should be the result of its action in the premises. I therefore propose, as a remedy, that persons owning slaves should bear their proportion of the public burden, and that slaves should be enlisted *pari passee* [*passu*] with the *free* persons of color. This cannot be done unless the act of Congress above referred to warrants it. The act gives the President power to employ *all* persons of African descent to put down the rebellion – not all *free* persons. Those persons therefore of African descent held to service in this State are clearly within the words of the act, and that their "relation" is not, and was not, intended by Congress to be a bar to their military service is plain from analagous statutes respecting the enlistment of white persons. The fundamental idea of all the laws of the Statute book respecting this matter is that military service is the equal duty of all persons who enjoy the protection of or owe obedience to the laws – the servant as well as the master. Hence Congress allows the enlistment of minors who, by law and natural right, owe service to the parent, and no compensation is made to the father for the lost service of his boy between the ages of 18 & 21   Again the law of Maryland establishes the relation of Master and Apprentice. Without the Statute such relation could not exist. It is the mere creature of law. Yet the act of Congress does not exempt the indentured youth from service nor does it provide a compensation for the master. Higher and above, paramount to all such relations, is the claim of the country for military service; and all such ties and obligations, whether by force of law or by contract, are supposed by Congress to be made or enjoyed in the full view of the well known duty of military service. I need not suggest that Slavery exists in this State upon no higher basis than the law. The service of a child to his parent, of an apprentice to his master, of a hireling to his employer, is a legal obligation. One law is not superior to another. Statutes are of equal force, and as it is the duty of all persons to perform military service in one of these relations, the others have no claim to exemption. Perhaps it would be as well to remove an erroneous impression, which seems to be an obsticle in the way of dealing with this matter; and that is that the relation of master and slave has more of natural right or of the accidents of property than the relations to which we have likened it. It is what the Constitution of Maryland calls it and it is nothing more – "The relation of Master and Slave". The right to hold the Slave may be of more value than the right to the services of an apprentice. It may be the subject of inheritance, and not cease with the life of the party to whom service is due, as in the case of the parent and child; but the value of a thing does not alter its legal status or definition. The law deals with it in

Maryland precisely as it deals with the relation of master and apprentice. If a man cruelly beats his apprentice the law dissolves the relationship. If a man cruelly beats his negro, the law dissolves that relationship also, and the negro is free. If a man brings a party owing service into this State, intending to sell him to some one out of the State, the act of Assembly manumits the party and annuls the obligation to service. And as the law of Maryland views the matter, so the act of Congress views it as an obligation to service to which the military duty of the person owing service is paramount. The law of Maryland never loses sight of the fact that the party owing service is a person. The law of Congress regards him likewise as a person and that he owes military service. If the Department agrees with me in these views the duty of the Government is clear. A few years ago the Legislature of Maryland, under the influence of ultra pro-slavery councels, submitted to the people of a large portion of the State for acceptance a law compelling the free persons of color of this State to enter the relation of servitude again or be sold to the highest bidder. Our people knew that the free people of color would forsake the State rather than return again to bondage, and looked upon the law as an attempt to deprive them of the services of the free population, and compel them, the non-slaveholding community, to hire the surplus slave population. The law was indignantly rejected. I submit that the Government, if it pursues the course now practiced, will be in effect putting in force a Statute which the people of Maryland in the heyday of slavery in this State refused a place on the Statute Book. A leading slaveholder has, I am informed, made a request that the Government allow a bounty or sum of money by way of compensation to the owner of slaves who shall enlist them in the service of the U.S. The objection to this course is that it is partial and unjust. The Government makes no such allowance to a poor father whose son is enlisted, nor to a mechanic whose apprentice is drafted. And also that it renews a proposal of the President to compensate our slaveholding fellow citizens who would favor emancipation, against which proposition the vote of every representative from our slaveholding districts was recorded six months ago, and they are renominated for Congress, thus approving their action. If, however, the Government, willing to yield the enforcement of strict law to what they may think a more conservative policy, shall adopt any such method and offer a bounty for the enlistment of slaves, it is to be hoped that such allowance will be made only to loyal people, and that with respect to persons owing service to disloyal men the paramount obligation of military service will be enforced. I hope, however, the

Government will view the matter as I do, and authorize the
Officer entrusted with this service to issue the following
proclamation. Very truly,

TLcSr   Hugh L. Bond.

Hugh L. Bond to Hon. E. M. Stanton, 15 Aug. 1863, Negro in the
Military Service, pp. 1484–88, ser. 390, Colored Troops Division, RG 94
[B-460]. Enclosed is a draft proclamation, addressed to all black men aged
eighteen to forty-five in Maryland, "invit[ing] and entreat[ing]" their enlistment in the U.S. Army. The proposed proclamation explicitly declared
that "not merely freemen, but also persons owing service or labor . . . will
be accepted . . . and protected against any person who may presume to
impede their patriotic purpose of offering their services to their country for
the suppression of this rebellion." Baltimore newspapers published Bond's
letter in early September 1863, provoking a heated counterargument by
Maryland's governor, which also appeared in the public press. Governor
Augustus W. Bradford charged Bond with seeking to effect emancipation
through slave enlistments.

72: Civilian Recruiting Agent to the Superintendent of Maryland Black Recruitment

Frederick city [*Md.*] Aug 19th *1863*.
Dear friend   Under the circumstances I thought best to write to
you again not having heard from you either as to my dispatch or
letter. I tried to inform you that I had been very successfull at
and in the vicinity of this place   as I came here to meet my
appointment on Sunday morning a colord freind at Liberty informd
me that 100 good men would leave carrolls mannor for Union
Bridge that night, preparatory to going to camp at Baltimore on
Monday. I fully expected to be there to ship them by the
afternoon train of Monday. although having rode 20 miles in the
morning and spoke twice that day I started for union Bridge and
had rode some 10 miles, when I was overtaken by a private from
Major Coles cavalry, who stated that Col Malsby wished to see me,
and therefore I would have to return to Frederick. I told him I
could not do so and asked him to show his authority   he answered
that he had no order from Col Maulsby. I rode on   he then
became abusive and said he would go with me if I went to hell
&c, to which I paid but little attention. after riding about half a
mile, he stoped. I went on slowly having a poor travelling
Horse. I soon left the main road intending if possible to get to
union Bridge and arrange for sending forward the men, but they

came up with me and after seeing the writ I at once submited to the civil authority, and returned to this place. they demanded 1000$ bail I made no effort to get as almost every person had gone to bed, & being compartively a stranger I thought it not likely that I could obtain the bail. on Monday I sent for an attorney who frankly told me that he was a pro slavery man & was opposed to taking negros into the army. he examined my orders and told me I would have to get you here in order to prove their authenticity. his charge would be 50$ beside the court charges. I told him I would defer the matter untill I could write to you and obtain your answer. I thought to try the Habeus Corpus then, but shall defer untill I hear from you. they charge me with having enticed Slaves to leave their masters. it is true I have recruited some, but did not know they were such at the time. the only thing I am sorry for is that I cannot go on with my recruiting. Col we can raise a Brigade in Md. I am sure of it if we can have a chance   all, their [*slaves*] are running off and going to Washington or Baltimore. I have got the matter completely under way, they understand it, and if I had the chance I could send some 25 pr diem. on Sunday night 38 started from here, so one of the colord men told me yesteday, and there is 30 more who want to go to day   these last are all free men, and I shall try to get transportation for them by sending the order to the agt and get him to fill a blank if he will do so. I can then send them forward to you. I will give you notice with each squad, but if I fail in this I do not know what couse to take. Judge Bond I hope will come up to the work and give me such advice as may be necessary under the circumstances. I shall try to keep you posted each day. please send me a little money   I have used all I had, and must have some.   there are some, 8 Slaves in this Jail kept here by their masters who are all traitors, one of whom is in the Rebel Army. his slave named Martin V. Bucham is here and wants to join the army. they thowed up to my window yestrday the following note in a hankercheif with a stone in it.

> Copy   Col Creager, Sir, I have the honor to inform you that they a lot of Boys in hear that wants to enlist and go in the Army and they would make good soldiers and they all appear to want to go and fight, and be very glad to go, and if you will take them you will oblige the signers.

then follows 8 names.   had you not better send an order for them. in greate haste your sincere friend

J. P. Creager

pray for me that I may have true courage & strength to do my duty   God bless you all, and our good cause   Please answer this

at once and give me all necessary advice under the
circumstances   if I dare do it could recruit any amount right
here. give me authority to do so if you can. when will Gen
Schenck return. we want his aid now   the cold man is waiting to
take this to the office & I must conclude

ALS   J. P. C

J. P. Creager to Col. Wm. Birnie, 19 Aug. 1863, enclosed in Colonel
Wm. Birney to Adjutant General U.S. Army, 20 Aug. 1863, filed with
B-40 1863, Letters Received, ser. 360, Colored Troops Division, RG 94
[B-25]. Early in September, the Adjutant General's Office refused to order
Creager released from jail, on the grounds that the military lacked author-
ity in cases involving civilians. Earlier, Colonel William Birney had urged
the War Department to take action, arguing that the employment of
civilians had "been unavoidable, there being no officers available for the
purpose," and concluding that recruiting depended "to a great extent"
upon Creager's release, "publicly and by military authority." (A.A. Genl.
C. W. Foster to Col. Wm. Birney, 9 Sept. 1863, vol. 4, p. 337, Letters
Sent, ser. 492, Volunteer Service Division, RG 94 [BB-7]; Colonel William Birney to Adjutant General U.S. Army, 28 Aug. 1863, filed with
B-40 1863, Letters Received, ser. 360, Colored Troops Division, RG 94
[B-25].)

73: Eastern Shore Recruiting Agent to the Secretary of War

Centreville, Queen Anns Co., Md. Augst 22^{d} 1863
Dear Sir: While I believe in the wisdom, and justness of intention
on the part of the Government in all its efforts to put down the
rebellion, you will allow me to call your attention to one thing
which is very unjust, unfair, and which bears very hard on a large
majority of the loyal men of Maryland, viz. the drafting and
recruiting free colored men and leaving out the slaves.
In this (Queen Anns) County, nearly all the slave holders are
disloyal men and are doing all they can against the Government,
while nearly all of the non-slaveholders are loyal and true men to
the Government. By taking away the free colored men, you take
away the labour from the very men who are doing their utmost to
sustain the Government, and give every advantage to the men who
oppose the Government. It ought not to be so. In nearly every
case between master and slave, the slave is the only loyal man and
anxious to fight for the country, but is prohibited from doing
so. Can you not remove the barrier so that all the slaves who wish
to, may join the army also? Under existing laws, the disloyal men
of this county will be benefitted rather than hurt by the draft. If

they happen to be drafted they will either pay the three hundred
dollars, commutation money, or put in substitutes, and soon more
than get their money back by the exorbitant prices they will
demand for the hire of their slaves. But if you will allow the
slaves to go, you strike a deeper blow against the rebellion than
can be given in any other way.

Sincerely hoping that you will give the matter due
consideration, and speedily order the recruiting of slaves, I am,
with great respect, your humble and obedient servant.

William T. Chambers

P.S. If it is not too heavy a tax on your time and patience, I
should be happy to receive a response from you.

ALS   W. T. C.

William T. Chambers to Hon. Edwin M. Stanton, 22 Aug. 1863, C-125
1863, Letters Received, ser. 360, Colored Troops Division, RG 94 [B-27].
Two days later, Chambers reported to the superintendent of black recruitment in Maryland that civil authorities were obstructing his efforts to recruit free blacks, on the grounds that "when a free colored man hires himself for a year, or a shorter period of time, he is a slave for the length of
time he hires himself, and that I have no right to recruit him, though it
may be his desire to volunteer." (Wm. T. Chambers to Col. Wm. Birney,
24 Aug. 1863, C-134 1863, Letters Received, ser. 360, Colored Troops
Division, RG 94 [B-616].)

74: Superintendent of Maryland Black Recruitment to the Bureau of Colored Troops, Enclosing a Writ by a Justice of the Peace

Baltimore, August 26, 1863.

Sir, The scheme to obstruct and arrest the enlistment of U.S.
Colored Troops in Maryland is prosecuted with activity by a few
political schemers; while I have had every reason to believe that
the great majority of loyal men in the state are ready to favor and
promote the measure. The arrest of my agent, J. P. Creager,
acted as was anticipated: it intimidated the people of color, giving
them the impression that the United States was powerless to
protect them against their enemies in this state. That act alone
caused me to lose between one and two hundred recruits who were
ready to come to the rendezvous at Baltimore. It perplexed and
disheartened the many respectable gentlemen who had, in different
parts of the state, volunteered to aid me in gathering in the men
willing to enlist. Nearly all of them have since been deterred by

menaces from the further prosecution of the work; and the business of recruiting is going on but slowly. Encouraged by their success, the enemies of the enlistment of U.S. Colored Troops have within the last week resorted to the most inhuman outrages against the families of free men of color who have enlisted: the cornfields of these poor people have been thrown open, their cows have been driven away and some of the families have been mercilessly turned out of their homes. I shall immediately take measures to lay before you in an authentic shape the facts of some of these outrages designed to intimidate the men of color from enlisting.

I have the honor at this time to bring to the notice of the Brevet Brigadier General Commanding the acts in Queen Ann's County of the opponents of colored enlistment. On or about the 19th inst., John Singer, a free man of color, was arrested, when on the point of leaving for Baltimore with the avowed intention of joining the U.S. Colored Troops, on a pretended writ, of which I annex a copy. Such a writ, I am advised by counsel learned in the law, is not known to the law of Maryland. The men who were concerned in this arrest avow their intention to prevent enlistments by issuing the writ in all similar cases. I therefore request that Louis Hergremather, Clement McConner and Charles Chambers may be at once arrested and brought to trial for obstructing enlistments in the Army of the United States. Your obedient servant,

ALS

William Birney

[*Enclosure*] [*Queen Annes Co., Md.*] 18th day of August. 1863. The State of Maryland To Clement McConnor. greeting Whereas, application has this day been made to me by Charles Chambers, agent of H. S. Mitchell, that John Singer a free Negro after hiring himself to said H. S. Mitchell has left his house, and quit the service of said H. S. Mitchell before the expiration of the time the said hiring was to terminate without reasonable and proper cause.

You are therefore hereby commanded immediately to apprehend the said John Singer and bring him before me the subscriber on the 19th day of inst. ensuing the date hereof, or some other justice of the peace of Queen Ann's Co. in case of my absence, resignation or death, to be dealt with according to law.

HDcSr

(Signed) Louis Hergremather, J.P.

Colonel William Birney to Capt. C. W. Foster, 26 Aug. 1863, enclosing writ for apprehension of John Singer, 18 Aug. 1863, filed as B-40 1863, Letters Received, ser. 360, Colored Troops Division, RG 94 [B-25]. Endorsement.

75: Governor of Maryland to the U.S. Postmaster General

Baltimore Sep. 11 1863

My Dear Judge. Whilst the progress of our army every where just now is calculated to fill us with joy & hope I can not enjoy it as I would like, witnessing as I do the excitement and alarm existing here from what may almost be called the kidnapping of our slaves. It sometimes really almost seems that there is a determination somewhere to get up if possible, something of a Civil War in Maryld. just as we are about to subdue it every where else. I went to Washington two weeks ago on this subject and regretted that you were absent. I had an earnest Conversation with the President and Mr Stanton, but I fear to little purpose, for though they both declared that the enlistment of slaves had not been determined on and no one had been authorized to enlist them, the practice not only continues but seems from what I see and hear to be every day increasing. They are being sent over from the Eastern Shore by scores and some of the best & most loyal men are among the sufferers.

I will not trouble you with many details, but refer only to the last Committee which waited on me yesterday. –   They were four Gentlemen from St Michaels District in Talbot County, represented to me as of undoubted loyalty. The District itself, as perhaps you know, is notorious throughout the Shore for its early and inflexible loyalty. They said that a few days ago they went on board the Steamer when she was about to leave her landing, to see if their Slaves were not on board. They found a large number of slaves from the County huddled together in the Bow of the Boat armed with uplifted Clubs prepared to resist any close inspection. One of these gentlemen – and in his relation he was very calm & dispassionate – approached the officer having them in charge & told him that he had come merely to ascertain whether his Slave was among those on board – and respectfully asked to be allowed merely to see whether he was there told him at same time that if he found him, he had no idea of demanding him, or interfering with the officer's possession of him or interfering in the slightest manner with his purpose. That he merely wanted to be able to identify his negro, that he might have some proof of his being taken by the Government in case it should think proper to pay for such – *And this request was denied.* – Now my dear Judge is it not almost a mockery to talk of paying loyal owners any thing, if the Contraband Camps are closed against them, and their negroes after being taken by the recruiting officers are at the very threshold of their own homes suffered to crouch together, conceal themselves from the possibility of identification, to club off their owners who make any such attempt, and then carried off before their face to—no one knows where?

I understand that the President & Secretary of War will say that such recruiting is unauthorized— Then why in God's name permit it? It seems to me to be most obviously due not only to the Citizen but to the Government itself that some open and positive stand should be taken on the subject and that nothing should be suffered to be done indirectly that is not directly ordered. Let the practice be openly recognized or openly repudiated. — And let such recruiting either be expressly ordered or positively forbidden— I write to you with freedom on this subject and as to a Marylander understanding our Condition and capable of appreciating the effects of such proceedings in such a community— I beseech you to stop them, if it be possible. You can hardly estimate the damage we are Suffering. — These complaints come not from the Secessionists or the Democrats—they are comparatively quiet, and I doubt not are Chuckling in their hearts over the practice, But our most loyal men, men who are willing and anxious to sustain the Government—Aye to sustain the Republican party sooner than again put themselves in the grasp of the Democracy. — But I tell you, and mark my prediction—if these practices are not speedily stopped we are given over in spite of all we can do, once more to the Democratic rule. — As things are now going nothing but Bayonets at the breast of the people can prevent it.

I have gone farther into the matter than I intended. — if you can by any possibility have a stop put to this slave enlistment—let me beg you to do it.

I sat down to write you chiefly about a Supplemental matter. — These gentlemen whom I saw last evening said to me: "We have come to you Governor at this time not so much to get pay for our slaves—if the Government stands in need of them let it have them; but we have come earnestly to entreat that a *negro regiment* which they threaten to bring down from Baltimore and quarter in our neighbourhood may not be allowed to come. Our people are in a state of utter Consternation at the propect of such a thing. — Whilst we are willing that the Government shall take from us any thing it needs, for God's sake let it not suffer us to be pillaged by a Regiment of negroes."

I give you Judge the language as nearly as I can of one of the Committee—a plain straightforward, sensible, loyal Farmer. I wish you could have heard him. And can not this poor boon at least be granted? Can not this Regiment be kept here where it is? or must it without the shadow of necessity be sent across the Bay

only further to inflame, terrify and disgust our Citizens? Truly
this would seem to be adding insult to injury. – Will you my
dear Sir, see the President and if you can do nothing else, keep at
least this negro Regiment at home. Yours very Truly
ALS   A W Bradford

A. W. Bradford to Hon. M. Blair, 11 Sept. 1863, President 164 1863,
Letters Received from the President & Executive Departments, RG 107
[L-164]. Endorsement.

76: Eastern Shore Provost Marshal to the Secretary of War

Easton [*Md.*], Sept. 21st *1863*
Dear Sir, I enclose a letter from Judge Bond. When I recd. it, I
was in Balto and expected to go to Washington. I was however
prevented and take this method it to express what I should have
said if I had seen you personally.

The enlistment of slaves has been quite rapid in Talbot. Some
three hundred have enlisted and left Easton within the last five
days and many more are now in Town to leave by steamer
tomorrow. The loyal almost universally approve their
enlistment – the disloyal utter no objection but seem to regard it as
a matter of course. They say openly if it be authorized by the
administration they deem it useless to object. The only excitement
we have had (and it was very slight) was some days after the first
squad left the county. A report was circulated that Gov Hicks[1]
had been to Washington and had been informed that no such
authority had been given to any one – representing that the
President was totally opposed to its continuance and would not
permit further enlistments. Rebel sympathisers at once indulged
in some threats against the particular individuals who had invaded
their rights contrary to the will of the administration. A few days
later a special steamer arrived, and several hundred have enlisted in
open day and quietly left our public wharf for Balto.

I have no hesitancy in saying that if the President would issue
his proclamation – setting forth that it is the will of the
Administration to accept all slaves who are willing to
volunteer – there would be at once a universal acquiescence on all
sides – particularly if it was known that loyal citizens would be
compensated and the district receive a credit on the quota of
troops required. Talbot has already furnished near 400 slaves and
free persons of color since the enrollment of her citizens and will

before the end of this week furnish probably two or three hundred more if the enlistment of slaves is continued as it should be. Poor men are rejoiced at the prospect of being exempt from draft. Loyal slave owners are glad of a last chance to receive some compensation for a property rendered worthless by the Rebellion and the cause of emancipation receives a constant accession of supporters. Nothing which has ever occurred has so strengthened the party favoring emancipation.

I trust therefore the Government will speedily develop its policy in this respect. The present doubt and uncertainty is the only source of trouble on the subject   Very Respectfully Your obt. Servant

ALS   John Frazier Jr

Capt. John Frazier Jr. to Honbl. E. M. Stanton, 21 Sept. 1863, F-500 1863, Letters Received, RG 107 {L-163}. The enclosure mentioned is a note of introduction from Judge Hugh L. Bond.

1 Former Maryland governor, Thomas H. Hicks, an Eastern Shore resident.

77: Secretary of War to the President and a Memorandum by the President

Washington City, October 1st 1863

Mr. President: In answer to the communication of his Excellency, A. W. Bradford, Governor of Maryland, of the 28th ultimo, referred to me, I have the honor to report:

That, during the last visit of Governor Bradford to Washington, he favored this Department with an interview, in which the subject of his communication of the 28th of September was pretty fully discussed, and I had supposed a harmony of views arrived at. The following propositions were understood to have received the assent of Governor Bradford: — First, that free persons of color in Maryland should be enlisted; second, that slaves should be enlisted by consent of their owners; third, that, if it were necessary for the purposes of the Government that slaves should be enlisted without regard to the consent of their owners, there would be no objection to a general regulation by which loyal owners of slaves could receive just compensation for the labor or service of such slaves, upon filing in the Department deeds of manumission — disloyal owners not being entitled to any such compensation.

Shortly after this interview, letters were received from General

Andrew Johnson, Governor of Tennessee, desiring that regulations should be made for the enlistment of colored persons within that State, and, after full communication with him, similar terms were assented to in respect to the State of Tennessee, where it is understood enlistments are now being made upon that basis. A general order regulating the subject-matter has been delayed for the purpose of having an understanding with Governor Johnson, so that the same principles might be applicable, so far as circumstances admitted, to the States of Tennessee and Maryland, both of which stand in similar relations to the General Government in the present war. There is a necessity applicable to the States of Maryland and Tennessee, requiring the enlistment of colored soldiers, free or slave, in a peculiar degree, and not so applicable to other States excepted from the proclamation of emancipation. The State of Maryland is in the midst of the war in the East. White soldiers are suffering from the malarious influences of the locality at Fortress Monroe, and require all the power of the Government to supply their places by black troops. The State of Tennessee is now the centre of the war in the West, and the Government requires the use of every loyal soldier, without regard to color, or whether bond or free, in that State. In the State of Kentucky, military authority has impressed the slave population to the amount of six thousand and upwards, for the purpose of making military roads; but, there being no enemy there, it is not so essential that they should be enlisted as troops in that State, as that they should be employed in labor for the supply of other troops. There is therefore, in my judgment, a military necessity, in the State of Maryland and in the State of Tennessee, for enlisting into the forces all persons capable of bearing arms on the Union side, without regard to color, and whether they be freemen or slaves. It is the desire of the Department, in conformity with the views which, under your direction, have heretofore governed it, to make such regulations as shall do justice to all loyal persons in any way affected by the measure. Governor Bradford was requested to receive the claims of any persons whose slaves were enlisted in Maryland, and present them to the War Department, in order that they might be investigated, and such compensation made as the laws and rules of the service would admit. It has also been reported to the Department that recruiting officers have uniformly, without exception, given to persons claiming slaves who have been enlisted, a descriptive list, upon which they might prove their property and make their claims. If there has been any departure from this course, it is without sanction, and, upon being specified, prompt redress will be administered.

In view of the military necessity of organizing colored troops in Maryland and Tennessee, it is proposed to issue the accompanying General Order. I have the honor to be, Very respectfully, Your obedient servant,

HLcS   Edwin M. Stanton

[*Washington, October 2?, 1863*]

To recruiting free negroes, no objection.

To recruiting slaves of disloyal owners, no objection.

To recruiting slaves of loyal owners, *with their consent,* no objection.

To recruiting slaves of loyal owners *without* consent, objection, *unless the necessity is urgent.*

To conducting offensively, while recruiting, and to carrying away slaves not suitable for recruits, objection.

TEc   [*Abraham Lincoln*]

Edwin M. Stanton to Mr. President, 1 Oct. 1863, M-101 1863, Letters Received Irregular, RG 107 [L-133]; [Abraham Lincoln] memorandum, [2? Oct. 1863], Negro in the Military Service, p. 1644, ser. 390, Colored Troops Division, RG 94 [B-466]. Lincoln's memorandum, which was transcribed in the 1880s by the compilers of the document collection, the Negro in the Military Service, from the same file as Stanton's letter, is no longer in that file. The file does not contain the letter from Governor Bradford referred to in Stanton's letter. It does include a draft version of the order issued on October 3, 1863, by the War Department, Adjutant General's Office, as General Order No. 329. (*Official Records,* ser. 3, vol. 3, pp. 860–61.)

78: Western Shore Slaveholders to a U.S. Senator from Maryland and Endorsement by the Superintendent of Maryland Black Recruitment

Upper Malboro [*Md.*]. Wednesday, Oct 28. 1863
Dear Sir   Your letters to Major Lee gave us great relief. But the negro troops have *not* been withdrawn. The promise made to you last friday has not been kept. They are still harassing us, plundering us, abducting our negroes. So far from being withdrawn the field or their raid upon is much extended; now all way up the Patuxent. Yesterday a steamboat of them came up to Hill's landing, the head of navigation of the river, opposite this place. The negroes in the fields refusing their persuasions to go

with them, they threaten them, that they will return to-morrow, thursday, and carry them off by force. We beg your prompt and urgent interposition. Judge Blair, we trust, will aid you. The officer of the adjutant general's department, whom he told our deputation in Washington, last Wednesday, would be despatched that day to the Patuxent, never came at all. Very truly, your friends and obt. sevts

Thos Clagett Jr	C C Mapson
Thos. Hodgkin	W^m. B. Hill
Shelby Clark	J. F. Lee
R. H. Lasscer	Saml. H. Berry

HLS

[*Endorsement*] Newtown, Md. Nov. 8 /63. The authors of the within letter are reckless in their statements. I intend to recruit up the Patuxent but never have done so. Above Benedict, where my stockade camp is located, there never has been a recruiting station or party. The "steamboat of them" (negro troops) contained *three* colored soldiers placed on board to prevent slaveholders from burning the boat. There was one officer on board. The object of the trip was to observe the landings, with a view to future recruiting under order No. 329 and to give the regular pilot of the boat the advantage of the instruction of a Patuxent river pilot who accompanied him. There was no *"harrassing," "plundering"* or *"abducting,"* terms which I understand Senator Johnson's correspondents to apply to the Government recruiting of Colored Troops for the defence of the country.

The threats to return next day and "carry them off by force" are the coinage of Messers Hodgkin and his associates. The officer & men on the boat fully understood they were *not* to return next day. The boat has never returned there nor has there since that date been a colored soldier or an officer of the U.S. Colored Troops up the Patuxent above Benedict for any purpose whatever.

The Western Shore slave owners are more unscrupulous than the same class elsewhere. Two of them killed my Lieutenant, the unfortunate and noble-hearted White, others helped off the murderers, nearly all of them justified the murder; and now, we have strong grounds for suspecting that four of my soldiers, who have died suddenly – after an hour's convulsions – have been poisoned by the emissaries of these men.

When there is sufficient loyalty and public virtue on the Western Shore to make it unpopular to run the blockade or to harbor rebel officers and spies, it will be time enough for its inhabitants to claim peculiar privileges from Government and to oppose the increase of the U.S. Army. At present, nearly all the loyal men here are among the class which I have been sent here to recruit. William Birney, Colonel 2^d U.S.C.T., Recruiting Officer.

Thos. Clagett Jr. et al. to Hon. Reverdy Johnson, 28 Oct. 1863, filed with B-40 1863, Letters Received, ser. 360, Colored Troops Division, RG 94 {B-462}. Other endorsements; that of November 11, 1863, by Major General Robert Schenck, certified that Colonel Birney's statement was "litterally correct & deserved." President Lincoln on October 21, 1863, had protested to General Schenck about reports that armed black troops were "frightening quiet people" along the Patuxent River. When informed by Schenck that black recruiting squads had indeed been stationed at landings along the Patuxent but that the only "disorder" had been the murder of a white officer by two secessionists, Lincoln telegraphed: "It seems to me we could send white men to recruit better than to send negroes, and thus inaugerate homicides on punctillio." (A. Lincoln to Major General Schenck, 21 Oct. 1863 & 22 Oct. 1863, Negro in the Military Service, pp. 1687, 1692, ser. 390, Colored Troops Division, RG 94 {B-461}; Maj. Genl. R. C. Schenck to Mr. Lincoln, 21 Oct. 1863, Telegrams Collected by the Office of the Secretary of War (Bound), RG 107 {L-165}.)

79: Endorsement by the Superintendent of Maryland Black Recruitment to the Bureau of Colored Troops

Camp Stanton [*Md.*], Jan. 28, 1864.
No slaves whatever have been mustered by me against their will; and no free persons. Every person prior to muster has full opportunity to say whether or not he will enter the service or not. I do not keep my recruits under guard.

Slaveholders have frequently offered me their slaves, provided I would take them by force. I have uniformly declined having any thing to do with forcing them, although if the slaveholders had brought the men to me, I should have taken them, the orders recognising their right to enlist them.

Nine owners out of ten will insist upon it that their slaves are much attached to them and would not leave them unless enticed or forced away. My conviction is that this is a delusion. I have yet to see a slave of this kind. If their families could be cared for or taken with them, the whole slave population of Maryland would make its exodus to Washington.

AES   Wm Birney

Endorsement by Brig. General Wm. Birney, 28 Jan. 1864, on Chs. E. Worthington to Major C. W. Foster, 15 Jan. 1864, W-69 1864, Letters

Received, ser. 360, Colored Troops Division, RG 94 [B-15]. Birney wrote this statement in reply to the assertion of Charles Worthington, a Frederick County slaveholder, that his slaves had been enlisted unwillingly.

80A: States Attorney of Prince Georges County to the Governor of Maryland

(Copy)   Upper Marlboro' [*Md.*], 15" March 1864
Sir. My having been confined to a sick bed for the past week will be my apology for not having before called your attention, officially, to the following circumstance: —

On the afternoon of the 8th inst. a large number of negro troops, from Birney's Camp at Benedict, arrived at this place, under the command of one Lt. Col Perkins and other white officers and took possession of the Court House for quarters. The next morning a squad of the negroes was sent into the County Jail, of which they had previously demanded the keys, and set at liberty 21 of the prisoners—leaving only one person behind, a white man charged with Larceny— of those released, one was a white man brought here recently from Washington under a Requisition from your Excellency. *Eleven* were confined on various criminal charges, some being already under indictment and awaiting trial. The charges varied from Arson to Larceny, abducting slaves &c. one of the negroes released was actually under *conviction* of Arson—his sentence having been respited by the Court until April Term

As soon as our Sheriff reached the village, he hastened after the military who had started for Annapolis. The Lt. Col. had stated that his orders were only to take out the *able bodied* negroes &c. and that the Jailer was responsible for the escape of the others, *yet all of them were released by a large armed squad,* and at the very point of the bayonet. Still the sheriff followed on to Queene Anne, hoping to have restored at least the women & boys &c.

But he met with no success, was roughly treated, and even threatened with personal violence.

The occurrence of so unprecedented an outrage within 18 miles of the National Capital, ought not probably to pass unnoticed   I had thought of communicating the facts to Mr Johnson of the Senate, and to our member in the House of Representatives—But upon reflection, I supposed I should best discharge myself of my duty in the premises by placing you in possession of the facts, and leaving the whole matter to your superior experience and discretion

Your Excellency will not fail to observe that the *practical working* of this affair is to invite the negroes to the perpetration of any crime and to offer practical protection and indemnity to them. It seems imposible that this man could have acted under orders   Very Respectfully Yr Obt Servt

(Signed) Edward W Belt

One of the negro women released and taken along by them was under indictment for attempting to poisen a white family

The troops and prisoners went from here to Annapolis

HLcSr

Edward W. Belt to Governor Bradford, 15 Mar. 1864, enclosed in A. W. Bradford to Abraham Lincoln, 16 Mar. 1864, M-94 1864, Letters Received, ser. 2343, Middle Dept. & 8th Army Corps, RG 393 Pt. 1 [C-4140]. Governor Bradford forwarded this copy of the States Attorney's letter to President Lincoln, seeking prompt punishment for the "outrage" and orders to prevent a recurrence.

80B: Officer of a Maryland Black Regiment to the Superintendent of Maryland Black Recruitment

Head Quarters 19th U.S.C.T [*Md.*] March 28th 1864

Sir   In reply to certain communications sent me to day through your Head Qr[s], I have the honor to state, that on the 6th day of March 1864, pursuant to Special Orders No 56 dated Head Quarters Camp Stanton, March 4th 1864, and signed by order of Brig General Birney, and guided by a certain letter of instructions received from you, on the 6th day of March 1864 I left Camp Stanton Benedict M[d] having under my command Co. H 19th U.S.C.T. 80 men, under the immediate command of Captain Jordan 30th U.S.C.T. and the Camp Provost Guard, 27 men commanded by Lieutenant D. B. Holmes 19th U.S.C.T.

On the afternoon of the eighth, as we were approaching Upper Marlboro, Prince Georges County, I detailed an officer, with a squad to take one road, while with the principal command I pursued another, both leading to Marlboro, the County seat of Prince Georges County. The directions which I gave, were nearly as follows "Take this road, stopping at the plantations along it, and enlisting all the able bodied men, who are willing to come, and if you arrive at Malboro before I do, as the Weather is bad, put your men in some public building, if equally convenient put them in the Court House.

I arrived at Marlboro about 5 o'clock P.M. and found the detachment sent off, already located in the Court House, the rest of the command were also put there for the night with a strong guard around it to prevent any straggling of the men.

After the men were made comfortable for the night, I went to the Hotel, where I found a note from one Shelby Clark signing himself as Provost Marshall of Prince Georges County, stating that he had heard that the Jail would be opened, and requesting that it should not be done; I said I would see that the Jail should not be opened without proper authority, and remarked that he must have heard very soon, as at that time the command had not been in the town more than half an hour, all of which time the men had been under a guard, and I think that none of them had been in the streets at all. I however gave orders that no one should trouble the Jail, and during the night there was no disturbance.

Hearing that there were some able bodied Negroes, confined in the Jail for running away and assisting others to run away, in the morning I sent an officer with the Jailor to see if this was the case, and if so to enlist them, if they were willing into the Military service of the United states, giving directions that none others should be liberated by *Military authority*. The officer who was detailed for this purpose sent, requesting that I would come personally and see just what was in the Jail. as I went up I found the Court yard filled with people of all colors ages and sexes, but the door fast. I knocked and it was opened by the Jailor. inside I found the Jailor, the officer whom I sent to enlist the men with some two or three of the other officers of my command, and I think Acting Ass^r Surgeon Campbell U.S.A

The lower part of the Jail was in two rooms about ten feet square each, in the front room were about a dozen women with their children, all colored, who were confined there by orders of their so-called masters for safe keeping. I was informed by the Jailor (the only County Official I could see) that many of them had been there since the War broke out, and that their masters were some of them in the Rebel Army. The door of this room, when I entered the building was opened into the hall, but immediately on my entry, the Jailor, at my suggestion: closed and locked it.

At this time a guard was posted in the Court Yard, to prevent disturbance.

In the back room were eight able bodied men (Colored) all chained to one large staple in the centre of the room, by both legs, with Chains like ordinary cast chains, each manacle had been put on hot and rivetted down with a hammer and anvil. I was told that one of these men, belonged to the notorious murderer

Colonel Southoron and had been there two years just because his master thought he would run away if he had a chance. The filth and stench was so utterly inhuman, that I had but little time to discriminate, although I was informed; and since then even in the communications referred to above; I have no reasons to think that any of them were confined for any greater offence than either trying to escape or assisting others to do so. I at once sent for a blacksmith, and told him to cut the chains off these men, saying I will not have any man enlisted into the Military Service of the United States with *irons* on"

At this time the Mr Clark calling himself Provost Marshall, although without any insignia of rank, came to me and asked by what authority do you release these people"? I answered, I do not recognise your authority to ask what my orders are, but I have released no one but the able bodied men, if any others have got out it has been through the neglect of the County Officer here. "Will you" said he "deliver up the women and children"? I answered "I have [*not*] released, neither do I take any woman or child under my protection, if you wish to, you can go and get them. My commission debars me from delivering them up to you, by act of Congress approved. But, as I shall put no obstacle in any ones way, so I shall not raise my hand to help, the men are enlisted and no one without a specific order can get them, the women take if you wish, no soldier shall interfere. at this time I was called away on other duty, and left an officer in charge.

Shortly after reaching "Queen Anne" on the afternoon of the 9th instant the Sheriff, or a man claiming to be such came into Camp, for the purpose of identifying and retaking the woman and children who had escaped from the Jail. He remained in Camp about an hour during which time there was no disturbance whatever: the result of his visit is set forth in the accompanying report of Lieut D. B. Holmes 19th U.S.CT. acting Provost Marshall of the Camp   I have the honor to be Very Respectfully Your Obedient Servant

HLcSr   "*signed* Joseph Perkins

Lt. Col. Joseph Perkins to Col. S. M. Bowman, 28 Mar. 1864, P-71 1864, Letters Received, ser. 2343, Middle Dept. & 8th Army Corps, RG 393 Pt. 1 [C-4136]. The report of Lieutenant Holmes confirmed the details of Perkins's explanation, adding that the only "offensive remarks" made at the jail "were words expressive of my abhorrence of the administration of Laws which would confine in such manner human beings called slaves, for trying to run away from such a Country." (Lt. D. B. Holmes to Col. S. M. Bowman, 5 Apr. 1864, H-88 1864, Letters Received, ser. 2343, Middle Dept. & 8th Army Corps, RG 393 Pt. 1 [C-4136].)

81: Affidavit of a Maryland Free Black

Balto April 13th 1864

The Petition of William Jackson (Colored) humbly shows –

That on Monday the 28th day of March 1864 I was approached by an officer of the United States Army accompanied by a file of soldiers, while sitting with my family *at my home* in Annarunde County State of Maryland –

I was asked by the officer my name & age and whether I wished to volunteer in the army and get the bounty of $400 – or to be forced to go and get nothing –

I replied that my name was William Jackson and my age 36 years. That I did not wish to enter the army, and would not volunteer for any consideration of bounty, because of the del[icate] and uncertain state of my health, arising from the fact of my having been subject for the past ten years to constantly returning attacks of Epileptic fits. That I was totally unfit for military duty and could only expect to drag out a few months of a miserable existance, an incubus upon the United States Government If I was forced to enter its service

The officer declined to receive my statement, recorded my name at once upon his book as a recruit, and ordered me to follow him.

With difficulty and by solemnly pledging myself to report to him that evening at 4 oclock I obtained leave to remain at my home until the hour for reporting arrived. I immediately went to the two Physicians in my neighborhood Drs Waters & Hall one or the other of whom had been attending me for ten years or longer and obtained from each of them the certificates, (annexed herewith as part of this petition) – showing the fact of my having been subject to Epileptic attacks for many years, and of my being incompetant for military duty by reason of this painful and dangerous disease

At the hour named viz 4 oclock P.M. March 28th I reported myself to Capt Read on board the Steamboat Cecil. as I had obligated myself to do. I stated my case and handed him my certificates. he said, I looked able to perform military duty and he would not take any certificate to the contrary.

I then begged leave to go back to my family and remain all night, pledging myself to report next day at 12 oclock. This permission was granted me. The next day at eleven oclock, I reported to the Captain and asked leave to go to Baltimore that morning and seek to obtain an exemption from the government

surgeon before whom the recruits were examined. I pledged
myself solemnly (and offered the Captain three or four hundred
dollars security – from good Union men for the faithful discharge of
my pledge) that I would report my self in Baltimore within ten
days if I was not exempted in the mean time   I obtained
permission and came to Baltimore accordingly on the 29th day of
March   I was not allowed to go before the examening surgeon for
two days but as soon as he would see me I reported to him and
was pronounced fit for service and ordered on duty to the Camp
near Baltimore where I have ever since and still am detained
against my will.

And further that I have never at any time received or agreed to
receive any money by way of bounty or compensation since I have
been taken unwillingly from my home and detained in my present
situation.

Your petitioner therefore upon the above recited facts prays that
he may be discharge from performing service in the United States
Army for which he is entirely unfit by reason of his delicate health
and peculiar desease

his

HDSr   Wm × Jackson

mark

Affidavit of Wm. Jackson, 13 Apr. 1864, J-82 1864, Letters Received,
ser. 360, Colored Troops Division, RG 94 [B-90]. Endorsements, attachment. Sworn before a justice of the peace. The physicians' certificates are
not filed with the affidavit. Endorsements indicate that President Lincoln
ordered Jackson's discharge on May 21, 1864.

82A: Maryland Slave Owner to the Headquarters of the Post of Annapolis

Anne Arundel Co., M[d] St. Margaret's, May 28th 1864.
Sir: Absence from home on day of the reception of your letter
prevented a reply by the *first* mail. – I hasten, on return, to
answer to say: – I was present when a band of some 8 or 10
negros and 1 white man came to a field where a negro man of M[r]
Thomas Pumphrey's was plowing; they surrounded the man, and
compelled him, with presented bayonets, to accompany them; and
I see them take him off. – I likewise heard M[r] Pumphrey ask

them if they tho't that was right? They replied, inquiring, "Do you not like it"? He remonstrated. They threatened him, *to serve him in the same way.* I saw one of the negros go to the fence, and on it level a gun, at Mr Pumphrey, while he was complaining

My own losses consist in the absence from work of my negros, concealing themselves, as did in like manner, nearly all the negros in this neighborhood, for several days, during all the time the Press Gang was in this neighborhood. –

To Dr Wm Hammond, (an old practitioner) who asked of these men their authority for seizing the negros, they replied by putting their hands on their swords, and saying "by this and by our muscle". – Dr Hammond has the words from their own mouths.

Numerous acts of a similar kind can be proved by other gentlemen, who have suffered losses. –

I also know that free negroes were carried off by them, to wit: Andrew Johnson & Horace Walker & others. – Some of them have escaped and got back. –

It is not necessary for me to repeat the fact that it is understood that *for money,* the slaves have been offered to be returned to some of the sufferers   I am with much respect, yr. obt. svt.

ALS   Henry Tydings. –

Henry Tydings to Lieut. Jno. S. Wharton, 28 May 1864, filed with H-309 1864, Letters Received, ser. 360, Colored Troops Division, RG 94 [B-464]. Tydings's statement had been solicited by the army post commander at Annapolis after he received a complaint from twenty-two Anne Arundel County whites, including Tydings, that a party of black soldiers was on the north side of the Severn River, "impressing all Negroes free and Slaves against their wishes, . . . shooting at and otherwise maltreating such as endeavour to escape; so that the Negroes have all deserted the farms and the owners are left in most cases without help of any kind." (Saml. T. Redgrave et al. to Col. Adrian R. Root, 4 May 1864, filed with H-309 1864, Letters Received, ser. 360, Colored Troops Division, RG 94 [B-464].) In the same file are several additional statements from Anne Arundel whites.

82B: Superintendent of Maryland Black Recruitment to the Headquarters of the Middle Department

Balt. M^d May 11$^{''}$ 1864

Sir: I have the honor to submit the following report in regard to the allegations of Saml. T. Redgrave and others

The officer referred to was. Capt Reed. 19th USC.T. He says, he lay with his boat at Annapolis three days, and gave his name to all who inquired of him. He says further, that he was informed the negroes in the district referred to, had been told not to enlist, that they would be sold to Government for breast works &c and that he directed many of them to be brought up so he could see them, and talk to them personally some friendly citizens assisting; that after seeing them and disabusing their minds of needless fear, they cheerfully enlisted. It is my custom to talk to the men before I muster them in, and in no instance have I finally mustered a recruit who expressed the least unwillingness

It is my opinion that Negro recruiting in Maryland is hurtful; negroes by force of circumstances and the costoms of the county have heretofore performed all the labor, and able bodied negroes between 20 & 45 have become exceedingly scarce, and whenever the U.S. gets a soldier, sombody's plow stands still; or sombody has lost a slave or servant of somekind

The only way to prevent these outrages is to stop recruiting entirely   I have the honor to be Very Respy Your Obedt Servant

HLS   S. M. Bowman

Col. S. M. Bowman to Lt. Col. Lawrence, 11 May 1864, filed with H-309 1864, Letters Received, ser. 360, Colored Troops Division, RG 94 [B-464]. Endorsements.

83: Superintendent of Maryland Black Recruitment to the Bureau of Colored Troops

Baltimore. – June 22nd, 1864.

Sir: I have the honor to acknowledge the receipt of a letter addressed by M[r]. H. F Krutz of Cambridge, M[d] to Hon: T. H. Hicks endorsed by the President, to the Secretary of War, and by him directed to be forwarded to me for my statement. It refers to colored soldiers recruited by me in this State. –

The controversy between the County Commissioners and myself, relates to the cash bounty due to these men the moment they were mustered into the U.S. Service, and which has not been paid, although they have been in the service several months. It is the duty of the Commissioners to pay the free-men –

They object, *first:* – That they ought not to pay on powers of attorney – well knowing this is the only mode in which they can pay.

2nd   That they ought not to pay at all, until these men shall prove themselves free, which involves an impossibility

Against these propositions I have insisted that it is only right that these men shall be paid, but I do not insist and have not insisted. they should be paid in any particular way. But I have insisted, and do insist unless these men are paid by the counties to which they are credited they should be transferred to the City of Baltimore which City offers to pay them bounty equal to that due them from the counties, and I have stated to these County Commissioners that unless they contrived some way to pay the men credited to Dorchester County, I had no doubt the Secretary of War would order the transfer, for it would be a cruel shame to allow these men to represent Dorchester Co. in the field, while their families are starving by reason of the non-payment of bounty justly due. I did not present the powers of attorney to the Commissioners because I was told in advance they would not pay on powers of attorney.

My anxiety to see these people paid grows out of my knowledge of the needy and helpless condition of many of their families whose distressing stories I am doomed to hear day after day; and for the further reason that they were persuaded to enlist by promises of prompt payment of bounty, and the tardy action of the State Authorities places me in the position of having deceived these men and makes me the seeming instrument of their disappointment and distress.

Soon after relieving Gen¹ Birney it became apparent that without extraordinary exertions, but few colored men could be enlisted in this State. I resolved to do all that could be done; I called a convention of negro preachers and prevailed upon them to open their churches for our use; I procured speakers to address them; sent out migratory recruiting parties into every neighborhood; published in all the papers; plastered huge posters on fences, walls, barn doors and wood piles, and set the black people crazy on the subject of enlisting, and the result was two fine regiments and eight hundred men besides for the Navy in about 40 days. A large proportion of these are free blacks whose enthusiasm and confidence were such that they left their families wholly unprovided for, having been assured by my officers and by myself that their bounty would be paid them as soon as mustered in or very soon thereafter. Hundreds of them could not have been induced to enlist except by this assurance   The poor creatures believed that we were their friends and would not deceive them; they were proud of their uniforms; proud to become soldiers in the service of the U.S. –

But it turned out they were ordered to the field before the

bounty was paid. It will be remembered I plead earnestly to have them remain until after they were paid, but the answer was. "The exigencies of the public service require these regiments to be sent forward." –

When the order came the men theretofore cheerful proud and enthusiastic became suddenly dissatisfied and dispirited. They felt, and had reason to feel they had been wronged and deceived. –

The best thing to be done under the circumstances, that we could think of, was to have powers of attorney executed to collect their bounty for them, and disburse it according to the wishes of the men. Mr Hill the Secretary of State of Maryland undertook to collect for some of them; but both officers and men desired that I should do it and accordingly many of the powers were made out to me. At the same time the men gave directions for the payment over to their families by signing a printed form a copy of which is sent herewith.

Under all the circumstances I could not well refuse to do all in my power to procure the bounty for the men who naturally looked to me for it. The business was not desirable by any means but my hope was to collect it at once, pay it over, and close the accounts, which could have been done 'ere this if the state authorities had been disposed to pay. –

So far from doing what the President in his endorsement deprecates, the thing is all the other way. I have advanced and disbursed for the benefit of the families of the men enlisted by me not only in the City but throughout the state more than half a years salary. In one county alone, Somerset I disbursed three hundred dollars to relieve the families of colored men, while the Commissioners of that county have never to my knowledge paid one of those men the bounty they hold in their hands nor advanced a farthing for the benefit of their families.

It is easy to complain of me. But I submit if these gentlemen who run to the President with complaints and pour into his mind their suspicions would address themselves to the matter of paying the negro soldiers some way or other, what is justly due them they could complain with better grace. But I state it as a fact that Senator Hicks nor any officers of the State Government have manifested the least anxiety on the subject, or the least willingness to co-operate with me in the premises.

It is the duty of the Comptroller to pay the enlisted slaves the bounty due to them, but no expedient to induce payment has been successful and of the four thousand slaves now in the field doing soldiers duty for Maryland not half a dozen of them have received one farthing. –

Early in this month I reported to Genl Goldsborough

(Comptroller) that about eighty enlisted slaves belonging to the different regiments were here and enquired whether or not they would be paid their cash bounty ($50 each) in case I would send them to Annapolis. His answer was not to send them but furnish a list of their names and he would cause them to be paid here. The names were immediately furnished and there the matter rests. —

But the cases of free colored men are hardest. They were mostly poor — many of them had large families — we took from them all the protectors these families had and while we have the men in the U.S. Service, women and children are suffering. It is no fiction. We have unconsciously brought great distress upon these people and I beg the Secretary of War to adopt the only means of reparation in his power: viz., to allow all free colored men whose bounty has remained due and unpaid three months to be transferred to the City of Baltimore where their bounty will be paid immediately. — I am Sir, Most Respectfully, Your Ob^r Servant,

HLS

S. M. Bowman

Col. S. M. Bowman to Major C. W. Foster, 22 June 1864, filed with W-500 1864, Letters Received, ser. 360, Colored Troops Division, RG 94 [B-69]. Endorsements. The printed form mentioned by Bowman is not enclosed. In the same file is the June 17, 1864, complaint of G. F. Kurtz to former Maryland Governor Thomas H. Hicks that prompted Bowman's letter. Kurtz accused Bowman of refusing to credit Dorchester County for its black volunteers unless Bowman himself collected their bounties, on the soldiers' powers of attorney. Local officials had adopted a policy of recognizing only those powers of attorney held by a "known wife or child" of a black recruit. Hicks forwarded the complaint to President Lincoln, who sent it to the Secretary of War with an endorsement expressing his "wish" that "our officers not . . . be scrambling to get other people's money into their hands."

MISSOURI

84: Missouri Farmer to His Father

Farmington M^o June 19, 1863

My Dear Pa   I have just returned from the Harvest Field where I have been making a pretty good shocker. We are getting along very well indeed considering all the drawbacks we have had to encounter. We have almost finished the two smaller fields & will begin on the large field of Mediterranean tomorrow. There has been considerable excitement here among the negroes, owing to the fact that a recruiting party from the 3[d] Mo Cavalry are here endeavouring to raise men for the black brigade: They seem to be by no means particular however; either as it regards sex, or age, as they are willing to take men, women & children, the oldest & the youngest alike. I fully expected to awake and find all of ours preparing to leave me this morning. Night before last several of the men came to the Cabins, collected the Negroes together and lectured them for several hours, the consequence was that they (the negroes) could not resist the glowing pictures presented to them, & they had all about come to the conclusion to leave in a body. Seven or Eight of the men dined with me yesterday & requested me have all of the Negroes brought in from the Farm & that he (the Lieut) would make a plain statement to them in my presence of what was wanted of them & what duties they were expected to perform, and all that volunteered might go and all that refused should remain. I agreed to this, preferring an open statement to secret persuasion. We did so, but as soon as the negroes found that they were required to fight & be separated from their families, they did not desire to go. This spokesman happened to be the same man who had lectured them the night before. And the Negroes say that he used very different arguments – in my presence, from those which he presented the night before. Dick Glenday was the only one, that was willing to volunteer, & his courage failed him this evening. This morning all went back to Harvesting. The soldiers have not gone yet: a large portion have gone to Big River for Recruits. If they will lett our negroes alone the will remain at home satisfied. But there is no telling what they may do – if constantly plied with the most seductive persuasions. They have about stripped Cooks Settlement & Fredericktown of negroes – The crops are rotting in the Fields for want of Harvest hands – Farmers are offering 3 dollars per day; but they cannot be got.

But I must close, as it is growing late. I will write to you again tomorrow. I have heard nothing of the stolen mare – The children are getting well very rapidly. All join me in love – Yours Affectly

ALS   E. P. Cayce

[*Endorsement*] Respectfully referred to Majr Genl Schofield with the statement that the conduct of the soldiers who pretend to be recruiting for negro regiments is most intolerable. Such conduct has no sanction either in any consent of mine or in any act of Congress or in any military order   H. R. Gamble Gov of Mo

[*Endorsement*] Hd Qurs 2^d Brig^d Cavl Divis 3^d Camp in the Field July 5th 1863 Respectfully returned with the information that in my absence a recruiting detail for a negro Brigade, was sent from my Regt. 3^d Cavl. Mo. Vols. – I have never known by whose authority – Doubt whether by any competent authority. Nevertheless, the conduct of the recruiting officer, – such as going to the house of a loyal man & forcibly taking his Slaves, horses & waggons – is an act of lawlessness, that can not be surpassed. Such Acts should be held to immediate & severe account. The rule of ethics which can tolerate the above, could as easily sanction the taking of liberty or life of a loyal man. I recommend, that all such recruiting officers be at once ordered to duty with their Regts. J. M. Glover Col Comg.

E. P. Cayce to Mr. M. P. Cayce, 19 June 1863, C-17 1863, Letters Received, ser. 2593, Dept. of the MO, RG 393 Pt. 1 [C-117]. Other endorsements, none of which provides the name of the recruiting officer or the authority for his actions.

85: Commander of the District of the Border to the Headquarters of the Department of the Missouri

St Louis M^o, Aug 3^d 1863.

Sir. In that part of Missouri included in the District of the Border, and especially in the Counties of Lafayette Johnson and St Clair, there are large numbers of negroes who have been slaves of men engaged in rebellion since the passage of the act of July 17, 1862, and who are by its provisions declared free. Many of them have escaped from their masters farms to adjacent military stations – but many more are being still held and worked as slaves. They nearly all feel unsafe where they are, and wish to get to Kansas where they will be able to support themselves, and enjoy the freedom declared theirs by the act of Congress. And a large majority of the adult males would willingly enter the service as soldiers if opportunity offered.

These negroes are not received as passengers on the steamboats running on the Missouri, as the owners of the boats fear the penalties of the State laws against those who carry off slaves. And they dare not travel by land, lest they be murdered on the road. The guerrillas have shown a singular and inhuman ferocity towards them. You will recollect the brutal murder of numbers of them on the "Sam Gaty" just before you assumed command of the Department. Two or three weeks ago, two Companies of the 4th Missouri set out from Lexington to Independence and were followed by several hundred negroes. On getting out of the town, the commanding officer told the negroes that they could not keep up, & were in danger of being murdered – whereupon all turned back except three men, one woman, one girl, and one boy, who kept on and succeeded in keeping up with the Cavalry during the first days march. On the second day, however, falling behind, they were attacked by a party of bushwhackers who killed all but one man. He escaped, though mortally wounded, and went through the woods at night to Independence where he is now in hospital.

It is a general beleif among thoroughly loyal men in my District that the guerrillas are encouraged, aided, and fed, by many of the slaveholding farmers of the Counties named above, with the understanding that they are to prevent the escape of all negroes. The facts within my knowledge bearing on the subject all tend to confirm that opinion – and I beleive it correct. The beleif that such league exists, and that the guerrillas are being supported and used by men enjoying in person & property the protection of the Government, for the purpose of preventing these freedmen obtaining actual liberty, leads all classes of loyal citizens in my District to regard with less disfavor those raids into Missouri which, though generally accompanied by robberies and pillage, yet give actual freedom to negroes who have a right to it under the law and are prevented attaining it by the means I have named.

For the purpose of giving these negroes protection, and opportunities for employment and self support, and for entering the service of the United States; and also for the purpose of removing a chief cause of disquiet and trouble in my District; I ask permission to give military escort out of those Counties to such negroes as wish it, and as were slaves of persons engaged in rebellion on or since 17th July 1862.

And I further ask authority to enlist in the service and organize in Companies free negroes in my District, for duty in Kansas or wherever you may direct.

It may be well to add that there is no danger that the women or children thus removed will suffer for want of means of support. We have had large numbers in Kansas where they have all had ready employment and earned comfortable livelihoods. I

believe there is not a negro pauper in the State. I am, Colonel,
Very Respectfully Y^r Obdt Svt

ALS   Thomas Ewing Jr

Brig. Genl. Thomas Ewing Jr. to Lt. Col. C. W. Marsh, 3 Aug. 1863,
B-604 1863, Letters Received, ser. 2593, Dept. of the MO, RG 393 Pt. 1
[C-114]. On August 14, 1863, department headquarters granted Ewing
permission to give "practical freedom" to slaves clearly entitled to such
under the confiscation acts, by escorting them out of western Missouri into
Kansas. Ewing's instructions were to enlist able-bodied men into the army
and assist others in securing employment. The orders enjoined "special
care" against interference with slaves of loyal masters. Ewing issued orders
effecting the policy on August 18. (*Official Records*, ser. 1, vol. 22, pt. 2,
pp. 450, 460–61.)

86: Commander of the Department of the Missouri to the Adjutant General's Office

Saint Louis Sept 29th 1863.

Colonel: I enclose herewith a copy of a letter received on the 26th
inst, from Brig Genl Thomas, Adjutant General, asking me to
afford facilities for raising another colored regiment in Missouri,
and my reply. I have thought it advisable to transmit these to the
Hon. Secretary of War with a few additional remarks for his
consideration and such instructions as he may be pleased to give.

In July last, Genl. Thomas, at my request, gave Col. Pile
authority to raise colored troops in Missouri subject to the approval
of the Governor of the state. The Governor gave his consent with
the condition that the laws of Mo. should not be violated—a very
difficult condition to comply with. It was however observed as far
as practicable, and a regiment was soon raised, mustered in and
sent to Helena.

Col. Pile then obtained permission to raise another regiment to
rendezvous at Keokuk Iowa. Recruiting officers were appointed,
by whom I know not, and sent into Missouri bearing copies of the
authority I had given to those engaged in raising the regiment in
St. Louis together with a similar one from Genl Thomas. These
recruiting officers went through the northern part of Mo. with
armed parties of negroes enlisting all who would go with them
without regard to their [*the*] loyalty of their masters and in some
instances I am informed forcing them away. Of course this could
not fail to produce intense excitement and I was compelled to put
a stop to it.

Genl. Ewing has authority, given by the Secretary of War, at my request, to raise one regiment in his district. He has been able to make but little progress so far, but I have no doubt will raise the regiment in time.

The first regiment raised absorbed all the negroes fit for military duty who had been collected at the various posts in Mo. and which included nearly all those at that time remaining in the state who were *unquestionably* entitled to their freedom under the Confiscation act. Nearly all those now remaining in the state belong either to loyal men or men who cannot be proven to have committed any act of disloyalty since the 17^{the} of July 1862. If it be admitted that a man who was, to any extent disloyal before that time may be a loyal man now, it is impossible to decide without judicial proceedings whether the act of July 17^{the} applies or not in a large majority of cases that arise. Moreover under the confused notions as to what constitutes loyalty, which now exist, the officers engaged in recruiting are about as likely to decide one man to be disloyal as another.

I believe the able bodied negroes in Missouri will be worth more to the Government as soldiers than they are to their masters as laborers, and that this is the general opinion among slave owners in the state. Moreover I believe it would be a great benefit to the state as well as to the negro to have him transformed from a slave into a soldier.

I respectfully suggest that it might be wise policy to enlist all able bodied negroes in Mo. who may be willing to enter the service giving to their masters receipts upon which those who established their loyalty may base a claim upon the Government for the value of the services lost. Those masters whose loyalty is undoubted might perhaps be paid immediately out of the substitute fund, and the doubtful cases left for future settlement.

If the Government decide to adopt such policy I shall be glad to carry it out. Very respectfully Your Obt Sevt.

HLcSr

J. M. Schofield

Major General J. M. Schofield to Col. E. D. Townsend, 29 Sept. 1863, vol. 14/24 DMo, pp. 260–61, Letters Sent, ser. 2571, Dept. of the MO, RG 393 Pt. 1 [C-387]. The letter from Adjutant General Lorenzo Thomas is not included in the same volume, but it was published in *Official Records,* ser. 3, vol. 3, p. 848. Schofield's reply to Thomas outlined the "difficulties and embarrassments" that had led him to suspend black recruitment in Missouri, argued that the black men who were "clearly proper subjects for enlistment" had nearly all left the state, and complained that recruiting officers inevitably disregarded the claims of loyal slave owners. Any further black recruitment in Missouri, Schofield argued, would require presidential authority to enlist the slaves of loyal masters. Schofield added that while he would execute such a policy if so instructed, a postponement for two to three months would be wise, to avoid interference with crop harvesting. Adjutant General Thomas, by contrast, contended that recruitment of Missouri blacks "has been conducted with discretion, and I have no doubt but that Colonel Pile could readily raise another colored regiment in that State, if the Commanding General of the Department would afford the proper facilities." (Adjt. Gen'l. L. Thomas to Col. E. D. Townsend, 7 Oct. 1863, enclosing Maj. Genl. J. M. Schofield to Brig. Genl. L. Thomas, 26 Sept. 1863, A-84 1863, Letters Received, ser. 360, Colored Troops Division, RG 94 [B-610].)

87: Testimony by the Superintendent of the Organization of Missouri Black Troops before the American Freedmen's Inquiry Commission

[*St. Louis, Mo. November 29, 1863*]

Q   What do you think the total number of slaves in Missouri?

A   From all the information I can gather, there are from 60 to 70,000.

Q   I suppose it would be a safe estimate to say one-fifth able-bodied men?

A   Fully that. There are from 12 to 14 000 able-bodied men.

Q   What part of the State are they chiefly in?

A   In the central portions of the State. In the 9th Congressional District there is a large number.

Q   How many able-bodied men do you think there are in the 9th district?

A   From 1500 to 1800.

Q   How many recruits have you got from there?

A   From that district, altogether, as a rough estimate, say 300 men.

Q   How is that district as to loyalty?

A   At the breaking out of the rebellion, it was almost wholly disloyal. In the progress of the war, there has been developed a small loyal party, but rebels and rebel sympathizers are now largely in the majority in that district, especially in Calloway, Ordway, Cooper and Howard counties. They have always been infested by bushwhackers and midnight marauders, and it is not safe even now for Union men to live in some portions of those counties.

Q   In a general way, you think the non-slaveholders are loyal?

A   All; with scarcely an exception.

Q   What is the total number you have recruited in Missouri?

Black Enlistment

A   I have organized two regiments. All the recruiting has been done under my direction until since the publication of order 135.

Q   Now, recruiting is confined to Provost Marshals and their assistants?

A   Yes, Sir.

Q   At what rate do you consider that you are getting them now?

A   Last week was the first week of operations under order 135. We received, last week, forty men. I don't think that is a fair sample, however, of what will be done under that order. I think they will come in more rapidly than that would indicate.

Q   Do you anticipate any great increase under the present plan, with the matter restricted to the Provost Marshals?

A   That will depend entirely upon how rigid the instructions are that are sent out to them. I cannot form an intelligent opinion upon that subject until I see Col. Marsh, and ascertain what his decision is upon these points. The present Provost Marshals, who have control of those portions of the State where there are the largest number of slaves, and where recruiting could be most effectually carried on, I know to be indisposed to carry out the order. They will enlist such as they are called upon to enlist, or such as come to them; but they will take no trouble to extend a knowledge of the order to the slave population, or to induce them to come in. I know there are influences being brought to bear to change the Provost Marshals in certain localities, and in fact, to change the Provost Marshal General of the Department. If the district and assistant provost marshals in those districts in the central part of the State were men who thoroughly sympathized with the movement, and were heartily in earnest in the work of enlisting colored troops, they could be enlisted very rapidly under order 135.

Q   How rapidly, do you think?

A   I should think that, commencing from the time when you could get the men on the ground, and get orders and instructions to them, so that they could fairly inaugurate the system, they could send in five hundred a week. I have no doubt about that. I could do it, give me the ropes.

Q   What would you consider the most efficient mode of hastening this thing on? Would it be necessary or expedient to appoint a recruiting officer in connection with the Provost Marshals?

A   If I were going to do it, my opinion of the best method is this: To have the Provost Marshals enlist, in accordance with the provisions of order No. 135, but to appoint men for Provost Marshals who are thoroughly in earnest in the work; then send out

233

one recruiting officer, selected for his business qualities and energy, who would be an efficient man in such work, to act in conjunction with the Provost Marshal, and circulate round through the country. I would have for each District & Assistant Provost Marshal a recruiting officer.

Q How many of these officers are there in the State?

A I don't know the precise number. I should say from sixty to seventy. I would have the enlistment papers made out as directed in order 135, by the Provost Marshals, but send out recruiting agents to go from plantation to plantation, and send guards with them, if necessary. I have learned this fact recently, that in the counties of Calloway & Howard, and up in the region where there are large numbers of slaveholders living close together, they are arming themselves and procuring ammunition, to intimidate the negroes from coming in to enlist, and keep patrols out during the night to watch the roads; and it is reported to me, on authority that I deem reliable, that several have been shot during the last ten days, who were attempting to make their way to some military post where there is a Provost Marshal to enlist them. My judgment is, that every able-bodied colored man in the State is worth far more to the gov't as a soldier than as a slave working in the field of a rebel sympathizer; and in such neighborhoods as it became necessary, I would have a body of cavalry, not to force the slaves to enlist, but to protect them in coming to a Provost Marshal if they wanted to enlist.

Q You consider an armed force necessary, in order that the negroes should really have a choice?

A Yes, Sir, I know that to be so. There are great numbers of negroes in the State who are deterred from enlisting by the representations that are made to them. Those interested in retaining them at home tell them all kinds of stories; that if they enlist in the army and are taken prisoners, they will be hung by the rebel authorities; that they will be put in the front of the battle by the United States authorities; that they will be maltreated as soldiers; that they will get no pay; that they are just as likely as not to be sold into slavery at the South, or be sent down South and never come back—and all such stories. But there is another class of slaveholders in the State who are encouraging enlistments.

Q What proportion of slaveholders in the State should you suppose to be loyal?

A Not over one in twenty. That proportion is large enough. When I use the term "loyal," I mean *loyal*. I don't mean a neutral, nor a man who avoids the law by staying at home.

Q   Have you any means of judging what proportion of the slaveholders have left the State as secessionists?

A   I have not; a very large number, however.

Q   One-half, do you think?

A   No, not one half; a third, I should say, as approximate.

Q   Do you know whether any instructions have been sent by the Provost Marshal General to the District Provost Marshals as to the mode of carrying out this order?

A.   There was a very short circular sent out with the order and the blanks, simply calling attention to the order, and giving instructions with regard to one or two points in it, but no instructions or orders to the Provost Marshals to use their influence or efforts to get recruits. They were simply instructed to enlist those that came to them.

Q   Were there any instructions to make the order known to the slaveholders and the slaves themselves?

A   In the original draft of the order, as drawn up by Col. Marsh, Asst. Provost Marshal General, there was a paragraph (but this is rather an office secret) directing the Provost Marshals to use all possible efforts to circulate the provisions of this order among slaveholders and slaves, and in every possible way to contribute to the success of the measure; but that direction was stricken out by order of the Provost Marshal General.

. . . .

HD

Excerpt from testimony of Col. Wm. A. Pile, [29 Nov. 1863], O-328 1863, Letters Received, ser. 12, RG 94 [K-204]. Topical labels in the margin are omitted.

88: Testimony by a St. Louis City Official before the American Freedmen's Inquiry Commission

[*St. Louis, Mo. November 30, 1863*]

I was on the train coming from Jefferson City last Sunday, on which there were twenty or thirty negroes coming down to enlist. As I had frequently visited the region of country from which they came, in former years, I went round among them, to see if I knew any of them. One of them, who came from near Waverly, in Lafayette Co., and belonged to a man named Hinton, who has four sons in the rebel army, recognized me, and I asked him how he got away. He said it was by lying by in the woods by daylight, and travelling at night. He told me that it was worth a negro's life, almost, to try to get away. He said the bushwhackers had killed three who were trying to get off to enlist; and he made this remark, that since order 135 was issued, the masters have got a fresh supply of guns and ammunition. He did not know where they came from, but supposed they came from Lexington. I asked him if they were United States guns, and he said, no, they were shot guns and rifles. One negro told me that he had carried off his master's gun and ammunition, and that if there was a recruiting office opened in Carroll, Ray, Lafayette, Howard and Saline Counties, and protection afforded to the slaves, every able bodied negro could be enlisted in those counties. He said he had left three grown men on the place where he lived, and they were coming away the first opportunity. He told me there was but one slaveholder in his county that was a loyal man, in the sense of being in favor of the Proclamation. I know the character of those places, and I know you would need a detachment of as many as 300 men at Waverly, and Cambridge, in Lafayette and Saline counties, if recruiting offices were opened there; and 600 men could not be better employed than on that service; they would treble their number in a short time.

. . . .

HD

Excerpt from testimony of R. A. Watt, [30 Nov. 1863], O-328 1863, Letters Received, ser. 12, RG 94 [K-205]. Topical labels in the margin are omitted.

89: Missouri Slave Owner to the Provost Marshal General of the Department of the Missouri

Union Franklin County Mo. December 30th 1863

Sir   I feel it to be my duty to write and give you a brief statement of how things are conducted at this place, and in doing so I deem it due to yourself, and the people of this County, and not in a spirit of fault finding, but that the *evil* may be remedied. I will refer briefly to the course pursued by Col. G. Krumsick in recruiting *Negroes*. It has been his custom, when a *Negro* enlist, to give him a pass for – say – five or ten days. The *Negro* returns to his former *master* only to abuse and threaten to burn him up and all he has. Our fellow Citizen, Doct Childs has met with this fate, all he had has been burnt up   Col Krumsick has in his employ, a man by the name of Bandizen. Yesterday he had about fifty *Negroes* in town all drunk, threatening to destroy the town and every one in it. Mr Whitson has a boy that enlisted, returned with a furlough, found his master laying dangerously ill, threatened to burn down his house, for no reason, but the desire of Mr Whitson for his *Slave* to enter the service. And I am now standing *guard* over my house fearing it will be burnt down, all because I prefer my Negroes should enter the service, at leaste to laying around the *groceries*. A pest to Society.

I would reccommend the discontinuance of granting furloughs or passes. Also that the recruiting, should be done by men of some character, and respect for the good of the Country I only object to the course of Co^l Krumsick in granting furloughs, and in appointing such men as Bandizen to recruit. I am your. Obt. Servt.

ALS   A. W. Maupin

A. W. Maupin to Lt. Col. James O. Broadhead, 30 Dec. 1863, M-4 1863, Letters Received, ser. 2786, Provost Marshal General, Dept. of the MO, RG 393 Pt. 1 [C-187].

90A: Affidavit of a Pike County Slave

[*Louisiana, Mo.*] Janry 4″ 1864.

Aaron Mitchell, colored man, belongs to Thomas Waugh, Says
  I was present last October, about the 8″ or 10″, when Alfred a colored man of James Stewart was Shot. Alfred, myself, Mrs Beasley's Henry and a girl named Malvina had Started to Hannibal a few days before to Enlist. We were arrested near Frankford, by George Tate, Joseph Brown, Robert Huff and John Cash taken to Frankford, kept there all night, and the next day we were taken back to our homes near Prairieville. They took Henry home to Mrs. Beasly and whipped him. They then took me and Alfred to Stewarts, and whipped us both. I was first taken home to Mr Waugh's & learning that Mr Waugh was at Stewarts, they took me there. Just before we got to the house I heard a pistol fired I was about 200 yards off when I heard it. When I got there, I saw Alfred lying in a little ice house in the yard. He was dead. He had been Shot through the heart, the ball coming to

the Skin on his back. Ja⁵ Stewart, Henry Pollord, James Calvin Mr. Gee, the overseer, Wᵐ Richardson, Tho⁵ Waugh, Samel Richardson, Walker Johnson, Geo Tate, and Bob Huff were standing, looking at him.

HD

Affidavit of Aaron Mitchell, 4 Jan. 1864, Unentered Letters Received, ser. 2594, Dept. of the MO, RG 393 Pt. 1 [C-183]. According to an endorsement by Deputy Provost Marshal P. Draper, dated February 13, 1864, the affidavit was sworn before him but not signed, "under the impression on my part that no testimony of a negro would ever be used, except as mere source of information." On January 9, 1864, the provost marshal for Pike County reported the same incident to Department of the Missouri headquarters, adding a report that after the would-be enlistee had been severely whipped, "the owner (who I am informed is a widow woman) offered to give any one five dollars who would kill the negro, whereupon one of the party steped forward and drew his Revolver and Shot him through the heart, killing the boy almost instantly –" He requested a mounted force to investigate and to arrest the guilty parties, which request was granted in an endorsement by the assistant provost marshal general of the department. (Jeff. A. Mayhall to Col. C. W. Marsh, 9 Jan. 1864, M-38 1864, Letters Received, ser. 2786, Provost Marshal General, Dept. of the MO, RG 393 Pt. 1 [C-202].)

90B: Petition by Pike County Whites to the Commander of the Department of the Missouri and Resultant Investigation Report

[Louisiana, Mo. February 1864]

TO MAJOR GENERAL W. S. ROSECRANS. COMMANDING DEPARTMENT OF THE MISSOURI. The subscribers citizens of the city of Louisiana and vicinity, in Pike County, Missouri respectfully beg to call your attention to certain abuses, existing in our county and we doubt not elsewhere, and which we believe grow out of, Either a want of perspicuity in existing orders and consequent misconstruction of those orders, or from a want of disposition to execute them.

Some two or three months since Leiut Jefferson A Mayhall 3ʳᵈ M.S.M. was appointed Asst. Pro. Marshall at this place, with orders to recruit Negros under General Order Nᵒ 135, and at once entered earnestly on his duties. It soon became apparent that from many sections of the County, the Negros failed to come in, as was alleged by the few that did come in, because they were prevented

by their owners, in some cases by actual violence, others by threats
of violence, in others by the locking up the clothing, and in some
cases by the owners promising rewards or bounties to them not to
Enlist. These facts being communicated to the Pro. Mar General,
the Order Dated Dec 19th 1863 (a copy of which is herewith
handed) was sent to him. In compliance with this order, he sent
out his small guard to make inquiry as to the facts, and to notify
the Negroes of their right to Enlist without hindrance. A large
number did come immediately and enlisted, proving conclusively
and for some of the reasons assigned, they had been
prevented. Many Women and children the families of those who
had Enlisted, escaped from their owners, and came into this place
in the most deplorable condition, many of them in a condition of
almost *Nudity* at the coldest season during the present Winter, and
found temporary shelter and employment among the Loyal Citizens
of this place.

Again Lieut Mayhall the Asst Pro Marshall here receives an
order from the Provost Marshall General, (of which we hand copy
herewith dated January 22nd 1864) prohibiting the sending out of
men for the purpose contemplated by the former order, but
directing him to send out and notify such persons as were
necessary to prove the fact of obstructions to Negroes coming in to
Enlist &c. We beg to submit, that, in Missouri the testimony of
Negroes is not to be received under any circumstances, and it is
not probable that any white person would be permitted to witness
any such obstructions, except those implicated.

Again, the copy of letter from H. V. P. Block to Pro Mar
General (herewith dated January 15. 1864) was forwarded by that
officer with his order of January 22 to the Asst Pro Marshall
here. Mr. Block asserts in the above named letter "that Col
Marsh" (Pro Marshal General) *"told me I could offer any under my
control any inducement I choose to remain"* By sending the copy of
that letter, we presume the Pro. Mar. General avows the truth of
this statement. We submit whether this be not an open violation
of the Law and orders, which prohibits any person from dissuading
men from voluntering in the United States service.

We understood the object of General Order N°. 135. to be to
obtain recruits and that every reasonable means of giving
information to the Negroes of their right to Enlist without
molestation, the pay to be given them, and the acquirement of
their freedom &c were not only the right of the Asst Pro Marshal
here, but his duty. The effect of the last order from the Pro.
Mar. General, has been to suspend Enlistments of Negroes
altogether.

We earnestly desire the Enlistment of all of them that will do so, but they will not do so, if their families are to be abused, beaten, seized and driven to their former homes in the night and deprived of reasonable food & clothing because of their Enlistment   These sceines have been enacted here in our streets by day and night during the past two weeks by the owners of the women and children, families of recruits, that have come here for shelter scarce one of these owners ever having made a pretense of loyalty

We do not desire to add to the perplexities of your position. We therefore earnestly hope that such clear and specific orders as to the duties of recruiting officers may be given, that they may not be mistaken. That the provisions of general order N°. 135 may be conducted and carried out in good faith, as we suppose it was intended, to secure the Enlistment of all who desired. We beg further that if, under the Law, the families of recruits are to be protected from violence in consequence of the Enlistment of their Husbands and Fathers it may be so stated in clear and unequivoical terms. If those families are entitled to freedom on the enlistment of the recruits, or only at the end of his term of service, that this also may be decided, so as to put an end, so far as may be, to all disquiet among the Negroes. That if the families of recruits are to be surrendered up to their owners notwithstanding all the brutal treatment they may receive, that this also may be fully stated, so there shall be no misapprehension on the subject. Attempts of Negroes to reach recruiting stations for the purpose of Enlistment, prior to the issuing of order N°. 135, have resulted, in one instance at least, in this county, in the deliberate shooting of one of them, no notice of which was ever taken by inquest or otherwise by the parties having knowledge of it, until the guilty party had ample time to make his escape. We think it is time indeed to put an end to such brutality.

We beg to state that we believe our Asst Pro. Marshal Lieut Mayhall has endeavoured to execute his orders, to the utmost of his ability, so far as it was possible to do so from their apparently conflicting character. We have the Honor to be very respectfully, Your fellow Citizens.

HDS   [*132 signatures*]

Saint Louis, Feby. 17th 1864

General. I have the honor to submit the following as the result of my investigations in Pike County Mo. in relation to the recruiting of Colored Men. — From causes enumerated by citizens of Pike County in their memorial to you, it is next to impossible to obtain strictly legal evidence in the matters in question. The evidence which I submit herewith is the best whereof the case admits, and I deem it worthy of full credence.

1. In the Southern part of Pike County, armed patrols guard the roads at night to prevent negroes from going off. The white inhabitants there are so generally disloyal that no evidence except that of negroes, can be obtained as to the true state of things there.

2. The negroes are terrified and intimidated from enlisting, by threats of violence to themselves and families in case they enlist; by severe and barbarous treatment of colored men, caught en route for recruiting Stations; by the barbarous treatment of the wives of men who have enlisted; by the actual murder of the negro Alfred, who was caught running away to enlist. —

3. The clothing, boots and shoes of negroes, are locked up at night in many cases, to prevent them from going off.

4. The motives and purposes of the government in calling upon Colored men to volunteer are misrepresented, and infinite falsehoods are told as to the treatment they will receive.

5. Added to the above the Assist. Prov. Marshal is stationed at Louisiana, while the Negroes are chiefly in the lower part of the County, from twenty to thirty miles below his station.

As an evidence of the terror held over able-bodied Negroes, it may be mentioned, that the Negroes who do enlist generally escape at night; not one in twenty, attempts to get away in the day time. It may be mentioned also that while the Negroes of loyal men have already nearly all gone into the Service, nine-tenths of those that remain belong to men of disloyal sentiments. The Negro population in Pike County in 1860 was 4055; of these there should have been 811 fit for the Service. About 100 men have gone out of the State to enlist, 245 have been enlisted and sent to Benton Barracks by Lt Mayhall   in all 345 enlisted, leaving yet in the county 466 able-bodied Colored men. This calculation is thought by citizens in Louisiana to be very nearly correct.

I have the honor to enclose sixteen statements concerning the above facts from parties in Pike County. Judge Fagg, Mayor Smith, Capt. Draper, Dr. Jones, Mr. Templeton, Mess. Williams and Bryson are all gentlemen of the very highest respectability, and who are known as having always been, unwaveringly good Union Men. I have the honor to be, General Very Respectfully Your obt. Servt

ALS   A. Jacobson

Wm. Fuller et al. to Major General W. S. Rosecrans, [Feb. 1864], and Lt. Col. A. Jacobson to Major Genl. Rosecrans, 17 Feb. 1864, J-49 1864,

Letters Received, ser. 2593, Dept. of the MO, RG 393 Pt. 1 [C-158]. The 132 signatures on the petition all represent names of men (although a few give only initials rather than full names) and are written in different hands—although often several signatures in a row appear to have been added by a single writer. The enclosures mentioned are not in the file.

⬯

91: Superintendent of the Organization of Missouri Black Troops to the Headquarters of the Department of the Missouri, with Reports from an Officer in a Missouri Black Regiment and from a Local Provost Marshal

Benton Bks Mo Feb 11th 1864

Maj   Enclosed you will find several communications and reports relative to the treatment of the wives and children of colored soldiers by their Masters, that I desire to submit for the consideration of the Maj Genl Comdg this Department.

I have information from a variety of sources that numbers of the wives and children of these enlisted colored men are being smuggled across to Kentucky and sold,—and many others are suffering most brutal and inhuman treatment.

Men who have been home on furlough report that their families have been sent away and they can get no information as to their wherebouts.

I most earnestly request that something be done to remedy these evils.

Hundreds of able bodied men are deterred from enlistment by fears of their families being abused or sold to Kentucky   I have the honor to be Very Respectfully Your Obt Servt

HLS   W^{m}. A. Pile

[*Enclosure*]   Benton Barracks Mo Feb 1st 1864

Sir,   Complaint has been made to me, by Martin Patterson, of Co. "H," 2^{d} Missouri Vols of A.D. that he has direct and reliable information from home that his family is receiving ill treatment from James Patterson their master, of Fayette, Howard Co. Mo

He says, that his wife is compelled to do out door work,—such as chop wood, husk corn &c. and that one of his children has been suffered to freeze, and has sinc died

Further complaint has been made by Wm Brooks that his wife and children are receiving ill treatment from Jack Sutter their

242

master, of Fayette, Howard Co. Mo. He says that they are
required to do the same work that he formerly had to do, such as
chopping wood, splitting rails &c

The said Martin Patterson and Wm Brooks request that
permission be granted to remove their families to Jefferson
City   Yours Respectfuly

ALS   William P Deming

[*Enclosure*]   Louisiana Mo Feby 4th 1864
Dear Sir   Lewis Emerson and Anthony Fleener discharged for
disability, have returned to this place and their Masters claim
them as their property— they have claimed protection of me, and
as it is something new to me, I wish You to inform me whether
they are to receive protection and whether anyone has a right to
demand their papers.

I also wish to call your attention to the fact that the Soldiers
(Colored) wives and families are being awfully abused, particularly
those belonging to Rebels—

Some twenty five or more of the wives of men who have
enlisted here came into Louisiana and called upon me to protect
them, and I assure you I was doing all I could for the poor
unfortunates, but on Thursday evening I received an order from
the Pro Mar Genl, to drive all the Woman and children out of the
Quarters, and to notify their Masters to come and get them—but
before I received the order some of the Copper heads of this
vicinity had posted the Rebels and when they came in after them,
you I am confident, never saw such a scene in your life. I hope I
may never witness the like again.

Genl, for the sake of down trodden humanity, use your
influence to have the negro recruiting Stoped—or else protect the
families of the poor Soldiers who are enlisting to defend the
Government. If the Government calls on the negro to fight her
battles—in Gods name protect their wives and children while they
are in the army. I will be down in a short time and will tell you
of the sights I have seen since I have been here. the orders I have
has completely put a stop to the recruiting business, and if you
can do anything to have Genl Orders No 135 carried out I can
recruit 300 men in this county, besides those I have already sent
down. I am Genl very Respectfully Your Obedient Servant

ALS   Jeff A Mayhall

Brig. Genl. Wm. A. Pile to Maj. O. D. Greene, 11 Feb. 1864, enclosing
1st Lieut. William P. Deming to Brig. Genl. Pile, 1 Feb. 1864, and

Lieut. Jeff. A. Mayhall to Brig. Genl. Pile, 4 Feb. 1864, P-91 1864, Letters Received, ser. 2593, Dept. of the MO, RG 393 Pt. 1 [C-159]. Other enclosures.

92A: Missouri Slave Woman to Her Soldier Husband

Mexico Mo Dec 30th 1863

My Dear Husband   I have received your last kind letter a few days ago and was much pleased to hear from you once more. It seems like a long time since you left me. I have had nothing but trouble since you left. You recollect what I told you how they would do after you was gone. they abuse me because you went & say they will not take care of our children & do nothing but quarrel with me all the time and beat me scandalously the day before yesterday – Oh I never thought you would give me so much trouble as I have got to bear now. You ought not to left me in the fix I am in & all these little helpless children to take care of. I was invited to a party to night but I could not go   I am in too much trouble to want to go to parties. the children talk about you all the time. I wish you could get a furlough & come to see us once more. We want to see you worse than we ever did before. Remember all I told you about how they would do me after you left – for they do worse than they ever did & I do not know what will become of me & my poor little children. Oh I wish you had staid with me & not gone till I could go with you for I do nothing but grieve all the time about you. write & tell me when you are coming.

Tell Isaac that his mother come & got his clothes   she was so sorry he went. You need not tell me to beg any more married men to go. I see too much trouble to try to get any more into trouble too – Write to me & do not forget me & my children – farewell my dear husband from your wife

ALS   Martha

[*Endorsement*] Benton Bks Mo Jany 9th 1863 Lt. Hussey is directed to send the man to whom this letter was sent, to me that I may get his Masters name &c in order to redress the wrongs complained of Wm A Pile Brig Genl Comdg

[*Endorsement*] Geo – Cardwell[1] Mexico – Mo has Seven
Children – oldest 14 years of age Virginia Francis Richmond James
Billy Joseph Benj – 13 m[s]

Martha to My Dear Husband [Richard Glover], 30 Dec. 1863, enclosed in
Brig. Genl. Wm. A. Pile to Maj. O. D. Greene, 11 Feb. 1864, P-91
1864, Letters Received, ser. 2593, Dept. of the MO, RG 393 Pt. 1
[C-159].

1 Owner of Martha and her children.

92B: Superintendent of the Organization of Missouri Black Troops to the Commander of the Department of the Missouri

                                    Benton Barracks Mo Feb 23[d] /64
Genl   Richard Glover (a colored Soldier) Enlisted in Mexico Mo
Dec 14th /63 and was mustered into Co. "A" 2nd Mo Vols
A.D. –   Some three weeks after his Enlistment I learned through
Several Sources that his wife and Six children were being cruelly
treated by Geo W Cardwell his former master
  I directed my Adj Genl to write him a letter remonstrating
against this treatment and Saying, unless it was desisted from the
military authorities would have to interfere
  One week ago to day Mr Cardwell brought Glovers wife and
three youngest children to this city – kept them closely housed at
the Scobee House – went with the woman to the Pro Mar Genls
office to get a pass to take them to Kentucky –   The woman at
first refused to give her consent to go and was taken back to the
Scobee House – and by threats of Selling her children and putting
her in Jail unless she consented to go to Kentucky – She was so
frightened and terrified that She consented to go and mr Cardwell
obtained a pass issued Feby 19" for Martha and her children to be
taken to Kentucky
  I learned the facts of this case yesterday and that Cardwell
would start on the five oclock train for Kentucky
  I went in person immediately to the Scobee House took
possession of the woman and children – procured a revocation of the
permit and now hold the parties Subject to your order
  I am informed by Capt Pollion and Dr Martin who are reliable
Union men from Mexico that Cardwells family are openly and
bitterly rebel – that Cardwell pretends to be Loyal but associates
constantly with the worst rebels in the County – that a Box of

goods for paynes rebel Co was secreted in Cardwells house in the early part of the war

Wm Smithey a man who attends to Cardwells matters in his absence, whipped Glovers wife most cruelly on monday Dec 28th with a leather Strap from Buggy Harness, and this when she is Pregnant and near confinement

The facts in regard to the threats used to induce the woman to consent to go to Kentucky can be proved by Mr Watson John Baldwin and others

This is not an isolated case, but only a sample of many Similar ones that have occurred during the last two months and I most respectfully and yet most earnestly protest against this infamy in the name of God Justice and humanity

Believing that you will do all that you have power to do, to correct these infamous evils, I most respectfully and earnestly request

1st   That instructions be given the Pro Marshals of the Dept to grant no passes, to any man, to take the wife child or parent of a colored Soldier out of this State and they be held responsible for granting improper passes

2nd   That the Pro Mar Dept be required to furnish a report of all passes given for Slaves, to be taken out of the State during the last three months – giving name of the Slave, and owner, with their Residence date of permit and person to whom granted in order that I may ascertain, how many of the wives and children of colored Soldiers have been taken from the State, by Government authority and also from their former masters learn where they were taken – If this can be done, I will send reliable persons to ascertain their present where abouts and condition, –

I claim that it is due these men and the Loyal heart of the people of this State, that they know what has become of their families

3^d   That orders be sent out for the arrest of all persons, prowling over the state for the purpose of buying and smuggling to Kentucky the wives and children of these, Sable "Patriots" and true Heroes" And that all persons aiding or assisting them be arrested and Summarily punished   I have the honor to be Very Respectfully Your obt Servt

HLcS   W^m A Pile

Brig. Genl. Wm. A. Pile to Maj. Genl. Rosecrans, 23 Feb. 1864, enclosed in Brig. Genl. Wm. A. Pile to Maj. O. D. Greene, 17 Mar. 1864, P-197 1864, Letters Received, ser. 2593, Dept. of the MO, RG 393 Pt. 1 [C-160].

93: Army Commissary Officer to the Secretary of War

Lexington Missouri January 21, 1864

Sir/ In an unofficial way I have the honor, as I also consider it a duty to inform you, that colored men who enlisted in the service here left their wives and families, with the assurance, that their reenslavement was impossible. Civil officers are now returning them, to their owners   I went to the Provo Marshal to see if he would give them free papers   I found the but's and if's so numerous that nothing can be done for them here. without aid comes from Washington they will all be reenslaved, and an effectual bar be put in the way of enlisting Col^d men with wives —

This Provo has what our former one was declared to lack — viz "a proper respect for the feelings of this community

I would like that my name as communicator of these facts, should be kept out of sight — for two reasons   one is that I am taking upon myself something that does not legitimately belong to me   The other that Bushwhacking is far from being extinct   Very Respectfully Your obedient Servant

ALS   John Gould

[*Endorsement*] Hd. Qrs Dept of the Mo Office Pro Mar Genl. St Louis. Feb. 9. '64   Respt returned to the Major Genl. Commanding with the information, that under existing laws and regulations no remedy is known for the evils complained of. Communications of the same import are almost daily rec'd at this office from Asst. Pro. Marshals setting forth the further fact that appeals are often made to them for protection by the families of enlisted men, who represent that they are about to be sold to Kentucky slave traders on account of the enlistment of one of their number. The policy of selling families or the threatening so to do seems to have been adopted to deter enlistments and so soon as it becomes generally understood that the military authorities cannot interfere enlistments of men having families will be entirely at an end. The erroneous impression that the families of colored volunteers are freed by virtue of the enlistment prevails largely among the blacks and leads them to seek the military posts and which in turn has led the owners to resort to the civil authorities for their return. Capt. Gould seems to fall into the same error when he speaks of the return of slaves within the State to their owners, "as reenslavement." S S Burdett Act'g. Pro. Mar. Genl.

[*Endorsement*] Hd Qrs Dept of the Mo St Louis Mo Feb'y 13th /64 Respectfully returned to the Adj't Genl of the Army—attention invited to the endorsement of the Provost Marshal General of the Dept The subject of enlistments of Slaves is engaging my earnest attention and I sincerely hope that any abuses in connection therewith or any neglect of duty on the part of authorized agents for the enlistments thereof will soon be corrected— In the meantime it is but justice to my predecessor at the Command of the Dept to state that the system of enlistment of colored recruits initiated by him, has it is thought effected its purpose as well as any system which could have been proposed until the experience of time has enabled involuntary errors to be corrected— The number of colored recruits obtained is it is thought, as great as could possibly have been expected under any system— It is not known that any law of Congress or orders of the War Dept have proclaimed the freedom of the families of slaves enlisted into the service but if it be so I desire to be so instructed— If it be deemed proper I desire to say that I think justice would serve to indicate that it should be so—but I am unaware that I have any authority to act in accordance with such opinion W. S. Rosecrans Maj Genl Comdg

Captain John Gould to Hon. E. M. Stanton, 21 Jan. 1864, G-71 1864, Letters Received, RG 107 [L-34]. Other endorsements. A draft reply to Gould from the War Department, on February 22, 1864, in the same file, conceded that "it is a matter to be sincerely regretted, that there is at present no law which forbids such families from remaining in slavery."

94: Superintendent of the Organization of Missouri Black Troops to a Missouri Congressman

(Copy)   Benton Barracks Mo February 26" 1864
My Dear Sir I regret to have to inform you that the treatment, which the families of colored soldiers are receiving at the hands of their masters in this State, has almost suspended enlistment under Order No 135. Many of these families have been taken to Kentucky clandestinely, and many more by permission from Government Officers.

I herewith enclose to you a letter addressed to Maj Genl Rosecrans on this subject, containing as a sample of many others, a statement of one case (see Record of letter sent Feb 23[d] /64). The General promises to act on the suggestions given, and to correct the evils as far as lies in his power, but there is no remedy but *emancipation immediate* and *unconditional*

We cannot wait for the routine of "Amendments to the Constitution": we want an *immediate* remedy. Can one be provided at Washington?

If this can be done, it is very important that a new Department of "Freed-men's affairs" be created; and that we have a bureau of this Depart in Mo with Head Qrs at Saint Louis, and that subdivisions be established in different parts of the State with a view to the protection and supervision of these freed people; so that they can be looked after and hired out at fair wages to such *Loyal persons* as may wish to have their services. by this means the labor will be retained in the State, placed in the hands of *Loyal Men;* and these unfortunate people will be greatly *benefitted* and *blessed.*

I deem some practical, immediate remedy for these evils of the utmost importance: having been instrumental in causing the enlistment of these men, I cannot see their families thus treated, if any possible remedy can be reached. May I ask your special attention to this matter and that you will urge the necessity of *immediate action* looking to the accomplishment of a remedy? Hoping that you will do so, and thanking you for many favors and courtesies extended to me in the past, I have the honor to remain Very Respectfully Your Obt Servt

HLcSr   (Signed) Wm A. Pile

Brig. Genl. Wm. A. Pile to Hon. Henry T. Blow, 26 Feb. 1864, enclosed in Brig. Genl. Wm. A. Pile to Maj. O. D. Greene, 17 Mar. 1864, P-197 1864, Letters Received, ser. 2593, Dept of the MO, RG 393 Pt. 1 [C-160]. Copies of the enclosures mentioned are in the same file. General Pile had earlier written to Benjamin Gratz, U.S. senator from Missouri, asking him to seek an order from President Lincoln liberating black soldiers' parents, wives, and children, and, if that effort proved unavailing, to seek congressional legislation emancipating soldiers' families: "I claim that it is the plain and *imperious* duty of the Government to protect the families of these colored soldiers and every humane consideration urges that this be done immediately. I appeal to you Sir: in behalf of these suffering Patriots. . . ." (Brig. Genl. Wm. A. Pile to B. Gratz, 9 Feb. 1864, vol. 746/1912 DMo, p. 61, Letters Sent, ser. 2890, Organization of U.S. Colored Troops, Dept. of the MO, RG 393 Pt. 1 [C-212].)

95: Petition of Missouri State Legislators to the Commander of the Department of the Missouri

Jefferson City [*Mo.*] Feb 13th 1864

Sir   The undersigned members of the General Assembly of Missouri: would respectfully call your attention, to the fact: that, a large number of negros have left their masters or owners, and are now wandering about: many of them out of employment, and in a destitute condition: and likely to become a nusiance to the neighborhoods in which they have located.

Believing it but right, and just, that such as are able, who have left their owners, and have not enlisted, should be compelled to do so at once. We would therefore respectfully ask, that such steps be taken, as will force every colored man who is suitable for service, and who has left his owner, *to enlist*

HDS   [*178 signatures*]

Robert Bailey Jnr. et al. to Maj. Genl. Rosencrantz, 13 Feb. 1864, B-126 1864, Letters Received, ser. 2593, Dept. of the MO, RG 393 Pt. 1 [C-152]. An accompanying letter (Robt. Bailey Jr. to Maj. Genl. Rosecrans, 13 Feb. 1864) described the signers of the petition as "men of all parties, and from all sections of the State." In Washington County, Missouri, slaveholders asked the local provost marshal to forcibly enlist their slaves, who had "left them and gone to work for themselves." The compliant provost marshal ordered all black men to report to his office but later insisted that he enlisted only those who were willing. (1st Lieut. A. N. Grissom to Lieut. Col. C. W. Marsh, 20 Mar. 1864, Letters Received, ser. 2786, Provost Marshal General, Dept. of the MO, RG 393 Pt. 1 [C-196].)

96: Local Provost Marshal to the Provost Marshal of the District of Central Missouri

Lexington Mo Aug 3rd 1864

Capt   I wish to Make Some inquiries in refference to recruiting negroes. There is a great many here that have left their masters and they are either loafering about town or at work for themselves. I have made all the effort that can be made to recruit them, unless they are forced in they will not go in the army. Wages is high and demand for hands keep the negroes out of the Army. Is there any way by which these negroes can be recruited. It seems that neither master nor Slave is willing to enlist. If the master would Say recruit the Slave I woul recruit him. But there Seems to be in the minds of the most of the Slave-holders in this Section that all is not lost yet. The time is a comming in their estimation when they will have the power and they will get all their negroes back and be able to keep them at home Yours Respectfully

ALS   J M Gavin

Lieut. J. M. Gavin to Capt. R. L. Ferguson, 3 Aug. 1864, A-162 1864, Letters Received, ser. 2786, Provost Marshal General, Dept. of the MO, RG 393 Pt. 1 [C-194]. General William A. Pile, superintendent of the Organization of Missouri Black Troops, had reported to Adjutant General Lorenzo Thomas on May 21, 1864, that black enlistments had nearly ceased, with only 200 recruits received during the preceding month. Pile estimated that 3,000 to 4,000 able-bodied black men yet remained in Missouri, "but the time to enlist them has gone by": slave owners had succeeded in "getting them interested in the summer's farming" by offering contracts and shares of crops, and stories of the recent Fort Pillow massacre further deterred volunteers. (Brig. Genl. Wm. A. Pile to Brig. Genl. L. Thomas, 21 May 1864, P-163 1864, Letters Received, ser. 360, Colored Troops Division, RG 94 [B-53].) On the basis of this and other reports, Thomas transferred Pile to battlefield duty, convinced that Missouri slaves were "employed by their owners at fair wages" and that additional black troops could not be raised in the state "without strong armed parties to pass through the country." (*Official Records,* ser. 3, vol. 4, pp. 433–34, 501–2.) After an investigation trip to Missouri in early August 1864, the judge advocate of the Army informed the Secretary of War that "recruiting of colored troops in Missouri may be regarded, for the present as virtually closed." Considering the five regiments already enlisted, the large number of black men who had escaped to Kansas, and those who had been removed to Confederate states by their masters, he estimated that enough black men remained in the state for no more than a single regiment, "and from the very high price of labor, & the extraordinary efforts made to retain them in agricultural pursuits, these, with limited exceptions, are not likely voluntarily to enter the military service." (J. Holt to Hon. E. M. Stanton, 5 Aug. 1864, J-39 1864, Letters Received Irregular, RG 107 [L-130].)

KENTUCKY

97: Southern Kentucky Slaveholders to the President

Hopkinsville Ky. [*January 1864*]

To The President of the United States. The present condition of our part of Kentucky, to wit, Christian and adjoining counties, imperatively demand, as we think, that we should make known to you, as our National Executive, some of the facts, by which we are surrounded, and we most earnestly appeal to you for some relief in behalf of the Loyal men of our county, they have been most faithful to you, and have had the most implicit confidence that you would, to the extent of your honor as President, protect them in their allegiance to the Government, that you would not allow their Negroes to be taken from them without at least giving them some timely notice, that they might prepare for so great a change, by the establishment of a recruiting office for Colored Troops at Clarksville Tenne. on the border of our County, and the many inducements that are presented to the Negroes, they are made to leave their masters, all classes of them, and go there, no man has been so fortunate as to get one of them back, no matter how Loyal he may have been; As a sample of the suffering of the Loyal men here, we beg leave to present you with the case of an individual, one of our most respectable citizens, *B. C. Ritter* of *christian county; who, in the beginning of this War donated hundreds of dollars for the Union Cause, and who spent several months in public speaking and afterwards in recruiting for the Federal army, and finally, was for five months a refugee, and dared not return to his family, and on account of his efforts to sustain you in puting down the Rebellion, the Southern Soldiers took from him and destroyed his property to the value of from Ten to twelve thousand dollars; and very recently nine of his most valuable Negroes have been induced to go to Clarksville Tenne, and in his efforts to get them back, he has had no more success than the vilest Rebels in our Country, and he (now an old man) left with a large number of helpless females, both white and black, and not less than fifteen children, all entirely helpless as to doing any thing for a support.*

In the exercise of our "right of petition" we appeal to you with all earnestness for the relief of our suffering, but still Loyal people, by ordering the return of their Negroes, if you will not grant this full relief; then we ask their return, at least long enough to enable them to prepare their crops for market, which they cannot do without them.

And if nothing else can be done, we appeal to you, with renewed energy and earnestness in behalf of our fellow citizen B. C. Ritter; whose individual case we have given you. No man has labored, to the extent of his abilities, more faithfully and patriotically to sustain you in putting down this Rebellion, and if such citizens are to be sacrificed, and ruined, by that Government which they have been trying to sustain and uphold, with what confidence can any man pay Taxes, or do other acts to sustain a Government, that will not protect and sustain him. *"The price of allegiance and fealty, is the protection secured"*

We humbly and respectfully submit the above to your favorable consideration, with the hope that you may, in the exercise of your executive power, grant our petitions, and give to Loyal men a hope of protection, *from their impending ruin*

HDS   [*19 signatures*]

E. S. Edmunds et al. to the President, [Jan. 1864], W-42 1864, Letters Received, ser. 360, Colored Troops Division, RG 94 [B-426]. Endorsements. Kentucky Congressman George H. Yeaman presented the petition to President Lincoln. In December 1863, Governor Thomas E. Bramlette had endorsed a similar complaint with the indignant remonstrance that the Emancipation Proclamation "expressly excepted Kentucky but the repeated operations of indiscreet men along the border produces many hard and very unjust cases of improper interference with loyal citizens of Ky." (Endorsement, 4 Dec. 1863, on J. S. Golladay to Genl. J. T. Boyle, 20 Nov. 1863, G-103 1863, Letters Received, ser. 360, Colored Troops Division, RG 94 [B-423].)

98: Adjutant General of the Army to the Secretary of War

Louisville, Kentucky February 1, 1864.

Sir: Being informed at this place that the slaves of Kentucky on the borders of Ohio, Indiana, Illinois and Tennessee, were constantly crossing the lines and quite a number of them enlisting in organizations were for the distant states of Massachusetts and Michigan, I determined to see the Governor of this state, and suggest the organization of Regiments within its limits, and thus obtain a credit for the Negroes in the States quota. The plan to be similiar to that adopted for Missouri. I, accordingly, repaired to Frankfort and had a full conversation with Governor Bramlette, detailing my plan that the state might receive credit for the Colored Troops, and that the owners of the slaves might receive from the Recruiting officers, certificates for all slaves who might enlist. The Governor stated that the State was undoubtedly loyal and would support the Government, but that the Slavery question had caused great excitement in the state, and he dreaded any agitation at present, and sincerely hoped that the authorities at Washington would take no steps in the matter, believing that any movement to raise Colored Troops in the State, would be injurious to the Union cause, which, of late, had so greatly increased. I assured him that such being his views, I would take no steps to organize Regiments at this time, without I received instructions from you. He then referred to assurances given by the President to him, that Recruiting would not be ordered. He further said that he was receiving many complaints from the vicinity of Paducah, where it was stated that recruiting had recently commenced, and that he should call the attention of the War Department to the subject, as the excitement of the people in the 1st Congressional District, was very great. I informed him that a Regiment of Heavy Artillery had been authorized for the Garrison of Paducah.

I conversed freely with very many Senators and Representatives, at Frankfort, and the expression of sentiment was universal, agreeing fully with the views of the Governor.

The citizens of Kentucky, by a large majority, are loyal, and the Legislature eminently so, but with politicians there are many shades of difference only known to themselves, and which I could not comprehend. They regard the institution as virtually dead and feel that it would be of benefit to the State, to be entirely rid of Slavery; but, the people, while progressing in the right direction, have not schooled themselves to believe that the time has arrived for decisive action on their part for the entire abolition of slavery.

My presence at the State Capitol was the occasion of quite an excitement amongst all classes, male and female, – the opinion being freely expressed that I could only be there to take their negroes from them and put arms in their hands. I was, however, received with great kindness, and when my views were known, all were perfectly satisfied.

I think it would be injudicious to attempt raising troops in this state at present, and it might be well to suspend operations at Paducah, and let me, if necessary, raise a Heavy Artillery Regiment for its garrison elsewhere. I desire instructions on the subject

I shall leave tomorrow for Nashville, where communications will reach me. General Grant expected to arrive here tonight from St. Louis. I have the honor to be Very Respectfully, Your Obedient Servant

HLc   *[Lorenzo Thomas]*

Adjutant General [Lorenzo Thomas] to Hon. Edwin M. Stanton, 1 Feb. 1864, Letters & Telegrams Sent by L. Thomas, ser. 9, RG 94 [V-104].

99: West Kentucky Unionist to a Kentucky Congressman

Smithland [*Ky.*] February 1864

Dear Sir   Dr. F A McNeil Chaplain of the Post at Paducah and W. H. Shook Esq, the Special Confidential Agent of the Treasury Department, informed me as well as other prominent men who are glad to be called your Constituents that Col. R. D. Cunningham of Paducah has mustered in about 200 colored men in his Regiment, according to the order of the Hon E. M. Stanton. But he complains that the Order only Extends at Paducah and Vicinity. And he told Mr Shook of Caseyville that if he had sufficent Authority he would come up to this Rank *Seceesh Hole* and get some recruits

Now, my dear Sir I ask if the order of Sect Stanton is good for the Government, in Paducah why is it not Equally so in Smithland and in fact all through the 1st Congresion District — Of course such nigger union men as Blunt, Hodge, H. F. Givens Dr. Saunders and B Barner of this town will cry out and say it is a great violation of the C O N S T I T U T I O N of *Kai*ntucky. While in thier hearts they sigh for Jeff. Davis and his hellish crew, to win, so as to save thier niggers — But — Sir the true unconditional Union me[n], who had the honer, to work for your Election, will now, Stand up for you, and we wish you to assist us in having the order Extended, through the 1st District of Ky. Embracing 14 counties 7 on the East, & 7 on the West side of the Tennessee River

Mr Shook further informed me confidentially that the Kentucky Conservative Copperheads had made up a purse, and hired some weak kneeded, Union man to go on to Washington & Endeavor to have the order of Sect. Stantons, *revoked,* so that no more Negroes, should be mustered or conscripted in Kentucky — Now as your friend and the friend of the Government I ask is it not right that Rebel Sympathizers negroes, should be taken to put Down this infernal rebellion and restore the Government to its former Dignity & power. Therefore I would respectfully request you to assist the true Union men of your district in having the order of Sect. Stanton to Extend over this whole Congressional District, as I am informed there are many men anxious to recruit Colored Regiments, if they can get the Authority to do so   I am very Respectfully Your Obt Sevt

ALS   J. L Seaton

J. L. Seaton to Hon. Lush. Anderson, Feb. 1864, filed with C-444 1864, Letters Received, ser. 360, Colored Troops Division, RG 94 [B-424]. Seaton, a civilian, was deputy provost marshal in Smithland. The army post commander and five citizens appended their signatures to the letter, with statements of concurrence in its sentiments.

100: Final Report by the Provost Marshal of the 4th District of Kentucky

[*Lebanon, Ky. June 15, 1865*]

. . . .

THE ENROLMENT OF COLORED MEN. –

The amendment to the original enrolment act, approved February 24th 1864, requiring the enrolment of colored persons was received with great disfavor in Ky. Armed resistance was threatened, politicians and rebel sympathisers appealed to an excited populace to resist the law, and high officials consulted about the proprety of retaining Ky. troops, then in the state on veteran furlough, to aid in suppressing all attempts at its execution.

. . . .

Instructions from the Board required enrolling officers to visit the houses of each slave, and procure from *him* his age, etc. At the same time a circular letter was issued, in which it was stated, that – "In order to expedite the work (enrolment under Sec 24) to give the lesat [*least*] possible inconvenience to the owners of slaves and to make the enrolment, as perfect as possible the following regulations are announced: –

"All parties male or female 'holding persons to service' residing in any of the specified sub-districts, will, on the day allotted to that district call upon the enrolling clerk and report to him the names of his or her male negroes. – the enrolling officer being judge of the slaves that are to be enrolled."

Owners of slaves preferred reporting their slaves at designated points to having abolition(!) officers call at their kitchens.

. . . .

THE HISTORY OF COLORED VOLUNTEER RECRUITING.

The enrolment of colored persons under the act amending enrolment Act approved February 24th 1864 had just been finished, when Brig. Genl. Burbridge, then in command of the Dist. of Ky. issued Genl. Order. No 34 Hd. Qrs. Dist. Ky. Series 1864 authorizing the recruiting of free negroes and of slaves at the "request" of their owners. This order was more vehemently opposed, if possible, than the law authorizing the enrolment of colored persons. Provost Marshals and their deputies were constantly denounced; the people were arroused by the seditious speeches of such men as *Wolford* and Lt Gov. *Jacob:,* and those men who shewed favors to the executors of the law were banished from society. The President was denounced as a "tyrant" the Government as a "tyranny," and Prov. Mar's as the "petty instruments in the hands of a despot." Of course, as was forseen, slave-holders refused to give their slaves permission to enlist in the army. These slaves, however, flocked to my Hd. Qrs. begged to be recruited, and returned to their masters to be met with torrents of abuse, and the merciless lash.

(1)   On the 10th day of May 1864 seventeen (17) colored men from Green Co. Ky. presented themselves at my Hd. Qrs. for enlistment. They were kindly received, furnished with passes home, and with notes to their owners asking that the negroes be permitted to enlist. A mob of young men of Lebanon followed these black men from town, seized them and whipped them most unmercifully with cow-hides. Further than this they declared that "negro enlistments should not take place in Lebanon". Upon my arresting them I was threatened with a mob.

(2)   About the same time a colored man presented himself to a Deputy Prov. Mar. in Adair Co. to be enlisted. He was seized by the young men of the place, tied to a tree and subjected to the most unmerciful beating.

(3)   A colored man, while *en route* to my Head Quarters in order to enlist was seized in Taylor Co, badly whipped, and consigned to jail as a runaway.

(4)   Negro men were chased and killed in Nelson Co, for attempting to enlist.

(5)   In Green Co. violent speeches were made, the Depty Prov. Mar. threatened, and negroes knocked down when they spoke of enlisting.

(6)   In Spencer Co. the D.P.M. was severely beaten with clubbed guns, and chased from his home for attempting to do his duty.

(7)   In LaRue Co, a Special Agent was caught, stripped, tied to a tree and cow-hided for enlisting slaves.

It became absolutely necessary for the protection of the slave to enlist him without the consent of the owner. Those who knew the *animus* of Ky slaveholders, soon saw that mild measures would do no good, and that indeed, leniency to the slaveholder was death to the slave, and punishment to the loyal man.

Slaves had already began to leave the state for the purpose of enlisting in Indiana and Tennessee. The poor man saw that the determined opposition of the slaveholder would prevent the filling of the state's quota with colored recruits, and he, therefore, became loud in his calls for the removal of those restrictions which were running off Kentuckians to fill the quotas of other states. Just as the draft under call of February and March 1864 was about to be executed, the people became frightened, and cried out "enlist the negro — dont draft — " Therefore on the 13th day of May 1864 the Prov. Mar. Genl. of Ky directed me "to receive all negroes who may offer themselves regardless of the wishes of the owner."

It is not possible to depict the anger of the slaveholder or to repeat his denunciations, upon the publication of this order. So thoroughly infuriated were many of the people that public sentiment justified *M'Cann,* an Irish laborer in cutting off the left ears of two colored boys who were attempting to reach my Hd. Qrs. to enlist. Not less than eight negroes were killed in Nelson Co, for leaving their masters with the intention of volunteering. About this time Ex-Col *Wolford* and Lt Gov. R. T. *Jacob* visited the southern part of Ky, for the purpose of making speeches. These speeches were simply seditious, and so infuriated the people that the Board of Enrolment could not have remained in Lebanon but for the presence of Federal bayonets.

The 13th Ky. Cavalry was ordered to Lebanon about the 7th of June 1864. Many of the members of this regiment had been particularly active in preventing colored enlistments in Adair Co, and its Colonel had been under arrest for permitting an enrolling officer to be run from his camp in Cumberland Co Ky. When it arrived in Lebanon it announced that "negroes should not be enlisted." A negro man was forced from my camp for recruits, in my absence from my office, and upon attempting to escape the guard over him, was shot at. Maj. *Hu[s]t,* Lt *Cunningham,* Lt. *Shipman,* and others of this regiment denounced me, threatened to retake the negro man from camp with their regiment, and were so violent in their demonstrations that I ordered Lt *Horten* Comdg' Co. "B" 23. V.R.C., then on duty at my Hd. Qrs to prepare to protect the recruits. An attempt was made in the afternoon of the 19th of June to assassinate me by shooting at me from a hotel window. Disaffected citizens secretly gave aid and assistance to this seditious and badly disciplined regiment. Negroes did not dare to present themselves in the town of Lebanon and of course all recruiting ceased, during the time this regt, was stationed at my Hd. Qrs.

My experience in this connection was the experience of all of my employees. Every possible indignity was offered them, while the members of the Board of Enrolment were constantly insulted. It is fortunate for me that I can say that not one of the employees of this office refused or failed to do his duty when so thoroughly tried.

The treatment of the slaves in Ky, during the summer of 1864, the indignities offered the executors of the law of the land; the denunciations of the President and the machination of slave holders for the benefit of treason during the same time, admirably exemplified the barbarities of slavery.

. . . .

HDS

Jamˢ M. Fidler

Excerpt from Captain Jams. M. Fidler, historical report, [15 June 1865], enclosed in Capt. Jams. M. Fidler to Brvt. Col. W. H. Sidell, 15 June 1865, KY 4th Dist., Historical Reports, ser. 50, Pro. Mar. Gen. Central Office, RG 110 [R-68].

101: Provost Marshal of the 2nd District of Kentucky to the Assistant Provost Marshal General for Kentucky

Owensboro [*Ky.*], June 20. 1864

Major. I have the honor to report to you that on last evening an Enrolling Officer for Hancock Co. Ky. presented Thirty (30) Negroes at these Head Quarters for Enlistment— I ordered the negroes out of the street into the Public Square, which I had used as a Rendezvous because I could not rent a Building for the purpose, when about One Hundred (100) six months men,[1] raw & unorganized, who were encamped there, were drawn up into line by their Recruiting Officers, with their guns cocked ready to shoot any one who should attempt to enter positively asserting that the negroes should not enter— This demonstration was made in the presence of some Three Hundred (300) some of whom excited Citizens who had been encouraging the enlisted men to resistance by giving them the assurance of assistance to the extent of One Thousand (1000) men if necessary. I received this information from reliable, loyal men who were in the Crowd observing what was going on— I consulted with Lt. Woodward, who has the Command of the Camp, as to what course to pursue & he said that he could not control his men in this matter— I immediately placed the negroes in a large, well ventilated room in the Jail for safety— An hour after this the Sheriff demanded & obtained the Jail Keys from the Jailor, & took them out of town. The negroes cannot be enlisted, & can only be fed by conveying the food throug a grated window. With an excited community & a

259

demoralized & unorganized body of raw Recruits to contend with, I feel that the lives of the Surgeon & myself are in imminent peril, Head Quarters endangered & the interests of the Government at the mercy of Guerrillas & the opponents of the Negro Enlistments. The forces sent here for temporary duty remained but about Three (3) weeks, & by the time their influence had obtained quiet, they were ordered away— I make this communication from a sense of duty, & think that the interest of the Government demand immediate notice & protection— While writing the above, I have received a message from the Citizens that the negroes will be released from Jail if I will enlist them & send them off immediately— This speaks for the community which surrounds me, & it would seem that my official acts require their approval— I am Major Very Respy. Your Obt. Servt.

HLcSr   (Sign^d) J. R. Grissom

Capt. J. R. Grissom to Major W. H. Sidell, 20 June 1864, Letters Received, ser. 3994, KY Chief Mustering & Disbursing Officer, RG 110 [R-25]. Endorsements.

1 "Six months men" were white Union troops recruited in Kentucky for a six-months' term of service.

102A: Adjutant General of the Army to the Post Commander at Paducah, Kentucky

Louisville, Ky., July 17, 1864.

Sir: I have received your telegram of the 15th inst., reporting that Colonel H. W. Barry refuses to obey the order respecting the old men, women and children in his Camp at Paducah.

I am sorry for the position the Colonel has taken, but am willing to believe he has done it from conscientious motives, he supposing that by a compliance with the order, he would be violating the articles of War, prohibiting the rendition of fugitive[1] I enclose the Order referred to, No. 24, which I issued out of feelings of humanity, and after full consultation with General Burbridge, commanding the District of Kentucky. The presence of so many of this class of persons at Camp Nelson, was productive of evil, and so it will be at every place designated for the reception of Colored men, if they are permitted within our lines. In the States in rebellion, the case is different, for there the President has by proclamation, declared the negroes free, and when they come to our lines, they are to be received and not returned to their former owners. In Kentucky slavery exists by law, and this the Federal authorities under the Constitution recognize. The President, under his authority to raise armies in cases of rebellion, has decided to take the able bodied negroes of Kentucky as soldiers, and I am here to organize them. He has not decreed that any others shall be taken, and I cannot take any other slaves but those capable of being put into the Army. When he directs any other class to be taken, I am ready to obey his mandate. Kentucky being a State in which Slavery exists by law and the Constitution, I conceive that the owners have a right to take possession of the slaves whenever found in the State, except such as have been taken for Military purposes. If the Slaves succeed in leaving the State, then no officer would be justified in their rendition.

I will thank you to present these views to Colonel Barry, and if he still persists in his course, you will prefer charges against him for disobedience of orders, and apply to the proper commander for a General Court Martial.

In regard to the combination of the officers of the Regiment to sustain the course of their Colonel, you will do well to refer them to the Regulations against such a measure. Each officer must act individually for himself, and not enter into combinations. They are young in the service, and I hope they will see their course leads to insubordination, which will not be countenanced.

Please report to me by letter at this place. I am, Sir, Very Respectfully Your Obedient Servant

HLc   [*Lorenzo Thomas*]

Adjutant General [Lorenzo Thomas] to Colonel S. G. Hicks, 17 July 1864, L. Thomas Letters & Orders, Generals' Papers & Books, ser. 159, RG 94 [V-36].

1 By an act of March 13, 1862, Congress added a new article of war prohibiting the use of military forces "for the purpose of returning fugitives from service or labor who may have escaped from any persons to whom such labor or service is claimed to be due." (*Revised Army Regulations*, appendix, p. 529.)

102B: Commander of a Kentucky Black Regiment to the Commander of the District of Western Kentucky

Fort Anderson Paducah Ky July 20th 1864

Sir: I have the honor to make the following statements in reference to my arrest. – On the 16th inst. I recd. special Order N° (101) from Post Hd. Qr's. Paducah Ky. – and immediately visited Colonel Hicks, to have an understanding in referance to said Order. – In the Course of the Conversation I inquired, if the Carrying out of the order was to be general: and if the wives and Children of Colored Soldiers in my Command were to be returned by ME to their *masters*. – He answered, "the order includes all; – further you in *person,* with the assistance of your *officers* and *men* Shall Search your Camp, and vicinity thereof, and investigate all Cases Sent to you by *me,* and return to their *masters* all persons implied in this order: – I remarked "Colonel, I cannot return to Slavery, the wives and Children of men, whome your acknowledge, fought so gallantly, and saved yourself and Command, from *massacre,* and further, I was sent here by, and through the influence of Hon. Lucien Anderson, for the purpose of protecting union people, whether *Black* or *white,* with the assurance, that with his influence in my favor I Should not be deterred, although opposition was expected from officers in administration. – I further declared that I could not consistently comply, and assist in the enforcement, of the order. – I was then by His order, (Col Hicks) placed in arrest. – I have the honor to be General very respectfully Your Most Obd't Servt.

HLS   H. W. Barry

Col. H. W. Barry to General [E. A. Paine], 20 July 1864, enclosed in Brig. Genl. E. A. Paine to Maj. W. H. Morgan, 21 July 1864, P-74 1864, Letters Received, ser. 2869, Dist. West TN, RG 393 Pt. 2 No. 183 [C-2223]. In the covering letter, General Paine expressed surprise "that the wives and children of some of the colored soldiers who fought so bravely here, had been forced out of the lines and forced . . . to return to rebel masters." Paine also enclosed Colonel S. G. Hicks's Special Order No. 101, dated July 14, 1864, requiring that Colonel Barry "cause all the aged, and infirm negro men, those unfit for duty as soldiers, and all the women and children pertaining to or ajacent to his encampment to be at once returned to their masters." On July 24, the War Department instructed Adjutant General Thomas not to disperse the black dependents at Paducah, and the next day Thomas so instructed Colonel Hicks and ordered Colonel Barry's release from arrest. (Adjutant General [Lorenzo Thomas] to Colonel S. G. Hicks, 25 July 1864, L. Thomas Letters Sent, Generals' Papers & Books, ser. 159, RG 94 [V-36].)

102C: War Department to the Adjutant General of the Army

Washington, D.C. July 28th *1864.*

General, I have the honor to acknowledge the receipt of your telegram of the 26th instant, and in reply thereto I am directed by the Secretary of War to say that although the law prohibits the return of slaves to their owners by the military authorities, yet it does not provide for their reception and support in idleness at military camps. The interests of the service and the preservation of discipline would therefore seem to require that indigent colored people should be discouraged as much as possible from casting themselves upon the military authorities for a support.

A sound discretion in this matter should be exercised by all officers commanding rendezvous. I have the honor to be, General, Very Respectfully, Your Ob'd't Servant,

HLS   C. W. Foster

Assist. Adjt. Gen'l. C. W. Foster to Brigadier General L. Thomas, 28 July 1864, A-93 1864, Letters Received by Adjutant General L. Thomas, ser. 363, Colored Troops Division, RG 94 [V-36]. Thomas's July 26 telegram had questioned the War Department's new policy: "Am I to receive all the indigent colored men women and children coming into the Camps in Kentucky?" (Adjutant General [Lorenzo Thomas] to Colonel E. D. Townsend, 25 July 1864, L. Thomas Letters & Orders, Generals' Papers & Books, ser. 159, RG 94 [V-36].) The copy received by the Bureau of Colored Troops is dated July 26 and omits some of Thomas's words. (A-251 1864, Letters Received, ser. 360, Colored Troops Division, RG 94 [B-433].)

103: Judge Advocate General of the Army to the Secretary of War

St Louis July 31st *1864.*

. . . .

The recruiting of colored troops, in Kentucky is proceeding most satisfactorily. About ten thousand have already been enlisted, & this number, it is believed, will be doubled in Sixty days. They have for some time been coming in at the rate of about a hundred per day. When we consider the perils &

menaces, which these downtrodden men have to brave in making their way to the recruiting stations, we cannot but regard the example of their courage & loyalty & zeal as among the noblest & most cheering signs of the times. The commencement of the recruiting of colored troops in Ky. was signalised by disgraceful outrages perpetrated in the twin, & it would seem inseperable interests of treason & slavery. Slaves escaping from their masters, with a view of entering the military service were waylaid beaten, maimed & often murdered. This shameful condition of things, however, has disappeared, under an improved public sentiment, & from the vigor & success with which the government has continued to press its policy. The popular opinion is rapidly reaching the conclusion that the policy of recruiting colored troops is too firmly established to be resisted, & that it is the interest, as it certainly is the duty of Kentucky to acquiesce in it. The feeble opposition which still remains is fostered mainly by unscrupulous politicians, who hope to make out of this popular irritation a certain amount of political capital to be invested in the approaching presidential election. Upon the whole the recruiting of colored troops in Kentucky, must be held to be a decided success thus far, & to be full of encouragement for the future. The service under the vigilant & faithful administration of Maj Sidell & his subordinates, is marked by energy & discretion, & promises soon to bring to the support of the government a numerous & zealous body of soldiery, of a class whose courage & loyalty have been conspicuous on so many fields.

. . . .

HLS   J. Holt

Excerpt from J. Holt to Hon. E. M. Stanton, 31 July 1864, J-39 1864, Letters Received Irregular, RG 107 [L-130]. Portions not printed describe Kentucky as "in a deplorable condition," with large portions of the state "completely overrun with guerrillas, who plunder farm Houses & fields, & villages at will, & often murder the helpless victims of their robberies." Holt also reported the existence of a "treasonable association" in Kentucky, Ohio, Indiana, Illinois, and Missouri.

104: Kentucky Slaveholder to the President

Fairview, Jefferson Co, Ky July 1864

My Dear Sir: I can assure you it is with great diffidence that a lady of my humble abilities presumes to address your Excellency;

but the motives by which I am actuated must be my apology on the present occasion.

I addressed a letter to your Excellency a week ago which was forwarded through the urbanity of Capt. P. H Smith Prov. Mar. of Ky; but fearing it may not have reached you in consequence of the recent rebel raids in the vicinity of Washington, I have determined to send a second letter containing the substance of the first, with some additional remarks. At the commencement of the rebellion my husband and self took a decided stand on the side of the government and have remained firmly fixed ever since; though we are entirely surrounded by bitter rebel sympathizers. I have earnestly advocated your views of gradual emancipation and ardently desired that Kentucky would accept your proposition of compensated emancipation; for I then thought, and still think, it was the best policy that she could adopt. I have been in favor of gradual emancipation from my *earliest youth,* when I was a school-girl at the Capital of this state and listened to the earnest and eloquent appeals of Kentucky's great statesmen the immortal Clay in behalf of colonization.

Entertaining such views I have brought up from infancy and have been educating four servant boys – three of them, my own, and one belonging to my Mother – preparatory to sending to Liberia when I thought they were competent to take care of themselves. Two of those boys have enlisted in a coloured regiment being organized in this state, and it is for the purpose of obtaining their release that I now address your Excellency. I am fully persuaded that they were induced to enlist through the excitement of the times, and not of their own free-will; for up to the time of their leaveing home which was the day previous to their enlistment, they said that they never intended to go into the army unless compelled by the draft. I believe my case is an isolated one. In the Barracks where three thousand blacks are enlisted, I was told that not one of them had the promise of freedom by their masters. My servants being young and inexperienced, did not appreciate their high priviliges but rushed into the army without any reflection, and solely as they have since confessed to me, because they saw others going with whom they associated.

The eldest one, twenty years of age, who enlisted by the name of James Minor, belongs to my Mother, and was manumitted by my Fathers will fourteen years ago to take effect at her death. He is her only means of support and she is a widow of seventy years of age, has been afflicted with Rheumatism for fifteen years, and has been entirely helpless as an infant for the last three years.

The youngest boy, Alex, eighteen years of age, belonging to

myself has been her constant nurse for eight years. Her grief is so excessive in consequence of his loss, united with the loss of her own servant whom she regards with the affection of a son that she is almost deprived of reason and I fear it will eventually cause an entire derangement of mind. The eldest of my three servants left two months ago, when the drafting of the negroes commenced; and as we have received no intelligence of him, we suppose he has been taken in the army. Our servants have been our principal support, and we have but one left, a boy of twelve years of age. My husband is in the decline of life and has not sufficient health to labour for the support of his family. We have no children to fall back upon, my health very delicate and so affected with nervousness, that I am dependant on my husband to pen this letter.

In view of all these things I have resolved to throw myself on your mercy and appeal to you as a philanthropist and a christian, as I trust you are, to authorize the release of my servants if it is in your power; and if not, I beseech you to use your influence with the Secretary of War in my behalf; and not suffer all my domestic happiness to be impaired, and all my hopes to be blighted that I have cherished for so many years in regard to their present and future welfare. If you should be so merciful as to send an order for their release — which I hope and believe the feelings of your heart will prompt you to do — I want you, if you please, to have it so fixed that they cannot reenlist without our consent.

I feel assured that if you will comply with my *earnest request,* God will approve, and the prayers of a venerable and pious Mother, united with mine, will be daily offered at a throne of grace for your present and everlasting happiness. Yours with much respect

HLSr   Elizabeth A. Minor

Elizabeth A. Minor to Hon. A. Lincoln, July 1864, M-536 1864, Letters Received, ser. 360, Colored Troops Division, RG 94 [B-430]. Endorsements. An army officer forwarded the letter on July 19, 1864. In the same file is an earlier, and very similar, letter from Minor to Lincoln, dated July 11. Also filed is a reply from the Bureau of Colored Troops, July 23, 1864, informing Minor that "the reasons given in your request are considered insufficient, and to discharge them [the former slaves], would establish a precedent injurious to the interests of the service and not warranted by the circumstances of the case."

105: Commander of a Company of Kentucky Black Troops to the Commander of the District of Kentucky

Henderson Ky. Sept 17th 1864

Sir   I have the honor to acknowledge the receipt of your Telegram of the 16th inst. in which complaint is made by Mr Ira Delano that men belonging to this Command have been Stealing Negro Women and Children and Shiping them acrost the River.

Immediately upon our arrival at this Place (Monday Morning the 12th inst Col Moon foresaw that trouble would be likely to arise on that point and immediately took measures to prevent it. He issued Orders to the Ferryman and Fisherman in this vicinity prohibiting them from carrying Persons acrost the River without a permit from these Head Qrs. and there has been no permit granted to Colored Men Women or Children.

As Recruiting has been very brisk here many Women and Children follow after their Husband's and Father's laboring under the impression that they would be allowed to accompany them but when they were informed of their error many have taken my advice and returned to their Masters of their own accord and all others that have been found wandering in this vicinity have been promptly returned to thier Owners. On the 15 inst I was informed by Mr M Priest that two Skiff's had been procured and took ten Women and Children acrost the River. I immediately had all the Boats collected at one point and placed them under Guard   (Since I have heard of none crossing.

Notwithstanding we are Recruitin from forty to sixty Men daily we have no runaway Women or Children around our Head. Qrs. as those who have returned have discouraged others from coming.

It would be well for me to State that 9/10 of the inhabitants are very much prejudiced against Colored Troops and Negro enlistment   they do not hesitate to throw all the obstacles in our way that they can without committing themselves. The County appears to be filled with roving Bands of Guerrillas which prevent many from coming in to Enlist. I have made ten recoinoisences since I have been here for the purpose of dispercing these marauding Bands but owing to their fleet Horses I was unable to Capture any of them but it payed me well for my trouble as it opened the way for the Colored men to come in. Col Moon left Night before last for Owensboro Ky with one hundred and forty Recruits   since He left we have Recruited one hundred an four making in all two hundred and forty four.

I have the honor to report that the discipline of this Command is strictly enforced and I have been frequently complimented for

267

the good conduct of both Officers and men by the few well disposed Persons in this vicinity. Among the number is, Ex. Gov Dixon Mr Wm S. Holloway and Mr Priest and others. Mr Dixon told one of my Officers that the Colored Troops behaved themselves better than the White Soldiers did. such a confession coming from a disinterested Person I trust will go far to show that the complaint made by Mr Ira Delano has been greatly exaggerated on account of a few Servents entering the Service.

I have told Him as well as all others in this vicinity I should be happy to have Him report any misconduct on the part of this Command and I would punish the offender's accordingly. I would be thus enabled to correct the evil. And rest assured that I shall endeavor to do my duty so as to Command the respect of my Commanding Officer's, Also the well disposed Citizens of this Place. Very Respectfully you Obt Servt

ALS   John L. Bullis

Capt. John L. Bullis to Major Genl. Burbridge, 17 Sept. 1864, Letters Received, 118th USCI, Regimental Books & Papers USCT, RG 94 [G-169]. Bullis commanded a recruitment party from the 118th USCI.

106: Affidavit of a Kentucky Black Soldier's Widow

Camp Nelson Ky 25" March 1865

Personally appeared before me J M Kelley Notary Public in and for the County of Jessamine State of Kentucky Patsey Leach a woman of color who being duly sworn according to law doth depose and say –

I am a widow and belonged to Warren Wiley of Woodford County Ky. My husband Julius Leach was a member of Co. D. 5" U.S.C. Cavalry and was killed at the Salt Works Va. about six months ago. When he enlisted sometime in the fall of 1864 he belonged to Sarah Martin Scott County Ky. He had only been about a month in the service when he was killed. I was living with aforesaid Wiley when he died. He knew of my husbands enlisting before I did but never said any thing to me about it. From that time he treated me more cruelly than ever whipping me frequently without any cause and insulting me on every occasion. About three weeks after my husband enlisted a Company of Colored Soldiers passed our house and I was there in the garden and looked at them as they passed. My master had been watching me and when the soldiers had gone I went into the kitchen. My

master followed me and Knocked me to the floor senseless saying
as he did so, "You have been looking at them darned Nigger
Soldiers" When I recovered my senses he beat me with a
cowhide When my husband was Killed my master whipped me
severely saying my husband had gone into the army to fight
against white folks and he my master would let me know that I
was foolish to let my husband go he would "take it out of my
back," he would "Kill me by picemeal" and he hoped "that the
last one of the nigger soldiers would be Killed" He whipped me
twice after that using similar expressions The last whipping he
gave me he took me into the Kitchen tied my hands tore all my
clothes off until I was entirely naked, bent me down, placed my
head between his Knees, then whipped me most unmercifully until
my back was lacerated all over, the blood oozing out in several
places so that I could not wear my underclothes without their
becoming saturated with blood. The marks are still visible on my
back. On this and other occasions my master whipped me for no
other cause than my husband having enlisted. When he had
whipped me he said "never mind God dam you when I am done
with you tomorrow you never will live no more." I knew he
would carry out his threats so that night about 10 o'clock I took
my babe and travelled to Arnolds Depot where I took the Cars to
Lexington I have five children, I left them all with my master
except the youngest and I want to get them but I dare not go
near my master knowing he would whip me again. My master is
a Rebel Sympathizer and often sends Boxes of Goods to Rebel
prisoners. And further Deponent saith not.

Her

HDcSr   Signed Patsey   Leach

mark

Affidavit of Patsey Leach, 25 Mar. 1865, filed with H-8 1865, Registered
Letters Received, ser. 3379, TN Asst. Comr., RG 105 [A-6148].

107: Affidavit of a Kentucky Black Soldier

Camp Nelson Ky November 26, 1864
Personally appered before me E. B W Restieaux Capt. and Asst.
Quartermaster Joseph Miller a man of color who being duly sworn
upon oath says
I was a slave of George Miller of Lincoln County Ky. I have
always resided in Kentucky and am now a Soldier in the service of

the United States. I belong to Company I 124 U.S.C. Inft now Stationed at Camp Nelson Ky. When I came to Camp for the purpose of enlisting about the middle of October 1864 my wife and children came with me because my master said that if I enlisted he would not maintain them and I knew they would be abused by him when I left. I had then four children ages respectively ten nine seven and four years. On my presenting myself as a recruit I was told by the Lieut. in command to take my family into a tent within the limits of the Camp. My wife and family occupied this tent by the express permission of the aforementioned Officer and never received any notice to leave until Tuesday November 22" when a mounted guard gave my wife notice that she and her children must leave Camp before early morning. This was about six O'clock at night. My little boy about seven years of age had been very sick and was slowly recovering My wife had no place to go and so remained until morning. About eight Oclock Wednesday morning November 23" a mounted guard came to my tent and ordered my wife and children out of Camp The morning was bitter cold. It was freezing hard. I was certain that it would kill my sick child to take him out in the cold. I told the man in charge of the guard that it would be the death of my boy I told him that my wife and children had no place to go and I told him that I was a soldier of the United States. He told me that it did not make any difference. he had orders to take all out of Camp. He told my wife and family that if they did not get up into the wagon which he had he would shoot the last one of them. On being thus threatened my wife and children went into the wagon My wife carried her sick child in her arms. When they left the tent the wind was blowing hard and cold and having had to leave much of our clothing when we left our master, my wife with her little one was poorly clad. I followed them as far as the lines. I had no Knowledge where they were taking them. At night I went in search of my family. I found them at Nicholasville about six miles from Camp. They were in an old meeting house belonging to the colored people. The building was very cold having only one fire. My wife and children could not get near the fire, because of the number of colored people huddled together by the soldiers. I found my wife and children shivering with cold and famished with hunger They had not recieved a morsel of food during the whole day. My boy was dead. He died directly after getting down from the wagon. I Know he was Killed by exposure to the inclement weather I had to return to camp that night so I left my family in the meeting house and walked back. I had walked there. I travelled in all twelve miles Next morning I walked to

Nicholasville. I dug a grave myself and buried my own child. I
left my family in the Meeting house – where they still
remain   And further this deponent saith not

HDcSr
                                                his
                        (Signed) Joseph   Miller
                                               mark

Affidavit of Joseph Miller, 26 Nov. 1864, filed with H-8 1865, Registered Letters Received, ser. 3379, TN Asst. Comr., RG 105 [A-6148].
Publication of this and other affidavits in the Northern abolitionist press,
together with protest through military channels, resulted in the establishment of a "refugee home" at Camp Nelson for black soldiers' families.

108: White Unionist to a Kentucky Congressman

                              Irvine Kentucky Decr. 5th 1864
Sir: The result of the Nov. Election in Ky., demonstrates the fact
to my mind that the people of Kentucky are so wedded to the
Institution of Slavery, that they will never make any disposition of
it or adopt any system of Emancipation until it is uprooted and
rendered worthless by some power capable of consumating such an
object. This can easily be done, and promote the best interest of
the Gov. in the mientime, by enlisting into the Federal service
every able bodied male slave in the state   This once accomplished;
the Masters would soon be found trying to releave themselves of
the duty (burthen they call it) of maintaining the Slave women
and children and thus the Abolition of Slavery in Kentucky would
soon be accomplished. I am satisfied that a large majority of your
Constituants would rejoice to learn that such a line of policy had
been adopted by the Administration at Washington.
    It may be claimed by the opponents of the Administration,
that, such a policy would be oppressive. Let them claim it. No
milk and Cider policy will be attended with success. If we would
be successfull in our undertaking we must adopt and closely persue
a rigorous and determined policy, adopting such measures and
employing such means as will most certainly accomplish the object
in view. I am truly your friend and Obedient Servant –
ALS   H. C. Lilly

H. C. Lilly to Hon. W. H. Randall, 5 Dec. 1864, L-349 1864, Letters
Received, ser. 360, Colored Troops Division, RG 94 [B-431]. An endorse-
ment by Congressman W. H. Randall identifies Lilly as former colonel of a
Kentucky cavalry regiment.

❦

109A: Kentucky Slaveholder to the Secretary of War

Henderson Ky. March 14th 1865.

My Dear Sir— I trust you will excuse me for thus presuming to
address you   I beg to assure you that nothing else than as I
conceive my duty & humanity towards those, who have up to the
present time, been by the laws of the land considered mine & still
look up to me as their *friend* & protector induces me to do so—   I
have then three negroes—one man & two boys, who are at this
time in Camp here, having been, as the proof very conclusively
Shews, *forced* into the Service at the *point of the bayonet & against
their free will & consent*—   If they had gone in of their own accord,
I would not have said a word, or if they had been according to
Law drafted regularly into the Service as three others of mine were
last fall, whilst I should have been sorry to have seen them go off
reluctantly, I should still have acquiesced as cheerfully & been as
obedient to the law as any other man—   But when boys that I
have raised come as these do every day now, and with tears
beseech me to see *justice* done them, I can not refuse—and
especially when I know that it is in *violation* of the law under
which it is pretended that these Boys have been enlisted that they
are held to service where they are—   It is not I assure you my
Dear Sir, in expectation of any value which their services may be
to me in future, that I am prompted to the course I take, for as
far as the relation of master & slave is concerned I consider that as
done away, tho, not one of mine has yet run away or left me of
their own accord—   But if these in whose behalf I am now writing
were to leave me as soon as released from their present condition, I
should still make the same appeal, which I trust will be
successful—

I beg then in a few words more to draw your attention to five
Statements which I very lately enclosed to Hon. Geo. H. Yeaman,
going to shew that Humphrey Charles & Richmond Green have
been as I have said above forced into the service & of course in
violation of the law made & provided in such cases—   These
Statements & affidavits—are one from the Provost Marshal, Thos.
F. Cheaney here one . . . ¹ Clay, one from M. M. Catlin, a fourth
from Dallas Snead, & lastly from one of the negroes (Humphrey to
which the other two have added theirs) themselves—   I learn from
an attorney in Louisville, that the cases of the enlistments here,
have very recently been refered to you & this is the immediate
cause of my addressing you now—   If by any means these papers to

which I have alluded should not have reached your notice, or
should be out of place, I could furnish you duplicates which I have
retained — at all events I pray you will give the matter yr
attention at as early a moment as yr convenience will allow, & if
consistent with your sense of propriety cause an order to be at once
issued directing their discharge from the service — that they may go
where they please — and to this I need add no more than that I am
very Respectfully yr ob^d Servt

E. H. Green.

Humphrey Green 35 year old, with a broken ankle.
Richmond Green 17 year old in Novr last.
Charles Green   17 "   " the present month.

ALS

E. H. Green to Hon. E. M. Stanton, 14 Mar. 1865, G-110 1865, Letters
Received, ser. 360, Colored Troops Division, RG 94 [B-148]. Endorse-
ments. The letter and affidavits mentioned as having been sent to
Congressman George Yeaman also charged that Green's three slaves had
been forced into the army against their will. (E. H. Green to Hon. Geo.
H. Yeaman, 24 Feb. 1865, and enclosures, filed as A-47 1866, Letters
Received, ser. 360, Colored Troops Division, RG 94 [B-421].)

1 Edge of letter torn; approximately three words missing.

109B: Endorsement by a Post Commander, Enclosing Affidavits of Kentucky Black Soldiers

Henderson Ky May 31st 1865.
    Respectfully forwarded. The complainant, Mr E. H. Green is
one among the many notorious Rebel sympathizers of Henderson
Ky. and a bitter enemy towards the organization of Colored
Troops. It seems from the records of this office that the men
referred to were enlisted by Leut Col J. Glenn of the 120" U.S.C.
Inf. There are no officers present who know anything concerning
the matter. Refer to affidavits herewith enclosed.

AES   Jas. N. McArthur

[Enclosure]   State of Ky Co of Henderson 30th day of May 1865
    Humphrey Green private Co "D" 120" U.S.C.I. being duly
sworn deposeth and sayeth that I was asked by Lt Col John Glenn
to enlist. I replied I had rather not, I had the rheumatisam. He
then told me he would have one of his officers put me in jail, if I

did not, and that he guessed I would enlist when I got out. I then told him I would rather enlist than be put in jail. Lt Col. Glenn gave us (myself, Richmond and Charles.) whiskey to induce us to enlist. I do not want to be discharged. I will not go back to E. H. Green. No price would induce me to go back to my master. I never went to Mr Green to ask him to get me out

HDSr

his
Humphrey X Green
mark

[*Enclosure*]   State of Ky. Co of Henderson 30th day of May 1865
Charles Green, Corp "D" Co. 120 U.S.C.I. being duly sworn deposeth and sayeth: that on or about the 20th day of January 1865, some colored soldiers came to the residence of E. H. Green, in the Co. of Hopkins State of Ky. and found me at a pond back of the house. asked me if I wished to enlist in the service. I replied "No Sir." They then said well come up town (meaning Nebo) and see the Colonel meaning Lt Col. Glenn. They then took me up to Lt Col. Glenn, who told me to fall into line which I did. He then brought me to town and put us in quarters with the other men. When Col. Glenn wanted me to enlist he had me brought up to his office. I told him I did not want to enlist. Lt Col. Glenn asked me "What in hell was the reason," I did not want to go. He then turned around to the Sergeant who stood by and told him to "take this damned nigger to the jail," that "I was but a damed Secesh nigger anyway." I then replied, "Well rather than go in jail I will join. I was mustered at Louisville by Capt Womack. I made no objection to being mustered in. I do not want now to be mustered out. I am perfectly satisfied. On or about the 18″ of May 1865, E. H. Green asked me how I was getting along, and was I satisfied I replied I was very well satisfied Mr Green then replied I am glad. I never went to Mr Green or anyone else and with tears in my eyes beseech him to see justice done me. I never cried to anyone but my mother. I would not take five hundred dollars and go back to E. H. Green as a slave

HDSr

his
Charles X Green
mark

Endorsement of Col. Jas. N. McArthur, 31 May 1865, on E. H. Green to Hon. E. M. Stanton, 14 Mar. 1865, enclosing affidavits of Humphrey Green and Charles Green, 30 May 1865, G-110 1865, Letters Received, ser. 360, Colored Troops Division, RG 94 [B-148]. Other endorsements. Affidavits sworn before the adjutant of the 120th USCI. Also enclosed is a third affidavit, by Richmond Green, which similarly denies that he went to his former master with tears in his eyes, begging to be discharged from the army. That affidavit furthermore reported no threat of jailing, but rather that he volunteered "to fight for freedom."

✑✦☙

110: Order by the Commander of the Department of Kentucky

Louisville, Kentucky, March 12, 1865.

GENERAL ORDERS, No. 10. The General commanding announces to the colored men of Kentucky that by an act of Congress passed on the 3d day of March, 1865, the wives and children of all colored men who have heretofore enlisted, or who may hereafter enlist, in the military service of the Government, are made free.

This act of justice to the soldiers claims from them renewed efforts, by courage, fortitude, and discipline, to win a good name, to be shared by a free wife and free children. To colored men not in the army it offers an opportunity to coin freedom for themselves and posterity.

The rights secured to colored soldiers under this law will, if necessary, be enforced by the military authorities of this Department, and it is expected that the loyal men and women of Kentucky will encourage colored men to enlist in the army; and, after they have done so, recognize them as upholders of their Government and defenders of their homes, and exercise toward the helpless women and children made free by law that benevolence and charity which has always characterized the people of the State. BY COMMAND OF MAJOR GENERAL PALMER:

PD

General Orders No. 10, Headquarters Department of Kentucky, 12 Mar. 1865, enclosed in Maj. Genl. John M. Palmer to Hon. E. M. Stanton, 3 Apr. 1865, K-44 1866, Letters Received, ser. 360, Colored Troops Division, RG 94 [B-263].

III: Affidavit of a Kentucky Black Soldier and His Wife

Camp Nelson Ky March 29, 1865

Personally appeared before me J M Kelley Notary Public in and for the County of Jessamine State of Kentucky William Jones a man of color who being duly sworn according to law doth depose and say—I am a soldier in the 124th U.S.C. Infty. Before enlisting I belonged to Newton Craig Scott County Ky My wife belonged to the same man. Desiring to enlist and thus free my wife and serve the Government during the balance of my days I ran away from my master in company with my wife on Saturday March 11th between nine and ten Oclock at night. Our clothes were packed up and some money we had saved from our earnings we carried with us. On our way to Camp Nelson we arrived at Lexington about Three Oclock next morning Sunday March 12" 1865 where we were accosted by the Capt of the night watch James Cannon, who asked us where we were going. I told him I was going to see my daughter He said I was a damned liar, that I was going to Camp Nelson. I then told him that I was going to Camp whereupon he arrested us, took us to the Watch House where he searched us and took our money from us taking Fifty eight (58) dollars from me and eight (8) dollars from my wife. I told him that the money was my own that I desired to have it, He told me that he would send it with the man who would take us back to our master and when we got there we should have it. I said I would rather die than go back to master who said he would kill any of his niggers who went to Camp. Cannon made no reply but locked us up in the Watch house where he kept us all that day and night and on Monday morning March 13" 1865 he sent us back to our master in charge of an armed watchman whose name I believe was Harry Smith. When we arrived at my masters master was away from home and Smith delivered us to our mistress. I asked Smith to give me my money. He said Cannon had given him none but had kept the whole to himself. I ran away from home that day before master came home. I have never received a cent of the money which Cannon took from me. I have three sons and one son-in-law now in the service of the United States. I want to get my money back. And further Deponent saith not

his
(Signed) William   Jones
mark

Marilda Jones wife of the above deponent being duly sworn upon
Oath says. I have heard the affidavit of my husband read as above
and know the Statement therein contained to be true

her

HD_cS_r   Signed   Marilda   Jones

mark

Affidavits of William Jones and Marilda Jones, 29 Mar. 1865, filed with
H-8 1865, Registered Letters Received, ser. 3379, TN Asst. Comr., RG
105 [A-6148].

112: Commander of an Army Recruitment Rendezvous to the Commander of the Department of Kentucky

Maysville, Ky., April 25 1865

Sir The civil authorities are doing all in their power to annul
Genl. Order No. 10 Head Quarters Dept. Ky. by permitting cases
to be tried, where parties have employed the wives and children of
colored soldiers made free under the provisions of said *order,* and
the courts here have in one instance given damages to the amount
of one thousand dollars ($1000.00)[1] There are in this city about
fifty (50) wives and children of soldirs who are employed by
parties who wish to keep them but cannot as they are liable to a
heavy fine for doing so under the *state decisions.*[2] These parties ask,
of me, protection. How shall I give it. Shall I arrest the party
who brings suit. The officer who serves the *writ,* the Jury who
give damages, or the Judge who charges the Jury to find damages

The effect of these decissions is to drive every person from the
State who claim freedom under the order. I am Genl. Very
Respectfully Your Obedient Servt.

ALS   W. A. Gage

Lieut. Col. W. A. Gage to Maj. Genl. J. M. Palmer, 25 Apr. 1865,
G-137 1865, Letters Received, ser. 2173, Dept. of KY, RG 393 Pt. 1
[C-4329]. Endorsement.

1 Kentucky's slave code, like that of other slave states, made it illegal to
hire a slave without the master's consent. By applying that law to the
employers of black soldiers' wives and children, the civil authorities controverted the freedom of the soldiers' families.
2 A decision by State Circuit Judge L. W. Andrews in late March 1865
denied the power of the U.S. Congress to liberate slaves in Kentucky and

277

declared unconstitutional the joint resolution of March 3, 1865, that had freed the wives and children of black soldiers. The case arose in the following manner: after passage of the congressional resolution, the slave wife of a black soldier left her master and secured employment with another white man. The "master," represented by U.S. Senator Garrett Davis, thereupon sued her new employer in the state courts. Judge Andrews rejected the employer's plea that the woman was free under the resolution of Congress and rendered judgment against him, levying a fine and requiring return of the woman to slavery. General John M. Palmer, commander of the Department of Kentucky, reported this decision to the Secretary of War, informing him that most of Kentucky's circuit judges, as well as those on the state's highest court, would no doubt follow Judge Andrews's interpretation. Palmer sought the "views and wishes" of the War Department but proposed to "see that the particular woman adjudged by Judge Andrews to be a slave is put beyond his control." In the meantime, Palmer continued to enforce the congressional joint resolution: he ordered the arrest of "all persons who forcibly restrain the wives and children of enlisted men of their liberty" and even jailed two masters who were charged with beating black soldiers' wives. (Maj. Genl. John M. Palmer to Hon. E. M. Stanton, 3 Apr. 1865, enclosing undated clipping from *Cincinnati Enquirer,* K-44 1866, Letters Received, ser. 360, Colored Troops Division, RG 94 [B-263].

5

Confederate Recruitment

FROM THE BEGINNING of the war, a few Southern blacks and whites advocated enlistment of black freemen and slaves into the Confederate army.[1] As in the North, some black freemen hoped to gain new privileges by aiding the dominant class in its moment of crisis. Lower South free people of color, with a long tradition of military service, petitioned for enrollment, and both New Orleans and Mobile enlisted them in Native Guard units.[2] But Southern whites did not extend to their slaves the same prerogative of bearing arms offered to a select group of free blacks. If by arming free blacks Lower South Confederates hoped to retain the loyalty of their society's middle caste, they initially harbored few illusions about thus ensuring the fidelity of the slaves. Indeed, most whites feared that making slaves soldiers would swell black aspirations for freedom and fuel slave unrest. Still, while dismissing notions about wholesale slave enlistment, some whites reasoned that selective enrollment of a few blacks in every Confederate regiment promised not racial equality but the opportunity to remove the most dangerous bondsmen from the countryside. Somewhat inconsistently, they added that sending black soldiers against the enemy would teach the "nigger-loving" Yankees a lesson about the South's peculiar institution and the loyalty of the slaves. Although Confederate leaders routinely rejected requests to enlist black soldiers, they took special delight in observing that slaves would gladly defend their masters.

In the summer of 1863, the Northern decision to recruit blacks not only within the free states but also among the South's slaves renewed Confederate interest in black enlistment. With defeat at

---

[1]   Published works on Confederate recruitment include: Nathaniel W. Stephenson, "The Question of Arming Slaves," *American Historical Review* 18 (Jan. 1913): 295–308; Charles H. Wesley, "Employment of Negroes as Soldiers in the Confederate Army," *Journal of Negro History* 4 (July 1919): 239–53; James M. McPherson, *The Negro's Civil War: How American Negroes Felt and Acted During the War for the Union* (New York, 1965), pp. 241–44; Robert F. Durden, *The Gray and the Black: The Confederate Debate on Emancipation* (Baton Rouge, La., 1972).

[2]   *Official Records*, ser. 1, vol. 15, pp. 556–57; ser. 4, vol. 1, pp. 1087–88, and vol. 2, pp. 197, 941. See also the muster rolls of the Louisiana Native Guard, Muster & Pay Rolls, ser. 18, Adjt. & Insp. Gen., RG 109 [F-600].

Gettysburg, the fall of Vicksburg, and the steady decimation of rebel ranks, some Confederate patriots lost patience with those who would give their sons but not their slaves to the fight for Southern independence. Convinced that black enlistment provided the only means to preserve the Confederacy, they brushed aside the notion that black slaves could not or would not fight and instead insisted that the slave experience and the peculiar physiological and psychological character of black people would make them ideal soldiers. Besides, if the South did not utilize slave soldiers, the North had already demonstrated that it would.

Slave enlistment also offered an antidote to growing dissension within the Confederacy. The nearly universal draft of nonslaveholding whites and the exemption of planters and their overseers under the so-called "twenty-nigger" law angered yeoman soldiers. Knowledge that their wives and children lacked food and protection compounded their battlefield frustrations. During 1863 and 1864, nonslaveholders deserted in growing numbers. Some Southerners advocated enlisting slaves as a means of dispelling yeoman unrest by allowing some soldiers to return home and ease the subsistence crisis. To ensure the loyalty of the disenchanted yeomanry, others went even further. One Alabama farmer proposed that each Confederate soldier be given a slave who would be a servant in camp and a comrade in battle.

The manifest absurdity of this proposition demonstrated the inevitable link between black enlistment and emancipation. As the debate over the transformation of slaves into soldiers grew more intense, so too did the discussion of making bondsmen into freemen. Confederate interest in emancipation coincided with hopes that liquidation of slavery might bring European recognition and military intervention. These concerns impelled a few Southern leaders to think the previously unthinkable. In January 1864, some officers of the Army of Tennessee, led by General Patrick R. Cleburne, suggested that the Confederacy might transform weakness into strength by freeing and enlisting slaves.[3] The proposal never received a full hearing, but the same desperate shortage of manpower that Cleburne faced in the field soon forced the Confederate leadership in Richmond to pursue a similar course. In November 1864, Confederate President Jefferson Davis called for the enlistment of slaves and a "radical modification" of the status of blacks in Southern society.[4] Observing that slaves could hardly be expected to fight in Confederate service with only the promise of future freedom when simply crossing into Union lines would secure liberty, other Confederate

[3] *Official Records*, ser. 1, vol. 50, pt. 2, pp. 586–92.
[4] *Official Records*, ser. 4, vol. 3, pp. 797–99.

leaders stripped away the ambiguity of Davis's call and urged immediate freedom upon enlistment.

The debate over black enlistment within the Confederacy forced
Southern leaders, as it had earlier forced Northern policy makers, to
consider the possibility of emancipation. Some former defenders of
slavery, like J. H. Stringfellow, recognized the inevitability of emancipation and considered how planters could maintain their position
without slaves. In so doing, they not only confirmed the importance
of blacks to the Union war effort, but also set forth a scheme of
reconstruction in which blacks would gain legal freedom, perhaps
fighting for the Confederacy, but little else. "If we emancipate,"
Stringfellow assured Jefferson Davis early in 1865, "our independence is secured, the white man only will have any, and all political
rights, retain all his real and personal property, exclusive of his
property in his slave, make the laws to control the free negro, who
having no land, must labor for the land owner; and being an adequate *supply of labor,* must work for the land owner on terms about
as economical as tho owned by him."

Still, opposition to black recruitment remained intense. But in
February 1865, when General Robert E. Lee openly endorsed Davis's plea, public opinion turned sharply.[5] To strengthen his hand,
Lee invited soldiers in the Army of Northern Virginia to register
their opinion as to the advisability of recruiting slaves and to express
their position about fighting alongside blacks. In the plebiscite that
followed, Confederate officers expressed nearly universal support for
Lee's position. Enlisted men, anxious for able bodies of almost any
description to reinforce their depleted ranks and pushed to the point
of desperation sustaining the South's bid for independence, supported the measure with equal enthusiasm. Though some harbored
fears about the future role of blacks in Southern society, they expressed confidence in General Lee's ability to decide what was best
for the cause.

Thus, in the end if not in the beginning, some Southern whites
linked black liberty to their own independence. Still, the Confederate Congress vacillated. Finally, only a month before final defeat,
the legislature authorized black enlistments, and Davis, by executive
authority, provided means by which slave recruits would gain their
liberty.[6] But if white soldiers connected their freedom from Yankee

---

[5] Durden, *The Gray and the Black,* chap. 7; *Official Records,* ser. 4, vol. 3, pp.
1012–13; for rumors that the Confederate army had already begun accepting
blacks, see 1' Lt. Samuel Miller to Capt. P. F. Young, 9 Nov. 1864, Letters
Received & Other Papers of the Provost Marshal, ser. 1599, Post of Fernandina,
RG 393 Pt. 4 [C-364].

[6] *Official Records,* ser. 4, vol. 3, pp. 1161–62.

thralldom to black emancipation, blacks suffered no such confusion. Few joined the ranks of the failing Confederacy.

113: Alabama Farmer to the Confederate President

The State of Ala. Monroe County Bells Ldg May th 4 /1861
Dear Sir i havs to in form you that thire is a good meny pore men with large famely to susport An if they have to go in to the Army there famelys will sufer   thire is a Nother question to rise with us the Negroes is very Hiley Hope up that they will soon Be free so i think that you Had Better order out All the Negroe felers from 17 years oald up   Ether fort them up or put them in the army and Make them fite like good fells for wee ar in danger of our lives hear among them   So i Will close with my Best love to you
ALS   Wm H Lee

Wm. H. Lee to J. Davis, 4 May 1861, #957 1861, Letters Received, ser. 5, Sec. War, RG 109 [F-33].

114: Confederate Patriot to the Confederate Secretary of War

Athens Ga 4th May 1861
Dear Sir

. . . .

Some of our people are fearful that when a large portion of our fighting men are taken from the country, that large numbers of our negroes aided by emissaries will ransack portions of the country, kill numbers of our inhabitants, and make their way to the black republicans; There is no doubt but that numbers of them believe that Lincoln's intention is to set them all free. Then, to counteract this idea, and make them assist in whipping the black republicans, which by the by would be the best thing that could be done, could they not be incorporated into our armies, say ten or twenty placed promiscuously in each company? In this way there number would be too small to do our army any injury, whilst they might be made quite efficient in battle, as there are a great many I have no doubt that would make good soldiers and would willingly go if they had a chance. They might be valued as you would a horse or other property, and let the government pay for them provided they was killed in battle, and it should be made

known to them that if they distinguish[d] themselves by good
conduct in battle, they should be rewarded. Could some plan of
this sort be thought expedient and be carried out with propriety,
it would certainly lessen the dangers at home, and increase our
strength in the field, and would I have but little doubt, be
responded to by large numbers of our people in all the States. It
is however only a suggestion, but one that I have thought might
merit your consideration. Very Respectfully your humble Servant
ALS   John J. Cheatham

Excerpt from John J. Cheatham to Hon. L. P. Walker, 4 May 1861,
#605 1861, Letters Received, ser. 5, Sec. War, RG 109 [F-127]. The
omitted portion warns of the danger to Confederate ports from the Union's
use of floating batteries.

115: Arkansas Slaveholder to the Confederate Secretary of War

Helena Ark   July 17.th 1861 –
Dr Sir   I wrote you A few days Since, for myself & many Others
in this district – to ascertain if we could get Negroe
Regiments – Recvd. for Confederate Service – officered of course By
White *Men,* all we ask is *arms, Clothes* & provision[s] – & usual pay
for Officer[s] & not one cent pay, for *negroe*[s] –   our negroe[s] are too
good – to fight – Lincoln hirelings – but as they pretend to Love
negroe[s] – so much – we Want to show them – how much – the *true
Southern* Cotton *patch* negro Love them in RETURN   The North
Cannot complain at this –   they proclaim Negro equality from the
Senate Chamber – to the pulpit & teach it in their school[s], & are
doing all they can To turn the Slaves – upon Master, Mr[s] &
children –   & now Sir – if you can Receive the negroe[s] – that Can be
Raised – we Will Soon give the Northern theives a gorge of the
Negroe[s] – Love for them – *that* will never – be forgotten
   You well know – I have had Long epperience With
negro – character –   I am satisfied they Are Easy disciplined &
Less – trouble than whites In Camp – & will fight desperately as
Long As – they have a single *white* officer – Living –   I know one
Man that will furnish & arm one Hundred of his own & his son
for their Capt –   The Sooner we bring a strong negro force against
the hirelings – the Sooner we Shall Have peace in my humble
Judgement,
   Let me hear from you. yr. old friend
ALS   W. S. Turner

W. S. Turner to Hon. L. P. Walker, 17 July 1861, vol. 1, Documents
Printed in *The War of the Rebellion*, ser. 4, General Records CSA, RG 109
[F-150]. While noting that during the American Revolution "Washington,
himself, recommended the enlistment of two negro Regiments in Georgia,"
and that "almost every slave would cheerfully aid his master, in the work
of hurling back the fanatical Invader," the Confederate assistant secretary of
war rejected Turner's offer on the grounds that there was a "Superabun-
dance of our own color, tendering their services to the Government. . . ."
(A. T. Bledsoe to W. Y. Turner, 2 Aug. 1861, ch. IX, vol. 1, pp. 732–
33, Letters Sent, Sec. War, RG 109 [F-201].)

116: Mississippi Slaveholder to the Confederate President

Louisville Miss July 20th /63

Dear Sir   Visburg is gone and as a consequence Mississippi is
gone and in the opinion of allmost every one here the Confederacy
is gone. I can myself see but one chance, but one course to
pursue to save it, and I fear it is now too late for even that to
check the tide that is overwhelming us. It is simply by your own
authority, and without waiting for congress to give you authority,
to call out every able bodied *Negro* man from the age of sixteen to
fifty years old. They will go readily and cheerfully. The owners
would gladly give them up and afford every facility in getting
them off. On every road leading from the western Country there
is a constant stream of negroes running into Ala & Georgia & the
Carolinas. They will destroy all the food in those states like an
army of locusts. This if nothing else would starve us into
subjection in a few months   It is precisly what our enemy
want. Take our nego men away and thereby relieve us of a
dangerous element. Force the young white men, who are running
off with them, into the army and we, the old men will take care
of the negro women and children and make corn. Act
promptly   the negro men will all go to the enemy if not taken to
our own army   I believe fully half of them had rather go into our
ranks than the Yankees   They want to be in the frollick & they
will be one way or the other. Away with all squeamesness about
employing negroes in civilized warfare. Our enemies are doing it
as rappidly as they can and we are left no other alternative. – If
you knew with what pleasure I would send off every negro man I
have tomorrow morning you would not dismiss this hastily. I am
only one of the masses and what I say I believe nearly every slave

holder in the South would say and do. With the highest
considerations of respect I am verry truly youre friend.
ALS   O G Eiland

O. G. Eiland to President Davis, 20 July 1863, B-581 1863, Letters Received, ser. 5, Sec. War, RG 109 {F-122}. Endorsement.

117: Georgia Slaveholder to the Confederate President

Fairburn Geo July 29th /63

Dear Sir: I propose to make a suggestion to you, upon which, if
you have not already thought, your wisdom will readily perceive
the importance, and practicability of it.

Viewing the very alarming condition of our country; the success,
that has very recently attended the movements of the enemy,
together with our increasing weakness, makes it clear to my mind
that something *else* must be done. It is doubly true, that you have
done more than the world could have reasonably expected — all
things considered. It is no less evident, however, that much more
remains to be done, and that in less time. Every State of this
Confederacy is now invaded, every family, very nearly, bereaved of
some of its most precious inmates, all the young men now in the
field, many old ones there, and more called for; and after all that
are called for shall have been mustered in, even then, our army
will be much less than the one we have to meet. When we view
these things in an impartial light, we are forced to conclude that
the Confederacy must *go down,* or our army must be increased and
that largely. Where is the increase to spring from? Our white
population will so soon be exhausted. — We are shut out from all
the world beside, and instead of receiving help from other nations,
we cannot get the simple boon of recognition. Then, it seems
clear to me, that we are forced to call out the black male
population from 18 to 45 or 50 years. What is the use, or how
would it enhance our future greatness, to kill up all the white
male population and leave the country thronged with women, and
none to protect them, but a few old men? How shocking must be
the spectacle to those who look to the rising generation, to behold
a vast country peopled by live women, and *dead men.* The
patriotic men of the south have given up all their sons, and why
not give up their negroes. They have lost some of their sons, and
will loose all their negros if we are subjugated. The enemy has

marched his black soldiers down upon us, and many of them the property of those against whom they are sent to fight, – let us meet him upon his own principle. Put the hardy black man into the army, by squads in each company already formed. – Let them be place under the men from their own states, counties & districts, – than they will be under men who know them, and can control them in a way that will render them very useful to the army.

I have conversed with many of our wealthy farmers who are willing, *yea anxious* to put their negroes into the war. They donot wish to leave their negros at home rolling in their fat while their sons are suffering for their country. The crys from suffering widows and orphans demand it, humanity, in behalf of our bleeding country, calls loudly for help, *and there is no other help.* I make these suggestions with all due regard for your excellency's judgement, and should you not regard them as worthy of notice, I shall be content to let it pass unnoticed – Hoping that you will not regard me over presumptious I subscribe myself, Yr's Respectfully

ALS   J. H. M. Barton

J. H. M. Barton to President Davis, 29 July 1863, B-588 1863, Letters Received, ser. 5, Sec. War, RG 109 [F-74]. Confederate Secretary of War James A. Seddon noted in an endorsement that "several of such papers have been rec'd."

118: Georgia Farmer to the Confederate President

                              Greenville Merriwether Co Ga Septr 16th '64
Mr President. Is it not time now to enlist the negroes? I have been in favor of it ever since the enemy commenced it, & have feared no effort would be made on our side until it was too late. It is now our only resource to augment the army. – My plan is to conscribe them & force them into the army, all between Sixteen & fifty-five, upon the condition, if necessary, of freedom after the war. I have not been alarmed until now. I assure you Sir. that if the question were put to the people of this state whether to continue the war or return to the union, a large majority would vote for a return – I am almost inclined to believe that they would do it if *emancipation* was the *condition*. It occurs to me if you will call congress together & pass a bill to raise a negro force of two or even one hundred thousand, it would have a good effect upon the election at the North, if nothing more –

Has Congress & the authorities ever had this subject under consideration? I learn our army is falling back to Macon! In a very short time every able bodied negro in the abandoned section will either be a Soldier in the yankee army or employed in some way to contribute to our destruction. It seems to me this subject is well worthy your consideration if it is not now too late to do anything— I fear it is— Sir I am seriously alarmed! The cries of Starving women & children will make cowards of us all. — The policy of Sherman is to crowd our people together in the lower part of the State until want drives us to terms.

By Christmas he will have an army of fifty thousand negroes in his army— ought we not to hold on to all the territory we can until the drafting season is over— Their large bounties & the promise of freedom, will put all our negroes into their army   Your &c

ALS   F. Kendall

F. Kendall to Mr. President, 16 Sept. 1864, K-73 1864, Letters Received, ser. 5, Sec. War, RG 109 [F-125]. Endorsement.

119: **Confederate Governor of Louisiana to the Confederate President**

Shreveport, La., Sep. 26 1864

My Dear Sir   Your letter of the 1st ultimo is only received today. Hastening to reply, I have the honor to inform you that your disposition of the matter relating to my State officers, sought to be transferred, is entirely satisfactory. Some time ago I turned over to Gen. E. Kirby Smith all my State forces and I am doing all I can to 'hold up his hands' & strengthen the confederacy. That officer has done, and he is still doing, all in his power to develope the military resources of the Dept & render them available whenever & wherever resistance to invasion shall be needed or a blow can be given.

I fully appreciate, My Dear Sir, all you say in regard to the urgent need of troops in Virginia & Georgia, & would most cheerfully lend my influence to send you aid from this Department, if we could possibly spare them. Since the date of your letter the enemy have been constantly & steadily reinforcing their several commands west of the Mississippi, until they have at present thirty-five thousand troops in Arkansas and ten thousand in Louisiana   Already they have crossed the Atchafalaya and we are this day Skirmishing with their advance columns. I consider that the movement of Price & Magruder into Arkansas & Missouri has already saved Mobile & perhaps Hood's Army for it has drawn this large force from the East Bank of the Miss. River to this side.

We expect to give you a good account of ourselves in the coming contest which bids fair to be a most active fall campaign. Our troops and people are in fine spirits & more determined than ever to Submit to no compromises whatever, but to fight the war out.

The time has come for us to put into the army every able-bodied negro man as a soldier. This should be done immediately. Congress should at the coming session take action on this most important question. The negro knows that he cannot escape conscription if he goes to the enemy. He must play an important part in this war. He caused the fight & he will have his portion of the burden to bear. We have learned from dear-bought experience that negroes can be taught to fight & that all who leave us are made to fight against us. I would free all able to bear arms & put them into the field at once. They will make much better soldiers with us than against us & swell the now depleted ranks of our armies. — I beg you to give this your earnest attention.

With assurance of my friendly regard & very high esteem, I remain very respectfully yr obt St

HLS   Henry W. Allen

Gov. Henry W. Allen to Hon. James A. Seddon, 26 Sept. 1864, enclosed in Major General Ed. R. S. Canby to Major General H. W. Halleck, 12 Oct. 1864, C-610 1864, Letters Received by General Grant, ser. 105, Headquarters in the Field, RG 108 [S-35]. Endorsement. Allen's letter had been intercepted by Union forces at St. Joseph, La.

120: **Alabama Farmer to the Confederate President**

Autaugaville ala Oct 25th 1864.

Honered Sir   let me Drop in my views as regards our negro strength   it seams to me we might make them very available in this war if they were properly placed in the servis   I dont think it would work well to put them in as co & redgiment but mix them & the Best weigh to do that would be to impress every male slave betwen the age of 18 & 45 years of age [for] & during there natural life without any compensation allowing each owner to

288

reserve [one] of his choice   Then give to each soldier in the confedracey a negro man to be his property [&] let that slave be his servant in camp & in batle to be a soldier by his masters side & by thus doing I think every negro would do good fighting & it would interest many of our soldier in slavery & they too would feal better & fight better & stop deserting & stragling for most of men must have a dollar & cent view of matters to give them energy & action coupled on to Liberty   you can see from what I have hear said what I mean for in my umble opinion your superiors nover has lived   Your umble servant

ALS   Theodore Nunn

Theodore Nunn to Jeff. Davis, 25 Oct. 1864, N-79 1864, Letters Received, ser. 5, Sec. War, RG 109 [F-120]. Endorsement. The left margin is tattered, obliterating a few letters.

121: South Carolina Farmer to the Confederate Secretary of War

Fountain pond SC octre 25th /64

Sir   I have had it in contemplation of writing you for some time on various subjects of favoritisms abuses of public trusts reforms needed &.c. but being an humble and private individual I have been detered from doing so till the present time   I have concluded to make the venture.

the first thing I have on my mind is the subject of arming and puting in service our negroes   I for one have been in favor of that measure and have advocated it for the last twelve months   lately I have seen in some of the newspapers the outlines of a bill to be offered at the next session of our Congress for this purpose   I hope it will be carried through at once and I would advocate a called session of our congress to take action on the matter as soon as possible   I see by the outlines of the bill proposed that all able Bodied negroes from 18 to 45 years of age be conscripted and put in service   I hope this will be done without any exemptions whatever for this reason   the man that has but one negroe fellow is as much interested as the man that has one hundred   let none be exempt Mechanics or artizans of any Description   we have a law in this state where a man owns one road hand that hand is exempt from being sent to work on our fortifications on our coast   the result of that law is I know of several men that owned

289

two or three or more road hands to hire them out and divide them out in such away as to evade the law and send no hands to work on our fortifications   hence the injustice of alowing any exemptions whatever   besides it is fair to presume and I know it to be so that where there is one negroe fellow on a place there is younger negroes woman and children &c —

the next thing that has lay on my mind for a long time is the abuses and favoritisms of the conscription Bureaus of the country and enrolling offices &.c. at the vilages all over the country assesors tax collectors &c —   I have in my minds eye at this time of one assesors office where there are three able Bodied men fit for service when one old man and a decriped soldier could do the work   also of an enrolling office where there are five or six stout able bodied men   one a soldier on a wooden leg could do the work besides able stout men stuck in soft places at every village in the country   their places could be filled by old men and decriped soldiers   I now think of another case or cases   quarter masters commisaries and men runing about over the country as pressing officers hunting up supplies &.c. all of which could and should be done by disabled soldiers &c   these abuses should be remedied and that instantly or we are a gone people   what does the poor soldier say trudging suffering and fighting through this war   my family at home suffering while my rich neighbor with his thirty or forty negroes and fine plantations faring sumptously every day or stuck in some solft place and has never as much as lifted a finger in support of this cruel war   to my knowledge there are such cases   they have skulked out one way or another

one other matter and I have done for this time and that is in regard to prisners   I would if I had my way parole and send through our lines the last yankee prisner we hold except the officers and a few prominent men   they would do us more good to be sent home than a hard fought battle & a great victory   my word for it they would not return to fight us   besides thousands of them would take the oath and fall into our ranks and fight for us   besides I would rather fight what few might return than to feed them   these are my sentiments and I have to say that I have suffered as much and lost as much by this war ans any man in this district and am still as ready as any man to carry it through to a succesful end. I am yours most respectfully &c

Wᵐ McNeely

PS. if you wish any references I refer you to Col. E P Jones agt SC res richmond va   Senator orr from this congressional Dist Honl James Farrow W. D. Simpson

ALS

Wm. McNeely to Honl. Jas. A. Seddon, 25 Oct. 1864, M-537 1864, Letters Received, ser. 5, Sec. War, RG 109 [F-118].

122: Proslavery Theorist to the Confederate President

Glenn Allen   Henrico [*Va.*]   Feby 8th 1865
My dear Sir   Impelled by the perils of our country, and the thousand conflicting theories as to the cause, and cure; to continually have these things before me; I have been amazed to see, that no one thus far has concieved, or if concieved, had the boldness to present in my judgment, the only solution of all these perils and difficulties.   I address you because you have already taken a long stride in the right direction & because I believe your mind has already reached the true solution, but owing to peculiar circumstances has hesitated to enunciate it.   The history of this war demonstrates the wonderfull fact, that the Confederate states mainly subsists both of the immense armies engaged in the conflict, and actually after furnishishing *all* the soldiers to our army, contributes about one half of those making the army of its enemies, and should the war continue for annother year, the south will probably furnish *two thirds* of the army of her foes.   These facts which cannot be controverted show certainly any thing but *weakness, or inferiority* on the part of the south; but it does show that a change of policy in relation to the conduct of the war, and that a radical one must be adopted, or we shall be destroyed.   Let us look at a few facts.   The Yankees have now in their service 200 000 of our ex-slaves, and under their next draft, will probably have half as many more.   We have not *one* soldier from that source in our ranks.   It is held by us that *slaves* will not make soldiers, therefore we refuse to put them in the service & I think are correct in so doing.   But while we thus think, and thus act, our enemies are creating, in addition to their *white force which we have found to our cost in the last year, to be quite as large as we could manage,* an auxiliary army of our own escaped slaves, of three or four hundred thousand men.   Now however we may decry the negro as a soldier every one knows that if the white troops of the yankees are numerous enough to hold all ours in check, then this negro army can, at will, ravage and destroy our whole country, and we will be absolutely conquered by our own slaves.   We allege that *slaves* will not fight in our armies, escaped slaves fight & fight bravely for our enemies, therefore a freed Slave will fight.   If at the begining

of this war, all our negroes had been free, does any one believe the Yankees would have been able to recruit an army amongst them, does any one know of a solitary free negro escaping to them and joining their army. If our slaves were *now* to be freed would the Yankees be able to raise another recruit amongst them? If freedom and amnesty were declared in favour of those already in the Yankee lines, would they not almost to a man desert to their old homes? Would not our *freed* negroes make us as good soldiers as they make for our enemies? Again suppose we free a portion of our slaves & put them in the army, we leave *all the rest* as a recruiting field for the enemy, from which we cannot get a single soldier and thus we see one half of our *entire* population of no avail to us, but on the contrary ready at every oportunity to join the ranks of our enemies. Now sir Southern soldiers are the best that ever drew a blade in the cause of liberty, but there are some things which *they* cannot do; they cannot fight our battles against overwhelming numbers, and raise the necessary supplies for the army and the women and children at home, and yet sir this is what they will be called upon to do if this war is protracted for two years longer. I ask sir then in view of these *facts* if the prompt abolition of slavery, will not prove a remedy sufficient to arrest this tide of disaster? The Yankee army will be diminished by it, our own army can be increased by it & our labour retained by it. Without it, if the war continues, we shall in the end be subjugated, our negroes emancipated, our lands parcelled out amongst them, and if any of it be left to us, only an equal portion with our own negroes, and ourselves given only equal (if any) social and political rights and privileges. If we emancipate, our independence is secured, the white man only will have any, and all political rights, retain all his real and personal property, exclusive of his property in his slave, make the laws to controll the freed negro, who having no land, must labor for the land owner; and being an adequate *supply of labor,* must work for the land owner on terms about as economical as tho owned by him.

We cannot consent to reconstruction even if they repeal all their laws, and withdraw all their proclamations in regard to us, our Lands & our Negroes, because they now have, or at any session of their congress can make the necessary number of states, to alter the Constitution, in a constitutional manner, and thus abolish slavery, and interfere in any other way they think proper. But even if the present administration should pledge any thing we may ask, it binds no one but themselves, during their own term of service, which you of course understand better than I do and suppose they should even promise and stand by their promise to pay us for our negroes, lost or to be emancipated, how will they pay us. They cannot by direct taxation, but only in levying an export duty on our products, Cotton, Tobacco & Naval stores: and this war has shown them & the world, if not us, how much they will bear, Cotton commanding one dollar pr pound, Tobacco three dollars, Tar two hundred dollars pr Barrel &c &c. To pay their war debt & for our negroes would make a debt of six (thousand) millions or probably eight the interest of which at five pr ct, would take four hundred millions of revenue to pay, and to raise something additional to extinguish the principal, would require an additional hundred million, thus you see an export duty to this extent would be levied & could easily be raised upon our own products; twenty cents upon cotton which would make the price about 32 or 33 cts, the world would pay, because they must have it & have bought it for much more, would bring an annual income of about four hundred million without countg the duty on Tobacco & Naval Stores but even with this most favorable view of the case we should loose the whole of our own war debt which is or will be say two thousand million   of course this would be repudiated & justly by our enemies if we consent to reconstruction   Whereas if *we* emancipate we save the two thousand million, & we can pay for the negroes four thousand million more, and the export duty on cotton alone (which we should have levied if we go back into the Union) will pay the interest upon this at 5 pr ct and leave a hundred million as a sinking fund to extinguish the principal in some 30 or 40 years & the slave owner have all his labour on his farm that he had before; (for having no home & no property to buy one with, he must live with & work for his old owner for such wages as said owner may choose to give, to be regulated by law hereafter as may suit the change of relation)   And this six thousand million is not a debt we tax ourselves to pay, but the world pays it. The speculator who buys the cotton & pays the duty, makes the manufacturer pay him his ten or fifteen pr ct nett profit on his gross outlay, the manufacturer makes the merchant pay him his ten or fifteen pr ct on his gross outlay, the merchant charges the retail dealer his ten or fifteen pr ct on his gross outly, and so on till the *shirt* is made *and he who wears it out pays the duty & all the diferent pr centages upon it.* Thus *we* will pay to the extent of our consumption of the exported article when manufactured & returned to us, a mere nothing when compared to the immense gratuity, six thousand million which the World makes to us, & which they so justly should be made to hand over to us, for the cold blooded, heartless indifferance with which thay have contemplated the bloody,

293

inhuman, barbarous, and apparently hopeless contest in which we have been engaged, and which they at any moment could have arrested by a word.

By emancipation I think we would not only render our triumph secure as I have attempted to prove, in & of itself but in all future time the negro in place of being useless in time of war as a soldier, & really dangerous as we have seen to our cost, continues to be an element of strength. And I think we may *reasonably* hope that the nations of the earth would no longer be unwilling to recognise us, for surely no people ever before strugled so long, and under so many dificulties, and endured so many privations so uncomplainingly as we have without finding some friendly hand outstretched to encourage or to help; and there can be no other reason than that we are exclusively & peculiarly a nation of slaveholders. I think that even amongst our enemies numbers would be added to those who are already willing to let us go in peace, for we should thus give the lie at once & forever to the charge that we are waging a war only for negro slavery, and the heart of ever honest lover of human liberty throughout the world would sumpathise with the men who for their cherished rights as freemen, would wage such an unequal contest as we have waged & besides sacrefising all their earnest convictions as to the humanity & righteousness of slavery were willing to sacrefice their property interest of four thousand millions to secure their independence, which might all be saved so far as the *promises* of our enemies are concerned, by reconstruction. In my judgement, the only question for us to decide, is whether we shall gain our independence by freeing the negro, we retaining all the power to regulate them by law when so freed, or permit our enemies through our own slaves to compell us to submit to Emancipation with equal or superior political rights for our negroes and partial or complete confiscation of our property for the use & benefit of the negro And sir if the war continues as it is now waged, and we are forced, by the overwhelming odds of the Yankees and our own slaves in arms against us, into submission it would be but an act of simple justice for the Yankee Govt to see to it that their negro allies are at least as *well* provided for in the way of homes, as those who have been arrayed in arms against them.

I have always believed & still believe that slavery is an institution sanctioned if not established by the Almighty and the most humane & beneficial relation that can exist between Labor & Capital, still I think that this contest has proven that in a military sense it is an element of weakness & the teachings of providence as exhibited in this war dictates conclusively & imperitively that *to*

secure & perpetuate our independence we must emancipate the negro.
P.S. We should then get rid of the only impediment in the way
of an exchange of prisoners thus getting 30 or 40 thousand more
men in the field

I have given you what I conceive to be the only solution to our
dificulties. How to effect this is a serious difficulty. Men are
reluctant, in fact it might be imprudent, to discuss this thing
publickly; but we know that in great crises men think & act
rapidly, or at least should do so. If congress could be convinced of
the correctness of this course they could in Convention with the
Governors of the States devise some method, by which conventions
of the states could be held and the necessary measures adopted;
first by law of Congress if necessary provide for paying the owners
for them   I have not found a single slave holder with whom I
have conversed but is willing to submit to the measure if deemed
necessary by the proper Authorities   Indeed I have no doubt of
the power of Congress as a military necessity, to impress all of the
able bodied male negroes & pay for them giving them their
freedom & providing for paying for the rest upon the condition of
manumission, but the other course would be least
objectionable   We burn an individuals cotton, corn or meat to
keep it from the enemy so we can take his negro man & set him
free to keep him from recruiting the enemys army.

I have written you this much, hoping it may aid you in some
way. I have shown what I have written to no one, nor
communicated my intentions to any one. If you think what I have
written worth anything, make what use of if you chose, if not just
stick it between the bars of your g[rate.] What I have written is
with an [honest] endeavour to aid you in guiding our ship through
the perils & darkness which surround her & from no feeling of
dissatisfaction or distrust as to yourself, for you have all my
sympathies & all of my trust & confidence   With diffidence & the
warmest admiration & Respect I remain Your friend

                                                      J H Stringfellow
Written very hurriedly & with no effort at arrangement but only
as "food for thought"   JHS

I opened the envelope to say that my communication was
written before I heard of the return of our commissioners, & that I
am more than sustained by their report, and the action of the
Yankee Congress on the slavery question, & now we have only to
decide on or between *Emancipation for our independence,* or
Subjugation & Emancipation coupled with negro equality or
superiority, as our enemies may elect   JHS
ALS

J. H. Stringfellow to [Jefferson Davis], 8 Feb. 1865, S-57 1865, Letters Received, ser. 5, Sec. War, RG 109 [F-128]. Endorsement. A marginal notation instructs President Davis to read the last postscript first.

123: Commander of an Alabama Confederate Regiment to the Headquarters of the Confederate Army of Northern Virginia

Hd. Qrs. 15th Ala. Regt [*Va.*] Feb 14th 1865

Col   With this find a paper which in a great degree explains itsself. It is the work of the enlisted men alone and was handed to me after they had signed it. I then submited it to the Officers all of whom who are present with the Regt signed it. There are present for duty two hundred effective men   out of that number you will see that one hundred and forty three signed this paper and of that hundred & forty three and to whose names are annexed cross marks there are eighty eight (88) men who are willing to take the negroes in the ranks with them. The Officers present all consent to takeing them in ranks. The man who sent me the paper tells me that several more would have signed if they had thought it would have any effect towards brining about the desired object of puting the negroes in the army. Thinking that Gen[l]. R. E. Lee might like to get all the information he could as to the feeling in the Army on this subject, I concluded to have a copy of the paper made for his use and send it to you with the request that you hand it to him   Some of the congressmen seem to be very tender[foot?]ed on this point but I think here is the evidence that at least one Regt means political independence at any price. It is due that I should state that the eighty eight men who are willing to take the negroes in the ranks are among the best men in the Regt. Many of them are young men of good families in point both of position and property. I am satisfied that there are Two other Regts in this (Laws) Brig that are anxious to have negroes put in the army but of course I can not speak as definitely as of my own Regt. These two Regts are the 4th & 44th Ala. I send the original paper as signed by the men in pencil. With the request that you hand these papers to Gen[l] Lee   I am Colonell Resptfy

ALS   A. A. Louther

Col. A. A. Louther to Lt. Col. W. H. Taylor, 14 Feb. 1865, A-140 1865, Letters Received, ser. 12, Adjt. & Insp. Gen., RG 109 [F-334].

Endorsements. Enclosed is an undated resolution, signed by soldiers and officers of the 15th Alabama Regiment, which declares that "seeing the determination of the Federal govenment to finally subgugate us confiscate our Lands and property free our slaves . . . the time has come for the arming and putting {blacks} into the Confederate service. . . ."

124: Resolution of a Virginia Confederate Regiment

Head Qurs. 6th Regt. V^a Infy [*Va.*] 15th Feby 1865

An expression of opinions being asked in this Command upon the subject of receiving negroes in the Army as arms bearing men in a separate organization; the following resolution was presented and passed —

Resolved — That we are ready and willing to receive as co-laborers in the great struggle for liberty in which we are now engaged, our negroes, whenever such a course shall seem necessary, to our leaders and the Government — and that while we abide their judgement upon the matter, we must be permitted to urge such action, as shall add strength to our thinned, though determined ranks — Respy Forwarded

HDS   Geo. T. Rogers

Resolution of the 6th Virginia Infantry, 15 Feb. 1865, enclosed in Brig. General D. A. Weisiger to Lt. Col. W. H. Taylor, 17 Feb. 1865, filed with V-47 1865, Letters Received, ser. 12, Adjt. & Insp. Gen., RG 109 [F-252]. In a covering letter, General David A. Weisiger reported that among the five regiments in his brigade, three approved slave enlistment, one was "decidedly opposed," and one refused to recommend any action. Weisiger noted that "The sentiment is rapidly changing, however, a few weeks will I think find the command almost unanimously for the Employment of negroes."

125: Resolutions of a Virginia Confederate Regiment

Hd Qrs 18th V^a Infantry [*Va.*] Feb: 20th 1865

Resolved 1st   That the 18th V^a Infantry, reposing the most implicit, & unlimited confidence in the wisdom, skill & patriotism of our beloved General in Chief, will cheerfully acquiesce in the arming of any portion of our slaves for the defence of our Common Country whenever in his opinion this grave action on the part of Congress becomes necessary in order to successfully resist the further progress of a devastating & remorseless foe—*provided* that such armed slaves shall *form a separate & distinct Corps, & shall not be incorporated with our skeleton Regts*—

Resolved 2nd   That believing that freedom is not a boon to the negroe we are in favor of offering freedom to those only who elect it—

HD

[*Endorsement*] Col. W. H. Taylor A.A.G.   Col. The above resolutions were adopted by my Regt this morning, about 325 Officers & men present, with *only fourteen* dissenting votes. We agree to leave the whole matter with Gen'l Lee, but prefer that the slaves when armed shall constitute a separate Corps— I am Col Very resply Yr obt Sevt H. A. Carrington Col 18th V^a Inftry

Resolutions of the 18th Va. Infantry, 20 Feb. 1865, filed with P-206 1865, Letters Received, ser. 12, Adjt. & Insp. Gen., RG 109 [F-255].

126: **Report by a Committee from a South Carolina Confederate Brigade**

[*Va. February 23, 1865*]

The joint Committee of two persons from each Regiment respectfully submit the following report as expressing the "sense" of the officers and men in the several Regiments composing Brattons Brigade relative to the proposition to employ negro soldiers in our army.

Report. We have no data on which to base a correct opinion as to the military necessities requiring the enlistment of the negro as a Soldier in to our Armies   We have not sufficient information to determine whether, or not it has become a military necessity. If no such necessity exists we would prefer not to employ the negro. We will willingly submit to, and cheerfully acquiese in, any measure for the protection, and defence of the country, the Commanding General and authorities may concur in recommending and the Congress in their wisdom may deem proper to adopt. If it is, or if it becomes necessary to employ the negro to secure our Independence as a people, and our existence as a Government, and a nation we unhesitatingly say we would overcome any objections, or prejudices or repugnance we might have or feel to the enlistment of the negro, or serving with him. As to the political expediency of employing the slaves as soldiers in our army – the effect this would have on their loyalty to their masters, the influence it would have on the institution of Slavery and as to whether the negro would in the immergency be of more service to the country as a soldier or as a laborer, we decline to express an opinion.

As "Slave-holders we are willing if it is necessary for the good of the country, to surrender our negroes to the Government for the purpose of making Soldiers of them. Having the fullest confidence in the wisdom, integrity, and patriotism of our General-in-Cheif – we will cheerfully yeild our acquiesence in support of any military measure he may recommend for the defence and protection of the Country.

The joint Committee recommend the sending of a copy of this report to each regiment that they may accept or reject it by vote.

Signed F. G. Latham

     "   O. A. Wylie

     "   S. B. Clowney

Vote of the respective Regiments

1st So Ca Regiment	Unanimously in favor of report	
2nd " " Rifles	224 in favor	59 opposed
5th " " Regiment	81 " "	128 "
6th " " Regiment	283 " "	41 "
Pal S. Shooters	201 " "	78 "
	789	306

HDSr

Report of Capt. F. G. Latham et al., 23 Feb. 1865, filed with G-207 1865, Letters Received, ser. 12, Adjt. & Insp. Gen., RG 109 [F-336]. Endorsement. In the same file are several other reports of regimental votes taken on the subject of enlisting black soldiers in the Confederate army; all indicate a large majority in favor.

PART 2

The Structure of Black Military Life: Limits and Opportunities

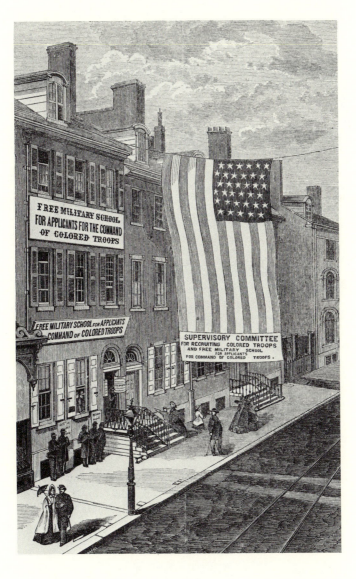

6

Black Officers

FROM THE START, proponents of black enlistment claimed the right of blacks to hold military office as a logical outcome of armed service.[1] The appointment of blacks to noncommissioned positions met little opposition, but the commissioning of black officers faced stiff resistance. The two ranks differed fundamentally in authority and responsibility. While commissioned officers from lieutenant up assumed an exalted status superior to that of all enlisted men, non-commissioned officers (sergeants and corporals) remained within the enlisted ranks.[2] Everyone in the army followed orders, but commissioned officers generally gave them while noncommissioned officers, like other enlisted men, usually stood at the receiving end. Similarly, all officers enjoyed some authority, but the authority of non-commissioned officers never extended beyond the regiment and usually not beyond the company, while that of commissioned officers, depending on rank, reached far beyond those narrow bounds. By

[1] Published works on black officers include: Joseph T. Wilson, *The Black Phalanx: A History of the Negro Troops in the War of the Rebellion, 1861–1865* (New York, 1888), pp. 176–79; Herbert Aptheker, *To Be Free: Studies in American Negro History* (New York, 1948), pp. 80–81, 212 n. 8; John W. Blassingame, "The Selection of Officers and Non-Commissioned Officers of Negro Troops in the Union Army, 1863–1865," *Negro History Bulletin* 30 (Jan. 1967): 8–11; Mary F. Berry, "Negro Troops in Blue and Gray: The Louisiana Native Guards, 1861–1863," *Louisiana History* 8 (Spring 1967), 165–90; in addition, for a list of all the officers who served in black regiments see *Official Army Register*, pt. 8.

[2] A War Department order of September 6, 1862, provided for the following officers in a volunteer infantry regiment, which consisted of ten companies, each with sixty-four to eighty-two privates.

Regimental commissioned officers (also called "field and staff" officers): colonel, lieutenant colonel, major, surgeon, two assistant surgeons, chaplain, adjutant (a lieutenant), quartermaster (a lieutenant).

Commissioned officers for each company (also called "line" officers): captain, first lieutenant, second lieutenant.

Regimental noncommissioned officers: sergeant-major, quartermaster sergeant, commissary sergeant, hospital steward.

Noncommissioned officers for each company: first sergeant, four sergeants, eight corporals.

The organization of volunteer cavalry and artillery regiments differed primarily in including more company officers, because there were twelve instead of ten companies. (*Official Records*, ser. 3, vol. 2, pp. 518–20.)

virtue of their ability to issue orders and their wide range of authority, commissioned officers possessed discretion and power that not
even the highest-ranking noncommissioned officers could match.
Moreover, the commissioned ranks enjoyed a variety of special rights
and privileges in return for the responsibilities they bore. For example, different regulations governed the conduct of enlisted men
and officers and different punishments – generally harsher for the
former than the latter – weighed upon violators of the rules.

Commissioning a black man would not only confer upon him the
prerogatives of "an officer and a gentleman," but would also allow
him broad authority which, in a given situation, might extend over
white soldiers and indeed over white officers. While federal officials
found it useful to place blacks in command over other blacks, they
had no desire to revolutionize American race relations by placing
blacks in command of whites. The War Department order that established the Bureau of Colored Troops in May 1863 allowed blacks
to enter noncommissioned ranks but pointedly made no mention of
commissioning black officers. Later, when the commissioning of
blacks became a matter of debate, Union officials maintained that
placing blacks in positions where they would be equal to some
whites and superior to others would not be for the good of the
service.[3] Despite intense lobbying by the proponents of black officers, the War Department refused to bridge the military's chasm
between "man" and "gentleman."

Still, the initial enlistment of black soldiers had seemed to bolster
the case for black commissioned officers. Early in 1863, abolitionist
Governor John A. Andrew of Massachusetts, believing that the appointment of black commissioned officers would aid enlistment in
his 54th Massachusetts Volunteers and would speed the nation down

---

[3] *Official Records,* ser. 3, vol. 3, pp. 215–16. In December 1864, C. W. Foster,
assistant adjutant general and the dominant figure in the Bureau of Colored
Troops, provided the nearest thing to an official rationale for army policy respecting black officers. Foster, like other officers, had no objection to "giving a
colored man the reward due to service and merit," provided it could be done
"consistently with the interests of the service." He then added: "Let us suppose a
colored man comissioned as an officer of a colored regiment. The accidents of the
service must give him rank above, and often put him on duty with white officers
of his own and also of other regiments. The real question presented then is. – are
white officers and men prepared to acknowledge and obey the colored man, or
officer, as a military superior? If they are ready to treat such an officer with the
respect and deference due from the inferior in rank to the superior in rank, there
can certainly be no harm in giving the colored man a commission. If, on the
other hand such action should be in advance of public opinion, and of army
ideas and convictions, would not the bestowal of commissions upon colored men
introduce in the army, a disturbing element which might be of serious injury to
the service?" ([C. W. Foster] to Colonel, 13 Dec. 1864, filed with S-97 1864,
Letters Received, ser. 360, Colored Troops Division, RG 94 [B-394].)

the road toward racial equality, pressed Secretary of War Edwin M. Stanton for approval. Stanton denied the request. But because congressional legislation did not prohibit such appointments, Andrew remained hopeful. Six months earlier, Senator James H. Lane, chief recruiter in Kansas, had acted without official sanction and commissioned blacks to help him fill the ranks of the 1st Kansas Colored Volunteers. Lane also pressed for War Department approval and, for a while, thought it had been granted.

While the North debated the use of black officers, a precedent established in Confederate Louisiana helped decide the case. Early in 1862, Governor Thomas O. Moore mustered into the state militia a regiment of free people of color, complete with free black company officers, many of whom claimed descent from the free men of color who had served with General Andrew Jackson half a century earlier. Composed of New Orleans's *gens de couleur* elite – light-skinned, educated, propertied, and cosmopolitan – the Native Guard regiment, as it came to be known, saw no Confederate service. In fact, when Union General Benjamin F. Butler captured New Orleans in the spring of 1862, the Native Guards refused to flee with their white comrades. Instead, they offered Butler their services in the Union cause. Butler expressed admiration for the mulatto officers, praising their intelligence, urbanity, and sincerity, but he nonetheless declined the offer. By September, however, military necessity forced him to "call upon Africa." He mustered both officers and men of the Native Guard regiment into federal service and made plans to organize two additional regiments with black officers.

Scarcely had Butler begun to implement this policy when he was relieved of command in the Department of the Gulf. His replacement, General Nathaniel P. Banks, assumed command in December 1862. Banks, who as governor of Massachusetts had in 1859 vetoed a measure opening the state militia to blacks, immediately voiced qualms about the three black regiments. He judged them "demoralized from various causes," and he felt that they "engaged in controversy with white troops to such an extent that . . . it was impracticable for them to continue in service." Banks blamed the black officers for these alleged difficulties, deeming them contentious and "unsuited for this duty." He determined to purge the regiments of their black leadership.[4]

By early 1863, Banks began to force the black officers out of service.[5] By his actions if not his words he encouraged white soldiers

---

[4] Draft of [Nathaniel P. Banks] to Abraham Lincoln, 12 Aug. 1863, Copies of Letters Sent, ser. 1741, Dept. of the Gulf, RG 393 Pt. 1 [C-610].

[5] As Banks pressed the Native Guard officers out of service, he also asserted authority over the organization of all black troops in the Department of the Gulf. On May 1, 1863, he established the Corps d'Afrique, to consist of eighteen

to defy and disdain the black officers, and, as a consequence, many of the latter, especially in the 1st Regiment, resigned. He moved more directly against the officers of the 3rd Regiment, apparently summoning them to his headquarters and, in effect, advising them to resign. Nearly all did so. For the officers in the 2nd Regiment, Banks devised an especially ingenious plan. He ordered a board of examination, which included some white officers of inferior rank, to pass judgment on the qualifications of the blacks. Most resigned rather than submit to such an indignity. Several, however, refused to withdraw in the face of Banks's intimidation. Captain Robert H. Isabelle, for example, appeared before the board and passed its examination in February 1863. But the following month he resigned in protest against continued discrimination by his white fellow officers. The only major in the officer corps, Francis E. Dumas of the 2nd Native Guard Regiment, also withstood initial pressure to resign, but by July 1863, he, too, had left the service.

Despite intense opposition from above, a few black officers survived the purge. In October 1863, Colonel Chauncey J. Bassett of the 1st Regiment, a white commander more sympathetic to black officers than some of his comrades, recommended black lieutenants Alfred Bourgeau and James H. Ingraham for promotion to captain. Surprisingly, the recommendation passed with approval up the ladder of command, and the two black lieutenants secured the higher rank.[6] Furthermore, as late as March 1864, some black officers of the 1st Regiment had yet to face review before an examining board. However, with their superiors outspoken in their opposition to black officers, with disrespect from white officers and enlisted men unabated, and with the meeting of their review board imminent, their days were numbered. They had all resigned by the summer of 1864.

Nonetheless, the drama dragged on even after the curtain had dropped, and the issue of Native Guard officers continued to exert powerful influence on the black military experience in Louisiana. For example, in the wake of Union victories at Port Hudson and Vicks-

---

regiments of 500 men each. (*Official Records*, ser. 1, vol. 15, pp. 716–17.) On June 6, he ordered incorporation of the four Louisiana Native Guard regiments as the first four infantry regiments of the Corps d'Afrique and subsumed the five regiments in General Daniel Ullmann's brigade as the 6th, 7th, 8th, 9th, and 10th infantry regiments Corps d'Afrique. (*Official Records*, ser. 1, vol. 26, pt. 1, p. 539.)

6 Lieut. Col. C. J. Bassett to Capt. G. B. Halsted, 8 Oct. 1863, Applications for Commissions, ser. 1936, Records of Boards of Examiners for Commissions, Dept. of the Gulf, RG 393 Pt. 1 [C-1053]. No less surprising, in the midst of the purge, when black officers of the 2nd Native Guard Regiment protested receiving less pay than white officers, Banks endorsed their petition favorably and forwarded it to the War Department. (See *Freedom*, ser. 2: doc. 156a.)

burg in July 1863, on the heels of the first wave of resignations, and in the midst of a relentless stream of requests from the resigned officers for permission to raise companies for which they would serve as officers, Banks decided to raise two sixty-day regiments. To spur enlistments without the impressment that had so complicated plantation recruitment, Banks authorized recruitment by the former black officers whom he had but recently drummed out of the service, promising that, if successful, they would be recommissioned. It appears that blacks filled all the company offices in both sixty-day regiments.[7] Banks had learned that with the promise of commission, free men of color could recruit much more successfully than whites, especially when both recruiting officers and enlistees understood that they would serve together after muster into service. Even Banks proved capable of laying aside his objections to black officers when manpower shortages so demanded.

Other commanders learned this lesson at their own pace. Late in 1864, Banks's successor in command of the Department of the Gulf, General Stephen A. Hurlbut, found himself in the same predicament that Banks had earlier experienced. Constrained by a recent ban on forcible conscription, Hurlbut had to devise a plan to promote voluntary enlistments. In October 1864, he authorized the formation of two black regiments from the New Orleans area and invited the former Native Guard officers to raise companies, assuring them that merit alone would guide the decisions of the examination board for officers. Several of the former black officers insisted upon appearing before the board before they recruited their companies, but Hurlbut hesitated. When the blacks pressed their case, insisting they could not recruit successfully without commissions, the general decided to scuttle the entire operation rather than accede to the demand of the officers and recruits. He revoked the officers' authorizations to recruit and in the process destroyed the hope of raising the regiments with volunteers. Hurlbut concluded that he would rather suffer continuing difficulties in obtaining black recruits than enlist black officers into the service.

Banks's purge of the Louisiana Native Guard officers in the early months of 1863, coming just as large-scale black enlistment began in the North and the occupied South, dismayed proponents of commissions for blacks. It dashed hopes that the Native Guard precedent would provide grounds for the War Department to establish a black officer corps. Instead, it revealed the full measure of official opposition to black officers. At the same time, the purge fired the determination of both black spokesmen and their white allies to see some black officers commissioned. Governor Andrew of Massachu-

[7] *Official Army Register,* pt. 8, pp. 317–18.

setts assumed the lead in pressing their case before Washington officials. As if searching for the line of least resistance, Andrew — with
the cooperation of the sympathetic colonels of his 54th and 55th
black regiments — sought War Department permission to commission
a small number of highly qualified freeborn blacks. In March 1864,
he exercised a governor's authority to appoint officers for state volunteer regiments and commissioned Sergeant Stephen A. Swails a
lieutenant in the 54th Massachusetts. Swails, freeborn and nearly
white in complexion, had distinguished himself in battle and commanded the respect and admiration of his superior officers. Andrew
chose his test case carefully, but apparently not carefully enough.
Under express War Department orders, General John G. Foster,
commander of the Department of the South under whom the 54th
and 55th served, refused to discharge Swails as an enlisted man so
that he could accept the promotion, even though Foster appreciated
Swails's good character and distinguished service.

By early 1865, black protest, coupled with the undeniable success
of black soldiers in the field, persuaded several prominent Northerners, including Vice-president Hannibal Hamlin, Henry Wilson,
James A. Garfield, and even Nathaniel P. Banks, to support commissioning blacks as officers. Anticipating a favorable War Department response to the changing mood, Foster reversed his earlier
stance and expedited Swails's promotion — on the grounds of his intelligence, his character, and his light color. The War Department
approved. In the wake of Swails's success, Peter Vogelsang and
Frank M. Welch also obtained commissions in the 54th Massachusetts, and John F. Shorter, James M. Trotter, and William H. Dupree became lieutenants in the 55th.[8]

James H. Lane's black Kansas officers experienced difficulties
similar to those of Governor Andrew's Massachusetts men. Hardly a
man to await official approval, Lane appointed blacks as recruiters
for his 1st Kansas Colored Volunteers in the summer of 1862 and

[8] But many high Union officials remained opposed to commissioning blacks. In
February 1865, writing in response to the proposed appointment of black second
lieutenants in a newly formed black regiment, Adjutant General Lorenzo Thomas
reiterated: "I do not deem it advisable that colored men should be appointed
Second Lieutenants or to any other commissioned office in a Regiment. the reasons against this are too numerous and apparent to mention, arising both out of
their association as such on an equality with white men holding similar positions
in other Regiments which must at nearly all times be on duty with them, and of
the effect upon the enlisted men in the Regiment. This was tried by Gen'l
Butler in a Regiment raised by him at New Orleans, the result was so injurious
to the service that white men were afterwards substituted as rapidly as vacancies
occurred — in several instances the colored officers themselves seeing the difficulty resigned, and I think all are now out of that Regiment." (Endorsement, 23
Feb. 1865 on Henry Wilson to Col. Foster, 4 Feb. 1865, W-94 1865, Letters
Received, ser. 360, Colored Troops Division, RG 94 [B-597].)

commissioned them as company officers when they had filled their units. The War Department grudgingly mustered the regiment into service more than a year after Lane had assembled it but refused to commission any black officers. William D. Matthews, a black whom Lane had appointed captain, protested. White officers in the regiment petitioned the department on his behalf, but the department refused to act and never acknowledged Matthews's captaincy. But for his receiving a commission in 1864 as a lieutenant (along with another of Lane's black officers, Patrick H. Minor) in the independent light artillery battery raised by black abolitionist H. Ford Douglas, Matthews's recruitment effort would have gone entirely unrewarded.

War Department objections to black commissioned officers did not extend to the approximately two dozen black chaplains and surgeons who served in the Union army, in large measure because those officers stood outside regimental command structures. The abolitionist-sponsored New England regiments and the early North Carolina "African Brigade" boasted black chaplains. Other black ministers, notably Henry M. Turner, Garland H. White, and Francis A. Boyd, gained commissions as chaplains by virtue of their special service as recruiters. But regulations required the election of chaplains by regimental officers; consequently black chaplains remained subject to the prejudicial whims of white officers. In Boyd's case, such opposition blocked his commission as chaplain of the 109th U.S. Colored Infantry for most of his term of service.

Moreover, for most of the war, chaplains occupied an undefined area with respect to rank. Only in April 1864 did Congress formalize the rank of chaplain, but the legislation set no firm equivalent to other officer ranks. While the law implied that chaplains stood somewhere between the ranks of major and captain, it clearly stipulated that chaplains occupied positions "without command."[9]

If surgeons escaped the ambiguity of rank that chaplains suffered, they experienced many of the same forces of opposition. War Department orders fixed the rank of surgeon as the equivalent of major, but surgeons, like chaplains, did not share the prerogatives of command. Moreover, most black surgeons served under contract rather than enjoying regimental appointments and saw fixed duty stationed at particular hospitals or camps, where they more closely approximated hired War Department employees than regimental officers. Nonetheless, because they could outrank other army physicians, white as well as black, black surgeons stood vulnerable to the general hostility of white officers, especially white surgeons. Some white doctors simply refused to serve alongside blacks and peti-

[9] *Official Records,* ser. 3, vol. 4, pp. 227–28.

309

tioned for their removal. When black surgeons like Alexander T. Augusta stood their ground, white physicians bombarded them with petty insults and refused them the courtesies military etiquette demanded. More often than not, the War Department acceded to the protests of the whites.

Because chaplains and surgeons exercised no regimental command functions, the War Department readily appointed black men to these offices. In so doing, it hoped to defuse criticism of the absence of black commissioned officers without threatening the white officer corps. Yet partisans of the black officer issue did not mistake the mere appearance of black officers for the reality of command, and they continued to press for the appointment of black company and regimental officers. Against their continuing demands, the War Department held firmly to the white chain of command, determined to keep it untarnished by the addition of black links.

Other than the unknown number of blacks who "passed" and filled officer positions in white regiments, scarcely a hundred blacks served as commissioned officers, roughly two-thirds serving as Louisiana Native Guard officers and another quarter as chaplains and surgeons.[10] The six Massachusetts officers did not receive commis-

---

[10] For the case of a black man who passed as white and served as captain in a Pennsylvania white regiment, see Edwin Belcher to Maj. Genl. O. O. Howard, 5 Nov. 1867, B-217 1867, Letters Received, ser. 15, Washington Hdqrs., RG 105 [A-408]. As nearly as can be determined from military service records, the following list includes all the black commissioned officers who served in black regiments during the Civil War:

1st Louisiana Native Guard (subsequently designated 73rd USCI): Captains: Alfred Bourgeau, Andrew Cailloux, Edward Carter, John DePass, Joseph Follin, James H. Ingraham, Alcide Lewis, James Lewis, Henry L. Rey. Lieutenants: Emile Detiége, William Harding, Louis D. Larrien, Victor Lavigne, Jules Mallet, Morris W. Morris, Ehurd Moss, Oscar Orillion, Paul Porée, Eugene Rapp, Henry Louis Rey, Charles Sentmanat, Hyppolite St. Louis, Louis A. Thibant, Charles Warfield.

2nd Louisiana Native Guard (subsequently designated 74th USCI): Major: Francis E. Dumas. Captains: William B. Barrett, William Belley, Arnold Bertonneau, Hannibal Carter, Edward P. Chase, Robert H. Isabelle, P. B. S. Pinchback, Samuel W. Ringgold, Joseph Villeverde, Samuel J. Wilkinson. Lieutenants: Alfred Annis, Jr., Louis De Gray, Peter O. Depremond, Alphonso Fleury, Jr., Calvin B. Glover, Solomon Hayes, Ernest Hubeau, Joseph Jones, Rufus Kinsley, John W. Latting, Jules P. Lewis, Theodore A. Martin, Ernest Morphy, Octave Rey, Jasper Thompson, Frank L. Trask, George F. Watson, Joseph Wellington.

3rd Louisiana Native Guard (subsequently designated 75th USCI): Captains: Leon G. Forstall, Peter A. Gardener, Charles W. Gibbons, Jacques A. Gla, John C. Holland, Samuel Laurence, Joseph B. Oliver. Lieutenants: Alfred Bourgeau, Charles Butler, Chester W. Converse, Octave Foy, William Hardin, Valdes Lessassier, Ernest Longpré, Jr., G. B. Miller, James E. Moore, E. T. Nash, Joseph G. Parker, Louis Petit, Hypolite Ray, Charles Schermerhorn, G. W. Talmon, A. F. Tervalon.

sions until 1865, all except Swails after war's end. In the independent artillery battery (roughly the equivalent of an autonomous infantry company), Douglas, Matthews, and Minor constituted the entire commissioned officer staff, but their exclusive service at Fort Leavenworth, Kansas, significantly reduced both their scope of command and their interaction with other black troops. Two of the highest-ranking black officers, Major Martin R. Delany and Captain O. S. B. Wall never saw active field service. Commissioned in the closing months of the war, they recruited briefly for the 104th U.S. Colored Infantry but, almost immediately after the regiment's muster, left on detached service with the Freedmen's Bureau. Moreover, at precisely the time that it approved their commissions, the War Department delayed considering the application of black Ohio recruiter, John M. Langston, for appointment as colonel of a black regiment. After the fighting stopped, the department informed Langston that it had no vacancies for black officers. Even as it took the first meaningful steps toward admitting blacks to commissioned offices, the War Department hedged its actions to prevent blacks from attaining significant authority and responsibility.

The War Department kept the black officer corps small and its experience limited. It allowed no black officer a significant line command and, when it appointed any black officers, chose only from a small select group, mostly Northern free blacks, few of whom were former slaves, none emancipated by the war. Black soldiers could not aspire to rise within the ranks, nor did many have the opportunity to serve under men of their own color, a fact that magnified the role black noncommissioned officers would play. Similarly, black civilians only rarely had the opportunity to see

54th Massachusetts Volunteer Infantry: Lieutenants: Stephen A. Swails, Peter Vogelsang, Frank M. Welch.

55th Massachusetts Volunteer Infantry: Lieutenants: John F. Shorter, James M. Trotter, William H. Dupree.

104th U.S. Colored Infantry: Major: Martin R. Delany. Captain: O. S. B. Wall.

Independent Battery, U.S. Colored Light Artillery: Captain: H. Ford Douglas. Lieutenants: William D. Matthews, Patrick H. Minor.

Surgeons: Anderson R. Abbott, Alexander T. Augusta, John V. De Grasse, William B. Ellis, William Powell, Charles B. Purvis, John Rapier, Alpheus Tucker.

Chaplains: John R. Bowles, Francis A. Boyd, Samuel Harrison, William H. Hunter, William Jackson, Chauncey B. Leonard, George W. Levere, Benjamin F. Randolph, David Stevens, Henry M. Turner, James Underdue, William Waring, Garland H. White.

This list is compiled from the *Official Army Register,* pt. 8; Carded Records, Volunteer Organizations: Civil War, ser. 519, RG 94; Personal Papers, Medical Officers & Physicians, ser. 561, Record & Pension Office, RG 94; Pension Application Files, RG 15.

black men with shoulder straps – the symbol of military authority – and few white soldiers or civilians had their racial preconceptions jarred by confronting a black man in command. Nonetheless, even the limited number of black officers made an important impact. The qualities that propelled black officers into their positions of military leadership despite long-standing opposition continued to distinguish them at war's end. Delany, Swails, Turner, and Augusta, among others, saw service with the Freedmen's Bureau, and still others remained in the South as teachers, doctors, and ministers.

The experience gained in the military launched many of these men into active political roles, although none more prominently than Captain P. B. S. Pinchback, Reconstruction lieutenant governor and, for a brief period, acting governor of Louisiana. The Civil War officer experience, however limited, proved important to the development of black leadership. But, for a combination of reasons, including racially motivated distrust of the capacity of blacks for command in combat and discomfort with having blacks outrank whites, the War Department chose to limit that experience to a tiny fraction of qualified black soldiers.

LINE OFFICERS

127: Testimony by the Former Commander of the Department of the Gulf before the American Freedmen's Inquiry Commission

[*Boston, May 1, 1863*]

. . . .

Let me give you a little history of the first colored regiment in this country. On the fifth of August [*1862*], we had the battle of Baton Rouge, and after that, it was reported that Breckinridge, assisted by Villepegue was coming down to take New Orleans. I wrote very strongly to the Department at Washington for reinforcements, but just at that moment, the retreat from Richmond was going on, and I got nothing but an order to hold New Orleans at all hazards – as though I wouldn't do *that*! I then wrote, if I could not get white help, I should call on Africa for assistance. They took no notice of that. I had read carefully two of the daily journals of New Orleans, published since the rebellion, and I ascertained that they had raised a colored regiment. The people at New Orleans wondered very much at my intimate knowledge, as they were pleased to say, of their affairs, & that I knew who was who. It all came of a reasonably retentive memory, and a very careful reading of two of their daily journals for two years past. I learned, in this way, that they had raised a colored regiment, and at last I got hold of the order under which it was raised. I then found that one of the captains was my translator in the Provost Court of German, Spanish and French – Mr. Souvenier. I sent for him, and asked him – (he was a colored man; hardly a mulatto) – "You were a captain in the colored regiment?" "Yes, Sir." "Are the other captains of that regiment here?" "Yes Sir." "Why didn't you go away with the rest of the Confederate forces, when they ran away?" "We didn't choose to go." The whole regiment stayed. "You had white field officers?" "Yes, Sir." "But," I said, "how came you, free colored men, fighting here for the Confederacy – fighting for slavery?" "Ah!" said he, "we could not help it. If we had not volunteered, they would have forced us into the ranks, and we should have been suspected. We have property and rights here, and there is every reason why we should take care of ourselves." "Didn't you do it out of loyalty to the Confederate Government?" "Not at all; there are not five men in the regiment fighting on the side of the Confederacy." "Are you willing to enlist on our side?" "Yes." "Will you get the captains and other officers to come here, and see if you can find your men?" "Yes, Sir." These men had been drilled, but without muskets. They would not let them have arms – either because they were afraid to trust them, or because they did not have the arms to give them. He brought in the captains and some lieutenants, – fifteen or sixteen, I think, – and I found them all very glad to take service with us. I then ordered a recruitment, and in ten days, I had a regiment a thousand strong of these men – I had arms for them, for I had taken about 7000 from the people of New Orleans. I wrote to the Department repeatedly to say whether I was right in taking this course, but they said nothing for two months; and when they did reply, they said the whole matter was left to the discretion of the Commanding General. That was all the ratification I got – but that was ratification enough. These men enlisted, and I appointed the officers from the ranks, giving them white field officers. I immediately had applications to recruit a second regiment, and I enlisted a second regiment. There, too, the field officers were white, except one, the Major, whom I had promoted from the first regiment – Major Dumas. I think he is some distant relation of Alexander Dumas. He is a man who would be worth a quarter of a million, in reasonably good

313

times. He speaks three languages besides his own – reckoning French and English as his own, – and is a gentleman who understands these matters as well as you or I do. He was quite willing to fight, and being senior captain of the first regiment, I made him Major of the second, to give them hopes of promotion. He had more capability as Major, than I had as Major-General, I am quite sure, if knowledge of affairs, and every thing that goes to make up a man, is any test. Then I enlisted a third regiment, and a battery of heavy artillery. Up to the time of completing the raising of the second regiment, – the Government not having sanctioned it, – my officers were rather shy; but when it was known that the Government sanctioned it, I had a pile of applications to be officers in the third regiment that thick [some six or eight inches][1]; and that regiment was made up partly of white line officers and partly of black, precisely as I found intelligence. If I found an intelligent black man, who had recruited his company, and who understood what he was about, and would make a good officer, he was commissioned; if I found an intelligent white man, whose heart was in the matter, and who would make a better officer than the next black man, I gave him the appointment; and I never heard of any difficulty about their serving together in peace and quietness. Certain it is, that I could have officered – white & black intermingled – a dozen regiments with the applications I had.

Now, then, I have heard, since I have returned, that all these colored officers have been required to resign, and have resigned, upon the ground that A, B, C, or D – principally, I believe, Billy Wilson's Zouaves – won't associate with them, won't stand on an equality with them. Certainly, they are not on an equality with them, as far as I understand it. I agree to that proposition. There is no such thing as equality between the First Regiment Louisiana Volunteers and Billy Wilson's Zouaves, in any thing.

Q You wouldn't do so much injustice to the Colored regiment as to place them on an equality?

A. Every man must draw his own conclusions as to which is the mountain & which is the valley.

Q Did you have any difficulty about the white field officers?

A. I never did. They said they wanted men who had had experience, and I appointed them from the white regiments. I will give you an instance of intelligence on the part of a black captain. These colored men who came to me said – "We have no equality here. We are free, and our fathers were free before us, but we have no equality." They showed me the original commissions issued by Jackson to black men, and I have them now. One gentleman's father was an engineer, and he has the certificate of Gov. Claiborne and Gen. Jackson to his capability. I said to these men—"I don't understand, if you are in earnest about this, why you black people have not risen against your masters. You are ten to one—forty to one. If you are really in earnest, and willing to fight for your rights, why have you not risen, and, aided by the United States, got your liberty?" There was one man, quite black, who was their spokesman, and he said—"General, I don't like to argue with you about this." "Oh," said I, "speak freely, Sir." "Ah, but you are the General." "But," said I, "when I ask a question, I always put myself on a equality with the man who answers it—just speak freely." "Well," said he, "to which of the commanders of the United States army should we apply for assistance, in case we make an insurrection?" I felt that I was answered, as completely as I was ever answered in my life.

. . . .

HD

Excerpt from testimony of Major General B. F. Butler before the American Freedmen's Inquiry Commission, [1 May 1863], O-328 1863, Letters Received, ser. 12, RG 94 [K-86]. General Butler's testimony distorted somewhat the chronology of his relationship with the Native Guard officers. On May 25, 1862, he had reported to the Secretary of War that he had recently held an interview with the officers, and even though "in color, nay, also in conduct, they had much more the appearance of white gentlemen than some of those who have favored me with their presence claiming to be the 'chivalry of the South,' " he declined their offer of service. (*Official Records*, ser. 1, vol. 15, p. 442.) Butler agreed to recommission the officers only after his archrival on the question of arming blacks, General John W. Phelps, informed Butler that he had recently spoken with a deputation of Native Guard officers about their entering Union service. (See *Freedom*. ser. 2: doc. 10.) After having decided to enlist the officers and their men, Butler could not resist commenting again to the Secretary of War on the lightness of their skins: "the darkest . . . will be about the complexion of the late Mr. Webster." (*Official Records*. ser. 1, vol. 15, p. 559.)

1 Brackets in manuscript.

128: Commander of the Department of the Gulf to the Adjutant General of the Army

New-Orleans, Feby 12 1863.

Sir; In compliance with the instructions contained in the letter from the Adjutant General's Office of January 16th 1863, I have the honor to state that the number of persons of African descent enrolled in the military service in this Department is as follows

1st	Louisiana	Native	Guards,	Infantry	955
2d	"	"	"	"	976
3d	"	"	"	"	996
Co "A"	"	"	"	Artillery	129
4th	"	"	"	in process	
		of organization,	recruits		195
					3251

The three regiments first named have ten companies each, their field and Staff Officers are white men, but they have negro company Officers, whom I am replacing, as vacancies occur by white ones, being entirely satisfied that the appointment of colored officers is detrimental to the Service.

It converts what, with judicious management and good officers, is capable of much usefulness, into a source of constant embarrassment and annoyance. — It demoralizes both the white troops and the negroes. The officers of the 4th regiment will be white men. It is progressing favorably. Very Respectfully Your mo Ob't Serv't

HLS
N. P. Banks

Maj. Genl. N. P. Banks to Brig. Genl. L. Thomas, 12 Feb. 1863, G-148 1863, Letters Received, ser. 496, Volunteer Service Division, RG 94 [BB-5]

129A: Black Officers in a Louisiana Black Regiment to the Commander of the Department of the Gulf

New-Orleans, Feb. 19th *1863.*

General,   The following circumstances renders It an Imparitive duty to ourselves, to herewith tender our Ressignations, unconditional and Immediate.

At the time we entered the army It was the expectation of ourselves, and men, that we would be treated as soldiers. we did not expect, or demand to be putt on a Perfect equality In a social point of view, with the whites, But we did most certainly expect the Priviledges, and respect due to a soldier who had offered his services and his life to his government, ever ready and willing to share the common dangers of the Battle field.   This we have not received, on the contrary, we have met with scorn and contempt, from both military and civillians. If we are forced to ask for Information, from the generality of white Officers, we Invariably, receive abrupt, and ungentlemanly answers, when in maney Instances It is their legitimate business to give the Information required. To be Spoken to, by a colord Officer, to most of them, seams an Insult. Even our own Regimental commander has abused us, under cover of his authority. Presuming upon our limited Knoledge of military Discipline, all combine to make our Position Insupportable.

General, This treatment has sunk deep Into our hearts. we did not expect It and therefore It is intolerable. we cannot serve a country In which we have no more rights and Priviledges given us.

Therefore, we most Respectfully beg of you, to accept This Tender. We have the honor, Sir, to be most Respectfully your obedient servants,

HLS   [*16 signatures*]

Capt. J. A. Gla et al. to Maj. Gen. N. P. Banks, 19 Feb. 1863, service record of Leon G. Forstall, 75th USCI, Carded Records, Volunteer Organizations: Civil War, ser. 519, RG 94 [N-1]. The signatures are those of seven captains, three first lieutenants, and six second lieutenants, all of the 3rd Louisiana Native Guard. Earlier in the month, two of the petitioners had submitted individual letters of resignation on the same grounds as those expressed in the collective petition. Their regimental commander, Colonel John A. Nelson, endorsed both resignations approvingly and almost identically, describing each officer as "of no use to the Survice And entirely unfit for the position He occupys having no military Knowledge or any controle over His Command." (Capt. Saml. Laurence to Major General Nathaniel P. Banks, 4 Feb. 1863, with undated endorsement of Col. John A. Nelson, service record of Samuel Lawrence, 75th USCI, Carded Records, Volunteer Organizations: Civil War, ser. 519, RG 94 [N-34]; Et. Longpré Jr. to Major General N. P. Banks, 5 Feb. 1863, with undated endorsement of Col. John A. Nelson, service record of Ernest Longpré, Jr., 75th USCI, Carded Records, Volunteer Organizations: Civil War, ser. 519, RG 94 [N-35].)

129B: **Black Former Officer in a Louisiana Black Regiment to the Secretary of War**

New Orleans May 30th 1863

Dear Sir—   The ex-Officers of the Third Louisiana Native Guards having organized an Association for the furtherance of our race,

317

both in civil and Military Institutions in this Department And individually wishing to reenter the service of the United States And having made numerous applications to the authorities in this department and not being positively denied the right to be Officers when we have shown ourselves to be competent, but are always told that the power was not vested in them by the Secretary of War; I as corresponding secretary of the Association of ex-Officers, do by this method apply to you for information on the subject.

About the 12th of February there was a Special Order Issued from Head Quarters department of the Gulf (or represented to be issued from that source) for all the colored Officers of the Third Regiment to report to Maj. Gen¹ Banks in person forthwith, in compliance with said order we acted; The said order was read privately to us by our Colonel, no colored Officer having the pleasure of seeing said order, When we arrived in New Orleans and reported to Maj. Genl Banks, he General Banks asked us why we came and what was our trouble. We answered him, that as a body we had no complaints to make, but some one or two had their aggrievances to lay before his notice; At the second interview the General asked us if we had concluded to resign, one said resign, and we all agreed because he General Banks was the first to propose resigning – and we thought that he wished us to do so. The General told us to write a general resignation and he would accept it, we did as we were requested to do. He then issued Order No 50 Discharing from service Honorably all colored officers belonging to the Third Louisiana Native Guards Regiment, Said Special Order No 50 was not made public as other orders are. For said Order No 50 was transmitted to Baton Rouge by one of the resigned Officers to General Grover the Commander of that Post. When we arrived at Baton Rouge we found men already appointed in our places without our Colonel being officially informed that we had resigned For the simple Reason that we carried Special Order No 50 with us, And left by the first transport going to that Post. Our Colonel informed us before leaving our Regiment that it was his opinion that we were going to be mustered out of the service. this also increased our anxiety to resign our positions – Sir – In our opinion had our Resignations been sent to you, you would not have accepted provided you had have examined our causes for resigning. And if it had been accepted by you there would have been an official Notice to that effect printed in an official paper. Every Order that is issued in this Department is printed in an official Journal But Special Order No 50 discharging Seventeen commissioned officers From one Regiment was not made public; so secretly was it

conducted that officers of other Colored Regiments are not aware
that we have resigned –

All this Honorable Sir – Goes to show us that we are not wanted
in this Department only as soldiers – But sir, put us to the test
of a board of examination and if we do not pass we are satisfied to
give up troubling the Authorities for positions – General Ullman
has offered us non-commissioned offices[1] – But after once holding a
commission and still retaining that commission we would not like
to accept a warrant. The army Regulations says all officers must
be mustered out of service, and we have not been mustered out of
the service for we still retain our commissions.

Honarable Sir. What we wish to know, is, Will we be allowed
to re-enter the Army again as Officers, if we are competent? Are
we properly discharged? Are we liable to Conscription? And if so,
we want the privilege of serving under Colored Officers for we
never would make good Soldiers under any other, for these reasons,
Colored men in this Department, who are born free, are all
educated and they know that there are men of color capable of
leading them. They are naturally ambitious and of course would
like a show for promotion. With white Officers we have not that
chance. The highest we can get as an orderly Segeant, when we
are capable of holding that position without being promoted. to
it. If you wish free and intelligent men, give us Colored Officers
& you shall have them, In Regiments where there are white
Officers you can scarcely find any of the Non-Commissioned
officers that can either Read or write & those that can, have been
offered large pay from the Officers pay. to get them – Whilst on
the other hand almost every private can read & write – I
respectfully transmit this to your Honor. hoping to receive an
early reply I Remain most respectfully Your Obedient Servant

Joseph G. Parker.

P.S. Please direct answer Care of Mr Thomas Burns No 55
Common Street. N.O.

ALS

[*Endorsement*] New York, Nov[r] 25" 1863. Respectfully
returned. The statements contained in this communication are so
generally inaccurate that I can only remark upon the most
prominent points presented.

The officers referred to herein were commissioned by Major
General Butler while he commanded the Dept. of the Gulf, except
perhaps a few whose commissions may have been signed by Gen[l]
Banks at Gen[l] Butler's request just after the latter was relieved,
and they – as were all the company officers of the three colored

regiments raised previous to the time when Gen[l] Banks arrived at New Orleans, – are free men of color.

The arrival of the 3[d] Louisiana Native Guards at Baton Rouge early in this year led to much ill-feeling among the officers and men of some of the white regiments, resulting often in controversy, and on several occasions in violence. By their arrogance and intolerant self-assertion, the officers of this regiment had conclusively shown that they were not the men to pioneer this experiment, even before they proceeded to demonstrate their hostile and uncompromising spirit by seeking occasions to force their complaints upon the Dep[t] Commander. It was then that General Banks sent for them, heard their complaints, and addressed them, urging patience, and dignified toleration. *At once* the spokesman of the party announced their determination to resign. The Comd'g General requested them to consider the matter carefully; not to be hasty; to see him again on the morrow. They came with their resignations written; which were at once accepted, in Special Orders, as is the custom.

Special Orders are never published in the newspapers, unless designed to reach persons out of the military channels of communication. I furnished these officers, myself, with an extra copy of the order in their case, to be presented by them to their Commanding Officer.

It will be seen that these officers commenced their evidently pre-conceived intention to quit the service, as soon as they found the Comdg General indisposed to take sides in a partisan quarrel, to the prejudice of good order and military discipline.

I may add that the colored officers of the 2[d] Louisiana Native Guards were brought before an Examining Board, at the request of their regimental or battalion commander, and were, with two or three exceptions, found incompetent, and mustered out of service.

No general action was taken with respect to the 1st Louisiana Native Guards, (at least before my illness), but the vacancies were, except at first and for a brief period, filled with white men.

Whatever may be the general merits of the question, no candid mind can doubt that, in its practical operation, the experiment of officering colored troops with colored men, has, *in these three cases,* proved a distressing failure: nor that this failure is due to the incompetency, or bad character of the appointees and their nervous and uncontrollable anxiety to discount the future of their race.

I regret that I have not been strong enough to attend to this matter before. All of which is respectfully submitted. Richd B. Irwin[2] A.A. General

Ex-2d Lieut. Joseph G. Parker to Honorable E. M. Stanton, 30 May 1863, P-26 1863, Letters Received, ser. 360, Colored Troops Division, RG 94 [B-39]. The Adjutant General's Office referred Parker's letter to General Nathaniel P. Banks, commander of the Department of the Gulf, on July 22, 1863. Banks waited until September 23, 1863, to forward the case to Irwin, who, in turn, waited until November 25 to write his endorsement. Other endorsements.

1 General Daniel Ullmann was at the time organizing a brigade of black troops under express authority from the War Department. The Department forbade him to commission black officers, although he could offer warrants as noncommissioned officers to blacks. (*Official Records*, ser. 3, vol. 3, pp. 14, 99–103; Brigadier General Daniel Ullman to Governor John A. Andrew, 28 Feb. 1863, Negro in the Military Service, pp. 1115–16, ser. 390, Colored Troops Division, RG 94 [B-483].)

2 Irwin was General Banks's adjutant at the time of the resignations; hence his familiarity with the case.

130A: **Black Officers in a Louisiana Black Regiment to the Commander of the Department of the Gulf**

[*Ship Island, Miss. March 2, 1863*]

Sir, at a meeting of the colored officers of the 2nd Regiment Louisiana Native Guards. At Ship Island. Miss. on the second day of March. AD. 1863. For the purpose of adopting some policy that will secure Justice to ourselves and alike to the country we have pledged ourselves to serve. The following resolutions were unanimously adopted.

1st Owing to the limited opportunities we have had Since we have been in the service; having done the heaviest guard duty ever known, from the 1st day of November 1862, until the 10th day of January 1863. on the New Orleans & Opelousas Rail Road. and since our arrival at Ship Island, we have been continually erecting Batteries, Magazines, and Fortifications, working both day and night, consequently we have not been able to acquire that perfect knowledge of Military, that would fit us to go before a board of examination.

2nd After mature reflection we are convinced that the board of examination which we understand is to be instituted for the examination of the colored officers of this Regiment, is but a preliminary step to our being mustered out of the Service. The greatest proof of which, is that the only White Line officer in the companies that have come before the board, at Fort Pike, was not Subjected to an Examination. It is evidently known by every officer of this Regiment that he is far inferior to the Majority of the Colored Officers, Either in civil or Military knowledge.

3rd It having come to our knowledge that an order has been issued by Major Genl N. P. Banks for the payment of the colored Troops and their Field Officers Excluding the Colored Line Officers. We cannot see the Justice of this order. As we have expended all the means we possessed and many of us have gone largely in debt in order to support ourselves and Families, most of which are now in want and destitution. Humanity demands that we be paid as speedy as possible. Aside from Justice and right.

4th That we view the exclusion of the colored Line officers from pay in that order as an ill omen

5th When we recieved authorizations to recruit our companies it was implicitly understood and plainly set forth in General B. F. Butlers order N° 63 that the Line Officers were to be colored men. In view of this fact many of our Friends and Relatives were induced to enter the ranks as private soldiers. To leave them to the mercies of other Commanders would be to us heavy and grievous.

6th From the many rumors that have reached us we are led to believe that it is the intention of the General to relieve us from our present Commands, Which we will most willingly submit to, if the good of the service require it. As we have been told such is the prevailing impression at Headquarters. However pleasing such a course may be to our enemies it is our impressions, will work to the opposite of the results aimed at. For once the fact is made known that there is no chance of promotion, the ambitious inspirations which lead all men to brave deeds, will be dead, hence the colored men will lose all interest, all energy, and become careless, indifferent and neglectful.

7th In conclusion we beg leave to state. By accepting our present positions we have alienated ourselves from our former Friends and employers. And many of us have given up lucrative positions. And if we are forced to resign at the present time will experience great difficulty in obtaining Situations now. where it was comparatively easy heretofore. Yet with all these difficulties staring us in the face, we will abide your decision and most respectfully beg to know what is to be the future disposition of us, As anything will be prefarable to the state of uncertainty in which

we now are. We have the honor to be most respectfully Your
Obedient Servants

HLS   [*18 signatures*]

Capt. P. B. S. Pinchback et al. to Major Genl. N. P. Banks, [2 Mar.
1863], Letters Received, 6th USCI, Regimental Books & Papers USCT,
RG 94 [G-287]. Next to the name of one signer, Joseph Villeverde, appears the notation "one of the veterands, of 1814." Though the officers
served in the 2d Louisiana Native Guards (later the 74th USCI), their
petition is misfiled among the papers of the 6th USCI. Other black officers
in the same regiment began tendering their resignations individually on the
day of the Ship Island meeting. (Capt. Arnold Bertonneau to Captain
Wickham Hoffman, 2 Mar. 1863, service record of Arnold Bertonneau,
74th USCI, Carded Records, Volunteer Organizations: Civil War, ser.
519, RG 94 [N-24]; 1st Lt. Ernest Morphy to Captain Wickham Hoffman, 3 Mar. 1863, service record of Ernest Morphy, 74th USCI, Carded
Records, Volunteer Organizations: Civil War, ser. 519, RG 94 [N-27];
First Lieutenant Octave Rey to Captain Wickham Hoffman, 2 Mar. 1863,
service record of Octave Rey, 74th USCI, Carded Records, Volunteer Organizations: Civil War, ser. 519, RG 94 [N-30].)

130B: Black Officer in a Louisiana Black Regiment to the Headquarters of the Department of the Gulf

Fort Pike [*La.*] March 3^{d} 1863

Sir   I have the honor to respectfully tender my resignation to the
office of 2^{d} Lieutenant of Co H 2^{d} Regt La Vols Native guards for
the following Reasons

When I Joined the united States army I did so with the sole
object of laboring for the good of the union supposing that all past
prejudice would be suspended for the good of our Country and
that all native born americans would unite together to sacrefice
their blood for the cause as our fathers did in 1812 & 15 to save
our native soil from her threatened doom

But after five or six months experience I am Convinced that the
same prejudice still exist and prevents that Cordial harmony among
officers which is indispensable for the success of the
army   Consequentely I respectfully tender this resignation Subject
to your approval hoping that the blessings of god will Ever smile
upon the flag of my Country   Respectfully Your obeident Servant

ALS   R. H. Isabelle

2d Lieut. R. H. Isabelle to Capt. Wickham Hoffman, 3 Mar. 1863, service record of Robert H. Isabelle, 74th USCI, Carded Records, Volunteer Organizations: Civil War, ser. 519, RG 94 [N-26]. Endorsements.

130C: **Black Officer in a Louisiana Black Regiment to the Commander of a Louisiana Black Brigade, and Reply by the Brigade Commander's Adjutant**

Ship Island [*Miss.*] May 17th 1863.

Sir: I have the honor to address you with these few lines, on a subject of great importance to me. It has been told to me that it was your intention to remove all of the colored officers under your command, now Sir I have put myself to a great deal of trouble and expense in getting up my company, and was one of the first residents who waited upon Maj. Genl. Butler, who was then in command of the Department of the Gulf, and offered my services to the Government, and just as soon as the General issued his order I went to work and raised my Company, which consist of all bona fide freed men, and not contrabands. Gen'l; Sir: you can judge how it will cut my pride as a soldier to give up my command of them who I have once led in the Battlefield, and they proved themselves brave and true soldiers, and worthy of chosing me for their Commander, some of them are near friends of mine and have been my companions, when we were civilians, and I would hate to part with them, as bad as they hate for me to leave them. And I assure you, General that with the right men in the right place, you would be proud of all colored officers who are under your command, but Sir. if it is your intention to move them I will cheerfully submit if it is for the good of the country. but Sir: it will cut the pride of many brave colored men who have offered their services to the Government, they have sworn to protect — with their lives —

In conclusion, General, I hope sir, you will excuse me for being so bold as to take the liberty of writing to you on this subject and hope sir, that you will, (Should this meet with your approbation) return me an answer, for it is better to resign than be dismissed. hoping sir that I have said nothing to offend I Remain Sir Most Respectfully, Your Obedient Servant

HLcSr

(sd) W. B. Barrett

New Orleans. La. May 26th 1863.
Captain: The General commanding desires me to say in answer to
your letter of the 17th inst. that he has come to no determination
whatever upon the subject respecting which you addressed him.
He does not intend to take the matter up until the command of
the Regiments now organized has been turned over to him by
Major: Gen. Banks. Very Respectfully

HLcSr

sd. Moses C. Brown

Capt. W. B. Barrett to Brigadier Genl. Ullmann, 17 May 1863, and
Moses C. Brown to Capt. W. B. Barrett, 26 May 1863, service record of
William B. Barrett, 74th USCI, Carded Records, Volunteer Organizations:
Civil War, ser. 519, RG 94 [N-22]. Barrett was a captain in the 2nd
Louisiana Native Guard.

130D: **Black Officer in a Louisiana Black Regiment to
the Commander of the Department of the Gulf**

Ship Island Miss July 7th 1863
Sir   I have the honor to respectfully beg leave to tender the
resignation of my commission as a Captain in the 2d Regt of
Native Guards volunteers of the State of Louisiana for the
following reasons.
    That a Board of Examination has been formed to investigate the
Military Capacity of the *Colored Officers* of this Regiment and that
the officers detailed to compose said Board are in the Majority of
inferiour rank (1st Lieutenants of the same Regiment) whose
promotion would be Effected by our dismissal   Respectfully
Submitted

HLS

S W Ringgold

[*Endorsement*] Head Quarters Defences N.O. N.O. July 17"
1863   Respectfully forwarded.   When this board was appointed
there were no officers of higher rank competent to sit on the
board   If a new board is appointed of Officers of Superior rank,
they cannot be selected from Officers at Ship Island   W H
Emory   B.G.C

Capt. S. W. Ringgold to Maj. Genl. N. P. Banks, 7 July 1863, service
record of Samuel Ringgold, 74th USCI, Carded Records, Volunteer Organ-

izations: Civil War, ser. 519, RG 94 [N-31]. Another endorsement. Captain Samuel J. Wilkinson of the same regiment submitted a letter of resignation nearly identical to Ringgold's. General Emory endorsed both identically on July 17. (Capt. Samuel J. Wilkinson to Maj. Genl. N. P. Banks, 6 July 1863, service record of Samuel J. Wilkinson, 74th USCI, Carded Records, Volunteer Organizations: Civil War, ser. 519, RG 94 [N-32].)

130E: Black Officer in a Louisiana Black Regiment to the Headquarters of the Department of the Gulf

Ship Island Miss February 11th 1864

Sir. I have the honor herewith to tender my resignation as 2nd Lieut of Co "F." 2nd Regt Corps d:Afrique on the account of the predjudices which exists in my Regiment; as well as the entire Service against Colored Officers, and being myself a colored Officer I wish that my resignation be excepted.

I certify that I am not indebted to the United States on any account whatever, and that I am not responsible for any Government property, except what I am prepared to turn over to the proper officer, on the acceptance of my resignation, and that I was last paid by Maj Morse, U.S. Paymaster to include the 31st day of Oct 1863. Very Respectfully Your Ob^{dt} Servt

ALS   Solomon Hayes

[*Endorsement*] Head Quarters Ship Island [*Miss.*] February 15th 1864 Approved and respectfully forwarded. This Officer is ignorant, unable to learn, & though a black has neither the respect or confidence of his men. He has labored to create a feeling against his Superior officer in the Company to which he is attached, & has so conducted himself that if his resignation be not accepted it will be necessary to prefer charges & place him in arrest. I refrained from doing so in the hope that the service may be sooner rid of him than would be possible by the forms of trial. W M Grosvenor Col 2^d Inf CdA Comd^g Post

2nd Lieut. Solomon Hayes to Maj. Drake, 11 Feb. 1864, service record of Solomon Hayes, 74th USCI, Carded Records, Volunteer Organizations: Civil War, ser. 519, RG 94 [N-25]. Other endorsements.

131A: Black Officer in a Louisiana Black Regiment to the Post Commander of Fort Macomb, Louisiana

Fort Macomb La. Sept. 5th 1863.

Sir. I hereby tender my resignation as 1st L^{nt} of C° D 1st R^{gt} La. Vols. free colored N. Guards, to take effect immidiately, for the followings reasons

The Company has been divided into two companies and transferred to the 20th Corps d'Afrique. Besides it seems to be the policy of the Government not to recognize the contracts made with the 1st La. Vols. free colored N. Guards by Gen'l Butler while in command of the Dept of the Gulf.

Believing that my honor as a gentleman and as a soldier demands that I leave the service for the above reasons. I have the honor to remain Your most obidient servant

ALS   Jules Mallet

1st Lnt. Jules Mallet to Capt. A. E. Buck, 5 Sept. 1863, service record of Jules Mallet, 73d USCI, Carded Records, Volunteer Organizations: Civil War, ser. 519, RG 94 [N-49]. Endorsements by the commanders of Fort Macomb and of the Defenses of New Orleans approved and forwarded Mallet's resignation. One of Mallet's fellow black officers submitted an identical letter of resignation to the post commander, and it was similarly approved. (2d Leut. Victor Lavigne to Capt. A. E. Buck, 5 Sept. 1863, service record of Victor Lavigne, 73d USCI, Carded Records, Volunteer Organizations: Civil War, ser. 519, RG 94 [N-49].)

131B: Black Officer in a Louisiana Black Regiment to the Headquarters of the Department of the Gulf

Port Hudson [*La.*], February 18th 1864

Sir: I respectfully tender my immediate and unconditional resignation because daily events demonstrate that prejudices are so strong against Colored Officers, that no matter what be their patriotism and their anxiety to fight for the flag of their native Land, they cannot do it with honor to themselves. Very respectfully, Your obedient servant

ALS   Joseph Follin

[*Endorsement*] Head Quarters 1st Inf C.d.A Port Hudson La Feb 18th 64 Respectfully forwarded approved as the advanced age &

health of this Officer in my opinion render him disqualified for the Service   C. J. Bassett   Col Comdg

[*Endorsement*]   Head Qurtrs 1″ Big 1″ Div C d'A   Port Hudson La Feb 18″ 1864   approved & respectfully forwarded   W^m H Dickey   Col Commandg

[*Endorsement*]   Head Quarters 1st Division C.d'A.   Port Hudson Feb. 19. 1864   Respectfully forwarded.   Daniel Ullmann   Brig. Gen. Comdg.

[*Endorsement*]   Head Quarters Corps d Afrique   Feby 25. 1864   Respectfully forwarded approved on the ground that this officer is not competant for His position   Geo. L. Andrews   Br Gnl Vols   Comdg Post

Capt. Joseph Follin to Asst. Adjt. Genl. George B. Drake, 18 Feb. 1864, service record of Joseph Follin, 73rd USCI, Carded Records, Volunteer Organizations: Civil War, ser. 519, RG 94 [N-18]. General Ullmann appears to have been an unenthusiastic participant in the black officers' resignations. Although he forwarded Follin's resignation without comment, more frequently he disapproved such requests. (See, for example, his endorsement of March 3, 1864, on Captain Alfred Bourgeau to A.A. Adjt. Genl. George B. Drake, 1 Mar. 1864, service record of Alfred Bourgeau, 73rd USCI, Carded Records, Volunteer Organizations: Civil War, ser. 519, RG 94 [N-15].) In contrast, General George L. Andrews, commander of the Corps d'Afrique, opposed black officers virtually without reservation. As early as November 1863, he informed the president of the examining board for officers in the Department of the Gulf that he could not "at present under any circumstances approve the application of any colored person for a commission in the Corps d'Afrique." (Brig. Gen. Geo. L. Andrews to Col. C. C. Dwight, 4 Nov. 1863, vol..45/74 DG, Letters Received, ser. 1930, Records of Boards of Examiners for Commissions, Dept. of the Gulf, RG 393 Pt. 1 [C-1052].) In a typical endorsement approving the resignation of a black officer, Andrews wrote: "This is a colored officer who is notoriously both incompetent and inefficient. His resignation is probably tendered to escape being discharged on the recommendation of the Board of Examiners. Under all the circumstances I respectfully recommend that it be accepted." (Endorsement on 1st Lieut. Ehurd Moss to Lieut. Col. Richard B. Irwin, 8 Mar. 1864, service record of Ehurd Moss, 73rd USCI, Carded Records, Volunteer Organizations: Civil War, ser. 519, RG 94 [N-20].) See also Andrews's endorsement on the application of a black soldier for examination for a commission, *Freedom*, ser. 2: doc. 132c.

132A: **Black Former Officers in a Louisiana Black Regiment to the Commander of the Department of the Gulf**

New Orleans   April 7th *1863*

Sir   we the undersigned in part resigned officers of the Third (3rd) reg[t] La vol native guards and others desiring to assist in putting down this wicked rebelion. And in restoring peace to our once peaceful country. And wishing to share with you the dangers of the battle field and serve our country under you as our forefathers did under Jackson in eighteen hundred and fourteen and fifteen – On part of the ex officers we hereby volunteer our services to recruit A regiment of infantry for the United Satates army –   The commanding Gen[l] may think that we will have the same difficulties to surmount that we had before resigning.   But sir give us A commander who will appreciate us as men and soldiers, And we will be willing to surmount all outer difficulties   We hope allso if we are permitted to go into the service again we will be allowed to share the dangers of the battle field and not be Kept for men who will not fight   If the world doubts our fighting give us A chance and we will show then what we can do–   We transmit this for your perusal and await your just conclusion. And hope that you will grant our request   We remain respectfuly your obedient servants

Adolph. J. Gla	James. E. Moore
Samuel. Lauence	William. Hardin
Joseph G Parker	William. Moore
Joseph. W. Howard	Charles. A. Allen
Charles. W. Gibbons	Dan[l] W. Smith J[r]

ALS

Adolph J. Gla et al. to Majr. Genl. N. P. Banks, 7 Apr. 1863, G-35 1863, Letters Received, ser. 1920, Civil Affairs, Dept. of the Gulf, RG 393 Pt. 1 [C-697]. The following month one of the signers of the petition made an additional appeal to raise troops, stating in part: "I Joseph. G. Parker 2nd Lieut of Co C third Regiment Louisiana Native Guards do Hereby agree or propose to Raise a Company of Cavalry of picked men of full stature who are free Born intelligent men who have been used to the saddle from infancy never having done any thing Else since they were old enough But Catch wild attakapas Cattle and hunt. They are men who understand the use of the Lassoe so well that they will wager to Catch a beef at full speed by any one of his feet." (Ex 2nd Lieut. Joseph G. Parker Jr. to Brigadier Genl. Daniel Ullman, 22 May 1863, service record of Joseph G. Parker, 75th USCI, Carded Records, Volunteer Organizations: Civil War, ser. 519, RG 94 [N-1].)

132B: Black Former Officer in a Louisiana Black Regiment to the Commander of a Louisiana Black Brigade

New Orleans June 12th 1863

Sir   Permit me to inform you that there more than one thousand free colored citizens in this city who are anxious to Enlist in the united states army to share their blood & lives in the common cause of their country.   among them are some who are very wealthey, having graduated in Eroupe as well as having considerable experience of the Military tactics, being capable of passing before a board of examination to prove their qualifications as to they being lines officers.

This is all they ask.   is the privilege of selecting their own lines officers or for you to select from our own race such persons as you might find qualified   this privilege our fathers enjoyed in 1812 & 15 and as the late battles of East Pascagoola Miss & Port Hudson has proved that the colored officers are capable of commanding as officers

I hope that you will pardon me for my familarness but as I feel that it is the duty of every man to come forward and aid in putting down this unholy rebellion and save our country from her awful threatened doom.   I have no doubt but that we can raise a regiment in less than one week of able bodid well educated men

Hoping that this applicaton will meet with your due consideration   Respectfully Your humble Servant

ALS   R. H. Isabelle

[*Endorsement*]   We certify that Lieut Robert H. Isabelle passed a board of Examination held at Fort Pike La Febuary 10th 1863 persuant to Special Orders No 34 from Head quarters Dept of the gulf. the board finding him qualified for his position   Alfred. G. Hall Lt Col 2^d Regt La Vols N.G. President   Elliot Bridgeman Capt 31 Mass Vols Comdg Fort Pike   Geo. S. Darling Capt 31 Mass Vols Recorder

Late 2d Lieut. R. H. Isabelle to Brig. Genl. Ullman, 12 June 1863, service record of Robert H. Isabelle, 74th USCI, Carded Records, Volunteer Organizations: Civil War, ser. 519, RG 94 [N-26].

132C: Louisiana Black Soldier to the Headquarters of the Department of the Gulf

Port Hudson [*La.*] Nov ^{the} 19 1864

Sir   I have the honor to apply to the Genl Commanding
Department of the gulf for an order for me to appear before a
board of Examiners as to my qualification as a line officer in one
of the regiments now forming at New Orleans   I have been a
soldier in the U.S. servies Two years and feel myself qualified to
hold the possition   Very Respectfully Your obdt Servt

ALS   Solomon Moses

[*Endorsement*] Head Quarters USC Troops Dept of the Gulf Port
Hudson [*La.*]. Nov. 28 /64 Respectfully forwarded. if colored
officers are to be allowed in the new organizations – I see no
objection to this man's application being granted. So far as my
own opinion may be required as to the advisability of admitting
colored commissioned officers, I am for the present opposed
thereto, 1st because with existing prejudices few or no good
white officers will enter a regiment with colored officers, and there
are not enough colored men who are qualified to fill *all* such
positions; at least I feel justified in such an inference, from the
fact that few of the colored officers I have seen were efficient, and
it is not easy to find even those well qualified for
non-commissioned officers, from lack of education. 2^d All well
qualified colored men are greatly needed in the non-commissioned
staff of regiments. Geo. L. Andrews Brig. Gen Vols Commdg.

Privit Solomon Moses to Asst. Adjt. Genl. Geo. B. Drake, 19 Nov. 1864,
service record of Solomon Moses, 76th USCI, Carded Records, Volunteer
Organizations: Civil War, ser. 519, RG 94 [N-3]. Other endorsements.

133: Superintendent of Recruitment in the Department of the Gulf to the Headquarters of the Department of the Gulf, Enclosing Recruitment Authorization and a Letter from Department Headquarters to a Black Former Officer of a Louisiana Native Guard Regiment

New Orleans Novem' 18# *1864.*

Major: I have the honor to enclose herewith, a letter from your office to Mr James Lewis with endorsement made by him thereon. Also, the letter authorizing him to recruit for the 1st Regiment U.S. Col^d Vol Infantry.

In regard to the enclosed papers, I would earnestly recommend that Mr Lewis be at once ordered before the board of examination for applicant for commission, In a previous communication on this subject (Novem 11th Inst) I called your attention to the fact that in my opinion it was absolutely necessary to have at least, one applicant commissioned or assured that a commission would be issued to him upon his recruiting a command.

I am convinced, that unless such action is taken it is only an useless expense to continue the recruitment of this regiment – so far, only fifty six (56.) accepted recruits have been received at the Depot, most of whom have been recruited by M^r. Jordan Noble, who is about the only person who seems to be satisfied that the conditions set forth in General Orders, No. 154,[1] will be respected. The other Recruiting Agents represent that the men think that after they are enlisted they will be sent to other regiments, and white officers placed over them. All the parties authorized to recruit affirm that if they were sure that they would be commissioned (if found competent) and if they could satisfy the persons desiring to enlist of that fact – they could easily recruit a command.

Assuring them verbally that the order will be strictly complied with; does not seem to satisfy them, if a few could be examined and given certificates, entitling them to muster upon the recruitment of a sufficient number of men. I have no doubt that the regiment could be organized in a very short time.

In connection with this subject, I would respectfully state that it is my opinion that if these persons are to undergo the same examination as white persons (other than the mere knowledge of tactics, company and regimental duties) there will be very few of them who will pass. I remain, Major: Very respectfully, your obd't sv't,

HLS

Sheldon Sturgeon.

[*Enclosure*]   NEW ORLEANS,   Nov. 1." 1864.
MR.   James Lewis, New Orleans,   SIR: —   YOU ARE HEREBY
AUTHORIZED TO RECRUIT FOR CO   REGIMENT
UNITED STATES COLORED INFANTRY, AUTHORIZED BY
GENERAL ORDERS NO. 154, CURRENT SERIES, FROM THESE
HEADQUARTERS.
     IF WITHIN   DAYS FROM THE DATE OF THIS LETTER
THERE SHALL HAVE BEEN THE MINIMUM NUMBER REQUIRED
BY LAW, OF ACCEPTED RECRUITS ENLISTED FOR SAID
COMPANY, YOU WILL BE APPOINTED AS   an officer   OF THE
SAME, SUBJECT TO THE APPROVAL OF THE WAR
DEPARTMENT, PROVIDED YOU PASS THE EXAMINATION
PRESCRIBED BY EXISTING ORDERS.
     YOU WILL REPORT THROUGH THE COMMANDING OFFICERS
OF THE DEPOT RECRUITING SERVICE, UNITED STATES
COLORED TROOPS, TO THE SUPERINTENDENT VOLUNTEER
RECRUITING SERVICE, DEPARTMENT OF THE GULF, FOR
ORDERS AND INSTRUCTIONS. BY COMMAND OF MAJOR
GENERAL HURLBUT:

Geo. B. Drake

Authorization No. 11
PD

[*Enclosure*]   *New Orleans,* Nov. 16th 1864.
Sir: — Upon the recommendation of Capt. S. Sturgeon, Supt. of
Volunteer Recruiting Service of the Department, who states that
he has reason to believe that you do not intend to act in
accordance with the provisions of the letter from these Head
Quarters, (addressed to you on the 1st inst.) authorizing you to
raise recruits for a Regiment of United States Colored
Infantry: — said letter of authorization is hereby revoked. The
same to be returned. By Command of Maj. Gen'l S. A. Hurlbut
HLS   Geo. B. Drake

[*Endorsement*] New Orleans Nov 17th 1864   Respectfully
Returned   Sir   I would have no difficulty in Recruting a company
Provided I have Passed the Board of Examination,
     I have Served the Unted States two years faithfully and was
honorably Discharge. My accounts have been acknowledged
Correct. in Washington.
     I Resigned because I was orderd to appear before a Board of

Examiners and I was told by a member of that Board that because I was a colored man that It was not the intention of the Board to Pass any Colored Officer.

in order to do myself and Recruits Justice I would Respectfully ask to go before the Board before I Recruit.

I have the honor to be very Respectfully your obt Servt   James Lewis. Late Capt 1ˢᵗ La vol Regt Native Guards

Capt. Sheldon Sturgeon to Maj. Geo. B. Drake, 18 Nov. 1864, enclosing Major Geo. B. Drake to Mr. James Lewis, 1 and 16 Nov. 1864, service record of James Lewis, 73rd USCI, Carded Records, Volunteer Organizations: Civil War, ser. 519, RG 94 [N-19]. The recruitment authorization of November 1, 1864, is a printed form with manuscript insertions.

1 The order, issued on October 27, 1864, by General Stephen A. Hurlbut, recently appointed department commander, authorized recruitment of two regiments of black volunteers from the New Orleans area for one year's service. To spur enlistments, the order invited the former officers of the Native Guards to raise companies, on the understanding that they would serve as officers of their companies after producing vouchers of their loyalty and standing. The order pledged that "In the selection of officers and non-commissioned officers, no test will be required but that of qualification, to be established by the Board of Examiners, now in session. . . ." (General Orders No. 154, Headquarters, Department of the Gulf, 27 Oct. 1864, Orders & Circulars, ser. 44, RG 94 [DD-9].)

134A: Officers of a Kansas Black Regiment to the Kansas Commissioner of Recruitment

Camp Henning, Fort Scott, Kansas. January 9ᵗʰ 1863
To Gen James H. Lane:— The Undersigned, Officers of the 1st
K. C. V. having heard with great regret, rumors to the effect that
the officers now commanding Co D. of this regiment, are not to
be mustered on account of their color, and not for any valid reason
of non-efficiency and capacity, do hereby most respectfully ask
that, for the sake of justice to individuals, of the principle
concerned, and for the harmony & efficiency of the regiment, that
no such action be taken, unless there be imperative orders from
the War Department against the mustering of Colored
officers. We each of us feel justified in declaring Captain Wm D.
Matthews, commanding said company, to be among the most

thorough and efficient officers in our organization; a soldier in every sense of the term, drilled, disciplined and capable. we have now been in camp with him for five months, and have at all times found him a worthy gentleman, and excellent officer. We give it as our conviction, that to Captain Mathews, among the most prominent, is due a large share of our [*success*] in maintaining this organization intact through the trials and difficulties of the last five months. We therefore ask in simple justice to him & ourselves that no action be taken detrimental to his rights.

HDS   [*21 signatures*]

Capt. J. M. Williams et al. to Gen. James H. Lane, 9 Jan 1863, filed with K-138 1864, Letters Received, ser. 360, Colored Troops Division, RG 94 [B-91].

134B: **Officer in a Kansas Black Regiment to the Kansas Commissioner of Recruitment**

Camp Henning [*Kans.*] January 12th 1863

General:– I beg you will not consider this note as an intrusion. But because of the interest which I am aware you so largely feel in our organization, I address you. Captain Mathews deserves better treatment than that which it w[d] seem is to be dealt out to him. Every officer is a unit on this point. General! *we* could not have held this organization together without Matthews. We have won, with you, a great triumph. All of us are your sincere friends – and I know I speak the sentiment of all when I say that we look to Gen Lane with confidence to see that no wrong be done the principles for which all have worked. Capt Mathews will do credit in the future as in the past, & public men need not fear that with the hurrying radical tendencies of the struggle, that the prominence of colored men as officers will affect their popularity. Gen Butler has already appointed them in Louisiana. As an individual, I for one shall work earnestly, with all the power I can, to secure that fair play for Capt Matthews which I demand for myself.

General – We want to form part of the Indian Division, provided it have a radical cheif. cannot Col. Phillips have command? It would be a good thing for his brains will make any movement successful, while his modesty will not make a success offensive to any one. Besides it will be gratefully accepted by the radicals here

335

to see Col P. in a position becoming his merits, and received through your influence

Excuse my frankness & believe Me   Respectfully Yours Truly

Richard J Hinton

P.S. Col Williams would suit us better even than Col P. & without doubt is capable. He is your faithful friend, you are aware.

Jan 12th – The muster took place today. Capt Matthews was not mustered and Major Weed, I understand states that he will not even give him a Recruiting Commission, so as to enable him to legally recover his deserters & gain new men. He can do as much or more than any one man to complete our organization. I trust that justice will be done him   RJH

The whole thing amounts simply to the idea, that "niggers" shd not be mustered as officers and not as to any question of competency

ALS

Richard J. Hinton to General [James H. Lane], 12 Jan. 1863, filed with K-138 1864, Letters Received, ser. 360, Colored Troops Division, RG 94 [B-91]. In 1864, William D. Matthews received a commission as lieutenant in a black light artillery battery organized in Kansas, but his compiled service record makes no mention of his earlier service with the 1st Kansas Colored Volunteers; hence, it appears that the War Department denied him the earlier commission. (Service record of William D. Mathews, Indpt. Batt'y. U.S. Col'd. L. Art'y., Carded Records, Volunteer Organizations: Civil War, ser. 519, RG 94 [N-9].) For Matthews's request for a commission in the 1st Kansas Colored Volunteers, see *Freedom,* ser. 2: doc. 14.

❧

135: Governor of Massachusetts to the Secretary of War

Boston 3^d Feby 63

Congressional bill passed house representatives does not prohibit colored officers in colored Regiments. Will you withdraw prohibition so far as concerns line officers assistant surgeons & chaplain of my proposed colored Regt. It will avoid difficulty. Power would not be used except possibly for few cases of plainly competent persons, reccommended by the field officers who shall be gentlemen & soldiers of highest merit & influence

HWSr   John A. Andrew

John A. Andrew to Hon. E. M. Stanton, 3 Feb. 1863, Telegrams Collected by the Office of the Secretary of War (Bound), RG 107 [L-303]. The Secretary of War replied that the question was presently under consideration by Congress and, while he preferred that the President have discretion in the matter, he would await Congress's decision. (Edwin M. Stanton to Governor Andrew, 13 Feb. 1863, Telegrams Collected by the Office of the Secretary of War (Bound), RG 107 [L-303].)

136: U.S. Senator from Massachusetts to the Secretary of War, Enclosing a Telegram from the Governor of Massachusetts to the Senator

[*Washington, D.C. February 9, 1863*]
My dear Sir   I tried to see you yesterday, (but did not succeed) in order to ask attention to the enclosed despatch from Govr Andrew.
   There are colored persons in Mass. members of the Bar &c   Faithfully yours,
ALS   Charles Sumner

[*Enclosure*]   Boston   Feby 7th 1863.
   Get me leave to commission Colored Chaplains assistant surgeons & few second Lieuts.   my discretion may be trusted.   The mere power will be useful   An interdict including member mass med society speaking four languages and member suffolk Bar is prejudicial.
HWSr   John. A Andrew

Charles Sumner to My dear Sir, [9 Feb. 1863], enclosing John A. Andrew to Charles Sumner, 7 Feb. 1863, S-129 1863, Letters Received Irregular, RG 107 [L-116]. In the same file is another telegram from Governor Andrew to Senator Sumner, dated February 9, 1863, pressing the question of appointing black officers: "What is Decided about Copeland. What about My Commissioning Colored Chaplain assistant surgeon & Few second Lieutenants." Sumner forwarded it to the War Department with the following endorsement: "Here is another telegram from Govr Andrew. Pray answer him directly." A search of the War Department's copies of letters and telegrams sent revealed no reply to Governor Andrew.

137: Michigan Newspaper Editor to the Secretary of War

Detroit, Aug 17, 1863.

Dear Sir, Gov. Blair has, at last, consented to the raising of a Colored regiment, and given me authority "to raise and organize" it. A copy of his authority to me is herewith enclosed. I am also furnished with "General orders" Nos. 110, 143, 144[1] and copy of instructions from the U.S. Adjutant General's office to the Governor. I should be gratified to receive a little more information than I can obtain here, and more specific instructions as to the payment of *necessary* expenses in the raising and organizing such a regiment. Will the Department allow the appointment of *Colored men for Commissioned Officers who are competent and pass an Examination* before a Board appointed, as provided in orders before me? I have several *good* men of color who are ready and willing to sumbit to such examination – indeed, they are *anxious,* & to abide the result cheerfully, and do not want position so much as to have *good* officers, and are influenced more by the popularity it would give to colored regiments among their own class than by other considerations. On this account, and the increased facility it would give to raising the regiment, I am anxious to give them an opportunity to be examined and to have commissions if found worthy, and it is not inconsistent with the determined policy of the Gov't. I give you the names of a few: O. C. Wood, John D. Richards, Charles Webb, R. L. Cullen. I have quite a number of others, which I will forward, if not objected to. I can but think the policy of giving *Company* offices to *competent* colored men would be a good one.

I have to request that 1st Lieut. George W. Waldron, now adjutant of 5th Michigan Infantry, and George S. Clay, a Lieutenant in the 15th Michigan Infantry, have permission to appear before an Examining Board, – the first named for Major, at the Washington Board, & the second for Captain, at the Cincinnati Board, as a matter of convenience to them. I will forward other names as soon as I can hear from you in reply. The prospect is flattering for the early filling up of the regiment, as soon as preliminaries are arranged. Very Respectfully Your ob't serv't

ALS   H. Barns

H. Barns to Hon. E. M. Stanton, 17 Aug. 1863, B-131 1863, Letters Received, ser. 360, Colored Troops Division, RG 94 {B-414]. A draft reply from the Bureau of Colored Troops, in the same file, states that

"Colored men will not be commissioned to command colored troops at present." (A.A. Genl. C. W. Foster to H. Barns, 24 Aug. 1863.)

1 War Department General Orders: No. 110 (29 Apr. 1863) prescribed the organization of volunteer regiments and companies; No. 143 (22 May 1863) established the Bureau of Colored Troops; and No. 144 (22 May 1863) outlined procedures for selecting officers of black troops. (*Official Records,* ser. 3, vol. 3, pp. 175–76, 215–16.)

138: Maryland Black Sergeant to the Secretary of War

Camp "Stannton" [*Md.*] Feb. 3^{d} 1864.

Sir, About one month Since I took the liberty to Write you With regard to the Chances of Colored men geting before the Examining Board for Officers of these Troops; but have not recieved an answer as yet upon this Important question.

As I am acting on the behalf of many men in the army and Some out of it, I am over-anxios to set the question Square before the people. So far as I am Concerned as an Individual it makes but little difference; I am Willing to trust to My future Conduct in the the Field to make my record; But there are others that Should Know Whether the highest position to be attained is that of Sergeant. I am Sir, With Great Respect Your Servant,

ALS   Wm U. Saunders

Q.M. Sergt. Wm. U. Saunders to Hon. Sec. Stannton, 3 Feb. 1864, S-127 1864, Letters Received, ser. 360, Colored Troops Division, RG 94 [B-22]. Saunders served as quartermaster sergeant in the 7th USCI.

139: Two Northern Black Sergeants to the Secretary of War

[*Morris Island?, S.C.*] September 11th 1864

Deare Sir   Having From my Childood A Desire to Serve My Country more Especerly Since this Wicked Rebellion has Proluted this Sacred Soil of our Beloved And most Glorrious Country –

Not having any motive only to try And [Quince?] this Rebellion from the face of the Earth And Sir I Can See no other mode then to Crush it With a Strong arm and bring the Rebellious People to a Sence of theair Duty –

Deare Sir I Hope that you will Not think me Imprudent by Wrighting you this letter But Sir I must Confess that I feel

Somewhat Interrested In the behalf of My bleeding Country And Sir I Feel like offering my life upon the bleeding alter Of My Country as a Sacrafise In behalf of that Glorrious baner that Waves over the brave and the free

Deare Sir My Motive in Wrightin to you Is Simply this Will your Hon Grant myself and Friend the Promoshion to Raise a light battry For the Defence of our Goverment a battry of Colard Men for Sir I am very Confident that In a verry Shorte time that We Could Have it Ready for to go Fourth and Defend the union, Secondly Will your *Hon* – Grant us to Have Colard officers Comishioned By Your *Hon* – for Sir We Deem it our Duty to try And to Help Reclaim our bleeding Country Sir I Have Stood by this glorrious union this far and Will Continiour to the End I Have fought and bleed and Ready to Die for my Countys *Honor*

Should your Hon Deem it Prudent to Reply to your Humble Servant I Will Be More then Happy to get your oppinion Upon the Matter Hoping Deare Sir To Heare From you Soon We Will Remain your Humble Servants

J. H. W. N. Collins

John Shaffer

HLS

First Sergeant J. H. W. N. Collins and 5 Sergeant John Shaffer to Honble Edwin M. Stanton, 11 Sept. 1864, C-789 1864, Letters Received, ser. 360, Colored Troops Division, RG 94 [B-99]. The letter and both signatures are in the same hand. The two sergeants served in the 54th Massachusetts Infantry.

140: Petitioners to the Secretary of War

[Washington, D.C.? January? 1865]

SIR: In view of the recent Proclamation of the President calling for 300,000 volunteers, and appreciating the necessity of an immediate response to this call, we would respectfully petition that permission be given to raise a number of *colored regiments,* to be officered *exclusively* by *colored men.*

In regard to the policy of this measure, we would respectfully urge that while many of the noblest of our race have sprung to arms with alacrity in defence of the Government, many others, equally loyal, have hesitated because one of the greatest incentives to enlistment, and the greatest stimulus to the strict performance of a soldier's duty – the hope of promotion – has been denied them.

We confidently believe that the removal of this bar to a soldier's ambition would result in an uprising of the colored people, unsurpassed even by the enthusiastic response to the President's first call.

In regard to the capability of colored men to perform the duties of commissioned officers, we would respectfully suggest that there are hundreds of non-commissioned officers in colored regiments who are amply qualified for these positions, both by education and experience, and that others of our educated men, anticipating the granting of commissions to colored men by the Government, have applied themselves to the study of military tactics, in order that men properly educated might not be wanting to accept them.

And your petitioners will ever pray, &c. Lewis H. Douglass, late Sergeant Major 54th Massachusetts Volunteers. James T. Wormley, Sergeant 5th Massachusetts Cavalry. Benjamin Owsley, Sergeant 27th Colored Troops. Charles R. Douglass, late Sergeant 5th Massachusetts Cavalry Volunteers. John H. Rapier, A.A. Surgeon U.S. Army. William R. Ellis, A.A. Surgeon U.S. Army. Thomas J. White David E. Wycoff, late Sergeant 108th New York Volunteers. James R. Martin, A. R. Abbott, A.A. Surgeon U.S. Army.

PD   [*185 signatures*]

Louis H. Douglass et al. to Hon. E. M. Stanton [Jan.? 1865], D-51 1865, Letters Received, ser. 360, Colored Troops Division, RG 94 [B-584]. In addition to the above names, which were printed on the document, nearly 200 men signed the petition. Among these leading abolitionists, antislavery politicians, generals, and other public figures were Senators Charles Sumner, Henry Wilson, and Edwin D. Morgan; Congressmen James A. Garfield, William D. Kelley, and Thomas D. Eliot; the mayors and councilmen of St. Paul, Minn., Keokuk, Iowa, and Hartford, Conn.; African Methodist Episcopal Bishop Daniel A. Payne; abolitonists Frederick Douglass, Charles Lenox Remond, and James McCune Smith; journalist Horace Greeley; and Generals James S. Negley and Nathaniel P. Banks. General Franz Sigel endorsed the petition as follows: "I endorse the above petition, believing that difference of race, color or nationality should be no obstacle to the appointment or promotion to the rank of commissioned officer if the applicants are otherwise qualified to command. – It would be a sign of progress . . . and justice in this Government and a great vindication of the colored race, if the above problem could be solved satisfactorily, which I do not doubt, it can." Minnesota Governor Stephen Miller added: "I believe that so soon as the men having the necessary military experience and capacity can be found, Colored men should upon merit be eligible to the command of colored companies and Regiments. In other words that color should be no barrier to such promotion."

141A: **Northern Black Sergeant to the Headquarters of the Department of the South**

Morris Island. S.C. Oct 15th 1864

Capt   I have the honor to transmit for the information of the Maj Genl Com^dg Dep^t, the following.

That I was commissioned a Second Lieutenant in the 54th Reg^t Mass. Vol. Infty, by Gov. John A. Andrew. March 11th 1864. That I reported for duty as such May 12th 1864.

And would respectfully ask a Discharge from the service (as an Enlisted Man) by reason of Promotion, for the purpose of being mustered on my commission   I am sir Very Respectfully your Obidient Servant

ALS   Stephen A. Swails

[*Endorsement*] HEADQUARTERS, Dept of the South Hilton Head, S.C. October 23^d 1864   Respectfully returned, a similar application was returnd June 2^d disapproved, as this man is of African descent. The action of the Maj. Gen. Comg. was approved by the Hon. Secy of War. By Command of Maj. Gen. J. G. Foster   W. L. M. Burger Asst. Adj. Genl.

1st Sergt. Stephen A. Swails to Capt. W. L. M. Burger, 15 Oct. 1864, S-97 1864, Letters Received, ser. 360, Colored Troops Division, RG 94 [B-394]. Other endorsements include those by Swails's company, regiment, post, and district commanders, all of whom approved his application for discharge. The earlier application for Swails's discharge, mentioned in Captain Burger's endorsement, has not been located, but in the same file as Swails's October 15, 1864, letter is a request dated June 19, 1864, from Colonel Edward N. Hallowell, Swails's regimental commander, asking the governor of Massachusetts to press the case. Charles W. Foster of the Bureau of Colored Troops endorsed that letter on June 28, 1864, approving General John G. Foster's refusal to discharge Swails for promotion. In mid-September 1864, with the Swails case deadlocked, Colonel Hallowell caustically commented: "Sergeant Stephen A. Swails is not yet mustered as an officer because he is believed to have African blood in him! How can we hope for success to our arms or Gods blessing in any shape while we as a nation are so blind to Justice?" (Col. E. N. Hallowell to Governor John A. Andrew, 19 Sept. 1864, Letters Sent, 54th Mass. Vols., Regimental Books & Papers USCT, RG 94 [G-234].)

342

141B: **Commander of the Department of the South to the Governor of Massachusetts**

HILTON HEAD, S.C., November 18th 1864

Sir: Sergeant Stephen A. Swails, of the 54th Mass. Vols, having received a commission, as Second Lieutenant, from you, applied on the 15th of October for a discharge from the service as an enlisted man, for the purpose of accepting the position as Second Lieutenant in accordance with your authority.

The matter was referred to Washington, and there decided that he could not be mustered in as an officer, owing to his being of African descent; and consequently was not entitled to a discharge.

I understand that Serg^t Swails has, on several occasions, distinguished himself in battle, and was severely wounded at "Olustee."

All the officers of his regiment have the highest respect for him and are anxious to have him made an officer of their regiment.

I have given Serg^t Swails a furlough, and write this in testimony of his good conduct, and to assure you that in refusing to discharge him as an enlisted man, I have acted under particular orders from the War Department. Very respectfully, Your obedient servant,

HLS

J. G. Foster

[*Endorsement*] COMMONWEALTH OF MASSACHUSETTS. EXECUTIVE DEPARTMENT, BOSTON, Dec. 2, 1864. Sergeant Swails, although not of white Caucassion blood, is a man of character, & intelligence, a soldier of superior merit, a gentleman and worthy the recognition of gentlemen. Such is the testimony of the field officers of his regiment. The foregoing letter of the Major General Commanding the Dept in which the regiment is serving adds high testimony to what was already known of the soldier's desert. The letter is respectfully sent to the Secretary of War, & the subject of Swails' promotion is again called to his attention with the remark that I have not hitherto understood that the Department of War had ever decided that a man, merely because he is "of African descent" cannot be discharged to accept promotion. I think and hope that Maj Gen — Foster is misinformed thereon.

And I respectfully insist that Mr Swails, having fairly earned promotion & having the capacity and talent to command men, ought not to be delayed in his muster in as a 2nd Lieutenant. I understood that the War Dept. long since left the Commanders of

Depts. the discretionary power in these cases to discharge for promotion. John A. Andrew, Governor of Massachusetts.

[*Endorsement*] War Dept. A.G. Office, Dec. 13",
1864. Respectfully returned to Colonel J. A. Hardie Inspector General U.S. Army, and the following report submitted
   The records of this office show that Sergt. Swails, a colored man, was appointed a 2^d Lieut. 54th Regt. Mass. Vols. some time prior to June, 1864. The matter first came up on letter from the commanding officer 54th Mass. Vols. to Governor Andrew, in which the Governor was informed that Major General Foster had refused to discharge Swails from service as an enlisted man to accept appointment. This letter the Governor forwarded to this Office through one of his Staff Officers. The subject as thus presented was submitted by me to the Secretary of War, who approved Major General Foster's action, and directed that Swails be not mustered into service as an officer. To carry out these instructions I referred the papers in the case to Major General Foster, with the remark that his action, in declining to discharge Sergt. Swails, to accept appointment, was approved by the Secretary of War. C. W. Foster A.A. Genl. Vols.

Major General J. G. Foster to Governor John A. Andrew, 18 Nov. 1864, filed with S-97 1864, Letters Received, ser. 360, Colored Troops Division, RG 94 [B-394]. Other endorsements.

141C: War Department Memorandum

[*Washington, D.C. January 1883*]
   It is shown by the records of this office that this officer [*Stephen A. Swails*] was commissioned 2nd Lieutenant by the Governor of Mass March 11, 1864; that he was then 1st Sergeant of company F 54th Mass Vols, absent in General Hospital for treatment for wounds received in the battle of Olustee Fla Feby 20th 1864; that he rejoined his regiment May 12, 1864, and on the 14th of the same month was assigned to duty as 2nd Lieutenant of company D; that he remained on duty as acting 2nd Lieutenant "awaiting muster" (a part of the time in command of the Co.) until Oct 20th 1864, when, in accordance with instructions from superior authority, he was relieved from duty as 2nd Lieutenant and placed

on detached service at Regimental Hd Qrs as 1st Sergeant, and that he continued on duty as 1st Sergeant, detached, or absent by proper authority, until January 17, 1865, when he was mustered into service as 2nd Lieutenant. It is further shown that from the 30th of March 1864 until his muster into service under his commission there was a legal vacancy in his company for a 2nd Lieutenant and that the delay in his muster in that grade was by reason of his color, he being partially of African blood. For this reason the Department Commander declined to discharge him for promotion and his action was approved by the Secretary of War, whose personal attention was called to the case. This action, as appears from memoranda filed with the papers (vide "unofficial" statement herewith from the then Chief of the Bureau for Colored Troops), was prompted by the opinion that it was contrary to public policy to receive persons of African descent into the service as Commissioned Officers. On the 15th of Jany 1865, however, Maj Genl Foster commanding the Department of the South, made the following statement:

"Sergt Swails is so nearly white that it would be difficult to discover any trace of his African blood. He is so intelligent and of such good character that after a fair trial I now recommend his being allowed to serve as a commissioned officer."

Upon this recommendation the Acting Adjutant General of the Army (Colonel E. D. Townsend), being then at Head Qrs Department of the South, issued the following order:

War Department *Hilton Head SC,* Jan'y 15, 1865.

S.O:

Authority is hereby given the Commanding General Dept of the South to discharge Sergt S. A. Swailes, 54th Mass Vols (colored) and to muster him into service as Second Lieutenant of the same regiment, to which he has been commissioned by the Governor of Masstts.

By order of the Sec War

E. D. T.
A.A.G.

Genl Foster.

Upon this authority Swails was mustered into service, as stated, to date Jan'y 17, 1865. He now claims recognition and pay as 2nd Lieutenant from the date of his commission – March 11, 1864. The laws and regulations governing the subject of musters, independently of the special circumstances and action in his case, would justify his recognition as 2nd Lieutenant from the date he was assigned to duty as such – *May 14, 1864.*

HD

345

Memorandum in case of Stephen A. Swails, late 2nd Lieutenant 54 Mass. Vols. (Colored), filed with S-97 1864, Letters Received, ser. 360, Colored Troops Division, RG 94 [B-394]. A War Department endorsement of January 29, 1883, ordered that Swails be recognized as 2nd Lieutenant from May 14, 1864. Other endorsements. The "unofficial" Bureau of Colored Troops statement referred to is a December 13, 1864, endorsement by C. W. Foster. (*Freedom*, ser. 2: doc. 141b.) Swails's military service record contains a copy of an order from the Adjutant General's Office (Special Orders No. 27, 1 Feb. 1883) authorizing Swails's pay as lieutenant from May 14, 1864. (Service record of Stephen Swails, 54th Mass. Inf. [Col'd.], Carded Records, Volunteer Organizations: Civil War, ser. 519, RG 94 [N-45].) Paradoxically, in 1895 the War Department's Record and Pension Office ruled that Swails's appointment dated from April 28, 1865. (Col. F. R. Ainesworth to the Auditor for the War Department, 14 June 1895, filed with S-97 1864, Letters Received, ser. 360, Colored Troops Division, RG 94 [B-394].)

142: Ohio Congressman to the Secretary of War, Enclosing a Letter from a Black Recruiter to the Secretary of War; and a Reply from the Bureau of Colored Troops to the Recruiter

Hiram [*Ohio*]. March 28, 1865
Dear Sir. Enclosed please find the application of John M. Langston of Oberlin. for a commission in the army. His a graduate of the College. and has been a practicing lawyer for the last ten years— He is an exceedingly fine speaker & has taken an active part in recruiting colored men— He has probably done much more in that way than any other Colored man in the U.S.

I am glad you have broken the ice and commenced giving commissions to colored men   It is very important that those who are commisioned should not fail—and I know of no colored man in the U.S. and but few if any men—who could succeed so well as he would in command of a regiment—

I therefore respectfully recommend that he be appointed a Colonel of Colored troops—   Very Respectfully Your O'b't Servt,
ALS   J. A. Garfield

[*Enclosure*]   Oberlin [*Ohio*] March 20. 1865.
Sir: I am a Colored resident of the State of Ohio. Though a colored man I have been according to Ohio Law a voter for the

last ten years. Since the outbreak of our terrible Rebellion I have been as actively ingaged in the Recruitment of Colored Troops for the service as a colored man could be. I recruited the 5th U.S.C.T., under Maj Geo L. Stearns, raising myself the money out of which the Bounty Fund was made for this Regiment, and buying and presenting to them Regimental Colors. I, also, assisted in recruiting the 54 & 55 Regiments of Massachusetts Volunteer Infantry. I desire, Sir, to make myself more useful to the Government. I think if I had a respectable rank, in the service, I could make myself of special use in the Recruitment and Organization of colored Troops. I therefore ask to be commissioned as a Colonel, if compatable with the rules and regulations of the service. Permit me to ask your early attention to this matter, and a reply as soon as practicable. I have the honor to be Your most obedient servant,

ALS   John M Langston.

Washington, May 17, 1865.

Sir: In reply to your letter of March 20″ 1865, asking for an appointment as Colonel of Colored Troops, I am directed to say that recruiting has ceased, and there is no vacancy to which you can be appointed. I am, Sir, Very Respectfully, Your Obedient Servant.

HLcS   C. W. Foster

J. A. Garfield to Hon. E. M. Stanton, 28 Mar. 1865, enclosing John M. Langston to Hon. E. M. Stanton, 20 Mar. 1865; A.A. Genl. C. W. Foster to John M. Langston, 17 May 1865, all filed with W-276 1865, Letters Received, ser. 360, Colored Troops Division, RG 94 [B-158]. Endorsement, another enclosure.

143: Commander of the District of Wilmington, North Carolina, to the Bureau of Colored Troops

Wilmington, N.C., August 21st, *1865.*

Colonel   I have the honor to call your attention to a communication from Maj. Philip Weinmann 37th U.S.C.T dated August 5th 1865 – which recommends Q.M. Sergt. John. L. Hodges for promotion as 2nd Lieut. in the 37th Regiment U.S.C.T. – fowarded from these Hd. Qrs. August 8th 1865 "Approved".

I would respectfully state as a matter of justice to the Government, and for the information of the War Dept. – that the said Sergt. Hodges is a colored man, – a fact not known at Post or Disctrict Head Quarters, when the paper in question was forwarded by them. In deference to the previous practice and supposed policy of the Government in this matter I desire to change my endorsement upon Maj. Weinmann's recommendation to *"Disapproved"* – I am Colonel Very respectfully Yr. Obt. Sert
ALS   J. W. Ames

[*Endorsement*] Head Quarters Dept N Caro–   Raleigh N. Caro– Aug. 25th 1865   Respectfully forwarded   The endorsement from these H^d Q^r of Aug 22^d 1865 – was made under the impression that Q^r Mr Sergt Hodge was a white man. I respectfully withdraw my recommendation in the case – & desire to change the endorsement to "Disapproved"   Thos H. Ruger Bvt Maj Genl Comdg

Bvt. Brig. Genl. J. W. Ames to Brevet Colonel C. W. Foster, 21 Aug. 1865, W-738 1865, Letters Received, ser. 360, Colored Troops Division, RG 94 {B-306}. Another endorsement. According to his military service record, Hodges did not rise above the rank of quartermaster sergeant. (Service record of John L. Hodges, 37th USCI, Carded Records, Volunteer Organizations: Civil War, ser. 519, RG 94.)

CHAPLAINS AND SURGEONS

144: Black Acting Chaplain to the Secretary of State

                    Camp Casey Washington City May 18th 1864
dear sir   please parden me for troubling you with business that is not Immediately connected with your office, yet it being justice to myself & of interest to my comrads in the military service of the government, I hope your honor will at once pardon me for the liberty I take in writing you such a letter. You will judge from past correspondence whilst in Canada that I was anxious to serve my country to the best of my humble ability. I have recruited colored men for every colored regiment raised in the north forsaken my church in ohio & canvassed the intire north & west urging my

people to inlist & have succeded in every instant at various times were told that I would have the chaplaincy of some one of the colored Regiment. I nearly recruited half the men in the 28th U.S. Colored Infrantry Regiment raised in Indiana Gov O. P. Morton of Ind promised to give me the office *but* could not as it was transfered from the volunteer serv to that of the regular Army. my officers have me acting as a chaplain but no man seeke my commission. I pray you will see me justified after having done as much as I have in raising such troops. I refer you to Gov Andrew of Mass Todd of ohio Morton of Ind Seymore of New York & Spridge of Rhode I— I also joined the regt as a private to be with my boys & should I fail to get my commission I shall willingly serve my time out, but I know you can get me my commission if any other gentleman in the world can & at the same time feel quite certain that should you vail to give my humble plea due consideration no other will. I pray you will aid me sprining from so humble an origin as myself namely that of being the body servant of Robert Toombs. please let your humble servant hear from you as soon as possible. May heaven Bless you & family in all your future pursuits I am dear sir your very humble servant

ALS   Garland. H. White

[*Endorsement*] I knew the writer of the within when he was a slave of Robert Toombs in Washington and I knew him afterwards a fugitive in Canada. I commend his case respectfully to the Hon. Secretary of War. William H. Seward

Acting Chaplain Garland H. White to Hon. Wm. H. Seward, 18 May 1864, service record of Garland H. White, 28th USCI, Carded Records, Volunteer Organizations: Civil War, ser. 519, RG 94 [N-6]. Other endorsements. Other records in the same file indicate that pursuant to White's election as chaplain by the officers of the regiment, he was mustered as chaplain on November 1, 1864, his appointment effective retroactively to October 25, 1864.

145A: Black Sergeant to the Commander of the Department of Virginia and North Carolina

[*Virginia*] Nov 4th 1864

General, Sir: I have come with all respect, to lay before you confidentially, for your Consideration; from the exalted standpoint which you occupy A grievance which in my humble estimation demands redress. Your servant has for one year been a Minister, of the Gospel, and from my early youth I have been desirous of laboring in that manner, for nine years I have been a member of the first Christian Church, in Louisville Ky. which is a White Congregation, Metropolitan, and highly respectable. being a model of Churches, in the United States and in England. our pastor Elder D. P. Henderson preached in augusta Georgia, seven weeks, after that state, passed the Ordinance o secession, and upheld for the lawful government in the midst of Rebel Bayonets. he obtained for me last June, from the Missionary society in Cincinnati, of which he is life Director, the appointment of Missionary. To labor for the instruction of Contrabands. I told him that for the present I Considered the Army my sphere of Labor. And if the society Considered me qualified for the position of Missionary; I was qualified for that of army Chaplain in a Regiment of the same Class of persons. where upon he told me he would see Colonel Hammond the commander of the Barracks at Louisville and obtain the appointment for me. he saw Colonel Hammond, who told him I could get the appointment on the Commendation of the Eldership of the Church whereupon the Commendation of the Eldership, was given in written form, and is now on the Records of the Church. In my regiment I have faithfully filled the post of Chaplain, and Color sergeant. I have procured a thousand and over six hundred Books, in Cincinnati for the instruction of the Regiment and one hundred and fifty dollars worth of Sanitary goods. I enlisted last June under the solemn promise from Colonel Hammond, witnessed by Dr T. S. Bell. Elder D. P. Henderson, and that I would be appointed to the Chaplaincy of one of our Colored Regiments.

I am desirous of serving our Government in any capacity, but this being my true calling, I can be more useful in this capacity than in any other. this matter is under a just God, most Respectfully submitted to your Consideration. I have the Honor sir, to remain your most obedient serv't

ALS   Francis A. Boyd

350

Serg't. Francis A. Boyd to General [Benjamin F. Butler], 4 Nov. 1864, service record of Francis A. Boyd, 109th USCI, Carded Records, Volunteer Organizations: Civil War, ser. 519, RG 94 [N-36]. On November 23, 1864, General Benjamin F. Butler appointed Boyd chaplain of the 109th USCI, which had been organized in Kentucky and in which Boyd had been serving as sergeant. (Appointment certificate, 23 Nov. 1864, filed with V-134 1864, Letters Received, ser. 360, Colored Troops Division, RG 94 [B-133].)

145B: Black Chaplain to the Commander of the Department of Virginia and North Carolina

Head Quarters, 109th U.S.C. Troops [*Virginia*], Jan' 5th 1865. Sir   the enclosed statement, has not been answered up to this Date, it was sent to the Colonel Tuesday Jan' 3rd between the hours, of six and eight p.m.   I have reason to believe that it has been entered upon the Field and Staff, muster, and pay roll, that I was appointed Chaplain in this Regiment, by Major General Butler, against the express wishes of the Field and Staff officers.   I have been coolly and contemptuously treated by the Officers of this Regiment with some exceptions,   predjudices are Dark, and Bitter, and I feel that my life is in peril   not long after my appointment, the evening of the same Day, that I recieved my Commission, the Colonel said that he understood that it was an impression, at Headquarters, that he had made promises of the Chaplaincy to me and that these promises placed his honor in peril, and the Man, who placed his honor in peril imperilled his life.   but know oh General that it was not Colonel O. A. Bartholomew, but Colonel Hammond of Taylor Barracks, Louisville Ky who made the promise   I send enclosed some Documents, from Louisville, and I Desire your protection. in the name of a long Down trodden and oppressed but truly loyal people.   With great respect Your most obed't serv't

ALS   Francis A. Boyd

Chaplain Francis A. Boyd to Major General B. F. Butler, 5 Jan. 1865, service record of Francis A. Boyd, 109th USCI, Carded Records, Volunteer Organizations: Civil War, ser. 519, RG 94 [N-36]. The statement that Boyd refers to as having been sent to Colonel Bartholomew on January 3 is not in the file; the enclosures from Louisville, which are in the file, include a letter from Boyd's half-brother, George Taylor, describing his efforts to gather the necessary documentation of Boyd's ordination, and letters of testimony from prominent white church leaders in Louisville. Boyd also wrote repeatedly to President Lincoln about his commission, referring to the President as "the patron of universal Liberty," whom "the Colored people, look upon . . . as their Friend." (Chaplain Francis A. Boyd to A. Lincoln, 12 Jan., 25 Feb., and 9 Mar. 1865, all filed with V-134 1864, Letters Received, ser. 360, Colored Troops Division, RG 94 [B-133].) In the letter of February 25, Boyd described a conversation with the adjutant general of the military division under which his regiment served. The adjutant general offered Boyd a position as clerk, which Boyd refused because the War Department had not yet ruled on his appointment as chaplain. Boyd then informed the adjutant of his regiment about the clerkship offer, declaring it "an insult to me, and my race, and that my race, were the only people, who were loyal as a class in the United States. therefore, if any among them rose upon their merits, no one had a right to try, to defraud them out of their office. . . ."

145C: Black Chaplain to the President

City Point V.A. May 12th 1865.

your excellency   I have the honor to communicate, at this fitting season, the dawn of peace the following story of the circumstances of my enlistment and my position as a Soldier. thinking that, I could serve God my race & country best in the sphere which I considered my true calling a minister, I determined upon the enlistment of colored troops in my native state – Kentucky to enter the army as Chaplain if I could but as a soldier, if not. to this end, I visited Colonel Hammond Com'd'g Taylor Barracks Louisville Ky who assured me I could be appointed Chaplain, but that I must enlist to recieve such appointment, not knowing the law on the matter and confiding in his word I enlisted June 23rd 1865 [1864]. After enlistment I need only to say that my hopes built upon the promises made me were blasted, as color sergeant I served with my regiment performing the duties of Chaplain & post master also even after the Chaplain Rev. Mr. Tarr, has taken his office until the 2d of December, 1864, at which time I was assigned to duty as Chaplain of the Regiment by the Colonel, General Butler having appointed & commissioned me to the office, upon the representation, of the facts to him   I filled my office honorably and industriously as my Colonel himself acknowledged up to the 25th February 1865, when upon a declaration being made by him to the War department it was revoked, and I was reduced to the ranks by order of Maj. General Ord. I have the

name of doing my duty faithfully in every position And I have
been offered the position of Hospital steward and orderly sergeant,
by the Colonel of my regiment, but I refused to accept it for the
sake of the service, because it would look bad to see a man who
had been a commissioned officer on his staff and whose only
dishonor was the color of his skin, holding the place of a
noncommissiond officer, therefore knowing as I do that alarm and
distrust exists among the Colored Troops who have witnessed these
proceedings, and to convince them that Justice holds sway, and
that this the hour of peace, is the hour of Judgement do appeal to
you to grant me an honourable position, in the army as I do not
by any means which to leave the service until I have shown what I
can do, and that a colored man, is capable of doing anything
under proper instruction that a white man can do. I am twenty
four years of age, and within I send you my church Letter, as a
sort of credentials Very respectfully Your obe't se'v't
ALS   Francis A. Boyd

[*Enclosure*]   Louisville Ky Feb 22^d 1865.
We the undersigned accredited ministers of the Christian Church
do hereby certify that Francis. A. Boyd is a regularly ordained
Minister of Said Church, of present good Standing and we do
hereby recommend his appointment as a Chaplain in the Military
Service of the United States. Said Francis A. Boyd, is a member
of the Christian Church, Corner of 4th & Walnut streets in the
City of Louisville Ky.
                    D. P. Henderson Pastor Christian Ch.
                    D. G. Stewart, a minister
                    Moses Smith, A minister
                    J E Noyes A Minister
HDS   Benjamin Skim Elder

Private Francis A. Boyd to Your Excellency [Andrew Johnson], 12 May
1865, enclosing a statement by Pastor D. P. Henderson et al., 22 Feb.
1865, filed with V-134 1864, Letters Received, ser. 360, Colored Troops
Division, RG 94 [B-133]. Documents in the same file contain additional
information regarding Boyd's case. In February 1865, Colonel Orion A.
Bartholomew, commander of Boyd's regiment, obtained a War Department
order revoking Boyd's commission as chaplain on the grounds that he had
not been elected to the position by the field officers and company commanders of the regiment, as regulations prescribed. Boyd returned to the
ranks as a private. In November 1865, the officers elected him chaplain,
but, because the regiment had fallen below strength, he could not be

mustered into the office. Boyd left service with his regiment in March 1866, still ranked as a private, even though he claimed that he had performed chaplain's duties from November 1865 until the regiment's muster out. Additional information in the file indicates that in 1867 Boyd claimed retroactive chaplain's pay for the time he served in that capacity. The claim dragged on for over twenty years. In 1886, former General Benjamin F. Butler wrote to the War Department on Boyd's behalf, and two years later a Kentucky congressman introduced a resolution in the U.S. House of Representatives to grant Boyd the pay he claimed. The bill apparently died in the House Committee on War Claims.

~~~

146A: Black Physician to the President

Toronto Canada West Jan 7" /63

Sir, Having seen that it is intended to garrison the U.S. forts &c with colored troops, I beg leave to apply to you for an appointment as surgeon to some of the coloured regiments, or as physician to some of the depots of "freedmen." I was compelled to leave my native country, and come to this on account of prejudice against colour, for the purpose of obtaining a knowledge of my profession; and having accomplished that object, at one of the principle educational institutions of this Province, I am now prepared to practice it, and would like to be in a position where I can be of use to my race.

If you will take the matter into favorable consideration, I can give satisfactory reference as to character and qualification from some of the most distinguished members of the profession in this city where I have been in practice for about six years. I Remain Sir Yours Very Respectfully

ALS   A. T Augusta

A. T. Augusta to President Abraham Lincon, 7 Jan. 1863, service record of Alexander T. Augusta, 7th USCI, Carded Records, Volunteer Organizations: Civil War, ser. 519, RG 94 [N-47]. Augusta signed the letter as "Bachelor of Medicine Trinty College Toronto." Other letters in Augusta's military service record contain additional information regarding his request for appointment. On the same day that he applied to the President, Augusta wrote a nearly identical letter to Secretary of War Edwin M. Stanton, seeking to "be of use to my race, at this important epoch." In late March 1863, the Army Medical Board in Washington, D.C., ruled that Augusta's entry into U.S. service would be "an evident violation of her Britannic

Majesty's Proclamation of Neutrality," inasmuch as Augusta was not only "a person of African descent" but also "an alien & a British Subject." (M. Clymer to Brig. Gen. Hammond, 23 Mar. 1863.) Augusta, now in Washington, suggested that his case "was not fully understood by the Board." He explained that his original letter of application had made no secret about his color and that he expected to serve in a black regiment. He asked for favorable consideration of his case, concluding, "I have come near a thousand miles at a great expence and saccrifice, hoping to be of some use to the country and my race at this eventful period. . . ." (A. T. Augusta to the President and Members of the Army Medical Board, 30 Mar. 1863.) Upon reconsideration, the board found Augusta "qualified for the position of Surgeon in the negro regiment now being raised." (Surg. W. Moss to Brigadier General Wm. A. Hammond, 1 Apr. 1863.)

146B: **Commander of a Washington, D.C., Contraband Camp to the Secretary of War**

Washington DC May 16th 1863

The bearer D[r] A S Agusta Surgeon U S A reported to me, as commander of this Camp, to be assigned by me to duty in the Camp. Knowing that D[r] Agusta ranked as Major, & that I ranked only as Captain, I felt as a loss as to what I should do, douting my right to assign to duty an officer who ranked me. I referred him to D[r] C B Webster Surgeon in charge of the Contraband Camp Hospital who being a Contract Surgeon was embarrassed by the same consideration. D[r] Augusta returned to you & an order came to me, from the Head Qrs of the Military Governor asking why I had not assigned D[r] Augusta to duty, to which I replied stating the reason assingned above, & the reply to that from Gen Hitchcock, Acting Military Governor, is an order of which the enclosed paper is a copy

The usual routine, according to my understanding for such matters is for the Surgeon General to order Medical officers to Report to some Medical Director, & for the Medical Director to assign such officer to his post of duty. The Surgeons in the Contraband Camp Hospital report immediately to Medical Director Abbott, who appoints or removes them at discretion If your wish is for D[r] Augusta to be assigned to duty in the Camp Hospital, Medical Director Abbott is the proper channel through which to have it done. If you wish him to be on duty only in the Camp, then I suppose I have the power to assign him & will do so, but I have not heretofore understood that there was any necessity for a physician in Camp apart from and independent of the

355

Hospital. All of which is respectfully submitted. Yours Most
Respectfully

ALS   James J Ferree

[*Enclosure*]   Military District Washington
Special Orders No 109   May 15th 1863

(EXTRACT)

13 Surgeon A S Augusta U S Vols having reported in
conformity with Special Order No 191 Head Quarters Dept
Washington is assigned to duty at the Camp for Colored
persons   He will report to Capt Ferree in charge   By command of
Maj Gen Hitchcock
Copy

HDc

James J. Ferree to Hon. E. M. Stanton, 16 May 1863, enclosing extract
from Special Orders No. 109, Headquarters Military District Washington,
15 May 1863, A-811 1863, Letters Received, ser. 12, RG 94 [K-65].

146C: White Army Surgeons to the President

Camp Stanton near Bryantown Md. [*February 1864*]
Sir, We the undersigned, Medical Officers in the Regiments of
Colored Troops, under command of Brig. Gen. Wm Birney at this
camp, have the honor most respectfully to ask your attention to
the following Statement.

When we made applications for positions in the Colored Service,
the understanding was universal that *all* Commissioned Officers
were to be white men. Judge of our Surprise and disappointment,
when upon joining our respective regiments we found that the
Senior Surgeon of the command was a Negro.

We claim to be behind no one, in a desire for the elevation and
improvement of the Colored race, in this country, and we are
willing to sacrifice much, in so grand a cause, as our present
positions, may testify. But we cannot in *any* cause, willingly
compromise what we consider a proper self respect. Nor do we
deem that the interests of either the country or of the Colored
race, can demand this of us. Such degradation, we believe to be
involved, in our voluntarily continuing in the Service, as
Subordinates to a colored officer. We therefore most respectfully,
yet earnestly, request, that this *unexpected, unusual,* and most

356

unpleasant relationship in which we have been placed, may in *some way* be terminated. Most Respectfully Your Obt. Servants,

J. B. McPherson   E. M. Pease

Chas C Topliff   Joel Morse

HLS   M O Carter   Henry Grange

Surgeon J. B. McPherson et al. to President Abraham Lincoln, [Feb. 1864], M-118 1864, Letters Received, ser. 360, Colored Troops Division, RG 94 [B-11]. Augusta had been assigned to duty as surgeon in the 7th USCI on October 2, 1863. The petitioners, surgeons and assistant surgeons in the 7th, 9th, and 19th USCI regiments, were all commissioned and assigned after Augusta and thus ranked inferior to him. The War Department did not respond to their petition in writing but did transfer Augusta away from his regiment to the recruitment rendezvous for black troops in Baltimore. While on detached duty examining black recruits, Augusta retained his rank as surgeon in the 7th USCI. In May 1864, Joel Morse, assistant surgeon in the 7th USCI, renewed the request to have Augusta permanently reassigned. With his own path to advancement blocked by Augusta's continued affiliation with the regiment, Morse wrote a long, impassioned letter to Senator John Sherman. Morse protested Augusta's appointment to a position in which he outranked white officers, appealing to Sherman "to right this *wrong*, which to my mind is *grave, unjust*, and *humiliating;* and more particularly so, when our Government had so extensively declared its intentions to be, *not to place* any of the colored race in the capacity of Commissioned officers." Morse vowed that "if Surgeon Augusta were to return to the regiment to day, I should resign immediately; not from any personal feeling against him, but from principle. I have not the Slightest objection to Dr. Augusta's holding the position of Surgeon, but it should be an independent one, as for instance, the one he was first appointed to last year at Washington, as a Surgeon of Volunteers, in charge of Contraband Camp, or as Surgeon of Some General Hospital for Colored Troops." Morse claimed not to object in principle to black officers, but he did object to mixing them with whites: "if a Sufficient number of intelligent and educated colored men can be found to officer a regiment, complete from Colonel down to Second Lieutenant, I say well and good, appoint them, and have a colored regiment complete, in officers as well as men, either make the officers all white or all black, I for one do not care which; but this thing of amalgamation or miscegennation in the appointment of officers *I do not believe in.*" Morse added apologetically: "Perhaps when I shall have attained to perfect Manhood, in the full sense of the word, I shall just as cheerfully assent to having my most intimate associate & superior officer a colored man, as a white one; but I am free to confess that I do not expect to attain that State of perfection, in this life." (Asst. Surg. Joel Morse to Hon. John Sherman, 14 May 1864, service record of Alexander T. Augusta, 7th USCI, Carded Records, Volunteer Organizations: Civil War, ser. 519, RG 94 [N-47].) For the remainder of the war, Augusta remained on detached duty while retaining his formal affiliation with the 7th USCI. On March 13, 1865, Augusta received the brevet rank

357

of lieutenant colonel, thereby becoming the highest-ranking black officer of the Civil War era. After the war, Augusta served as a surgeon with the Freedmen's Bureau, for the most part heading the freedmen's hospital at Savannah, Georgia. (Service record of Alexander T. Augusta, 7th USCI, Carded Records, Volunteer Organizations: Civil War, ser. 519, RG 94 [N-47]; medical officer records of Alexander T. Augusta, Personal Papers, Medical Officers & Physicians, ser. 561, Record & Pension Office, RG 94 [KK-1]; U.S., *Official Army Register*, pt. 8, p. 176.)

147A: Pastor of a Washington, D.C., African Methodist Episcopal Church to the Secretary of War

Washington August 1st 1863

Dear Sir, Having been connected with the movement of raising colored troops, from its commencement in this city,

And having by repeated Solicitations, concluded to go as the chaplain of the first colored regiment, the organization was commenced in my church,

And having at the request of cols Birney and Holman sent in my application, endorsed by five regularly ordained ministers,

And having been kept in suspense for some time, expecting the position of chaplain, from the promises made by the above named colonels, and the desire expressed by the Soldiers, and several of the officers of Said regiment,

Your honor would greatly relieve me, by informing me ONCE FOR ALL whether it is the intention of the government to have colored chaplains or not,

By answering this questain, pleasing your honor, you will settle my own mind on the subject, and enable me to inform my congregation what they may depend on   your humble servant

ALS   H M Turner

H. M. Turner to Hon. E. M. Stanton, 1 Aug. 1863, filed with T-18 1863, Letters Received, ser. 360, Colored Troops Division, RG 94 [B-44]. In the same file is another letter from Turner to Stanton, dated August 24, 1863, again seeking a chaplain's commission. Turner maintained that the colonel and all the men of the 1st USCI, as well as the chief recruiter of black troops in Washington, had encouraged him to apply for the position. Moreover, he argued that he had been serving in effect as the regimental chaplain, preaching to the men regularly since the regiment was organized. He also mentioned that since his letter of August 1, he had been drafted.

147B: **Secretary of the Treasury and an Illinois Congressman to the Secretary of War**

[*Washington, D.C.*] Sep. 4. [*1863*]

Dear Sir, Allow me to introduce the Revd H. M. Turner, the colored minister of whom I spoke the other day, and whom you said you would direct to be appointed Chaplain of a Colored Regiment. He has been very useful in raising the first Colored regiment raised here & Sent to North Carolina and thinks he could be useful in raising the tone of the men now forming the second. Yours truly

S P Chase

HLS
O Lovejoy

S. P. Chase and O. Lovejoy to Hon. E. M. Stanton, 4 Sept. [1863], filed with T-18 1863, Letters Received, ser. 360, Colored Troops Division, RG 94 [B-44]. The body of the letter is in Chase's hand. In the same file are Turner's commission as chaplain in the 1st USCI, dated Nov. 6, 1863, and his acceptance of the same date.

147C: **Black Chaplain to the Secretary of War**

Front of Petersburgh V^a June 30th 1864

I have been appointed by Chaplains Hunter of the 4th U S col Troops, Asher of the 6th U.S.C.T. and Green of the 37th U S col Troops. in conjuction with my own endorsement, to petition your honor, to set a part some mark that will designate the position of Chaplain, we not having any badge or mark by which we are known, subjects us to a thousand inconveniencies, especially at Hospitals where we are the most needed, unless the gaurds know us personally, we are often treated below a private, not allowed to enter where we have important business, and some times driven away unless we show our Chaplain's appointment. We most respectfully ask for some special mark, either a strap on the shoulder, or a stripe on the arm, And we will every pray your most truly

ALS
H. M. Turner

Chaplain H. M. Turner to Hon. E. M. Stanton, 30 June 1864, T-334 1864, Letters Received, ser. 12, RG 94 [K-2]. Chaplains Hunter, Asher, and Green were all white.

147D: Black Chaplain to the Secretary of War

Atlanta, Ga, Dec 15th 1865

Sir, As per appointment I reported to the 138th U.S.C. Troops. several Days ago, But to my great Surprize, I found a Chaplain already appointed to the same Regiment, and Mustered into Service, He was appointed by the General commanding the department,

Yet I was received very courteously by all the officers, and treated with evey mark of respect, especially by the colored troops, many of whom had heard me preach years ago,

But my appointment Stands useless by virtue of another filling the posision assign me, Major General Wilson, however, Says, my sirvices in the department are highly necessary, but owing to my assignment being to a Special Regiment, and the place filled by another, I could not be mustered into service, Notwithstanding, it is much regreted by several officers that I were not appointed, and turned over to the Freedmen Bureau, where I could have assisted them in their [*effort*] to enlighten the colored people directly.

But the special point to which I desire to call you attention, is that while in rout to my regiment, I addressed about 30,000 freed people, through VIRGINIA NORTH CAROLINA and SOUTH CAROLINA, At many of which gatherings, were large numbers of white persons (ex rebels) who treated me in every instance with profound respect, Several of whom took me to their houses, and furnished me carriages free of charge, while others would aid me with ideas and advice for the freed men, which were actually good. I even had white churches thrown open for me in Columbia S,C, and the pulpits given without any demuring whatever,

Since my arrival in Georgia, I have addressed large crowds, and am still at work, And I do not feel that I could in the face of any decency ask you for another position, I have asked for two, and received them, *and to abuse favors is ingrattitude,* But one request I desire to make, and if you will grant that, I hope to never be your petitioner again, In consideration that I am a poor man, and have a large family to support, I can not afford transportation,

And I do most respectfully ask your honor for an order from your own hand, to get transportation to any point, for the purpose of *Preaching, lecturing* and *establishing Schools, Literary Societies* &c, &c, among the freed people.

I am willing to risk my wife and children at the mercy of my friends, for the good of my race five or six months, and thus give my time regardless of pay or any compensation to the cause of humanity.

The reason I write to you is, I know you are a friend to my people, and one word from you all will obey, but others are uncertain, Unless I find a *brother Mason,* in command who invaribly will oblidge, I shall wait in Atlanta Ga for your reply, be that yea or na,

Please send through the P.O. as I am at no military Quarters.

Should you question my capacity to labor with the freed men, you may read the views of Proff Fowler of N.Y. For that reason I send you this Portrait in the Phrenological Journal   Your humble servant

ALS   H. M. Turner

Chaplain H. M. Turner to Hon. E. M. Stanton, 15 Dec. 1865, T-474 1865, Letters Received, ser. 631, GA Asst. Comr., RG 105 [A-428]. Endorsements. The phrenological journal portrait is not in the file. Turner's commission as chaplain in the 1st USCI had expired with the regiment's discharge in September 1865, hence some of the confusion surrounding his appointment to the 138th USCI. The Freedmen's Bureau eventually arranged the requested transportation, and Turner traversed the state of Georgia, preaching and teaching under the Bureau's auspices before entering the political arena in the fall of 1867. (See, for example, R. L. Rhodes to Maj. Genl. Tillson, 18, 25, and 31 Dec. 1866, filed as "Georgia R.R.," Unregistered Letters Received, ser. 632, GA Asst. Comr., RG 105 [A-428].)

7

Fighting on Two Fronts: The Struggle for Equal Pay

IN THE EARLY YEARS of the war, when blacks and their abolitionist allies first petitioned for the recruitment of black freemen and slaves in the Union army, they gave little consideration to the question of treatment after muster. Black military service offered the opportunity to strike a blow against slavery and to lay the groundwork for the reconstruction of the Republic on the basis of racial equality. Drawn by these heady possibilities and forced to fend off imputations of black docility and cowardice, proenlistment strategists did not foresee that military service would itself bear the stain of inequality they hoped to eradicate.[1]

Blacks understood that they had a special interest in the war's outcome that white soldiers could not claim. Nonetheless, they expected to share every material aspect of soldierly life on an equal footing with whites. The first recruiters of black troops—notably Senator James H. Lane in Kansas, General Benjamin F. Butler in Louisiana, and Generals David Hunter and Rufus Saxton in South Carolina—promised such equality, as did Massachusetts Governor John A. Andrew. On the basis of Andrew's reported assurances from Secretary of War Edwin M. Stanton, the governors of Connecticut, Rhode Island, Ohio, and other Northern states made similar promises. The federal government ultimately violated virtually every pledge of equal treatment, but no transgression caused as much hardship or so blatantly insulted the dignity of black soldiers as the policy of discriminatory pay.

The general poverty of the black community made the pay question an especially sensitive issue. Most Northern freemen toiled as

---

[1] Published accounts of the pay struggle include: Thomas Wentworth Higginson, *Army Life in a Black Regiment* (Boston, 1869), pp. 280–92; Joseph T. Williams, *A History of the Negro Troops in the War of the Rebellion, 1861–1865* (New York, 1888), pp. 151–60; Luis F. Emilio, *History of the Fifty-fourth Regiment of Massachusetts Volunteer Infantry, 1863–1865,* 2d ed. (Boston, 1894); Dudley Taylor Cornish, *The Sable Arm: Negro Troops in the Union Army, 1861–1865* (New York, 1956), pp. 181–96; James M. McPherson, *The Negro's Civil War: How American Negroes Felt and Acted During the War for the Union* (New York, 1965); chap. 14; Herman Belz, "Law, Politics, and Race in the Struggle for Equal Pay During the Civil War," *Civil War History* 22 (Sept. 1976): 197–222.

day laborers and owned little property. Probably many had never earned more than the $13 per month, plus clothing allowance, that the army offered white volunteers.[2] Newly emancipated slaves were even more impoverished, since few escaped bondage with more than the clothes on their backs. Thus black soldiers needed regular wages to support themselves and their families, and a few extra dollars a month could mean the difference between subsistence and destitution. Although few blacks enlisted solely for the money, their expectation of soldiers' wages reinforced their aspiration for equality. Poverty and principle proved an explosive mixture.

Under such circumstances, black soldiers felt betrayed by the War Department's decision early in June 1863 to pay them three dollars less per month than white soldiers, and to deduct from the remaining ten dollars an additional three dollars for clothing.[3] In justifying its policy, the War Department cited recent congressional legislation. Two 1862 acts, the Militia Act and the Confiscation Act, authorized the President to use blacks in national service, but only the former fixed a standard of pay.[4] Reasoning that black enlistments fell under the provisions of the Militia Act, which expressly authorized black military service, rather than the Confiscation Act, which applied more generally to any employment of contrabands, the department decided to pay the soldiers $10 per month as stipulated by the former. The department ignored its own pledges of equal pay, as well as those of Hunter, Butler, Andrew, and others. The War Department also overlooked the March 1863 Enrollment Act's guarantee of pay on a par with volunteers for drafted men, even though some Northern blacks were being drafted.[5] The meager army pay appeared all the more inequitable because black civilians working for military departments could earn as much as $25 monthly by virtue of the Confiscation Act's omission of pay restrictions.

The government's default on its pledge to pay black recruits at the same rate as whites deeply insulted black soldiers and their officers. It challenged their rights as citizens at a time when they assumed that military service would affirm racial equality. It revealed starkly that racial prejudice pervaded Northern as well as Southern society. The pay question generated an awareness that

[2] *Revised Army Regulations,* pp. 361–62 for pay; pp. 169–70, 517 for clothing allowance.
[3] *Official Records,* ser. 3, vol. 3, p. 252.
[4] Both acts were approved July 17, 1862. The relevant sections are section 11 of the Confiscation Act and sections 12, 13, and 15 of the Militia Act. (*Official Records,* ser. 3, vol. 2, pp. 276, 281–82.)
[5] Section 11 of the Enrollment Act stated "That all persons thus enrolled . . . when called into service shall be placed on the same footing, in all respects, as volunteers for three years, or during the war, including advance pay and bounty as now provided by law." (*Official Records,* ser. 3, vol. 3, p. 90.)

black soldiers had to fight two wars: one against Southern secession, the other against Northern discrimination.

The decision to pay black soldiers according to the restrictive provisions of the Militia Act fell with special intensity upon black noncommissioned officers. Promotion above the rank of private earned them no added monthly pay; they received only the $10 specified by the Militia Act for all black soldiers. Meanwhile, white privates and corporals earned $13 per month; company sergeants, $17; first sergeants, $20; and regimental sergeants, $21.[6] The white officers who organized and commanded black regiments lamented the stultifying effect of uniform pay for blacks upon the development of a black noncommissioned officer corps. Black men in the noncommissioned ranks not only shared that perspective, but also felt the sting of the discriminatory pay provision in monetary terms and smarted at the knowledge that the highest-ranking black sergeant earned less than a white private. Like all black soldiers, they condemned the policy that consigned them to inferior status purely on account of their ancestry. Taking advantage of their wider literacy, black noncommissioned officers penned memorials that swelled the larger chorus of protests emanating from the black enlisted ranks.

The War Department's decision also affected the black commissioned officers serving in the Department of the Gulf. Though General Nathaniel P. Banks maneuvered to eliminate them from the officer corps, he permitted black officers to draw the same pay as their white counterparts as long as they remained in service. When the War Department announced its policy of paying all blacks only $10, black officers sent an indignant protest to the Secretary of War, but the lower rate stood. The War Department similarly refused black surgeons and chaplains payment on a par with whites of the same rank. Like all blacks affected by the policy, surgeons and chaplains denounced discriminatory treatment.

The 54th Massachusetts regiment, recruited from all over the North by Governor Andrew on the promise of equality, sprang to action first. Sent to South Carolina in May 1863 for service under the sympathetic General Hunter, the regiment by July still had not received any pay whatsoever. Colonel Robert G. Shaw, who would die in the 54th's assault on Fort Wagner late in July, informed Governor Andrew at the beginning of the month that he would prohibit paymasters from distributing the inferior $10 compensation. Rather, he demanded that his men be mustered out of service.[7] After they had proved their mettle at Fort Wagner, the

---

[6] *Revised Army Regulations,* pp. 358–63.
[7] Robert G. Shaw to Governor Andrew, 2 July 1863, in Emilio, *Fifty-fourth Regiment,* pp. 47–48.

men themselves also refused to accept discriminatory pay. They further rejected Andrew's offer to use state funds to make up the difference between what he had promised and what the War Department offered. Most felt insulted that Andrew should think their objection a matter of money rather than of principle. A deputation from the governor in December 1863 could not shake the men's determination, and they reaffirmed their resolve to accept nothing less than equal pay from the War Department.

The Massachusetts soldiers' protest began as a result of the betrayal of the promise of equal pay made at the time they enlisted. As vast numbers of black volunteers entered the service during the second half of 1863, they, too, viewed the matter of discriminatory pay as a stigma of inferiority and protested against it. Yet no black soldiers matched the level of opposition expressed by the early regiments. Like the Northern units, the South Carolina regiments had enlisted under express War Department guarantees of equal pay,[8] and, even more galling, they had drawn at least one payment at the regular volunteer rate before the lower pay standard for black troops went into effect. Not surprisingly, then, opposition to the discriminatory pay policy centered in the South Carolina Sea Islands, where both the Massachusetts and South Carolina black regiments served. As the Massachusetts protest intensified during the summer and fall of 1863, the South Carolina troops kept pace. Laying specific claim to Secretary of War Stanton's written promise of equal pay, they and their officers petitioned the War Department to reinstate the equal rate of $13 per month. When the War Department did not satisfy the claim, they too took a principled stand and refused to accept the $10 offered them.

Their principles proved expensive. Soldiers daily received letters describing the hardships their families endured. Many learned of kin lodged in poorhouses for want of money to support themselves. Such reports shortened tempers and fueled unrest. For a time during the fall of 1863, the Massachusetts men teetered on the brink of mutiny, and only the most strenuous efforts of their officers averted violence. While freeborn Northerners threatened precipitate action, former slaves in the 3rd South Carolina Volunteers pressed their case to the limit. In mid-November 1863, led by Sergeant William Walker, the men of one company stacked their arms before the tent

---

[8] On August 25, 1862, Secretary of War Stanton authorized General Rufus Saxton to enlist 5,000 black troops and expressly indicated that such soldiers should "receive the same pay and rations as are allowed by law to volunteers in the service." (*Official Records,* ser. 1, vol. 14, p. 377.) Massachusetts Governor John A. Andrew maintained that Stanton had given him verbal assurances to the same effect (see *Freedom,* ser. 2: doc. 28), but Stanton's letter to Saxton is the only written War Department promise of equal pay to the early black regiments.

of their regimental commander, Colonel Augustus G. Bennett, and refused to do any further duty until the pay matter was settled in their favor. They adamantly refused to heed Bennett's warning that their action constituted mutiny, punishable by death. Despite his sympathy for their cause, Bennett formally charged the men with mutiny, and in February 1864 a firing squad executed Sergeant Walker in the presence of his entire brigade.

Northern black troops felt especially betrayed by the inferior pay policy, and they too protested their discriminatory pay. Michigan soldiers stationed on the Sea Islands in close proximity to the Massachusetts and South Carolina regiments also adopted the tactic of refusing to accept discriminatory pay. Farther away, on the coast of Texas, the only Rhode Island black regiment, the 14th Heavy Artillery, followed the same course and in March 1864, their protest ended in tragedy. After the men of one company refused to accept their pay, their commander court-martialed some two dozen noncommissioned officers and privates. Ensuing sentences of imprisonment for as much as one year at hard labor generated seething unrest, which soon erupted in a confrontation between a white lieutenant and a black enlisted man. The lieutenant killed the man on the spot; the regimental commander sustained the officer's action without even a reprimand and placed all the enlisted men under close guard until they capitulated. As long as it remained unsettled, the pay issue exposed and aggravated the entire range of discrimination that blacks experienced in the military and heightened the militance of black soldiers.

Support from high-ranking officers helped sustain the protest in some regiments and forestalled prosecution of larger numbers of angry soldiers. Technically, refusal to accept pay constituted mutiny, which, as both the Walker case and that of the 14th Rhode Island Artillery demonstrated, could meet summary and deadly punishment. Fortunately for the men of their regiments, commanders Robert G. Shaw and Edward N. Hallowell of the 54th Massachusetts, Norwood P. Hallowell and Alfred S. Hartwell of the 55th Massachusetts, James M. Williams of the 1st Kansas Colored Volunteers, and Thomas W. Higginson of the 1st South Carolina Volunteers, as well as Lane and Andrew, all came from abolitionist backgrounds. Similarly, Generals Hunter, Saxton, and Butler had been antislavery men. Furthermore, most regimental commanders— regardless of their backgrounds and despite their opposition to certain tactics of the protesters—endorsed the principle of equal pay. Without such allies, the soldiers' protest would have been arrested at the outset with a few exemplary executions.

In their tenacious pursuit of equality, black soldiers made the pay issue a symbol of the larger struggle for racial justice. Their cause sparked wide reaction throughout the North, mobilizing the entire spectrum of abolitionist opinion, as well as the sympathy and organized efforts of free black communities, in defense of equality. The protest spread as black enlistments escalated. By late 1863, all quarters joined the protest against discriminatory pay. In his annual report to the President in December 1863, even Secretary of War Stanton recommended that Congress remove the binding restrictions of the Militia Act so that black soldiers could collect the same pay as whites.[9]

Struggling to settle an issue so potentially explosive, Congress cast about for a solution that would extricate it from the contradictory provisions of the Confiscation and Militia Acts and at the same time offer a measure of justice to black soldiers. In the spring and early summer of 1864, the spirit of insubordination again arose as black soldiers throughout the South, especially the Massachusetts regiments stationed in South Carolina, lost patience with congressional dawdling on the pay issue. While their superiors threatened harsh punishment for insubordinate acts, Colonels Hallowell of the 54th and Hartwell of the 55th reiterated Colonel Shaw's earlier plea to have the men mustered out of service if the government abrogated its contractual obligation of equal pay, and Hartwell left on a special mission to Washington to plead the case of the black soldiers. In mid-June 1864, Congress at last responded, passing a military appropriations bill that authorized equal pay for all black soldiers retroactive to January 1, 1864, and continuing thereafter. In an attempt to settle the claims of the Northern regiments, the law makers also ruled that all black soldiers free on April 19, 1861, when the war began, were entitled to receive the pay allowed by law at the time of their enlistment, leaving to the Attorney General the determination of the applicable law. In July 1864, Attorney General Edward Bates ruled that the restrictive Militia Act did not govern the case of the free black soldiers and that the Confiscation Act – by virtue of its absence of pay constraints – provided for pay equal to that of white soldiers, that is, $13 per month. At the beginning of August, the War Department implemented Bates's ruling and ordered regimental commanders to ascertain, by administering an oath, who of their men had been free at the start of the war.[10] The

---

[9] *Official Records,* ser. 3, vol. 3, p. 1132.

[10] The pay provisions formed section 2 of the Appropriations Act of June 15, 1864. (*Official Records,* ser. 3, vol. 4, p. 448.) On June 20, 1864, Congress increased the pay of all soldiers, black and white, effective May 1, 1864. A private's compensation rose from $13 to $16 per month. (*Official Records,* ser. 3, vol. 4, p. 448.) Under these two acts, black privates thus became entitled to receive $13 per month beginning January 1, 1864, and $16 per month beginning May 1, 1864. The provisions equalizing the pay of black and white soldiers

"Quaker Oath" devised by Colonel Edward N. Hallowell of the Massachusetts 54th, simply required black soldiers to swear that at the start of the war "no man had the right to demand unrequited labor of you."

The congressional action began to defuse the pay issue, and the 54th and 55th Massachusetts regiments held an ecstatic celebration of their victory.[11] But the freemen's sweet success had a bitter taste to soldiers who had been slaves when the war began. They deeply resented the April 19th clause. The South Carolina regiments—those with the strongest case for equal pay—took no pleasure in seeing their claim annihilated on an arbitrary technicality. Hence they continued to press their demand, refusing to accept any pay for another nine months.

In a March 1865 enrollment act, Congress finally acknowledged Stanton's August 1862 order to Saxton as contractually binding on the War Department and recognized as legitimate the claim to equal pay from day of enlistment of the South Carolina regiments.[12] The legislation also empowered the Secretary of War to decide similar cases on an individual basis. Three months later, in reply to a petition from the Kansas officers, the department ruled against Lane's regiment, presumably on the grounds that Lane lacked proper authority to offer equal pay at the time he organized the regiment. That decision closed the Kansas soldiers' case.

By virtue of its policy of inequality, the Union government inadvertently enriched the black military experience. Unequal pay incited black soldiers to challenge discrimination with the same vigor and determination they used to fight slavery. The issue united soldiers of various backgrounds in a common struggle, even though it did not necessarily abolish perceived differences between freeborn and slaveborn. The struggle produced leaders from among the ranks and captured the support of Northern black communities and segments of white public opinion, both in Washington and throughout the North. In turn, the protest, and its largely successful outcome, shaped the thoughts and actions of black soldiers returning home to commence a new struggle for freedom.

---

also for the first time allowed black noncommissioned officers to receive higher pay than privates, at the same rate as white noncommissioned officers of comparable rank. Attorney General Bates announced his opinion on July 14, 1864, and the War Department implemented the decision about the pay due to free black soldiers in Circular No. 60, issued August 1, 1864. (*Official Records*, ser. 3, vol. 4, pp. 490–93, 564–65.)

[11] *Christian Recorder*, 12 Nov. 1864; Emilio, *Fifty-fourth Regiment*, pp. 227–28.

[12] Section 5 of the Enrollment Act of March 3, 1865, provided for retroactive equal pay to those regiments enlisted under explicit Presidential or War Department promise to that effect. (*Official Records*, ser. 3, vol. 4, p. 1223.)

148: Governor of Massachusetts to a Virginia Assistant Superintendent of Contrabands

Boston, May 23, 1863

My Dear Sir:

. . . .

The only letter from Mr. Stanton which has been received by me was the one sent by the hand of General Wild not many days since, covering an opinion of Mr. Whiting, the solicitor of the Department, which letter purported to be the reply to my recent inquiries and suggestions in regard to the proposed brigade of colored men to be raised under General Wild. I received it one evening, ran my eye over it, and over the opinion, and seing that it bore relation to General Wild's business (in which I was interested, to be sure, and was assisting as well as I could) but not to my own special affairs, I passed the papers immediately over to General Wild

. . . .

I know, as a matter of memory, that the subject of compensation of the colored troops, was distnctly spoken of and fully and explicitly stated, by the Secretary of War, in our conversations together, and in the same connection with the subject of appointing colored officers and the payment of twenty-five dollars of the United States bounty. And I know that their pay, &c., was distinctly agreed to be the same pay, &c., awarded to our other volunteers.

. . . .

The only difference, so Mr. Stanton said, which he would make, as against our colored volunteeers, was in regard to commissions. He verbally required me not to commission any colored men as officers. The written order does not allude to that point, however, at all. On the face of the order our colored volunteers are precisely like the white volunteers.

. . . .

One regiment already mustered in with the State bounty in their pockets and much money expended by us on it, now awaits only the readiness of the transport when it will sail for the South. Unless they are paid like other troops then they will have been cruelly misled. My statement delaring their position as to pay and all the rights of soldiers, save that I could not promise promotions to the places of commissioned officers, were

promulgated by a speech in print. And these men enlised on the
faith of these representations.

    . . . .

    I am very truly and faithfully, Yours, &c., &c., &c.,

TLcSr   John A. Andrew

John A. Andrew to John Wilder, 23 May 1863, Negro in the Military
Service, p. 1264–65, ser. 390, Colored Troops Division, RG 94 [B-455].
Ellipses and misspellings appear in the transcript prepared by the Adjutant
General's Office for the Negro in the Military Service compilation, appar-
ently from Massachusetts state records.

149: Governor of Ohio to the Secretary of War and Subsequent Correspondence

                              Columbus O. June 21, 1863
Hon. E. M. Stanton, My Colored Reg't. is progressing
handsomely.
    They are expecting the usual pay & bounty allowed white
Soldiers. Will they get it?

HWSr   David Tod

                         Washington City, June 27 1863
Governor Tod   A careful examination of the Acts of Congress by
the Soliciter of the War Department has led him to the conclusion
that the Government can pay to Colored troops only ten dollars
per month and no bounty – a months advance pay will be
authorised. For any additional pay or bounty colored troops must
trust to State contributions and the justice of Congress at the next
Session. Upon this basis the organizations have been made,
Elsewhere.

HWSr   Edwin M Stanton

                         Columbus O. July 14 1863.
E M Stanton   Assuming that you agree with me that a Colored
soldier should have the same pay as a white one why can you not
authorize me to raise a Reg't. of Colored troops under the law
providing for the raising of white troops. The item of pay is a
most serious obstacle in my way.

HWSr   David Tod

David Tod to E. M. Stanton, 26 June 1863; Edwin M. Stanton to Governor Tod, 27 June 1863; Telegrams Collected by the Office of the Secretary of War (Bound), RG 107 [L-210]; David Tod to E. M. Stanton, 14 July 1863, Telegrams Collected by the Office of the Secretary of War (Bound), RG 107 [L-200]. Receiving no reply to his telegram of July 14, Governor Tod wired Stanton again on July 18, seeking authorization to raise a regiment under the July 22, 1861, congressional act, which stipulated that volunteer soldiers would "in all respects, be placed on the footing, as to pay and allowances, of similar corps of the Regular Army." Tod argued that such authorization would obviate "the difficulty as to pay which is an insurmountable objection." (David Tod to E. M. Stanton, 18 July 1863, Telegrams Collected by the Office of the Secretary of War (Bound), RG 107 [L-200]; *Official Records,* ser. 3, vol. 1, pp. 380–83.) A search of the War Department's files of letters and telegrams sent revealed no reply to Governor Tod's requests.

150: Chairman of the Pennsylvania Committee for Recruiting Colored Regiments to the Secretary of War

Philadelphia July 30th 1863

. . . .

In raising a regiment of colored men in twenty seven days, the Committee took special care to inform each recruit that his pay would be but ten dollars per Month from which three dollars per month, would be deducted for clothing, but they were able at the same time, by the liberality of the Citizens Bounty Fund of Philadelphia, to pay Ten dollars bounty to each recruit.

Within the past few days, two other classes of recruits have been mustered in viz: drafted men who expect to be paid Thirteen dollars per month, without deduction for clothing, and a bounty the same as shall be paid to drafted white men, and a few substitutes for drafted white men. The latter class has been mustered in at Pittsburgh before, it is presumed, Provost Marshal General Fry's Circular No 54 was received,[1] This class besides expecting the same pay as the drafted white men for whom they are substitutes have doubtless received a premium to become substitutes The Committee understand that hereafter colored men will not be received as substitutes for white men, but there will still exist the glaring anomaly of the patriot colored *Volunteer* being paid by the law of July 1862[2] but Ten dollars per month, less Three dollars per month for clothing, and the drafted (perhaps unwilling) colored men being by the terms of section "of the Act commonly called the Conscription act"[3] placed on the same footing in all respects, with volunteers for three years or during the war, including advance pay and bounty as now provided by law!

This must prove most detrimental to the service and positively embarrass the recruiting of Volunteer Colored Troops

Bearing in mind all the circumstances connected with the legislation on this subject and especially the legal opinion given by the highest law officer of the government to the effect that free colored men are *Citizens,*[4] the Committee not only hope, but firmly believe, that it will be found by the Government that the legislation approved July 17th 1862[5] limiting the pay of "persons of African descent" "who may have been received" into the service of the United States" for certain purposes and used as soldiers only by implication is by the act approved 3[d] March 1863[6] absolutely supercede[d] so far as regards the pay of colored soldier as compared with that of white soldiers   By the act of July 1862 it is held that even women, boys and decripid men, in fact all classes of persons of African descent can be employed by the United States and when so employed are entitled to the pay therein stipulated,   under the promise of pay, the Committee have been compelled to recruit the 3[d] regiment United States colored troops from the free colored men of the loyal States, But now a new class viz drafted colored men are mustered in and sent to camp. These men must be "able bodied male citizens of the United States" and be a part of what is "declared to constitute the national forces and shall be liable to perform military duty in the service of the United States, when called out by the President, for that purpose; according to the terms of the Conscription act, else, they could not be drafted. If then these colored men do thus constitute part of the national forces, *all* able bodied colored men likewise constitute a part of those forces and as part of said forces they may volunteer when invited by the Government, as they have promptly done upon the official invitation of the War Department, By the 11th sec of Conscription act no distinction is made in the pay of the drafted colored man and the drafted white man nor in any part of the act is there any distinction or allusion whatever made to men of color. Either they are not subjects of the draft at all or if subjects of the draft then, by the express terms of the act, they are absolutely entitled to be "placed on the same footing in all respects with volunteers for three years or during the war, including advance pay, and bounty as now provided by law" Assuming, in the enlightened state of public and departmental feeling, in regard to the rights of men of color, that the act will be interpreted by the war department, that colored men are subjects of the draft the question becomes pertinent, does not this sweeping act, by defining what Constitutes the national forces and enrolling colored men, as part of said forces lift them clearly out of the restraining provisions of the act of July 1862

Have not colored men been thus placed on the same level with white men so far as regards "military duty in the services of the United States" and as such entitled to the same pay bounty &c: This is most undubitably the common sense conclusion of the people who say, on all sides "if the colored man is to be a soldier, let him have the same pay, bounty, rations and treatment, that white soldiers receive

The Committee are happy in the belief that the Equity and justice of such treatment to colored soldiers by the Government is recognized as well in the highest official circles as by the people, If by a just bold, liberal and wise policy the legislation of 62 and 63 apparently conflicting, can be reconciled so far that colored troops may be distinctly assured that their pay, advance pay and bounty shall be the same as are paid to white volunteers, a larger ratio of the able bodied of the colored race, will, in the judgement of the Committee volunteer for the war, than of the able-bodied of the white race, The colored men will gladly renounce their lowly avocation for the ennobling pursuit of arms, and devote their stalwart frames to the common defence, Upon the manifold advantage, arising from the enlistment of colored troops – to the industrial interests of the north in relieving them from a further drain upon skilled artisan' and mechanics – to the South, in imparting to the illiterate negro's of that section, in the most practicable manner, the blessings of freedom, of Education, and of moral and religious training – to the nation in furnishing it with obedient and brave soldiers, with capacity to Endure a semi-tropical climate unharmed: and, above all, in promoting the growth of, a correct public sentiment in regard to the future welfare of the millions of the race amongst us as the Committee forbear to enlarge.

With the Earnest prayer that the Administration will determine the question of pay of Colored Troops on the everlasting principles of justice, the Committee confidently await its decision

On behalf of the Committee I have the honor to be Very Respectfully your obt servt

HLS   Thomas Webster

Excerpt from Thomas Webster to Hon. E. M. Stanton, 30 July 1863, W-68 1863, Letters Received, ser. 360, Colored Troops Division, RG 94 [B-46]. For the rest of Webster's letter see *Freedom*, ser. 2: doc. 34.

1 Circular No. 54, issued on July 20, 1863, ordered that, because existing laws treated black soldiers differently from white soldiers in the matter of

pay, bounty, and other allowances, men of African descent could be accepted as substitutes only for other black men. (*Official Records,* ser. 3, vol. 3, p. 548.) 2 The Militia Act.

3 The Enrollment Act (or, as Webster refers to it, the Conscription Act), which instituted the draft, defined the "national forces" – those liable for enrollment and draft – as "all able-bodied male citizens of the United States, and persons of foreign birth who shall have declared on oath their intention to become citizens . . ., between the ages of twenty and forty-five years. . . ." (*Official Records,* ser. 3, vol. 3, p. 88.)

4 The opinion of Attorney General Edward Bates, issued on November 29, 1862, is printed in Edward McPherson, *The Political History of the United States of America, during the Great Rebellion* (Washington, 1865), pp. 378–84. 5 See note 2. 6 See note 3.

151: Father of a New York Black Sergeant to the Secretary of War, Enclosing a Letter from His Son to an Unidentified Recipient

Scio Allegany County State of New York Oct. 29th 1863.
Dr Sir I have a son now in the service of the U.S. who was drafted from this town in the month of July last. (he is colored.) and after being taken from this place to rendezvous at Elmira was sent to Washington and is now First Duty Sargent. (at Camp Casey) in Co. G. 2nd. U.S. colored troops. he has recd one month pay at $7. now what I wish to know, is whether the sum of Seven dollars, per month is all that colored drafted men from this state are entitled to. my son supposed & so did I that he would receive the same pay, as white Soldiers he is a truly loyal Boy and says, he will serve his Country faithfully. but thinks there must be something wrong in relation to his receiving only Seven dollars per month. pay. I inclosed a letter, he wrote home, making inquiry as to the matter. your reply will settle the matter and will be appreciated, by, a colored man who, is willing to sacrafice his son in the cause of Freedom & Humanity Yours Very Respectfully

ALS   Aaron Peterson

[*Enclosure*]   Camp Casey [*D.C.*] Oct 24 [*1863*]
sir   i take this Liberty to wright to you to let you no how soldiering goes with it all goes very well and i am content with every thing but my pay and i never can bee, contented untill i get my rits   i am first duty sargt and my pay should bee 17 dolars a month and i think it is hard to bee abliged to poot up with sevan

dolars   i thought you might giv me some infamation about it if
you will pleas rite to me   i am willing to bee a soldier and serve
my time faithful like a man but i think it is hard to bee poot off
in sutch a dogesh maner as that

it haint enough to pay postage on my letters so i shall hav to
send this with out a stamp for i haint money enough to buy a
stamp

remember me to the boys   Yours

Hiram A Peterson

7 dolars a month and half rations is rather hard

Excuse my boldnes but pleas answer this and obelege   yours
Sargt H A Peterson

ALS

Aaron Peterson to Hon. Edwin M. Stanton, 29 Oct. 1863, enclosing
Hiram A. Peterson to Mr. Babcok, 24 Oct. [1863], P-98 1863, Letters
Received, ser. 360, Colored Troops Division, RG 94 [B-40].

152: Testimony by the Superintendent of the Organization of Missouri Black Troops before the American Freedmen's Inquiry Commission

[St. Louis, Mo. November 29, 1863]

. . . .

Q   What wages do the colored soldiers receive?

A   The system adopted by the Paymaster General in this
Department is, $7.00 a month in money, and $3.00 a month in
clothing allowance – making $10.00 a month in all.

Q   How does that compare with the payments to white
soldiers?

A   The white soldiers get $13.00 a month in money and $3.50
clothing allowance.

Q   What do non-commissioned officers among the colored
troops get?

A   The same as the privates. The system of pay, I think,
should be revised, beyond all question. It is very important, to
render these regiments efficient, that there be an increase of the
pay of non-commissioned officers. The duties of those offices
require that those who fill them shall be able to read and
write. With the same pay for non-commissioned that privates
receive, there is not the same motive furnished to the men for
application and study to qualify themselves for those positions,

375

that ought to be held out by the Gov't to these men. I understand that one of the purposes of the Gov't in enlisting the negro is to prepare him, through his term of service as a soldier, for his position as a freeman; to elevate these people from a condition of slavery to a condition of freedom. If that be the policy of the Gov't, every inducement should be offered to them to improve themselves—to apply themselves to study, to learn to read and write, and to qualify themselves for the discharge of their duties as soldiers, and ultimately their duties as citizens. By a revision of the system of paying them, and by increasing the pay of non-commissioned officers, an increased motive to application would be furnished the negro, not only to learn his duty as a soldier, but to learn to read and write, & thereby to prepare himself for his duties as a citizen.

Q   What do white sergeants receive?

A   The Commissary and Quartermaster's sergeants, and Hospital stewards receive $21.00 a month, besides $3.50 for clothing.

. . . .

This matter of a change of pay I regard as very important. There is no making efficient regiments out of these people and reaching the end desired—that is, completely and thoroughly—upon the present system of remuneration. I know, that the idea has been very generally presented to the soldiers, on their enlisting (though no promise has been made to them) that there would be a change in this matter of pay.

. . . .

HD

Excerpt from testimony of Col. Wm. A. Pile before the American Freedmen's Inquiry Commission, [29 Nov. 1863], O-328 1863, Letters Received, ser. 12, RG 94 [K-204]. Topical labels in the margin are omitted.

153: Massachusetts Black Sergeant to the Adjutant General's Office

Morris Is S.C. Jan. 14, 1864

Sir   I am a Sergeant of Co "F," 54th Regiment Massachusetts Volunteers. I enlisted at Readville Mass, April 8th 1863, as a "volunteer from Massachusetts, in the force, authorized by an Act of congress of the United States, approved on the 22nd day of July, A.D. 1861, entitled, "An Act to authorize the employment of

Volunteers to aid in enforcing the laws, and protecting public property." This act distinctly states in Section 5, That the officers, non commissioned officers, and privates, organized as above set forth, shall, in all respects, be placed on the footing, as to pay, and allowances, of similar corps of the Regular Army." I was accepted by the United States, and mustered in with the company to which I belong, April 23, 1863, by Lieut. Robert P. McKibbon, mustering officer; since that time I have performed the duty of a soldier, and have fulfilled my part of the contract with the Government. But the Government having failed to fulfill its part of the agreement, in as much as it refuses me the pay, and allowances of a Sergeant of the regular Army. I therefore, hereby respectfully demand to be mustered out of the service of the United States. I am Sir Very respectfully your Obt Servant

HLS   Stephen A. Swails

[*Endorsement*] Hd Qrs Dept of the South Hilton Head SC. Jan 23. 1864 Respectfully forwarded to A.G.O.

The tone of this communication is disapproved

I have already, on a former occasion recommended that the Colored troops have the same pay and allowances provided by law for the white soldiers. I deem it important that such should be the Case— Q. A. Gillmore Maj Gen Com

1st Sergt. Stephen A. Swails to Colonel E. D. Townsend, 14 Jan. 1864, S-97 1864, Letters Received, ser. 360, Colored Troops Division, RG 94 [B-394]. Other endorsements by Swails's commanders, from the company through the district levels, simply approved and forwarded his request. Swails was later commissioned a lieutenant in the 54th Massachusetts Volunteers. (See *Freedom*, ser. 2, doc. 141c.)

154: Black Sergeant to the Secretary of War

Fort Halleck Columbus—Ky. Aprile 27th 1864

I Sir by way of Introduction was made 1ˢᵗ· Sergeant of *Co.* C which was then denominated as 2ⁿᵈ *Tenn* Heavey Artillery now as 3ᵈ United States Heavey Artillery, as I wish to state to you, the facts which can be Relied, upon as I am fully able to prove if necessary I may say to you this *Reg.* is a *coloured* one of Southern Birth consequently have no Education, not so with my self I was Freeborn and Educated to some extent which makes me know   we know that we have never had our Just Rights, by the Officers who command us, the white officers of other *Reg.* here persuaded me to Join when there were no *Reg.* of coloured here to Join so I consented and being the first to sign my name in this *Reg.* They promiced to pay us the same wages as was paid the whites & Rations & clothing the same they have given us clothing & Rations sufficient for the time but have not paid us our Money according to promice the white privates tell us we Should get the same pay as they do but none of us has yet we never have been paid more than Seven Dollars per Month they now say that is all we are allowd by the Govornment of the United States Many of these people have Families to support and no other means of doing it than what they get in this way. Such of those that are not able Bodied men are employed on Govornment work and are paid Ten Dollars per Month We who belong to this *Reg.* have done more work than they on Fatigue and other wise the very Labour that was appointed for them we have had to toil day and night when necessity demands it, I may say to you at the presant our Regimental officers are nearly played out they have been Turned out and their places have not been furnished with other commanders now *Hon.* Secretary of war I wish to ask you not only for my own Satisfaction but at the Request of my *Reg.* is Seven Dollars per month all we Soldiers are to get or may we Expect in the final settlement to get our full Rights as was promiced us at the first

If we are to Recieve as much as White Soldiers or the Regular thirteen Dollars per Month then we Shall be Satisfied and on the field of Battle we will prove that we were worthy of what we claim for our Rights

With this Statement I may close by Requesting your Answer to this for the many Anxious and disappointed men of this *Reg.* I am Sir your obedient Servant

W^m. J. Brown

PS) Direct yours to me in care of *Co.* C. 3^d U States Heavey *Arty.* Care of *Lieut.* Adams of *Co.* A. 3^d *U.* States Heavey *Arty.*
ALS

Wm. J. Brown to Honourable Secretary of War, 27 Apr. 1864, B-582 1864, Letters Received, ser. 360, Colored Troops Division, RG 94 [B-84].

155: Michigan Black Soldier to the Chief Justice of the United States and a Report by the Soldier's Company Commander to the Adjutant General of the Army

General Hospitle Beaufort SC June 25th *1865.*
Dear, Sir, I am under the painfull necesity of writing you a few
lines for Redresse   I hav been in The Sirvice of the united states
since Nov fifth one thousand eight hundred and sixty four and hav
never recieve pay but twice once in June sixty four and then in,
August   What you paid me in June was seven doll. Per
months   I hav not recieved my Back pay From the government
yet   I am a man of faimley a Wife and two small children   I was
foold in the first place   my famley Recieves no Relief from my
state as was Promesed me For I was stolen from my town of
Enrollment and creaded to the city of Detroit, state of Michigan
by H. Barnes the one that got up the Regiment for the state of
Michigan   I could tell you Of a great deal of rascality that has
Ben a going on in the Regtment that I belong if it was nesicary
but I only want obliging my self   as you are one of the head of
our great governent I write you for assistance   I want them to
Give me my discharge and let me go and worke and suporte my
Familey for they are nearly starved and hav not suitabal cloathing
to hide thair neckedness   my familey depends upon my daily labor
for their suporte   when I enterd the service i felt it my Duty to
go   I meryed along all to my duty untill about the last two
months   I hav ben in the Hospitle   I went with out Pay nearly
all of the time I hav ben out   now the ware is over I think that
it is no moore than wright that I should Have my Discharge as I
was sick and in the hospitle before the order was Ishued to
discharge men in hospitle   Some of the officers has eaven taken
the mens Discharge papers away from them in the 32nd USC
Troops   Is that right   some officers will not send the mens
discriptive list to them   that is the case with me   If I hav don
wrong in writing to my superior i pray Pardon me For so doing
But I should like to Recieve some money from the governent and
go and see after my fanliey   Nomore From your moste humble
Servent and Solgier

George G Freeman

I am a colord man one that has no advantage
ALS

Near Winnsboro S.C. Aug 17 /65

Gen   I have the honor to make the following Report in relation
to certin Complaints and Charges made by letter to the "U S
Chief Justice" by Priv George G. Freeman of my Co E 102 USCT
which letter with the several endorcements theron is herewith
enclosed

Priv Freemans first Complaint is that he was accredited to some
ward in the City of Detroit Mich by Conl Barnes and was thereby
deprived of certin local appropriations which were generally made
by the several towns in the State of Michigan to the famillies of
those who enlisted during the late war

The Complaint is well founded with these exceptions   1st Priv
Freeman was accredited to a certin ward in the City of Detroit at
his own request because he was aware he could get a larger Bounty
in the City of Detroit than he could in a rural District where his
famlily resided   2^{d} His enlistment and Muster Papper show that
instead of Conl Barnes having had any thing to do with his
enlistment & credit he was enlisted by Capt W T Bennett late of
the 102 USCT

He Complains also that he never has recieved any Pay but twice
since his connection with the Regement and that he has "never
recieved any back Pay" by which he no doubt means the difference
between $7,00 per month (which was the origonal pay of Colored
Soldier) and $16.00 per which is the allowence at the present time

The *facts* are as follows   The first time the Regement was ever
paid off was in May 1864   at this time Priv Freeman refused to
accept his pay because the Regement was being paid off at $7,00
per month   He also used his utmost endevours to persuade others
to refuse their pay and so far suceeded that only nine out of sixty
recieved their pay at all And as I was creditably informed at the
time councelled the men of his Co "to stack their arms" and not
do any more duty until it should be known that they were to
recieve more than seven dollars per month   He afterward recieved
his pay twice the last time being in the month of August
1864   At the first Muster thereafter (Aug 31 1864) though being
at the time 1st Sergt of his Co he absented himself from Camp
without leave and was mustered on the Muster & pay Roll absent
from Camp without leave & reduced to the Ranks therefor by
order of the Mustering Officer Conl Henry L Chipman   He could
not of course draw any pay on those Rolls on which the Co was
paid about the 25th of October 1864 And neither his Co nor the
Regement to which he belongs was paid thereafter until about the
15 of June 1865 at which time he was absent in Hospital

In relation to his being in hospital without his Descriptive list I would Report as follows

About the 1st of March 1865 while in Camp with his Regement near the City of Charleston S.C. he again absented himself from Camp without leave and went to the City of Charleston S.C. where he caught a verry lothsome type of Syphilis and was shortly thereafter and while his Regement was on a march near Georgetown S.C. and when the Co Books & Records were not present to be consulted sent to Gen Hospital at Charleston S.C. on account of his being unable to discharge his duty by reason of the disease above aluded to

As soon as his Co & Regement again got into Camp where access could be had to the Books & Records of his Co his Descriptive List was promptly transmitted to the Surgeon in charge of the Hospital   In relation to his statement that he has "never recieved justice in the Regement" I am inclined to report that he nevr will until he is dishonorably Discharged the Service for willfully contracting a loathsome disease which has for a long time made him a charge upon the Government & rendered him totally unfit to perform his duty as a soldier   I have the honor to be Your obt servent

ALS   E J McKendrie

George G. Freeman to U.S. Chief Justice, 25 June 1865, and Capt. E. J. McKendrie to Brig. Gen. L. Thomas, 17 Aug. 1865, F-155 1865, Letters Received, ser. 360, Colored Troops Division, RG 94 [B-243]. Endorsements. In the same file is another letter from Freeman, dated Sept. 5, 1865, which renews his request for pay.

156A: Louisiana Black Officers to the Secretary of War

[*New Orleans   October 1863*]

The Memorial of the Undersigned officers and Men belonging to the Second Regiment of Native Guards. Respectfully represents.

That your memorialists, free colored citizens of the state of Louisiana, were invited to volunteer to serve in the volunteer forces of the United States, by General order No. 63, issued by Major General B. F. Butler lately Commanding the Department of the Gulf, and dated at his head Quarters, on the twenty second day of

August 1862, and in which, using the language of the order itself, it was declared that, all "who shall enlist in the Volunteer Service of the United States, shall be duly organized by the appointment of proper officers and accepted, *paid,* equipped, armed and rationed, as are other volunteer troops of the United States."

Your memorialists further respectfully represent that relying upon the promises thus made by the Commanding General, they cheerfully enrolled themselves under the flag of the Union, and have ever since faithfully performed their duty, in a manner which they are proud to say has met the public approval of their Commanding General, but to their disappointment, they are now informed that they are to be placed in regard to pay, on a different footing from other volunteers, and are to be paid only   , instead of   Dollars a month, a difference which they consider unjust in view of the circumstances and promises under which they enlisted, and which operates as a severe privation to the families of the Men, who relied, before enlisting, for the most part on their daily labor for support.

Your Memorialists look with Confidence to the justice of their Government, and respectfully pray that their case may be taken, at an early Moment, under consideration, and the proper order given to allow them the same pay as other volunteers.

All of which is respectfully Submitted.

P. B. S. Pinchback	S. J. Wilkison
W. B. Barrett	Joseph Jones
H C Carter	Louis De Gray
S. W. Ringgold	John W. Latting
E. P. Chase	Jasper Thompson

HDS   P O Dapremons

[*Endorsement*]   Hd. Qrs. Dept. of the Gulf New Orleans, Oct. 26. 1863 Approved and respectfully forwarded to the Secretary of War. N. P. Banks Maj. Gen. Com'g.

Capt. P. B. S. Pinchback et al. to Honorable Edwin M. Stanton, [Oct. 1863], G-104 1863, Letters Received, ser. 360, Colored Troops Division, RG 94 [B-403]. The blank spaces left for the amounts of money appear in the manuscript. The signers were all captains and lieutenants who, by virtue of an earlier decision of General Nathaniel P. Banks, received the same monthly pay as their white counterparts—that is, $60 for captains, $50 for first lieutenants, and $45 for second lieutenants. (Banks's policy is reported in Addl. Paymaster H. O. Brigham to Col. T. P. Andrews, 14 July 1863, #632/20, Letters Received, ser. 7, RG 99 [CC-3]; rates of pay appear in *Revised Army Regulations,* p. 361.) Presumably this petition greeted the first appearance of the paymaster armed with the regulations of June 1863 that required payment of all blacks in the army at the rate of $10 per month, less $3 for clothing.

156B: Statement by the Commander of a Louisiana Black Regiment

Port Hudson, La, Oct. 3^{d}, 1863.

On Saturday afternoon, October 3rd, 1863, this Regiment was paid off, from the date of enrollment of the enlisted men, by Major Palmer, Paymaster, U.S. Army, now on duty in this Department.

The Sergeants, Corporals, and Privates, received equal pay, viz:—Seven (7) Dollars, per man, per month.

This being their first payment, (having been taken from their homes,) and the most of them having families to maintain, they felt necessitated to receive what the Paymaster tendered.

They have been mustered into the service of the United States, as United States Soldiers; they have been called upon, and still are, to do all the duties of such, and to undergo all the hardships and privations, as such. And they were told that they were to receive the same pay as white troops—told by their Officers that they were to receive the pay of their grades in accordance with the Regulations for the government of the Armies of the United States.

It does not seem to be in accordance with the principles of Justice, Equity, and Honor, that these Soldiers of the United States Army, should receive less pay per month, for the same services, than any other United States Soldiers, of the same grade and class; and in their name and on their behalf, I most earnestly and respectfully protest, and pray that this evident injustice, may be speedily rectified, that the seeds of discord and discontent, may not be sown nor take root. Very Respectfully Submitted,

Jno. C. Chadwick

One copy sent Maj. Genl. Banks, Comdg. Dept.
"　　"　　"　Brig. Genl. Andrews, " C. d-A.
"　　"　　"　Maj. Palmer, P.M. U.S.A.

ADS

Statement by Major Jno. C. Chadwick, 3 Oct. 1863, C-242 1863, Letters Received, ser. 360, Colored Troops Division, RG 94 [B-32]. Charles W. Foster, head of the Bureau of Colored Troops, forwarded Chadwick's statement to the Solicitor of the War Department on October 27, 1863. In summarizing the complaint, Foster misconstrued it, indicating that Chadwick referred to equal pay for white noncommissioned officers serving with black troops, when in fact Chadwick had protested discriminatory pay for black soldiers at all levels. The Bureau of Colored Troops received the letter back from the Solicitor, without comment, on June 28, 1864, and filed it.

156C: Louisiana Black Soldier to the Secretary of War

Fort Jefferson Tortugas Fla. May 1865

Sir I have the honor to respectfully request that I may be released from imprisonment I have ben in imprisonment six months and over. and if I should remain here six years. I could not be more sory of having done rong then I am know. althou I though mysalfe somewhat justified doing what I have done, at the time. I persume you honor has been enform in what manner of treatment the 73. U.S.C.T. has ben subject to doing the short-period of the first years servise. when I enlisted I had no other entention then perform my duty faithfully as a soldier. and would fermily have done so if we had not ben treatted in such ill manner and was subject to all kinds of missrepresentations. My crme was (dissertion) not wishing to justify mysalf althou I though at the time that one breack of enlissment was quite sufficient to justify another perticulurly when it was transacted on the part of the gov. Althou most of us are free men and was before the war yet the most of us have nothing more then is required to support our family from day to day as we labor for it. althou I am now but seventeen years old I have my old mother to support and as such expectted that the gov. or its agents in this department would comply with its agreement I could have something to support my relitives. I persume your honor has been enformed that Gel Buttler promas my regt $13.00 per month $58.00 Bounty and I suppose his promasses should have been kept if a genl promas or assureance is paid no respect to how much less could there be expectted of a poor soldier (pri.) I do not wish to justify my[self] in and act of dissertion for I dont think it write wrere a soldier can get a redress to his grevences other wise but we tried every way and could not get no redress after having been some 8. moth in servise when pay day came we were in dept to the gov. at the rate thay ware to settle with us. I hope you will comply with my request should you require my cerviseses any longer into U.S. servise I am willing to act in any capasity your honor may see fit to have me to perform Very Respectfully Your obt servt

ALS   Warren D. Hamelton

Warren D. Hamelton to Hon. E. M. Stanton, May 1865, H-285 1865, Letters Received, ser. 360, Colored Troops Division, RG 94 [B-139]. The 73rd USCI, formerly the 1st Louisiana Native Guard, was the first black regiment Major General Benjamin F. Butler organized in Louisiana.

157A: Massachusetts Black Corporal to the President

Morris Island [*S.C.*]. Sept 28th 1863.
    Your Excelency will pardon the presumtion of an humble individual like myself, in addressing you. but the earnest Solicitation of my Comrades in Arms, besides the genuine interest felt by myself in the matter is my excuse, for placing before the Executive head of the Nation our Common Grievance: On the 6th of the last Month, the Paymaster of the department, informed us, that if we would decide to recieve the sum of $10 (ten dollars) per month, he would come and pay us that sum, but, that, on the sitting of Congress, the Regt would, in his opinion, be *allowed* the other 3 (three.)   He did not give us any guarantee that this would be, as he hoped, certainly *he* had no authority for making any such guarantee, and we can not supose him acting in any way interested. Now the main question is. Are we *Soldiers*, or are we LABOURERS. We are fully armed, and equipped, have done all the various Duties, pertaining to a Soldiers life, have conducted ourselves, to the complete satisfaction of General Officers, who, were if any, prejudiced *against* us, but who now accord us all the encouragement, and honour due us: have shared the perils, and Labour, of Reducing the first stronghold, that flaunted a Traitor Flag: and more, Mr President. Today, the Anglo Saxon Mother, Wife, or Sister, are not alone, in tears for departed Sons, Husbands, and Brothers. The patient Trusting Decendants of Africs Clime, have dyed the ground with blood, in defense of the Union, and Democracy. Men too your Excellency, who know in a measure, the cruelties of the Iron heel of oppression, which in years gone by, the very Power, their blood is now being spilled to maintain, ever ground them to the dust. But When the war trumpet sounded o'er the land, when men knew not the Friend from the Traitor, the Black man laid his life at the Altar of the Nation, – and he was refused. When the arms of the Union, were beaten, in the first year of the War, And the Executive called more food. for its ravaging maw, again the black man begged, the

privelege of Aiding his Country in her need, to be again refused, And now, he is in the War: and how has he conducted himself? Let their dusky forms, rise up, out the mires of James Island, and give the answer. Let the rich mould around Wagners parapets be upturned, and there will be found an Eloquent answer. Obedient and patient, and Solid as a wall are they. all we lack, is a paler hue, and a better acquaintance with the Alphabet. Now Your Excellency, We have done a Soldiers Duty. Why cant we have a Soldiers pay? You caution the Rebel Chieftain, that the United States, knows, no distinction, in her Soldiers: She insists on having all her Soldiers, of whatever, creed or Color, to be treated, according to the usages of War. Now if the United States exacts uniformity of treatment of her Soldiers, from the Insurgents, would it not be well, and consistent, to set the example herself, by paying all her *Soldiers* alike? We of this Regt. were not enlisted under any "contraband" act. But we do not wish to be understood, as rating our Service, of more Value to the Government, than the service of the exslave, Their Service is undoubtedly worth much to the Nation, but Congress made express, provision touching their case, as slaves freed by military necessity, and assuming the Government, to be their temporary Gaurdian: – Not so with us – Freemen by birth, and consequently, having the advantage of *thinking,* and acting for ourselves, so far as the Laws would allow us. We do not consider ourselves fit subjects for the Contraband act. We appeal to You, Sir: as the Executive of the Nation, to have us Justly Dealt with. The Regt, do pray, that they be assured their service will be fairly appreciated, by paying them as american SOLDIERS, not as menial hierlings. Black men You may well know, are poor, three dollars per month, for a year, will suply their needy Wives, and little ones, with fuel. If you, as chief Magistrate of the Nation, will assure us, of our whole pay. We are content, our Patriotism, our enthusiasm will have a new impetus, to exert our energy more and more to aid Our Country. Not that our hearts ever flagged, in Devotion, spite the evident apathy displayed in our behalf, but We feel as though, our Country spurned us, now we are sworn to serve her.

Please give this a moments attention

ALS   James Henry Gooding

Corporal James Henry Gooding to Abraham Lincoln, 28 Sept. 1863, enclosed in [Harper & Brothers] to [Abraham Lincoln], 12 Oct. 1863, H-133 1863, Letters Received, ser. 360, Colored Troops Division, RG 94 [B-408].

157B: **Commander of a Massachusetts Black Regiment to the Governor of Massachusetts**

Morris Is. S C Nov. 23rd 1863

Governor. Copies of Your address, delivered to the Legislature of Massachusetts Nov. 11, 1863 have been recieved in this regiment. Such parts of it as reccommend the General Court to authorize the payment to the enlisted men of the 54th Mass. Vols. of that portion of the lawful Monthly pay of United States Volunteers which has been or may be refused them by the Paymaster of the United States, are received unfavorably by the enlisted men of this Regiment. They were enlisted and mustered into the Service of the United States with the understanding that they would be treated in all respects as other Soldiers from Massachusetts. They will refuse to accept any money from the United States until the United States is willing to pay them according to the terms of their enlistment. They feel that by accepting a portion of their Just dues from Massachusetts and a portion from the United States, they would be acknowledging a right on the part of the United States to draw a distinction between them and other Soldiers from Massachusetts, and in so doing they would compromise their self respect. They enlisted because *men* were called for, and because the Government signified its willingness to accept them as such *not* because of the money offered them. They would rather work and fight until they are mustered out of the Service, without any pay than accept from the Government less than it gives to other soldiers from Massachusetts, and by so accepting acknowledge that because they have African blood in their veins, they are less men, than those who have saxon.

Thanking you in behalf of the men; for the kind spirit you have always manifested in your efforts to establish their Just rights   I remain Very Respectfully. Your Obdt. Svt.

HLcSr   (Sgd) E. N. Hallowell

Col. E. N. Hallowell to Governor John A. Andrew, 23 Nov. 1863, Letters Sent, 54th Mass. Vols., Regimental Books & Papers USCT, RG 94 [G-232].

387

158A: Officers of a South Carolina Black Regiment to the Adjutant General of the Army

Hilton Head SC Nov 21st 1863

General   We the undersigned Officers of the Third Regiment of South Carolina Infantry do most respectfully beg leave to call the attention of the President of the United States regarding the circumstances attending the payment of Colored Troops in the Department of the South. The Paymasters make a distinction based on their color and refuse to pay the Soldiers of African desent the stipulated wages of United States Volunteer Troops.

The colored Troops raised in this Department under Genl R Saxton were enlisted with the promise of the same pay clothing and rations as is accorded to other soldiers in the United States Service.

In the first organization of the regiments they received this amount, subsequently it was reduced and it has again been reduced this present month

Whatever may be the policy of the Government in regard to colored Troops raised in other insurectionary States we rely on the plighted honor of the Government that no discrimination be made in this Department of any class of Soldiers on account of their color or Nationality.

The cause of the present reduction of pay now offered to the colored Troops has been based on an Act of Congress of July 1862 but which at that time bore no reference to colored enlisted men but only to those otherwise employed by the Government.

We respectfully request therefore an explanation of the interest and purpose of this Act to be forwarded to the Paymaster of this Department in order that the colored Troops may be paid their just dues. The cause of much grievance to the colored Troops of this Command arrises mainly from the partiality Shown to men of their own Nationality employed in the Several Departments   Numbers are now employed in the Quartermaster and Commissary departments on wages varying from Twelve to Twenty five Dollars per Month with rations, but the soldier who at any time may be called on to lay down his life in the Nations cause is offered in this Department but Seven Dollars per Month with clothing and rations and without any relief for his family. Under the draft of all able bodied Negroes most of them had to give up these more lucrative employments for the Army

388

and their places are filled at present by lately arrived refugees from the rebel States

We do therefore pray the favorable consideration of the President of the United States and have the honor to be Very Respectfully Your Obedient Servants

HLS   [*13 signatures*]

[*Endorsement*] Beaufort So. Ca. Nov 29" 1863   Memorial from the Commissioned officers of the 3d So Ca Vols. Asking for an increase of pay— Respectfully forwarded and recommended   the men of this regiment have performed valuable service and were enlisted before the law of Congress reducing the pay of colored Soldiers to ten dollars per month was passed   I hope that the Dept. will think proper to recommend to Congress the propriety of giving these soldiers the full pay of thirteen dollars per month   R Saxton Brig. Genl. Mil Gov.

Lt. Col. A. G. Bennett et al. to Brig. Genl. L. Thomas, 21 Nov. 1863, B-454 1863, Letters Received, ser. 360, Colored Troops Division, RG 94 [B-1]. A note below the signatures indicates that the signers constituted all the commissioned officers in the regiment except four who were absent sick. Saxton's contention that the soldiers entered service before passage of the July 1862 law apparently refers to the original enlistment of blacks in General David Hunter's regiment during May 1862.

158B: Commander of a South Carolina Black Regiment to the Headquarters of the Department of the South and the Commander of U.S. Forces at Hilton Head to the Superintendent of Contrabands in the Department of the South

Hilton Head SC November 30" 1863.

Captain   I have the honor most Respectfully to request that the families of men of 3^d S.C. Infty be furnished with rations until such time as their pay will be raised and enable them to furnish means for their support. In making this request I would respectfully call the attention of the General Comdg^s to the following facts.

On the Organization of this regiment the families of the men, received rations by Genl D. Hunter's orders, those rations have from time to time been curtailed, and now they are entirely taken away, some of the men have large families unable to procure sufficient food and are in a deplorable condition. – The pay of the men being only seven dollars ($7) per month, and being obliged to remain in Camp to attend to their military duty they are unable to render the least assistance towards the support of those who are depended upon them; while Colored men employed in the *Quartermaster's* Department receive from 10 to 25 dollars per month, with ample opportunity for the cultivation of the soil, do receive full rations for their families thereby causing great dissatisfaction among the men of this Command   Hoping that the above will meet with the approval of the General Comdg, I am Capt Very Respectfully Your most Obt Sert

HLS   Aug's. G. Bennett

[*Endorsement*] Hd. Qrs. Dept. South Folly Isl. S.C. Dec. 2'
1863 Respectfully returned. If the families of these men are suffering from destitution, application for subsistence stores should be made to Brig Gen'l Rufus Saxton, Military Governor, who is authorized by the Secretary of War to provide for such cases. By com^d of Maj. Gen. Q. A. Gillmore, Ed W Smith A.A. Gen'l

Hilton Head, Port Royal, S.C. December 5th 1863.
General – I have the honor to forward herewith a communication from Lieut Col Aug G Bennett comd'g 3' So Ca Infty, with an endorsement by Lt Col E. W. Smith Assist Adj't General Dept of the South.
  There is no doubt that the families referred to in this communication are in a suffering condition & that measures should be taken for their immediate & permanent relief. I have the honor to be General – Very Respcty Your Obt Servant

HLS   W^m B Barton

[*Endorsement*] Beaufort – So: Car: Decr 11$''$ – 1863 – Genl Saxton is of the opinion that a habit of dependence upon the Government for food and clothing ought to be discouraged among the freedmen, even at the risk of some suffering.
  Genl Saxton issues rations only to those in extreme destitution, unable to help themselves, and having no relatives who can support them. He would be very glad to see the colored soldiers in this Department paid fully and fairly, as other soldiers are, but he does not think it best to regard as "destitute" persons the families of men who are receiving seven dollars a month, besides rations and clothing for themselves. By order of Brig^r Genl Saxton Mil: Gov: E. W. Hooper Capt – & A.A.A. Genl.

Lieut. Col. Aug's. G. Bennett to Captain Wm. L. M. Burger, 30 Nov. 1863, and Col. Wm. B. Barton to Brig. Genl. R. Saxton, 5 Dec. 1863, Letters Received, 21st USCI, Regimental Books & Papers USCT, RG 94 [G-80]. Another endorsement.

158C: **Court-Martial Testimony by the Commander of a South Carolina Black Regiment**

Hilton Head, S.C. Jan. 11. 1864

Lt. Col. A. G. Bennett 3ᵈ S.C. Vols, a witness for the prosecution, was duly sworn.

Question by Judge Advocate: Please state your military rank and position.

Answer: Lt. Col. 3ᵈ S.C. Vol. Infy.

Question by Judge Advocate: At what place was the third Regt S.C. Vols encamped, on or about the 19ᵗʰ Nov. 1863?

Answer: At camp called camp Bennett, to the left of Genl Hospital, Hilton Head S.C.

Question by Judge Advocate: On that day did you see the accused [*Sergeant William Walker*]?

Answer: I did.

Question by Judge Advocate: State his conduct as far as it came under your observation on that day, and what occurred in relation thereto?

Answer: On the morning of Nov. 19. 1863, when a portion of the command was in a state of mutiny, I noticed the accused, with others of his company and regiment stack his arms, take off his accoutrements and hang them on the stack. I inquired what all this meant, and received no reply, and again repeated the question, when the accused answered by saying, that they "would not do duty any longer for seven dollars per month." I then told the men the consequences of a mutiny, and what they might expect. I told them if they did not take their arms and return to duty, I should report the case to the Post Commander and they would be shot down. While saying this, I heard the accused tell the men not to retake their arms, but leave them and go to their street, which command of his they obeyed. Again, later in the day, in the evening, I ordered the accused in arrest, and told him not to leave his tent without my permission, if he did, I should confine him to the Provost Guard. The next morning, Nov. 20ᵗʰ 1863, I received information he had broken his arrest, by leaving his tent and going into another tent & company street. I then ordered him to the Provost Guard House.

Question by Judge Advocate: Where was the accused, at the time you told the men to take their arms, and told them the consequences if they did not?

Answer: He stood on the right of the line when I first saw him—he afterwards moved to the rear, moving back and forth.

Question by Judge Advocate: Who gave you the information that accused had broken his arrest?

Answer: Capt. Abeel Co "D" 3^{d} Regt S.C. Vols.

Question by Judge Advocate: Do you know the object of the accused passing to and fro to the rear of the company or line—if so, state how and what was the reason?

Answer: He was advising the men "to go back to their quarters without their arms."

. . . .

HD

Excerpt from testimony of Lt. Col. A. G. Bennett, 11 Jan. 1864, proceedings of general court-martial in the case of Sergeant William Walker, 3rd SC Vols., MM-1320, Court-Martial Case Files, ser. 15, RG 153 [H-27].

158D: Court-Martial Statement by a South Carolina Black Sergeant

Hilton Head, S.C. Jan 12, 1864

The accused, in presenting to the Honorable the Court his defence to the charges preferred against him admits that there are many points on which he is justly blamable, and for which he cannot hope to escape without punishment. But when the Honorable Court take into consideration the circumstances connected with the gravest charge made aginst him—that of *Mutiny*—he trusts that an enlightened understanding of the matter may plead for him in extenuation of a crime which was more an error of judgment, (as evidenced by the fact that nearly the whole of his regiment acted in like manner as himself,) than a wilful desire to violate the law.

Before the organization of this Regiment to which I am now attached, I was a Pilot on the U.S.S. gun-boat *Wissahican,* and received from Admiral Dupont, then commanding the squadron a "pass" to come ashore and visit my family. While here the subject of joining the army was proposed to me—and although by my "pass" I was exempted from conscription – I yet, on the promise solemnly made by some who are now officers in my regiment, that I should receive the same pay and allowances as were given to all soldiers in the U. S. Army, – voluntarily entered the ranks. For an account of the treatment that has been given to the men of the 3^d Reg't S.C. Vols. by a large majority of their officers, nine-tenths of those now in service there will be my witness that it has been tyrannical in the extreme, and totally beneath that standard of gentlemanly conduct which we were taught to believe as pertaining to officers wearing the uniform of a government that had declared a "freedom to all" as one of the cardinal points of its policy. This treatment, prepared the way for the events that occurred when it was announced to us that we could receive but $7 per month pay.

As to my conduct on the 19th day of November last, when the Regiment stacked arms and refused farther duty, I believe that I have proved conclusively by the testimony of the non-commissioned officers and men of my company that I did not then exercise any command over them – that I gave no word of counsel or advice to them in opposition to the request made by our commanding officer – and that, for one, I carried my arms and equipments back with me to my company street. I respectfully suggest that these men are less apt to be mistaken, than officers who feared that they were facing a general mutiny, and were ignorant of the next movement that might be made by the excited crowd before them – but an assemblage who only contemplated a peaceful demand for the rights and benefits that had been guaranteed them.

. . . .

My case, in connection with the events of the 19th of November last, is the case of that of all the other members of Co. "A." On military law, and the rules of the service, we are entirely ignorant. Never, since the organization of the company, have the "Articles of War" been read to us nor any part of the "Regulations" even. We have been allowed to stumble along, taking verbal instructions as to the different parts of our duty, and gaining a knowledge of the services required of us as best we might. In this way many things have occurred that might have been made entirely different had we known the responsiblity of our position.

In conclusion the undersigned asks respectfully that the Honorable Court will give his case as favorable a consideration as the rules of the service and the responsibility devolving upon each member of it will permit.

his
William × Walker
mark

HDSr

Excerpts from statement of Sergt. William Walker, 12 Jan. 1864, proceedings of general court-martial of Sergeant William Walker, 3rd SC
Vols., MM-1320, Court-Martial Case Files, ser. 15, RG 153 [H-27]. The
court found Walker guilty of mutiny, mutinous conduct, conduct prejudicial to good order and military discipline, and breach of arrest, and sentenced him to be executed.

158E: Order for the Execution of a South Carolina Black Sergeant

H. Q. Dist. of Florida Feb. 28″ 1864

Genl. Orders No. 8   The sentence of the G.C.M. in the case of
Sergt. Wm. Walker, of Co. "A" 3″ S.C. Vols. as promulgated in
G.O. No. 29 H.Q. Dept. So. of Feb. 6″ 1864 will be carried into
effect, & he will be "shot to death with musketry," at 9 o'clock,
A.M. Feb. 29″ 1864 under the direction of the Provost Marshal of
the Dist. in the presence of the Brigade to which his Regt. is now
attached. By order of Brig. Gen T. Seymour

HD

General Order No. 8, H.Q. Dist. of Florida, 28 Feb. 1864, filed with
service record of William Walker, 21st USCI, Carded Records, Volunteer
Organizations: Civil War, ser. 519, RG 94 [N-7].

158F: Superintendent of Black Recruitment in the Department of the South to the Provost Marshal General of the Department of the South

Hilton Head, S.C., June 3ᵈ 1864.

Colonel   I have the honor to acknowledge the receipt of a
communication from you, dated June 2ᵈ, in which you ask me to
state what I know of the mutiny, in the late 3ᵈ S.C. Vol. now the
21ᵗʰ U.S.C.T. which accured last fall, at Hilton Head, S.C. that
you can report upon the guilt or innocence of those now in
confinement at the Provost Guard House.

The conversation I had with Lt. Col. Bennett, in command of
the Regiment, is all I knew of the facts in the case: as I
understand it is this: The 3ᵈ S.C. Vol was organized by Gen.
Hunter, in the spring of ,63. as Fatigue men, with a promis that
they should have $13.ᵈ per. month, The men immediately placed

in camp, with inferior clothing, having no care, worked hard and with little or no instruction; they were commanded by inferior officers, a portion whom have been dismissed from service: When the paymaster came to pay them they were offered but $7.00 & not knowing what they were doing, supposing they could stop doing duty, as they had done when at work, if they pay did not suit them; they stacked arms, & refused to *longer* be *soldiers:* as soon however, as the worthless officers left & good officers took charge, & explained to the men, thir obligation *all at once entered willingly to their duties:* The Regiment is one of the best now, we have, & it under Lt. Col. Bennett, The pints I make are these:

1st The men were guilty of no crime, as they did not know they were doing wrong, consequently no wrong was committed.

2^{d} The partial manor with which these men were tried and the irregularities of the records, has rendered it impossible for these men to have Justice: Humanity calles that they should be released from their long confinement; & the best interest of the service will be promoted by having these men in the ranks with muskets in hands, rather than being kept on public expence were they are.

3^{d} Maj Gen. Gillmore ordered these men all be returned to duty, in January last, when the men were consolidated with my own Regiment, hence they augh not to suffer from these long & vexatious delays, & their pay should at least commence January 1" 1864, but I urge as the colonel of the Regiment, that they all be returned to duty with *no* stopage of pay.

Hoping Col, that this matter may soon come up, I will close with the reget that I can furnish you with no more facts. I wish to be understood as casting no reflections upon the Officers with the Reg^{t} now, as they are good, faithful & efficient. I have the honor to be Col. Very Respectfully Yr. Obt. Servt

ALS   M. S. Littlefield

Col. M. S. Littlefield to Col. P. P. Brown Jr., 3 June 1864, Letters Received, 21st USCI, Regimental Books & Papers USCT, RG 94 [G-81].

⟨flourish⟩

159: Commander of a Rhode Island Black Artillery Regiment to the Office of the Governor of Rhode Island

Fort Esperanza, Texas. April. 16. 1864.

Col; I have the honor herewith to acknowledge the receipt of yours of the 13th Feby. I am indeed pleased that his Excellency

the Gov. is gratified with the reports in regard to this
Battalion. But I very much fear he will be obliged to change his
mind, as we have had a little trouble in this Batt. Every man in
this Batt. was told, when he enlisted, that it was upon the same
footing as white soldiers; that he was to have thirteen (13) dollars
pr. month. Trouble has been brooding for a long time, but we
kept it down until the 17th March, when Co. A. refused in a body
to answer to their names at Monthly Inspection by the Act. Asst.
Inspector Genl. giving as a reason that they would not be
mustered to take seven (7) dollars pr. month. After the matter
was explained to them, they answered. I preferred charges against
the noncommissioned officers and twenty (20) privates; all of
whom have been sentenced to hard labor at Fort Jefferson Florida
of from three (3) months to one year. The non-commissioned
officers for one year; which, in my opinion is not sufficient
punishment, as it was a case of mutiny. On the 30. March, I left
the Island in company with Major General McClernand on a visit
to Brownsville, Matamoras &ce. I returned on the 12th
April. The Batt. was left under command of Capt. Fry; and
during my absence 2nd Lieut Potter was obliged to shoot one of
the men, for which he was justified. Some of the men then stated
that they would kill every white officer in the command and that
Mr. Potter should not stay on the Island. Capt Fry, instead of
shooting these men reported it to Maj. Gen'l. Dana who ordered
out two light batteries and two white Regts. to put down a
mutiny in this camp. The whole Batt. was then placed under
arrest and ordered down the Island, and kept under guard of a
white Regt. for twenty four hours; after which they returned to
duty; and every thing has since been in perfect order. The men
needed a lesson and received one. I do not attach any blame to
the conduct of Capt. Fry in the matter as it is not everybody who
can, in cold blood, kill a man. But I should have sustained Mr.
Potter, if I shot every man in the Regt; a fact which the men
know perfectly well. It is only fear which will keep this class of
men in their place and make good soldiers. and the moment they
find an officer is afraid of them, they will over run him and put
him down. I have now two Officers who are not worth the price
of their shoulder-straps. Lieut. Wheeler resigned last month; he
was a good Officer, and I was exceedingly sorry to have him
leave. Lt. Gay has also resigned on account of sickness. I am very
short of Officers and I trust their places may be filled with good
Officers as soon as possible. My command is about broken
up. Co. A. left yesterday for Aransas Pass to take charge of the
guns at that place; it is about eighty (80) miles from here. Co. B.
is in charge of the two (2) fortifications at McHenry's Bayou; two

(2) miles from the Fort, Co D. at the Interior line of Works, one (1) mile from the Fort; and Co. C. at Fort Esperanza, where I make my Head Quarters. I have charge of all the works on the Island that are completed. I have never as yet received any official notice of a senior officer to me in this Regt. If there is such I would like to be notified that I may make the proper reports to him. There are two (2) men of this Batt. now in Prov[*idence*] with Col Viall. I would like very much to have them sent to me. I know nothing more to inform you of, as regards this Batt. All trouble is now at an end. To Major Engley I lay all blame; as he swindled every man he enlisted.

Trusting that the health of his Excellency the Gov. is good, as also your own   I have the honor to be With Respect Your Obt. Svt.

J. J. Comstock, Jr.

HLcSr

Major J. J. Comstock Jr. to Col. Chas. E. Bailey, 16 Apr. 1864, Letters Sent, 11th USCHA, Regimental Books & Papers USCT, RG 94 [G-57]. The War Department's policy regarding recruitment for the 14th Rhode Island Heavy Artillery stated: "Colored persons offering themselves for enlistment should be distinctly informed that they will not receive any bounty or premiums, except the enlistment fee of two dollars, and that their pay will be ten dollars per month, from which monthly pay the cost of their clothing will be deducted." (Quoted in Lt. Henry P. Worcester to Captain A. P. Davis, 31 Oct. 1863, Miscellaneous Papers, 11th USCHA, Regimental Books & Papers USCT, RG 94 [G-28].)

❦

160A: Commander of the Northern District of the Department of the South to the Headquarters of the Department of the South

Folly Island S.C. June 2nd 1864

I consider it my duty to lay before the Major General Commanding the fact that two regiments of this Command have not been paid since they entered the service of the United States, now one year ago.

This unhappy state of affairs seems to have been brought about by some misunderstanding between the United States and the State of Massachusetts in regard to colored Troops. For this misunderstanding the enlisted men cannot be held responsible, and they consequently should not be made to suffer for it.

397

Letters have been constantly arriving for six months in these regiments, in which the wives of the enlisted men describe their sufferings, and the sufferings of their families, – children have died because they could not be supplied with proper food, and because the Doctor could not be paid, or medicines obtained from the Druggist; – wives have proved untrue to their husbands and abandoned their offspring. Mothers advise their sons to throw down the musket and come home, it being impossible for them to live longer without their support.

The effects of such letters on the minds of the enlisted men of these regiments may be easily imagined, and it reflects to the credit of the officers as well as the men that the efficiency of the regiments has not materially suffered under these trying circumstances.

I have ordered Colonel A. S. Hartwell of the 55th Mass Vols, to explain the case personally to the General Commanding and to beg the General to send him North, in order to procure an order from the Paymaster General for the payment of these regiments as soon as possible upon the law to that effect being passed.

Sending the Colonel, North, for that purpose, would at least have the certain effect of Keeping the men quiet while awaiting his return, and of convincing them that something was being done on their behalf which would prove decisive, whereas now many of them do not believe they will ever receive any pay. I have the honor, to be, Very Respectfully Your Obd't Servt

HLcSr   (signed) A. Schimmelfennig

Brig. Gen'l. A. Schimmelfennig to Captain W. L. M. Burger, 2 June 1864, vol. 58 DS, pp. 148–49, Letters Sent, ser. 2413, Northern Dist., Dept. of the South, RG 393 Pt. 2 No. 145 [C-1672].

160B: Commander of a Massachusetts Black Regiment to the Secretary of War

Folly Island, S.C. June. 13. 1864.

Sir. Application is respectfully made that this Regiment be mustered out of the service of the United States, for the reason that the men have not been paid according to the contract made by Government.

It is respectfully submitted that this Regiment was enlisted as Massachusetts Volunteer Infantry under the act of July 1861, by his Excellency the Governor of Massachusetts on the authority of the Hon. Secretary of War, empowered by which authority the officers and agents of this Regt. promised the men all the pay, rations &c. allowed by the said Act; that this Reg't began to be organized on the 13th day of May 1863, and from that to the present time has received no pay from Government, and no tender of payment according to the terms of the contract. There has been tender of pay of seven ($7. −) dollars per month according to the Act. of July, 1862, and not accepted by the men for the reason that they were not enlisted under that agreement, but under Act allowing them thirteen ($13. −) dollars per month. I have the honor to be Very Respectfully Your Ob'd't serv't

HLS   Alfred S. Hartwell

[*Endorsement*] Head Quarters Dept South Hilton Head S.C. June 17″ 1864 Respectfully forwarded, Col Hartwell applied to me two weeks since to be sent North for the purpose of making arrangements for the payment of his Regiment, representing at the time that he thought it could be effected by having their claims put before the authorities in a proper light. Being anxious to secure to the men the pay they were entitled to by their contract with the Officer by whom they were enlisted I gave him the desired permission, − Before he left, I learned that Col Hallowell of the 54th Regt Mass Col. Vols was an officer better qualified for the undertaking and as his regiment was situated in the same way concerning pay, having been enlisted under the same authority, at the same time, and as they had already distinguished themselves, I revoked the order, and sent Col Hallowell in his place. It appears that these regiments was enlisted by the authority of Gov. Andrews of Mass. under representation from their officers, that they were to have the same compensation as was paid white troops, when the regiment was mustered for pay their friends sent an agent here with funds to make up to them the difference between the Government pay of Colored and White soldiers. This the men declined to take refusing at the same time the pay from Government, this was a year ago. Under this arrangement they could have had their *full* pay at any time during the past twelve months. They are both (the 54″ Mass Col'd Vols & 55th Mass Col'd Vols) good regiments, and are now doing duty on Morris Island. Some of the men having showed a disposition to mutiny, have been severely punished which put a stop to further trouble. J. G. Foster. Maj. Gen'l Comd'g

Col. Alfred S. Hartwell to the Secretary of War, 13 June 1864, H-407 1864, Letters Received, ser. 360, Colored Troops Division, RG 94 [B-

399]. Other endorsements. In the same file is a copy of the Bureau of Colored Troops reply, dated June 29, 1864, which informed Foster that the pay of black soldiers was under advisement, according to the provisions of the congressional Equal Pay Act of June 15, 1864.

160C: Circular from the Commander of a Massachusetts Black Regiment, Enclosing a Letter from an Officer of the Regiment

Folly Island, S.C., June 14th, 1864.
Circular: This circular, with the accompanying letter of Lt. Col. Fox, will be read by the Commanding Officer of each company to his men at the next roll-call; by the officer of the Day to the Guard and Police, and by every commissioned officer of the regiment in charge of a detachment or picket as early as possible. These views of Lieut. Col. Fox meet the entire approval of the Commanding Officer, who has already forwarded to the Secretary of War a request that the regiment be mustered out of the service of the United States on the ground of non-fulfillment of contract.

Many feel uncertain whether to trust the reports of the papers and of the private letters of the action of Congress in reference to the matter. Whatever that action is, or shall be, must shortly be known, as Congress will soon adjourn, and the course that the War Department takes will undoubtedly be decided by that action. By order of A. S. Hartwell, Colonel Commanding

TDc

[*Enclosure*]   [*Folly Island, S.C.*] Tuesday, June 14th, 1864.
Colonel: It having come to my knowledge that erroneous opinions are held by a portion of the regiment as to what I consider the proper course in our present position; I have the honor to make the following statement of my views: —

The State of Massachusetts, the responsible party in the enlistment of our regiment, having offered to make good as far as possible the promises made by her agents, and that offer having been declined under the express understanding that it was preferred to await the action of Congress, no possible claim to be discharged the service on the ground of non-payment can be made, until the present Congress has refused to provide for the pay of the regiment agreeably to the terms of their enlistment, or has adjourned taking no action.

Should Congress refuse by vote or adjournment, to sustain the action of the State of Massachusetts, the claim to be mustered out of the service can then be made only to the Secretary of War, through the proper Military channels, on the ground of 'enlistment under false pretences.'

Nothing can be more certain than that mutinous conduct or refusal to do duty would result in the extreme penalty of the law to the ringleaders, and the probable disarming of the entire regiment and their employment at hard labor on Military works during the remainder of their term of service. Once mustered into the service of the United States any man or body of men can only leave it in the maner provided by regulation. I have the honor to be, Respectfully, Your obedient servant,

TLcSr

Chas. B. Fox

Circular, Headquarters 55th Mass. Vols., 14 June 1864, enclosing Lieut. Col. Chas. B. Fox to Col. A. S. Hartwell, 14 June 1864, Negro in the Military Service, pp. 2623–24, ser. 390, Colored Troops Division, RG 94 [B-474].

160D: Soldiers of a Massachusetts Black Regiment to the President

Folly island South Carolina July 16th 18.64
Sir   We The Members of Co D of the 55th Massachusetts vols Call the attention of your Excellency to our case
  1st   First We wase enlisted under the act of Congress of July 18.61 Placing the officers non Commissioned officers & Privates of the volunteer forces in all Respects as to Pay on the footing of Similar Corps of the Regular Army   2nd   We Have Been in the Field now thirteen months & a Great many yet longer   We Have Recieved no Pay & Have Been offered only seven Dollars Pr month Which the Paymaster Has said was all He Had ever Been authorized to Pay Colored Troops   this was not acording to our enlistment   Consequently We Refused the Money   the Commonwealth of Massachusetts then Passed an act to make up all Deficienceys which the general Government Refused To Pay But this We Could not Recieve as The Troops in the general service are not Paid Partly By Government & Partly By State   3rd   that to us money is no object   we came to fight For Liberty justice & Equality. These are gifts we Prise more Highly than Gold   For these We Left our Homes our Famileys Friends & Relatives most Dear to take as it ware our Lives in our Hands To Do Battle for God & Liberty

401

4th after the elaps of over thirteen months spent cheerfully &
willingly Doing our Duty most faithfuly in the Trenches Fatiegue
Duty in camp and conspicious valor & endurence in Battle as our
Past History will Show

P 5th therefore we Deem these sufficient Reasons for
Demanding our Pay from the Date of our inlistment & our
imediate Discharge Having Been enlisted under False Prentence as
the Past History of the Company will Prove

6th Be it further Resolved that if imediate steps are not
takened to Relieve us we will Resort to more stringent mesures

We have the Honor to Remin your Obedint Servants   The
members of Co D

HLS   [*74 signatures*]

Sergt. John F. Shorter et al. to the President of the United States, 16 July
1864, L-211 1864, Letters Received, ser. 360, Colored Troops Division,
RG 94 [B-103]. The names of five sergeants and six corporals are among
the signatures. Most signers appear to have signed their own name.

160E: Wife of an Ohio Black Soldier to the Governor of Massachusetts or the President

                         Piqua Miama Co ohio Sep 12 1864
Sir i write to you to know the reason why our husbands and sons
who enlisted in the 55 Massichusette regiment have not Bin paid
off i speak for my self and Mother and i know of a great many
others as well as ourselve are suffering for the want of money to
live on   when provision and Clotheing wer Cheap we might have
got a long But Every thing now is thribbl and over what it was
some thre year Back   But it matters not if Every thing was at the
old Price i think it a Piece of injustice to have those soldiers
there 15 months with out a cent of Money   for my part i Cannot
see why they have not th same rite to their 16 dollars per month
as th Whites or Even th Coulord Soldiers that went from ohio   i
think if Massichusette had left off Comeing to other States for
Soldiers th Soldirs would have bin Better off and Massichusette
saved her Credit   i wish you if you pleas to Answer this Letter
and tell me Why it is that you Still insist upon them takeing 7
dollars a month when you give the Poorest White Regiment that
has went out 16 dollars   Answer this if you Pleas and oblige Your
humble Servant

ALS   Rachel Ann Wicker

Rachel Ann Wicker to Mr. President Andrew, 12 Sept. 1864, W-734 1864, Letters Received, ser. 360, Colored Troops Division, RG 94 [B-72]. Endorsement. Massachusetts Governor John A. Andrew received the letter first, but, reasoning that Wicker intended it for President Abraham Lincoln, he forwarded it to the War Department. In the same file is a draft letter from the Adjutant General's Office to Andrew, dated October 10, 1864, which indicates that the 55th Massachusetts regiment was momentarily to receive its pay in compliance with the congressional act of June 15, 1864.

160F: Commander of a Massachusetts Black Regiment to the Governor of Massachusetts

> Morris Island [*S.C.*] September 19. 1864

Dear Sir   I respectfully request that Charles F Ivy of Brighton Mass. now a Sergant in F Co 2nd Mass Heavy Artillery stationed at Fort Stephenson N.C. be commissioned a second Lieutenant in this regiment.

Sergeant Stephen A. Swails is not yet mustered as an officer because he is believed to have African blood in him! How can we hope for success to our arms or Gods blessing in any shape while we as a nation are so blind to Justice?

The men now expect to be paid according to the terms of their enlistment, about the first of October. I administered the following oath to them "You do solemnly swear that on or before the 19th day of April 1864 [*1861*], no man *had the right* to demand unrequited labor of you so help you God." None of them objected to taking the oath, and I mustered them accordingly. The Paymaster has written me he will bring the money to us in about two weeks, he has it all ready and is only waiting to make the necessary calculation upon the rolls. The men have been deceived so often in this matter, they are not willing to send the money home in the usual manner but say they would "rather have it in their own hands first." Adams Express Co has kindly promised to send an agent along with the Paymaster to receipt for such sums as they may conclude to send. Pay day will be our day of thanks giving and prayer, for we will have won a victory, as important to our race as the taking of Atlanta was to the nation.

Six Companies of the regiment now form part of the Guard over the Camp of Rebel officers. Prisoners of War situated under the guns of Fort Wagner and near the grave of their beloved Colonel Shaw. Some of thess same rebel officers were in Fort Wagner on the memorable night when we assaulted it and say they saw Colonel Shaw fall, shot by one of the 57th N.C regiment.

Our men are proud of the honor of guarding these Rebels but they do not like to *see* them starved even in retaliation, when off duty they say it is all right, but when on duty if a man begs them for something to eat, it is hard not to be allowed to yield to the feeling which prompts them to do good to those who despitefully use them. The Rebel ration is for Breakfast one cracker Dinner two crackers 1/2 lb meat 1/5 pint beans Supper one cracker, no Tea or Coffee   Very Respectfully Your Obt Servant

HLcSr   (Sgd) E N Hallowell

Col. E. N. Hallowell to Governor John A. Andrew, 19 Sept. 1864, Letters Sent, 54th Mass. Vols., Regimental Books & Papers USCT, RG 94 [G-232].

161: Officers of a Kansas Black Regiment to the Secretary of War

Little Rock, Arkansas July 5th 1865.

Sir   The undersigned Officers of the 79th U.S Colored Infantry (late 1$''$ Kan Col'd Vol) would respectfully represent that in the months of August and September 1862 they were commissioned and mustered as recruiting officers, under and by authority of Hon James H. Lane, then acting as Commissioner of Recruiting in the state of Kansas; that acting under the authority above mentioned and by orders from the said James H. Lane Recruiting Commissioner they enlisted a large number of persons of African descent who were afterwards, at various times between the 13th day January and 2nd day of May 1863, mustered into the U.S. service in the above named regiment; (then known as the 1$''$ Kan Col'd Vol); that when they entered upon their duties as recruiting officers as aforesaid, they were instructed that the persons so enlisted would receive the same pay and allowances, that were or might be paid and allowed to other volunteers in the Military service of the United States; that in accordance with such instructions, the men so enlisting were instructed that they would receive the same pay and allowances, allowed by law to other regiments in the U.S. service; That from the date of enlistment, to may 1st 1864, the enlisted men so enlisted as aforesaid were paid

404

ten ($10) dollars per month for their services, three dollars of which was in clothing.

Wherefore in view of the above facts we would respectfully request: that in accordance with Sec. 5, Act of Congress, Approved March 3th 1865, an order be issued directing the Pay Department to cause the enlisted men of said regiment, enlisted as aforesaid, to be paid the same pay and allowance paid and allowed, to other regiments in the U.S. service at and during the period, dating from the date of their original enlistment to include the 30" day of April 1864

J. M. Williams	Benj G Janes
R G Ward	D. M. Sutherland
John K. Graton	Ransom Ward
E. Huddleston	A. J. Armstrong
B Hitchcock	L. A. Thrasher

HLS

Col. J. M. Williams et al. to Hon. Secretary of War, 5 July 1865, W-558 1865, Letters Received, ser. 360, Colored Troops Division, RG 94 [B-298]. Endorsements. The same file contains a draft reply from the Bureau of Colored Troops, which denied the request on the grounds that Lane's "'instructions' above referred to did not emanate from the sources specified in the Act of Congress herein cited, and the payment requested cannot, therefore, under existing law, be ordered." (A.A. Genl. C. W. Foster to Major Genl. J. J. Reynolds, 24 July 1865.) For earlier pay difficulties experienced by the Kansas regiment, see *Freedom*, ser. 2: doc. 16.

8

Black Soldiers and Their Officers

BELIEVING that only white officers could bend former slaves to the demands of military life and lead black soldiers into battle, the War Department refused to commission blacks until late in the war and then only in very small numbers.[1] For the most part, relations between officers and soldiers in the black regiments followed the familiar pattern of American race relations: whites as superiors and blacks as inferiors. Yet, even within this tired formula enormous variation existed.

The abolitionist proponents of black enlistment rejected notions of black inferiority and sensed that the selection of officers of impeccable credentials would at once silence critics and spur the success of black regiments. Massachusetts Governor John A. Andrew recruited men of known abolitionist principles to lead the 54th and 55th Massachusetts regiments, as did Kansas Senator James H. Lane for his 1st Kansas Colored Volunteers. For similar reasons and upon Andrew's recommendation, Edward A. Wild took command of the North Carolina "African Brigade" which bore his name, and Thomas W. Higginson of Massachusetts and James Montgomery of Kansas received commands in the South Carolina Colored Volunteers, recruited by antislavery Generals David Hunter and Rufus Saxton.[2]

---

[1]   The free black officers of the Louisiana Native Guard whom General Benjamin F. Butler mustered into service and whom General Nathaniel P. Banks purged were a brief exception to this generalization. See *Freedom,* ser. 2: doc. 127–132.

[2]   In establishing criteria for choosing officers in the black regiments he was organizing, Captain Reuben D. Mussey, commissioner for the organization of black troops in middle and east Tennessee, insisted that in addition to meeting the standards of commissioned rank, "No person is wanted as an officer in a Colored Regiment who 'feels that he is making a sacrifice in accepting a position in a Colored Regiment,' or who desires the place simply for higher rank and pay. It is the aim of those having this organization in charge to make Colored Troops equal, if not superior, to the best of White Troops in Drill, Discipline, and Officers. It is more than possible that Colored Troops will hereafter form no inconsiderable portion of the permanent army of the United States, and it should be the aim of every officer of Colored Troops to make himself and his men fit for such an honorable position. It can be no 'sacrifice' to any man to command in a service which gives Liberty to Slaves, and Manhood to Chattels, as well as Soldiers to the Union." (Circular, Head-Quarters, Com'r. Org'n. U.S. Col'd.

The abolitionists who officered the early black regiments came from a variety of backgrounds. Many had grown up in the war against slavery and battled side by side with William Lloyd Garrison and Charles Sumner. Others, like David Branson of Mississippi, had powerful unionist commitments and were not easily intimidated by the sneers directed toward "nigger officers." Indeed, such slander only intensified their sense of mission and their determination to see the "experiment" succeed. Some, like Colonel Isaac F. Shepard, who had a white soldier whipped for abusing his black troops, risked their careers to protect their men. But rapid growth of black enlisted ranks, especially after May 1863 when the War Department's Bureau of Colored Troops began operation, outpaced the number of abolitionists available to officer black regiments.

Establishment of the bureau not only marked the wholesale expansion of black recruitment but also constituted a minor revolution in the selection of Union officers. On the assumption that authority to raise regiments conveyed the power to appoint officers, state governors had regularly chosen officers for the volunteer units raised in their states. The inauguration of recruitment by the Bureau of Colored Troops placed the entire officer selection mechanism for black regiments in the hands of the federal government.[3] To secure officers readily, the bureau offered to both white officers and white enlisted men the prospect of promotion in rank if they accepted commissions in black regiments. But, in order to ensure high quality in the new officer corps and guard against the dangers inherent in a system that propelled privates to lieutenants, sergeants to captains, and captains to colonels almost overnight, the bureau required that prospective officers pass examinations before receiving appointments.[4] In so doing, the federal government closed the patronage route to commission in black regiments.

Troops, 15 Feb. 1864, enclosed in Col. R. D. Mussey to Maj. C. W. Foster, 10 Oct. 1864, M-750 1864, Letters Received, ser. 360, Colored Troops Division, RG 94 [B-468]).

[3] Of the five black regiments raised by Northern governors – the 54th and 55th Massachusetts Volunteer Infantry, the 5th Massachusetts Colored Cavalry, the 29th Connecticut Volunteer Infantry, and the 14th Rhode Island Colored Heavy Artillery – only the Rhode Island unit received a new regimental designation under the Bureau of Colored Troops, becoming the 8th U.S. Colored Heavy Artillery (later redesignated the 11th USCHA). (*Official Army Register,* pt. 8, pp. 147, 159, 313–16.) According to the provost marshal general, however, only the 54th and 55th Massachusetts Volunteers remained under state jurisdiction throughout their service. (*Official Records,* ser. 3, vol. 5, p. 661.)

[4] As early as July 1861, the Adjutant General's Office authorized boards of examination to review the qualifications of volunteer officers, but that order applied to officers who had already entered service and did not detract from the power of the governors to appoint whomever they wished. (*Official Records,* ser. 3, vol. 1, p. 349.)

In December 1863 the Supervisory Committee for Recruiting Colored Troops, recognizing the critical need for qualified officers, established the Free Military School in Philadelphia to prepare prospective officers for examination. The directors of the school screened applicants closely, categorically excluding "Such as are intemperate; such as seek the service for lack of a better business; such as have been, while in the military service, frequently sick at the hospital; and such as are proved to be ill whenever there is a hard march on hand, or a battle in prospect." Thomas Webster, chairman of the Supervisory Committee, proudly described the students as "enthusiastic in their views regarding the duties of the colored race to the government in this war, and the duties of the people and the government to this race." "A large proportion of them," according to Webster, were "men of liberal education, culture and excellent social position." The school operated entirely on the basis of voluntary contributions and, hence, never enjoyed financial stability. After exhausting its resources, it closed in September 1864. In its nine-month existence, the Free Military School boasted 484 graduates who served as officers in black regiments. Shortly after closing, the school – renamed the U.S. Military School for Officers – reopened on a tuition basis. The school survived through the rest of the war, preparing officers for service with black troops and providing a precedent for the training of officers outside the established military academies.[5]

The boards of examination intended that men knowledgeable in military tactics and possessing the requisite personal qualities of officers should lead black soldiers. However, the boards did not question prospective officers about either their racial attitudes or their motives for volunteering with black troops, and, as a consequence, officers differed widely in commitment to their work. Some shared the antislavery vision of the early abolitionist officers and accepted service with black troops as a challenge both to their adherence to the cause of racial equality and to their beliefs in the inherent capabilities of former slaves. Others cared little about black advancement or even emancipation and instead sought only promotion and the pay and perquisites that attended higher rank. Embarrassed by their affiliation with "nigger troops," many of these officers viewed their speedy advancement as meager compensation for the stigma of such association. They resented the difficulties associated with com-

[5] On the Free Military School, see Thomas Webster to Hon. Edwin M. Stanton, 22 Apr. 1864, enclosing printed pamphlet, *Free Military School for Applicants for Command of Colored Troops* (Philadelphia, 1864), W-392 1864, Letters Received, ser. 360, Colored Troops Division, RG 94 [B-439]. On the U.S. Military School, see the printed pamphlet, *U.S. Military School for Officers* (Philadelphia, 1865), enclosed in John H. Taggart to Hon. E. M. Stanton, 4 Apr. 1865, T-92 1865, Letters Received, ser. 360, Colored Troops Division, RG 94 [B-595].

manding former slaves and the added burdens of instruction and paperwork that resulted from the ignorance of their men and especially from the shortage of literate noncommissioned officers. A few slave owners even numbered among the new officer corps. In sum, many officers carried the racial prejudices commonplace in American society. While experience with black soldiers would modify the views of most, some officers maintained active contempt for blacks throughout their term of service.

The diverse social views of the officer corps in the black regiments guaranteed a wide range of treatment of enlisted men. Whereas some officers felt a special sympathy for former slaves, on the assumption that the "law of kindness" should replace the slave master's domination by force, others believed an iron rule the only way to command men accustomed to the lash. At times, in their zeal to impress black soldiers with the necessity of abiding by military regulations, the strict disciplinarians ran roughshod over their men. Of course, officers in white regiments often behaved no differently. Many officers of black troops learned their habits of command while serving with whites and treated their black subordinates no more harshly than they had their white ones. Commissioned rank conferred enormous power, which any officer might abuse. But racial contempt fueled the arbitrary use of authority and encouraged some white officers to abuse black enlisted men. While only a minority beat their men, bucked and gagged them, or tied them up by their thumbs, many more demeaned black soldiers by demanding that they act as body servants and by ridiculing their ignorance of military ways. The racial contempt implicit in such behavior often stemmed from other than strictly malicious motives and manifested itself in other ways. Well-meaning white officers who believed that blacks, fresh from slavery, were less than adults, manifested a similar contempt when they regularly intruded into the personal and social lives of their men.

Racist officers did not confine their contempt strictly to blacks in uniform but expressed similar scorn for blacks in civilian garb. Taking little heed of the family feelings of their men, they often treated soldiers' wives as prostitutes. While black soldiers played the liberator's role, their officers all too often showed greater sympathy for former masters. Such behavior imbued black troops with distrust of their officers and magnified the ironies of fighting a war for black freedom in the midst of pervasive racial prejudice.

While officers of antislavery lineage, alive to the special needs of former slaves, attempted to instruct their men in the rudiments of reading and writing, others took advantage of the soldiers' illiteracy and general ignorance of military regulations. Payday provided just another opportunity for conscienceless officers to separate the men

409

from their money. At times, such sharpers played the banker, taking money from black soldiers on promise of depositing it for them and then swindling them out of their savings. At other times, officers borrowed heavily from their men and later neglected to repay. The War Department naturally frowned on such practices and routinely stopped the pay of guilty officers awaiting discharge. Nonetheless, the department moved slowly, and, when officers left service before soldiers lodged their complaints, the soldiers had no alternative but to seek redress through civil action, an uncertain undertaking at best. Even an occasional black officer borrowed from his men without scruple of repayment.

All in all, white officers and black soldiers frequently held expectations of each other that exceeded possible realization. Officers hoped to command men eager to fight for freedom, to improve themselves morally and intellectually, and to do credit to themselves and their race. But, in the uncertainty and drudgery that characterized much of military life, soldiers often failed to meet these standards. Similarly, black enlisted men expected officers to accord them the dignity of soldiers and the rights of free men, to sympathize with the needs of their families, to understand the difficulties posed by their recent emergence from slavery and, if possible, to help them prepare for lives as free men. But unsympathetic and incompetent officers grew demoralized and turned their frustrations upon the soldiers, often treating them as little more than brutes. The realities of military life frequently reinforced racial preconceptions of both white officers and black enlisted men.

In a sense, relations between white officers and black enlisted men bore the brunt of the earliest transition from slavery to freedom. Laboring under such a heavy burden caused men on both sides to revert to familiar patterns of behavior that, even while they offered psychological comfort, proved obsolete for dealing with the new realities of freedom. The searing experience eventually wrought changes in the racial perspective of both white officers and black soldiers. Black soldiers discerned the differences between slave society and free society as exemplified by military experience. Even though officers often wielded greater power than slave masters, formal rules and higher authority circumscribed the actions of military officers in ways that far exceeded the power of antebellum civil officials to curb the prerogatives of slave owners. Many blacks who entered the army calling every white man "boss" or "captain" soon learned the distinctions in the rank of corporals, captains, and colonels and the rights common soldiers had before each. They learned that in free society they could appeal to higher authority for redress of grievances on a scale utterly unthinkable under slavery. While military regulations sacrificed some of the slave system's qualities of personal mediation of power (which could intervene on the side of leniency as well as on the side of brutality), soldiers recognized that in the army their more impersonal relationship to authority rested on their being elevated to the status of persons themselves. Few preferred slavery to freedom.

The crucible of war transformed white officers as well as black enlisted men. If some officers in black regiments clung to their racial beliefs and saw them sadly confirmed, most returned home after the war aglow with praise for their men and skeptical of the neat stereotypes cast by nineteenth-century racist ideology. Many who had reluctantly and disdainfully taken command of black troops emerged as champions of the new order. Their own racial preconceptions had crumbled when black soldiers fought as bravely as white soldiers and learned to perform other soldierly duties on a par with whites. These officers helped bolster the growing mood of racial tolerance in the North that black military service itself had set in motion. Newly committed to the cause of racial equality, they numbered prominently among the army officers who served with the Freedmen's Bureau in the South after the war. Such officers represented both a continuation and an expansion of the emancipation process from the army of liberation to the freedpeople at large and to Northern whites as well.

162: Provost Marshal of Norfolk and Portsmouth, Virginia, to the President

Norfolk V^a Feb 18. 1861 [*1863*].

Mr Lincoln, you will not of course remember me. I called upon you recently & urged you to appoint Brig Genl Viele to a Maj. Generalship. I wish now to call your attention to another matter, which I think is about to become one of vast importance. It is in regard to the organization of the Negro solders, supposing there is to be any such organization. Mr Lincoln, I assure you, that the great failure in the conduct of this War so far, has been that the decided majority of our officers of all grades have no sympathy with your policy; nor with any thing human. They hate the Negro, more than they love the Union. You would probably suppose that such men would not seek or accept positions in the Negro Regts: not so however. There is a regular cabal here among the very worst class of Negro hating officers, to secure & parcel out to themselves & others like themselves, all those places. Whether this is a part of a great general conspiracy, or not, I cannot positively say, but I am inclined to think it is. These men have at this moment two agents in Washington under pay sent there from here—to secure their appointments in this force, all the way down from Brigadier to Captain. For Gods sake dont let this black army fall into such hands; for these reasons—

1st They will grossly maltreat the poor creatures.

2nd They will turn this force against the Govt should there be a coup de etat in favor of McClellan or any other Democratic Military Chieftain—which I do not think *entirely* beyond the bounds of possibility.

3rd At the least they will render the force worthless, as they do our [. . .] white armies—

4th They are very generally dishonest, & they will have vast opportunities to plunder out of both government and people— All of which is submitted with the greatest Respect

ALS   A E Boney

Major A. E. Boney to Mr. Lincoln, 18 Feb. 1861 [1863], B-25 1863, Letters Received, ser. 360, Colored Troops Division, RG 94 [B-417].

163: Order by the Commander of a Louisiana Black Brigade

New Orleans, June 10, 1863.

GENERAL ORDERS No. 7.

. . . .

II. The General Commanding brings to the particular notice of the officers of this command, that they are engaged, by the orders of the Government, in a special, peculiar and difficult service. They have been selected as possessing qualities which, it is supposed, eminently qualify them for this duty, namely: accurate knowledge of the drill, long experience in the field, patience, diligence, and patriotism. They will find the constant exercise of all these qualities necessary.

You are brought into contact with a race, who, having lived in an abnormal condition all the days of their lives, are now suddenly elevated into being soldiers of the United States, fighting against their oppressors, as well for their own liberties as for the integrity of the Republic. They are to be moulded by you into drilled and well-disciplined troops. You cannot display too much wisdom in your conduct, both as regards yourselves and them. *Let the law of kindness be your guide.* Thus acting, you will soon obtain their confidence; you will then find them docile, impressionable, fully

imbued with the spirit of subordination (one of the highest
attributes of a soldier), possessed of a deep appreciation of kindly
treatment and of keen perceptions, which enables them quickly to
discover any flaw in the conduct of their superiors.

You have the materials, crude though they now may be, but
perfectly malleable, to make the best of soldiers. It remains with
you to say whether such shall be the result. Perform your duty
conscientiously, and our beloved and once happy country will not
only have a body of soldiers, who will enthusiastically aid her in
fighting her battles, but she will also have the proud satisfaction
of knowing that she has, at last, taken a practical step towards the
elevation of a hitherto degraded and oppressed race.

III. The General Commanding learns that the malignant
enemies of the Union and the people of the United States, are
busily engaged in endeavoring to persuade the colored population
of the South, that if they recruit as soldiers in the armies of the
Republic, they will, at the close of the war, be returned to slavery
by the Government.

It is to be expected, in this unholy war between truth and
falsehood – humanity and oppression – justice and injustice – freedom
and slavery – regulated liberty and unrestrained despotism, that the
atrocious instigators of this foul and unnatural rebellion, together
with their secret aiders and sympathizers, who have the oath of
allegiance on their lips and treason in their hearts, should, to
sustain themselves, resort to every device which the arch enemy of
mankind suggests to their willing minds.

This is one of those devices.

Let not the colored men of the South be deceived by any thing
that may be said by those who are at once their, and the
UNION'S foes.

The General Commanding, therefore directs his officers of all
grades, to assure every colored man whom they recruit, that if he
shall, by virtue of the authority delegated to the General, be
regularly enlisted into the service of the United States, and shall
bear himself as a true and faithful soldier until the end of the term
of his enlistment, he has the sacred honor of the United States
pledged, that the whole power of this Government, moral and
physical, shall be exerted to secure to him and to his posterity for
ever, the inestimable blessings of freedom.

It is not in the power of the General Government, under the
Constitution, to remand a single human being, once freed, to
slavery, "otherwise than in punishment of crimes, whereof the
party shall have been duly convicted."

Beside, this war, in its consequences, has reached a point
beyond the power of man. The first gun that was fired at Fort

Sumter sounded the death-knell of slavery. They who fired it were the greatest practical abolitionists this nation has produced. The decree went forth from that hour that slavery should quickly cease to exist on this North American continent.

Come, then, colored men of the South, enlist in the armies of the United States. Your brethren at Port Hudson have shown to the world that they can and will fight, and have displayed as dauntless courage as ever illuminated a battle field. Emulate their noble example, and fight under the glorious banner of the Republic, which will be to you, in the great FUTURE, as it has been in the PAST to millions of the white race, the symbol of every temporal blessing.

Truth, Justice and GOD are on our side. THEY WILL PREVAIL. By command of DANIEL ULLMANN, *Brigadier General Commanding.*

PD

General Orders No. 7, Headquarters Brig. Gen. Ullmann's Brigade, 10 June 1863, vol. 206/424 DG, pp. 5–6, General Orders & Special Orders, ser. 2146, Ullmann's Brigade, 19th Army Corps, RG 393 Pt. 2 No. 122 [C-1051]. The first section of the order, omitted here, pertains to injuries resulting from the accidental discharge of firearms.

164: Adjutant General of the Army to the Secretary of War

Goodrichs Landing La October 5th 1863

Sir   When I first commenced the organization of negro regiments on the Mississippi River Colonel Isaac F. Shepard, commanding the 3rd Regiment Missouri Volunteers, presented himself with high Testimonials and requested authority to raise some troops, and expressed a desire, although then Colonel of a white Regiment, to take the Colonelcy of a colored one, looking forward of course, to further advancement, should his zeal, activity and services justify a recommendation from his superior officers. I gave him the 1st Mississippi, and he went to work with an energy which showed that his heart was in the business. I should have asked his promotion some time since, but, when in Washington understood he had ordered a white soldier whipped by blacks, which caused great indignation against him in the army here. You may recollect I personally brought the case to your notice and it was determined not to appoint him Brigadier General.

Since my return here, I have examined the case and find that

Colonel Shepard, when in command of the Colored Troops, near white regiments, acted with judgement and forbearance, when the white soldiers committed acts of wantonness against the negroes and their families. To his numerous complaints to the commanding officer no action was had, and finding it useless to make any more, the flagrant case under consideration coming up, one calling for the severest punishment, even to the loss of life, he had the culprit tied up to be flogged. The punishment inflicted was very light and Colonel Shepard soon stopped it   The Colonel asked a court of inquiry, which was granted the proceedings of which I have seen, and they cast no censure upon him.   General Grant dismissed the case without notice, and ordered the Colonel to duty.   I have conversed with the President of the Court Brig Genl P. Kilby Smith who speaks in high praise of Colonel Shepard of his capacity for command.

Brig Genl. Hawkins, his present commander, also commends him for his soldierly bearing, military capacity and high moral capacity.

Colonel Shepard was made a Colonel by the late lamented General Lyon at the battle of Wilson Creek in which grade he has continued to the present time   He was with General Sherman in the first attack upon Vicksburg and received honorable mention from that General.

His case is a special one, he being the only Colonel who presented himself for a command in colored troops which gave him no additional rank at a time when I needed the support and co-operation of high officers.   His services with the negroes have been valuable and no one has rendered better service in elevating them and fitting them for all the Duties of Soldiers

I therefore now respectfully recommend him for the appointment of Brigadier General, and if appointed request that the commission may date from the 7th of June, the battle of Millikens Bend, where though in arrest for the case above stated, he accompanied his regiment to the ramparts and encouraged his men during that bloody fight whilst unable to give a command.   I have the Honor to be Very Respy. Your Obed Servt

HLcS   L Thomas

Adjutant General L. Thomas to Hon. Edwin M. Stanton, 5 Oct. 1863, L. Thomas Letters & Orders, Generals' Papers and Books, ser. 159, RG 94 [V-21]. Shepard received the promotion.

415

165: Soldiers in a Louisiana Black Regiment to the Headquarters of the Department of the Gulf

Alexandria [*La.*] March 28th 1864

Sir we the noncommissioned officers musicians and privates belonging to the 1st Inft C. d.A with regret make the following report hopeing that we may derive some good by laying our Complaint before the Commanding General as we believe thair is no General in the field who will Simpathize with his men when they have been wronged as Genl Banks will and now yestoday March 27th 1864 the Colonel Commdnding the brigade ordered our flag to be Sent to port Hudson the flag what we faught under at Port Hudson and General banks raised his hat to on the right of port hudson the Col Commanding the Brigade Col Wm H. Dickey Said it was a dam pettiecoat and A disgrace to the brigade he also Cursed our Regt and Said we wer the dam Smart Nigers

hoping that this may meet with the Sympathies of the commanding general and that we may have our flag returned and other wrongs Stoped we humble beg pardon if we are in the wrong we remain very respectfully you obt Servts and dutiful Soldiers

HL   1st Regt Infty Corps d A

[*Endorsement*] Hd Qrs 1st Brigade 1st Div C d A Alexandria [*La.*] March 29th 1864 Respectfully rturned. The Flag Brought out by this Regt was old faded and Ragged and bore no resemblance to the colors prescribed by Regulations— The Regt has at Port Hudson Two fine colors. I ordered the commanding officer to return his old colors and have one of these brought up— no such language as is mentioned in the communication has ever been used by me Wm H Dickey Col Comgd

1st Regt. Infty. Corps d'A. to A.A.A. Genl. G. Norman Lieber, 28 Mar. 1864, Letters Received, 73rd USCI, Regimental Books & Papers USCT, RG 94 [G-50]. Another endorsement.

166: Company Officers of a Mississippi Black Regiment to the Regimental Commander

Camp 52nd U.S.C. Infty [*Miss.*] Dec. 7" 1864

Col. The undersigned officers of your command desire to call your attention to the fact that certain *Company Commanders* permit their *1st Sergeants,* (COLORED) to occupy tents on the line with the *officers,* which we *protest* against as being out of place and *decidedly disagreeable* to us. We would most Respectfully ask, that *all colored* persons other than *officer's Servants* be sent to their own side of the color line[1] to quarter. Respectfully,

N. G. Clement	Benj. A. Lee
M van B Haskins	P. J. Gosnell
Clarendon Kelly	Peter A Simmons

HLS

N. G. Clement et al. to Col. Geo. M. Ziegler, 7 Dec. 1864, Letters Received, 52nd USCI, Regimental Books & Papers USCT, RG 94 [G-194]. Clement and Kelly did not indicate their army rank; the other four were captains.

1 The color line was an imaginary line along which the national and regimental flags were placed when a regiment was encamped. (See the prescribed camp arrangements in *Revised Army Regulations,* pp. 76–80.)

167: Chaplain of a Louisiana Black Regiment to the Commander of a Louisiana Black Brigade

Morganzia [*La.*] Dec. 19 1864

Dear Sir: If it is not too great an intrusion upon your time, I wish to address you unofficially, with regard to a matter that seems to me of grave importance. In the scout from which the 73^d & 92^d U.S.C.I. have just returned, I was witness to abuses practised by officers upon the men, such as cursing and vilifying, in the most shameful language, striking and kicking, – with a manner that indicated it was practised habitually, – which is evidently against military order, and would not be practised upon white soldiers. But as these colored troops are in a state of pupillage, it would seem fitting that they above all others should be impressed with the dignity and justice of military law. The discipline of the service ought to present to them a contrast to the irresponsible cruelties of slavedriving, instead of a too faithful reproduction of them. For my own part, I came into the service

417

under a deep conviction, as a citizen – to speak of no higher obligation – of the heavy responsiblity our government assumed in becoming the guardian of these millions of freedmen, and from a desire to contribute my help as one man, towards the great work of leading them up from their enforced degradation to manhood and citizenship, and I recognize the military service, in its legitimate operation, as an excellent school for this end. But such treatment as I have referred to, only adds to their former degradation the humiliating thought, that it comes from those who have professed to be their only friends. After such proof of bad faith, what hope or ambition can be left in them? I am well assured that all effort towards their elevation in this generation or the next, will be futile, unless there is an end to the plantation style of government; that is, so far as the army is their school.

I am aware, sir, that there is a specific method of proceeding, against specific military offences, but I am uncertain whether there is a disposition in the governing powers of the army to take cognizance of this class of offences, and enforce a better principle. I am ready to take any responsiblity that will lead to practical results. With the highest respect. – I remain, sir, Your obedient Servant

ALS

Saml L. Gardner

Chaplain Saml. L. Gardner to Gen. Ullman, 19 Dec. 1864, D. Ullmann Papers, Generals' Papers & Books, ser. 159, RG 94 [V-2].

168: Court-Martial Testimony by the Commander of a Kentucky Black Regiment

[*Louisville, Ky. May 29?, 1865*]

. . . .

You gentlemen who have been raised with Negroes know their disposition, know that they are treacherous by nature, & difficult to command. They were armed right among their former masters, for instance a slave would come in to day & enlist, to-morrow, he would be upon the Picket Post, and halt his master & demand of him a pass before he could get into Town. This thing was very unpleasant, to the people of the southern portion of Ky. they did not like it & I must acknowledge myself that I would rather be halted & questioned by a white man than by a negro, especially if that negro had formerly been my slave. The most serious specification I say is in regard to permitting, allowing, & giving permission to my men to fire indiscriminately through the Town, endangering the lives of citizens. You have heard the testimony in regard to this point. I have adopted every measure in my power to prevent it, & it cannot be expected that I could arm a lot of slaves among their former masters & bring them down to strict military discipline all at once. When I went to Henderson the last time I took 30 men & 3 officers, there was a detatchment there of the 118" Regt U.S. Colored Infantry. I had some difficulty with those men. Men comeing from the East & New England States looked upon us who were raised in the state of Ky as disloyal men, & upon the state of Ky. as a disloyal state. The officers of the 118" were disposed to let their men trespass & do every thing that was wrong. We were rebels. I kept them in subjection until they were relieved & my own men were armed among their former masters– Until then you did not hear of a complaint.

. . . .

I have had some experience in commanding colored troops. I have been a resident of the state of Ky for 15 years, & have had a great deal to do with negroes, & you will find it a great deal easier to command troops already disciplined than to take charge of illiterate, ignorant revengeful, blood-thirsty negroes, & bring them down in the space of 2 or 3 months to regular disciplined soldiers.

. . . .

I can explain the reason for a great deal of this firing. The hardest thing in the world to learn negro soldiers is to learn them to shoot with that acuracy of regular soldiers–they are more awkward with a gun than with any thing else. I had orders to expend as much amunition as I deemed necessary in target practice, in teaching my men how to shoot, we had a good deal of target practice firing & besides the guard discharged their guns at 9-o'clock in the morning. They went down to the river & shot into the bank– Of course the noise may have offended or unstrung the nerves of some Union ladies in Henderson who were very much in favor of negro troops & officers– Yet it is singular that so many outrages have been committed by my troops & no body hurt, except young Wortham, & I considered that a very great outrage. When I have said that I have not controlled my troops, I had reference to that particular affair. The testimony is that I would & could controll them– I knew it would take very severe measures, which measures I adopted.

. . . .

HD

Excerpts from exhibit "C", proceedings of general court-martial in the case of Lt. Col. John Glenn, 120th USCI, 29? May 1865, MM-2404, Court-Martial Case Files, ser. 15, RG 153 [H-10]. According to the charges and specifications, Lieutenant Colonel John Glenn permitted the enlisted men of his regiment "to be guilty of lawless and outrageous conduct," and he "was unable to control his men." The judge advocate, in his summation to the court, asserted that "the very worst thing for our cause is this running at large of negro soldiers throughout the state with inefficient officers in command permitting them to do as they choose. . . . It requires a man of more ability to com'd a regt of negro troops than of white ones, and requiring a man of ability none but such should have the position, and inefficient men should be got rid of as fast as possible." The court found Glenn guilty of "conduct prejudicial to good order and military discipline" but sentenced him only to forfeit rank, pay, and allowances for two months.

169: Black Chaplain of a New York Black Regiment to the Adjutant General of the Army

Beaufort S.C. May 31st 1865

Sir— In accordance with Ser. 3^d Gen. Orders 158, April, 1864, I submit the following report of the Moral and Religious condition of this regiment, for the present month. –

Maximum Strength of regt –		1018.
Whole Number of whom belong to Regimental Church per last report –		76.
Conversions Since –		18.
Whole Number at present –		94.
" "	Ordained ministers among enlisted men –	2.
" "	Exhorters	4.
" "	learning to read & write, Arith. & Gram. &c –	250.
" "	in Guard House during present month –	4.
" "	detected Stealing " " "	1.
" "	gambling " " "	0.
" "	playing cards on Sabbath " "	3.
" "	White Com Officers on duty at present –	28.
" "	habitually profane Com. Officers –	10.

Religious meetings are frequent and tolerable well attended. Many manifest an interest in meetings. The Regimental School is taught by a teacher furnished by Am. Miss. Society.

Many of the men manifest much interest in learning, and great good is being done in this respect, and many of these men will return to their homes better Scholars, and better morally. The greatest ostensible evil in this regiment is, profanity. Some of the white Com. Officers, *persist* in this evil habit, which makes it very difficult for the Chaplain to check it on the part of the men. The poor oppressed negro of this land needs the most wholesome example set before him to elevate him, but this is one bad example, set by those whom he looks up to for example, and one which confirms him in his degredation. Would That for humanity's Sake it could be Stoped!

All of which is most respectfully submitted,

ALS   B. F. Randolph

Chaplain B. F. Randolph to Brig. Gen. L. Thomas, 31 May 1865, R-462 1865, Letters Received, ser. 12, RG 94 [K-530].

170A: Soldiers in an Independent Kansas Black Light Artillery Battery to Their Black Commanding Officer

Fort Leavenworth [*Kans.*] June 19th 1865

Sir   We the undersigned members of Indpt Cold Battery trusting on you as an officer who desires to see Justice done to all men we therefore Respectfully request you to use your Influence to have us mustered out of Service for the following Reasons

1st   That we were pressed into Service by force of numbers without any Law civil or millitry to sanction it   many of us were knocked down and beaten Like dogs   others were dragged from our homes in the dead hour of [*night*] and forced into a Prison without Law or Justice   others were tied and thrown into the river and held there untill forced to subscribe to the Oath   Some of us were tied up by the thumbs all night   we were starved beaten kept out all night untill we were nearly frozen and but one alternative to join the service or nearly suffer death

2nd   The Exigencies of the war are past and as our services are no longer needed to put down the Rebellion as our enlistment was Illegal and unjust therefore we Respectfully request to use your influence to have us discharged from this service that we may return to our famillies some of whom have not seen them for five or six months and having no means to send them they are in a Suffering Condition and we therefore Request you to use your influence to have us discharged from service   We are Captain Very Respectfully Your Obt Servants

HLSr   [53 *signatures*]

Gabriel Grays et al. to Capt. H. Ford Douglas, 19 June 1865, filed with D-76 1865, Letters Received, ser. 360, Colored Troops Division, RG 94 [B-396]. Endorsements. The petition and all signatures are in the hand of Gabriel Grays; the other men made their marks after their names.

170B: Black Commander of an Independent Kansas Black Light Artillery Battery to the Headquarters of the Post of Fort Leavenworth, Kansas

Fort Leavenworth Kan. June 20th 1865
Sir In response to this communication from the men of this Battery I have the honor to most respectfully call the attention of the Major General Commanding the department to the following statement of facts.

This Battery was raised while Major General Curtis was in command of the Department. More than (75) per. cent of the men who now belong to it, are the victims of a cruel and shameless conscription. Not under the ordinary forms which are usually resorted to, but in opposition to all civil and military law. Before I became connected with the company I have seen men dragged through the streets of Leavenworth from their wives and little ones who were dependent upon them for their daily bread—mid winter, and placed on the bleak knob of Fort Sully, and there starved until from shere exhaustion they were compeled to swear into the service. These facts I am prepared to substantiate by more than a thousand witnesses. Now General since the necessity for their service no longer exists,—I would most respectfully request that this Battery be at once mustered out of the service. I am General Very Respectfully Your Obt. Servant
ALS   H. Ford Douglas

[*Endorsement*] Hd Qrs Post Fort Leaven'th June 20th 1865   Respectfully forwarded to General R. B. Mitchell Com'dg District. I Concur with Capt Douglass that his Company Should be Mustered Out. They Are of No Service to the Govt at all. Everything Seems to be in disorder in Capt Douglass' Command especially his Accounts and it appears necessary to appoint a Committee to Settle the Liabilities of Capt Douglas to the Gov^{t} and to his Men. Capt Douglas has borrowed Money from his Men. from $225. down to ten, and before this Organization is disolved a Settlement Must be Made. There is Some Good

Soldierly Material in this Command that Might be retained and transferred to other Regiments of that kind   It is my Opinion that the Interests of Government requires that Something be done Soon   Gust. Heinricks.   Lt Col Comdg Post

[*Endorsement*] Adjt. Genl's Office. July 5", 1865. Respectfully submitted to Lieutenant General Grant, Commanding Armies of the United States.

In the month of November, 1864, Major General Curtis, then commanding the District of Kansas, applied to the War Department for authority to recruit and organize a Light Artillery Company, to be composed of colored men and officered by colored men – the officers to be appointed upon his nomination. Said Company was recruited and mustered into service December 23", 1864, and is known as "Independent Battery U.S. Colored Artillery (Light)."

It appears from the papers herewith that the Company was not raised by volunteer enlistment, nor by draft, but that the men were run down, seized by force, and barbarously practiced upon in various ways, until from exhaustion or terror they consented to take the oath of enlistment. The result is such as might be expected; simply a collection of dissatisfied men, without order and without discipline.

The officers, (Colored men) could have had no experience, and the fact that they are largely indebted to the enlisted men of the Company for money borrowed, would seem to indicate that they are men of little character and less integrity. In view of the record, it is respectfully recommended that the company be mustered out of service, and that the honorable muster-out of service of the officers be withheld until they shall have refunded all the monies borrowed from the enlisted men of the command. C. W. Foster A.A. Genl. Vols.

Capt. H. Ford Douglas to 2d Lieut. Jno. Barber, 20 June 1865, filed with D-76 1865, Letters Received, ser 360, Colored Troops Division, RG 94 [B-396]. Other endorsements. Both General Grant and the Assistant Secretary of War approved Foster's recommendation.

171: Pennsylvania Black Soldier to the Secretary of War

> Camp Near Brownsville. Texas On the Riogrande River
> July the 20th A.D. (1865)

Sir   i Seat myself to Rite you a few lines to inform you of my
Health Wich is Good at Present and I hope When these few Badly
Written lines Reach you they Will find you in the Best of
Health.   Sir last night there was about a Dozen of my fellow
Soldiers Desired to have Worship as they usualy have Been Doing,
and no one interrupted them Untill last Night.   and there Was a
lieutenant By the Name of Stacy.   he told them if they Wanted to
Pray they must Go out on the Perade Ground about a half amile
from camp   i am not a member of the church But i Do not like
to See the Peopple of God Disturbed   they Pray for all in
artharity their families &c   Sir Do you think it is Right, that
they Should be molested.   Sir we have Some new men in our
Regt. that we Got Since Richmond was Taken and they Dont
understand how to Drill as Well as the old Soldiers and the
officers Will Smote them over the Head with all theire might and
they even Beat the older Soldiers, Who have Proved themselves on
the Different Battle fields. Petersburgh July 30 /64 and many
other Places.   Do you think it is right that we Should Be thus
used.   When we joined the 9th A.C. at annoppolis M.D. in 64,
Gen. Burnside Rode through our Camp and told us that he
wanted us to Be Good Soldiers for he had Some Work for us to
Do   last Summer While we was in his Corps, there was not a
man Struck With a Sword.   But as Soon as we was transferred into
the 25th Corps there Was men tied up So high that they lost the
use of their arms.   Capt Brown just Believes in Beating men with
there Swords also Capt Wright and Capt Dill went to the extent
to Break his Sword over a mans Back   if a Private Soldier Goes to
Colonel he Gets no Satisfaction.   there is men who has Been in
Bondage   we cant expect them to Do as well as a man that has
Been free.   when we was on the Boat Capt Dill, Struck a Private
and kicked him, and the Soldier Defended the Blows of[f] So as to
keep the capt. from knocking him Down the hatch way.   they Put
hand Cuffes on him and they have had them on him evry Since we
Strted from City Point Va.   there is a Dozen Pair of them in the
Reg^t   will you Please to intercede for us.   Mr Staunan Do you
Remember a colored man By the Name of Jacob Prisby who lived
in Stubenville Ohio.   i Dont Doubt But what he has Done some
Work for you Before the War   I live with his Brother Peter

Prisby in Washington Co. Pa. Just 2 miles from Stubenville
ohio I mus close   From

ALS   Simon Prisby

Simon Prisby to Honerable E. M. Staunton, 20 July 1865, P-429 1865,
Letters Received, ser. 360, Colored Troops Division, RG 94 [B-281].

172: Anonymous Kentucky Black Soldier to the Secretary of War

                    Bryant Station Lexington Ky Oct the 22. 1865
Mr E M Stanton   We are here and our wives and children are
laying out doers and we have no chance to get a home for
them   we havent had Six days furlough to See our wives and we
have been in the army fourteen months   these officers are laying
here and learning us nothing   instead of them learning us
Something they are Robing us out of our money   they are taken
our rations and Selling them and are Keeping the money   i think
it is mighty hard for us to Stand that after just coming from
under bondage   their are men that has never had the chance to
learn anything   they will give them change for a one dollar for a
fifty dollars in Stead of teaching them better   that is the way they
treat them. we come in three years or Sooner discharge. we
would be willing to Serve three years longer   under these
circumstances it would disheartin any one and haf to pay thirty
dollars for a ten days pass   when our wives comes to the camp to
See us they are not allowed to come in camp and we are not
allowed to go and See them   they are drumed of[f] and the
officers Says go you damed bitches   you know that it is to much
they are treated So by these officer   they ought to be a friend to
us and them to   the major makes his Brages that he will keep
these dam niggers in until he makes a fortune   they have us
cleaning up farms and cutting up Stumps for these citizens and
they pay the officers for it and they are allowing these citizens to
run over us   if we Say anything to them we are put in jail and
two or three months pay docked from us   if you please to allow
us the privelege of going home to Situate our familys for the
winter   we hate to See them laying and Stroling around but we
cant help our Selves   we are able to Situate them by labor if they
will allow us the privelege   we have payed nine hundred dollars
for the rasing of our brass band   now they want to claim the

instruments off of us   its now more than what i masters would
have done   the lost of this fifth regiment is over thirteen hundred
dollars by these officers   i think it is mighty hard for us to lay
here and they fool with us that way and when they here of us
being mustered out they Says that they will right to washington
and they will holde us   they Say if they cant holde us any other
way they will move us out of the State   Shame Shame Shame how
we are treated   they will not let us trated out Side of the
Sutlers   if we do they want to punish us   things that the Sutler
has got that is onely worth a dollar they charge us Seven or eight
dollars   if you want to by anything out Side they Say know god
dam you go to the Sutlers and by

I must bring my letter to a close   5. U.S."C." Cav   your most
devoted Soldier until death

HL

Unsigned to Mr. E. M. Stanton, 22 Oct. 1865, A-420 1865, Letters
Received, ser. 360, Colored Troops Division, RG 94 [B-200].

173A: Officer in a Northern Virginia Black Regiment to the Adjutant General of the Army

Quincy Florida   November 14, 1865

Sir— I have just received information that 1st Lt O. A. Carpenter
Co H 2nd Regt U.S.C.I has been discharged

I have the honor to Report that said officer has been mustered
by me on the Rolls of said Co Absent without leave since April
30th 1865   He has also ($2000) two thousand dollars belonging to
the enlisted men of Co H 2nd U.S.C.I which they gave him for
safe keeping

I respectfully ask that if he has not received his full pay that he
be debarred from doing so untill he refunds the money to the
men   Most Respectfully Your Obt Servt

ALS   Edward Pease

Capt. Edward Pease to Brig. Genl. Thomas, 14 Nov. 1865, filed with
B-875 1865, Letters Received, ser. 360, Colored Troops Division, RG 94
[B-221]. Pease served in the 2nd USCI. The file contains other records in
Carpenter's case.

173B: Black Former Soldier to the Adjutant General of the Army

Crownsville, Md   Aug 25" 1871

Sir   Will You Please interceed for my money thats in the Hands
of Lieut Carpenter. look on Lieut Carpenter. Count Book in
Company. H. 2nd District Colored Regiment & you will find. the
Amount. After you find you will Please write to the Lieut
immedialtely & get it for me. & assoon as you get an Answer
from him please write to me & let me kow what he ses about
it. You can tell the Lieut that I have been to see you. & you told
me where he was   if you get it let me know whether you have
sent it by the Adams Express. to Annapolis or not so that if you
sends it there I can go there & get it. Also Wm Bumbry
Requested me to ask you to get his money from Lieut
Carpenter   he has about $40 (forty dollars) belonging to him,   he
(Bumbry) has been very sick & is much in need of it now.

   Wm Bumbry lives in Union town maryland. I would have
writen to you before now but I have been very sick & could not
write.

   You can Direct Your Letters to Crownsville Anne arundel Co
Maryland   Yours truly

John B Bowie

P.S. I am much in want of it now, & if you get it sir, I will
Recompence you for it. Direct to Wm Bumbry Union town
Maryland

ALS

John B. Bowie to the Adjutant General, 25 Aug. 1871, filed with B-875
1865, Letters Received, ser. 360, Colored Troops Division, RG 94 [B-
221]. In the same file is a draft reply from the Adjutant General's Office,
September 7, 1871, which advised Bowie to write to Carpenter but warned
that "In case of his failure to pay on your application, a resort to the civil
courts would appear to be your only remedy."

174: Louisiana Black Soldier to the President

Fort Livingston La. January 28th 1866 –

Sir: Your most humble and obedience servant, Prince Albert, Private of Company. "C." 10th United States, (Cold) (Heavy) (Artillery,) Here stationed at Fort Livingston La.

Has an opportunity of seen and observing the Conducts of The Commanding officer. at Fort Livingston La, Towards the cruel treatment of my self said P. Albert   I am Severely punish on the 28th Ult. for not fishing oysters, on the 27th January 1866, For said commanding officer   on (the 27. inst. Said commanding officer send an order from His Hd. Qrs. for said Prince Albert. and Privts. Edward Brinkley, and Priv. Levi Boucry and Priv. Theropolite Monorvice. all where of said Co. "C." 10 U.S. (Cold) (Hvy) (Arty)   And been on Saturday. I had my arms and equipage and &c. to clean For inspections on the Sabbath morning. on (the 28th Inst.)   I has refused going after oysters for said commanding Officers Mess. and I where on well., and I did not procur an by his Order. And on the 28th Ult. after Inspection, said Commanding Officer After march the Co. on Its Street to dismisted the Co. order Said P. Albert to report myself to the Sergeant of the guard.   And I obeyed his Ordered. and said Commanding officer ordered. The Sergeant of The guard to Stand me on a barrel with my knabsack   And I where not to Set down on the barrel. or was I to have. Nothing to eat at all until I where to be humbled to Said Commanding officer.   I said Prince Albert where standing on a barrel, By ordered of said Commanding officer. from ten (10) O'clk. A.M. During all the night in all of the night air.

And at 7. P.M. the Sergeant of the guard marched Me up to The Hd. Qrs. of said Commanding Officer.s.   And when I arrived, said Comdg. officer said I most ask him Pardon. for disobeying. his Orders., and I refuesed, to asked, Pardon for not going after oysters. but said Comdg. officer. said He did not standed me on a barrel for not going after oysters By His Orders but where for speaking into ranks on (the 28th inst.)   And I did spoke into ranks when said Comdg officer ordered. Me to reported my Self To The Sergeant of The guard.   and I. Said Prince Albert. did asked Him Pardon for speaking Into ranks: and again inpresent of the Sergeant of the guard, Said Comdg. officer. said I where to asked Him Pardon The second time for not obeying His Orders. of not going, After Oysters for Him, and I refuesed Asking Him Pardon The Second time

And I Told Said Comdg. Officer That where not any of my

Duties for To Fished Oysters for Him., and I told Him I came Here to do millitarie duties., and not for to Hunt Oysters. I enlisted for To do millitarie duties. And Said Comdg. Officer ordered The Sergeant of the Guard to Stand me on the barrel again for all night Again, in all of the Heavy Dew of the Night and Night air also: And said Comdg. officer are not using The Co. as an Officer ought too. Here on The 28th Inst., Said Comdg. officer ordered Private Theropolite Monorvice Of Said Co. to go and fish oysters for said Comdg. offr., Mess. and He Shall Have a furlough, and this said Priv. Theropolite Monorvice did accordingly. there are men of families in the Co. Cant never get a furlough to see their Familis, also said Prince Albert Has never Had a Furlough Sence into The Service of the U.S., I Have The Honor To be Your most obt. Servant,

ALS   Prince Albert.

Priv. Prince Albert to Andrew Johnson, 28 Jan. 1866, P-66 1866, Letters Received, ser. 360, Colored Troops Division, RG 94 [B-275].

175: Black Former Quartermaster Sergeant to the Freedmen's Bureau Agent at Louisville, Kentucky

Louisville Ky February 21 1866
Sir   I have the honor to Call your attention to [my] Report   on or about the 23rd day of April (1865) I adressed a Communication to a Paper Published in New York called the Anglo Affrican   in Substance it was Like this   the treatment in Our Regiment is very harsh

The Regiment was out on Battalion Drill yesterday When one of the Officers Struck One of the Men Under his Command with his Sword and Cut a Gash in his Eyebrow Large Enough to Lay a Pen holder in   Last fall a Certain Captain Struck one of his men with his Sword and Knocked the Breath out of him   the Major is home on Leave at Phila,   I would Like to See, the Major Return with the Spread Eagles in Stead of the Leaves[1]   the Major is a Good Officer and Deserves Promotion

The treatment we Receive from Our Pretended Friends I think is very Rough

and I hope God will Save me from Such friends

Sir this was the Sum and Substance of the Letter   Lt. Col John J. Bishop Sent for me and asked me if I was the author of a Certain Letter Bearing the Date of April 23th (1865) in the Anglo Affrican.   I told him I was

Several days after this the Col Ordered me Under arrest   the Officer of the Day Capt Benton Tutle Took my Revolver from me. the Col Visited me, and told me that I would Be tried for the Violations of the articles of war

he the (Col) Referred me to the 222nd Paragraph Revised Regulations (1863)[2]   I never Prior to that knew there was Such an article in the Regulations   the next thing, Or, Charge was Carrying a Loaded Pistol against the Orders of my Superior Officer   I will Say on my honor Sir that I Never heard Such an order Prohibiting the Carying of Pistols   an Officer Swore that there was an Order to that Effect But it Could not Be found in the Regimental Order Books where all Regimental Orders are Copied   there was in the Regiment five Officers in the Regt that wanted me Reduced   thay waited on the (Col and he told them that he Could not Reduce me But if they would Get the majority of the Officers in the Regt to Sign the Petition he would do it   But Sir they Could not Get half of the Officers to Sign the Petition   So they Let that drop, and, the. Col John J. Bishop urged 2nd Lt. Wilbur F. Dubois to Prefer those Charges against me and he done So   the. Col. Said that it would not do for him to Prefer the Charges, for, fear that I would have Some influence in having him tried for Embezzlement   I can Say this and tell the truth that Lt. Col. John J. Bishop had not Bought Neither Sugar Tea Coffee Bread nor flour nor Meat for the Period of Six Months Untill I Stopped Issuing to him and then those Charges were Preffered against Me   the Charges I Know were Sent to Maj Genl. Jos. Hooker. I Understood he disaproved for Some Reason of Wich I am Unable to State   So then the Regt was Transfered from the Northern Dept., and Ordered to the Dept of Miss   those Charges were Renewed again

there was two Officers in the Regt that wanted to Sell me a Pistol   One of the Officers was None Other than a field Officer   the Col John J. Bishop Stole a Barrel of White Sugar from a Citizen   that Man the Proper Owner of the Sugar, Come, Looking for the Same But he was told By a Certain Officer that it was not   the Col Knew that this man was Looking for the Sugar and he had the Sugar Moved in to his Private Quarters for fear that it would Be discovered   he Ordered three Per. Cent of all the Sugar and Coffee that was issued to the Regt for a Post fund and the Same three Per Cent of Coffee and Sugar he Sent to his family living in indianapolis   those things I know to Be So   he also allowed a deserter from the 18th Regt U.S.C.I. to follow the 108th U.S.C.I. to Rock Island Ill and then Enlist in another Regt of Col Inf for a Large Bounty   and Sir I could Mention Plenty of Similar Cases if Necessary   all that I have Stated I can Prove and the Best of Proof there was one Witness that was Brought Up to Swear against Me was an Orderly Sargent that was made Sware against me By his Superior Officer and Company Commander   he that is his Captain told him that if he did not Sware against me he would Reduce him to the Ranks   those five Officers have Lived Off of their Companys for one year, and a half to my Knoledge   I Never told the men any thing farther than this   I told them the Officers had no Right to Live off of their, the (Men) Rations   they had no Right to Curse them and Beat them with Sword and allow the Men to Get from the Sutlers $(1200 and) 1500 worth of Goods Per Month and then the Soildiers Money All Gone to the Sutler   the Regt would Get four Months Pay and the Sutler Get Eight Months Pay

Oh Captain Sir I Could not Relate half the Rascality that Occurs in my Regt

I think that I have been treated Unjust   false Evidence was taken against Me   Everything done to Get me Out of the Regt So as the Officers Could have full Sway in their Nefarious Crimes

Officers would take their Company Rations and Give to Confederate Prisoners and the Company would have to Go with Out and if they Said anything about it they the (Men) were Tied Up by the thumbs for Claiming their Rights   this Sir is what they Call inSubordination   A just Claim   there is Some Officers in the 108th U.S.C.I. that Better Officers Can not Be found in the Service of the U.S.A.

for three months after I enlisted I acted in the Place of all the N.C.S. Except One and that was Hospital Steward   all the While I was in the regiment I acted Qr Master Sergt and Commisary Sargt.   I had a man detailed to help me in the Commisary and he was taken from me to tend to the (Col^s Private horses.   I had all the work to do My Self   When Ever I would ask for men the Col would Say that there was no need of Such help   what there was to do I Could do it my Self   from the Effect of Such treatment Sir I am Unable to work at anything that will Cause me to Stoop from the fact Sir that I Strained my back Lifting barrels and boxes while in the Service of the United States   the hospital Steward Simon Vanderheyden Left the Regt on the account of the treatment towards him

At one time Last winter I lost a barrel of Sugar by not having a Sufficient detail to Guard the Commissary Stores and by that means one Company went with out their Sugar   So as a Natural Consequence the Captain had no Sugar to put in his Coffee wich made him quite Rathy   he Could not control his Passions for Sweetness   he had to Expend Something near to a quarter of a dollar of his months wages for Sugar   So he told the Quarter

Master of the Regiment that if I Spoke to him this Captain he would Blow my Brains out I Related the facts to the Col and he Said that he could not do anything with out I Preferred Charges against the Captain the Captain abused me Like a dog because I would not Give him forage for a horse wich he had Captured from the Confederate army and of wich he had no Right to in the world the horse had Been turned in to the Quarter Master of the Regiment with a lot of Other horses and then I Received an Order from the (Col) that I would Chose a horse for my own Use and the Rest I would Turn Over to the quarter master at this Place wich I done and I Showed the horse to the (Col) this Captain Come up and Claimed the horse and the horse was Given up to the Captain by Order of the (Col there had been nothing But Wholesale Robbery and theft from the Organization of the Regt Up to the (17th) day of August (1865)

I liked the Service U.S.A. very much and would have liked to Served my term of Service Out But I was Deprived of it by Claiming Justice at the hands of my Superior Officers fiffty Pages of foolscap would not contain half of the Under Ground work that is done in the Regt if was Penned Very Respectfully Sir I Remain your most Obt Servt

ALS   Chas. H. Davis

Late Q.M. Sergt. Chas. H. Davis to Capt. E. D. Kennedy, 21 Feb. 1866, enclosed in Capt. E. D. Kennedy to H. H. Burkholder, 20 Feb. 1866, Unregistered Letters Received, ser. 1209, Louisville KY Supt., RG 105 [A-4530]. In the same file is a letter from the adjutant of Davis's regiment who described him thus: "He was very well calculated to fill the position which he held, were it not for one thing. He was at times very insubordinate, often using language, in the presence of the enlisted men that was calculated to incite insubordination among them also, and in fact caused more trouble to Officers and enlisted men than any other individual in the regiment." (1st Lieut. Morris Stafford to Capt. E. D. Kennedy, 11 Feb. 1866.) Other documents in the file indicate that a court-martial found Davis guilty of conduct prejudicial to good order and of using disrespectful language concerning his superior officer. He was sentenced to be reduced to the ranks and to be imprisoned for one year, with forfeiture of pay. He was, however, released in January 1866.

1 An eagle was the insignia of a colonel; a cluster of gold leaves, the insignia of a major.
2 The 222nd paragraph is not relevant to this case. The appropriate paragraph is the 220th: "Deliberations or discussions among any class of military men, having the object of conveying praise, or censure, or any mark of approbation toward their superiors or others in the military service . . . are strictly prohibited." (U.S., War Department, *Revised United States Army Regulations* [Washington, 1863], p. 38.)

9

Military Discipline, Punishment, and Justice

DETAILED regulations ordered nearly every aspect of a soldier's life and prescribed his duties and responsibilities. The Articles of War, legislated by Congress, established general standards of military conduct and defined the most serious violations of military law. Army regulations, issued by the War Department, elaborated upon congressional directives and precisely specified every army procedure, from the layout of a camp to the composition of a military court, from the contents of a soldier's knapsack to the mode of carrying out an execution.[1] Additional orders emanated from the War Department; from department, army corps, brigade, post, and regimental commanders; and, within each company, from the captain, lieutenants, and noncommissioned officers. These laws, regulations, and orders were read to soldiers when they enlisted and during regimental assemblies and drills.[2] Some soldiers acquired copies of the regulations and studied them privately. But no soldier, regardless of how well or poorly he knew the rules, could escape the force of military authority.

The labyrinth of rules and regulations all led to one central obligation: obedience to the commands of superior officers. In its opening paragraph, the *Army Regulations* declared: "All inferiors are required to obey strictly, and to execute with alacrity and good faith, the lawful orders of the superiors appointed over them."[3] Army procedures and etiquette confirmed this authority of superior officers in countless rituals of deference. Symbols of rank, modes of address, and forms of punishment, as well as numerous prerogatives of command, all operated to establish and preserve the distinction between those who ordered and those who obeyed. Furthermore, military regulations undergirded the obligation of obedience with the threat

---

[1] *Revised Army Regulations.* The Articles of War are included as an appendix, pp. 485–502. All references hereafter are to this 1863 edition of the regulations.

[2] Article 10 required that the Articles of War be read to every soldier upon enlistment and that he swear to obey them. Article 101 provided that they "be read and published" once every six months "to every garrison, regiment, troop, or company." (*Revised Army Regulations,* appendix, pp. 486–87, 501–2.)

[3] *Revised Army Regulations,* p. 9.

of force. They defined as the most serious offenses those actions that challenged military authority: contempt or disrespect for a commanding officer, refusal to obey orders, desertion, violence toward a superior officer, and mutiny. For such offenses the army held out the penalties of death or lengthy imprisonment. A challenge to the order of a superior called down the full force of military law.[4]

All soldiers thus found themselves embedded in a system that demanded absolute obedience. But obedience took on an added dimension in black regiments, for, with a few exceptions, the officers who exercised day-to-day command were white. Although sergeants and corporals, the noncommissioned officers, ordinarily rose from the ranks of the black soldiers,[5] they nonetheless remained enlisted men, subject to army regulations and procedures markedly different from those applicable to commissioned officers. Although invested at times with considerable authority over privates, noncommissioned officers stood with the privates on one side of the great divide that loomed between enlisted men and commissioned officers.[6] In the black regiments the divide of color reinforced that of rank.

Ex-slave soldiers thus exchanged obedience to a white slave master for obedience to white officers, and to some the new relationship differed little from the old. But most black soldiers recognized a fundamental change in the source of authority, and they pressed upon commanders their view of the new conditions. While the rule of slavery had been personal and arbitrary, the rule of the army rested, at least in theory, on abstract law. If black soldiers stood answerable to military law and regulations, so did white soldiers, and so, as well, did white officers. Furthermore, army regulations demanded obedience only to the "lawful orders" of superiors. The same paragraphs that enjoined obedience upon soldiers required officers to exercise military command "with kindness and justice to inferiors," specified that punishments be "strictly conformable to military law," and forbade superiors "to injure those under them by tyrannical or capricious conduct, or by abusive language."[7] Black soldiers who listened to readings of the regulations held their commanders accountable to these restrictions no less than they heeded admonitions of obedience.

Just as both officers and men stood subject to military law, so

---

[4] Articles 6, 7, 8, 9, and 20 of the Articles of War, *Revised Army Regulations,* appendix, pp. 486, 488.

[5] For the argument in favor of black noncommissioned officers, see *Freedom,* ser. 2: doc. 205c.

[6] For symbolic embodiment of the distance between enlisted men and commissioned officers in the physical arrangement of regimental camps, see the diagrams and instructions in *Revised Army Regulations,* pp. 76–80.

[7] *Revised Army Regulations,* p. 9.

both enjoyed its protections. While army regulations promised sober penalties for serious offenses, they also attempted to safeguard the procedural rights of the accused. Officers at the rank of brigadier general or above convened general courts-martial to hear the graver charges, including all carrying the death penalty. Only commissioned officers sat upon the panel of thirteen judges, but the defendant could call witnesses, cross-examine the prosecution's witnesses, testify in his own defense, and appeal convictions to higher military authorities. Death sentences required the concurrence of two-thirds of the court, and, in all cases, the general officer who had convened the court-martial had to approve its proceedings before sentences were announced and effected. The convening officer could pardon convicted defendants or mitigate any sentence except death, in which case he could delay the execution pending appeal to the President of the United States. He could also overturn a conviction entirely on procedural grounds. Such general courts-martial offered accused black soldiers many of the procedural rights that free people enjoyed under the common law and the Constitution and, of course, many more rights than slaves could claim.[8]

For the majority of black soldiers who had formerly been slaves, army justice provided their first experience with the law and formal judicial procedures. On the plantation, masters exercised undisputed personal authority, setting rules and punishing infractions arbitrarily. Justice rarely exceeded the bounds of the plantation, except when no less arbitrary patrollers came to the slave owner's assistance, or when slaves committed serious crimes that brought them before county and state courts. But in the army ex-slaves quickly learned to take advantage of the rules and procedures of formal law. Soldiers convicted before courts-martial, for example, regularly petitioned sympathetic commanders, War Department officials, and the President himself. While only literate soldiers could appeal their cases in writing, prisoners who could write often served as scribes for their less-educated fellow inmates. Samuel Roosa, a New York black soldier imprisoned at Fort Jefferson, Florida, during late 1864 and early 1865, appears to have written several such letters.[9] Other soldiers had sympathetic company officers appeal on their behalf, often successfully. Sheldon Penock, a Kentucky black soldier convicted of mutiny, managed to

---

[8] Articles 64 through 90 of the Articles of War specified the composition, procedures, powers, and protections of courts-martial, including the rights of the accused. Army regulations provided further details about the conduct of military courts. (*Revised Army Regulations*, pp. 124–27 and appendix, pp. 495–99.)

[9] See, for example, Charles Boltamore to Abraham Lincoln, 17 Jan. 1865, filed with W-87 1865, Letters Received, ser. 360, Colored Troops Division, RG 94 [B-156]; and Warren D. Hamelton to Hon. E. M. Stanton, May 1865, H-285 1865, Letters Received, ser. 360, Colored Troops Division, RG 94 [B-139].

have his old master petition the authorities, a tactic that secured his release from prison even though the master's version of his crime differed entirely from that of the court-martial evidence. In general, appeals fell upon more receptive ears once the war had ended and demobilization of the army was underway.

Even free blacks acquired new rights under military law. Military justice offered both freeborn and ex-slave soldiers a privilege hitherto denied most black people in the United States, that of testifying under oath in open court against a white defendant. Accorded the same procedural rights as white enlisted men, black soldiers were accepted as competent witnesses against both white enlisted men and white officers. Dozens of black soldiers, for example, offered testimony against white officers that resulted in convictions on charges of swindling or of illegal recruitment practices. The ability of blacks to testify against whites in military courts marked a significant advance over civil procedures, even those in many Northern states. For most black soldiers, that privilege abruptly ended with discharge from military service. Back in civilian life, they had to struggle to regain the right of testimony. Many black soldiers did not again experience such unobstructed access to the witness stand.

According to the Articles of War, general courts-martial had jurisdiction over all capital cases and over all charges against commissioned officers. Lesser infractions by enlisted men fell to regimental or garrison courts-martial, appointed by the commanding officer of a regiment, fort, or garrison. Composed of three commissioned officers, these lower courts-martial could by law inflict punishments no greater than imprisonment for one month, assignment to hard labor for one month, or a fine of one month's pay.[10] The Articles of War also designated the regimental court-martial as the main avenue of redress for any enlisted man who felt wronged by a commissioned officer. Regulations provided that an aggrieved soldier complain to his regimental commander, who was then required to summon a regimental court-martial to hear the soldier's charge. And from the regimental court-martial, either party could appeal to a general court-martial.[11] Not surprisingly, the protection offered by the regimental court-martial was more impressive in theory than in practice, if only because the three judges came from the same regiment as the accused and could hardly rule impartially upon charges against a fellow officer. Moreover, enlisted men with complaints against the regimental commander himself could expect little from the prescribed grievance procedure.

[10] Articles 66 and 67, Articles of War, *Revised Army Regulations*, appendix, pp. 495–96.
[11] Article 35, Articles of War, *Revised Army Regulations*, appendix, p. 491.

Although army regulations provided for transmission of regimental court-martial proceedings to the superior department commander "without delay," sentences often passed immediately into execution, without benefit of review.[12] Ordinarily regimental punishments were relatively minor. But special conditions in the field sometimes provoked severe retribution without the usual embellishments of justice. On their own authority, regimental commanders assembled "drum-head" courts-martial even upon serious charges technically beyond the purview of regimental justice.[13] In such cases, punishment was swift—often the same day as the trial—and extended even to the firing squad, with no possibility of appeal. During the Civil War six black soldiers met their deaths by decision of drum-head court-martial. All six were charged with rape.[14] Under such circumstances, a drum-head court-martial might easily become little more than a legal lynching. No records survive of the proceedings in these six cases, and it is likely that none were created by such summary courts.[15] Thus the exigencies of war often circumscribed severely the rights theoretically accorded all soldiers before the army's formal institutions of justice.

On a day-to-day basis, most infractions of army regulations remained within the company command and did not come to the notice of either regimental or general courts-martial. Because War Department regulations did not prescribe particular punishments for petty offenses, company officers enjoyed great latitude in dealing with violators of the rules.[16] Most trivial breaches of discipline merited routine punishment, for example, serving extra tours of guard

---

[12] *Revised Army Regulations*, p. 126.

[13] In addition to limiting the punishments permissible by sentence of a regimental court-martial (see note 10), the Articles of War expressly provided that "No person shall be sentenced to suffer death but by the concurrence of two-thirds of the members of a *general* court-martial. . . ." (emphasis added). (Article 87, Articles of War, *Revised Army Regulations*, appendix, pp. 498–99.)

[14] *List of U.S. Soldiers Executed by United States Military Authorities during the Late War,* 5981-A-85, Letters Received, ser. 409, Enlisted Branch, RG 94 [FF-1]. This list includes only one white soldier executed by authority of a "drum-head" court-martial. His offense was desertion.

[15] No proceedings in the six "drum-head" courts-martial are filed in the appropriate regimental records, RG 94; in the court-martial case files of the Judge Advocate General's Office, RG 153; or in the service records of the individual soldiers, RG 94.

[16] Army regulations did specify the legal punishments that could be inflicted by sentence of a court-martial: "death; confinement; confinement on bread and water diet; solitary confinement; hard labor; ball and chain; forfeiture of pay and allowances; discharges from service; and reprimands, and, when non-commissioned officers, reduction to the ranks." In August 1861, Congress outlawed whipping as a military punishment. Otherwise, neither the Articles of War nor army regulations declared standards for punishment of minor offenses. (*Revised Army Regulations*, pp. 126, 528.)

duty. But both army tradition and the temptations of power gave rise to a full range of punishments. At one extreme these included ritualized exaggerations of a soldier's duties, such as walking a beat shouldering a log instead of a musket, standing at attention for hours on a barrel head, wearing a sign describing the offense while being drummed out of camp, and riding a wooden horse (a rail perched several feet above ground). At the other extreme, however, punishments like kicking, cuffing, striking with swords, whipping, tying up by the thumbs, and bucking and gagging could border on sadism.[17]

Officers in white regiments employed such punishments no less than did officers in black regiments, yet black soldiers held them in special contempt. They not only found them personally humiliating, but they also likened them to slave modes of correction. Men fighting in the army of liberation to destroy human bondage considered the persistence of slave punishments intolerable. They contested such treatment at every level and expressed to company officers their willingness to accept forms of punishment other than those characteristic of slavery. When recalcitrant officers refused to adopt other modes, black soldiers took their complaints up the chain of command. But the limited channels of redress often left them frustrated.

Frustration bred unrest. Sensing this, many commanders banned such carryovers from plantation days as tying up by the thumbs and bucking and gagging, and Congress had prohibited whipping as a military punishment.[18] Yet, company officers still exercised considerable discretion, and violations of the proscriptions abounded. In many regiments, soldiers continued to press against the bounds of military discipline. Eventually their protests led to violations of orders, to assaults upon the "slave-driving" officers, and ultimately to mutiny. Then the full weight of military regulations crashed down upon the mutineers, superseding their protest and often resulting in their death before a firing squad.

One of the earliest cases of mutiny among black soldiers occurred in December 1863 at Fort Jackson, Louisiana, as a result of the whipping of two drummers by the commander of the 4th Louisiana

---

[17] A man tied up by the thumbs hung from a pole or tree limb at such a height that only his toes touched the ground, putting all his weight upon his thumbs. An offender who was bucked had his wrists tied together in front of him, his arms placed over and around his knees (while in a sitting position), and a stick passed beneath his knees and over his arms. Gagging the mouth with a piece of wood or other article usually accompanied bucking. For a full description of common military punishments, see Bell Irvin Wiley, *The Life of Billy Yank: The Common Soldier of the Union* (Indianapolis, 1951), chap. 8 and illustrations opposite p. 118.

[18] The August 5, 1861, act of Congress is extracted in *Revised Army Regulations*, p. 528.

Native Guard, Lieutenant Colonel Augustus W. Benedict. Soldiers in this regiment had long detested Benedict for his use of abusive punishments. His outright assault upon the two drummers, coming soon after Adjutant General Lorenzo Thomas had personally promised to dismiss any officer who maltreated the men, provoked wholesale insubordination. Before their officers could persuade them to return to order, many of the soldiers of the 4th Louisiana engaged in a wild shooting spree, calling for retaliation against Benedict. General Nathaniel P. Banks, commander of the Department of the Gulf at the time, had a vested interest in the 4th—the first black regiment raised after his purge of the black officer corps. From Banks's standpoint, Benedict's action threatened his all-white officer policy. Furthermore, Banks's recruiters had repeatedly promised black enlistees that they would under no circumstances be subjected to punishment by whipping. Banks therefore took considerable interest in the case, recommended prompt punishment for Lieutenant Colonel Benedict, and reduced to imprisonment the death sentences of the convicted mutineers. Only Banks's involvement in the case spared the protesters from the death penalty that other black mutineers would face.

While many mutinies grew out of altercations with insensitive and sometimes sadistic officers, other grievances sometimes prompted black soldiers to refuse to do duty, a stance that officers could construe as a challenge to their authority. The issue of equal pay proved a potent source of insubordination. When Sergeant William Walker of the 3rd South Carolina Colored Volunteers had his company stack their arms and refuse to do further duty until the army promised equal pay, the regimental commander charged the men with mutiny. Walker ultimately suffered execution for his leading role. Some black mutineers did not even get a hearing. When enlisted men in the 14th Rhode Island Heavy Artillery refused to perform duty until the pay issue reached settlement, a violent confrontation with an officer resulted in the fatal shooting of the most vociferous protester. The regimental commander sustained the execution without investigation, inasmuch as all commissioned officers retained the right to enforce summary justice upon men who refused to obey orders.[19]

The magnitude of their power over enlisted men led some officers to abuse their authority. And few suffered serious penalties for excessive zeal, or even cruelty, in punishing wrongdoing among the enlisted ranks. Because commissioned officers occupied the exalted status of gentlemen, they theoretically suffered as much from besmirched reputations as enlisted men did from physical punishment.

---

[19] See *Freedom,* ser. 2: doc. 158c–f, 159.

Rather than suffer imprisonment or death, officers convicted of serious infractions were generally dismissed from the service or temporarily suspended from command.[20] They might even avoid punishment altogether: a colonel who had punished enlisted men by having them run a gauntlet suffered no penalty when one man died as a result of the beating he had taken.[21] Black soldiers understood that all members of the army – enlisted men and officers alike – had to obey regulations, and they could see little justice in the exoneration of officers who committed offenses for which enlisted men would suffer long imprisonment or worse. When their pleas for redress went unanswered, they took matters into their own hands.

The resulting confrontations exposed many of the daily tensions in relations with officers. Angry soldiers overcame the respect for authority and the fear of punishment that usually kept them silent in the face of discrimination and abuse. Giving vent to their long pent-up feelings, they displayed their animosity toward officers whose behavior violated the trust that soldiers felt necessary to the proper working of the military apparatus. Moreover, since nearly all officers were white, the soldiers' anger also revealed the racial hostility that so often lay simmering beneath the surface of relations between white officers and black troops. Suspicious of the motives of their white officers, black soldiers took umbrage at treatment that they believed would not have been accorded white soldiers. On one occasion the army's judge advocate general acknowledged this sensitivity of black soldiers to language and actions that could be taken as "a grievous insult to their color." He recommended executive clemency for several men who, "jealous of every act of their white superiors, which might be . . . interpreted as a slur upon their race," had refused to obey orders.[22] Under such circumstances, confrontations between white officers and black soldiers could take on the character of race riots.

When racial tension flared, black noncommissioned officers carried a special burden. As sergeants and corporals, they bore particu-

---

[20] The Articles of War required that a commissioned officer convicted of "conduct unbecoming an officer and a gentleman" be dismissed from the army. And if his crime was cowardice or fraud, they specified that, in addition, his name, his home residence, and the fact of his conviction "be published in the newspapers in and about the camp, and of the particular State from which the offender came. . .; after which it shall be deemed scandalous for an officer to associate with him." (Articles 83, 84, and 85, Articles of War, *Revised Army Regulations,* appendix, p. 498.)

[21] General Court-Martial Orders, No. 265, War Department, Adjutant General's Office, 30 Aug. 1864, Orders & Circulars, ser. 44, RG 94 [DD-7].

[22] Endorsement by Judge Advocate General J. Holt, 6 Mar. 1866, on Peter Birts et al. to General Thomas, 4 Dec. 1865, A-50 1866, Letters Received, ser. 360, Colored Troops Division, RG 94 [B-206].

lar responsibility to enforce obedience to orders and to check insubordination. Yet, as both black men and enlisted men, they experienced mistreatment by the white officers and shared the privates' perception of the injustices of military life. To escape this dilemma they sometimes sought to distance themselves from the privates and magnify their meager privileges as "non-coms." But more often, common origins and shared experiences with other enlisted men led them to place their allegiance squarely with other black soldiers. Indeed, the privates regularly turned to their noncommissioned officers as natural protest leaders. Black noncommissioned officers who tried to temper resistance to white superiors suffered accusations that they betrayed their race. But if noncommissioned officers concurred in the protests – and even if they tried to channel grievances into legitimate modes of complaint – they could find their actions interpreted as inciting mutiny. Many black noncommissioned officers paid a high price for their efforts to obtain justice for themselves and their fellow enlisted men.

After the war ended and black soldiers awaited discharge, they saw no excuse for officers to continue inflicting demeaning punishments. Having won the war against slavery, they were determined to excise all remaining vestiges of the hated institution and felt more than ever the oppression of slave forms of correction. In one of the last major mutinies of the wartime era, Kentucky soldiers in the 25th Army Corps, en route by sea from Virginia to Texas, objected to their comrades' being tied up or ironed to the hatch for having dirty rifles. Claiming that shipboard conditions prevented cleanliness, they cut one man down, eventually returning to their quarters only after their officers threatened to have the guard open fire upon the mutineers. Even more than during the war, black soldiers in the postwar army bristled under the continued burden of being punished like slaves.

The very distinctions that black soldiers drew between punishments incidental to slavery and those acceptable in freedom reveal the significance of their involvement in the institutions and procedures, however limited, of military justice. Exercise of even circumscribed formal rights, as well as access to appeal procedures, left a deep impression upon black soldiers. As a result of their military experience, they understood that their freedom divested whites of the legal right to exercise the arbitrary authority of slaveholders. With the establishment of the Freedmen's Bureau, blacks had specially tailored judicial procedures available to them, and soldiers led the way in taking advantage of such opportunities. But even in the Bureau's absence, former soldiers seized upon the rights of citizens before the civil courts of the respective states and the United States. Their knowledge of the military judicial system provided advance training for entering complaints before such courts, confidence in testifying against whites, and determination to appeal adverse decisions to higher authority. Although only a small proportion participated in courts-martial, all black soldiers gained a general exposure to formal military regulations, which helped prepare them for civilian life in a society at least nominally ruled by law. Out of uniform they continued their protest against slave forms of punishment. They used both their consciousness of armed victory over their former masters and their understanding of the protections offered by the law to challenge all efforts to prolong human bondage. And in time, former soldiers and other freedpeople joined in demanding the right to participate in the creation, administration, and adjudication of the law.

176: Testimony by Officers of a Louisiana Black Regiment before a Military Commission

Fort Jackson [*La.*], Decr 12, 1863

. . . .

Colonel Charles W. Drew, Fourth Regiment Infantry, Corps d'Afrique, being duly sworn testified as follows.

Question— Please state your name, rank and the nature of your command

Answer: My name is Charles W. Drew, Col. 4th. Regt. Corps d'Afrique, and commanding the Post, which includes Ft Jackson and Ft St Phillip.

Question Were you in command on the 9th inst.

Answer— I was.

Question— Please state in detail what unusual events, if any, occurred on that day.

Answer— The first unusual event that I noticed occurred about five O'Clock P.M. I saw Lieut Colonel Benedict, of the 4th Regt. Infantry Corps d'Afrique strike one of the Drummers with a whip, two or three times—at the same time reprimanding him. He made use of an expression like this, "I have had a great deal of trouble with you already, and I am going to stop it." He then walked off. I turned towards him when I saw him strike him, intending to reprimand him there, but he turned off, and I thought it best to delay it, instead of reprimanding him in the presence of the men. I went to my quarters and was sitting at my desk as nearly as I can judge about half past six, when the Adjutant who had come into my room said, "There is a disturbance among the men, I think they are taking their arms." I replied "no I think not" He then went to the door and upon opening it ascertained that they were. I immediately went out into the Parade when they commenced firing into the air, and shouting. I soon discovered from their language that it was in consequence of Lieut Colonel Benedict's action. I immediately turned and ordered him to his quarters, and with my officers, who were all present endeavored to quell the disturbance. I soon got enough of them quieted so that I could talk to them and told them to go to their quarters and put up their guns, as I wished to talk to them, but would not do it whilst they had them. At this time I should think about thirty had gone outside the Fort towards the river, continuing the firing. Nearly all those inside went to their quarters and put up their guns upon my assuring them that I would see that justice was done them. The firing had been going on then about half an hour. I formed the men into a hollow square and had commenced talking to them when some of those from outside the Fort, came in saying, "Dont give up your guns" and demanding Lieut Col Benedict, making so much disturbance that I directed the officers to form their companies in the company streets, as it was impossible to talk to them there. Very soon everything inside became quiet again. I should think that nearly one half the regiment was engaged in the disturbance, the other half trying to quiet them. I had tattoo beaten, I think about eight O'clock that night – much earlier than usual, when everything was quiet, and nearly all the men answered to their names at roll call.

. . . .

Lieut Col Benedict had been stationed at Fort St Phillip, but came to Fort Jackson the day before, and was placed in command of the regiment by me, which at this time was all at Fort Jackson, numbering five hundred men.

Question – You say that when you went out on the parade during the disturbance you soon discovered from the language used, that the disturbance was in consequence of Lieut. Col. Benedict's action in whipping a music boy. – Please state what that language was.

Answer – It was language something like this. "Give us Col Benedict, we did not come here to be whipped by him. Kill Col Benedict. Shoot him." and other language to the same effect.

Question – Were the guns fired, aimed at any person?

Answer – I do not know of a single gun being aimed at any person. They were all apparently fired into the air. I heard one man – a soldier – cry out "Kill all the damned Yankees."

. . . .

Question – Did the disturbance seem to have any organization, or was it a mob raised without premeditation and plan.

443

Answer— So far as I know it was raised on the spur of the moment. I have since understood that there was discontent with Lieut. Col. Benedict by the men who were under him at Fort St. Phillip, part of whom had been transferred to Fort Jackson and were in the disturbance.

. . . .

Question— Please state more definitely the conduct of the men when you ordered them to their quarters and whether they refused or neglected to obey your orders.

Answer— When I first came into the parade I immediately ordered them to stop firing and go to their quarters. Some of them stopped firing and gathered around me, saying, "we don't want to hurt you, "It is Col. Benedict we are after. While others replied "We will not stop firing until we have him." and continued the firing. I then told them that Col Benedict had done wrong, but that was no excuse for their conduct. They must go to their quarters and put up their arms and I would talk to them, and see that justice was done them. One of the officers came to me and said that they thought I wanted them to put their guns away and turn the guns of the Fort upon them. I took advantage of this information to tell them that if they would go to their quarters, I would take no farther steps at that time, and most of them went to their quarters and put up their guns. Those who went outside the Fort violated the rules in doing so, and forced the guard.

. . . .

Question— Have the men ever made any complaints to you previous to the disturbance of the 9th inst, and if so, please state what they were and how made.

Answer— I remember no complaint's except in the case of pay. Their individual complaints I make them go to their company commanders with, and let them refer them to me. About the last of October one company immediately after being paid turned out and were coming towards my quarters, where the Paymaster was. I ordered them to their quarters, and arrested two Sergeants who I understood were instrumental in starting the thing. I afterwards sent for them and told them the consequences that must follow from such action and explained to them as I had instructed the company officers to do before that the amount of their pay was not definitely settled and would not be until Congress convened. Upon the promise of future good behavior I released them. Afterwards the company sent me word that they were very sorry, and such a thing should not occur again.

. . . .

Major William E Nye, Fourth Infantry Corps d'Afrique was then duly sworn by the Judge Advocate. . . .

Question – Do you know what was the cause of the disturbance.

Answer – I should judge it was the whipping of those men by Lt Col Benedict.

Question – What men do you refer to when you say "Those men."

Answer – I refer to the two drummer boys named Harry Williams, and Munroe Miller. I do not know whether the latter is the correct name – I only know him by that. He is the one I saw Lt Col Benedict whip. I did not see him whip Williams. I saw him strike Miller three or four times with as nearly as I could judge from the distance a mule whip – such as used on carts – a whip with a stock and lash. He did not strike very severely

. . . .

Question – For what purpose did the men go out of the Fort to the Levee.

Answer – My impression is that they thought that Lt Col Benedict, was either on the "Suffolk" or would attempt to get there and that they were after him. I think they would have killed him if they had caught him.

. . . .

Question – Was there ill-feeling towards Lt Col Benedict before this –

Answer – My impression is that there was, but I do not know personally. I think it was on account of some punishment inflicted upon men.

Question – What are the punishments in your reg't. Do you punish without Court Martial, and how.

Answer – Confinement in the Guardhouse, carrying Ball and chain, and in one instance a man was tied up by his thumbs. Unless charges are preferred within twenty four hours or before the next Guard-mounting, the new Officer of the Day has orders to release him – the prisoner –

. . . .

Fort Jackson [*La.*] Decr. 13th 1863

The Court met pursuant to adjournment. Present all the members.

The proceedings of the previous day were then read and approved.

The examination of Captain James Miller was then resumed.

Question – You say that the men said that they knew what Gen Grant said to them meaning Adjutant General Thomas, who made a speech here to them. To what portion of the speech did they allude. Can you give the words.

445

Answer – General Thomas addressed the Officers and told them how to treat the men. He then addressed the men and told them that if the officers maltreated them in any way or struck them he would dismiss them The address was made at Fort St Phillip in the presence of both officers and men. Lieut Col Benedict was not present on duty. He might have been present, not on duty. This was about the first week in September

. . . .

Second Lieutenant Edward D. Mooney, 4th Regiment Infantry, Corps d'Afrique, was then duly sworn by the Judge Advocate. . . .

Question – Were you stationed at Fort St Philip and if so during what time.

Answer – I was stationed there from the twenty third day of August until the 8th of December.

Question – Who was in command during that time

Answer – Lieut Col Benedict part of the time and Captain Knapp part of time.

Question – How did Lt Col Benedict treat the men under his command.

Answer – He treated them tolerably well as a general thing. He might have been a little hasty sometimes.

Question – Were you ever as Officer of the Day or Guard required by Lt Col Benedict to inflict any unusual punishment

Answer – I was officer of the day once and Officer of the Guard once when I had to inflict by Lt Col Benedict's order a punishment that was unusual to me.

Question – What were those punishments

Answer – On the 7th of August at Baton Rouge when officer of the Guard I was ordered by Lt Col Benedict to take two men, have their shoes and stockings taken off and to lay them on the ground, straighten their legs and arms out and stake them – tie them down. Then he told me to go to the Commissary and get some molasses and cover their faces, feet and hands with molasses. He told me to keep them there during the day and night, and said he did not care if I kept them there until they died. They belonged to Company B. 4" Infantry Corps d'Afrique. I do not remember their names. Lt Colonel Benedict was commanding the regiment at that time. I understood him at the time that the men had been stealing some corn to roast, but I do not know certainly. They were kept tied down from ten A M until 7 P.M. or 7 1/2 P M They were tied down again the next morning and I turned them over to the officer of the Guard that relieved me.

On the 25th of August I think when at Fort St Phillip he had a man tied down in the same way. I saw him so tied down. He was tied down when I took charge of the Guard and remained so until between two and three that day. I do not know what his offence was. His face was not smeared with Molasses.

Question – Did you know of any ill feeling towards Lt Col Benedict existing among the men prior to the disturbance of the 9″ instant

Answer – Yes Sir I do – When we came to divide the Regiment many asked to remain at Fort St Phillip so that they would not have to be under Lt Col Benedict.

Question – What was the cause of the ill-feeling.

Answer – His general ill-treatment of them all, kicking and knocking them about.

. . . .

The Commission then having been cleared the Judge Advocate submits the question whether it is advisable and necessary to take the evidence of any of the enlisted men (colored) of the regiment, which was decided in the negative.

. . . .

Question – Please state your name, rank and the Command you held on the 9″ instant.

Answer – Augustus W Benedict, Lieutenant Colonel, Comd'g, 4th Regiment Infantry Corps. d'Afrique.

Question – Please state what steps were taken to quell the disturbance at Fort Jackson on the 9th instant.

Answer – As quick as the outbreak occurred Col Drew and myself proceeded to the parade ground and ordered the men to disperse and go to their quarters. They refused to do it and we expostulated with them – tried to quell them by reasoning and talking with them. This failed for that instant but finally succeeded. No force was resorted to. . . .

Question – Do you think the outbreak could have been put down if force had been resorted to at the first commencement of it

Answer – Not by any force that the white Officers present could have used.

Question – Had you noticed any disposition among the men to mutiny previous to the disturbance on the 9th.

Answer – Not during the time I was in command. I was only placed in command the day before.

. . . .

Question – What proportion of the regiment do you suppose were disposed to do right

Answer – I should think four fifths but I do not think they could have been relied upon in putting down the others

Question – What did you say to the men on the parade to quiet them.

Answer— The only remark that called for an answer from me was "We want to be treated as soldiers" I replied "Those boys were bad boys and I treated them as such" and they then cried "don't shoot," "don't Shoot."

Question— What offence had the two boys to whom you refer, committed.

Answer— The immediate offence was going to a sentinel and telling him the Sergeant of the guard had permitted them to go out and going out on that pretence.

The examination of Lt Col Benedict was here closed.

. . . .

HD

Excerpts from proceedings of a military commission convened at Fort Jackson, La., 12–13 Dec. 1863, G-527 1863, Letters Received, ser. 12, RG 94 [K-569]. In the same file is the commission's report (13 Dec. 1863), which described Lieutenant Colonel Benedict's whipping of the two drummers as the "immediate cause" of the "disturbance" at Fort Jackson, "aggravated by his previous conduct toward the men of the regiment, and the severe punishments to which he had been in the habit of resorting." The commission concluded that "the conduct of the men was more owing to an ignorance of their rights and the proper means of redress than to any preconcerted plan of revolt." When General Nathaniel P. Banks, commander of the Department of the Gulf, reported the "unpleasant affair" at Fort Jackson to General-in-Chief Henry W. Halleck (11 Dec. 1863), he explained that black soldiers and laborers "have been constantly assured . . . that under no circumstances whatever were they to be subjected to the degrading punishment of flogging. This has always been made a condition by them, and they have always received this assurance from the officers of the Government." (*Official Records,* ser. 1, vol. 26, pt. 1, pp. 456–57.) Later in December, Benedict and thirteen enlisted men faced court-martial. Benedict was found guilty of "inflicting cruel and unusual punishment, to the prejudice of good order and discipline," and was sentenced to dismissal from the service. The court found eight enlisted men guilty of mutiny, sentencing two to execution and six to imprisonment at hard labor for terms ranging from one to twenty years. One man was convicted merely of "insubordinate conduct" and received a sentence of hard labor under guard for one month. General Banks approved the court-martial's findings and sentences, but suspended the two executions "until further orders," confining the prisoners at Fort Jefferson, Florida, instead. The proceedings of the court-martial are no longer in the files of the Judge Advocate General's Office; notation indicates that they were sent to General Banks in April 1864 but were never received. (General Orders No. 90, Headquarters, Department of the Gulf, 30 Dec. 1863, NN-1301, Court-Martial Case Files, ser. 15, RG 153 [H-14].) The two executions were never carried out. (*List of U.S. Soldiers Executed by United States Military Authorities during the Late War,* 5981-A-85, Letters Received, ser. 409, Enlisted Branch, RG 94 [FF-

1]; service records of Abraham Victoria and Frank Williams, 76th USCI, Carded Records, Volunteer Organizations: Civil War, ser. 519, RG 94 [N-41].)

177: Commander of the District of North East Louisiana to the Commander of a Mississippi Black Regiment

Goodrichs Landing [*La.*] Dec. 24, 1863.

Col, In answer to your telegram relative to the men creating a mutiny this date I have instructed you to prefer charges and send them here for trial. In quelling the mutiny or in the heat of it the shooting of one or all of them would have been proper and I would have commended you for so doing, but after the men have been arrested and all quieted, such a procedure would not be justifiable, unless in case of being on a march when a drum-head Court could dispense justice summarily. I will have them tried as rapidly as possible by the court now in session here. Very Respectfully Your Obdt. Servt.

HLS

John P. Hawkins

Brig. Genl. John P. Hawkins to Col. R. H. Ballinger, 24 Dec. 1863, Letters Received, 53rd USCI, Regimental Books & Papers USCT, RG 94 [G-200]. The letter is addressed to Millikens Bend, Louisiana, where Colonel Ballinger commanded the 3rd Regiment of Mississippi Volunteers of African Descent (53rd USCI).

178: Charges and Testimony in the Court-Martial of a Mississippi Black Soldier

[*Vicksburg, Miss.*] June 15th 1864.

. . . .

The accused, Private John, Mitchell of the 53[d] Regt. U.S. Colored Infantry was arraigned on the following charge and specification.

Charge. Desertion.

Specification. – In this that the said Private John, Mitchell, Company "B" 53[d] Regiment U.S. Colored Infantry, having been duly enlisted as a soldier in the United States Army did desert the same from Milliken's Bend La. on or about the 22nd day of November 1863. and did remain absent from his company and

449

Regiment until on or about the 15th day of April, 1864, when he was arrested and brought back as a prisoner. –

. . . .

Captain William, Hubbard, 53[d] Regt. U.S. Colored Infantry a witness on the prosecution was duly sworn

. . . .

Question   "How do you know that the accused is a soldier in Company 'B,' 53[d] U.S. Colored Infantry?"
Answer   "I was present when he was mustered-in."
Question   "Where was you, and where was the accused on or about the 22nd day of November, 1863?"
Answer   "At Millikins Bend, La. I think the accused deserted on that day."

. . . .

Question   "When did you again see or hear anything of the accused?"
Answer. "On or about the 15th day of April, 1864, on board the steamboat 'Shenango.'
Question   "How was the accused reported on your reports from the 22nd day of November, 1863 to the 15th day of April 1864?"
Answer   "He was reported as a deserter."
Question   "Under what circumstances did you see the prisoner on board the steamer 'Shenango' on the 15th day of April 1864?"
Answer   "I heard that he was there employed, and went down with a guard to arrest him."
Question   "State how he was employed on board Steamer 'Shenango'?
Answer   "I think he was employed by the clerk of the boat as cabin boy, I saw the clerk pay him when I took him away."

. . . .

The prisoner gave the following statement in defence. – "I told the Captain previous to going away that I should leave his Company and go to some other if he continued to kick and cuff me about as he had been doing: I told him that I was willing to go into any other company in the Regiment."
The evidence of both parties being thus in possession of the Court, the Court was cleared for deliberation, and having maturedly considered the evidence adduced, find the accused John, Mitchell Private Company "B" 53[d] U.S. Colored Infantry as follows: –
On the Specification of the Charge. *"Guilty."*
Of the Charge – *"Guilty"*
And the Court do therefore sentence the said John, Mitchell, Private Company "B" 53[d] U.S. Colored Infantry, *"to forfeit all pay*

now due, or which may become due for the next four (4) months, and be kept at hard labor under charge of a regimental guard with a ball weighing twelve (12) pounds attached to his right leg with a chain four (4) feet long."

HD

[*Endorsement*] Headquarters, 1ˢᵗ Division U.S. Colored Troops Vicksburg, Miss. June 20ᵗʰ 1864. The Proceedings in the foregoing case are respectfully returned to the Court for reconsideration of the sentence. The Prisoner was absent five months until arrested, and by his own statement he shows his desertion was premeditated. There is nothing in the evidence to palliate the guilt, and by comparity there should be no letting up on the extreme punishment prescribed by the Articles of War. Desertions have been too common in this command and they will become more frequent unless Soldiers are made to understand the severe punishment they must suffer for not being faithful to their oath of service to the Government. They know very well they should not desert. It is time they learned as well the just punishment due a deserter. John P. Hawkins Brig. Genl. Comdg.

[*Endorsement*] 2″ o'clock P.M. June 22ⁿᵈ 1864. In accordance with the above indorsement, marked and appended, the following named members of the Court met to revise the sentence passed in the foregoing case of Private John, Mitchell, Company "B" 53ᵈ U.S. Colored Infantry for "Desertion". . . .

The Court after a mature deliberation do sentence Private John, Mitchell, Company "B," 53ᵈ U.S. Colored Infantry, *"to be shot to death with musketry at such time and place as the commanding general shall direct. Two thirds of the members of the Court concurring therein.*

[*Endorsement*] The proceedings finding & sentence in the foregoing case are approved Vicksburg Miss. June 25. 64 John P. Hawkins Brig. Genl Comdg. Division

[*Endorsement*] Head Qrs Dist of Vicksburg June 28ᵗʰ 1864 The proceedings finding and sentence in the foregoing case are approved and respectfully forwarded for action of Department commander – with a recommendation that the sentence be commuted to loss of pay now due & to hard labor four months with ball & chain attached to his leg H. W. Slocum Maj Genl Cmdg

[*Endorsement*] H^d Qrs Dept and Army of the Tenn, Before Atlanta, Ga, July 30th 1864   Proceedings, findings and sentence approved and confirmed.

P^{vt} John Mitchell "B" Co 53^d Regt U.S.C. Infy will be shot to death with Musketry on the 15th day of September 1864, between the hours of 9 o'clock A.M. and 3 o'clock P.M. at Vicksburg, Miss.

The Commanding Officer of Post Vicksburg is charged with the execution of this order   By order of Maj Genl O. O. Howard   Wm T. Clark   AA General

Excerpts from proceedings of general court-martial in the case of Private John Mitchell, 53d USCI, 15 June 1864, LL-2350, Court-Martial Case Files, ser. 15, RG 153 [H-50]. Mitchell was executed on September 15, 1864. (*List of U.S. Soldiers Executed by United States Military Authorities during the Late War,* 5981-A-85, Letters Received, ser. 409, Enlisted Branch, RG 94 [FF-1].

179: Order by the Commander of a Division of Black Troops

Vicksburg, Miss. August 28" 1864.

General Orders No 36.

I   The following punishments will not be used in this Division:
Tying men up (stretched up), by the hands, wrists or thumbs; bucking and gagging, the latter may, however, be used when a man will not stop talking, or making a noise after being ordered to stop; making men undergo punishment, carrying knapsack, accoutrements or gun; extra tours of guard duty.   By order of Brig. Gen'l J. P. Hawkins.

HD

General Orders No. 36, Hd. Qrs. 1st Division, U.S. Cold. Troops, 28 Aug. 1864, Issuances, 53rd USCI, Regimental Books & Papers USCT, RG 94 [G-198].

180: Imprisoned Louisiana Black Sergeant to the President

Fort Barrancas Florida Oc^t 7 1864

To. The. Honorable Abrham Lincon   I your Partishener W^m D Mayo 1st Sarg^t C^o D. 86 cullard Infentry of L.A. will now state to

you the condishons I am in being confined in the Provost Guard
House under the sentanc of A Genl Cort Marshal held hear on the
8^{inst} of Aug last   this centence being to serve a turm of one year
and 9 months hard Labour without pay on Tortugas Island   the
charges bein against me is 1st disobediants of Orders which I can
prove I am not guilty of by over 25 of the same Reg^t charge 2nd
Breach of Arest which I plead guilty to under those
surmstances,   thare was a Private John Vier suffering punishment
in the way of Riding a Wooden Horse   the word came to me that
he had falen from the horse dead   I was excited and Humanity
hurid me to his asistince at once not remembering that I was
under arest untill My Capt ordred me back to my quarters which I
returned to amediatly   charge 3^d Mutinus conduct in that I W^m D
Mayo gathered some 6 or 8 men and said I would not serve under
Capt Miller any longer which they faild to prove and which I can
say before God and Man I never uterd   one thing more I will
draw your attention to is I was denyed the privaleges of having
some 25 witesness who I could of Prooved my entire inocences by
and alowed but 2 only   thare being two comishend Officers
against me I was suposed of course to be guilty.   under this
unlawfull and unjust punishment I can. but Apeal to your Honner
for Justice in this case   in a pucenarury point of view I say
nothing however I will say one thing.   I am getting towards 50
years of age and my Wife is over fifty and Goverment will hav to
suport while I am reely willing and able to as enny good Loyal
man can   I hav ben always ben faithfull and don My Duty as a
Souldier should and concequencely I want Justice don me in return
by hir   when I was sent to the Guard house I was deprived of My
own private property   I had the Army Regulations that I bought
and paid for with my own money, and charged me with reading
that which a Nigar had no buisness to know.   now Dear Sir I
Apeal to a Greate Man a man that is governing this Nation to
govern the Justice and punishment that is delt out to one of its
Faithfull subjects   I Remain Your Obediant Servent

ALS   W^m. D. Mayo

1st Sargt. Wm. D. Mayo to the Honerable Abrham Lincon, 7 Oct 1864,
M-250 1865, Letters Received, ser. 12, RG 94 [K-528]. In the same file
is a copy of the order publishing the charges and findings of the general
court-martial that tried Mayo. According to the charges, Mayo refused to
execute orders from his captain to have his company police the camp
grounds. Then, after being placed under arrest for disobedience, Mayo left
confinement without permission and "did parade some eight or ten privates
of the afforsaid Company . . . telling them that he loved his men and
would live by them and die by them, and would Stand no such work from

any Captain, and would never go into a fight with Capt. Miller." The court-martial found Sergeant Mayo guilty of disobedience of orders, breach of arrest, and mutinous conduct, and sentenced him "[t]o be reduced to the ranks, his chevron, buttons, and all insignia of rank to be cut off, and that he be drummed out of camp in the presence of his Regiment" and to serve the remainder of his term of enlistment in confinement at hard labor, with loss of pay. (General Orders No. 36, Hdqrs. D. W. Florida, 30 Aug. 1865 [1864].) According to endorsements, the Bureau of Military Justice was unable to locate a record of Mayo's trial in its files, but based on this order "and in absence of any evidence of injustice in the findings," the judge advocate general recommended against pardon. Also in the file is his draft letter to Mayo (13 May 1865), stating that investigation revealed "no grounds to justify the exercise of Executive clemency in your behalf."

181: Order by the Commander of a Missouri Black Regiment

Brazos Santiago Texas, November 9th 1864

General Orders No 36   The Lieut. Col. comdg, has learned with regret that several officers of this command have been in the habit of abusing men under their command by striking them with their fists or swords. & by kicking them when guilty of very slight offences. This is as unmanly and unofficer like as it is unnecessary. –   An officer is not fit to command who cannot control his temper sufficiently to avoid the habitual application of blows to enforce obedience. Men will not obey; as promptly, an officer who adopts, the customs of the slave driver to maintain authority, as they will him who punishes by a system consistent with the character and enormity of offences and the spirit of the age. The time for enforcing authority with the sword is in case of willful disobedience of orders, mutiny, or cowardice in action; which in the ordinary course of events, will rarely occur.

While censuring the officers referred to, their commander makes due allowance for the fact that, generally; the men who have received such punishment have been of the meanest type of soldiers; lazy, dirty, & inefficient and provoking to any high spirited officer: But he is satisfied never-the-less, that such treatment will not produce reform in them; while it has an injurious effect on all good men, from its resemblance to their former treatment while slaves. By Order of Lieut. Colonel David Branson Comdg. Regt.

HD

General Orders No. 36, Hd. Qrs. 62nd U.S. Cold. Inf., 9 Nov. 1864, Orders, 62nd USCI, Regimental Books & Papers USCT, RG 94 [G-255].

182: Imprisoned Mississippi Black Soldier to the President

Vicksburg miss. November the 26 /64

Dear Sir   itestifie that David Washiton a Bugler of Co B thurd US Colerd Calalry   My Capt fell out with me fer what I dont know   he struck me   I came up to the courthouse and reported him   Genl. Slomkum made me stay at the courthouse untill my capt get hear   it was too days before my capt came up   the capt he then came up frome campt and reported me feradeserter   I was put in geail on the 7^the of August 1864   I am put prson fer twelve month all lowents and pay stoped   the cort says it can not do me enny good as my cpt reported me as a dezerter and Genal. Slomkem. was not hear at time of my tryl   if he had bin hear I wood came clear   I am agood solger all ways has done what is right   my cap^t drew apistole on me   iam will to do what right yet my comeny will so to   I drop thes fewlines asking fer Jested [*justice*]   I ought not to be in prson if I had Jested done me   I am a colerd man   I have no edication   I dont know nothing at all abought law   I am willing to do all I can for you as solger or a man if you pleas doe all you can fer me   pleas let me hear from you   I am respectfully yours

David Washiton

in Vicksburg miss in prson

ALS

David Washiton to Mr. A. Lincon, 26 Nov. 1864, W-4 1865, Letters Received, ser. 360, Colored Troops Division, RG 94 [B-159]. The Judge Advocate General's endorsement recommended against clemency. In the same file is a draft letter from the War Department (22 Dec. 1864) informing Washington that the Secretary of War "finds no sufficient grounds for interference." At Washington's general court-martial, Captain Andrew Emery testified that the bugler's difficulties began when he failed to appear at assembly. Later, Washington asked permission to gather witnesses who would prove that he had not been absent, but instead of doing so, he complained to the colonel of the regiment that Emery had tied him up by the thumbs "without cause." Upon learning of Washington's actions, Emery proceeded to tie him up by the thumbs, despite the bugler's resistance and his declaration that he would complain again to the colonel. Within an hour, an unidentified person cut down Washington, who fled to Vicksburg. The court-martial found Washington guilty of desertion and insubordination and sentenced him to one year's imprisonment at hard labor, with loss of all pay and allowances. (Testimony of Capt. Andrew Emery, 26 Aug. 1864, proceedings of general court-martial in the case of Bugler David Washington, 3rd USCC, LL-2783, Court-Martial Case Files, ser. 15, RG 153 [H-28].)

183: Louisiana Black Soldier to the Commander of the Defenses of New Orleans

New Orleans December 6ᵗʰ 1864

General   I have the honor of addressing you upon a subject of painfull interest – To complain of wrongs which I feel assured you need but to become aware of – to correct.

Lieut Brown 77ᵗʰ Regt U.S.C.I. Company A daily treats the men of company with such excesive cruelty that they can no longer submit to the degredation heaped upon them.

I have been compeled to walk a *"beat"* untill I have deposited the excrement of my body in my pants

He has also threatened to kill me and I do not consider my life safe while under his command

Hopeing that you will see justice done I am your Obediant Servant

ALS   Newton Rucker

Private Newton Rucker to Brigadier Gen'l. T. W. Sherman, 6 Dec. 1864, Letters Received, 77th USCI, Regimental Books & Papers USCT, RG 94 [G-105]. Endorsement. The names of three other privates in Rucker's company are appended as witnesses.

184: Order by the Commander of a Pennsylvania Black Regiment

Head Quarters 41 U.S.C.T. [*Va.*] Decenber 15ᵗʰ 1864

General Order No 8   When a soldier mutilates himself by firing his gun so that the bullet passes through some part of his person not permanently injuring him – for the purpose of getting rid of duty – he shows himself to be a *villain* false to his oath a *coward* who does not dare to face his duty and do it – a scoundrel and a fool – Such a man is a disgrace not only to the service but to humanity and is not fit to be ranked with or to enjoy the priveleges of men. Such a creature will be hereafter so regarded. And it is ordered. That when any man of this Regiment shall mutilate himself purposely. – He shall perform double duty for one month thereafter as little regard as the nature of the case will allow being paid to the wound he has inflicted upon himself. He shall have his meals seperately served to him and no

man of his Company or Regiment shall be permitted to speak to or associate with him under pain of similar punishment— He shall not be considered fit for the compan of honest men and good soldiers and the work to which he shall be assigned shall be that so far as possible which is the most disagreeable and filthy as being the best calculated for one who is by nature a liar and a coward— This shall continue for one month more or less in the discretion of the Commanding Officer That such a man shall be distinguished from all others and that every such man may be avoided he shall have one painted board attached to his breast marked in large letters *Liar* and a similar one upon his back marked *Coward*— and any man seen to speak to one so branded except in the way of duty— or to eat with him, or to sit or walk with him shall be severely and similarly punished The gun may be accidentally discharged— but this can never be done without gross carelessness, and any such accident is liable to severe punishment. A man may be wounded without his intention by such accidental discharge but this is worse carelessness and will be still more severely punished. But when the discharge is purposely made with the intention of self mutilation— or where the person is injured or wounded purposely, by any other means, — the punishment will be as herein ordered— Or this punishment may be changed or made more severe and humiliating as the Commanding officer may deem best. By command of Col L F Haskell
HD

General Order No. 8, Head Quarters 41 U.S.C.T., 15 Dec. 1864, Orders, 41st USCI, Regimental Books & Papers USCT, RG 94 [G-264].

185: Order by the Commander of a Kentucky Black Regiment

White Bluffs Tenn. Jan. 30" 1865

Generals Orders No. 3. Company Commanders will divide their Companies into squads— each squad to be placed under the special charge of a Non-Com-officer of the Company, who will be held responsible for the good order, cleanliness, obedience and prompt conduct of the men. Any Non-Commissioned Officer whose squad is habitually neglectful of the above named requirements will be reduced to the ranks. Company Commanders will see that the orders of the Non-Commissioned officers are respected with the same promptness as their own and will sustain them by such measures as may be necessary to secure discipline and obedience.

It is desirable that the men exhibit somewhat more promptitude and spirit in the execution of orders. To this end Company Com'd'rs are to see that dilatoriness is punished as a greivous offense in such way as to prevent a repetition but without any appearance of anger or feeling on the part of the officer. Men must be made to feel that it is law and orders that have been violated when an offense is brought to punishment, not merely the directions of the individual officer. As an effectual and prompt mode of punishment, tying up by the thumbs is recommended when any corporeal punishment is deemed necessary, as, if properly administered it never fails to subdue the delinquent and will not inflict any serious or permanent injury. By command of Lieut. Col. Henry Stone

HD

General Orders No. 3, H'd. Qr's. 100" U.S. Colored Infantry, 30 Jan. 1865, Orders, 100th USCI, Regimental Books & Papers USCT, RG 94 [G-134].

186: Order by the Commander of a Mississippi Black Regiment

Vicksburg, Miss., Feb'y 17", 1865.

General Orders, No. 7.

I. In future, the Officer of the day will make very close inspection of barracks, kitchens and clothing.

II. The habit of putting clothing under blankets and knapsacks will be at once discontinued.

Any man found with clothing under his blanket, knapsack or bunk, will be tied up by the thumbs for two hours, for violation of orders.

Frequent inspections of quarters by Company officers should be made during the day.

III. This order will be read to the men at "retreat" for four days, so that none may be ignorant of its existence. By order of Col. Geo. M. Ziegler

HD

General Orders, No. 7, Head Quarters 52d U.S. Cold. Infantry, 17 Feb. 1865, Orders, 52nd USCI, Regimental Books & Papers, RG 94 [G-248].

187: Imprisoned Louisiana Black Soldiers to the Secretary of War

Military Prison   Alton Ills.   Feb 20th 1865

Dear: Sir. We The undersigned Members of Company F. 49th E. Col.[d] Infantry stationed at Vicksburg Miss. our charge being mutiny by stacking arms. & refusing to do duty in Said comp or regiment. at the time of doing This we were not aware what the consequences of Mutiny would be. we did not intend to any way injure The government but it was for The purpose of resenting the repeated ill treatment of our officers. They were useing us in the most shamefull manner. our intentions when we enlisted was to do our duty as soldiers should & we refrained from doing what we did untill the cruelty of those in command of us compelled us to do something   we had reported to the Col. several times in regard to the treatment we were receiving but he paid no attention to us & therefore had no other recourse but to do as we done   There is no set of Men More willing to serve the United States Than ourselves & we intended to fight for The country expecting to be treated as human beings

Our sentenced is for life   we think it to hard for doing or commiting our act which we did not understand what would be the result. we now see our folly in doing what we did & allso are aweare that we should be punished to some extent. we are willing to go into the service for three years longer if you will grant our pardon   we would far rather serve three years in The tented field than one month in prison. we hope you will carefully consider the circumstances we are placed under & our not being acquiainted with the prosribed laws & regulations of The United States   we think our ignorance of them should gain our pardon & in future we promise to faithfully preform our duty towards the United States as soldiers should do & obey all orders coming from our superior officers promptly   hopeing you will take an interest in our case as soon as possible or convient we close by Remaining Yours Respetifully

HLSr   [*16 signatures*]

Price Warefield et al. to Hon. E. M. Stanton, 20 Feb. 1865, filed with S-196 1865, Letters Received, ser. 360, Colored Troops Division, RG 94 [B-150]. The petition and all signatures are in the same hand. According to court-martial testimony, the imprisoned black soldiers stacked their arms in front of the tent of their captain and announced their refusal to do further duty "until we can have the promise of better treatment from you." The soldiers, including three noncommissioned officers, especially protested that the captain "had broken open some of their boxes and had treated them as though they were thieves." The court-martial found twenty men guilty of mutiny. Two, judged to be the ringleaders, were sentenced "to be shot to death with musketry"; seventeen received sentences of imprisonment at hard labor for life; one was sentenced to confinement at hard labor, with ball and chain, for the remainder of his term of enlistment. (Testimony of Capt. James P. Hall, 20 June 1864, proceedings of general court-martial in the case of Sergeant Giles Simms et al., 49th USCI, LL-2492, Court-Martial Case Files, ser. 15, RG 153 [H-29].) After the two death sentences were carried out in September 1864, regimental officers and post, department, and district commanders forwarded numerous letters and endorsements recommending release of the other men, arguing that the two executions sufficed to impress upon the men their obligation of strict obedience. These appeals in late 1864 and early 1865, filed with the soldiers' own petition, resulted in a War Department order releasing the men and returning them to duty on May 4, 1865.

188: Proceedings of a Regimental Court-Martial in a Kentucky Black Regiment

Smeedville, Tenn., March 22nd 1865,

. . . .

4. Burrill Clark, Co. G., 100th U.S.C. Infy.

Charge 1st Conduct prejudicial to good order and military discipline.

Specification: In this, that said private Burrill Clark, Co. G. 100th U.S.C. Infy. having been duly posted as a sentinel, was found sitting down on his post when visited by the Corporal of the Guard, between the hours of 12 and 2 A.M.

Charge 2nd Disobedience of orders.

Specification: In this, that private Burrill Clark, Co. G. 100th U.S.C. Infy, having been duly posted as a sentinel, was found sitting down contrary to orders; instead of halting the relief agreeable to instructions he only jumped up and said "hello!"

All this, at Smeedville, Tenn., on or about the 15th of March, 1865.

To these charges and specifications, the accused pleaded guilty.

The finding was guilty.

Sentence:— To stand on a stump not exceeding one foot in diameter, six hours a day, for three successive days, wearing a knapsack weighing not less than ten pounds, and carrying a rail in the position of shoulder or support arms during that time; and the remainder of his term of punishment to be kept at hard labor under charge of the guard.

5. Private Geo. Torand, Co. G. 100th U.S.C. Infy.

Charge; Disobedience of Orders.

Specification: In this, that said private Torand Co. G. 100th U.S.C. Infy, did commit a nuisance on or near the parade ground.

This at Smeedville, Tenn., on or about March 18. 1865.

To this charge and specification the accused pleaded guilty.

The finding was guilty.

Sentence: — To be tied up by the thumbs for two hours.

6. Private Ned Bowman, Co. G. 100th U.S.C. Infy.

Charge 1st Absence without leave.

Specification. In this, that private Ned Bowman, Co. G. 100th U.S.C. Infy. did go out of camp without leave.

This at Smeedville, Tenn., on or about March 18. 1865.

Charge 2nd. Drunkenness.

Specification: In this, that said private Ned Bowman did get drunk, while absent without leave.

This at Smeedville, Tenn., on or about March 18, 1865.

To these charges and specifications the accused pleaded guilty.

The finding was guilty.

Sentence: To be confined at hard labor, under charge of the guard, for thirty days, wearing a ball and chain, and with a placard tied on his back with the word "Drunk" on it, in large letters; and to be kept on bread and water during half that time.

7. William Johnson, private Co. "A," 100th U.S.C. Infy.

Charge: Absence without leave.

Specification: In this, that private William Johnson Co. A. 100th U.S. Colored Infantry, did go out of camp without leave.

This at Smeedville, Tenn., on or about March 18. 1865.

To this charge and specification the accused pleaded guilty.

The finding was guilty.

Sentence: — To be confined at hard labor under charge of the guard for fourteen days, and to be kept on bread and water during his term of punishment.

HDSr   Henry Stone

Excerpt from proceedings of a field officers court-martial, 22 Mar. 1865, Letters Received, 100th USCI, Regimental Books & Papers USCT, RG 94 [G-137]. Endorsements. In the three omitted cases—men charged with sitting down while on sentinel duty and being absent from camp without leave—the court specified similar punishments.

189: Testimony in the Court-Martial of Eight
Tennessee Black Soldiers

[Memphis, Tenn. April 22, 1865]

. . . .

Sergeant John. W. Chandler duly sworn—

Ques   State your name, rank, Company & Regiment?

Ans   John. W. Chandler Farrier Co. "F" 2ᵈ U.S. Col'ᵈ Artillery
(Light)—acting first Sergeant of the Company . . . .

Ques   State whether if you know there was any difficulty or
disturbance in your Company on or about the evening of the 30ᵗʰ
day of March 1865?

Ans   There was—

Ques   State whether either or all of these men were engaged in
it and if so give their names?

Ans   I know of Sergeant Tolliver Sergeant Hall and Corporal
Jones, George Bryant and Isaac Reeves.   That is all that I know of
myself—

State if you know with whom they had the difficulty and what
it was about?

Ans   When I first came it was with Catain Marion, Sergeant
Price, and my self—   I was ordered by Sergeant Price acting
Lieutenant to go up to the Stables and tie up a Corporal or rather
untie him and Buck and gag him.   While I was in the act of
Bucking and gaging him Sergeant Price came there and the
Corporal told him the Bucking and gaging was nothing he was
Bucked and gagged before and then he told me to not Buck and
Gag him but to make a Spread Eagle of him by tying him to the
Spare wheel of the caisson.   I tied him to the spare wheel—   The
men were down wattering the horses at the time and I went down
to the Barracks before they returned.   After they came from water
I was in my tent and I heard a noise out in the front of the
Captains quarters and I thought it was the men who had been on
daily duty that had marched down there to get their dram as
usual   As soon as I got around there where the men were Sergeant
Tolliver seized me by the collar and drew back to hit me and told
me I had tied up that man for them damned white sons of
Bitches—   I told him that what I did I had done by the orders of
the Captain and the Sergeant acting Lt—and said if he did not like
it to go and see the Captain about it and he replied God dam the
Captain that he was not going to have the white Sons of Bitches
to come there and do what their own officers had never done.   I
told him that the next man that put his hands on me about it I

was going to shoot   I did not care who it was   At that time the
Captain stepped to the door and told them to hush their noise and
go to their quarters. He told Sergeant Tolliver especially – and he
told the Captain by God he was not going and said he was going
to have satisfaction right then and looked around to the men and
said would they see that he was righted –   Then Sergeant Hall
spoke up and said yes – we have got to fight it out and we might
as well fight it out here as any where else –   Then Captain Marion
came down out of his quarters and took hold of Sergeant Tolliver
and took him around behind the quarters and was going to tie
him up – and I went round the oppostc side of the Barracks and
went into my tent –   I heard hollowing and whooping out there
and I went there and just as I got to the fence the Captain said to
the men to go back to their quarters and told them three or four
times which none of them did except one that I saw and that was
Corporal Jones   he went back into the quarters and pulled of[f]
his jacket and came back with a pistol in his hands waving it
about and said just let him tie him up and I will shoot the son of
a bitch. The Captain then sent me to his quarters for his
pistol –   I brought it to him and gave it to him and he cocked it
and bursted a cap at some body – I dont know who it was and
then threw it down upon the ground by him and attempted again
to tie up Sergeant Tolliver and he then again said, I want you
men to go to your quarters and the cook Thomas Hill went and
George Bryant was standing on the same side of the fence the
Captain was with a club in his hand and said to Hill "what are
you runing for   the Captain aint but one man and he could not
tie up the whole company nor he could not arrest the whole
company   The Captain then called Bryant to come to him and he
replied he would not do it nor he did not do it. That was the
end of that so far as I know –   I went to my tent and in about
three or four minutes – a short time I heard some one say there
comes the Provost Guard and they have got Jim Jones –   Isaac
Reeves was standing at my tent door talking with me when I
heard that and he run from my tent door just as I started to where
the men were and said three or four times, let us go and charge
the Captains tents and get their pistols and go out and fight their
Provost Guard and then I started around on the other side of the
Barracks from the crowd and I saw the Provost Guard haveing six
or seven –   McDowell started after them and said he was going to
follow them men to "hell". Sergeant Warren called after him to
come back and he said he would not do it. I called him and he
told me to go to hell he was going to see them men out – he
would follow them to hell as long as he had started –

. . . .

Sergt. Tolliver would state to the court that on the day when the disturbance took place, he went to water the horses and when he returned with his party he found Corporal Haskins of the Co. tied up to a caisson. He asked what it was for; and some of the men told him that he was tied up on account of the Sutler, and that John Chandler, a colored Sergt. of the Company, and who had never omitted an opportunity to oppress and domineer over them had tied him up. He told the boys that if Chandler tied him up, they would take him down, and carry him to the officers; and if they then found that they had ordered it done, they would tie him up again; otherwise they would let him go.

When Capt. Marion first ordered him to go to his quarters, he did so. When afterwards the captain came to tie him up, he told the Captain that he would like to talk with him; but the Captain said he would not have any talk. He had been a non-commissioned officer ever since being in the company. It had never been the practice in the company to tie up non-commissioned officers. He had always borne a good name in the company, and had been accustomed to the respect of his officers, and to the respect and obedience of the men. Is it strange, then that in the heat of the excitement he should have struggled to get away, and to escape the suffering of such an indignity in their presence.

. . . .

Sergeant Hall would state to the court, that he does not attempt to justify his conduct on that occasion; and that while he does not expect an acquittal at their hands, he cannot but hope that they will see in his case many extenuating circumstances. It had not been customary in his company to tie up non-commissioned officers. And when this was done, at the instigation of the sutler and by order of a non-commissioned officer who had recently been detailed to their company from another battery, it is not surprising that it should have caused a general excitement among the men, and that expressions should have been used and threats made, which under ordinary circumstances would deserve severe punishment. He does not deny using expressions which he should not have used — but he claims, (and there is no evidence to the contrary), that he did not untie nor instigate the untying of Haskins, and when he discovered that the act complained of by the men was sanctioned by Captain Marion he said no more; but when the Captain ordered the crowd to disperse he returned to his proper duty as stable sergeant and ordered some of the men on duty under him to go with him. He remained at his duty, and was arrested by order of Captain Marion while engaged in issuing feed. He therefore rests his case with the judgment of the court, again begging leave to remind them that those parts of the specfication wherein it is alleged that he by force and violence released the prisoner and attempted to overpower the provost guard are not true and have not been proven against him.

. . . .

HD

Excerpts from proceedings of general court-martial in the cases of Sergeant J. Hall et al., Co. "F", 2d USCA (Light), 22 & 25 Apr. 1865, MM-2179, Court-Martial Case Files, ser. 15, RG 153 [H-9]. The excerpts from testimony taken on April 22 are not reproduced here in the same order that the testimony was given. The court found Sergeants Tolliver and Hall guilty of mutiny and sentenced them to imprisonment at hard labor for terms of four and three years, respectively. Their sentences further specified that four months of each year be spent in solitary confinement and that the prisoners subsist on bread and water during the first ten days of each month of solitary confinement. The court also convicted Corporal Jim Jones, who received a sentence identical to that of Sergeant Hall, and two privates, who were sentenced to three years' confinement at hard labor. Two privates and a bugler were found not guilty.

190A: Testimony in the Court-Martial of Kentucky Black Soldiers

[Indianola, Texas October 4, 1865]

. . . .

Captain Samuel W. Campbell 109th U.S.C.T. a witness for the prosecution being duly sworn, says:

. . . .

Question by J.A.: State to the Court what language, if any, the prisoner [*Private Edward Hawes*] made at a disturbance among the soldiers of the 109th U.S.C. Troops, on board the Steamer "Thoˢ A Scott." tending to create mutiny, on or about the 6th day of June 1865.

Answer: It was about 10 o'clock at night when I first saw this man; he had about eight or ten men around and he was talking to them. I was up at the bow of the boat, near the Pilot-House. I went over where they were and heard this man remark: "That he be damned if he ever saw an inspection on board a transport

before, or heard of it;" he swore that the officers came out of their
nice rooms with damned dirty swords, and it was impossible to
keep any thing clean on the boat, for he had a pair of white
gloves that he had never had on his hands in his pocket and they
were dirtier than if he had worn them several times on land; "he
did not think it was right, he said, to tie up men and put them
on guard for having dirty guns"   He continued talking for about
fifteen minutes: he had some eight or ten around him and was the
principal spokesman.

· · · ·

Question by J.A: What was the cause of the disturbance you
have mentioned?

Answer: Two men of Co "D" were put on guard for keeping
dirty guns; they wouldnt try to keep them clean like the
rest: Capt Keene told the "Officer of the day" to release them at
such an hour; when the "officer of the day" came to release them
they began saucing him, and when asked their names gave him
ficticious ones; he tied them both up for it, and by some means
one of them got loose and refused to be tied a second time: he
swore he wouldnt be tied up by the "officer of the day", They
called up two of the guards and they couldn't tie him; and some
officers went and got a pair of "Hand-cuffs" and put on him; he
was then tied to the deck.

After he was tied there sometime the 1st Sergt of Co "D" and a
crowd of men came to release the ones tied up; and the 1st Sergt.
called Captain Keene and demanded the release of them two men.

I believe that was the cause of the disturbance.

Afterwards the men gathered in groups talking about it and
were not quieted until after 10. o'clock. Some tried to bring it on
again as this man did.

· · · ·

HD

[*Indianola, Texas*] October 19th 1865.

· · · ·

Captain A. H. Keene, 109th U.S.C. Inf. a witness for the
prosecution being duly sworn says:

· · · ·

"The disturbance was occasioned by one of my Company being
tied up for neglect of duty   During the first of the evening that
day there was a party visited me composed of men from
Companies on the boat. The prisoner [*Sergeant Samuel Green*] was

at the head of the party and came to the cabin door where the
officers were setting in the cabin, and called for me. I stepped out
of the cabin near the aft hatch way and the prisoner said 'Captain
those men must be released. if they are not released it will raise
the devil' or words [*to*] that effect. and he further said that. 'We
came from home to get rid of such treatment as this. referring to
the prisoners who were confined on deck.' I dont remember of his
saying anything else or taking any part in the release of the
prisoners. He made some remarks which I cant remember showing
sympathy with the prisoners,"!

Question by J.A. "What was the bearing of the prisoner when
he visited you, and made use of the remarks specified?"

Answer "I considered it at the time to be disrespectful and I
considered the words in the form of a demand instead of a request,
and accompanied with a threat that if the prisoners were not
released it would raise the devil."!

. . . .

1st Sergeant James Dahoney, Co "D" 109th U.S.C. Inf. a witness
for the defence being duly sworn says:

. . . .

Question by accused [*Sergeant Samuel Green*]. "State all you
know in regard to the circumstances of the party visiting Capt.
Keene?"

Answer. "When the men rose in the first place I talked with
them and they got very calm. Sergt. Tyler Co. 'D' came around
and raised them again. I quieted them down the second time and
he came and raised them again   I quieted them down the third
time and he came for. them. Sergt. Tyler. said that. 'Sergt
Dahoney is a damned coward and that he could get twelve (12)
men without calling on Company 'D' and cut the men loose who
were tied. he raised the men then and I could do nothing with
them and then the orderly of the Company Sam. Green says that
he would go down to the Captain and see if he couldent do
something with them and he went down to the Captain but I
could not hear what he said. I followed on after him myself with
Corp'l Milene. Segt Green called the Captain out of his
room. when he called him out of the room Sergeant Tyler and his
gang were there and I could not get up near them!"

Question by accused. "Did not accused use every means in his
power to quiet the men?"

Answer "Yes sir! he came up and talked to them and tried to
get them down   he said 'boys you dont know what you are
adoing, you go and cut one of them down and he will try and kill
you a few moments afterwards,   then he said, 'I advise you every

467

one to leave those boys alone' that is all I heard pass from him, he could not do as much with the men as I could!"

Question by accused "Did not accused visit Capt. Keene for the purpose of preventing a disturbance on the boat?"

Answer. That is what he told me he was agoing to do. all I heard him say was that he would go and see the Captain and see what could be done about it!"

. . . .

The accused [*Sergeant Samuel Green*] having no further testimony to offer. made the following remarks in his defence —

"The boys asked me if I was going into the fuss and I asked them what, and they said cutting the boys loose and I asked them were they tied up and they told me they were. and I replied to them that they would have to do like I did when I got into difficulty and they asked me how I done. and I told them I got out the best way I could. Then they went on and I told them that all armies had to have regulations and all men were sworn in to obey orders. it was no use for them to cut up about the boys for if they cut the boys loose, they would want to fight them I told them that just such men as they were cutting up about started the rebellion in the commencement and I dident see the use of 10 men rebelling against a regiment or a regiment against the United States Army. I told them that it had not been but a few weeks since the Colonel had talked to us about such things and now it was awful to think about let alone to do it. Then some wild fellow said. that. some men who upheld the officers were no better than they were and that they could destroy them as well as the officers. I replied that I dident tie the men and dident have it done and that I wasent going to have any thing to do with them I remarked to Sergt Dahoney and Corporal Milene that I would go and report to the Captain about the thing. I went down and the Captain asked if it was our Company who was making the disturbance and I said it wasent ours any more than it was the balance of the men, and he said you go and try and delay the men and I will go and see the Lieut Colonel. as we parted. I said. 'Yes Captain I think it would be better than have any fuss here on the ship out on the water. the Lieutenant Colonel came out and said 'Sergt. you take the men to their quarters and I went to them and said. 'Come on away from there' and I went up to the bow of the boat. The Captain came and requested me to get the men to their quarters and he would see the Lieut Colonel and do all he could to get the prisoners released, and he said nothing more to me. I have been hard at work ever since I was arrested!"

. . . .

HD

[*Indianola, Texas*] September 30th 1865

. . . .

1st Lieutenant John M. Schoonmaker. 109th U.S.C.Inf. a witness for the prosecution being duly sworn: says:

. . . .

Question by J.A. "State to the Court what language, if any, you heard the prisoner [*Private Sandy Fenqua*] use at that time?"

Answer. "I found him near the bow of the boat, and he said 'he would see wether they had a right to tie up our men or not.' And while I was talking to some of my men. he said. 'The damned white sons of bitches think they can do as they please with us. they have lied to us long enough. He made other threatening remarks These came from him while I was talking to a Sergeant of my Company!"

Question by J.A. "What was the cause of the disturbance?"

Answer. Two men of Co. "D" of our regiment were tied up, on the boat, and there seemed to be an effort on the part of the men to cut them down!"

Question by J.A. "What was its character, merely a disturbance or a mutiny?"

Answer. Its character was mutiny I should judge, as some men of my company loaded their guns!"

. . . .

HD

[*Indianola, Texas*] October 24th 1865.

. . . .

Capt. Samuel W. Campbell. 109th U.S.C. Infantry a witness for the prosecution being duly sworn says:

. . . .

"There were two men of Co "D" of the 109th U.S.C. Infantry tied up and were being punished and some fifteen (15) or twenty (20) men of the regiment made an effort to release them, they released one. and were ordered back by the officers to the bow of the boat. About an hour after the demand was made for the release of the prisoners. I went up to the bow of the boat and heard Lieut. Schoonmaker talking to his men, and this man [*Private Peter Blinco*] was going down the hatchway and I heard him make the remark that he 'would die for his race before they should be imposed upon' That is all I know in regard to this man!"

. . . .

HD

469

[*Indianola, Texas*] October 18th 1865.

. . . .

Corporal Dick Young, Co "D" 109th U.S.C. Inf. a witness for the prosecution being duly sworn says:

. . . .

"There was an inspection on the boat and the Captain put Allen Johnson in confinement for something about his gun and the officer of the Day tried to tie him up and he said the officer of the day shouldent tie him. After they tied him up there were several men came down where they were tied and wanted to get the men loose, and orderly Green went down & said he wanted to see the Captain— he took the Capt off to one side and I dont know what he said to him. while he was talking to the Captain the prisoner [*Private Sheldon Penock*] came up and cut Allen Johnson, the prisoner who was tied, loose!"

. . . .

Corporal Martin Wethers. Co "D" 109th U.S.C. Infantry a witness for the prosecution being duly sworn says:

. . . .

Question by J.A. "State to the Court all you know in regard to that mutiny and the part taken in it by the prisoner [*Private Sheldon Penock*]?"

Answer "The prisoner came down in the hold after his gun and he got it and loaded it, and he went up on top and said he'd shoot any one who interfered with those who were going to cut loose Armsted Martley and Allen Johnson of Co "D" 109" U.S.C. Inf. who were tied up for having dirty guns!

. . . .

HD

[*Indianola, Texas*] October 2[d] 1865.

. . . .

1st Lieut John M. Schoonmaker 109th U.S.C. Infantry a witness for the prosecution being duly sworn says:

. . . .

Question by J.A. "State to the Court what language, if any, Private George Mudd Co "F" 109th U.S.C. Inf used at a disturbance among the soldiers of the 109th U.S.C. Infantry on board the Steamer Thomas A Scott on or about the 6th day of June 1865?"

Answer. "I went to the bow of the boat to talk to my Company to quell the disturbance, and while talking to my Company. George. spoke up and said. 'These officers think they

470

can do just as they have a mind to with us. now the war is over but we will show them and I think he said if we have to kill every one of them!"

Question by J.A. "Did he try to excite the disturbance in any other way than by using the language spoken of?"

Answer. "That was all, he stood quiet leaning up against the railing!"

Question by J.A. "What was the cause of the disturbance spoken of?"

Answer "There were two men of Co 'D' of our regiment being tied up and punished and there was a demand made by the 1st Sergt. of Co 'D' for their release there was a crowd gathered around the prisoners and Capt. Keene notified Col. Bates of it and he ordered them to their quarters. after that I buckled on my belt and ordered them away, the crowd went back before me. I ordered Co "F," every man, to their quarters, when I got amongst them. I also went on to state to those who were loyal what their duties were, and that called forth the remarks of the prisoner. After it was quieted down we found that one of the prisoners was released and the rope cut on the other!"

. . . .

HD

Excerpts from proceedings of general court-martial in the cases of Private Sheldon Penock et al., 109th USCI, 30 Sept.–14 Oct. 1865, MM-3244, Court-Martial Case Files, ser. 15, RG 153 [H-32]. The court found Sergeant Green and Private Blinco not guilty, but convicted the others of inciting, participating in, or failing to suppress mutiny. Five men were sentenced to confinement at hard labor during the remainder of their terms of enlistment, Private Penock receiving the additional punishment of wearing a twenty-four-pound ball and chain during the first six months of imprisonment. Four men received sentences of confinement at hard labor for terms varying from one to ten months.

190B: Former Master of an Imprisoned Kentucky Black Soldier to the President

Greensburg Ky Apl 16th 1866—

Dear Sir— Among, the thousands, of *"prayers, & petitions"*—from, as many, of the citizens, of the United States, of America, please receive, this, from one, of your *many endorsers,* in behalf, of an old *servant,* of mine, and my house, who it seems, from "disobeying some order", in the army, was sentenced, to hard labor, at Fort

Pickens, Florida, for the term, of Eighteen months. The charge, preferred against him, was the cutting loose, of a fellow soldier, who was, *tied*, by command, of an officer, full exposed, to the fire, of the enemy, near Richmond. Believing, he would most assuredly, be killed, by the enemy, this negro soldier, for whom, I petition, ventured, to cut him loose, for which cause the sentence as. above. He was among, the first, who left in Kentucky, and although, he ran away, from me, his lawful owner, yet I would do, what I can, for his release. There was, a strong affection, between master, and slave. His name, is Shelton Penick, and is in confinement, at Fort Pickens – Pensacola, Fla, where, he, has served, about, one year, of the time, for which, he, was sentenced. Should, this elicit, any notice, and should you, in your mercy, see proper, to pardon, the offence, for the remainder, of the time you will have added, *one more,* to your many, good deeds, and will much oblige, Your Petitioner –

ALS   B. W. Penick.

[*Endorsement*] War Department   Bureau of Military Justice   June 3$^\text{d}$ 1866   To the Secretary of War   For the President: –   The within named Sheldon Penock, Vo'l. Co. "D"., 109$^\text{th}$ U.S.C. Infy, was tried by a G.C.M. convened at Indianola, Texas, convicted of *"Violation of the 7th Article of War"*:[1] & sentenced, "To forfeit all pay & allowances now due or that may become due him. To be confined at hard labor during the remainder of his term of service, & to have a twenty four (24) pound ball attached to his right leg by a chain four (4) feet long during the first six (6) months of said confinement, at such place as the Commanding General may direct and to be dishonorably discharged the service at the expiration of his term of service": This sentence was confirmed & "Fort Pickens, Pensacola Harbor," designated as the place of imprisonment.

The offense of which the accused was convicted was the cutting loose prisoners tied up for a military offense on board the Stmr: "Thomas Scott" and aiding & encouraging others to mutinous conduct.

His former master petitions for the remission of his sentence, representing that it was in the belief that the soldier cut loose would be killed – (he being exposed to the fire of the enemy –) that he committed the offense & that he has served out about one year of the time for which he was sentenced.

It appears from the proceedings that the prisoner was sentenced, October 19$^\text{th}$ 1865, he has consequently been confined less than eight months. There is nothing in the record to sustain the allegation of the petitioner that the soldier who was cut loose, was exposed to the fire of the enemy. Admitting however such to be the fact, the impulse of humanity which led this soldier to the violation of the military law, may be received as a palliation of the offense.

In this view of the case, and in consideration of the severe imprisonment he has already suffered, it is respectfully recommended that the remainder of his sentence be remitted. J. Holt. Judge Advocate General

B. W. Penick to Honor. Andrew Johnson, 16 Apr. 1866, filed with A-111 1866, Letters Received, ser. 360, Colored Troops Division, RG 94 [B-209]. Other endorsements, including that of President Andrew Johnson (7 June 1866) remitting the unexecuted portion of Sheldon Penock's sentence and ordering his release from confinement.

1 "Any officer or soldier who shall begin, excite, cause, or join in, any mutiny or sedition . . . shall suffer death, or such other punishment as by a court-martial shall be inflicted." (*Revised Army Regulations,* appendix, p. 486.)

191: Imprisoned Pennsylvania Black Soldier to the Governor of Pennsylvania

Tartugas Florida January ^{the} 13: 1866

Govanor   being Plaiced In the Most Panfull Situation I will State the Case   on the 29 October One of the Members of the Regtment was tied up to A trea fore Not having a Clean Gun   he was tied ther About 1/2 Day   one of the Members of the *Co* went And Ast [Leone?] to have him taken down   the Roap broked and the Man fanted & then the Officer of th Day Tied him Up again   one of the Member of the Regtmet went to ast the Lt. Conal to Lett him Down   then the Lt Conal drew his Revolver And fired three Shots killing one man & wonded Another   then Some of the Members went out with thare Guns after the Lt Colnel Shot thoes Two men   then Some of the Members fired on Lt Colnel Shot two of his fingers off   the man That Shot the Lt Col. went Home the Next Mornig or to after they Sent the Lt Col a way with 4 Copanys   the Officr of the Day was Sent Away the Day It hapen   the Lt Col Nor The Officr of the [Day] Was Present at th courtmartial   They Just took Sutch men as they

Susptioned   All the Charges that they had against mee was that I
Said the Pole Should bee cut Down   I Belong to Co E. 3 USC
Troops from P^a   My Name is John Miller   I worked Fore Dr
Willson and Rent Elliot. A Brotherlow Son of the Govonor   I was
Drafted on th 16 Day March 1865   I hope that Yo will ond Do
ass mutch ass Yu Cane fo No Govoner Ever done more fore the
Comforat of thare then Yo did   Frome Your Most Humbel
Servent

ALS   John Miller

John Miller to Govanor, 13 Jan. 1866, P-49 1866, Letters Received, ser.
360, Colored Troops Division, RG 94 [B-274]. Pennsylvania Governor
Andrew G. Curtin forwarded the letter to the War Department. According
to testimony at the court-martial of Miller and fourteen other soldiers of
the 3rd USCI, the mutiny at Jacksonville, Florida, on October 29, 1865,
stemmed from opposition to the continued punishment of a prisoner. One
private, Jacob Plowden, reportedly disputed the authority of officers to tie
men up by the thumbs, arguing that "white soldiers were not tied up that
way, and no other colored soldiers only in our regiment." Other testimony
described Private Miller as "very fiery, walking from one part of the crowd,
to the other, talking loudly, using language calculated to lead the men to
cut down the man undergoing punishment. He said he never saw any
thing of that kind in the city of Philadelphia." A group of unarmed soldiers advanced toward the prisoner, upon which the lieutenant colonel fired
three shots at them, felling one man. Amid general cries of "one of us is
shot, get your muskets . . . shoot the son of a bitch," some soldiers ran for
their guns and fired them into the air and, according to some testimony,
also at the lieutenant colonel. Other soldiers, however, interceded and
quelled the disturbance. No testimony implicated Miller in the shooting.
The court found Miller and thirteen other men guilty of mutiny, sentencing six to death and the others to confinement at hard labor for terms
varying from two months to fifteen years. Miller's sentence was two years
at hard labor. The six executions were carried out on December 1, 1865.
(Proceedings of general court-martial in the case of Private Joseph Nathan-
iels et al., 3rd USCI, 31 Oct.–2 Nov. 1865, OO-1477, Court-Martial
Case Files, ser. 15, RG 153 [H-47]; *List of U.S. Soldiers Executed by the
United States Military Authorities during the Late War,* 5981-A-85, Letters
Received, ser. 409, Enlisted Branch, RG 94 [FF-1].)

192: **Imprisoned Mississippi Black Soldier to the Secretary of
War and the Court-Martial Charges against Him**

Fort Jefferson Fla May 28th 1866.
Sir. I most humbly beg leave to represent, that I am a private of
Co "C" 5th US Colored Artillery. That in the month of July last I

was very severely punished by the Commanding Officer of my company for a very light offense against the rules and discipline of war. That after undergoing for 2 hours the torture of being hung by the wrists I was let down and my Lieutenant threatened to shoot me because I could not move. That I was put in the guard house and charges preferred against me for disobedience of orders, and a few days afterwards set at liberty and returned to duty. Rearrested again for the same offense for which I had already been punished and after a confinement of 3 months before my trial took place, I was tried by a General Court Martial and sentenced to 2 years hard labor and to forfeit all pay and allowances due or to become due me for said period of two years.

Since nearly one year, Sir, I have been confined, and although being inocent I suffered greatly. I lived in the hopes that my release would be ordered, but I hoped in vain, and must give up all hopes of being restored to liberty before my time is up if some generous person does not take some steps in my behalf.

I therefore apply to you Honorable Sir, trusting in your Kindness and well Known generosity towards unfortunates and I most humbly beg to be released from confinement.

The charge brought against me was altogether wrong and if my witnesses had been allowed to give their testimony in Court I have no doubt but I would have been honorably acquitted. I would respectfully state that my conduct in my regiment has always been good, that I have a family to support, a mother a wife and four children who are suffering greatly on account of my imprisonment, and if with my release, you would order my full pay and allowances to be restored you would confer on me a favor for which I will be everlasting grateful.

Trusting that this letter will meet with your approbation I remain, Honorable Sir, Your most humble servt

his
John × Higgins
mark

HLSr

Vicksburg, Miss., Nov. 11, 1865.

GENERAL COURT MARTIAL ORDERS No. 12.

. . . .

Private *John Higgins,* Company C, 5th United States Colored Artillery (Heavy).

CHARGE I, "Conduct prejudicial to good order and military discipline."

Specification, "In this, that the said *John Higgins,* private of Company C, 5th United States Colored Artillery (Heavy), when

475

ordered by his commanding officer, *Walter W. King,* 1st
Lieutenant 5th United States Colored Artillery (Heavy), to get
canteens of other men and fall in with the squad and get water,
used very improper Language, to wit: "The colored soldiers are
imposed upon, and kept cooped up like dogs. I have soldiered
long enough not to be kept under guard. White soldiers are not
kept under guard, but allowed to do as they please." This in
camp at Grenada, Mississippi, on or about the 24th day of July,
1865.

CHARGE II, "Mutiny."

Specification, "In this, that said *John Higgins,* Company C, 5th
United States Colored Artillery (Heavy), hearing his Commanding
Officer, *Walter W. King,* 1st Lieutenant 5th United States Colored
Artillery (Heavy), give orders to the sergeant of the guard, used
the following language in a threatening manner: "I have done
nothing to be punished for. I will kill the first guard that lays
hands on me." This in camp at Grenada, Mississippi, on the 24th
day of July, 1865.

CHARGE III, "Inciting mutiny and sedition."

Specification, In this, that the aforesaid private *John Higgins,*
Company C, 5th United States Colored Artillery (Heavy), when in
presence of the guard, did use the following language in a
threatening manner: "God damn any nigger that will stand by
and see another tied up for nothing. It is time we took our own
part; we have been run over by our officers long enough; if we
don't take our own part, nobody else will take it for us. The
niggers are all a set of damned cowards, or they would not be
imposed upon so;" and other menacing words, tending to make
mutiny in the command. This in camp at Grenada, Mississippi,
on or about the 24th day of July, 1865.

. . . .

PD

John Higgins to Hon. E. M. Stanton, 28 May 1866, H-174 1866, Letters
Received, ser. 360, Colored Troops Division, RG 94 [B-253]; excerpt from
General Court Martial Orders No. 12, Headquarters Department of Missis-
sippi, 11 Nov. 1865, filed with Maj. Genl. Geo. H. Thomas to Adjutant
General U.S.A., 13 Apr. 1866, A-126 1866, Letters Received, ser. 360,
Colored Troops Division, RG 94 [B-210]. The court-martial found Hig-
gins guilty of all charges and specifications, except the words "I will kill"
in the second specification, and sentenced him to confinement at hard labor
for two years, with loss of all pay and allowances. In the same file is a War
Department order dated June 28, 1866, releasing Higgins from confine-
ment. On April 13, 1866, the commander of the Military Division of the
Tennessee had requested the release of several imprisoned men, including
Higgins, whose regiments had been mustered out.

193: **Imprisoned New York Black Soldier to the President on behalf of an Imprisoned Louisiana Black Soldier**

Fort Jefferson Turtugas Fla. January 24th 1864 [*1865*]

Sir   I have the honor to respectfully call your attention to a few remarks which I hope may receive your libral consideration.

I am a prisener here at fort Jefferson turtugas fla. I was sentence here for the short period of six months   I will not mention the injustice I received at the discretion of my court martrial. for I have but such short period to remain here that I deem it hardly nessessary to enter into the merits of the case. but I shall speek inbehalf of a great number of poor but patriocic colored soldirees who have become victoms to a cruel ponishment for little arror. I will attemp to state in bref the circumstences connected with the case of Jack Morris of Co. "F" 73th U.S. Colored Infy. who enterd the U.S. servise on the 27th day Sept 1862 and was erressted on the 27th day of June 1864. and sentencd. on about the 20th day October 1864 at Morganza. having served some two years allmost fathfully without even as much as being once ponish in the lease. He was trie and held to answer the charge of leveing his post   he had often been told by his officers he said not to leve his post the consequence of which he know not   he having call siveral times for the corporal of the guard but without responce   with respects to you sir It being case of necesity he thought that it would not be a killing circumstance as much as he did not go out sight and hearing of his post   he was absent but five minits and when he returned the corpral ask him where he had been   he told him after which he was poot immediately under arrest. and received a sentence of two years hard labor at this post   he is a man of famely and has not had no pay sinc he has been in servise but once and then he received but few months pay at seven dollars per month which of couse couldnot efford his famely much releaf. I am well awere that every breach of military regulations which officers or soldiers are guilty of is ponishable at the discretion of a propper court martrial but I do say and appeal to your honor that there aut to be a liberal consideration and allowance made for ignorence   the person refered to enfect most all of the colored troop recruted in this department with few excepttion are egnorent men who know nothing more then the duties of hard labor and as slaves was held for that perpose and where not permtted to even as much as hendle there masters book. much less having the privelage of reading or even allow the use of a small elementry speling book and of corse are as total egnorent of the regulations as a poor while efrican is of

477

gramer or elgebra. I appeal to your honor and most respectfuly
request in the name of him who has at his command the
destination of all nations that his sentence may be repreved. he
says he dont mind the ponishment that he is receiving here but he
would like to be where his serviseses may be of some use to the
contry and the proceeds of which may be used for the support of
his famely which is in great need of it   in this department it is
different from the most of the military post   the famely of the
(colored) soldiers perticularly the poor who are depending upon
there husband for support   the most of the inhabitince perticular
the welthey portion are so prejudice against the famely of colored
soldiers in the US servise that thay wont even give them
employment for no prise to sustain if posible the old hipocrittical
idea that free colored people wont work and of cours the soldiers
families have to suffer   in other states infact in most of the
northern states there is releaf fonds but here there is none, and if
the only support are taken away by death or any other cause thay
must suffer and that severely. for I have been and eye witness to a
grate many cases not only deprved of there homes on the a/sc^t
[*account*] of little means to pay there house rent but baught at
abased by passes by insulting words such as (now you see what the
yenkees will do for you had you not better stay with your
masters.) the soldier seeing his famely subject to such crual
ponishment and ill treetment does feel some what discuraged when
he is ill treeted by thoes who is his only relience is for justice and
his present existence for I have never have saw a more solom lot a
priseners then I saw here from like circumstances   (all thay have
to say that the yankes treat me more woser then the rabs)   for my
part I cant complane   I have had evry respect shown me since I
have been in the servise with but few exceptions   I even was
allowed while under arrest as a freehold cittizon of the state of
New York to cast my vote on a ritten form for that perpose for
the first time for the candidate of my choise and as we hale the
election of the fondor of the proclamation of emencipation we as
poor priseners with undanted patriocism to the cause of our contry
look foward towards washing[*ton*] to here something in behalf of
poor priseners   we know that your four years of administration has
been as berdensome as it has victorious and no dought you have
but lettle time to listen to the grate many pleas that comes
through such scorce   we do feal as union soldiers that we may ask
with that positive assureanc that we will be herd   all we can say
that we are sory that we have become victoms to a millitary crime
and do senserely repent and ask to be forgiven   we cant do no
more   where we to remain here 5 years we should be know less

sory then we are know. Very respectfully your humble & obt
servt

ALS   Samuel Roosa

[*Endorsement*] War Department, Bureau of Military Justice,
February 28, 1865. Respectfully returned to the President.

The enclosed communication of Samuel Roosa, Private Co C,
20th U.S.C.T. a prisoner at Fort Jefferson Fla. contains an appeal
for clemency in the case of a fellow prisoner, Jack Morris, Private
Co F. 13th [73rd] U.S.C.T. based upon the idea that special
leniency should be exercised in punishment inflicted upon Colored
recruits from Southern States, on account of their ignorance, and
the fact that their families are entirely dependent upon them for
support; the local authorities providing no relief, and the citizens
refusing to employ them because their husbands are in, the Union
Army. The particular plea in the case of Morris is that his offence
was of a trivial character, having left his post as sentinel, for a
necessary purpose, after vainly attempting to call the Corporal of
the guard to his relief.

Morris was tried for "stealing" and "deserting his post."

He pleaded "Guilty" to the first offence, and was clearly proven
to be guilty of the second, having left his Post for the purpose of
stealing from the Sutlers tent, over which he was placed as guard.

He was sentenced to two years confinement, with forfeiture of
pay during that time—a sentence which was warranted by the
circumstances, and should be fully executed. J. Holt. Judge Adv
General.

Samuel Roosa to Abraham Lincoln, 24 Jan. 1864 [1865], filed with P-133
1865, Letters Received, ser. 360, Colored Troops Division, RG 94 [B-
181]. Other endorsements. In the same file is a copy of the court-martial
proceedings in the case of Private Jack Morris, 73rd USCI. Morris pleaded
"guilty" to stealing one can of preserved fruit from the sutler's tent. Although Morris pleaded "not guilty" to desertion of his post, the Corporal
of the Guard testified that he found Morris absent from his assigned guard
duty.

PART 3

Black Military Life: On Duty

Duties: "Instead of the Musket it is the Spad and the Wheelbarrow and the Axe"

THE ENLISTMENT of blacks into the Union army closed one debate only to open another. The strongest white proponents of black enlistment, including Governor John A. Andrew, Generals David Hunter, Benjamin F. Butler, and Rufus Saxton, and Senator James H. Lane, urged black enlistment not merely to defeat the Confederacy but also to demonstrate black manhood and lay the basis for emancipation. Black abolitionists like Frederick Douglass and black recruiting agents like Martin R. Delany, Henry M. Turner, and John M. Langston similarly made this argument central to their appeal for volunteers in Northern black communities. While they received increasing support from men who cared nothing for black freedom or racial equality, the abolitionists who sponsored black enlistment never lost sight of their original goal. John A. Andrew, for example, demanded that the 54th Massachusetts be sent to an active theater where they could participate in "operations of a brilliant sort," and he maneuvered to have the regiment placed in David Hunter's lowcountry command. When Secretary of War Edwin M. Stanton threatened to send the Massachusetts regiment to Louisiana under General Nathaniel P. Banks, Andrew bombarded the Secretary with telegrams until he dropped the plan. Eventually, the 54th and 55th Massachusetts served with distinction along the south Atlantic coast.[1]

At first few federal policy makers shared Andrew's concerns; instead, most took a narrow view of the role that black soldiers would play in putting down the rebellion. Doubting the military prowess of "African" people, especially when confronted by their former masters, they planned to employ newly enlisted black soldiers at menial labor or in relief of white troops holding stationary positions far from the line of battle. Black enlistment would increase the number of soldiers who might be sent against the rebels, but fighting the war would remain the white man's business. This policy

[1] Major Genl. J. G. Foster to Hon. Edwin M. Stanton, 5 May 1863, #2371 1863, Letters Received Irregular, RG 107 [L-126] (see *Freedom,* ser. 2: doc. 44); Gov. John A. Andrew to Hon. E. M. Stanton, 16 May 1863, Telegrams Collected by the Office of the Secretary of War (Bound), RG 107 [L-202].

nicely suited white racial preconceptions; indeed, it confirmed the role whites assigned to blacks in antebellum society, North and South. It also reflected the deep-seated, if self-serving, belief that blacks could better withstand the rigors of labor under the hot tropical sun. Black enlistment into the Union army offered no threat to the racial ideals of most federal officials.

While the partisans of black soldiers as fighters and of black soldiers as laborers staked out their positions along the forbidding terrain of American racial ideology, the course of the war intertwined these two distinct positions in peculiar and unexpected ways. Some racist officers wanted black soldiers confined to fatigue duties, but others, finding that a black soldier could stop a bullet as well as a white one, cheerfully sent black troops into battle. At the same time, some abolitionists blanched at battle carnage and tempered their insistence that black soldiers be sent into the thick of battle; others viewed sacrifice even in the face of hopeless odds as the quickest and surest path to acceptance and craved opportunities to lead the attack. But more important, as the war dragged on and blacks became a larger proportion of the federal force, the overarching considerations of manpower utilization dictated the employment of black troops. Racial ideology continued to influence decisions, but military necessity both created and limited alternatives. How black soldiers served came to depend more on the circumstances of the Union army than on the views of its commanders. In a sense, the war made the best generals into racial pragmatists, regardless of their views on the capabilities of blacks.

Preeminent among these pragmatic generals was Adjutant General Lorenzo Thomas, whom Stanton dispatched to the Mississippi Valley in the spring of 1863 with orders to recruit black troops and provide for contrabands. Enjoying a long association with prominent Southern planters and sharing unreservedly their beliefs about black people, Thomas nonetheless considered himself first a professional soldier. Racial presuppositions flavored Thomas's policy, but he subordinated them, in considerable measure, to the larger military strategy of lining the Mississippi River with a population loyal to the Union. The extension of Union lines and the transformation of the rebellion into a war of attrition occurred at just the moment blacks first entered the service in large numbers. That, more than racial philosophy, governed Thomas's decision to enlist blacks into artillery and infantry units and employ them in garrisoning Mississippi River fortifications, railroads, Union-controlled plantations, and contraband camps. From Thomas's point of view, the employment of raw black recruits in garrison duty not only freed seasoned veterans for action against the enemy but also protected contrabands, Northern lessees, and Southern unionists from Confederate guerrillas. As an added dividend, it encouraged black recruitment by allowing former slaves to remain near their families as plantation and contraband camp guards.[2] While Thomas's decision appeared to favor those who saw black soldiers as laborers in blue uniforms, Thomas recruited blacks to fight as well as to dig. He refused requests to disperse black soldiers among white regiments as permanent laboring units. And he continued to organize recruits into infantry, artillery, or even cavalry regiments as strategic needs demanded.

Despite its intent, Thomas's policy encouraged some Union commanders to substitute black soldiers for whites in fatigue details. In many places black soldiers found themselves doing little but constructing fortifications, digging trenches, and loading and unloading wagons and ships. White officers commonly assigned them the most loathsome duties such as cleaning latrines and ship bunkers, and then cursed them for doing the odious work. Even the officers of engineer regiments, charged with building fortifications and the like, found extraordinary the amount of labor assigned to black units. In other areas outside Thomas's immediate control, black soldiers similarly suffered excessive assignment to fatigue duties. In the South Carolina Sea Islands, black soldiers were even ordered to prepare and police the camp of a white regiment. Protests from the abolitionist officers of Edward A. Wild's "African Brigade," then stationed in the lowcountry, ended that particular practice but not the regular assignment of blacks to menial duties.

Unremitting labor took its toll on black soldiers. It wore out their clothes, lowered their morale, and broke their health. It allowed them little time for drill or training in the martial arts. Their consequent lack of military bearing and their bedraggled, ragamuffin appearance only confirmed the belief that blacks could not be sent into armed combat. An inspection report of the black troops stationed in the Sea Islands in December 1863 concluded that some black units continued to bear a disproportionate share of the drudgery despite a direct order by the department commander, but it nonetheless justified the practice on grounds that black soldiers remained "inferior in drill and discipline." Such circular reasoning locked blacks into the role of military menials: they could not fight because excessive fatigue duty prevented them from drilling, and because their lack of proper training rendered them unsuitable for battle, they might as well keep on digging.

Protests continued. General Daniel Ullmann, recruiting black soldiers in the Department of the Gulf, put the question directly to Senator Henry Wilson, chairman of the Senate Military Affairs Committee: are these men to be laborers or soldiers? Later he addressed Adjutant General Thomas in the same vein. Black soldiers

[2] For a full discussion of this question, see *Freedom*, ser. 1.

took their complaints directly to the President and, when given the opportunity, backed their protest with clear evidence of their military abilities. After the battles of Fort Wagner and Port Hudson in early summer 1863, there could be little justification for assigning blacks the role of the drudge.[3] In June 1864, with Union manpower needs increasing, Thomas issued Order No. 21 directing an equitable division of fatigue labor between white and black soldiers and urging military commanders to bring black soldiers to the highest degree of military preparedness.

Patterns established early in the war and supported by centuries of white domination did not change easily. In August 1864, when Colonel Edward N. Hollowell, commander of the 54th Massachusetts, assigned black clerks to the Ordnance Department, the officer in charge returned them with the admonition that black soldiers would be accepted only as cooks and laborers. Although growing numbers of black troops saw combat during the last year of the war, others continued to shoulder a shovel. "Instead of the Musket it is the Spad and the Wheelbarrow and the Axe," one black soldier bitterly observed.

Events at the post of Morganzia, Louisiana, during the summer of 1864 demonstrate the grim consequences of the earlier discriminatory policy. In July 1864, soon after Thomas issued Order No. 21, the officers of several black regiments stationed at Morganzia protested the assignment of their troops exclusively to fatigue duty, noting that the white soldiers were rarely so engaged. The post commander at first denied the accusation. Later he acknowledged the truth of the complaint, but denied knowledge of Thomas's order. Finally, after additional protests, he acknowledged both the abuses and Thomas's order, but argued that nothing could be done to remedy the situation. Through the steaming summer months, black soldiers continued to toil on the fortifications with the apparent approval of General Nathaniel P. Banks, commander of the Department of the Gulf, and General Edward R. S. Canby, commander of the Division of West Mississippi. The black units had no time for drill, so it mattered little that they were issued worthless arms or that they were excluded from military exercises, including routine weekly inspections. Among whites, only military prisoners wearing ball and chain followed a similar regimen, a comparison which galled and demoralized black soldiers and their officers. The discriminatory duties assigned black regiments stationed at Morganzia were also extended to other black units who moved into the area, suggesting endemic racism within the post command. By the end of the summer, continuous labor had left its mark, especially

[3] See *Freedom,* ser. 2: doc. 212a–b.

among border-state soldiers who had little resistance to lowland diseases. A medical board convened in October 1864 found that more than a third of three Missouri black regiments – the 62nd, 65th, and 67th U.S. Colored Infantry – had perished since enlistment, mostly from various undiagnosed diseases. The condition of those remaining was none too good. The board recommended that nearly 200 soldiers be discharged for medical reasons. Soon thereafter, the appointment of General Daniel Ullmann as post commander improved conditions somewhat. He moderated "heavy labor, in mud and water," corrected unsanitary conditions, and revised the soldiers' diet. But by then the damage was done.

The pattern of discrimination evident in the employment of black troops at Morganzia represented the extreme at which white racism could combine with military necessity in an area where Union lines were relatively secure and little fighting remained to be done. Throughout the Union command, however, even after blacks had proven themselves in battle and federal officials had certified their equal status within the army, some field officers could not shake their preconception that black soldiers might better dig than fight. Black soldiers and their officers protested, but remedies came slowly and imperfectly, leaving many broken both in spirit and in body.[4]

[4] As late as mid-June 1865, company commanders of the 15th USCI, stationed at Nashville, protested the excessive fatigue duty assigned to their men. (Capt. Cyrus N. Gray et al. to Lieut. F. M. Whitelaw, 13 June 1865, Letters Received, 15th USCI, Regimental Books & Papers USCT, RG 94 [G-294].

194: **Adjutant General of the Army to the Secretary of War**

Cairo Illinois, April 1 1863

Sir – On the 30th ultimo I made an inspection of that class of population known as contrabands, and respectfully make the following report.

The present numbers in the barracks provided for them are 281 males & 545 females 704 children total 1530, and are in charge of Chaplain J B. Rogers 14th Regiment Wisconsin Volunteers. The camp was organized in the month of August 1862, and Mr Rogers took charge of them the 27th. of September following. He appears to be a humane man, gives his personal attention to them and sees to their wants. The barracks are indifferent and too limited in capacity, consequently the blacks are too much crowded. The sickness has been great and very many have died. The prevalent diseases are Pneumonia, measles and small pox. There are three hospitals, one for males one for females and

one pest house. Whole number in them 145, in pest house
46. Besides these are many sick in their quarters   They are
attended by two physicians and a steward.

Clothing, except a few blankets, have been furnished by friends
at the north, chiefly by the society of Friends. The adults receive
full rations from the Subsistence Department, corn meal in lieu of
flour when possible and rye instead of coffee. children acending to
age draw one half and one forth rations. Fuel is cut by themselves
and drawn by the public teams.

A school was established for the children whole number
receiving instruction 400, average attendance 90. They were
taught gratuitously by Mr Job Hadly wife and niece for eleven
weeks, now taught by a sprightly young contraband who can read
and write very well. The improvement of the children is reported
to have been very satisfactory— Besides the foregoing the
Quartermaster employs 133 at $10 per month and one ration,
thereby causing quite a saving to the Government, as white labor
costs $30 per month— a few are employed in other Departments
of the Government, and some find work in private families in the
city.

The chaplain has gained the confidence of these people, and
when this is attained they can very readily be moulded to any
useful purpose. Mr Rogers states that of the males under his
charge capable of bearing arms he could raise a company of about
fifty. He has already organized some as a guard, who make
vigilant and most obedient sentinels. A stranger perhaps could not
do this. Mr Rogers is desirous of raising a Regiment, but I doubt
whether his health would enable him to take and keep the field.

This place is not at all suited for these people, their being no
field for their employment; and they [would] not be of much or
any expence if placed in situations where they could cultivate the
ground. An order has just been received to transfer them to Island
N° 10, an excellent measure, for there they can, at little expense,
cultivate corn and other articles. Some kind of shelter will have to
be provided, and some fencing, as I learn the timber has been cut
from the Island and used for military purposes.

In the last few days I have thought much of the best manner in
which to take charge of and usefully employ, these descendants of
Ham, for their own good and for the benefit of the government
which has declared them free. It will not answer to collect them
in large bodies, employ only what our armies require for laborers
and teamsters, and let the rest of the men with the women and
children look to the Quartermaster and Commissary of Subsistence
for clothing and food; nor will it do to send them in numbers into
the free states, for the prejudices of the people of those states are

against such a measure, and some of the states have enacted laws against the reception of free negroes! Such prejudice is particularly the case with those of Irish and German descent. It would be unwise to place them in the border slave states (except such as might be necessary for military purposes) as they might again, to some extent, be reduced to slavery, or kidnapped and carried as slaves far beyond our lines. Therefore these people must, in great measure, continue in the Southern States now in rebellion, and in rear of our lines as our armies advance until a new home beyond our boundaries can be found; and they should be put in positions to make their own living   The men should be employed with our armies as laborers and teamsters, and those who could be induced to do so, or conscripted if necessary, be mustered as soldiers, and the others with the women and children placed on the abandoned plantations to till the ground. The negro Regiments could give protection to these plantations, and also operate effectively against the guerillas. This would be particularly advantageous on the Mississippi River, as the negroes, being acquainted with the peculiar country lining its banks, would know when to act effectively. They could also garrison positions, and thus additional regiments could be sent to the front. These negroes, knowing where cotton is secreted, should be encouraged to bring it to the banks of the river, where it could be taken possession of by a government agent, placed in the transports returning empty and delivered at St Louis or some place on the Ohio river for sale on government account. If the plan meets your views and those of the President, a competent and faithful agent should be appointed and go to work vigorously as the spring will rapidly open. Competent men must also be selected as overseers. I confess that this is a difficult subject to handle, and I offer the foregoing views with diffidence. Still under your instructions I feel bound to offer them. I have the honor to be Very Respcy Your obt servt

L Thomas

P.S. I understand that the abandoned plantations are generally amply provided with farming implements, &c.

ALcS

Adj't. Genl. L. Thomas to Honble. Edwin M. Stanton, 1 Apr. 1863, L. Thomas Letters & Orders, Generals' Papers & Books, ser. 159, RG 94 [V-124].

195: Adjutant General of the Army to a Brigade Commander

Memphis Tenn. May 19th 1863.

Sir   I have received your letter of yesterdays date, but cannot approve of your plan of attaching a company of blacks to each Regiment of your brigade for fatigue duty. My instructions are to arm them as soldiers and organize them into Regiments and Brigades. I have stated to General Hurlbut and other commanders that I will authorize as many Regiments in the 16th Army Corps as can be organized in a reasonable time, the roster complete for each to be furnished to me. I am Sir Very Respectfully Your obd^t ser^t

HLcS   L Thomas

Adjutant General L. Thomas to Col. Wm. W. Sanford, 19 May 1863, L. Thomas Letters & Orders, Generals' Papers & Books, ser. 159, RG 94 [V-18].

196: Commander of U.S. Forces at Hilton Head, South Carolina, to the Headquarters of the Department of the South

Hilton Head S.C. May 19th 63

Colonel   I would respectfully ask that the eight companies of the 6th Conn Vols, now on Folly Island S.C., may be ordered back to this Post & if it be necessary, that you will detail another Regiment to take their place. I would also request that the extra duty men of the 6th Conn Vols & 8th Maine Vols now at Beaufort S.C. in the Quartermasters depts & Genl Hospitals may be relieved in order to join their respective commands at this Post, in consequence of the heavy details which have to be made from the Regiments of this Post, to do the necessary work and in view of the approaching hot weather I would most respectfully & earnestly request that the details be made from the Colored Troops, by so doing I am fully convinced that It will add much to the health & General efficiency of the command. If this request is granted I will guarantee that no abuse of any kind shall occur, or if any should occur that the offenders shall be immediately punished, and for the second offense in the same Regiment or Detachment, that Regiment or detchmt shall be made to do all shuch work for a certain length of time. By adopting such rules I am sure we shall have no trouble, & that the troops may be kept in good

condition. I have the honor to be Colonel Most respectfully Your
obt servant

HLc   {*John S. Chatfield*}

Colonel {John S. Chatfield} to Lt. Col. Chas. G. Halpine, 19 May 1863,
vol. 95/189 DS, pp. 108–9, Letters Sent, ser. 548, Post of Hilton Head,
RG 393 Pt. 4 [C-1634].

197: Commander of the District of Southeast Missouri to the Commander of the Department of the Missouri

Pilot Knob, Mo., July 23^{d} *1863.*

General– If Col Guylee's Regiment of "American citizens of
African descent" are to be organized in Missouri I would suggest
they be sent down *here* for that purpose– I could use them to
good advantage on the fortifications, and in the fatigue department
at this Post– There is quite a squad of recruits here for that Reg^{t}
and it would seem to me to be *best* that the whole party should be
away from St. Louis, and *where* they can apply themselves to
something aside from *rations*– I am Genl Very Respectfully Your
Ob^{t} Servant

ALS   Clinton B. Fisk

Brig. Genl. Clinton B. Fisk to Maj. General J. M. Schofield, 23 July
1863, Letters Received, 56th USCI, Regimental Books & Papers USCT,
RG 94 [G-203].

198A: Officer in a South Carolina Black Regiment to the Regimental Commander

Seabrook S.C. August 3rd 1863

Colonel, I have the honor to acknowledge the receipt of statement
made by Mr John Hays in relation to the manner in which the
very ardous fatigue duty has been performed by the Detachment of
the 3rd S.C. Infantry stationed at this point.

By reference to morning reports you will find I have present and
for duty 89 Men, of this number I have been forced to detail each
day 12 men for guard duty–the old and new Guard making 24

besides non commissioned officers each day, leaving for duty 65 Men. I will not go back many days to show how much duty these men have performed, the three past days will serve as sample of each days work since I have been in command. Friday morning furnished 30 Men; Friday night furnished 30 Men; Saturday Morning furnished 30 Men Saturday Night furnished 30 Men; Sunday Morning furnished 30 Men; Hours 7 A.M to 12 M; 1 P.M to 6 P.M. You will observe that the men have been on duty *over* 3 times within the same number of days. Beside these regular details I have furnished men for other duty drawing sand; loading wood; water and pumping out vessels assisting the crews of the vessel. The duty performed is of the hardest kind, in some instances triming the *"bunkers"* on board vessels. My men are nearly used up. I have quite a number sick, at times I have had to put the sick on duty in order to make out the number called for.

Several complaints have been made to me of the manner in which Mr Hays treats the men while on duty. that of calling them *Black sons of bitches* threatening to shoot them has been the pith of his orders while on duty.

I have examined into the charges made against Lieutenant Reed and find them slightly exaggerated. Mr Hays ordered him to take off the *guard* and march them down for duty. Upon my return in the afternoon I asked Mr Degan if a night detail was wanted, and he answered me that he did not know, that Mr Hays would send up if one was required, none was ordered. I am confident that the charges against Lieut Reed are made against him more from personal feeling than from any neglect of public duty. Lieut Reed disclaims every and any intention of speaking disrespectfully of Col Ellwell. He has the highest opinion of him as a military man & gentleman.

I could wish that I had more explicit orders in relation to the duty to be performed here whether I am to perform other duties than the coaling of ships

The labor is so ardous and constant that it will be impossible to perform it much longer with the force at present under my command. My men are giving out   Respectfully Your Most Ob^t Servt

ALS   Edmund R Fowler

Capt. Edmund R. Fowler to Lieut. Col. A. G. Bennett, 3 Aug. 1863, Letters Received, 21st USCI, Regimental Books & Papers USCT, RG 94 [G-79]. Endorsement. Hays's statement is not filed with Fowler's report.

198B: Commander of a North Carolina Black Regiment to the Commander of a Black Brigade

Folly Island [*S.C.*] Sept. 13th 1863.

General   It is reported to me on good authority that men of my command ordered to Morris Island on fatigue duty, are put to work laying out and policing camps of white soldiers on that Island. I am informed that to day a detachment of 60 men properly officered, having been ordered to report to a Major Butts of some New York Regiment were set to work levelling ground for the Regimental Camp, digging wells &c pitching tents and the like.

Since the commencement of the war I have never before known such duty imposed upon any Regiment; it being (unless I am greatly in error) the custom of New York and other Regiments to pitch their own tents and lay out their own camps a privilege, by the way, which my men have had little time to enjoy by reason of constant detail on fatigue.

As you are aware — the fatigue duty of my regiment has been incessant and trying — so that my sick list has increased from 4 or 5 to nearly 200 in a little over one month; and I respectfully protest against the imposition of labors which by no principle of custom or right devolve upon my command. I respectfully protest against this particular imposition because of its injurious influence upon the men in another respect.

They have been slaves and are just learning to be men   It is a draw-back that they are regarded as, and called "d- - -d Niggers" by so-called "gentleman" in uniform of U.S. Officers, but when they are set to menial work doing for white regiments what those Regiments are entitled to do for themselves, it simply throws them back where they were before and reduces them to the position of slaves again.

I therefore request that you will entertain this my protest; and, if you find no objection to the matter or manner of the same, will forward it through the proper Channel to the General Commanding the Department —   If these men do their duty in the trenches, and in the field, I do not believe that he will make them hewers of wood and drawers of water for those who do no more. I am General Very Respectfully Yours

HLcSr   James C. Beecher

[*Endorsement*]   H'd Qr's African Brigade   Folly Island   Sept. 14. 1863   approved and respectfully forwarded.

I have given instructions that the officers of fatigue details from my command shall disregard such orders hereafter.

But I forward the complaint trusting that *all* such *abuses* will in future be authoritatively corrected from Hd. Qrs   Sgd   Edwd A. Wild   Brig Genl. Col^d Vol's

[*Endorsement*]   Hd Qrs Folly Island Sept. 15th 1863   This protest is forwarded notwithstanding it is somewhat wanting in proper respect due to his superior in its manner and style — on account of the important military principle which it asserts —   If it be true that the troops are engaged in preparing camping grounds for others their being so employed can not but exercise an unfavorable influence with the minds both of the white and black troops.   If possible I deem it desirable that opportunities be given to drill and instruct the colored troops in their duties as soldiers.   I am aware that hitherto the amount of fatigue imposed upon this command and has prevented this being done   I hope however that in the future a fair opportunity may be givein for instructions"   sgd   I Vogdes   Brig Gen Comdg

Col. James C. Beecher to Brig. Genl. Edward A. Wild, 13 Sept. 1863, Letters Received, 35th USCI, Regimental Books & Papers USCT, RG 94 [G-182]. On September 17, 1863, General Quincy A. Gillmore, commander of the Department of the South, prohibited the use of black soldiers "to prepare camps and perform menial duties for white troops." (General Orders, No. 77, Department of the South, Headquarters in the Field, 17 Sept. 1863, Orders & Circulars, ser. 44, RG 94 [DD-2].) A month later, Gillmore noted that the officers of his command continued to impose "improper labors upon colored troops." He reiterated the importance of General Orders No. 77 and reminded his command that "Colored troops will not be required to perform any labor which is not shared by the white troops, but will receive in all respects the same treatment, and be allowed the same opportunities for drill and instruction." (General Orders No. 105, Department of the South, Headquarters in the Field, 25 Nov. 1863, S-1573 1863, Letters Received, ser. 12, RG 94 [K-103].)

198C: Special Inspector to the Adjutant General's Office

Washington D.C.   Dec 20th 1863.
Colonel.   In compliance with orders from Adj. Genl's office dated Nov 25th 1863, I left New York for Hilton Head S.C. on the steamer of the 29th, arrived at Hilton Head on the 3rd of Dec. and returned to New York on the steamer of the 15th.

I enquired carefully into the alleged discrimination made

between the white and colored troops in the Dept. of the South, and have the honor to report, that, at the time of my visit, no material distinction was made, both were employed with some slight exceptions, on guard, picket and fatigue duty in proportion to their numbers.

I found great dissatisfaction existing among the officers of all the colored regiments with the exception of the 1st S.C. Vols. in Genl Saxton's command, on account of the undue proportion of fatigue duty required of the colored troops during the past campaign. This dissatisfaction was not shared by Col. Littlefield com^{dg} the colored brigade in Genl Vogdes division, nor by Col Montgomery com^{dg} the colored brigade in Genl Terry's division. They considered the interests of the service necessitated the discrimination.

The reasons given for this discrimination at the Headq^{rs} of the two divisions were as follows:

1st That during the months of August and September, the sickness among the white troops amounted to upwards of 30 per cent, being one third greater than the sickness among the colored troops

2nd That the colored troops being inferior in drill and discipline were assigned, during the operations against Fort Wagner an inferior position.

3rd That the different staff officers at Dept Headqrs were in the habit of applying for details of colored troops preferring them for their industry and docility. Genl Gillmore stated that out of 23.500 days work done under superintendence of Col. Serrell of the N.Y. Eng. reg^t 9.500 had been done by the colored troops.

The 3rd S.C. Vols. at Hilton Head had until within a few weeks, been employed simply as labourers; they were awkward in the use of their arms, not well equipped and provided with tents unfit for use. The regiment is now in camp being drilled.

The 1st S.C. Vols. at Beaufort is in every respect a model regiment; in drill, discipline and soldier like appearance equal to the best white reg^{ts}.

The only fatigue duty with the exception of the repairs to the fortifications of Morris Isl^d, now being performed in Charleston Harbour are the works on Long Isl^d, carried on by a permanent detail of 125 colored soldiers from Genl Vogdes division.

At the time of my visit the colored troops were suffering more from sickness than the white, the proportion being 12 per cent of the former to 8 per cent of the latter. The white troops suffer from fever and dysentery in the summer, the colored from lung diseases in the winter. The Northern colored reg^{ts} suffer from both.

I saw the colored troops constantly drilled, they were well armed, equipped and provided with camp equipage with the exception of the 3rd S.C. I have the honor to be Very respectfully Your ob^t serv^t

ALS   R. T. Auchmuty

Capt. R. T. Auchmuty to Col. E. D. Townsend, 20 Dec. 1863, A-31 1863, Letters Received Irregular, RG 107 [L-93].

199: Commander of a Louisiana Black Division to the Chairman of the Senate Committee on Military Affairs

Port Hudson [*La.*], Dec. 4. 1863

My dear General; I have long had it in view to write to you, as the Head of the Military Committee of the Senate, on a subject of grave importance, namely, the organization of colored troops. You are well acquainted with my status in the premises.

I have had every opportunity, during the last seven months to examine this policy in all its bearings.

The first point to settle is whether it be intended to make these men soldiers or mere laborers – if the latter, the mode pursued is the right one, and I have nothing more to say. If the former – then there are some vital changes to be made. I fear that many high officials, outside of Washington, have no other intention than that these men shall be used as diggers and drudges. Now, I am well satisfied, from my 7 months intercourse with them that, with just treatment, they can be made soldiers of as high an average as any in the world. Their qualifications in most respects are equal to any and in one, superior, to wit, – their habit of subordination.

All that is necessary is to give them a fair chance, *which has not been done.* Since I have been in command, such has been the amount of fatigue work thrust upon the organization, that, it has been with the utmost difficulty, that any time could be set aside for drill. Months have passed, at times, without the possibility of any drill at all. The amount of actual labor performed by these men has been enormous. Much of it was done by them in the trenches, during the siege of this place, whilst more exposed to the severe fire of the enemy than any other of our troops. They

496

discharged their duties with cheerfulness alacrity and marked courage.

Then again, I have been forced to put in their hands arms almost entirely unserviceable, and, in other respects, their equipments have been of the poorest kind. But there is another injustice done to these men, which they appreciate as well and feel as keenly as any body. It is a mistake to think that these poor fellows do not understand these matters *just as well as we do*. They are all the constant subject of conversation among them. The point is this, while other soldiers are fed, clothed, have superior arms, and are paid $13 per month, and the non-commissioned officers receive respectively $17. & $20., they are fed, have unserviceable arms and receive $10. per month, from which is deducted $3 for clothing, and no addition whatever for noncommissioned officers, and have no clothing allowance.

Now, General, I assure you that these poor fellows, with all their warm enthusiastic patriotism, and it is even greater than that of most other troops, are deeply sensible to this gross injustice.

It breaks down their "morale" to an extent which I who command and come into constant contact with them daily deplore. Instead of thus lowering their "morale" it should be our effort, by just treatment in every respect, to rouse their pride and establish among them a high standard.

I have succeeded thus far in soothing them by representing that I have an abiding conviction that Congress will early in its next session do them justice. I think that it would be sufficient to pass a Bill giving the Privates $10. per month, with clothing allowance of other troops, and the noncommissioned officers the same pay as whites.

500 Citizens of New Orleans, free, most of them well educated, offered to enlist under my command on the above terms. The service suffers greatly, because I could not accept the offer, as it would have enabled me to remedy one of the chief difficulties with which we have to contend—namely, the procuring of non-commissioned officers, who can read and write.

There is one other notion that must be eradicated—i.e., that *anybody* can command negro troops. So far from this—they require a superior grade of officers, though I well know that those prophets, who declare that negroes never will make soldiers, are striving to force their prophecies to work out their own fulfilment, by appointing ignoramuses and boors to be officers over men, who are as keensighted as any to notice the short comings of those placed over them. Men have been made Field Officers in this section, who are not fit to be non commissioned Officers. Men so

497

ignorant that they cannot write three consecutive sentences without violating orthography and syntax.

My own judgement is, that in the great future before us we shall have to draw largely from this element for soldiers, and the sooner we set about it in earnest the better. This will be best accomplished by establishing the better Regiments on the same footing and permanence as the Regular Army – if not actually a part of it. The thorough discipline of that branch of the service is needed in this organization, both for officers and men.

I desire to assure you in conclusion, General, that my faith in this movement grows stronger day by day.

The obstacles which have opposed its progress in the South West are altogether exceptional and have no necessary connection with it. The changes above suggested, and a strong hand in the War Departmt, will sweep them away like cobwebs. Notwithstanding the persistant hostility, open and covert, which strove to defeat my mission here as a Pioneer, the progress made in the right direction is emminently encouraging, and I feel strong to carry it out to a successful issue, if the right help shall come from Washington.

I shall be glad if you will submit this letter to the Honorable, the Secretary of War. I am, My dear General, your very faithful friend and obedient servant

HLS   Daniel Ullmann

Brigadier General Daniel Ullmann to Honorable Henry Wilson, 4 Dec. 1863, U-3 1868, Letters Received, ser. 360, Colored Troops Division, RG 94 [B-470]. Ullmann spoke from experience. On June 30, 1863, he had reported to Adjutant General Lorenzo Thomas that his troops had been employed "since the first days of June in 'digging.' They have been of great service in this respect – the officers and men often passing twenty consecutive hours in the trenches." (Brig. General Daniel Ullmann to Adjutant General U.S.A., 30 June 1863, U-5 1863, Letters Received, ser. 360, Colored Troops Division, RG 94 [B-467].) Ullmann continued to petition against the use of black soldiers merely as military laborers, and he begged the opportunity to lead them in battle: "With the strong prejudice which exists, in high places, in this Department, against the employment of this class of troops, they will *never,* under present auspices, have an equal and fair chance to show themselves *as soldiers.*" (Brig. General Daniel Ullmann to Brigadier General L. Thomas, 16 Apr. 1864, U-1 1864, Letters Received by Adjutant General L. Thomas, ser. 363, Colored Troops Division, RG 94 [V-85].)

200: Commander of a Tennessee Black Regiment to the Commissioner for the Organization of Black Troops in Middle and East Tennessee

Gallatin Tenn. 6 Dec 1863.

Captain I feel so great an interest in the success of the Regt which I have the honor to command and of the entire Corps D'Afrique that I can not refrain from making another effort to secure the return of the 14" Reg. to this point. I send you a communication which I desire to be forwarded to Maj. Gen[l] Thomas, asking that the Regiment be ordered back to Gallatin and I would most earnestly ask that Maj Stearns be urged to use his influence with Sec. of War, to secure this permit. The raising of Negro Regiments in this Dept is an experiment as yet and its success depends largely upon the impression made upon the public mind, by those regiments now formed and organizing, during the present winter. The public mind in the army and out of it is now interested. During my recent visit to Chattanooga, Gen[ls] Carlin, Reynolds, and Thomas besides numerous Colonels, and many soldiers inquired of me with interest what progress was being made in raising Col[d] Troops – and what promise they give of becoming good soldiers. Gen[l] Carlin said he would love to see them tried along with other soldiers when *their failure* would not entail defeat. Maj Gen[l] Thomas expressed the opinion that "they will fight well behind fortifications." was not *sure* that they would fight in the field. The entire Army – and the county at large is watching the course of Col[d] Regiments ready to condemn or applaud. It behooves the friends of this movement to secure a favorable decision from the great tribunal public opinion. This can not be done by making laborers of these troops. The best of soldiers must need work and commanders of negro regiments are willing that the troops under their command shall do their part in all army labor, but while they will cheerfully perform any labor incident to camp life – or required by the exigencies of the time, they feel that it is degrading to single out Col[d] Troops for fatigue duty while white troops stand idly by. Such treatment savors too much of the old regime, and if persisted in will utterly ruin the prospect of the work of making soldiers here of black men. Negroes will not enlist for this purpose neither will efficient officers enter the service. The class of men who are willing to take hold with all their energies to drill and discipline a body of soldiers will not for any consideration consent to become overseers for black laborers. Rather would they carry their rifles in the ranks of fighting men.

499

The Government professes to know no distinction among its soldiers arising from color, and it demands of our enemies that they shall make no distinction. It persistently refuses to exchange until the so-called Confederate Government consents to give up man for man. But if the Government allows its own Genls to make a wide distinction in favor of white soldiers, how can it expect our enemies to do any better?

The friends of Col^d Soldiers do not ask for them any favors either from the Government or Rebels – they only ask of the Gov't that col^d soldiers be allowed to do soldiers work.

I am not particularly solicitous that the 14″ Reg. be ordered to Gallatin, though it seems to me that there are reasons favoring this disposition of the Reg't for the present.

There is work for soldiers to do at this Post. The ordinary Guard and Picket duty must be performed, forage collected &c. The entire country is infested with gurillas stealing and murdering. They must be hunted down or driven out. The Reg't stationed here during this Winter could perform these duties and make in addition great advancement in drill.

There is another consideration of weight in the fact that systematic efforts made by a col^d regiment stationed here, could result in gathering in large numbers of black men from the country around.

The General commanding at Gallatin takes a lively interest in the success of the enterprise – and has given all the aid and assistance in his power to render the black soldiers here efficient – honorable in the eyes of loyal men and a terror to traitors. With firm hopes that our cause is right and will succeed, I am Captain With high regard Your O'b't Ser't

ALS   Th. J. Morgan

Lieut. Col. Th. J. Morgan to Capt. R. D. Mussey, 6 Dec. 1863, Miscellaneous Records, 14th USCI, Regimental Books & Papers USCT, RG 94 [G-293].

201: Order by the Adjutant General of the Army

LOUISVILLE, KY., JUNE 14, 1864.

GENERAL ORDERS, No. 21. The incorporation into the army of the United States of colored troops renders it necessary that they should be brought as speedily as possible to the highest state of discipline. Accordingly, the practice which has hitherto prevailed, no doubt from necessity, of requiring these troops to perform most of the labor on fortifications, and the labor and fatigue duties of permanent stations and camps, will cease, and they will only be required to take their fair share of fatigue duty, with the white troops. This is necessary to prepare them for the higher duties of conflicts with the enemy.

Commanders of colored troops, in cases where the troops under their commands are required to perform an excess of labor above white troops in the same command, will represent the case to the common superior through the regular channel. By order of the SECRETARY OF WAR.

PDSr

L. THOMAS, *Adjutant General.*

Adjutant General L. Thomas, General Orders No. 21, 14 June 1864, A-589 1864, Letters Received, ser. 12, RG 94 [K-544]. As Adjutant General of the Army, Thomas regularly issued orders in the name of the Secretary of War, but Secretary Edwin M. Stanton sometimes reversed him, particularly in matters of policy. In a handwritten endorsement added to this copy of Order 21, Thomas appealed to the War Department, "It is very important that I be sustained in this order."

202: New York Black Soldier to the President

New Orleans Camp Parpit Louisiana [*August*] 1864
My Dear Friend and x Pre   I thake up my Pen to Address you A fiew simpels And facts   We so called the 20th u.s. Colored troops we was got up in the state of New York so said By A grant of the President. we Dont think he know wether we are white or Black   we have not Bin Organized yet And A grate meney Brought Away without Being Musterd in, and we are treated in a Different maner to what others Rigiments is Both Northern men or southern Raised Rigiment   Instead of the musket It is the spad and the Whelbarrow and the Axe cuting in one of the most horable swamps in Louisiana stinking and misery   Men are Call to go on thes fatiuges wen sum of them are scarc Able to get Along the Day Before on the sick List And Prehaps weeks to And By this treatment meney are thowen Back in sickness wich thay very seldom get over. we had when we Left New York over A thousand strong   now we scarce rise Nine hundred the total is said to Be   we lost 1.60 men who have Left thire homes friends and Relation And Come Down hear to Lose thire Lives in For the Country thy Dwll in or stayd in   the Colored man is like A lost sheep   Meney of them old and young was Brave And Active. But

has Bin hurrided By and ignominious Death into Eternity. But I
hope God will Presearve the Rest Now in existance to Get Justice
and Rights   we have to Do our Duty or Die and no help for
us   It is true the Country is in A hard strugle   But we All must
Remember Mercy and Justice Grate and small. it is Devine. we
All Listed for so much Bounty Clothing and Ration And 13
Dollars A month. And the most has fallen short in all thes
Things   we havent Recived A cent of Pay Since we Bin in the
field. Instead of them Coming to us Like men with our 13
Dollars thay come with only seven Dollars A month wich only A
fiew tuck it   we stand in Need of Money very much indeed And
think it is no more than Just an Right we should have it   And
Another thing we are Cut short of our Ration in A most Shocking
maner. I wont Relate All now But we Are Nerly Deprived of All
Comforts of Life   Hardly have Anough Bread to Keep us From
starving   six or 8 ounces of it to Do A Soldier 24 hours on Gaurd
or eney other Labor and About the Same in Meat and Coffee   sum
times No meat for 2 Days   soup meat Licqour with very Little
seazing the Boys calls hot water or meat tea for Diner   It is A
hard thing to be Keept in such a state of misery Continuly   It is
spoken Dont musel the ox that treads out the corn. Remember we
are men standing in Readiness to face thous vile traitors an
Rebeles who are trying to Bring your Peaceable homes to
Destruction. And how can we stand them in A weak and starving
Condition

HL

Unsigned to My Dear Friend and x Pre., {Aug.} 1864, filed with R-268
1864, Letters Received, ser. 360, Colored Troops Division, RG 94 {B-57}.
This unsigned letter is filed with another letter in the same hand which
was written by Nimrod Rowley, a soldier in the 20th USCI.

203: Commander of a Massachusetts Black Regiment to the Headquarters of the Department of the South and an Exchange between the Ordnance Department of the Department of the South and the Commander of the Massachusetts Black Regiment

Morris Island {S.C.} Aug 24. 1864

Sir   I wish respectfully to submit to the Major Gen'l Comd'g
Dep't South the enclosed letter which is a true copy of one sent by
Lieut J. R. McGinness Chief of Ordnance Dept South to Capt

James W. Grace of my Regiment, and I respectfully request that
all officers and enlisted men now detailed from my regiment in the
Ordnance Dep't be returned to their respective companies, and that
no others be detailed for duty in that Dept till the Chief of
Ordnance is willing to treat them as United States soldiers. I have
the honor to be Sir Very Respectfully your Obt Servant

HLcSr   (Sgd) E N Hallowell

[*Enclosure*]   Hilton Head [*S.C.*], Aug 3, 1864
Sir   It having been reported at this Office that you have on duty
as clerk in the Ordnance Office Morris Island a Negro from the 54
Mass Vols, you are hereby ordered to relieve the said Negro at
once and have him returned to his regiment.

Should you be unable to procure the services of a white soldier
to act in that capacity you are authorized to engage the services of
a Civilian not paying him however a salary of more than $60. per
month with one Gov't ration per day but no Negroes will be
allowed to hold any positions in the Ord Dept with my consent
other than that of cook or laborer   Respectfully Your Obt Servant

HLcSr   (Sgd) J. R. McGinnis

Morris Island S.C. Aug 7th 1864
Sir. Having been informed that no soldier from my Regiment can
be used in the Ordnance Department excepting as a Cook or
Laborer, I respectfully request that the enlisted men now detailed
to report to Capt. J. W. Grace. A.O. Officer at this Post, be
returned to their companies. Very respectfully

HLcSr   (sig'd) E. N. Hallowell

Col. E. N. Hallowell to Captain W. L. M. Burger, 24 Aug. 1864, enclosing 1st Lt. J. R. McGinnis to Captain James W. Grace, 3 Aug. 1864;
Col. E. N. Hallowell to Captain R. H. L. Jewett, 7 Aug. 1864, Letters
Sent, 54th Mass. Vols., Regimental Books & Papers USCT, RG 94 [G-
262]. Hallowell commanded the 54th Massachusetts Volunteers. Both of-
ficers and men of the Massachusetts black regiments persistently contested
discriminatory duty assignments. In September 1863 Colonel Norwood P.
Hallowell, commander of the 55th Massachusetts Infantry and brother of
Edward N. Hallowell, had been "severely reprimanded" for withholding
his regiment from fatigue detail. (Special Order No. 28, Head Qrs. Brig.
Genl. Wild, 1 Sept. 1863, Orders, 35th USCI, Regimental Books &
Papers USCT, RG 94 [G-239].)

204: Aide-de-Camp of a Division in the 16th Army Corps to the Adjutant General of the Army

Vicksburg Miss., November 3rd 1864.
General: In forwarding the Muster Rolls of the 50th & 52^{d} Colored Regiments, I have the honor to make the following statement in regard to the Inspection Remarks on said Rolls, which, without some explanation show very badly for the Commanding Officers of those Regiments.

The bad condition of Clothing, Arms and Accoutrements is mainly attributable to the heavy guard and fatigue duty that is required of these troops, giving them no chance for improvement in Discipline, Instruction and the duties of a soldier, or time to clean and take proper care of their arms and accoutrements.

I enclose Semi-Weekly Report of the Brigade to which these Regiments belong. Out of the eight hundred and forty-two (842) privates for duty, seven hundred and eighteen (718) are on duty! With this proportion of the Command on guard and fatigue, day after day, is it to be wondered at, that when they appear on Inspection, their Arms, Clothing and accoutrements are in bad condition, and the men present an unsoldierly appearance?

The fact is, that with so much work the officers become careless and despondent, and do not take the pride in making their men good and efficient soldiers, they would under more auspicious circumstances. Very Respectfully, Your Ob'd't, Servant,
ALS   O. J. Wright

Capt. O. J. Wright to Brig. General L. Thomas, 3 Nov. 1864, Letters Received, 50th USCI, Regimental Books & Papers USCT, RG 94 [G-100]. The muster rolls referred to are not enclosed.

205A: Commander of a Missouri Black Regiment to the Headquarters of the Department of the Gulf

Morganzia, La July. 7th 1864.
Sir   In obedience to General Orders No. 21. dated Louisville Ky. June. 14, 1864, and signed L. Thomas, Adjt. Genl. I have the honor to report that the colored troops under my command *are*

required to perform an excess of labor above white troops stationed at this post.

Since the arrival of my command at this place on the 21st day of June 1864, all men fit for duty, not on camp guard or police have been worked from 8 to 10 hours daily on the fortifications; except Sundays, one day for review, and half a day for muster & inspection. No white troops have been worked on these fortifications during said period except those held as prisoners; undergoing punishment. Very Respectfully, Your Obt Servan

ALS   David Branson

[Endorsement] H^d Qrs U.S. Forces Morganzia La July 12″ 1864 Respectfully forwarded   The Colored Troops are the only troops permanently stationed at this Post. It is not true that they have performed any more than their share of the Labor—since the order referred to was issued— The white troops have unloaded all the stores used at the Post, have done all the guard duty, except that of the negro camps, have been on expeditions ect ect. There is no foundation for the complaint— The number of negro troops is greater than the whites. when those under marching orders and the cavalry is deducted. Some of the colored regiments were raised for the express purpose of making fortifications and they have no right to complain when they are engaged in making one for their own defence   M. K. Lawler, Brig Gen Comdg

[Endorsement] This complaint has no special application to the circumstances of the case. The white troops at Morganzia constitute a part of the reserve force of the Division held in readiness to move at any hour. A part has already been sent to the Army of the Potomac and another part to the Dept of the Arkansas. The colored troops at that place constitute its permanent garrison, were selected for that purpose & directed to throw up the works necessary to enable them to hold it. Respectfully forwarded. Ed. R. S. Canby M.G.C. Hd Qrs. Div. of W. Miss. July 19, 1864

Lt. Col. David Branson to Lt. Col. R. B. Irwin, 7 July 1864, Letters Received, 62nd USCI, Regimental Books & Papers USCT, RG 94 [G-224]. Other endorsements.

205B: Commander of a Louisiana Black Regiment to the Headquarters of the Commander of U.S. Forces at Morganzia, Louisiana

Morganzia, La. July 20th [*1864*]

Sir: I very respectfully invite the attention of the Brig. Gen. Comdg. to the following order of the War Dept.[1]

. . . .

For upwards of four months my command has been constantly employed at fatigue duty to the exclusion of all military exercises of whatever nature, not excepting *even Sunday morning Inspections.*

I am now required to furnish for fatigue duty every available man of my command for eight hours each day, Sundays excepted.

This I know to be "an excess of labor above white troops" in this command, and so far, a violation of the above order.

I hereby protest against any further disregard of the above order so far as it shall affect my command. I have the honor to be, sir, Very respectfully Your Ob't serv't,

ALS   Jno. L. Rice

[*Endorsement*] Head Quarters, United States Forces, Morganza, La. July 27" 1864. Respectfully returned; Until the reciept of this communication, the General Commanding was not aware of any such order as what the within purports to be. He has never recieved an official copy of it from superior Head Quarters, nor been officially notified by competent authority of its publication, and on this ground alone he might justly refuse to acknowledge the obligation which it aimes to impose, but aside from this the facts in the case leave but little cause for complaint.

The 75" U.S. Colored Infantry arrived here on the 19" Inst. – For labor performed by this regiment prior to that time, the General Commanding is not responsible, and the amount of work performed at other stations, cannot be permitted to outweigh what the exigencies of the Service may require at this.

The General Commanding assumed control of the Forces at Morganzia the 6" inst. at which time it seemed to be the general understanding as regards division of labor, that the Colored Troops were to work on the Fort, leaving all the other duties of fatigue, picket, scouting and defense to the white troops. There was then no complaint although the white troops numbered 16,000; and the Colored 16.00, or in the proportion of 10 to 1, much less should there be complaint now when there are but 14,00 white Infantry to 22,00 colored.

The cavalry at this Post, since the 6th, have worked hard. The Infantry—cut down to 1400, have performed all the fatigue duty, discharging stores from boats, and armaments and material for the Fort, also camp, headquarters and very heavy picket-guard duty, besides acting as escorts, and policing: Finally, the exigencies of the service, and the safty of the Post, require that they should be held at all times in readiness to defend our extensive camp.

Under these circumstances, while he willingly concedes the correctness of the principle involved, he cannot admit the justice of the protest, or direct any change, in the present division of labor. By Command of Brig. Gen. Lawler, B. Wilson Assistant Adjutant General.

Lieut. Col. Jno. L. Rice to Asst. Adjt. Genl., 20 July [1864], enclosed in Lieut. Col. Jno. L. Rice to Brig. Gen. L. Thomas, 20 Sept. 1864, R-19 1864, Letters Received by Adjutant General L. Thomas, ser. 363, Colored Troops Division, RG 94 [V-91].

1 Omitted passage is a copy of Adjutant General Lorenzo Thomas's General Order 21, issued July 14, 1864, which prohibited inequitable assignment of black troops to labor and fatigue duties. (See *Freedom,* ser. 2: doc. 201.)

205C: Assistant Inspector General of Black Troops to the Assistant Inspector General of the Department of the Gulf

Port Hudson La Aug 30th 1864.
Colonel: In compliance with Circular No 9 from your office calling for tri monthly reports on particular matters appertaining to the execution of orders and the efficiency of the command. I have the honor to submit the following statement in relation to the colored troops in the Department.

With regard to the execution of orders by the colored troops I have the honor to report it to be generally prompt and to the best of the ability of officers and men. In relation to the execution of orders from superior authority in relation to colored troops, I respectfully report that Gen. Orders. No. 21 from the Secretary of War dated Louisville June 14th 1864. and republished in Gen. Orders No. 108 current series from Department Head Quarters is not enforced at Post of Morganzia, where all the fatigue duty on fortifications is performed by colored troops and prisoners sentenced to hard labor. This duty is reported to be incessant to the exclusion of all opportunities for drill or instruction. The difficulty of making soldiers of these men, in face of the constant practical assertion of their unfitness for anything but that labor which is shared with them only by the wearers of ball and chain, is self evident. Those regiments which have had the good fortune to escape these consequences of the association with white troops show an infinite superiority in all soldierly qualities.

The utterly unreliable and often worthless arms which have been issued to the colored troops have been already the subject of many reports. This matter has been now refferred to Gen. Andrews and inspection reports will shortly be forwarded to Department Head Quarters which it is presumed will result in their exchange.

It is hoped that when the matter of consolidation of Regiments is fairly over some uniform system for appointment and promotion may be established throughout the Department if not throughout the Army. If the provisional commissions or appointments issued by Department Commanders could be in due time followed or replaced by appointments in the name of the President or Secretary of War and issued from Washington it would in my opinion influence many good officers to enter this branch of the service. The matter is a trifle, it is acknowledged but when motives are evenly balanced, trifles will decide.

With all deference for the judgment of superiors it is nevertheless respectfully recommended that the practice authorized by Brig Gen Thomas of appointing white 1st Sergeants for colored regiments be not extended to other colored troops in the Dept. In the first place colored soldiers of sufficient intelligence to qualify themselves for this position if held out to them can in my opinion be easily obtained. Secondly the class of white soldiers willing to take this position are in my opinion those who conscious of inability to pass the examination required for an officer hope in this way to attain promotion, in which if they do not speedily succeed they become discontented and ashamed, and lastly because the introduction of a quasi third estate will tend to render confused and indistinct that sharp social distinction between the officer and the enlisted man without which the permanent efficiency of troops is very rare   I have the honor to be Very Respectfully your Ob^{t} Servt

HLcSr

(sig) S. M. Quincy

Col. S. M. Quincy to Lieut. Col. Wm. S. Albert, 30 Aug. 1864, vol. 188/362 DG, pp. 4–6, Letters Sent by the Inspector General, ser. 2126, U.S. Forces Port Hudson, RG 393 Pt. 2 No. 118 [C-880].

205D: Commander of a Louisiana Black Regiment to the Adjutant General of the Army

Morganza La Sept 20" 1864

Sir: I take the liberty to transmit herewith a communication with the endorsements thereon, which I addressed to Hd. Qrs. U.S. Forces Morganza July 20"[1]

The paper sufficiently explains the state of affairs which called it forth.

Since it was written the abuse complained of has assumed a still more aggravated character

On the 5" of August "Gen. Order No. 21" was republished and generally distributed from Hd. Qrs. Dept. of the Gulf. Nothwithstanding this my whole available command has been kept constantly at fatigue duty up to this time, from five (5) to eight (8) hours every day Sundays excepted. During all this time the white troops have performed no fatigue duty except to unload Com. & Q.M. stores, although most of the time they have been largely in excess of the colored troops.

My regiment also performs its share of picket duty and has done so since early in August. It has also taken part in expeditions against the enemy, so that now the "division of labor" which was thought to be so equitable in July cannot well be urged against my protest.

I am aware that in sending this paper *direct* I incur the risk of punishment but I console myself with the thought that if I suffer, the colored troops in this department will perhaps be benefited.

I think, sir, abundant testimony can be taken among officers of the 1st Brig. U.S. Col'd Troops now at this post, to convince you that the brigade has, during the last six months, suffered an amount of injustice sufficient to utterly demoralize any equal body of white troops.

The officers are very much disheartened and have almost ceased to look for that day of deliverance which they have so long expected.

I still hope to see justice done these troops altho' I have hitherto made many appeals in vain. I have the honor to be, sir, Very respectfully your ob't serv't

ALS   Jno. L. Rice

Lieut. Col. Jno. L. Rice to Brig. Gen. L. Thomas, 20 Sept. 1864, R-19 1864, Letters Received by Adjutant General L. Thomas, ser. 363, Colored Troops Division, RG 94 [V-91]. Thomas referred Rice's letter to General

Edward R. S. Canby, commander of the Military Division of West Mississippi, who in turn referred it to General Michael K. Lawler, post commander at Morganzia. Lawler reiterated his previous stand and observed
that at the time the complaint was originally made "there was no good
reason for it." He added, "At present the Colored Forces at this place in
their proportion do the same duty as white troops." Other endorsements,
enclosure.

1 See *Freedom,* ser. 2: doc. 205b.

205E: Commander of a Louisiana Black Brigade to the Headquarters of the Post of Morganzia, Louisiana

Morganzia La Sept 24 1864

Lieut   I have the honor to report the safe return of my
command   Col. Guppy of the 23^{d} Wis Infty hving other troops
directed the march which continued all night. Soon after daylight
we reached the point of our destination which was Morgans Ford
on the Atchafalaya river where we found quite a force under
Command of Col Spicely 24th Ind Infty and who treated me
courteously and gentlemenly throughout the time I was under his
command.

For two days we worked at fatigue, building Lunettes for the
artillery and cutting roads in the woods so they could be
approached under cover. Some officers apparently acting by
authority Seemed hardly able to find enough for the Colored troops
to do   Lt Col Pearsall of the 99th Engineers who was in charge of
the works became disgusted and returned to Morganzia.

Some beef procured by a detail from my command from over
the river by permission of Col Spicely for the benefit of the troops
who were suffering some with Scurvy was in my temporary absence
taken by a cavalry officer who represented it to be by my
order. I am very sorry to say there are persons wearing the
uniform of a United States officer who will not scruple to tell a
falsehood to gain some petty advantage and use his uniform to
decive a "Poor nigger" and afterwards tell his smartness (shame) to
his fellows and then with the air of a clown look around for
applause

The evening before we left some buildings on the opposite side
of the river were burned. There seemed a general disposition to
accuse the colord troops of doing it and Col Spicely seemed to
believe the report and would probably have officially so reported if
I had not positively assured him to the contrary from indisputable

evidence in my possession, but they could not accuse them of
burning the buildings the night before they came the ruins of
which were still smouldering and which was just as wanton an act
as the other.

Some white solders on the road were catching fowls and no
effort was made to stop them   when some officers sent in some of
their men to get water, a white guard was sent immediately to
arrest them to prevent, as was aledged, their plundering, yet no
stop was put to the operation of the others.

On the return but few men were unable to march and keep up
and not a dozen had to be carried and in this respect they far
exceeded the white troops.   In fact they ma[r]ch as well as any
white troops with which they have come in contact.

Some Sixteen recruits were obtained and about one hundred and
fifty "contrabands". A patient and systematic effort would
probably bring to light many recruits but great pains are taken to
hide this class of persons on the approach of our forces.   The
migration of so many women and children is not encouraged as
they are an incumbrance to the army and it is not beneficial to
themselves. If some officers with a few mounted men were
permitted to accompany the cavalry many more recruits could be
obtained but as it is when they go they have no interests and in
fact discourage the coming of these persons.

The policy of breaking up brigades and then mixing white and
black regiments to form a new one for raiding purposes
temporarily is exceedingly injudicous and productive of much evil
and disorganization and but little good can ever come of it.

No white troops lifted an ax or a spade while out on that trip
to work yet the colored troops marched as far, done as much guard
duty and would probaly fought as hard as the other troops as they
carried as much ammunition and were as well armed and while the
rest lay in the shade we were hard at work.

The constant violation of the orders of the War Dept by so
many Commanders falling temporarily in command of colored
troops has been the subject of remark and complaint so long that
it seems useless to complain again or to mention it for I have
almost ceased to expect justice from any one for if they will not
obey and respect the published orders of the Secretary of War
neither will they those of Genl. Canby for he has republished this
order that prohibits colored troops being required to do an excess
of work or fatigue duty over and above those with whom they are
associated

The *work* is no objection to either officers or men but the
manner and the circumstances under which it is required   the Slur

and Stigma of *inferiority* is what displeases so many officers and makes it so difficult to keep our best officers for they *will* not command troops that the Government allows *inferiority* to become attached to, for they say if the Government wants bosses or overseers let them so be employed from those who want the position but while they bear commissions they want only their *fair share* of fatigue but will do any amount of fighting.

The people along the road of this raid and the one previous seemed terror stricken at the sight of black troops and in future if every raid is answered by black troops you will Soon not hear of one this side of the Atchafalaya river yet they behaved in a soldierly manner and was at all times under strict discipline.

The distance between this place and the Atchafalaya river is so small on a straight line that a couple of regiments could probably in a week make a good road between two points   The value of holding the line of that river is so manifest to one who will look at the subject that probably only very great interests elsewhere have so far prevented but with this road the same force that holds the Mississippi could hold that and give quiet and Security from Turnbuls Island to Bayou Lafourch and yet be as available in three hours as if at Morganzia

An intrenched camp on the west side of that river to cover the operation of the cavalary up and down and towards Opelousas flanked by batteries on the East bank would make the position impregnable and no raid need be apperhended from the certainty of its destruction if attempted.

The force now at Morganzia would answer the purpose and when they are withdrawn concentrate the troops between here and Brashear City rail road and its occupation would include within our lines a very rich country from which considerable supplies for the enemy are now being drawn and the abundance of timber would enable us to quickly and cheaply construct a telegraph and keep the wagon road in good order. I have the honor to be Very respectfully your obedient Servant

ALS   H. N. Frisbie

Col. H. N. Frisbie to Lieut. O. A. Rice, 24 Sept. 1864, D. Ullmann Papers, Generals' Papers & Books, ser. 159, RG 94 [V-1].

205F: Commander of a Louisiana Black Division to the Headquarters of the Military Division of West Mississippi

Morganza, La. Oct. 29th 1864.

Sir: I have the honor to forward, for the information of the Major General Comdg the M. Division, the accompanying documents, consisting of an order instituting a Medical Board, and the report of the same.

The three Regiments named were raised at St Louis, Missouri, last winter and spring, and have since been under my command and at Port Hudson & at this place. The extraordinary amount of sickness and mortality in them presented such a remarkable contrast to the condition of the other colored Regiment, under my Command, that I considered it my duty to have the matter investigated.

The reasons are, I doubt not, correctly set forth in these documents. I desire to state in connection with them that I have never been able to procure sufficient Medical attendance, Surgeons, Hospital stewards & nurses, for these Regiments, nor has it ever been possible to obtain any but a very limited supply of vegetables.

I respectfully suggest that these Regiments either be filled up or consolidated   I have the honor to be your obt servant

HLc
[Daniel Ullmann]

B.G.V. [Daniel Ullmann] to Lieut. Col. C. T. Christensen, 29 Oct. 1864, V-29 1864, Letters Received, ser. 1976, U.S. Forces Morganzia LA, RG 393 Pt. 2 No. 104 [C-880]. Enclosed are tables compiled by the medical board in October 1864, itemizing causes of death and discharge in each of three black regiments stationed at Morganzia, as well as further discharges recommended by the board. The information is consolidated in the accompanying table.

Causes of Death and Discharge in Three Black Regiments

	62nd USCI	65th USCI	67th USCI	Total
Original number in regiment	1,019	1,104	1,035	3,158
Deaths				
Fevers	39	75	50	164
Eruptive diseases	11	8	59	78
Respiratory diseases	43	28	119	190
Digestive diseases	64	56	113	233
Casualties	1	0	3	4
Other diseases	27	22	45	94
Unstated diseases	177	335	99	611
Total deaths	362	524	488	1,374
Discharges by regimental surgeon				
Imbecility	1	0	0	1
Respiratory diseases	3	1	0	4
Hernias	9	11	0	20
Chronic rhumatism	3	3	0	6
Other diseases	5	18	0	23
Unstated diseases	5	6	0	11
Total discharges	26	39	0	65
Recommended for discharge	54	82	53	189
Number remaining in regiment	577	459	494	1,530

The order constituting the board is not enclosed, nor is any report of the board other than the tables. One month earlier, an inspector from the headquarters of the Department of the Gulf had also found the health of black soldiers at Morganzia poor. He blamed conditions on "the very inferior *personnel* of the men, who it would seem, must have been recruited without proper medical examination." (Ass't. Inspect. Gen'l. Wm. S. Abert and Lieut. J. Chas. Robinet to Maj. Geo. B. Drake, 24 Sept. 1864, A-994 1864, Letters Received, ser. 1756, Dept. of the Gulf, RG 393 Pt. 1 [C-556].)

206: Anonymous Louisiana Black Soldier to the Secretary of War

Jack Son Ville Florida March the 7th 1866th
I have take My pen in hand purposely for to form you of my present Condition   I have been in the United State Service Going on three yeares And from the times the Regiment were in Augurated in New or Leans Louisiana in the years of 1863 and ser from the times that the Regiment was Made up in New orleans Augest the 27th 1863   well from New orleans the Regiment went to Bray Shear City Louisiana and there the Regiment was working Days and Night Loading and unloading the Steams Boats and from that to Bilding up forts there At Bray Sheare City and Do Regular Gard Duties there untill the 9th of March in the years of 1864   and from there we went on An Experdition toward pleaseant Hill and we were on the field from the 9th of March untill the 27th of May in the years of 1864 but after the Battle of pleasen Hill we Reatreated to Grandicoo   there we was Cuten Down trees and Billing up Fortiforcation   Well from there Down to Alexandria Louisiana and there we was Billing A Dam Cross the river So the Guns Boats Come Down   And ther we were working Days And Nights Untill the Guns Boats was Able to Come Down And from there we Reatreated to Moganzea Louisiana and there the 99th U.S.C.T. Regiment was Billing up forts from the first of June untill the 18th of January in the years of 1865th   And from there the 99th Regiment landed At forte Jefferson Florida And we lef it and went to the battle of Natchar Bridge and while on that Experdition as we were Going we had Sixty Round of Carchage and 2 Days Ration in our harvest Sack and our Robber Blanket woolen Blank and two pece of Artiliry to hall Through all that Mud and water   and from there to point Rossy and there we was Billing up Fort from the 11th of March untill the last of April   And from there we went to [City?] [. . .] And A partay of Us went to work [S]assay Creek Florida working on the Rail Road and Some Days with Nothing to Eat only what we Could Get from the Citizens by paying our Money for it   and here we is at Jack Son ville Florida working on the whoft from 7 oClock AM untill 12 M and from 1. p.M. to 5 pM And working very hard in Deed Loading And unloading Steame Boats And loading and unloading wagons with woods and So forth and with hardly Anything to Eat Much   And here we is in Jack son ville Fla working from Monday Morning to Saturday Evening but we Dont work any of Night but work the hold week & Dont have one Day so we may wash our Close and Cleans our Musket   with All that

we have to Go on Enspection Every Sunday and if our Guns or
Clothes is not Cleans we have A Large piece of wood to tote all
Day   and sir I am Going to tell you one thing About the
Disperseation of the 99th Regiment officers how they is the
Meaning [Lote] of officers that is in the holds of the Union   they
Even Dont like to hear any Metting And they try to keep Us as
Egnorence as they Can but I thank God And My God promus to
help me and I Believe that He will Help Me As long As I live
and Even when I come to Die he will Come and Stand by
Me   Though our offices treat Us very mean in Deed yet I hope
God will be with them for they have A Strct Account to Give for
there Bavaore [*behavior*] here   And So this is from Co A. 99th.
U.S.C.T. and we All Enhope that we will Recieve Some
Satisfaction from you Ser And we Enhope that you will think Nufe
of us as to Answerd this Letter Ser if you please Ser for we ar here
As poor Cretchers what is in A Greate Distress   All that is About
our officers being so bad but Never the less we will Get out some
of these Days if God will help us

HL

Unsigned to Edward M. Stanton, 7 Mar. 1866, A-52 1866, Letters Received, ser. 360, Colored Troops Division, RG 94 [B-207]. The letter is
written on a blank Confederate quartermaster's form. The writer's regiment
was originally organized in August 1863 as the 15th Infantry, Corps
d'Afrique. It was designated an engineer regiment in February 1864, becoming the 5th Regiment Engineers, Corps d'Afrique, and subsequently,
in April 1864, the 99th USCI. (*Official Army Register*, pt. 8, p. 280.)

Combat: "To Strike a Manly Blow for the Liberty of Your Race"

IN THE EYES of most Northern whites military enlistment would not transform docile slaves into fearless soldiers.[1] Black spokesmen and their white abolitionist allies challenged this belief and yearned for the opportunity to demonstrate their military prowess on the field of battle. Shedding the blood of the Southern chivalry would not only belie notions of racial inferiority but also secure the freedom promised by the Emancipation Proclamation and give firm foundation to black demands for equality. Yet to the extent that success under fire would elevate blacks, failure would degrade them. For both whites and blacks, much rode on black battlefield performance. Both skeptics and proponents watched the first black units closely for evidence of martial talents. Nearly all observers remarked upon the pride the new soldiers took in armed service and their expertise in disciplined drill. Even scoffers who belittled black military prowess openly acknowledged the superiority of black soldiers in executing drillfield evolutions, although they usually attributed such skills to habits of subordination and aptitude for imitation. But however reassuring to the advocates of black enlistments, parade-ground polish did not guarantee success in battle.

The Kansas, Louisiana, and South Carolina black regiments recruited in 1862 offered the earliest tests of black men under arms. In Kansas, James H. Lane's troops entered the fray against Confederate guerrillas late in 1862. That fighting resulted in the war's first loss of life by black soldiers in Union uniforms, but distance and the character of frontier warfare devalued these exploits in the public eye. The Sea Islands of South Carolina presented a different situation. There the ex-slave soldiers recruited by General Rufus Saxton boasted abolitionist officers whose talents with the pen equaled their talents with the sword, guaranteeing wide publicity for black accomplishments. In late 1862 and early 1863, South Carolina Colored Volunteers raided the coastal rivers from Port Royal to northern Florida, liberating hundreds of slaves from the interior, securing supplies for the army, and augmenting their own ranks. They engaged enemy soldiers, withstood fire from Confederate batteries, and

[1] For the quotation in the title, see *Freedom,* ser 2: doc. 343.

evened old scores with their masters. As their officers freely acknowledged, the ex-slaves' unrivaled familiarity with the local terrain ensured the success of these expeditions. Proud of the performance of his men and convinced of their unbounded potential as soldiers, the commander of the 1st South Carolina Volunteers, abolitionist Thomas W. Higginson, wrote stirring descriptions of his regiment's operations for the Northern press. The cool demeanor of the South Carolina regiments under fire convinced sympathetic observers that black soldiers could meet the enemy with courage. It remained only for uniformed blacks to engage successfully in formal battle against Confederate forces for the verdict to be conclusive.

Before long black soldiers had that chance. In May 1863, just as the federal government launched large-scale recruitment of blacks, men from three previously enlisted Louisiana black regiments participated in an assault upon the strongly fortified Confederate post of Port Hudson, on the Mississippi River north of Baton Rouge. The 1st and 3rd Louisiana Native Guards, led largely by black company officers, shared the field with a newly organized black engineer regiment, as well as with white units. Confronting an entrenched enemy, the black soldiers charged repeatedly, braving artillery fire and regrouping after repulse to mount further assaults. Although the Union forces failed to capture the Confederate works, the black soldiers won encomiums from their white comrades-in-arms and even from General Nathaniel P. Banks, never excessive in his praise of black abilities. Banks assured his superiors that the manner in which the Louisiana black soldiers had withstood combat fully justified the policy of placing them under arms.

In early June 1863, hard on the heels of Port Hudson, the Confederates attacked black troops at Milliken's Bend, Louisiana. The outnumbered Union forces consisted of a white regiment from Iowa and two newly organized Louisiana black units, the latter ill-trained and poorly armed. In the first charge the ex-slaves did not handle their guns well. As the enemy advanced, however, they met the rebels with fixed bayonets and rifle butts and held them back in fierce hand-to-hand fighting that made even seasoned officers blanch. Forced at length to retreat before the Confederate onslaught, the Union soldiers managed, however, to hold the line until Navy gunboats forced the enemy to withdraw. Reports of the battle at Milliken's Bend praised the courage of the black soldiers and went far to reduce skepticism within Union ranks. A Confederate battle report went further, asserting that the black soldiers had resisted the charge "with considerable obstinacy, while the white or true Yankee portion ran like whipped curs. . . ."[2]

---

[2] *Official Records,* ser. 1, vol. 24, pt. 2, p. 467.

In July 1863, the 54th Massachusetts Volunteers matched the exploits of the Louisiana black regiments with an assault on a stronghold in the outlying defenses of Charleston. Recruited from throughout the North and only recently arrived in South Carolina, the Massachusetts regiment joined white units in an ill-fated attempt to capture Fort Wagner. Assigned the frontal position in a direct assault at the insistence of their commander, the Northern black soldiers suffered withering enemy fire and ruinous casualties. They nevertheless reached the Confederate parapet, only to be driven back after still further losses. The bloody outcome of the assault suggested to many observers that the Massachusetts blacks had in fact been sent into deliberate slaughter by commanders who valued black lives less than white. The fallen black soldiers, who shared death and a common grave with their colonel, abolitionist Robert G. Shaw, earned heroic status in exchange for their sacrifice. Together, Fort Wagner, Milliken's Bend, and Port Hudson had demonstrated beyond cavil that black soldiers—whether Northern freemen, Southern freemen, or former slaves—could withstand the rebel's most murderous fire.

In fending off imputations of docility and cowardice, the first black regiments that took the field both modified white opinion and electrified black freemen and bondsmen. As the war dragged on, pride in the achievements of Port Hudson, Milliken's Bend, and Fort Wagner helped swell black enlistments and strengthen black demands for equality within the army and without. By their sacrifice, black soldiers irreversibly transformed the meaning of the war.

But even as thousands of new black soldiers donned the Union uniform, the strategy of the war changed dramatically, and black soldiers entered an army that offered fewer opportunities for battlefield glory. With the fall of Vicksburg and Port Hudson in July 1863, the Union army had gained control of the Mississippi River, dividing the Confederacy and leaving miles of river fortifications to garrison, Union-supervised plantations and contraband camps to guard, and long lines of transportation and communication to protect. For the remainder of the war, these duties fell largely to units of the U.S. Colored Troops. While the drama of the western theater shifted to General William T. Sherman's relentless advance upon Atlanta, followed by his free-wheeling march to the sea, tens of thousands of black soldiers labored far from the battlefront to make such movements possible, supporting seemingly endless supply lines and protecting Sherman's armies from rearguard Confederate attack and guerrilla disruption. Sherman took no black troops with his advancing forces, arguing that he preferred to rely upon seasoned veterans rather than untried recruits, but also not bothering to disguise his unshakeably low opinion of black men in uniform.

Excluded from Sherman's army, black soldiers in the western theater nonetheless saw scattered action during 1864. Black troops participated in General Banks's ill-starred Red River expedition early in the year, with black engineers constructing dams that permitted the retreat of stranded Union gunboats. At forts in Kentucky, Tennessee, Mississippi, and Alabama, black garrisons met attacks by Confederate forces under General Nathan B. Forrest, a prominent antebellum slave trader. Anxious to make his mark and intimidate the black regiments and white Southern loyalists who manned many of the Mississippi Valley fortifications, Forrest urged his soldiers to fight ferociously. In April 1864, perhaps taking his orders too literally, Forrest's men slaughtered the largely black Union garrison at Fort Pillow, Tennessee, after it had surrendered. A wave of outrage swept the Northern army and the Northern public, and black soldiers everywhere added Fort Pillow to their battle cries.[3] "Remember Fort Pillow" bitterly attested to the fate that might follow surrender and spurred black warriors to fight with special desperation. When, for example, the Union commander at Athens, Alabama, surrendered to General Forrest in September 1864, black soldiers among the garrison pleaded that the battle continue, preferring a fight to the death over capture by Forrest's men.

In addition to countless armed encounters with rebel guerrillas during 1864, black soldiers in the western theater also fought in actions designed to capture or disrupt Confederate saltworks, ironworks, and transport networks. And when Confederate General John Hood, repulsed by Sherman's smashing advance into Georgia, turned to invade Tennessee, black soldiers helped shatter Hood's forces at the battle of Nashville in December 1864. That battle, which extinguished Confederate hopes in Tennessee, tested many black units for the first time. Such confrontations, although less stirring than the dramatic engagements of 1863, continued to transform the consciousness of black and white alike. Many white soldiers held firm to their contempt for blacks while readily accepting that black bodies could stop rebel bullets, but common engagement against the Confederate foe pushed some white soldiers to a positive appreciation of black abilities. In October 1864, newly recruited Kentucky ex-slaves marched into battle at Saltville, Virginia amid insults from their white comrades. They marched out to respectful silence after proving their mettle under fire. Similarly, after the battle of Nashville, a Tennessee recruiter responsible for enlisting many of the battle's black casualties, captured something of the equalitarian implications of black participation when he noted that

---

[3] For a demand by a Northern black civilian that the North retaliate for the murder of black soldiers at Fort Pillow, see *Freedom,* ser. 2: doc. 235.

black and white bodies lay side by side upon the bloodied field. "Death," he proclaimed, "had known no distinction of color. . . ."[4]

In the eastern theater, the character of warfare also changed in 1864 and 1865. With Ulysses S. Grant's assumption of command in the spring of 1864, the Union armies massed for a grinding endurance contest against the Confederate forces under Robert E. Lee. After carnage at the Wilderness and Cold Harbor, Grant marched the Army of the Potomac to join the Army of the James. By the summer of 1864, Grant's forces stood immobilized in trench lines around Petersburg and Richmond, the conflict a stalemate. For ten months, the behemoths faced each other in grueling siege operations. Stand-up battles with troops advancing across open fields gave way for the most part to trench construction, picket duty, reconnaissance, and short advances – only to dig new defenses. In the rifle pits of the armies of the James and the Potomac, thousands of black soldiers held portions of the Union lines. Their ranks included most of the free black regiments recruited in the North, as well as black regiments from Maryland, the District of Columbia, Virginia, and North Carolina. In the fall of 1864, newly recruited black troops from Kentucky joined their comrades before Petersburg. At the end of the year, consolidation of the black regiments created the all-black 25th Army Corps, commanded by General Godfrey Weitzel, which represented the largest concentration of black soldiers engaged in any one theater during the war.

While most black troops in the East sweated in the trenches before Petersburg and Richmond, some saw other action in 1864 and 1865. Along the South Atlantic coast, black soldiers participated in the battles of Olustee, Florida, and Honey Hill, South Carolina, and numbered among the first Union troops to march victoriously into Charleston. In December 1864 and January 1865, black regiments from the Army of the James took part in expeditions against Fort Fisher, North Carolina. But throughout the last year of the war, costly and often dispiriting siege warfare in Virginia claimed the energies of the vast majority of black soldiers.

In the task of holding and fortifying their lines, all Union soldiers entrenched before Petersburg and Richmond wielded the pick and shovel more often than the musket. But charges abounded that blacks dug the trenches only for whites to occupy them. And when a rare opportunity for dramatic action arose at the battle of the Crater in July 1864, the black troops initially promised a leading position were instead ordered into reserve. General Grant later as-

---

[4] Col. [Reuben D. Mussey] to Capt. C. P. Brown, 21 Dec. 1864, vol. 221 DC, pp. 364–68, Letters Sent by the Commissioner, ser. 1141, Organization of U.S. Colored Troops, Dept. of the Cumberland, RG 393 Pt. 1 [C-50].

serted that he changed the battle order to forestall charges of using blacks only as cannon fodder.[5] Instead, he let white soldiers lead the assault across a crater formed by a failed attempt to explode the rebel works. Blacks followed the charge, after Confederate fire had littered the field with their dead and wounded white comrades. Unable to advance or find shelter in the open crater, they too suffered decimation. When the carnage ended, the black soldiers might well have regretted not having had the lead.

After a weary winter in the trenches, the black soldiers of the 25th Army Corps looked to the spring campaign of 1865 with renewed hope of participating in the final defeat of the rebel armies. Some fought in the scattered engagements that marked the opening of the struggle, but most continued to fortify the Union line and press the enemy's entrenchments. When at last the Union forces broke through rebel lines and the Confederates evacuated Petersburg and Richmond, thousands of black soldiers followed the retreating enemy and entered the long-besieged cities. They arrived in Petersburg to the cheers of welcoming slaves and ranked among the first Union soldiers to occupy Richmond. Although dispute later raged as to which units had reached the Confederate capital first, the news that initially raced across the telegraph wires placed black soldiers in the van. Receiving that word, Massachusetts Governor John A. Andrew exulted: "The colored men received late, got in first, and this is Scripture fulfilled."[6]

---

[5] Grant testified before a congressional committee on December 20, 1864: "General Burnside wanted to put his colored division in front, and I believe if he had done so it would have been a success. Still I agreed with General Meade in his objection to that plan. . . . that if we put the colored troops in front . . . and it should prove a failure, it would then be said, and very properly, that we were shoving those people ahead to get killed because we did not care anything about them." (U.S. Congress, "Report of the Joint Committee on the Conduct of the War: Battle of Petersburg," *Senate Reports,* 38th Cong., 2nd sess., no. 142, p. 111.)

[6] *Official Records,* ser. 1, vol. 46, pt. 3, p. 543.

207: Commander of a South Carolina Black Regiment to the Superintendent of Contrabands in the Department of the South

On board Steamer "Ben Deford." [S.C.] Feb. 1. 1863. General. I have the honor to report the safe return of the expedition under my command, consisting of four hundred and sixty two Officers and men of the 1st Reg[t] of South Carolina Volunteers who left Beaufort on January 23d, on board the Steamers "John Adams," "Planter," and "Ben Deford."

The expedition has carried the regimental flag and the President's Proclamation far into the interior of Georgia and Florida. The men have been repeatedly under fire; have had infantry, cavalry, and even artillery arrayed against them, and have in every instance, come off, not only with unblemished honor, but with undisputed triumph.

At Township, Florida, a detachment of the expedition fought a cavalry company, which met it unexpectedly on a midnight march through pine woods, and which completely surrounded us. They were beaten off, with a loss on our part of one man killed and seven wounded, while the opposing party admits twelve men killed (including Lieut. Jones, in command of the company) besides many wounded. So complete was our victory, that the enemy scattered and hid in the woods all night, not venturing back to his camp, which was five miles distant, until noon next day; a fact which was unfortunately unknown until too late to follow up our advantage. Had I listened to the urgent appeals of my men, and pursued the flying enemy, we could have destroyed his camp; but in view of the darkness, his uncertain numbers and swifter motions, with your injunctions of caution, I judged it better to rest satisifed with the victory already gained.

On another occasion, a detachment of about two hundred and fifty men, on board the "John Adams," fought its way forty miles up and down a river, regarded by the Naval commanders as the most dangerous in the department – the St. Mary's – a river left untraversed by our gunboats for many months, as it requires a boat built like the "John Adams" to ascend it successfully. The stream is narrow, swift, winding, and bordered at many places with high bluffs which blazed with rifle shots. With our glasses, as we approached these points, we could see mounted men by the hundred, galloping through the woods, from point to point, to await us, and though fearful of our shot and shell, they were so daring against musketry, that one rebel actually sprang from the shore upon the large boat which was towed at our stern, where he was shot down by one of my sergeants. We could see our shell scatter the rebels as they fell among them, and some terrible execution must have been done, but not a man of this regiment was killed or wounded, though the Steamer is covered with bullet marks, one of which shows where our brave Captain Clifton, commander of the vessel, fell dead beside his own pilot house, shot through the brain by a Minie ball. Major Strong, who stood beside him, escaped as if by magic; both of them being unnecessarily exposed, without my knowledge.

The secret of our safety was in keeping the regiment below, except the gunners; but this required the utmost energy of the officers, as the men were wild to come on deck, and even implored to be landed on shore and charge on the enemy.

Nobody knows anything about these men, who has not seen them in battle; I find that I myself knew nothing; there is a fiery energy about them beyond anything of which I have ever read, unless it be the French Zuaves. It requires the strictest discipline to hold them in hand; during our first attack on the river, before I had got them all penned below, they crowded at the open ends of the steamer, loading and firing with inconceivable rapidity, and shouting to each other "Never give it up." When collected into the hold, they actually fought each other for places at the few port holes from which they could fire on the enemy. Meanwhile the black gunners, admirably trained by Lieut's Stockdale and O'Neil, (both being accomplished artillerists) and Mr. Heron of the gunboat, did their duty without the slightest protection and with great coolness, amid a storm of shot.

This river expedition was not undertaken in mere bravado. Capt. Sears, U.S.A., the contractor of Fort Clinch, had urged upon the War Department, to endeavor to obtain a large supply of valuable bricks, said to remain at the brick yards, thirty miles up the St. Mary's, from which Fort Clinch was originally supplied. The War Department had referred the matter to Col Hawley, who approved my offer to undertake the enterprise. Apart from this it was the desire of Lieut. Hughes, U.S.N. commanding U.S. Steamer "Mohawk," now lying at Fernandina, to obtain information regarding a rebel steamer, the "Berosa," said to be lying still farther up the river, awaiting opportunity to run the blockade. Both objects were accomplished; I brought away all the bricks, and ascertained the "Berosa" to be worthless.

I have the honor to state that I have on board the "Ben Deford" 250 bars of the best new railroad iron, valued at $5000, and much needed·in this Department. This was obtained on St. Simons and Jekyll Islands, Georgia, from abandoned rebel forts, a portion of it having been previously blown up, and collected by Captain Steedman of the "Paul Jones." I have also eight large sticks of valuable yellow pine lumber, said to be worth seven hundred dollars, which came from St Mary's, Georgia. There is, also, a quantity of rice, resin, cordage, oars and other small matters, suitable for army purposes. On board the "John Adams" there is a flock of 25 sheep from Woodstock, Florida.

I have turned over to Capt. Sears about 40,000 large sized bricks, valued at about a thousand dollars, in view of the present high freights. I have also turned over to Judge Latta, civil Provost Marshal at Fernandina, four horses; four steers, and a quantity of agricultural implements, suitable for Mr. Helper's operations at that location.

I have seen with my own eyes, and left behind for want of means of transportation (and because brick was considered even more valuable) enough of the choicest Southern lumber to load steamers like the "Ben Deford" – an amount estimated at more than a million feet, and probably worth at Hilton Head, fifty thousand dollars. I also left behind, from choice, valuable furniture by the houseful, pianos, china, &c. all packed for transportation, as it was sent inland for safe keeping. Not only were my Officers and men forbidden to take any of these things for private use, but nothing was taken for public use save articles strictly contraband of War. No wanton destruction was permitted, nor were any buildings burned, unless in retaliation for being fired upon, according to the usages of war. Of course, no personal outrage was permitted or desired.

At Woodstock, I took six male prisoners, whom I brought down the river as hostages, intending to land part of them before reaching Fernandina, and return them on parole, But in view of the previous attack made upon us from the banks, this would have seemed an absurd sketch of magnanimity, and by the advice of Col. Hawley, I have brought them for your disposal.

At the same place we obtained a cannon and a flag, which I respectfully ask for the regiment to retain. We obtained also some trophies of a different description from a slave jail, which I shall offer for your personal acceptance; three sets of stocks, of different structure, – the chains and staples used for confining prisoners to the floor – and the key of the building. They furnish good illustrations of the infernal barbarism against which we contend.

We return at the appointed time, although there are many other objects which I wish to effect, and our rations are not nearly exhausted. But the "Ben Deford" is crowded with freight and the ammunition of the "John Adams" is running low. Capt. Hallett has been devoted to our interest, as was also, until his lamented death, the brave Capt. Clifton. Of the "Planter" I have hitherto said nothing, as her worn out machinery would have made her perfectly valueless, but for the laborious efforts of Capt. Eldridge, and her engineer, Mr. Barker, aided by the unconquerable energy of Capt. Trowbridge of Co. A., who had the command on board. Thanks to this, they were enabled, during our absence up the St. Mary's, to pay attention to the salt works along the coast. Finding that the works at King's Bay, formerly destroyed by this regiment, had never been rebuilt, they proceeded five miles up "Crooket River," where salt works were seen. Capt. Trowbridge, with Capt. Rogers, (Co. F.), and thirty men, then marched two miles across a marsh, drawing a boat with them; then sailed up a creek and destroyed the works. There were twenty two large boilers, two store houses, a large quantity of salt, two canoes, with barrels, vats, and all things appertaining.

I desire to make honorable mention, not only of the above officers, but of Major Strong, Capts James, (Co. B.) Randolph (Co. C.) Metcalf (Co. G.) and Dolly (Co. H.). Indeed every officer did himself credit, so far as he had opportunity, while the cheerfulness and enthusiasm of the men made it a pleasure to command them.

We found no large numbers of slaves anywhere, yet we brought away several whole families, and obtained, by their means, the most valuable information. I was interested to observe that the news of the President's proclamation produced a marked effect upon them, and in one case it was of the greatest service to us in securing the hearty aid of a guide who was timid and distrustful, until he heard that he was legally free, after which he aided us gladly and came away with us.

My thanks are due for advice and information to Capt. Steedman U.S.N. of the Steamer "Paul Jones", to acting Master Moses U.S.N. of the barque "Fernandina," to acting Lieut. Budd U.S.N. of the Steamer "Potomskee," for information and counsel, and especially to Lieut. commanding Hughes, U.S.N. of the Steamer "Mohawk" for twenty tons coal, without which we could not have gone up the river.

I may state, in conclusion, that I obtained much valuable information, not necessary to make public, in regard to the location of supplies of lumber, iron, rice, rosin, turpentine and cotton; and it would afford the Officers and men of this regiment great pleasure to be constantly employed in obtaining these supplies for the government, from rebel sources.

But they would like still better to be permitted to occupy some advanced point in the interior, with a steamer or two like the "John Adams," and an adequate supply of ammunition. We could obtain, to a great extent, our own provisions, could rapidly enlarge our numbers, and could have information, in advance, of every movement against us. A chain of such posts would completely alter the whole aspect of the war, in the seabord slave States, and would accomplish what no accumulation of Northern regiments can so easily effect.

No officer in this regiment now doubts that the key to the successful prosecution of this war lies in the unlimited employment of black troops. Their superiority lies simply in the fact that they know the country, while white troops do not; and moreover that they have peculiarities of temperment, position, and motive, which

belong to them alone. Instead of leaving their homes and families
to fight, they are fighting for their homes and families; and they
show the resolution and the sagacity which a personal purpose
gives. It would have been madness to attempt, with the bravest
white troops, what I have successfully accomplished with black
ones. Everything, even to the piloting of the vessel, and the
selection of the proper points for cannonading, was done by my
own soldiers; indeed the real conductor of the whole expedition up
the St. Mary's was Corporal Robert Sutton of Company G.
formerly a slave upon the St. Mary's River, a man of extraordinary
qualities, who needs nothing but a knowledge of the alphabet to
entitle him to the most signal promotion. In every instance when
I followed his advice, the predicted result followed, and I never
departed from it, however slightly, without finding reason for
subsequent regret. I have the honor to be, General, Very
respectfully, Your obedient Servant,

HLcSr   (signed) T. W. Higginson.

Col. T. W. Higginson to Brig. Gen. Saxton, 1 Feb. 1863, vol. 14, Union
Battle Reports, ser. 729, War Records Office, RG 94 [HH-1].

208: Superintendent of Contrabands in the Department of the South to the Secretary of War

                        Beaufort, South Carolina, April 4, 1863.
Sir: — I have the honor to report the return of the First and
Second Regiments of South Carolina Volunteers from Florida. The
expedition was in every way successful, and had it not been
withdrawn, would in a short time have cleared the State of Florida
of the rebel troops, and secured large amounts of cotton and other
valuables to the Government. We had complete and undisputed
possession of Jacksonville and Pilatka, and Col. Montgomery was
moving into the interior when the order of recall from General
Hunter was received. This was deemed necessary by him in view
of his operations in the vicinity of Charleston As might be
expected, the moral effect of the presence of these colored soldiers
under arms was very great, and caused a perfect panic among the
rebels throughout the State. The colored soldiers behaved bravely
in all their various actions with the enemy, and in no case did
they display any inferiority in point of courage to other soldiers.
  I am glad to report that the hostility which at one time existed
among the white troops in this Department against the

employment of colored troops, has passed away, and they are now perfectly willing to go into action with them.

I shall urge upon the commanding officer of this Department the importance of re-occupying Florida as soon as the Charleston expedition is over. It may require a somewhat larger force at first to re-gain that we have abandoned. Should the Charleston expedition be successful, such force can be recruited there. With the St. Johns. River for a base of operations, the entire State can be readily occupied by our forces, and restored to the Union. Had the expedition been allowed to remain in Florida, I am confident that its success would have fully equalled your expectations. I am, Sir, With great respect, Your Obt. Servant,

HLS
R Saxton

Brig. Genl. R. Saxton to Hon. Edwin M. Stanton, 4 Apr. 1863, S-499 1863, Letters Received, RG 107 [L-158].

209: Officer in a Louisiana Black Regiment to the Commander of a Louisiana Black Brigade

Baton Rouge [*La.*] May 29th /63.

General. feeling deeply interested in the cause which you have espoused, I take the liberty to transmit the following, concerning the colored Troops engaged in the recent battles at Port Hudson.

I arrived here the evening of the 26th Inst, was mustered and reported to Maj. Tucker for duty—

During the night I heard heavy connonadeing at Port Hudson. Early next morning I obtained permission and went to the front. But was so much detained, I did not reach our lines until the fighting for the day had nearly ceased— There being no renewal of the engagement the following day—I engaged in removing and administering to the wounded, gathering meantime as much information as possible concerning the battle and the conduct of our Troops. My anxiety was to learn all I could concerning the Bravery of the Colored Reg. engaged, for their good conduct and bravery would add to your undertakings and make more popular the movement. Not that I am afraid to meet unpopular doctrins, for I am not. But that we may show our full strength. the cause should be one of general sanction.

I have ever believed, from my idea of those traits of character which I deemed necessary to make a good soldier, together with their history, that in them we should find those characteristics necessary, for an effective army. And I rejoice to learn, in the late engagements the fact is established beyond a doubt.

The following is (in substance) a statement personally made to me, by 1ˢᵗ Lt. Co. F. 1ˢᵗ R. La. Native Guard who was wounded during the engagement.

"We went into action about 6. A.M. and was under fire most of the time until sunset.

The very first thing after forming line of battle we were ordered to charge— My Co. was apparrently brave. Yet they are mostly contrabands, and I must say I entertained some fears as to their pluck. But I have now none— The moment the order was given, they entered upon its execution. Valiantly did the heroic decendants of Africa move forward cool as if Marshaled for dress parade, under a most murderous fire from the enemies guns, until we reached the main ditch which surrounds the Fort. finding it impassible we retreated under orders to the woods and deployed as skirmishers— In the charge we lost our Capt. and Colored sergeant, the latter fell wraped in the flag he had so gallantly borne— Alone we held our position until 12. o'clock when we were relieved—

At two o'clock P.M. we were again ordered to the front where we made two separate charges each in the face of a heavy fire from the enemies Battery of seven guns—whose destructive fire would have confuse and almost disorganized the bravest troops. But these men did not swerve, or show cowardice. I have been in several engagements, and I never before beheld such coolness and darring—

Their gallantry entitles them to a special praise. And I already observe, the sneers of others are being tempered into eulogy—"

It is pleasant to learn these things, and it must be indeed gratifying to the General to know that his army will be composed of men of almost unequaled coolness & bravery—

The men of our Reg. are very ready in learning the drills, and the officers have every confidence in their becoming excellent soldiers.

Assureing you that I will always, both as an officer of the U.S. Army and as a man, endeavor to faithfully & fully discharge the duties of my office, I am happy to Subscribe Myself, Very Respectfully, Your Most Obt. Servt,

ALS   Elias D. Strunke

Capt. Elias D. Strunke to Brig. Genl. D. Ullman, 29 May 1863, D. Ullmann Papers, Generals' Papers & Books, ser. 159, RG 94 [V-9]. Strunke was an officer in the 5th Regiment U.S. Volunteers (later redesignated 82nd USCI), one of the black regiments under General Daniel Ull-mann. Two decades later, when Ullmann wrote a report of his military service for the Adjutant General's Office, he recounted the battlefield performance of the three black regiments at Port Hudson on May 27, 1863: "They were on our extreme right where the ground was very broken and covered with an exceedingly tangled abattis. They made six or seven charges over this ground against the enemy's works. They were exposed to a terrible fire and were dreadfully slaughtered." Acknowledging that "it may be doubted whether it was wise to so expose them," Ullmann argued that "the conduct of these Regiments on this occasion wrought a marvellous change in the opinion of many former sneerers." (Bt. Major General Daniel Ullmann to Gen. Richard C. Drum, 16 Apr. 1887, Generals' Reports of Service, ser. 160, RG 94 [JJ-6].) General Nathaniel P. Banks, Union commander of the assault on Port Hudson, exemplified the transformation in attitudes toward black soldiers, asserting in his official battle report that "Whatever doubt may have existed heretofore as to the efficiency of organizations of this character, the history of this day proves conclusively . . . that the Government will find in this class of troops, effective supporters and defenders." (M.G.C. N. P. Banks to Major General Halleck, 30 May 1863, vol. 26, Union Battle Reports, ser. 729, War Records Office, RG 94 [HH-2].)

210: Adjutant General of the Army to the Chairman of the Senate Committee on Military Affairs

Washington, May 30, 1864.

Dear Sir: On several occasions when on the Mississippi river I contemplated writing to you respecting the colored troops, and to suggest that as they have been fully tested as soldiers their pay should be raised to that of white troops, and I desire now to give my testimony in their behalf. You are aware that I have been engaged in the organization of freedmen for over a year, and have necessarily been thrown in constant contact with them.

The negro in a state of slavery is brought up by the master from early childhood to strict obedience, and to obey implicitly the dictates of the white man, and they are thus led to believe that they are an inferior race. Now, when organized into troops, they carry this habit of obedience with them; and their officers being entirely white men, the negro promptly obeys his orders. A regiment is thus rapidly brought into a state of discipline. They are a religious people, another high quality for making good soldiers. They are a musical people, and thus readily learn to march and accurately perform their maneuvers. They take pride in being elevated as soldiers, and keep themselves neat and clean, as well as their camp graounds. This I know from personal inspection, and from the reports of my special inspectors, two of my staff being constantly on inspecting duty.

They have proved a most important addition to our forces, enabling the generals in active operations to take a large force of white troops into the field; and now brigades of blacks are placed with the whites. The forts erected at the important points on the river are nearly all garrisoned by blacks—artillery regiments raised for the purpose—say at Paducah and Columbus, Kentucky; Memphis, Tennessee; Vicksburg and Natchez, Mississippi, and most of the works around New Orleans. Experience proves that they manage heavy guns very well. Their fighting qualities have also been fully tested a number of times, and I am yet to hear of the first case where they did not fully stand up to their work. I passed over the ground where the first Louisiana made the gallant charge at Port Hudson, by far the stronger part of the rebel works. The wonder is that so many made their escape. At Milliken's Bend, where I had three incomplete regiments, one without arms until the day previous to the attack; greatly superior numbers of rebels charged furiously up to the very breast-works. The negroes met the enemy on the ramparts, and both sides freely used the bayonet, a most rare occurrence in warfare, as one or other party gives way before coming in contact with the steel. The rebels were defeated with heavy loss. The bridge at Moscow, on the line of railroad from Memphis to Corinth, was defended by one small regiment of blacks. A cavalry attack of three times their number was made, the blacks defeating them in the three charges made by the rebels. They fought them hours, until our cavalry came up, when the defeat was made complete, many of the rebel dead being left on the field. A cavalry force of one hundred and fifty attacked three hundred rebel cavalry near the Big Black with signal success, a number of prisoners being taken and marched to Vicksburg. Forrest attacked Paducah with seven thousand five hundred. The garrison was between five and six hundred; nearly four hundred were colored trops, very recently raised. What troops could have done better? So, too, they fought well at Fort Pillow until overpowered by greatly superior numbers.

The above enumerated cases seem to me sufficient to demonstate the value of the colored troops. I make no mention of the cases on the Atlantic coast with which you are perfectly familiar. I have the honor to be, Very respectfully, Your obedient servant,

TLcSr   L. Thomas

Adjutant General L. Thomas to Hon. H. Wilson, 30 May 1864, Negro in the Military Service, pp. 2596–98, ser. 390, Colored Troops Division, RG 94 [B-609].

211: Commander of the District of Northeast Louisiana to the Headquarters of the Department of the Tennessee

Young's Point, La., June 12", 1863.

Colonel: I have the honor to report, that in accordance with instructions recieved from me, Colonel Leib, Commanding 9" La. A.D. made a reconnaisance in the direction of Richmond, on June the 6th starting from Milliken's Bend at 2 A.M. He was preceeded by two Companies of the 10" Illinois Cavalry, Commanded by Captain Anderson, whom he overtook three miles from the Bend. It was agreed between them that the Captain should take the left side of Walnut Bayou, and pursue it as far as Mrs. Ame's Plantation, while Colonel Leib proceeded along the Main Richmond road to the Railroad Depot, three (3) miles from Richmond, where he encountered the enemies Pickets and advance, which he drove in with but little opposition, but anticipating the enemy in strong force, retired slowly toward the Bend. When about half way back, a squad of our Cavalry came dashing up in his rear, hotly pursued by the enemy. – Colonel Leib immediately formed his regiment across an open field, and with one volley, dispersed the approaching enemy. Expecting the enemy would contest the passage of the Bridge over Walnut Bayou, Colonel Leib fell back over the bridge, and from thence to Milliken's Bend, from whence he sent a Messenger informing me of the success of the expedition, and reported the enemy to be advancing. I immediately started the 23" Iowa Vol. Inft. to their assistance, and Admiral Porter ordered the Gun-Boat "Choctow" to that Point.

At three (3) o'clock the following morning the enemy made their appearance, in strong force, on the Main Richmond road, driving the Pickets before them. The enemy advanced upon the left of our line – throwing out no skirmishers – Marching in close column, by division, with a strong Cavalry force on his right flank. Our forces – consisting of the 23d Iowa Vol. Inft. and the African Brigade, in all, 1061 men – opened upon the enemy when within musket-shot range, which made them waver and recoil; a number running in confusion to the rear, the balance, pushing on with intrepidity, soon reached the Levee, when they were ordered to "charge," with cries of "No Quarters!" The African Regiments being inexperienced in use of arms – some of them having been drilled but a few days, and the guns being very inferior – the enemy succeeded in getting upon our works before more than one or two volleys were fired at them. Here ensued a most terrible hand to hand conflict, of several minutes duration, our men using the bayonet freely and clubbing their guns with fierce obstinacy, contesting every inch of ground, until the enemy succeeded in flanking them and poured a murderous enfilading fire along our lines – directing their fire chiefly to the officers, who fell in numbers. Not 'till they were overpowered, and forced by superior numbers, did our men fall back behind the bank of the river, at the same time pouring volley after volley into the ranks of the advancing enemy

The Gun-Boat now got into position and fired a broad-side into the enemy, who immediately disappeared behind the Levee, but all the time keeping up a fire upon our men

The enemy at this time appeared to be extending his line to the extreme right, but was held in check by two Companies of the 11" La. Inft. A.D., which had been posted behind cotton bales and part of the old Levee. In this position the fight continued until near noon, when the enemy suddenly withdrew. Our men seeing this movement, advanced upon the retreating column, firing volley after volley at them, while they remained within gun-shot. The Gun-Boat "Lexington" then paid her compliments to the "flying foe," in several well directed shots, scattering them in all directions. I here desire to express my thanks to the officers and men of the Gun-Boats "Choctaw" and "Lexington" for their efficient services in the time of need. Their names will long be remembered by the officers and men of the "African Brigade," for their valuable assistance on that dark and bloody field.

The officers and men deserve the highest praise for their gallant conduct, and especially Colonel Glasgow of the 23ᵈ Iowa, and his brave men, and also Colonel Leib, of the 9" La., A.D., who by his gallantry and daring, inspired his men to deeds of valor, until he fell, seriously, though not dangerously wounded. I regret to state that Col. Chamberlain, of the 11" La. A.D., conducted himself in a very unsoldierlike manner.

The enemy consisted of one (1) Brigade, numbering about 2,500, in command of General McCullough, and two hundred Cavalry. The enemies loss is estimated at about 150 killed, and 300 wounded. It is impossible to get anything near the loss of the enemy, as they carried killed and wounded off in ambulances. Among their killed is Colonel Allen, 16" Texas.

Enclosed please find tabular statements of killed, wounded and missing—in all 652. Nearly all the missing Blacks will probably return, as they were badly scattered

The enemy, under General Hawes, advanced upon Youngs Point whilst the battle was going on at Milliken's Bend, but several well-directed shots from the Gun-Boat's compelled them to retire.

Submitting the foregoing, I remain Yours Respectfully,

HLS   Elias S. Dennis

Brig. Genl. Elias S. Dennis to Colonel John A. Rawlins, 12 June 1863, enclosed in Maj. Gen. U. S. Grant to Brig. Gen. L. Thomas, 16 June 1863, vol. 24, Union Battle Reports, ser. 729, War Records Office, RG 94 [HH-3]. Enclosures.

212A: **Testimony by a Special Correspondent of the *New York Tribune* before the American Freedmen's Inquiry Commission**

[*New Orleans February? 1864*]

. . . .

Gen. Gilmore had little confidence in negro troops when he assumed command of the Department [*of the South*]; Col. Turner was Chief of Staff; Maj. Smith was assistant Adjutant General; his generals were Terry, Seymour, Strong, Vogdes, Stevenson, Gordon and Wilde; the colored troops were in Strong's brigade; the bombardment of Fort Wagner [*South Carolina*] commenced at 11 A.M. from the iron-clad fleet and all the shore batteries; the action continued until about an hour before sunset, with occasional replies from Wagner and Sumter; Gen. Seymour had command; Gen. Gilmore with his staff, the leading colonels, and the correspondents of the press, were on the observatory, 2 1/2 miles from Sumter and 1 3/4 from Wagner. An hour before sunset, Gen. Gilmore (who had been most of the time on the observatory) came down and asked Gen. Seymour (who was lying on the ground) if he thought the fort could be taken by assault. Gen. Seymour replied: "I can run right over it. I can camp my whole command there in one night." Said Gen. Gilmore: "Very well. If you think you can take it you have permission to make the assualt. How do you intend to organize your command?" Gen. Seymour answered: "Well, I guess we will let Strong lead and put those d- - -d niggers from Massachusetts in

the advance; we may as well get rid of them, one time as
another. But," said he, "I would give more for my old company
of regulars than for the whole d- - -d crowd of volunteers." Gen.
Gilmore laughed, but ordered the movement to take place. Gen.
Seymour's command were soon formed in line of battle on the
beach in front of the town; 1 3/4 miles from Wagner. The
division was organized by placing Gen. Strong in advance, Col.
Putnam second and Gen. Stevenson in reserve. The whole column
moved together up to a house about a mile from Fort Wagner, in
open daylight and in full view of the enemy from all the forts;
there all halted but the brigade of Gen. Strong; he marched up at
double quick towards the fort, under a most terrific fire from Forts
Gregg and Sumter and all the James Island batteries, losing on the
way 150 killed and wounded. The first brigade assaulted at dusk,
the 54th Massachusetts in the front. Col. Shaw was shot just as
he mounted the parapet of the fort. Notwithstanding the loss of
their Colonel, the regiment pushed forward, and more than
one-half succeeded in reaching the inside of the fort. Three
standard bearers were shot, but the flag was held by the regiment
until their retreat. The regiment went into action commanded by
their Colonel and a full staff of officers; it came out led by Second
Lieut Higginson—a nephew of Col. H—he being the highest
officer left to command, all ranking being either killed or
wounded. Gen. Strong's brigade was led out by Maj. Plimpton of
the 3d New Hampshire. Gen. Strong received a mortal wound
almost at the commencement of the action; Col. Shaw was killed,
and all the other colonels severely wounded. The 1st brigade
having been repulsed with such severe loss, the second brigade was
then ordered to move. Col. Putnam led his brigade gallantly;
carried the flag of the 7th New Hampshire into the fort, which he
held for half an hour without being reinforced. The enemy
succeeded in bringing to bear against him ten or twelve brass
howitzers, loaded with grape and canister, when the slaughter
became so terrible that he was forced to retire, after having lost
nearly all his officers. About fifty of the 54th Massachusetts were
taken prisoners; none have been exchanged; I believe all reports as
to the harsh treatment of our colored prisoners are untrue; I have
reason to think that they are treated as prisoners of war. Gen.
Gilmore and staff ridiculed negro troops; the evident purpose in
putting the negroes in advance was to dispose of the idea that the
negroes could fight; Major Smith advised Gen. Gilmore to put the
negroes at the head of the assaulting party and get rid of
them. On the previous week Gen. Terry had made favorable
mention of the 54th Massachusetts for gallantry on James
Island. Many of Gen. Terry's officers spoke of them unfavorably

before and favorably since the action referred to. The regiment is now at Morris Island; numbers four hundred men; is in Col. Littlefield's brigade and is commanded by Major Hallowell. Gen. Seymour was not in the advance at Fort Wagner, but early in the action received a very slight wound in his heel, not drawing blood, immediately after which he retired to the south end of Morris Island and remained there all night; next morning he congratulated the remaining officers upon their escape, and charged the failure of the assault upon the d- - -d negroes from Massachusetts. He is now an ardent admirer of negro troops. These facts are personally known to me, and I am willing to swear to their truth.

. . . .

HD

Excerpt from testimony of Nathaniel Paige before the American Freedmen's Inquiry Commission, [Feb.? 1864], O-328 1863, Letters Received, ser. 12, RG 94 [K-217]. Earlier portions of the testimony explain that the witness had gone to coastal South Carolina when General Quincy A. Gillmore assumed command there. The testimony also describes the North Carolina, South Carolina, and Massachusetts black regiments as equal to white troops in the Department of the South and, indeed, better disciplined; asserts that the prejudice against black troops "seems entirely to have passed away"; and argues that literate black soldiers "are well qualified for commissioned officers."

212B: Commander of a Massachusetts Black Regiment to the Commander of the Attack on Fort Wagner

Morris Island S.C. Nov 7th 1863

Genl. In answer to your request that I furnish a report of the part taken by the 54th Mass Vols in the late assault upon Fort Wagner, I have to state

During the afternoon of the 18th of July last the 54th Mass Vols Col R. G. Shaw commanding landed upon Morris Island and reported at about 6 o'clock P.M. to Brig Genl G. C Strong. Col Shaw's command present, consisted of a Lieut Col of the field, a Surgeon, Adjutant and Quartermaster of the Staff, Eight Captains and Eleven Sabaltern officers of the line, and six Hundred enlisted men.

Genl Strong presented himself to the Regt. and informed the men of the contemplated assault upon Fort Wagner, and asked them if they would lead it. They answered in the affirmitive. The Regt was then formed in column by wing, at a point upon the beach, a short distance in the advance of the Beacon House. Col R. G. Shaw commanded the right wing and Lt Col E. N. Hallowell, the left. In this formation, as the dusk of the Evening came on; the Regt advanced at quick time, leading the column, the enemy opened upon us a brisk fire, our pace now gradually increased 'till it became a run. Soon cannister and musketry began to tell upon us. With Col Shaw leading, the assault was commenced. Exposed to the direct fire of cannister and musketry and as the ramparts, were mounted, to a like fire on our flanks, the havoc made in our ranks was very great.

Upon leaving the ditch for the parapet, they obstanetly contested with the bayonet our advance. Notwithstanding these difficulties the men succeeded in driving the enemy from most of their guns, many following the enemy into the Fort. It was here upon the crest of the parapet that Col Shaw fell; here fell Capts Russel and Simpkins; here were also most of the officers wounded. The Colors of the Regt reached the crest, and were there fought for by the enemy, The State Flag then torn from its staff, but the staff remains with us. Hand Grenades were now added to the missels directed against the men.

The fight raged here for about an hour, when compeled to abandon the Fort the men formed a line about 700 yds from the Fort, under the command of Capt Lius Emilio – the 9th Captain in the line – the other Captains were either killed or wonded. The Regt then held the front until relieved by the 10th Conn Regt, at about 2 o'clock A.M. of the 19th.

The assault was made upon the South Face of the Fort. So many of the officers behaved with marked coolness and bravery, I cannot mention any above the others. It is due however to the following named enlisted men, that they be recorded above their fellows for especial merit.

Sergt Robert J. Simmons Co B
" William H Carney Co C
Corpl Henry T Peal Co F
Private Geo Wilson Co A

The following is the list of casualties

Col R. G. Shaw	killed
Lt Col E. N. Hallowell	wounded
Adjt G. W. James	do
Capt S Willard	do
Capt C. J. Russel	missing supposed to be killed
do W. H Simpkins	do do

537

do Geo Pope	Wounded
do E. L. Jones	do
Capt. J. W. M Appleton	Wounded
do O. E. Smith	do
1st Lieut R. H. L. Jewett	do
" W. H. Homans	do
2d Lieut C. E. Tucker	do
2d " J. A. Pratt	do
Enlisted Men	
Killed	9
Wounded	147
Missing	100
Total	256

I have the honor to be Very respectfully your Obt Serv't

E. N. Hallowell

HLcSr

Col. E. N. Hallowell to Brig. Genl. T. Seymour, 7 Nov. 1863, Letters Sent, 54th Mass. Vols., Regimental Books & Papers USCT, RG 94 [G-270].

ᴥ

213: Commander of a Confederate Brigade to the Commander of a Confederate Cavalry Division

Hd Qrs Ten Brigade [Miss.] March 5. 1864

Dr Genl   Genl Richardson joined me yesterday with 500 Effective Men. Our forces united made 1300. and as the Yankee force in Yazoo City was only 2000. We determined this morning to move in and make a reconnoisance and if possible take the place. My Brigd was in front & stormed & took all the redoubts around the City but one and invested that completely. Genl Richardson moved around & occupied the City driving off the Gun Boat Capturing all their stores much cotton & many Horses & mules. Goods &c— The men at once loaded themselves with plunder—and began to hunt the rear— I demanded the immediate & unconditional surrender of their last redoubt which was occupied by the 11 & 109 Ill Infty—& some Negro Troops— We squabbled about the terms of the capitulation. as I would not recognise Negroes as Soldiers or guarantee them nor their Officers protection as such— And while negotiations were going on & the time given them to determine was drawing well nigh to a close.

538

two Transports came up with reinforcements & the Negroes who
had run down the River in the commencement of the fight
returned & pressed our forces so hard that we were compelled to
withdraw the force between the redoubt & the City and they
refused to surrender— It was then 4 PM—and night came on
before the place could be assaulted with Troops in proper style or
with well regulated lines. So We determined to draw off—and are
now at our old camp (The Ponds) At one time we had their
supplies, Cotton. & 30 or more wounded in our possession. Genl
R burned the cotton, & we have a good many prisoners & much
plunder now. The Commissary stores could not be burned— The
fighting was very desperate. The hardest & hottest part of the
engagement was made by the 14th Tenn under Maj Thurmond, in
driving the Enemy & the Gun Boats from Town. Major T. was
killed. Lt Garrin 6th Texas—Lt Howel 3^{d} Texas were
wounded. Our loss in killed & wounded will not exceed
50. Several of the Battery were wounded—None killed— I will
make a report tomorrow of loss & gain—

The Troops are much encouraged by the result of the days
operations. Genl R. will remain with me Tomorrow. I will move
back as you direct to Burton & establish [Courrir] Line &c to
Canton— Cant you come over & see me Soon— Can get up some
sport for you now any day— Very respec &c

ALS
                                                                L S Ross

Brig. Genl. L. S. Ross to Brig. Genl. W. H. Jackson, 5 Mar. 1864, vol.
32, Documents Printed in *The War of the Rebellion*, ser. 4, General Records
CSA, RG 109 [F-152].

214A: Superintendent of the Organization of Tennessee Black Troops to an Illinois Congressman

                                        Memphis, Tenn., April 14th 1864.
My Dear Sir   Before this letter reaches you you will have learned
of the capture of Fort Pillow & of the slaughter of our troops after
the place was captured. This is the most infernal outrage that has
been committed since the war began— Three weeks ago I sent up
four co's of colored troops to that place under Maj Booth a most
brave & efficient [*officer*] who took command of the Post— Forest
& Chalmers with about 3000 devils attacked the place on the 12th
at 9 am & succeeded after *three assaults,* & when both Maj Booth

& Maj Bradford of the 13th Tenn Cav'y had been killed, in capturing the place at 4 P.M. — We had in all less than 500 effective men 2/3 of whom were colored — The colored troops fought with desperation throughout. After the capture our colored men were literally butchered — Chalmers was present & saw it all — out of over 300 colored men — not 25 were taken prisoners & they may have been killed long before [this]. There is a great deal of excitement in turn in consequence of this affair expecially among our colored troops — If this is to be the game of the enemy they will soon learn that it is one *at which two can play*

The gov't will no doubt take cognizance of this matter immediately & take such measures as will prevent a recurrance —

It is reported that Forest will move on this place in a few days — I dont believe it — I am hurried & can write no more today — I am feeling dreadfully over the fate of my [brave] officers & men — Like all others I feel that the blood of these *heroes must be avenged.*

Forest will probably try to get out of west Tenn as soon as he can — We have reinforcement coming in & we shall soon be on his track In haste sincerely Your friend

ALS   [*Augustus L.*] Chetlain

Brig. Genl. [Augustus L.] Chetlain to Hon. E. B. Washburn, 14 Apr. 1864, President 259 1864, Letters Received from the President & Executive Departments, RG 107 [L-174]. Endorsement.

214B: Commander of a Tennessee Black Light Artillery Battery to the Headquarters of the 16th Army Corps

near Memphis, Tennessee April 27th 1864 —
Colonel I hereby have the honor to submit the following report with regard to the section of my Battery, which was on detached service at Fort Pillow, Tenn., and partook in the action at said place on the 12th inst. —

The most reliable information, I have been able to gain, is the report of "John Kennedy" a private of my Battery, who returned, wounded, to this place, two days after the engagement

The section consisted of 1 commissioned officer and 34 enlisted men — Only 2 enlisted men have as yet returned to this place — Private Kennedy informs me, that, the garrison fought well, repulsed two attacks and were in good hopes to be able to hold the fort — The fight continued for eight hours — He saw 6

men killed of my Battery, 5 of whom were killed after the
surrender, having been previously wounded during the action, and
lying in their tents— He heard them ask for mercy, but the
rebels did not listen to them, but shot some of them through their
heads and bodies, knocking others to death with their
muskets— He saw a black woman, who was wounded during the
action, shot through the head and killed, by one of the
rebels— During the last attack when the rebels were climbing the
works and entering the fort he heard Major Bradford give the
command "Boys save your lives," to this he heard Lieut Bisehoff of
the 6th U.S. Heavy Artillery (Colored), object, saying to the
Major, to order the men to remain at their guns and continue to
fight the ennemy, but the Major turning around and seeing the
ennemy coming in from all sides in overwhelming number,
replied, that it was useless.

Kennedy, then, together with some others ran for the river, but
within 2 feet of the same, he was shot through both legs and fell
down— He saw Lieut. A. M. Hunter the com'd'g officer of the
section with others in the river, he saw the rebels fire at them but he
does not know with what effect for he was captured at same moment
and dragged away— The rebels turned his pockets inside out, and
robbed him of what little valuables he had— He was then brought to
the rear about a mile from the fort, and kept there over night
together with some other prisoners, about 50 as he believes, black
and white— Unable to move on account of his wound, he was tied to
a tree and lashed with a gun-sling— He saw 3 colored soldiers
butchered to death by the rebels— They were knocked in their heads
with muskets until they expired— He saw some few rebels, officers
and privates, who tried, to prevent these outrages— He saw only one
officer, who he knew amongst the prisoners, Lieut Bisehoff 6″ U.S.
Heavy Artillery (Colored)— He states that after Major Booth was
killed, the troops were drawn from the rifle-pits to the inner-work by
Major Bradford, and that the thought was prevailing amongst the
prisoners, that, if they had remained at the rifle-pits our troops would
have been able to hold the fort.— Kennedy was held as a prisoner to
the day after the fight when he managed to escape. The detached
section from my Battery consisted of 1 commissioned offr and 34
enlisted men and the casualties are the following, viz.

Killed:	enlisted men	6.	
Wounded:	Dᵒ	Dᵒ	3. (hospital in Cairo,)
Dᵒ:	Dᵒ	Dᵒ	1. (hospital in Memphis.)
Escaped:	Dᵒ	Dᵒ	1. (with the Battery.)
Prisoners:	Dᵒ	Dᵒ	5
	Total accounted for	16. —	

541

1 Commissioned officer (1st Lieut. A. M. Hunter) and 18 enlisted men missing with *no* information about their fate— I have the honor to be, Colonel, very respectfully Your most obedient servant
ALS   Carl Adolf Lamberg

Captain Carl Adolf Lamberg to Lieut. Col. T. H. Harris, 27 Apr. 1864, vol. 32, Union Battle Reports, ser. 729, War Records Office, RG 94 [HH-5]. Endorsements.

214C: Adjutant of the Commander of Fort Pillow to the Secretary of War

Nashville, Tenn. 17th, January 1865.
Sir: I have the honor to acknowledge the receipt of your communication of the 31st. ultimo, and in accordance with the direction therein contained to make the following report of the battle of Fort Pillow:

On the 12th, day of April, 1864, the Federal forces stationed at Fort Pillow, Tenn, consisted of one batallion of the 6th U.S. Hvy. Art'y, C.T.; one battery 2nd U.S. Light Art'y. C.T.; and the 13th Reg't. West Tenn. Vols. (Cav'y.) which was there recruiting—having four companies mustered into the U.S. Service and the fifth Company ready for muster. The men composeing this company had been enlisted by Capt. John L. Poston and repeated applications had been made to have them mustered into the U.S. Service, but no mustering officer could be sent for that purpose. Our entire Garrison numbered some Five Hundred and fifty effective men, with Six pieces of artillery—the whole under command of Major L. F. Booth, of the 6th U.S. Hv'y. Art'y. C.T. In addition to this force the U.S. Gun Boat "New Era"—Capt. Marshal—was stationed off Fort Pillow, and participated in the engagement, but owing to the high bluffs, and in consequence the long range she was obliged to take with her guns, but little assistence was rendered the garrison from this quarter.

At half past five o'clock on the morning of the 12th, of April 1864, our pickets were attacked and driven in by the advance of the enemy under command of General Forrest. Our Garrison immediately opened fire on the advancing rebels from our artillery at the fort, while companies "D." and "E." of the 13th, West Tennessee Cavalry were deployed as skirmishers which duty they performed until about eight o'clock A.M., when they were compelled to retire to the fort after considerable loss in which Lieut. Barr of Company "D" was killed. The fireing continued without cessation principally from behind logs, stumps, and under cover of thick underbrush and from high knolls until about nine o'clock A.M., when the rebels made a general assault on our works, which was successfully repulsed with severe loss to them and but slight loss to our garrison. We, however, suffered pretty severely in the loss of Commissioned Officers by the unerring aim of the rebel sharpshooters – and among this loss I have to record the name of our post Commander – Maj. L. F. Booth – who was killed almost instantly by a musketball through the breast. Major W. F. Bradford of the 13th, West Tenness Vols. Cav'y being the next ranking officer then assumed command of the Garrison and directed the remainder of our operations.

At about eleven o'clock A.M., the rebels made a second determined assault on our works, In this attempt they were again successfully repulsed with severe loss. The enemy succeeded, however, in obtaining possession of two rows of barracks running paralell to the south side of the fort and distant about one hundred and fifty yards. These barracks had previously been ordered to be destroyed, but after severe loss on our part in the attempt to execute the order, our men were compelled to retire without accomplishing the desired end save only to the row nearest the fort. From these barracks the enemy kept up a murderous fire on our men, despite all our efforts to dislodge him. Owing to the close proximity of these buildings to the fort, and to the fact that they were on considerably lower ground our Artillery could not be sufficiently depressed to destroy them or even render them untenable for the enemy. Musketry and Artillery fireing, continued, however, on both sides with great energy, and although our garrison was almost completely surrounded all attempts of the enemy to carry our works by assault were successfully repulsed – notwithstanding his great superiority in numbers.

At half past three o'clock P.M., fireing suddenly ceased in consequence of the appearance of a white flag displayed by the enemy. The party bearing the flag was halted about one hundred and fifty yards from the fort, when we were informed by one of the party, that they had a communication from General Forrest to the Commanding officer of the U.S. forces at Fort Pillow. I was ordered out accompanied by Captains Bradford and Young to receive this communication which I took back to the fort while the party bearing the same remained for an answer. As nearly as I can remember the communication was as follows:

"Head Quarters Confederate Cavalry
near Fort Pillow, Tenn. 12" Apl. 1864.

Maj. L. F. Booth
Com'd'g. U.S. Forces at Fort Pillow
Major:
Your gallant defence of Fort Pillow has entitled you to the
treatment of brave men. I now demand the unconditional surrender
of your forces at the same time assureing you that you will be
treated as prisoners of war. I have received a new supply of
ammunition and can take your works by assault and if compelled to
do so you must take the consequences
Very Res'p'y. Your Obt. Servt
(signed) N. B. Forrest
Maj. Genl. Com'd'g Confed Cav'y".

To this communication I was ordered to make the following reply,
which I placed in a sealed envelope, addressed to Maj. Gen'l.
Forrest and delivered to the party in waiting:

"H'd. Qr's. U.S. Forces
Fort Pillow, Tenn. 12" Apl. 1864.

Maj Gen'l N. B. Forrest
Comd'g. Confed. Cavalry
General:
Yours of this inst. is received and in reply I have to ask one
hour for consultation and consideration with my Officers and the
Officers of the Gun Boat
Very Respy Your Obt. Servt.
(signed) L. F. Booth
Maj. Com'dg. U.S. Forces."

Desireing to conceal from the enemy the fact of the death of
Maj. Booth, and cause him to believe that he was still in
command, it was deemed not only proper, but advisable that I
append his name to the Communication.
I again repaired to the fort, where I had been but a few minutes
when the party bearing the white flag again made its appearance
with a Second communication and I was again sent out to meet
the same.
This time just as an Officer was in the act of handing me the
communication, another officer galloped up and said: "That gives
you twenty minutes to surrender; *I* am General Forrest." This I
took back to the fort, the party remaining as before for an
answer. It read as follows:

"H'd. Qu'rs. Confed. Cav'y
Near Fort Pillow. 12" Ap'l. 1864.

Maj. L. F. Booth
Com'd'g. U.S. Forces at Fort Pillow
Major:

I do not demand the surrender of the Gun Boat; twenty minutes
will be given to you to take your men outside the fort and
surrender; if in that time this demand is not complied with I will
immediately proceed to assault your works and you must take the
consequences.

Very Resp'y Your Obt. Serv't
(signed) N. B. Forrest
Maj. Genl. C.S.A."

After a short consultation with the Officers of the Garrison it was
unanimously voted not to surrender. In accordance with this
decision I was ordered to write and deliver to the party in waiting
the following communication:

"H'd. Qr's. U.S. Forces
Fort Pillow, Tenn. 12" Apl. 1864.

Maj. Gen'l. N. B. Forrest
Com'd'g. Confed. Cav'y.
General:

I will not surrender

Very Resp'y. Your Obt Servt
L. F. Booth
Com'dg. U.S. Forces Fort Pillow"

This I delivered to General Forrest in person, who broke open the
envelope in my presence, and after a hasty perusal of its contents
refolded it when we simply saluted and each went our way.

During the cessation of fireing on both sides in consequence of
the flag of truce offered by the enemy, and while the attention of
both Officers and men was naturally directed to the south side of
the fort where the communications were being received and
answered, Forrest had resorted to means the most foul and
infamous ever adopted in the most barbarous ages of the world for
the accomplishment of his design. Here he took occasion to move
his troops partially under cover of a ravine and thick underbrush
into the very position he had been fighting to obtain throughout
the entire engagement up to three and half o-clock
P.M., Consequently when the final decision of the Garrison had
been made known, the rebel charge was immediately sounded,
when, as if riseing from out the very earth on the centre and
North-side within twenty yards of our works, the rebels received
our first fire – wavered, rallied again and finally succeeded in

545

breaking our line and in thus gaining possession of the fort. At
this juncture one Company of the 6th. U.S. Hv'y. Art'y. C.T.
rushed down the bluff—at the summit of which were our
works—and many of them jumped into the river, throwing away
their arms as they fled. Seeing that through a gross violation of
the rules of civilized warfare the enemy had now gained possession
of our works, and in consequence that it would be useless to offer
further resistence, our men threw down their arms and
surrendered. For a moment the fire seemed to slacken. The scene
which followed, however, beggars all description. The enemy
carried our works at about four o'clock P.M., and from that time
until dark and at intervals throughout the night, our men were
shot down without mercy and almost without regard to
color. This horrid work of butchery did not cease even with the
night of murder, but was renewed again the next morning, when
numbers of our wounded were basely murdered, after a long night
of pain and suffering on the field where they had fought so
bravely. Of this display of Southern Chivalry, of this whole sale
butchery of brave men—white as well as black—after they had
surrendered; and of the innumerable barbarities committed by the
rebels on our sick in Hospital and the bodies of our dead, I do not
deem it necessary further to speak, inasmuch as the "Committee
on the Conduct of the War" has made a full and acurate report of
the same, in which the barbarities practiced by the rebels at Fort
Pillow are shown to have been horrid in the extreme and fully
confirming even the most seemingly exagerated Statements.[1]

The fate of Maj. Wm F. Bradford, for a while involved in some
degree of doubt and obscurity seems now to be clearly
established. Subsequent events show beyond a reasonable doubt
that he was brutally murdered the first night of his capture. Of
the Commissioned Officers of the 13th. West Tennessee Vols.
Cavalry—(now the 14th. Regt) all were killed, save 1st Lieut.
Nichalos D. Logan of "C" Company—who died in prison at
Macon, Ga. on 9th. June 1864.—and myself—the Adjutant of the
regiment. The rebels were very bitter against these loyal
Tennesseeans, terming them "Home-made Yankees" and declareing
they would give them no better treatment than they dealt out to
the negro troops with whom they were fighting.— At about ten
o'clock A.M. the day following the capture of the fort, while the
U.S. Gun Boat No. 28, from Memphis, was shelling the enemy,
who, at the same time was engaged in murdering our
wounded—Forrest sent a flag of truce to the Commander granting
him from that time until five o'clock P.M., to bury our dead and
remove the few surviveing wounded—he having no means of
attending to them.

This proposition was accepted; and under it myself with some fifty-nine others – all that were left of the wounded – were carried on board the transport "Platte Valley" and taken to Mound City, Ill., where we received good care and medical treatment in the U.S. General Hospital at that place. But one Commissioned Officer of the Garrison besides myself lived to get there, and he – Lieut Porter – died soon afterwards from the effect of his wound.

Of the number – white and black – actually murdered after the surrender I cannot say positively. However, from my own observation as well as from prisoners who were captured at Fort Pillow and afterwards made their escape, I cannot estimate that number at anything less than Three Hundred.

From what I could learn at the time of the fight, as well as from escaped prisoners since then, relative to the Confederate loss in the attack and capture of Fort Pillow, I am confident that Five Hundred men in killed and wounded would not be an over estimate. The Confederate forces engaged, as nearly as I could ascertain, numbered some seven Thousand men under Command of Generals Forrest, Chalmers and M‘Cullough.

The bravery of our troops in the defence of Fort Pillow, I think cannot be questioned. Many of the men, and particularly the colored soldiers, had never before been under fire; yet every man did his duty with a courage and determined resolution seldom if ever surpassed in similar engagements.

Had Forrest not violated the rules of civilized warfare in taking advantage of the flag of truce in the manner I have mentioned in another part of this Report – I am confident we could have held the fort against all his assaults during the day, when, if we had been properly supported during the night, by the Major General Commanding at Memphis, a glorious victory to the Union cause would have been the result of the next days operations.

In conclusion it may not be altogether improper to state that I was one of the number wounded – at first considered mortally – after the surrender; and but for the aid soon afterwards extended to me by a Confederate Captain – who was a member of an Order to which I belong (Free Masonry) I would in all probability have shared the fate of many of my comrades who were murdered after having been wounded. This Captain had me carried into a small shanty where he gave me some brandy and water. He was soon ordered to his Company, and I was carried by the rebels into the barracks which they had occupied during the most of the engagement. Here had been collected a great number of our wounded – some of whom had already died. Early the next morning these barracks were set on fire by order of a rebel Officer

547

who had been informed that they contained Federal wounded: I
was rendered entirely helpless from the nature of my wound – the
ball having entered my right side, and, rangeing downwards,
grazed my lung and deeply imbedded itself in my hip (where it
still remains) out of easy reach of surgical instruments. In this
condition I had almost given up every hope of being saved from a
horrible death when one of my own men who was less severely
wounded than myself succeeded in drawing me out of the building
which the flames were then rapidly consumeing.

As to the course our Government should persue in regard to the
outrages perpetrated by the rebels on this as well as on a number
of occasions during the existing rebellion I have only to express my
belief that some sort of retaliation should be adopted as the surest
method of preventing a recurrence of the fiendish barbarities
practiced on the defenders of our flag at Fort Pillow. I am,
Sir: Very Respectfully Your Obt. Servt.

ALS   Mack J. Leaming –

Lieut. Mack J. Leaming to Hon. Edwin M. Stanton, 17 Jan. 1865, vol.
32, Union Battle Reports, ser. 729, War Records Office, RG 94 [HH-4].

1 U.S. Congress, Joint Committee on the Conduct and Expenditures of the
War, "Fort Pillow Massacre," *House Reports,* 38th Cong., 1st sess., no. 65.

215: Commander of a Black Division to the Commander of the Department of Virginia and North Carolina

Camp Hamilton Va April 29" 1864
General   In view of the approaching campaign, and more
especially on account of the recent inhumanities of the enemy
perpetrated upon troops of like character to those of my command,
I deem it my duty to urge that these troops shall be more
efficiently armed, to enable them to defend themselves and lessen
their liability to capture.

There certainly out to be no objection to arming these troops
with as effective a weapon as any that are placed in the hands of
white Soldiers, who are to go into battle with none of the peculiar
disadvantages to which my men will be Subject

The present arms of several regiments in the division are
inferior, in kind and manufacture.

The Springfield Rifled musket of the Bridesburg manufacture is an unreliable gun. The contract Enfield Rifle is also unreliable, and one Reg't is armed with the Old Harpers Ferry smoothbore.

Now these arms will perhaps answer for troops who will be well cared for if they fall into his hands. But the troops who cannot afford to be beaten, and will not be taken, the best arm should be given that the country can afford.

The retaliation we should at present adopt is to arm our colored troops with Spencers Repeating Rifle, and I request that my Division or a part of them may be armed with a repeating or breech-loading fire-arm. I am General. Very Respectfully Your Ob't Serv't

HLc   [*Edward W. Hinks*]

Brig. Gen. [Edward W. Hinks] to Maj. General B. F. Butler, 29 Apr. 1864, vol. 33/66 1/2 25AC, pp. 8–9, Letters Sent, ser. 1659, Hinks' Division 18th A.C., RG 393 Pt. 2 No. 73 [C-3150].

⁓ᔕᐁᗘᔖ⁓

216A: Commander of a Black Brigade to the Headquarters of the 4th Division, 9th Army Corps

Before Petersburg, Va., July 31st 1864.
Sir; In obedience to orders I moved my Brigade, on the morning of the 30th inst., down the covered way immediately in rear of Col. Humphrey's Brigade of the 3rd. Div. – On arriving at the meadow, I was halted by the stopping of Col. H's Brigade – After remaining here sometime I, in accordance to orders, moved by the Brigade of the 3rd. Division, at a flank as directed, across the field through the crater made by the explosion of the mine. Great difficulty was experienced in passing through this crater, owing to it's crowded condition – living, wounded, dead and dying crowded so thickly that it was very difficult to make a passage way through. By the great exertions of the Officers, and heroic determination of the men, my Brigade finally made it's way through and was halted beyond by the Rebel line of entrenchments, which was filled with troops of the 1st, 2nd and 3rd Divisions – behind this line it formed in good order – The 43rd Reg^{t}. U.S.C.T. moved over the crest of the crater towards the right – charged the enemy's entrenchments and took them, capturing a number of prisoners, a rebel stand of colors, and recapturing a stand of National Colors – This line was part of the continuous line connecting with the crater. The balance of my

Brigade was prevented from advancing into this line by the number of troops of the 1st, 2nd and 3rd Divisions in front of them. This position left my Brigade very much exposed to the fire of the enemy, and it was so exposed at least an hour. Owing to the crowded lines of troops of the stated Divisions, immediately in front it was impossible to get my Brigade on. Just as the troops in front were about to make a charge, a white color bearer with his colors, crossed the work in retreat. The troops gave way and sought shelter in the crater—where was concentrated a terrific fire from the enemy's batteries and entrenchments. My Brigade held it's position, until pushed back by the mass of troops, black and white, who rushed back upon it, and until the enemy occupied the works to it's left, and the opposite side of the entrenchments; when becoming exposed to a terrific flank fire, losing in numbers rapidly and in danger of being cut off, it fell back behind the line temporarily occupied by part of the 18th Corps, where it originally started from.

Too much praise cannot be awarded to the bravery of both officers and men— The former fearlessly led, while the latter as fearlessly followed, through a fire hot enough to cause the oldest of troops to falter. The Field Officers particularly distinguished themselves. Col. Delavan Bates, Commanding 30th U.S.C.T. fell, shot through the face, at the head of his Reg^t, whilest his Major, Ja^s. C. Leeke stood on the ramparts urging the men on, with the blood, from a wound through his breast, gushing from his mouth. Lieut. Col. H. Seymour Hall, Com'd'g 43rd Reg^t lost his right arm bravely leading his regiment— His Adjutant, 1st Lieut. James O'Brien deserves honorable mention, having displayed the most heroic courage and daring, standing on the summmit of the crater cheering the men on, amidst a terrific fire of shot and shell. He received a severe wound through the breast. Capt. D. W. Wright 43rd, in charging the rebel line with his men, personally captured a stand of rebel colors and five prisoners, bringing all safely to the rear, although receiving a wound, through the right arm. Col. O. P. Stearns, Com'd'g 39″ put his regiment into the fight with great coolness and ability—his officers and men bravely did their work. L't Col. Charles I. Wright, Comd'g 27th remained on the rebel works with part of his command, until the enemy occupied the opposite side, and until but few men remained with him, when he directed them to retire through the ravine on the right— He received two shots—neither of which disabled him sufficiently to leave his command— Where so many displayed such bravery and fearlessness it is difficult to enumerate—suffice it to say that all did their duty.

I have to regret the loss of 1st Lieut. William Washburn of 35th

Mass. Vol^s. Act'g Aid-de-Camp on my staff, a valuable officer, who was wounded in he neck and taken prisoner while delivering an order to the Brigade. My Staff behaved well—were constantly busy and of great assistance in manouvreing the Brigade.

Had it not been for the almost unpassable crowd of troops, of the leading Divisions, in the crater and entrenchments, Cemetery Hill would have been our's, without a falter upon the part of my Brigade! I am Sir Very Respectfully Yr. Obd't Ser't

ALS

J. K. Sigfried,

[*Attachment*]   Before Petersburg, Va. July 31st 1864.

Report of Killed, Wounded and Missing in 1st Brig. 4' Div. 9' A.C. July 30 1864.

	Killed.		Wounded.		Missing.		
	Com. Off.	En. men	Com. Off.	En. men	Com. Off.	En. men	Aggregate
27' U.S.C.T.	1	11	1	36	2	100	151
30' do	-	18	5	107	5	79	214
39' do	-	12	9	101	-	63	185
43^d do	1	17	6	77	2	128	231
Totals	2	58	21	321	9	370	781

J. K. Sigfried Col.
48' Regt. P.V.V.I.

HDSr

Colonel J. K. Sigfried to Capt. Geo. A. Hicks, 31 July 1864, vol. 40, Union Battle Reports, ser. 729, War Records Office, RG 94 [HH-10]. Sigfried's brigade included black regiments organized in Maryland, Ohio, and Pennsylvania.

216B: Commander of a Black Brigade to the Headquarters of the 4th Division, 9th Army Corps

[*before Petersburg, Va.*] August 2^d 1864.
Sir. With regard to the fight of July 30th 64. I have the honor to state that soon after daylight in the morning, this Brigade entered the covered way leading to the front of that part of the line occupied by the 9 Corps. following the first Brig. of our Div. We were held about half an hour in this way. & then went at double

quick into the exploded Fort & into the rifle pits on our right. Here I lost Lt Col. Ross commanding the leading Reg^t & the two officers of his Reg^t next him in rank. The loss here was heavy in getting into position. There was a white Division in the pits into which we were ordered. The instant I reached the 1st Brig. I attempted to charge, but the 31$''$ was disheartened at its loss of officers & could'nt be gotten out promptly. Capt. Dempcy & Lt Pennell & myself then attempted to lead them but the fire was so hot that half the few who came out, of the works were shot Here Lt Pennell was killed & riddled through & through. He died with the Flag in his hand doing every thing an officer could do to lead on the men. His appearance & actions were splendid I might say heroic, sacrificing deliberately & knowingly his life, in the hope of rendering his country some service. A partially successful attempt was then made to separate the 28th & 29th Reg^t U.S.C.T. from the white troops, of one of the Brigades of the 1st Division 9 Corps, previous to attempting another charge. I then sent word that unless the enfilading Fire on my right was stopped by the moving of a force in that direction, at the moment in which I moved, that no men could live to reach the crest. Immediately after this I was ordered by Brig Genl Ferrero to advance in concert with Col Sigfried & take the crest. I ordered the 29$''$ this time to lead which it did gallantly closely followed by the 28th & a few of the 23^d when it was at once engaged by a heavy charging column of the enemy & after a struggle driven back over our rifle Pits. At this moment a panic commenced The black & white troops came pouring back together. A few, more gallant than the rest, without organization but guided by a soldier's instinct remained on the side of the Pits nearest our line, & held the enemy at bay some ten or fifteen minutes. until they were nearly all shot away.

The 19 U.S.C.T. being in rear was unable to enter the line, but moved up until it rested the left & right Flanks of the right & left wings rested on the line, & its own line ran to the right of the exploded Fort. They remained there unable to strike a blow but received heavy losses. About one hundred of the men of this Reg^t with some of the officers went into the Crater & remained there for hours expending all their own ammunition & all they could take from the cartridge boxes of the wounded & dead men that lay thick together in the bottom of this Pit. After the repulse the Brigade was reformed just in rear of our (now) front line & lay there until 2.30 P.M. It was then filed around to the right by a little hill & then lay until sunset when we marched to & reoccupied the ground we had left in the morning.

Whether we fought well or not the scores of our dead lying as thick as if mown down by the hand of some mighty reaper & the terrible loss of Officers can best attest.   Nearly all the Officers who came under my eye, were fighting with bravery & coolness.

My staff did good service   Capt Dempcy, A.A.A.G. was conspicuous brave & hard at work, throughout the whole affair.   It would be invidious to mention individual cases of Reg^t Commanders when all so far as I could see behaved admirably.   I desire however to pay a passing tribute to Lt. Col. Bross 29 U.S.C.T. who led the charge of this Brigade.   He was the first man to leap over the works & bearing his colors in his own hands he fell never to rise again.   I would also speak of the Gallant & genial Maj The^o H Rockwood 19″ U.S.C.T. who when the Reg^t was ordered forward sprang upon the Parapet the first man & fell cheering his Reg^t on.   Such men cannot easily be replaced nor the void they leave in our hearts readily filled   I am Capt Very Respt'fly Your Obt Servant

ALS   H G. Thomas

Col. H. G. Thomas to Capt. Hicks, 2 Aug. 1864, vol. 40, Union Battle Reports, ser. 729, War Records Office, RG 94 [HH-10]. Thomas's brigade included black troops organized in Maryland, Virginia, Indiana, Illinois, New York, and Connecticut.

217: Statement by Officers of Three Alabama Black Regiments and a Tennessee White Regiment

Enterprise Mississippi.   October 17^h 1864.

We the undersigned officers of the United States service who were surrendered to Maj Genl N B. Forrest at Athens Ala on the 24^h day of September 1864 by Col W Campbell com'dg the post feel it incumbent upon us to make known to the public, the precise situation of affairs in the fort, at the time, in order that the responsibility of the surrender may rest upon the proper persons and also to place upon record our judgement as to the necessity for the surrender.

The Fort was a strong one well built one thousand three hundred and fifty (1350) feet in circumference, seventeen (17) feet from the botton of the ditch to the top of the parapet and encircled by both a palisade, and an Abbattis of felled trees.   It was considered by inspecting Officers to be the strongest work between Nashville and Decatur.

The garrison at the time of surrender consisted of detachments from the 106[h] 110[h] and 111[h] Regiments USCI numbering in the aggregate 469 efficient men. In addition to the Colored troops there were 150 men belonging to the 3[d] Tenn Cav'y and two (2) 12 pounder howitzers. On the night of the 23[d] and 24[h] the Col Com'dg caused nearly if not quite all the Commissary stores at the post to be moved into the fortifications— These stores were thought ample for a siege of ten days. A well in the fort afforded a sufficient supply of water. As for the ammunition there was at the time about 70000 rounds of EB cartridges and an ample supply for the carbines of the Cavalry men. For the howitzers there were 12 rounds each Our pickets were driven in at half past Five (5) PM of the 23rd and from that time until long past dark there was a good deal of skirmishing the night was past in making preparations to receive the enemy and getting provisions into the Fort.

On the morning of the 24[h] about 7 oclock the enemy opened fire on the fort throwing solid shot and shell from a Battery planted on the Buck Island road, shortly after they opened on us another Battery from the Browns Ferry road. From these two Batteries the enemy threw 55 or 60 shots of this number of shots 24 struck in the Fort or Buildings in the fort causing the death of one man only "a non-combattant" and wounding one soldier.

At 9 Oclock AM the enemy sent in a Flag of truce demanding the surrender of the place this was refused by Col Campbell. Genl Forrest then again demanding the surrender of the place this was refused by Col Campbell. Gen'l Forrest then again demanded the surrender of the place stating that he had ample force to take it and offering to show his force to Col Campbell. Col Campbell then called a council of officers commanding detachments in which council we are informed but two officers voted in favor of a surrender, neither of whom had a command in the Fort. Of the 45 officers present in the Fort at the time this council was held but eight (8) were consulted and of these eight there were several who had no command present with them in the fort whilst officers who had the largest numbers of men under their charge were excluded. Col Campbell after reviewing the forces of the enemy returned to the fort saying "The jig is up pull down the Flag," thus surrendering the best fortification on the line of the Nashville and Decatur Rail Road.

We also feel it our duty to make mention of the bravery and disposition of the soldiers in the Fort, both white and Black. It was everything that any officer could wish of any set of men, so far from there being any disposition on the part of the men to surrender or to avoid a fight it was just the reverse. Officers had to exert all their authority even to threatening to shoot their own men to restrain them from exposing themselves.

The soldiers were anxious to try conclusions with Gen'l Forrest believing that in such a work they could not be taken by ten times their number. When told that the fort had been surrendered and that they were prisoners they would scarcely believe themselves, but with tears demanded that the fight should go on preferring to die in the Fort they had made to being transferred to the tender mercies of Gen'l Forrest and his men. Another thing should be taken into consideration, which is that we were on the point of receiving reinforcements. While the truce was in operation and during the time occupied by Col Campbell in viewing the enemy's force firing was heard on the Nashville and Decatur Rail Road, this force came from a force of our troops [s]ent to our relief from Decatur consisting of detachments from the 18^h Mich and 102nd Ohio Infty numbering 360 men commanded by Lieut Col Elliott of the 102nd Ohio who was severely wounded.

These brave men had forced their way through three lines of the enemy, were within musket range of the Fort when our Flag was lowered. The surrender of the fort allowed Gen'l Forrest to throw a portion of his force between the fort and them compelling them to surrender after a hard fight of three hours duration during which they lost one third of their number in killed and wounded – And after they had arrived almost at the very gates of our Fort. In conclusion we do not hesitate to say over our signature that the surrender was uncalled for by the circumstances was against our wishes and ought not to have been made.

HDcSr   (signed) [*32 signatures*]

[*Endorsement*] We also respectfully request that a thorough and immediate investigation of the above statements be made that our names may not be placed on the list of *cowards* in the general suming up of our Nations History. Very Respectfully &c. signed Officers that were surrendered.

[*Endorsement*] We would also respectfully request permission be granted us to publish the original statement of which verbatim copy. Very Respectfully (sig) Robt McMillan 1st Lt 110' US Col'd Inf Parole Camp Benton Barracks St Louis Mo. If permission should be granted please forward papers to the above named Officer.

Statement of Maj. S. W. Pickens et al., 17 Oct. 1864, filed with Colonel Wallace Campbell to Lieutenant J. D. Hazzard, 24 Nov. 1864, vol. 39, Union Battle Reports, ser. 729, War Records Office, RG 94 [HH-8]. Other endorsements. The signers include officers from the 3d Tennessee Cavalry and the 106th, 110th, and 111th USCI. Apparently in response to demands for an investigation of his conduct, Colonel Campbell resigned from the service. (*Official Records*, ser. 1, vol. 39, pt. 1, p. 530n.) For the fate of black soldiers captured by the Confederates at Athens, Alabama, see *Freedom*, ser. 2: doc. 238.

218: Commander of a Tennessee Black Regiment to the Commissioner for the Organization of Black Troops in Middle and East Tennesee

Chattanooga Tenn Oct. 8th 1864

Colonel. It affords me pleasure to tell you of the good conduct of the 14th at Pulaski. on the 27th. The regiment faced the enemy twelve hours. The men lay in line, quietly, and confidently, awaiting his approach. He came "with banners" to the sound of shot and musketry. The men of the 14th looked on as if they were witnessing a parade, and to my questions they replied. "Col. dey never git the old 14th out o' here. Dey not break dis line."

The skirmishers were very cool and deliberate. Capt. Bakers Co. "A – did excellent work, and inflicted considerable loss on the enemy, suffering but little themselves. Four of my men were wounded.

A Federal Cavalryman was killed in front of Baker's line. Two comrades – The enemy was pressing" – asked the colored skirmishers to assist in getting the body Four of them steped out at once – advanced, opened and kept up a brisk fire untill the white soldiers bore away their fallen companion. This was a fine exhibition of the spirit of a true soldier.

One of the 16th stood out without shelter and took deliberate aim at a Johnny, whose gun fired at him at the same instant.

Did I tell you how manly Henry Prince of A. Co. died at Dalton? He was the first man killed in the regiment. As the line of battle was about to advance, Lieutenant Keinbarts, said, "boys" it may be slavery or Death to some of you to day" Henry said "Lieutenant, I am ready to die for Liberty." The line moved. The vows were scarce uttered until a ball pierced his heart and he was dead!

God accepted the sacrifice.

Two others who were wounded at Dalton, have died of their wounds. I am Col. Respectfully Your Obt Servt. & Friend,

HLcSr   Thomas J Morgan

Col. Thomas J. Morgan to Col. R. D. Mussey, 8 Oct. 1864, enclosed in Col. R. D. Mussey to Major C. W. Foster, 10 Oct. 1864, M-750 1864, Letters Received, ser. 360, Colored Troops Division, RG 94 [B-468]. Morgan commanded the 14th USCI.

219: Superintendent of the Organization of Kentucky Black Troops to the Adjutant General of the Army

Lexington Ky Oct 20 /64

General   I have the honor to forward herewith a report of the operations of a detachment of the 5th U.S. Colored Cavalry during the late operations in Western Virginia against the Salt Works.

After the main body of the forces had moved, Gen'l Burbridge Comdg District was informed I had some mounted recruits belonging to the 5th. U.S. Colored Cavalry, then organizing at Camp Nelson and he at once directed me to send them forward.

They were mounted on horses that had been only partly recruited and that had been drawn with the intention of using them only for the purpose of drilling. Six hundred of the best horses were picked out, mounted and Col Jas. F. Wade 6th. U.S.C. Cav'y was ordered to take command of the Detachment.

The Detachment came up with the main body at Prestonburg Ky and was assigned to the Brigade Commanded by Colonel R. W. Ratliff 12th O.V. Cav.

On the march the Colored Soldiers as well as their white Officers were made the subject of much ridicule and many insulting remarks by the White Troops and in some instances petty outrages such as the pulling off the Caps of Colored Soldiers, stealing their horses etc was practiced by the White Soldiers. These insults as well as the jeers and taunts that they would not fight were borne by the Colored Soldiers patiently or punished with dignity by their Officers but in no instance did I hear Colored soldiers make any reply to insulting language used toward [them] by the White Troops.

On the 2^{d} of October the forces reached the vicinity of the Salt Works and finding the enemy in force preparations were made for battle. Col Ratliffs Brigade was assigned to the left of the line and the Brigade dismounted was disposed as follows. 5th U.S.C.

557

Cav. on the left. 12th O.V.C. in the centre and 11th Mich. Cav. on the right. The point to be attacked was the side of a high mountain, the Rebels being posted about half way up behind rifle pits made of logs and stones to the height of three feet. All being in readiness the Brigade moved to the attack. The Rebels opened upon them a terrific fire but the line pressed steadily forward up the steep side of the mountain until they found themselves within fifty yards of the Enemy. Here Col. Wade ordered his force to charge and the Negroes rushed upon the works with a yell and after a desperate struggle carried the entire line killing and wounding a large number of the enemy and capturing some prisoners There were four hundred black soldiers engaged in the battle. one hundred having been left behind sick and with broken down horses on the march, and one hundred having been left in the Valley to hold horses. Out of the four hundred engaged, one hundred and fourteen men and four officers fell killed or wounded. Of this fight I can only say that men could not have behaved more bravely. I have seen white troops fight in twenty-seven battles and I never saw any fight better. At dusk the Colored Troops were withdrawn from the enemies works, which they had held for over two hours, with scarcely a round of ammunition in their Cartridge Boxes.

On the return of the forces those who had scoffed at the Colored Troops on the march out were silent.

Nearly all the wounded were brought off though we had not an Ambulance in the command. The negro soldiers preferred present suffering to being murdered at the hands of a cruel enemy. I saw one man riding with his arm off another shot through the lungs and another shot through both hips.

Such of the Colored Soldiers as fell into the hands of the Enemy during the battle were brutally murdered. The Negroes did not retaliate but treated the Rebel wounded with great kindness, carrying them water in their canteens and doing all they could to alleviate the sufferings of those whom the fortunes of war had placed in their hands.

Col. Wade handled his command with skill bravery and good judgement, evincing his capacity to command a much larger force. I am General Very Respectfully Your Obedt. Servant

HLS   James S Brisbin

Col. James S. Brisbin to Brig. Gen. L. Thomas, 20 Oct. 1864, vol. 39, Union Battle Reports, ser. 729, War Records Office, RG 94 [HH-9]. The 5th and 6th U.S. Colored Cavalry regiments were both recruited in Kentucky.

220: Order by the Commander of a Tennessee Black Regiment

Chattanooga Tenn Nov 23rd 1864

General Order No 50   The Colonel commanding desires to express
to the Officers and men of the 14″ U.S.C.I. his entire satisfaction
with their conduct during the 27″ 28″ 29 and 30″ days of
October, in the defense of Decatur Ala— On the march, on the
skirmish line, in the charge, they proved themselves
Soldiers— Their conduct has gained for the regiment an enviable
reputation in the Western army, noted for its fighting
qualities— The blood of those who fell has hushed the mouths of
our Enemies while the conduct of those who live Elicited praises
and cheers from *all* who witnessed it— It is no small event for a
black regiment to receive three hearty cheers from a regiment of
white men; and yet the 14th deserved the compliment. It is sad to
lose the Officers and men who have been so long intimately
connected with the regiment, but it had been better for *all* to
have gone with them to honorable graves, than for the regiment to
have failed to do its duty— There were many instances of personal
bravery and devotion shown by the Regiment shown by the
Enlisted men— The Colonel was especially pleased with these and
will not forget those who thus distinguished themselves—Sergeant
Major, George Griffith, 1st Serg't Thos McClellan, Serg't King,
Serg't Graffenberg, Corp'l Seuter and those who bore and stood by
the Colors did admirably— Companies F and G. never before been
under fire and yet they behaved, like Veteran Soldiers— One year
ago the regiment was unknown, and it was considered by most of
the army and a large number of the people of the United States
very doubtful whether Negroes would make good soldiers and it
was esteemed no honor to be an Officer in a black
regiment— Today the regiment is known throughout the army
and the North and is honored— The Col commanding is proud of
the regiment and would not {*exchange*} its command for that of the
best white regiment in the U.S. service— He again thanks the
men for their bravery and the earnestness they have manifested in
their work and the Officers for their ready co-operation with him
in advancing the interests of the Command, but he cautions them
that very much remains to be done   By Order of Thomas J.
Morgan Col 14″ U.S.C. Infantry—

HD

General Order No. 50, H'd. Q'r's. 14th U.S. Col'd. Infantry, 23 Nov.
1864, General Orders, 14th USCI, Regimental Books & Papers USCT, RG
94 [G-252].

221: Commissioner for the Organization of Black Troops in Middle and East Tennessee to the Headquarters of Tennessee Black Troops

Nashville Tenn. Dec 21st 1864.

Captain   I have the honor to state that General Tillson reports a gain of 12 men in the 1st U.S.C. Art'ly during the last week, and that recruiting operations in this vicinity, have been wholly suspended by the presence of the enemy.

In the operations which have had so successful an issue, and one so full of joy to every loyal heart, the Colored Troops have sustained the part assigned them with distinguished bravery and honor

I have already reported the good behavior of these troops upon several reconnoissances mad upon our left prior to the battles of Thursday and Friday. In these reconnoissances, the troops engaged the 12th 13th 14th 16th 44th and 100th Regiments gained the commendations of General Steedman Commanding our left, and other Generals in this command who saw them.

On Thursday, General Thomas marched out of our line and delivered battle.

The extreme left of our line was two brigades of Colored troops, Col. Morgan's and Col. Thompson's. A day or two prior to the battle the 16th U.S.C. Infty Col. Gaw had been detached from Morgan's brigade, as guard to pontoon train, and the 17th U.S.C. Infty had been assigned to it.

The real attack of Thursday's battle was made by our right. –   a vigorous feint was made by our left which carried a rebel line of works, and developed a considerable force of the enemy.   Both brigades were engaged, Morgan's having the heaviest work of it, and taking an advanced position which was untenable, and from which it was compelled to fall back.

Through the entire day these men were under a heavy and effective fire of artillery and musketry: there was no flinching.

Col. Shafter's Regiment the 17th U.S. Col. Infty had its baptism of battle, its first engagement, its loss was 119 men killed and wounded.

Capt's Aldrich and Ayers killed, Capt's Bateman, Heimbach, and Freeland wounded, 1st Lieutenant Clark wounded and missing, and 2^{d} Lieutenant Sumner wounded

On Friday morning the enemy had fallen back from their position of Thursday some two or three miles, changing so as to cover the Franklin and Granny White pikes, their lines of retreat.

The Colored Troops moved across the country from their

position of Thursday, encountering but slight resistance till they reached a point on the Franklin pike some five miles from the city, at the range of hills known as the "Oranton Hills"; upon one of these, the Rebels had a battery of four pieces, sheltered by a strong earthwork, a field Post in short. The colored brigades were still on the left of our line, joining the 4th Army Corps on the right.

General Steedman had with these troops, a small force of detachments of white troops, and two batteries.

Heavy skirmish and artillery firing was kept up by our troops from their arrival at the place about 1 o'clock p.m. till after 3 o'clock p.m. when Col Post's brigade of Wood's Corps, the fourth, and Col. Thompson's, were ordered to charge upon the fort. The charge was gallantly made, but was unsuccessful, the ground up which the troops moved was obstructed with brush and tree tops, the slope was very gradual, and consequently the hill of itself afforded no protection to the men, and the dried leaves strewn upon the ground made walking difficult, while the fire of the enemy poured upon them in torrents. Our men fell back. An hour later, a successful charge was made by the left of A. J. Smith's and the right of Wood's line upon a more accessible point in the enemy's works, a half a mile or more from the fort, and the day was won. Our entire line advanced capturing guns, prisoners, small arms &c &c.

I rode over the ground in front of the Fort. Black and white dead lay side by side. Death had known no distinction of color, nor had Valor, for the blacks were as near the enemy's line, as were the whites. Some three hundred must have been killed and wounded in that charge, probably more from Thompson's brigade. The following are as near as I could ascertain the casualties

KILLED

1st Lieutenant George Taylor	13th USC Infty
2d Lieutenant James A Isom	13th " " " "
1st Lieutenant J. M. Woodruff	13th " " " "

These were officers in the same company, and lay within twenty feet of each other, not thirty yards from the enemy's works.

WOUNDED

1st Lieutenant P. B. Dickson	13th U.S.C. Infty
2d Lieutenant L. B. Parks	13th " " " "
Major Finch	12th U.S.C. Infty
2d Lieutenant D. Dease	12th " " " "

Capt's Wright Dickson and Streight of the 100th U.S.C. Infty Lieut Grosvenor 101st U.S.C.I. A.A.A.G. on Col. Thompson's Staff.

Col. Hottenstein of the 13th U.S.C.I. was wounded but so slightly as not to relieve him from duty.

During the reconnissance prior to the battle, Capt. Headon 12th U.S.C. Infty was wounded severely.

There were many instances of conspicuous bravery during the charge of Friday. The color-bearer of the 13th U.S.C. Inf. advanced to the enemy's works and was shot down; another of the color guard went on with the flag and he was shot, and so till five color-bearers were shot. The last color-bearer shook the flag over the rebel works but it was snatched from his hand, and he was shot. Every one of the color-guard was either killed or wounded.

The wounded men bore their sufferings with a degree of patience and fortitude which has elicited the encomiums of all who saw them, and what is more they want to get well and try it again.

Hospital accommodations here for colored Troops are very insufficient, but Dr. Brinton is doing all he can to make them comfortable.[1] The battles of Thursday and Friday have demonstrated that the Colored Troops in this department are brave, well disciplined and have good officers, and that henceforth in the army they will have their place beside all other troops. Another proof of the wisdom of our Government, in arming the Blacks has been given

The Colored Troops are now in the pursuit of Hood, and as soon as they can be reached, I will endeavor to obtain full lists of their casualties. I have the honor Captain to be Very Resp'y Your Obd't Servant

[Reuben D. Mussey]

P.S. I ought perhaps to add that on the extreme right of our interior line, a position was assigned me, and the incomplete regiments under my command, but our services were not needed.

HLc

Col. [Reuben D. Mussey] to Capt. C. P. Brown, 21 Dec. 1864, vol. 221 DC, pp. 364–68, Letters Sent by the Commissioner, ser. 1141, Organization of U.S. Colored Troops, Dept. of the Cumberland, RG 393 Pt. 1 [C-50]. All the black regiments mentioned by Mussey were recruited in Tennessee, except the 100th USCI, recruited in Kentucky but organized in Tennessee. At the conclusion of the campaign against the Confederate army of General John Hood, the commander of the 100th USCI, Colonel Henry Stone, commended his regiment for the plaudits they had won from their commanding generals, George H. Thomas and James B. Steedman. "For the first time in the memorable history of the Army of the Cumberland," he rhapsodized, "the blood of white and black men has flowed freely together for the great Cause which is to give freedom, unity, manhood and peace to all men, of whatever birth or complexion. . . ." (General Orders No. 5, Head Quarters, 100th Regt. U.S. Colored Infantry, 2 Feb. 1865, General Orders, 100th USCI, Regimental Books & Papers USCT, RG 94 [G-273].)

1 For a description of the inadequate medical care afforded the black soldiers wounded at the battle of Nashville, see *Freedom,* ser. 2: doc. 270.

222: Chaplain of a Louisiana Black Regiment to the Adjutant General of the Army

Before Blakely, Alabama, April 1st 1865
Sir: I have the honor herewith to submit my Report of the "general history and moral condition" of 47th Regt. U.S.C.I. for the month ending the 31st day of March 1865.

At the opening of the month, this regiment was disembarking at Barrancas Florida; at its close, it had just arrived before Blakeley Alabama. The former had been selected as a place for organizing an expedition which should make its way into the interior of Florida and carry out such plans as were known only to the originators of the enterprise. Time from 1st to the 19th ult. was consumed in preparation, in drill, in practicing upon the construction of field defences and in the ordinary duties of camp. After a completeness and thoroughness of organization which promised victory in due time, this expedition, consisting of one division of white troops, under Genl Andrews, one division of colored troops under command of Genl. J. P. Hawkins, one brigade of cavalry under Genl. Lucas and three batteries, left Barrancas, Sunday March 19th commanded by Maj. Genl Steel. At night we camped at Pensacola Fla. The next morning the men were provided with every thing necessary for a severe march. Here we broke all connection with our base and entered the country of the enemy.

Omitting further details, we pass to notice some results of this march upon the regiment and the colored troops in general, whose military services, for the most part, have heretofore consisted of garrison duties

1st We notice the ready manner in which the men adapted themselves to *field service.* Those whose burden was too heavy, abandoned such articles as forethought suggested would be least needed. Many exhibited a ready skill and tact in the various methods resorted to for the purpose of personal comfort and protection against storms and in caring for their health and their arms. The spirit also, manifested was a good one. By persons, whose time has mostly been spent in the monotonous duties of camp life, a march was regarded as an episode; and entered upon with a spirit of cheerfulness prompted in part by a love of novelty. And had the country through which we passed been other than an uninhabited, uninhabitable pitch-pine forest growing out of a bottomless marsh, the zest and cheerfullness of the march would have been pleasant to witness, beguiling the weary length of the swampy way. It was, owing to this same easy conformity to circumstances and the tractable spirit of the men that, in addition to the ordinary hardships of a march, they built miles of "corduroy" road over swamps, without a word of complaint. When parched corn, beef and half rations of salt composed their diet scarce a word of murmur was heard. When we consider all these things, we see endurance was not wanting. They are men possessed not only with a cheerful and willing spirit – easily handled, but have also corresponding physical strength. He whom drill has disciplined, hardships have hardened into veterans.

2nd Another development of the march we speak of with conscious pride. It is the high degree of discipline attained by these colored troops. For the high standard set up, praise must be awarded to the officers; but for the manner in which these men have attained to that standard, they are deserving of high commendation. Their obedience to orders is prompt and unquestioned. During the march, when hunger or pillage were the only parts of the alternative, hunger was preferred to disobedience of orders. Their conduct contrasted strikingly with their white comrads. Yet they were not eager to follow the example of others when that example was pronounced incorrect. They denied themselves liberties granted others, that their wills might conform to the will of their superiors. And is not this the highest type of a soldierly mind?

Finally I have never witnessed such a friendly feeling between white and colored troops. During the whole march I have not heard a word of reproach cast upon a colored soldier. But on the other hand, I have seen the two divisions exchange gifts, and talk with each other with apparent equality. All seemed to realize that they were marching from victory to victory beneath the same flag; – that their arms were alike raised in defence of our endangered liberties. The white soldier seemed ready to welcome to his side any aid which looked to the rescue of his broken Union; and the "might that slumbered in the sable man's arm" was ready to strike for the country whose privileges and blessings he yet hopes to enjoy.

The moral condition of the regiment is all we could expect it to be during the irregularity of a march. I have heard but little profanity, far less than among white troops. Whenever occasion has offered for religious services, I have found a good spirit and an attentive audience. Many realize and speak of the uncertainty of life and dangers of a soldier's life.

Many feel keenly their separation from their wives and families, and solicitude on their account. This anxiety is increased as they cannot, like white soldiers, have communication with their families by writing. In this respect they are dependent upon their officers. Their families also are more helpless owing to the fact that the able-boddied men are nearly all in the army. I have the honor to be, General, Your Ob't Serv't

ALS   C. W. Buckley

Chaplain C. W. Buckley to Brig. Genl. L. Thomas, 1 Apr. 1865, B-656 1865, Letters Received, ser. 12, RG 94 [K-508]. Endorsements.

223: Commander of a Pennsylvania Black Regiment to the Headquarters of His Brigade Commander

        near Petersburg Va April 20 1865
Sir, I have the honor to make the following report of the part taken by the 8th U.SCT in the late campaign

The regiment crossed the James river at Varnes Landing March 27. 1865 – the following day marched to Hatcher's Run, and then encamped before the defences of Petersburg. On the 31st was ordered as a support to Genl Turner's prov^l division, 24th AC. – the day after massed for an attack on the defences of Petersburg. On the morning of the 2nd entered the outer line of works which had been abandoned by the enemy and marched at once to the interior and principal line protecting the city; – massed for an attack on one of the main forts – sent forward Capts. Newland and Camp with their companies as skirmishers who advanced handsomely and close up to the enemy's works, during their skirmishers, – this under a brisk fire of musketry and shells. The order for attack was countermanded. Early on the morning of the 3rd the regiment was deployed as skirmishers with orders to press the enemy's works and ascertain if they were still present and develop their strength. The line advanced just before daylight and found the enemys works abandoned – took possession of three pieces of artillery and several cassions and waggons left in the works. Capt. Camp. Co. I. was first to enter the line immediately followed by Major Pell. The regiment was at once advanced on and into Petersburg receiving a number of deserters and most cheering and hearty welcome from the colored inhabitants of the city whom their presence had made free. Same day (3rd) marched to Sutherlands Station on the Cox Road. The day after was train guard. On the 5th 6th & 7th made seven marches. Reported to Genl Foster on the 8th and made a long and most exhausting march of thirty five (35) miles. April 9th moved out of camp at 3. A.M. and shortly afterwards were ordered to the support of Sheridan's Cavalry which was retreating in disorder, and attempting to break through our line   Formed line of battle, arrested the progress of the enemy; – Capt Newland at once deployed his company as skirmishers, and assisted in driving back the enemys skirmishers and line of battle. Soon after marched to another position on the left where it remained to ap^l 11. On that day marched for Petersburg arriving at the defences of the city April 17. 1865.

   It is impossible to name any officers as having specially distinguished themselves; – all were so zealous and efficient in the discharge of their duties. I am Sir, with great respect Your obedient Servant,

HLS   S. C. Armstrong

Col. S. C. Armstrong to Lt. Lyon, 20 Apr. 1865, vol. 46, Union Battle Reports, ser. 729, War Records Office, RG 94 [HH-12].

Prisoners of War

CONFEDERATE POLICY MAKERS, like Southern whites generally, regarded black men in arms against their masters as rebels.[1] The enlistment of black soldiers in Union-occupied South Carolina and Louisiana in 1862 met with cries of outrage from Confederate leaders, who condemned Union Generals David Hunter and John W. Phelps and warned that all Union officers captured at the head of insurrectionary slaves would be executed as felons rather than treated as prisoners of war.[2] For black soldiers, Confederate officials offered an even more certain fate. Initially, Confederate field officers debated whether captured blacks under arms should be shot or hanged, with most opting for hanging. Secretary of War James A. Seddon, determined not to grant former slaves the rights accorded prisoners of war and less troubled by means than ends, approved summary execution without specifying the method. But in December 1862, President Jefferson Davis, with a nice concern for due process, settled the debate. He ordered Confederate commanders to turn captured black soldiers over to the various state governments to be dealt with according to the appropriate state statutes.[3] All Southern states had laws prescribing death to black insurrectionists – usually by hanging.

Confederate policy denying prisoner-of-war status to captured black soldiers or their white officers had been well established by the early months of 1863, when the federal government began large-scale black recruitment. Eliminating any doubts that remained, the Confederate Congress, at the urging of Jefferson Davis, issued a joint resolution in May 1863 restating Confederate policy: officers of black regiments would be treated as criminals and soldiers

---

[1]   Published accounts of the issue of black prisoners of war include: Dudley Taylor Cornish, *The Sable Arm: Negro Troops in the Union Army, 1861–1865* (New York, 1956), chap. 9; James M. McPherson, *The Negro's Civil War: How American Negroes Felt and Acted During the War for the Union* (New York, 1965), pp. 216–22; and Leon F. Litwack, *Been in the Storm So Long: The Aftermath of Slavery* (New York, 1979), pp. 87–93.

[2]   *Official Records*, ser. 1, vol. 14, p. 599.

[3]   *Official Records*, ser. 2, vol. 5, p. 797.

who had been slaves would be turned over to state authorities.[4] Still, some confusion remained. Confederate policy did not provide for captured free black soldiers. Some state officials, particularly the governor of South Carolina, wanted to treat free and formerly enslaved soldiers alike, and at first Richmond policy makers appeared to agree. But by 1864, they seemed to have reversed themselves. While never officially granted the rights of prisoners of war, black freemen appear to have been treated much as were captured white soldiers.

Even as a coherent policy emerged, many Confederate field commanders remained ignorant of the official stance. When they questioned the Confederate War Department, the response did not always conform to the policy the President and Congress had promulgated. In April 1863, Secretary of War Seddon, answering a query from the field, ordered that captured blacks be put to work on Confederate fortifications. Later that year, when General E. Kirby Smith of the Trans-Mississippi Department suggested eliminating the problem of black prisoners of war simply by not taking them alive, Seddon moved quickly to cool Smith's murderous enthusiasm. While agreeing that a few examples might be made, Seddon thought it better to return the "deluded victims" of Yankee perfidy to their masters. This confusion and vacillation reflected growing concern among Confederate policy makers that the Union would retaliate or that European public opinion would be alienated at a time when the Confederate government still hoped for French or British intervention in the South's favor. While they did not retract their policy, Confederate War Department officials privately admitted that the issue embarrassed them, and they discouraged state officers from publicly trying and executing black soldiers. Confederate field commanders, also fearing Union retaliation and having no taste for the executioner's role, took comfort in this unofficial turn toward moderation and either returned black soldiers to their masters, sold them into slavery, or placed them at work as slaves on Confederate fortifications. While falling short of the draconian implications of official Confederate policy, such enslavement violated the conventions of warfare and sent freemen as well as freedmen into bondage.

Official Union policy shared with its Confederate counterpart simplicity of statement and clarity of meaning: the federal government would afford black soldiers the same protection guaranteed white ones. Secretary of War Edwin M. Stanton tendered these assurances to Massachusetts Governor John Andrew at the onset of black recruitment.[5] In April 1863, the codification of United States Army

---

[4] *Official Records,* ser. 2, vol. 5, pp. 940–41.
[5] See *Freedom,* ser. 2: doc. 28.

laws for the conduct of land warfare gave Stanton's sentiment the stamp of official policy,[6] and in July President Abraham Lincoln added the weight of his office to Stanton's pledge, promising to retaliate in kind for every Union soldier murdered or enslaved, by executing or placing at hard labor one captured Confederate soldier. Yet, like Confederate officials, Union policy makers and army officers found it difficult to implement their stated policy. Although the Union government ended all prisoner exchanges with the Confederacy when the South excluded black soldiers from the exchange, it hesitated to execute prisoners or place them at hard labor for fear of inviting counterretaliation by the Confederacy not only against black prisoners but against white ones as well.[7] So the threats and counterthreats continued through the remainder of the war, with each side accusing the other of various barbarities, but with neither side willing to act consistently on its own stated policy.

With both Confederate and Union policy makers paralyzed by the implications of their official positions, it fell to field commanders to establish standards of treatment for black prisoners of war. As early as May 1863, a confrontation between Colonel James M. Williams, commander of the 1st Kansas Colored Volunteers, and Major T. R. Livingston, a Confederate battalion commander, demonstrated how brutal and deadly such events would be. But whatever action Confederate commanders adopted, the official Confederate stance encouraged abuse that went beyond enslavement. Some Confederate officers and enlisted men adopted the official policy for their own and summarily executed black prisoners of war. Others acted similarly in the heat of battle. Men taught from birth to give little value to black humanity needed scant encouragement to vent their frustrations on captured black soldiers. Such abuses appear to have increased during the war as hope of Confederate victory slipped away and as ragtag Confederate soldiers faced a better-fed and better-equipped black fighting force. They doubtless reached their high point at Fort Pillow, Tennessee, where Confederate soldiers, led by General Nathan B. Forrest, slaughtered hundreds of black soldiers after they had surrendered.[8]

Union officers responded to such atrocities with horror and disbe-

---

[6] Section III, paragraph 58, of the "Instructions for the Government of Armies of the United States in the Field" stated: "The law of nations knows of no distinction of color, and if an enemy of the United States should enslave and sell any captured persons of their Army, it would be a case for the severest retaliation, if not redressed upon complaint. The United States cannot retaliate by enslavement; therefore death must be the retaliation for this crime against the law of nations." (*Official Records,* ser. 3, vol. 3, p. 155.)

[7] Cornish, *Sable Arm,* pp. 168–72.

[8] See *Freedom,* ser. 2: doc. 214a–c.

lief. A few acted boldly to protect the soldiers of their command. In the fall of 1864, when General Benjamin F. Butler found that Confederate forces had been using captured black soldiers to construct fortifications along the James River, he placed an equal number of prisoners of war at work on Union earthworks, inducing protest from the Confederate commander, Robert E. Lee, and a threat of counterretaliation, but, ultimately, the removal of black prisoners of war from forced labor. Most Union officers, however, found their revulsion tempered by their skepticism about the reports of atrocities and by their respect for military protocol. Rather than seek immediate redress, they forwarded their complaints to their superiors. While the War Department queried its Confederate counterpart on the validity of various claims, the horror of such atrocities lost its force. President Lincoln never saw need to redeem his pledge to retaliate for the murder or enslavement of black soldiers, and field commanders did so only sporadically.

Black soldiers and civilians had a longer memory. Fort Pillow and similar affairs left an indelible mark in the minds of black fighting men. They fought with a special ferocity knowing that they could never predict what surrender might bring.[9] Black civilians shared their fear and anger. They condemned the government that failed to protect its own soldiers, and they begged Lincoln and the War Department to respond forcefully to the abuse of black prisoners of war. But to no avail. Black soldiers came to realize that, while they might have more to gain in the war than whites, they also had more to lose.

[9] See *Freedom*, ser. 2: doc. 217. Responding to Confederate complaints that black soldiers had sworn an oath to avenge Fort Pillow, a Union commander observed that Confederate attempts "to intimidate the Colored troops by indiscriminate slaughter has signally failed and that instead of a feeling of terror, you have aroused a spirit of courage and desperation that will not down at your bidding." (Maj. Gen. C. C. Washburn to Maj. Genl. N. B. Forrest, 19 June 1864, filed with L-831 1864, Letters Received, ser. 12, Adjt. & Insp. Gen., RG 109 [F-329].)

224: Commander of an Alabama Confederate Regiment to the Headquarters of the Confederate District of the Gulf

Pollard [*Ala.*] Nov 8, 1862.

Captain   I have the honor to call attention to the fact that on the enemy's late expedition (in considerable force) to Milton, a number of armed . . .[1] [through] the town shoulder [to] shoulder with the [white] abolition soldiers. These facts are reported to me by Genl

J Morton of Fla & by Capt Leigh of the Florida Cavalry. Capt
Leigh when he obtained the information was scouting with his
Company, in the direction of Milton. I have given orders to
shoot, wherever & whenever captured, all negroes found armed &
acting in concert with the abolition troops either as guides or
brothers in arms. I respectfully request instructions as to the
treatment to which white Abolition Officers & private soldiers of
Genl Dow's command shall be subjected – hereafter if
captured. – Respectfully

ALS   Jno. R. F. Tattnall

[*Endorsement*] Head Qrs Dist. of the Gulf Mobile [*Ala.*] Nov.
11, 18[62]   Respectfully referred for the instructions of the War
Department in the premises. I have written Colonel Tatnall as
follows:
   "Meantime, hang instead of shooting, any negroes caught
bearing arms in Abolition . . .² [acting?] as guides, unless [there]
be evidence that their employment with the enemy was
voluntary. You will perceive, that when force has been used to
make a captured negro shew the enemy any particular road, or
object, the same guilt is not involved." John W. Forney Maj.
Gen. Commanding

Col. Jno. R. F. Tattnall to Capt. S. Croom, 8 Nov. 1862, T-964 1862,
Letters Received, ser. 12, Adjt. & Insp. Gen., RG 109 [F-274]. According to other endorsements, the Confederate Adjutant and Inspector General's Office submitted Tattnall's letter, with Forney's endorsement, to the
Secretary of War and President Jefferson Davis. According to an undated
notation, the Secretary of War directed that a copy of his letter of November 30, 1862, to General Pierre G. T. Beauregard be forwarded to Forney,
instructing Forney to act in accordance with its instructions. That letter is
printed immediately below as document 225 of this volume.

1 Letter torn at fold; one full line missing.
2 Edge torn; approximately four words missing.

225: Confederate Secretary of War to the Commander of the Confederate Department of South Carolina, Georgia, and Florida

Richmond Nov 30ᵗʰ 1862

General   The question as to the Slaves taken in federal Uniform
and with arms in their hands as presented to you by the letter of

Brig. Genl. Mercer of the 14th inst., and by you forwarded to this Department has been considered on conference with the President. Slaves in flagrant rebellion are subject to death by the laws of every slave holding State, and did circumstances admit, without too great delays, and Military inconveniences, might be handed over to the civil tribunals for condemnation. They cannot be recognized in anyway as soldiers subject to the rules of war and to trial by Military Courts, yet for example, and to repress any spirit of insubordination, it is deemed essential that slaves in armed insurrection should meet condign punishment, summary execution must therefore be inflicted on those taken, as with the slaves referred to by Genl Mercer, under circumstances indicative beyond doubt of actual rebellion. To guard however against the possible abuse of this grave power under the immediate excitement of capture, or through over zeal on the part of subordinate officers, it is deemed judicious that the discretion of deciding and giving the order of execution should be reposed in the General Commanding the Special Locality of the capture. You will therefore instruct Brig Gnl Mercer to exercise this discretion of decision and summary execution in the case of the Slaves referred to by him and any others hereafter captured under like circumstances. I have the honor to be Very Respectfully Yrs

HLcSr   James A Seddon

James A. Seddon to Gen. G. T. Beauregard, 30 Nov. 1862, ch. IX, vol. 8, p. 237, Letters Sent, Sec. War., RG 109 [F-551]. General Hugh W. Mercer, commander of the District of Georgia, wrote Seddon in response to a petition by the planters of Liberty County, Georgia. The slaveholders complained that large numbers of their slaves had fled bondage, joined the Union army, and returned to recruit still others. They suggested that "a few executions of leading transgressors among them by hanging or shoot-ing" would provide a "punishment adequate to their crime & adequate to fill them with salutary fear of its commission." (R. Q. Millard et al. to Brigadier General Mercer, [Aug. 1862] enclosed in Brig. Genl. H. W. Mercer to Geo. W. Randolph, 5 Aug. 1862, M-7867 1862, Letters Re-ceived, ser. 5, Sec. War, RG 109 [F-1000].)

226: Confederate Secretary of War to the Commander of the Confederate Department of Mississippi, Tennessee, and Louisiana

Richmond April 8, 1863.

Genl. Your letter of 26th ult asking instructions in regard to a negro captured on the U.S. Steamer Mississippi has been received.

In answer you are respectfully informed that the negro can be put to work in any of the workshops of the Government or on the Fortifications or in any manner that may be regarded by you as advisable.

The Department has determined that negroes captured will not be regarded as prisoners of War. Very Respectfully Your Obdt Servt

HLcSr

Jas. A. Seddon

Jas. A. Seddon to Lt. Genl. J. C. Pemberton, 8 Apr. 1863, ch. IX, vol. 11, p. 128, Letters Sent, Sec. War., RG 109 [F-552].

227: Commander of the Department of the South to the Confederate President

HILTON HEAD, Port Royal, S.C., April 23rd 1863.

The United States flag must protect all its defenders, white, black or yellow. Several negroes in the employ of the Government, in the Western Department, have been cruelly murdered by your authorities, and others sold into slavery. Every outrage of this kind against the laws of war and humanity, which may take place in this Department, shall be followed by the immediate execution of the Rebel of highest rank in my possession; man for man, these executions will certainly take place, for every one murdered, or sold into a slavery worse than death. On your authorities will rest the responsibility of having inaugurated this barbarous policy, and you will be held responsible, in this world and in the world to come, for all the blood thus shed.

In the month of August last you declared all those engaged in arming the negroes to fight for their country, to be felons, and directed the immediate execution of all such, as should be captured. I have given you long enough to reflect on your folly. I now give you notice, that unless this order is immediately revoked, I will at once cause the execution of every rebel officer, and every rebel slaveholder in my possession. This sad state of things may be kindly ordered by an all wise Providence, to induce the good people of the North to act earnestly, and to realize that they are at war. Thousands of lives may thus be saved.

The poor negro is fighting for liberty in its truest sense; and M[r] Jefferson has beautifully said, – "in such a war, there is no attribute of the Almighty, which will induce him to fight on the side of the oppressor."

You say you are fighting for liberty. Yes you are fighting for liberty: liberty to keep four millions of your fellow-beings in ignorance and degradation; – liberty to separate parents and children, husband and wife, brother and sister; – liberty to steal the products of their labor, exacted with many a cruel lash and bitter tear, – liberty to seduce their wives and daughters, and to sell your own children into bondage; – liberty to kill these children with impunity, when the murder cannot be proven by one of pure white blood. This is the kind of liberty – the liberty to do wrong – which Satan, Chief of the fallen Angels, was contending for when he was cast into Hell. I have the honor to be, very respectfully, Your mo. ob. serv.

HDcS   D. Hunter

Major Gen. D. Hunter to Jefferson Davis, 23 Apr. 1863, enclosed in Maj. Gen. D. Hunter to Hon. E. M. Stanton, 25 Apr. 1863, S-1563 1863, Letters Received, ser. 12, RG 94 [K-101].

228: Correspondence between the Commander of a Confederate Battalion and the Commander of a Kansas Black Regiment

Camp Jackson [*Kans.?*] May 20th 1863

honored sir   I hev five of you Solgers prisoners Three Whight and two Black men   The whight men I propose Exchainging with you if you hev eny of My Men or uther confedorate Solgers to exchainge for Them   as for the Negrows I cannot Reccognise Them as Solgers and In consiquence I will hev to hold them as contribands of ware   if My proposels Sootes your you will Return ameadately my men or uther confedorate Solgers and I will send your your men   [*You*] arested a citizion of this Naborhood by the name of Bishup   If that is your mode of Warefair to a Rest civil citizions who air living at home and trying to Rase a crop for their familys Let me know and I will try to play to your hand   Mr Bishup was onece arested taking to Fort Scott Examoned Released and past home a civil citizion   Sum of your men Stated that he was burnt up in Mrs Radors House but I am sadisfied that you are to high toned a jentleman to stoope or condecend to such Brutal deeads of Barbarity. I remain yours truly

HLcSr   T. R Livingston

Camp Hooker Ks. May 21st 1863 —

Sir. Yours of the 20th inst. is at hand. You have in your custody
as I believe Privates, Pipkins & Whitstine of the 2^{d} Kansas
Battery, for which I will exchange two Confederate Soldiers   now
prisoners in my camp. In regard to the other white man now a
prisoner with you, I do not know of any man belonging to my
command not otherwise accounted for — and you can arrange for his
exchange at Fort Scott.

In regard to the colored men, prisoners, beloning to my Regiment,
I have this to say, that it rests with you to treat them as prisoners of
war or not but be assured that I shall keep a like number of your men
as prisoners untill these colored men are accounted for. And you can
safely trust that I shall visit a retributive justice upon them for any
injury done them at the hands of the confederate forces. And if
twenty days are allowed to pass without hearing of their exchange I
shall conclude that they have been murdered by your Soldiers or
shared a worse fate by being sent in chains to the slave pens of the
South, and they will be presumed to be dead: In regard to Bishop I
have to say that he was known as a paroled prisoner of war, he was
taken in arms against our forces, and was convicted of having shot a
wounded prisoner, disarmed and at his mercy. he was shot and
shared the fate of other Soldiers for whom spades could not be found
to dig their graves. And if this be "brutal barbarity" compare it to
the fiendish treatment he himself visited upon one of my men and of
the bodies of club bruised, and brain bespattered corpses of my men
left on the prairie by your men and leave it to a candid world who
profits by the comparison. Sir these men are enlisted and sworn into
the service of the United States as soldiers, and I doubt not the
Government I have the honor to serve will take the necesary steps to
punish her enemies amply for any such gross violation of all rules of
civilized and honorable warfare, and you can rest assured that
knowing the justice of the course. I shall not long wait for orders in
the premices, but will act as I have a right to upon my own
judgement, and myself assume the responsibility and if you take
exceptions to this course of proceedure you are at liberty to "play to
my hand" as best suits your pleasure or convenience. "But I will
promise to follow suit or trump"   If these two men appear in Camp
(Pipkins and Whitstine) unharmed by your forces, I will conduct
beyond my lines two Soldiers of the confederate army in exchange for
them. You will of course furnish them with exchange papers, and
your men will be furnished accordingly, or if you choose to send a
man with them, he will be allowed to return with the men exchanged
for.

HLcSr   J. M. Williams.

575

Camp Chester Mo. May 23^d /63

Sir   I send you by Mr Wheley, H. Pipkins and David Whitstine which you will please send my two Confederate Soldiers in return for them. I have yet in my custody a private Soldier by the name of W. Y. Akers belonging to the 6th Kansas Co. (K). If it suits your views you can send me a man for him for which I will send him to you, as soon as I recieve my man. I have a better oppinion of your Government in regard to the treatment of prisoners and citizens than you appear to have from the tenor of your letter. For they very well know that my Government is very able to retaliate, and have it in there power to do so at least three two one. though they do not allow such conduct. I understand that you have a confederate soldier in your hands that is somewhat crippled   if it suites you, you can send him for one as I want you to have able bodied men in your possession.

HLcSr

T. R. Livingston

Camp Ben Butler [*Kans.?*] May 26th 1863

Sir   I desire to call your attention to the fact that one of the colored prisoners in your camp was murdered by your Soldiers. And I therefore demand of you the body of the man who committed the dastardly act. And if you fail to comply with this demand, and do not within forty eight hours, deliver to me this assassin. I shall hang one of the men who are now prisoners in my Camp.

Further, you must understand that when I burn a dwelling in a rebel country, it is notice to the occupants thereof to remove beyond the Federal lines, and failing to do which they will be summarily dealt with, and if afterwards found quartered upon any Union mans premices, they will be treated as thieves and marauders and neither age nor sex shall shield them from the full measure of punishment due to such Criminals.

I enclose herewith a copy of a letter from Gen Blunt, to one Col Parker – and I feel myself bound by its directions, and fully competant to execute same. I repeat to you that I am not agoing to lie here hunting a rebel force, who have no specific character or purpose and who are supported by persons living within our lines. Tell them from me to put their house in order, for if I cannot find the force and have a fair stand up fight, I will destroy them by taking from them the means whereby they live   Yours &c –

J. M. Williams

"P.S." You need not excuse the murder of the colored man by
claiming that it was beyond your power to prevent it. If you are
fit to command, you can control your men. And I shall act from
the belief that the murder was committed by your consent and
will recieve no excuse therefor   J. M. Williams.

HLcSr

Camp, Diamond Grove, Mo. May 27th 1863 –
Sir   yours of the 26th is at hand and contents noted   I confess my
surprise at an officer of your rank should have fixed such
conditions to your demand as you are doubtless aware that the one
who committed the offence charged is not a member of any
company over which I have any controle but was casualy at my
camp & became suddenly inraged and an altercation took place
between him and Deceased which resulted in way I very much
regret & that said offenders whereabouts is to me unknown.
Consequently making it impossible for me to comply with your
demand; and as to threats of retaliation upon prisoners of mine
that you hold, I am not aware that you have any belonging to my
command   consequently the innocent will have to suffer for the
guilty and I much regret that you compel me to adopt your own
rule, but had much rather be governed by the established usage of
civilized warfare   Sir your letter with acompanying Letters from
Gen Blunt, will be immediately layed before the Government of
the Confederate States unless immediately retracted by you & your
answer will be anxiously looked for. In regard to your threats a
gainst boath sects, carries with it its own condemnation, and needs
no reply to. In regard to the little attack made upon your train
yesterday, it was by some forces on their way to my command   If
I had have been there myself or some of my old trained Spikes it
would have been a sure thing though I hope we will meet before
long and then I will show you how I can Shuffle the cards. I have
the honor to remain yours most obedient

HLcSr   T. R. Livingston

Maj. T. R. Livingston to Col. Williams, 20 May 1863; Col. J. M. Williams to Maj. T. R. Livingston, 21 May 1863; Major T. R. Livingston to
Col. Williams, 23 May 1863; Col. J. M. Williams to Maj. T. R. Livingston, 26 May 1863; and Major T. R. Livingston to Col. Williams, 27 May
1863, Letters Sent, 79th USCI (new), Regimental Books & Papers USCT,
RG 94 [G-118]. The letter of General Blunt to Colonel Parker mentioned
in Williams to Livingston, 26 May 1863, is not in the letterbook. The
correspondence continued, with Livingston, still angry about Bishop's

death, threatening that Union prisoners might "meet the same unfortunate fate as a penalty for attempting to escape" and Williams urging the Confederate commander to meet him in open battle. Livingston ignored that challenge and instead observed that there would be no gain for "white men and jentalmen to eaquillize them Selvs to com out hand to hand against a lot of eatheuoppieons commanded by a lot of low down thieving white men." (Major T. R. Livingston to Col. Williams, 8 June 1863; Col. J. M. Williams to Maj. T. R. Livingston, 8 June 1863; and T. R. Livingston to Col. Williams, 13 June 1863, Letters Sent, 79th USCI (new), Regimental Books & Papers USCT, RG 94 [G-118].)

229: Commander of the Confederate Department of the Trans-Mississippi to the Commander of the Confederate District of Louisiana

Shreveport La June 13th 1863

General. I have been unofficially informed, that some of your troops have captured negroes in arms— I hope this may not be so, and that your subordinates who may have been in command of Capturing parties may have recognized the propriety of giving no quarter to armed negroes and their officers, in this way we may be relieved from a disagreeable dilemma, if they are taken however, you will turn them over to the State authorities to be tried for crimes against the State, and you will afford Such facilities in obtaining witnesses, as the Interests of the Public service will permit. I am told that negroes found in a state of insurrection may be tried by a Court of the Parish in which the crime is committed, composed of two Justices of the Peace and a certain number of Slaveholders, Gov. Moore has called on me and stated that if the report is true, that any armed negroes have been captured, he will send the attorney General to Conduct the prosecution, as soon as you notify him of the Capture. I have the honor to be General Your Obt Servt

HLcSr

Signed— E. Kirby Smith

Lt. Genl. E. Kirby Smith to Maj. Genl. R. Taylor, 13 June 1863, enclosed in Lt. Genl. E. Kirby Smith to Genl. S. Cooper, 16 June 1863, S-1373 1863, Letters Received, ser. 12, Adjt. & Insp. Gen., RG 109 [F-256]. Pleading ignorance of Confederate policy, Smith forwarded this letter to Samuel Cooper, Confederate adjutant and inspector general. Cooper, in turn, requested clarification from Secretary of War James A. Seddon. Seddon suggested "a different policy in regard to the negroes. Considering them as deluded victims, I would have them received to Mercy & returned to their owners. A few examples might perhaps be made, but to refuse them quarter would only make them agst their tendencies fight desperately." An assistant in Cooper's office forwarded Seddon's comments to Smith. (A.A.G. H. L. Clay to Lieut. Genl. E. K. Smith, 13 July 1863, ch. I, vol. 38, p. 326, Letters & Telegrams Sent, Adjt. & Insp. Gen., RG 109 [F-275].)

230: Governor of South Carolina to the Commander of the Confederate Department of South Carolina, Georgia, and Florida

Charleston. July 22^d 1863

Sir: I am informed that on the 11th inst on James Island certain "negro slaves" of different Confederate States were "captured in arms" "in insurrection" against the lawful authority of the State of South Carolina and associated with them were a number of armed free negroes from the Federal State of Massachusetts, and that in the night of the 18th inst there were captured "in arms" on Morris Island certain other "negro slaves" of different Confederate States as also certain other armed free negroes of Federal States and also certain "commissioned officers of the United States" "found serving in company with armed slaves in insurrection, against the authority" of South Carolina.

By Proclamation of the President of the 23^d December 1862 among other things it was ordered "that all negro slaves captured in arms be at once delivered over to the Executive Authorities of the respective States to which they belong to be dealt with according to the laws of said States." Also, "That the like orders be executed in all cases with respect to all commissioned officers of the United States, when found serving in company with armed slaves in insurrection against the Authorities of the different States of this Confederacy." "The observance and enforcement" of the above orders by the officers of the Confederate States army is required by an order from the office of the Adjutant and Inspector General of the 24th December 1862.

No action having been as yet taken on your part so far as I am informed to carry into effect the above orders, I deem it my duty to the State to call your attention to the matter and ask that you will turn over to me the said commissioned officers and slaves to be dealt with according to the laws of this State.

The expression in the order as to turning over slaves in arms namely "to the Executive authorities of the respective States to which they belong" was used by the President under the supposition, I presume, that the slaves would be found "in insurrection" in the States to which they belong and that he could but mean that they are to be turned over to the Executive Authorities of those States in which the offence might be committed. But if you should differ from me in this opinion I then request that you will retain them here till the question shall be decided by the President and till my demand for their delivery to me can be made according to law on the Governors of the States to which they respectively belong.

The point as to free negroes is for the present reserved till I can correspond directly with the War Department as to their disposition; and I request that they also be retained. I am Sir Very Respectfully your obedient Servant

HLS   M. L. Bonham

[*Endorsement*] Secry of War   The question presented in this file of papers is whether persons of colour belonging to the army of the U.S. & captured by the Confederate troops are to be surrendered to the State authorities of the state in which the capture is made when there is no testimony to show that these persons, had been *slaves* in these *state*

The ground on which the claim of the State rests is not apprehended. J. A. C[*ampbell*] A.S.W.

[*Endorsement*] The Resolutions of Congress are explicit that negroes captured in arms shall be surrendered to the authorities of the States in which they are taken   14 Augt 63 J A Seddon Secy of War

M. L. Bonham to General G. T. Beauregard, 22 July 1863, filed with S-1509 1863, Letters Received, ser. 12, Adjt. & Insp. Gen., RG 109 [F-311]. Other endorsements. Governor Bonham put the slave soldiers on trial in the Charleston District provost marshal's court and, much to his dismay, the court ruled it had no jurisdiction in the case. Meanwhile, Confederate officials, including Jefferson Davis, growing fearful of possible federal retaliation, urged against public trial and executions. Bonham complied, but noted that "in cases of slaves of this State offending in a like manner . . . the offending have been executed." (*Official Records,* ser. 2, vol. 7, p. 673; vol. 6, pp. 169, 245–46, 1081–82.) Governor Bonham wanted the free black soldiers, as well as the fugitive-slave soldiers, turned over to the state. He solicited the opinion of South Carolina's attorney general, Isaac W. Hayne, who assured him that state law held a Negro to be a slave until proven otherwise; hence, "in the absence of evidence to the contrary color alone is prima facia evidence that a negro captured in arms in South Carolina is a slave." Unfortunately for the governor, interrogation of the captured soldiers by William H. Trescot and J. M. Middleton revealed that some had been born free. Governor Bonham then invoked an 1805 South Carolina law whereby freemen supporting slave insurrection could be charged with treason and subject to the death penalty. (I. W. Hayne to Governor Bonham, 18 July 1863; Testimony of Negro Prisoners in the Charleston Jail, [20 July 1863]; and M. L. Bonham to Hon. Jas. A. Seddon, 23 July 1863, all filed with S-1509 1863, Letters Received, ser. 12, Adjt. & Insp. Gen., RG 109 [F-311].) The governor's reasoning at first satisfied Confederate Secretary of War James A. Seddon but later made Seddon uneasy. At his urging, the free Negro soldiers were not placed on trial, and, a year later, Seddon admitted that it would be "considered best" to make a distinction between former slaves and free black soldiers. While the former were to be returned to their owners, the latter would simply be held like other captives but not "formally recognized in any official dealing with the enemy as prisoners of war. . . ." (*Official Records,* ser. 2, vol. 7, pp. 703–4; vol. 6, pp. 139–40, 190–94, 245–46; vol. 7, p. 673.)

231: Union Naval Officer to the Commander of the Mississippi Squadron

U.S.S. "Louisville" Grand Gulf [*Miss.*] June 16– 63. Sir— The following persons were received on board this vessel— June 14– 1863. James Henry–and William D. Shoemaker, deserters from 12th Arkansas Reg^{t} Sharp shooters— Thomas Cormal, deserter from Major Harrisons Battery Light Artillery–also his wife June 15– 1863. George Ferris, from Rodney, Jeff Co Miss. –deserter from Capt Powers detachment of Sharp Shooters—

Thomas Cormal witnessed the hanging at Richmond La. of the white Captain and negroes, captured at Millikens Bend—

Gen Taylor and Command were drawn up to witness the execution. It is also reported by this man, that the Sargent who commanded a company of Contrabands, and who was captured by Harrisons Cavalry some weeks ago was also hung at Perkins Landing I have the honor to be, Sir Your Most Obd^{t} Servt

HLcSr   (signed) E. K. Ewen

Lt. Commander E. K. Ewen to Act'g. Rear Admiral David D. Porter, 16 June 1863, enclosed in Maj. Gen. U. S. Grant to Brig. Gen. L. Thomas, 22 June 1863, #551 1863, Letters Received Relating to Military Discipline & Control, ser. 22, RG 108 [S-7].

232: Mother of a Northern Black Soldier to the President

Buffalo [*N.Y.*] July 31 1863

Excellent Sir   My good friend says I must write to you and she will send it   My son went in the 54th regiment. I am a colored woman and my son was strong and able as any to fight for his country and the colored people have as much to fight for as any. My father was a Slave and escaped from Louisiana before I was born morn forty years agone   I have but poor edication but I never went to schol, but I know just as well as any what is right between man and man. Now I know it is right that a colored man should go and fight for his country, and so ought to a white man. I know that a colored man ought to run no greater risques than a white, his pay is no greater his obligation to fight is the same. So why should not our enemies be compelled to treat him the same, Made to do it.

My son fought at Fort Wagoner but thank God he was not taken prisoner, as many were   I thought of this thing before I let my boy go but then they said M^r. Lincoln will never let them sell our colored soldiers for slaves, if they do he will get them back quck   he will rettallyate and stop it. Now Mr Lincoln dont you think you oght to stop this thing and make them do the same by the colored men   they have lived in idleness all their lives on stolen labor and made savages of the colored people, but they now are so furious because they are proving themselves to be men, such as have come away and got some edication. It must not be so. You must put the rebels to work in State prisons to making shoes and things, if they sell our colored soldiers, till they let them all go. And give their wounded the same treatment. it would seem cruel, but their no other way, and a just man must do hard things sometimes, that shew him to be a great man. They tell me some do you will take back the Proclamation, don't do it. When you are dead and in Heaven, in a thousand years that action of yours will make the Angels sing your praises I know it. Ought one man to own another, law for or not, who made the law, surely the poor slave did not. so it is wicked, and a horrible Outrage, there is no sense in it, because a man has lived by robbing all his life and his father before him, should he complain because the stolen things found on him are taken. Robbing the colored people of their labor is but a small part of the robbery   their souls are almost taken, they are made bruits of often. You know all about this

Will you see that the colored men fighting now, are fairly treated. You ought to do this, and do it at once, Not let the thing run along   meet it quickly and manfully, and stop this, mean cowardly cruelty. We poor oppressed ones, appeal to you, and ask fair play. Yours for Christs sake

Hannah Johnson.

[*In another hand*] Hon. Mr. Lincoln   The above speaks for itself   Carrie Coburn

ALS

Hannah Johnson to Hon. Mr. Lincoln, 31 July 1863, J-17 1863, Letters Received, ser. 360, Colored Troops Division, RG 94 [B-34].

233: War Department Order Publishing an Order by the President

Washington, July 31, 1863.

GENERAL ORDERS, No. 252. The following order of the President, is published for the information and government of all concerned:

EXECUTIVE MANSION, *Washington, July* 30, 1863.
It is the duty of every Government to give protection to its citizens, of whatever class, color, or condition, and especially to those who are duly organized as soldiers in the public service. The law of nations, and the usages and customs of war, as carried on by civilized powers, permit no distinction as to color in the treatment of prisoners of war as public enemies. To sell or enslave any captured person, on account of his color, and for no offence against the laws of war, is a relapse into barbarism, and a crime against the civilization of the age.

The Government of the United States will give the same protection to all its soldiers; and if the enemy shall sell or enslave any one because of his color, the offence shall be punished by retaliation upon the enemy's prisoners in our possession.

It is therefore ordered, that for every soldier of the United States killed in violation of the laws of war, a rebel soldier shall be executed; and for every one enslaved by the enemy or sold into slavery, a rebel soldier shall be placed at hard labor on the public works, and continued at such labor until the other shall be released and receive the treatment due to a prisoner of war.

ABRAHAM LINCOLN.
BY ORDER OF THE SECRETARY OF WAR:
PD

General Orders, No. 252, War Department, Adjutant General's Office, 31 July 1863, Orders & Circulars, ser. 44, RG 94 [DD-1].

234A: Commander of U.S. Forces at Port Hudson, Louisiana, to the Commander of a Confederate Cavalry Brigade

Port Hudson La Aug 5th/63

Sir I have been informed by several eyewitnesses that two of the Colored Soldiers of this command have been recently hanged at or near Jackson La by the men of your command. I am also further informed that some of the Colored Soldiers of this command were, while prisoners of War badly beaten and otherwise Ill-treated. I cannot doubt that these outrages were committed without your authority, but it is my duty to call upon you to disavow these acts and to punish the perpetrators thereof. I would also suggest, the expediency of reminding the men of your command that while it may be difficult to discover and bring to justice those concerned in such crimes, particularly when, as it is certainly probable, they are at least not repressed by some of your junior Officers as they might be — it is not at all difficult to retaliate severely upon the prisoners in our hands and upon those that may be taken hereafter —

The severest measures of retaliation will certainly be adopted on my part if such outrages should be again committed or if those herein mentioned are not disavowed and the perpetrators properly dealt with. I am Sir Respectfully Your Obdt Servt.

HLcSr

Signed Geo. L. Andrews.

Brig. Genl. Geo. L. Andrews to Brig. Genl. J. A. Logan, 5 Aug. 1863, enclosed in Brig. Genl. Geo. L. Andrews to Maj. G. N. Lieber, 14 Sept. 1863, A-488 1863, Letters Received, ser. 1756, Dept. of the Gulf, RG 393 Pt. 1 [C-518]. Also enclosed is the reply of the Confederate commander, John L. Logan, denying that Confederate soldiers had hanged or mistreated any black prisoners. (Col. Jno. L. Logan to Brig. Genl. Geo. L. Andrews, 8 Aug. 1863.) Upon inquiry about the incident from the Department of the Gulf headquarters, Andrews forwarded copies of the correspondence. In the covering letter, he reviewed Logan's denial and other evidence and concluded that, while Confederate soldiers had shown great contempt for captured black soldiers and their officers, he had no proof of the alleged hangings. Without "clear and decisive evidence," he was unwilling to retaliate in kind.

234B: Confederate Cavalry Officer to the Commander of a Confederate Cavalry Brigade

Hd Qr Cav Comd. [*La.*] Sept 2nd 1863
Col. In compliance with the enclosed order I would Say— A
Squad of Negroes were (In arms) were captured at Jackson La
   The morning after the affair at Jackson Col Griffith and myself
ordered the Negroes Several hours in advance of the comd—So as
to arrive in camp at the proper time— Finding the Guard took
the rong road—myself & Col Griffith rode in advance of the
comd—So as to notify them of the fact & order them back— On
the rout back four of the Negroes attemted to escape. I ordered
the Guard to shoot them down. in the confusion the other
Negroes attemted to escape likewise— I then ordered every one
shot, and with my Six Shooter I assisted in the execution of the
order. I believe few ascaped most of them being Killed instantly
   There was not any Federal prisnors with the Negroes— I am
Col. Yours Respetfy
ALS   Frank Powers

Col. Frank Powers to Col. Jno. L. Logan, 2 Sept. 1863, enclosed in Col.
Jno. L. Logan to Col. B. L. Ewell, 3 Sept 1863, #1454 1863 Letters &
Telegrams Received, ser. 93, Dept. of MS & East LA, RG 109 [F-300].
The order Powers refers to is not enclosed. In his covering letter to the
headquarters of General Stephen D. Lee, cavalry commander in the Confederate Department of Mississippi, Alabama, West Tennessee, and East Louisiana, Colonel John L. Logan reviewed Powers's admission and other similar evidence. "My own opinion," he concluded, "is that the negroes were
summarily disposed of." Nonetheless, General Lee closed the case on September 17, 1863, with an endorsement: "Do not consider it to the interests of the service that this matter be further investigated at present—as a
Court of Enquiry or Court Martial will afford the only means of gaining
correct information."

234C: Commander of U.S. Forces at Port Hudson, Louisiana, to the Union Commissioner for Exchange of Prisoners

Port Hudson La Feb'ry 7th 1864
General   A long and serious illness has prevented my answering
your communication of Dec 2nd 1863—which reached me after
much delay—until now. The letter from an officer at this Post to
which you refer was unauthorized and the statements therein made
were then unsupported by any evidence   There have been many

rumors and many statements based upon heresay evidence to the effect that our colored soldiers have been hung or shot by the rebels – but until very recently I have had no positive evidence of the facts. A man from Jackson La. has recently made a statement at Baton Rouge under oath that just after the affair at Jackson last August between a detachment of colored troops from this place and a large force of rebels under General Logan – he saw a rebel Lieutenant Shattuck shoot some wounded colored soldiers, there lying on the ground – This is confirmed by the statements under oath of two colored men, who came from Jackson last week   They also stated that captured colored soldiers were at that time taken into the wood by rebel soldiers who afterward stated that they had shot them – And these colored men say that they afterward found in that direction the bodies of several colored soldiers. At the time of the affair above mentioned I sent a communication to the rebel general Logan informing him of rumors and reports concerning the shooting hanging and ill treatment of colored soldiers and calling upon him to disavow such acts and punish the perpetrators. – He replied denying that such acts had been committed   This matter has been reported to Maj Genl Banks, and the papers recently obtained have been sent to him, and I am informed that a communication on the subject is to be sent immediately to the rebel commander in this Department. I am satisfied that rebel soldiers with the connivance and assistance of their Officers, have abused and shot some of our captured colored soldiers   I am of the opinion that no officers (captured), of colored troops have been shot, but that they have been abused more or less. As already observed it is only within a few days that I have been able to obtain any positive reliable evidence of the perpetrators of these outrages, although I have made every effort to obtain such evidence. All the rebel prisoners claim to know nothing of the matter. – I learn that the Texan troops in Western Louisiana openly state that they will take no colored soldiers prisoner   This Statement is made by Texan refugees. – I believe I have now given you the substance of the information in my posession on this subject. I am General Respectfully Your Ob'd't Ser'v't

[*George L. Andrews*]

Brig. Genl. [George L. Andrews] to Maj. Gen. E. A. Hitchcock, 7 Feb. 1864, vol. 172/335 DG, pp. 213–14, Letters Sent, ser. 2100, U.S. Forces Port Hudson LA, RG 393 Pt. 2 No. 118 [C-518].

235: New York Black to the Secretary of War

New York April 18ᵗʰ 1864

Sir: Some Sixty or Seventy thousand of my down trodden and despised brethren now wear the uniform of the United States and are bearing the gun and sword in protecting the life of this once great nation   with this in view I am emboldened to address a few words to you in their behalf if not in behalf of the government itself. Jeff Davis issued a threat that black men fighting for the U.S. should not be treated as prisoners of war and the President issued a proclamation threatening retaliation. Since then black soldiers have been murdered again and again yet where is there an instance of retaliation. To be sure there has been a sort of secrecy about many of these slaughters of colored troops that prevented an official declaration to be made but there is now an open and bold murder, an act following the proclaimed threat made in cold blood gives the government an opportunity to show the world whether the rebels or the U.S. have the strongest power. If the murder of the colored troops at Fort Pillow is not followed by prompt action on the part of our government. it may as well disband *all its colored troops* for no soldiers whom the goverment will not protect can be depended upon   Now Sir if you will permit a colored man to give not exactly advice to your excellency but the expression of his fellow colored men so as to give them heart and courage to believe in their goverment you can do so by a prompt retaliation. Let the same no. of rebel soldiers, privates and officers be selected from those now in confinement as prisoners of war captured at the west and let them be surrounded by two or three regiments of colored troops who may be allowed to open fire upon them in squads of 50 or 100, with howitzers loaded with grape. The whole civilized world will approve of this necessary military execution and the rebels will learn that the U.S. Govt. is not to be trifled with and the black men will feel not a spirit of revenge for have they not often taken the rebels prisoners even their old masters without indulging in a fiendish spirit of revenge or exultation. Do this sir *promptly and without notice to the rebels at Richmond   when the execution* has been made then an official declaration or explanation may be made. If the threat is made first or notice given to the rebels they will set apart the same no. for execution. Even that mild copperhead Reverdy Johnston avowed in a speech in the Senate that this govt. could only be satisfied with man for man as an act of retaliation. This request or suggestion is not made in a spirit of vindicativeness but simply in the interest of my poor suffering confiding fellow negros who are even now assembling at Annapolis and other points to reinforce the army of the Union   Act first in this matter   afterward explain or threaten   the act tells   the threat or demand is regarded as idle.   I am Sir with great respect Your humble Servant.

ALS   Theodore Hodgkins

Theodore Hodgkins to Hon. E. M. Stanton, 18 Apr. 1864, H-868 1864, Letters Received, RG 107 [L-45]. For the Fort Pillow murders, see *Freedom,* ser. 2: doc. 214a–c.

236: Commander of the Department of Virginia and North Carolina to the Commander-in-Chief of the Union Armies, Enclosing the Affidavit of a Black Soldier

In the field [*Va.*] July 12th 1864

General.   I have the honor to forward the sworn testimony of Sam[l] Johnson as to the occurrences at Plymouth [*N.C.*] after its capture—

The man is intelligent, was examined by me, and duly cautioned as to the necessity of telling the exact truth, and this, is his reiterated statement, in which I have confidence as to its main features and substantial accuracy—

It seems very clear to me that something should be done in retaliation for this outrage—   Many prisoners have been taken from the 8th N.C. Reg[t]—   The 6th, is still at Plymouth—

Were I commanding independently in the field I should take this matter into my own hands, but now deem it my duty to submit it to the better and cooler judgment of the Lieut Gen Com'dg—   For myself, at the present moment, I am far too much moved by the detail of these occurrences, to act in the matter—   I have the honor to be Very Respectfully Your obedient servant

HLS   Benj F Butler

[*Enclosure*]   In the field [*Va.*] July 11th 1864—

Sam[l] Johnson being duly sworn deposes and says:

I am Orderly Serg[t] of C[o] D— 2nd U.S. Colored Cavalry—   In about April last I went to Plymouth N.C. in C[o] with Serg[t] French, a white man, who acted as recruiting Officer, to take charge of some recruits, and was there at the time of the capture of Plymouth by the Rebel forces—

When I found that the city was being surrendered I pulled off my uniform and found a suit of citizens clothes which I put on, and when captured I was supposed and believed by the Rebels to be a citizen— After being captured I was kept at Plymouth for some two weeks, and was employed in endeavoring to raise the sunken vessels of the Union Fleet.

From Plymouth I was taken to Weldon and from thence to Raleigh N.C. where I was detained about a month and then was forwarded to Richmond where I remained until about the time of the battles near Richmond when I went with Lieut Johnson, of the 6th N.C. Regt as his servant to Hanover Junction.

I did not remain there over four or five days before I made my escape into the lines of the Union Army and was sent to Washington D.C and then duly forwarded to my Regt in front of Petersburg—

Upon the capture of Plymouth by the Rebel forces, all the negros found in blue uniform or with any outward marks of a Union soldier upon him was killed— I saw some taken into the woods and hung— Others I saw stripped of all their clothing, and they stood upon the bank of the river with their faces riverwards and then they were shot— Still others were killed by having their brains beaten out by the butt end of the muskets in the hands of the Rebels—

All were not killed the day of the capture— Those that were not, were placed in a room with their officers, they (the Officers) having previously been dragged through the town with ropes around their necks, where they were kept confined until the following morning when the remainder of the black soldiers were killed—

The Regiments most conspicuous in these murderous transactions were the 8th N.C. and I think the 6th N.C.

his
Samuel ✕ Johnson
mark

HDSr

Maj. Gen. Benj. F. Butler to Lieut. Gen. U. S. Grant, 12 July 1864, enclosing affidavit of Samuel Johnson, 11 July 1864, V-92 1864, Letters Received by General Grant, ser. 105, Headquarters in the Field, RG 108 [S-30]. Affidavit sworn before an army provost marshal.

237: Order by the Commander of the Department of Virginia and North Carolina

In the Field [*Va.*], October 13, 1864.

GENERAL ORDERS, No. 126. It being testified to the
Commanding General by a number of refugees and deserters from
the enemy, that from one hundred to one hundred and fifty
soldiers of the United States, captured in arms by the Confederates
on the lines near Chapin's Bluff, have been taken from Libby
Prison and otherwheres, and placed to labor on the entrenchments
of the enemy's lines in front of their troops, the Commanding
General on the 13th day of October, notified the Confederate
Agent of Exchange, Robert Ould, of the outrage being perpetrated
upon his soldiers, and informed him that unless the practice was
stopped, retaliation in kind would be adopted by the Government
of the United States.

Being assured by Gen. Ewell, Commanding Confederate forces
on the North side of the James, that an answer to this
communication, if any, would be sent by eleven o'clock, A.M.,
to-day; and it being now past twelve, (noon,) and no answer
having been received,

IT IS ORDERED: That an equal number of Prisoners of War,
preferably members of the Virginia Reserves, by and under whose
charge this outrage is being carried on, be set to work in the
excavation at Dutch Gap, and elsewhere along the trenches, as may
hereafter seem best, in retaliation for this unjust treatment of the
soldiers of the United States so kept at labor and service by the
Confederate authorities.

It being also testified to by the same witnesses, that the rations
served to the soldiers of the United States, so at labor, is one
pound of flour and one third of a pound of bacon daily, it is
ordered that the same ration precisely be served to these
Confederate Prisoners so kept at work, daily, and no other or
different.

It being further testified to, that the time of labor of the
soldiers of the United States, so at work under the Confederates, is
ten hours each day; these Confederate prisoners so kept at work,
will be made to work, and work faithfully, daily during the same
period of time.

This order will be read to the Prisoners set to work, the first
time they are mustered for labor, in order that they may know
why, it is that they do not receive that kind and courteous
treatment they have heretofore from the United States, as Prisoners
of War.

Upon any attempt to escape, by any of these Prisoners so kept at work, they will be instantly shot. By command of Major General BUTLER:

PD

General Orders, No. 126, Head Quarters Department Virginia & North Carolina, Army of the James, 13 Oct. 1864, Orders & Circulars, ser. 44, RG 94 [DD-13]. Upon the withdrawal of captured Union soldiers from Confederate fatigue duties, General Benjamin F. Butler ordered the removal of Confederate prisoners from similar duties on October 20, 1863. (General Orders, No. 134, Head Quarters Department of Virginia and North Carolina, Army of the James, 20 Oct. 1864, Orders & Circulars, ser. 44, RG 94 [DD-13].) Butler's action had been authorized by General Ulysses S. Grant, and Grant directly informed General Robert E. Lee, commander of the Confederate Army of Northern Virginia, of his decision. Lee responded with a full explication of Confederate prisoner-of-war policy, noting that under the still extant fugitive slave law, Confederate forces returned slaves to their masters. The captured black soldiers in question had been placed at work by error and would be withdrawn until their masters could be located. Thus, in Lee's mind, Confederate policy had not been altered. Lee forwarded a copy of his letter to Confederate Secretary of War James A. Seddon, who seemed much relieved that counterretaliation had not been necessary. Confederate President Jefferson Davis observed that Lee's "gentlemanly bearing" contrasted favorably with Grant's crude threats. Grant, for his part, accepted the withdrawal of black prisoners of war from the Confederate fortifications as satisfaction enough and observed, "I have nothing to do with the discussion of the slavery question, therefore decline answering the arguments adduced to show the right to return to former owners such negroes as are captured from our Army." (*Official Records*, ser. 2, vol. 7, pp. 1010–12, 1015–16, 1018–19, 1029–30.)

238: Affidavit by an Alabama Black Soldier

[*Nashville, Tenn.*] 30th day of January, 1865

STATEMENT OF PRIVATE JOSEPH HOWARD
CO. "F," 110th REGT, U.S. C'D INFY.

I was taken prisoner at the surrender of Athens, Ala., Sept. 24, 1864. We were marched to Mobile, Ala., stopping at various places on the route. We were twelve days going to Mobile. After we were captured, the rebels robbed us of everything we had that they could use. They searched our pockets – took our clothing, and even cut the buttons off what little clothing they allowed us to retain. After arriving at Mobile, we were placed at work on the fortifications there, and impressed colored men who were at work when we arrived, were released, we taking their places. We were kept at hard labor and inhumanly treated. If we lagged, or faltered, or misunderstood an order, we were whipped and abused – some of our own men being detailed to whip the others. They gave, as a reason for such harsh treatment, that we knew very well what they wanted us to do – but that we feigned ignorance – that if we were with the Yankees we would do all they wanted &c. For the slightest causes we were subjected to the lash. We were very poorly provided for with food, our rations being corn-meal and mule meat, and occasionally some poor beef.

On the 7th of December, I stole a skiff and went down Mobile River to the Bay, and was taken on board one of our Gunboats. I was taken to Fort Morgan on the Gunboat, and reported to the Commanding Officer, who, after hearing my story, furnished me a pass and transportation to New Orleans. Form there I was sent to Cairo, thence to Louisville, and from there, here.

his
(signed) Joseph X Howard
mark

HDcSr

Affidavit of Private Joseph Howard, 30 Jan. 1865, enclosed in Col. R. D. Mussey to Capt. C. P. Brown, 31 Jan. 1865, M-2 1865, Letters Received by Adjutant General L. Thomas, ser. 363, Colored Troops Division, RG 94 [V-88]. Affidavit sworn before an assistant to the Commissioner for the Organization of Colored Troops at Nashville.

239: Mississippi Citizen to a United States Commissioner

[Vicksburg, Miss.] Aug. 14th 1865

Mr G. G. Adam; Yesterday an order dated H'd Q'rs Western Dist. Miss. Aug. 13th 1865 came under my notice, for the transportation to Memphis Tenn. of Priv^s. John Powell & Joe Ewing of the 59th U.S.C.I.

The order represented these men as "having been released from captivity by the rebels."

The long time that has elapsed since all men held as prisoners of war by the rebels *should* have been restored to their liberty led me to question these colored men concerning their imprisonment. They made a statement substantially as follows: – We were taken, about eight months ago, by Wheeler's men; by them I was sold to a man who lives at Kosciusko, Miss. for $5.000

By him I was set to work in the steam-mill at that place that was used for the rebel army.

After the surrender last spring the mill referred to was kept in use for the inhabitants of the country round about; and we were forced to remain by the man who had bought us. I tried to run away from them and was shot, by them in the act of running away, and wounded.

We then stayed, under cumpulsion, at that labor until yesterday two weeks ago. (that was the 29th of July) when a force of United States Soldiers came to garrison the town of Kosciusko. Then the man who had bought us from Wheeler's men permitted us to leave. Thence we came to this place on our way to our regiment. The name of the man who bought us was Lawyer Joe Taylor.

The above statement is *substantially* true, as to the facts set forth to me by the colored soldiers who made it. I am not *entirely* certain that the name of the perpetrator of the wrong was given just as I have here written it — My recollection of the *exact words* that they used not being perfect.

ALS   Elias Shull

Elias Shull to Mr. G. G. Adam, 14 Aug. 1865, S-1 1865, Registered Letters Received, ser. 2188, Jackson MS Acting Asst. Comr. of the Northern Dist. of MS, RG 105 [A-9314]. Endorsement.

PART 4

Black Military Life: Off Duty

13

Camp Life

LIKE THEIR WHITE COMRADES, black soldiers spent only a fraction of their time fighting or doing fatigue duty. Instead, the timeless routines of military life dogged them, filling their waking hours with countless minor but necessary tasks. Between reveille and taps, black soldiers spent hours drilling, performing guard and picket duties, cleaning weapons, polishing shoes and buttons, policing camp, and standing long hours in the hot sun while the officer of the day droned regulations and orders.

Military tasks notwithstanding, soldiers also enjoyed a considerable amount of leisure time. They occupied and entertained themselves in quiet moments alone and in raucous groups, singing, praying, reading, gambling, and swapping stories. Many attended regularly organized regimental schools, gaining their first formal education. Such leisure time enabled soldiers to maintain their links with loved ones at home and to associate with both their comrades in uniform and black folk in nearby communities. In so doing, black soldiers in some measure constructed a life of their own, apart from and often incomprehensible to their white officers. Yet, even during their free moments, soldiers could not fully escape the military regimen. Officers interdicted behavior they considered objectionable, and chaplains warred against gaming and profanity, repeatedly reminding men of the standards of respectability to which they should aspire.[1]

As soldiers sat around campfires, recounting past experiences in slavery and speculating on their future in freedom, comrades-in-arms became fast friends. Many of these friendships lasted long after discharge, although some ended tragically in battle or fatal illness.

---

[1] Monthly reports by the chaplains of black regiments to the Adjutant General's Office provide general accounts of camp activities, with special attention to religion and education. Their comments about the moral condition of the soldiers describe gambling, profanity, and other camp vices. (See, for example, Chaplain G. A. Rockwood to Lieut. F. H. Evans, 31 Oct. 1864, R-890 1864, Letters Received, ser. 12, RG 94 [K-550]. On gambling, see the proceedings of the general court-martial in the case of Corporal George Ringo, 13th Kansas Volunteers, 13–27 Apr. 1865, MM-2035, Court-Martial Case Files, ser. 15, RG 153 [H-43]. See also *Freedom*, ser. 2: doc. 253.

Inevitably and sadly, funerals became a regular part of the soldier's routine, as did writing the loved ones of fallen comrades. Although less dramatic than heroic conquests and less monumental than miles of fortifications constructed, such activities formed every bit as important a part of the soldier's experience.

240: Order by the Commander of a Louisiana Black Regiment

Port Hudson La Augt 7th 1863.

GENERAL ORDERS *No 16*

1st On and after the 10th Inst the following Roster of daily exercises will be strictly observed in this command

Reveille-(roll call)	5 o.clock AM	Co or Battallion drill	4 to 5.45 P.M
Breakfast	5.30 " "	Retreat Parade (roll call)	6 "
Squad drill	6.30 to 8 "	Supper	7 "
N.C. officers "	9.30 " 10.30	Tattoo (roll call)	9 "
Guard Mount	9 " "	Taps (lights out)	9.30 "
Dinner (roll call)	1 o.clock P.M.		

The customary company inspection will be held at 9. AM each Sunday —

The above hours will be strictly observed under personal responsibility of the Officer of the Day —

2nd In compliance with the Reg^t [*Requirements*] of Act [*Article*] 3, G.O. No 11, Head Qrs U.S. Forces Port Hudson La. July 27th 1863, Officers Comd'g Companies are instructed to keep the grounds occupied by their respective companies & the vacinity in a state of neatness & cleanliness —   The streets are to be visited at least three times per week by an officer of the company & to be thoroughly cleaned —

3rd On the saturdays of each week only the morning drill will be observed & the rest of the day devoted to general policing, every 2nd and 4th Saturday of each month immediately after morning drill the arms are to be stacked in the company street, the equipments hung upon them and the Tents taken down for a thorough airing and cleaning — until 3 o clock in the afternoon —

4th Every Saturday afternoon between the hours of 4 & 6.30 the Five right flank companies and on Saturday morning the Five left flank companies between the hours of 6 & 8.30 will be marched to the River in a body — under the charge of a Lieut for the purpose of bathing. The officer in charge will not premit the men to straggle or go into the water while heated with marching or to remain in the water for more than 20 minutes —

5th Company Commanders will pay the greatest attention to the instruction of their N.C Officers, at least one or two good men should from each Company be drilled with the N.C. Officers to fit them to hold positions as N.C Officers. Only good sober and intelligent men are to be chosen for N.C Officers – At least one or two good men, (the ones selected to drill with the N.C Officers) should be instructed in reading & writing –

6th On every Tuesday & Friday of each week the N.C. Officers and Privates chosen for promotion will be drilled by the Reg'tl Adg't in Company and Battallion moovements at the prescribed hours

7th The names of all N.C. Officers will be sent to these Head Qrs in order of priority of enlistment, and with all necessary remarks and information, on or before the 15th inst. There will be an examination of the N.C Officers on the 31st inst or as soon thereafter as practicable when all those worthy will receive their Warrants of promotion, while those found wanting will be reduced to the ranks

8th Officers are again reminded of the great importance of enstilling into the minds of their men, a thorough and sincere respect towards rank – and their duty of manifesting the same – by the proper salutes, and every enlisted man guilty of negligence in saluting Officers, whether of this or any other Regiment they meet with, will be severly punished –

9th The state of the Co Kitchens, and its vacinity and the proper cooking the soldiers meals must form a matter of the greatest importance, to every Officer. The food should be inspected often, and at different hours of the day –

10th All Teams, Horses & Mules, except those properly belonging to the Reg[t] or Officers of the Reg[t] are to be turned into the Reg'tl Q.M. by 10 o clock am the 10th inst, for the purpose of being given up to the Post Q.M. This order is to be strictly complied with, as the formation of the Co saving fund depends upon a consciencious compliance therewith. All necessary teaming will be provided by the Q.M. of this Reg[t] –

11th Although at present engaged in Infantry drill, it is still the hope, and sincere belief of the Lt Col Comd'g that this Reg[t] is yet to bear the proud title of the "1st Colored Cavalry Reg[t]" until that time comes, let every one put his shoulder to the wheel and do his utmost to be the best Reg[t] Soldiers! – the eyes of the world are upon you – to you the friends of your long oppressed race look for the proof of that manliness which they hold to be just as much your gift from Almighty God as that of any white man. To you, your late oppressors, and now enemy's look with terror, and fear, foreseeing the time when you will be their equals,

599

and masters, upon the same soil where not long ago, a great
majority of you, held as their slaves. Show by your actions that
you are worthy of being called freemen, and citizens of this great
Country. You have Officers who have faith in your
manhood. They have left their homes and come among you,
knowing they are liable of being hung by the rebel gov' should
they be taken prisoner   and why? Because they instruct you to be
soldiers. Because they teach you how to fight for liberty they
would wish to enjoy. Respect those Officers, obey them and help
them, and be grateful to them. The Comd"g Officer embraces
this opportunity to thank both Officers and men in this command
for the promptness, cheerfulness and good will which they have
performed their various duties, assigned them. may the actions of
the past be the best assurance of our future success, and then
indeed we will be first, if not in name in the attributes that are
invariably found in brave soldiers good patriotic and useful
citizens. Let us remember our brave comrads who died in the
great & successful capture of this late Rebel stronghold and with
their example before us, and their names upon our lips for a
prayer, unitedly strive to accomplish our glorious share in the
crushing of this unholy rebellion, and save this "land of the brave"
and now more than ever before "Home of the free" – By order L.
L. Zulavsky Lt Col Comdg

HDc

General Order No. 16, Head Quarters 10th Regt. Corps d'Afrique, 7
Aug. 1863, Orders, 82nd USCI, Regimental Books & Papers USCT, RG
94 [G-128]. Contrary to Lieutenant Colonel Zulavsky's hope, the regiment
remained one of infantry.

241: Maryland Black Soldier to the Mother of a Dead Comrade

Near Petersburge [*Va.*] August 19th 1864
Dear Madam   I receave A letter from You A few day Ago inquir
in regard to the Fait of Your Son   I am sarry to have to inform
You that thear is no dobt of his Death   he Died A Brave Death
in Trying to Save the Colors of Rige[*ment*] in that Dreadful
Battil   Billys Death was unevessally [*mourned*] by all but by non
greatter then by my self   ever sins we have bin in the Army we
have bin amoung the moust intimoat Friend   wen every our
Rige[*ment*] wen into Camp he sertan to be at my Tent and meney
happy moment we seen to gether Talking about Home and the

Probability of our Living to get Home to See each other Family and Friend   But Providence has will other wise and You must Bow to His will   You and His Wife Sister and all Have my deepust Simppathy and trust will be well all in this Trying moment

You Inquired about Mr Young   He wen to the Hospetol and I can not give You eney other information in regard to Him

Billys thing that You requested to inquired about I can git no informa of as in the bustil of the Battil every thing was Lost

Give my Respects to Samual Jackson and Family not forgeting Your self and Family   I remain Your Friend

ALS   G. H. Freeman

G. H. Freeman to Madam, 19 Aug. 1864, enclosed in Rebecca Guy to the Adjutant General of the Army, 11 Mar. 1865, G-42 1865, Letters Received Relating to Recruiting, ser. 366, Colored Troops Division, RG 94 [B-348]. The covering letter, from the wife of the dead soldier, Corporal William Guy, requests a certificate of his death so that she may apply for a pension. She enclosed Freeman's letter as evidence of her husband's death. Also enclosed is a piece written by a fellow black soldier for the *Lyceum Observer* describing Corporal Guy's gallant death.

242: Officer in a Maryland Black Regiment to the Headquarters of the General-in-Chief of the Army

Near Petersburg Va. Aug. 13. 64

General: I desire to obtain the order of the Lt. Gen. Commanding to remove the 39th U.S.C.I. to some convenient post in the rear to offer an opportunity for discipline and drill. A short history of the organization of the regiment will best convey to your mind the necessities of such an opportunity being granted. And what I say in regard to the 39th is also true of the 19th & 30th The regiment was recruited in Baltimore Md. between the 18th and 31st day of March, and the recruits were used for recruiting parties in the state of Maryland until the 10th day of April 1864 when the organization was completed by bringing the recruits together and assigning individual recruits to the different companies. At that time the regiment numbered 979 men, and in a few days, (I think the 13th by an order from the War department 267 men were transferred to the Navy. To enable the Navy department to enlist the men final statements and discharges for each individual, had to be made out. The necessary labor in making out these papers occupied one whole day.

Then an order from the Executive of the State of Maryland came requiring powers of attorney to be made for each individual to enable the families of soldiers to receive the local bounties offered by the state to those enlisting in the United States service. This occupied two days.

Up to this date there was assigned to the regiment a second Lieutenant to each company whose time was occupied day and night in clothing and equipping his command. Hardly had this been accomplished when the order came to join the 9th Army Corps at Annapolis Md. and on the 18th day of April the regiment left Baltimore for the place of rendezvous. Accouterments were drawn for and delivered to the men at Annapolis and on the 23rd day of April the regiment with the 9th Army Corps started upon the march to Alexandria Va. receiving their arms while marching through Washington City D.C. On the 26th day of April the regiment marched to Fairfax C.H. and on the next day marched to Manassas Junction where it remained five days, and where the majority of the officers reported to the regiment.

From the 5th day of May owing to the continual marchings and fatigue which we have necessarily been required to perform no opportunity has been allowed to drill or discipline, and in fact from the organization, the lack of officers and the press of business has forbidden more than an attempt at regimental drill, while anything more than the most simple evolutions are out of the question. Target practice, except for the five days at Manassas Junction has been out of the question, and this for men who have never been allowed the handling, much less the use of fire arms, has proven to be to short to enable many to determine as to whether the explosive part of the cartridge is the powder or the ball, Many believing that because it is the ball that kills [*it*] should be put into the gun first. A few put in two or more loads at a time, while many are as apt to shoot at a right shoulder shift as at an aim. There are a few however who have been used to fire arms who are as good shots as the best. They do not yet perfectly comprehend the facings many facing to the left when the order given should be right and vice versa. So much the opportunity for drill and their profit thereby: and this is not all, I together with others who have been connected with colored troops, have become accustomed to their awkwardness and it does not impress us so forcibly as it will a casual observer.

As to discipline I know not where to begin to describe defects. To them every one is Captain or Boss and no amount of correction has so far rectified their knowledge of rank. Those who have been accustomed to be the Masters servant arrogate to themselves privileges unbecoming in a soldier and frequently after

performing some light military duty seem to expect the reward to
which they have been accustomed for slight favors for their masters
Visitors. It is a hard matter to convince many that they have not
the right to wear an officers uniform, when they are able to pay,
for it. The labor which the officers are necessarily called upon to
do (for there are no men who can perform the duties of Company
clerk) precludes the posibility of correcting all these things in as
arduous campaign as this has been.

These men lack the intelligence of the white race   They
comprehend what they are fighting for, but it must take time to
enable them to as fully understand their duties as the white race
does. I fully believe the material for good soldiers exists in the
regiment, but that it takes longer to develop it, there can be no
question   I am General Very respectfully your obt. Servt.

ALS   Quincy McNeil

[*Endorsement*]   Head Qrs 39th USCI   Near Petersburg Va   Aug 13.
1864   Constitutionally averse to recommending to Superior
Officers I yet most heartily *approve* the within request.   The want
of more Co & Battalion drill is painfully evident whenever an
attempt is made to maneuver the Regt   moreover the little
learned in the art of firing while at Manassas seems to have been
almost entirely forgotten

Approved subject to the exigencies of the service unknown to
me and Respfly forwarded   O P Stearns   Col Comdg Regt

[*Endorsement*]   Head Quarters 4th Division 9 A.C.   Before
Petersburg Va   August 21st 1864   Respectfully forwarded, with
the statement that the condition of the 39th U.S. Colored Troops
is no worse than any other Regiment in the Division.   They are all
composed of raw recruits and thus far have had very little
instruction.

It is respectfully recommended that as soon as the exigencies of
the service will permit, the whole Division be placed in such a
position as will allow opportunity for instructions

A large proportion of Commissioned Officers were lost in the
last assault rendering the labor of those that are left very
onerous   Edwd Ferrero   Brig. Genl. Comd'g

Maj. Quincy McNeil to Brig. Gen. Jno. A. Rawlings, 13 Aug. 1864,
Letters Received, 39th USCI, Regimental Books & Papers USCT, RG 94
[G-189]. Another endorsement.

243: Chaplain of a Mississippi Black Regiment to the Adjutant General of the Army

Vicksburg Miss September 30th 1864.

Sir;— In Reporting to the War Department the "Moral Condition and General History" of the 50th Reg. U.S. Colored Infantry for the Month of September 1864, I have the honor to Submit the following viz—

The Camp of the Regiment has been at Vicksburg, Miss. Portions of the Regiment have been detached, guarding Rail Road. Other portions have been on Fatigue, Guard and Picket, Building Barracks and an Expedition. The Men are in good spirits—doing well, and continually improving. Sickness has however, increased during the month in about the same ratio as the increase of heavy fatigue duty.

The burial of the dead is properly attended with Religious Services and Military Escort. The regular Sabbath Services have been somewhat interrupted on account of the Chaplains illness and preperations for the Expedition. The daily evening prayer meetings, and the School also, to some extent. I hear more profanity when on marches than when in Camp, both from Officers and Privates. I have little or no expectation that the Privates will leave off swearing untill their Officers do. — I think if there was no profane language used by Generals, there would not be as much, by the inferior Officers and Privates, and I recommend that the experiment be tried, beginning at all higher Head Quarters where Officers are guilty of violating the Third Article of War.[1] As Congress requires that all Commanding Officers must render Chaplains such facilities as will aid in the moral good of a Regiment, I Suggest that the example of Officers would be a very efficient aid in this, and in other respects also.

The Marriage relation of Forty Three Couple of this Reg., has been legalized, according to the Order of the Secretary of War, Some of whom had lived togather according to the slave system Thirty years without legal Marriage. I discourage all the young men's marrying while they are in the army and urge marriage upon all those who, already, have families.

I think I witness a very decided improvement in the social and domestic feelings of those married by the authority and protection of Law. It causes them to feel that they are beginning to be regarded and treated as human beings. I am, Sir, Most Respectfully Your Obedient Servant

ALS   Ja^s Peet

Chaplain Jas. Peet to Brig. Gen'l. L. Thomas, 30 Sept. 1864, P-1203 1864, Letters Received, ser. 12, RG 94 [K-549]. Endorsements. In his report for October 1864, Chaplain Peet described other activities of the regiment's enlisted men while in camp: "During the Summer months and dry weather it has been a practice among the Soldiers, to spend the evenings, one party dancing, and the other holding prayer meetings; but during the rainy weather, neither party has considered it agreable to hold a meeting or dance in a mud puddle; there has consequently, been a decrease of both." (Chaplain Jas. Peet to Brig. Gen'l. L. Thomas, 1 Nov. 1864, P-1316 1864, Letters Received, ser. 12, RG 94 [K-549].)

1 Article 3 prohibited profanity among both officers and enlisted men and stipulated a fine of one dollar for each offense by a commissioned officer. (*Revised Army Regulations*, appendix, p. 485.)

244: Inspector General of the Northern Division of Louisiana to the Assistant Inspector General of the Department of the Gulf

Baton Rouge, La. April 3^d 1865.

Colonel, In compliance with instructions, I made an inspection of the arms of the 81st U.S.Cd. Infty., while at Port Hudson lately and find their condition to be as stated in Inspection Report of Capt. Geo. E. Wentworth (late Inspector at that Post, copy of which I have the honor to enclose. I fully concur in the disposition which he recommended, as I found them to be very defective yet beautifully clean; as good care having been taken of them, as though they were the most perfect arm manufactured.

I do not think any Regiment of Regulars or Volunteers can show a cleaner stand of arms than those now in the hands of the 81st U.S. Colored Infantry; and I cheerfully recommend, that a new stand of Springfield Rifled Muskets be issued to Lieut. Col. Gaskill, commanding that Regiment, as soon as practicable. I am Colonel Very Respectfully Your Obt Servt

HLcSr

Jno. C. Chadwick

Lt. Col. Jno. C. Chadwick to Lt. Col. W. H. Thurston, 3 Apr. 1865, vol. 188/362 DG, pp. 109–10, Letters Sent by the Assistant Inspector General, ser. 1925, Northern Division of LA, RG 393 Pt. 2 No. 100 [C-881]. The 81st USCI was organized in Louisiana.

245: Order by the Commander of a North Carolina Black Artillery Regiment

Morehead City N.C. April 18 1865

Circular Order No. 9   Company Commanders are again reminded of the necesity of Keeping their Cook Houses, Quarters and the suroundings thoroughly neat and clean.   More than half the diseases prevalent among Soldiers can be avoided by a strict attention to the rules of health.   Tents should be spread open and blankets thoroughly aired every day.   Poles should be immediately placed between the tents upon which blankets and clothing can be aired.   Bones, old clothes and decaying Subsistance Stores should be buried or burned.   Slops from the Cookhouses must be emptied into the water.

The sweepings of the Streets containg as they do a large amount of sand should be used for filling the swampy ground near the centre of the color line.   This must not be placed in heapes but spread over the surface.   The men must be encouraged to bathe frequently and to keep their clothing clean and neat.   The Company Streets will be considered to extend to the waters edge, and Company Commanders will be held responsible that it is kept clean.   They will warn their companies that committing a nuisance of any kind near the camp will be most rigorously punished, and that the sinks alone must be used to receive filth and garbage.

HD

Circular Order No. 9, Hd. Qrs. 14 U.S.C. Arty., 18 Apr. 1865, Orders, 14th USCHA, Regimental Books & Papers USCT, RG 94 [G-62].

246: Testimony in the Court-Martial of Two Maryland Black Soldiers

[*Indianola, Tex.*]   October 24th 1865

. . . .

1st Sergeant Mitchel Bailey. Co "F" 7th U.S.C. Inf. a witness for the prosecution being duly sworn, says: . . . .

Question by J.A. "Were you present in the camp of the 7th U.S.C. Inf. at Indianola Tex. between the hours of 10. P.M. August 19th 1865 and 2. A.M. August 20th 1865

Answer. "Yes sir!"

Question by J.A. "Was there a disturbance in the camp among the men at that time?"

Answer   "Yes sir!"

Question by J.A.   "State to the Court all you know in regard to that disturbance and the part taken in it by the prisoner [*Private William H. Thomas*]?"

Answer.   "All I know is that when I woke up I heard a fuss in the Company street with the prisoner in   the prisoner was struck with the 'power' and was praying in a very loud tone of voice!"

Question by J.A.   What do you mean by the "power"?

Answer.   "Struck with religion," I guess he had religion by the way he was going on"!

Question by J.A.   "How did he come to get religion so late in the evening?"

Answer.   "There was a prayer meeting in the fore part of the evening, and I suppose he was excited over it!"

Question by J.A.   "Did he try to enrage the men against their officers?"

Answer.   "I didnot hear him if he did!"

Question by J.A.   "Did he make use of any disrespectful language toward his officers?

Answer.   "Not in my presence!"

Question by J.A.   "Was it understood among the men of his company that there was to be no noise or disturbance after taps?

Answer.   "Yes sir!"

Question by J.A.   "Was the prisoner ordered to return to his tent and stop his noise?"

Answer   "Yes, sir!"

Question by J.A.   "Did he obey that order?"

Answer.   "No sir!"

Question by J.A.   "Who ordered him to his quarters?"

Answer   "The commanding [*officer*] of his company Lieut. McCusky!"

Question by J.A.   "Did he stop his noise when ordered to do so by Lt. McCusky?"

Answer.   "No sir, he still kept on praying!"

Question by J.A.   "Are you entirely certain that the prisoner is the same man who was ordered to return to his tent and stop his noise?"

Answer.   "Yes sir!"

The accused declined to Cross Examine

Question by the Court   "How does a man act who has the 'Power'?"

Answer.   Shout and pray, some have their senses and some dont. I never experienced it myself!"

Question by the Court.   "How was it in this mans case? did he appear to know what he was doing?"

Answer. "He did not appear to have his senses about him in this instance, he did not obey any orders!"

Question by Court. "What has been the general conduct of the prisoner?

Answer. "Very good conduct!"

Question by the Court. "Did he make any remarks to Lieut. McCusky, when he ordered him to his quarters?"

Answer. "I didnot hear him"!

Question by Court. "Were you near enough to have heard him in case he had said anything to Lt. McCusky?"

Answer "Yes sir"!

Question by Court. "Did you consider the conduct of the prisoner insubordinate?"

Answer. "No, sir!"

The accused declined to Cross Examine

"The Prosecution Here Closed"

The accused having no testimony to offer made the following remarks in his defence— "Gentlemen, I didnot use any disrespectful language toward my officers. I have always tried to obey them ever since I have been in the regiment, and was at that time carried away by the 'Power of the Almighty. I didnot know or think anything about law. I wasent thinking of such a thing!"

. . . .

HD

[*Indianola, Tex.*] October 26th 1865

. . .

Lieut. Colonel. O. E. Pratt. 7th U.S.C. Inf. a witness for the prosecution being duly sworn says, ...

Question by J.A. "Were you present in the camp of the 7th U.S.C. Inf. on or about August 19th 1865 between the hours of 10 P.M. and 12 P.M."?

Answer. "I was!"

Question by J.A. "Was there a disturbance among the men of the regiment at that time?"

Answer. "There was!"

Question by J.A. "State to Court all you know in regard to that disturbance and the part taken in it by the prisoner [*Private Richard Frisby*]?"

Answer. "About 10 P.M on the 19th of August hearing a noise in camp I went out to see what it [*was*] and found that it was in Company 'F'. The prisoner who was then acting as Sergeant was one of the principle ones in the disturbance, and I ordered him to stop his noise and go into his quarters, he refused, he was then taken to Head Quarters, and then I ordered him several times to stop his noise he refusing all the time, at last I gagged him and that ended his performances!"

Question by J.A. "What was the cause of the disturbance?"

Answer. "Religious excitement!"

Question by J.A. "Was there an order existing in the regiment at that time against making noise and disturbance after taps?"

Answer. "Yes sir!

Question by J.A. "Did the prisoner use his influence to create noise and disturbance among the men?"

Answer "He did, by setting the example and refusing or neglecting the disturbance!"

Question by J.A. "Was he at all defiant in his bearing or manner?"

Answer. "I think he was!"

Question by J.A. Are you positive that the prisoner is the same man who refused to obey your order?"

Answer "Yes sir.

"The accused declined to cross examine"

Question by the Court "Was the prisoner under the influence of religious excitement?"

Answer. "I think religious excitement was the cause of the disturbance!"

Question by the Court. "Did he appear to be concious of what he was doing or saying?"

Answer "He did!"

Question by the court. "What language did he make use of when he refused to obey your order?"

Answer "I can't recollect the exact language it was a repetition of some indistinct utterances I dont know what!"

Assistant. Surgeon. Z. P. Dennler 7th U.S.C. Inf. a witness for the prosecution being duly sworn says.

. . . .

Question by J.A. "State to the Court all you know in regard to that disturbance and the part taken in it by the prisoner?"

Answer. "About 10 or 11 P.M. I was awakened by quite a tremendous noise down in the camp; my quarters are some distance from camp but I was awakened. I got up and dressed my self and by the time I got dressed the prisoner was up to Col Pratt's quarters. he was crying and saying he was being "prostituted for Christ's sake." he make considerable noise but that remark struck me very forcibly. I believe the Col throw some water into his face to try and cool him down, but he didnot. The Colonel asked some one if they could not stop him but none were successful, he turned to me and asked me if I couldnot stop him and I told him I thought I could. I got about four inches of roller bandage, it was about two inches across and got it into his mouth, he didnot make any more noise!"

Question by J.A. "Was he ordered by Lt. Col Pratt to stop his noise?"

Answer "He was!"

Question by J.A. "What was the cause of the disturbance?"

Answer. "Religious excitement!"

Question by J.A. "Did the prisoner appear to be concious of what he was doing or saying?"

Answer. "I should say the man must have been concious, I dont know why he shouldent have been concious. He was excited!"

Question by J.A. "Did the prisoner appear to have what is called the 'Power'?"

Answer. "He was laboring under strong spiritual excitement, if that is what you call the power he had it?"

"The accused declined to Cross-Examine"

. . . .

HD

Excerpts from the proceedings of a general court-martial in the cases of Private William H. Thomas and Private Richard Frisby, 7th USCI, 24 & 26 Oct. 1865, MM-3244, Court-Martial Case Files, ser. 15, RG 153 [H-34]. Thomas, accused of mutinous conduct, disrespect toward an officer, and disobedience of orders, was found guilty of the third charge and sentenced to one month's confinement in the guard house with loss of pay and allowances. The court found Frisby guilty of both disobedience of orders and mutinous conduct and sentenced him to six months' imprisonment at hard labor. The court-martial tried other men in the regiment upon similiar charges stemming from the same "religious excitement."

14

Education

FEW OF THE BLACKS who enlisted in Union ranks had any formal education, and only a small portion could read or write.[1] Most of these had been free before the war, and they were concentrated in regiments from the Northern states, a few border-states, and Louisiana.[2] Illiterate soldiers could not perform all the duties necessary to keep a modern army moving. Officers had to accompany them on the most routine missions to read sign posts and prevent wily impersonators from countermanding legitimate authority. The shortage of literate blacks to serve as noncommissioned officers also threatened to bury white commanders under an avalanche of paper work.[3] Thus the same military necessity that impelled black enlistment also necessitated that at least some black soldiers be taught to read and write.

Military necessity was not the only motive in the establishment of regimental schools. Most Americans believed that education was the birthright of a free people. It allowed men and women to rise to the full measure of their abilities, and it provided the best source of social discipline. In one form or another, Union officers shared these sentiments. Antislavery idealists who led the early black regiments saw education as a means for blacks to shed the shackles of bondage and enjoy the full benefits of liberty after the war. But even those officers who did not share the abolitionist vision often pressed their soldiers to attend classes so that they would not be, as one officer termed it, "common niggers."

[1] Published works on the education of black soldiers include: Dudley Taylor Cornish, "The Union Army as a School for Negroes," *Journal of Negro History* 37 (Oct. 1952): 368–82, and John W. Blassingame, "The Union Army as an Educational Institution for Negroes, 1862–1865," *Journal of Negro Education* 34 (Spring 1965): 152–59.

[2] Soldiers had to sign their names or make their marks to verify receipt of uniforms and other equipment. Extant registers, although often compromised by clerks who simply signed everyone's name, indicate that most black soldiers made their mark and only a few could sign their own name. (Clothing Account Books, Regimental Books & Papers USCT, RG 94.)

[3] See Brig. Genl. John P. Hawkins to Brig. Genl. L. Thomas, 19 Aug. 1864, H-48 1864, Letters Received by Adjutant General L. Thomas, ser. 363, Colored Troops Division, RG 94 [V-75].

For the most part, officers did not have to press very hard. Black soldiers desired to read and write so they could communicate with their families, and, like whites, they too saw education as a means to improve themselves. They petitioned for regimental schools, purchased their own books, and paid teachers from their own funds. When teachers were not available, they taught each other, drawing on the knowledge of the few who had attained scraps of a formal education. In some units, blacks formed literary societies and established regimental libraries. "Cartridge box and spelling book are attached to the same belt," noted one regimental chaplain.

Regimental schools that would provide basic education had no precedent in the American army, and the War Department offered little direction for their development. Schools for black soldiers sprang up haphazardly and depended, in large measure, on the concern of commanding officers. Although many ignored the educational needs of their men, some – pressed by black soldiers – developed systematic programs to teach basic skills and provide for military advancement. General Godfrey Weitzel, commander of the black 25th Army Corps, ordered his officers to erect schoolhouses for their men and taxed sutlers within his command to ensure the success of these efforts.[4] As Weitzel's orders suggest, direction of these educational programs fell to regimental and company officers who controlled the soldier's daily routine. Some officers emphasized the instruction of only a few black soldiers to relieve themselves of onerous clerical duties; others aimed for universal literacy, occasionally adding a sprinkling of the liberal arts. Pedagogical practices varied as widely as interest in education itself. While some officers used the carrot of free time and military advancement to encourage the participation of enlisted men, others wielded the stick, making school attendance mandatory and threatening to demote illiterate black noncommissioned officers. And, like other educators, some used a bit of both approaches.

Regimental chaplains generally directed the army schools. Their commitment also varied widely. The Reverend Henry M. Turner, a militant black abolitionist deeply imbued with the importance of education, pressed his superiors for books, time, and tents to operate his school. Other chaplains used their connections with missionary organizations to secure financial support and teachers from the North. Still others disdained their charges, believed blacks inherently inferior, and saw no purpose in educating the soldiers.

[4] Circular, Hd. Qrs. 1st Div. 25th AC., 20 Jan. 1865, Letters, Orders, & Reports Received by the 1st–3d Divisions, ser. 533, 25th Army Corps, RG 393 Pt. 2 No. 9 [C-4500]; General Orders No. 38, Headquarters 1" Div. 25 A.C., 10 May 1865, Letters, Orders, & Reports Received by the 1st–3d Divisions, ser. 533, 25th Army Corps, RG 393 Pt. 2 No. 9 [C-4501].

The chaplains generally linked black education with their own concern for the moral and spiritual condition of their men. For many, true education and true religion were one. In the spring of 1864, Congress ordered army chaplains to report monthly on the spiritual and moral condition of their units.[5] The order flowed slowly through the chain of command, but by the beginning of 1865 the chaplains' reports flooded the Adjutant General's Office. These monthly summaries reveal a good deal about the nature of army education and the religious life of black soldiers as seen by the men who bore primary responsibility for their educational and spiritual affairs.

Even under the most concerned company officers and chaplains, education was subordinate to other military duties. The absence of direct War Department instructions and the press of the war gave education a low priority. Few commanders invested in education when orders to break camp would mean that a carefully constructed school house had to be left behind, along with books, blackboards, and civilian teachers. Wartime educational efforts appear to have been more concerned with producing a few literate noncommissioned officers than with uplifting the masses. But in late 1864, as the fighting ended in some theaters, regimental schools began to function with greater regularity.

These educational efforts had mixed results. At the end of the war, most black privates still could not sign their names. This was especially true in the regiments raised among the plantation slaves of the Lower South. But, even in these regiments, some literate noncommissioned officers could be found. Among the Northern, largely free black regiments, about one-quarter of the privates could sign their names when they were discharged, and literacy was nearly universal among the noncommissioned officers.[6] Some Southern, and probably slave, regiments also made remarkable progress. The 62nd U.S. Colored Infantry, raised in Missouri in late 1863 as the 1st Missouri Colored Infantry, ordered to the Department of the Gulf in 1864, and incorporated into the 25th Army Corps at war's end, exemplified the achievements of interested enlisted men and concerned officers. Upon leaving the regiment in January 1866, its commander boasted that "of four hundred and thirty one men, ninety nine have learned to read and write understandingly; two hundred and eighty-four can read; three hundred and thirty seven can spell in words of two syllables, and are learning to read, not more than ten men have failed to learn the alphabet."[7]

[5] *Official Records*, ser. 3, vol. 4, pp. 227–28.
[6] Muster-out payrolls required soldiers to sign their names or make their marks to verify receipt of wages. (Payrolls, Records of the Second Auditor, RG 217.)
[7] See *Freedom*, ser. 2: doc. 342.

247: Provost Marshal of Assumption Parish, Louisiana, to the Headquarters of the Provost Marshal General of the Department of the Gulf

Napoleanville, La., April 7th 1865

Sir   I have the honour to State that Comp I. 26th Ind. Vols having been relieved from duty as Provost Guards at this office, I requested of Gen[l] Cameron Comdg District of Lafourche to furnish me with another Guard, he complied with my request by sending me a Sergt one Corp[l] and Six privates of The 78th Regmt, U.S. (Col) Infantry. They are of no use to me whatever. Consequently I respectfully request that I may have detailed the necessary Guard for duty at this office from some white Regiment. I need good steady and intelligent men that have some experience and judgement. My present Guard does very well for usual guard duty. but they are not fit for the duties of this office. I need some one that are at least able to read, and I have none that can read or write. If I send them in the country to make arrests they are just as apt to get the wrong as the right Person, if they get any at all. And under such circumstances I am unable to stop the Thieving business that is carried on in this Parish. There has been at the least calculation Fifty mules stolen within the last two months in this Parish and I have not been able to catch the rogues yet. I have made some arrests but have not been able to get satisfactory evidences as yet. the man that I wanted the most Escaped. The guard went to him and showed him their summons   of course he read it and told them it was for some other man and he would show them where he lived, the man he referred them to not being at Home they returned without any and thus the rascal Escaped. I do not object to this guard on account of they being colored, but for the reason that they are inefficient for this duty. I have tried them until I am quite satisfied that they will not answer for this duty. There are other reasons why I should have a change. The Johnny Rebs make their apppearance every few days   They are Spying about to get informations and if there is any chance for smuggling this is a point that is as well if not the best adapted to that business as any in the district. There has been four Smugglers captured within the last month whose goods came from New Orleans with permits properly Signed   Still the goods were intended for the Rebs. I have these classes of persons to watch, and besides this I have the duties of my office to attend to, that of Local Special agent, Assistant Superintendant of Free Labor, which in my opinion is good and sufficient reasons that I should have more efficient

assisstance   If it is impossible to make a change I shall do all in
my power to give satisfaction to all and Justice to my
Government   I have the Honor to be Very Respectfully Your
obedient Servant

ALS   J W Greene

Capt. J. W. Greene to 1st Lt. W. D. Putnam, 7 Apr. 1865, Letters &
Telegrams Received, ser. 774, Dist. of LaFourche, RG 393 Pt. 2 No. 13
[C-855]. Endorsements indicate that Greene's request was granted.

248: Kentucky Black Sergeant to the Tennessee Freedmen's Bureau Assistant Commissioner

Nashville Tenn   October 8th 1865

Sir   I have the honor to call your attention To the neccesity of
having a school for The benefit of our regement   We have never
Had an institutiong of that sort and we Stand deeply inneed of
instruction the majority of us having been slaves   We Wish to
have some benefit of education To make of ourselves capable of
buisness In the future   We have estableshed a literary Association
which flourished previous to our March to Nashville   We wish to
become a People capable of self support as we are Capable of being
soldiers   my home is in Kentucky Where Prejudice reigns like the
Mountain Oak and I do lack that cultivation of mind that would
have an attendency To cast a cloud over my future life after have
been in the United States service   I had a leave of abscence a few
weeks a go on A furlough and it made my heart ache to see my
race of people there neglected And ill treated on the account of the
lack of Education being incapable of putting Thier complaints or
applications in writing   For the want of Education totally ignorant
Of the Great Good Workings of the Government in our
behalf   We as soldiers Have our officers Who are our protection
To teach how us to act and to do   But Sir What we want is a
general system of education In our regiment for our moral and
literary elevation   these being our motives We have the Honor of
calling your very high Consideration   Respectfully Submitted as
Your Most humble serv^{t}

ALS   John Sweeny

1st Sergeant John Sweeny to Brigadier General Fisk, 8 Oct. 1865, S-82
1866, Registered Letters Received, ser. 3379, TN Asst. Comr., RG 105
[A-6329]. Endorsement. Pencilled on the letter is the notation "Will send
Teacher as soon as possible." Sweeny, a free black from Green County,

Kentucky, enlisted in Nashville in September 1863, giving his occupation as "boatman." Upon muster-out in January 1866, he returned to his home county and taught at a school whose pupils included many wives and children of other black soldiers still in service. (Service record of John Sweney, 13th USCI, Carded Records, Volunteer Organizations: Civil War, ser. 519, RG 94 [N-4]; John Sweney to Gen. [Clinton B. Fisk], 10 Apr. 1866, S-175 1866, Registered Letters Received, ser. 3379, TN Asst. Comr., RG 105 [A-6333]; John Sweney to Mr. Fiddler, 15 Nov. 1866, F-412 1866, Letters Received, ser. 1068, KY Asst. Comr., RG 105 [A-4243]; John Sweney to Captain Fiddler, 8 Dec. 1867, enclosed in Jams. M. Fidler to Bvt. Col. Ben. P. Runkle, 12 Dec. 1867, F-382 1867, Letters Received, ser. 1068, KY Asst. Comr., RG 105 [A-4243].)

249: Order by the Commander of a Louisiana Black Regiment

Port Hudson, La. Mch 15th 1864.
General Orders No 9   With a view to introducing greater regularity in the management of, and a greater promptness in the attendance to school – the following regulations will be strictly obeyed on, and after wednesday the 16th inst

1st   all the Non "Com" Officers except those specially excused or on duty will attend school under pain of reduction to the ranks for 4 weeks for the first offence, and entire loss of rank for the second offence.

2nd   As we do not posess the means for instructing every man in the Regt company commanders will select from their companies, such privates as in their opinion deserve instruction, and are capeable of improving thereby, not exceeding 25 from each company and the attendance of these men at school will become, obligatory as with the N.C.O.

3rd   Company Commanders will furnish Lt J. E. Young with a complete list of their N.C.O. & such privates as they may appoint for instruction, at each class the roll will be called, and absentees accounted for by the senior N.C.O. of each company.

4th   There will be a class exclusively for Sergeants and the two best corporals from each company, under the management of Chaplain Camp from 8.30 until 9.30 AM, and for the other corporals & privates from 7.15 until 8.30 PM under the guidance of Lt Young.   By command of Col L L Zulavsky   Comdg
HD

General Orders No. 9, Head Quarters 10th Regt. Infty. Cd'A., 15 Mar. 1864, Orders, 82nd USCI, Regimental Books & Papers USCT, RG 94 [G-129].

250: Order by the Commander of a Missouri Black Regiment

Morganzia, La. July 3rd 1864.
General Order No 31   All non-Commissioned officers of this
command who shall fail to learn to read by or before the 1st day of
January 1865 will be reduced to the ranks and their places filled
by persons who can read.   In the position of Sergants preference
will be given to men who can both read & write and are otherwise
good soldiers.   All soldiers of this command who have by any
means learned to read or write, will aid and assist to the extent of
their ability their fellow soldiers to learn these invaluable arts,
without which no man is properly fitted to perform the duties of a
free citizen   By order of Lt. Col. David Branson Comm'd'g Regt.
HD

General Order No. 31, Hd. Qrs. 62d U.S. Cold. Infty., 3 July 1864,
Orders, 62nd USCI, Regimental Books & Papers USCT, RG 94 [G-253].
Six months later, Branson reduced five noncommissioned officers to the
ranks for failing to comply with this order. (General Orders No. 3, Hd.
Qrs. 62nd. U.S. Colored Infantry, 12 Jan. 1865, Orders, 62nd USCI,
Regimental Books & Papers USCT, RG 94 [G-253].)

251: Order by the Commander of a Rhode Island Black Regiment

New Orleans La. Oct 17. 1864
General Orders No 37. Schools of instruction for
non-commissioned officers will be organized as soon as possible in
each battalion of the Eleventh Regiment U.S.C. Arty. (Hy) under
the direction of a competent officer selected by the Battalion
Commander.
   II. Such schools shall be held not less than three times in each
week at such times and places as the battalion Commander shall
designate
   III   The course of instruction will be as follows: Reading
Writing and Arithmetic through division; Tactics, – Casey's shool
of the soldier thorough; Heavy Artillery Tactics to include forming
detachments; posts and duties of men at the piece; name and use
of implements; loading, pointing, firing &c; such subjects in
Gen. Regulations as are necessary to a correct and intelligent
performance of every duty required of non-Commissioned officers,
such as making morning reports, provision returns &c, &c.

IV. The necessary text books will be purchased and the expence charged to the battalion fund.

V. Instructors will be expected to be energetic and zealous in the performance of their duties and will strive to imbue their pupils with the same spirit. By order of Col J. Hale Sypher 11th U.S.C.A. (Hy) Comdg

HD

General Order No. 37, Head Quarters Eleventh Regt. U.S.C.A. (Hy.), 17 Oct. 1864, General Orders, 11th USCHA, Regimental Books & Papers USCT, RG 94 [G-32].

252: Chaplain of a Louisiana Black Regiment to the Commander of a Black Division

Port Hudson La April 8th 1864

General: I have the honor to report that I have visited the schools established and organized by you in the regiments of the 2[d] Brigade of your Division, and respectfuly submit the following statement of their condition.

There are, at the present time, four schools in successful operation. The buildings, which also serve as Churches and Lecture rooms, are large and comfortable structures, neatly whitewashed, and fitted with well made seats, desks and blackboards. The attendance of the men has been as regular as was consistent with the performance of their military duties, and they have made rapid progress in learning to read and write.

I am sure that I never witnessed greater eagerness for study; and all, who have examined the writing books and listened to the recitations in the schools, have expressed their astonishment and admiration. A majority of the men seem to regard their books as an indispensable portion of their equipments, and the cartridge box and spelling book are attached to the same belt. There are nearly five hundred men in the four regiments of the Brigade which bears your name, who have learned to read quite well, and also quite a large number who are able to write. A short time ago scarcely one of these men knew a letter of the alphabet. Many of the Sergeants who came into the regiment six months ago, entirely ignorant of the alphabet, are now able to make out their own Rolls. Instruction to a considerable extent has also been given in the Geography of the Country, especially as regards the States,

618

their capitals, rivers, population &c. The accomplishment of so much, under the circumstances, is an additional proof of the intellectual capacity of the race. Their extreme eagerness & ability to improve is established.

Chaplains Chase Camp and Paterson have cheerfuly cooperated in the organizing & conducting of the schools, and especial mention may be made of Messrs Seymour Young and North, who were appointed by you as Instructors. In the death of the last-named officer, the Corps and especially the 9th Regt suffers a serious loss.

This excellent movement for the instruction of our soldiers, inaugerated by yourself and rendered successful by your exertions & by a timely supply of books obtained from the North through your influence, deserves the approbation of every friend of the Freedmen, and your personal efforts in their behalf, will be gratefully remembered by us all in the future. I am, very respectfuly Your obt servt

ALS   E. S. Wheeler

Chaplain E. S. Wheeler to Brig. Genl. Ullmann, 8 Apr. 1864, D. Ull-mann Papers, Generals' Papers & Books, ser. 159, RG 94 [V-12].

253: Orders by Two Commanders of a Missouri Black Regiment

Brazos Santiago, Texas. October 29th 1864

General Orders No 35   Hereafter when any soldier of this command is found to be, or to have been, playing cards, he will be placed, standing, in some prominent position in the camp with book in hand, and required then and there to learn a considerable lesson in reading and spelling; and if unwilling to learn, he will be compelled by hunger to do so.

When men are found gambling in any way, the money at stake will be seized and turned into the Regt. hospital fund. No freed slave who cannot read well has a right to waste the time and opportunity here given him to fit himself for the position of a free citizen.

This order will be read twice to this command, and copied in each order book   By order of Lieut. Col. David Branson. Comdg. Regt.

HD

Brazos Santiago Texas January 25th 1865.
General Orders *No. 4.* The Regimental Council of
Administration having appropriated Fifty Dollars for the purchase
of premiums for the encouragement of the enlisted men of this
Regiment to learn to write it is hereby ordered. That a gold pen
be given to the Sergeant in each Company, who shall learn to
write the best by the fourth day of July 1865

That a gold pen be given the Corporal in each Company who
shall learn to write the best by the 4th day of July 1865. That a
good book be given the private of each Company who shall learn
to write the best by the 4th day of July 1865.

These rewards to be publicly given by a committee chosen as
judges of the writing, and the names of men gaining prizes to be
mentioned in orders   By order of Major J. K
Hudson Commanding Regt
HD

General Orders No. 35, Head Qrs. 62nd Regt. U.S. Cold. Inf., 29 Oct.
1864, Orders, 62nd USCI, Regimental Books & Papers USCT, RG
94 [G-254]; General Orders No. 4, Hd. Qtrs. 62nd Regt. U.S. Cold.
Infantry, 25 Jan. 1865, Orders, 62nd USCI, Regimental Books & Papers
USCT, RG 94 [G-256]. Prize winners were announced in General Orders
No. 13, Head Quarters 62nd Regt. U.S. Colored Infty., 31 July 1865,
Orders, 62nd USCI, Regimental Books & Papers USCT, RG 94 [G-256].

254: Chaplain of a Pennsylvania Black Regiment to the Adjutant General of the Army

[*near Richmond, Va.*] January 31st 1865
Sir:— I have the honor to report to you for the month ending as
above, and will also beg you to consider the work of my office
during the preceeding time, the months, Nov. and Dec. 1864,
inclusive in this report, with this explanation: Not until very
recently was I aware of an Order according to Sec. 3. Act of
Cong. approved April 9th 1864, making it the duty of Chaplains
to report monthly. In the absence of anything to the contrary, I
was governed by Published Regulations 1863. Hereafter I shall
furnish you my reports agreeable to existing order.

Immediately after becoming chaplain of this Regt. I commenced
the work of canvassing it, with a view to acquaint myself with its
history, and more particularly to prepare the way for my

labors. The Officers of the Reg^t afforded me all necessary
assistance in the satisfactory accomplishment of this purpose.

The average number present of the command is about (450)
Four Hundred and Fifty, including non-commissioned officers and
privates. A majority of this number, about (325) Three-Hundred
and Twenty Five were Free Men of Color before enlisting: They
are principally from the State of Penna. The remainder are
Freedmen, and generally from the States Maryland and Kentucky.

Upon examination I found that (70) Seventy of the whole
number were able to read; but very few could understand
intelligently what they did read. There were (30) Thirty who
could write their own signature, and attend themselves to their
own correspondence; but their composition was not correct in any
of the essentials. Those who had so far, although very imperfectly,
acquired some education were with few exceptions Free Men of
Color. The others were unacquainted with the alphabet. This
occasions no surprise, as the miserable institution of Slavery where
ever existing studies to prevent intellectual culture in the enslaved,
and is altogether unfavorable to such pursuits.

Agreeable to instructions, suitable and convenient School Houses
are to be erected here in each Regt. for the benefit of our co^{ld}
Troops. In consequence of frequent changes of situation the co^{ld}
troops of this Regt. were hitherto prevented enjoying school
conducted in a suitable house. In several instances the building
was erected, but we were required to leave before the work fairly
commenced. However I have been ministering to their instructions
without the house by supplying them with books, &c, and
exercising the superintendance of the work. Officers and others
have cheerfully assisted me. I supplied the Regt. with a sufficient
number of "First Lessons" for Beginners published by the Amer.
Tract. Soc., and "First Reader" and "Second Reader," published by
Amer. Sun$^{dy.}$ Sch. Union, besides the New Testament Scriptures,
and copies of the Freedmen, Christian Banner, and in fact all the
different religious papers coming to the army through the
Christian Commission. I also recieve regularly direct from the
Amer. Tract Soc. of Boston suitable and valuable reading
matter. All have made very commendable progress. They apply
themselves closely whenever their duties permit. I find the
Freedmen especially appreciate most sincerely these advantages so
unjustly denied them in their servitude. The question of education
in the case of the colored race is not truly debatable. I am
satisfied they will make surprisingly rapid progress, as those do
who have the facilities granted them.

We have again in course of erection a School House which we
expect to finish in a few days. This convenience will allow us to

adopt practically the best system, and we intend therefore to organize our co^{ld} Troops of this Regt. each man in a class suitable to his studies. For the improvement of the non-commissioned officers, and the benefit of such improvement to the Regt. as well as to themselves, we intend to organize them in classes separated from the others, and bestow on them our special attention for the time being. With a view to success in this whole work, we will need more teaching force. We expect and will no doubt recieve the aid of Officers of the Regt. in this particular.

Said School House will also be used as a house of divine worship for the Regt. where services will be conducted as often and regularly as practicable. Heretofore in our public services we suffered some interruption which was made unavoidable by the inclemency of the weather, and by military moves. We very gladly accepted an invitation lately extended by the Christian Commission to join them in services conducted in their Large Tent in this Corps. We are pleased to mention that our colored Soldiers are generally very attentive hearers to the preaching of the Gospel. Many in this Regt. profess faith in the Redeemer, and give evidence of the sincerity of their christian profession. We hope others, their companions in arms may be induced shortly to enlist under the Banner of the Cross, and thus become soldiers of the Heavenly Country, with the same distinguished bravery they are manifesting in this sacred cause now.

Suitable religious service has been conducted in the burial of all soldiers who died present with the command.

Permit me herewith to acknowledge the uniform kindness and courtesy extended me by Col. Yeoman, Com^{dg} this Regt. and all the other officers under him, Brig. Genl. Thomas, Com^{dg} the Brigade, Brig. Genl. Wild, Com^{dg} the Division, as well as all others of the Dept. to whom I have had occasion to apply for aid facilitating my work. They are intelligent military gentlemen, and true friends and supporters of the cause of education and christianity among our colored Troops. Respectfully submitted by Your Ob^t servant.

ALS   J. M. Mickly

Chaplain J. M. Mickly to Adjt. Genl. U.S.A., 31 Jan. 1865, M-296 1865, Letters Received, ser. 12, RG 94 [K-525]. Endorsements.

255: Chaplain of a Louisiana Black Regiment to the Regimental Adjutant

Vicksburg, Miss., Feb. 1st 1865.
Sir: Agreeably to orders and my own duty, I have the honor to forward my report for the month ending 31st Jan. 1865.

The ninth day of the current month is the first anniversary of my entrance into military service. The present thus is a favorable time to make comparisons, and to note the progress which has been made. In reporting from month to month, it frequently happens, that the progress made in the regiment is not very apparent. But when we compute time by the year and not by the month, the change is vast and apparent to all.

During the past year, great progress has been made in a military aspect. This fact is evident to an observer at dress parade, and in the increased attention bestowed upon the minor duties of daily routine. The men are not only more manly, but far more soldierly. Their guns are uniformly cleaner, their brass brighter, their personal cleanliness and general appearance has vastly improved.

The improvement in an educational view is also very marked. One year ago, but a few, not more than fifteen in the regiment knew the alphabet thoroughly. But now the converse is true. The teacher, who is now employed in the regiment, has been connected with it for three months, and during that time, she has found but *one* person who does not know the alphabet.

In the religious life of the regiment, there has been great change; here even where we would least expect it; for history testifies to the reluctance with which any race give up their religious forms and customs, or their language. The haughty Norman strove, in vain, for years, to supplant the religion and language of the ancient Britons. But here we find a people, so tractable, with such unlimited confidence in their liberators, as to yield up set forms of expression, religious customs and manners, familiar from infancy for those of *another race*. This is due to no instruction given on these points, nor any effort to make a change. It simply shows the necessary tendency of the human mind to grow into the likeness of those with whom we are brought in contact. These colored people are easily moulded and shaped by the stronger minds which press upon theirs, and which command them.

During the year past, a deep and abiding foundation has been laid for a vast change in moral sentiment, in No. 15 Special Orders, Sect. of War legalizing marriages among the Freedmen. A

623

revolution is rapidly going on among them in reference to the sacred nature and binding obligations of marriage. One more measure in this direction is greatly needed, – a court with power to grant divorces, on legal and scriptural grounds. The demand is urgent, that evil consequences may be avoided. One instance has come to my knowledge, in my own regiment, where a divorce should be granted, and that for reasons expressly stated in Scripture. It would be well and safe to apply to such persons the doctrine held by the christian church, during all ages, on this subject.

As I have witnessed the progress of freedom for the past year, – when slavery was abolished and forever prohibited in all the territories, – when the negro was admitted to equal rights in United States Courts as parties to suits and as witnesses, – as "the Statute book was cleansed of every support of slavery," – as state after state has declared emancipation, – as I now witness how christian men and women are following our loyal and conquoring armies with the agencies of mental and moral instruction, to fit and prepare the freedmen for the duties of a new and higher life, every chamber of my heart is filled with rejoicing. Such tidings are grateful to our ears. My response, and that of my fellow officers to such legislation, is, the colored race is worthy of it. Respectfully Submitted.

ALS   C. W. Buckley

Chaplain C. W. Buckley to Lt. Austin R. Mills, 1 Feb. 1865, B-284 1865, Letters Received, ser. 12, RG 94 [K-508]. Endorsements.

256: Order by the Commander of a Louisiana Black Regiment

Vicksburg Miss 11" April 1865,

General Orders No 13   In consequence of the heavy duty the men have been compelled to perform for several months past they have been very irregular in their attendance at school and in many instances as it is thought needlessly so, The following regulations in the school of this regiment will be observed in future. Each relief of the guard every day, will be instructed one hour by Chaplain Merrill and he will also be required to visit the companies once a day, to encourage the men to attend school.

Church will only be held when in his opinion it will be for their best interests, as education is believed, should be the paramount object in elevating these soldiers to the true status of manhood. The school will continue as heretofore during the day and evenings under charge of Miss Pinkham, who will teach the soldiers belonging to the regiment, their wives, and children and any persons who may come from outside, so long as they do not interfeare, with those belonging to this regiment—

The officers are enjoined to do all in their power, to compel the men to attend as well as to encourage Miss Pinkham who has always labored with commendable zeal and energy, for the improvement of the men and regiment. The good results that have followed, must be clear to all. And we must conclude that, much more may yet be accomplished, with due exertion on the part of all.

Officers should indelibly fix on the minds of their men, by repeated lectures the importance of learning to read write and spell, and that it is only by education that they ever will attain a higher standard of manhood, than the commmon "Nigger." Two hours each day might be spent by the most of the men, profitably in school instead of sleeping around in places they ought not to be.

Chaplain Merrill will have full supervision of all the schools of this regiment   By Order of Capt James P. Hall Comdg
HD

General Orders No. 13, Head Quarters 49th USCI, 11 Apr. 1865, General Orders, 49th USCI, Regimental Books & Papers USCT, RG 94 [G-114].

257: Order by the Commander of a Kentucky Black Regiment

Smeedsville, Tenn June 2nd 1865
General Orders No 21   Hereafter, Company drills will not be required in the afternoon— Instead of drills, a school will be held in each company: The company commanders will find the men of their companies who are sufficiently instructed to teach their comrades, and will see that lessons are properly taught, and that the men give their attention. The men may buy the necessary books, or company commanders will purchase them from the company fund. It is believed that every man will devote his attention faithfully to this work. The surest and only step to respectable life, as Freemen, is intelligence. The best way to win the respect of all, and to render themselves worthy of the right which Freedom confers, is for every man to acquire the best

Education he can. Let it be deemed a disgrace for any man, in this Regiment, to leave the service without, at least knowing how to read. Every facility will be given in carrying out this important work. By Command of Lt. Col. Henry Stone

HD

General Orders No. 21, H'd. Qrs. 100" U.S.C. Infantry, 2 June 1865, Orders, 100th USCI, Regimental Books & Papers USCT, RG 94 [G-136].

258: Black Chaplain of a District of Columbia Black Regiment to the Adjutant General of the Army

Roanoke Island N.C. June 29th 1865

Sir. I have the honor to submit the following report, as embracing the moral and religious condition of my regiment.

After we left the Fort of Richmond, and started on the Fort Fisher expedition, our campaign was so constant and uncertain, and being a part of the time detailed on extra duty, which subjected our religious exercises to so many disappointments, I thought it unnecessary to forward any more reports, untill so much of our active duties, should be over, as would enable us to have some assurrance, that our religious efforts and plans would not always be thwarted by unavoidable disappointments.

During this intermedium, however, we have had preaching, prayer meetings, and other moral or religious exercises, as frequently, as circumstances would permit, so much so, that no one could frame for an excuse, that his identity with sin, was founded upon the ground, that he was not taught better.

But for the last six weeks, our regimental church, has been systematically carried on, and I beleive benefically disposed of. It gives me great pleasure to still acknowledge the religious integrity of several in the regiment, as well as the profound anxiety manifested by several others, who are yet strangers to Christ, in obtaining the pearl of Great Price.

Should it please God to let us remain in our present quarters for a reasonable time, surrounded with our present favorable conveniences, I cherish the hope, that many will be added to the lists of the faithful, and many others, if not actually purged by Grace, brought to so comprehend their future destiny, as to lay the base of a reformatory course of action. Upon the whole the moral and religious aspects of the regiment, will tally quite favorable with any in the service.

Having constantly kept the subject of education before our soldiers, I flatter our literary success unequalled considering our time and chance. But at present, all literary efforts must remain at a partial stand still, owing to want of books, to supply the heavy demand, for whom it appears almost impossible to procure them.

Had my repeated application for *leave of absence,* been granted, I intended to have supplied this want, even, at my own expense. But as it was not granted, I hope it will not be an outrage upon the *right of Petition,* to most respectfully request, that you have my regiment furnished with at least (500) five hundred spelling books.

The most of these books too, should be of the advance kind, As a large portion of the Troops, who can read and write some, need to be much better drilled in spelling. And hundreds for whom I had gotten books, had them destroyed in their knapsacks, by the sinking of a boat in the Cape Fear River. I claim this favor for my regiment, upon the ground, that she is the mother of colored Troops, and that in nine battles, regardless of skirmishes, she has never faltered, give way, or retreated, unless ordered by the General Commanding. Her record for bravery, courage, or invincibleness dffies the redicule of the world. I challenge mortal man to stain her career with one blot of cowardice. Therefore as a means to make brave soldiers, good and intelligent citizens, I must respectfully ask for 500 spelling books. I hope this application may meet a speedy and favorable consideration.

The health of our regiment is excellent at this time. Military decorum and soldierly deportment, are peculiarly characteristic of our officers as a general thing. I have the honor to be your servant

ALS   Henry M Turner

Chaplain Henry M. Turner to Adjutant General U.S. Army, 29 June 1865, T-736 1865, Letters Received, ser. 12, RG 94 [K-537]. Endorsements. Chaplain Turner served in the 1st USCI, which he, as minister of Israel African Methodist Episcopal Church in Washington, D.C., had helped recruit in the spring of 1863. It was the first black regiment organized under the auspices of the Bureau of Colored Troops, hence Turner's reference to "the mother of colored Troops."

259: Chaplain of a Kentucky Black Regiment to the Adjutant General of the Army

Brownsville Texas, Sept. 11, 1865,

General, I have the honor to send you another monthly report. To do so is not only an incumbent duty, but also a peculiar pevilege of which I shall always with profound pleasure avail myself. In a periodical production which has special though not exclusive reference to the moral condition of men much variety cannot be reasonable expected, but it shall be our endeavour to render it as attractive and as interesting as we possible *can*. There has been as you are by this time doubtless aware during the last month an unusual amount of sickness in Camp and as a legitimate consequence much suffering has been experienced and many deaths have occured among the men of this Regiment. The most prevailent disease with which these Soldiers were affected was [Scurbutus] which for a while assumed an epidemical and alarming character threatening to render unfit for duty a large portion of this excellent Regiment. Disease suffering and mortality have been among us to an extent without precedent in our military history and by these afflictive dispensation of Divine Providence we have been taught a solemn and instructive lesson, which all would do well to remember, and which some [I am] persuaded will not soon forget. By the use of appropriate remedies especially the *Agate Americana* the health of the Regiment has for some weeks exceedingly improved, some of the most obstinate cases have yielded to judicious medical treatment and many who recently seemed the hopeless victims of inveterate maladies are now getting better and by the Goodness of *God* will soon be well again.

There is an ardent and universal desire among these men for books, especially those of an elementary character. Books of this sort cannot here be procured the desire of these Freedmen cannot be gratified, and we are consequently obliged to use to the best advantage the few facilities now within our power. Many of these Colored men possess minds of the very highest order, and were they plased in circumstances favorable to mental Culture and intellectual developement they would exhibit such talents such aptness to acquire useful knowlege make such proficiency in the arts and sciences as would forever confound their implacable enemies, and gladden the hearts of their genuine friends.

Nearly all the men of my Regiment can spell and read with more or less accuracy, many can write with considerable mechanical excellence and carry on an epistolary correspondance with their friends at home. This valuable attainment is not only a gratification to me but by it I am also relieved from an amount of labor in the form of letter writing which when I became Chaplain of this Regiment was almost intolerable oppressive. Though these men have improved as much perhaps as could be expected since their chains were broken and since they entered the Army of the United States, are still as a general thing lamentable ignorant, their literary and theological attainments are narrow superficial, and often preposterously *absurd* and it will take a consider time under the most auspicious circumstance before they can intelligently discharge the duties which devolve on all American Citizens. The moral condition of ths Regiment still continues comparatively Good. The means of grace are regularly dispinsed and are generally attended by a large congregation of attentive and devout worshippers. My whole time is devoted to the mental the moral culture the temporal and eternal welfare of these men, and my prayers to God daily are that with all other favors recently and I may so say wonderfully confered, they may possess moreover the glorious liberty of the sons of God. For sobriety attention to orders, the diligent and conscientious performance of duty for good discipline-military and religious attainments this Reg. will favorable compare if not altogether excell any other now in the celebrated Army of the Rio Grande.

This Regiment is now commanded by Colonel Thomas L. Sedgwick an accomplished and excellent Officer who is ever willing to render me prompt, and effectual aid in the discharge of my manifold and arduous duties. To his cordial and generous cooperation I am greatly indebted for whatever success has attended my labors among both officers and men. I have the honor to remain your obedient servant

ALS   Thomas Stevenson

Chaplain Thomas Stevenson to Brig. Gen. L. Thomas, 11 Sept. 1865, S-2274 1865, Letters Received, ser. 12, RG 94 [K-535]. Endorsement. Stevenson served with the 114th USCI.

260: Chaplain of a New York and Connecticut Black Regiment to the Adjutant General of the Army

Roma Texas Oct 1ˢᵗ /65

Sir. I have the honor to report that the general condition of this Reg. has I think improved for the month past. The efforts of the Officers have not been fruitless. As we have now become acclimated, and comfortably settled in summer quarters, our duties

have become more regular and agreeable. Nearly six hundred
dollars has been raised in the Reg. with which to procure a
regimental library, and primary books and reading matter for the
men of the Reg. so that the leisure time of the ensuing season
may be pleasantly and profitably occupied. I am able to give a
cheering report of the religious and moral state of the
Reg. Besides the Regular service on the Sabbath, the men meet in
prayer meetings. every evening in the week save one, and, I think
are truly sincere. To show regard for the welfare of their friends
they have remitted home full one quarter, I think of their pay for
the past six months. I am Very Respectfully Your Obt Servt

ALS   A. Alvord

Chapln. A. Alvord to Adjutant General U.S.A., 1 Oct. 1865, A-1209
1865, Letters Received, ser. 12, RG 94 [K-510]. Endorsements. Augustus
Alvord served as chaplain to the 31st USCI, which was partially organized
in New York and completed in the field in Virginia, after consolidation
with an incomplete Connecticut black unit.

261: Chaplain of a Kentucky Black Regiment to the Adjutant General of the Army

                                   Camp Nelson Ky. Nov. 30. 1865 –
Dear Sir: I have the honor of making and forwarding to you my
1ˢ Monthly Report.

The 119. was organized in Kentucky, and about half the men
are freed men of Ky. There are perhaps 400 men in the Regt.
from other States, Tennessee, N. & S. Carolina, Georgia, and
Virginia are all represented. So far as I am acquainted more than
half the men have families. Since my connection with the Regt. it
has been so much scattered, that I had not opportunity of serving
more than three companies, which were stationed at Jeffersonville,
Ind. During the month of November I wrote 150 letters for the
Soldiers to their families, and friends, preached on all seasonable
occasions, distributed all the reading matter that could be made
use of, and spent to average two hours each day in teaching the
men to read & write. School books are furnished by Freedmen's
Aid Com. and sold at figures which will cover cost. It is thought
better to teach the men to spend a part of their money judiciously
in buying books &c. than to give the books to them. Nearly all
the Freedmen are eager to learn to read and write. Many of the
119 have already learned to read, without any instructor, quite a
number are advanced to the 2ᵈ and 3ᵈ Readers, (McGuffies

series). The discipline of the Army seems necessary in training them to correct habits. The question appears to be "will it not be cheaper to keep the Freedmen in the Army, than to turn them loose without either experience of education." There certainly is an intention, on the part of a numerous class in Ky to do all they can to harass and oppress the Freedman and his family. If discharged from the service, many of them would go to their old homes, and masters, and would be virtually under a worse system of servitude than that from which they have just emerged. If taught to read and write, and he have the benefit of experience and discipline, when he is discharged, will take his family and go where he can be an independent man. The standard of morals is above what I conceived it to be. Perhaps 1/5 of the Regt. are members of some evangelical church, and there are to be found examples of sound piety. So far as I am able to judge all the officers are practically and sentimentally moral. I am sorry to report that several of the Officers occasionally indulge in uncalled for profanity. Several Officers are exemplary professors of the Christian faith.

Officers of the Regt. have afforded me every facility for the discharge of my duty, and appear ready at all times to Co-operate with the Chaplain.

There are officers in the 119″, who in the estimation of Military Men, are worthy of promotion. All the Officers, so far as known to me, are on intimate terms with each other. I know of no clashings or jealousies. All of which make the chaplaincy of the 119″ a pleasant position. I am Sir, Most respectfully Your ob^d. Servant

ALcS   J. R. Reasoner

Chaplain J. R. Reasoner to Adjt. Genl. U.S.A., 30 Nov. 1865, Letters Received, 119th USCI, Regimental Books & Papers USCT, RG 94 [G-175].

262: Chaplain of an Arkansas Black Regiment to the Adjutant General of the Army

De Vall's Bluff, Ark. Feb. 28, 1866.
Sir. Since my last Report (Jan 31) I have continued on duty in this regiment as its Chaplain. In only one particular have the matters belonging to my sphere of action exhibited change that requires mention. The Schools that for some months have been maintained are closed. The Colonel (L. W. Whipple), as well as

others, has for some time felt that the presence of persons not assigned by law to the organization, and yet holding intimate relations to its men, perhaps making them feel that their duties are irksome and needless, is unadvisable. As the discipline and drill of this Regiment are unusually thorough, I cannot doubt the propriety of this feeling, though regretting (as does he) its result in this instance

The enlisted men of this Regiment have paid since last October for Schools (not including books &c) $728, as follows.

Co.	B	$165	
"	D	27	
"	E	25	
"	F	115	
"	G.	82	
"	I	75	
"	H	4	
"	K	235	Total $728

Cos. A and C are on detached service, as was Co. H until recently.

Besides this, they have paid $60 to maintain in Town, during the past two months, a School for Colored children, organizing a Society for that purpose, and conducting it with liberality and public spirit. Thus the amount raised by them during the period referred to lacks but little ($12) of $800. I have the honor to be, Respectfully Your obedient servant

ALS

Joel Grant

Chaplain Joel Grant to Brevet Major General L. Thomas, 28 Feb. 1866, filed with W-836 1865, Letters Received, ser. 360, Colored Troops Division, RG 94 [B-400].

15

Health

SICKNESS STALKED the Union army, slaying soldiers of all sorts by the thousands, but disease took an especially high toll of black troops. Whereas nearly two white soldiers died of disease for every one who fell in battle or died of wounds, the ratio among black soldiers was roughly ten to one. Some of this disparity resulted from the comparatively late entry of black soldiers into the war and their proportionately smaller combat role. Still, the fact remains that while approximately one of every twelve white soldiers died of disease, roughly one in five black soldiers did.[1] And, according to an official estimate, for every disease-related death, five men were seriously ill.[2] Conditions varied enormously from place to place, but in Virginia during the closing months of the war, for example, the medical director of the Army of the James calculated that sickness struck four black soldiers for every white stricken and that black deaths from disease outnumbered white by seven to one.[3]

The catastrophe had a variety of sources. Many black recruits

[1] The ratios derive from the following approximations:

	White	*Black*
Total in service	1,900,000	179,000
Killed in battle and mortally wounded	107,000	3,000
Died of disease	162,000	33,000

Original estimates of total numbers of soldiers appear in *Official Records*, ser. 3, vol. 4, p. 1270; and original estimates of deaths in U.S., War Department, Surgeon General's Office, *The Medical and Surgical History of the War of the Rebellion* (Washington, 1870), pt. 1, vol. 1, p. xxxvii. Revised estimates, from which the above approximations derive, appear in William F. Fox, *Regimental Losses in the American Civil War, 1861–1865* (Albany, N.Y., 1889); Thomas L. Livermore, *Numbers & Losses in the Civil War in America: 1861–65* (1900; reprint ed., New York, 1969); and E. B. Long, *The Civil War Day by Day: An Almanac 1861–1865* (New York, 1971), pp. 710–11. The estimate of 1,900,000 total white soldiers who served represents a reduction of the official total of 2,500,000 white enlistments to account for reenlistments. The figure of 179,000 total black soldiers who served coincides with the total of black enlistments, on the assumption that few blacks had the opportunity to reenlist given the comparatively late acceptance of blacks into the army.

[2] *Official Records*, ser. 3, vol. 5, p. 669.
[3] See *Freedom*, ser. 2: doc. 273.

came ill prepared for soldiering. Slavery left them weak and susceptible to disease, and the Union recruitment dragnet placed many
men under arms who would otherwise have been disqualified. Even
when examining physicians noticed the poor physical condition of
black recruits, they often approved the marginally healthy anyway.
Although the Union army's need for troops often forced such actions, motives of genuine concern also played a part. Fugitive slaves
rejected for military service could fall victim to vengeful masters and
slave catchers, so examining physicians often enlisted the runaways,
regardless of health, to secure their liberty. Yet, admitting such
unhealthy men to service had dire consequences. Many black recruits
could not withstand the rigor of military life. Even before they faced
the enemy such soldiers stood in mortal danger. In the crowded
conditions of army camps, contagious diseases spread quickly, especially among those who had little resistance.

Once the recruits entered service, maintaining their health became the responsibility of regimental surgeons and regimental commanders and their superiors. While the full complement of regimental officers included one surgeon and two assistant surgeons, few
black regiments enjoyed the luxury of three medical officers. Regimental commanders petitioned for medical assistance, but the deficiency of qualified medical personnel that plagued the entire Union
command by the summer of 1863 dimmed any hope of success.

As they watched the health of their men deteriorate, commanders
often contended with either indifference or prejudice among their
superiors. The War Department gave no special consideration to the
medical, sanitary, and dietary needs of black soldiers. In addressing
problems of mobilization, organization, and deployment, department policy makers simply assumed that the standard medical pre-
cautions and regular rations would do as well for black soldiers as
they did for white ones. This seemingly equalitarian policy worked
to the detriment of black soldiers both because it failed to provide
for their special needs and because it allowed white officers too
much latitude in implementing policies based on what they perceived as physiological differences between whites and blacks. Assuming that blacks could naturally withstand the rigors of labor in
hot sun and lowland environment better than whites, some Union
commanders removed white troops from unhealthy posts and assigned black ones in their stead. They also ordered black soldiers
disproportionately to fatigue duty on the same assumption. In such
circumstances, blacks often fared as miserably as the whites whom
they replaced. Their health broke under incessant labor just as surely
as their clothing tattered. Moreover, as sick men fell, the labor
burden on healthy men increased, further taxing their resistance and
giving fresh impetus to the cycle of disease. Then the commanders

responsible retreated to convenient explanations offered by the pano-
ply of racial stereotypes that had motivated their original orders,
and, ignoring the mounting casualties from disease, they took no
action to ameliorate the deteriorating health of their soldiers.

The standard army ration represented the War Department's understanding of contemporary nutritional knowledge. Consisting of a
combination of meat, starches, and a variety of vitamin sources, the
ration was intended to guarantee the health of the average soldier at
the least possible cost.[4] The ration authorized a variety of protein
sources but, in line with the eating habits of Northern whites, favored beef above other meats. For Northern blacks entering the
service, the ration posed no particular difficulty, inasmuch as they
generally shared the culinary preferences of their white fellow
Northerners. For Southern black soldiers, in contrast, the standard
ration represented a sharp departure from their customary regimen
of pork, cornbread, and green vegetables. As disease spread, black
soldiers, who understood in their own way the connection between
diet and health, indicted the army ration as one source of deteriorating health. Efforts to change the ration of black troops in line with
slave dietary patterns came into conflict with the eating habits of
Northern blacks. Meanwhile, the shortage of fresh vegetables
pleased the palates of neither white nor black soldiers, Northern or
Southern. Moreover, it unleashed a virtual epidemic of scurvy,
which respected neither color nor place of origin. As diet-related
disease continued to decimate the ranks of black soldiers, commanders found a variety of excuses – administrative and ideological –
not to tamper with the standard ration.

The imperfect state of mid-nineteenth century medical knowledge
similarly exacerbated the health problem by giving full play to a
confused logic about physical differences allegedly attributable to
race. As some race-conscious observers maintained, blacks did enjoy
immunities to certain diseases. Some had their origin in genetic
differences between the peoples of West Africa and Northern Europe, such as the resistance to malaria among the former that mod-

[4] The official daily ration per man, as prescribed by the army regulations of 1861,
included twelve ounces of pork or bacon (or twenty ounces of fresh or salt beef),
and eighteen ounces of bread or flour (or twelve ounces of hard bread, or twenty
ounces of corn meal). In addition, each man received a portion of beans (or rice,
or potatoes), mixed vegetables, coffee (or tea), sugar, salt, vinegar, candles, and
soap allotted to each one hundred rations. In August 1861, Congress increased
the ration of bread, added rations of pepper and (when practicable) molasses, and
made rice and potatoes part of the standard allotment (instead of using them as
substitutes for beans). In July 1864, Congress legislated a return to the earlier
ration. (U.S., War Department, *Revised Regulations for the Army of the United
States* [Philadelphia, 1862], p. 243; *Revised Army Regulations*, pp. 244, 526;
Official Records, ser. 3, vol. 4, p. 449.)

ern medicine has attributed to the sickle cell trait. But, along with special immunities, blacks also carried special susceptibilities. Some of these had their origin in lack of exposure to certain communicable diseases, such as measles, to which the rural and relatively immobile plantation-based slave population had never established resistance. Acceptance of baseless racial stereotypes and ignorance of substantive differences provided racist officers with a rationale for their actions and handicapped the most sympathetic officers in their search for explanations of high disease mortality among black troops.

As a result of soaring mortality rates and the Union command's impervious indifference, individual commanders began casting about for some solution that might improve the health of their men. Officers of abolitionist background moved first to allay the health crisis. They isolated three key components: unbalanced diet, inadequate shelter, and excessive fatigue duty. And in their carefully constructed arguments for policy changes, they refuted the War Department's logic of benign neglect.

Faced with the heavy labor required of their men and the soldiers' own apparent preference for pork, several officers proposed that the diet of Southern black soldiers include more pork and less beef, more corn and less wheat, and more vegetables of all kinds. Often they found support for their views among commissary officers willing to encourage such modifications provided that they cost less. Whatever the intention of this policy, it sometimes met opposition from Northern black soldiers – long accustomed to a beef and wheat diet – and other black troops who viewed pork and corn as the slave regimen. Through it all, sympathetic commanders insisted that their men could not withstand constant labor in the hot sun in unhealthy atmospheres with unsuitable shelter any more than white soldiers could. They demanded change in the discriminatory policies that cost so many black lives in noncombat pursuits. Yet, this well-intentioned benevolence produced no uniform policy and, despite occasional improvements, did little to benefit the general health of black soldiers.

If disease stalked blacks in their regiments, the relentless pursuit of victims did not stop at the hospital door. In fact, given imperfect knowledge of the causes of most wartime diseases, care at established medical facilities often merely aggravated ill health and even hastened death. Again, racism compounded a problem all soldiers faced. Exasperated by their inability to reverse the high morbidity and mortality rates, some medical officers accused blacks of feigning sickness in much the same way that masters and overseers accused slaves of shirking work. They mistreated, abused, overworked, or neglected such soldiers, thereby contributing to further deterioration of their health.

While hospitalized soldiers could not escape the disabilities common to blacks in the army, they did reap some rewards to compensate for their additional suffering. Many took advantage of religious services and educational opportunities, both much more accessible in hospitals than in the field. For the first time, many soldiers found the leisure to write to their friends and families. At army hospitals, sick and wounded soldiers met agents of the U.S. Sanitary Commission and the Christian Commission, who provided them with writing equipment and assistance in composing letters. With such materials and advice readily available, some hospitalized soldiers seized the opportunity to send complaints about poor facilities or abusive treatment to the War Department. And, like Spotswood Rice, a former slave from Missouri, a few found the courage to write to the owners of wives and children, threatening to liberate by force family members not freed immediately.[5] While removed from the daily demands of army life, hospitalized soldiers could reflect upon the meaning of the war, the role of black soldiers in the war effort, and the rewards that blacks throughout the country could expect to reap as a result of military service. Such reflections accompanied many hospitalized soldiers to their graves, but for others, they offered diversion from pain and motivation to recover and rejoin their regiments in the field or their families at home.

[5] See *Freedom,* ser. 2: doc. 299a–c.

263: Testimony by the Superintendent of the Organization of Missouri Black Troops

[*St. Louis, Mo. November 29, 1863*]

. . . .

Q How do the rations of the white soldiers suit the colored men?

A They are not adapted to them, in my judgment. The rations could be changed, and the issue of subsistence modified, to cost the Gov't less, and yet be much better adapted to the negro, in consideration of his former habits.

Q Do you think the negroes suffer in consequence of the change of food?

A I am certain of it; especially in the derangement of the stomach & bowels. They have lived on corn bread all their lives, which they have baked themselves, mixing it simply with water and a little salt.

Q What specific change would you recommend?

A I would recommend the issue of corn meal, and a change of camp and garrison equipage to enable them to use it. This change I think is essential and important.

Q Would you recommend any change of meat?

A I would recommend the issue of more pork and less beef. Beef does not agree with them. I have often found that the men under my charge had less diarhoea when they could get corn bread and either fresh or salt pork, than when they used wheat bread, especially hard bread.

Q Have you made any estimate as to the cost of the rations you propose compared with those now furnished?

A The corn bread could cost a little over half what the wheat does, and the pork would cost perhaps an eighth less than the beef.

Q At all events, it would not be more expensive?

A No, Sir.

. . . .

HD

Excerpt from testimony of Col. Wm. A. Pile before the American Freedmen's Inquiry Commission, [29 Nov. 1863], O-328 1863, Letters Received, ser. 12, RG 94 [K-204]. Topical labels in the margin are omitted.

264: Chief Quartermaster of the Department of the Gulf to the Commander of the Department of the Gulf

New Orleans, La. Dec 22nd 1862

General The Forts below the city, as wood & Pike on the lakes, St Phillip and Jackson on the river, with Ship Island & land Spits now held by white troops, it appears to me, might be two thirds, or more, garrisoned by negroes, with both propriety and policy. The whites suffer terribly by disease and the men become weak. The negroes do not so suffer, are very strong and would fight should it ever be necessary. They can thus be drilled and made very useful soldiers. The white companies associated with them at these deadly forts ought to be exchanged frequently. Ship Island not being exposed to attacks could be easily held by the Blacks. They would besides make good sailers. I make this suggestion because I think it will save our men and made the colord corps useful Most Truly Yours

ALS

S. B. Holabird

638

Col. S. B. Holabird to Major General Banks, 22 Dec. 1862, H-47 1862, Letters Received, ser. 1956, Field Records Banks' Expedition, Dept. of the Gulf, RG 393 Pt. 1 [C-823].

265: Medical Inspector of Black Troops to the Headquarters of the Superintendent of the Organization of Tennessee Black Troops

Memphis Tenn May 30th 1864

Sir   On the 26th inst the 4th U.S. Heavy Artillery was inspected when with an aggregate of 936 present there were 111 sick, A ratio of over 12 pr 100. A little explanation however will show that the present Sanitary condition of the regiment is better than these figures seem to indicate.

The past winter was one of unusual severity for this region of country and during that season a comparatively large force was stationed at Columbus, Ky. and the 4th H. Arty *being negros* were made to perform all the labor required at the landing, government store houses &c in loading and unloading steamboats and storing supplies. This excessive labor and exposure combined reduced the standard of vitality in the men so as soon to swell the Sick List of the regiment to an unusual extent and many of those now in hospital are there because their physical powers were so broken down then as not to permit of their being put on duty since. Some of them will not be of Service again during their present term of enlistment.

There is yet another cause for the large number of men reported unfit for duty and that is that at the time of recruiting such was the anxiety to fill up the number necessary for a regimental organization that sufficient care was not taken in the examination of recruits, and many were admitted who should have been rejected as being physically disqualified for performing the duties of a soldier. Such of those as have not already died may almost be considered as fixtures at the Regimental Hospital

Among the causes having a disturbing influence upon the sanitary condition of the regiment may be considered that of location. Fort Hallack occupies the summit of a hill or bluff upon the river-bank and almost completely surrounded by low swampy lands. Such situations are considered more unhealthy than the lower lands in the same vicinity.

There are two companies garrisoning a small detached work

(Fort Quimby)   They are quartered in huts but to crowded as to allow only about 150 feet (cubic) of breathing space pr man, Whilst 400 cubic feet is considered as the minimum that should be allowed in barracks.

The police of quarters and grounds is good, and both medical and line officers appear to take much interest in procuring the comfort and well-being of the men   I have the honor to be most Respectfully your obdt Servt

ALS   John Rush

Surg. John Rush to Capt. George Mason, 30 May 1864, Letters Received, 4th USCHA, Regimental Books & Papers USCT, RG 94 [G-14].

266: Anonymous Louisiana Black Soldier to an Unidentified Washington Official

Brazos Santiago Texas August 20th 1864

Dear Sir   I take honor to inform you of the Ill treatment towards the Colored Soldiers in the line of medical attendance. hear on this Island the Sick are lying everyother tent covered with Sand all Over and are not able to wipe it from thier faces and they friends that they have here with them are on duty every day Guard pickett and on the breast works So they can not assistance and the doctors visits them about three times a week, and they do more harm then Good for they Poison the Soldiers. they are called doctors but they are not. They are only Students who knows nothing about issueing medicins   Dr Webbs and Peaz and Saunds are call murderers   they have mad many threats and have carried them in to exicution, for he told one Soldier of Company B. to Report to the Captain for duty and if he didt then he would never   the man told him he was not able so he had him buck and gagded until 12. o.clock and then told the captain to Releace him and Send to the hospital and he gave him Som medicin and the next morning he was a Chorps   Most of the men are complaining of Swollen legs and with pain in leg and have to walk with a Stick and they Curses them. the officers See all this and dont Seem to pay any attention to it and there was One man of Company D. 87. crawl out of his tent to ease him Self   Dr Peaze came up at the time and Cursed him and kick him in to his tent   that night he died. and they was another in the hospital dieing and he Seem to Suffer very much and Dr Peaze Cursed him and told him god damn him if he was a going to die and dont So much fuss about it   So my Dear friend for us and for the Sake of

640

our Cuntry do not throw this a Side unnoticed   I can not make
the Complaint of all the men in this and if you will Send Some
officer to investicate the mater you will find out matter
Correctly   nothing more   yours respectfuly

P.S.   please do not let the letter fall into they hands for there is
So many ways to Seek revenge and they may find out who inform
you of they misdeeds   my writing is none of the best for Slaves
are poorly learned   yours Res---tly
HL

Unsigned to Sir, 20 Aug. 1864, A-332 1864, Letters Received, ser. 360,
Colored Troops Division, RG 94 [B-79]. Endorsement.

267: Battalion Commander in a Rhode Island Black Regiment to Regimental Headquarters

Plaquemine, La.,   October 3, 1864.
Lieutenant, – I have this day received an order from the Colonel
Commanding requiring me to report to Head-Quarters my opinion
as to the effect that will be produced in my Battalion by the issue
of corn-meal, instead of flour.

It is my opinion, and also that of my officers whom I have
consulted, that the change will be very disagreeable to the men,
and in a sanitary point of view, detrimental to their health.

The men composing the Battalion were free blacks from the
North, and previous to entering the service, were accustomed to
the same kind of food as the white soldiers were, who are now
serving in this Department.

They have also been apprised that by an Act of Congress, they
are entitled to the same pay, allowances, clothing, *rations,* etc. as
white troops and they will naturally feel that the distinction made
is unjust.

The effect will be to dispirit them, and also to discourage the
officers in their endeavors to bring this Battalion up to the highest
standard of discipline and effectiveness. I enclose the certificate of
Ass't Surg. Mecomey   Very Resp'y Your Ob't Servant.
HLcS   Richard G Shaw

Maj. Richard G. Shaw to 1st Lieut. J. Cary Whiting Jr., 3 Oct. 1864,
Letters Sent, 11th USCHA, Regimental Books & Papers USCT, RG 94
[G-58].

268: Anonymous Black Noncommissioned Officer to an Unidentified Washington Official

Jackson ville Florida octobor the 18, 1864

I have taken honourabul opportnunity to Embrace you with the honour that you have issued your law to all the department to pick out all men that Was not abel and the is A Larg number of men in the first north Calala regiment and it is a pitty to See how the offices are treeting those men as are Sick   the doctor have got Some are Lame and Sume Blind and Sume with arm Broken and the doctor and ffices Are press the poor Sick and Lame men on duty and the men are not Abel to march three mild   the are full of pane and the Command offices dont See to those men and I say those men Can not pay fer What th duty tha can du and i think that it is right for those men that can not du ful duty Shud B taken out for doctor marce has good many Lame men and affleted and sum are About to Louse they eyes   cant see good   and the mager doctor marce has got them there or press them to du duty and the officers are press the men and the officers is not much feand to those men   it seem like the officers want to kill those men and those men is not fettain for the surves   and the fficers try to keep those lame men and when they know that those men is not abel for duty and sum are Been in the regiment About ten months and are Been wounded in Battle of luster [*Olustee*] and are not well yet   it is A petty treet those men like those officers du for we all know that the (35 US regiment is the Best regiment that we have in our army   now i will Close my letter

out of Another regiment   this is what i have seen in the 35
[*In the margin*] this Letter are wretten by fficers
HL

Unsigned to unidentified official, 18 Oct. 1864, A-400 1864, Letters Received, ser. 360, Colored Troops Division, RG 94 [B-81]. The 35th USCI was originally designated the 1st North Carolina Volunteers.

This letter are written by officers

Jacksonville Florida October the
1st 1864 (?) US I have
taken honnested oppertunity
to embrace you with the honour that
you have issued your law to all
the department to picket
all men that was not abel
aby And the is a verry
number of men in the first
northcalald regiment and it
is a pitty to see how the officers
are treeting those men it all
sick the doctor have got some are
game and some blind
And some with arm Broken
And the doctor and officers
are make the poor sick and
game men on duty and
the men all not abel to
marsh half mild the are
full of pane and the commment
officers dont see to those men an

269: Northern Black Soldier to the Adjutant General
of the Army

Camp Wm Penn [*Pa.*] Nov the 28th 1864

Honored Sir   This is the Second letter that I have Sent in relation
to this matter   I will at first direct your attention to one
particular point which is this   there has been a number of Sick
men of various deseases who have been Kept here for months after
months under the treatment of the Doctor   they can not be
Cured   they are Still lying here in the Same Condition   one of
the men that has been here lingering got to be So bad that they
Sent him to the hospital   he was there three days when he
died   previous to his Death he wanted to go home   he is a man
of family But he did not get to See them   I wish to know if that
is human treatment   I do not Consider it treatment for a dog   it
is ridiculous a perfect Shame   I only wish and pray that Some of
you gentlemen that has Some Sympathy for human being to come
and examine   I wish those that has feelings for to See   I
Sometimes think that it is on Account of our Color   if we was in
Comfortable quarters So that we Could improve in health it would
be a great deal better for us   the Doctor that we have Cannot do
us any good   therefore we Shall never have our health while we
remain here in this State   the reasons why that I write to you I
do not think that [you] are aware of all these transactions   I am
confident that there is Some other remedy besides keeping us here
in this horrible condition   last Sunday when at inspection of the
Barracks the Major called the Straglers in line   at the presence of
the Major one of the men took a fit   he asked a few questions in
relation to this man   they told him that the same man had been
here for months in the Same Situation, fits every other day   there
has been men discharged here that was able to do duty and we
that are afflicted have to remain there I suppose untill we are
either dead or our time out   we have to work as long as we can
stand and then in bed they are here not able to do
anything   Some has been here Since march on cructhes   all the
time they will not allow them to go home to see how there family
is getting along   I scarcely know how to give you a discription of
how things are going on   I would rather be in my grave than to
Stay here in this Barracks   I hope that you attend to this
matter   Some of the men are actually loosing the use of their
limbs   they will not allow our friends to visit us   I expect to
here from Some of you   you will attend to this matter
immediately   Your Obedient Servant

ALS   John H. Wilkison

John H. Wilkison to Honored Sir, 28 Nov. 1864, W-945 1864, Letters Received, ser. 360, Colored Troops Division, RG 94 [B-189]. Endorsement.

270: Adjutant General of the Army to the Assistant Surgeon General

> Nashville, Tenn., January 16, 1865.
> Sir: A complaint having been made by a Captain of Colored Troops, that the wounded soldiers of his Company, in Hospital were neglected, I made an inspection of Hospital No. 16., containing a large number of sick and wounded of the Colored Troops. I directed Surgeon Sargent, of my Staff, to make an inspection, and sent for the superintendents of Hospitals, Surgeon J. H. Brinton, who was present; also Acting Asst. Surgeon J. S. Giltner. Surgeon Sargent's report is enclosed, with statements of the two other officers named above.
>
> I have inspected many Hospitals but have never seen one that was not in good order, except this one.
>
> The building was unsuitable, but that, I judge, was unavoidable. It was taken a year ago as a Contraband Hospital, and then used for sick Colored Soldiers likewise. In that time it ought to have been put in a more habitable condition; — Still, of this I do not complain, because the Quartermaster's Department was erecting suitable buildings. What I complained of were the filthy condition of the wounded, and the bedding. Words of mine cannot describe the utter filthiness of what I saw. I will instance one or two cases: — A soldier wounded Dec. 15, with leg amputated, was on a bed, the clothing of which had not been changed up to yesterday, and he was still in the dress in which he was carried from the battle-field, everything saturated with blood — and he complained that the lice were eating him up. Another was shirtless, having discarded his shirt ten days previous, on account of its filthy condition. Other instances could be given but let this suffice.
>
> Had these men been white soldiers, think you this would have been their condition? No! And yet the Black fell side by side with the White with their faces to the Foe, at the very apex of the abbatis. One man was cared for in every respect: — the other suffered in filth for weeks.
>
> The excuse given that the water was cut off by an irresponsible person, two weeks previous, is futile. — The Military authorities

were at hand to arrest any abuse, besides there were laundries at the other Hospitals, which could be used, and the river was near, and the quartermasters ready to furnish any requisite number of washerwomen. Any necessary amount of bedding could have been obtained on proper application. I conceive, however, that no excuse whatever is admissible in the case. I at first intended to ask the dismissal of the two officers, but, find that Dr. Giltner has worked very hard, night and day, and made himself sick thereby; and that Surgeon Brinton has but recently assumed his present high and responsible duties, – and have concluded to refer the whole case to you. If you will express to them your dissatisfaction, it, with the severe rebuke I gave them, will be sufficient. I must ask, however, that another Medical officer be placed in chief charge of the above Hospital, instead of Doctor Giltner. You can judge whether, by further experience, Surgeon Brinton will be able fully to superintend the Hospitals at Nashville. Very Respectfully Y'r Obedient Servant

HLc   [*Lorenzo Thomas*]

Adjutant General [Lorenzo Thomas] to Colonel R. C. Wood, 16 Jan. 1865, L. Thomas Letters & Orders, Generals' Papers & Books, ser. 159, RG 94 [V-50]. The items mentioned as enclosed were not copied into the letter book.

271: Anonymous Indiana Black Soldier to the Secretary of War

                            Camp Wm Penn Chelton Hill Pa Jan 21, 1865
Dear Sir I am nesseriley compelled to write you a few Lines I hav bin in This camp Just four Months and half of That time I hav Bin unable for duty My Left Leg is very Badley Afected from an old cut and The Surgent here hav Bin giving Me harts ham Leinament to Rub it withe and it is well Mixt with Turpintine I hav Bin useing it till I hav almost Lost the use of My Leg I hav tole him often that it was getting worse but he will driv Me off Like a dog and Say That he cant do any thing for Me I then went to The Hospitle surgent and had him to Examan Me and he Says That thare can Be but Litle Remady for Me and that he could do nothing for Me unless I could gett a Ticket from The other Surgent and then he did not think that he could do Me Much good as it is an old cut I am sined to the Eighth Regemant U.S.C.T. I ast Col Lewis Wagner if Thare would Be any chance

of an Indiana man getting Money here and that I was drafted in Madison town Ship Jefferson. Co. Indiana and for the period of one yeare and that My familey had nothing to Liv on   I also tole him that I wanted to go to My Regt where I can gett My Money and Send to My wife   But he would not Let Me go with My company and yeat they Make Me do duty Every day and as My god woul hav it I found that My descriptive Role cant Be found   I was drafted on the 21 day of Septembar 1864 and I am hapy to Say notwithstanding the unjesteness that is dun to us as Black Men By Those who hav sworn to do Just to all Men Thare has not Bin one Indiana Colored Solder who hav deserted out of This camp and yeat we ar treated Like Slaves   dear Sir if I was a white Man I would be discharged Sum time a go but I am a Black Man and they hav giving Me over to the quartermaster and they think we will not Let the negro no what is the Matter and keepe him here to wate on us   dear Sir My helth is the onley Thing that has cept Me from the armey   they would not take Me as a volinteare But they taking Me as a drafted Man   now sir if you concidor that the above is Just I am compelled to differ with you   yeat we ar fighting as white Men ar and numbering with Thear dead   I am Sir very Respecflly your obdiant Servant
HL   Colored Colders Letter

Colered Colder to Mr. Edward M. Stanton, 21 Jan. 1865, A-37 1865, Letters Received, ser. 360, Colored Troops Division, RG 94 [B-112]. A few days later, in a letter to President Lincoln, the soldier renewed his plea for discharge, citing his continued sickness and his wife's need for his support. (Colored Solder to Honerble Mr. Presordent U.S., 4 Feb. 1865, A-136 1865, Letters Received, ser. 360, Colored Troops Division, RG 94 [B-113].)

272: Pennsylvania Black Soldier to the President

[*City Point, Va.*] Feb the 2 1865
Mr Abebrem Lenken the Presdent of the U.S. stats   I will rite you A few Lins to let you now that I am not Well and i Can not rite to Day for i am sick but i am in Good hops that you will rede this   i have ben sick Evy since i Come her and i think it is hard to make A man go and fite and Wont let him vote and wont let him go home when he is sick   We had Boys her that Died that Wood gout well if thy Could go home   thy Can Come back as Well as A whit man   i hope you will give us some pleser of our life   give us A chenc of A man   i Will rite no more this

time   i Dont wont you to get mad with what i say for i Dont mene any harme   rite soon if you pleze and let me no how you feel   so No More this time

my wife is left A long and no helf and thy wont let me go home   Derect you letter to City Point 8 Reg U.S.C.T. 25 Corps 2ⁿ Briggad 2ᶰᵈ Divsion Com. B   re Derict to

ALS   Zack Burden

Zack Burden to Mr. Abebrem Lenken, 2 Feb. 1865, B-1 $\mathfrak{r}\mathfrak{o}$ 1865, Letters Received, ser. 360, Colored Troops Division, RG 94 [B-118].

273: Special Examining Board to the Headquarters of the Department of Virginia

Head-Quarters, 25th Army Corps [Va.], February 12, 1865. Colonel, The Undersigned, a Board, appointed by Special order, No. 37, of the 6th inst., from Head Quarters, Department of Virginia, beg leave to report.

On the question, "Should the ration vary in different regiments?" we report negatively.

The question *"What should compose the ration for the U.S. Colored Troops?"* has received our most careful consideration.

If we were called upon to recommend a ration for the use of troops in camps of instruction or of rendezvous for recruits, we would be inclined to make several important changes in the present issue. The army ration differs so widely in several particulars from the ordinary diet of the people as to require the exercise of more than ordinary judgment to prevent sickness among recruits arising from a total and sudden change of their habits of life. The derangement of the physical system by a change of food without any transition is the abundant cause of sickness among those new to the army. It seems to be well established that those recruits whose food has been for some time the same as that used by soldiers do not suffer much from sickness. The men who have labored in large numbers under contractors on the public works soon enjoy the immunity of the veteran. A larger mortality occurs among the young men who come from our northern farms; but the severest effects are witnessed among the class known as "contrabands," the freedmen from the rebellious or the border states, who do not obtain in the army a single article of their usual diet. Habituated to subsist on corn-meal, fresh fish, yams,

648

potatoes and on the varied vegetable products of their garden
patches, they have suffered greatly from being placed suddenly
under the regimen of the army ration. Diseases of the stomach
and bowels have been common among this class, and they have
fallen victims to fevers of the types common in the army. Their
physical systems have been low in tone from want of the habitual
nutrition and have been without strength to react against
disease. That the mortality among this class does not result from
color but from a too rapid change in nutriment and habits of life
is evident from the fact that there is no perceptible difference
between the colored and white soldiers who come from the north
and whose food has not differed widely before entering the army.

As most of the colored troops in the 25th Corps have been
enlisted for several months, we propose to confine our
recommendations to the ration to be used by soldiers seasoned to
the field. The changes we have to advise are, therefore,
inconsiderable being intended to obviate the slight tendency to
scurvy perceptible among the enlisted men. All of them can be
effected within the terms of War Department General Orders, No.
226, of July 8th, 1864.

Paragraph 5 of that order is as follows: "When deemed
necessary, fresh vegetables, dried fruit, molasses, pickles, or other
proper food, may be purchased and issued *in lieu* of any component
part of the ration of equal money value."

This puts it in the power of the Commissary Department to
make all such purchases of food as the health of the troops may
require, provided it does not pass the limits of the money value of
the present ration. It empowers the military commander to make
within the same limits, the changes he may deem necessary. He
can order, if he should think proper, more *vegetable food* and *greater
variety* which are the only changes the board thinks necessary in
the present ration.

We are unanimous in recommending the more frequent issue of
corn-meal and increase in the quantity of hominy and molasses and
freeer purchases of vegetables.

The fund for the increase and purchases recommended can be
formed by dropping portions of some articles now issued. *Vinegar*
and *coffee* are rarely altogether consumed by any troops; and the
black troops are not accustomed to coffee in such large
quantities. The issue of candles is too large, especially in the
summer season; and a portion of the fresh beef may well exchanged
for vegetables.

The following economies on the present ration seem to us
practicable:

	cts
One half, vinegar, value at 100 rations,	.20
One fifth, coffee, " "	93.6
One fifth, candles, " "	09.5
Four oz., salt or fresh beef, "	4.50.
Total Savings,	$5.73.1

The amt. saved to be expended as follows:

	cts.
Hominy, add ten lbs. on 100 rations, value,	.52.5
Dried fruit, add five lbs " "	.65.
Molasses, add two gallons " "	1.76.
Fresh vegetables, " "	2.79.6
	$5.73.1

We would earnestly recommend that the largest *variety* permitted in the present ration be carefully maintained by the Commissary Department in the issue.

The following variety seems to be practicable without any change in the existing orders:

> Corn meal, three times a week;
> Flour or soft bread, twice a week;
> Hard bread,   twice "   "   ;
> Pork or Bacon,   three "   "   ;
> Fresh Beef,   twice "   "   ;
> Mutton,   once "   "   ;
> Mackerel, or if estimated for, Codfish once a week

We respectfully submit the above views for the consideration of the Major General Commanding Department.

C. A. Heckman*
William Birney
George Suckley

*Gen. Heckman authorised me to sign his name to the above report, after he had heard the first draught read. W^m. Birney, Brig. Gen. U.S.V.

HLS

[*Endorsement*] Office of Medical Director Head Quarters Dept. of Virginia, ARMY OF THE JAMES. *In the field,* March 9th 1865. Respectfully returned. The within report having been referred to me partially as Medical Director, and partly because the only officer now present in the army who composed the Board

framing it, for opinion and slight correction, I have the honor to
return it with the following recommendations:

That the Ration as issued to colored troops be: – two issues of
fresh beef weekly, one pound at each issue: three issues of pork or
bacon weekly, 3/4 of a pound to the issue: one issue of mutton
weekly one pound to the ration: one issued of salt fish (pickled)
weekly, eighteen ounces per ration.

Three issues of corn meal weekly one pound per ration. Two
issues of flour weekly, one pound per ration: three quarters of a
pound of hard bread twice a week.

The full Regulation allowance of beans: coffee six pounds
(instead of eight) per hundred rations. Sugar the regulation issue:
vinegar one half the regulation issue: Candles one fifth less than
the regulation ration: soap the full ration: Salt, full ration. Pepper
full ration.

The following additional articles are recommended: Hominy ten
pounds per hundred rations: Dried fruit five pounds per hundred
rations: Molasses two gallons per hundred rations.

The cost of the Government Ration as established by law, as I
compute it, is about 35 1/2 cents per man. The cost as
announced from Washington is at present 35 cents.

The money value of the articles proposed amounts to about 33
1/2 cents per individual exclusive of the diminution caused by the
saving of two ounces of flour and one quarter of a pound of corn
meal from each ration of those articles. Without these latter
savings being counted we have a clear margin daily of 1 1/2 cents
per man for the purchase of succulent fresh vegetables – or
desiccated vgts. *With* them the margin for these expenditures is
nearly three cents per man daily, which at present rates would give
more than one pound of potatoes daily to the man, or an
equivalent in other vegetable nutriment, or other anti-scorbutics.

I recommend that the report of the Board be adopted with the
slight modifications herein indicated.

The low state of health of our colored troops and their proneness
to disease and death (sickness as four to one, and deaths as seven
to one as compared with the white troops) show that there is some
radical evil which requires correction. We average in this army
about eight deaths daily among colored troops.

In my opinion the principal cause of disease among these people
is the Army ration, to which they have hitherto been
unaccustomed. In this opinion I am borne out by the views of
officers of experience with colored troops, and of Medical Officers
of learning, experience, and common sense. George
Suckley Surgeon US Vols Medical Director, Army of the James:

Note. It is well to state that the issue of mackerel once each week makes a difference of eleven 1/16 cents per man weekly, as a saving, making a handsome margin for vegetable food, which seems to have been over-looked by Captain Masser, CS US Vols., in his calculations. Geo. Suckley Surgeon & Med^l Director.

[*Endorsement*] Hdqrs 25th A.C. March 10th 1865 My experience with and observations made after two years service with and near colored troops, leads me to approve the endorsement of Dr. Suckley G. Weitzel Maj Genl US Vols

Brigadier General C. A. Heckman et al. to Lieut. Col. E. W. Smith, 12 Feb. 1865, enclosed in M.G. E. O. C. Ord to Col. M. R. Morgan, 10 Mar. 1865, O-34 1865, Letters Received, ser. 517, 25th Army Corps, RG 393 Pt. 2 No. 9 [C-4504]. Another endorsement. General Heckman was temporary commander of the 25th Army Corps; General Birney was a division commander in the 25th Army Corps; and Surgeon Suckley was medical director of the Army of the James.

274: Black Chaplain of a Hospital for Black Soldiers to the Adjutant General of the Army

Alexandria, Va. April 30th *1865.*
Sir I have the honor to report for the Month Ending April 30th /65. In accordance to orders received from Surgeon R. O. Abbott Medical Director U.S.A.

I received my appointment from our late beloved President of the United States Aug. 1864. and was assigned to duty at this Hospital by Surgeon R. O. Abbott U.S.A.

I have been on duty all of the Month past, and have to the best of my ability performed these duties as a faithful Christian Chaplain, and have not been engaged in the performance of duties which are not connected with this Hospital. As Soldiers in the US Service we mourn the loss of our Noble Chief Magistrate. We have looked to him as our earthly Pilot to guide us through this National Storm, and Plant us Securely on the Platform of Liberty, and Equal Political right, but God in his wise Providence has removed him. Brave men weep for him who is no more, "Man" Dies but "God" lives.

I have endeavored to act both the part of A Chaplain, and Teacher, Trusting by divine assistance to be instrumental in the accomplishment of Some good As Chaplain I have held divine Services at LOuverture Branch Hospital, four times a week, and at

Grace Church Branch three times a week, which have been well attended, and at times with increased interest. one has given evidence of a change of heart, through the regenerating power of God, and two have been reclaimed, from a backsliden State, to the enjoyment of spiritual blessings. Agreable to request, I have administered the ordinance of Baptism to one young man, who has Given good evidence of conversion, but with all these Privileges the hearts of many seem hardened in Sin, and though far from the enjoyment of Christ, and his blessings, love their distance well.

The School is not as prosperous as in Months Past; The necessary change incident to Hospital life, renders it imposible to have the same class of men to instruct longer than a few weeks, consequently the progress is not as manifest as it otherwise would be. I am amply supplied with books through the kind donations of friends from the North and West.

I have organized a Literary Society, for the Moral and intellectual improvement of our Soldiers, which promises good. Its exercises are Declamation dissertation Oral discussion, and a paper called the "Day Star" to which all contribute who can write.

I have distributed nine hundred copies of Religious Papers during the past Month. I think that many enjoy reading these papers, and although I cannot See much good has been accomplished yet I trust that a good impression is being made upon the minds of our Soldiers, which will finally result in good to the Soul.

I have Committed to the grave with appropriate religious services, Ten Soldiers and Two Civilians, Seven died in hope of Bliss, beyond the grave, and five died impenitent. though desiring to become Christians, they died without a knowledge of Jesus Christ. Through the untiring efforts of our much esteemed surgeon in charge, and his assistants, The LOuverture Hospital Stands No 1. in point of excellence in Phisical Treatment and Wholesome Discipline. I have the honor to be Very respectfully Your Obt Servant,

ALS   Chauncey Leonard

Chaplain Chauncey Leonard to Adjutant General Lorenzo Thomas, 30 Apr. 1865, L-287 1865, Letters Received, ser. 12, RG 94 [K-524].

275: Anonymous Maryland Black Soldier to the Secretary of War

New Berne *N.C.* October 2nd 1865

Kind & Hornorible Sir   i am Veary Happy that it is my good Fourchan & i am Sorry Dear Sir that i hafto availe myselfe of this Sorrowfull opportunity but i Reealy thought that when i came out into the Servus that We Would be Honestly Dealte with but i find Since i have come out that there has bin a Vase Differrances & a Conciderble Change in my officers   We came out in 1[8]63 as Valent hearted men for the Sacke of our Surffring Courntury & Since that Time things has chings a Round. We have Never Refuces of Douing any Duty that We war call on to Dou & when Ever We war orded to go we always Whent Like men but Mr E. M. Stanton we Never bin Treated as men Since we have bin out in the field   We have bin cut Down to Only 75 men out of one 1000 Strong but we have Never bin forchenent as to Ever be call off of the field. & We are now in a Veary Hard & a Dreadfull condishion   for the Last three months we have bin a Surffring in a Tearrable condision   Ever Since we have bin a Laying hear at this awlffull & Deserble & Forceaken Place We have bin a Surffring in the wors Kind of a manner. We havent a 150 men for Duty & the officers are a Reporting 400 men for Duty & they cant Raies a Relefe of guard   We have men that bin on Duty now for Near Two months havent bin Releve from guard & when we Put men on guard in Town we hafto Leve them there for a Weeke at a Time & i Know that it tis not milertary to Keepe men on guard Longer 48 Hours at the Longes. & we have bin a careing has high as five & Six men to the Hospital a in a Day   & Day a after We have bin a Douing the Likes & i Supose as Long as we Shall Stay hear in this forcaken Plasce we Shall contineua to So to Doue it. We have come out Like men & we Expected to be Treeated as men but we have bin Treeated more Like Dogs then men. Sir alow me to Say that i hope that the Time Shall Soon come when Shall all be Eacklize as men hear   our Hospital is full of sick men & our camp is a Laying one halfe of the men that are in campe ar Cripples & Still they are Reporting 400 men for Duty. & they are Even Puting the fiffers & Drummars on guard. i have Read the Reagulations Enough to Know that it is Rong but i Supose that because we are colored that they think that we Dont no any Better   & the officers have wa[i]ters & they Send them to the companys for there Rations & i Dont think in my Small judgment that a officer has any Right to Send his wa[i]ter to the company for Rations   if he is not able to Bord him he would better Dou

654

without any. & if thare is any Reagulation in this; Kind of
Buisness then i will Sey that i arnt United States Soldier nor Dont
Know any thing army Reagulations. if we Ever Expect to be a
Pepple & if we Dont Reply to some one of a thourety we Shall for
Ever be Troden Down under foot of man. We have made Two
Sutlars Rich Since We have bin out in the Servus We would
Like to Know if it Lawfull for us to Set Up or to Reastablish
Some three Specturlaters & to Set them upe for Buisniss. by them
a Seialing there goods at Duble Prices Which we have bin a
Paying Double Priceses for things from our Sutlars Ever Since we
have had them. Where we Lay now a Person cant go a Houndred
yeards from camp without geting into a Swamp We are
Surounded with Ponds chills & fevers & Deseasses of Every Kind &
i hope that it whont be but a Short Time befor We Shall be
Remove from hear or Some thing Don for us for the Better. Even
our chaplain who Should be ar Best freind & to Lookeout for our
wellfear has Even gone intou Buisness of Spectulation & in my
Small Judgment i think that it would be Prudent to Dischage
them all Let go Back to Where they come from Worke foor there
Liveing as they heartofor have Don for all they are after is a
makeing money   it tis not the Love for there counntary that they
whant Stay for but it only for the money

   Pleass to Excuse bad writing & also mistakes   Hoping to hear
from you Sir i have the Hornor to be Repectifully Your o.b.
Serviant   this is from Two of the Old 1863 Soldiers to which you
have our warmest & well wishess   this is from the Camp of 4th
Reg^t U.S.C.T.

HL

Unsigned to Mr. Edwin M. Stanton, 2 Oct. 1865, A-396 1865, Letters
Received, ser. 360, Colored Troops Division, RG 94 [B-198].

16

A Brothers' War: Black
Soldiers and Their Kinfolk

THE FAMILY STOOD at the center of antebellum black life, slave and free.[1] When black men shouldered arms for the Union, they continued no less to be husbands, fathers, sons, and brothers. Indeed, in some respects military service intensified the significance of kinship bonds and family responsibilities. Familial ties influenced the initial decision to enlist, shaped perceptions of a soldier's duties and rights, and created both new opportunities and new difficulties for the men and their kin. A war so intimately connected with the fate of black people inevitably affected black soldiers' families.

Black men contemplating enlistment had to weigh the opportunity to strike a blow for freedom and the prestige gained by military service against the demands of family. For Northern and border-state freemen, who first faced this choice in 1863, the economic needs of their families rendered the decision especially difficult. Free blacks had long been limited to the most menial occupations, and the security of their families depended upon the income of all adult members. Prolonged absence of husbands and sons, and the possibility of irrevocable loss through death in the service, thus threatened the fragile economic base of black domestic life, while also imposing the emotional pain of wartime separation. Drafted free blacks, torn from their families with less ceremony, faced similar difficulties without even the possibility of choice. Still, military service offered potential gains. Army pay promised to be more regular than the ordinary wages of most casual laborers, and free-state bounties, tendered as inducements to volunteer, often equaled a year's wages. Black families balanced these economic considerations with ideological, emotional, and personal ones as they debated enlistment, but for the men who joined the army, as for those who remained at home, family ties continued to frame their actions. Kinsmen frequently enlisted together, creating military units in which brothers, cousins, fathers, and sons marched side by side. The characterization

---

[1] Published accounts of black family life during the Civil War include: Herbert G. Gutman, *The Black Family in Slavery and Freedom, 1750–1925* (New York, 1976) and C. Peter Ripley, "The Black Family in Transition: Louisiana, 1860–1865," *Journal of Southern History* 41 (August 1975): 369–80.

of the war as a "brothers' war" had a distinctive meaning for many black families.

Wartime inflation worsened the always-precarious material circumstances of free black households, and an absent soldier's pay could not be depended upon to alleviate his family's plight. Perhaps no army practice contributed more blatantly to the distress of free black families than the failure to pay soldiers promptly. Many soldiers remained unpaid for months on end. That the army pay, when received, was for much of the war less than that of white soldiers only aggravated nerves rubbed raw by the impoverished conditions of loved ones at home. Black soldiers and their relatives deluged the War Department with pleas for assistance to hard-pressed families; most petitions shunned charity, seeking merely the pay to which a soldier was justly entitled or the release from service of a soldier whose family desperately required his support.

Free blacks in the Union-occupied South faced even greater difficulties than those in the Northern states. Many free black men had married slave women and could live with or visit their families only at the slave owner's sufferance. When such men enlisted in the federal army, masters revoked visitation privileges and even vented their fury by abusing the soldiers' enslaved relatives. In New Orleans, home of a large community of *gens de couleur,* the slave families of enlisted freemen faced, in addition, a special form of urban harassment – eviction notices.

The federal government's decision to recruit slaves as well as free blacks increased the number of families exposed to retaliation by angry masters. In those parts of the Confederate South where slave owners remained in residence after Union occupation – notably Louisiana and Tennessee – enlistment left the families of slave soldiers under the control of their masters. By the terms of the second Confiscation Act, the 1862 Militia Act, and the Emancipation Proclamation, some of these families held claims to freedom, but others belonged to Unionist masters exempt from the liberating provisions. Whatever their legal position, most continued to labor under conditions not markedly different from those of bondage. Still other black soldiers donned federal uniforms only after first escaping from slavery in Confederate-held territory. Successful flight often meant leaving behind family members less able to hazard a difficult journey. Relatives thus consigned to continued servitude stood constantly at risk of punishment because their men had joined the army of liberation.

Nearly all families of border-state black soldiers likewise remained in bondage. Exempted from the Emancipation Proclamation by virtue of their adherence to the Union, border-state slave owners found sustenance for their authority in law and military policy, as well as in practice. Their power unchallenged, these masters manipulated slave family ties first to discourage enlistments and then to vent their wrath against the tens of thousands of men who nevertheless dared to join the army. Masters threatened to turn out helpless family members and often refused to support dependents once the able-bodied men had enlisted. They also cut rations, assigned slave women and children to tasks ordinarily performed by men, and punished them for communicating with soldier husbands and fathers.

The abuse of family and friends angered black soldiers, many of whom had but recently felt the sting of the master's lash. Generally they expected the army to intervene on their families' behalf, and they regularly carried reports of ill treatment to sympathetic officers, some of whom reproved culpable masters by letter or appealed to superiors for punitive action. With an assumption of simple entitlement and justice, some black soldiers requested that the army forcibly liberate their still-enslaved kin. Others, propelled by the new power and authority acquired with the wearing of Union blue, threatened offending masters directly. Such challenges at once contested the moral basis of human bondage and confirmed the worst fears of the slaveholders. The threat of unilateral black action forced federal officials to confront the question of freedom for the slave families of black soldiers. But while many army officers did what they could to compel decent treatment, federal authorities moved slowly. Congress did not formally declare the freedom of all black soldiers' families until March 1865.

Many slave families escaped bondage intact. On the coasts of South Carolina, North Carolina, and Virginia, masters fled at the approach of the Union army, leaving their slaves behind. Throughout the Mississippi Valley and from the interior of the eastern slave states, slave families often managed to flee together into Union lines or to reconstitute themselves after individual escapes. These circumstances eliminated the prospect of retaliation by masters if the men enlisted, but cast black families upon the uncertain mercy of the Union army.

Having maintained family integrity through slavery and its collapse, blacks proved reluctant to entrust family security to their Yankee liberators. Army recruiters soon discovered that willingness to enlist hinged upon offers of protection for families. As a result, in the Union-occupied South the government promised either to care for black women, children, and elderly dependents in contraband camps or to supervise free labor arrangements with local planters and Northern lessees, specifying wage payments and prohibiting abuse. To stimulate black enlistment, some recruiters stipulated that black soldiers would serve as contraband camp guards, thereby assuring blacks that their families would remain together and formalizing the role of family protector. General Benjamin F. Butler, never hesitant to seize the initiative, issued perhaps the fullest pledge of family protection in December 1863. His order promised Virginia and North Carolina blacks that the family of every enlistee would receive a certificate entitling dependents to government support while the men served in the army. Despite such guarantees, the integrity of black family life seldom ranked among the military's highest priorities, and promises often went unfulfilled. With the cessation of fighting in the spring of 1865, the army violated Butler's explicit bargain, although protests from black soldiers and Northern missionaries secured temporary respite from termination of ration issues.

In the absence of reliable federal support, thousands of black soldiers' families improvised homes in the vicinities of the camps or garrisons where the men were stationed. In south Memphis, on the outskirts of Vicksburg, at the fringes of nearly every military post where black soldiers performed duty, sprawling "villages" of shanties and cabins housed soldiers' kinfolk. Women, children, and the aged supported themselves as best they could, often as laundresses, cooks, and in other army-related employment. Proximity to the husband's camp facilitated family visits and permitted husbands to assist in the families' precarious maintenance. The swollen population of these shanty towns made it difficult, however, for everyone to earn a living, and army policy continually disrupted family life. In the eyes of army officers, these black families constituted a perpetual nuisance, an ever-present source of "demoralization," which distracted the men from their duties. Certainly, men whose families lacked adequate food and shelter performed their duties less than assiduously. They took unauthorized leave to attend to domestic needs; on occasion they stole army rations or other property to feed, clothe, or house their families; they even resorted to violence to protect loved ones. Repeated army attempts to remove the families from jerry-built settlements to more distant and closely regulated camps brought resistance by the families and forcible intervention by the soldiers.

Army officials displayed their lack of concern for black family life in other less brutal, but nonetheless painful ways. Ridiculing the idea that black men and women knew anything of marital obligations, white officers disparaged the concern and affection soldiers lavished on their families and vilified the soldiers' wives as "whores" and "bitches." In callous disregard of the intimate ties and obligations of their men, some officers restricted contact between black soldiers and their families, while installing their own wives and mistresses near camp.

Even under the best of circumstances, army life created new difficulties for black families. General illiteracy, especially within the units composed of former slaves, hampered communication among relatives separated by great distance, while army movements and heavy duties limited time for letter writing. Irregular news from loved ones compounded the anxieties of a soldier's life and the concerns of those at home. Still, many families managed to correspond with enough frequency that any unexplained hiatus in communication immediately spawned fears of illness, capture, or death. Wives, mothers, and other relatives took their worries to the War Department and other government officials; anxious inquiries about a soldier's safety revealed both the accustomed regularity of family correspondence and the alarm created by lack of news.

Wartime separation inevitably strained family relationships, and some never recovered. Death severed many marriage bonds. Among the living, one or both partners might choose to abandon established relationships. Distanced from their homes, some black soldiers formed new affections, and by the same token, some wives grew attached to other men. Invoking strongly held convictions against adultery, both soldiers and their wives frequently alleged a spouse's prior infidelity as justification for their own new liaisons. Others remained unattached and bore their grief alone. In many cases, estranged wives sought assistance from the army or Freedmen's Bureau in securing support from former husbands for themselves and the children of now-defunct unions. Similarly, some soldiers tried to remove their children from the custody of wives who had betrayed them.

If army service rent the fabric of some black marriages, other husbands and wives seized wartime opportunities to place their relationships on firmer legal footing. Thousands of black soldiers and their wives publicly reaffirmed marriages established during slavery, often unions of long duration. Army chaplains and Northern missionaries took special interest in formalizing the marriage relations of black soldiers, but the ex-slaves themselves pressed for ceremonies and legal registrations that at once celebrated the new security of black family life and brought their most intimate ties into conformity with the standards of freedom.

Unmarried black soldiers also affirmed the significance of marriage and kinship relations. As in most armies, the Union's black troops were younger than the general population. Often military service took them great distances from where they had been born and raised. Far from home and often lonely, many youthful black soldiers courted and married while in the service. In doing so, they confirmed traditional domestic values and established families of their own. Army chaplains customarily discouraged such alliances, urging young single soldiers to postpone marriage until the end of the war. Other white officers saw in the courtships of black soldiers nothing more than licentiousness and even labeled the soldiers' wives and sweethearts "common place women of the town." Despite the absence of official endorsement, young black soldiers and their new wives, mostly ex-slaves, ratified kinship beliefs forged during slavery. With their marriages they carried the family values of slaves into the first generation of freedom.

SOLDIERS' MOTHERS, WIVES, AND WIDOWS

276A: Marriage Certificate Issued by a Black Army Chaplain to a Black Soldier and His Wife

(See page 662)

276B: Black Soldier to His Wife

Camp 1ˢᵗ U.S.C.T. Near Hampton [*Va.*] apl the 2[2] 1864
My Dear wife   I thake this opportunity to inform you that I am
well and Hoping when thoes few Lines Reaches you thay my find
you Enjoying Good Health as it now fines me at Prisent   Give
my Love to all my friend   I Recived you Last letter and was verry
Glad to Hear fome you   you must Excuse you fore not Riting
Before this times   the times I Recive you Letter I was order on a
march and I had not times to Rite to you   I met witch a Bad
mich-fochens I Ben [S]ad of   I Lost my money   I think I will
com Down to See you this weeck   I thought you Hear that I was
hear and you wood com to see me   Git a Pass and com to see me
and if you cant git Pass Let me know it   Give my Love to mother
and Molley   Give my Love to all inquaring fried
   No more to Say   Still Remain you Husband untall Death
                                                    Rufus Wright
Derect you Letter to foresess Monre VA
ALS
(*cont. p. 663*)

276A: Marriage Certificate Issued by a Black Army Chaplain to a Black Soldier and His Wife

MARRIAGE CERTIFICATE.

This is to Certify,

That Mr. *Rufus Wright*
of *Richmond, Va.* and
Miss *Elizabeth Turner*
of *Portsmouth, Va.* were lawfully joined in
HOLY WEDLOCK, on the *Third* day
of *December* in the year of our Lord one
thousand eight hundred and *Sixty three,*

May the God of all grace enable you faithfully to fulfil the
solemn covenant made in His presence, and after having lived
together in a state of holy joy and pious friendship, may you meet
in Heaven in perfect happiness never to be terminated.

H. M. Turner Pastor of the
Evang. Lutheran Church in *Chaplain U. S. Army*

Sold by T. NEWTON KURTZ, 151 Pratt-st., Baltimore, Md.

PDS

(276B *cont.*)

wilson Creek Va May 25th 1864

dear wife   I take the pleasant opportunity of writeing to you a
fiew lines to inform you of the Late Battle we have had   we was a
fight on Tuesday five hours   we whipp the rebls out   we Killed
$200 & captured many Prisener   out of our Regiment we lost 13
Thirteen Sergent Stephensen killed & priate out of Company H &
about 8 or 10 wounded   we was in line Wednesday for a battele
But the rebels did not Appear   we expect an Attack every
hour   give my love to all & to my sisters give my love   to Miss
Emerline tell John Skinner is well & sends much love to
her.   Joseph H Grinnel is well & he is as brave a lion   all the
Boys sends there love them   give my love to Miss
Missenger   You must excuse my short Letter   we are most
getting ready to go on Picket   No more from your Husband
ALS   Ruphus Wright

Rufus Wright to Dear wife, 2[2] Apr. 1864, and Ruphus Wright to dear
wife, 25 May 1864, filed with affidavit of Elisabeth Wright, 21 Aug.
1865, Letters & Orders Received, ser. 4180, Norfolk VA Asst. Subasst.
Comr., RG 105 [A-7945].

276C: Affidavit of a Black Soldier's Widow

Norfolk [*Va.*] August the 21 1865

    This is to certify That Elisabeth Wright Appeared Before me J W
Cook Notary and Counsiler Fore The Freedmen In This
Department By Permission Of Maj General Miles And Swore to

276A (facing page)

Marriage certificate, 3 Dec. 1863, filed with affidavit of Elisabeth Wright,
21 Aug. 1865, Letters & Orders Received, ser. 4180, Norfolk VA Asst.
Subasst. Comr., RG 105 [A-7945]. Printed form with manuscript insertions. Henry M. Turner, who married the couple, was chaplain of the
regiment in which Rufus Wright served, the 1st USCI, which was organized in the District of Columbia in the spring of 1863. Apparently
Wright met his future wife after joining the army, possibly while on duty
in the Portsmouth, Virginia, area. He had enlisted at Mason's Island, Virginia, in July 1863, giving his residence as Edenton, North Carolina. At
that time he was twenty-three years old and unmarried. (Service record of
Rufus Wright, 1st USCI, Carded Records, Volunteer Organizations: Civil
War, ser. 519, RG 94 [N-40].)

The Fowling Statements and the Said Testimony Was Confermed
By Seargant Frank Turner 5th Sergant Co {I} Wich Said Decased
Belong to Captain William Brazzee Col John Holman Commading
Regiment 18 Armey Core Maj B F Butler commanding   Having
Stated That Her Husband Was Killed in June 1864 Before
Petterburgh Rufus Wright And She The Said Widdow – Elisabeth
Wright has Never Received Pay Or Allowances From the
Goverment And know Ask to Receive The Pay That May Be Due
The Said Rufus Wright Her Husband   I have The Honnor To
Remain Your Most Obedient Servant

Elisabeth   her mark   ✕   Wright
Witness   his mark   Frank   ✕   Turner

P.S. The Papers in Testimony I here With Enclose To Be Retured
with you Convenience

HDSr

Affidavit of Elisabeth Wright, 21 Aug. 1865, Letters & Orders Received,
ser. 4180, Norfolk VA Asst. Subasst. Comr., RG 105 {A-7945}. Endorsements. The enclosures mentioned are the marriage certificate and letters
printed above. Private Rufus Wright died in the U.S. General Hospital at
Ft. Monroe, Virginia, on June 21, 1864, of an abdominal wound received
in action at Petersburg on June 15. (Service record of Rufus Wright, 1st
USCI, Carded Records, Volunteer Organizations: Civil War, ser. 519, RG
94 {N-40}.)

✤

277: Mother of a Pennsylvania Black Soldier to the President

Carlisles [Pa.] nov 21 1864

Mr abarham lincon   I wont to knw sir if you please wether I can
have my son relest from the arme   he is all the subport I have
now   his father is Dead and his brother that wase all the help
that I had   he has bean wonded twise   he has not had nothing to
send me yet   now I am old and my head is blossaming for the
grave and if you dou I hope the lord will bless you and me   if
you please answer as soon as you can if you please   tha say that
you will simpethise withe the poor   thear wase awhite jentel man
told me to write to you   Mrs jane Welcom if you please answer it
to

he be long to the eight rigmat co a u st colard troops   mart
welcom is his name   he is a sarjent

AL   [Jane Welcome]

[Jane Welcome] to abarham lincon, 21 Nov. 1864, W-934 1864, Letters Received, ser. 360, Colored Troops Division, RG 94 [B-188]. In the same file is a draft reply from the Bureau of Colored Troops stating that "the interests of the service will not permit that your request be granted." (Asst. Agt. C. W. Foster to Mrs. Jane Welcome, 2 Dec. 1864.)

278: Relative of Several Philadelphia Black Soldiers to the Secretary of War

Philad[a] February 8th 1865

Honl Sir   I am in great trouble of mind about my husband   it is reported that he is dead   he has been gone over a year and I have not hear from him   his name is Samuel or Sandy Brown Co. C. 25th regiment U.S. Colored Troops Penn   he went with his brother and five cousins to list   they are all in same Co. and regiment   none of them have been heard from only reports that they were dead which causes their wifes great grief. You will be doing charity by letting us know there whereabouts if alive so that we may write to them. Their names are Samuel or Sandy Brown Co. C. 25th regt Daniel Brown. Asa Miller. Daniel Horsey. George Horsey. Samuel Horsey George H. Washington   they all belong to same C[o] and regiment, other [dide?]   We have not received a cent from them since they left   we are all bad off   it would do us a great favor if you would give the information as soon as your time will permit   I am your obedient servant

Sarah Brown

care of Peter Kelly N[o] 511 South 6th Street

ALS

Sarah Brown to Honl. E. M. Stanton, 8 Feb. 1865, B-67 1865, Letters Received Relating to Recruiting, ser. 366, Colored Troops Division, RG 94 [B-338].

279: Wife of a Michigan Black Soldier to the Secretary of War

Detroit May 11 1865

Dear sir   I have taken the Liberty to write you afew lines which I am compelled to do   I am colored it is true but I have feeling as well as white person and why is it the colored soldiers letters cant pass backward and fowards as well as the white ones   Mr

Stanton   Dear sir I think it very hard We cant get any letters and
I wish would please look in this matter and have things arranged
so we can hear from our Husband if we cant see them   I have not
heard from my Husband in three months   John Bailey is my
husband   he was Drum major of the 100th united States Colored
Troops   he went from Detroit   he is the man Senator Howard
wrote to you about last summer and tryed to get afurlogh for
him   Then he was sick   I have hurd through others he was very
sick and since that I have heard he was dead   if he is living I
wish you would please grant him afurlogh to come home   he was
promised one when he went away and he has been gone over a year
and I do wish you would be so kind as to let him come home if
he is living   I wish you would look oar your Books and see if he
is alive   I dont know who to write to only you   President Lincoln
is gone and he was our best friend and now we look to you and I
hope God will wach over and protect you through this war
    please write me as soon as you get this   Direct to Mrs Lucy
Bailey 190 Congress Street 190

AL   *[Lucy Bailey]*

[Lucy Bailey] to Secrary Stanton, 11 May 1865, B-313 1865, Letters Received, ser. 360, Colored Troops Division, RG 94 [B-135]. In the same
file is a draft reply from the Bureau of Colored Troops which reports that
"John Bailey Co 'G' 100th U.S. Colored Troops deserted his regiment June
18th 1864. Nothing further is known in regard to him at this office."
(A.A.G. C. W. Foster to Mrs. Lucy Bailey, 16 May 1865.)

280: Virginia Freedman to the Secretary of War

                        Charles City County Va May 14th 1865.
Hon. Sir. will you be so obligeing as to give me information of
my nephue Theodore Mason Colored Born in the City of
Richmond, Va. I think he Enlisted in the Army about the time
they were Commencing to Enlist men for the Colored Troops. if
you can give me any information about him being into the Army
now or was Ever into It you alway may call me your
Debter   what makes me ask for this information is that ware I
live there is some Colored Troops Buried and on one of the graves
is marked Theodore Mason Colored Soldier wich makes me think
it is my Nephue   if you can give me news that my Nephue still
lives you will make this old Darkey Happy again   Hon Sir you
must Excuse my materiel for writing as this is the gift of a Union

Soldier[1] my address Hon Sir Is Erasmus Booman Charles City
County. Va [via] Wilson Landing   Hon Sir if you will condesent
to contencs this from one in truble you will recive the Blessing of
a aged man near the Dread Portales of the unseen future   Hon Sir
I remain your obeident Servant

ALS   Erasmus Booman

Erasmus Booman to Hon. Edward M. Stanton, 14 May 1865, B-258
1865, Letters Received Relating to Recruiting, ser. 366, Colored Troops
Division, RG 94 [B-362]. A notation on the outside of the letter reads
"Not answered."

1 The letter is written on lined blue paper with no distinguishing marks.

281: **Wife of a Virginia Black Soldier to the Secretary of War**

                            Hampton Fortress Monroe Va July 10th 1865
Respected Sir   I pen you this pamplet of a letter praying your
honor to so arrange my Husband William Massey (Colored. 1st
U.S.C T Com. G. Infantry) Money that when he is discharge I
may receive Sufficient to meet my wants   I am his lawful wife
and he has neglected to treat me as a husband should. and unless
your honor So arranges his money as to privelledge me to meet my
wants, he never will as he is nothing but a Spendthrift   I have
not received a cent of money from him Since last March /65 – then
he gave me twenty six dollars all of which he took back again   he
has left me in detrimental circumstances and I know not how to
meet my present wants   I have toiled and am still striving to earn
my bread but as I feel myself declineing daily. I think it no more
than right than that he should be made to do what he has never
yet done and that is to help me to support myself as I helped yes
not only helped but naturally did support him before he came in
the army   I would not ask for any one to attend to his money
matters for him. were it not for the fact that he seems to be to
slothfull as to attend to it for him and myself   please attend to it
for me and my prayers to Allmighty God for your honor shall be
that God may prolong your life and enlarge your feild of good and
at last when this mortal tenemant shall dissolve. prepare for you a
mansion in the realms of unclouded day   With due respect to
your Excellency I remain faithfully your Humble Colored Servant

                                                        Mrs Catherine Massey

667

When you Receive this please answer as soon as you can make conveneint   Direct thus Mrs Catherine Massey Hampton Fortress Monroe Va

ALS

Mrs. Catherine Massey to Hon. Edwin M. Stanton, 10 July 1865, M-475 1865, Letters Received, ser. 360, Colored Troops Division, RG 94 [B-266].

282: Wife of a New York Black Soldier to Her Husband

McGranville [*N.Y.*] July 26th [*1865*]

My Dear Husband   I received a letter from you to day. and was vary glad to hear of your good health, and also that you had received two letters from me. but Oh Husey I have sad news for you   littel Fay is vary sick   he was taken sick tusday morning had a vary hard stumake ake didnot eat hardley any breakfast but he begd so hard for me to let him go to school that I concented but I have been vary sory that I did. when he got home from school he never eat any super and went wright to bead   he said he was sick all over   I give him some P S [Townsdson?] sasuprilea and thought he would be better in the morning but befor dark he was taken out of his head   I had hard wourk to keeap him in the bed talking evry thing you could think of with . . .^{1} feaver and vometed and bowel complaint   in the morning he was no better   Mr Forshee was going up to Cortland and I toled him to tell Dr Ball to come and see him   he got [*here*] wendsday about three Oclock   he said he was a vary sick boy. he said he must not eat anything but water porudge   you must not wory to much about him   he is not dngrious yet and I hope he will be better in the morning. but Oh how I wish you could be hear   Fay wants you to get a furlou and come home just as soon as you can. you say in your last letter that thear is no order for the 54 to be musterd out. Dr Hendrick said thear was an order the day after you left for the 54 Reg to be musterd out imeadetley. and Bill was up hear tusday and he said the same   I thought you was on your way home   wall I must close   I shall have to tend to Fay. may the Lord be with you and keep you in all your ways. the rest of us are well   write soon

[*Etta Waters*]

[*In the margin*] and may the Lord hasten you home. be faithuf to God and tell them littel Orphen bosy of Jesus. E. A.

ALI

[Etta Waters] to My Dear Husband, 26 July [1865], Letters Received, ser.
4109, Dept. of the South, RG 393 Pt. 1 [C-1388]. A corner of the letter
is torn, obliterating all of another marginal notation except the name "Etta
Waters."

1 Corner of letter torn; one or two words missing.

283: New York Black Soldier to an Unidentified Official

U S Genar hospital fort monroe VA hampton VA
Sptember th 26th 1865

My kind friend i Take my pen in hand to Let yoo know that i
am not Well at present but I hop that these few Lines may find
you the Same I Want to ask yoo a few questions if you Will
allow me to if yoo Wont yoo please to Let me go home alittle
While I Want to go home for a While to stay for my mothr is
Sike and Would Lieke go hom on furlough for 30 deys I Want
to go home Very much to see my [*mother*] if you please Let me
go home my mothr is sicke for I have not seen her for tow
years my mothr is old and Lik to go and he for While I have
maid aplication for furlough on the fifth of Sptember and it has
not Come yet for the doctor of my Ward singed my aplication but
they dont Care for us her in the hospital i want to get home
once more to See my poor old mothr my mothr is fifty 3 years
old and She is hall i have got my mother Lives in poor Shanty
and has not any one to get Wood for her next winter i wish that
you let me have a furlough for 30 days if you please to Grant me
my furlough I Cant thank you anough for my [*mother*] has not seen
my face for two years i think it iS high time that try and go and
see her please to write and let me know if please thy Wont make
out a furlough my mother is Sik and the family is all diying
off if i Stay much longer I Will not See any of my folks to
home My mother lost all her Children this fall Whill I Was in
the Serveice U.S. thy can have all my money if they want it if
they for I did not Comme out for the money for I Was a fraid of
geting drafted and I thought that Would enlist When that order
was given out for to muster out all in the hospital I Was put
down for muster out and thy have not Let me go yet the doctors
ar very mean they Wont give us our discharge at all
  My father is dead My mother farther is deaed my mothr is
Widow and So here left alone for Ever Yours respctfully obedient
Servent
ALS   Richard Henry Tebout

Richard Henry Tebout to My kind friend, 26 Sept. 1865, T-151 1865, Letters Received Relating to Recruiting, ser. 366, Colored Troops Division, RG 94 [B-382]. At the end of the letter are several stray words, mostly repetitions of the author's signature, which are omitted here. Tebout also added that he was a member of the 31st USCT and that he was from Schoharie County, New York. In the same file is another and very similar letter from Tebout, of the same date, also addressed merely to "my kind Friend." It adds the information that he was nineteen years old and had been wounded at the battle of Petersburg. Endorsements indicate that the surgeon in charge of the Fortress Monroe hospital ordered Tebout to report to New York for muster out of service.

284: North Carolina Black Soldier to His Wife and the Wife's Affidavit

Wilmington N.C. Nov. 28th, 1865.

Dear and most affectionate wife   I have again taken my seat this afternoon to write you a few lines to inform you that I am in splendid health at this time and I hope that this letter will find you the same, Sister Julia has got married and has now got a fine little child since you seen her   Mr. Newkirk is the name of the gentleman that has won her affectionate heart. I wrote to you a few weeks since, but I have not received any answer from it as yet. I am in the thirty seventh Regiment of United States Colored infantry in Camp, one and a half miles from the city of Wilmington N.C. I hope that you will take the matter in to deep and earnest consideration to write and let me know how you are and how you are getting along at home   my respects to all of the family at home, I am doing pretty well at the present time. I have expected to get out of the service before this hour, but ah not yet, I hope you will write to me soon as you get this letter as I am extremly anxious to hear from you and the family   also my respect to all that feel themselves at the least interested in my welfare in the service of the United states Colored Troops in the state. Direct to Soloman Sanders C° A 37th U.S.C.I. Wilmington, N. Carolina   Your affectionate husband

Soloman Sanders

Wite soon

[*In the margin*] *Write to me Soon,*

ALS

State of North Carolina County of Franklin 22^d day of May 1866
  Marina Saunders, Freedwoman, being duly sworn says that she
lives near Wake Forest College, some eight miles from here, that
she is married & has five children the oldest, eleven years of age,
that her Husband is a Soldier in the 39$''$ U S Col'd Troops, & is
now stationed at Wilmington N.C   That she has never received
any money from him since he has been in the Army   That she is
a hard working woman, but owing to the size of her family she is
obliged to take all her earnings in provisions & that she has found
it next to impossible to obtain food enough for herself &
children.   She earnestly requests to be aided with some provisions,
in order that she may get some cash, with which to buy clothes
for her children

her
Marina X Sanders
mark

HDSr

Solomon Sanders to Mrs. Merina Sanders, 28 Nov. 1865, and affidavit of
Marina Sanders, 22 May 1866, Letters Received, ser. 2794, Oxford NC
Asst. Supt., RG 105 [A-979]. Affidavit sworn before a local Freedmen's
Bureau officer. According to endorsements, the Freedmen's Bureau superintendent at Raleigh, North Carolina, forwarded Marina Sanders's affidavit
on June 4, 1866, "with the suggestion that transportation be furnished to
this woman, to enable her to take her family to Wilmington where the
husband can support them," but on June 8 the Freedmen's Bureau assistant
commissioner for the state returned the affidavit marked "Disapproved."
The statement in the affidavit that Marina Sanders's husband belonged to
the 39th USCI is apparently in error.

285: Officer in a Tennessee Black Regiment to the Freedmen's Bureau Superintendent at Memphis

Fort Pickering [Memphis, Tenn.] Decbr 20 1865

Major: Private Saml. Bolton of this Company wishes to lodge
complaint against his Mother-in-law, who is the alleged cause of
much trouble between himself and his wife. He desires her to
move out of his house and she refuses to do so. Very Respectfully
Your obt sevt

ALS

M Mitchell

Capt. M. Mitchell to Major [A. T. Reeve], 20 Dec. 1865, Unregistered Letters
Received, ser. 3522, Memphis TN Supt., RG 105 [A-6515]. Endorsement.

286: A Freedmen's Bureau Superintendent of Marriages to the Freedmen's Bureau Agent at Alexandria, Virginia

Freedmen's Village, Va. June 1ˢᵗ 1866.

Dear Col: I have the honor to report to you concerning my efforts as Supt. of Marriages in 5ᵗʰ Dist Va. from April 25th, to May 31ˢᵗ, (inclusive) 1866.

My appointment from the Freedmen's Bureau, is dated April 18– 1866. From that time to the 25th, I was so much engaged in closing my obligations to the Philadelphia Committee of Orthodox Friends, relating to several schools of Freedmen (Fort Strong, and other localities), that I could give only a passing, and occasional notice to the marriage subject.

On the evening of April 25th, I preached on the subject of Marriage to the soldiers at Fort Corcoran, 107. U.S.C.I. co. A & co E. Capt. Goff of co. A. and commander of the Fort, was present, and assisted me, by reading the Circular on Marriage,[1] explaining it — and adding earnest remarks, which exerted much influence on the minds of the soldiers. I record for him my *thanks* for such timely, and efficient assistance. I addressed the soldiers at that Fort several other times, on the same theme: these occasions included two Sabbath evenings. At the close of service on one of those evenings — Corporal Murray (of co A), said: —

"Fellow Soldiers: —

I praise God for this day! I have long been praying for it. The Marriage Convenant is at the foundation of all our rights. In slavery we could not have *legalised* marriage: *now* we have it. Let us conduct ourselves worthy of such a blessing — and all the people will respect us — God will bless us, and we shall be established as a people." His character is such, that every word had power.

I have preached & lectured, or *talked* publicly five times at Freedmens Village. From Apr 26 to May 30th, gave fifteen certificates: six to soldiers of 107 USCI Fort Corcoran; three to 107. Vienna Fairfax county — one-107 Freedmens Village — one 107 Alx- - -; and four couples of citizens, all of Alexandria co. Nearly three weeks of sickness prevented me from accomplishing more. Yesterday, 31ˢᵗ of May, we gave seventy nine certificates in Freedmens Village. We have much more to do. Rev R S Laws, Rev D A. Miles & lady teachers, much help me. Spent last Sabbath with Capt Ross, of Vienna & the way is open for work in that region. Yours

ALS   J. R. Johnson

J. R. Johnson to Col. S. P. Lee, 1 June 1866, Unregistered Letters Received, ser. 3853, Alexandria VA Supt., RG 105 [A-9975]. The soldiers of the 107th USCI, to whom Johnson preached and issued marriage certificates, were almost all former slaves recruited in Kentucky and transferred to Virginia in October 1864.

1 Circular No. 11, from Colonel O. Brown, Virginia Freedmen's Bureau assistant commissioner, dated March 19, 1866. The circular quoted two February 17, 1866, acts of the Virginia General Assembly, which established procedures for blacks to obtain marriage licenses and have their marriages legally recorded and also legalized husband and wife relationships established during slavery. Assistant Commissioner Brown instructed Freedmen's Bureau agents to "cause the above quoted laws to be read at all religious and other meetings of the colored people until they are sufficiently informed of the important change effected by legislation in their domestic relations." He ordered bureau agents to register the names of freedmen and women who were "cohabiting together as man and wife" on February 17, 1866, and to "take pains to explain to colored persons . . . that they are firmly married by the operation of the law. . . ." (General Orders, Special Orders & Circulars, ser. 3800, VA Asst. Comr., RG 105 [A-8293].)

287: Affidavits of a Kentucky Black Soldier's Wife, the Soldier, and a Witness

[Louisville, Ky.] 6" day of July 1866

Sarah Fields (colored) being first sworn says that she was married to Jackson Fields (a colored man) about three weeks before Christmas in the year (as she supposes) 1863 that she had one child by him in the regular time of nine months to first August 1864 That eleven months after the child was born her husband enlisted in the army— During all the time named they slept together without missing but very few nights That the child spoken of above died in a short time after Jackson enlisted— That she now has another child by him which is about one year old— That she has Known no other man since they married That she has remained in Woodford County ever since and learning that her husband after his discharge was living in Louisville Ky and she came down and on yesterday found him living with another woman to whom he says he has been legally married— She went to his house (situated in the suburbs of the city known as Limerick) and he would not recognize her as his wife and did not recognize the fact of his being the father of the child she alleges to be his but took hold of her and showed her off his lot into the street   That her husband enlisted in the month of October in the army

her
Sarah × Fields
mark

HDSr

[*Louisville, Ky.*] 6' day of July 1866

Jackson Field (colored) being sworn states that he enlisted in the army in September 1864 and that he was discharged in April 1866   He says he did live with Sarah Fields as his wife before going in the army and that he has not seen her since until yesterday   That after he was discharged from the army he concluded to remain in Louisville

That he wrote one letter to Sarah while he was in the army and that he got other soldiers who were writing home to their friends to say to her as his wife that he was well—   He states that Susan Taylor a cousin of Sarah came to the camp at Munfordsville to see her husband and told him that his wife was acting badly and was living with another man named John who then belonged to Mr Buford of Woodford County   That after being in Louisville after his discharge he saw another woman and asked her to marry him to which she consented and he applied to the County Court Clerk of Jefferson County Ky and procured a License and they were married and are now living together

his
Jackson × Field
mark

HDSr

[*Louisville, Ky.*] 7" day of July 1866

Susan Taylor (Colored) being first sworn says that she has been acquainted for many years with Sarah Fields and Jackson Fields   That she witnessed their marriage in the usual manner of slaves marrying between three or four years since   that he continued to live with her as his wife until he enlisted in the army

That she never heard any reports that Sarah was unfaithful to Jackson during the time he was with her   that since he enlisted she has heard it said that Sarah was unfaithful but she cannot say anything of her own knowledge—   She never witnessed any wrong conduct in Sarah   That when she visited her husband while his regiment was at Munfordsville she saw Jackson who was in the same regiment and he asked her concerning the conduct of his wife

674

and she answered that she had heard that she was not doing right
but she had not seen any wrong conduct herself

HDSr

her

Susan ✕ Taylor

mark

Affidavits of Sarah Fields, 6 July 1866, Jackson Field, 6 July 1866, and
Susan Taylor, 7 July 1866, #68 1866, Letters Received, ser. 1208, Louisville KY Supt., RG 105 [A-4486]. Endorsements. Sworn before the Freedmen's Bureau superintendent for the Louisville subdistrict. On July 7,
1866, the superintendent gave judgment that Jackson Field pay $50 to the
plaintiff Sarah Field "to assist in supporting her child of which he is the
father." (Entry 26, 7 July 1866, vol. 152, p. 117, Register of Complaints,
ser. 1216, Louisville KY Supt., RG 105 [A-4486].) Not satisfied with
that decision, Sarah Fields on the same day entered a complaint at the
Office of the Assistant Commissioner of the Kentucky Freedmen's Bureau,
also in Louisville, swearing that her husband had deserted her and married
another woman, "and that she wants to get her husband back to help her
make a living for herself and two children." The Assistant Commissioner's
Office referred the new affidavit to the Louisville bureau agent, who reported that he had already decided the case; the assistant commissioner
then confirmed the earlier decision. (Statement of Sarah Fields, 7 July
1866, #68 1866, Letters Received, ser. 1208, Louisville KY Supt., RG
105 [A-4486], and endorsements.)

288: Mother of a West Virginia Black Soldier to the Adjutant General's Office

Berkeley Springs Morgan County W. V[a]. Dec[r] 24th 1866.
Dr Sir I received your very prompt reply to my letter of the 6th
Nov[r] /66. making inquiry about my son Gus: Wells of C[o]. I. – 38
Regimt US Troops of Volunteers, and your answer to me is that
Gus: Wells Died in Hospital at Brownsville Texas. during the
month of October 1865. Now my dear Sir as a fond mother I am
still in doubt about his death thinking that it might be another
Gus: Wells that has died: as there is a colored soldier here who
says he left him well at Brownsville after that date and he has lead
me to believe what he tells me is the truth I therefore have
concluded that there might be another of the same name *dead* and
not my *son:* if it is a mistake I know you can find it out and let
me know— I hope you will make the search and gratify a poor
distressed mother. it will give me satisfaction to know his color

his age his height, &c which I suppose his officers have down on their Books and if I am Satisfied in my distressed mind that my son is dead I will go to Texas & Bring him Home: I hope you will give me the name of the Hospital Doctor. and let me know if I can get him   please let me know the distance to Texas and what it would cost   now dear Sir I hope you will not consider me putting you to too much trouble in making these inquiries about my son when you consider that I am a fond mother and now a distressed mother being in doubts about the death of my son   as I have said there may be *one* of the same name in the same Regement who has *died* at that time   if so you can soon find out and let me know. the Doctor of the Hospital I suppose can give full information   I will be under many obligations for any further information from you and this will relieve a fond but distressed mothers mind   please tell me know if he died with a wound or natural sickness   I am your Humble and obedient Servant

Martha Wells

in great Haste.

ALS

[*Endorsement*] Augustus Wells, Pvt. Co "I" 38 U.S.C.I. Died at Post Hospl. Brownsville Texas. October 2^{d} 1865. Chronic Diarrhoea

Martha Wells to Assistant Adjutant Genl. T. W. Taggard, 24 Dec. 1866, W-209 1866, Letters Received Relating to Recruiting, ser. 366, Colored Troops Division, RG 94 [B-391].

289A: Affidavit of a Kentucky Black Soldier's Sister-in-Law

Louisville, Ky. April 3^{d} 1867

Minta Smith colored being sworn says that she is married to a man named Alexander Smith and lives in the city of Louisville. That her husband's Brother Harrison Smith enlisted in the Army some time in March or first of April 1865   That Harrison Smith had one child a boy now about seven years old. That some time about the first of December 1865 she asked the mother's permission to take the child to her house for a while and she agreed to it

That a short time afterwards the mother was taken down with the small Pox and by the authorities was sent to the Pest house and was there about one month. That after getting from the Pest house she (the mother) frequently came to the house of this affiant to see her and to see the child and once during the first of this year she asked that the boy be returned to her. This affiant said to her she was not able to take care of the boy and as the Father had several times expressed the wish that the boy should remain with her she hoped that it would be done. That during the last high water the houses in the neighborhood where they were living were all overflowed and the most of the tenants had to remove to other houses and during the time of removal from the overflow the mother again got possession of the boy and will not let her the affiant have him again

That about ten months since the mother of the boy commenced living with a man by the name of James Downs colored and that for the last four months they have kept house and lived together as man and wife without being married

That Harrison Smith sent his wife the mother of the boy money at different times until he heard that she had taken up with and was living with the man Downs and that soon after he heard that he wrote to this affiant to take his boy and take care of him until he the Father came home   This last letter is dated at Fort Bliss Texas March 9 /67 and is herewith filed

her

Minta X Smith

mark

HDSr

Affidavit of Minta Smith, 3 Apr. 1867, #169 1867, Letters Received, ser. 1208, Louisville KY Supt., RG 105 [A-4509]. Sworn before a Freedmen's Bureau officer.

289B: Kentucky Black Soldier to His Sister-in-Law

fort bliss texas March th 9 1867
My dear sister   I write you this letter to let you no I am
well   Mintey I ask of you in this letter to go and take my boy
from my wilf as sh is not doeing write by him   take him and
keep him untill I com home   if sh is not willing to gave him up
go to the fried mands bury [*Freedman's Bureau*] and shoe this
letter   it is my recust for you to have him   I doe not want her to
have my child with an another man   she is not living writ to rase

677

children   I feel for my child becase I no I have agod mother   I
would lik for my child to be rased well   take god cear of him   I
will be hom next fall if I live   asholder stand abad chanc but if
god spars me I will be home   I have nothing more to say but I
still remain your true brother

Harison smith

write soon

ALS

Harison smith to my dear sister, 9 Mar. 1867, filed with #169 1867,
Letters Received, ser. 1208, Louisville KY Supt., RG 105 [A-4509].

289C: Affidavit of a Kentucky Black Soldier's Wife

Louisville, Ky. April 3^d 1867

Harriet Ann Bridwell colored being sworn says that some eight
years since she married Harrison Smith

That they were married according to the usages and customs
among slaves. That by him she had two children one of which is
dead and the other now over seven years of age and the one in
controversy between Minta Smith and herself   That after her
husband Harrison Smith enlisted in the army she could not keep
up and support herself and her child and she under these
circumstances was induced to accept the offers of protection made
her by James Bridwell sometimes called Downes and she is now
living with and keeping his house as his wife although they have
not been married by license obtained from the proper authority

She further says she is willing to Deliver the child to his Father
but she does not want others to have him before the Father comes
home   She says that she asked Minta Smith more than once for
the child and Minty would answer her that she (meaning me) was
not able to take care of the child and to let her [*keep*] him until
the Father came home

her
Harriet Ann × Bridwell
mark

HDSr

[*Endorsement*] Bureau R.F.&A.L. Gen. Office Louisville Sub Dist.
Ky Louisville 3^d April 1867. Respectfully forwarded to Brig.
General Sidney Burbank Asst. Com Sta. Ky. for Orders.

The Father now Serving in the Army asks that the child be kept for him by claimant, so as not to be ruined by its Mother's shame. Under the circumstances I recommend that the child be delivered to claimant until its Father's return, before its ruin is complete. In the absence of: C. H. Frederick 1st Lt. 45$''$ Inf. Supt Louisville Sub Dist Ky A. Benson Brown. 1st Lieut 43^{d} Inf. Ass't. Supt.

[*Endorsement*] Bureau RF&A Lands. Asst Comrs Office State of Ky Louisville April 5 1867. Respectfully returned to Lieut C. H. Frederick Sub Asst. Comr &c Louisville, KY who will, if he is satisfied that the mother is a prostitute, return the child to Minta Smith (cold) within mentioned. By order of Bvt Brig Genl S. Burbank, Asst. Comr State of Ky John Ely Bvt Brig Genl USV. Chief Supdt.

[Endorsement] Child in question turned over to Minta Smith   8$''$ April 67   Brown

Affidavit of Harriet Ann Bridwell, 3 Apr. 1867, filed with #169 1867, Letters Received, ser. 1208, Louisville KY Supt., RG 105 [A-4509]. Sworn before a Freedmen's Bureau officer.

289D: Proceedings in the Louisville Freedmen's Bureau Court

[*Louisville, Ky.*] May 28 [1867]

In The case of Minta Smith colored against the mother of the child of Hamilton Smith now in the army and stationed at EL. Passo Texas. on the 8$''$ of last month the child was awarded to Minta under the instructions of the Father in a letter exhibited by her. To day the mother comes and exhibits letters from the Father which are properly Post marked and in which he says he wants the mother to have the possession of the child and the child at the present being with the mother she is permitted to keep it untill further advised

HD

Entry 63, 28 May [1867], vol. 153, p. 55, Proceedings of Freedmen's Court, ser. 1217, Louisville KY Supt., RG 105 [A-4509].

SOLDIERS' WAGES AND THE BLACK FAMILY

290: Wife of a New Jersey Black Soldier to the President

Mt Holly [*N.J.*] July 11 1864

Sir, my husband, who is in Co. K. 22nd Reg't U.S. Col^d Troops. (and now in the Macon Hospital at Portsmouth with a wound in his arm) has not received any pay since last May and then only thirteen dollars. I write to you because I have been told you would see to it. I have four children to support and I find this a great strugle. A hard life this!

I being a col^d woman do not get any State pay. Yet my husband is fighting for the country. Very Resp'y yours

ALS   Rosanna Henson

Rosanna Henson to Abraham Lincoln, 11 July 1864, 993/DB2, Letters Received, ser.7, RG 99 [CC-1]. Endorsement.

291: New York and Delaware Black Soldiers to the President

New Orleans Louisiana Camp Parpit [*August*] 1864

My Dear and Worthy Friend MR. President. I thake this oppertunity of interducing my self to you By wrteing thes fiew Lines To let you know that you have Proven A friend to me and to all our Race   And now i stand in the Defence of the Country myself Ready and Willing to oBay all orders & demands that has A tendency to put Down this Rebelion In military Life or Civel Life. I Enlisted at Almira state of N. York, shemoung County Under *Mr* C. W. Cawing Provose Marshall And [*when*] I Enlisted he told me i would get 13 Dollars Per. Mounth or more if White Soldiers got it   he expected the wages would Raise And i would get my pay every 2 Months   hear i am in the survice 7 months And have Not Recived Eney Monthly Pay   I have a wife and 3 Children Neither one of them Able to thake Care of Themselfs and my wife is sick   And she has sent to me for money   And i have No way of geting Eney money to send to her Because i cant Get my Pay. And it gos very hard with me to think my family should be At home A suffering have money earnt and cant not get it   And I Dont know when i will Be Able to Releave my

suffering Family   And another thing when I Enlisted I was
promised A furlow and I have Not had it   Please MR Lincom
Dont think I Am Blameing you for it   I Dident think you knew
Eney thing About it   And I Dident know eney Other Course to,
thake To obtain what I think is Right   I invested my money in
Percuring A house an home for my wife and Children   And she
write to me she has to work and can not surport the Children
with out my Aid   When I was At home i could earn from 26 to
28 Dollars A Month   When I Enlisted it told i was to have the
same Bounty Clothing and Ration as the Soldier and 325 Dollars
wich the 25 Dollars i Never got   I Dont Beleave the Goverment
wants me eney how   In fact i mean the New York 20th
Regiment   The Reason why i say so is Because we are treated
Like A Parcels of Rebs   I Do not say the Goverment is useing us
so   I [*do not*] Believe the Government knows Eney thing About
how we are treated   we came out to be true union soldiers the
Grandsons of Mother Africa Never to Flinch from Duty   Please
Not to thinks I Am finding fault with the rules of the
Goverment   If this Be the rules i am willing to Abide by
them   I wonce Before was a Slave 25 years   I made escape
1855   Came In to York state from Maryland   And i Enlisted in
the survice got up By the union Legue Club   And we ware
Promised All satisfaction Needful   But it seem to Be A
failure   We Are not treated Like we are soldiers in coleague
Atall   we are Deprived of the most importances things we Need
in health and sickness Both That surficint Food And quality   As
for The sick it is A shocking thing to Look into thire
conditions   Death must Be thire Doom when once they have to
go to the Hospital   Never Return Again   such is the medical
Assistance of the 20th Rig n.y   your sarvent under Arms sincerely
    George Rodgers
    Thomas Sipple Wilmington Delaware.
    Samuel Sampson
Mr President   I Surtify that this I is jest what mr Rodgers sais
and my other frend mr Sipele
    Nimrod Rowley Elmira Chemong CO. N.Y.
Pease excuse your Needy Petishners   We most heartly wish you
the intire victory over All Your Enemys. And A spedy sucsess To
the Commander-in Chief of the Army And Navy   And may Peace
Forever Reighn

HLS

George Rodgers et al. to Mr. President, [Aug.] 1864, R-268 1864, Letters Received, ser. 360, Colored Troops Division, RG 94 [B-57]. The
letter and all the signatures appear to be in Rowley's hand.

292: Wife of a Michigan Black Soldier to the Secretary of War

Detroit Michigan May 27 instant 1865

Sir   I take the privelige of writing to you asking A favour of you if it is in your power to grant that is to give my Husband John Wesley Wilson A furloah   My Husband belonges to the 102d U.S. Colored regiment and is the leader of the regimental Band now Station at Beaufort S.C. or will you please to give me Transporation to Beaufort S.C. if had money I would not ask you for a Pass   John Wesley Wilson has not recevied any pay from the government for nine mounths and it leaves me compleatly distitute   I have no support except what I earn by my own labor from day to day   the relief fund that I have been receiving has been cut of[f] through prejudices to Color and it leaves me compleatly distitute of means for my support   Michigan has no respect for her Colored Soldiers or their famileys. My Husband has been in the army one year and half and i am very anxous to see him and by giving me Transportation to Beaufort S.C. you would Confer a great favour on your well wisher   Your Obedient Servent

ALS   Mrs John W. Wilson

Mrs. John W. Wilson to Hon. E. M. Stanton, 27 May 1865, W-416 1865, Letters Received, ser. 360, Colored Troops Division, RG 94 [B-151].

293: Northern Black Soldier to a State Military Agent with Accompanying Documents

Alexandria [*Va.*], July 20th 1865

Dear Sir, Will you assist me? My circumstances and the circumstances of my family are such that I feel it my duty to ask for my discharge. I enlisted on the 5th of October last at Detroit, Mich. and never have received a cent since I have been in the service. My family are sick and absolutely naked, having no clothes to wear. They are also threatened with being turned into the street. Now I respectfully ask for my discharge that I may be able to attend to the wants of my family – or if I cannot obtain my discharge I earnestly petition for my pay. Very truly yours

HLSr   John Turner

Washington, D.C., Aug 7th 1865

Sir, I respectfully refer to you the case of the bearer, John Turner, 102d U.S. Col. Troops, whose wife has quite recently died and who has a family of children left on his hands, with no home and no one to look after them. He has just received orders to go the Regiment, leaving, as he says, his children in the street destitute and homeless. He respectfully asks to be discharged or detained till he can make proper provisions for them. Very Respectfully Your Obt Servant.

ALS   D. E. Millard

Louverture Gen. Hos'l. Alexandria Va Aug 9th 1865.

Let this certify that Mrs John Turner wife of Priv. John Turner Recruit of 102 Regt U.S.C.T. and recently a patient at this Hospital, died in this City of "Dysentery"— Also that she left three children William 6 months of age, Nancy 3 years of age and James 8 years of age all of whom are now in this City.

ADS   S. D. Twining

John Turner to Mich. Mil. Agt., 20 July 1865, D. E. Millard to Major Gen. C. C. Augur, 7 Aug. 1865, and certificate of A.A. Surgeon S. D. Twining, 9 Aug. 1865, all filed as M-519 1865, Letters Received, ser. 360, Colored Troops Division, RG 94 [B-268]. Endorsements. Turner's letter is in Millard's handwriting. A draft letter from the Adjutant General's Office, in the same file, indicates that Turner received a discharge. ([C. W. Foster] to Major Gen. C. C. Augur, 12 Aug. 1865.)

294: Commander of a Kentucky Black Regiment to a Military Railroad Superintendant

Victoria Texas Aug 12, 1865

Col: I have the honor to submit the following statement relative to my Regiment as regards pay. The enlisted men have not been paid since Oct 31, 1864 now nearly 10 months. A very large number of the men have families now residing in Paducah Ky. dependent upon them for support.

The soldiers having formerly been slaves and recruited at a time when the sentiment in Kentucky was bitterly opposed to the arming of colored troops their women and children were driven from their homes and followed their husbands to the recruiting depot at Paducah Ky. and thereforth became dependent upon the wages of the husband and the soldier to supply them with the necessaries of life: and to my own knowledge they are constantly writing to them to send them money and having no means to satisfy their demands it has a tendency to discourage the soldier.

I am confident that if these men can be paid they will not only be much more cheerful and happy but will also prosecute the work of building the Military Rail Road upon which they are now engaged with much more vigor and energy

I would therefore most respectfully and earnestly request in behalf of these men, that you use your influence towards having them paid   I have the honor to be Colonel Very respectfully Your Obdt Servant

HLcSr   H W Barry

Col. H. W. Barry to Brevet Col. W. H. Greenwood, 12 Aug. 1865, Letters Sent, 8th USCHA, Regimental Books & Papers USCT, RG 94 [G-26]. Colonel Barry commanded the 8th USCHA, recruited in the Paducah, Kentucky, area. In late September 1865, Barry reported that his men had still not been paid. The approach of "the inclement season of the year" prompted him to reproach the paymaster: "shall the soldiers of my Regt have to submit to hear the pleadings of their wives and Children without being able to give them anything, to keep them from freezing & starving." (Col. H. W. Barry to Chief Paymaster Military Division of the Gulf, 23 Sept. 1865, Letters Sent, 8th USCHA, Regimental Books & Papers USCT, RG 94 [G-26].)

SOLDIERS' FAMILIES IN SLAVERY

295: Commander of a Louisiana Black Regiment to the Headquarters of the Department of the Gulf

New-Orleans, Oct 14th *1862.*

Sir. I beg respectfully to call your attention to the case presented by Auguste Perrauld – a private in Co B – 1st Regt La Native Guards free Colored.

He says that his mother who is married to a free man of Color in this City is owned by Oscar Perrauld living in the Parish of St Bernard.

For many years she has been allowed her time and permitted to live in the city with her husband, but now that her son, who is free, has entered the service, he has evinced his indignation, by causing the woman to be arrested and put in the Police Jail.

I respectfully ask that an order for her discharge be given. Respectfully

ALS   S. H. Stafford

Head-Quarters, 1st Reg't L^a N.G. [*La.*] January 4th, 1863. Sir: When this Regiment was organized, it was with the promise of bounty, advance pay and rations for families.

Shortly after the arrival of Maj. Giddings, 14th Infantry, mustering and disbursing officer, he received the order of the War Department, dated sometime before, but which had not before then been received in this Depart., discontinuing the bounty.

This Reg't, therefore, never received either bounty or advance pay.

Since then, upon representations made to the War Departm't by Maj. Gen'l Butler, the bounty and advance were awarded to the 2nd Louisiana (white) which was not mustered till long after we were. It is respectfully urged that enlisted under the same contract and expected to render equal service, justice requires that the same measure should be meted to us as to other troops.

I am persuaded that the attention of the Commanding General has but to be called to this matter, to ensure from him such representations to the War Department as will cause prompt orders in this behalf to the disbursing officer.

The Government expects the full performance of his contract on the part of the soldier, and it ought not to fail in the conditions on its part to be performed.

I respectfully request that enquiry be made into the action of the Relief Committee which is charged with the distribution of the rations to families.

I am told that the quantities distributed by them are far below the standard and that some of the articles comprising a ration are wholly withheld.

The withholding of the promised bounty and advance, coupled with the fact that though the payrolls up to 31st Oct. have been for some time past in the hands of the pay-master, no payment of any kind has yet been made them, has forced the families to fall into arrears of rent.

In Confederate times and before these men entered the U.S. service, the landlords were quite complaisant to their tenants, but the moment these troops were raised they awoke to the importance of collecting their rents and have since practiced every means of annoyance to their families.

A practice had largely obtained among owners of female slaves to secure for them free men as husbands – some of these husbands are in my Reg't.

When it appeared that they had entered the service, they were forbidden by the owners of their wives the permission and privileges before accorded them, and such treatment is practiced upon their wives and children as to exasperate them as has in some instances tended to breaches of the peace.

Almost daily complaints of both the kinds of oppression above alluded to are made to me and applications are constantly made for leave to visit the city to enable the soldiers to make some provision for their families.

Being forced to refuse such applications, I have nevertheless promised to ask the attention of the Gen'l Commanding to these evils, and respectfully urge that some means be taken to prevent their recurrence. Respectfully Your obed't serv't.

HLc
[S. H. Stafford]

Col. S. H. Stafford to Major General B. F. Butler, 14 Oct. 1862, S-19 1862, Letters Received, ser. 1756, Dept. of the Gulf, RG 393 Pt. 1 [C-502]; [Col. S. H. Stafford] to Lieut. Col. R. B. Irwin, 4 Jan. 1863, S-92 1863, Letters Received, ser. 1756, Dept. of the Gulf, RG 393 Pt. 1 [C-502]. On November 6, 1862, General Benjamin F. Butler, commander of the Department of the Gulf, ordered suspension of all court processes for eviction of families of Union soldiers on account of rent past due. Butler's edict quoted a Confederate noneviction order issued in New Orleans in March 1862 and, with evident irony, simply applied that measure to the families of Union servicemen. (General Orders No. 90, Headquarters Department of the Gulf, 6 Nov. 1862, Orders & Circulars, ser. 44, RG 94 [DD-3].)

296: Missouri Slave Woman to Her Soldier Husband

Paris Mo Jany 19, 1864

My Dear Husband   I r'ecd your letter dated Jan'y 9th also one dated Jany 1st but have got no one till now to write for me. You do not know how bad I am treated. They are treating me worse and worse every day. Our child cries for you. Send me some money as soon as you can for me and my child are almost naked. My cloth is yet in the loom and there is no telling when

686

it will be out. Do not send any of your letters to Hogsett
especially those having money in them as Hogsett will keep the
money. George Combs went to Hannibal soon after you did so I
did not get that money from him. Do the best you can and do
not fret too much for me for it wont be long before I will be free
and then all we make will be ours. Your affectionate wife

Ann

P.S. Sind our little girl a string of beads in your next letter to
remember you by. Ann

HLSr

[*Endorsement*] Andy if you send me any more letters for your wife
do not send them in the care of any one. Just direct them plainly
to James A Carney Paris Monroe County Mo. Do not write too
often   Once a month will be plenty and when you write do not
write as though you had recd any letters for if you do your wife
will not be so apt to get them. Hogsett has forbid her coming to
my house so we cannot read them to her privately. If you send
any money I will give that to her myself. Yrs &c   Jas A Carney

Ann to My Dear Husband, 19 Jan. 1864, enclosed in Brig. Genl. Wm.
A. Pile to Maj. O. D. Greene, 11 Feb. 1864, P-91 1864, Letters Received, ser. 2593, Dept. of the MO, RG 393 Pt. 1 [C-159]. The letter is
addressed to "Andrew Valentine Co E 2nd Mo Colored Inft A D Benton
Barracks St Louis Mo." Both letter and endorsement are in James Carney's
hand.

297: Officer in a Missouri Black Regiment to the Superintendent of the Organization of Missouri Black Troops

Benton Barracks Mo Feb. 6th 1864

Sir— I have received information—by Sergt Whitson of my
Company just from St. Clare—that the wives of Simon Williamson
& Richard Beasley has again been whiped by their Master most
unmercyfully. Their Master is one John Crowder and lives about
three miles this side of the village of St Clare in Franklin
County. He refuses to let them go to the Post Office to get their
letters, and if any one comes to them and brings them letters and
reads them to them he is shure to whip them for it if he knows
it. Williamson & Beasley are members of my company and are
good Soldiers. If any thing could be done to relieve their families

it would afford me a good deel satisfaction and relieve them from a good deel of anxioty. Very respectfully your Ob't. Serv't.

ALS   A. J. Hubbard

Capt. A. J. Hubbard to Brig. Genl. Pile, 6 Feb. 1864, enclosed in Brig. Genl. Wm. A. Pile to Maj. O. D. Greene, 11 Feb. 1864, P-91 1864, Letters Received, ser. 2593, Dept. of the MO, RG 393 Pt. 1 [C-159].

298: Assistant Provost Marshal at Fulton, Missouri, to the Provost Marshal General of the Department of the Missouri

Fulton M° March 28ᵗʰ 1864

Colonel. The wife of a colored recruit came into my Office to night and says she has been severely beaten and driven from home by her master and owner. She has a child some two years old with her, and says she left two larger ones at home, She desires to be sent forward with her husband; says she is willing to work and expects to do so at home or elsewhere; that her master told her never to return to him; that his men were all gone, and that he could not, and would not support the women. What is proper for me to do in such cases? I know many such will occur. Several persons have asked me the question. "What are we to do with the women and children"? the men are in the army; we cannot raise enough for them to eat. I am well convinced that threats are made, that in case the men go away, the women will be turned out of door. The owner of the woman refered to, is an aged man, a most inveterate rebel, and has, or did have when the war commenced, four sons in the rebel army. I am Colonel Very Respectfully Your Obedient Servant

ALS   Hiram Cornell

Capt. Hiram Cornell to Col. J. P. Sanderson, 28 Mar. 1864, C-258 1864, Letters Received, ser. 2786, Provost Marshal General, Dept. of the MO, RG 393 Pt. 1 [C-192]. An endorsement by the provost marshal general states, "This is but one of dozen's of similar applications of like character."

299A: Missouri Black Soldier to His Enslaved Daughters

[Benton Barracks Hospital, St. Louis, Mo., September 3, 1864]
My Children I take my pen in hand to rite you A few lines to
let you know that I have not forgot you and that I want to see
you as bad as ever   now my Dear Children I want you to be
contented with whatever may be your lots   be assured that I will
have you if it cost me my life   on the 28th of the mounth. 8
hundred White and 8 hundred blacke solders expects to start up
the rivore to Glasgow and above there thats to be jeneraled by a
jeneral that will give me both of you   when they Come I expect
to be with, them and expect to get you both in return.   Dont be
uneasy my children   I expect to have you. If Diggs dont give you
up this Government will and I feel confident that I will get
you   Your Miss Kaitty said that I tried to steal you   But I'll let
her know that god never intended for man to steal his own flesh
and blood. If I had no cofidence in God I could have confidence
in her   But as it is If I ever had any Confidence in her I have
none now and never expect to have   And I want her to remember
if she meets me with ten thousand soldiers she {will?] meet her
enemy   I once *[thought]* that I had some respect for them but now
my respects is worn out and have no sympathy for
Slaveholders. And as for her cristianantty I expect the Devil has
Such in hell   You tell her from me that She is the frist Christian
that I ever hard say that aman could Steal his own child especially
out of human bondage
  You can tell her that She can hold to you as long as she can   I
never would expect to ask her again to let you come to me because
I know that the devil has got her hot set againsts that that is
write   now my Dear children I am a going to close my letter to
you   Give my love to all enquiring friends   tell them all that we
are well and want to see them very much and Corra and Mary
receive the greater part of it you sefves   and dont think hard of us
not sending you any thing   I you father have a plenty for you
when I see you   Spott & Noah sends their love to both of
you   Oh! My Dear children how I do want to see you
HL   *[Spotswood Rice]*

[Private Spotswood Rice] to My Children, [3 Sept. 1864], enclosed in F.
W. Diggs to Genl. Rosecrans, 10 Sept. 1864, D-296 1864, Letters Received, ser. 2593, Dept. of the MO, RG 393 Pt. 1 [C-154] The first
fourteen lines of the letter appear to be in Private Rice's handwriting, but

the remainder is in another hand. Rice, a tobacco roller and the slave of Benjamin Lewis, had enlisted in early February 1864 at Glasgow, Missouri. On the date of this letter, he was hospitalized with chronic rheumatism. (Service record of Spotswood Rice, 67th USCI, Carded Records, Volunteer Organizations: Civil War, ser. 519, RG 94 [N-5].)

299B: Missouri Black Soldier to His Daughter's Owner

[*Benton Barracks Hospital, St. Louis, Mo., September 3, 1864*]

I received a leteter from Cariline telling me that you say I tried to steal to plunder my child away from you   now I want you to understand that mary is my Child and she is a God given rite of my own and you may hold on to hear as long as you can but I want you to remember this one thing that the longor you keep my Child from me the longor you will have to burn in hell and the qwicer youll get their   for we are now makeing up a bout one thoughsand blacke troops to Come up tharough and wont to come through Glasgow and when we come wo be to Copperhood rabbels and to the Slaveholding rebbels for we dont expect to leave them there root neor branch   but we thinke how ever that we that have Children in the hands of you devels we will trie your [vertues?] the day that we enter Glasgow   I want you to understand kittey diggs that where ever you and I meets we are enmays to each orthere   I offered once to pay you forty dollers for my own Child but I am glad now that you did not accept it   Just hold on now as long as you can and the worse it will be for you   you never in you life befor I came down hear did you give Children any thing not eny thing whatever not even a dollers worth of expencs   now you call my children your pro[*per*]ty   not so with me   my Children is my own and I expect to get them and when I get ready to come after mary I will have bout a powrer and autherity to bring hear away and to exacute vengencens on them that holds my Child   you will then know how to talke to me   I will assure that and you will know how to talk rite too   I want you now to just hold on to hear if you want to   iff your conchosence tells thats the road go that road and what it will brig you to kittey diggs   I have no fears about geting mary out of your hands   this whole Government gives chear to me and you cannot help your self

ALS   Spotswood Rice

Spotswood Rice to Kittey diggs, [3 Sept. 1864], enclosed in F. W. Diggs to Genl. Rosecrans, 10 Sept. 1864, D-296 1864, Letters Received, ser. 2593, Dept. of the MO, RG 393 Pt. 1 [C-154].

299C: Missouri Slave Owner to the Commander of the Department of the Missouri

                                        Glasgow Mo   Sept. 10″ 1864
Sir   Enclosed I send you two Letters written one to my Sister the
other to two colo girls one beloning to her & the other to
myself.   and I write this to ask the favour of you to send the
scoundrel that wrote them down to the army   I do not think that
he should be allowd to remain in the state   he wrote to my sister
to let his child come down to see him and he would send her
back   she was hired out   she went to see the person that hired
her to let he go but they refused.   The scoundrels wife & ten
children were alowed to go to him and the other would have been
sent whenevr I could be satisfied that her Mother had goton in
situation to support her.   I am and have been [*loyal*] from the
commencement of this wicked rebellion and I may say all I had
was in slave property which I connclud at the commencement was
defunct never to be resusitated   Six men are in the United States
service and I have told the bal[*ance*] when they wished to go just
say so and I would give them a pass   and under all these
circumstances my family all being of the same politics of myself
and to be thus insulted by such a black scoundrel is more that I
can stand   for refference Mr John D Perry   B. W. Lewis   James T
Bunch & William Spear of firm of Wm Spear & Co
Tobaconists   hopeing You will give this subject the attention it
deservs I remain Your obt Servt
ALS   F W Diggs

Postmaster F. W. Diggs to Genl. Rosecrans, 10 Sept. 1864, D-296 1864,
Letters Received ser. 2593, Dept. of the MO, RG 393 Pt. 1 [C-154].
Enclosed are the two letters from Private Spotswood Rice. Endorsement.

300: Louisiana Black Sergeant to the Commander of a Louisiana Black Brigade

                                        Barrancas Fla.   Dec 27. 1864
Sir   I beg you the granterfurction of a Small favor   will you ples
to Cross the Mississippia River at Bayou Sar La. with your
Command & jest on the hill one mile from the little town you

will finde A plantation Called Mrs Marther. H. Turnbuill & take
a way my Farther & mother & my brothers wife with all their
Childern & U take them up at your He^d Quarters. & write to
me   Sir the ar ther & I will amejeately Send after them. I wishes
the Childern all in School. it is beter for them then to be their
Surveing a mistes. Sir it isent mor then three or four Hours
trubel   I have bain trying evry sence I have bin in the servis it is
goin on ner 3. years & Could never get no one to so do for
me   now I thinks it will be don for you is my Gen. I wishes
evry day you would send after us. our Regt. ar doing all the hard
fightin her   we have disapointe the Rebes & surprizeed theme in
all. importan pointes   they says they wishes to Captuer the 82nd
Regt that they woul murdar them all   they Calls our Reg^t the
Bluebellied Eagles   Sir my Farthers Name Adam Harris   he will
Call them all to gether. & tel him to take Cousan Janes Childarn
with hime

Joseph. J. Harris

Sir I will remain Ob your Soldiar in the U.S.A.

ALS

1st Sgt. Joseph J. Harris to Gen. Ullman, 27 Dec. 1864, D. Ullmann
Papers, Generals' Papers & Books, ser. 159, RG 94 [V-4]. Harris had
made a similar request of General Daniel Ullmann just one month earlier.
In that letter he enumerated the relatives to be forcibly liberated, beginning with his father, a driver, who was "Hed" of the family: "Adam Harris, Mother Jonea, Brothers Wife Clarries & her Childern, Grand children
Lusinda & Casiel, My Suster Anner & her childe." His brother had died
since Harris departed for the army. Sergeant Harris warned Ullmann that
"Very probly they may not want to come but pleas not ask them about
their wills becaus their Misstes have led them to beleive that there is no
liven in the Lines of the Yankees." (Firt Sergt. J. J. Harris to Breg. Gen.
Ulman, 6 Nov. 186[4], D. Ullmann Papers, Generals' Papers & Books,
ser. 159, RG 94 [V-4].)

301: Kentucky Black Soldier to the Secretary of War, Enclosing Letters from the Soldier's Wife and from Her Owner

U.S. Gen. Hospital, Hampten, V.A. January 26th 1865

Sir. I the under-Sined, Respectfully ask for the liberation of my
Wife and children now residing in the State of Ky. Boone County.
I enclose two letters Received from there   one is supposed to be
from my Wife   the other is from a man claiming to be my Wifs

master by the name of Jerry, *Smith.* You can see by the contents
of his letter forbidding me not to write, Saying that he only gave
her to me on my good conduct Of which he Says I have not
fullfiled   it is not necessary for me to say anymore   you can see
his letter, –

And as I am a *Soldier.* willing to loose my life for my Country
and the liberty of my fellow man I hope that you will please be So
Kind as to attend to this   please lett me know, or send me your
Reply and oblige your humble Servent,   yours very Respectfully

ALS   Aaron Oats

[*Enclosure*]   [*Union, Ky.*] December the 22 64
Dar husban   I receive your letter dated December the 7 64 which
gave me much pleasure to hear that you ar alive and well   I mus
state that I and mother and the children ar all well hopping thet
these few lines may still find you well still   I am at home and far
as well as usial   I shall content myself and wait for the time to
come as you thought you could not get a ferlough   I must state
that there is another one was Born sence you left but I suppose
you heard of it   if you have not I will tell you hernane is effis
tell [pood?] as they call him can run half as fast as you can and
fat asever   your sisters ar all well   Johns mother states that, she
wish that John would right and if he wont Right when you right
again send all the perticklers About him whether he is live ordead.

N.B you stated in your letter that you sent me too letters and
your picture but I never receivd either

so I must conclude my short letter by saing that I send my love
to you all and keep the Best part for your self   so no more till
death

HLSr   Lucrethia

[*Enclosure*]   [*Union, Ky. January 10, 1865*]
   When your letter came to hand it was red and answerd and
when I went to put it in the office ther was another at hand Equal
as insolent as the other so I concluded to send you a few lines
apon my own responsibelity and, not to wright any more with out
you will have some Respect for me   ~~if you dont they will not be
red nor answered~~   my darkes has too much Sence to be foold in
such away   ther has been agreat menny woman and children have
left and returned back again   one instant in my nabohood   Henry
corben's mandy you nod her   dan had encoyd her and six children
over in cincinnati out on walnut hill and there she and three
children starved to death   the oldest that could travel came home

and got his master to bring them home to keep them from
starvation and too of the youngest had ate flesh of ther fingers   N
B Lucretia dont belong to you   I only gave her to you for wife
dureing good behaviour and you have violated your plede, my
darkes olways tells me when they want to leve me   they will tell
me   they say that if they ar to be deliberated they want it don
honorable

this lettere was rote the 22 of December but taken it back to
answer you my self I neglected to put it in the office till now this
being the 10 of January 1865   But my darkes is as well now as
they wer then and doing better than when you was hear   now,
they ar wated on   when you was hear they had you to wait
on   so no more

HL   [Jerry Smith]

Private Aaron Oats to Hon. Ed. M. Stanton, 26 Jan. 1865, enclosing
Lucrethia to Dar husban, 22 Dec. 1864, and [Jerry Smith] to Aaron Utz,
10 Jan. 1865, O-6 1865, Letters Received, ser. 360, Colored Troops Division, RG 94 [B-178]. The letter from Lucrethia and the unsigned letter
from her master are in the same handwriting, presumably that of the
master.

302: Affidavit of a Kentucky Black Soldier's Wife

Camp Nelson Ky 25th March 1865
Personally appeared before me J M Kelley Notary Public in and
for the County of Jessamine State of Kentucky Frances Johnson a
woman of color who being duly sworn according to law doth
depose and say —

I am the wife of Nathan Johnson a soldier in Company F. 116th
U.S.C. Infty. I have three children and with them I belonged to
Matthias Outon Fayette County Ky. My husband who belonged to
Mary Outon Woodford Co. Ky enlisted in the United States
service at Camp Nelson Ky. in May 1864. The day after my
husband enlisted my master knew it and said that he (my
husband) and all the "niggers" did mighty wrong in joining the
Army. Subsequent to May 1864 I remained with my master until
forced to leave on account of the cruel treatment to which I was
subjected. On Wednesday March 8th 1865, my masters son
Thomas Outon whipped me severely on my refusing to do some
work which I was not in a condition to perform. He beat me in
the presence of his father who told him (Thos Outon) to "buck me
and give me a thousand" meaning thereby a thousand
lashes. While beating me he threw me on the floor and as I was

694

in this prostrate and helpless condition he continued to whip me endeavoring at one time to tie my hands and at another time to make an indecent exposure of my person before those present. I resisted as much as I could and to some extent thwarted his malignant designs. In consequence of this whipping suffered much pain in my head and sides. The scar now visible on my neck was inflicted at that time. After such treatment I determined to leave my master and early on the following morning – Thursday March 9" 1865 I stealthly started for Lexington about seven miles distant where my sister resided. On my arrival there I was confined on account of sickness produced by the abuse I had received from my masters son as aforementioned.

During Friday March 10" 1865 I sought a lodging for myself and children – Towards evening I found one and about 7 o'clock at night I left for my masters intending to take my children away. About 9. O'clock I arrived there much fatigued, went to the Cabin where my children were, no one but the colored folks knowing that I was present, got my children with the exception of one that was too sick to move, and about 10" o'clock P.M. started for a neighboring Cabin where we remained during the night. At day break next morning I started for Lexington. My youngest child was in my arms, the other walked by my side. When on the Pike about a mile from home I was accosted by Theophilus Bracey my masters son-in-law who told me that if I did not go back with him he would shoot me. He drew a pistol on me as he mad this threat. I could offer no resistance as he constantly kept the pistol pointed at me. I returned with him to his (Bracys) house carrying my children as before I remained at Bracys all day. My sick child was moved there during the day. I tried to find some chance of running away but Bracey was watching me. He took my eldest child (about seven years of age) and kept her as an Hostage. I found I could not get away from Bracey's with my children, and determined to get away myself hoping by this means to obtain possession of them afterwards. I knew Bracey would not give me my children or allow me to go away myself so at daybreak on the following morning Sunday March 12" I secretly left Bracey's, took to the woods in order to elude pursuit, reached Lexington and subsequently arrived at Camp Nelson. My children are still held by Bracey. I am anxious to have them but I am afraid to go near them knowing that Bracey would not let me have them and fearing least he would carry out his threat to shoot me. And further the deponent saith not

her
(Signed) Frances X Johnson
mark

HDcSr

Affidavit of Frances Johnson, 25 Mar. 1865, filed with H-8 1865, Registered Letters Received, ser. 3379, TN Asst. Comr., RG 105 [A-6148]. Sworn before a notary public.

303: Indiana Black Recruiter to the Secretary of War

New Albany. Ind. April 1st 1865

Sir. I. H. G. Mosee. take my pen in hand to inform you of the hardships and troubles of Colored Soldiers Wives here. it makes my heart bleed to see how they are treated. some are starving some are robbed out of all their poor husbands leave for them those persons are the so called Contrabands. they have made their way to this place and no Men with them or the greater part of them the most of them have come from Kentucky We, the Colored people of this place do all we can to help these poor people and I thought by applying to you that we would be a great deal better off if such Conduct could by any means be prevented if one Colored Man had Military Orders to see after such persons this would be stopped. such as Kidnaping and carrying Soldiers Wives and Children back into Kentucky and going into their houses stealing what they have and because the Colored Women have not got a White Witness they cant do any thing they can stand and look at their own property but cant get it because they have no White witness or Military Man to speak in their favor. as fast as Contrabands come they will take him and put him in jail and tell him he cant get out unless he goes as a Substitute and sell him for one thousand. dollars and give him one hundred or one hundred and fifty. they tell him they will give him five hundred dollars until he is Mustered in and then pay him what they please. he may have a Wife and Children then they will say to him give me your Money and I will give it to your Family or I will give you fifty dollars and carry the balance to your Family but not a dollar will the Family get and so they go I cant tell you (sir) how bad it is I know you will put a stop to this and if you will give me orders I will go any length for such poor people. I was licensed by J. H. Almy. to recruit for the. 29th and 30th Regiments of Colored Volunteers. I will send you my license and you can see what I have been doing. you will please to return them to me again. and if your (Honor) will send me such papers I will be pleased to serve for the Benifit of the Colored population of this place. if ever the poor Colored people wanted a Beaureau it is here. your humble servant

ALS   H. G. Mosee

H. G. Mosee to Secratary Stanton, 1 Apr. 1865, M-248 1865, Letters Received, ser. 360, Colored Troops Division, RG 94 [B-170]. An enclosure from New York City, on stationery printed "Headquarters Connecticut," authorizes Mosee to recruit black soldiers. (Wm. H. Craig to H. G. Mozee, 9 June 1864.)

304: Wife of a Kentucky Black Soldier to Her Husband

Green Cty Ky. July the [6] 1865

Dear Husband   i set my self down to write you a few lines to let you know that Mr Reed twoke to me and my three children to live with him to live and R. L. Moor and Mr. Frank Coward come hear to day and beat me nearly to death   he says that he will kill any man that will take me in to a house to live with him   Pharoah this is roat by Sarah M Reed[1]   i want you to hand this to your captain Stranger   i want to know of all you that is a friend to the cullard people that you have got thar husband in survice i want you to come to greens burg and treat old Coward just like he did Pharoah wife to day   and he said that if i said one word that he would searve me the same way   he knocked hear down and old dick more hell hear and Coward beat hear nearly to death   he took the older girl with him home and he said to jane that before she should live with me he would killer de[ad] and all of the Reeds that was on top of earth in less than one weak   i would ceap you wife but R L more says that he will kill every woman that he knows that has got a husband in the army   he said that i was no better than a negro rage and i think that i am just as good as he is   i never treated nothing as he did Pharoah wife to day   i want you to come to greens burg and let me see you and tell you all about it   i think we will have to leve hear on the acount off the rebels that is hear for if a man ever leaves his wife and children at home by thar selves thay are abusded by some one of them   you must do some thing for Mr Frank coward in return to his treatment to day to Pharoah wife   i never was so abused in my life by no man   my husband is not at home to day   i have two children in the uion army and we have two children that was killed in the union army and i think that aught to have some peace at home when my husband leaves me at home   do pray do come to our relieaf at home   nothing more but this   your wife

jane coward

rote by Sarah M Reed

HLSr

jane coward to Dear Husband, [6] July 1865, Letters Received, 125th USCI, Regimental Books & Papers USCT, RG 94 [G-179]. Endorsement. Coward's husband was Private Pharoah Marshall of the 125th USCI.

1 At this point in the letter the voice changes from that of Jane Coward, wife of the black soldier Pharoah, to that of Sarah Reed. The latter, who penned the letter, was evidently the wife of the Mr. Reed who had taken in Jane Coward and her three children.

305: Letters to a Louisiana Black Soldier from His Wife and Sister and a Report from His Company Officer to the Louisiana Freedmen's Bureau Assistant Commissioner

Roseland Plantation [*La.*] July 16th 1865

My Dear Husband   I received a letter from you week before last and was glad to hear that you were well and happy.

This is the fifth letter I have written you and I have received only one —   Please write as often as you can as I am always anxious to hear from you.   I and the children are all well — but I am in a great deal of trouble as Master John Humphries has come home from the Rebel army and taken charge of the place and says he is going to turn us all out on the Levee unless we pay him (8.00) Eight Dollars a month for house rent —   Now I have no money of any account and I am not able to get enough to pay so much rent, and I want you to get a furlough as soon as you can and come home and find a place for us to live in.   and besides Amelia is very sick and wants you to come home and see her if possible   she has been sick with the fever now over two weeks and is getting very low —   Your mother and all the rest of your folks are well and all send their regards & want to see you as soon as you can manage to come —   My mother sends her compliments & hopes to see you soon

My children are going to school, but I find it very hard to feed them all, and if you can not come I hope you will send me something to help me get along

I get all the work I can and am doing the best I can to get along, but if they turn me out I dont know what I shall do —   However I will try & keep the children along until you come or send me some assistance

Thank God we are all well, and I hope we may always be so   Give my regards to all the boys.   Come home as soon as you can, and cherish me as ever   Your Aff wife

HLSr   Emily Waters

698

Black Military Life: Off Duty

Roseland Plantation [*La.*] July 30th 1865

My Dear Brother   I learn by Hannibal that you are well and
happy— Mother and all the rest of us are well but we are in deep
trouble— Your wife has left Trepagnia and gone to the city and
we dont know where or how she is, we have not heard a word
from her for four weeks

Master John has come home and is going to turn us all out of
doors unless we pay him $3.00 per month rent, and we have no
way to earn the money and it is coming mighty hard on
us   David has left and gone some where— He has been gone over
two weeks and we dont know what has become of him—

My little boy has been very sick, but is getting quite well
now— Moses is well and sends his regards, Aunt Rosalie and
Aunt Liddie both send their love & best wishes

Moses wants you to send him a pair of soldiers pants if you
can— Hopeing to hear from you soon   I am Your Aff Sister

HLSr

Alsie Thomas

Fort St. Philip. La. Aug. 1st, 1865.

Sir. I am an officer in a co. of 140 men. – have been with them
continually Since their organization as a Co., and most of the time
the Sole officer with them. Feeling an interest in the advancement
and prosperity of the colored race and always sympathizing with
them in their trials and Sufferings, which are now very great,
owing to the peculiar condition of the country, and their people,
those under my immediate charge have learned to look to me for
consolation in regard to many matters not Strictly military. I
always do what I can but frequently that is nothing at all. One of
the most frequent complaints brought to me is the mistreatment of
Soldiers wives, and in Some cases their ejectment for non-payment
of rent by *returned rebels* who seem to be resuming their old
positions all over the country. This of course is inhuman as well
as contrary to Genl. Orders. No. 99. H^d Qrs. Dept. of the Gulf.
June 30th, 1865, which declares that the families of Soldiers in the
Service of the Gov't. either on land or water, Shall not be ejected
for rent past due, and no collections of rent forced until further
orders. This is a very humane provision but owing to the
ignorance of many colored persons it is *very* often violated. Those
who know of the provision do not know how to go to work to
receive their rights under it, frequently, and when they do attempt
it they are often snubbed by those who they feel a right to expect
as their friends. Truly, the colored race are passing through an
ordeal that will test every virtue they possess, and it will not be

astonishing if, in many cases they fail to meet the expectation of an uncharitable world.

My object in writing you this letter is to call your attention to a Mr. John Humphrey, who I am told is a returned rebel officer, now living on Roseland Plantation, St. Charles Parish, who is Said to have made innumerable threats and at least one attempt to put out the family of one of my Soldiers. — *for non-payment of rent.* — I gave the man a furlough and he got home Just in time to find a *Provost Guard* at his house for the purpose of ousting his wife and children. These look like Strange proceedings viewed at this distance with my understanding of the law. The fact is, persecution is the order of the day amongst these returned rebels, against the colored race in general, and Soldiers families *in particular*. And I am grieved to Say that many wearing the U.S. uniform are too easily bought body and Soul over to the evil designs and purposes of these same individuals. It seems to me that your Bureau and its agents are the "forlorn hope" of the colored people. — These rebels Strongly object to these agents, and declare that they will only keep up a confusion and disturbance, continually. That means that they do not intend to manifest the "good faith" for which Genl. Howard hopes, but intend to take Such a course with the colored people as will *oblige* the interference of the agents of your Bureau.

These are my views, although I owe you an apology for expressing them at Such length. If it pleases you I shall be glad to lay the frequent cases which arise in my Co. before you, as I know your voice is very potent   With great respect I am Your Most Obt. Servt.

ALS   Hugh P. Beach.

Emily Waters to My Dear Husband, 16 July 1865, and Alsie Thomas to My Dear Brother, 30 July 1865, enclosed in 2nd Lieut. Hugh P. Beach to Mr. Thomas W. Conway, 1 Aug. 1865, B-28 1865, Letters Received, ser. 1303, LA Asst. Comr., RG 105 [A-8553]. Waters's and Thomas's letters are written in the same hand. There is no indication which of the contradictory rent figures is correct. The men served in the 10th USCHA.

306: Commander of the Post of Port Hudson, Louisiana, to the Louisiana Freedmen's Bureau Assistant Commissioner and the Latter's Reply

Port Hudson, La., October 2nd *1865.*

I have the honor to acknowledge the receipt of your letter of 20th ult in answer to my telegram of the 18th ult. I cannot agree with the sentiments therein expressed for if Colored Soldiers and their families are to be treated like and expected to take care of themselves as white Soldiers and their families in the north then is your Bureau a useless incumbrance and the sooner it is shut up and its agents sent home the better but it is because the colored Soldiers families and their friends are *totally unlike* in condition to the white Soldiers families and friends that your Bureau is here to day and if you allow planters to turn off and shut up the cabins of these soldiers families before provisions are made for them elsewhere and especially months before any one else wants to hire them, then has your Bureau utterly failed in its functions contemplated in its establishment. In regard to the question of food I am positive that outside of the Parishes around New Orleans and immediately on the River not one in fifty Planters furnishes food but require labor and they feed themselves from their little gardens, pigs, chickens and eggs

In this particular case no clothing food or pay has been furnished for two years. It seems to me proper to require Planters when they have persons on their place not wanted to request their removal through the Bureau, but to turn them off at their pleasure and keep their pigs chickens and cooking utensils and leave them on the levee a week in a starving condition is an injustice towards the families of these soldiers that the Noble Republic grateful for the services of these men in its hour of peril will not permit at the hands of any of its agents

And no one knows better than yourself how hard it is to get a Boat to take on any of these people on Board. the Boats are run wholy in the interest of the white men as controlled by the sentiment of the south, and just let a Boat show any favor to this class of people and see how much freight they would get after the cry of Abolitionist was raised against it. *Why!* they had better have the yellow fever on board

It is the general purpose among the Planters to turn off very soon nearly all those upon their places and already Baton Rouge & Port Hudson are so crowded that there is no room for more, and yet the complaints of cruelty and injustice are so numerous that

701

but few of them can be attended to and I hear the same state of things extends elsewhere

In the north the land is in many hands, little villages everywhere – homes and residences already provided or plenty of friends who have them, and a sentiment favorable to the soldiers, their families, and cause, are scattered every where over the north and prevades the entire community. But here how different. The land is in few hands, few villages where homes are to be had and those already crowded. The whole people who control these things *very* hostile to these men, their families, and cause. And yet you say these men must do as the white Soldiers of the north do. But, how are they to do it? where are the homes to be had? Now I wish to look at practical measures and discard merely theory or extremes in such measures as may be taken to make these people wholy self supporting in the shortest possible time which I conceive to be the object of your Bureau, and to this end will cheerfully co-operate with you. To you personally I renew the assurance of my respect and esteem and remain a friend

HLS   H. N. Frisbie

New Orleans Octo 5th 1865.

Colonel: Your communication of the 2^d, instant is received and more fully explains the matter in regard to the injustice done to the wives of your colored soldiers & their families, than the telegram of the 18th.

I am not pleased with the tone of your letter; and I deeply regret the suffering which you inform me has ensued – . In my letter I stated that we could not compel planters to retain those women if their husbands were not on the place, unless contracts had been made with them. This is so. While I am proud of the services which the colored man has rendered to his country, I can see no reason why, with the pay which he receives from the Government; and the amount which can be earned by an industrious woman their families cannot be supported and maintained in at least a comfortable manner. The comparisons between the condition of the white soldier and the black, and the country North and South I consider unnecessary. I did not labor to prove that the negroe and the white possessed equal advantages; that I meant to convey the idea that with a little economy and industry the family of the black soldiers could be maintained without expense to the Government. Very Respectfully Your Obd^t Servant

HLcS   Thomas W Conway

Col. H. N. Frisbie to Thomas W. Conway, 2 Oct. 1865, F-37 1865,
Letters Received, ser. 1303, LA Asst. Comr., RG 105 [A-8567]; Asst.
Comr. Thomas W. Conway to Col. H. N. Frisbie, 5 Oct. 1865, vol. 15,
p. 395, Letters Sent, ser. 1297, LA Asst. Comr., RG 105 [A-8567].

307A: **Letters between a Kentucky Black Soldier and His Wife**

Nashville Tenn Aug 12th 1865

Dear wife   I Received your letter that was writen on the 8th to
day and was glad to hear that you was well and that the children
was well also. I am well as to health and well Satisfide all to
Seeing you and as I can't tell when I can come to see you my
wishes is for you to come and See me   I am in earnis a bout you
comeing and that as Soon as possiable   it is no use to Say any
thing a bout any money for if you come up here which I [*hope*]
you will it will be all wright as to the money matters   I want to
See you and the Children very bad and my love for you and the
Children is as great to day as it ever was. I can get a house at
any time   I will Say the word So you need not to fear as to
that   So come wright on just as Soon as you get this. I also wish
you to get George to give you Some money to bare your exspences
here. and if you cant get off you must write to me a gain and I
will try and Send you Some money   I want you to tell me the
name of the baby that was borm Since I left   that is if you can't
come up here. and I want you to bring my son George with you
for I want him. and if it Suits you you can leave your daughter
Elisabeth there with George. I am your affectionate Husband
untill Death

Norman Riley

Write Soon

ALS

Nashville Tenn Aug 26 *1865*

Dear and affectionate Wife   I Seat myself to write you a few lines
to let you know that I am well hoping that these lines may fine
you the same. Dear wife I would like you to come down if you
Possible can   I wrote to you some time a go to come and you did
not come and I dont know the reason for I have not got any letter

703

from you to hear how you was nor to know cause of you not
comeing. I cant tell when I shall get out of service and I want to
See you very bad and if you [want] to See me you will have to
come and see me and I would like for you to come for I think
that you can make a great deal more here then you can. and you
George I think very hard of you for not coming and Seeing me for
you know that I cant come and See you and therefore you ought
to come and See me and if you dont feel like coming down here I
want [you] to come and bring my family and you can go back if
choose.

now if you cant come I want you to write me an answer to this
as Soon as you Receive it. I have Nothing more at Preasent but I
Remain Your Most affectionate Husband Untill Death.

Derect your letter as headed above in care of Capt. F. P. meigs
(Box 115)

Norman Riley

Write Soon   yes I have got a house all Ready for you and if cant
come I Shall reant it out a gain in the coure of ten days so good
by

ALS

Clarksville Tenn Aug 28. /65

Dear husband   It is with pleasure that I Seat myself for the
perpose of Writing you afew lines. acknoklage the recept of your
letter. which came to hand in Dew time. it finding [me] very Well
as I trust this may find you. I am sorry to Inform you. that your
brother George is very badly Wonded   he went out After my
things and Jessie Boyd also. Jessie went with him. he was also
shot. but not so bad as Geo. and George wants that you should
come down To see him if you posible Can. do so   he thinks that
if you cannot come now. you Need not to come at all for he is
very badly wounded   I guess you would like to know the reson
why that I did not come when you wrote for and that is because
that I hadnot the money and could not get it. and if you will
send me the money. or come after me I will come   they sent out
Soldiers from here After old Riley. and they have got him in Jale
In Bolling Green K.Y. and one of his Sons. Kernealious I think.
was woulded by the Colord Soldiers. and they have his brother
Elias here in Jale. dear husband If you are coming after me. I
want you to come before it Get too cold. that I cant Travel   I
dont want you to Rent that house out. for if there is a better
chance to make a living there. then what there is here. I want to
get up there.

George was badly Shot through the Back. the shot still remains

704

in him and Jessie boyd was shot through the thigh. I seen Uncle
Moses Riley. Sunday and he told me to give you his best respect.
and tell you that he was well and doing very well. dear husb I
havenot got my things from home yet but I shell. as soon I
can. having nothing more to Write. I shell close hopeing to hear
from you soon   I Remain as ever your affectionate and Loving
Wife

ALS   Catherine Riley

Nashville Tennessee Septr 22nd *1865*
Mr Dear Wife   I again the pleasure of writing to you To let you
know that I am In the enjoyment of Good health. I would like to
know the reason why you did not answer my last two letters. I
am very anxious to hear from you. and particularly to know if you
are coming Here. if you are coming I would like for you to come
immediately, as there is A man here about. to buy a house and he
has no person to go into it to take care of the things. also let me
know if George has got well or not   I am very anxious to hear
from him   I want you to write to me inside of an hour after you
receive this and let me know what you are going to do   I will
now conclude hoping to hear from you son   I remain your
affectionate & Loving Husband

HLSr   Norman Riley

Norman Riley to Dear wife, 12 Aug., 26 Aug., and 22 Sept. 1865, filed
with R-101 1866, Registered Letters Received, ser. 3379, TN Asst.
Comr., RG 105 [A-6171], endorsements; Catherine Riley to Norman
Riley, 28 Aug. 1865, M-80 1865, Registered Letters Received, ser. 3379,
TN Asst. Comr., RG 105 [A-6171]. Norman Riley apparently took his
wife's letter describing the shooting of his brother George and another man
to his company officer, who forwarded it to the Tennessee and Kentucky
Freedmen's Bureau assistant commissioner, asking bureau action against the
former master if the civil authorities should fail to prosecute. (Endorsement
by Capt. F. P. Meigs, 4 Sept. 1865.)

307B: Freedmen's Bureau Agent at Clarksville, Tennessee, to the Headquarters of the Kentucky and Tennessee Freedmen's Bureau Assistant Commissioner

Clarksville Tenn Decr 19. 1865
Sir   I have the honor to call your attention to the following
statement and ask your advice thereon

On the 9th ult I gave Catherine Riley, the wife of a soldier, an order to James Riley of Logan Co Ky. for her child which the said Riley still claimed as his Slave. She got the child & started on her return to this place & when about three miles from said Rileys, he overtook her, & did unlawfully beat her with a club, & left her senseless on the ground after which he returned home with the child. Catherine Riley reported to me the following day. and substantiated the above facts by competent witnesses & at the time was all covered with blood. could scarcely talk & was barely able to stand alone. The above facts have also been told to me by a neighbor of the said James Riley— I sent a guard for him but he could not be found, as he had gone from home & taken the said child with him, as he remarked. to a neighbor, to "put the child out of the reach of the d- - -d Yankees Not long since this same man Riley shot a negro soldier, & ran away from home to prevent his being arrested.

Cases of the above kind are reported to me about every day, but many of them I cannot attend to on account of not having soldiers to enforce my orders at a distance

I respectfully refer this matter to you & ask your advice thereon Resp[ct] Your ob[t] Servt

ALS   W. G. Bond

W. G. Bond to Brvt. Lieut. Col. J. H. Cochrane, 19 Dec. 1865, B-203 1865, Registered Letters Received, ser. 3379, TN Asst. Comr., RG 105 [A-6089]. Bond's successor as Freedmen's Bureau agent in Clarksville later reported that James Riley was arrested and tried before him on charges of having "maltreated" Catherine Riley. He found James Riley guilty and levied a fine of $100, including $48.80 in damages to the freedwoman. (Joshua Cobb to Brevt. Maj. Genl. C. B. Fisk, 28 Feb. 1866, Narrative Reports of Operations, ser. 3388, TN Asst. Comr., RG 105 [A-6089].)

307C: Affidavit of a Kentucky Black Soldier's Wife with an Endorsement by the Freedmen's Bureau Agent at Clarksville, Tennessee

State of Tennessee   Montgomery County   5 day of May 1866

Catherine Riley being duly sworn and examined on oath makes complaint & says that Norman Riley late of Logan Co. Ky & the slave of John Riley in the fall of 1856 did marry this affiant according to the forms & ceremonies practiced among colored people and her the said Cathrine then & their had for wife. That affiant has had four (4) children by him three of whom are now

living. That she has ever been faithful in marrige relations. And
that the said Norman Riley afterwards and while he was so
married to this affiant as aforesaid to wit in the year 1865 at the
City of Nashville in the State of Tennessee he the said Norman
Rily feloniously & unlawfully did marry & take to wife one other
colored woman whose name is unknown to this affiant—this affiant
his former wife being then & now living, against the power &
dignity of the State & contrary to the forms of the Statute in such
case made & provided—

Wherefore affiant prays that he be arrested & dealt with
according to law

her
Catherine × Riley
mark

[In the margin, in another hand] This man works at Roaring
Springs Ky. This is such a flagrant case that it is desirable to
send this to Gen Fisk— Will Dr Cobb please swear this woman &
send this to Gen Fisk.

5' day of May 1866

Affiant further says that she presented the above affidavit to Dr
Cobb Bureau Agent of the freedman here who refused to swear her
to it. She further says that the above affidavit is true & she prays
that Gen Fisk will help her. She says that Dr Cobb told her that
if her husband when *arrested* should swear that the children were
not all his, it would send this affiant to State Prison

her
Catherine × Riley
mark

HDSr

[Endorsement] Bureau R F and A Lands Office Supt for
M[ontgomery] County Tennessee Clarksville May 24th
1866 Respectfully Returned with the following
statements— That sometime in April last the colored woman in
question (Catharine Riley) made to me substanially the statements
contained in the paper herin enclosed marked A.— But knowing
that some of Catharines children were bright mulattoes, and some
quite black, I could not see how she could sustain these statements
and would advise her with the letters (the same herin enclosed)
and a letter which I would give her, to go before the Supt of the
Bureau at Cadiz Trigg County Ky who would have her husband
brought before him, and then face to face, with her the difficultly
could be settled. I saw no more of Catharine until, about the 5th

of Apl—when she came to my office with the paper marked A. drawn up by or in the office of Messr Buck & McMullin, with a request from them that I should sware her as to the statements therein contained but on reading over the paper I was convinced that it would be improper for her to make oath to the same—and stated to her that should she do so she would lay herself liable to prosecution for perjury   And here I would state that Doctor A. C. Swartzwelder of your city being present and his attention being called to the case after asking the woman (Catharine) a few questions—became himself convinced from her answers that it would be wrong for her to be sworn to the statements contained in said paper—and that further in a few hours after this—the Doctor and myself in making a visit to the contraband camp—happened to call at the cabin occupied by said Catharine and her children—and the Doctor's attention was called to the Mulattoe & Black children of said Catharine, all of whom she was about to and has since sworn to be the children of Norman Riley—and the Doctor then & there told her it would not do for her to sware to the Statements of said paper   The next I heare of the matter is on the receipt of the enclosed papers from your office with request to report on the facts and from which I learn that the simple woman, from advise of her lawyer—went before the County Court clerk and made oath to the correctness of the contents of said paper—   I have only to add that I know of no better way to adjust this matter than the one herin already suggested by me to the woman Catharine   all of which is respectfully submitted   Joshua Cobb   Supt BRF and A Lands for Montgomery County Tenn

Affidavit of Catherine Riley, 5 May 1866, R-101 1866, Registered Letters Received, ser. 3379, TN Asst. Comr., RG 105 [A-6171]. Other endorsements. Affidavit sworn before a clerk in the law office of Buck & McMullin, Clarksville, Tennessee. The marginal notation was presumably added by the lawyer or his clerk. The paper marked "A," to which Cobb refers in his endorsement, is Catherine Riley's affidavit.

SOLDIERS' FAMILIES WITHIN UNION LINES

308: Order by the Commander of a Missouri Black Regiment

Helena Arkansas Feb 3rd 1865

Genl Orders No 41

(I)   Information has been received at these Head Quarters, that the enlisted men of this command, are much in the habit of marrying Common place women of the town, this must be stopped at once –

(II)   All Marriage Certificates given by the Rev J. I. Herrick, Minister of the Gospel and Post Chaplain, are annulled from this date – Any soldier allowing any Minister or calling on any Minister or Chaplain to marry them after this date, without first obtaining written permission from their Company Commander and submitting the same for approval at these Head Quarters will be severely punished for every such offence –

(III)   Company Commanders will forward at once all Certificates of Marriage in their Companies, given at this Post, with their approval or disapproval; to these Head Quarters, for approval or otherwise –

(IV)   The names of all soldiers who have their wives with them who were married prior to December 14th 1863 will be forwarded to these Head Quarters. All Marriages and Soldiers having their wives with this command will be recorded at these Head Quarters.

(V)   No soldier will send for his wife or cause her directly or indirectly to come to this command – without first getting the approval of his Company Commander, and forward the same for action at these Head Quarters. Company Commanders will cause all on their part to be firmly but kindly executed, and reporting the name of any Soldier whose wife comes with or without permission. Marriages that are disapproved of, the Soldiers will not be allowed to Stay out of Quarters nights – By order of John G Hudson Col Comdg

HD

Genl. Orders No. 41, Head Quarters 60th U.S. Cold. Inft., 3 Feb. 1865, Issuances, 60th USCI, Regimental Books & Papers USCT, RG 94 [G-221].

309: Page from a Marriage Register

[*Vicksburg, Miss. 1864*]

386

Date.	Name of Male.	Place of Residence.	Name of Female.	Place of Residence.	Age-Years.	Color.
1864.						
July 17	William Montgomery	K, 5th U.S.C.H.A.	Vicey Ann	Yazoo City, Miss.	23	Blk
" 25	John McYoung	66th U.S.C.I.	Sarah James	Ill.	42	Mul.
" 31	Wilson Martin	Vicksburg, Miss.	Mary Martin	Vicksburg, Miss.	73	"
"	Henry Marshall	F, 53d U.S.C.I.	Hannah Marshall	"	51	Blk
August 1	Eclipse Mitchell	K, 52 "	Adelia Coleman	"	40	"
" 4	Collins Moore	Vicksburg, Miss.	Susan Statham	"	24	Sld
"	~~Eclipse Mitchell~~	~~K, 52 U.S.C.I.~~	See above, Aug. 4. Married twice.			
July 10	Mat Martin	Bolivar, Miss.	Mary J. Leadbury	Carroll, La.	23	Mix'd
" 31	Henry Miller	47th U.S.C.I.	Ann M. Chainey	Lake Washington	49	"
August 14	John A. McComb	St. Coupee, La.	Suretia Harris	Vicksburg, Miss.	46	Blk
" 21	James Mullens	K, 5th U.S.C.H.A.	Margaret Taylor	"	20	"
Sept. 4	Lamb Wosely	G, 52d U.S.C.I.	Jane Wosely	do	39	do
" 4	James F. Murphy	G, 118th U.S.C.I.	Esther Anne Burns	do	24	do
" "	Thomas Worgan	A, 5th U.S.C.H.A.	Frances Green	do	41	do
" 11	Manuel McDaniel	B, 50th U.S.C.I.	Harriet McDaniel	Washington Co. Miss.	36	do

HD

Vicksburg marriage register, vol. 43, pp. 386–87, Registers of Marriage, ser. 2073, MS Asst. Comr., RG 105 [A-9533]. Volumes 43, 44, and 45

MALE.							FEMALE.						Name of Officiating Minister. and Witness.
Blk	Blk				15	Blk	Blk	Blk					Joseph Warren Charles Warren
White	"				20	"	"	"	1 force				Walter C. Yancey E. Fuller Parent
"	"	16 force	5	56	"	"	"	8 death	1				Joseph Warren Henry Marshall
Blk	Blk	10	"		40	"	"	"	18	"	13		" Riley Gordon
"	"	1	"		17	Mul.	Mul.	Mul.					" Charles Gordon
"	"				25	Blk	Blk	Blk	4	"	2		" Amanda H. Geet
Mixed	Mixed				19	Mixed	Mixed	Mixed	1	"			G. N. Carruthers Walter C. Yancey
Blk	"	6	"	2	29	"	Blk	"	1 Choice				Charles W. Buckley Lewis Robinson
Blk	Blk	10	"	2	32	Blk	Blk	Blk	5 death		2		S. H. Sayler D. B. Hawkes
"	"				25	"	"	"					Joseph Warren Charles Warren
do	do	1 force	1	40	do	do	do	7 force	2	6			James A. Hawley Euphine Mosely.
do	do				21	do	do	do					Thomas Calahan Asa Merrill.
do	do				49	do	do	do	11 death				Joseph Warren Malvina Curliss.
do	do				41	do	do	do					Jos Warren Elvira Thomas.

in this series contain entries for over 1,400 marriages of ex-slaves, recorded at Vicksburg, Natchez, and Davis Bend, Mississippi, in 1864 and 1865.

310: Chaplain of an Arkansas Black Regiment to the Adjutant General of the Army

Little Rock Ark Feb 28th 1865

The movements of the 54th during the month has interfered to some extent with our Sabbath services; and has also, rendered it impracticable to continue the day school. On reaching this post from, Ft Smith, the Reg[r] was divided, and five companies sent out towards Brownsville, to guard the Rail Road. These have been ordered back to Little Rock and the ten companies, are now camped, on the north side of the river, doing guard, & provost, duty in & around Little Rock: As soon as a building can be procured, I design to open a day school for such as are disposed to attend.

Weddings, just now, are very popular, and abundant among the Colored People. They have just learned, of the Special Order No' 15. of Gen Thomas[1] by which, they may not only be lawfully married, but have their Marriage Certificates, *Recorded;* in a *book furnished by the Government.* This is most desirable; and the order, was very opportune; as these people were constantly loosing their certificates. Those who were captured from the "Chepewa"; at Ivy's Ford, on the 17th of January, by Col Brooks, had their Marriage Certificates, taken from them; and destroyed; and then were roundly cursed, for having such papers in their posession. I have married, during the month, at this Post; Twenty five couples; mostly, those, who have families; & have been living together for years. I try to dissuade single men, who are soldiers, from marrying, till their time of enlistment is out: as that course seems to me, to be most judicious.

The Colord People here, generally consider, this war not only; their *exodus,* from bondage; but the road, to Responsibility; Competency; and an honorable Citizenship— God grant that their hopes and expectations may be fully realized. Most Respectfully

A. B. Randall

ALS

Chaplain A. B. Randall to Brig. Gen. L. Thomas, 28 Feb. 1865, R-189 1865, Letters Received, ser. 12, RG 94 [K-529].

1 Adjutant General Lorenzo Thomas's order provided: "Any ordained minister of the Gospel, accredited by the General Superintendent of Freedmen, is hereby authorized to solemnize the rites of marriage among the Freedmen." (Orders No. 15, 28 Mar. 1864, L. Thomas Letters & Orders, Generals' Papers & Books, ser. 159, RG 94 [V-63].)

311: Tennessee Black Soldier to the Commander of the Military Division of the Tennessee and a Report by the Commander of a Tennessee Black Regiment

Bridgeport Ala N 19th 1865

Dear Ser   We are here at this place under the cormand of Colonel luster   genel I rite you thes few lines to let you know the condishon that we are living   we are guarded there night and day no even permitted to go to the spring after a drink of water onley by companys   wether Corprel Sargent they hav all got in to such a comfuse ment they say they will not stand it any longger   I say to you less than ten days there will be over half the men gon from the regment if they is not treatted better   they keep they bys hand cuf evver day and night and I cant see what it is for   if they do any thing to be hand cuff for we wold not exspec any thing eles   mens wifes comes here to see them and he will not alow them to come in to they lines uur the men to go out to see them after the comg over hundred miles   but evver offiscer here that has a wife is got her here in camps & one mans wif feel jest as near to him as anurther   a colard man think jest as much of his wife as a white man dus of his   if he is black they keep us hemd up here in side the guarde line and if our wife comes they hav to stand out side & he in side and talk a cross they lines   that is as near as they can come   they treat this hold reg ment like it was prisners   we volenterd and come in to the servest to portec this govverment and also to be portected our selves at the same time but the way colonel luster is treating us it dont seem like to me that he thinks we are human

I rite these few lines to you to see if we cant get some releaf   yours truly a friend

George Buck Hanon

ALS

Bridgeport Ala Decr 14th /65

General   I have the honor to acknowledge the receipt of a communication addressed to the Major Genl com^{dg}, professing to be signed and written by "George Buchhanon 40th U.S.C.I."

Altho' no such man can be found in the rolls of the regiment nor any name approximating to it, neither can any man be found to father the document, yet in obedience to the order contained in your endorsement, I subjoin the following statement.

The sum & substance of the complaint set forth against me seems to resolve into this, that I am endeavoring to maintain discipline in a regiment of U.S. troops committed to my care, and that I prevent the camp of the said regiment from becoming a brothel on a gigantic scale. To this I plead guilty.

The marital relationship is but little understood by the colored race, and, if possible still less respected.

I have from time to time caused a careful inquiry to be made by company commander's with the view to ascertain the number of men who are married by any process known to civilization, or even those who by long cohabitation might be looked on as possessing some faint notions of constancy and decency. Even with this lax view not more than one in four who claim to have wives can support that claim.

In fact the larger proportion of the enlisted men change their so called wives as often as the regiment changes stations.

The immorality developed after last pay day required a strong effort to repress it. Large herds of colored prostitutes flocked to Bridgeport from both ends of the line, but the guard regulations not suiting them, the greater proportion soon left for "fresh fields & pastures new."

It is just within the bounds of possiblity that some virtuous wives may have been amongst the number so excluded from camp, but I gravely doubt it.

The Rev[nd] John Poucher, Chaplain of my regiment is doing his best to correct the vices so prevalent amongst colored soldiers, but the habits of licentiousness not only permitted but greatly encouraged by the former owners of these men are hard to eradicate.

The charge of guarding parties going for water is partly true. Water has to be brought from a considerable distance, the road to it lies thro' the line of stores erected here for the express purpose of robbing soldiers, the proprietors of which having laid in a stock of whisky in anticipation of pay-day did, both on and on the day after that day, make nearly the entire regiment drunk.

I was compelled to adopt severe measures with store keepers and soldiers, since which there has been no trouble on that subject.

It is also true that I keep some of the men hand-cuffed, and only regret I cannot have some of them shot. Deserters who have twice escaped and who are constantly trying to escape, men who draw their bayonets on officers, and who stab their comrades are I think fit subjects for irons whilst awaiting trial.

On the subject of leave from camp &c I submit the following rules. All men not on duty may leave camp without passes between company drill and dinner roll call or from 10 A.M. to 12. M, and again from 12.30 to 1.30 P.M, making in all three hours daily. I have a vivid recollection of the time when I did not spend that time from my regiment in one year, and think that three hours daily is sufficent for these men of tender and domestic feelings to enjoy in the bosoms of their families.

Prowling over the country between tattoo & reveille is entirely stopped, in fact it never existed, and that is of course the time the badly disposed men want to commit outrages. I have the honor to be, General, Very respectfully, Your obed' Servt

ALS   F. W. Lister

George Buck Hanon to Genel thoms, 19 Nov. 1865, and Col. F. W. Lister to Brigr. Genl. W. D. Whipple, 14 Dec. 1865, Letters Received, 40th USCI, Regimental Books & Papers USCT, RG 94 [G-190]. Endorsements.

⁓⊰⊱⁓

312A: Affidavit of a Northern Missionary

Camp Nelson Ky Dec. 16" 1864

Personally appeared before me E B W Resticaux Capt and A.Q.M. Abisha Scofield who being duly sworn upon oath says. I am a clergyman of the congregational denomination and have been laboring among the Freedmen at Camp Nelson Ky. under the auspices of the American Missionary association since the 20th of Sept 1864. The families of the colored solders who were in Camp lived in cabins and huts erected by the colored solders or at the expense of the women. During my labors among them I have witnessed about fifty of these huts and cabins erected and the material of which they were constructed was unserviceable to the Government. I have had extensive dealing with these people and from my observation I believe that they supported themselves by washing cooking and &c.

Until the 22nd of last November I never heard any objection made by the military authorities of the Post to the women and children of colored soldiers residing within the limits of the

715

camp. On Tuesday the 22nd of November last the huts and cabins in which the families of the colored soldiers lived were torn down and the inhabitants were placed in Government wagons and driven outside the lines. The weather at the time was the coldest of the season. The wind was blowing quite sharp and the women and children were thinly clad and mostly without shoes. They were not all driven out on one day but their expulsion occupied about three days.

When they were driven out I did not know where they were to be taken and on the following Sabbath Nov 27" I went in search of the exiles. I found them in Nicholasville about six miles from Camp scattered in various places. Some were in an old Store house, some were straying along and lying down in the highway and all appeared to be suffering from exposure to the weather. I gave them some food. I received the provisions from Capt T. E. Hall A.Q.M.

The food was absolutely needed. On Monday Nov. 28 I saw and conversed with about sixteen women and children who had walked from Nicholasville in the hopes of getting into Camp. The guard refused them admittance. I told the guard that the order by which the women and children were expelled had been countermanded. The guard told me that he had strict orders not to admit them   They were not admitted. Among the number was a young woman who was quite sick and while I was conversing with the guard she lay on the ground. A day or two after this they were allowed to return to Camp. They were then very destitute most all complaining of being unwell. Children trembling with cold and wearied with fatigue. Since that time they have been crowded in a school room in Camp and their condition has been most abject and miserable, whereas they were pretty comfortable before they were driven out. While out of Camp they incurred disease and are now suffering from the effects of this exposure   As a clergyman I have no hesitation in pronouncing the treatment to which these poor people have been subjected as exceedingly demoralizing in its effects in addition to the physical suffering it entailed. And further this deponent saith not

HDcSr   (Signed) Abisha Scofield

Affidavit of Abisha Scofield, 16 Dec. 1864, filed with H-8 1865, Registered Letters Received, ser. 3379, TN Asst. Comr., RG 105 [A-6148]. Sworn before an assistant quartermaster at Camp Nelson. Several affidavits by other Camp Nelson missionaries and by black soldiers and their wives are in the same file.

312B: Superintendent of the "Refugee Home" at Camp
Nelson, Kentucky, to the Freedmen's Bureau Commissioner

Camp Nelson [*Ky.*] June 22nd 1865

General, I have the honor to submit for your consideration the
following statement of facts relative to the "Home" for the wives
and children of colored soldiers which was established in this
Camp by order of the Hon. Secy. of War.

First as to its origin. Last Autum and Winter there were
congregated in this Camp some four hundred woman and children
the families of colored soldiers   They in most instances were
forced to leave their former homes by the ill treatment to which
they were subjected on account of the enlistment of their husbands
and fathers in the Army — On or about the 20$''$ of Nov. 1864 the
officer then in command of this Post ordered these people to be
expelled. The Provost Marshal executed the order even to the
tearing down of the rude cabins they had formerly occupied. No
provision had been made for them. The weather was intensely
cold   To have seen them would have melted to pity any heart not
already hardened by familiarity with such suffering   For miles the
roads were lined with these poor sufferers. Many died; and many
contracted diseases from which, but few ever entirely
recovered. Be pleased to bear in mind that these were the families
of soldiers who were even then in the field fighting for that
Government which was causing all this suffering to their people. I
have been for a long time identified with these poor and suffering
people and was everywhere known as their friend. They begged of
me to interfere on their behalf. I did so. I telegraphed to Gen
Burbridge, then at Cumberland Gap. He sent the substance of my
dispatch to the Secy. of War, The order expelling them from
Camp was promptly countermanded and the officers stationed at
Camp directed to provide them with food and shelter. Being then
in Camp I was directed to superintend the work and organize a
Home for these poor people.

This, General, was the origin of the "Home." I have been in
charge of it from that day to the present. I am aware that I have
incurred the ire of the slaveholder. For this I care not. I am well
aware that they have boasted that they would have me sent out of
the State. This I have laughed at. The time, I apprehend has
gone by for a man to be tried, convicted, and condemned
unheard. I am aware that they have boasted that you would break
up this Home. This I did not believe until you have at least
listened to the other side of the question. I pledge myself to show
that this Home is almost the only protection the poor colored

woman has. Not a day passes during which free colored women are not imprisoned and whipped by the slave power in Kentucky. Not a day passes during which I am not entreated by some poor defenceless wife or child to interfere for their protection against the fury of their master. I beg you to examine this subject carefully ere you decide to discontinue this "Home"; this "city of refugee" to which they can flee and be safe.

For myself I ask nothing. I have no desire to remain one hour as Superintendent of this institution. But I do ask, in the name of the plighted faith of the government that there shall be some protection for these poor, defenceless creatures. Protection from the present prejiduce growing out of the fact that these colored men for once in their lives dared to act for themselves; and offered themselves as a shield for the protection of the institutions of the country. As an illustration of this prejudice let me say that the wife and the child of a colored soldier cannot have a burial in some places in Ky. Only this day a colored woman walked from Nicholasville six miles, bringing in her arms the *body of her dead child* because the Chivalry in Nicholasville, through prejiduce refused it burial! The child was brought to me and I had it buried. Remember, I beseech you that this was the child of a soldier, and that soldier away from his family, in the field fighting for that Government that did not or could not protect the body of his own child from insult. I beg your candid and careful perusal of the accompanying affidavits particularly those of Joseph Miller and Albert A. Livermore

Pardon me for troubling you but I felt the importance of the subject demanded this hasty presentation, I most respectfully ask for an investigation before I am condemned. If I cannot prove the facts as I have represented them, then let my enemies triumph

Justice is all I ask and that I have a right to demand I have the honor to be General Very Respectfully Your Obedient Servant

ALS   T. E. Hall

T. E. Hall to Major Genl. Howard, 22 June 1865, filed with H-8 1865, Registered Letters Received, ser. 3379, TN Asst. Comr., RG 105 [A-6149]. Endorsements, enclosures. The affidavits mentioned are among the enclosures.

313: Commander of a Tennessee Black Regiment to the Headquarters of the Department of the Mississippi and a Report by the Superintendent of Freedmen in West Tennessee

Memphis. Tenn. Jan. 11th 1865

Sir. There are several hundred negro women living in Temporary huts, between the camp of this regiment and the city, who have no visible means of support, and who are, for the most part, idle, lazy vagrants, committing depredations, and exercising a very pernicious influence over the colored soldiers of this Post. They are generally in a destitute condition, and their wants are partially supplied by soldiers of colored regiments who claim them as wives. The influence of these women over the members of my regiment is such, that I have great difficulty in keeping my men in camp nights, and have to be continually watchful and vigilent and enforc the severest penalties, in order to maintain any thing like satisfactory discipline, and attention to duties on the part of my men. They also carry off rations from the companies in spite of the utmost vigilence of company commanders, and also carry off axes, shovels, spades, and picks, wherever they can be found, to use in building, and maintaining these households. The soldiers of my regiment also steal each others clothing for their families to wear and dispose of. I am compeled to enforce punishments continualy. for offences relating in some manner to these women. Soldiers who are out nights are of no use while out of camp, and of very littl use for active duty when in camp. The most serious obsticle I have to contend with in enforcing discipline arrises from this increasing evil. As long as these women are allowed to remain where they are, it will be impossible to enforce that discipline which is requisite for efficiency, in my regiment; and I earnestly request for the benefit of the service, and for the sake of humanity, that these families be removed to Presidents Island where they will be much better cared for, and where they will be no detriment to the service, and society at large. I am very respectfully Your Obdt. Servt.

HLS

John Foley

Memphis, Tenn., 24 Jany *1865.*

Captain: I have the honor to state, that in attempting to carry out the request made by Lieut Col Foley, in the inclosed communication, I detailed a guard of (12) Twelve men from Companies "B" and "K" 63^d U.S.C.I. who with all the teams at my disposal, I sent with Lieut Bush to accomplish the work— The Lieut commenced with a will, but has had very poor success on account of not having a stronger detail— The people are unwilling to be moved, and will give no assistance themselves, but lock their doors, and run to their husbands in the various military organizations for protection— The husbands swear their families shall not be moved to the Island and in some instances have come out under arms to prevent it

Owing to these and various other circumstances, all the men that I can send to the work are necessary for guards—

I would therefore request that a detail of (20) Twenty men with (4) Four non-commissioned officers, be ordered to report at this office, for fatigue duty, daily—Sundays excepted—until the work of removal is accomplished.

The removal of this class of dependent and almost helpless people, together with the necessary provisions for their immediate comfort, is no light and withall a very unthankful job, and as my facilities are so circumscribed, I think that I may without presumption, ask the cooperation of all those who are alike interested— I am Capt Very Respectfully Your Obt. Servt.

T A Walker

I would also request a guard of ten men to accompany the detail called for   T A Walker Capt & Supt Freedmen

ALS

Lieut. Col. John Foley to Lieut. Col. T. Harris, 11 Jan. 1865, filed with Capt. T. A. Walker to Capt. J. S. Lord, 24 Jan. 1865, Unregistered Letters & Reports Received, ser. 2870, Dist. of West TN, RG 393 Pt. 2 No. 183 [C-2203]. Endorsements. Foley commanded the 61st USCI. Efforts to remove black soldiers' families from the area near the Memphis garrison had begun at least as early as March 1864, as had the soldiers' resistance to such plans. (Col. J. G. Kappner to Lieut. Geo. A. Mason, 4 Mar. 1864, Letters Received, 3rd USCHA, Regimental Books & Papers USCT, RG 94 [G-9].) In April 1864, Lieutenant Colonel John Phillips, superintendent of freedmen in the district of West Tennessee offered employment on plantations near Helena, Arkansas, stating that "under existing orders the families of Colored Soldiers must be made self-supporting and I assure them in all kindness that it is for their interest to go voluntarily." He added that from Helena "they can have daily communication by Boat with their husbands at Memphis." (Circular, Office Supt. Freedmen West Tenn., 4 Apr. 1864, Letters Received, ser. 2910, Organization of U.S. Colored Troops, Dist. of West TN, RG 393 Pt. 2 No. 183 [C-2204].) By July 1864, army policy focused upon relocating the families to President's Island, in the Mississippi River. (Lt. Col. A. L. Mitchell to Major W. H. Morgan, 28 July 1864, filed with P-320 1864, Letters Received, ser. 2869, Dist. of West TN, RG 393 Pt. 2 No. 183 [C-2222].)

314A: Virginia Black Soldier's Wife to the Commander of the Department of Virginia and North Carolina

Portsmouth Va February 28th 1864

Sir the fowlling order No 49 in your department was orderd that all the Soljurs[s] wives of collor should be supplied with rations and wood if they ware in the need of it. my husband is the first U S volunteer Col) cavalry at fort moroe. I have made sevel reports for wood and have bin objectad in Portsmouth at the quartermaster department. Sir you will plase to attend to it as I am in the need of some wood Yours

ALS Ann Sumner

Ann Sumner to Major Genl. Buler, 28 Feb. 1864, S-95 1864, Letters Received, ser. 5063, Dept. of VA & NC, RG 393 Pt. 1 [C-3028]. Endorsements. General Benjamin F. Butler referred the letter to the quartermaster at Portsmouth, who reported that since he had received no orders to furnish wood to such applicants, he referred all requests to the superintendent of Negro affairs. The order to which Sumner refers was actually numbered as General Order 46, issued by General Butler on December 5, 1863. It specified that the family of each black recruit "so long as he shall remain in the service and behave well, shall be furnished suitable subsistence, under the direction of the superintendent of Negro Affairs, or their assistants; and each soldier shall be furnished with a certificate of subsistence for his family as soon as he is mustered." (General Orders No. 46, Head Quarters Dept. of Va. and North Carolina, 5 Dec. 1863, vol. 52 VaNc, General Orders Issued, ser. 5078, Dept. of VA & NC, RG 393 Pt. 1 [C-3062].)

314B: Commander of the Department of Virginia to the Commander of the District of Eastern Virginia

Richmond, Va., May 12th *1865.*

General. In reply to your note on the subject of issuing rations to families of negro soldiers, I have to reply that it is not deemed proper to stop the issue suddenly by any general order, simply because it might raise a cry at the North, but you can issue orders to the various superintendants to open intelligence offices, in each, to gather the unemployed women and hire them out, and in case no means of employment offers, to try and find work for them, as nurses to hospitals, to make clothing or wash for prisoners, or for the other negroes, detail them as laundresses for the Companies of the 25th Corps in the field, and send them to the Companies where they have, or claim to have husbands, or if every other source of labor fails, gather these women and children into buildings and open a grand *general* washing establishment for the city, where clothing of any one will be washed gratis.

A little hard work and confinement will soon induce them to find employment, and the ultra philanthropists will not be shocked. Very Respectfully Your Obedient Servant

HLS   E. O. C. Ord

Major General E. O. C. Ord to Brig. Genl. George H. Gordon, 12 May 1865, Unregistered Letters & Telegrams Received, ser. 3799, VA Asst. Comr., RG 105 [A-7526].

314C: Commander of the District of Eastern Virginia to the Virginia Freedmen's Bureau Assistant Commissioner

Norfolk, Va. June 6th, 1865.

Sir: I understand that you are feeding with Government rations, from fifteen hundred to two thousand colored persons, families of colored soldiers, many, if not all of these persons being able to gain a livelihood by work.

You claim that such an indefensible proceeding is justified by a contract with the colored soldier, made upon enlistment, by Major General Butler, which contract, you state, was made in 1863, and is contained in General Orders No. 46, dated, Head Quarters 18th Army Corps, Department of Virginia and North Carolina, Fort Monroe, V,a, Dec. 5th, 1863, and is, in terms, as follows: that the colored soldier shall receive $10. Bounty, $10. Pay per month, and support of his family.

You are aware that early in 1864, Congress raised the pay, clothing and rations of the colored soldier to an equality with the white soldier.

I do not consider the United States Government, through its agent, Maj. Genl. Butler, bound by the contract of Dec. 5, 1863, since the pay of the colored soldier was raised; the reasons for the contract failing, and the necessity no longer existing, you will at once discontinue an issue so pernicious in its effects to the colored persons, so unwarranted by precedent, and so exhaustive upon the public treasury.

None of these families will receive rations after the tenth of this month, unless they are such as, in Northern towns, would be admitted to the county poor house.

You will immediately advise all interested of this order. A copy will be sent to the Commissary General of Subsistence. Respectfully

HLcS

Geo H Gordon

Brig. Genl. Geo. H. Gordon to Capt. O. Brown, 6 June 1865, vol. 88/174 VaNc, pp. 168–69, Letters Sent, ser. 1622, Dist. of Eastern VA, RG 393 Pt. 2 No. 72 [C-3129]. Just one day earlier, the adjutant general of the army had also strongly recommended that rations no longer be issued to black soldiers' families, "for so long as they receive this bounty from the Government, they remain in idleness, and make little or no effort to help themselves." He acknowledged that when blacks were first enlisted, support of their families "may have been necessary" because their pay was so low, "but now, when their pay is equal to that of a white soldier, they are abundantly able to provide for their families." (Adjutant General [L. Thomas] to Hon. Edwin M. Stanton, 5 June 1865, L. Thomas Letters & Orders, Generals' Papers & Books, ser. 159, RG 94 [V-56].)

314D: Commander of a Black Cavalry Brigade to the Headquarters of the 25th Army Corps

[Brazos Santiago, Texas June 1865]

The majority of the 1st and 2^d Regt^s USC Cavalry are residents of Portsmouth & Norfolk & vicinity, and the 2 USC.C. having met their families and Children (nearly 1000 as I am informed) they were unwilling to leave them unprovided with money or rations. Consequently they became excited and decidedly insubordinate. At which juncture Major Dollard Comd'g instead of being with his men on shore to rule and prevent outrage, retired to the Cabin of the Steamer and some time after called the Line Officers away from their Commands, probably for consultation thus leaving the men on shore unrestrained by their presence.

During the excitement some (20) twenty Men deserted and left with their families, but in a few hours order was restored and the leaders of the Mutiny I took from the Boat – placed in irons, and have them in custody

All the men appearing contented before seeing their families, and even afterward promptly obeyed all orders in arresting their comrades but were enraged at the threat of using white troops to coerce them, as was offerred by Major Dollard 2^d USC.C. –

723

I found the same feeling of discontent and insubordination in the 1s Regt USC Cavalry. Many were wishing to see their families and being unable to make any provision for their support from not having been paid and rations having been stopped to Soldiers wives—

Major Brown, Comd'g 1″ USC.C. while this state of affairs prevailed left his Command and was absent at Norfolk all night leaving his Arms on the dock at Fort Monroe, and his Troops in charge of his subordinate officers who found it necessary to shoot (not fatally) one man and turn over to me six more whom I ironed.

With the exception of Major Brown 1″ USCC and Major Dollard 2 USC.C. the officers of the Brigade both Staff and Regimental were all prompt and dutiful, and for their close attention to duty, and sober, earnest labor in the prompt and thorough embarkation of this Command, (no boat being detained an hour) they merit my warmest thanks, not one being behind time or neglecting an order a course of conduct which if pursued by their superiors would I am convinced have prevented any disturbance whatever, for every man left Camp as cheerfully as ever before.

I should have placed both Major Brown and Major Dollard in arrest but for the apparant encouragement to the insubordinate enlisted men—

I have mentioned the condition of the families &c not as an excuse for the conduct of the men but showing the cause of the excitement and the stupidity of permitting them the inflamatory stimulus of free intercourse with the howling multitude—

We arrived at Mobile Bay the 23ᵈ inst having had a smooth voyage of seven (7) days where (Fort Morgan) we found orders to proceed to Brazos Santiago, Texas.

A Report of the voyage from Mobile Bay to Brazos Texas will be forwarded as soon as practicable. I remain Very Respectfully Your Obedient Servant

HLfS

Geo. W. Cole

Brevet Brig. General Geo. W. Cole to [25th Army Corps Headquarters], [June 1865], Miscellaneous Letters, Orders, Reports & Circular Letters Received, ser. 518, 25th Army Corps, RG 393 Pt. 2 No. 9 [C-4507]. The 1st USCC and 2nd USCC sailed from Norfolk, Virginia, for the Southwest about June 10, 1865, the day General George Gordon's order cutting off rations went into effect. On June 17 the Virginia Freedmen's Bureau assistant commissioner reported that "mismanagement" had produced the "mutiny" of black troops about to leave for Texas. He cited "recent District orders reducing the ration one half, the non payment of a part of the troops for the past eight or ten months, together with stories set afloat by the inhabitants that they were to be 'colonized in Texas' (of which these people have a great horror)." (Capt. O. Brown to Maj. Genl. O. O. Howard, 17 June 1865, B-169 1865, Letters Received, ser. 15, Washington Head-quarters, RG 105 [A-7460].)

1 The first page or pages are missing. The events described in the surviving portion of the letter took place as several regiments from the 25th Army Corps, recently shipped down the James River to Norfolk, Virginia, awaited embarkation for Texas.

314E: Anonymous Virginia Black Soldiers to an Unidentified Washington Official

Brazos Santiago Texas, Dec 1865

Sir   here is my Compliment & wishes to be pertectd by the War Department

1ˢᵗ U S Colred Cavalry   sir Wee present to you our sufering at present Concerning our Famileys wich wee are now informed that Commisserys has been Closed a gainst them as though wee were rebeling a gainst U S. and has Came to be a great Wonder & a great Contemplation a mung the men of this regt and wee would be happay to find some one to pertect us in thes Case   Wee have been on Dayley fetig from the Last of Juli up to this Day without a forlough or any comfort what ever & our wifes sends Letters stateing thir suferage saying that they are without wood without wrashions without money and no one to pertect them   Wee have Done the best that wee can do and trys to obey orders and would pleassed to know the Cause of our Dishonorble in treatment   Wee have been exspecting to be musered out of the Army. Why because wee knew the men wich wee have taken for our friends was acquinted with what Liberty. wee have been granted up to this time and for that cause wee thought that it would please any good hearted man to turn us out of servis to the pertecttion of our be loved wifes   and if there be any man North or south Let him say to Day what shell be our pertecttion for this Day wee Disiaer to know.

here wee have come in as U S. Soldiers and are treated as Slaves   never was wee any more treated Like slaves then wee are now in our Lives   I well remember before the Closeing of the war that men who was fighting a gainst the U S. how thir wifes were pertected and if our wifes were half pertected as they were wee would be happy men. Wee are said to be U S Soldiers and behold wee are U S Slaves   Wee are now well acquinted with earley

Dec 1865 Brazos Santiago, Texas.
to U S C C Sir here is my
Compliments & Wishes to be perfected
by the War Department
of U S Colred Cavalry Sir we
present to you our Sufering
at present concerning our
familys Wich we are now
informed that Commissderys has
been Closed against them as
though we were rebeling against
U S. and has came to be a great
Wonder & a great Contemplation
among the men of this regt
and we would be happy
to find some one to protect
us in thes Case we have been
on Easey fetig from the Last
of fute up to this Day
without a forlough or any Comfort
whatever & our Wifes sends
Letters stateing thier Suferage

riseing and Late bed time and such things wit wich has been don here of Late is a shame to. be. don before the men of the south

Wee had rather pay for our next years serviss and be turned out then to stay in and no pertecttion granted to our wife

Sir wee would be verey much pleased to be Dis banded from the field and if the War Department Can not spar us or spar the time. wee. will. pay them for one years. servis. in the beside what soldiering wee have done   Wee onley wish the pertecttion of our wifes and as we has been all ways been so acomodated with the Law for any thing that wee do young [*wrong*] wee now wish to be comodated for what wee have done right   and if I have said any thing young I pray to be exc. your obeient U S Servts

also wee cant get a forlough unless paying $60 Dollars and wee thinks verey hard of it

HL

Unsigned to Sir, Dec. 1865, A-8 1866, Letters Received, ser. 360, Colored Troops Division, RG 94 [B-203]. The 1st U.S. Colored Cavalry was organized in Virginia and served in that state until transferred to Texas in June 1865.

313A: **Assistant Superintendent of Negro Affairs at Roanoke Island, North Carolina, and Several Missionary Teachers to the Freedmen's Bureau Commissioner**

Roanoke Island. N.C. June 5" 1865

General   In behalf of suffering humanity which it is not within our power to relieve, we appeal to you trusting that the necessity of the case may be sufficient reason for addressing you personally and directly

There are about thirty five hundred blacks upon this island, the larger part of whom are dependents of the following classes, viz. Aged and Infirm, Orphan children and soldiers wives and families. Of these about twenty seven hundred have (including children) drawn rations from the Government, and by this assistance and the exertions of benevolent Societies they have been cared for, though not without extreme suffering in many instances up to the present time.

Those who are able to work have proved themselves industrious and would support themselves, had they the opportunity to do so, under favorable circumstances. The able bodied males with few exceptions are in the army, and there are not many families on the Island that have not furnished a father, husband or son, and in numerous instances, two and three members to swell the ranks of our army. And these left their families and enlisted with the assurance from the Government that their families should be cared for, and supported in their absence.

The issue of rations has been reduced, so that only about fifteen hundred now receive any subsistence from the Government. The acre of ground allotted to each family has been cleared and tilled, to the best of their ability—but this has only produced a very small part of what has been, and is required for family consumption.

We know that it is not the design of the government to support those who will not work, in idleness, nor is it the wish of those who make this representation as this would [be] an evil not Second to slavery itself

Nor is it to complain of the spirit of the government towards this unfortunate class, but to state the facts of their condition as they exist and bespeak such assistance as humanity shall dictate to the infirm and helpless, and such support as may be justly claimed for the families of soldiers whose wants the Government is bound to supply until they can be placed in a position to be able to Sustain themselves.

If it is the design of the Government to return these families to their former masters to be supported and cared for by them, this design has not been explained to them, and no facilities have been afforded them to leave the island, while the sweeping reduction of the rations brings hundreds suddenly face to face with starvation.

There are numerous cases of orphan children who have been taken in, and afforded a shelter while subsistence was furnished, who are now cast off because they have nothing to eat.

There are many who are sick and disabled whose ration has been cut off, and these instances are not isolated, but oft recurring and numerous. It is a daily occurrence to see scores of women and children crying for bread, whose husbands, Sons and fathers are in the army today, and because these things are fully known, and understood by those whose duty it is to attend to, and remedy them and disregarded by them. we appeal to a Source more remote and out of the ordinary channel.

We do this with a feeling that the emergency demands immediate action to prevent suffering which justice, humanity, and every principle of christianity forbids

With the hope of immediate investigation which Shall bring with it a Speedy relief, We remain Your Obt Ser'ts

W^m A Green	Susan Odell
Caroline A Green	Mrs. R. S. D. Holbrook
Amasa Walker Stevens	Ella Roper
Mrs S. P. Freeman	E. P. Bennett
Esther A. Williams	Kate L. Freeman

HLS

728

Chaplain Wm. A. Green et al. to Maj. Genl. O. O. Howard, 5 June 1865, Unregistered Letters Received, ser. 2453, NC Asst. Comr., RG 105 [A-643].

315B: North Carolina Black Soldiers to the Freedmen's Bureau Commissioner

[*City Point?, Va. May or June 1865*]

Genl   We the soldiers of the 36 U.S.Col Reg^t Humbly petition to you to alter the Affairs at Roanoke Island. We have served in the US Army faithfully and don our duty to our Country, for which we thank God (that we had the opportunity) but at the same time our family's are suffering at Roanoke Island N.C.

1   When we were enlisted in the service we were prommised that our wifes and family's should receive rations from goverment. The rations for our wifes and family's have been (and are now cut down) to one half the regular ration. Consequently three or four days out of every ten days, thee have nothing to eat. at the same time our ration's are stolen from the ration house by Mr Streeter the Ass^t Sup^t at the Island (and others) and sold while our family's are suffering for some thing to eat.

2nd Mr Steeter the Ass^t Sup^t of Negro aff's at Roanoke Island is a througher Cooper head a man who says that he is no part of a Abolitionist. takes no care of the colored people and has no Simpathy with the colored people. A man who kicks our wives and children out of the ration house or commissary, he takes no notice of their actual suffering and sells the rations and allows it to be sold, and our family's suffer for something to eat.

3rd Captn James the Suptn in Charge has been told of these facts and has taken no notice of them. so has Coln Lahaman the Commander in Charge of Roanoke, but no notice is taken of it, because it comes from Contrabands or Freedmen   the cause of much suffering is that Captn James has not paid the Colored people for their work for near a year and at the same time cuts the ration's off to one half so the people have neither provisions or money to buy it with. There are men on the Island that have been wounded at Dutch Gap Canal, working there, and some discharged soldiers, men that were wounded in the service of the U.S. Army, and returned home to Roanoke that Cannot get any rations and are not able to work, some soldiers are sick in Hospitals that have never been paid a cent and their familys are suffering and their children going crying without anything to eat.

729

4th our familys have no protection the white soldiers break into our houses act as they please steal our chickens rob our gardens and if any one defends their-Selves against them they are taken to the gard house for it. so our familys have no protection when Mr Streeter is here to protect them and will not do it.

5th. Genl we the soldiers of the 36 U.S. Co Troops having familys at Roanoke Island humbly petition you to favour us by removeing Mr Streeter the present Asst Supt at Roanoke Island under Captn James.

Genl prehaps you think the Statements against Mr Streeter too strong, but we can prove them.

Genl order Chaplain Green to Washington to report the true state of things at Roanoke Island. Chaplain Green is an asst Supt at Roanoke Island, with Mr Holland Streeter and he can prove the facts. and there are plenty of white men here that can prove them also, and many more thing's not mentioned   Signed in behalf of humanity

Richard Etheredge
Wm Benson

HLS

Sergt. Richard Etheredge and Wm. Benson to Genl. Howard, [May or June 1865], Unregistered Letters Received, ser. 2453, NC Asst. Comr., RG 105 [A-648]. Another soldier in the 36th USCI reported to his brigade commander, just before the regiment was shipped from Virginia to Texas, that the issue of rations to his family at Roanoke Island had been cut off. He protested that "when I inlisted in the united states Service the Goverment made Promis for to have them Taken Care off." General Alonzo G. Draper, the brigade commander, forwarded the letter up the chain of command with the following endorsement: "The colored soldiers recruited in this Department under Maj. Gen. Butler had the pledge of the government that their families should receive rations." When the complaint reached General O. O. Howard, commissioner of the Freedmen's Bureau, he referred it to the North Carolina Freedmen's Bureau assistant commissioner with instructions to continue ration issues to soldiers' families until further orders. (Frank James to Genrell A. G. Draiper, 4 June 1865, and endorsements, Unregistered Letters Received, ser. 2453, NC Asst. Comr., RG 105 [A-647].)

PART 5

Black Soldiers in Postwar America

17

Black Soldiers in the Postwar Army of Occupation

WITH WAR'S END, War Department officials began demobilizing the huge volunteer army while retaining enough soldiers to occupy the defeated South. Both the shortage of men in the regular army and the abundance of volunteers, whom the war's final campaigns had drawn to the various Confederate states, guaranteed a preponderance of volunteer troops in the occupation army. Thus necessity and convenience combined to ensure that the defeated South would face uniformed black, as well as white, victors. That experience would have a lasting impact on both former masters and former slaves.

Because whites entered the army earlier than blacks, their terms of enlistment generally expired sooner; demobilization therefore left the postwar Union army blacker than the wartime forces. At the end of the war, blacks composed about 11 percent of the approximately 1,000,000 Union soldiers, but by the fall of 1865, when the entire army had shrunk to some 227,000 men, blacks made up roughly 36 percent of the total.[1] Generally, Southern black soldiers remained close to where they had enlisted, in areas that had boasted large antebellum black populations and that had fallen under federal control earliest. In October 1865, for example, Mississippi and Louisiana hosted more than 27,000 black soldiers between them, and Kentucky and Tennessee accounted for another 22,000. Thus, more than half of the 83,000 black troops in the army at that date served in those four states. Except for the coastal strip that Union forces had initially occupied, states like Alabama, Florida, Georgia, and South Carolina experienced little wartime black recruitment until the Union army spread across their territory in the closing months of the war. As a result, black troops constituted only a small portion of postwar federal forces in those states.[2]

---

[1] The end-of-the-war figure was calculated from official estimates of 123,156 black soldiers among the 1,052,038 soldiers in the entire Union army. (*Official Records*, ser. 3, vol. 5, p. 138, and vol. 4, p. 1283.) Estimates from September 1865 derive from figures of 83,079 blacks in an army of 226,611 men. (*Official Records*, ser. 3, vol. 5, p. 114.)

[2] *Official Records*, ser. 3, vol. 5, p. 114.

Although the War Department retained most Southern black soldiers where they had enlisted and served, it intervened to send others far afield. For example, the department moved masses of troops from Virginia to the Rio Grande border of Texas shortly after the Confederate surrender in the East. These soldiers from the eastern theater were sent to defeat the Confederate troops west of the Mississippi, to cut off Jefferson Davis's anticipated escape across the border, and to counter French-backed Monarchist forces in Mexico. The black 25th Army Corps, considered too undisciplined and too poorly officered for occupation duty in Virginia, figured prominently among those troops reassigned.[3] The move transplanted some 10,000 black soldiers—mostly from Kentucky, Maryland, Virginia, North Carolina, and the North—to Texas, taking them far (or farther) from their homes, and leaving Virginia, the state with the largest antebellum slave population, virtually bereft of black liberators.

Army policies not only concentrated black soldiers in some parts of the South and removed them entirely from others, but also shaped the composition of the black occupation force. During the fall of 1865, the War Department determined to disband all Northern-raised black regiments regardless of the demobilization orders governing the larger command structures to which they belonged.[4] As a result, by the end of the year, the army of occupation no longer included those black soldiers with the longest experience in freedom. Thus the army's patterns of assignment and discharge influenced both the experience of black soldiers in the postwar world and their relations with the Southern population, white and black.

Union occupation forced many Southern whites into daily contact with black soldiers. In the urban South, blacks often served as provost guards, in effect policing the cities. On sidewalks and in public houses and buildings, whites met black soldiers claiming equality if not superiority. Such encounters frequently produced verbal or physical confrontations which, at times, led to more widespread disturbances. In the rural South, black soldiers came into contact with plantation laborers and, with the enthusiasm of former slaves turned liberators, pressed to eradicate the remnants of slavery. In thousands of ways, black soldiers communicated to freedmen and freedwomen the meaning of the war, the role black people played in defeating the Confederacy and destroying slavery, the new rights liberty allowed, and the new responsibilites it demanded. While they rarely joined freedpeople in redressing old wrongs and in evening scores with former masters, black soldiers regularly helped organize and

---

[3] *Official Records*, ser. 1, vol. 46, pt. 3, pp. 990, 1005–6; vol. 48, pt. 2, pp. 476, 525–26, 647, 716–17.
[4] *Official Records*, ser. 3, vol. 5, p. 108.

build schools, churches, and other social institutions in the black communities where they served. In one Arkansas town, black soldiers even paid for and constructed a home for black orphans.

Black soldiers also encouraged freedpeople to expand the horizons of freedom and stood armed and willing to defend from retaliation fellow blacks seeking to make freedom a reality. "After fighting to get wrights that White men might Respect by Virtue of the Law," black soldiers would tolerate no abuse of their people. Because they had seen more of white society than most plantation hands and had gained familiarity with the workings of the Union army, black soldiers stood prepared to help former slaves articulate their grievances and direct them to appropriate authorities. In this regard, the War Department's decision to disband the Northern black regiments had a profound effect on the freedpeople's quest for equality under the tutelage of black soldiers: the struggle proceeded without the self-confident and self-conscious Northern black liberators who generally had the highest literacy rate and the longest term of service of all black soldiers and who had taken such prominent part in the struggle for equal pay and equal treatment in the army.

To the extent that black soldiers relished their role in the army of occupation, white Southerners loathed it. More than any other post-bellum figure, the black soldier represented the world turned upside down: the subversion of slavery, the destruction of the Confederacy, and the coming of a new social order that promised to differ pro-foundly from the old. At best, whites reacted to black soldiers with silent contempt; often that contempt found active manifestation. Some whites struck out at black soldiers, attacking them in the manner Southern whites traditionally used to deal with violators of their code of racial etiquette. But disgruntled whites who contemplated violence against armed blacks courted danger, especially when the intended victims wore the uniform of the victorious Union army. An assault on a black soldier, even if it was an immediate success, might bring down upon a community the full force of federal military power. And if Union authorities often responded slowly, black soldiers did not take kindly to the abuse of their comrades and frequently preferred immediate retaliation to dilatory official action.

Unable to intimidate black soldiers, whites charted a different course. They accused black soldiers of sowing insubordination among their laborers and fomenting insurrection with extravagant tales of land distribution and high-flown notions of equality. Viewing the disruption of their labor force as tantamount to the destruction of Southern society, former masters conjured up all their deep-seated fears of the horrors of Haiti. They pressed for immediate removal of black soldiers from the South, especially those attached to Freedmen's Bureau offices who assisted bureau agents in adjudicating labor disputes and investigating blacks' complaints of mistreatment.

Southern white protesters found support among some Union commanders who believed that the presence of black troops undermined labor discipline and jeopardized harmonious relations between former masters and former slaves. Such army officers kept tight rein on their black troops, limiting them to their posts and warning them of their responsibilities as Union soldiers. Some even recommended the removal of black units from areas of pronounced white opposition. In Virginia, for example, General Henry W. Halleck, commanding at Richmond after the Confederate defeat, ordered all black troops into a camp for instruction to overcome an alleged lack of discipline that he felt ill fitted them for occupation duty. At bottom, Halleck sought to forestall their potentially disquieting effect on Virginia's black labor force during the rapidly ending planting season. Within weeks he proposed their reassignment to Texas, thus removing approximately 10,000 perceived troublemakers from Virginia.[5]

Most officers, including General Godfrey Weitzel, commander of the 25th Army Corps, defended the performance of their men, commending their discipline and restraint under trying circumstances.[6] While the presence of black soldiers undoubtedly emboldened freedpeople to press their newly won rights to the full extent, army inspectors generally acknowledged the good behavior of black troops. Still, Southern whites found enough sympathetic ears to hasten the demobilization of most black regiments and to remove blacks in the army of occupation far away from disruptive contact with freedpeople and embarrassing contact with whites. As a result, by October 1866 only 12,985 men and officers of black volunteer regiments remained in service, and by October 1867 not a single black volunteer still served.[7]

The record that black soldiers compiled during the Civil War ensured them, however, a place in the peacetime regular army. The congressional act of July 1866 reorganizing the regular army provided for two black cavalry regiments and four black infantry regiments.[8] Recruited to a large extent from among Civil War veterans,[9] these regiments played a prominent, if ironic, role in sub-

---

[5] *Official Records,* ser. 1, vol. 46, pt. 3, pp. 1016, 1062, 1148.

[6] *Official Records,* ser. 1, vol. 46, pt. 3, p. 1160.

[7] *Official Records,* ser. 3, vol. 5, pp. 1029, 1047.

[8] Negro in the Military Service, pp. 4678–84, ser. 390, Colored Troops Division, RG 94 [B-484].

[9] For enthusiasm of Kentucky black volunteers about reenlistment in the regular army, see Lieut. Colonel A. Duncan to Genl. W. T. Sherman, 12 Mar. 1866, D-9 1866, Letters Received, ser. 2484, Mil. Div. of the Miss., RG 393 Pt. 1 [C-2300].

duing the Indian peoples of the West and, at the end of the century, defeating the Philippine insurrectionists. In the long run, the regiments continued to bear witness to the fighting capabilities of black soldiers, which Civil War service had established beyond doubt, just as they testified to the persistence of race segregation and inequality even after the destruction of slavery. They served both as symbol of past injustice and hope of future equality.

In the short run, black soldiers in the postwar army heightened awareness among both blacks and whites of the meaning of emancipation and the black soldiers' role in hastening it. Freedpeople continued to look to black troops as a source of inspiration, protection, and direction as they made their way in the new world of freedom. Southern whites likewise continued to see black soldiers as symbols of Southern defeat and sources of resistance in their attempts to restore the old order. As symbols of both liberation for blacks and humiliation to whites, black soldiers would play a central role in the reconstruction of Southern life.

316: Commander of U.S. Forces at Petersburg, Virginia, to the Commander of the 25th Army Corps

Petersburg &c Va May 13″ 1865

General   Many complaints are made at these H^d Qrs of depredations committed by soldiers of the 25″ Army Corps. – Consisting principally in the destruction of buildings and the exciting of the colored people to acts of outrage against the persons and property of white citizens –

It is asserted that the buildings are destroyed that the boards and timbers may be used to build huts and quarters for the soldiers, and the bricks of chimneys are carried off, probably for the same purpose – Colored soldiers are represented as having straggled about, advising Negroes not to work on the farms, where they are employed, and been told by the soldiers, that if they had not arms to use against their former masters, that they "the Soldiers" would furnish them.

Such acts must create discord and discontent, and should be stopped at once.

Beleiving that these facts need only to be brought to your knowledge to insure their correction –   I have the honor to be Respectfully Your Obt Servt

HLcS

Geo L Hartsuff

Maj. Genl. Geo. L. Hartsuff to Maj. Genl. G. Weitzel, 13 May 1865, vol. 99/202 VaNc, p. 183, Letters Sent, ser. 1683, Headquarters, U.S. Forces Petersburg, RG 393 Pt. 2 No. 75 [C-3152]. In defense of his men, General Godfrey Weitzel, commander of the 25th Army Corps, wrote to General Ulysses S. Grant's headquarters on May 16, 1865, denying all charges of irregularity and declaring, "The behavior of my entire corps during the last month has been most excellent." Two days later, General Edward O. C. Ord, commander of the Department of Virginia, endorsed Weitzel's statement: "I do not consider the behavior of the colored corps from what I have heard to have been bad, considering the novelty of their position and the fact that most of their company officers had come from positions where they were unaccustomed to command, and this was perhaps the first great temptation to which their men were exposed. In the city of Richmond their conduct is spoken of as very good." (*Official Records*, ser. 1, vol. 46, pt. 3, pp. 1160–61.)

317: Headquarters of the District of Wilmington, North Carolina, to the Commander of the Post of Wilmington

Wilmington, N.C. June 27th 1865

Colonel, The Brevt Brig Gen. Comd'g directs me to call your attention to the fact that complaints are made of the discipline and behavior of the Detachment of the 27th U.S. Colored Troopes under charge of Capt. E. F. McMurphy stationed on the line of the Wilmington and Goldsboro Rail Road.

These complaints are made by good reliable citizens and are well authenticated and are mainly as follows

1st That these soldiers are in the habit of leaving their posts and roaming through the country, visiting the houses of citizens, demanding meat, vegetables and other articles of food and committing depredations upon their Gardens and Fields.

2nd That upon the representations of the colored people residing in the neighbourhood that they have been wronged by their former masters or the persons they are labouring for these soldiers assume the responsibility of redressing their wrongs, and administering justice betweean the Freedman and his former master, an assumption of authority entirely unwarranted. There has been complaints of the same character made previous to this, and particular instructions have been given to the officers comd'g the detachment in regards to restraining their men, enforceing discipline and confineing them to the performance of the duties that wer assigned them, – namely – the guarding of the Rail Road, and ass't the Police Guard of the County in making arrests and

preserveing order when called upon. The Gen. directs that you
send instructions to Capt. M'Murphy and the officers under him
again in regard to the duties required of him and that his men be
held in proper restraint and discipline. Also inform him that in
case any more complaints are made of the bad behaviour of the
men under his command his name will be forwarded to the War
Dept. for dismissal from the service as incompetant to command or
enforce discipline. The Gen. desires that you give particular
attention to this matter   Very Respct. &c.

HLS   Edwin. O. Latimer

Capt. Edwin O. Latimer to Lieut. Col. A. G. Chamberlain, 27 June 1865,
vol. 178 VaNc, p. 152, Letters Sent, ser. 1821, Dist. of Wilmington, RG
393 Pt. 2 No. 90 [C-3172].

318: Report by an Army Officer to the Commander of the Post of Beaufort, South Carolina

[St. Helena Island, S.C. July 23, 1865]

MEMORANDUM OF EXTRACTS FROM SPEECH BY MAJOR
DELANEY,[1] AFRICAN, AT THE BRICK CHURCH,
ST. HELENA ISLAND, S.C. SUNDAY JULY 23rd 1865.

I came to talk to you in plain words so as you can understand
how to throw open the gates of oppression and let the captive
free— In this state there are 200. m. able, intelligent, honorable
negros, *not an inferior race,* mind you, who are ready to protect
their liberty, The matter is in your own hands. Yes I will fight
them and take them man by man, I want to tell you one thing,
do you know that if it was not for the black man this war never
would have been brought to a close with success to the Union,
and the liberty of your race if it had not been for the negro? I
want you to understand that— Do you know it, do you know it,
do you know it, cries of yes. yes. yes.— they can't get along
without you. Yankees from the north who come down here to
drive you as much as ever it [*was*] before the war. Its slavery over
again northern, universal U.S. slavery. But they must keep their
clamps off, If I were a slave I would be the most worthless one
on the plantation, I would not do anything. They (i.e. before the
war) have often told you, Sam, you lazy nigger, you don't earn
your salt. If you don't do better I'll sell you to the first trader
that comes along, at the same time they are making their

thousands annually on every one of you, And so it is with these yankees from the north, they don't pay you enough. I see too many of you are dressed in rags and shoeless. these yankees talk smooth to you, o, yes! their tung rolls just like a drum, (laughter) but its slavery over again as much as ever it was, I expect Gen. Saxton back very soon, he is working with me, when this matter will be settled – I mean about lands – when you can plant and work your own farms. – Don't be anxious for large places, 40 acres is Enough   cotton will bring 30. & for two years to come   that is putting it at a low estimate   (Here he explained a mathematical calculation showing that they could make $900. per year on this staple.) and then your little cabins will be floored, barns built, and carpet will take the place of bare floors. (The last paragraph is well. A.W.Jr.) – But you must only deal with the Govr. accredited agents, recognize none but authorized cotton agents. – I know that cotton has been raised by you, these fellows have told you they would send it north and sell it for you – months pass, and when you ask for money they will tell you the cotton is not yet sold. – There are good yankees and when you come across a good yankee he is smart, (Here followed a description of a yankee, the figure is yellow trousers, & claw hammer coat, dealing in wooden hams and nutmegs,) (and calculated to impress the negros with feelings of indignation towards the white people from the north now residing here, engaged in the products of this climate.) But what I don't like, and what we won't have is these fellows from the north, who were nothing at home, and ape the southerner, with a big broad brim hat, he has his overseer too, a chuckleheaded slave driver on the fence or in the crotch of a tree, and say Sam or Jim do this, do that, light my pipe, as lazy as any southerner or overseer was. –

They promise you, 30^c task, you are to get 1/3 crop – and I will see that you get it – You must not think that you are yankees. You are negros the same as I am, (he gave the idea that the real yankee is smart – but those here were not conscientious.) "There is something rotton in Denmark" –

ADS   Alexander Whyte Jr.

Memorandum by 2d Lieut. Alexander Whyte Jr., 23 July 1865, W-17 1865, Registered Letters Received, ser. 2922, SC Asst. Comr., RG 105 [A-7084]. Throughout the memorandum, Whyte interspersed "xxx" (omitted here), which he apparently intended to serve as ellipses or breaks in Delany's thoughts. Colonel Charles H. Howard, post commander at Beaufort, forwarded Whyte's memorandum to General Rufus Saxton, South Carolina Freedmen's Bureau assistant commissioner, on July 28, 1865, noting that "It is the opinion of Lt. Whyte (who was sent by me to listen to the speech . . .) that the general tone of the speech was such as to produce *discontent* among the Freedmen." By the beginning of 1866, Delany took a different approach and, in his capacity as agent of the Freedmen's Bureau, defused as much discontent among Sea Island freedpeople as he had reportedly fomented earlier. (See Maj. Genl. D. Sickles to Brig. Genl. E. D. Townsend, 30 Jan. 1866, filed with D-135 1863, Letters Received, ser. 360, Colored Troops Division, RG 94 [B-393].)

1 Major Martin R. Delany of the 104th USCI, a South Carolina black regiment. A Virginia-born free black who moved to the North as a child, Delany had been active as a recruiter of black troops in the Midwest during the war (see *Freedom,* ser. 2: doc. 37) and at the very end of the conflict became one of the Union army's small number of black commissioned officers. On the date of this speech he was serving on detached service with the Freedmen's Bureau.

319: **Inspector General of the Army to the Chief of the Bureau of Colored Troops**

Washington, D.C. August 25th 1865.
Extracts respectfully furnished for information of Chief of Bureau of Colored Troops.

Jas A Hardie
Inspector General U.S.A.

"From Insp. Reports of the *Dept. of La.* for the month of July '/65   *Eastern Dist of La. . . . Post Donaldsonville. . . .*
20th *U.S.C.I.* "During the past month this Regiment has paid strict attention to drill, and has made a very marked improvement, their movements are quick and generally correct   Officers now show life and zeal changing the whole tone of the organization. While the *Genl Commanding* has had occasion to *reprimand* some of the doing of Guard,(?) yet I must report guard duty well done, and where fault exists it is where guards are sent to report to *Officers outside the Regiment* and not relieved every day, and in my opinion the Officer having the guard in charge is most to blame. The Inspector has generally found the guards that are relieved every day efficient. In a *city* of this size *Colored Troops* on guard labor under many embarrassments, and more particularly these men, who were mostly *free before the War* and received more or less education in the free States. − Not being used to *personal abuse* before wearing the U.S. uniform they will not submit to it now, from *Citizens* they may be guarding or who may be passing their Posts: and it is my opinion that when citizens learn to respect the

uniform of the *United States Soldier* there will be less complaint about Guard duty."

. . . .

HDS

Excerpt from Inspector General Jas. A. Hardie to Brevet Col. C. W. Foster, 25 Aug. 1865, I-26 1865, Letters Received, ser. 360, Colored Troops Division, RG 94 [B-254]. Endorsements. Omitted are inspection reports of other black regiments at posts in Louisiana. The 20th USCI was organized in New York.

320: Michigan Black Sergeant to the Commander of the Department of South Carolina

Columbia S.C August 7th /65

Dear Sir   With Due Respect to you, after Coming to this pleasant City and Getting somewhat acquainted I find the freedmen are Shamefuly abused   for instance one Andrew Lee a Collord man Come in from the Country to Report some White men for Going into his house and Breaking open his trunks with a pretinse of searching for a hog that they Claimed to have lost. The Said Andrew Lee Went General Horton Commanding Post and Entered Complaint   after hearing Andrew Lees Complaint he General Horton told Lee to Go off and that he General Horton had ought to put Lee in the Guard house and that those men had a Wright to search his house   This is a queer state of things Brought about to allow those Miscreants to plunder houses Without Some officer or Written authority   Sir I am only a sergeant and of Course Should be as silent as posible But in this I Could not hold my temper After fighting to get wrights that White men might Respect By Virtue of the Law   Sir I Would further say to you try and Give those things Due Considderation   No More But Remain Yours With Respect and true friend to the Union

ALS   E S Robison

Sergt. E. S. Robison to Major General Q. A. Gilmore, 7 Aug. 1865, Letters Received, ser. 4109, Dept. of the South, RG 393 Pt. 1 [C-1382]. Endorsements indicate that General Quincy A. Gillmore ordered an investigation, which was conducted and reported, but the report does not appear in the files. Sergeant Robison served in the 102nd USCI.

321: Provost Marshal of Nottaway Court House, Virginia, to the Headquarters of the Subdistrict of Roanoke

                                 Nottoway Court House Va. Aug 26th 1865
Lieut: I have the honor to Submit the following report for the
week ending Saturday, August 26th 1865.
   Whilst troops were stationed at this place, I am pleased to say
there was not a single complaint made by the citizens against
them   they have said frequently that thier behaviour was better
than that of white troops who have been stationed here previously;
this is the testimony of people living in and around the Court
House, still they objected to having them here for fear that thier
presence would have a demorilazing effect on the colored people
which fear I thought was unfounded   true the Freed people
assembled at the barracks for the purpose of attending Church and
school (there was no other buildings suitable for that purpose than
those occupied by the Soldiers) but for no other purpose and for
any man to say that idleness was fostered there, makes a false
statement,

                                · · · ·

ALS   Thos C Bennett

Excerpt from 1st Lieut. Thos. C. Bennett to Lt. [J. F. Usher?], 26 Aug.
1865, Letters Received, ser. 1688, District of the Nottoway, RG 393 Pt.
2 No. 75 [C-3152]. The remainder of the report comments on sentiments
among local whites, the condition of blacks, and crop prospects.

322: Statement by a Tennessee Black Sergeant

                                 Memphis, Tenn., [*September 11*] 1865
   Sergt Joe. Brown. Co. D. 3^d US (Hy) states I was sitting in my
own door on Sunday night the 10" of Sept., about dark. And a
policeman who lives opposite to me on corner Brown-Avenue and
Causey Streets Named Sweatt. said to me I wish I could get a
chance to kill all the Damned Nigger Soldiers. and I said you cant
kill me — he then stepped back a few paces and ran up and struck
me with his *club*, on the head — at that time another Policeman
came up and he struck me several times. and they thru me down
and stamped me in the back while lying on the ground. My shirt
was torn off and I was badly bruised. The man who I rent of saw
this and knows the Policeman — Thy tried to take me to the

station House and told them I would not go – and about this time the Patrol came along and took me to *Irving Block*. –

I had commited no offence at the time the Policeman came for which to be arrested. I was sitting in the door with this man Tom talking quitly.

HD

Statement by Sergt. Joe Brown, [11 Sept.] 1865, Affidavits & Statements, ser. 3545, Memphis TN Provost Marshal of Freedmen, RG 105 [A-6589].

323: Testimony by a Provost Marshal's Employee before a Military Commission in the Case of a Louisiana Black Soldier

Mobile, Alabama September 18th 1865.

Robert S. Thompson, citizen of Mobile Ala. a witness for the prosecution was duly sworn and testified as follows. "I recognize the prisoner [*Sergeant William Barcroft*] to be the same soldier who was with a crowd of soldiers & citizens making a disturbance on the Eighth day of this month (September) between 4 and 5 o'clock in the afternoon. I am, in the employ of the Provost Marshal in the city of Mobile. I left my office at 4 o'clock p.m & started down Dauphin St. I met some colored men both soldiers and citizens standing on the corner of Dauphin & Hamilton Sts. They were making so much fuss on the corner that I ordered them to go on about their business. I passed this crowd and went about half way down the block where I met the prisoner and some seven or eight other negroes, one of them had a musket and another had a bottle of whisky. I do not know that it was the prisoner who had the whisky. It was another black man who had the musket. Part of the squad seemed to be considerably under the influence of liquor, using very improper language, uttering threats against the white population at large and cursing everybody as damned rebels. The prisoner made the remark to the squad of soldiers that he was their officer and if they would only follow him, he would kill every white son of a bitch in town or lead them to hell and that there were colored men enough in Mobile to take it now and that they would have it in a week. I followed the party up to the corner of Dauphin & Hamilton Sts where the other squad of colored men was. I intended to get a guard from the Provost Marshals Office to disperse the crowd. The squad on the corner told this second squad with which the prisoner was that I had already ordered them away and the men of the second squad, the prisoner being one, said they did not care a damn for any policeman in the city. I had previously exhibited my badge of office as a policeman of the City. The negroes remarked that they were soldiers of the United States Army and didn't care a damn for anybody and that they would do as they pleased. I told them that I also was an Officer of the United States Government and that my particular authority was over them more than with citizens to see they kept order in the City. They then started towards Government Street cursing me as they went. I crossed the Street to the Provost Marshal's Office and called for a Guard. I commanded the prisoner and the squad of negroes with him, to halt. They refused to stop. I fired a shot at them and ordered them to stand. Before the guard could get out of the office, the squad broke and ran. The prisoner ran down through Government St. I followed him. A white soldier intercepted him, caught him and brought him back. Several others were finally caught & brought back, but I cannot swear positively that they belonged to the same party. The Provost Marshal examined into the case – put the prisoner in arrest & sent him out to the Camp of his Regiment.

Q. by Recorder   Did the prisoner wear his side arms or appear to be on duty with either of the squads you have alluded to?

Answer.   He did not appear to be on duty. The balance of the party seemed to me to be a detail for fatigue duty with one sentinel in charge of them, but the prisoner seemed to be in command of the soldiers certainly had full control over them, was making remarks to the colored citizens and soldiers around him and as I look at it seemed to be trying to raise and excite an insurrection by his language.

HD

Testimony of Robert S. Thompson, 18 Sept. 1865, proceedings of military commission in the case of First Sergeant William Barcroft, 86th USCI, MM-2824, Court-Martial Case Files, ser. 15 [H-3]. Barcroft was charged with inciting insurrection. Defense witnesses testified that Thompson did not show his "policeman's badge," that Barcroft had not been drinking, and that they did not hear the threatening language allegedly spoken by Barcroft. Barcroft did not testify in his own defense. The commission found him innocent of inciting insurrection, but guilty of "gross misconduct to the prejudice of the peace and good order of the city" and sentenced him to be reduced to the rank of private and to forfeit pay for six months. On October 10, 1865, however, the judge advocate general of the army disapproved the proceedings and annulled the sentence, because Barcroft should have been tried by a court-martial rather than a military commission.

745

324: Commander of the Military Division of the Atlantic to the Secretary of War

Philadelphia. Pa. September 20th 1865.
Sir, In compliance with your instructions dated the 21st ultimo, I proceeded to make an inspection of the States of South and North Carolina and Virginia, and have now the honor to submit the following report

1. SOUTH CAROLINA.
. . . .

COLORED TROOPS.

At the period of my inspection Major-General Gillmore had, under the orders of the War Department, mustered out of service the regiments of colored troops enlisted at the north, leaving in his command about five regiments organized in the southern states.

These Regiments were inspected by my order, and found to be in not very good condition, owing to gross neglect and fraud on the part of the medical and other officers recruiting them, and to the want of efficient subaltern officers, these being generally appointed by the military Commander of the Department from such material as he had at his disposal at the time the regiments were raised. Major General Gillmore reported that a large number of the men of these regiments had been pronounced by a medical board, as physically disqualified for service. These he was having discharged; and after he had eliminated all such cases, he would present a plan for consolidating the five regiments into either two or three, according to the number of men left. A careful examination satisfied me that the charges against the colored troops, mentioned in your letter of instruction,[1] were groundless. It is undoubtedly true that the colored troops fraternize more with the laboring population than white soldiers – their camps, moreover, are a great source of attraction to the negroes, and in this way may produce some evil by tempting the laborers to leave their work, and visit the camps. The superior condition of the soldier, in point of pay and physical comfort, over the laborer, is perhaps, also, injurious in its effect on the laboring population leading to discontent. But all these arguments against the employment of colored troops in the abstract, and are believed moreover to be very trifling in their results, and are not sufficient in my judgment to justify the discontinuance of this class of troops. It is undoubtedly true that the people of the South are very much prejudiced against these troops, that they really believe they are actively employed disorganizing the laboring population, and not to be relied on in the event of being called on to suppress a negro insurrection, the chronic terror of the South; but I could get no evidence to justify these fears and prejudices. Still, as I was satisfied from the reasons given above that these troops were, for the purposes for which troops are now required in the South, inferior to the white troops, I directed Major General Gillmore, after consolidating the regiments as proposed, to move them to the seaboard, where they can be usefully employed garrisoning the fortifications, and where they will be measurably removed from contact with the whites.

. . . .

HLcSr   (Sd.) George G. Meade.

Excerpt from Major General George G. Meade to Honorable E. M. Stanton, 20 Sept. 1865, vol. 1 DAt, pp. 53, 55–56, Letters Sent, ser. 430, Mil. Div. of the Atlantic, RG 393 Pt. 1 [C-4157]. In the omitted portion of the report Meade comments at length on military and freedmen's affairs in South Carolina, North Carolina, and Virginia.

1 "Complaints have been made that this class of troops are insubordinate, and lax in discipline; that they are discontented, turbulent, and present a threatening aspect to the people of the Department in which they are employed. No specific facts upon this subject have come to the knowledge of this Department, and whether there is any occasion for such complaints is a matter upon which the President desires accurate information. . . ." (Edwin M. Stanton to Major Genl. George G. Meade, 21 Aug. 1865, vol. 59, p. 294, Letters Sent, RG 107 [L-311].)

325: Mississippi Planter to Three State Legislators

Panola [*Miss.*]. Oct 22^d, 1865

Gentlemen. I wish to call your attention to a serious & growing evil, with the hope that you will give it your earliest attention, that something may be done to remove it from our midst— The Negro Soldiery here are constantly telling our negroes, that for the next year, The Goverment will give them lands, provisions, Stock & all things necessary to carry on business for themselves, — & are constantly advising them not to make contracts with white persons, for the next year. — Strange to say the negroes believe such stories in spite of facts to the contrary told them by their ~~masters~~ employers. — The consequence is they are becoming careless, & impudent more & more, for they are told by the

soldiers that they are as good as the whites & that they have come
here for their protection & that they shall not be
hurt. – furthermore I have good cause to believe that our negroes
are told that when the soldiers are withdrawn, that the whites will
endeavor to enslave them again – & that they are urged to begin at
an early day, perhaps about Christmas, a massacre of the whites,
in order to ensure their freedom, & that if the whites are got out
the way here, that then they will have no further apprehension – &
that this Country will then be given to them by the northern
people forever as an inheritance. – & Gentlemen to ignorant persons
situated as the negro is such arguments seem quite plausible. – In
truth the people of the South are in very great danger, more so
than many suppose – I have been born & reared in the midst of
negroes. I know their nature well, & have never, yet been
deceived in my estimate of them. I am no alarmist, but I tell you
most seriously that the whole south is resting upon a volcano – &
that if the negro troops are not removed from our mids pretty
Soon – that trouble of the direst kind will befal us – They will
stimulate the negroes to insurrection & will then lend them a
helping hand – It is well Known here that our negroes through
the country are well supplied with fire arms, muskets, Double
Barrel, shot Guns & Pistols, – & furthermore, it would be well if
they are free to prohibit the use of fire arms until they had proved
themselves to be good citizens in their altered state. – Gentlemen
I do not write you these views hastily. – I have well considered
them, & thcy appear more & more convincing day by day – I
have talked with many of our citizens upon this matter – they
appear anxious & say something ought to be done – but no one
feels disposed to move in the matter. – Get the negro Soldiery
removed from our midst & no danger will follow – our negroes will
be quiet, will hire for another year. – & will do their duty in many
cases very well – Let the Soldiery remain – & our negroes will
refuse to hire will grow more & more insolent & will without a
doubt – (relying upon the help of the Soldiery which they will be
sure to get) will endeavor by universal Massacre to turn this fair
land into another Hayti. – Our only hope of escape from the evils
above enumerated & many others, is to get the negro troops
removed from the State. Cannot it be done? – I think with Such
men as Gov Sharkey – & others like him making application to the
President to that effect, that the South can be Saved from Anarchy
& bloodshed – Please to enlist youselves with Dr Mosely in this
matter, for much indeed depends upon it for the weal or woe of
our selves our wives & our little ones – I remain Your friend,
truly &c

E. G. Baker

P.S. Esq Ballard has just told me that a squad of colored Soldiers
met him near his house this morning & without any
provocation—his not even speaking a word—they called him a
damned old rebel & threatened to kill, him; they did the same to
Wiley Baker a few minutes before using the most vulgar abusive
language to him— they have several times arrested citizens
walking about the streets of a night attending to their own
business—their camp being down near the old mill,— they are
generally drunk when they act So—but the Lt who commands
them when complained to merely says that he does not authorise
them to do so & there the matter ends— they are also killing up
the hogs robbing potatoe, patches,—parading (mustering) up &
down the streets in the most offensive manner.— If things go on
this way much longer there will be a collison between the citizens
& the black rascals let the consequences be what they
may— Please to give the matter of their removal from our midst
your earliest & most serious attention—& you will have the most
lastings feelings of gratitude for your efforts in behalf of the whole
country—Your friend—B.
ALS

E. G. Baker to Messrs. Irby & Ellis & Mosely, 22 Oct. 1865, enclosed in
Governor Benj. G. Humphreys to Genl. M. F. Force, 3 Nov. 1865, H-
371 1865, Letters Received, ser. 2433, Dept. of MS, RG 393 Pt. 1 [C-
2089]. Mississippi Governor Benjamin G. Humphreys forwarded this and
other reports of anticipated insurrection to the commander of the Northern
District of Mississippi, asserting in his covering letter that "unless some
measures are taken to disarm them [the freedmen] a collision between the
races may be speedily looked for. . . . That the colored troops are the cause
of the mischief is not doubted."

326: Order by the Commander of a Kentucky Black Regiment

Okolona Miss Oct 25 1865,

Regtl Orders No 137   Sergt Eli Helen and Corporal Joseph
Ingram Co K having been selected by the Colored Citizens of
Okolona and vicinity as collecting agents for the fund to establish
a school for colored children, are hereby granted permission to visit
Okolona in the execution of their duties as such

This order to continue in force during their good behavior   By
order of Col John S Bishop
HD

Regtl. Orders No. 137, Head Quarters 108" U.S.C.I., 25 Oct. 1865, Order Book, 108th USCI, Regimental Books & Papers USCT, RG 94 [G-157].

327: Company Officer in a Kentucky Black Regiment to the Headquarters of the Regiment

Battery Rodgers, Va— November 15th 1865—
Sir: I have the honor to make the following statement, relating to Serg't Thoˢ MᶜDougal of Co. "F" 107th U.S.C.I. who received a Furlough of thirty days on the 1st of October 1865, to visit his family in Ky.; and would respectfully request that it be forwarded to the proper authorities in order that *justice* may be done in his case.

After reaching Louisville Ky. Serg't MᶜDougal got an order from Gen'l Palmer, — in charge of the Freedman's Bureau of Kentucky, — to move his family to Louisville— His wife is living with her old master Hillary Johnson, Judge of the county of Larue Ky, and living in the town of Hodgensville. he is an old rebel and one of some note in that County. — Serg't MᶜDougal was arrested by Johnson soon after reaching Hodgensville, his order taken from him and he lodged in the County jail, where he has been confined since October 24th 1865, on account of trying to free his family from bondage.

The above is a true statement of the case at it has reached me.

Serg't MᶜDougal is a superior Non-com. Officer and his services are much needed in this Company. I am sir, very respectfully, Your obedient servant,

ALS   F. B. Clark

[*Endorsement*] Hd Qrs 107ᵗʰ U.S.C Inf'y Fort Corcoran Vᵃ. Nov 21ˢᵗ 1865 Respectfully forwarded. Quite a number of instances have occurred where men of this Regiment have been incarcerated in prison upon the most frivolous pretences. The Regiment was organized in Kentucky; and when the men return home to provide for their families they are often shamefully treated by their former masters. Especially is such the case in the interior districts of the state, where the disloyal element strongly preponderates, and where it is impossible for colored soldiers to obtain justice from magistrates who despise the Federal uniform—particularly so when worn by their former slaves. I would respectfully request that some action be taken to have Sergt McDougall released, so that he can return to his regt as soon as practicable   D. M. Sells. Lt. Co^l. Comdg

[*Endorsement*] H^d Qrs Dept of Ky Louisville Nov 30 1865 Respectfully returned to Col C W Foster AAG with the remark that the case of Sergeant McDougal illustrates in an eminent degree the peculiar ideas of loyalty honesty, and justice which animates certain of the judicial officers of Kentucky   The facts as I have ascertained them are substantially as follows. McDougal went to the house of Johnson who is county Judge of Larue County Ky and formerly owned McDougals wife and demanded her   Johnson refused to give her up without my order which was promptly given   He then removed his family from Johnsons house and in doing so inadvertently took with them the clothes of some other colored child of the value of 75. cts as I am advised   When these clothes were demanded of him he said "There they are take them   I knew nothing about them supposed they belonged to my children" which I am assured by respectable people is true. Judge Johnson however had him arrested for larceny brought before himself and committed him to jail in default of bail   (The Judge it is reported takes the astute distinction that though the act of Congress may free the wives and children of soldiers "it does not divest the owner of the title to the clothes they wear")   I at once took steps to investigate the case found the facts as before stated with the additional fact that a loyal man had become McDougals bail and the court just at hand   As the soldier was in civil custody upon colorable process authorised for a scandalous purpose in a rascally way I determined to wait the action of the Court trusting that justice would be done   The court met on last Monday—   The result of its action will be promptly reported

   I may add that the colored soldiers who return to this state are persecuted and outraged in many ways. John M Palmer Maj Genl Comd^g

Capt. F. B. Clark to Lieut. E. T. Lamberton, 15 Nov. 1865, C-771 1865, Letters Received, ser. 360, Colored Troops Division, RG 94 [B-227]. Other endorsements. In January 1866 General Palmer, commander of the Department of Kentucky, reported that the grand jury of Larue County had failed to indict Sergeant McDougal, who was then living with his family in Hodgensville. (Major General John M. Palmer to Col. C. W. Foster, 26 Jan. 1866, vol. 2 DKy, Letters Sent, ser. 2164, Dept. of KY, RG 393 Pt. 1 [C-4344].)

328: Commander of a Military Sub-District to the Headquarters of the Military District of Charleston

Georgetown SC, November 19th 1865

Captain: – In compliance with verbal instructions from the Bvt. Maj. Gen. Commanding the District, I have the honor to submit the following statements in regard to the effects of the presence of Colored Troops in this Sub-District.

I have endeavored by frequent conversations with the best informed people, especially planters, to ascertain the true ground of the objection to Colored Troops, and submit the results of my inquiries and such additional facts and remarks as it is believed are likely to throw light on the subject. –

I. The earliest ground of objection was that the freedpeople were looking forward to the arrival of Colored Troops with the expectation that their advent would enlarge their privileges, and obtain the realization of their expectations of obtaining possession of the lands of the country. I have no doubt there existed such a feeling among the colored people, and the only way to remove it was to send Colored Troops. I am satisfied that it no longer exists and could furnish conclusive evidence of the fact, if necessary.

II. The presence of the Colored Troops is not as pointedly a means of Military power against the Freedpeople as the white inhabitants think the condition of things demands. They desire that the presence of the Military Authorities should be recognized by both the blacks and the whites, as a disposition having reference wholly to an existing or anticipated turbulent or insurrectionary state among the blacks, in the same [*way*] that it would have been [*recognized*] had the Military power been called into the field to repress rebellion on the part of the blacks. They perceive, very correctly, that this impression would be created more rapidly if Colored Troops were removed and white soldiers substituted in their place. So far as my experience extends, I think that the military force in this Sub-Dist. should not be so Employed as to be interpreted as a menace to any portion of the community, but a reserved safeguard for the maintenance of the public peace against all offenders. My dispositions have been made in accordance with this idea, the military force being in garrison near Battery White, a mere harbor defence, and the reserve employed to visit and inspect Plantations, carrying nothing but side arms.

I have been here upwards of a month, in a District where the number of blacks are at least twelve or fourteen to one white, and the first occasion to use military force has not arisen. Of course the presence of a reserve force ready at command to enforce law has been essential and in my judgement will for a long time be essential to the maintenance of good order, not because there is a universal disposition among the people of this District to resist the force or the amount of difficulty, but because society is disorganized to an extent inconsistent with the preservation of property by ordinary civil methods.

III. The apprehension is general among resident whites, that in case of insurrection the colored Troops will fraternize with the black population against the whites. In the first place there is no indication of any insurrectionary effort or feeling. It is true the blacks have larger expectations than it will be possible to gratify – a not unusual state of things in political bodies, but they look to memorializing and influencing the government as a means of securing their desires. In the second place, if an insurrectionary state existed it would be a gratuitous and dishonorable assumption to hold in the absence of evidence, that soldiers who have served two years and upwards in the field against public enemies, have been obedient, brave and vigilant, would desert the flag of their government to assist in insurrection. So long as government places confidence in its Colored Troops, they will be an honor to the service. While I am not prepared to say what would be the effect if such a mark of distrust as that implied by the measure recommended by the citizens of the state. In addition to this, the effect of such distrust on officers who have labored individually to make Colored Troops worthy of the confidence of the government would be most depressing.

IV. It is thought that the presence of Colored Troops will interfere with the successful inauguration of the system of labor under consideration by the Legislature of the State, and the adoption of which is looked forward to as the future policy of the state.

The series of enactments popularly known as "The Code" appears to embody the principle of requiring all negroes to labor, except those having business as Shopkeepers or Mechanics, under written Contracts, subject to the penalty of being treated as vagrants, and punished by compulsory service. The power of fixing the value of labor, in the absence of the agreement of the parties, rests with the District Judge in whose selection the blacks have no voice. As this will pracically prove to be an attempt to compel labor at prices fixed by public authority, not selected by one of the parties to the transaction, I think the objection last stated should be extended to embrace all troops of the United States of whatever color.

Having Stated, as fairly as I am able to do it, all the grounds of

753

objection that have been communicated to me, I beg leave to state a few advantages that I believe will arise from the presence of Colored Troops.

I. They are an example of subordination and obedience to authority, and respect for the government, of the greatest importance, especially to the freedpeople.

II. They are so far in sympathy with the freedpeople that when they have an opportunity they endeavor to cultivate the importance of placing trust in the government by obeying implicitly its orders. The services they are called upon to perform, being so obviously directed to the advancement of the true interests of the people of color, they are rendered freely and cheerfully without reluctance, while volunteer Troops being anxious to return to their homes, feel that this service is a burden, and in many instances an imposition upon them.

III. They submit more cheerfully than Volunteer Troops to the necessary exclusion from villages and places where amusement and entertainment are to be found.

IV. They are, as a class, temperate.

In submitting the foregoing facts and views, I merely intended to communicate the impressions of my mind, the result of careful and impartial observation, believing that, without assuming that my sphere of observation and accuracy of judgement is broad enough to sustain all the considerations that should have weight in so important a question, the truth of these observations can be verified as far as this Sub-District and its Military Garrison is concerned. Very Respectfully Your Obdt. Servant

HLcSr   (signed) A. J. Willard

Lt. Col. A. J. Willard to Capt. Geo. W. Hooker, 19 Nov. 1865, vol. 156 DS, pp. 25–28, Letters Sent, ser. 2389, 4th Subdist., Mil. Dist. of Charleston, RG 393 Pt. 2 No. 142 [C-1615].

329: Mississippi Black Soldier to the Freedmen's Bureau Commissioner

Vicksburg. Miss. De^c 16th 1865.

Sir   Suffer me to address you a few lines in reguard to the colered people in this State,   from all I can learn and see, I think the colered people are in a great many ways being outraged beyound humanity,   houses have been tourn down from over the heades of women and Children – and the old Negroes after they have worked

754

there till they are 70 or 80 yers of age drive them off in the cold
to frieze and starve to death.

One Woman come to (Col) Thomas, the coldest day that has
been this winter and said that she and her eight children lay out
last night, and come near friezing after She had paid some wrent
on the house Some are being knocked down for saying they are
free, while a great many are being worked just as they ust to be
when Slaves, without any compensation, Report came in town this
morning that two colered women was found dead side the Jackson
road with their throats cot lying side by side, I see an account in
the Vicksburg. Journal where the (col) peple was having a party
where they formily had one. and got into a fuss and a gun was
fired and passed into a house. they was forbidden not to have any
more but did not heed. The result was the house was fired and a
guard placed at the door   one man attemped to come out but was
shot and throed back and burned   five was consumed in the
flames, while the balance saught refuge in a church and it was
fired and burned. The Rebbles are going a bout in many places
through the State and robbing the colered peple of arms money
and all they have and in many places killing.

So, General, to make short of a long story I think the safety of
this country depenes upon giving the Colered man all the rights of
a white man, and especialy the Rebs. and let him know that their
is power enough in the arm of the Govenment to give Justice, to
all her loyal citizens –

They talk of taking the armes a way from (col) people and
arresting them and put them on farmes next month and if they go
at that I think there will be trouble and in all probability a great
many lives lost. They have been accusing the colered peple of an
insorection which is a lie, in order that they might get arms to
carrie out their wicked designs –

for to my own knowledge I have seen them buying arms and
munitions ever since the lins have been opened and carring them
to the country. In view of these things I would suggust to you if
it is not incompatible with the public interest to pass some laws
that will give protection to the colered men and meet out Justice
to traters in arms.

For you have whiped them and tried them and found out that
they will not do to be depended upon, now if you have any true
harted men send them down here to carrie out your wishes
through the Bureau in reguarde to the freedmen. if not get
Congress to stick in a few competent colered men as they did in
the army and the thing will all go right, A trouble now with the
colered peple on account of Rebs. after they have rendered the
Government such great survice through the rebellion would spoil

755

the whole thing—and it is what the Rebles would like to bring a bout, and they are doing all they can to prevent free labor, and reasstablish a kind of secondary slavery   Now believe me as a colered man that is a friend to law and order, I blive without the intervention of the General governmt in the protection of the (col) popble that there will be trouble in *Miss.* before spring   please excuse this for I could not have said less and done the subject Justice. infact I could say more, but a hint to the wise is soficient   If you wish to drop me a line Direct Calvin. Holly. *Vick* Miss Box 2^{d} yours Most Respectfully,

ALS   Calvin. Holly., colered

Privt. Calvin Holly to Major General O. O. Howard, 16 Dec. 1865, H-72 1865, Registered Letters Received, ser. 2052, MS Asst. Comr., RG 105 [A-9050]. After his signature Holly indicated that he was serving on detail at the office of Colonel Samuel Thomas, Freedmen's Bureau assistant commissioner in Mississippi.

330A: Black Minister to the Secretary of War

                                        Columbus Ga Feb. 14th 1866,
Sir, I assume the liberty of laying before your honor, some fact connected with a fray which took place in the Streets, Monday evening the 12 inst, I was standing, conversing with a gentleman when the report of three shots attracted my attention Just below me, I soon heard a colored Soldier was shot, large crowds of rebels gathered around the scene crying out kill the negro, kill the negro, others Said get your guns boys, hells to play, the negroes are rising &c, &c, fearing Something would occur Serious, I walked to where the colored troops were Quartered, by this time the wounded Soldier arrived in a wagon at the barracks covered with blood, The colored soldiers seeing the conditions of their comrade, began to curse and sware, But the officers stood in the door and kept them in, for I verily believe, if they had got out Just at the moment a serious issue would have resulted,

But the point to which I wish to call your attention, is this, The rebels are trying to blame the colored Soldiers for raising a row, and publishing a thousand faulshoods, Here is the testimony of the wounded Soldiers given to me upon oath,

I James Gant Co F 103, U.S.C.T. was walking up street, and

heard a white man say "God damn black son of a bitch"   And I
turn and looked at him, not saying a word, and walked on the
couse I was going, and the next thing I knew, I heard a pistol fire,
and a ball went through my hand, two more balls instantly
followed going through each of my arms, at this point the white
man run, I never Said a word, never rubed against him, nor
looked at him, till he cursed me, all of which I do positively
affirm,

Several other persons present declare the same thing; Now Mr
Stanton read these extracts and look at the published lies of these
slanderous rebels, Besides every body almost say that this Lindsay
is a drunken Sot, His brother was shot dead by another rebel a
few months ago, for his devilish conduct, and the life of this one
was threatened by rebels several times   Now because he shot a
negro, these Columbus papers are making him a great and good
man,

These rebels here are the meanest wretches on earth, The lives
of the white teachers have been threaten several times, Colored
people in five miles of this place dare not own their
freedom, Every body tells me, not to go out side of Columbus to
lecture, But I could not tell you half the condition of things, in a
short letter,

But I do hope, and all the colored pray, that you will not
remove this garrison, They want white soldiers, So they can buy
them over, to ill treat the colored as they have done, I trust you
will order a Strong garrison of Colored Soldiers to remain here, for
fifty white rebels have told me, the negroes never bother them,
unless they commence with them, And while there is almost a
universal dislike to Negro soldiers, yet many say, the negroes
never interferes with them first,

The fact is, when colored Soldiers are about they are afraid to
kick colored women, and abuse colored people on the Streets, as
they usually do,

For fear I may trespass upon your time I will Say no
more, Your humble Servant

H M Turner

I am not stoping here permanently, I am only here lecturing

ALS

H. M. Turner to Hon. E. M. Stanton, 14 Feb. 1866, T-35 1866, Letters
Received, RG 107 [L-1]. Endorsements. Turner enclosed three newspaper
clippings, two describing the altercation and one reporting a city council
resolution requesting removal of the black garrison. James Gant's regiment,
the 103rd USCI, was organized at Hilton Head, South Carolina.

330B: Governor of Georgia to the President, Enclosing a Petition from the Mayor and Other White Citizens of Columbus to the Governor

Milledgeville Georgia February 15th 1866

Sir: It has become my duty again to ask your attention to a subject adverted to in a former communication, viz: the keeping in our midst colored troops. After many of them had been withdrawn and the policy of their withdrawal seemed likely soon to be consumated, our people felt great relief, and on many localities where there remained no military force at all, law and order were strictly observed – peace and quiet prevailed – and good business relations, mutually advantageous, were established between white and colored people. Suddenly, in certain places, as in the Cities of Macon and Columbus, colored troops were introduced, and settled as if for indefinite occupation. In the latter City, a most unfortunate disturbance of the public peace, has already occurred, which from all the information in my possession, I verily believe originated in the grossly improper and insulting conduct of some of those troops. The circumstances are briefly referred to, in the inclosed communication which is the immediate cause of this to you. A majority of the signers, are known to me personally or by reputation, as respectable, intelligent, moral men, such as any City or State might be proud of.

Their statements are altogether reliable. Believe me, Sir, the presence of these troops among us is unfavorable to the public peace and tranquility. When out of the immediate presence of their officers, their conduct is often intolerably insulting, and not unfrequently going to the extent of personal violence. I have myself, when quietly riding in my carriage with my Wife, on the high-way, in the absence of all provation, by word, by jesture or by look, been cursed by them and ordered to get out of the road with that carriage, they wanted the whole road. My old blood, did not boil over quite; but the hot blood of a young man can hardly bear being rudely thrust from the pavement, or seeing a lady wantonly insulted. If it be supposed that these troops are kept in proper subjection by their officers, I respectfully affirm that as a general rule, it is not so.

Mr President, I believe you have full authority in the premises, I know your kindly feelings and purposes towards us and I entreat you, if it do not contravene any policy you deem necessary, to relieve us of this portion of the United States Military. I have the honor to be Very respectfully your Obt Servant

HLS

Charles J. Jenkins

[Enclosure]   *[Columbus, Ga. February 13, 1866]*
Dear Sir   The undersigned citizens of Columbus Georgia
respectfully represent to you the following facts and urgently solicit
your intervention in their behalf.

The garrison of united States troops, being the 151 Reg. Illinois
Infty on duty at this post since about the 15th Aug. last took their
departure about the 15th Jany last. Since that time peace & order
have prevailed in our community as previously it did. Within ten
days just past a garrison of about 100 U.S.C. Troops have come
into the city. Their conduct since has been characterized by a
disregard of moral and legal restraints robbing and insulting our
citizens both male & female upon the public streets and in a
collision resulting therefrom one of the colored soldiers was shot
upon the street yesterday. After this the Colored Troops fired
indiscriminately into the street wounding one of our peaceable &
orderly citizens necessitating the amputation of his leg.

Our community is a loyal and law-abiding one, rendering
willing obedience to the laws & regulations of the State & the
United States, and anxious to do justice alike to all classes of
people. We do not refuse subjection to the military authority
properly and lawfully exercised among us. We respectfully ask
your excellency to represent these facts to the President of the U.S.
and solicit from him such action in our behalf as the proprieties of
the case may in his Judgment seem to call for.

Respectfully submitted to your candid consideration
HLS   *[38 signatures]*

Governor Charles J. Jenkins to President Andrew Johnson, 15 Feb. 1866,
enclosing F. G. Wilkins et al. to Governor Charles J. Jenkins, [13 Feb.
1866], W(D)-84 1866, Letters Received Relating to Military Discipline &
Control, ser. 22, RG 108 [S-23]. Endorsements. Governor Jenkins also
enclosed letters from several Georgians and resolutions from the state legislature requesting restoration of confiscated property and termination of
military intervention in civil processes.

330C: Freedmen's Bureau Subassistant Commissioner at Columbus, Georgia, to the Headquarters of the Georgia Freedmen's Bureau Assistant Commissioner

Columbus Ga. March 8. 1866.
Captain: In regard to the enclosed communication of Mr. H. M.
Turner I have the honor to state, that his report of the fray, which

occurred here on the 12th ult. and the condition of things in the
Country in regard to the Freedpeople, is true, although a little
exaggerated. C. Lindsay, who shot the colored soldier, is a man of
good family, but known as a ruffian and to be of bad
character. He had been in a state of intoxication all day, and
made the remark that he would shoot one of these d- - - niggers
before night. – The town was in a state of exitement all the time
since the colored troops came here, which feelings were not a little
stimulated by the bitter and slanderous accounts in the "Daily
Sun", a newspaper in this town. The citizens felt degraded and
insulted by being guarded by colored troops, and when the affair
took place, hundreds rushed in the street, armed with revolvers
etc. cursing and swearing to attack the troops and drive every
"Yankee" out of town. Some had even the impudence to
sourround Lieut. Mulligan of the Detachment, in the street, and
pointing their pistols at his head, demanded the surrender of
Lindsay. The officers deserve much credit for the manner in which
they acted; they used their utmost to keep the men in quarters,
who were frantic with exitement and determined to take immidiate
revenge. Lt. Col. Bogart, of the same Regiment and Comdg Mil.
Dist. at Macon Ga. arrived here the second day after the
occurrence, and made a full investigation of the whole
affair. What steps he has taken in regard to it, I am unable to
tell. The troops were soon afterwards removed and a Detachment
of the 176th N.Y.V. under Command of Lt. Col. C. Lewis took
their place. Lindsay escaped to Cuba, they say, but others think
that he is still living in the Country. – Since that time things
have gone on very well here in town; the best relations exist
between the Civil and Military Authorities. The Freedpeople feel
secure and protected, and are little molested by the Whites. *Only
two* colored men were shot since, one of the offenders was arrested
and turned over to the Civil Authorities for trial; the other one
escaped, and I have been unable to apprehend him. But in the
Country things are very different, especially since the troops have
been removed. The lower class of the white population seem to
have their own way and the freedpeople are little protected against
the outrages of this class. Every day I hear complaints, and the
condition of the freedmen grows worse from day to day. No
wonder that they leave the country and come here in town, to
work for much less wages or their mere living, than accept the
best inducements in the country. Here they are protected, but
beyond 10 miles from town they must live in continual fear of
their lives and property. I do the best I can under the
circumstances and with the means at my command; but it is very

difficult, on account of the distance and without mounted troops, to rectify such abuses and bring the guilty party to punishment. I am with much respects Your ob't. serv't.

ALS   Fred. Mosebach

Capt. Fred. Mosebach to Capt. W. W. Deane, 8 Mar. 1866, filed with T-35 1866, Letters Received, RG 107 {L-1}. Mosebach made this report in response to Henry M. Turner's letter of February 14, 1865, forwarded by the War Department for investigation. The following summer Mosebach reported twice on continuing developments in the case. On July 13, he reported that Cooper Lindsay had returned to Columbus, but the civil authorities would not prosecute him, inasmuch as most whites considered Lindsay "their benefactor and the immediate cause of having been relieved from the garrison of colored troops." On July 24, he recounted the events of the shooting, described Lindsay as a man of good family, although personally inclined toward rowdyism, and provided the names of six witnesses to the fray. Mosebach also noted that, since the black soldiers had been mustered out of the army, Columbus city officials contemplated prosecuting them. (Capt. Fred. Mosebach to Capt. W. W. Deane, 13 July 1866, and Capt. Fred. Mosebach to A.A. Gen'l. A. Ramsey Ninninger, 24 July 1866, vol. 222, pp. 42–43, 47–48, Letters Sent, ser. 832, Columbus GA Subasst. Comr., RG 105 [A-223].)

331: Freedmen's Bureau Chief Superintendent for the District of Kentucky to the Headquarters of the Kentucky and Tennessee Freedmen's Bureau Assistant Commissioner

Louisville Ky   April 9th 1866.

. . . .

The presence of a few troops under the immediate orders of the Chief Superintendent, was found to be absolutely essential to insure the respect of the white people for the Superintendents, and their agents and the enforcement of the rules and regulations of the Bureau. I accordingly made application to Maj. Genl Palmer Comdg. Depart of Kentucky, for two companies of troops which he furnished me from the 119th U.S.C.I., one company of this detail, I posted at Lexington, and details of thirty men each under command of a commissioned officer, were posted at Maysville & Covington.

The presence of these troops caused a marked change for the

better in the sentiments of the people toward the Bureau, and gave confidence to the many good men (white people) who accept the present condition of affairs, and are willing when assured of protection, by the United States authorities, to aid by their influence and action, in the just and proper administration of the laws of the U.S. establishing this Bureau. These troops are also employed to protect the colored people in many of the counties of that sub Dist. particularly in Scott Owen Harrison Nicholas Bath, Montgomery, Estell and Madison, from the fiendish outrages committed by white people, who are in many cases banded together under the cognomen of "Regulators" "Nigger Killers" &c operating in said counties. These scoundrels are generally returned rebel soldiers of the lowest grade of white humanity, working at no respectable employment, the graduates of the corner groceries and grog dens of their regions.

The outrages committed by these people have been numerous; many of them have resulted in death, a special report of which was furnished to the Assistant Commissioner, by his special Agent Peter Bonesteel Esq. Since the rendition of that report and befor I moved my Hd. Quarters to this place, two murders, one of which was a colored soldier, who had been discharged from the 114th U.S.C.I. have been reported from Montgomery County, by the Superintendent H. C. Howard at Mt. Sterling who states that the good people of the County, are rendering him valuable assistance to procure the arrest of the murderers, and that the civil authorities have recently signified their willingness to co-operate.

The Freedmen are in the main well employed, at fair wages, throughout that Sub Dist. and were it not for the terrorism incited by the lawless bands heretofore mentioned there would be no difficulty in finding good homes and competent employment for every freedman in that section. As yet however, many of the well disposed white people who reside at places remote from the stations where troops are posted are afraid to employ black men, particularly those recently mustered out of the U.S. Military service for fear of injury to their persons or property, by the self styled regulators.

. . . .

HLcSr   (Signed) John Ely.

Excerpt from Brvt. Brig. Genl. John Ely to Captain H. S. Brown, 9 Apr. 1866, Unregistered Letters & Telegrams Received, ser. 928, Mil. Div. of the TN, RG 393 Pt. 1 [C-29]. Endorsement. Omitted portions of the report describe the condition of freedmen in Kentucky.

332: Adjutant of a Missouri and Arkansas Black Regiment to the Executive Committee of the Indiana Yearly Meeting of Friends

Helena Ark June 11 1866.

Gentlemen: Your favor of the 14th of April 1866 in which you accept the trust of taking charge of the Orphan asylum established in Philips Co Ark. by subscription of the Officers and men of this Regiment has been recieved and a copy furnished each soldier. Under the energetic Management of Your Agent and trusty lady, Mr & Mrs Clark, the institution progresses finely and I have no doubt its beneficial results will be seen and acknowledged soon even by its opponents. The Amount of work that has been done on the grounds by the Soldiers is immense, from an allmost unbroken forrest it has been cleared fenced and a large part of it planted, and four substantial buildings erected suitable for the wants of the children and those who have the Care of them. It is contemplated to dedicate the Institution on the next 4th of July in a public manner with proper exercises. And in behalf of the Regiment I extend herewith to you an invitation to be present if convenient   Very Truly Yours

ALcS   S J Clark

1st Lieut. S. J. Clark to Joseph Dickenson and Timothy Harrison, 11 June 1866, Letters Sent, 56th USCI, Regimental Books & Papers USCT, RG 94 [G-258]. The soldiers who had constructed the orphanage were members of the 56th USCI, organized in St. Louis, Missouri, as the 3rd Regiment Arkansas Volunteers.

333: Kentucky Black Soldiers to the President

White Ranch [*Tex.*] July 3rd 1866

Dear President   I have the honer to address the as followes   the few remarks i wish to say and to inform you of is this   the Condition of our familys in Kentucky and the Condition of our self   we Kentuckians are men that Came out in this great and noble cause   we did come out like men   we have stood up to geather with Comrades and have proved not only to the people but to the world that we have been faithfull and prompt to all dutys   we have fulfilled all posts that we have been put and then as for a Regiment Commander to treat the soldiers so mean as we have been treated i think it is out of the question   My President and vice i think as a dutyfull as the 116th Regiment of U.S. Coloured Infantry have not had no more quarters shown them then what as been i dont think it is right for i think that there are not the tenth part of quarters shown us that is intended for us for if our officers and field officers would take the Law as it is given to them and use it they have not the power to use such ill treatment   Mr President and vice we learn by the papers that the sum of three Hundred dollars that was promised us when we inlisted in the service we would not get it   but if the Govener should turn out the men of our standing barehanded i would like to know how you would expect for us to live ear after   we are a nation that was poor and had nothing when we came to the service   we had neather house nor money no place to put our familys   now these poor nation of colour have spent the best part of his days in slavery   now then what must we do   must we turn out to steal to get a start   we left our wifes and Children no place for them to lay there heads   we left them not counted on Eaqual footing as the white people   they where looked on like dogs and we left them with a willing mind to exicute our duty in the army of the United States war to eather to make us a nation of people eather in this generation or the next to come   now Mr President i wish you to ansure this letter and let us know we are to do as this Regiment is labouring under a great mistake untill you let us know what we are to do and you will releive our mind a great deal and we will remain your affectionate Brother Soldier   Direct to

1est Sargint Wm White

1 " Do Mc Meail

2 " Do Taylor

[Corpor]arl Thomass

HLSr

Sargint Wm. White et al. to Dear President, 3 July 1866, P-199 1866, Letters Received, ser. 360, Colored Troops Division, RG 94 [B-272]. Endorsements referred the complaint through several military channels, until it reached Lieutenant Colonel Chas. Kireker, commander of the 116th USCI. On November 6, 1866, he returned the petition with the statement that "there are no men of the names of the signers of the enclosed communication in this regiment." For an earlier petition from the same regiment and apparently from some of the same men, see *Freedom*. ser. 2: doc. 341.

18

Home from the War:
Discharged Black Soldiers

FEDERAL DEMOBILIZATION began almost immediately after the Confederate surrender and moved quickly to discharge the volunteer soldier force. Demobilization generally took place by seniority of service, although, because muster-out orders covered army corps rather than individual regiments, some new units were disbanded before veteran ones. Within five months of the surrender, the War Department had discharged nearly one-third of the black volunteers, and within eighteen months, more than nine-tenths. The black volunteer force that had stood at roughly 123,000 in July 1865 shrank to approximately 83,000 three months later. By the fall of 1866, fewer than 13,000 black soldiers remained in service, and all were discharged by the fall of 1867.[1]

Nonetheless, many black soldiers believed that the demobilization process took too long. With the fighting ended, they longed to leave the service and return to civilian life. Because they had enlisted on the assumption that they would serve for three years or the duration of hostilities, many could neither understand nor accept the seemingly endless delays that encumbered discharge. One soldier, repeatedly frustrated in his attempt to be discharged, at last exploded, "We have fought like men and now ar treatid like dogs. . . ."[2] The travail of slavery added to the anxiety black soldiers suffered while awaiting discharge, inasmuch as former slaves worried about the safety, even the exact whereabouts, of their loved ones in ways that did not concern free men. Black troops stationed near their families saw at close range the physical deprivation and suffering that their families endured at the hands of former masters or new employers. Even when federal authorities afforded black dependents the protection of contraband camps, the dilapidated facilities and critical shortages of food and clothing that characterized those refuges convinced black soldiers that the welfare of their wives and children demanded their immediate return to civilian life.

Lingering pockets of slavery in portions of the South added to the

---

[1] *Official Records*, ser. 3, vol. 5, pp. 114, 138, 1029, 1047.
[2] Wm. H. McClintic to Hon. Secaretary, 26 June 1865, M-437 1865, Letters Received, ser. 360, Colored Troops Division, RG 94 [B-175].

burden of some black soldiers. Unlike its border-state neighbors, for example, Kentucky did not abolish slavery during the war, and its loyalty to the Union exempted it from the Emancipation Proclamation. Moreover, many Kentucky masters defied the March 1865 congressional resolution that freed the immediate families of blacks in the armed forces. Even when wives and children obtained their liberty, soldiers still worried about other kinfolk who, excluded from the resolution's promise of freedom, remained legally the property of their "loyal" masters. To make matters worse, the final battles of the war took many Kentucky regiments far from home. Several units served in the Virginia campaign with the black 25th Army Corps, which was then transferred to Texas when fighting ended in the East. In December 1865, ratification of the Thirteenth Amendment at last extinguished slavery's legal standing, but physical separation continued to deny soldiers knowledge of their families' welfare and left their worry undiminished.

Once discharged, black soldiers attempted to collect the bounties promised them at enlistment, payments they had hoped would guarantee family security in their absence and perhaps provide a head start at war's end. A bounty of several hundred dollars, even if collected in installments, would go far toward the purchase of the land, mules, and equipment necessary for a new life in freedom. For once black soldiers did not lack assistance. Claim agents, many of them former recruiting officers, established offices at every major army post to aid black veterans. Many agents honestly attempted to help their clients through the tangled web of bounty eligibility, but others, taking advantage of the confused state of the law and the ignorance of the soldiers, cheated without compunction.[3] In desperation, former soldiers sought assistance at military posts and Freedmen's Bureau offices. Responding to the swelling ranks of black claim seekers, the bureau created a special claim branch in 1866,

---

[3] In June 1864, the act equalizing pay between black and white soldiers approved bounty payments to black soldiers who had been free before the war or had enlisted under the President's draft call of October 1863. Only a small fraction of the black fighting force met these requirements, and in July 1864, to encourage black enlistments, Congress offered graduated bounties to new black volunteers on the same scale as whites: $100 for one-year enlistments, $200 for two-year enlistments, and $300 for three-year enlistments, in each case payable one-third at enlistment, one-third midway through the term of service, and one-third at discharge. The same act legitimated claims for such bounties by the widows, children, and mothers (in that order) of deceased soldiers. In May 1865, the provost marshal general devised a calendar of bounty eligibility depending upon date of enlistment. All blacks—slave and free—who enlisted after July 1864 could claim a bounty according to term of service, but slaves who had enlisted before that time could lay no such claim. In the eyes of the War Department, the slave's freedom itself was adequate bounty. (*Official Records*. ser. 3, vol. 5, pp. 658–60.)

which survived until 1872 – four years after most other bureau operations terminated – and formed the nucleus of its successor, the Freedmen's Branch of the Adjutant General's Office. Yet, despite these efforts, most black veterans and their families met countless obstacles in their effort to collect the money they believed due them. By virtue of the slow payment process in legitimate cases and the prolonged investigation necessary in disputed cases, many bounties remained uncollected for years.

Like other Union soldiers, blacks left the army amid great fanfare. Officers recounted their exploits, praised their accomplishments, and congratulated them on behalf of a grateful nation for a job well done. The applause grew louder when the black veterans returned home to family and friends. Often entire black communities turned out to greet the black liberators, their own conquering heroes. Savoring such approval, some former slaves continued to wear their blue uniforms, and even those who had enjoyed no special status before the war were called upon for their advice on personal and community matters. Some veterans, especially the handful who had served as commissioned officers and the more numerous sergeants and corporals, actively sought positions of leadership and directly transferred their experience in the wartime struggle for liberation to the postwar struggle for equality.

If the self-confidence of returning black veterans comforted the black community, it worried the white one. As part of John Brown's army and the Union occupation force, black soldiers symbolized Southern defeat. But whereas armed and organized soldiers enjoyed the protection of the federal military establishment, as well as the force of their own numbers, individual returning veterans were vulnerable to assault by angry, frustrated Confederate partisans.

Former Confederate soldiers felt the presence of black veterans most keenly. Cut adrift from the old antebellum world, unable to find a place in the new postbellum one, traumatized by fear of losing status, and angered by "foreign" military occupation, they frequently formed the nucleus of regulator gangs that roamed the South in the wake of Lee's surrender, avenging Confederate defeat and reasserting the old order. They vented their wrath on the most obvious and, in some ways, the most available symbol of the new order – discharged black soldiers – and threatened, assaulted, and murdered returning veterans almost at will. When alert black veterans managed to escape the regulators, their families frequently suffered in their stead. While many respectable whites deplored the uglier aspects of regulator violence, few took steps to curtail it. Indeed, many white officials seemed to take special pleasure in turning the tables on abused soldiers, accusing and even convicting them of some petty offense that allegedly had provoked the initial assault.

Assaults on Union blue and the equation of Union military service with subversion indicate the deeply symbolic nature of the violence black veterans everywhere confronted. Behind the symbols stood the stark reality that former soldiers with their sense of pride, their expectations of full citizenship, and their military experience offered real protection to the black community and impeded white attempts to reinstitute the old order. Nothing made that reality clearer than the return of black veterans who had purchased their arms at the time of discharge. Tossing aside Constitutional guarantees, whites moved quickly to disarm returning black soldiers. In some places, like Mississippi, planters and local officials acted in concert as part of a calculated state policy. Elsewhere, employers, local officials, and vigilantes acted on their own authority to disarm blacks. Everywhere, however, the attempt to disarm returning black soldiers added to the level of postwar violence as black veterans resisted being stripped of the means of self-protection and one of the most important symbols of their new status.

Southern whites uniformly despised the presence of former black soldiers, but demographic and political conditions shaped their opposition in different ways. In lowcountry South Carolina and Georgia, for example, the overwhelming numerical preponderance of blacks protected black veterans from the full fury of white hostility. Numerical dominance offered similar protection in the lower Mississippi Valley, although gangs of former Confederate soldiers and other regulators assiduously pursued returning black soldiers. In the upcountry from Virginia to Mississippi, however, where whites dominated numerically and enlistment had often been a solitary act prefaced by flight from slavery, isolated black veterans fell easy prey to regulator bands and vengeful former masters.

Black soldiers returning to the border states suffered by far the most widespread and systematic postwar terror. Maryland, Tennessee, and Missouri had each charted a wavering course toward emancipation, with black enlistment playing a major role in slavery's demise. The war and the transition from slavery to freedom left their white populations deeply embittered and sharply divided; Confederate sympathizers commonly turned upon blacks as scapegoats. Kentucky, unlike the other border states, had never accepted emancipation on its own and considered federally mandated liberation a betrayal of its wartime Union loyalty. There, unionists enraged at having lost their slaves despite their fidelity joined forces with rebels equally enraged at having lost their slaves as the price of defeat, and both vented their frustration on returning black soldiers. In some communities, whites assaulted black veterans as they alighted from trains. In other places, whites denied returning soldiers access to their families, to employment, and to the equal protection of the law. Moreover, the pattern of demobilization meant that discharged soldiers could not take advantage of either their collective armed might or their numerical preponderance in the black male population. Because individual regiments were mustered out sporadically over the first two postwar years, black soldiers often returned home in the most vulnerable circumstances, either individually or in small groups.

Federal officials could do little to halt the vicious physical abuse. In February 1866, after months of investigation, General Clinton B. Fisk, head of the Freedmen's Bureau in Kentucky and Tennessee, reported on the treatment of Kentucky blacks. Many of the estimated 25,000 returned black soldiers, he concluded, "were enlisted against the wishes of their masters, and now, after having faithfully served their country, and been honorably mustered out of its service, and return to their old homes, they are not met with joyous welcome, and grateful words for their devotion to the Union, but in many instances are *scourged, beaten, shot at,* and driven from their homes and families. . . ."[4] When Fisk submitted his findings to the Kentucky state legislature, that body accused him of fabricating bloody incidents to besmirch the state's reputation. The violence that continued for years afterward revealed the brutal consequences of the black man's role in the war for freedom and Union.

Assaults against black veterans did not diminish the importance of the black military experience; instead, they confirmed its importance. Having traveled broadly and enjoyed a wide range of experience generally denied the slave, former soldiers brought a new worldliness and sophistication to the black community. They had seen white men powerless as well as powerful, and they had seen black men powerful as well as powerless. They had confronted the impersonal rules that regulated military life as well as the slave owner's paternalistic justice and mastered both. They had acquired literacy and the intangible qualities of battle-forged leaders. Black veterans quickly put their experience to work. Throughout the South they founded schools, led churches, and took their places as community leaders.

The political importance of the black military experience became apparent at the end of the war. Black veterans—many of them still wearing their Union uniforms—played a prominent role in the host of state and local conventions freedmen held during 1865 and 1866. Not surprisingly, the published addresses and resolutions of these meetings almost without fail predicated their case for extending full citizenship rights to Southern blacks upon the military record of

---

[4] Brevet Major General Clinton B. Fisk to Major General Howard, 14 Feb. 1866, K-60 1866, Letters Received, ser. 15, Washington Hdqrs., RG 105 [A-6023].

black soldiers.[5] When Radical Reconstruction began, former soldiers continued to play an important role, joining forces with white Republicans to advance the transformation of the South initiated by Confederate defeat. Some former soldiers, including Stephen A. Swails in South Carolina, Henry M. Turner in Georgia, William U. Saunders in Florida, and P. B. S. Pinchback (along with several of his fellow officers in the Native Guard regiments) in Louisiana, served in prominent elective office during Reconstruction. Countless other former soldiers served in local elective offices, in appointive offices, and as officers in state and local Republican organizations. Black veterans in the North organized along similar political lines. In Iowa they held a soldiers' convention to map political strategies for the postwar era, and in the Northeast they formed the Colored Soldiers' and Sailors' League for the same purpose.[6] Like their Southern counterparts, they also became staunch Republicans. Through such political forums, former soldiers extended their influence to statewide and, at times, national constituencies.

Brandishing a finely honed sense of their own role as liberators, former soldiers moved to the front ranks in the struggle for land, economic autonomy, and racial justice. The knowledge that they had subdued the rebellion and secured Union victory added force to their demands for equal treatment and the full rights of American citizens. When confronted by hostile whites, they commonly announced – in defiance of the obvious risks that such assertiveness entailed – that they had fought under the stars and stripes, had worn Union blue, and feared no man, whatever his color. As former masters had anticipated, the pride and sense of accomplishment black soldiers brought home from the war proved contagious. Under the soldiers' example and tutelage, both Northern free blacks and Southern freed blacks insisted that black people had fought for their liberty and, consequently, should share in the fruits of victory. That insistence animated postwar demands for land, full citizenship rights, and social justice.

[5] *Proceedings of the Colored People's Convention of the State of South Carolina* (Charleston, 1865); *Proceedings of the Freedmen's Convention of Georgia* (Augusta, 1866); *Proceedings of the First Convention of Colored Men of Kentucky* (Louisville, 1866).
[6] *Christian Recorder*, 18 Nov. 1865, 12 Jan. 1867.

DISCHARGE

334: **Rhode Island Black Corporal to the Superintendent of Public Printing**

Fort Banks La [*May 1865*]

Sir   I take this opportunity of writing to you, informing you of my being quite well and hope this will find yourself and family in the enjoyment of good health   I am now situated at the above named place about nine miles, from New orleans   [*From*] the company, I am some three miles distant doing picket duty at a canal leading to the Lake from which place the principal part of the Fish pass for the New Orleans market an excellent position I must admit   but amid all these Comforts even the pleasure of Gathering Blackberries they are at this time abundant hundreds of Gallons May be gathered here, also Strawberries has been for some time in existence vegetables in abundance and many other things to please one who is disposed to be inactive,   such is not my case,   Garrison duty becomes a bore,   it seems as if we are to continue to hold this Fort,   Such is the reputation of the Company that the Citizens desire them to remain and do the duty of Guards in this vicinity   Mr Defreese My principal Object for writing to you is to inquire if it would be worth while for me through your influence to apply for a discharge   My motive is to get an honourable one, and my reasons are first my spiritual disires and opportunitys are brought under subjection   secondly since all the strong holds of the enemy has been reduced or subjugated and thirdly it has been shown by many examples the Love of Country and the willingness of Colored men to protect and defend to the utter most the interest felt and determination to stand by her as long as the God of heaven seen fit in his allwise providence to give them strength to Battle for the right, and that all men might worship God and none to molest him nor make him afraid,   My mission has so far been to my entire satisfaction and more has been done in such a short space of time, than I could have expected, and I now feel that all that I can do has been done,   I am no aspirant to office   even the one I now hold I rejected untill the Capt Compelled me to accept of it,   As I have informed you in times past I desire to see some signs of a future for Our afflicted Race   the time has so far dawned, through God and Abraham the Second that I am satisfied to say time will bring all things to bear

Mr Defreese kind Sir were it not for my age I would seek to

771

become more, interested in Military life but I have no desire to continue only as long as I am immediately needed and then return where I can enjoy my spiritual comforts which I have been deprived of for nearly 18 months, we have many men in this Battalion from Washington and all have done Honour to the District with not an acception. Our Officers are soldiers and Gentleman Strict disciplinarians in duty and are willing to educate from primer to Geography and many have been benefitted by their instruction many who could not understand or knew a letter in the Book are now Capable of writing their name. You will please be kind enough to remember me to all hands particular to Ephraim

My kindest regards to your children particularly Mr Morris and Mr Rollin Defreese and also Anna respectfully yours

Moses Foskey

You will please answer if you think it necessary, or at all events if convenient you will Oblige Me

ALS

Corp. Moses Foskey to Mr. J. D. Defreese, [May 1865], enclosed in Jno. D. Defrees to Lieut. Col. Saml. Breck, 20 May 1865, D-155 1865, Letters Received, ser. 360, Colored Troops Division, RG 94 [B-131]. Other records in the file indicate that the request for discharge was denied.

335: Anonymous Northern Black Soldier to the Secretary of War

[*New Berne, N.C. July 1865*]

Sir   I adress you with a few lines in reference to colored troops doing duty in North Carolina who, are, troops organized in Northern State. for instance their is the 6th U.S.C.T. from Camp William Penn at Pennsylvania 4th U.S.C.T. from Baltimore, Md., 5th U.S.C.T. from Ohio 1st U.S.C.T from. Washington D.C., who, Have Served the goverment faithfully two years, & the most of them free men, amongst them are a large number of farmers, & Mechanic who, could get employment if they were Mustered out of the Service   they Have been Loyal, in all respects   as, soon as the call for colored. Troops was made they rallied around the countries Standard & gave themselves to their country & now Since their is No More fighting to be done are desirous of turning Home to their families after two years Hard Service in the field.   while their was fighting the colored troops in Division was

Satisfied. if war was to break out again they would Serve 3 years longe without finding fault. Mr Secty our division at one time belonged to the old 18″ A.C. under command of Gen. E. W. Hinks & on the 15″ & 16″ of June 1864, Stormed the works in front of Petersburgh & gave the rebs a brush at Spring Hill, Virginia, & The 6th U.S.C.T. & 4th U.S.C.T. worked, in Dutch gap canal, from begining to end, & on the 29th of September 1864 attacked the rebels at Deep bottom we Under Command of Brvt Maj. Gen. C J Paine   it is well known How the colored troops Showed their devotion for their country, & at Fort Fisher the same division was attached to the 10″ A.C in North Carolina & Participated in all the engagement the Corps Had in North Carolina. & Have never flinched yet. we are attached to 10″ A C yet, &, Now Mr Secty dont you think we, Have done our duty as, men & soldiers, & if you can Shorten our time as, their is an order to muster out more troops. I, speak, of the 1st 6th 4th 5″ U.S.C.T. Please do all you can, for those four Regiments

HL   A. Loyal. Citizen & Friend to all

A Loyal Citizen & Friend to all to Hon. Edward M. Stanton, [July 1865], A-278 1865, Letters Received, ser. 360, Colored Troops Division, RG 94 [B-192].

336: Anonymous Missouri Black Soldier to the Secretary of War

Chattanooga Ten. August th 22 1865

Sir I have the honor of Reporting Sevral condishtion to you about difference Circumstance   the Colored Men of these 44th & 16th & 18th there Wives is Scatered abut over world without pertioction in Suffernce condishtion & there Husband is here & have not seen there Faimlys for 2 years & more   we would be under ten thousand obligations to you if pervid Some plain for Our benfit   the greats Duites that is performed at this Place is Poleasing Ground   Some of us has not heard from our Wivies for 2 & a half [*years*] & Some of theses Familys I am very sure that is worse then I Repersent them to be   the all says the would be willing to fight there Enemy but at the present time is no fighting on this side of the Rior Grand   the says that dont want to go their whilce thire Familys is in a Suffernce condishtion but to Fight in the U.S.A. the all say the will do it without Truble   the think under the present [*circumstances*] of their Familys

773

the ought to be permitt to go & see after Familys   I was late
from Mo. & Ka. & anoumber of them that I saw all most Thread
less & Shoeless without food & no home to go   sevral of there
Masters Run them off & as fur as I can see the hole Race will fall
back if the U.S. Goverment dont pervid for them Some way or
ruther   the is noumbers of them here at this place suffering for
the want of Husband Care   the Ration is giving to them dose not
degree very well with Childern   recording to there Enlistments
there times is out for the war is over   the Enlist 3 years or during
[*the war*]   well the war is over   the is some talk of consolidating
Regiments   Some of the Officers says if the men will Stack ther
Arms the will Stand at the head of there Companys until the
fall   I glorys in there Spunk   I am a friend to the U.S.
Goverment but [*not*] to Col. L. Johnson of the 44th
U.S.C.I   please reply to this   Col Johnson if he Don't look out
he will git apple cart tumbled   he has been kicking some of the
Boys but the say the will stop that or stop his life & I am will to
report the case before hand   I am very respectful and & &

these three Regiments that I Speak of has a very notion to Stack
there Armys because there times of Enliting is out   the say the
Enlited 3 years or during the War & the war is over & there times
is out.

HL

Unsigned to Mr. E. M. Santon, 22 Aug. 1865, A-345 1865, Letters Received, ser. 360, Colored Troops Division, RG 94 [B-195]. The regiments
mentioned were raised in Missouri and Tennessee.

337: Michigan Black Soldier to a United States Senator from Michigan

                                        Clarksville, Texas, Sept. 14 /65.
Sir: As an inhabitant of the State of Michigan I have the honor to
respectfully claim your attention, and more, as one who
precipitated himself into the chasm which the perfidious leaders of
rebellion inaugurated with the vain hope of severing this great
Republic, and rearing a government based on Chattel Slavery, I
am confident that you will use your influence, which your
magnanimity always prompts you to do, when the alleviating the
condition of humanity calls it forth.
    Now that Rebellion has been effectually crushed and the

authority of the Government not only tolerated but re-established in all the seceded States, I most respectfully request that you take into consideration the facts which will be laid before you by the person delivering this letter, and apply to the Honble. Secretary of War for my discharge from the service of the United States.

Having manfully performed all the arduous duties of a soldier which devolved upon me while the destiny of the Country was yet uncertain, under adverse circumstances, and painful disadvantages, and that peace has again brightened our sky, the pecuniary circumstances of an aged grand mother and several orphan sisters whose sole dependence is on my earnings, prompts me to solicit, with your influence, my honorable discharge. Be assured, Sir, that in condescending to bestow on me and my orphan sisters this favor, your names will ever be remembered and the prayers of those suffering children shall never cease to ascend the throne in your behalf. I am, most Respectfully, Your Obdt. Humble Servt.

ALS   Elijah Reeves.

Musician Elijah Reeves to Honble. Z. Chandler, 14 Sept. 1865, R-209 1865, Letters Received, ser. 360, Colored Troops Division, RG 94 [B-289]. An endorsement by Senator Zachariah Chandler recommends Reeves's discharge. A copy of the Bureau of Colored Troops reply to Chandler, in the same file, indicates that Reeves's regiment, the 5th Massachusetts Cavalry, was en route to Boston for final payment and discharge. (A.A.G. C. W. Foster to Hon. Z. Chandler, Oct. 25, 1865.)

338: Iowa Black Sergeant to the Secretary of War

Louisville. Ky Nov 19" 1865

Dear Sir   I have the honor to be your obdent Servant   I am a colord man   my name is Alex Shaw   I have ben conected with the U.S.A for 3 years   I was a "spye" for Col Hog Lt. Col. of the 2 Ills cav. for 6 monthes   I all so have Recuted 300 colord troopes for the U.S.A. then geoind this Regement of hevay artery on the 16" of October 1863   I acted ordely Sergent until January 1" 1865 then I was appointed first sergent of my Co By My Capt. Capt. Edward Kemeys   I never have ben under a Rest sence I ben In the Severace   My helth is falling fast   I have a Mother who is a bout 70 years of age a wife and one child. I am the onley Menes of seeport   I have a farm in Iowa of 80 acers I wish to go to as the war is over now   I am a free man and was be for the Rebelion   all so I have Lost 1000 Dolars of Propetey By the

775

Rebelion a bout all I had   I am willing to serve my countary
until Deth   I dont think My countary needs me anay Longer   if
so I will be willing to seve   so I Most Respectfly ask for a
Discharg from the armey of the U.S. as My helth is falling   all so
My Capt. is not Present with his co   he is abesent sick or he
wood have Rote my appelaction   I Remain your obdet Servernt
until Deth.

ALS   Alex Shaw

Little Rock arknasas Feb 8 1866
Dear Sir   I have the Honor to be your obdet Severnt   Mr Stanton
Sir   I have severid the armey for 4 years Nerley   I have a faimly
that is in desetutuion   I cant Seeport them in the armey and is
the War is over I Wish to get out of Serverice and I have a desire
that trubles me very mutch   I had some propety before the
Rebelion but the Rebbles distroeid all that I had   My faimily has
the Small Pox   I have no money to assist them   I have done a
great *Eal* for the Cause and I now humblley honestley ask you to
give me a Discharge   I have asked you or Ritten to you for one
severel times but it semes like I cant heer from you   for my sake
and my Suffering faimily grant it   I have looked for the Regement
to be Mustard out but the time semes Long   My adress is Alex
Shaw Post office Little Rock Arknasas   I Remain your obdet
Severnt till Deth

ALS   A A Shaw

Pine Bluff Ark Nov. 12th 1866
Dear Sir   I have the Honor to be your obbdt Sevrnt   Mr Stanton
Please alow me to make my wants nowen to you   I am a Colord
man   my name is Alex Shaw   I was borne in the state of
Kentuckey once was a slave was sette free in 1855 then was sold
in to slavery a gain & Remained until the Rebbleion brok out &
affter the act was passed to Raise colerd trups I einlisted In the 4
Regement of hevey arterley & severed Faithfull until Feb 25
1866   I was in Different Eingagements was badely wonded very
badley for Life   I worked hard for the cause & was wronged out of
my wrights by men who had the Power & I have a famly & cant
Seport them   I was first Sergent of co. H 4 U.S. arty & Sir I
wish to No if you will Place me in some conditon that I may
Live   I think if the gov'ment will do anay thing for a colerd man
it shoud be me for I have stood By it in the darkest our when the
Conflict was Raggen & I thought you was the proper one to call

on is you air Looked on & Loved by the Colord Pople or by me
anay way   Please Lect me no if you can do anay thinge for
me   Wright sone if you please Sir   derict to Cairo Ills   I am Sir
your Obbdet Sevent

ALS   A. A. Shaw (colerd)

1″ Sergent Alex Shaw to Mr. E. M. Stanton, 19 Nov. 1865; 1″ Serget A.
A. Shaw to Mr. E. M. Stanton, 8 Feb. 1866, and A. A. Shaw to Hon. E.
M. Stanton, 12 Nov. 1866, all filed as S-938 1865, Letters Received, ser.
360, Colored Troops Division, RG 94 [B-294]. In all three letters, dots
which Shaw made after almost every word have been omitted. The file
includes two additional letters from Shaw to the Secretary of War, dated
December 18 and 30, 1865, which state the same facts and request discharge from the army. The 4th USCHA, in which Shaw served, was organized at Columbus, Kentucky.

339: Anonymous South Carolina Black Soldier to the Commander of the Department of South Carolina

Morris Island So Ca January 13 1866
My Dear Respictfully Friend General Sickels   it is with much
Honor we take to write to you about the Circumstances of our
case   now Genl do if you please Cir to this lookin to this [for
us]. now General the Biggest Majority of our mens never had a
Home Science this late wor Commence between the States   the
Greatist majority of them had Runaway from they Rebels master &
leave they wives & old mother & old Father & all they
parent   jest Run away from they Rebels master in the years 1862.
& 1863 & come Right in under the Bondage of Soldiers life living
& according to agreement & promised we was expected to get out
at the Closing of the wor, & then go back over the Rebels lands
to look & seek for our wives & mother & Father
   But General now to see that the wor is over & our Enlisment is
out the Greatist majority of by two months & the General
characters of our Regiment we do not think that the our
Goverment have knowit   for Instant I think if he had know the
General characters of our Regt he would let us go at the Closing
of this [war]   for instant look & see that we never was freed
yet   Run Right out of Slavery in to Soldiery & we hadent nothing
atoll & our wifes & mother most all of them is aperishing all
about where we leave them or abbout the Country & we hear on
morris Island Perishing sometime for something to Eate   Half of

777

our money got to use up in the Regtal Sutler for somthing to Eate
& we all are perrishing   our self & our Parent & wives all are
Suffering

& do General if you Please do see & Enterceed & see if you
cannot do any good to get us out of this if you please cir   for all
other Colored Soldiers that had a Home & is well situated at
Home is go back but we that never had a Comford Home we is
heer yet & we will have to buy our lands & places & by the time
we get out of this all the Goverment cheap. Property & all the
lands that would be sold cheap will be gone & we will have a
Hard struggle to get along in the U S   & then all the Southern
white Peoples will have us for alaughin & game after for our
Braverist that we did to Run away from them & come
asoldiers   they will be glad to see that we would not have but
very little money & we would not have any land, atoll for all the
cheap in things are going now   So do Gen you is the only one
that we know could do any good for us beside forwarded to
Washington.   So Please if you can do any good for us do it in the
name of god   it is a mejority of men of the 33 Regt USCT

HL

Unsigned to General Sickels, 13 Jan. 1866, Letters Received, 33rd USCI,
Regimental Books & Papers USCT, RG 94 [G-89]. Endorsements. The
same soldier wrote a similar letter to the commander of the Department of
the South in August 1865. (Unsigned to General Gilmore, [Aug. 1865],
Letters Received, 33rd USCI, Regimental Books & Papers USCT, RG 94
[G-88].) Lieutenant Colonel Charles T. Trowbridge, commander of the
33rd USCI, endorsed that earlier letter, describing the writer (whose name
was not revealed) as the most troublesome man in the regiment: "He has
deserted four times, & has repeatedly been confined & punished for writing
similar documents to Superior Head Quarters, *direct,* which upon investigation have always been found groundless."

340: Missouri Black Soldier to the Secretary of War

Helena Ark May. 15th 1866
Dear Sir   I imbrace this opertunity of writing you a few lines to
inform you that I am well at present hoping those few lines may
find you engoying the same gods blesing   I am a soldier of the
56th Colerd Infintry under Col— Benzona and have preformed my
duty as a soldier should   since I inlisted I have never ben abesent
at eny rool call   I inlisted January the 4th 1864 under Col Russel
Columbia boon County, Mo.   when I left my family I promised

them that I would come home on furloe   in August last I lost
two of my children   I asked for a leaf of absence and was
refused   thare has ben but one man furloed in my comand and he
was qtr master sargent and that was this year   in my redgement
we have a large magority Christians and I thank god for it   thare
has ben a grate meny of my felow soldiers who throgh grief and
anziety about their families have pined away and died   there has
severl Redgements who inlisted one year after we did mustered out
and gone home   we stood on the bank and shed teers to think
that we who had batled for our country over two years should still
be retained and deprived of the priviledge of seeing those who are
so dear to us   my actions have proved that I have ben true to my
government and I love it dearley now the war is over and I now
want to see those who are dearer to me than my life   thare is a
great many of my Brother Soldiers who have ben out since the
first Battle was faught in mo and have never seen their families   I
have nothing more to say   hoping that you will lend a listening
ear to an umble soldier I will close

ALS   James Herney

James Herney to Seceretary Stanten, 15 May 1866, H-154 1866, Letters
Received, ser. 360, Colored Troops Division, RG 94 {B-252}.

341: Kentucky Black Soldiers to the President and the Secretary of War

Whites Ranch   Texas   May 30 1866

Sir   I has the orner this morning to adress a few Lines to you
Consuring the condishion of our Famuleys of Kentucky. a humble
Good and faiful Soldier. the few remarks I wish to say is
this   the condishion of our Famuleys at home sum of them are
Suffren for wanting of healp and Needing of retention. and reson
Why I Wish to inform of this. is because that. I Know that my
own Famuley is Liven in old Kentucky under just as much Slave
as the was when I left her or before the war broke out. and agreat
mani of other Men's Famuleys is Liven the Same Life. Now M^r
President and Ceterry. When we in Listed in this great and Noble
coas. we did not heasertate the Least. But we came out like Men
and Stud with in the feeal. with Vengengs againts the amny
in-ten-erley [*intending?*] to eather to ful-fil our Dutys and to obay
all orders that was agreable to Millerterry or to the regerlation of
the United States en if not for victry so we did intended to waided
in Blood upto our chins. Now Mr President and Ceterry. we all

779

can Say this much and we do not Say it just for a Prise nor for a
large Name here after. for every word that is Spoken in this Letter
is true. the 116. U.S. Col.^d Regiment She has don. her duty, and
i thinks cording to the regerlations that is gaven by the House of
Congress of War we has ben Prompest to all dutys in the feeal or
on Picket dutys or Girson or fertig or any other dutys that may be
Put before us. and I dont think the quarters is Shorn to us that is
intended for us. it is very true thire has ben furlowes easherd
[*issued*]. but a Mighty few of them. What has ben easherd they
was easherd to the Men that the Officers Like the best. and the
good and duble [*dutiful?*] Soldier had to Stand Back. thire is
agreat Parshalege Shored in among the Men out here. thire was a
few furlowes easherd to 116 US Col Inf. about 17th of this. month
and I dont think it was don justis. f[*or*] thire was only two men a
lod out of a Company of the 116. Regiment. U.S. Col Inf. and
we has not any way to send our Money home   the men that gos
home they lives in adifrent part of the State. and thire is no
Purson that we could trust for we has sent large amounts of
Money to our famuleys. and they has not got it. and I larns that
thire is a Numbers of our famuleys has ben turned out of Doors,
and they has no Place to lay thire heads and we has no way to
healp them. Now Mr Prisident and Ceterry I think that a duble
Regiment as we has ben and has Prove it to the World. and then
to have nomore quarters Shorn to us then what has ben I dont
think it is right. it is true that all Soldiers Should obay all orders
wich the 116. Regiment. U.S. Col Inf. has don ever Sence we has
in the feeal. Only one thing I surpose you know all about it that
happen at city-point of. V.a.¹ but you know how that is. Where
thire is a hundred Sheaps thire must be a Black one. But this is
what Pleas me. is this   we has Stud up like men Man for Man. in
the time of action in the feeal of. V.a. and Never has flench nor
Dreded the time up to this Present moment. Mr President and
Ceterry. aflet a moment to think what a Condishion we
Kentuckys. came out upon the Condishion that we Left Our
Famuleys in. yest. But the way was oping that is very true. that
we Poore Nation of a Colered rast Might come out in our Native
State to afend for our Selfs and the Next Generration to come. See
how willely we come. and Left our States our Wifes and our
homes and children in such away that they may do the best they
can and to take cire of thire Selfs. ye. what kind of fixt was it
to. Now the old Servent he has no Propty he has no Money he
has no House to put them in to. What is they to do now when
they is turn out of House and home. I would like to Know how
would they go about takeing cire of thire Selfs and Children. when
this Poore old Soldier had nuthing to leave with them. No House

to put them in to. the old Servent has Spent the best of his days in Slavery. then must these Poore Creatchers be Sufferd to lye out of Doors Like Beast or sum brute. I says No. if our Govener is for us a Poore unhapy Soldier Wich has Stud. with Comrights to comrights. and Sholder. to. Sholder Marching Boldly in the feeal. And then Suffer his Soldiers Famuleys and Piarints. to Suffer with Such Punishment is that I thinks not. Now Mr President and Ceterry. you Need not to think that we holds you all asponerbul [*responsible*]. for Such treatment for we do not. We beleave the Govener is just. and if our feeal Offecers and Company Commanders would use the Laws a corden to the Law of the regerlations that is gaven to them by the House of Congress. why we dont think that Such treatment would be don and – Mr President. is it Law-ful for a Company Offecers to Detail Men Soldiers. out of thire Companys to wait upon them as a Servent. and Boot-blacker or a cook and keep them. I dont think thire is any. Such law is that. in the regerlations. and then at the same time gave them the Power to Punishe them at the ful Extent as if a Genel cort marshel might Punish a Soldier when he has don a great crime Now Mr President and Ceterry I hope that there is no harm in Doing this I Shall Close I remain your true Beleaver and Well Wisher

	G. E. Stanford	John Dannlus
	W. P. Southwith	Mc Feedlins
HDSr	Mc Mear	William Berry

Capt. G. E. Stanford et al. to Mr. President and the Ceterry of War, 30 May 1866, P-163 1866, Letters Received, ser. 360, Colored Troops Division, RG 94 [B-272]. All six signatures appear to be in the same handwriting as the petition. The military ranks of the signers are given as a captain, two sergeants, two corporals, and a private. However, the register of officers who served with volunteer regiments lists no captain named Stanford as having served with the 116th USCI. (*Official Army Register*, pt. 8, p. 297.) On July 3, 1866, four soldiers of the regiment addressed another petition to the President. Although employing similar – indeed, at points nearly identical – language, none of the signers of the July petition was the same as the above, with the possible exception of a "Sargint McMeail." (See *Freedom*, ser. 2: doc. 333.)

1 In May 1865, at City Point, Virginia, two black sergeants of Company "I," 116th USCI, led a group of men in refusing to serve any longer under their captain because he customarily punished the men by tying them up by the thumbs. The two sergeants were convicted of mutiny and executed. (Proceedings of the general court-martial in the cases of Sergeant Doctor Moore and 1st Sergeant William Kease, 18–19 May 1865, MM-2394, Court-Martial Case Files, ser. 15, RG 153 [H-37].)

FAREWELL TO ARMS

342: Commander of a Missouri Black Regiment to the Officers and Men of the Regiment

Ringgold Barracks Texas Jany 4th 1866

Officers   It is now more than two years since you became connected with the 62^d United States Colored Infantry; now about to be consolidated on account of its reduced numbers, into a battalion of four companies.

You came together strangers, from many different regiments, and from states widely separated. It was at a time when rebellion was strongest and treason most defiant. In connecting yourself with the regiment, you did not merely re-enter the army; you embraced an unpopular cause amid the threats of the enemies of the Union, and the sneers of many of its professed friends. More than this, you espoused the side of the slave, making his cause your own, well knowing that all the infernal cruelty and fiendish hatred of rebellions revenge, was to be upon you in case of failure. The black man had as yet had scarcely an opportunity to assert his manhood. His capacity for becoming a soldier was doubted by even many of its best friends. The prejudices of the great mass of the North were against him, and against you because of him. It was therefore with the confidence of support of only a few that you entered the black army. Officers coming together under such circumstances, and in such a cause must surely be earnest men.

How well you have maintained that character, let the history of the regiment tell. By your exertions it has been made in point of discipline and instruction, second to few of the more than two thousand regiments that have served in the war for the destruction of slavery, and the preservation of the country. Not alone in the presence of the enemy has it been tried. Amid the malaria of a deadly climate, the daily routine of duty went on while Death held high carnival, day after day, for months. The four hundred graves, many of them nameless are witnesses of how much it endured, and how bravely and sternly it suffered. Always everywhere, upon the march, in the camp, in the trenches, on the picket line, and on the field of action it has done its whole duty. I am sure you will point with pride to the records of the morning reports; they show but few arrests. Is there any regiment that has had less desertion? In acquiring the rudiments of a

common education, I think there has been on the part of some of
the men, a progress under the circumstances truly wonderful. Out
of four hundred and thirty one men, ninety nine have learned to
read, write and cipher, and are studying geography; two hundred
read and write understandingly; two hundred and eighty-four can
read; three hundred and thirty seven can spell in words of two
syllables, and are learning to read, not more than ten men have
failed to learn the alphabet. Habits of economy have been
cultivated, as is proved by the fact, that fifty-two men have each
saved $200 or more, and one hundred and thirty nine have saved
upwards of $100^{00} each from their past earnings, six months pay
being still due in addition.

Officers it is *your* work; by your watchfulness, your zeal, your
energy, and untiring labors, you have made soldiers out of
slaves – men out of those to whom the prejudices and the avarice of
the majority, had denied the capacity for manhood.

Do I say that it is the work of the officers? I should say,
rather, that under their instruction and direction, and by their
assistance, all this has been accomplished; for

Men of the Regiment   It is you yourselves, that have made
yourselves soldiers and men. The fortitude with which you have
endured every hardship; the patience with which you have
persevered in perfecting yourselves in every soldierly
acquirement – your patriotism – your fidelity – your earnestness, your
zeal for the acquirement of knowledge have won for you the
respect and confidence of those who know you best, and given you
a right to claim for yourselves, whatever is due to brave men and
freemen.

To you the hardships have been greatest. It is your comrades
that fill the coffinless graves. It was your families, that were, too
often left defenceless to the cruel uncertainties of a war, in which
your former masters were your enemies.

But as you had most to suffer, you had also most to gain. You
and your families are no longer chattels. You left cabins and
negro quarters; you can return if you choose to cottages and
homes. For your children instead of the auction block there will
be school houses; slave pens will be replaced by social gatherings;
and your wives shall have hereafter, a husbands protection, – not a
masters.

And now in closing my connection with you, as your fellow
soldier & commanding officer, I wish to give you a few words of
advice.

Some of you are about to leave the army, and the term of
service of the remainder will expire within a year. When you

return to your homes, you will find yourselves surrounded by circumstances entirely different from what they were when you entered the army. You will go home to freedom; with the freedom will come new responsibilities. It will devolve upon you to care for yourselves and your families. If you desire to have a home, you must provide one for yourself. Freedom does not mean idleness. You will therefore, like all others, find it necessary to labor. Save your money; every private soldier in the regiment should save at least $150°° during the next year; every non-commissioned officer should have a considerable larger sum. Avoid whisky drinking and grog-shops. Do not gamble, a gambler is fit for anything but an honest life. Every man should know how to read and write before the day comes for discharge. Learn all you can. Study arithmetic and geography when you shall have learned to read; take your books with you to the guard room; study at night – improve every leisure moment; you can all of you, if you choose, acquire enough education to be of great assistance to you.

When discharged I advise every one to get for himself a piece of land, for a home. *Buy* the land; you can all have from two hundred to five hundred dollars each, when you leave the service, if you will save your money: – and with the money you can buy a piece of land; upon the land build yourselves a home; your home need not cost you much – you can build it yourself, make it neat and comfortable not costly. If you have not a wife already, get one. Stay at home, raise your own grain and meat and make your own gardens. If your piece of land should be small – cultivate it the more: – it will not require many acres to support you and your family in comfort and plenty. I advise you to *buy* the land because it is a great deal better for you to live upon your land, than to hire land from another, or to work for another. Learn to calculate for yourselves, and to labor for yourselves. Do not go near the cities; keep away from steamboats and hotels: show to the world that you can be more and do better than be waiters.

Recollect that it is not the color which is hereafter to make the difference between men. You are to have an equal chance with the white man. You wish to be citizens? Show to the country then that you are capable of citizenship. Make yourselves better men than are those who would deny you what you have fought for. You who have been in the army must be instructors to those who have had no opportunity to emerge from the ignorance which the "barbarism of slavery" has put upon your race. Be industrious and frugal – be honest and faithful – be truthful – *learn to wait*. Obey every law, although for the time, the government for which your lives have been periled, may seem ungenerous and

784

unjust. Do not dishonor yourselves and dishearten your friends, by any act of violence or unlawful conduct.

Your worst enemy could not inflict upon you a greater injury, than you would do yourselves, were you to act in any other way than as peacable and law abiding men. Depend upon it, if you shall deserve citizenship, you will in the end receive it, with every right and every privilege enjoyed by those who now deny these rights to you.

A little less than two years ago, you passed through one of the great cities of the Union on your way to the field. As you marched through the principal streets there was scarcely a word of welcome or encouragement. Some looked curiously on to see the black regiment pass by – some looked on sullenly. Crossing the river on the ice, your right rested on the Illinois side, while your left was still in Missouri and thus, uniting slave soil with free, you marched out of bondage, with muskets on your shoulders. What a bond of Union! Has not the black man been indeed a bond of Union everywhere? And do you think, that the two hundred thousand Slaves, who have served in the army to put down a slave masters rebellion, are always to be the subjects of opprobrium and oppression, because of the leprous influence of slavery?

Soldiers, I tell you, you can well afford to wait; for the time is coming, and is not far distant, when those who enslaved you, shall be forced to acknowledge, that to have been a colored soldier, is to be a citizen, and to have been an advocate of slavery, is but another name for traitor. –

Officers and men of the 62$^\text{d}$ U.S. Colored Infantry; for the kindness and courtesy uniformly extended to me, on all occasions, during the two years I have been connected with you in the regiment, I render you my sincere thanks.

I bid you all, *"Farewell."*

HDcS   T. H. Barrett

Colonel T. H. Barrett to the Officers & Men of the 62d U.S. Colored Infantry, 4 Jan. 1866, vol. 22/51 25AC, pp. 103–8, Letters Sent, ser. 7038, 2d Div. 25th Army Corps, RG 393 Pt. 2 No. 483 [C-4502].

343: Order by the Commander of a South Carolina Black Regiment

Morris Is. S.C. Feb'y. 9th 1866

General Orders No. 1. Comrades: The hour is at hand when we must separate for ever, and nothing can ever take from us the pride we feel, when we look back upon the history of the 1st S.C. Vols;—the first black regiment that ever bore arms in defence of freedom on the continent of America—

On the 9th day of May 1862, at which time there were nearly four million of your race in a bondage sactioned by the laws of the land, & protected by our flag; on that day, in the face of floods of prejudice, that well nigh deluged every avenue to manhood & true liberty, you came forth to do battle for your country and your kindred. For long weary months without pay, or even the privilege of being recognized as soldiers, you labored on, only to be disbanded and sent to your homes without even a hope of reward. And when our country, necessitated by the deadly struggle with armed traitors, finally granted you the opportunity *again* to come forth in defence of her nation's life, the alacrity with which you responded to the call gave abundent evidence of your readiness to strike a manly blow for the liberty of your race— And from that little band of hopeful, trusting & brave men, who gathered at Camp Saxton, on Port Royal Island in the fall of 1862, amidst the terrible prejudices that then surrounded us, has grown an army of a hundred & forty thousand black soldiers, whose valor and heroism has won for your race a name which will live as long as the undying pages of history shall endure; & by whose efforts, united with those of the white man, armed rebellion has been conquered, the millions of bondmen have been emancipated, & the fundamental law of the land has been so altered as to remove forever the possibility of human slavery being re-established within the borders of redeemed America. The flag of our fathers, restored to its rightful significance, now floats over every foot of our territory, from Maine to California, & beholds *only freemen!* The prejudices which formerly existed against you are well-nigh rooted out.

Soldiers, you have done your duty, and acquitted yourselves like men, who, actuated by such ennobling motives, *could* not fail; & as the result of your fidelity and obedience, you have won your *freedom*— And Oh! how *great* the reward—

It seems fitting to me, that the last hours of our existance as a regiment should be passed amidst the unmarked graves of your comrades at Fort Wagner— Near you rest the bones of Colonel

Shaw, buried by an enemies hand, in the same grave with his black soldiers, who fell at his side; where in future, your children's children will come on pilgrimages to do homage to the ashes of those that fell in this glorious struggle.

The flag that was presented to us by the Revd Geo. B. Cheever & his congregation, of New York City, on the 1st of January 1863 – the day when Lincoln's immortal proclamation of freedom was given to the world – & which you have borne so nobly through the war, is now to be rolled up for ever, and deposited in our nation's capital. And while there it shall rest, with the battles in which you have participated inscribed upon its folds, it will be a source of pride for us all to remember that it has never been disgraced by a cowardly faltering in the hour of danger, or polluted by a traitors touch.

Now that you are to lay aside your arms, and return to the peaceful avocations of life, *I adjure you, by the associations and histories of the past, & the love you bear for your liberties, to harber no feelings of hatred toward your former masters,* but to seek in the paths of honesty, virtue, sobriety and industry, & by a willing obedience to the laws of the land, to grow up to the full sature of American citizens – The Church, the school house & the right forever to be free, are now secured to you, & every prospect before you is full of hope and encouragement – The nation guarantees to you full protection & justice, & will require from you in return that respect for the laws & orderly deportment which will prove to every one your right to all the privileges of freemen.

To the officers of the Regiment, I would say, your toils are ended, your mission is fulfilled, & we separate for ever. The fidelity, patience and patriotism with which you have discharged your duties to your men & to your country, entitle you to a far higher tribute than any words of thankfulness which I can give you from the bottom of my heart – You will find your reward in the proud conviction that the cause for which you have battled so nobly has been crowned with abundent success.

Officers & soldiers of the 33^d U.S.C. Troops, once the First South Carolina Volunteers, I bid you all farewell! By order of Lt. Col. C. T. Trowbridge Comdg. Regiment

HD

General Orders No. 1, Head Quarters, 33d U.S.C.T., 9 Feb. 1866, Orders, 33d USCI, Regimental Books & Papers. USCT, RG 94 [G-274].

344: Order by the Commander of a Kentucky Black Regiment

Devalls Bluff Ark April 16 1866

Order N° 43

I. *Officers & soldiers of the 6" U. S.C. Cav.* your services being no longer required by the Government of the United States, you will immediately be mustered out & disbanded.

Well and faithfully have you done your duty and in the name of the Govt I thank you for the valuable service rendered.

The battles of *Kingsport Marion & Saltville* will be forever honorable memories to you and your children.

When you black men enlisted, you were promised freedom and protection as a condition. On the 18" of December 1865 a requisite number of states having ratified a Consititutional Amendment, forever abolishing slavery in the United States the Sec of State issued a proclamation declaring it to be the law of the land. You are, therefore, legally as free as the white men of this county, and it is your duty to yourselves & your children to maintain your freedom.

Do not create imaginary wrongs for yourselves: be civil, polite, industrious, frugal, just & religious, and you will prosper. Save your money, buy property, and educate your children. If men speak disrespectfully of you, be silent, if the taunt you, tell them you are free: if they menace you, tell them you are a man: but if they beat, oppress, or strive to enslave you, resist. There are but two ways of maintaining freedom: by the bayonet & with the ballot. The Gov't will give you one or the other, or both.

Since the war closed, in this Dept, many white cavalry soldiers have deserted, but notwithstanding you were offered to labor on plantations, twice as much pay as you ever received from the Govt, not a single black soldier deserted. This is most creditable to your patriotism & good sense.

Go now, black soldiers, to your houses, & become orderly, sober & industrious citizens. When the Govt requires your services again, it will call for you, & you will come. The flag that now floats over us is as much yours, as it is mine, and, you must at all times be ready to defend it. Be as loyal to it in the future, as you have been in the past. Teach your children to love it as you have loved it, to fight for it as you have fought for it & if necessary to die for it as your brothers did at Saltville & Marion Ja^s S. Brisbin Bvt Col USA Lt Col 6" USCC Comdg Regt

HD

Order No. 43, Head Qrs. 6" U.S.C. Cav., 16 Apr. 1866, Orders, 6th
USCC, Regimental Books & Papers USCT, RG 94 [G-77].

PROMISES KEPT AND BROKEN

345: Broadside of a Black Claim Agent
(See page 790).

346A: Affidavit of a Discharged Virginia Black Soldier

State of Virginia City of Norfolk 20th day of October 1866
On this 20th day of October 1866, before me the undersigned a
Notary Public for the City aforesaid in the state aforesaid, duly
Commissioned and qualified and authorized by the law of said
state to administer oath for general purposes in said City,
personally appeared George Washington, who, being by me first
duly sworn deposes and says, that about the month of June last he
employed Chas C. Brown to prosecute his claim for Bounty, for
Services as a private in Co: G. U.S. Col^d Troops, [10th]
Reg^t That in the month of August following, the deponent called
upon the said Chas C. Brown to know what was coming to him,
that he might purchase some clothes which he much needed. The
said Brown wrote on a peice of paper, "Good for fifty dollars,"
which the deponent took to Messrs: Seldner & Co, Clothing
merchants of Norfolk, and purchased clothes to the amount of
forty nine 50/100 dollars. The said deponent then returned to M^r
Brown, in company with the Clerk of Messrs: Seldner & Co:, and
informed him of the purchase and the amount, and Mr Brown
assumed to pay the amount when the money due the said
deponent for bounty was received by him. About two weeks after
Mr Thos L. R. Baker sent for him and asked deponent what he had
got? The deponent informed Mr Baker, in answer to his inquiry,
what he had purchased and the amount, and how and when the
same was to be paid for. Mr Baker replied that deponent would be
(cont. p. 791).

345: Broadside of a Black Claim Agent

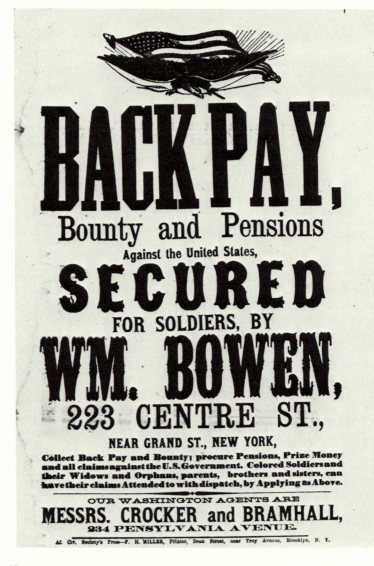

(*346A cont.*)

fucked* out of his money by Mr Brown. Mr Baker then requested
me to send to him all the men who had purchased clothing from
Seldner & Co:, that he intended to inform the Gov^t at Washington
of Mr Brown's course and to break him up. Mr Baker then drew
up a paper which he required the deponent to sign and swear to,
the contents of which the deponent does not know, but this is all
that passed between us.

his
George × Washington
mark

*Before putting down the word as used by the witness, I requested
him to reflect upon the language he attributed to Mr Baker, and
not to impute to him an outrage upon all that was decent. The
witness reitterated it, and said that it was the word used by M^r
Baker. Simon S. Stubbs Notary Public
HDSr

Affidavit of George Washington, 20 Oct. 1866, filed with W-709 1866,
Registered Letters Received, ser. 3798, VA Asst. Comr., RG 105 [A-
7737]. Sworn before a notary public.

346B: Local Storekeeper to the Freedmen's Bureau Agent at Norfolk, Virginia

Norfolk v.a October 23. 1866

Dear Sir Your letter requesting me to inform You whether the
bill for goods attached, said to have been bought of me by George
Washington formerly Private in Comp. G. U.S.C. Troops was
correct, is bevore me, I was very much suprised when I read Your

---

345 (facing page)
Printed broadside, [1866], Letters Received Relating to the Freedmen's
Savings Bank, ser. 157, Education Division, Washington Hdqrs., RG 105
[A-10593]. In the summer of 1866, Bowen, who had helped organize the
New York branch of the Freedman's Savings and Trust Company, proposed
that the government make black soldiers' claims payable to the bank rather
than to private claim agents, because black veterans lacked confidence in
the agents. (William Bowen to J. W. Alvord, 28 Aug. 1866, Letters
Received Relating to the Freedmen's Savings Bank, ser. 157, Education
Division, Washington Hdqrs., RG 105 [A-10593].)

letter and the bill as the letter is *entirely false*   I take the liberty
to enclose a true Copy of the bill of goods sold to George
Washington, to the corectness of which I have sworn before a
Notary Public, as also a Statement of George Washington himself,
also sworn to bevore a Notary Public,   My bill is copied exactly as
I have it in my book the total amount of which is forty nine
50/100 Dollars, and agreeing exactly with the amount of the order
given me by said George Washington and being less than the
amount stated in the Copy send me by You   it would hardly be
supposed that I would take an order for less than the amount of
the bill for the goods sold,   I am sure that this, my stainless
reputation here, and the certified Copies of the bill and order
enclosed, are sufficient to stamp the Statement of George
Washington as a fabricated falshood, yet I feel it but a Matter of
justice to myself to explain to You how I acted in selling goods to
those who have bounties due them upon orders to be paid out of
those bounties whenever paid to them –

Mr C C Brown Claims Agent acting here for the well known
firm of Wolf Hurt's Co in Washington, called on me severall
times to know if I would be willing to sell to those whose Claims
he knew to be good, a scertain Amount of Clothing upon orders
for a portion of their bounty Money,   He represented to me that
many of the men needed Clothing and boots & Shoes very badly,
and that though I would have to wait for the Money I would be
sure to get it finally,

I wrote to Mess Wolf, Hurts Co for advice and they answered
me that if they had Clothing they would sell, and furthermore
that Mr Brown their Agent was a very honest upright men who
would see justice done to All parties and in whom I could put
implicit Confidence,   I accordingly sold as much goods as my
Circumstances would permitt me to sell on Credit, and also made
arrangements with other parties here to sell them some Shoes and
boots as I do not deal in them myself and most of the men
assuring me that they stood sadly in need of them, some of them
showing me their toes sticking out of their boots,   I also had an
understanding with Mr Brown that none of the men, even those
who had the largest bounties due them should get more than
50.00 the highest 75 Dollars Worth of goods,   thus with George
Washington   he brought me a Note from Mr Brown to sell him
50 Doll worth of Goods,   he offered to sell me his order but I
refused to buy at all telling him that I would let *him have the*
worth of it in goods.   You can take his bill as a fair specimen of the
prices at which I sold the majority of goods,   I charged for good
salelable goods reasonable prices, and sold many not fashionable
but nevertheless very good garments for much less than their

actuall Value,   more particularly was such the Case with Military Goods,   I sold for instance to George Washington a pair good blue officer pants for $12 oo/ooo which could not be bought North or East for less than from 14–16 Dollars   in many instances I was obliged to give the men better goods than they realy wanted, such has been more particularly the Case with shirts and Undergarments of which my suply was at times entirely exhausted so I had to sell them both linen bosom and Woolen Overshirts which cost me from 30–54 Dollars per Dozend Drawers which cost me from 15–30 Dollars per Dozend –

No reasonable men could have expected me to sell goods on an indefinite Credit at the same rates as I would sell them for Cash,   I can however assure You that I acted in a most reasonable manner charging no more than a reasonable advance on my regular Cash retail prices, and I belief I can with safety say that Mess Lowenberg & Bro who furnished the boots & Shoes acted in the same Manner that I did, and Mr Brown would never accept and sighn an order without first asking the giver of the same if that was the amount they owed and if they were satisfied with their purchase

I would not imply ought against any men that I cannot prove, yet I must express my belief that the men themselves are not as reponsible for the Statemends they have made as much as those who encited them to it,   there are other Claims agents here who requested me to sell goods to their men, of whose conections I knew nothing, and whose orders I have consequently refused to exept,   As many of the men have given their claims to Mr Brown who otherwise might have taken them to other Agents I have strong reasons to fear that this statmends have been to injure me and through me Mr Brown –   I am very glad and greatly obliged to you Sir; for giving me this opportunity of explaining the whole matter to You as it realy is, though I regret very much to have been obliged to make the statemend such a lengthy one, and thereby occuping so much of you Valuable time in reading it   My cause is, that I have felt it my duty in justice to myself to make You this detailed Statemend, assuring You of my highest regards   I am dear Sir Very respectfully

ALS   S. W. Seldner

[*Enclosure*]   Norfolk v.a October 22. 1866
George Washington to S. W. Seldner Dr
Sept 14. 1 blue Jacket   14.00
          1   "   pants   12.00
          2 Shirts   5.50

2 pair drawers	4.00
1 Box paper Collars	50
1 linen Pocket Handershrif	75
1 pair Suspenders	75

	37.50
Shoes and Boots from Lowenberg & Bro	12.00
total	$49.50

Copy of order from G. Washington

Norfolk v.a Septemb 14. 1866   Mr C. C Brown will please pay to the order of S. W. Seldner forty nine 50/100 Doll. value received and oblige

Witness
L. C. Day

his
George ✕ Washington
mark

Accepted and payable out of any Money I may recieve from or for George. Washington

HD

C. C Brown

S. W. Seldner to Capt. Wm. P. Austin, 23 Oct. 1866, enclosing his account with George Washington, 22 Oct. 1866, filed with W-709 1866, Registered Letters Received, ser. 3798, VA Asst. Comr., RG 105 [A-7737]. Endorsement.

347: Discharged Maryland Black Soldier to a Freedmen's Bureau Claim Agent

Williamsport Washington Co MD oct ^{the} 8 /66

Sir   it is With Much Pleser That I seat my self Tu Rit you a few lines Tu Now if you can Git The Bounty That is Cuming Tu us & We hear That The ar Mor for us   if The ar Pleas Tu let us Now & if you Can git it With or Discharges   if you Can I shod lik for you Tu Du so   sum of The Boys ar Giting on Esey A Bout Thear Papars & The Monney Tu   The ar so Menney After Them Tu let Them git it for Them & The Tel Them That The Can git it suner   Nomor But I stil Reman your abdiant survent

ALS

Charles. P. Taylor

Charles P. Taylor to Mr. Wm. Fowler, 8 Oct. 1866, Unregistered Letters Received, ser. 1963, MD & DE Asst. Comr., RG 105 [A-9641]. Endorsement. Taylor identified himself as a former sergeant in the 4th USCI.

348: South Carolina Attorney to a U.S. Senator from Massachusetts, Enclosing a Petition from Former Soldiers of a South Carolina Black Regiment

Beaufort S.C. Jan^{ry} 28th 1867.

Dear Sir. Inclosed I send you a petition of colored Soldiers who three years ago bought real estate here paying one fourth of the purchase money down the bal. to be paid in three years which have now expired. These Soldiers almost to a man, are unable to pay the 3/4 of the purchase money now become due the U.S. & their houses are now liable to be sold at auction over their heads & if they are will in most cases go back into the hands of the original owners. All of these soldiers have *bounties due* them from the Government, & a good portion of them back pay. Now what they ask for is a postponement of the sale *one year* giving them a chance to get their money of the Government & they are willing to pay interest so the United States will lose nothing by the delay.

We have sent a petition also to the Secry of the Treasury & perhaps he has power to order the Tax Commissioners here to postpone the payment one year without the help of any legislation in the matter, but of that you know best. Your favorable consideration of the matter will very much oblige your colored friends in this department   I am dear Sir very truly yours

ALS   E. G. Dudley

[Enclosure]   Beaufort S.C Jany 23^d 1867

To the Honorable, the Senate, and House of Representatives, in Congress assembled   Respectfully represent the undersigned late soldiers in the U.S. Army, that they purchased dwelling Houses, and House lots upon which they have built houses, in the City of Beaufort, and State of South Carolina at the sale by the U.S. Direct Tax commissioners three years ago, paying one fourth of the purchase money down and the other three fourths to be paid in three years—   That we are unable to pay the balance of the purchase money which has now become due, and our houses are liable to be sold at auction, Thus depriving us of our homes, the improvements we have made, and the money which we have already paid. Our Bounty money we have not yet received, and many of us entitled to back pay, which, Bounty money, and back pay we have made application for, and expect to get in the course of the next twelve months. If these houses are sold at auction in all probability they will in most cases be bought in by the old owners, and thus go into disloyal hands. We therefore pray your

Honorable Body, to postpone the sale thereof one year, and charge interest on what is now due, so that the United States would suffer no loss by the delay and thus give us a chance to get our back pay and Bounty money, which are now in arrears and which we have mainly depended on for the payment of these arrearages, now due the Government. And your petitioners as in duty bound will ever pray

HDS   [*23 signatures*]

E. G. Dudley to Hon. Charles Sumner, 28 Jan. 1867, enclosing Israel Cohen et al. to the Senate and House of Representatives in Congress assembled, 23 Jan. 1867, 39A-H10.2, Committee on Military Affairs, Petitions & Memorials, ser. 582, 39th Cong., RG 46 [E-7]. Each signer apparently wrote his own name.

349: Two Louisiana Black Corporals to the Secretary of War

                                   Ship Island Miss Janary 31st 1867
Kind Sir   I want to tell you Some thing of my afairs, I was Enlisted On the 15th Day of August 1864   I was Received Under (Capt) Horace Kimball   I was Draft for One Years but I am kept Almost 3 Three Years and I am about to be Muster out Without any Bounty   not onley that their has been men has been Enlisted the Same the as me [*h*]as and Now is gone home   their is men out of Conpany H and Conpany I of the 10th both Companys   I Ask my (Capt) if I would get any Bounty   He said that He did not know if We would or not
   So theirfore if he did not know I though that I would write to you all to Say and find out   Sectary Sir my family is out Dore but I hope that you will if you please to fix So that I will get that what is for me   I Seves the U.S.(A) all This time then to be turned out without any bounty   Captain Jesse Lettis of the 10th USCA (Hy) Co F told me that He did Not Know if We would get any Bounty   i have no space to live after Serving the US.A. Almost 3 Three Years then to put me out with[*out*] anything   I am Sorry to know that.   Sectary Kind Sir I am not Insulting Sir I am jist tring to tell you my afiars   I have about 30 men of the Condishtion as me Enlisted the time I did and on the Sane terms for one year.
   We was musterd in by 1st (Lt) M[c]Calester at that time wich now He is now (Capt) of Company B of the 10th   He was the man

that Mustere us in the Army of the U.S. kind Sir I would Acquent you befor now but I did not know as much about as I know now.

Sectary Sir I think that I aught to been muster out about 17 Seventeen Month ago accordingly to my Enlisement   if you plase to let me know something about that – .   Yours Respectfully Servants

Philip Barrow
Anthony Dwayton

HLSr

Coporal Philip Barrow and Coporal Anthony Dwayton to Sectary, 31 Jan. 1867, D-9 1867, Letters Received, ser. 360, Colored Troops Division, RG 94 [B-313]. The letter and both signatures are in the same hand.

350: Affidavit of the Mother of a Deceased Kentucky Black Soldier

Louisville, Ky., July 30th 1867.

Mary Fields (colored) being duly sworn, states that she is the mother of Frank Walker (deceased) late Private Co "F" 28 U.S.C. Troops, and that she sold her claim for arrears of Pay and Bounty due her son Frank Walker, to J. H. H. Woodward Claim Agent at Louisville Ky. in January 1867, for the sum of one Hundred and fifty (150) Dollars, and that it was her understanding that if when the claim was allowed by the 2^d Auditor of the Treasury, it amounted to more than the sume above mentioned, She was to have all over that amount, except such amount as Mr Woodward was by law entitled to receive as fees for collecting the same, and that neither Mr Woodward or his Clerk explained to her that she would not receive any more than one hundred and fifty (150) dollars, if more than that sum was allowed by the 2^d Auditor. She further states that she has been informed that her certificate was No 282,408 and for $359 10/100, and that Mr Woodward has been paid the same.

She further states that neither Mr Woodward or his clerk explained to her that she was selling her claim, and she was not aware of the contents of the paper she had signed, until a short time after the transaction had been conducted, when she was informed by Mr A. A. Burkholder claim agent, that she had sold all interest in said claim.

She further states that she has been married to her present

797

husband about ten (10) years, but that he is not the father of
Frank Walker, who was the son of her first husband.

her
Mary × Fields
mark

Affidavit of Mary Fields, 30 July 1867, F-248 1867, Letters Received, ser.
1068, KY Asst. Comr., RG 105 [A-4352]. Sworn before a Freedmen's
Bureau officer. The 28th USCI was organized in Indiana. Mary Fields's son
was from Kentucky but crossed the Ohio River to enlist in Jeffersonville,
Indiana, on March 28, 1864, before black recruitment was permitted in his
home state. (Service record of Frank Walker, 28th USCI, Carded Records,
Volunteer Organizations: Civil War, ser. 519, RG 94.)

351: Discharged North Carolina Black Soldier to the Freedmen's Bureau Claim Agent at Baltimore, Maryland

East Newmarket Dorchester Co Md [*December 1870*]
Dear Sir I Receved yore kind leter Concerning my Discharge   in
1861 the manspation had not taken place but I was in the
prtection By the youion Troops an Sat free by Presadence Lincon at
the manspation I think in 1863 if I mis Stake not   Sir I was a
volentery Sirlder in 1862 inlested under Capt Crass incruting oficer
in Newbren NC Craveing Co an I never has Receve Eny Bounty
yeat   Nether eny Back pay Sir all tho I had the promoust of
bounty an all so back pay   But my Lord and Savor Jesus Christ is
Witness to day who knows All Things and Shall judge the world
at the Last day knows I have not Receve a cent of Bounty Nether
back pay   I was Born in the year 1846 July the 4   A volen terry
Sirlder A Slave up an Tell the manspation   my Regament paper
was to put in a frame an Set it up in a house an tell all the Batles
that I had been in   I Enlested for three years Sooner
Discharge   that was in case if the war Should End in Side of three
years the 35 US Should be Discharge   My Discharge was Stole in
the city of Charleston S.C. if you wish to kno the commanding
all I will send them to you Sir and every private Sirlder   I come
out the army in the year of 1865 the 22 of June
   I was a Slave all of my life Tell the year of 1863   if you Wish
to Know my Commanding Oficers an the mames of the private I
will sen The names all To you if you wish Sir   my Discharg paper
I Loss it at Charleston SC   Some [onas] Stole it Soon after I was
discharge in abote at the Walf S.C. Sir I cant mot write very well

an I lives so agreat wais of from eny one that can wrigh So I have
to try an do it my self   if you wish for me to come an State this
to you at Baltimore I will Come   sir will remain yore true obt
ALS   Charles Jones

Charles Jones to Lieut. S. E. Knower, [Dec. 1870], Case Files for Claims
of Bounty & Pay Arrearages, ser. 2000, Claim Division, MD & DE Asst.
Comr., RG 105 [A-4106]. Notations on the file wrapper indicate that the
Freedmen's Bureau agent received this letter on December 27, 1870. In the
same file is an earlier letter from Jones to the agent, dated October 17,
1870, which provides additional names relevant to his military career. Notations indicate that the agent had asked Jones for further information
about his antebellum status, whether he had volunteered or had been
drafted, and whether he had a copy of his discharge; hence Jones's December letter. The final outcome of the case is not known.

VICTIMS AND HEROES

352: Statement by a Discharged Virginia Black Soldier

                                        Alexandria [*Va.*], Aug. 11 /65
   John Berry of Alexᵃ Va., vs. Benjamin Triplet of Fauquier, near
Ashby's Gap, Va. Complaint of refusal to allow him to bring
away his family and of threatening his life as follows:
   Berry states that on Monday the 7ᵗʰ inst. he went to Triplets,
who said he went to the d- - -d yankes to fight against him — told
him that the war was not over yet — that the niggers were not
free. He asked him for his family, but Triplet told him he should
not have them — that nobody should take them away, and that if
anybody come into the yard he would shoot them. Berry has wife
and 6 children from 4 to 14 years of age.
HD

Statement of John Berry, 11 Aug. 1865, Miscellaneous Records: Court
Cases, ser. 3878, Alexandria VA Supt., RG 105 [A-10025]. Statement
taken by the Alexandria Freedmen's Bureau agent.

353: Freedmen's Bureau Agent at Brentsville, Virginia, to the Freedmen's Bureau Superintendent of the 10th District of Virginia

Prince W^m Co. V^a Brentsville Jan'y. 15" 1866.
Sir: I have the honor to inform you that a dastardly outrage was committed in this place yesterday, (Sunday,) within sight of my office, the circumstances of which are as follows. A freedman named James Cook was conceived to be "impudent," by a white man named John Cornwell; whereupon the whiteman cursed him and threatened him. The freedman, being alarmed, started away, and was followed and threatened with "you d- - -d black yankee son of a b- - -h I will kill you"; and was fired upon with a pistol, the ball passing through his clothes. He was then caught by the white man, and beaten with the but of a revolver, and dragged to the door of the Jail near where the affair occurred, where he was loosened and escaped. He came to me soon after, bleeding from a deep cut over the eye, and reported the above, which was substantiated to me as fact by several witnesses. I have heard both sides of the case fully, and the only charge that is brought against the freedman is "impudence"; and while being pounced upon as a "d- - -d Yankee," and cursed and called all manner of names, this "impudence" consisted in the sole offense of saying, that he had been in the union army and was proud of it. *No other "impudence" was charged against him.* I know the freedman well, and know him to be uncommonly intelligent, inoffensive, and respectful. He is an old grey-headed man, and has been a slave of the commonwealth attorney of this co. a long time. He has the reputation I have given him among the citizens here, and has rented a farm near here for the coming season. As an evidence of his pacific disposition, he had a revolver which was sold him by the Government, on his discharge from the army, which he did not draw, or threaten to use during the assault; choosing, in this instance at least, to suffer wrong rather than to do wrong.

To show you the state of feeling here among *many* people, (not all) in regard to such a transaction, Dr. C. H. Lambert, the practicing physician of this place, followed the freedman to me, and said, that "Subdued and miserable as we are, we will not allow niggers to come among us and brag about having been in the yankee army. It is as much as we can do to tolerate it in white men." He thought "It would be a good lesson to the niggers" &c. &c. I have heard many similar, and some more violent remarks, on this, and other subjects connected with the freedmen. I would not convey the impression however, that there

800

is the slightest danger to any *white* man, from these vile and cowardly devils. But where there are enough of them together, they glory in the conquest of a "nigger." They hold an insane malice against the freedman, from which he must be protected, or he is worse off than when he was a slave.

. . . .

ALS   Marcus. S. Hopkins.

Excerpt from 1ʺ Lieut. Marcus S. Hopkins to Maj. James Johnson, 15 Jan. 1866, H-59 1866, Registered Letters Received, ser. 3798, VA Asst. Comr., RG 105 [A-7408]. The remainder of the report describes other difficulties between blacks and whites and requests a horse and several mounted men. In an endorsement, Major James Johnson, superintendent of the 10th District, recommended assignment of at least one noncommissioned officer and one private to each provost marshal in his district. Another endorsement.

354: Discharged North Carolina Black Soldiers to the North Carolina Freedmen's Bureau Assistant Commissioner

Winton Hertford co: N.C [*January 1866*]
We as faithfull and regler Soilders of the US: States All free born men of color and of heartford county and State of NC and air willing to work for our liveing and do Justest to our Country in a time of the great Rebelion   we Ether had to be puled in this or escape for our lives   we then inlisted at Plymout NC nerly 2 years ago   we has bin doing duty a round Newburn and a very short time ago we was all regler discarge and had the privledge of bying us Shot guns to take home with us to use on our farms and when we all landed at Winton the 20 day December with our Shot guns Some 1 or 2 mought had pistols   1 I know Serg John Collings had 1 pistol which he got Recd for and when we got of the Boat and Started up the hill all Sober and under good behaver there we meet with Col Joshua garrett in command of the malisha formed in a line of Battle halted us and de maned of us our Shot guns of which he Sed he had orders to take guns from all persons of color by orders from the War department   we did not mislist against them but sur rendered them up to Col garrett and it apear that it was be cause we had bin in the US Servis that they taken our guns be cause they has not taken any except ours   and I myself Corpel John Bizzell after Reaching home Jesse Sowel in command of a Small Squad of men Some 4 or 5 at late ours of the night with they arms and I with non came to Serch my house   I asked

them What did they want to Serch for   all they would Say they
wanted to Serch   I turned them in as A gentleman   they
plundered my house and taken my aminishion belonging to my
gun that had bin taken   now we all as umble Servants of yours do
ask of you to a vord any further privlege being taken from us and
our guns if can be granted or pay for them if you pleas—

<table>
<tr><td></td><td>John Bizzell</td><td>Richard Weaver</td></tr>
<tr><td></td><td>Andrew Reynolds</td><td>Miles Weaver</td></tr>
<tr><td>HLSr</td><td>James Manly</td><td>Briant Manly</td></tr>
</table>

Corp. John Bizzell et al. to Col. E. Whittlesey, [Jan. 1866], Letters Received, ser. 2755, Newberne NC Supt. Eastern Dist., RG 105 [A-852]. The
petition and all signatures are in the same hand, apparently that of Bizzell.
The petitioners had served in the 14th USCHA; Bizzell, Reynolds, and
Richard Weaver are identified as corporals. In an endorsement of January 16,
1866, Captain F. A. Seely, Freedmen's Bureau superintendent for the Eastern District of North Carolina, referred the petition to Lieutenant George S.
Hawley, bureau agent for Gates and Hertford counties, for investigation,
adding, "There is no authority for the action of the police complained of."
Hawley returned the petition on February 13, reporting that the firearms
had been turned over to his office "and will be restored to their owners."
Other endorsements. In the same file is a second petition from the same
former soldiers to the North Carolina Freedmen's Bureau assistant commissioner, dated January 18, 1866. The discharged soldiers stated that "when
we left this Section & went to the Union, in time of rebellion, they said we
should never come back here again. We left our wives & children here & was
bound to come back to them, to take care of them." Upon their return, they
encountered great animosity, including searches of their houses, seizure of
firearms and ammunition, and even beatings, "& if there not a stope put to
it there will not bee any liveing in this Section." They reported that "The
whites tells us we cant have arms without paying liesens" and demanded to
know "if a solder out of the U.S.A. have got to pay liesens to carry arms."
The former soldiers appealed for restoration of their arms, all of which they
had purchased with their own money.

355: Superintendent of a Freedmen's Bureau Farm in St. Mary's County, Maryland, to the Headquarters of the District of Columbia Freedmen's Bureau Assistant Commissioner, Enclosing the Affidavit of a Discharged Maryland Black Soldier

Charlotte Hall St Marys C° Md Feby 7th 1866
Lieut   I have the honor to enclose herewith a Statement of another
Colored Soldier who has been beaten by returned rebels and their
friends. Some action ought to be taken to prevent such outrages.

The mans face presented evidence of hard usage, his nose swollen and his body cut. I have applied in vain to civil power for redress. it is very easy for them to say wait until the Grand Jury is in session and then present the guilty parties. The presentation is a farce and their laws the same. I have had all the experience I want in that line.

My people here are very indignant at the way in which their class is treated and I have been keeping a very close watch to prevent any outrages being committed. I overheard a few nights since while on my rounds at midnights, talking and on listening found that some were actually debating, whether it would not be justice to burn some of these wretches out. I tried to arrest the men but they were too quick for me and before I could summon the guard they were off.

I am a little afraid that my people may get mixed up with outside parties, and were any of them to be caught it would be enough to cause us to be charged with all the crimes committed in the County.

I hope we may soon be able to protect these men from the brutal assaults of these men of St Mary's C°. if the law will not protect them I fear they will protect themselves. I try by every means in my power to help these men and recommend them to put up for a time with the insults and contumely they receive, and tell them that their pilgrimage is short in this life, and that they will receive the crown if they bear the cross. I tell of the pains and sufferings of their Saviour who died that they might live &c but all of no use. they say they are willing to work and want to work but they are human and will not put up with abuse and flogging; and they go away leaving me in a very disgusted state of mind with Maryland and its laws and causing belligerent feelings to spring up that I have tried to bury—

But I hope I may soon be allowed to use Justice (Irish) with (out) mercy on them   Yours respectfully

ALS   Edward F O'Brien

[*Enclosure*]   St. Mary's Co. Md. 7ᵗʰ day of February 1866

STATEMENT OF ESSEX BARBOUR – COL. D.

While at Chaptico Md. on the 3″ day of February 1866, at the store of one Garner, I was beaten, without cause, by a number of men, the most prominent of whom was Bob Dent, and Clem Thompson, Dent striking me first with a large stone, in the head—& then hit my nose. The crowd got me on the ground and kept me there while Dent kicked me in the head & on the

shoulders, severly injuring me. I succeeded in regaining my feet &
ran away—followed closely by Dent who had a large club in his
hand, with which he meant to strike me.

Two men, Ripley Tibbet, & Wesley Shammid got upon their
horses & also followed, with the intention, which they expressed,
of shooting me. They chased me for about a mile, but I, by
getting out of the public road & crossing a swamp succeeded in
escaping from their clutches.

Repley Tibbit—one of my assailants—is a returned rebel soldier
& makes it his business to injure colored people, more especially
colored soldiers, such as me, at all times and places. He is a
dangerous man in any community, but more especially in that
which he now is, which is guided alone by prejudice to the blacks
and the government.

I have defended the country in the field and most respectfully
request that I be protected at home

his
(Signed) Isaac ✕ Barbour
mark

HDcSr

Edward F. O'Brien to Lieut. S. N. Clark, 7 Feb. 1866, enclosing affidavit
of Isaac Barbour, 7 Feb. 1866, #727 1866, Letters Received, ser. 456,
DC Asst. Comr., RG 105 {A-9743}. Affidavit sworn before O'Brien. Barbour had served in the 30th USCI.

356: Affidavit of a Discharged Kentucky Black Soldier

Paducah Ky 10th day of March 1866

Personally appeared before me Jacob Johnson late private "B" Co
4th U.S.C.A.H. who upon being duly sworn deposes and says he
was discharged from the U.S. Service on the 25th day of Feb'y
1866 and returned to his home at Columbus Ky on the 1st of
March 1866 bringing with him his arms consisting of a U.S.
musket purchased by him from the Govt and a pistol. — That his
arms were demanded of him by Esq Morton a justice of the peace
at Columbus Ky, but deponant refused to deliver the same, until
he had an opportunity to ascertain his rights in the premises. He
further deposes that all discharged col'd soldiers are required to
surrender their arms to the civil officers at Columbus including the
muskets purchased by them from the U.S. Gov't

his
Jacob ✕ Johnson
mark

HDSr

Affidavit of Jacob Johnson, 10 Mar. 1866, enclosed in Lt. Col. A. M. York to General C. B. Fisk, 10 Mar. 1866, Y-14 1866, Registered Letters Received, ser. 3379, TN Asst. Comr., RG 105 [A-6029]. Sworn before the Freedmen's Bureau superintendent at Paducah, Kentucky.

357: Discharged Maryland Black Soldier to the Freedmen's Bureau Commissioner

Near Centerville Queen Anns Co Md March 13th 1866

General. I hope you will parden me, for addressing this letter to you, But General we donot know who elce to look to but you. our case – Sir is this. the returned colard Solgers are in Many cases beten, and their guns taken from them, we darcent walk out of an evening if we do, and we are Met by Some of these roudies. that were in the rebbel army they beat us badly and Sumtime Shoot us, on last Wednesday evening the 7th our collard School teacher was collard and beaten, he got loos and ran and was Shot at. the party was Six white Men. and on Sunday evening the 11th Sum persons we think two in Number cam on horse back to our chirch a bout 11 oclock *P M* and Set fier to the chirch that we keep School in and burnt it to the ground.

Now – Sir – this is the way we get our freedom can you do any thing for us. for gods Sake do it we do not know where to go for Safty. I am Gen your Obt Servt

ALS   Charles A Watkins colard man

Charles A. Watkins to Gen. Howard, 13 Mar. 1866, W-76 1866, Letters Received, ser. 15, Comr., RG 105 [A-9704]. Endorsements.

358: Freedmen's Bureau Agent at Elizabethtown, North Carolina, to the North Carolina Freedmen's Bureau Assistant Commissioner

Elizabethtown, N.C., August 10th, *1866*

Sir. I have the honor to transmit the following report of an occurrence which happened in this place on Monday the 6th inst. The County Court met here on that day, & in consequence there was a large crowd collected here, many of them being intoxicated. While sitting in my Office about 10 A.M. a freedman came in and stated to me that while standing out side

805

some men came up to him & said "You damed nigger did you serve in the Yankee Army" He replied "yes" when one of the men struck him a violent blow. I, in compliance with G.O. No 3.[1] wrote a letter to a justice of peace then over at the Court House, gave it to the Negro & told him to carry it to the Justice who would probably give him a warrant. He took it & had been gone less than one minute when he came back with his head all cut open & also his face. He stated that while going over to the Court House, he was instantly surrounded by a crowd of men, one of whom seized the letter I wrote & tore it up and the rest hit him & struck him with a brick. I then went over to the Court House & got a warrant for the man who struck him first Bill Sutton. The case was heard in my office and as the man was hurt so badly as to be unable to appear I asked the Justice to postpone the case a few days until he *was* well enoungh to appear, but the Justice refused and discharged Bill Sutton & I had to pay the costs. The Office was filled with men who drew their pistols & made all sorts of threats. One man (Lenoard Tatum) said he had slayed many a God damed Son of a bitch of a Yankee & would slay more before he got done with it. My life was threatened &c. The man who tore up my letter to the Justice was Hays Bouie, The Freedman who was assaulted is called John Smith. In fact Gen, there is a bad state of affairs here amongst a certain class. There are a great many gentlemen in this Co. who approve my course but they take no method or system to put down these loafers. At the next session of Court which is in October I shall make application for Troops to protect me. I should have reported the case before but have been unwell with the chills and fever. I am Gen. Very Respectfully Your obd't Servt

ALS   Ed B Northup

1st Lt. Ed. B. Northup to Brevet Brig. Gen. Allan Rutherford, 10 Aug. 1866, Unregistered Letters Received, ser. 2453, NC Asst. Comr., RG 105 [A-664]. Endorsement.

1 General Order No. 3, issued by the North Carolina Freedmen's Bureau assistant commissioner on July 13, 1866, advised agents to refer all cases involving freedmen to the civil authorities, inasmuch as the governor had assured bureau officials that the law no longer discriminated against blacks on account of color. (General Orders & Circulars, ser. 2457, NC Asst. Comr., RG 105 [A-664].)

359: Affidavit of the Wife of a Discharged Georgia Black Soldier

[Griffin, Ga.] Sept. 25, 1866

Rhoda Ann Childs came into this office and made the following statement:

"Myself and husband were under contract with Mrs. Amelia Childs of Henry County, and worked from Jan. 1, 1866, until the crops were laid by, or in other words until the main work of the year was done, without difficulty. Then, (the fashion being prevalent among the planters) we were called upon one night, and my husband was demanded; I Said he was not there. They then asked where he was. I Said he was gone to the water mellon patch. They then Seized me and took me Some distance from the house, where they 'bucked' me down across a log, Stripped my clothes over my head, one of the men Standing astride my neck, and beat me across my posterior, two men holding my legs. In this manner I was beaten until they were tired. Then they turned me parallel with the log, laying my neck on a limb which projected from the log, and one man placing his foot upon my neck, beat me again on my hip and thigh. Then I was thrown upon the ground on my back, one of the men Stood upon my breast, while two others took hold of my feet and stretched My limbs as far apart as they could, while the man Standing upon my breast applied the Strap to my private parts until fatigued into stopping, and I was more dead than alive. Then a man, Supposed to be an ex-confederate Soldier, as he was on crutches, fell upon me and ravished me. During the whipping one of the men ran his pistol into me, and Said he had a hell of a mind to pull the trigger, and Swore they ought to Shoot me, as my husband had been in the 'God damned Yankee Army,' and Swore they meant to kill every black Son-of-a-bitch they could find that had ever fought against them. They then went back to the house, Seized my two daughters and beat them, demanding their father's pistol, and upon failure to get that, they entered the house and took Such articles of clothing as Suited their fancy, and decamped. There were concerned in this affair eight men, none of which could be recognized for certain.

her
Roda Ann × Childs
mark

HDSr

Affidavit of Roda Ann Childs, 25 Sept. 1866, vol. 270, pp. 41–42, Register of Complaints, ser. 893, Griffin GA Subasst. Comr., RG 105 [A-417]. Sworn before a Freedmen's Bureau agent.

360: Affidavit of a Discharged Kentucky Black Soldier

Louisville. Ky. Jan. 2nd 1867

Abraham Riley (Colord) beeing duly sworn says, I live at Legrange Oldham County Ky. Two weeks ago I was discharged from the Army and returned to Legrange where I lived previous to going into the army. Three men named, James Fitzgerrald, William Wells, and William Hite (white) met me and asked me what I came back there for, saying that no "Damned Blue Coat Nigger should live there, that either I or they must leave the place, and gave me three hours to get out of town. They said that none of Abe Lincolns free niggers could stay there and that I must go into a free state. They said that they would burn my house and drive my family away. I have not left Legrange, but am afraid that these men will come and drive me off.

his

Abraham X Riley

mark

HDSr

Affidavit of Abraham Riley, 2 Jan. 1867, R-1 1867, Letters Received, ser. 1068, KY Asst. Comr., RG 105 [A-4402]. Sworn before a Freedmen's Bureau inspector.

361: Freedmen's Bureau Agent at Christiansburg, Virginia, to the Freedmen's Bureau Superintendent of the 8th District of Virginia

Christiansburg Mont'y Co. Va. February 14th 1867.

Major— I have the honor to make the following Special report of the persecution by the civil Authorities of two returned Colored Soldiers, Thomas and Othello Fraction, late of the 40th US Colored Inft These Boys were formerly the Slaves of Robert T. Preston. of this county (a Rebel Colonel) and on account of their enlisting in the U.S. Service, met with the displeasure of the Said Preston; who threatened to Shoot them, Should they ever again return to his premises. Thomas on being advised of the threatening language used by Mr Preston; wrote him a letter, Stating in Substance, that in case of their return, they would not quietly Submit to be fired upon, but would be prepared to defend themselves – although they did not Suppose he would carry the threat into execution. February 1866, having received a Furlough to visit their Homes, they proceeded to the premises of Mr Preston, where their Parents still resided – But were not long on the place, before a Servant had reported to them, that they had better leave at once, as Mr Preston had been apprized of their presence, and had armed himself to do them bodily harm. On hearing this, they thought best immediately to leave the premises; and having Strapped on their Knapsacks, Started from the Cabin. A Short distance from the House Mr Preston overtook them, and raised his Pistol to fire, taking deliberate Aim; but the Cap Snapped, and the Pistol was not discharged. Then commenced a Series of Skirmishing, the colored men firing back, while Mr Preston received assistance from his friends. The Boy Thomas on receiving a wound at the hand of Mr Preston or one of his party, became disabled – and both of the Boys were Soon Secured. They were then incarcerated in Salem Jail, for attempting the life of Mr Preston, and remained in confinement three months, until released by order of Genl. Terry, Com'dg Dept. of Va. The full particulars of this case, I presume are on file at Dept. Hd. Quarters. Lieut Hiram L Hunt Stationed at Salem, Roanoke County Va, informs me that he investigated this case, and transmitted a Statement of all the proceedings to Richmond – and further he feels fully pursuaded that the Boys only acted in Self-defence; having been followed up and fired upon by Mr. Preston, when leaving his premises. He also thinks with his experience of the case, that they cannot get justice awarded them in Montgomery County.

Since their discharge from the Army, they have been living in the vicinity of Mr Preston's; but have never ventured upon his property, or molested him in any way, but tried to avoid meeting him as much as possible. On Wednesday the 6th inst, while working (one building a Log House for his Family – the other in the field) they were arrested by the Sheriff of this county, on a Bench warrant issued by Judge Fulton, Some four months Since, for the offence herein stated; and brought to Christiansburg for examination before a Magistrate. The case instead of being examined at once, was postponed until the following Saturday – and the Boys incarcerated in the county jail. On Saturday for Some trivial cause it was postponed until Wednesday of the present week – On Wednesday postponed again until Saturday; and thus three months may again elapse without a trial, while their Families are Suffering, and their Employers deprived of their labor. I would further State that one of the principle witnesses for the Boys is Somewhere in Richmond – another is in Salem, but neither of these have been Summoned to appear at the examination before the Magistrate, although their testimony goes to prove, that the Boys simply acted in Self defence. Bail has also been offered by responsible parties, for their appearances at any time, but rejected by the Magistrate, who appears affraid to take action in the case, lest he might offend "Col" Preston, who is a prominent Man of the county, and who, I understand is very anxious to have the Boys convicted and Sent to the Penitentiary.

Awaiting your instructions I remain Very Respectfully Your Ob't Servant

ALS   C S Schaeffer

[*Endorsement*] Bureau. R.F.&A.L. Hd. Qurs. Supt. 8 Dist, Dept Potomac, Wytheville Va., Feby 16th 1867. Respectfully referred to Bvt. Brig. Genl O Brown A.A.A. Genl, for instructions, The proceedings of the civil authorities in this case, especially in View of the former incarceration and investigation, and the release of the parties, appear from the within Statement of Bvt. Capt. C. S. Schaeffer, Asst. Supt. to be Very unjust and oppressive, The case has the appearance of being a revengeful and malicious prosecution, and the chances of Justice at the hands of the civil authorities appear to be Very Slight. – J H Remington Capt. & Bvt, Maj, V,R,C Supt 8th Dist.

Bv't. Captain C. S. Schaeffer to Bv't. Maj. J. H. Remington, 14 Feb. 1867, R-24 1867, Registered Letters Received, ser. 3798, VA Asst. Comr., RG 105 [A-7767]. Enclosure. Later in the month, Schaeffer reported that the Fraction brothers continued to have difficulty with Preston, who, insisting that he was proprietor of the church that they attended in common, ordered the Fractions to leave, declaring "that they and him could not worship at the same church, nor live in the Same town together." (Bv't. Captain C. S. Schaeffer to Bv't. Brig. Genl. O. Brown, 25 Feb. 1867, Narrative Monthly Reports on Manner of Justice to Freedmen, ser. 3806, VA Asst. Comr., RG 105 [A-7767].) The final outcome of the case is not known.

362: Nashville Blacks to the Union Convention of Tennessee

Nashville, January 9th, 1865:

PETITION OF THE COLORED CITIZENS OF NASHVILLE.

We the undersigned petitioners, American citizens of African descent, natives and residents of Tennessee, and devoted friends of the great National cause, do most respectfully ask a patient hearing of your honorable body in regard to matters deeply affecting the future condition of our unfortunate and long suffering race.

First of all, however, we would say that words are too weak to tell how profoundly grateful we are to the Federal Government for the good work of freedom which it is gradually carrying forward; and for the Emancipation Proclamation which has set free all the slaves in some of the rebellious States, as well as many of the slaves in Tennessee.

After two hundred years of bondage and suffering a returning sense of justice has awakened the great body of the American people to make amends for the unprovoked wrongs committed against us for over two hundred years.

Your petitioners would ask you to complete the work begun by the nation at large, and abolish the last vestige of slavery by the express words of your organic law.

Many masters in Tennessee whose slaves have left them, will certainly make every effort to bring them back to bondage after the reorganization of the State government, unless slavery be expressly abolished by the Constitution.

We hold that freedom is the natural right of all men, which they themselves have no more right to give or barter away, than they have to sell their honor, their wives, or their children.

We claim to be men belonging to the great human family, descended from one great God, who is the common Father of all, and who bestowed on all races and tribes the priceless right of freedom. Of this right, for no offence of ours, we have long been cruelly deprived, and the common voice of the wise and good of all countries, has remonstrated against our enslavement, as one of the greatest crimes in all history.

We claim freedom, as our natural right, and ask that in harmony and co-operation with the nation at large, you should cut up by the roots the system of slavery, which is not only a wrong to us, but the source of all the evil which at present afflicts the State. For slavery, corrupt itself, corrupted nearly all, also, around it, so that it has influenced nearly all the slave States to rebel against the Federal Government, in order to set up a government of pirates under which slavery might be perpetrated.

In the contest between the nation and slavery, our unfortunate people have sided, by instinct, with the former. We have little fortune to devote to the national cause, for a hard fate has hitherto forced us to live in poverty, but we do devote to its success, our hopes, our toils, our whole heart, our sacred honor, and our lives. We will work, pray, live, and, if need be, die for the Union, as cheerfully as ever a white patriot died for his country. The color of our skin does not lesson in the least degree, our love either for God or for the land of our birth.

We are proud to point your honorable body to the fact, that so far as our knowledge extends, not a negro traitor has made his appearance since the begining of this wicked rebellion.

Whether freeman or slaves the colored race in this country have always looked upon the United States as the Promised Land of Universal freedom, and no earthly temptation has been strong enough to induce us to rebel against it. We love the Union by an instinct which is stronger than any argument or appeal which can be used against it. It is the attachment of a child to its parrent.

Devoted as we are to the principles of justice, of love to all men, and of equal rights on which our Government is based, and which make it the hope of the world. We know the burdens of citizenship, and are ready to bear them. We know the duties of the good citizen, and are ready to perform them cheerfully, and would ask to be put in a position in which we can discharge them more effectually. We do not ask for the privilege of citizenship, wishing to shun the obligations imposed by it.

Near 200,000 of our brethren are to-day performing military duty in the ranks of the Union army. Thousands of them have already died in battle, or perished by a cruel martyrdom for the sake of the Union, and we are ready and willing to sacrifice more. But what higher order of citizen is there than the soldier? or who has a greater trust confided to his hands? If we are called on to do military duty against the rebel armies in the field, why should we be denied the privilege of voting against rebel citizens at the ballot-box? The latter is as necessary to save the Government as the former.

The colored man will vote by instinct with the Union party, just as uniformly as he fights with the Union army.

This is not a new question in Tennessee. From 1796 to 1835, a period of thirty-nine years, free colored men voted at all her elections without question. Her leading politicians and statesmen asked for and obtained the suffrages of colored voters, and were not ashamed of it. Such men as *Andrew Jackson,* President of the

United States, Hon. *Felix Grundy,* John Bell, Hon. *Hugh L. White, Cave Johnson,* and *Ephraim H. Foster,* members of the United States Senate and of the Cabinet, *Gen. William Carroll, Samuel Houston,* Aaron V. Brown, and, in fact, all the politicians and candidates of all parties in Tennessee solicited colored free men for their votes at every election.

Nor was Tennessee alone in this respect, for the same privileges was granted to colored free men in North Carolina, to-day the most loyal of all the rebellious States, without ever producing any evil consequences.

If colored men have been faithful and true to the Government of the United States in spite of the Fugitive Slave Law, and the cruel policy often pursued toward them, will they not be more devoted to it now than ever, since it has granted them that liberty which they desired above all things? Surely, if colored men voted without harm to the State, while their brethren were in bondage, they will be much more devoted and watchful over her interests when elevated to the rank of freemen and voters. If they are good law-abiding citizens, praying for its prosperity, rejoicing in its progress, paying its taxes, fighting its battles, making its farms, mines, work-shops and commerce more productive, whey deny them the right to have a voice in the election of its rulers?

This is a democracy—a government of the people. It should aim to make every man, without regard to the color of his skin, the amount of his wealth, or the character of his religious faith, feel personally interested in its welfare. Every man who lives under the Government should feel that it is his property, his treasure, the bulwark and defence of himself and his family, his pearl of great price, which he must preserve, protect, and defend faithfully at all times, on all occasions, in every possible manner.

This is not a Democratic Government if a numerous, law-abiding, industrious, and useful class of citizens, born and bred on the soil, are to be treated as aliens and enemies, as an inferior degraded class, who must have no voice in the Government which they support, protect and defend, with all their heart, soul, mind, and body, both in peace and war.

This Government is based on the teachings of the Bible, which prescribes the same rules of action for all members of the human family, whether their complexion be white, yellow, red or black. God no where in his revealed word, makes an invidious and degrading distinction against his children, because of their color. And happy is that nation which makes the Bible its rule of action, and obeys principle, not prejudice.

Let no man oppose this doctrine because it is opposed to his old prejudices. The nation is fighting for its life, and cannot afford to

813

be controlled by prejudice. Had prejudice prevailed instead of principle, not a single colored soldier would have been in the Union army to-day. But principle and justice triumphed, and now near 200,000 colored patriots stand under the folds of the national flag, and brave their breasts to the bullets of the rebels. As we are in the battlefield, so we swear before heaven, by all that is dear to men, to be at the ballot-box faithful and true to the Union.

The possibility that the negro suffrage proposition may shock popular prejudice at first sight, is not a conclusive argument against its wisdom and policy. No proposition ever met with more furious or general opposition than the one to enlist colored soldiers in the United States army. The opponents of the measure exclaimed on all hands that the negro was a coward; that he would not fight; that one white man, with a whip in his hand could put to flight a regiment of them; that the experiment would end in the utter rout and ruin of the Federal army. Yet the colored man has fought so well, on almost every occasion, that the rebel government is prevented, only by its fears and distrust of being able to force him to fight for slavery as well as he fights against it, from putting half a million of negroes into its ranks.

The Government has asked the colored man to fight for its preservation and gladly has he done it. It can afford to trust him with a vote as safely as it trusted him with a bayonet.

How boundless would be the love of the colored citizen, how intense and passionate his zeal and devotion to the government, how enthusiastic and how lasting would be his gratitude, if his white brethren were to take him by the hand and say, "You have been ever loyal to our government; henceforward be voters." Again, the granting of this privilege would stimulate the colored man to greater exertion to make himself an intelligent, respected, useful citizen. His pride of character would be appealed to this way most successfully; he would send his children to school, that they might become educated and intelligent members of society. It used to be thought that ignorant negroes were the most valuable, but this belief probably originated from the fact that it is almost impossible to retain an educated, intelligent man in bondage. Certainly, if the free colored man be educated, and his morals enlightened and improved, he will be a far better member of society, and less liable to transgress its laws. It is the brutal, degraded, ignorant man who is usually the criminal.

One other matter we would urge on your honorable body. At present we can have only partial protection from the courts. The testimony of twenty of the most intelligent, honorable, colored loyalists cannot convict a white traitor of a treasonable action. A white rebel might sell powder and lead to a rebel soldier in the presence of twenty colored soldiers, and yet their evidence would be worthless so far as the courts are concerned, and the rebel would escape. A colored man may have served for years faithfully in the army, and yet his testimony in court would be rejected, while that of a white man who had served in the rebel army would be received.

If this order of things continue, our people are destined to a malignant persecution at the hands of rebels and their former rebellious masters, whose hatred they may have incurred, without precedent even in the South. Every rebel soldier or citizen whose arrest in the perpetration of crime they may have effected, every white traitor whom they may have brought to justice, will torment and persecute them and set justice at defiance, because the courts will not receive negro testimony, which will generally be the only possible testimony in such cases. A rebel may murder his former slave and defy justice, because he committed the deed in the presence of half a dozen respectable colored citizens. He may have the dwelling of his former slave burned over his head, and turn his wife and children out of doors, and defy the law, for no colored man can appear against him. Is this the fruit of freeedom, and the reward of our services in the field? Was it for this that colored soldiers fell by hundreds before Nashville, fighting under the flag of the Union? Is it for this that we have guided Union officers and soldiers, when escaping from the cruel and deadly prisons of the South through forests and swamps, at the risk of our own lives, for we knew that to us detection would be death? Is it for this that we have concealed multitudes of Union refugees in caves and cane-brakes, when flying from the conscription officers and tracked by bloodhounds, and divided with them our last morsal of food? Will you declare in your revised constitution that a pardoned traitor may appear in court and his testimony be heard, but that no colored loyalist shall be believed even upon oath? If this should be so, then will our last state be worse than our first, and we can look for no relief on this side of the grave. Has not the colored man fought, bled and died for the Union, under a thousand great disadvantages and discouragements? Has his fidelity ever had a shadow of suspicion cast upon it, in any matter of responsibility confided to his hands?

There have been white traitors in multitudes in Tennessee, but where, we ask, is the black traitor? Can you forget how the colored man has fought at Fort Morgan, at Milliken's Bend, at Fort Pillow, before Petersburg, and your own city of Nashville?

When has the colored citizen, in this rebellion been tried and found wanting?

In conclusion, we would point to the fact that the States where the largest measure of justice and civil rights has been granted to the colored man, both as to suffrage and his oath in court, are among the most rich, intelligent, enlightened and prosperous. Massachusetts, illustrious for her statesmen and her commercial and manufacturing enterprises and thrift, whose noble liberality has relieved so many loyal refugees and other sufferers of Tennessee, allows her colored citizens to vote, and is ever jealous of their rights. She has never had reason to repent the day when she gave them the right of voting.

Had the southern states followed her example the present rebellion never would have desolated their borders.

Several other Northern States permit negro suffrage, nor have bad effects ever resulted from it. It may be safely affirmed that Tennessee was quite as safe and prosperous during the 39 years while she allowed negro suffrage, as she has been since she abolished it.

In this great and fearful struggle of the nation with a wicked rebellion, we are anxious to perform the full measure of our duty both as citizens and soldiers to the Union cause we consecrate ourselves, and our families, with all that we have on earth. Our souls burn with love for the great government of freedom and equal rights. Our white brethren have no cause for distrust as regards our fidelity, for neither death nor life, nor angels, nor principalities, nor powers, nor things present, nor things to come, nor height, nor depth, nor any other creature, shall be able to separate us from the love of the Union.

Praying that the great God, who is the common Father of us all, by whose help the land must be delivered from present evil, and before whom we must all stand at last to be judged by the rule of eternal justice, and not by passion and prejudice, may enlighten your minds and enable you to act with wisdom, justice, and magnanimity, we remain your faithful friends in all the perils and dangers which threaten our beloved country.

PD   [*62 signatures*]

Unidentified newspaper clipping of Andrew Tait et al. to the Union Convention of Tennessee, 9 Jan. 1865, enclosed in Col. R. D. Mussey to Capt. C. P. Brown, 23 Jan. 1865, Letters Received, ser. 925, Dept. of the Cumberland, RG 393 Pt. 1 [C-12].

363: Washington, D.C., Blacks to the U.S. Congress

[*Washington, D.C. December 1865*]

To The Honorable Senators and Members of the House of Representatives in Congress Assembled.

We, the Colored Citizens of the District of Columbia, do most respectfully memorialize your Honorable Bodies in our behalf to the following effect:

We would press upon your attention a principle universally admitted by all Americans, namely, that "Governments derive their just powers from the consent of the governed" The Colored American citizens of the District of Columbia are denied the benefits of this conceded principle, in being refused the right of suffrage in the District of Columbia, and therefore appeal to you for this franchise.

We respectfully submit to your Honorable Bodies, that a large portion of the Colored citizens of the District of Columbia are property holders; that they pay no inconsiderable amount of taxes; but are nevertheless as slaves to its distribution, unlike other tax-payers they see the proceeds of their labor taken and disposed of without a single voice.

We are intelligent enough to be industrious; to have accumlated property; to build, and sustain churches, and institutions of learning. We are and have been educating our children without the aid of any school-fund, and, until recently, have for many years been furnishing unjustly as we deemed, a portion of the means for the education of the white children of the District. We are intelligent enough to be amenable to the same laws, and punishable alike with others for the infractions of said laws. We sustain as fair a character in the Records of Crime and the statistics of Pauperism as any other class in the community, while unequal laws are continually barring our way, in the effort to reach and possess ourselves of the blessings attendant upon a life of industry, of self-denial, and of virtuous citizenship.

We also represent that out of a population of less than 15.000, we have contributed three full regiments, over 3.500 enlisted men, while the white citizens out of a population of upwards 60.000 sent only about 1.500 enlisted men for the support of the Union, the Constitution and the Laws. In all our Country's trials, our loyalty has never been questioned – our patriotism is unbounded. At our country's call we volunteered with alacrity, and that without the incentives of high pay, bounty and promotion.

We cherish fond hopes and laudable desires, and have honorable aspirations in connection with the future of our country. Your Honorable Bodies have done much for us within the past three years, for which you have the Sincere, over-flowing gratitude of our whole people. You have given us a free District, and a free Country. Still without the political rights enjoyed by every other man, the colored men of the District of Columbia are but nominally free.

Experience teaches that all reforms have their opponents. The same experience also teaches that apprehensions of evil arising from reforms founded in justice, are but seldom if ever realized. We would respectfully offer as an illustration the just act of the thirty seventh Congress by which Slavery was abolished in the District of Columbia. The opponents of that measure predicted most dire results to this community – which was to be the "White man's Hell," and ruin to the party whose liberation was proposed. There has been no realization of this prediction of evil, but, on the contrary, the happy results of this just measure are now manifest and conceded by all. As Freemen, – far from being a terror and a curse to the country, they are a terror to its enemies only. Experience likewise teaches that that debasement is most "humane which is most complete. The possession of only a partial liberty, makes us the more keenly sensible to the injustice of withholding those other rights which belong to a perfect manhood.

Without the right of suffrage, we are without protection, and liable to Combinations of outrage. The petty officers of the law respecting the source of power, will naturally defer to the one having a vote; and the partiality shown in this respect operates greatly to the disadvantage of the colored citizen.

These principles and Considerations are the basis upon which we predicate our claim for suffrage, and civil equality before the law, and for which we will ever pray. Respectfully submitted.

HDS   [2,500 *signatures*]

John Francis Cook et al. to the Honorable Senators and Members of the House of Representatives in Congress Assembled, [Dec. 1865], 39-A-H4, Committee on the District of Columbia, Petitions & Memorials, ser. 582, 39th Congress, RG 46 [E-2]. Approximately 2,500 names appear on the petition, each apparently in the hand of the signer.

364: Former Florida Black Soldiers to the Commander of the Military District of East Florida

Jacksonville Fla May 3^d 1866

Colonel, We the undersigned respectfully ask permission to form a Company in this Town the object being for the protection of ourselves, and as peaceable citizens of this place: or to respond willingly in quelling all riots or any disturbance to the peace of the town. Signed

Edward Bell	Henry Wiggins
Fulton McGuire	Alex Bascom
Alfred Jones	Weaver Brown
George Johnson	Wm Clark

HLcSr

Edward Bell et al. to Col. J. W. Sprague, 3 May 1866, J-33 1866, Letters Received, ser. 1691, Dept. of FL, RG 393 Pt. 1 [C-317]. All but one of the signers identified himself as a former noncommissioned officer in the 34th USCI (originally the 2nd South Carolina Volunteers); Wiggins is labeled "citizen." The commander of the Military District of East Florida forwarded the petition to General John G. Foster, commander of the Department of Florida, who in turn forwarded it to Florida Governor David S. Walker. Foster argued in favor of the petitioners, but Governor Walker insisted that the state militia law restricted military organizations to white men aged eighteen to forty-five. General Foster then appealed to the adjutant general of the army for a decision regarding possible violation of the 1866 Civil Rights Act. (Maj. Genl. J. G. Foster to Governor D. S. Walker, 7 May 1866; and Maj. Gen. J. G. Foster to Bvt. Maj. General L. Thomas, 10 May 1866, vol. 6 DFla, pp. 339–40 and 345, Letters Sent, ser. 1685, Dept. of FL, RG 393 Pt. 1 [C-305]; Govr. D. S. Walker to Maj. Genl. J. G. Foster, 9 May 1866, F-267 1866, Letters Received, ser. 1691, Dept. of FL, RG 393 Pt. 1 [C-305].) Evidently the military authorities took no further action in the case, and the black militia was never formed.

365: Former Northern Black Sergeant to the South Carolina Freedmen's Bureau Assistant Commissioner

St Mathewis PO SC Oct 10th 1866

General Sur   I feeal it my Duty to take a great Intress In Locating Lands in the Stat of Florida a coden to the act of congress an Aprovd by the President June th 21st 1866.[1] here is a larg number of freedmen Nambeing a bout 1000 hu wants to Gow with Me there and I feel it my duty to Do all I cen for them   I

hav labert her a mong them 12 months maken speches to them an
tring to lern them habats of In Dustrey and to live a truthful and
Verchus an onest life   they all Seem to take me as a father an
believ what i tell them   my desier is know to Locat lands for
them an Start January to them   I hav the formes of affidavit from
the land office in florida but I am darst to make a moov to git up
Emegrants to go to florida un Less feshel orders from you for the
sitisins of this plas is bitter a gance the freedmen saing they want
them to stay hear an worck for them for [maner?] nuthing   they
only give the 1/4 an 1/5 an have 1/3 of the crop an Evry minut
that is lost is chargd to them an when the End of the year coms
thos minuts amounts to days and they charg them 50 cents per
day an that Will leav the Pore negro with out Eney thing   I am
agt for A P Smuker ho has 4 Plantation an I hav taken knotes to
Evry thing   Sum of the peple will not get won sent

So I wood be glad if you will giv Me power to worke an I will
go at wants to ras a larg number of freedmen an Will be redy to
leav by the time ther contracts is out   I am Willing to Serv as
agt for them an go with them an live with them for 3 years till
they be cum setled   general foster is willing to ad me all he
can   So if you will a point me agt i will gow to orang burgh an
obin a office an will gow by your orders

I was up to Clombia fu days a gow an on my return I Saw 2
old horses and 2 old mules alsow 2 carts 4 Par of harness which ar
not in ues so iwas told which wood be Very usefill to help
transport Emigrants cross the cuntrey to floriday   than the stalk
[stock] is Very thin in deed an if i git them I wood hav to feed
them an ners them up for 2 months be for they cod do Eney good
for they ar Very thin   I thot that they wood be help to the
freedmen for the first year to make them Bread as hors power will
be [leas]   I wish to know what you wood let me hav them at   I
want them ondley for the Benefit of freedmen ho goes to
florida   this stalk is at the Goverment plantation at [Hopkin
tuenant?]   Now more at presant   your most obedient Servent

ALS   W^m M Viney

Wm. M. Viney to Bvt. Maj. Gen. R. K. Scott, 10 Oct. 1866, Unregistered Letters Received, ser. 2923, SC Asst. Comr., RG 105 [A-7064].

1 The Southern Homestead Act, which opened to homesteading by actual
settlers the remaining public lands in Alabama, Arkansas, Florida, Louisiana, and Mississippi. The act provided that these public lands be available
without discrimination on the basis of race or color and that until January
1, 1867, all applicants be required to make oath that they had not supported the Confederacy – thereby in effect restricting the provisions of the

act to freedmen and loyal whites for the first six months. (U.S., *Statutes at Large,* vol. 14, pp. 66–67.)

366: Mississippi Blacks to the Commander of the Department of the Gulf

Yazoo City [*Miss.*] January 20 1867
Dr Sir   by Request I Send you the Proceeding of [*this*] Place   the Law in regard to the freedman is that they all have to have a written contract   judge jones mayor of this place is enforcing of the Law   He says they have no right to rent a house nor land nor reside in town with[out] a white man to stand fer thim   he makes all men pay Two Dollars for Licience and he will not give Licence without a written contract   both women and men have to submit or go in Jail
His Debuty is taking the people all the time   men that is traverling is stoped and put in jail or Forced to contract   if this is the Law of the United States we will submit but if it is not we are willing to take our musket and surve three years Longer or [have] more liberty. We the undersigner Looke to you fer Protiction and hope you will give it   you can write to any whit man of this place and he can testify to same   Yours Respictfully
Sined by twelve 12 Men
Please to complies With the colard Freedman at Yazoo City, Miss
HL

twelve 12 Men to General Sheridan, 20 Jan. 1867, Unregistered Letters Received, ser. 2363, Vickburg MS Subcomr., RG 105 [A-9277]. On January 25, 1867, Department of the Gulf military headquarters forwarded this letter to the Freedmen's Bureau for investigation. In the same file is a response by the mayor of Yazoo City denying the charges and declaring the complaint of the freedmen "wholly, and utterly, unfounded." (D. Jones to Major Geo. W. Corliss, 15 Feb. 1867.) At the same time, however, another Yazoo City white resident sustained the statement of the freedmen and concluded: "The Freedmen are much discouraged by these persecutions, and say they will soon be slaves again unless some check is placed on the actions of the Civil authorities." (Wm. N. Darnell to Sir, 12 Feb. 1867, Unregistered Letters Received, ser. 2363, Vicksburg MS Subcomr., RG 105 [A-9277].)

367: Petition of Kentucky Former Black Soldiers to the U.S. Congress

[Kentucky, July 1867]

MEMORIAL.
TO THE HONORABLE SENATE AND HOUSE OF
REPRESENTATIVES, OF THE UNITED STATES OF
AMERICA, IN CONGRESS ASSEMBLED – COME GREETING:

The undersigned, citizens (colored) of the United States of America, respectfully present this our petition, to humbly ask your Honorable Assembly to grant us the right of Suffrage.

Your petitioners beg leave to say that they are residents of the State of Kentucky, by whose laws they are denied the right to testify in Court, &c. And they would further say, that many crimes have been committed upon them during the last year, for which they have failed to obtain redress. Colored men have been frequently murdered in cold blood by white citizens, and as we have not the right to testify against them, the criminals go unpunished.

They further beg to say that they are now and always have been loyal to the United States, and this *unquestioned* Loyalty subjects them to the malevolence of the friends of the "Lost Cause." It is objected by the opposers of Republicanism that we Negroes are too ignorant to prudently exercise the great boon of freedom. Gov. Clark, in his message to the Legislature of Kentucky in 1837, said that one-third of the adult white population were unable to write their names; ignorance was not considered a bar to the ballot in their case. It is believed that men vote their political convictions, not their intellectual acquirements. We are poor, but not paupers. In addition to all other tax, we pay tax on the following property, much of which has been acquired since freedom came to us: Fayette County, $91,800; Bourbon, $17,275; Boyle, $35,450; Jessamine, $8,500; Franklin, $53,730; and so in proportion through the entire State.

It is feared by friends and boastfully claimed by opponents, that if enfranchised, the negro would vote against the party that saved the Government. It is answered that many of your petitioners were *Soldiers;* they think they fought on the right side; *they* see no reason to change sides and vote against the *Liberty* for which they *fought.* It is believed by your petitioners that their enfranchisement will arrest the cruel spirit of robbery, arson and murder in Kentucky, as it most evidently has done in more Southern States.[1]

Hoping that this our humble petition may be kindly received, and our prayer granted, we will ever pray, &c.

PDSr   [*170 signatures*]

William Major et al. to the Honorable Senate and House of Representatives, [July 1867], HR40A-H10.3, Committee on the Judiciary, Petitions & Memorials, ser. 506, 40th Cong., RG 233 [D-10]. The printed form contains columns in which each signer listed his county of residence and his former regiment and company.

1 Unlike the states that had seceded and joined the Confederacy, Kentucky escaped inclusion in the Reconstruction Acts of March 1867, which, among other things, conferred the suffrage on black men. As a result, black men could not vote in Kentucky until ratification of the Fifteenth Amendment in 1870.

Index

825